EIGHTH EDITION

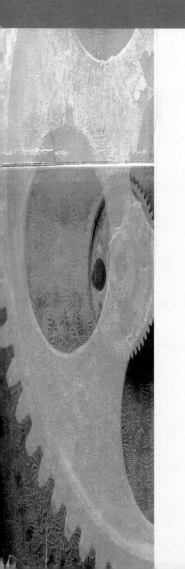

# STRATEGIC MANAGEMENT
## CONCEPTS & CASES

FRED R. DAVID

*Francis Marion University*

Prentice
Hall

Upper Saddle River, New Jersey 07458

*To Joy, Forest, Byron, and Meredith—my wife and children—*
*for their encouragement and love.*

**Library of Congress Cataloging-in-Publication Data**

David, Fred R.
   Strategic management: concepts & cases / Fred R. David—8th ed.
    p. cm.
   ISBN 0-13-026995-6
   1. Strategic planning—Case studies. 2. Strategic planning. I. Title.
   HD30.28 .D385 2001
   658.4'012—dc21                     00-047860

**Executive Editor:** David Shafer
**Editor-in-Chief:** James Boyd
**Assistant Editor:** Michele Foresta
**Editorial Assistant:** Kim Marsden
**Executive Marketing Manager:** Michael Campbell
**Marketing Assistant:** Elena Picinic
**Media Project Manager:** Michele Faranda
**Managing Editor (Production):** John Roberts
**Production Editor:** Renata Butera
**Production Assistant:** Keri Jean
**Permissions Coordinator:** Suzanne Grappi
**Associate Director, Manufacturing:** Vincent Scelta
**Production Manager:** Arnold Vila
**Manufacturing Buyer:** Diane Peirano
**Design Manager:** Patricia Smythe
**Art Director:** Cheryl Asherman
**Interior Design:** Donna Wickes
**Cover Design:** Amanda Wilson
**Cover Illustration/Photo:** © Corbis/Dave Teel
**Illustrator (Interior):** Electrographics
**Manager, Print Production:** Christina Mahon
**Composition:** Carlisle Communications
**Full-Service Project Management:** Carlisle Communications
**Printer/Binder:** R. R. Donnelley & Sons

10 9 8 7 6 5 4 3
ISBN 0-13-026995-6

**Books are to be returned on or before
the last date below.**

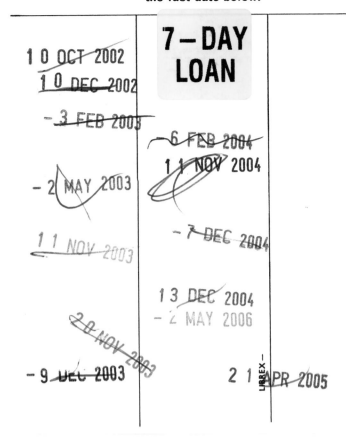

7 – DAY
LOAN

1 0 OCT 2002

1 0 DEC 2002

- 3 FEB 2003

- 6 FEB 2004

1 1 NOV 2004

- 2 MAY 2003

1 1 NOV 2003

- 7 DEC 2004

1 3 DEC 2004

- 2 MAY 2006

2 0 NOV 2003

- 9 DEC 2003

2 1 APR 2005

LIBREX –

# CONTENTS

## STRATEGIC MANAGEMENT CASES

### SERVICE COMPANIES

### MANUFACTURING COMPANIES

# PREFACE

The new millennium has ushered in a radically different and more complex business world than it was just two years ago when the previous edition of this text was published. An avalanche of e-commerce has changed the nature of business to its core. European companies purchased hundreds of American companies. Downsizing, rightsizing, reengineering, and countless divestitures, acquisitions, and liquidations permanently altered the corporate landscape. Thousands of firms globalized, and thousands more merged in the last two years. Thousands prospered, and yet thousands more failed. Many manufacturers became e-commerce suppliers, and many rival firms became partners. Long-held competitive advantages have eroded, and new ones have formed. Both the challenges and opportunities facing organizations of all sizes today are greater than ever.

Our mission in preparing the eighth edition of *Strategic Management* was "to create the most current, well-written business policy textbook on the market—a book that is exciting and valuable to both students and professors." To achieve this mission, every page has been revamped, updated, and improved. The prior Chapter 10 titled "International Strategic Management" has been replaced with every chapter now comprising 20 percent new global content. There is a new E-commerce Theme permeating each chapter in this edition. Chapter 2 in the prior edition becomes Chapter 5 in this edition. New strategic-management research and practice are incorporated throughout the chapters, and hundreds of new examples abound. There is a new Cohesion Case on America Online (AOL)—2000. A wonderful selection of new cases include such companies as eBay, E*Trade, Amazon.com, Compaq Computer Corporation, First Union Corporation, and Wachovia Corporation. The time basis for all cases included in this edition is to 2000, representing the most up-to-date compilation of cases ever assembled in a business policy text.

 ## SPECIAL NOTE TO PROFESSORS

This textbook meets all AACSB guidelines for the business policy and strategic management course at both the graduate and undergraduate level. Previous editions of this text have been used at more than five hundred colleges and universities. Prentice Hall maintains a separate Web site for this text at www.prenhall.com/davidsm. The author maintains the Strategic Management Club Online Web site at www.strategyclub.com. Membership is free to both professors and students.

Although structure of this edition parallels the last, dramatic improvements have been made in readability, currentness, and coverage. In keeping with the mission "to become the most current, well-written business policy textbook on the market," every page has undergone rethinking and rewriting to streamline, update, and improve the caliber of presentation. A net result of this activity is that every chapter is shorter in length, and there are now nine chapters instead of ten. New concepts and practices in strategic management are presented in a style that is clear, focused, and relevant.

## CHAPTER THEMES

Three themes permeate all chapters in this edition and contribute significantly to making this text timely, informative, exciting, and valuable. A new boxed insert for each theme and substantial new narrative appear in each chapter. The three themes follow.

### 1. Global Factors Affect Virtually All Strategic Decisions

The global theme is greatly enhanced in this edition because doing business globally has become a necessity, rather than a luxury, in most industries. Nearly all strategic decisions today are affected by global issues and concerns. For this reason, the previous Chapter 10 on "International Strategic Management" has been replaced by substantial new global coverage in each chapter. There is growing interdependence among countries and companies worldwide. The dynamics of political, economic, and cultural differences across countries directly affect strategic management decisions.

### 2. E-Commerce Is a Vital Strategic Management Tool

A new e-commerce theme is deeply integrated throughout the chapters in response to immense e-commerce opportunities and threats facing organizations today. Almost all products can now be purchased over the Internet. Business-to-business e-commerce is ten times greater even than business-to-consumer e-commerce. Accelerating use of the Internet to gather, analyze, send, and receive information has changed the way strategic decisions are made. Since the last edition, literally millions of companies have established World Wide Web sites and are conducting e-commerce internationally.

### 3. Preserving the Natural Environment Is a Vital Strategic Issue

Unique to strategic-management texts, the natural environment theme is strengthened in this edition in order to promote and encourage firms to conduct operations in an environmentally sound manner. Countries worldwide have enacted laws to curtail firms from polluting streams, rivers, the air, land, and sea. Environmental concerns are a new point of contention in World Trade Organization (WTO) policies and practices. The strategic efforts of both companies and countries to preserve the natural environment are described in this edition. Respect for the natural environment has become an important concern for consumers, companies, society, and the AACSB.

## TIME-TESTED FEATURES

This edition continues many of the special time-tested features and content that have made this text so successful over the last decade. Trademarks of this text strengthened in this edition are as follows:

### Chapters: Time-Tested Features

- The text meets AACSB guidelines which support a practitioner orientation rather than a theory/research approach. This text supports that effort by taking a skills-oriented approach to developing a mission statement, performing an external audit, conducting an internal assessment, and formulating, implementing, and evaluating strategies.

- The global theme permeating all chapters couches strategic-management concepts in a global perspective.
- A simple, integrative strategic-management model appears in all chapters and on the inside front cover of the text.
- A Cohesion Case (America Online—2000) appears after Chapter 1 and is revisited at the end of each chapter. This case allows students to apply strategic-management concepts and techniques to a real organization as chapter material is covered. This integrative (cohesive) approach readies students for case analysis.
- End-of-chapter Experiential Exercises effectively apply concepts and techniques in a challenging, meaningful, and enjoyable manner. Eighteen exercises apply text material to the Cohesion Case; ten apply textual material to a college or university; another ten send students into the business world to explore important strategy topics. The exercises are relevant, interesting, and contemporary.
- Excellent pedagogy, including Notable Quotes and Objectives to open each chapter, and Key Terms, Current Readings, Discussion Questions, and Experiential Exercises to close each chapter.
- Excellent coverage of business ethics aimed at more than meeting AACSB standards.
- Excellent coverage of strategy implementation issues such as corporate culture, organizational structure, marketing concepts, and financial tools and techniques.
- A systematic, analytical approach presented in Chapter 6, including matrices such as the TOWS, BCG, IE, GRAND, SPACE, and QSPM.
- The chapter material is again published in four color.
- The Web site www.prenhall.com/davidsm provides chapter and case updates, an online Study Guide, and support materials.

## Cases: Time-Tested Features

- The 2000 timeframe for cases offers the most current set in any business policy text on the market.
- The cases focus on well-known firms in the news making strategic changes. All cases are undisguised and most are exclusively written for this text to reflect current strategic-management problems and practices.
- The cases feature a great mix of small business, international, and not-for-profit firms organized conveniently by industry.
- Almost all cases provide complete financial information about the firm and an organizational chart.
- A split-paperback version including only cases is available.
- A special matrix provided here in preface compares all cases in the text on important criteria such as topics covered, size of firm, complexity of case, etc.

 ## NEW TO THIS EDITION

In addition to the special time-tested trademarks described above, this edition includes some exciting new features designed to position this text as the clear leader and best choice for teaching business policy and strategic management include:

## Changes in the Cases

- Thirteen brand-new, year 2000 cases focusing on companies in the news appear exclusively for the first time in this text. The cases are:

America Online (AOL)—The New
  Cohesion Case
E*Trade
eBay
Amazon.com
First Union Corporation
Wachovia Corporation
Lockheed Martin Corporation

Compaq Computer Corporation
Dell Computer Corporation
Research in Motion
M. D. Anderson Biomedical Services
  Department
Quorum Health Group
Reader's Digest Association
Reebok International

- Twenty-eight fully-updated cases from the last edition are included as follows:

The Limited
Wal-Mart Stores
Target Corporation
Mandalay Resort Group
Harrah's Entertainment
The Audubon Institute
Riverbanks Zoological Park and Botanical Garden
The Classic Car Club of America
RailTex
Greyhound Lines
Carnival Corporation
Southwest Airlines Co.
Central United Methodist Church
Elkins Lake Baptist Church

Harley-Davidson
Winnebago Industries
Avon Products
Revlon
UST
Pilgrim's Pride Corporation
H. J. Heinz Company
Hershey Foods Corporation
The Boeing Company
Apple Computer
Stryker Corporation
Biomet
Playboy Enterprises
Nike

## Specific Chapter Changes

- Chapter 1 titled "The Nature of Strategic Management"—New headings, sub-headings, and topics include: History of Strategic Planning, Pitfalls in Doing Strategic Planning, Why Some Firms Do No Strategic Planning, Guidelines for Doing Strategic Planning, Internet Ethics Issues, Nature of Global Competition, Advantages and Disadvantages of International Operations.
- Chapter 2 titled "The Business Mission"—Extensive new coverage of vision statements is provided including numerous examples. All-new example mission statements are provided and evaluated. New topics include Concern About Company Mission Across Continents and Vision Versus Mission. Chapter material is totally reorganized to improve caliber of presentation.
- Chapter 3 titled "The External Assessment"—Fully undated Web site references and narrative with all new examples. New headings include The Global Challenge, Politics in Mexico, Politics in Russia, Politics in China, Is the Internet Revolution Bypassing the Poor, Minorities?, What Country is the Most Wireless Nation? Expanded coverage of Competitive Intelligence and Cooperation Among Competitors is provided. New demographic trend information included.
- Chapter 4 titled "The Internal Assessment"—New headings, subheadings, and topics include: American Versus Foreign Cultures, Changing Role of Women in Japan, E-Stores Replacing Brick Stores. All new examples provided. Prior table giving internal audit checklist of questions now integrated throughout the chapter. Extensive new advertising and global material.

- Chapter 5 titled "Strategies in Action"—Previously Chapter 2, new headings include: Should Internet Sales Remain Tax-Free? Does the USA Lead in Small Business Start-ups?, The Nature of Long-Term Objectives, and Not Managing by Objectives. All new strategy examples are provided, including the lists of current divestitures, joint ventures, and mergers. Previous table titled Guidelines for Situations When Particular Strategies Are Most Effective has been replaced with appropriate integration throughout the chapter. Joint Venture is no longer grouped as a Defensive Strategy. Michael Porter's generic strategy material shifts and expands in coverage.
- Chapter 6 titled "Strategy Analysis and Choice"—New headings include: Industries Most Affected By Online Sales, Merger Mania in Europe, Boards of Directors. The long-term objectives material shifts to prior chapter. New year-2000 examples provided throughout. Extensive new coverage provided on governance. Matrix approach to strategy analysis and choice improved.
- Chapter 7 titled "Implementing Strategies: Management Issues"—New headings include: Restructuring Changes a Country, The Mexican Culture, The Russian Culture, The Chinese Culture, CEO's Becoming E-Commerce Leaders. Increased coverage of women in top management, natural environment issues, e-engineering, global issues, and e-commerce. All new examples provided.
- Chapter 8 titled "Implementing Strategies: Marketing, Finance/Accounting, R&D, and CIS Issues"—New coverage of Internet marketing, Internet advertising, market segmentation, New headings include: Europe Acquiring the USA, Business Reaction to Global Warming, New Trends in Firms Going Public. New examples provided throughout. Expanded coverage of global and e-commerce factors.
- Chapter 9 titled "Strategy Review, Evaluation, and Control"—New headings are The Best Companies in Britain, France, and Germany and Using Virtual Close for Strategy Evaluation. All new examples provided. Increased coverage of global factors and e-commerce issues.

 ## ANCILLARY MATERIALS

- *Instructor's Resource CD-ROM.* Includes improved PowerPoint slides offering professors easy lecture outlines for in-class presentations. Chapter headings and topics are highlighted on up to forty PowerPoint slides per chapter. The *Instructor's Manual* and Test Item File are also included.
- *Case Instructor's Manual.* Provides a comprehensive teacher's note for all forty-one cases. The teachers' notes feature detailed analyses, classroom discussion questions with answers, an external and internal assessment, specific recommendations, strategy implementation material, and an epilogue for each case. Each teachers' note is also provided on a PowerPoint slide for convenience to the professor.
- *Instructor's Manual.* Provides lecture notes, teaching tips, answers to all end chapter Experiential Exercises and Review Questions, additional Experiential Exercises not in the text, a glossary with definitions of all end-of-chapter key terms and concepts, sample course syllabi, and a test bank of nearly fifteen hundred questions with answers.
- *Twenty Color Case Video Segments.* To accompany the Cohesion Case, a color video prepared by America Online (AOL) is available to adopters free of charge. Shown near the beginning of the course, the AOL video can arouse students' interest in studying the Cohesion Case and completing Experiential Exercises that apply chapter material to this case. In addition, a collection of nineteen other color case video segments is available free of charge. The segments average fifteen minutes each and were professionally prepared by firms used in cases in this text.

- *PHLIP/CW—Prentice Hall Learning on the Internet Partnership (PHLIP).* This is a content-rich, multidisciplinary business education Web site created by professors for professors and their students. PHLIP provides academic support for faculty and students using this text, offering students the Student Study Hall, Current Events, an Interactive Study Guide, and Internet Resources. Instructors can choose from text-specific resources such as the Faculty Lounge, Teaching Archive, Help with Computers, and Internet Skills.
- *Standard Web CT—Free to Adoptors.* Standard Web CT, an online course from Prentice Hall, features Companion Web Site and Test Item File Content in an easy-to-use system. Developed by educators for educators and their students, this online content and tools feature the most advanced educational technology and instructional design available today. The rich set of materials, communication tools, and course management resources can be easily customized to either enhance a traditional course or create the entire course online.
- *Transparency Masters.* Approximately one hundred transparency masters are available with this text. These transparencies feature figures and key topics in the text and are provided as full-color acetates.
- *Printed and Computerized Test Bank.* The test bank for this text includes 737 True/False questions, 425 multiple-choice questions, and 202 essay questions for the text chapters. Answers to all objective questions are provided. The test questions given in the *Instructor's Manual* are also available on computerized test software to facilitate preparing and grading tests.

# MASTERING STRATEGY

*Mastering Strategy* is the first product in the *Mastering Business* series. It offers students an interactive, multimedia experience as they follow the people and issues of Cango, Inc., a small Internet startup. The text, video, and interactive exercises provide students an opportunity to simulate the strategic planning experience and chart the future activities for Cango.

## The Mastering Strategy Environment

Students will learn strategy concepts within the context of Cango, Inc., a fictitious Internet company that focuses its efforts in the entertainment arena of the e-commerce world. The company began by retailing books on the Internet and has branched out to offer CDs, videos, MP3 files, and customized players. Cango employs mostly recent college graduates enthusiastic about working with an online business and its possibilities for expansion. Currently, Cango is experiencing great growth, but little profit.

Thus, Cango employees are always on the lookout for new ventures. The company is considering hosting streaming video, e-books and e-book readers, and partnerships with other firms. One example would be a film studio so that Cango can serve the needs of independent filmmakers and tap into the growing popularity of home video hardware and software.

The company's goals are to get bigger, better, and to someday make a significant profit. In *Mastering Strategy,* the firm transforms from a small, independent company to one listed on the NASDAQ through the IPO process. The firm's founder and the management team must deal with all the implications of this change, both within the company and in the context of the external world of investors, the board of directors, and potential competitors.

## Employees

Liz is Cango's founder. She's a smart, enthusiastic, and driven CEO. She can be intimidating to some employees, but invokes a great deal of admiration from them as well. She received her MBA about five years ago, and holds a BA in Music. She left a traditional company to start Cango when she recognized that the Internet would take off. Liz is recognized in the industry as a pioneer who likes to play a role in every decision. She's a visionary with a very magnetic personality.

Cango currently has a total of thirty-two employees. There are six managers that comprise the senior management team at Cango.

Andrew is a recent marketing graduate and Cango's director of marketing. He is enthusiastic and creative in his work. He's also a fun guy who tends to dress and act in an avant-garde way. Other employees turn to him to lighten things up, or whenever they need a creative shot in the arm. He keeps his eye on what the competition is doing. He loves coming up with cool new ideas, and as far as Cango is concerned, he's always thinking, "What are we going to do tomorrow?"

Warren, the Director of Operations, has a background in economics. He focuses on how supply and demand, pricing, interest rates, and production costs affect Cango's new ventures. Warren has been with Cango since its inception. He is a realist and everyone knows that it is thanks to him that many neat ideas become realities. Warren is a sports buff and frequent sports analogies can be heard coming from him. His goal is to keep the firm on track.

The company's director of personnel is Maria. She has an MBA in human resource management and a BA in psychology. She is a people person who nonetheless has to make many of the hard decisions regarding hiring and firing. Many employees turn to her to discuss personnel issues as well as for advice and feedback. She finds that her role is to always be thinking, "How will this affect our workforce?" whenever new ideas or changes are on the horizon for Cango.

Clark is Cango's VP of finance. He frequently interfaces with actual and potential Cango investors. Whenever new ideas come up, he can be counted on to ask, "Are we making shareholders more money with this idea?" Clark is a married man with strong family values; he is extremely competent in his work. He tends to look at new opportunities with the approach of, "How does this idea add value to the firm?"

Cango's director of accounting is Ethel. She is detail oriented and has a bookkeeper/CPA background. The company depends upon her to always consider the potential costs of all the exciting new ideas that get floated around. She can be counted on to bring up questions that no one else wants to talk about. She spends most of her time dealing with the legalities, with auditing firms, etc. Cango's managers may not always want to hear what she has to say, but they admit—she's usually right.

There are several minor characters as well as many extras. Each employee brings a different set of personal and professional attributes to the young firm. The dynamics between all of these people is what will make Cango either a success or failure. How each copes with various decisions and problems is the basis for the *Mastering Strategy* project.

## Cango's Course of Action

In early episodes, students engage in the crux of strategic planning as they work with Cango to create vision and mission statements, grapple with the issues of social responsibility and engage in the detailed planning of a SWOT analysis. In later episodes, working from competitive and internal environmental analyses, students engage in strategic choice and the implementation issues that arise from selecting among various strategic options.

## Cango's IPO

Embedded in these analytical activities are events at Cango that add further spice to the decision-making process. Competitive environment realities move Cango towards an IPO. This change presents Cango's management team with options for investing capital in different strategic venues, including whether and how to diversify into a new line of business.

The threat of being acquired by a larger industry player appears, as do problems with managing the firm's value chain when demand forecasting is inadequate, and the struggle for the CEO to maintain power in the face of not meeting Wall Street's or the board of director's performance expectations. Embedded in all of these strategic issues are the human factors that are encountered when decisions about tangible and intangible resources, performance measurements, and power relationships are made.

## Episodes Within *Mastering Strategy*

The videos show the management team in action within their offices and on location at the company's warehouse, restaurants, public parks, parking lots and other areas. Here are brief summaries of each of the twelve episodes that comprise the *Mastering Strategy* project.

### Episode 1: Concept of Strategic Management

Elizabeth is named Business Leader of the Year and delivers a speech on how she and Cango came to be a success. For the first time in the company's history, she actually examines its development and her thinking along the way. Cango's management team meets to decide if the company should enter the online gaming marketing.

### Episode 2: Vision and Mission

Elizabeth struggles with the idea of taking Cango public, realizing that to do so she must have clear vision and mission statements for the company. She puts her ideas about the company on paper and gives her staff the opportunity to voice their own Cango vision.

### Episode 3: External Environment

The rumor on the street is that a rival Internet startup is looking to buy Cango. The team views this as a hostile takeover, and they also discuss the possible impact of another threat: government regulation of commercial Internet sites.

### Episode 4: Competitor Analysis

Cango's management team learns of another large company's plans to buy out the Internet entertainment industry. Cango isn't on the "hit list," but comes out against the action, calling the company a "bureaucratic behemoth." The team makes a list identifying and rating their competitors.

### Episode 5: Internal Analysis

Cango's board of directors questions Liz's leadership ability after the company stock takes a dive. An outside consultant's report verifies the board's concerns. Liz manages to convince the Board that she can change her leadership style and keeps her current position.

### Episode 6: Strategic Analysis and Choice

The IPO has raised $130 million and the management team meets to discuss how to use it. Some want the company to push into new markets, others are more cautious. The resolution is to move into the emerging online gaming market.

### Episode 7: Business Level Strategy in a Single or Dominant-Product Business

Liz and Andrew discuss the ramifications (including cost leadership, differentiation, and focus) of Cango entering the online gaming arena. An MP3 company offers Cango an exclusive distribution contract and a high commission for space on Cango's Web site.

### Episode 8: Corporate Level Strategy

Cango's management team discusses how the company can get into online gaming without having to start from scratch. The idea put forth is that Cango form an alliance with a well-known gaming company already on the market. The repercussions of this are debated.

### Episode 9: Strategic Implementation

Cango has acquired Webjouster, Inc., which specializes in interactive entertainment media. The two cultures clash, impacting employee productivity and satisfaction. Resolutions to this problem are discussed.

### Episode 10: Strategic Control

Cango's financial data shows the company's performance has been lackluster, and Liz is concerned that this information will create a negative response from the board of directors even though Cango has been successful in other ways.

*Episode 11: Leadership and Governance*

Cango's board of directors decides to "promote" Elizabeth to chair of the board and bring in a more seasoned CEO. In a passionate speech, Liz persuades the board to keep her as CEO. She vows to step back more from the day-to-day operations.

*Episode 12: International Management*

Warren discovers that the majority of Cango's Web sales are within the United States, and the management team decides if they should start targeting international customers. It is determined that no one at Cango has the expertise to tackle the issue of internationalization.

## Summary

*Mastering Strategy* can be ordered separately or packaged with this or other texts for an additional fee. Contact your local Prentice Hall sales representative for details.

### System Requirements

The *Mastering Business* CD-ROM takes no space on a PC's hard drive. It runs entirely from the CD-ROM. You will need an Internet browser program (Internet Explorer 4+ or Netscape 4+) and a media player (Windows Media Player or Quicktime Player).

### Using the CD-ROM

The program itself is very easy to use, but every computer starts CDs differently. Some begin playing CDs as soon as you put them in and close the tray. For others, there may be a desktop icon for you to click. Look on the *Mastering Strategy* CD-ROM for detailed instructions.

# SPECIAL NOTE TO STUDENTS

Welcome to business policy. This is a challenging and exciting course that will allow you to function as the owner or chief executive officer of different organizations. Your major task in this course will be to make strategic decisions and to justify those decisions through oral and written communication. Strategic decisions determine the future direction and competitive position of an enterprise for a long time. Decisions to expand geographically or to diversify are examples of strategic decisions.

Strategic decision making occurs in all types and sizes of organizations, from General Motors to a small hardware store. Many people's lives and jobs are affected by strategic decisions, so the stakes are very high. An organization's very survival is often at stake. The overall importance of strategic decisions makes this course especially exciting and challenging. You will be called upon in business policy to demonstrate how your strategic decisions could be successfully implemented.

In this course, you can look forward to making strategic decisions both as an individual and as a member of a team. No matter how hard employees work, an organization is in real trouble if strategic decisions are not made effectively. Doing the right things (effectiveness) is more important than doing things right (efficiency). For example, Compaq was prosperous in the mid-1990s, but ineffective strategies led to millions in losses in the late 1990s. Compaq Computer CEO Eckhard Pfeiffer lost his job for lack of an Internet vision [Del Jones, "Are Company Chiefs Paying Heed to Web?" *USA Today*, July 2, 1999, p. 5B].

You will have the opportunity in this course to make actual strategic decisions, perhaps for the first time in your academic career. Do not hesitate to take a stand and defend specific strategies that you determine to be the best. The rationale for your strategic decisions will be more important than the actual decision, because no one knows for sure what the best strategy is for a particular organization at a given point in time. This fact accents the subjective, contingency nature of the strategic-management process.

Use the concepts and tools presented in this text, coupled with your own intuition, to recommend strategies that you can defend as being most appropriate for the organizations that you study. You will also need to integrate knowledge acquired in previous business courses. For this reason, business policy is often called a capstone course; you may want to keep this book for your personal library.

This text is practitioner-oriented and applications-oriented. It presents strategic-management concepts that will enable you to formulate, implement, and evaluate strategies in all kinds of profit and nonprofit organizations. The end-of-chapter Experiential Exercises allow you to apply what you've read in each chapter to the AOL Cohesion Case and to your own university.

Use the Strategic Management Club Online Web site at www.strategyclub.com. The templates and links there will save you time in performing analyses and will make your work look professional. Work hard in policy this term and have fun. Good luck!

 ## ACKNOWLEDGMENTS

Many persons have contributed time, energy, ideas, and suggestions for improving this text over eight editions. The strength of this text is largely attributed to the collective wisdom, work, and experiences of business policy professors, strategic management researchers, students, and practitioners. Names of particular individuals whose published research is referenced in the eighth edition of this text are listed alphabetically in the Name Index. To all individuals involved in making this text so popular and successful, I am indebted and thankful.

Many special persons and reviewers contributed valuable material and suggestions for this edition. I would like to thank my colleagues and friends at Auburn University, Mississippi State University, East Carolina University, and Francis Marion University. These are universities where I have served on the management faculty. Scores of students and professors at these schools shaped development of this text. I would like to thank the following reviewers who contributed valuable suggestions for this eighth edition text:

Anthony F. Chelte, Western New England
   College
Leyland M. Lucas, Rutgers University
Joshua D. Martin, Temple University
Bob D. Cutler, Cleveland State University
Evgeny A. Lapshin, Tomsk State Pedagogical
   University, Russia

Cathleen Folker, University of
   Nebraska–Lincoln
Jeffrey J. Bailey, University of Idaho
David Dawley, Florida State University
J. Michael Geringer, California State
   University

Individuals who develop cases for the North American Case Research Association Meeting, the Midwest Society for Case Research Meeting, the Eastern Casewriters Association Meeting, the European Case Research Association Meeting, and Harvard Case Services are vitally important for continued progress in the field of strategic management. From a research perspective, writing business policy cases represents a valuable scholarly activity among faculty. Extensive research is required to structure business policy cases in a way that exposes strategic issues, decisions, and behavior. Pedagogically, business policy cases are essential for students in learning how to apply concepts, evaluate situations, formulate strategies, and resolve implementation problems. Without a continuous stream of update business policy cases, the strategic management course and discipline would lose much of its energy and excitement.

The following individuals wrote cases that were selected for inclusion with this text. These persons helped develop the most current compilation of cases ever assembled with a business policy text:

Claire Anderson, Old Dominion University
M. Jill Austin, Middle Tennessee State University
Robert Barrett, Francis Marion University
Phillip Bartlett, Francis Marion University
Henry Beam, Western Michigan University
Eugene Bland, Francis Marion University
Carol Braddock, Francis Marion University
Jim Camerius, Northern Michigan University
Thomas Carey, Western Michigan University
Johnnie Chamblee, Francis Marion University
Forest David, Francis Marion University
Satish Deshpande, Western Michigan University
Mary Dittman, Francis Marion University
Teresa Dullaghan, Francis Marion University
Ronald Earl, Sam Houston State University
Jule Eldridge, Francis Marion University
Caroline Fisher, Loyola University New Orleans
Steve Giordano, Francis Marion University

David Griffin, Francis Marion University
Christie Haney, Sam Houston State University
James Harbin, East Texas State University
Marilyn Helms, Dalton State College
Kay Lawrimore, Francis Marion University
Phillip Lynn, Francis Marion University
John Marcis, Coastal Carolina University
Maria Margiotis, Francis Marion University
Angela Page, Francis Marion University
Tyra Phipps, Frostburg State University
Paul Reed, Sam Houston State University
John Ross, Southwest Texas State University
Amit Shah, Frostburg State University
Frank Shipper, Arizona State University
Matthew Sonfield, Hofstra University
David Stanton, University of South Carolina
Charles Sterrett, Frostburg State University
Carolyn Stokes, Francis Marion University
Brian Williamson, Francis Marion University

Scores of Prentice Hall employees and salespersons have worked diligently behind the scenes to make this text a leader in the business policy market. I appreciate the continued hard work of all those persons.

I especially appreciate the wonderful work completed by the eighth edition ancillary authors as follows:

Bruce Barringer, *Instructor's Manual*
   University of Central Florida
Forest David, *Case Instructor's Manual*
   Francis Marion University
Amit Shah, *Test Item File and Companion Web Site Content*
   Frostburg State University

Tony Chelte, *PowerPoint Electronic and Overhead Color Transparencies*
   Western New England College
Forest David, *Case PowerPoints*
   Francis Marion University

I also want to thank you, the reader, for investing time and effort reading and studying this text. As we have entered the new millennium, this book will help you formulate, implement, and evaluate strategies for organizations with which you become associated. I hope you come to share my enthusiasm for the rich subject area of strategic management and for the systematic learning approach taken in this text.

Finally, I want to welcome and invite your suggestions, ideas, thoughts, and comments and questions regarding any part of this text or the ancillary materials. Please call me at 843-669-6960, fax me at 843-661-1432, e-mail me at Fdavid@Fmarion.edu, or write me at the School of Business, Francis Marion University, Florence, South Carolina 29501. I sincerely appreciate and need your input to continually improve this text in future editions. Drawing my attention to specific errors or deficiencies in coverage or exposition will especially be appreciated.

Thank you for using this text.

*Fred R. David*

# HOW TO LOCATE THE CASE COMPANIES

| | STOCK SYMBOL | STOCK EXCHANGE | TELEPHONE NUMBER | HEADQUARTERS ADDRESS | WEB PAGE ADDRESS |
|---|---|---|---|---|---|
| 1. E*Trade, Inc. | EGRP | NASD | 650-331-6000 | 4500 Bohannon Dr. Menlo Park, CA 94025 | www.etrade.com |
| 2. eBay Inc. | EBAY | NASD | 408-558-7400 | 2005 Hamilton Ave. San Jose, CA 95125 | www.ebay.com |
| 3. Amazon.com, Inc. | AMZN | NASD | 206-622-2335 | 1516 2nd Ave. Seattle, WA 98101 | www.amazon.com |
| 4. The Limited, Inc. | LTD | NY | 614-415-7000 | 3 Limited Pkwy. Columbus, OH 43216 | www.limited.com |
| 5. Wal-Mart Stores, Inc. | WMT | NY | 501-273-4000 | 702 S.W. Eighth St. Bentonville, AR 72716-8611 | www.wal-mart.com |
| 6. Target Corporation | DH | NY | 612-370-6948 | 777 Nicollet Mall Minneapolis, MN 55402-2055 | www.dhc.com |
| 7. Mandalay Resort Group | MBG | NY | 702-734-0410 | 3950 Las Vegas Blvd. Las Vegas, NV 89119 | www.mandalayresortgroup.com |
| 8. Harrah's Entertainment, Inc. | HET | NY | 901-762-8600 | 1023 Cherry Rd. Memphis, TN 38117 | www.harrahs.com |
| 9. First Union Corporation | FTU | NY | 704-374-6565 | 1 First Union Center Charlotte, NC 28288-0570 | www.firstunion.com |
| 10. Wachovia Corporation | WB | NY | 336-770-5000 | 100 N. Main St. Winston-Salem, NC 27105 | www.wachovia.com |
| 11. The Audubon Institute | N/A | N/A | 504-861-2537 | 6500 Magazine St. New Orleans, LA 70118 | www.auduboninstitute.org |
| 12. The Classic Car Club of America, Inc. | N/A | N/A | 847-390-0443 | 1645 Des Plaines River Rd. Suite 7 Des Plaines, Il 60018 | www.classiccarclub.com |
| 13. M. D. Anderson Biomedical Services Department | N/A | N/A | 713-792-7170 | Patient Care Facility M. D. Anderson Cancer Center Houston, TX 77030-4095 | www.mdanderson.org |
| 14. Quorum Health Group, Inc. | QHGI | NY | 615-371-7979 | 103 Continental Pl. Brentwood, TN 37027 | www.quorumhealth.com |
| 15. Greyhound Lines, Inc. | LDW | NASD | 214-849-8966 | 15110 N. Dallas Pkwy., #600 Dallas, TX 75248 | www.greyhound.com www.laidlaw.com |
| 16. Carnival Corporation | CCL | NY | 800-438-6744 305-599-2600 | 3655 N.W. 87th Ave. Miami, FL 33178 | www.carnivalcorp.com |
| 17. Southwest Airlines Co. | LUV | NY | 214-792-4000 | 2702 Love Field Dallas, TX 75235 | www.iflyswa.com www.southwest.com |
| 18. Central United Methodist Church | N/A | N/A | 843-662-3218 | 225 W. Cheves St. Florence, SC 29501 | www.centralumcsc.web.com |
| 19. Elkins Lake Baptist Church | N/A | N/A | 936-295-7694 | 206 Highway 19 Huntsville, TX 77340 | www.elbc.org |
| 20. RailTex, Inc. | RTEX | NASD | 210-841-7600 | 4040 Broadway, #200 San Antonio, TX 78209 | www.railtex.com |
| RailAmerica | RAIL | NASD | 561-237-1437 | 5300 Broken Sound Blvd., N.W. Boca Raton, FL 33487 | www.railamerica.com |

| | STOCK SYMBOL | STOCK EXCHANGE | TELEPHONE NUMBER | HEADQUARTERS ADDRESS | WEB PAGE ADDRESS |
|---|---|---|---|---|---|
| 21. Harley-Davidson, Inc. | HDI | NY | 414-342-4680 | 3700 W. Juneau Ave. Milwaukee, WI 53208 | www.harley-davidson.com |
| 22. Winnebago Industries, Inc. | WGO | NY | 515-582-3535 | 605 W. Crystal Lake Rd. Forest City, IA 50436 | www.winnebagoind.com |
| 23. Avon Products, Inc. | AVP | NY | 212-546-6015 212-282-5000 | 1345 Avenue of the Americas New York, NY 10105-0196 | www.avon.com |
| 24. Revlon, Inc. | REV | NY | 212-527-4000 | 625 Madison Ave. New York, NY 10022 | www.revlon.com |
| 25. Pilgrim's Pride Corporation | CHX | NY | 903-855-1000 | 110 South Texas St. Pittsburg, TX 75686 | www.pilgrimspride.com |
| 26. H. J. Heinz Company | HNZ | NY | 412-456-5700 | 600 Grant St. Pittsburg, PA 15219 | www.heinz.com |
| 27. Hershey Foods Corporation | HSY | NY | 717-534-6799 | 100 Crystal Dr. Hershey, PA 17033 | www.hersheys.com |
| 28. The Boeing Company | BA | NY | 206-655-2121 | 7755 E. Marginal Way S. Seattle, WA 98108 | www.boeing.com |
| 29. Lockheed Martin Corporation | LMT | NY | 800-568-9758 301-897-6000 | 6801 Rockledge Dr. Bethesda, MD 20817 | www.lockheedmartin.com |
| 30. Dell Computer Corporation | DELL | NASD | 512-338-4400 | 1 Dell Way Round Rock, TX 78682 | www.dell.com |
| 31. Apple Computer, Inc. | AAPL | NASD | 408-996-1010 800-692-7753 | 1 Infinite Loop Cupertino, CA 95014 | www.apple.com |
| 32. Compaq Computer Corporation | CPQ | NY | 281-370-0670 | 20555 State Hwy. 249 Houston, TX 77070 | www.compaq.com |
| 33. Research in Motion | RIMM | NASD | 519-888-7465 | 295 Phillip St. Waterloo, Ontario N2L 3W8 Canada | www.rim.net |
| 34. Stryker Corporation | SYK | NY | 616-385-2600 | 2775 Fairfield Rd. Kalamazoo, MI 49002 | www.strykercorp.com |
| 35. Biomet, Inc. | BMET | NASD | 219-267-6639 | Airport Industrial Pk. Warsaw, Indiana 46581 | www.biomet.com |
| 36. Playboy Enterprises, Inc. | PLA | NY | 312-751-8000 | 680 N. Lake Shore Dr. Chicago, IL 60611 | www.playboy.com |
| 37. Reader's Digest Association, Inc. | RDA | NY | 914-238-1000 | Reader's Digest Rd. Pleasantville, NY 10570-7000 | www.readersdigest.com |
| 38. Nike, Inc. | NKE | NY | 503-671-6453 800-806-6453 | 1 Bowerman Dr. Beaverton, OR 97005 | www.nike.com |
| 39. Reebok International, Ltd. | RBK | NY | 781-401-5000 | 100 Technology Center Dr. Stroughton, MA 02072 | www.reebok.com |
| 40. UST, Inc. | UST | NY | 203-661-1100 | 100 W. Putnam Ave. Greenwich, CT 06830 | www.shareholder.com/ust |

# INTRODUCTION

# HOW TO ANALYZE A BUSINESS POLICY CASE

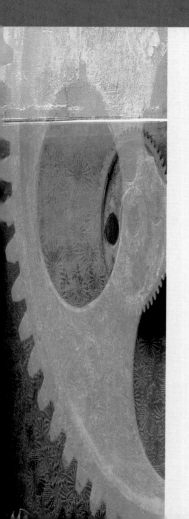

## OUTLINE

- What Is a Business Policy Case?
- Guidelines for Preparing Case Analyses
- Preparing a Case for Class Discussion
- Preparing a Written Case Analysis
- Making an Oral Presentation
- Fifty Tips for Success in Case Analysis

## OBJECTIVES

*After studying this chapter, you should be able to do the following:*

1. Describe the case method for learning strategic-management concepts.
2. Identify the steps in preparing a comprehensive written case analysis.
3. Describe how to give an effective oral case analysis presentation.
4. Discuss fifty tips for doing case analysis.

# NOTABLE QUOTES

The essential fact that makes the case method an educational experience of the greatest power is that it makes the student an active rather than a passive participant.

WALLACE B. DONHAM

Two heads are better than one.

UNKNOWN AUTHOR

Good writers do not turn in their first draft. Ask someone else to read your written case analysis, and read it out loud to yourself. That way, you can find rough areas to clear up.

LAWRENCE JAUCH

One reaction frequently heard is, "I don't have enough information." In reality, strategists never have enough information because some information is not available and some is too costly.

WILLIAM GLUECK

I keep six honest serving men. They taught me all I know. Their names are What, Why, When, How, Where, and Who.

RUDYARD KIPLING

Don't recommend anything you would not be prepared to do yourself if you were in the decision maker's shoes.

A. J. STRICKLAND III

A picture is worth a thousand words.

UNKNOWN AUTHOR

The purpose of this section is to help you analyze business policy cases. Guidelines for preparing written and oral case analyses are given, and suggestions for preparing cases for class discussion are presented. Steps to follow in preparing case analyses are provided. Guidelines for making an oral presentation are described.

## WHAT IS A BUSINESS POLICY CASE?

A *business policy case* describes an organization's external and internal condition and raises issues concerning the firm's mission, strategies, objectives, and policies. Most of the information in a business policy case is established fact, but some information may be opinions, judgments, and beliefs. Business policy cases are more comprehensive than those you may have studied in other courses. They generally include a description of related management, marketing, finance/accounting, production/operations, R&D, computer information systems, and natural environment issues. A business policy case puts the reader on the scene of the action by describing a firm's situation at some point in time. Business policy cases are written to give you practice applying strategic-management concepts. The case method for studying strategic management is often called *learning by doing.*

## GUIDELINES FOR PREPARING CASE ANALYSES

### The Need for Practicality

There is no such thing as a complete case, and no case ever gives you all the information you need to conduct analyses and make recommendations. Likewise, in the business world, strategists never have all the information they need to make decisions: information may be unavailable, too costly to obtain, or may take too much time to obtain. So, in preparing business policy cases, do what strategists do every day—make reasonable assumptions about unknowns, state assumptions clearly, perform appropriate analyses, and make decisions. *Be practical.* For example, in performing a pro forma financial analysis, make reasonable assumptions, state them appropriately, and proceed to show what impact your recommendations are expected to have on the organization's financial position. Avoid saying, "I don't have enough information." You can always supplement the information provided in a case with Internet and library research.

### The Need for Justification

The most important part of analyzing cases is not what strategies you recommend, but rather how you support your decisions and how you propose that they be implemented. There is no single best solution or one right answer to a case, so give ample justification for your recommendations. This is important. In the business world, strategists usually do not know if their decisions are right until resources have been allocated and consumed. Then it is often too late to reverse the decisions. This cold fact accents the need for careful integration of intuition and analysis in preparing business policy case analyses.

### The Need for Realism

Avoid recommending a course of action beyond an organization's means. *Be realistic.* No organization can possibly pursue all the strategies that could potentially benefit the firm. Estimate how much capital will be required to implement what you recommended.

Determine whether debt, stock, or a combination of debt and stock could be used to obtain the capital. Make sure your recommendations are feasible. Do not prepare a case analysis that omits all arguments and information not supportive of your recommendations. Rather, present the major advantages and disadvantages of several feasible alternatives. Try not to exaggerate, stereotype, prejudge, or overdramatize. Strive to demonstrate that your interpretation of the evidence is reasonable and objective.

## The Need for Specificity

Do not make broad generalizations such as "The company should pursue a market penetration strategy." *Be specific* by telling what, why, when, how, where, and who. Failure to use specifics is the single major shortcoming of most oral and written case analyses. For example, in an internal audit say, "The firm's current ratio fell from 2.2 in 2000 to 1.3 in 2001, and this is considered to be a major weakness," instead of, "The firm's financial condition is bad." Rather than concluding from a SPACE Matrix that a firm should be defensive, be more specific, saying, "The firm should consider closing three plants, laying off 280 employees, and divesting itself of its chemical division, for a net savings of $20.2 million in 2001." Use ratios, percentages, numbers, and dollar estimates. Businesspeople dislike generalities and vagueness.

## The Need for Originality

Do not necessarily recommend the course of action that the firm plans to take or actually undertook, even if those actions resulted in improved revenues and earnings. The aim of case analysis is for you to consider all the facts and information relevant to the organization at the time, generate feasible alternative strategies, choose among those alternatives, and defend your recommendations. Put yourself back in time to the point when strategic decisions were being made by the firm's strategists. Based on information available then, what would you have done? Support your position with charts, graphs, ratios, analyses, and the like—not a revelation from the library. You can become a good strategist by thinking through situations, making management assessments, and proposing plans yourself. *Be original.* Compare and contrast what you recommend versus what the company plans to do or did.

## The Need to Contribute

Strategy formulation, implementation, and evaluation decisions are commonly made by a group of individuals rather than by a single person. Therefore, your professor may divide the class into three- or four-person teams to prepare written or oral case analyses. Members of a strategic-management team, in class or in the business world, differ on their aversion to risk, their concern for short-run versus long-run benefits, their attitudes toward social responsibility, and their views concerning globalization. There are no perfect people, so there are no perfect strategists. Be open-minded to others' views. *Be a good listener and a good contributor.*

## PREPARING A CASE FOR CLASS DISCUSSION

Your professor may ask you to prepare a case for class discussion. Preparing a case for class discussion means that you need to read the case before class, make notes regarding the organization's external opportunities/threats and internal strengths/weaknesses, perform appropriate analyses, and come to class prepared to offer and defend some specific recommendations.

### The Case Method Versus Lecture Approach

The case method of teaching is radically different from the traditional lecture approach, in which little or no preparation is needed by students before class. The *case method* involves a classroom situation in which students do most of the talking; your professor facilitates discussion by asking questions and encouraging student interaction regarding ideas, analyses, and recommendations. Be prepared for a discussion along the lines of, "What would you do, why would you do it, when would you do it, and how would you do it?" Prepare answers to the following types of questions:

- What are the firm's most important external opportunities and threats?
- What are the organization's major strengths and weaknesses?
- How would you describe the organization's financial condition?
- What are the firm's existing strategies and objectives?
- Who are the firm's competitors and what are their strategies?
- What objectives and strategies do you recommend for this organization? Explain your reasoning. How does what you recommend compare to what the company plans?
- How could the organization best implement what you recommend? What implementation problems do you envision? How could the firm avoid or solve those problems?

### The Cross-Examination

Do not hesitate to take a stand on the issues and to support your position with objective analyses and outside research. Strive to apply strategic-management concepts and tools in preparing your case for class discussion. Seek defensible arguments and positions. Support opinions and judgments with facts, reasons, and evidence. Crunch the numbers before class! Be willing to describe your recommendations to the class without fear of disapproval. Respect the ideas of others, but be willing to go against the majority opinion when you can justify a better position.

Business policy case analysis gives you the opportunity to learn more about yourself, your colleagues, strategic management, and the decision-making process in organizations. The rewards of this experience will depend upon the effort you put forth, so do a good job. Discussing business policy cases in class is exciting and challenging. Expect views counter to those you present. Different students will place emphasis on different aspects of an organization's situation and submit different recommendations for scrutiny and rebuttal. Cross-examination discussions commonly arise, just as they occur in a real business organization. Avoid being a silent observer.

 ## PREPARING A WRITTEN CASE ANALYSIS

In addition to asking you to prepare a case for class discussion, your professor may ask you to prepare a written case analysis. Preparing a written case analysis is similar to preparing a case for class discussion, except written reports are generally more structured and more detailed. There is no ironclad procedure for preparing a written case analysis because cases differ in focus; the type, size, and complexity of the organizations being analyzed also vary.

When writing a strategic-management report or case analysis, avoid using jargon, vague or redundant words, acronyms, abbreviations, sexist language, and ethnic or racial slurs, and watch your spelling. Use short sentences and paragraphs and simple words and phrases. Use quite a few subheadings. Arrange issues and ideas from the most important to the least important. Arrange recommendations from the least controversial to the most controversial. Use the active voice rather than the passive voice for all verbs; for example, say, "Our team recommends that the company diversify," rather than, "It is recommended by our team to diversify." Use many examples to add specificity and clarity. Tables, figures, pie charts, bar charts, time lines, and other kinds of exhibits help communicate important points and ideas. Sometimes a picture *is* worth a thousand words.

## The Executive Summary

Your professor may ask you to focus the written case analysis on a particular aspect of the strategic-management process, such as (1) to identify and evaluate the organization's existing mission, objectives, and strategies; or (2) to propose and defend specific recommendations for the company; or (3) to develop an industry analysis by describing the competitors, products, selling techniques, and market conditions in a given industry. These types of written reports are sometimes called *executive summaries.* An executive summary usually ranges from three to five pages of text in length, plus exhibits.

## The Comprehensive Written Analysis

Your professor may ask you to prepare a *comprehensive written analysis.* This assignment requires you to apply the entire strategic-management process to the particular organization. When preparing a comprehensive written analysis, picture yourself as a consultant who has been asked by a company to conduct a study of its external and internal environment and make specific recommendations for its future. Prepare exhibits to support your recommendations. Highlight exhibits with some discussion in the paper. Comprehensive written analyses are usually about ten pages in length, plus exhibits.

## Steps in Preparing a Comprehensive Written Analysis

In preparing a comprehensive written analysis, you could follow the steps outlined here, which correlate to the stages in the strategic-management process and the chapters in this text.

| | | |
|---|---|---|
| *Step* | *1* | Identify the firm's existing mission, objectives, and strategies. |
| *Step* | *2* | Develop a mission statement for the organization. |
| *Step* | *3* | Identify the organization's external opportunities and threats. |
| *Step* | *4* | Construct a Competitive Profile Matrix. |
| *Step* | *5* | Construct an EFE Matrix. |
| *Step* | *6* | Identify the organization's internal strengths and weaknesses. |
| *Step* | *7* | Construct an IFE Matrix. |
| *Step* | *8* | Prepare a TOWS Matrix, SPACE Matrix, BCG Matrix, IE Matrix, Grand Strategy Matrix, and QSPM as appropriate. Give advantages and disadvantages of alternative strategies. |
| *Step* | *9* | Recommend specific strategies and long-term objectives. Show how much your recommendations will cost. Itemize these costs clearly for each projected year. Compare your recommendations to actual strategies planned by the company. |
| *Step* | *10* | Specify how your recommendations can be implemented and what results you can expect. Prepare forecasted ratios and pro forma financial statements. Present a timetable or agenda for action. |
| *Step* | *11* | Recommend specific annual objectives and policies. |
| *Step* | *12* | Recommend procedures for strategy review and evaluation. |

## MAKING AN ORAL PRESENTATION

Your professor may ask you to prepare a business policy case analysis, individually or as a group, and present your analysis to the class. Oral presentations are usually graded on two parts: content and delivery. *Content* refers to the quality, quantity, correctness, and appropriateness of analyses presented, including such dimensions as logical flow through the presentation, coverage of major issues, use of specifics, avoidance of generalities, absence of mistakes, and feasibility of recommendations. *Delivery* includes such dimensions as audience attentiveness, clarity of visual aids, appropriate dress, persuasiveness of arguments, tone of voice, eye contact, and posture. Great ideas are of no value unless others can be convinced of their merit through clear communication. The guidelines presented here can help you make an effective oral presentation.

### Organizing the Presentation

Begin your presentation by introducing yourself and giving a clear outline of topics to be covered. If a team is presenting, specify the sequence of speakers and the areas each person will address. At the beginning of an oral presentation, try to capture your audience's interest and attention. You could do this by displaying some products made by the company, telling an interesting short story about the company, or sharing an experience that you had related to the company, its products, or its services. You could develop or obtain a video to show at the beginning of class; you could visit a local distributor of the firm's products and tape a personal interview with the business owner or manager. A light or humorous introduction can be effective at the beginning of a presentation.

Be sure the setting of your presentation is well organized, with chairs, flip charts, a transparency projector, and whatever else you plan to use. Arrive at least fifteen minutes early at the classroom to organize the setting, and be sure your materials are ready to go. Make sure everyone can see your visual aids well.

### Controlling Your Voice

An effective rate of speaking ranges from 100 to 125 words per minute. Practice your presentation out loud to determine if you are going too fast. Individuals commonly speak too fast when nervous. Breathe deeply before and during the presentation to help yourself slow down. Have a cup of water available; pausing to take a drink will wet your throat, give you time to collect your thoughts, control your nervousness, slow you down, and signal to the audience a change in topic.

Avoid a monotone by placing emphasis on different words or sentences. Speak loudly and clearly, but don't shout. Silence can be used effectively to break a monotone voice. Stop at the end of each sentence, rather than running sentences together with *and* or *uh.*

### Managing Body Language

Be sure not to fold your arms, lean on the lectern, put your hands in your pockets, or put your hands behind you. Keep a straight posture, with one foot slightly in front of the other. Do not turn your back to the audience, which is not only rude but which also prevents your voice from projecting well. Avoid using too many hand gestures. On occasion leave the podium or table and walk toward your audience, but do not walk around too much. Never block the audience's view of your visual aids.

Maintain good eye contact throughout the presentation. This is the best way to persuade your audience. There is nothing more reassuring to a speaker than to see members of the audience nod in agreement or smile. Try to look everyone in the eye at least once during your presentation, but focus more on individuals who look interested than on persons who seem bored. Use humor and smiles as appropriate throughout your presentation to stay in touch with your audience. A presentation should never be dull!

## Speaking from Notes

Be sure not to read to your audience, because reading puts people to sleep. Perhaps worse than reading is memorizing. Do not try to memorize anything. Rather, practice using notes unobtrusively. Make sure your notes are written clearly so you will not flounder trying to read your own writing. Include only main ideas on your note cards. Keep note cards on a podium or table if possible so that you won't drop them or get them out of order; walking with note cards tends to be distracting.

## Constructing Visual Aids

Make sure your visual aids are legible to individuals in the back of the room. Use color to highlight special items. Avoid putting complete sentences on visual aids; rather, use short phrases and then elaborate on issues orally as you make your presentation. Generally, there should be no more than four to six lines of text on each visual aid. Use clear headings and subheadings. Be careful about spelling and grammar; use a consistent style of lettering. Use masking tape or an easel for posters—do not hold posters in your hand. Transparencies and handouts are excellent aids; however, be careful not to use too many handouts or your audience may concentrate on them instead of you during the presentation.

## Answering Questions

It is best to field questions at the end of your presentation, rather than during the presentation itself. Encourage questions and take your time to respond to each one. Answering questions can be persuasive because it involves you with the audience. If a team is giving the presentation, the audience should direct questions to a specific person. During the question and answer period, be polite, confident, and courteous. Avoid verbose responses. Do not get defensive with your answers, even if a hostile or confrontational question is asked. Staying calm during potentially disruptive situations such as a cross-examination reflects self-confidence, maturity, poise, and command of the particular company and its industry. Stand up throughout the question and answer period.

## FIFTY TIPS FOR SUCCESS IN CASE ANALYSIS

Business policy students who have used this text over seven editions offer you the following fifty tips for success in doing case analysis:

1.  View your case analysis and presentation as a product that must have some competitive factor to differentiate it favorably from the case analyses of other students.
2.  Prepare your case analysis far enough in advance of the due date to allow time for reflection and practice. Do not procrastinate.
3.  Develop a mind-set of "why," continually questioning your own and others' assumptions and assertions.
4.  The best ideas are lost if not communicated to the reader, so as ideas develop, think of their most appropriate presentation.

5. Maintain a positive attitude about the class, working *with* problems rather than against them.

6. Keep in tune with your professor and understand his or her values and expectations.

7. Since business policy is a capstone course, seek the help of professors in other specialty areas as needed.

8. Other students will have strengths in functional areas that will complement your weaknesses, so develop a cooperative spirit that moderates competitiveness in group work.

9. Read your case frequently as work progresses so you don't overlook details.

10. When preparing a case analysis as a group, divide into separate teams to work on the external analysis and internal analysis. Each team should write its section as if it were to go into the paper, then give each group member a copy.

11. At the end of each group session, assign each member of the group a task to be completed for the next meeting.

12. Have a good sense of humor.

13. Capitalize on the strengths of each member of the group; volunteer your services in your areas of strength.

14. Set goals for yourself and your team; budget your time to attain them.

15. Become friends with the library.

16. Foster attitudes that encourage group participation and interaction. Do not be hasty to judge group members.

17. Be creative and innovative throughout the case analysis process.

18. Be prepared to work. There will be times when you will have to do more than your share. Accept it, and do what you have to do to move the team forward.

19. Think of your case analysis as if it were really happening; do not reduce case analysis to a mechanical process.

20. To uncover flaws in your analysis and to prepare the group for questions during an oral presentation, assign one person in the group to actively play the devil's advocate.

21. Do not schedule excessively long group meetings; two-hour sessions are about right.

22. A goal of case analysis is to improve your ability to think clearly in ambiguous and confusing situations; do not get frustrated that there is no single best answer.

23. Push your ideas hard enough to get them listened to, but then let up; listen to others and try to follow their lines of thinking; follow the flow of group discussion, recognizing when you need to get back on track; do not repeat yourself or others unless clarity or progress demands repetition.

24. Do not confuse symptoms with causes; do not develop conclusions and solutions prematurely; recognize that information may be misleading, conflicting, or wrong.

25. Work hard to develop the ability to formulate reasonable, consistent, and creative plans; put yourself in the strategist's position.

26. Develop confidence in using quantitative tools for analysis. They are not inherently difficult; it is just practice and familiarity you need.

27. Develop a case-writing style that is direct, assertive, and convincing; be concise, precise, fluent, and correct.

28. Have fun when at all possible. It is frustrating at times, but enjoy it while you can; it may be several years before you are playing CEO again.

29. Acquire a professional typist and proofreader. Do not perform either task alone.

30. Strive for excellence in writing and technical preparation of your case. Prepare nice charts, tables, diagrams, and graphs. Use color and unique pictures. No messy exhibits!

31. In group cases, do not allow personality differences to interfere. When they occur, they must be understood for what they are and put aside.

32. Do not forget that the objective is to learn; explore areas with which you are not familiar.

33. Pay attention to detail.

34. Think through alternative implications fully and realistically. The consequences of decisions are not always apparent. They often affect many different aspects of a firm's operations.

35. Get things written down (drafts) as soon as possible.

36. Read everything that other group members write, and comment on it in writing. This allows group input into all aspects of case preparation.

37. Provide answers to such fundamental questions as what, when, where, why, and how.

38. Adaptation and flexibility are keys to success; be creative and innovative.

39. Do not merely recite ratios or present figures. Rather, develop ideas and conclusions concerning the possible trends. Show the importance of these figures to the corporation.

40. Support reasoning and judgment with factual data whenever possible.

41. Neatness is a real plus; your case analysis should look professional.

42. Your analysis should be as detailed and specific as possible.

43. A picture speaks a thousand words, and a creative picture gets you an A in many classes.

44. Let someone else read and critique your paper several days before you turn it in.

45. Emphasize the Strategy Selection and Strategy Implementation sections. A common mistake is to spend too much time on the external or internal analysis parts of your paper. Always remember that the meat of the paper or presentation is the strategy selection and implementation sections.

46. Make special efforts to get to know your group members. This leads to more openness in the group and allows for more interchange of ideas. Put in the time and effort necessary to develop these relationships.

47. Be constructively critical of your group members' work. Do not dominate group discussions. Be a good listener and contributor.

48. Learn from past mistakes and deficiencies. Improve upon weak aspects of other case presentations.

49. Learn from the positive approaches and accomplishments of classmates.

50. Join the Strategic Management Club Online at www.strategyclub.com.

## Current Readings

FIELEN, JOHN. "Clear Writing Is Not Enough." *Management Review* (April 1989): 49–53.

HOLCOMBE, M., and J. STEIN. *Presentation for Decision Makers* (Belmont, CA.: Lifetime Learning Publications, 1983).

————*Writing for Decision Makers* (Belmont, CA.: Lifetime Learning Publications, 1981).

JEFFRIES, J., and J. BATES. *The Executive's Guide to Meetings, Conferences, and Audiovisual Presentations* (New York: McGraw-Hill, 1983).

SHURTER, R., J. P. WILLIAMSON, and W. BROEHL. *Business Research and Report Writing* (New York: McGraw-Hill, 1965).

STRUNK, W., and E. B. WHITE. *The Elements of Style* (New York: Macmillan, 1978).

ZALL, P., and L. FRANC. *Practical Writing in Business and Industry* (North Scituate, MA.: Duxbury Press, 1978).

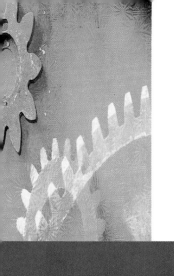

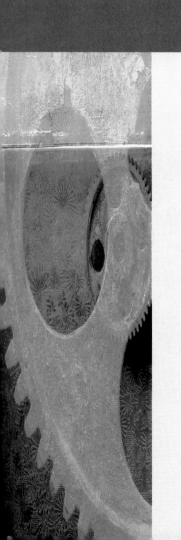

# STRATEGIC
# MANAGEMENT
## CONCEPTS

# *1* THE NATURE OF STRATEGIC MANAGEMENT

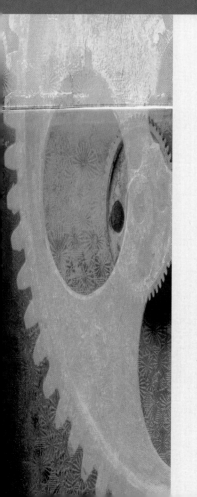

## CHAPTER OUTLINE

- What Is Strategic Management?
- Key Terms in Strategic Management
- The Strategic-Management Model
- Benefits of Strategic Management
- Why Some Firms Do No Strategic Planning
- Pitfalls in Strategic Planning
- Guidelines for Effective Strategic Management
- Business Ethics and Strategic Management
- Comparing Business and Military Strategy
- The Nature of Global Competition
- The Cohesion Case and Experiential Exercises
- The Cohesion Case: America Online, Inc., 2000

**EXPERIENTIAL EXERCISE 1A**
*Strategy Analysis for America Online (AOL)*

**EXPERIENTIAL EXERCISE 1B**
*Developing a Code of Business Ethics for America Online (AOL)*

**EXPERIENTIAL EXERCISE 1C**
*The Ethics of Spying on Competitors*

**EXPERIENTIAL EXERCISE 1D**
*Strategic Planning for My University*

**EXPERIENTIAL EXERCISE 1E**
*Strategic Planning at a Local Company*

**EXPERIENTIAL EXERCISE 1F**
*Does My University Recruit in Foreign Countries?*

## CHAPTER OBJECTIVES

*After studying this chapter, you should be able to do the following:*

1. Describe the strategic-management process.
2. Explain the need for integrating analysis and intuition in strategic management.
3. Define and give examples of key terms in strategic management.
4. Discuss the nature of strategy formulation, implementation, and evaluation activities.
5. Describe the benefits of good strategic management.
6. Explain why good ethics is good business in strategic management.
7. Explain the advantages and disadvantages of entering global markets.

# NOTABLE QUOTES

If we know where we are and something about how we got there, we might see where we are trending—and if the outcomes which lie naturally in our course are unacceptable, to make timely change.

ABRAHAM LINCOLN

Without a strategy, an organization is like a ship without a rudder, going around in circles. It's like a tramp; it has no place to go.

JOEL ROSS AND MICHAEL KAMI

Plans are less important than planning.

DALE MCCONKEY

The formulation of strategy can develop competitive advantage only to the extent that the process can give meaning to workers in the trenches.

DAVID HURST

Most of us fear change. Even when our minds say change is normal, our stomachs quiver at the prospect. But for strategists and managers today, there is no choice but to change.

ROBERT WATERMAN, JR.

If business is not based on ethical grounds, it is of no benefit to society, and will, like all other unethical combinations, pass into oblivion.

C. MAX KILLAN

If a man take no thought about what is distant, he will find sorrow near at hand. He who will not worry about what is far off will soon find something worse than worry.

CONFUCIUS

It is human nature to make decisions based on emotion, rather than fact. But nothing could be more illogical.

TOSHIBA CORPORATION

No business can do everything. Even if it has the money, it will never have enough good people. It has to set priorities. The worst thing to do is a little bit of everything. This makes sure that nothing is being accomplished. It is better to pick the wrong priority than none at all.

PETER DRUCKER

Executives, consultants, and B-school professors all agree that strategic planning is now the single most important management issue and will remain so for the next five years. Strategy has become a part of the main agenda at lots of organizations today. Strategic planning is back with a vengeance.

JOHN BYRNE

Planners should not plan, but serve as facilitators, catalysts, inquirers, educators, and synthesizers to guide the planning process effectively.

A. HAX AND N. MAJLUF

This chapter provides an overview of strategic management. It introduces a practical, integrative model of the strategic-management process and defines basic activities and terms in strategic management and discusses the importance of business ethics.

This chapter initiates several themes that permeate all chapters of this text. First, *global considerations impact virtually all strategic decisions!* The boundaries of countries no longer can define the limits of our imaginations. To see and appreciate the world from the perspective of others has become a matter of survival for businesses. The underpinnings of strategic management hinge upon managers' gaining an understanding of competitors, markets, prices, suppliers, distributors, governments, creditors, shareholders, and customers worldwide. The price and quality of a firm's products and services must be competitive on a worldwide basis, not just a local basis. A Global Perspective is provided in all chapters of this text to emphasize the importance of global factors in strategic management.

A second theme is that *electric commerce (e-commerce) has become a vital strategic-management tool.* An increasing number of companies are gaining competitive advantage by using the Internet for direct selling and for communication with suppliers, customers, creditors, partners, shareholders, clients, and competitors who may be dispersed globally. E-commerce allows firms to sell products, advertise, purchase supplies, bypass intermediaries, track inventory, eliminate paperwork, and share information. In total, electronic commerce is minimizing the expense and cumbersomeness of time, distance, and space in doing business, which yields better customer service, greater efficiency, improved products, and higher profitability.

The Internet and personal computers are changing the way we organize our lives; inhabit our homes; and relate to and interact with family, friends, neighbors, and even ourselves. The Internet promotes endless comparison shopping which enables consumers worldwide to band together to demand discounts. The Internet has transferred power from businesses to individuals so swiftly that in another decade there may be "regulations" imposed on groups of consumers. Politicians may one day debate the need for "regulation on consumers" rather than "regulation on big business" because of the Internet's empowerment of individuals. Buyers used to face big obstacles to getting the best price and service, such as limited time and data to compare, but now consumers can quickly scan hundreds of vendors offerings. Or they can go to Web sites such as CompareNet.com that offers detailed information on more than 100,000 consumer products.

The Internet has changed the very nature and core of buying and selling in nearly all industries. It has fundamentally changed the economics of business in every single industry worldwide. Slogans and companies such as e-Business, e-Services, e-Bay, e-Trade, e-commerce, e-mail, and e-Toys have become an integral part of everyday life worldwide. Business-to-business e-commerce is five times greater than consumer e-commerce. Fully 74 percent of Americans think the Internet will change society more than the telephone and television combined.[1] An Information Technology Perspective is included in each chapter to illustrate how electronic commerce impacts the strategic-management process.

A third theme is that *the natural environment has become an important strategic issue.* With the demise of communism and the end of the Cold War, perhaps there is now no greater threat to business and society than the continuous exploitation and decimation of our natural environment. Mark Starik at George Washington University says, "Halting and reversing worldwide ecological destruction and deterioration . . . is a strategic issue that needs immediate and substantive attention by all businesses and managers." A Natural Environment Perspective is provided in all chapters to illustrate how firms are addressing environmental concerns.

## WHAT IS STRATEGIC MANAGEMENT?

Once there were two company presidents who competed in the same industry. These two presidents decided to go on a camping trip to discuss a possible merger. They hiked deep into the woods. Suddenly, they came upon a grizzly bear that rose up on its hind legs and snarled. Instantly, the first president took off his knapsack and got out a pair of jogging shoes. The second president said, "Hey, you can't outrun that bear." The first president responded, "Maybe I can't outrun that bear, but I surely can outrun you!" This story captures the notion of strategic management, which is to achieve and maintain competitive advantage.

### Defining Strategic Management

*Strategic management* can be defined as the art and science of formulating, implementing, and evaluating cross-functional decisions that enable an organization to achieve its objectives. As this definition implies, strategic management focuses on integrating management, marketing, finance/accounting, production/operations, research and development, and computer information systems to achieve organizational success. The term strategic management in this text is used synonymously with the term strategic planning. The latter term is more often used in the business world, whereas the former is often used in academia. Sometimes the term strategic management is used to refer to strategy formulation, implementation, and evaluation, with strategic planning referring only to strategy formulation. The purpose of strategic management is to exploit and create new and different opportunities for tomorrow; long-range planning, in contrast, tries to optimize for tomorrow the trends of today.

The term strategic planning originated in the 1950s and was very popular between the mid-1960s to mid-1970s. During these years, strategic planning was widely believed to be the answer for all problems. At the time, much of corporate America was "obsessed" with strategic planning. Following that "boom" however, strategic planning was cast aside during the 1980s as various planning models did not yield higher returns. The 1990s however brought the revival of strategic planning, and the process is widely practiced today in the business world.

The term strategic management is used at many colleges and universities as the subtitle for the capstone course in business administration, Business Policy, which integrates material from all business courses. Consider joining the Strategic Management Club Online at www.strategyclub.com that offers many free benefits for business policy students.

### Stages of Strategic Management

The *strategic-management process* consists of three stages: strategy formulation, strategy implementation, and strategy evaluation. *Strategy formulation* includes developing a vision and mission, identifying an organization's external opportunities and threats, determining internal strengths and weaknesses, establishing long-term objectives, generating alternative strategies, and choosing particular strategies to pursue. Strategy-formulation issues include deciding what new businesses to enter, what businesses to abandon, how to allocate resources, whether to expand operations or diversify, whether to enter international markets, whether to merge or form a joint venture, and how to avoid a hostile takeover.

Because no organization has unlimited resources, strategists must decide which alternative strategies will benefit the firm most. Strategy-formulation decisions commit an organization to specific products, markets, resources, and technologies over an extended period of time. Strategies determine long-term competitive advantages. For better or worse, strategic decisions have major multifunctional consequences and enduring effects on an organization. Top managers have the best perspective to understand fully the ramifications of formulation decisions; they have the authority to commit the resources necessary for implementation.

*Strategy implementation* requires a firm to establish annual objectives, devise policies, motivate employees, and allocate resources so that formulated strategies can be executed; strategy implementation includes developing a strategy-supportive culture, creating an effective organizational structure, redirecting marketing efforts, preparing budgets, developing and utilizing information systems, and linking employee compensation to organizational performance.

Strategy implementation often is called the action stage of strategic management. Implementing strategy means mobilizing employees and managers to put formulated strategies into action. Often considered to be the most difficult stage in strategic management, strategy implementation requires personal discipline, commitment, and sacrifice. Successful strategy implementation hinges upon managers' ability to motivate employees, which is more an art than a science. Strategies formulated but not implemented serve no useful purpose.

Interpersonal skills are especially critical for successful strategy implementation. Strategy-implementation activities affect all employees and managers in an organization. Every division and department must decide on answers to questions such as "What must we do to implement our part of the organization's strategy?" and "How best can we get the job done?" The challenge of implementation is to stimulate managers and employees throughout an organization to work with pride and enthusiasm toward achieving stated objectives.

*Strategy evaluation* is the final stage in strategic management. Managers desperately need to know when particular strategies are not working well; strategy evaluation is the primary means for obtaining this information. All strategies are subject to future modification because external and internal factors are constantly changing. Three fundamental strategy-evaluation activities are (1) reviewing external and internal factors that are the bases for current strategies, (2) measuring performance, and (3) taking corrective actions. Strategy evaluation is needed because success today is no guarantee of success tomorrow! Success always creates new and different problems; complacent organizations experience demise.

Strategy formulation, implementation, and evaluation activities occur at three hierarchical levels in a large organization: corporate, divisional or strategic business unit, and functional. By fostering communication and interaction among managers and employees across hierarchical levels, strategic management helps a firm function as a competitive team. Most small businesses and some large businesses do not have divisions or strategic business units; they have only the corporate and functional levels. Nevertheless, managers and employees at these two levels should be actively involved in strategic-management activities.

Peter Drucker says the prime task of strategic management is thinking through the overall mission of a business:

> . . . that is, of asking the question, "What is our Business?" This leads to the setting of objectives, the development of strategies, and the making of today's decisions for tomorrow's results. This clearly must be done by a part of the organization that can see the entire business; that can balance objectives and the needs of today against the needs of tomorrow; and that can allocate resources of men and money to key results.[2]

## Integrating Intuition and Analysis

The strategic-management process can be described as an objective, logical, systematic approach for making major decisions in an organization. It attempts to organize qualitative and quantitative information in a way that allows effective decisions to be made under conditions of uncertainty. Yet, strategic management is not a pure science that lends itself to a nice, neat, one-two-three approach.

Based on past experiences, judgment, and feelings, *intuition* is essential to making good strategic decisions. Intuition is particularly useful for making decisions in situations of great uncertainty or little precedent. It is also helpful when highly interrelated variables exist, or when it is necessary to choose from several plausible alternatives. Some managers and owners of businesses profess to have extraordinary abilities for using intuition alone in devising brilliant strategies. For example, Will Durant, who organized General Motors Corporation, was described by Alfred Sloan as "a man who would proceed on a course of action guided solely, as far as I could tell, by some intuitive flash of brilliance. He never felt obliged to make an engineering hunt for the facts. Yet at times, he was astoundingly correct in his judgment."[3] Albert Einstein acknowledged the importance of intuition when he said, "I believe in intuition and inspiration. At times I feel certain that I am right while not knowing the reason. Imagination is more important than knowledge, because knowledge is limited, whereas imagination embraces the entire world."[4]

Although some organizations today may survive and prosper because they have intuitive geniuses managing them, most are not so fortunate. Most organizations can benefit from strategic management, which is based upon integrating intuition and analysis in decision making. Choosing an intuitive or analytic approach to decision making is not an either-or proposition. Managers at all levels in an organization inject their intuition and judgment into strategic-management analyses. Analytical thinking and intuitive thinking complement each other.

Operating from the I've-already-made-up-my-mind-don't-bother-me-with-the-facts mode is not management by intuition; it is management by ignorance.[5] Drucker says, "I believe in intuition only if you discipline it. 'Hunch' artists, who make a diagnosis but don't check it out with the facts, are the ones in medicine who kill people, and in management kill businesses."[6] As Henderson notes:

> The accelerating rate of change today is producing a business world in which customary managerial habits in organizations are increasingly inadequate. Experience alone was an adequate guide when changes could be made in small increments. But intuitive and experience-based management philosophies are grossly inadequate when decisions are strategic and have major, irreversible consequences.[7]

In a sense, the strategic-management process is an attempt to duplicate what goes on in the mind of a brilliant, intuitive person who knows the business and hinge it with analysis.

## Adapting to Change

The strategic-management process is based on the belief that organizations should continually monitor internal and external events and trends so that timely changes can be made as needed. The rate and magnitude of changes that affect organizations are increasing dramatically. Consider, for example, e-commerce, laser medicine, laser weapons, the aging population, and merger mania. To survive, all organizations must be capable of astutely identifying and adapting to change. The strategic-management process is aimed at allowing organizations to adapt effectively to change over the long run.

In today's business environment, more than any preceding era, the only constant is change. Successful organizations effectively manage change, continuously adapting their bureaucracies, strategies, systems, products, and cultures to survive the shocks and prosper from the forces that decimate the competition.[8]

Information technology and globalization are external changes that are transforming business and society today. On a political map, the boundaries between countries may be clear, but on a competitive map showing the real flow of financial and industrial activity, the boundaries have largely disappeared. Speedy flow of information has eaten away at national boundaries so that people worldwide readily see for themselves how other people live. People are traveling abroad more; ten million Japanese travel abroad annually. People are emigrating more; Germans to England and Mexicans to the United States are examples. As the Global Perspective indicates, U.S. firms are challenged by competitors in many industries. We are becoming a borderless world with global citizens, global competitors, global customers, global suppliers, and global distributors!

The need to adapt to change leads organizations to key strategic-management questions, such as, What kind of business should we become? Are we in the right fields? Should we reshape our business? What new competitors are entering our industry? What strategies should we pursue? How are our customers changing? Are new technologies being developed that could put us out of business?

 ## KEY TERMS IN STRATEGIC MANAGEMENT

Before we further discuss strategic management, we should define eight key terms: strategists, mission statements, external opportunities and threats, internal strengths and weaknesses, long-term objectives, strategies, annual objectives, and policies.

 # GLOBAL PERSPECTIVE

## Do U.S. Firms Dominate All Industries?

*The Wall Street Journal*'s annual ranking of the world's largest companies reveals that U.S. firms are being challenged in many industries. The world's ten largest insurance companies and banks are listed below in rank order. Note that U.S. firms do not dominate these two industries.

| Insurance Firms | Banks |
| --- | --- |
| Axa Group, France | Deutsche Bank, Germany |
| Allianz Group, Germany | UBS, Switzerland |
| Nippon Life, Japan | Bank of Tokyo-Mitsubishi, Japan |
| Zenkyoren & Prefectural Ins. Federations, Japan | Bank of America, U.S. |
| Dai-ichi Mutual Life, Japan | Fuji Bank, Japan |
| American International Group, U.S. | ABN Amro, Netherlands |
| Metropolitan Life Insurance, U.S. | HSBC Holdings, United Kingdom |
| Sumitomo Life, Japan | Credit Suisse Group, Switzerland |
| Zurich Financial Services Group, Switzerland | Bayerische Hypotheken & Vereinsbank, Germany |
| Prudential Corporation, United Kingdom | Sumitomo Bank, Japan |

Adapted from: "World Business," *The Wall Street Journal* (September 27, 1999): R30.

## Strategists

*Strategists* are individuals who are most responsible for the success or failure of an organization. Strategists have various job titles, such as chief executive officer, president, owner, chair of the board, executive director, chancellor, dean, or entrepreneur. Regarding entrepreneurs, there are now 9.1 million businesses owned by women. This represents 38 percent of all firms in the United States.[9] More than thirty million people nationwide are employed at female-owned firms.

Strategists help an organization gather, analyze, and organize information. They track industry and competitive trends, develop forecasting models and scenario analyses, evaluate corporate and divisional performance, spot emerging market opportunities, identify business threats, and develop creative action plans. Strategic planners usually serve in a support or staff role. Usually found in higher levels of management, they typically have considerable authority for decision making in the firm. The CEO is the most visible and critical strategic manager. Any manager who has responsibility for a unit or division, responsibility for profit and loss outcomes, or direct authority over a major piece of the business is a strategic manager (strategist).

Strategists differ as much as organizations themselves, and these differences must be considered in the formulation, implementation, and evaluation of strategies. Some strategists will not consider some types of strategies because of their personal philosophies. Strategists differ in their attitudes, values, ethics, willingness to take risks, concern for social responsibility, concern for profitability, concern for short-run versus long-run aims, and management style. The founder of Hershey Foods, Milton Hershey, built the company to manage an orphanage. From corporate profits, Hershey Foods today cares for over one thousand boys and girls in its School for Orphans.

Some strategists agree with Ralph Nader, who proclaims that organizations have tremendous social obligations. Others agree with Milton Friedman, an economist, who maintains that organizations have no obligation to do any more for society than is legally required. Most strategists agree that the first social responsibility of any business must be to make enough profit to cover the costs of the future, because if this is not achieved, no other social responsibility can be met. Strategists should examine social problems in terms of potential costs and benefits to the firm, and address social issues that could benefit the firm most.

## Vision and Mission Statements

Many organizations today develop a "vision statement" which answers the question, What do we want to become? Developing a vision statement is often considered the first step in strategic planning, preceding even development of a mission statement. Many vision statements are a single sentence. For example the vision statement of Stokes Eye Clinic in Florence, South Carolina, is "Our vision is to take care of your vision." The vision of the Institute of Management Accountants is "Global leadership in education, certification, and practice of management accounting and financial management."

*Mission statements* are "enduring statements of purpose that distinguish one business from other similar firms. A mission statement identifies the scope of a firm's operations in product and market terms."[10] It addresses the basic question that faces all strategists: What is our business? A clear mission statement describes the values and priorities of an organization. Developing a mission statement compels strategists to think about the nature and scope of present operations and to assess the potential attractiveness of future markets and activities. A mission statement broadly charts the future direction of an organization. An example mission statement is provided below for Microsoft.

> Microsoft's mission is to create software for the personal computer that empowers and enriches people in the workplace, at school and at home. Microsoft's early

vision of a computer on every desk and in every home is coupled today with a strong commitment to Internet-related technologies that expand the power and reach of the PC and its users. As the world's leading software provider, Microsoft strives to produce innovative products that meet our customers' evolving needs. At the same time, we understand that long-term success is about more than just making great products. Find out what we mean when we talk about Living Our Values (www.microsoft.com/mscorp/).

## External Opportunities and Threats

*External opportunities* and *external threats* refer to economic, social, cultural, demographic, environmental, political, legal, governmental, technological, and competitive trends and events that could significantly benefit or harm an organization in the future. Opportunities and threats are largely beyond the control of a single organization, thus the term *external.* The computer revolution, biotechnology, population shifts, changing work values and attitudes, space exploration, recyclable packages, and increased competition from foreign companies are examples of opportunities or threats for companies. These types of changes are creating a different type of consumer and consequently a need for different types of products, services, and strategies. Many companies in many industries face the severe external threat of online sales capturing increasing market share in their industry. For example, online grocery shopping accounted for $5 billion in sales in 1999, but it is expected to surge 116 percent to $10.8 billion by 2003—to the dismay of traditional grocers.[11]

Other opportunities and threats may include the passage of a law, the introduction of a new product by a competitor, a national catastrophe, or the declining value of the dollar. A competitor's strength could be a threat. Unrest in the Balkans, rising interest rates, or the war against drugs could represent an opportunity or a threat.

A basic tenet of strategic management is that firms need to formulate strategies to take advantage of external opportunities and to avoid or reduce the impact of external threats. For this reason, identifying, monitoring, and evaluating external opportunities and threats is essential for success. This process of conducting research and gathering and assimilating external information is sometimes called *environmental scanning* or industry analysis. Lobbying is one activity that some organizations utilize to influence external opportunities and threats.

## Internal Strengths and Weaknesses

*Internal strengths* and *internal weaknesses* are an organization's controllable activities that are performed especially well or poorly. They arise in the management, marketing, finance/accounting, production/operations, research and development, and computer information systems activities of a business. Identifying and evaluating organizational strengths and weaknesses in the functional areas of a business is an essential strategic-management activity. Organizations strive to pursue strategies that capitalize on internal strengths and improve on internal weaknesses.

Strengths and weaknesses are determined relative to competitors. *Relative* deficiency or superiority is important information. Also, strengths and weaknesses can be determined by elements of being rather than performance. For example, a strength may involve ownership of natural resources or an historic reputation for quality. Strengths and weaknesses may be determined relative to a firm's own objectives. For example, high levels of inventory turnover may not be a strength to a firm that seeks never to stock-out.

Internal factors can be determined in a number of ways that include computing ratios, measuring performance, and comparing to past periods and industry averages. Various types of surveys also can be developed and administered to examine internal factors such as employee morale, production efficiency, advertising effectiveness, and customer loyalty.

## Long-Term Objectives

*Objectives* can be defined as specific results that an organization seeks to achieve in pursuing its basic mission. *Long-term* means more than one year. Objectives are essential for organizational success because they state direction; aid in evaluation; create synergy; reveal priorities; focus coordination; and provide a basis for effective planning, organizing, motivating, and controlling activities. Objectives should be challenging, measurable, consistent, reasonable, and clear. In a multidimensional firm, objectives should be established for the overall company and for each division. Minnesota Power's long-term objectives are to achieve a 13 percent return on equity (ROE) in their core electric utility, 14 percent ROE on water resource operations, and 15 percent ROE on support businesses. Minnesota Power also strives to stay in the top 25 percent of electric utilities in the United States in terms of common stock's market-to-book ratio and to maintain an annual growth in earnings per share of 5 percent.

## Strategies

*Strategies* are the means by which long-term objectives will be achieved. Business strategies may include geographic expansion, diversification, acquisition, product development, market penetration, retrenchment, divestiture, liquidation, and joint venture. Strategies currently being pursued by Barnes & Noble, Starbucks, and Royal Numico are described in Table 1–1.

Strategies are potential actions that require top management decisions and large amounts of the firm's resources. In addition, strategies affect an organization's long-term prosperity, typically for at least five years, and thus are future-oriented. Strategies have multifunctional or multidivisional consequences and require consideration of both external and internal factors facing the firm.

### TABLE 1–1    Three Organizations' Strategies in 2000

**BARNES & NOBLE**

Barnes & Noble, the large bookseller, hesitated with an online strategy, while upstart Amazon.com captured huge market share in online bookselling. Despite huge capital expenditures and massive advertising in recent years, Barnes & Noble still remains barely more than one-tenth Amazon's size online. Barnes & Noble initially did not want to "cannibalize" its own core franchise. The lesson for other businesses may be that the Internet does not tolerate caution and hesitation. Many brick-and-mortar companies today "hesitate" with an online strategy because of perceived "cannibalism" with existing walk-in sales. Caution could spell disaster.

**STARBUCKS**

Headquartered in Seattle, Starbucks, the gourmet coffee company, is diversifying into noncoffee areas such as ice cream, candy, tea, specialty food, and even kitchen and home products. Starbucks is also expanding internationally by adding four hundred new stores in 1999 to its base of twenty-three hundred stores. The company has started selling products in supermarkets, as well as its own retail outlets, and this is causing discontent among some store managers. Starbucks has more than twenty-six thousand employees and annual sales of about $1.5 billion. Company profitability and stock performance are faltering.

**ROYAL NUMICO**

This large Dutch nutritional-products manufacturer recently acquired General Nutrition Companies (GNC), the leading American retailer and maker of vitamins and other supplements. Numico paid $1.7 billion for GNC creating the world's largest human nutrition company with annual sales over $3 billion. GNC has 4,203 retail stores and will now offer more patented products and more scientific data on products it sells. Numico now has more than 27,000 employees worldwide and much better control over distribution of its products.

### Annual Objectives

*Annual objectives* are short-term milestones that organizations must achieve to reach long-term objectives. Like long-term objectives, annual objectives should be measurable, quantitative, challenging, realistic, consistent, and prioritized. They should be established at the corporate, divisional, and functional levels in a large organization. Annual objectives should be stated in terms of management, marketing, finance/accounting, production/operations, research and development, and information systems accomplishments. A set of annual objectives is needed for each long-term objective. Annual objectives are especially important in strategy implementation, whereas long-term objectives are particularly important in strategy formulation. Annual objectives represent the basis for allocating resources.

Campbell Soup Corporation has an annual objective to achieve 20 percent growth in earnings, a 20 percent ROE, and a 20 percent return on invested cash. The company calls this ERC, for earnings, returns, and cash.

### Policies

*Policies* are the means by which annual objectives will be achieved. Policies include guidelines, rules, and procedures established to support efforts to achieve stated objectives. Policies are guides to decision making and address repetitive or recurring situations.

Policies are most often stated in terms of management, marketing, finance/accounting, production/operations, research and development, and computer information systems activities. Policies can be established at the corporate level and apply to an entire organization, at the divisional level and apply to a single division, or at the functional level and apply to particular operational activities or departments. Policies, like annual objectives, are especially important in strategy implementation because they outline an organization's expectations of its employees and managers. Policies allow consistency and coordination within and between organizational departments.

Substantial research suggests that a healthier workforce can more effectively and efficiently implement strategies. The National Center for Health Promotion estimates that more than 80 percent of all American corporations have No Smoking policies. No Smoking policies are usually derived from annual objectives that seek to reduce corporate medical costs associated with absenteeism and to provide a healthy workplace. Pullman Company in Garden Grove, California, charges smokers ten dollars more each month for health insurance than it charges nonsmokers. Smoking among American teens dropped from 20 to 18 percent from 1997 to 1998, while smoking among all Americans dropped from 30 to 28 percent during that time.[12]

## THE STRATEGIC-MANAGEMENT MODEL

The strategic-management process best can be studied and applied using a model. Every model represents some kind of process. The framework illustrated in Figure 1–1 is a widely accepted, comprehensive model of the strategic-management process.[13] This model does not guarantee success, but it does represent a clear and practical approach for formulating, implementing, and evaluating strategies. Relationships among major components of the strategic-management process are shown in the model, which appears in all subsequent chapters with appropriate areas shaped to show the particular focus of each chapter.

Identifying an organization's existing vision, mission, objectives, and strategies is the logical starting point for strategic management because a firm's present situation and condition may preclude certain strategies and may even dictate a particular course of action. Every organization has a vision, mission, objectives, and strategy, even if these

**FIGURE 1–1**

**A Comprehensive Strategic-Management Model**

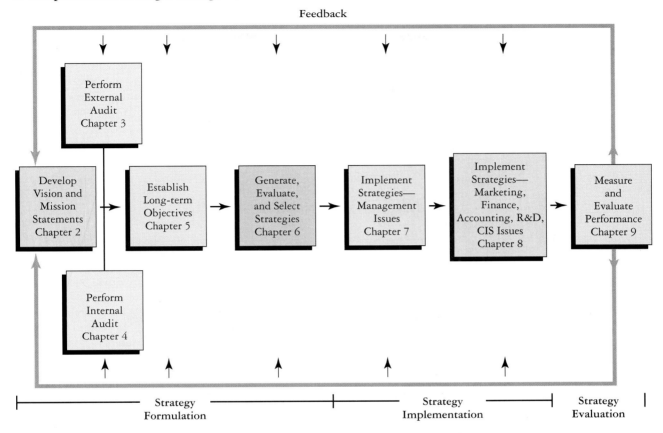

Source: Fred R. David, "How Companies Define Their Mission," *Long Range Planning* 22, no. 3 (June 1988): 40.

elements are not consciously designed, written, or communicated. The answer to where an organization is going can be determined largely by where the organization has been!

The strategic-management process is dynamic and continuous. A change in any one of the major components in the model can necessitate a change in any or all of the other components. For instance, a shift in the economy could represent a major opportunity and require a change in long-term objectives and strategies; a failure to accomplish annual objectives could require a change in policy; or a major competitor's change in strategy could require a change in the firm's mission. Therefore, strategy formulation, implementation, and evaluation activities should be performed on a continual basis, not just at the end of the year or semiannually. The strategic-management process never really ends.

The strategic-management process is not as cleanly divided and neatly performed in practice as the strategic-management model suggests. Strategists do not go through the process in lockstep fashion. Generally, there is give-and-take among hierarchical levels of an organization. Many organizations conduct formal meetings semiannually to discuss and update the firm's vision, mission, opportunities/threats, strengths/weaknesses, strategies, objectives, policies, and performance. These meetings are commonly held off-premises and called *retreats*. The rationale for periodically conducting strategic-management meetings away from the work site is to encourage more creativity and candor among participants. Good communication and feedback are needed throughout the strategic-management process.

Application of the strategic-management process is typically more formal in larger and well-established organizations. Formality refers to the extent that participants, responsibilities, authority, duties, and approach are specified. Smaller businesses tend to be less formal. Firms that compete in complex, rapidly changing environments such as technology companies tend to be more formal in strategic planning. Firms that have many divisions, products, markets, and technologies also tend to be more formal in applying strategic-management concepts. Greater formality in applying the strategic-management process is usually positively associated with the cost, comprehensiveness, accuracy, and success of planning across all types and sizes of organizations.[14]

 ## BENEFITS OF STRATEGIC MANAGEMENT

Strategic management allows an organization to be more proactive than reactive in shaping its own future; it allows an organization to initiate and influence (rather than just respond to) activities, and thus to exert control over its own destiny. Small business owners, chief executive officers, presidents, and managers of many for-profit and nonprofit organizations have recognized and realized the benefits of strategic management.

Historically, the principal benefit of strategic management has been to help organizations formulate better strategies through the use of a more systematic, logical, and rational approach to strategic choice. This certainly continues to be a major benefit of strategic management, but research studies now indicate that the process, rather than the decision or document, is the more important contribution of strategic management.[15] *Communication is a key to successful strategic management.* Through involvement in the process, managers and employees become committed to supporting the organization. Dialogue and participation are essential ingredients. The chief executive officer of Rockwell International explains, "We believe that fundamental to effective strategic management is fully informed employees at all organizational levels. We expect every business segment to inform every employee about the business objectives, the direction of the business, the progress towards achieving objectives, and our customers, competitors and product plans."

The manner in which strategic management is carried out is thus exceptionally important. A major aim of the process is to achieve understanding and commitment from all managers and employees. Understanding may be the most important benefit of strategic management, followed by commitment. When managers and employees understand what the organization is doing and why, they often feel a part of the firm and become committed to assisting it. This is especially true when employees also understand linkages between their own compensation and organizational performance. Managers and employees become surprisingly creative and innovative when they understand and support the firm's mission, objectives, and strategies. A great benefit of strategic management, then, is the opportunity that the process provides to empower individuals. *Empowerment* is the act of strengthening employees' sense of effectiveness by encouraging and rewarding them to participate in decision making and exercise initiative and imagination.

More and more organizations are decentralizing the strategic-management process, recognizing that planning must involve lower-level managers and employees. The notion of centralized staff planning is being replaced in organizations by decentralized line-manager planning. The process is a learning, helping, educating, and supporting activity, not merely a paper-shuffling activity among top executives. Strategic-management dialogue is more important than a nicely bound strategic-management document.[16] The worst thing strategists can do is develop strategic plans themselves and then present them to operating managers to execute. Through involvement in the process, line managers become "owners" of the strategy. Ownership of strategies by the people who have to execute them is a key to success!

Although making good strategic decisions is the major responsibility of an organization's owner or chief executive officer, managers and employees both must also be involved in strategy formulation, implementation, and evaluation activities. Participation is a key to gaining commitment for needed changes.

An increasing number of corporations and institutions are using strategic management to make effective decisions. But strategic management is not a guarantee for success; it can be dysfunctional if conducted haphazardly.

## Financial Benefits

Research indicates that organizations using strategic-management concepts are more profitable and successful than those that do not.[17] Businesses using strategic-management concepts show significant improvement in sales, profitability, and productivity compared to firms without systematic planning activities. High-performing firms tend to do systematic planning to prepare for future fluctuations in their external and internal environments. Firms with planning systems more closely resembling strategic-management theory generally exhibit superior long-term financial performance relative to their industry.

High-performing firms seem to make more informed decisions with good anticipation of both short- and long-term consequences. On the other hand, firms that perform poorly often engage in activities that are shortsighted and do not reflect good forecasting of future conditions. Strategists of low-performing organizations are often preoccupied with solving internal problems and meeting paperwork deadlines. They typically underestimate their competitors' strengths and overestimate their own firm's strengths. They often attribute weak performance to uncontrollable factors such as poor economy, technological change, or foreign competition.

Dun & Bradstreet reports that more than 100,000 businesses in the United States fail annually. Business failures include bankruptcies, foreclosures, liquidations, and court-mandated receiverships. Although many factors besides a lack of effective strategic management can lead to business failure, the planning concepts and tools described in this text can yield substantial financial benefits for any organization. An excellent Web site for businesses engaged in strategic planning is www.checkmateplan.com.

## Nonfinancial Benefits

Besides helping firms avoid financial demise, strategic management offers other tangible benefits, such as an enhanced awareness of external threats, an improved understanding of competitors' strategies, increased employee productivity, reduced resistance to change, and a clearer understanding of performance-reward relationships. Strategic management enhances the problem-prevention capabilities of organizations because it promotes interaction among managers at all divisional and functional levels. Interaction can enable firms to turn on their managers and employees by nurturing them, sharing organizational objectives with them, empowering them to help improve the product or service, and recognizing their contributions.

In addition to empowering managers and employees, strategic management often brings order and discipline to an otherwise floundering firm. It can be the beginning of an efficient and effective managerial system. Strategic management may renew confidence in the current business strategy or point to the need for corrective actions. The strategic-management process provides a basis for identifying and rationalizing the need for change to all managers and employees of a firm; it helps them view change as an opportunity rather than a threat.

Greenley stated that strategic management offers the following benefits:

1. It allows for identification, prioritization, and exploitation of opportunities.
2. It provides an objective view of management problems.
3. It represents a framework for improved coordination and control of activities.
4. It minimizes the effects of adverse conditions and changes.
5. It allows major decisions to better support established objectives.
6. It allows more effective allocation of time and resources to identified opportunities.
7. It allows fewer resources and less time to be devoted to correcting erroneous or ad hoc decisions.
8. It creates a framework for internal communication among personnel.
9. It helps integrate the behavior of individuals into a total effort.
10. It provides a basis for clarifying individual responsibilities.
11. It encourages forward thinking.
12. It provides a cooperative, integrated, and enthusiastic approach to tackling problems and opportunities.
13. It encourages a favorable attitude toward change.
14. It gives a degree of discipline and formality to the management of a business.[18]

## WHY SOME FIRMS DO NO STRATEGIC PLANNING

Some firms do not engage in strategic planning and some firms do strategic planning but receive no support from managers and employees. Some reasons for poor or no strategic planning are as follows:

- *Poor Reward Structures*—When an organization assumes success, it often fails to reward success. Where failure occurs, then the firm may punish. In this situation, it is better for an individual to do nothing (and not draw attention) than risk trying to achieve something, fail, and be punished.
- *Fire-fighting*—An organization can be so deeply embroiled in crisis management and fire-fighting that it does not have time to plan.
- *Waste of Time*—Some firms see planning as a waste of time since no marketable product is produced. Time spent on planning is an investment.
- *Too Expensive*—Some organizations are culturally opposed to spending resources.
- *Laziness*—People may not want to put forth the effort needed to formulate a plan.
- *Content with Success*—Particularly if a firm is successful, individuals may feel there is no need to plan because things are fine as they stand. But success today does not guarantee success tomorrow.
- *Fear of Failure*—By not taking action, there is little risk of failure unless a problem is urgent and pressing. Whenever something worthwhile is attempted, there is some risk of failure.
- *Overconfidence*—As individuals amass experience, they may rely less on formalized planning. Rarely, however, is this appropriate. Being overconfident or overestimating experience can bring demise. Forethought is rarely wasted and is often the mark of professionalism.

- *Prior Bad Experience*—People may have had a previous bad experience with planning, where plans have been long, cumbersome, impractical, or inflexible. Planning, like anything, can be done badly.
- *Self-Interest*—When someone has achieved status, privilege, or self-esteem through effectively using an old system, they often see a new plan as a threat.
- *Fear of the Unknown*—People may be uncertain of their abilities to learn new skills, their aptitude with new systems, or their ability to take on new roles.
- *Honest Difference of Opinion*—People may sincerely believe the plan is wrong. They may view the situation from a different viewpoint, or may have aspirations for themselves or the organization that are different from the plan. Different people in different jobs have different perceptions of a situation.
- *Suspicion*—Employees may not trust management.[19]

## PITFALLS IN STRATEGIC PLANNING

Strategic planning is an involved, intricate, and complex process that takes an organization into unchartered territory. It does not provide a ready-to-use prescription for success; instead, it takes the organization through a journey and offers a framework for addressing questions and solving problems. Being aware of potential pitfalls and prepared to address them is essential to success.

Some pitfalls to watch for and avoid in strategic planning are provided below:

- Using strategic planning to gain control over decisions and resources
- Doing strategic planning only to satisfy accreditation or regulatory requirements
- Too hastily moving from mission development to strategy formulation
- Failing to communicate the plan to employees, who continue working in the dark
- Top managers making many intuitive decisions that conflict with the formal plan
- Top managers not actively supporting the strategic-planning process
- Failing to use plans as a standard for measuring performance
- Delegating planning to a "planner" rather than involving all managers
- Failing to involve key employees in all phases of planning
- Failing to create a collaborative climate supportive of change
- Viewing planning to be unnecessary or unimportant
- Becoming so engrossed in current problems that insufficient or no planning is done
- Being so formal in planning that flexibility and creativity are stifled[20]

## GUIDELINES FOR EFFECTIVE STRATEGIC MANAGEMENT

Failing to follow certain guidelines in conducting strategic management can foster criticisms of the process and create problems for the organization. An integral part of strategy evaluation must be to evaluate the quality of the strategic-management process. Issues such as "Is strategic management in our firm a people process or paper process?" should be addressed.

Even the most technically perfect strategic plan will serve little purpose if it is not implemented. Many organizations tend to spend an inordinate amount of time, money, and effort on developing the strategic plan, treating the means and circumstances under which it will be implemented as afterthoughts! Change comes through implementation and evaluation, not through the plan. A technically imperfect plan that is implemented well will achieve more than the perfect plan that never gets off the paper on which it is typed.[21]

Strategic management must not become a self-perpetuating bureaucratic mechanism. Rather, it must be a self-reflective learning process that familiarizes managers and employees in the organization with key strategic issues and feasible alternatives for resolving those issues. Strategic management must not become ritualistic, stilted, orchestrated, or too formal, predictable, and rigid. Words supported by numbers, rather than numbers supported by words, should represent the medium for explaining strategic issues and organizational responses. A key role of strategists is to facilitate continuous organizational learning and change. Robert Waterman emphasized this, saying:

> Successful companies know how to keep things moving. If they share a habit pattern, it's the habit of habit breaking. Sometimes they seem to like change for its own sake. IBM's chief executive John Akers says, "IBM never reorganizes except for a good business reason, but if they haven't reorganized in a while, that's a good business reason." Successful companies are deliberate bureaucracy-busters. They delight in smashing pettifogging encumbrances that Harry Quadracci calls "playing office."[22]

R. T. Lenz offered some important guidelines for effective strategic management:

> Keep the strategic-management process as simple and nonroutine as possible. Eliminate jargon and arcane planning language. Remember, strategic management is a process for fostering learning and action, not merely a formal system for control. To avoid routinized behavior, vary assignments, team membership, meeting formats, and the planning calendar. The process should not be totally predictable, and settings must be changed to stimulate creativity. Emphasize word-oriented plans with numbers as back-up material. If managers cannot express their strategy in a paragraph or so, they either do not have one or do not understand it. Stimulate thinking and action that challenge the assumptions underlying current corporate strategy. Welcome bad news. If strategy is not working, managers desperately need to know it. Further, no pertinent information should be classified as inadmissible merely because it cannot be quantified. Build a corporate culture in which the role of strategic management and its essential purposes are understood. Do not permit "technicians" to co-opt the process. It is ultimately a process for learning and action. Speak of it in these terms. Attend to psychological, social, and political dimensions, as well as the information infrastructure and administrative procedures supporting it.[23]

An important guideline for effective strategic management is open-mindedness. A willingness and eagerness to consider new information, new viewpoints, new ideas, and new possibilities is essential; all organizational members must share a spirit of inquiry and learning. Strategists such as chief executive officers, presidents, owners of small businesses, and heads of government agencies must commit themselves to listen to and understand managers' positions well enough to be able to restate those positions to the managers' satisfaction. In addition, managers and employees throughout the firm should be able to describe the strategists' positions to the satisfaction of the strategists. This degree of discipline will promote understanding and learning.

No organization has unlimited resources. No firm can take on an unlimited amount of debt or issue an unlimited amount of stock to raise capital. Therefore, no organization can pursue all the strategies that potentially could benefit the firm. Strategic decisions thus always have to be made to eliminate some courses of action and to allocate organizational resources among others. Most organizations can afford to pursue only a few corporate-level strategies at any given time. It is a critical mistake for managers to pursue too many strategies at the same time, thereby spreading the firm's resources so thin that all strategies are jeopardized. Joseph Charyk, CEO of The Communication Satellite Corporation (Comsat), said, "We have to face the cold fact that Comsat may not be able to do all it wants. We must make hard choices on which ventures to keep and which to fold."

Strategic decisions require trade-offs such as long-range versus short-range considerations or maximizing profits versus increasing shareholders' wealth. There are ethics issues too. Strategy trade-offs require subjective judgments and preferences. In many cases, a lack of objectivity in formulating strategy results in a loss of competitive posture and profitability. Most organizations today recognize that strategic-management concepts and techniques can enhance the effectiveness of decisions. Subjective factors such as attitudes toward risk, concern for social responsibility, and organizational culture will always affect strategy-formulation decisions, but organizations need to be as objective as possible in considering qualitative factors.

 ## BUSINESS ETHICS AND STRATEGIC MANAGEMENT

*Business ethics* can be defined as principles of conduct within organizations that guide decision making and behavior. Good business ethics is a prerequisite for good strategic management; good ethics is just good business!

A rising tide of consciousness about the importance of business ethics is sweeping America and the world. Strategists are the individuals primarily responsible for ensuring that high ethical principles are espoused and practiced in an organization. All strategy formulation, implementation, and evaluation decisions have ethical ramifications.

Newspapers and business magazines daily report legal and moral breaches of ethical conduct by both public and private organizations. As the Natural Environment Perspective indicates, however, managers and employees of firms must be careful not to become scapegoats blamed for company environmental wrongdoings. Harming the natural environment is unethical, illegal, and costly; as more countries and companies realize this fact, export opportunities for pollution control equipment abound.

A new wave of ethics issues related to product safety, employee health, sexual harassment, AIDS in the workplace, smoking, acid rain, affirmative action, waste disposal, foreign business practices, cover-ups, takeover tactics, conflicts of interest, employee privacy, inappropriate gifts, security of company records, and layoffs has accented the need for strategists to develop a clear code of business ethics. United Technologies Corporation has issued a twenty-one-page Code of Ethics and named a new vice president of business ethics. Baxter Travenol Laboratories, IBM, Caterpillar Tractor, Chemical Bank, Exxon, Dow Corning, and Celanese are firms that have a formal code of business ethics. A *code of business ethics* can provide a basis on which policies can be devised to guide daily behavior and decisions at the work site.

The explosion of the Internet into the workplace has raised many new ethical questions in organizations today. For example, United Parcel Service (UPS) recently caught an employee actually running a personal business from his computer. A Lockheed Martin employee recently sent a religious e-mail to sixty thousand fellow employees that disabled company networks for more than six hours. Boeing is an example company that seemingly has accepted the inevitable by instituting a policy specifically allowing employees to use company faxes, e-mail, and the Internet for personal reasons for "reasonable duration and frequency without embarrassment to the company." In contrast, Ameritech has a policy

# E-COMMERCE PERSPECTIVE

### Business Ethics and the Internet

May employees use the Internet at work to conduct day-trading of personal stocks? May employees send e-mail to personal friends and relatives from the workplace? Is it ethical for employees to shop online while at work? May employees hunt for a new job while online at work? May employees play games online while at work? Before answering these questions, consider the following facts:

- Employee productivity can suffer immensely when many workers surf the Web at work.

- Unlike phone calls, e-mail can often be retrieved months or years later and be used against the company in litigation.

- When employees surf the Web at work, they drag the company's name along with them everywhere. This could be harmful to the company if employees visit certain sites such as racist chat rooms or pornographic material.

- Software packages are now available to companies that report Web-site visits by individual employees. Companies such as Telemate.Net Software Inc. in Atlanta produce software that tell managers who went to what sites at what times for how long.

- Some 27 percent of large U.S. firms have begun checking employee e-mail, up from 15 percent in 1977. BellSouth employees must regularly click "OK" to a message warn-

ing them against misuse of e-mail and the Internet, and alerting them that their actions can be monitored.

- Many companies such as Boeing grant Internet usage to employees as a perk, but many of those firms are finding that this "fringe benefit" must be managed.

Lockheed Martin now directs their employees onto the Internet for extensive training sessions on topics that include business ethics, legal compliance, sexual harassment, and day-trading. Lockheed even has an Internet ethics game, Ethics Challenge, which every single employee and manager must play once a year. During the first half of 1999, Lockheed discharged 25 employees for ethics violations, suspended 14 others, gave a written reprimand to 51 persons and an oral reprimand to 146 employees.

Soon after installing the Telemate software, Wolverton & Associates learned that broadcast.com was the company's third-most visited site; people download music from that site. And E*Trade was the company's eighth-most visited site; people day-trade stocks at that site.

Adapted from: Michael McCarthy, "Virtual Morality: A New Workplace Quandary," *The Wall Street Journal* (October 21, 1999): B1. Also, Michael McCarthy, "Now the Boss Knows Where You're Clicking," *The Wall Street Journal* (October 21, 1999): B1. Also, Michael McCarthy, "How One Firm Tracks Ethics Electronically," *The Wall Street Journal* (October 21, 1999): B1.

that says "computers and other company equipment are to be used only to provide service to customers and for other business purposes."

The E-Commerce Perspective focuses on business ethics issues related to the Internet. Merely having a code of ethics, however, is not sufficient to ensure ethical business behavior. A code of ethics can be viewed as a public relations gimmick, a set of platitudes, or window dressing. To ensure that the code is read, understood, believed, and remembered, organizations need to conduct periodic ethics workshops to sensitize people to workplace circumstances in which ethics issues may arise.[24] If employees see examples of punishment for violating the code and rewards for upholding the code, this helps reinforce the importance of a firm's code of ethics.

Internet privacy is an emerging ethical issue of immense proportions. There is a national push for industry assurances that children have parental permission before giving out their names, ages, and other private details to companies that run Web sites. Privacy advocates increasingly argue for new government regulations to enforce protection of young users.

## NATURAL ENVIRONMENT

### *You May Become a Scapegoat*

More than half of the five hundred major rivers in the world are polluted badly according to the World Bank and United Nations. The Amazon and the Congo are the two healthiest rivers. River pollution contributed to 25 million environmental refugees in 1999 according to the World Commission on Water. More U.S. firms today actively seek out environmental groups and the Environmental Protection Agency (EPA) to engage proactively in dialogue aimed at setting environmental standards for the firm and industry. The old, reactive, command-and-control approach to environmental affairs no longer is considered the most effective. Ciba-Geigy, Monsanto, Exxon, Amoco, and General Motors are just a few among thousands of firms that today actively engage trade associations; regulatory bodies; and state, national, and foreign legislatures in setting industry natural environment standards. Companies find that many environmentalists are highly competent technologically and operationally. Dialogue thus often results in new processes that significantly improve corporate efficiency as well as environmental effectiveness. Benefits of this activity far exceed public relations.

Before a firm engages an environmental group in discussions, the following seven recommendations can pave the way for success:

- Be sincere in wanting their input.
- Be willing to accept some advice.
- Be part of the issue, so you have credibility.
- Look at the larger interests; see the big picture.
- Staff the meeting with decision makers.
- Have a good corporate reputation.
- Reach out on other issues, also.

When organizations today face criminal charges for polluting the environment, firms increasingly are turning on their managers and employees to win leniency for themselves. Employee firings and demotions are becoming common in pollution-related legal suits. Managers being recently fired at Darling International, Inc., and Niagara Mohawk Power Corporation for being indirectly responsible for their firms' polluting water exemplifies this corporate trend. Therefore, managers and employees today must be careful not to ignore, conceal, or disregard a pollution problem or they may find themselves personally liable.

*Source:* Adapted from Gail Dutton, "Green Partnerships," *Management Review* (January 1996): 24–28. Also, Dean Starkman, "Pollution Case Highlights Trend to Let Employees Take the Rap," *The Wall Street Journal,* (October 9, 1997): B10. Pauline Jelinek, *"Many World Rivers Are Contaminated,"* USA Today (November 30, 1999): 4A.

Millions of computer users are worried about privacy on the Internet and want the U.S. government to pass laws about how data can be collected and used. Advertisers, marketers, companies, and people with various reasons to snoop on other people now can discover easily on the Internet others' buying preferences, hobbies, incomes, medical data, social security numbers, addresses, previous addresses, sexual preferences, credit card purchases, traffic tickets, divorce settlements, and much more. Many Internet users are ready for what they call "some law and order" in cyberspace.

Given the global nature of e-commerce, any U.S. government regulations to inhibit free flow of information will not carry much weight anyway in places such as Moldova, home of a phone-porn scam. But perhaps the United States at least should set a standard for e-commerce rules and regulations that other countries could consider adopting.

An ethics "culture" needs to permeate organizations! To help create an ethics culture, Citicorp developed a business ethics board game that is played by forty-thousand employees in forty-five countries. Called *The Work Ethic,* this game asks players business ethics questions, such as how to deal with a customer who offers you football tickets in exchange for a new, backdated IRA. Diana Robertson at the Wharton School believes the game is effective because it is interactive. Many organizations, such as Prime Computer and Kmart, have developed a code-of-conduct manual outlining ethical expectations and giving examples of situations that commonly arise in their businesses. Harris Corporation's managers and employees are warned that failing to report an ethical violation by others could bring discharge.

One reason strategists' salaries are high compared to those of other individuals in an organization is that strategists must take the moral risks of the firm. Strategists are responsible for developing, communicating, and enforcing the code of business ethics for their organizations. Although primary responsibility for ensuring ethical behavior rests with a firm's strategists, an integral part of the responsibility of all managers is to provide ethics leadership by constant example and demonstration. Managers hold positions that enable them to influence and educate many people. This makes managers responsible for developing and implementing ethical decision making. Gellerman and Drucker, respectively, offer some good advice for managers:

> All managers risk giving too much because of what their companies demand from them. But the same superiors who keep pressing you to do more, or to do it better, or faster, or less expensively, will turn on you should you cross that fuzzy line between right and wrong. They will blame you for exceeding instructions or for ignoring their warnings. The smartest managers already know that the best answer to the question "How far is too far?" is don't try to find out.[25]

> A man (or woman) might know too little, perform poorly, lack judgment and ability, and yet not do too much damage as a manager. But if that person lacks character and integrity—no matter how knowledgeable, how brilliant, how successful—he destroys. He destroys people, the most valuable resource of the enterprise. He destroys spirit. And he destroys performance. This is particularly true of the people at the head of an enterprise. For the spirit of an organization is created from the top. If an organization is great in spirit, it is because the spirit of its top people is great. If it decays, it does so because the top rots. As the proverb has it, "Trees die from the top." No one should ever become a strategist unless he or she is willing to have his or her character serve as the model for subordinates.[26]

No society anywhere in the world can compete very long or successfully with people stealing from one another or not trusting one another, with every bit of information requiring notarized confirmation, with every disagreement ending up in litigation, or with government having to regulate businesses to keep them honest. Akers stated that being unethical is a recipe for headaches, inefficiency, and waste. History has proven that the greater the trust and confidence of people in the ethics of an institution or society, the greater its economic strength. Business relationships are built mostly on mutual trust and reputation. Short-term decisions based on greed and questionable ethics will preclude the necessary self-respect to gain the trust of others. More and more firms believe that ethics training and an ethics culture create strategic advantage.

Some business actions *always* considered to be unethical include misleading advertising or labeling, causing environmental harm, poor product or service safety, padding expense accounts, insider trading, dumping banned or flawed products. In foreign markets, lack of equal opportunities for women and minorities, overpricing, hostile takeovers, moving jobs overseas, and using nonunion labor in a union shop.[27]

Ethics training programs should include messages from the CEO emphasizing ethical business practices, development and discussion of codes of ethics, and procedures for discussing and reporting unethical behavior. Firms can align ethical and strategic decision making by incorporating ethical considerations into long-term planning, integrating ethical decision making into the performance appraisal process, encouraging whistleblowing or the reporting of unethical practices, and monitoring departmental and corporate performance regarding ethical issues.

In a final analysis, ethical standards come out of history and heritage. Our fathers and mothers and brothers and sisters of the past left to us an ethical foundation to build upon. Even the legendary football coach Vince Lombardi knew that some things were worth more than winning, and he required his players to have three kinds of loyalty: to God, to their families, and to the Green Bay Packers, "in that order."

## COMPARING BUSINESS AND MILITARY STRATEGY

A strong military heritage underlies the study of strategic management. Terms such as *objectives, mission, strengths,* and *weaknesses* first were formulated to address problems on the battlefield. According to Webster's *New World Dictionary,* strategy is "the science of planning and directing large-scale military operations, of maneuvering forces into the most advantageous position prior to actual engagement with the enemy." The word "strategy" comes from the Greek *strategos,* referring to a military general and combining *stratos* (the army) and *ago* (to lead). The history of strategic planning began in the military. A key aim of both business and military strategy is "to gain competitive advantage." In many respects, business strategy is like military strategy, and military strategists have learned much over the centuries that can benefit business strategists today. Both business and military organizations try to use their own strengths to exploit competitors' weaknesses. If an organization's overall strategy is wrong (ineffective), then all the efficiency in the world may not be enough to allow success. Business or military success is generally not the happy result of accidental strategies. Rather, success is the product of continuous attention to changing external and internal conditions and the formulation and implementation of insightful adaptations to those conditions. The element of surprise provides great competitive advantages in both military and business strategy; information systems that provide data on opponents' or competitors' strategies and resources are also vitally important.

Of course, a fundamental difference between military and business strategy is that business strategy is formulated, implemented, and evaluated with an assumption of *competition,* whereas military strategy is based on an assumption of *conflict.* Nonetheless, military conflict and business competition are so similar that many strategic-management techniques apply equally to both. Business strategists have access to valuable insights that military thinkers have refined over time. Superior strategy formulation and implementation can overcome an opponent's superiority in numbers and resources.

Both business and military organizations must adapt to change and constantly improve to be successful. Too often, firms do not change their strategies when their environment and competitive conditions dictate the need to change. Gluck offered a classic military example of this:

> When Napoleon won it was because his opponents were committed to the strategy, tactics, and organization of earlier wars. When he lost—against Wellington, the Russians, and the Spaniards—it was because he, in turn, used tried-and-true strategies against enemies who thought afresh, who were developing the strategies not of the last war but of the next.[28]

## THE NATURE OF GLOBAL COMPETITION

For centuries before Columbus discovered America and surely for centuries to come, businesses have searched and will continue to search for new opportunities beyond their national boundaries. There has never been a more internationalized and economically competitive society than today's. Some American industries, such as textiles, semiconductors, and consumer electronics, are in complete disarray as a result of the international challenge.

Organizations that conduct business operations across national borders are called *international firms* or *multinational corporations.* The term *parent company* refers to a firm investing in international operations, while *host country* is the country where that business is conducted. The strategic-management process is conceptually the same for multinational firms as for purely domestic firms; however, the process is more complex for international firms because of the presence of more variables and relationships. Social, cultural, demographic, environmental, political, governmental, legal, technological, and competitive opportunities and threats that face a multinational corporation are almost limitless, and the number and complexity of these factors increase dramatically with the number of products produced and the number of geographic areas served.

More time and effort are required to identify and evaluate external trends and events in multinational corporations. Geographical distance, cultural and national differences, and variations in business practices often make communication between domestic headquarters and overseas operations difficult. Strategy implementation can be more difficult because different cultures have different norms, values, and work ethics.

The fall of communism and advancements in telecommunications are drawing countries, cultures, and organizations worldwide closer together. Foreign revenue as a percent of total company revenues already exceeds 50 percent in hundreds of U.S. firms, including Exxon, Gillette, Dow Chemical, Citicorp, Colgate-Palmolive, and Texaco. Joint ventures and partnerships between domestic and foreign firms are becoming the rule rather than the exception!

World trade centers are proliferating in the United States and abroad because of growing interest in foreign trade. These new world trade centers offer many specialized services, such as assisting small businesses in exporting or importing, and housing foreign banks, export firms, and law offices.

Fully 95 percent of the world's population lives outside the United States, and this group is growing 70 percent faster than the American population! The lineup of competitors in virtually all industries today is global. Global competition is more than a management fad. General Motors, Ford, and Chrysler compete with Toyota, Daimler Benz, and Hyundai. General Electric and Westinghouse battle Siemens and Mitsubishi. Caterpillar and Deere compete with Komatsu. Goodyear battles Michelin, Bridgestone, and Pirelli. Boeing competes with Airbus. Only a few U.S. industries, such as furniture, printing, retailing, consumer packaged goods, and retail banking, are not yet greatly challenged by foreign competitors. But many products and components in these industries too are now manufactured in foreign countries.

International operations can be as simple as exporting a product to a single foreign country, or as complex as operating manufacturing, distribution, and marketing facilities in many countries. U.S. firms are acquiring foreign companies and forming joint ventures with foreign firms, and foreign firms are acquiring U.S. companies and forming joint ventures with U.S. firms. This trend is accelerating dramatically. AT&T's former Chief Executive Officer, Robert Allen, said, "The phrase *global markets* is not empty rhetoric. Foreign competitors are here. And we must be there." Many U.S. firms have been spoiled by the breadth and plenty of home markets and remain ignorant of foreign languages and culture. For example, Hershey Foods, the leading pasta and chocolate producer in the U.S., derives only about 10 percent of its total revenues from outside the United States.

## Advantages and Disadvantages of International Operations

Firms have numerous reasons to formulate and implement strategies that initiate, continue, or expand involvement in business operations across national borders. Perhaps the greatest advantage is that firms can gain new customers for their products and services, thus increasing revenues. Growth in revenues and profits is a common organizational objective and often an expectation of shareholders because it is a measure of organizational success.

In addition to seeking growth, firms have the following potentially advantageous reasons to initiate, continue, and expand international operations:

1. Foreign operations can absorb excess capacity, reduce unit costs, and spread economic risks over a wider number of markets.

2. Foreign operations can allow firms to establish low-cost production facilities in locations close to raw materials and/or cheap labor.

3. Competitors in foreign markets may not exist, or competition may be less intense than in domestic markets.

4. Foreign operations may result in reduced tariffs, lower taxes, and favorable political treatment in other countries.

5. Joint ventures can enable firms to learn the technology, culture, and business practices of other people and to make contacts with potential customers, suppliers, creditors, and distributors in foreign countries.

6. Many foreign governments and countries offer varied incentives to encourage foreign investment in specific locations.

7. Economies of scale can be achieved from operation in global rather than solely domestic markets. Larger-scale production and better efficiencies allow higher sales volumes and lower price offerings.

A firm's power and prestige in domestic markets may be significantly enhanced with various stakeholder groups if the firm competes globally. Enhanced prestige can translate into improved negotiating power among creditors, suppliers, distributors, and other important groups.

There are also numerous potential disadvantages of initiating, continuing, or expanding business across national borders. One risk is that foreign operations could be seized by nationalistic factions, which occurred in Kuwait during the Gulf War and in Indonesia more recently. Other disadvantages include the following:

1. Firms confront different and often little-understood social, cultural, demographic, environmental, political, governmental, legal, technological, economic, and competitive forces when doing business internationally. These forces can make communication difficult between the parent firm and subsidiaries.

2. Weaknesses of competitors in foreign lands are often overestimated, and strengths are often underestimated. Keeping informed about the number and nature of competitors is more difficult when doing business internationally.

3. Language, culture, and value systems differ among countries, and this can create barriers to communication and problems managing people.

4. Gaining an understanding of regional organizations such as the European Economic Community, the Latin American Free Trade Area, the International Bank for Reconstruction and Development, and the International Finance Corporation is difficult and often required in doing business internationally.

5. Dealing with two or more monetary systems can complicate international business operations.

## CONCLUSION

All firms have a strategy, even if it is informal, unstructured, and sporadic. All organizations are heading somewhere, but unfortunately some organizations do not know where. The old saying "If you do not know where you are going, then any road will lead you there!" accents the need for organizations to use strategic-management concepts and techniques. The strategic-management process is becoming more widely used by small firms, large companies, nonprofit institutions, governmental organizations, and multinational conglomerates alike. The process of empowering managers and employees has almost limitless benefits.

Organizations should take a proactive rather than a reactive approach in their industry, and should strive to influence, anticipate, and initiate rather than just respond to events. The strategic-management process embodies this approach to decision making. It represents a logical, systematic, and objective approach for determining an enterprise's future direction. The stakes are generally too high for strategists to use intuition alone in choosing among alternative courses of action. Successful strategists take the time to think about their businesses, where they are with the businesses, and what they want to be as organizations, and then implement programs and policies to get from where they are to where they want to be in a reasonable period of time.

It is a known and accepted fact that people and organizations that plan ahead are much more likely to become what they want to become than those who do not plan at all. A good strategist plans and controls his or her plans, while a bad strategist never plans and then tries to control people! This textbook is devoted to providing you with the tools necessary to be a good strategist.

Success in business increasingly depends upon offering products and services that are competitive on a world basis, not just on a local basis. If the price and quality of a firm's products and services are not competitive with those available elsewhere in the world, the firm may soon face extinction. Global markets have become a reality in all but the most remote areas of the world. Certainly throughout the United States, even in small towns, firms feel the pressure of world competitors. Nearly half of all the automobiles sold in the United States, for example, are made in Japan and Germany.

We invite you to visit the DAVID page on the Prentice Hall Web site at **www.prenhall.com/davidsm** for this chapter's World Wide Web exercises.

## KEY TERMS AND CONCEPTS

Annual Objectives (p. 12)

Business Ethics (p. 19)

Code of Business Ethics (p. 19)

Electronic Commerce (p. 20)

Empowerment (p. 14)

Environmental Scanning (p. 10)

External Opportunities (p. 10)

External Threats (p. 10)

Host Country (p. 24)

Internal Strengths (p. 10)

Internal Weaknesses (p. 10)

International Firms (p. 24)

Intuition (p. 7)

Lobbying (p. 10)

Long-Range Planning (p. 5)

Long-Term Objectives (p. 11)

Mission Statements (p. 9)

Multinational Corporations (p. 24)

Policies (p. 12)

Strategic Management (p. 5)

Strategic-Management Model (p. 12)

Strategic-Management Process (p. 5)

Strategies (p. 11)

Strategists (p. 9)

Strategy Evaluation (p. 6)

Strategy Formulation (p. 5)

Strategy Implementation (p. 6)

Vision (p. 9)

Vision Statement (p. 9)

## ISSUES FOR REVIEW AND DISCUSSION

1. Explain why Business Policy often is called a "capstone course."

2. Read one of the suggested readings at the end of this chapter. Prepare a one-page written summary that includes your personal thoughts on the subject.

3. What aspect of strategy formulation do you think requires the most time? Why?

4. Why is strategy implementation often considered the most difficult stage in the strategic-management process?

5. Why is it so important to integrate intuition and analysis in strategic management?

6. Explain the importance of a vision and mission statement.

7. Discuss relationships among objectives, strategies, and policies.

8. Why do you think some chief executive officers fail to use a strategic-management approach to decision making?

9. Discuss the importance of feedback in the strategic-management model.

10. How can strategists best ensure that strategies will be effectively implemented?

11. Give an example of a recent political development that changed the overall strategy of an organization.

12. Who are the major competitors of your college or university? What are their strengths and weak-nesses? What are their strategies? How successful are these institutions compared to your college?

13. If you owned a small business, would you develop a code of business conduct? If yes, what variables would you include? If no, how would you ensure that ethical business standards were being followed by your employees?

14. Would strategic-management concepts and techniques benefit foreign businesses as much as domestic firms? Justify your answer.

15. What do you believe are some potential pitfalls or risks in using a strategic-management approach to decision making?

16. In your opinion, what is the single major benefit of using a strategic-management approach to decision making? Justify your answer.

17. Compare business strategy and military strategy.

18. What do you feel is the relationship between personal ethics and business ethics? Are they, or should they be, the same?

19. Why is it important for all business majors to study strategic management since most students will never become a chief executive officer nor even a top manager in a large company?

20. Explain why consumption patterns are becoming similar worldwide. What are the strategic implications of this trend?

21. What are the advantages and disadvantages of beginning export operations in a foreign country?

## NOTES

1. KEVIN MANEY, "The Net Effect: Evolution or Revolution?" *USA Today* (August 9, 1999): B1.

2. PETER DRUCKER, *Management: Tasks, Responsibilities, and Practices* (New York: Harper & Row, 1974): 611.

3. ALFRED SLOAN, JR., *Adventures of the White Collar Man* (New York: Doubleday, 1941): 104.

4. Quoted in Eugene Raudsepp, "Can You Trust Your Hunches?" *Management Review* 49, no. 4 (April 1960): 7.

5. STEPHEN HARPER, "Intuition: What Separates Executives from Managers," *Business Horizons* 31, no. 5 (September–October 1988): 16.

6. RON NELSON, "How to Be a Manager," *Success* (July–August 1985): 69.

7. BRUCE HENDERSON, *Henderson on Corporate Strategy* (Boston: Abt Books, 1979): 6.

8. ROBERT WATERMAN, JR., *The Renewal Factor: How the Best Get and Keep the Competitive Edge* (New York: Bantam, 1987). See also *Business Week* (September 14, 1987): 100.

Also, see *Academy of Management Executive* 3, no. 2 (May 1989): 115.

9. BILL MEYERS, "Women Increase Standing As Business Owners" (June 29, 1999): 1A.

10. JOHN PEARCE II and FRED DAVID, "The Bottom Line on Corporate Mission Statements," *Academy of Management Executive* 1, no. 2 (May 1987): 109.

11. LORRIE GRANT, "Grocery Chore No More," *USA Today* (July 21, 1999): p. B1.

12. JAMES ABUNDIS and SUZY PARKER, "Americans, Teens Smoking Less," *USA Today* (August 31, 1999): A1.

13. FRED R. DAVID, "How Companies Define Their Mission," *Long Range Planning* 22, no. 1 (February 1989): 91.

14. JACK PEARCE and RICHARD ROBINSON, *Strategic Management* 7th ed. Irwin (New York: McGraw-Hill Publishing Company, 2000): p. 8.

15. ANN LANGLEY, "The Roles of Formal Strategic Planning," *Long Range Planning* 21, no. 3 (June 1988): 40.

16. BERNARD REIMANN, "Getting Value from Strategic Planning," *Planning Review* 16, no. 3 (May–June 1988): 42.
17. G. L. SCHWENK and K. SCHRADER, "Effects of Formal Strategic Planning in Financial Performance in Small Firms: A Meta-Analysis," *Entrepreneurship and Practice* 3, no. 17 (1993): 53–64. Also, C. C. Miller and L. B. Cardinal, "Strategic Planning and Firm Performance: A Synthesis of More than Two Decades of Research," *Academy of Management Journal* 6, no. 27 (1994): 1649–1665. Also, Michael Peel and John Bridge, "How Planning and Capital Budgeting Improve SME Performance," *Long Range Planning* 31, no. 6 (October 1998): 848–856. Also, Julia Smith, "Strategies for Start-Ups," *Long Range Planning* 31, no. 6 (October 1998): 857–872.
18. GORDON GREENLEY, "Does Strategic Planning Improve Company Performance?" *Long Range Planning* 19, no. 2 (April 1986): 106.
19. Adapted from: www.mindtools.com/plreschn.html
20. Adapted from the Web sites: www.des.calstate.edu/limitations.html and www.entarga.com/stratplan/purposes.html

21. McCONKEY, 66.
22. ROBERT H. WATERMAN, JR., *The Renewal Factor: How the Best Get and Keep the Competitive Edge* (New York: Bantam, 1987).
23. R. T. LENZ, "Managing the Evolution of the Strategic Planning Process," *Business Horizons* 30, no. 1 (January–February 1987): 39.
24. SAUL GELLERMAN, "Managing Ethics from the Top Down," *Sloan Management Review* (Winter 1989): 77.
25. SAUL GELLERMAN, "Why 'Good' Managers Make Bad Ethical Choices," *Harvard Business Review* 64, no. 4 (July–August 1986): 88.
26. DRUCKER, 462, 463.
27. GENE LACZNIAK, MARVIN BERKOWITZ, RUSSELL BROOKER, and JAMES HALE, "The Ethics of Business: Improving or Deteriorating?" *Business Horizons* 38, no. 1 (January–February 1995): 43.
28. FREDERICK GLUCK, "Taking the Mystique Out of Planning," *Across the Board* (July–August 1985): 59.

## CURRENT READINGS

AGLE, BRADLEY R., RONALD MITCHELL, and JEFFERY A. SONNENFELD. "Who Matters to CEOs? An Investigation of Stakeholder Attributes and Salience, Corporate Performance, and CEO Values." *The Academy of Management Journal* 40, no. 5 (October 1999): 507–525.

ATHANASSIOU, N. and D. NIGH, "The Impact of U.S. Company Internationalization on Top Management Team Advice Networks: A Tacit Knowledge Perspective." Research Notes and Communications. *Strategic Management Journal* 20, no. 1 (January 1999): 83–92.

BREWS, P. J. and M. R. HUNT. "Learning to Plan and Planning to Learn: Resolving the Planning School/Learning School Debate." *Strategic Management Journal* 20, no. 10 (October 1999): 889–914.

CAMPBELL, ANDREW. "Thinking About . . . Tailored, Not Benchmarked: A Fresh Look at Corporate Planning." *Harvard Business Review* (March–April 1999): 41–51.

CROSSAN, MARY M., HENRY W. LANE, and RODERICK E. WHITE. "An Organizational Learning Framework: From Intuition to Institution." *The Academy of Management Review* 24, no. 3 (July 1999): 522–537.

DASCHER, PAUL E. and WILLIAM G. JENS, JR. "Executive Briefing/Family Business Succession Planning." *Business Horizons* 42, no. 5 (September–October 1999):2–4.

DESSLER, GARY. "How to Earn Your Employees' Commitment." *The Academy of Management Executive* 13, no. 2 (May 1999): 58–67.

EISENHARDT, KATHLEEN M. "Strategy as Strategic Decision Making." *Sloan Management Review* 40, no. 3 (Spring 1999): 65–72.

ELLERMAN, DAVID P., The World Bank. "Global Institutions: Transforming International Development Agencies into Learning Organizations." *The Academy of Management Executive* 13, no. 1 (February 1999): 25–35.

GLAISTER, KEITH W. and J. RICHARD FALSHAW. "Strategic Planning Still Going Strong." *International Journal of Strategic Management* 32, no. 1 (February 1999): 107–116.

HARRIS, LOYD C. and EMMANUEL OGBONNA. "The Strategic Legacy of Company Founders." *Internal Journal of Strategic Management* 32, no. 3 (June 1999): 333–343.

HOPKINS, H. DONALD. "Using History for Strategic Problem-Solving: The Harley-Davidson Effect." *Business Horizons* 42, no. 2 (March–April 1999): 52–60.

HOSKISSON, ROBERT E., MICHAEL A. HITT, WILLIAM P. WAN, and DAPHENE YIU. "Theory and Research in Strategic Management: Swings of a Pendulum." *Journal of Management* 25, no. 3 (1999): 417–456.

KOGUT, BRUCE, Books in Review. "What Makes a Company Global?" *Harvard Business Review* (January–February 1999): 165–175.

MARKIDES, CONSTANTINOS C. "A Dynamic View of Strategy." *Sloan Management Review* 40, no. 3 (Spring 1999): 55–64.

MARUCA, REGINA FAZIO, HBR Case Study. "Web Site Blues." *Harvard Business Review* (March–April 1999): 24–34.

MINTZBERG, HENRY and JOSEPH LAMPEL. "Reflecting on the Strategy Process." *Sloan Management Review* 30, no. 3 (Spring 1999): 21–30.

MINTZBERG, HENRY and JOSEPH LAMPEL. "Reflecting on the Strategy Process." *Sloan Management Review* 40, no. 3 (Spring 1999): 21–30.

MONCRIEF, J., Briefcase. "Is Strategy Making a Difference?" *International Journal of Strategic Management* 32, no. 2 (April 1999): 273–276.

PFEFFER, JEFFREY and JOHN F. VEIGA. "Putting People First for Organizational Success." *The Academy of Management Executive* 13, no. 2 (May 1999): 37–48.

PUFFER, SHEILA M., Interview. "Global Statesman: Mikhail Gorbachev on Globalization." *The Academy of Management Executive* 13, no. 1 (February 1999): 8–14.

REINHARDT, FOREST L. "Bringing The Environment Down To Earth." *Harvard Business Review* 77, no. 4 (July–August 1999): 149–159.

ROGERS, P. R., A. MILLER, and W. Q. JUDGE. "Using Information-processing Theory to Understand Planning/Performance Relationships in the Context of Strategy." *Strategic Management Journal* 20, no. 6 (June 1999): 567–578.

SUSSMAN, LYLE. "How To Frame a Message: The Art of Persuasion and Negotiation." *Business Horizons* 42, no. 4 (July–August 1999): 2–6.

TREVIÑO, LINDA KLEBE, GARY R. WEAVER, DAVID G. GIBSON, and BARBARA LEY TOFFLER. "Managing Ethics and Legal Compliance: What Works and What Hurts" *California Management Review,* 41, no. 2 (Winter 1999): 146–156.

WEAVER, GARY R., LINDA KLEBE TREVINO, and PHILIP L. COCHRAN. "Integrated and Decoupled Corporate Social Performance: Management Commitments, External Pressures, and Corporate Ethics Practices." *The Academy of Management* 42, no. 5 (October 1999): 539–552.

WEBLEY, SIMON. "Source of Corporate Values." *International Journal of Strategic Management* 32, no. 2 (April 1999): 173–178.

WETLAUFER, SUZY. "Organizing for Empowerment: An Interview with AES's Roger Sant and Dennis Bakke." *Harvard Business Review* (January–February 1999): 110–120.

WICKS, ANDREW C., SHAWN L. BERMAN, and THOMAS M. JONES. "The Structure of Optimal Trust: Moral and Strategic Implications." *The Academy of Management Review* 24, no. 1 (January 1999): 99–116.

# THE COHESION CASE AND EXPERIENTIAL EXERCISES

Two special features of this text are introduced here: (1) the Cohesion Case and (2) the Experiential Exercises. As strategic-management concepts and techniques are introduced in this text, they are applied to the Cohesion Case through Experiential Exercises. The Cohesion Case centers on America Online (AOL). As the term *cohesion* implies, the AOL case and related exercises integrate material presented throughout the text. At least one exercise at the end of each chapter applies textual material to the AOL case. The Cohesion Case and Experiential Exercises thus work together to give students practice applying strategic-management concepts and tools as they are presented in the text. In this way, students become prepared to perform case analyses as the policy course progresses.

Some Experiential Exercises in the text do not relate specifically to the Cohesion Case. At least one exercise at the end of each chapter applies strategic-management concepts to your university. As a student nearing graduation, you are quite knowledgeable about your university. Apply concepts learned in this course to assist your institution. More colleges and universities are instituting strategic management.

After reading the text and applying concepts and tools to the Cohesion Case through Experiential Exercises, you should be well prepared to analyze business policy cases. The objectives of the case method are as follows:

1. to give you experience applying strategic-management concepts and techniques to different organizations

2. to give you experience applying and integrating the knowledge you have gained in prior courses and work experience

3. to give you decision-making experience in real organizations

4. to improve your understanding of relationships among the functional areas of business and the strategic-management process

5. to improve your self-confidence; because there is no one right answer to a case, you will gain experience justifying and defending your own ideas, analyses, and recommendations

6. to improve your oral and written communication skills

7. to sharpen your analytical and intuitive skills

# THE COHESION CASE

## AMERICA ONLINE, INC., 2000
*David Stanton, University of South Carolina*
www.aol.com

The January 11, 2000, headlines of *The Wall Street Journal* read "You've Got Time Warner!" Headquartered in Dulles, Virginia, AOL's $156.14 billion acquisition of Time Warner has been approved. Thus the world's largest online company has joined forces with the world's largest media company in the biggest merger ever. The new company is called AOL Time Warner, Inc. and the stock symbol is AOL.

"AOL Anywhere." That's the vision of AOL founder and Chairman Steve Case. Or, as AOL's mission statement phrases it, "Our mission is to build a global medium as central to people's lives as the telephone or television . . . and even more valuable."

Impossible? With telephones everywhere and Americans watching seven hours of television a day, it is certainly a daunting challenge, especially for the company that only a few years ago faced a severe crisis in not being able to meet demand. However, AOL has embarked on a mission to cut its ties to the desktop computer and be everywhere for everyone, all the time, on myriad devices.

"We think average time online will continue to increase," says Case, "particularly with new devices and new kinds of networks, and being untethered from simply being in your den, turning on your desktop PC when you get home—to really having services anytime, anywhere. That's going to lift the overall usage and stimulate all kinds of wonderful things in people's lives, as well as stimulate all kinds of wonderful new revenue streams for AOL."

Prior to the merger, AOL was the world's most valuable media company. Its market value of $200 billion was larger than AT&T or the combined values of Disney, Time Warner, and News Corp. In December 1999, *The Wall Street Journal* named America Online's stock as the "Biggest Gainer of the '90s" with a nearly 80,000 percent gain. AOL's market value is approaching 50 percent of the market value of the world's most valuable company—Microsoft. AOL's nearly $5 billion in sales for 1999 was more than the total of the next twenty Internet companies. Its services in one form or another account for 39 percent of the time Americans spend online. AOL delivers more electronic messages than the U.S. Post Office delivers letters and packages. Case's goal is for AOL to surpass Microsoft and become the most valuable company in the world.

The company's plan to reach its vision has three basic elements. The first is to double the membership of the flagship America Online service and add even more members overseas and through its other branded services like Netscape, ICQ, and CompuServe. The second element is to develop new services, intended to increase the time users spend online and thereby grow advertising revenues. The third element is to extend the company's expanded services to television screens, handheld computers, cellular phones, and other devices.

### ■ HISTORY

In 1985, Steve Case founded what has become America Online. Then called Quantum Computer Services, the company operated online services under several names before consolidating them under the America Online name and changing the name of the company to America Online, Inc., in 1991. The company went public in 1992 at $11.50 per share.

Case was the right person at the right time—the beginning of the Information Revolution. When the company went public, it had fewer than 200,000 members. In less than seven years, membership grew a stunning 9400 percent to more than 19 million in 1999. It happened because people discovered that computers could be used as a basic medium of communication. Before the advent of online services, most computers were isolated units, useful only for the work that could be done on one machine. Many were connected to local area networks (LANs), or even to larger networks, but these networks themselves were isolated from each other. But everyone had a telephone. With a modem, a telephone line, and an online service like AOL, individuals were suddenly able to form virtual communities based on mutual interests, correspond via electronic mail, and access information at remote locations via computer.

A pivotal year for AOL was 1997. The company faced its worst problems since its founding, began to overcome them, and made deals that would change its structure dramatically. The company adopted $19.95 per month flat-rate pricing and passed the 9 million-subscriber mark. The year began with what was perhaps the most controversial episode in the history of the company—the near-collapse of its systems under the demand crush that flat-rate pricing generated. The problems generated enough complaints from users that attorneys in many states threatened legal action against the company for failure to deliver the service it was selling. After a barrage of negative publicity over busy signals, slow and unpredictable network performance, e-mail blackouts, and customer billing disputes, AOL's network overhaul improved the situation. At the peak of anti-AOL sentiment, there were more than one hundred sites on the World Wide Web devoted to everything that was wrong with America Online, including sites such as "AOL Sucks," "Why and How to Leave AOL," "AOHELL," "Yeah, Yeah, Another AOL Sucks Page," and "America On Hold."

In 1998, AOL acquired CompuServe and garnered a combined customer base of more than 12 million subscribers, dwarfing its biggest competitor—Microsoft Corp.'s Microsoft Network, with 2.3 million users. The addition of CompuServe's 850,000 European users made AOL the largest European online service. AOL also gained more than 300,000 CompuServe members elsewhere around the world.

Also in 1998, AOL acquired Mirabilis, LTD, which at the time was the premier provider of instant-messaging software. Mirabilis had 12 million registered trial users and had established a brand of instant-messaging software called ICQ ("I seek you.") that had become well known in a short time and had a large community of users. The acquisition was seen at the time as a key to the company's future strategy. "The question for us is not just acquiring ICQ for what it is today," AOL Chairman Steve Case said. "It is what ICQ can become in our efforts to expand on the Web."

In 1999, AOL acquired Netscape Communications Corp. in a complex deal that also involved an alliance with Sun Microsystems, Inc.

## ■ INTERNAL OPERATIONS

Once you are online with AOL, there are many opportunities to join interest groups such as chat rooms and forums, where you can discuss your interests with others. The exclusive content areas, called channels, organize the vast stores of information into a digestible form. America Online is the world's most popular online service. The service provides subscribers with a variety of interactive features—electronic mail, Internet access, entertainment, reference information, news, sports, weather, financial information and transactions, electronic shopping, and more. The service had record membership growth in fiscal 1999, with more than five million new subscribers. Its members average more than fifty-two minutes a day online, and it has more than one thousand advertising, e-commerce, and content partners.

America Online's primary market is the home computer user, and that market is growing. For the first time, the average American household is more likely to have a PC than not, and more than 60 percent of U.S. households with children have PCs. PCs are now a mainstream item, and nearly 40 percent of U.S. households are online.

AOL has four product groups organized into two business divisions. The Interactive Online Services business includes the Interactive Services Group, the Interactive Properties Group, and the AOL International Group. The Enterprise Solutions business is comprised of the Netscape Enterprise Group.

### Interactive Services Group

The Interactive Services Group develops and operates branded interactive services, including the AOL service, the CompuServe service, the Netscape Netcenter Internet portal, the AOL.COM Internet portal, and the Netscape Communicator software, including the Netscape Navigator browser. The Interactive Services Group generates most of the company's revenues, subscriber fees, which were $3.3 billion in 1999, nearly ten times 1995's $352 million in such fees. Advertising, commerce, and other revenue accounted for $1 billion, twenty times more than 1995's $50 million.

### Netscape Communicator

Netscape Communicator is a suite of software programs used to connect users to the Web and interact with other Internet users. It integrates browsing, e-mail, Web-based word processing, and group scheduling. The Netscape Navigator Web browser is the primary product and was at one time the dominant browser on the market. It has lost that position to Microsoft's Internet Explorer browser, but it still retains a substantial market share. Netscape had an 87 percent share in 1996 but dropped to 36 percent in 1999. The primary causes of the market share loss have been Microsoft's decision to give away its browser and repeated delays in the release of a new version of Communicator.

### ICQ

When AOL acquired ICQ, parent company of Mirabilis, the instant-messaging service had grown to more than fifty million users to become the world's largest and fastest growing. An average of ninety-four thousand new people were signing up daily, and the company had signed $100 million worth of e-commerce and marketing agreements.

ICQ's registered users have desirable demographics. Most are young (85 percent are under thirty-five) and single. Fewer than one in ten ICQ users were America Online subscribers, so the service greatly expanded AOL's customer base. Also, ICQ increased AOL's presence in worldwide markets. More than two-thirds of its users were outside the United States. ICQ had more than two million users in Brazil and nearly two million in China.

Instant messaging increases the amount of time individuals spend each day on AOL's various services, thus increasing its advertising and e-commerce reach. Many people leave the ICQ software on their computer screens whenever they are online. Its users on average keep the service on their computer screens for more than 2.5 hours daily, and actively use it for more than an hour a day. Thus, AOL gains a way to constantly promote its offerings on the user's computer screen, no matter where the user goes on the Web. Also, AOL is working with newly acquired Tegic Communications to bring AOL instant messaging to a broad range of mobile wireless devices.

In addition, AOL is developing ICQ.com itself into a Web portal in its own right, with expanded features including free e-mail, search capability, topic-specific content channels, and directory services. AOL has signed multiple agreements with third parties to build ICQ's user base and add features to the service. One such agreement is a four-year deal with Net2Phone, Inc. to provide Internet telephony (voice) services for America Online's ICQ service. Another is an agreement with Motorola, Inc. to deliver instant-messaging capabilities to cell phones. Marketing partnerships with other companies, such as eBay, Inc. and American Greetings, bring benefits to ICQ users while generating upfront payments to ICQ and continuing fees based on advertising impressions and e-commerce transactions.

### MovieFone

AOL MovieFone (www.moviefone.com) is the world's leading destination for moviegoers to find out what movies are playing, check theaters and showtimes, and purchase tickets. One in five moviegoers uses AOL MovieFone, and the service has more than 150 million users per year over the telephone and on the Web. AOL acquired MovieFone in 1999 and re-branded it AOL MovieFone. AOL is enhancing MovieFone to make it more convenient, and it plans to offer additional content and commerce opportunities. The service has been integrated into the AOL.COM and Netscape Netcenter, and the promotional trailers for MovieFone will be updated with AOL branding in movie theaters around the country.

### Spinner.com, Winamp, and SHOUTcast

The Internet is dramatically transforming the music business, and AOL has made strategic acquisitions to help it capture an increasing share of the more than $50 billion music market. AOL acquired the Internet music brands Spinner.com, Winamp, and SHOUTcast in 1999, through its acquisitions of Spinner Networks, Inc. and Nullsoft, Inc.

The Spinner.com Web site offers more than 250,000 songs on more than 120 channels of programmed music in various formats. Its music player turns your computer into a radio, displays song information as the song is played, and enables listener feedback and instant ordering of the music being played. The Spinner Networks broadcast more than ten million songs weekly with the typical user session lasting two hours. The site also offers music downloads that can be saved and played on portable digital music players using the popular MP3 format.

Nullsoft, Inc. is the developer of the Winamp digital music player software and SHOUTcast, a streaming audio system that enables individuals to broadcast their own digital audio content over the Internet. Winamp is the leading high-fidelity music player for Windows. Two-thirds of Winamp users are under age twenty-six, with one-third living outside the United States.

### AOL International Group

More than two-thirds of Internet users are expected to live and work in other countries by 2002, and AOL is aggressively expanding its international business, launching new services, and making changes in existing ones. The AOL International Group oversees the AOL and CompuServe operations outside the United States, as well as the Netscape Online service, which was launched in August 1999 as a free online service in the United Kingdom. Globally, members are able to access these services in more than one hundred countries. As of August 1999, the AOL and CompuServe services had more than three million members outside the United States.

AOL's basic international strategy is to build a global brand but with local implementations of the service. It has established joint ventures in each area, then built local management to make local decisions about the software, content, and pricing. AOL offers its AOL- and/or CompuServe-branded services through joint ventures or distribution arrangements in Australia, Austria, Canada, France, Germany, Japan, the Netherlands, Sweden, Switzerland, and the United Kingdom. AOL provides services in several European countries through joint ventures with Bertelsmann A.G. entitled "AOL Europe," and "CompuServe Europe" plans to extend these services into additional European markets. Germany's Bertelsmann is one of the world's largest media companies.

In Great Britain, Internet users are subject to heavy per-minute charges for local telephone calls. The high telephone charges stymied the growth of the Internet there until recently, when Freeserve Plc (NYSE:FRE) began offering service with no monthly service fees. Until then, AOL was Britain's largest ISP, but it quickly lost ground to Freeserve and other free services as the free-service model quickly became the dominant one in Great Britain.

AOL responded by launching its Netscape Online service for value-oriented consumers. Netscape Online has experienced strong growth. It offers instant messaging, Netscape's Web browser, as well as content and community features. Netscape Online software—co-branded with Woolworths—is available free of charge through the nearly eight hundred Woolworths stores across the United Kingdom.

In Germany, the company has introduced new AOL pricing plans. In August 1999, AOL Europe announced it would offer unlimited online access in Germany for a flat rate of 9.90 marks per month. The flat rate is intended to speed growth in Germany and undercut rival Deutsche Telekom A.G. In October 1999, AOL Germany announced that it had surpassed one million members, a first for an AOL property outside of the United States. AOL is also embarking on an aggressive expansion into other international markets, including Hong Kong, China, Brazil, Argentina, and Mexico.

### Netscape Enterprise Group

The Netscape Enterprise Group provides businesses a range of software products, technical support, consulting, and training services. These products and services enable businesses and users to share information, manage networks, and take their businesses online. Enterprise solutions revenues grew from $23 million in 1995 to $456 million in 1999 following the Netscape acquisition.

### Marketing and Distribution

To encourage people to join its flagship online service, AOL gives away an introductory package that includes the AOL software and a free one-month trial membership, which it promotes through a variety of traditional and new media outlets. There are many ways for people to get the introductory package. Millions of AOL 5.0 CD-ROMs have been distributed through more than five thousand retail outlets, including CompUSA, Circuit City, Office Depot, J&R Computer World, and Barnes & Noble. In addition, the software has been pre-installed on PCs from many manufacturers. It can be accessed through an icon on the Windows 95 and 98 and Apple Macintosh desktops. It can be obtained by calling 1-800-4-ONLINE or by downloading it from www.aol.com. It has even been distributed in boxes of Chex cereal, and it appears as a kind of bonus track on some music CDs. It is also estimated that well over 100 million copies have been distributed by bulk mail. AOL has been criticized for massive spending on some of these marketing methods, especially the shotgun mailings that are expensive and tend to yield higher percentages of short-term members who soon cancel their accounts.

America Online offers "tiered" pricing in the United States. The flat, unlimited-use rate is $21.95 per month. Those who pay in advance can opt for a one-year unlimited usage membership for $19.95 per month. Consumers who already have Internet service through an ISP can get AOL content for $9.95 a month, and those whose online usage is light may join AOL for $4.95 per month for three hours of service, with additional time costing $2.50 an hour. CompuServe membership is $24.95 per month with no additional hourly charge, or five hours for $9.95 per month, with additional time priced at $2.95 per hour.

### Services

AOL 5.0 includes a number of new features. "You've Got Pictures" was developed in partnership with Eastman Kodak and is supported by forty thousand Kodak dealers. The service allows members to receive their developed photos online, share them via e-mail, organize and store them online, and order reprints and gifts online. "My Calendar" is an interactive web-based calendar that helps members track appointments, key dates, and other personal events online. AOL Search is a new search product that enables AOL members to easily search the Internet and AOL's exclusive content without leaving the AOL service. AOL Plus enables members to connect to the AOL service through high-speed broadband technologies, including DSL, cable, satellite, and wireless. AOL Plus provides additional online content to members using broadband connections, including video, games, music, and online catalogue shopping features. AOL Radio delivers event-driven, live programming of such events as concerts, breaking news, sports, and celebrity events.

### Agreements

AOL has promised to buy $500 million worth of equipment from Sun by 2002. In return, Sun will use its sales force to sell Netscape electronic-commerce server software, agreeing to pay AOL $100 million a quarter over twelve quarters to build on and sell software developed by Netscape. The alliance is a quasi-independent company with more than two thousand employees gathered equally from Netscape and Sun.

AOL signed an agreement with Web career site Monster.com, making it the exclusive provider of job-hunting information on America Online, Inc. under a four-year, $100 million alliance. Monster.com and AOL will create co-branded sites allowing AOL members and visitors to search for jobs, apply online, research companies, and choose personalized geographic areas to help with their job searches. Recruiters also can use the co-branded sites to post jobs, search through Monster.com's resumes, screen candidates, and receive e-mails when matching resumes are posted.

In another deal, AOL and Net2Phone Inc. unveiled a three-year alliance to provide AOL Instant Messenger users with phone service over the Internet. AOL will work with Net2Phone to create AOL Instant Messenger–branded phone service and products, including a branded card that gives Instant Messenger users low-cost Internet-based phone service.

AOL has announced a deal to invest $800 million in cash and stock in PC maker Gateway, Inc., making AOL the default Internet service provider for the more than five million Gateway-made machines sold annually. It is AOL's most aggressive move to date in the growing sector of "computer service providers"—companies that aim to position themselves as one-stop shops for buying computing devices, online access, and applications for a single monthly fee. AOL also will assume management of Gateway's 600,000-subscriber Gateway.net online service, incorporating content and personalization tools from AOL's Web properties into the Gateway-branded service. The companies also plan to offer non-PC devices that integrate access to the AOL service.

AOL reached an agreement with Compaq Computer Corporation whereby the Compaq Presario Internet PCs will be equipped with modems and pre-installed AOL software with special broadband programming and features. With these computers, AOL members in DSL-available areas will be able to access AOL through a high-speed DSL connection without additional equipment, wiring, or phone jacks.

AOL formed a strategic alliance with Hughes Electronics, taking a major step forward in its "AOL Anywhere" strategy while gaining a valuable e-commerce partner and adding to its broadband capabilities. The partnership will help launch two new AOL services: AOL TV and high-speed broadband AOL Plus. AOL and Hughes will develop television set-top boxes to make AOL TV available to DirecTV customers. The two plan a major cross-marketing campaign for both AOL TV and Hughes's DirecTV. They will market AOL TV to the more than seven million DirecTV subscribers while marketing DirecTV to U.S. AOL and CompuServe members and consumers of America Online's Internet brands. The alliance also advances America Online's commitment to provide its AOL-Plus broadband service nationwide, making AOL-Plus available via Hughes's DirecPC satellite network.

AOL has agreements with several telecommunications companies to expand broadband access for its customers. Deals with SBC Communications Inc., Bell Atlantic Corp., and Ameritech Corp. together will bring high-speed asymmetrical digital subscriber line (ADSL) access services to 55 percent of the households served by AOL. DSL allows faster transmission of data through existing copper phone lines, and at present it is AOL's primary route to providing high-speed broadband services.

AOL has an agreement to invest $30 million in the online business of video rental and sales chain Blockbuster, Inc. as part a multi-year strategic alliance. The investment in Blockbuster.com will be used to jointly develop broadband programming and delivery. Blockbuster will have a continuous presence in the home-video area of AOL's entertainment channel, and AOL members will have direct access to home-video and entertainment information available on Blockbuster.com. Blockbuster, which claims sixty-five million active members, will distribute free AOL software at approximately four thousand Blockbuster locations in the United States. Blockbuster will also expand its promotion of AOL on its in-store television network, in TV advertisements, and in TV programs such as the Blockbuster Entertainment Awards.

AOL announced an alliance with electronics retailer Circuit City. AOL's products and services will be featured in the chain's 615 stores nationwide, and part of each store will be dedicated specifically to promoting AOL's dial-up service and upcoming broadband offerings. Circuit City also will incorporate promotion of AOL into its traditional advertising. The deal will also make AOL Circuit City's preferred Internet online service, and feature Circuit City as an anchor tenant in the Shop@online shopping destinations. Circuit City will be able to offer consumers everything they need for home connectivity, including access to the Internet via AOL. In addition, Circuit City will promote AOL and its in-store offerings in its print and television advertising programs and in other promotional and marketing campaigns. Circuit City is the nation's eleventh-largest brand advertiser and the leading specialty retail advertiser of consumer electronics, personal computers, and major appliances.

AOL and Wal-Mart have a wide-ranging strategic alliance to create a new co-branded Internet service provider and numerous cross-marketing initiatives between the two companies. The new co-branded Wal-Mart/AOL ISP will be a customized version of the CompuServe service priced for value-conscious consumers. The alliance is the largest yet in a string of deals between major retailers and established Web players.

Wal-Mart will promote both the Wal-Mart/AOL ISP and the America Online flagship interactive service, through print, radio, and television advertising, and in-store promotions in its more than twenty-nine hundred U.S. stores. Wal-Mart will also distribute AOL 5.0 software in its stores and is exploring ways to market other AOL products. Wal-Mart.com also will be available in the Shop@ areas across America Online's brands.

AOL and Wal-Mart also said that they would work together to expand local Internet access in smaller communities where it is currently not available. Wal-Mart said that only six of every ten towns where it operates stores have local Internet access. The alliance should help to provide more Wal-Mart communities with convenient, low-cost access to the Internet.

### Shop@AOL

Shop@AOL uses a highly visual, magazine-style design to bring together millions of products from more than 275 brand-name merchants, and offers a 100 percent guarantee of satisfaction and security. Since its launch in 1999, it has become the most popular shopping venue in cyberspace, offering features that please both consumers and merchants, while adding substantially to AOL revenues. Consumers like the service for a variety of reasons, including convenience, variety and security. Shop@AOL has a variety of features that make it one of the easiest ways to buy online. Shopping Search helps users find specific items, with links to the AOL merchant partners offering the product. Quick Checkout "wallet" technology safely stores ten credit card numbers and up to fifty shipping addresses online for use at any of the merchants on the service. Quick Checkout users see a "Buy Now" icon next to Shopping Search results and can click on it to immediately purchase the product.

Merchants like Shop@AOL because it is the most profitable way for many of them to sell online. A recent Forrester Research report praised Shop@AOL as the "Internet's Miracle Mile," saying "retailers repeatedly cite AOL deals as the most profitable." One "bricks-and-mortar" retailer told Forrester: "They are our best relationship by far, and all we have is a button on their shopping channel. It is the only portal that pays for itself—every dollar yields multiple dollars in return." The report predicted that "experienced retailers will vote with their feet and move the bulk of their spending to AOL, relegating other portals to performance-based deals." AOL's efforts have led to an extraordinary 95 percent merchant partnership renewal rate. From 1998 to 1999, AOL expanded its roster of online stores by nearly 150 percent, with many partners expanding their commitments to the service.

Shop@AOL offers merchants the broadest reach available online, reaching 70 percent of all those who visit online services or Web sites every month. The service is available through the America Online service, Shop@AOL.COM, Shop@CompuServe, Shop@Netscape, and Shop@Digital City. This broad reach generates large volumes of traffic for merchants. The percentage of people buying online in general went up to 42 percent in 1999 from 31 percent in 1998, and shopping appears to be growing even faster on America Online. More than 60 percent of America Online's twenty million members have made at least one online purchase, and thirty thousand members a day try online shopping for the first time. Online shopping by America Online members topped $2.7 billion in the September 1999 quarter.

*Financials*

AOL had net income of $762 million in 1999. The company had revenues of $4.777 billion, an increase of 54 percent compared to $3.091 billion in 1998. Expenses in 1999 were $4.319 billion, up only 36 percent from $3.211 billion in 1998.

Subscription services revenues increased from $2.183 billion to $3.321 billion, or 52 percent, over fiscal 1998. The increase was primarily attributable to a 38 percent increase in the average number of subscribers, compared to fiscal 1998, as well as an 8.2 percent increase in the average monthly subscription services revenue per subscriber. The average monthly subscription services revenue per subscriber increased from $17.95 in fiscal 1998 to $19.42 in fiscal 1999, primarily because of the April 1998 increase in the Flat-Rate Plan membership fee from $19.95 to $21.95.

Advertising, commerce, and other revenues increased by 84 percent, from $543 million in fiscal 1998 to $1 billion in fiscal 1999, with a backlog of committed revenues of $1.5 billion. More advertising on the company's America Online service and Netcenter portal and an increase in electronic commerce fees drove the increase. Advertising and electronic commerce fees increased by 114 percent, from $358 million in fiscal 1998 to $765 million in fiscal 1999.

Enterprise solutions revenues increased by 25 percent, from $365 million in fiscal 1998 to $456 million in fiscal 1999. The increase was because of an increase in product sales related to server applications and consulting services. Cost of revenues increased from $1,811 million to $2,657 million, or 47 percent, over fiscal 1998, and decreased as a percentage of total revenues from 58.6 to 55.6 percent. Sales and marketing expenses increased from $623 million to $808 million, or 30 percent, over fiscal 1998, and decreased as a percentage of total revenues from 20.2 to 16.9 percent. Product development costs increased from $239 million to $286 million, or 20 percent, over fiscal 1998, and decreased as a percentage of total revenues from 7.7 to 6.0 percent. General and administrative expenses increased from $328 million to $408 million, or 24 percent, over fiscal 1998, and decreased as a percentage of total revenues from 10.6 percent to 8.5 percent.

## ■ COMPETITION

AOL has a number of obstacles blocking it from achieving its founder's dream of being the world's most valuable company. Free and fee-based ISPs, Baby Bells, cable companies, Web portals, and television networks are some of their present competitors. Yahoo! Inc. has the single largest portal on the Internet, is stronger internationally, and has signed more deals to deliver Web content via handheld computers, smart phones, and pagers. However, one company in particular stands in AOL's way: Microsoft.

AOL has bested Microsoft more than once. The MSN online service was a failure while America Online was growing rapidly. MSN has had only mediocre results since its reincarnation as an ISP. And in 1998 and 1999, AOL bested Microsoft again in the field of instant messaging. With the 1998 acquisition of Mirabilis, AOL snatched a prime piece of the Internet. In 1999, Microsoft introduced its own new instant messaging software with the ability to exchange messages with AOL Instant Messenger users. AOL managed to block the attempt.

The instant messaging conflict was about who controls the consumer, and ultimately the Internet. Whoever dominates the instant messaging market can use that power to attract users to their other software and services. Microsoft's problem is that the overwhelming majority of instant messaging users already use AOL instant messaging network. New users want to be able to communicate with the most people possible, so they are very likely to use the service with the largest user base. If AOL can keep its system closed to competitors, it will have a natural monopoly on the instant messaging market. It is possible that it could avoid antitrust action by the U.S. government if it continues to offer the software and service for free. For now, the service is not profitable, but a closed instant-messaging system helps the company maintain a captive audience and build a platform for future audio and video services.

By mid-2000, AOL expects to launch AOL TV, a new rival to Microsoft's TV initiatives. With the help of partners DirecTV, Hughes Network Systems, Philips Electronics (PHG), and Liberate Technologies (LBRT). AOL is expected next year to start marketing a set-top box—using a non-Microsoft browser—that can bring both AOL's interactive service and DirecTV's satellite broadcasts to the same TV screen.

Currently bogged down in antitrust litigation, Microsoft nevertheless plans to accelerate the trend toward low-price or free Internet access. "We intend to be aggressive with access," said Brad Chase, vice president of Microsoft's new consumer and commerce Group and the point man for Microsoft's new strategy. "AOL might think about it as a profit center. That's not how we think about it." Microsoft has also tested $9.95 a month pricing and made deals with retailers and PC makers to offer customers $400 rebates in return for three-year MSN service contracts. AOL responded by matching the offer through its CompuServe 2000 service.

AOL also faces competition from free Internet access services. Currently, 1.5 million American households access the Web for free, while 41.4 million households go through another type of service, according to Jupiter Communications. By 2003, Jupiter estimates as many as 8.8 million households will use some kind of free service to access the Web. As connection costs come down, free access to the Internet may become common.

Consumer ISPs EarthLink and MindSpring merged in 1999 to create the second largest U.S. Internet provider. The newly formed EarthLink Network has 3 million subscribers. There are many other ISPs, large and small, that compete with AOL. It is likely that further consolidation will occur in this segment, providing stronger competition for AOL.

The Baby Bells are also an increasingly strong competitor. Regional Bell Operating Companies (RBOCs) and other telecommunications carriers are becoming more successful as consumer ISPs. During 1998, the combined subscriber base for these nontraditional service providers grew 137 percent compared to only 37 percent growth among traditional ISPs (including AOL, MSN, Mindspring, Earthlink, Prodigy, and Flashnet).

Cable providers also have begun to broaden their share of the overall consumer market. Cable subscriptions grew almost ten-fold, although their share of the overall U.S. consumer market remained low, accounting for only 1 percent by the end of 1998. Cable TV operators report that more than a million cable modems have been installed in users' homes, but this is still a small fraction of the over thirty-eight million households currently accessing online services.

Mergers and acquisitions of Internet sites soared to $33.4 billion in the first half of 1999, more than twenty-two times the 1998 first-half total of $1.5 billion, according to a report by the Webmergers.com unit of San Francisco-based New Media Resources.

*AOL—2000*

AOL has purchased MapQuest.com for $1.1 billion to enhance its AOL Anywhere strategy and to become the leader in online mapping. In another move, AOL and Gateway have introduced a line of low-cost Internet kitchen appliances that allow quick access to the Internet from kitchen appliances.

If the Time Warner–AOL merger is approved, executives of both companies vow that their megadeal will accelerate the arrival of high-speed Internet services, sometimes called broadband services, in homes and businesses. Fewer than two million American households in mid-2000 have the two main broadband-delivery technologies: cable modems, which deliver broadband services via cable-television lines, and digital subscriber lines, the phone companies' version of high-speed access. Thus this high speed market is almost untapped and provided the primary rationale for the merger itself.

AOL is developing software to allow its customers to receive their e-mail to and from Palm computers. AOL's purchase of Tegic Communications enhanced their entry into wireless communications. Time Warner owns the magazines *Time, People,* and *Sports Illustrated* as well as cable channels CNN and HBO; it also owns WB Network, Atlantic Records, and Warner Books. Some analysts believe that the sheer size of Time Warner which has seventy thousand employees compared to AOL's twelve thousand employees will sap AOL's creative energy and result in a bureaucratic giant. Time Warner, headquartered in New York, has annual revenue of about $27 billion compared to AOL's annual revenue of about $5 billion.

## ■ CONCLUSION

AOL's stock price has dropped sharply in 2000 as concern still lingers regarding the Time Warner merger. Some analysts contend that the rapid move to wireless communication makes the Time Warner acquisition a bad deal for AOL.

Prepare a three-year strategic plan for AOL's CEO Steve Case. Include proforma financial statements with your plan to reveal the expected results of your proposed strategies.

## CASE FIGURE 1    Company Highlights

| IN MILLIONS UNLESS OTHERWISE NOTED | Year Ended June 30 | | |
| --- | --- | --- | --- |
| | 1999 | 1998 | 1997 |
| Subscription Services Revenues | $ 3,321 | $ 2,183 | $ 1,478 |
| Advertising, Commerce, and Other Revenues | 1,000 | 543 | 308 |
| Enterprise Solutions Revenues | 456 | 365 | 411 |
| Total Revenues | $ 4,777 | $ 3,091 | $ 2,197 |
| Operating Income* | $ 578 | $ 66 | $ 6 |
| Net Income* | 396 | 59 | 10 |
| EPS (IN DOLLARS)* | 0.34 | 0.06 | 0.01 |
| EBITDA** | 968 | 302 | 111 |
| AOL Members (IN THOUSANDS) | 17,619 | 12,535 | 8,636 |
| Employees (IN WHOLE NUMBERS) | 12,100 | 8,500 | 7,400 |

\* on a fully taxed basis before one time charges
\*\* EBITDA: Earnings Before Interest, Taxes, Depreciation and Amortization

Source: AOL 1999 Annual Report, p.1.

## CASE FIGURE 2    AOL's Material Properties

| Location | Size | Owned/Lease | Purpose |
| --- | --- | --- | --- |
| Columbus, OH | 296,000 sq. ft. | Owned | Office Space |
| Dulles, VA | 590,000 sq. ft. (1) | Owned (2) | Corporate Headquarters |
| Dulles, VA | 180,000 sq. ft. | Owned | Technology Center |
| Manassas, VA | 220,000 sq. ft. | Owned | Technology Center (3) |
| Mountain View, CA | 1,054,000 sq. ft. | Leased | Office Space |
| Reston, VA | 265,000 sq. ft. | Owned (2) | Technology Center |
| San Francisco, CA | 36,000 sq. ft. | Leased | Office Space |
| Vienna, VA | 110,000 sq. ft. | Leased | Office Space |

(1) Two additional facilities are under construction at this site that, when completed, will add 380,000 sq. ft. to the current size. Both facilities are expected to be completed in 2000.

(2) This property is held subject to a mortgage.

(3) The Company acquired 25.5 acres of land in Manassas, Virginia in February 1999. The technology center to be located on the property is under construction and is expected to be completed in early 2000.

Source: AOL's 1999 Annual Report, p. 13.

CASE FIGURE 3    **AOL's Segment Information**

|  | *Year Ended June 30* | | | | | |
|---|---|---|---|---|---|---|
|  | 1999 | | 1998 | | 1997 | |
|  | *(Amounts in millions)* | | | | | |
| **Revenues:** | | | | | | |
| Interactive Online Services . . . . . . . . . . . . . . . . . | $4,321 | | $2,726 | | $1,786 | |
| Enterprise Solutions . . . . . . . . . . . . . . . . . . . . . . | 456 | | 365 | | 411 | |
|     Total revenues. . . . . . . . . . . . . . . . . . . . . . | $4,777 | | $3,091 | | $2,197 | |
| **Income (loss) from operations:** | | | | | | |
| Interactive Online Services (1) (2). . . . . . . . . . . . | $  955 | | $  412 | | $ (257) | |
| Enterprise Solutions (2) . . . . . . . . . . . . . . . . . . . | 6 | | (18) | | 98 | |
| General & Administrative. . . . . . . . . . . . . . . . . . | (408) | | (328) | | (220) | |
| Other (3) . . . . . . . . . . . . . . . . . . . . . . . . . . . . . . | (95) | | (186) | | (106) | |
|     Total income (loss) from operations. . . . . . . | $  458 | | $ (120) | | $ (485) | |
| **Revenues:** | | | | | | |
| Advertising and electronic commerce fees. . . . . . . | $  765 | 76.5% | $  358 | 65.9% | $  147 | 47.7% |
| Merchandise . . . . . . . . . . . . . . . . . . . . . . . . . . . . | 134 | 13.4 | 103 | 19.0 | 109 | 35.4 |
| Other . . . . . . . . . . . . . . . . . . . . . . . . . . . . . . . . . | 101 | 10.1 | 82 | 15.1 | 52 | 16.9 |
| Total advertising, commerce and other revenues . . | $1,000 | 100.0% | $  543 | 100.0% | $  308 | 100.0% |
| **Revenues:** | | | | | | |
| Subscription services. . . . . . . . . . . . . . . . . . . . . . | $3,321 | 69.5% | $2,183 | 70.6% | $1,478 | 67.3% |
| Advertising: commerce and other . . . . . . . . . . . . | 1,000 | 21.0 | 543 | 17.6 | 308 | 14.0 |
| Enterprise solutions . . . . . . . . . . . . . . . . . . . . . . | 456 | 9.5 | 365 | 11.8 | 411 | 18.7 |
| Total revenues. . . . . . . . . . . . . . . . . . . . . . . . . . | $4,777 | 100.0% | $3,091 | 100.0% | $2,197 | 100.0% |

*Source:* AOL's 1999 Annual Report, p. 18, 20, 26.

**CASE FIGURE 4**    **AMERICA ONLINE, INC.**
**CONSOLIDATED BALANCE SHEETS**

|  | June 30, | |
|---|---|---|
|  | 1999 | 1998 |
|  | *(Amounts in millions, except share data)* | |
| **ASSETS** | | |
| Current assets: | | |
| Cash and cash equivalents . . . . . . . . . . . . . . . . . . . . . . . . . . . . . . | $  887 | $  677 |
| Short-term investments . . . . . . . . . . . . . . . . . . . . . . . . . . . . . . . | 537 | 146 |
| Trade accounts receivable, less allowances of $54 and $34, | | |
| respectively. . . . . . . . . . . . . . . . . . . . . . . . . . . . . . . . . . . | 323 | 192 |
| Other receivables . . . . . . . . . . . . . . . . . . . . . . . . . . . . . . . . . | 79 | 93 |
| Prepaid expenses and other current assets . . . . . . . . . . . . . . . . . | 153 | 155 |
| Total current assets. . . . . . . . . . . . . . . . . . . . . . . . . . . . . . . . | 1,979 | 1,263 |
| Property and equipment at cost, net. . . . . . . . . . . . . . . . . . . . . . | 657 | 503 |
| Other assets: | | |
| Investments including available-for-sale securities . . . . . . . . . . . | 2,151 | 531 |
| Product development costs, net . . . . . . . . . . . . . . . . . . . . . . . . . | 100 | 88 |
| Goodwill and other intangible assets, net. . . . . . . . . . . . . . . . . . | 454 | 472 |
| Other assets . . . . . . . . . . . . . . . . . . . . . . . . . . . . . . . . . . . . | 7 | 17 |
| Total assets. . . . . . . . . . . . . . . . . . . . . . . . . . . . . . . . . . . . . | $5,348 | $2,874 |
| **LIABILITIES AND STOCKHOLDERS' EQUITY** | | |
| Current liabilities: | | |
| Trade accounts payable. . . . . . . . . . . . . . . . . . . . . . . . . . . . . . | $   74 | $  120 |
| Other accrued expenses and liabilities . . . . . . . . . . . . . . . . . . . . | 795 | 461 |
| Deferred revenue . . . . . . . . . . . . . . . . . . . . . . . . . . . . . . . . . | 646 | 420 |
| Accrued personnel costs . . . . . . . . . . . . . . . . . . . . . . . . . . . . . | 134 | 78 |
| Deferred network services credit. . . . . . . . . . . . . . . . . . . . . . . . | 76 | 76 |
| Total current liabilities. . . . . . . . . . . . . . . . . . . . . . . . . . . . . . | 1,725 | 1,155 |
| Long-term liabilities: | | |
| Notes payable . . . . . . . . . . . . . . . . . . . . . . . . . . . . . . . . . . . | 348 | 372 |
| Deferred revenue . . . . . . . . . . . . . . . . . . . . . . . . . . . . . . . . . | 30 | 71 |
| Other liabilities . . . . . . . . . . . . . . . . . . . . . . . . . . . . . . . . . . | 15 | 7 |
| Deferred network services credit. . . . . . . . . . . . . . . . . . . . . . . . | 197 | 273 |
| Total liabilities. . . . . . . . . . . . . . . . . . . . . . . . . . . . . . . . . . . | $2,315 | $1,878 |

*continued*

CASE FIGURE 4    **AMERICA ONLINE, INC.**
**CONSOLIDATED BALANCE SHEETS** *(cont.)*

|  | June 30, | |
|---|---|---|
|  | **1999** | **1998** |
| Stockholders' equity: | | |
| Preferred stock, $.01 par value; 5,000,000 shares authorized, no shares issued and outstanding at June 30, 1999 and 1998, respectively................. | — | — |
| Common stock, $.01 par value; 1,800,000,000 shares authorized, 1,100,893,933 and 973,150,052 shares issued and outstanding at June 30, 1999 and 1998, respectively.... | 11 | 10 |
| Additional paid-in capital ............................. | 2,703 | 1,431 |
| Accumulated comprehensive income—unrealized gain on available-for-sale securities, net....................... | 168 | 145 |
| Retained earnings (accumulated deficit).................. | 151 | (590) |
| Total stockholders' equity ............................ | 3,033 | 996 |
| Total liabilities and stockholders' equity ................. | $5,348 | $2,874 |

*Source:* AOL's 1999 Annual Report, p. 37.

CASE FIGURE 5    **AMERICA ONLINE, INC.**
**CONSOLIDATED STATEMENTS OF OPERATIONS**

|  | Year ended June 30, | | |
|---|---|---|---|
|  | **1999** | **1998** | **1997** |
|  | *(Amounts in millions, except per share data)* | | |
| Revenues: | | | |
| Subscription services .................................... | $3,321 | $2,183 | $1,478 |
| Advertising, commerce and other........................... | 1,000 | 543 | 308 |
| Enterprise solutions ..................................... | 456 | 365 | 411 |
| Total revenues ...................................... | 4,777 | 3,091 | 2,197 |
| Costs and expenses: | | | |
| Cost of revenues...................................... | 2,657 | 1,811 | 1,162 |
| Sales and marketing | | | |
| Sales and marketing.................................. | 808 | 623 | 608 |
| Write-off of deferred subscriber acquisition costs ............. | — | — | 385 |
| Product development.................................... | 286 | 239 | 195 |
| General and administrative .............................. | 408 | 328 | 220 |
| Amortization of goodwill and other intangible assets ........... | 65 | 24 | 6 |
| Acquired in-process research and development................. | — | 94 | 9 |
| Merger, restructuring and contract termination charges .......... | 95 | 75 | 73 |
| Settlement charges..................................... | — | 17 | 24 |
| Total costs and expenses............................... | $4,319 | $3,211 | $2,682 |

*continued*

CASE FIGURE 5     **AMERICA ONLINE, INC.**
**CONSOLIDATED STATEMENTS OF OPERATIONS** *(cont.)*

| | *Year ended June 30,* | | |
| --- | --- | --- | --- |
| | 1999 | 1998 | 1997 |
| Income (loss) from operations.............................. | 458 | (120) | (485) |
| Other income, net ...................................... | 638 | 30 | 10 |
| Income (loss) before provision for income taxes................ | 1,096 | (90) | (475) |
| (Provision) benefit for income taxes ....................... | (334) | 16 | (10) |
| Net income (loss)...................................... | $ 762 | $ (74) | $ (485) |
| Earnings (loss) per share: | | | |
| Earnings (loss) per share-diluted.......................... | $ 0.60 | $(0.08) | $(0.58) |
| Earnings (loss) per share-basic ........................... | 0.73 | (0.08) | (0.58) |
| Weighted average shares outstanding-diluted................. | 1,277 | 925 | 838 |
| Weighted average shares outstanding-basic .................. | $1,041 | $ 925 | $ 838 |

*Source:* AOL's 1999 Annual Report, p. 38.

# EXPERIENTIAL EXERCISES

**EXPERIENTIAL EXERCISE 1A ▶**

**Strategy Analysis for America Online (AOL)**

### PURPOSE

The purpose of this exercise is to give you experience identifying an organization's opportunities, threats, strengths, and weaknesses. This information is vital to generating and selecting among alternative strategies.

### INSTRUCTIONS

Step 1   Identify what you consider to be AOL's major opportunities, threats, strengths, and weaknesses. On a separate sheet of paper, list these key factors under separate headings. State each factor in specific terms.

Step 2   Through class discussion, compare your lists of external and internal factors to those developed by other students. From the discussion, add to your lists of factors. Keep this information for use in later exercises.

**EXPERIENTIAL EXERCISE 1B ▶**

**Developing a Code of Business Ethics for America Online (AOL)**

### PURPOSE

This exercise can give you practice developing a code of business ethics. Research was conducted to examine codes of business ethics from large manufacturing and service firms in the United States. The twenty-eight variables listed below were found to be included in a sample of more than eighty codes of business ethics. The variables are presented in order of how frequently they occurred. Thus the first variable, "Conduct business in compliance with all laws," was most often included in the sample documents; "Firearms at work are prohibited" was least often included.

1. Conduct business in compliance with all laws.
2. Payments for unlawful purposes are prohibited.
3. Avoid outside activities that impair duties.
4. Comply with all antitrust and trade regulations.
5. Comply with accounting rules and controls.
6. Bribes are prohibited.
7. Maintain confidentiality of records.
8. Participate in community and political activities.
9. Provide products and services of the highest quality.
10. Exhibit standards of personal integrity and conduct.
11. Do not propagate false or misleading information.
12. Perform assigned duties to the best of your ability.
13. Conserve resources and protect the environment.
14. Comply with safety, health, and security regulations.
15. Racial, ethnic, religious, and sexual harassment at work is prohibited.
16. Report unethical and illegal activities to your manager.
17. Convey true claims in product advertisements.
18. Make decisions without regard for personal gain.
19. Do not use company property for personal benefit.
20. Demonstrate courtesy, respect, honesty, and fairness.

21. Illegal drugs and alcohol at work are prohibited.
22. Manage personal finances well.
23. Employees are personally accountable for company funds.
24. Exhibit good attendance and punctuality.
25. Follow directives of supervisors.
26. Do not use abusive language.
27. Dress in businesslike attire.
28. Firearms at work are prohibited.[1]

### INSTRUCTIONS

**Step 1**  On a separate sheet of paper, write a code of business ethics for AOL. Include as many variables listed above as you believe appropriate to AOL's business. Limit your document to one hundred words or less.

**Step 2**  Read your code of ethics to the class. Comment on why you did or did not include certain variables.

**Step 3**  Explain why having a code of ethics is not sufficient for ensuring ethical behavior in an organization. What else does it take?

### NOTES

1. DONALD ROBIN, MICHAEL GIALLOURAKIS, FRED R. DAVID, and THOMAS E. MORITZ. "A Different Look at Codes of Ethics," *Business Horizons* 32, no. 1 (January–February 1989): 66–73.

**EXPERIENTIAL EXERCISE 1C ▶**

## The Ethics of Spying on Competitors

### PURPOSE

This exercise gives you an opportunity to discuss ethical and legal issues in class as related to methods being used by many companies to spy on competing firms. Gathering and using information about competitors is an area of strategic management that Japanese firms do more proficiently than American firms.

### INSTRUCTIONS

On a separate sheet of paper, number from 1 to 18. For the 18 spying activities listed below, indicate whether or not you believe the activity is Ethical or Unethical and Legal or Illegal. Place either an *E* for ethical or *U* for unethical, and either an *L* for legal or an *I* for illegal for each activity. Compare your answers to your classmates' and discuss any differences.

1. Buying competitors' garbage.
2. Dissecting competitors' products.
3. Taking competitors' plant tours anonymously.
4. Counting tractor-trailer trucks leaving competitors' loading bays.
5. Studying aerial photographs of competitors' facilities.
6. Analyzing competitors' labor contracts.
7. Analyzing competitors' help wanted ads.
8. Quizzing customers and buyers about the sales of competitors' products.
9. Infiltrating customers' and competitors' business operations.
10. Quizzing suppliers about competitors' level of manufacturing.
11. Using customers to buy out phony bids.

12. Encouraging key customers to reveal competitive information.
13. Quizzing competitors' former employees.
14. Interviewing consultants who may have worked with competitors.
15. Hiring key managers away from competitors.
16. Conducting phony job interviews to get competitors' employees to reveal information.
17. Sending engineers to trade meetings to quiz competitors' technical employees.
18. Quizzing potential employees who worked for or with competitors.

**EXPERIENTIAL EXERCISE 1D** ▶

**Strategic Planning for My University**

### PURPOSE

External and internal factors are the underlying bases of strategies formulated and implemented by organizations. Your college or university faces numerous external opportunities/threats and has many internal strengths/weaknesses. The purpose of this exercise is to illustrate the process of identifying critical external and internal factors.

External influences include trends in the following areas: economic, social, cultural, demographic, environmental, technological, political, legal, governmental, and competitive. External factors could include declining numbers of high school graduates; population shifts; community relations; increased competitiveness among colleges and universities; rising number of adults returning to college; decreased support from local, state, and federal agencies; and increasing number of foreign students attending American colleges.

Internal factors of a college or university include faculty, students, staff, alumni, athletic programs, physical plant, grounds and maintenance, student housing, administration, fund raising, academic programs, food services, parking, placement, clubs, fraternities, sororities, and public relations.

### INSTRUCTIONS

**Step 1** On a separate sheet of paper, make four headings: External Opportunities, External Threats, Internal Strengths, and Internal Weaknesses

**Step 2** As related to your college or university, list five factors under each of the four headings.

**Step 3** Discuss the factors as a class. Write the factors on the board.

**Step 4** What new things did you learn about your university from the class discussion? How could this type of discussion benefit an organization?

**EXPERIENTIAL EXERCISE 1E** ▶

**Strategic Planning at a Local Company**

### PURPOSE

This activity is aimed at giving your practical knowledge about how organizations in your city or town are doing strategic planning. This exercise also will give you experience interacting on a professional basis with local business leaders.

### INSTRUCTIONS

**Step 1** Use the telephone to contact business owners or top managers. Find an organization that does strategic planning. Make an appointment to visit with the strategist (president, chief executive officer, or owner) of that business.

**Step 2** Seek answers to the following questions during the interview:

a. How does your firm formally conduct strategic planning? Who is involved in the process?

b. Does your firm have a written mission statement? How was the statement developed? When was the statement last changed?

c. What are the benefits of engaging in strategic planning?

d. What are the major costs or problems in doing strategic planning in your business?

e. Do you anticipate making any changes in the strategic planning process at your company? If yes, please explain.

**Step 3**   Report your findings to the class.

**EXPERIENTIAL EXERCISE 1F ▶**

Does My University Recruit in Foreign Countries?

### *PURPOSE*

A competitive climate is emerging among colleges and universities around the world. Colleges and universities in Europe and Japan are increasingly recruiting American students to offset declining enrollments. Foreign students already make up more than one-third of the student body at many American universities. The purpose of this exercise is to identify particular colleges and universities in foreign countries that represent a competitive threat to American institutions of higher learning.

### *INSTRUCTIONS*

**Step 1**   Select a foreign country. Conduct research to determine the number and nature of colleges and universities in that country. What are the major institutions in that country? What programs are those institutions recognized for offering? What percentage of undergraduate and graduate students attending those institutions are American? Do these institutions actively recruit American students?

**Step 2**   Prepare a report for the class that summarizes your research findings. Present your report to the class.

# 2

# THE BUSINESS MISSION

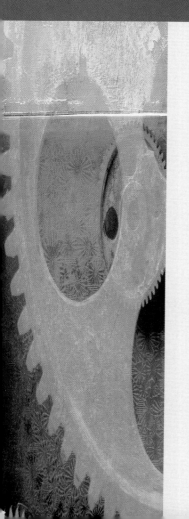

## CHAPTER OUTLINE

# CHAPTER OBJECTIVES

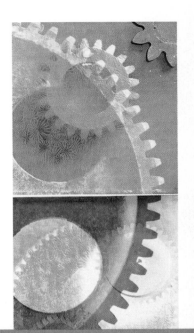

*After studying this chapter, you should be able to do the following:*

1. Describe the nature and role of vision and mission statements in strategic management.
2. Discuss why the process of developing a mission statement is as important as the resulting document.
3. Identify the components of mission statements.
4. Discuss how clear vision and mission statements can benefit other strategic-management activities.
5. Evaluate mission statements of different organizations.
6. Write good vision and mission statements.

# NOTABLE QUOTES

A business is not defined by its name, statutes, or articles of incorporation. It is defined by the business mission. Only a clear definition of the mission and purpose of the organization makes possible clear and realistic business objectives.

PETER DRUCKER

A corporate vision can focus, direct, motivate, unify, and even excite a business into superior performance. The job of a strategist is to identify and project a clear vision.

JOHN KEANE

Where there is no vision, the people perish.

PROVERBS 29:18

Customers are first, employees second, shareholders third, and the community fourth. That's the credo at H. B. Fuller, the century-old adhesives maker in St. Paul.

PATRICIA SELLERS

For strategists, there's a trade-off between the breadth and detail of information needed. It's a bit like an eagle hunting for a rabbit. The eagle has to be high enough to scan a wide area in order to enlarge his chances of seeing prey, but he has to be low enough to see the detail—the movement and features that will allow him to recognize his target. Continually making this trade-off is the job of a strategist—it simply can't be delegated.

FREDERICK GLUCK

The best laid schemes of mice and men often go awry.

ROBERT BURNS (paraphrased)

A strategist's job is to see the company not as it is . . . but as it can become.

JOHN W. TEETS, CHAIRMAN OF GREYHOUND, INC.

That business mission is so rarely given adequate thought is perhaps the most important single cause of business frustration.

PETER DRUCKER

This chapter focuses on the concepts and tools needed to evaluate and write business vision and mission statements. A practical framework for developing mission statements is provided. Actual mission statements from large and small organizations and for-profit and nonprofit enterprises are presented and critically examined. The process of creating a vision and mission statement is discussed.

We can perhaps best understand vision and mission by focusing on a business when it is first started. In the beginning, a new business is simply a collection of ideas. Starting a new business rests on a set of beliefs that the new organization can offer some *product or service*, to some customers, in some geographic area, using some type of technology, at a profitable price. A new business owner typically believes that the management philosophy of the new enterprise will result in a favorable public image and that this concept of the business can be communicated to, and will be adopted by, important constituencies. When the set of beliefs about a business at its inception is put into writing, the resulting document mirrors the same basic ideas that underlie the vision and mission statements. As a business grows, owners or managers find it necessary to revise the founding set of beliefs, but those original ideas usually are reflected in the revised statements of vision and mission.

Vision and mission statements often can be found in the front of annual reports. They often are displayed throughout a firm's premises, and they are distributed with company information sent to constituencies. The statements are part of numerous internal reports, such as loan requests, supplier agreements, labor relations contracts, business plans, and customer service agreements.

 ## WHAT DO WE WANT TO BECOME?

It is especially important for managers and executives in any organization to agree upon the basic vision for which the firm strives to achieve long term. A vision statement should answer the basic question, What do we want to become? A clear vision provides the foundation for developing a comprehensive mission statement. Many organizations have both a vision and mission statement, but the vision statement should be established first and foremost. The vision statement should be short, preferably one sentence, and as many managers as possible should have input into developing the statement.

Several example vision statements are provided below and in Table 2–1.

The Vision of the National Pawnbrokers Association is to have complete and vibrant membership that enjoys a positive public and political image and is the focal organization of all pawn associations.—National Pawnbrokers Association (http://npa.ploygon.net)

Our Vision as an independent community financial institution is to achieve superior long-term shareholder value, exercise exemplary corporate citizenship, and create an environment which promotes and rewards employee development and the consistent delivery of quality service to our customers.—First Reliance Bank of Florence, South Carolina

At CIGNA, we intend to be the best at helping our customers enhance and extend their lives and protect their financial security. Satisfying customers is the key to meeting employee needs and shareholder expectations, and will enable CIGNA to build on our reputation as a financially strong and highly respected company (www.cigna.com).

TABLE 2-1    Vision and Mission Statement Examples

THE BELLEVUE HOSPITAL

*Vision Statement*
The Bellevue Hospital is the LEADER in providing resources necessary to realize the community's highest level of HEALTH throughout life.

*Mission Statement*
The Bellevue Hospital, with *respect, compassion, integrity and courage,* honors the individuality and confidentiality of our patients, employees and community, and is progressive in anticipating and providing future health care services.

U.S. POULTRY & EGG ASSOCIATION

*Vision Statement*
A national organization which represents its members in all aspects of poultry and eggs on both a national and an international level.

*Mission Statement:*
1. We will partner with our affiliated state organizations to attack common problems.
2. We are committed to the advancement of all areas of research and education in poultry technology.
3. The International Poultry Exposition must continue to grow and be beneficial to both exhibitors and attendees.
4. We must always be responsive and effective to the changing needs of our industry.
5. Our imperatives must be such that we do not duplicate the efforts of our sister organizations.
6. We will strive to constantly improve the quality and safety of poultry products.

We will continue to increase the availability of poultry products.

JOHN DEERE, INC.

*Vision Statement*
John Deere is committed to providing Genuine Value to the company's stakeholders, including our customers, dealers, shareholders, employees and communities. In support of that commitment, Deere aspires to:

- Grow and pursue leadership positions in each of our businesses.
- Extend our preeminent leadership position in the agricultural equipment market worldwide.
- Create new opportunities to leverage the John Deere brand globally.

*Mission Statement*
John Deere has grown and prospered through a long-standing partnership with the world's most productive farmers. Today, John Deere is a global company with several equipment operations and complementary service businesses. These businesses are closely interrelated, providing the company with significant growth opportunities and other synergistic benefits.

MANLEY BAPTIST CHURCH

The Vision of Manley Baptist Church is to be the people of God, on mission with God, motivated by a love for God, and a love for others.
The Mission of Manley Baptist Church is to help people in the Lakeway area become fully developing followers of Jesus Christ.

U.S. GEOLOGICAL SURVEY (USGS)

The Vision of USGS is to be a world leader in the natural sciences through our scientific excellence and responsiveness to society's needs.
The Mission of USGS is to serve the Nation by providing reliable scientific information to

- describe and understand the Earth;
- minimize loss of life and property from natural disasters;
- manage water, biological, energy, and mineral resources; and enhance and protect our quality of life.

*Continued*

TABLE 2-1    **Vision and Mission Statement Examples** (*continued*)

MASSACHUSETTS
DIVISION OF BANKS

*Vision Statement*

To protect the public interest, ensure competition, accessibility and fairness within the relevant financial services industries, respond innovatively to a rapidly changing environment, and foster a positive impact on the Commonwealth's economy.

*Mission Statement*

To maintain a safe and sound, competitive banking and financial services environment throughout the Commonwealth and ensure compliance with community reinvestment and consumer protection laws by chartering, licensing and supervising state regulated financial institutions in a professional and innovative manner.

OHIO DIVISION OF HAZARDOUS WASTE MANAGEMENT

*Vision Statement*

Ohio's Division of Hazardous Waste Management is recognized as a leader among state hazardous waste management programs through our expertise, effectiveness, application of sound science and delivery of quality service to our stakeholders.

*Mission Statement*

The Division of Hazardous Waste Management protects and improves the environment and therefore the health of Ohio's citizens by promoting pollution prevention and the proper management and cleanup of hazardous waste. We provide quality service to our stakeholders by assisting them in understanding and complying with the hazardous waste management regulations, and by implementing our program effectively.

ATLANTA WEB PRINTERS, INC.

*Vision Statement*

- To be the first choice in the printed communications business. The first choice is the best choice, and *being the best* is what Atlanta Web *pledges* to work hard at being—*every day!*

*Mission Statement*

- to make our clients feel welcome, appreciated, and worthy of our best efforts in everything we do . . . each and every day.
- to be recognized as an exceptional leader in our industry and community.
- to conduct all our relationships with an emphasis on long-term mutual success and satisfaction, rather than short-term gain.
- to earn the trust and respect of all we work with as being a Company of honesty, integrity and responsibility.
- to provide an environment of positive attitude and action to accomplish our vision, by increasing positive feedback and recognition at all levels of the Company.
- to train and motivate our employees and to develop cooperation and communication at all levels.
- to use our resources, knowledge and experience to create win/win relationships for our clients, employees, suppliers, and shareholders in terms of growing compensation, service, and value.

CALIFORNIA ENERGY COMMISSION

*Vision Statement*

It is the vision of the California Energy Commission for Californians to have energy choices that are affordable, reliable, diverse, safe, and environmentally acceptable.

*Mission Statement*

It is the California Energy Commission's mission to assess, advocate and act through public/private partnerships to improve energy systems that promote a strong economy and a healthy environment.

## WHAT IS OUR BUSINESS?

Current thought on mission statements is based largely on guidelines set forth in the mid-1970s by Peter Drucker (www.cgs.edu/faculty/druckerp.html), often called "the father of modern management" for his pioneering studies at General Motors Corporation and for his twenty-two books and hundreds of articles. *Harvard Business Review* calls Drucker, now in his eighties, "the preeminent management thinker of our time."

Drucker says asking the question, What is our business?, is synonymous with asking the question, What is our mission? An enduring statement of purpose that distinguishes one organization from other similar enterprises, the *mission statement* is a declaration of an organization's "reason for being." It answers the pivotal question, What is our business? A clear mission statement is essential for effectively establishing objectives and formulating strategies.

Sometimes called a *creed statement,* a statement of purpose, a statement of philosophy, a statement of beliefs, a statement of business principles, or a statement "defining our business," a mission statement reveals what an organization wants to be and whom it wants to serve. All organizations have a reason for being, even if strategists have not consciously transformed this into writing. As illustrated in Figure 2–1, carefully prepared

## FIGURE 2–1

**A Comprehensive Strategic-Management Model**

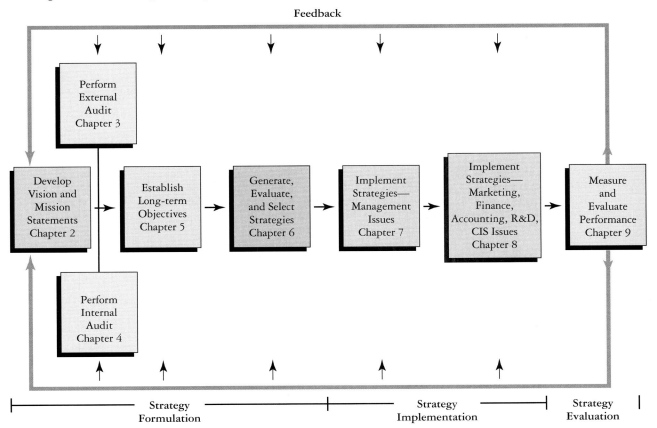

statements of vision and mission are widely recognized by both practitioners and academicians as the first step in strategic management.

> A business mission is the foundation for priorities, strategies, plans, and work assignments. It is the starting point for the design of managerial jobs and, above all, for the design of managerial structures. Nothing may seem simpler or more obvious than to know what a company's business is. A steel mill makes steel, a railroad runs trains to carry freight and passengers, an insurance company underwrites fire risks, and a bank lends money. Actually, "What is our business?" is almost always a difficult question and the right answer is usually anything but obvious. The answer to this question is the first responsibility of strategists. Only strategists can make sure that this question receives the attention it deserves and that the answer makes sense and enables the business to plot its course and set its objectives.[1]

Some strategists spend almost every moment of every day on administrative and tactical concerns, and strategists who rush quickly to establish objectives and implement strategies often overlook developing a vision and mission statement. This problem is widespread even among large organizations. Many corporations in America have not yet developed a formal vision or mission statement, but most do have formal mission statements.[2] An increasing number of organizations are developing these statements.

Some companies develop mission statements simply because they feel it is fashionable, rather than out of any real commitment. However, as will be described in this chapter, firms that develop and systematically revisit their vision and mission, treat them as living documents, and consider them to be an integral part of the firm's culture realize great benefits. Johnson & Johnson (J&J) is an example firm. J&J managers meet regularly with employees to review, reword, and reaffirm the firm's vision and mission. The entire J&J workforce recognizes the value that top management places on this exercise, and these employees respond accordingly.

## Vision Versus Mission

Many organizations develop both a mission statement and a vision statement. Whereas the mission statement answers the question, What is our business?, the *vision statement* answers the question, What do we want to become? Many organizations have both a mission and vision statement. Several examples are given in Table 2–1.

It can be argued that profit, not mission or vision, is the primary corporate motivator. But profit alone is not enough to motivate people.[3] Profit is perceived negatively by some employees in companies. Employees may see profit as something that they earn and management then uses and even gives away—to shareholders. Although this perception is undesired and disturbing to management, it clearly indicates that both profit and vision are needed to effectively motivate a workforce.

When employees and managers together shape or fashion the vision and mission for a firm, the resultant documents can reflect the personal visions that managers and employees have in their hearts and minds about their own futures. Shared vision creates a commonality of interests that can lift workers out of the monotony of daily work and put them into a new world of opportunity and challenge.

## The Process of Developing a Mission Statement

As indicated in the strategic-management model, a clear mission statement is needed before alternative strategies can be formulated and implemented. It is important to involve as many managers as possible in the process of developing a mission statement, because through involvement, people become committed to an organization.

A widely used approach to developing a mission statement is first to select several articles about mission statements and ask all managers to read these as background information. Then ask managers themselves to prepare a mission statement for the organization. A facilitator, or committee of top managers, then should merge these statements into a single document and distribute this draft mission statement to all managers. A request for modifications, additions, and deletions is needed next, along with a meeting to revise the document. To the extent that all managers have input into and support the final mission statement document, organizations can more easily obtain managers' support for other strategy formulation, implementation, and evaluation activities. Thus the process of developing a mission statement represents a great opportunity for strategists to obtain needed support from all managers in the firm.

During the process of developing a mission statement, some organizations use discussion groups of managers to develop and modify the mission statement. Some organizations hire an outside consultant or facilitator to manage the process and help draft the language. Sometimes an outside person with expertise in developing mission statements and unbiased views can manage the process more effectively than an internal group or committee of managers. Decisions on how best to communicate the mission to all managers, employees, and external constituencies of an organization are needed when the document is in final form. Some organizations even develop a videotape to explain the mission statement and how it was developed.

A recent article by Campbell and Yeung emphasizes that the process of developing a mission statement should create an "emotional bond" and "sense of mission" between the organization and its employees.[4] Commitment to a company's strategy and intellectual agreement on the strategies to be pursued do not necessarily translate into an emotional bond; hence strategies that have been formulated may not be implemented. These researchers stress that an emotional bond comes when an individual personally identifies with the underlying values and behavior of a firm, thus turning intellectual agreement and commitment to strategy into a sense of mission. Campbell and Yeung also differentiate between the terms vision and mission, saying vision is "a possible and desirable future state of an organization" that includes specific goals, whereas mission is more associated with behavior and with the present.

# IMPORTANCE OF VISION AND MISSION STATEMENTS

The importance of vision and mission statements to effective strategic management is well documented in the literature, although research results are mixed. Rarick and Vitton found that firms with a formalized mission statement have twice the average return on shareholders' equity than those firms without a formalized mission statement; Bart and Baetz found a positive relationship between mission statements and organizational performance; *Business Week* reports that firms using mission statements have a 30 percent higher return on certain financial measures than those without such statements; O'Gorman and Doran however found that having a mission statement does not directly contribute positively to financial performance.[5] The extent of manager and employee involvement in developing vision and mission statements can make a difference in business success. This chapter provides guidelines for developing these important documents. In actual practice, wide variation exists in the nature, composition, and use of both vision and mission statements. King and Cleland recommend that organizations carefully develop a written mission statement for the following reasons:

1. To ensure unanimity of purpose within the organization.
2. To provide a basis, or standard, for allocating organizational resources.
3. To establish a general tone or organizational climate.
4. To serve as a focal point for individuals to identify with the organization's purpose and direction, and to deter those who cannot from participating further in the organization's activities.
5. To facilitate the translation of objectives into a work structure involving the assignment of tasks to responsible elements within the organization.
6. To specify organizational purposes and the translation of these purposes into objectives in such a way that cost, time, and performance parameters can be assessed and controlled.[6]

Reuben Mark, CEO of Colgate, maintains that a clear mission increasingly must make sense internationally. Mark's thoughts on vision are as follows:

> When it comes to rallying everyone to the corporate banner, it's essential to push one vision globally rather than trying to drive home different messages in different cultures. The trick is to keep the vision simple but elevated: "We make the world's fastest computers" or "Telephone service for everyone." You're never going to get anyone to charge the machine guns only for financial objectives. It's got to be something that makes them feel better, feel a part of something.[7]

## A Resolution of Divergent Views

Developing a comprehensive mission statement is important because divergent views among managers can be revealed and resolved through the process. The question, What is our business?, can create controversy. Raising the question often reveals differences among strategists in the organization. Individuals who have worked together for a long time and who think they know each other suddenly may realize that they are in fundamental disagreement. For example, in a college or university, divergent views regarding the relative importance of teaching, research, and service often are expressed during the mission statement development process. Negotiation, compromise, and eventual agreement on important issues are needed before focusing on more specific strategy formulation activities.

> "What is our mission?" is a genuine decision; and a genuine decision must be based on divergent views to have a chance to be a right and effective decision. Developing a business mission is always a choice between alternatives, each of which rests on different assumptions regarding the reality of the business and its environment. It is always a high-risk decision. A change in mission always leads to changes in objectives, strategies, organization, and behavior. The mission decision is far too important to be made by acclamation. Developing a business mission is a big step toward management effectiveness. Hidden or half-understood disagreements on the definition of a business mission underlie many of the personality problems, communication problems, and irritations that tend to divide a top-management group. Establishing a mission should never be made on plausibility alone, should never be made fast, and should never be made painlessly.[8]

Considerable disagreement among an organization's strategists over vision and mission can cause trouble if not resolved. For example, unresolved disagreement over the business mission was one of the reasons for W. T. Grant's bankruptcy and eventual liquidation. As one executive reported,

There was a lot of dissension within the company whether we should go the
Kmart route or go after the Montgomery Ward and J. C. Penney position. Ed
Staley and Lou Lustenberger (two top executives) were at loggerheads over the
issue, with the upshot being we took a position between the two and that consequently stood for nothing.[9]

Too often, strategists develop statements of vision and business mission only when
their organization is in trouble. Of course, it is needed then. Developing and communicating a clear mission during troubled times indeed may have spectacular results and
even may reverse decline. However, to wait until an organization is in trouble to develop
a vision and mission statement is a gamble that characterizes irresponsible management!
According to Drucker, the most important time to ask seriously, "What do we want to
become?" and "What is our business?" is when a company has been successful:

Success always obsoletes the very behavior that achieved it, always creates new
realities, and always creates new and different problems. Only the fairy story
ends, "They lived happily ever after." It is never popular to argue with success
or to rock the boat. The ancient Greeks knew that the penalty of success can be
severe. The management that does not ask, "What is our mission?" when the
company is successful is, in effect, smug, lazy, and arrogant. It will not be long
before success will turn into failure. Sooner or later, even the most successful
answer to the question, "What is our business?" becomes obsolete.[10]

In multidivisional organizations, strategists should ensure that divisional units perform strategic-management tasks, including the development of a statement of vision and
mission. Each division should involve its own managers and employees in developing a
vision and mission statement consistent with and supportive of the corporative mission.

An organization that fails to develop a vision statement as well as a comprehensive
and inspiring mission statement loses the opportunity to present itself favorably to existing and potential stakeholders. All organizations need customers, employees, and managers, and most firms need creditors, suppliers, and distributors. The vision and mission
statements are effective vehicles for communicating with important internal and external stakeholders. The principal value of these statements as tools of strategic management are derived from their specification of the ultimate aims of a firm:

They provide managers with a unity of direction that transcends individual,
parochial, and transitory needs. They promote a sense of shared expectations
among all levels and generations of employees. They consolidate values over
time and across individuals and interest groups. They project a sense of worth
and intent that can be identified and assimilated by company outsiders. Finally,
they affirm the company's commitment to responsible action, which is symbi-
otic with its need to preserve and protect the essential claims of insiders for sustained survival, growth, and profitability of the firm.[11]

## CHARACTERISTICS OF A MISSION STATEMENT

### A Declaration of Attitude

A mission statement is a declaration of attitude and outlook more than a statement of
specific details. It usually is broad in scope for at least two major reasons. First, a good
mission statement allows for the generation and consideration of a range of feasible alternative objectives and strategies without unduly stifling management creativity. Excess

specificity would limit the potential of creative growth for the organization. On the other hand, an overly general statement that does not exclude any strategy alternatives could be dysfunctional. Apple Computer's mission statement, for example, should not open the possibility for diversification into pesticides, or Ford Motor Company's into food processing. As indicated in the Global Perspective, French mission statements are more general than British mission statements.

Second, a mission statement needs to be broad to effectively reconcile differences among and appeal to an organization's diverse *stakeholders,* the individuals and groups of persons who have a special stake or claim on the company. Stakeholders include employees; managers; stockholders; boards of directors; customers; suppliers; distributors; creditors; governments (local, state, federal, and foreign); unions; competitors; environmental groups; and the general public. Stakeholders affect and are affected by an organization's strategies, yet the claims and concerns of diverse constituencies vary and often conflict. For example, the general public is especially interested in social responsibility, whereas stockholders are more interested in profitability. Claims on any business literally may number in the thousands, and often include clean air, jobs, taxes, investment opportunities, career opportunities, equal employment opportunities, employee benefits, salaries, wages, clean water, and community services. All stakeholders' claims

# GLOBAL PERSPECTIVE

## Concern About Company Mission Across Continents

Researchers recently studied the mission statements of British and French firms. Results are summarized here.

Researchers found that a highly participative (French) approach to developing a mission statement is more effective in gaining employee commitment than a less participative (British) approach. Differences between British and French statements are rooted in or attributable to different cultural, social, and economic factors in the two countries. For example, in Britain the predominance of equity financing has lead companies frequently being bought and sold like commodities. In contrast, the traditions of family ownership are stronger in France, providing a sense of community and a better basis for development of shared mission statements.

British mission statements tend to be short, specific, and developed by top managers, whereas French mission statements tend to be long, general, and developed by all managers and employees.

A large study of chief executive officers (CEOs) around the world recently revealed management challenges in the year 2000. The table below provides the percentage of CEOs in each area that consider various topics to be a management challenge. Note that 38 percent of Japanese CEOs considered "engaging employees in the company mission" to be a major management challenge next year.

*Source:* Adapted from "Sharing the Vision: Company Mission Statements in Britain and France," *Long Range Planning* (February 1994): 84–94.

| Major Management Challenge in Year 2000 | U.S. | Europe | Japan |
| --- | --- | --- | --- |
| Customer Loyalty | 44% | 28% | 3% |
| Managing Mergers, Acquisitions, Alliances | 30 | 42 | 16 |
| Reducing Costs | 29 | 32 | 41 |
| Engaging Employees in Company's Mission | 28 | 32 | 38 |
| Competing for Talent | 26 | 9 | 3 |
| Increasing Flexibility and Speed | 24 | 39 | 31 |

Adapted from: Anne Carey and Alejandro Gonzalez, "What's Troubling CEOs?" *USA Today* (August 12, 1999): p. B1.

on an organization cannot be pursued with equal emphasis. A good mission statement indicates the relative attention that an organization will devote to meeting the claims of various stakeholders. More firms are becoming environmentally proactive in response to the concerns of stakeholders.

Reaching the fine balance between specificity and generality is difficult to achieve, but is well worth the effort. George Steiner offers the following insight on the need for a mission statement to be broad in scope:

> Most business statements of mission are expressed at high levels of abstraction. Vagueness nevertheless has its virtues. Mission statements are not designed to express concrete ends, but rather to provide motivation, general direction, an image, a tone, and a philosophy to guide the enterprise. An excess of detail could prove counterproductive since concrete specification could be the base for rallying opposition. Precision might stifle creativity in the formulation of an acceptable mission or purpose. Once an aim is cast in concrete, it creates a rigidity in an organization and resists change. Vagueness leaves room for other managers to fill in the details, perhaps even to modify general patterns. Vagueness permits more flexibility in adapting to changing environments and internal operations. It facilitates flexibility in implementation.[12]

# NATURAL ENVIRONMENT

### Is Your Firm Environmentally Proactive?

Conducting business in a way that preserves the natural environment is more than just good public relations; it is good business. Preserving the environment is a permanent part of doing business for the following reasons:

1. Consumer demand for environmentally safe products and packages is high.
2. Public opinion demanding that firms conduct business in ways that preserve the natural environment is strong.
3. Environmental advocacy groups now have over twenty million Americans as members.
4. Federal and state environmental regulations are changing rapidly and becoming more complex.
5. More lenders are examining the environmental liabilities of businesses seeking loans.
6. Many consumers, suppliers, distributors, and investors shun doing business with environmentally weak firms.
7. Liability suits and fines against firms having environment problems are on the rise.

More firms are becoming environmentally proactive, which means they are taking the initiative to develop and implement strategies that preserve the environment while enhancing their efficiency and effectiveness. The old undesirable alternative is to be environmentally reactive—waiting until environmental pressures are thrust upon a firm by law or consumer pressure. A reactive environmental policy often leads to high cleanup costs, numerous liability suits, loss in market share, reduced customer loyalty, and higher medical costs. In contrast a proactive policy views environmental pressures as opportunities, and includes such actions as developing green products and packages, conserving energy, reducing waste, recycling, and creating a corporate culture that is environmentally sensitive.

A proactive policy forces a company to innovate and upgrade processes; this leads to reduced waste, improved efficiency, better quality, and greater profits. Successful firms today assess "the profit in preserving the environment" in decisions ranging from developing a mission statement to determining plant location, manufacturing technology, product design, packaging, and consumer relations. A proactive environmental policy is simply good business.

*Sources:* Adapted from "The Profit in Preserving America," *Forbes* (November 11, 1991): 181–189; and Forest Beinhardt, "Bringing the Environment Down to Earth," *Harvard Business Review* (July–August 1999): 149–158.

An effective mission statement arouses positive feelings and emotions about an organization; it is inspiring in the sense that it motivates readers to action. An effective mission statement generates the impression that a firm is successful, has direction, and is worthy of time, support, and investment.

It reflects judgments about future growth directions and strategies based upon forward-looking external and internal analyses. A business mission should provide useful criteria for selecting among alternative strategies. A clear mission statement provides a basis for generating and screening strategic options. The statement of mission should be dynamic in orientation, allowing judgments about the most promising growth directions and those considered less promising.

## A Customer Orientation

A good mission statement describes an organization's purpose, customers, products or services, markets, philosophy, and basic technology. According to Vern McGinnis, a mission statement should (1) define what the organization is and what the organization aspires to be, (2) be limited enough to exclude some ventures and broad enough to allow for creative growth, (3) distinguish a given organization from all others, (4) serve as a framework for evaluating both current and prospective activities, and (5) be stated in terms sufficiently clear to be widely understood throughout the organization.[13]

A good mission statement reflects the anticipations of customers. Rather than developing a product and then trying to find a market, the operating philosophy of organizations should be to identify customers' needs and then provide a product or service to fulfill those needs. Good mission statements identify the utility of a firm's products to its customers. This is why AT&T's mission statement focuses on communication rather than telephones, Exxon's mission statement focuses on energy rather than oil and gas, Union Pacific's mission statement focuses on transportation rather than railroads, and Universal Studios's mission statement focuses on entertainment instead of movies. The following utility statements are relevant in developing a mission statement:

> Do not offer me things.
>
> Do not offer me clothes. Offer me attractive looks.
>
> Do not offer me shoes. Offer me comfort for my feet and the pleasure of walking.
>
> Do not offer me a house. Offer me security, comfort, and a place that is clean and happy.
>
> Do not offer me books. Offer me hours of pleasure and the benefit of knowledge.
>
> Do not offer me records. Offer me leisure and the sound of music.
>
> Do not offer me tools. Offer me the benefit and the pleasure of making beautiful things.
>
> Do not offer me furniture. Offer me comfort and the quietness of a cozy place.
>
> Do not offer me things. Offer me ideas, emotions, ambience, feelings, and benefits.
>
> Please, do not offer me things.

A major reason for developing a business mission is to attract customers who give meaning to an organization. Hotel customers today want to use the Internet, so as indicated in the E-Commerce Perspective, more and more hotels are providing Internet service. Note which hotels provide their mission statement on their Web site. A classic description of the purpose of a business reveals the relative importance of customers in a statement of mission:

> It is the customer who determines what a business is. It is the customer alone whose willingness to pay for a good or service converts economic resources into

# E-COMMERCE PERSPECTIVE

## *The Internet Rolls into Hotels*

After resisting the expense of placing computers in all rooms, hotel chains are hurriedly wiring every room for Internet access. Gordon Lamborne at Marriott says "customers have an insatiable demand for the Internet and demand access wherever they go." Marriott is completely wiring 100 of its 228 U.S. properties in 1999. A recently Greenfield Online survey concludes that 51 percent of traveling executives carry laptops and want instant Internet access at hotels. Wingate Inns, a 70-unit hotel chain, became the first national chain in fall 1999 to be fully wired for high-speed Internet access. Many hotels such as Marriott, Hilton, Hyatt, Radisson, Westin, and Sheraton charge a fee of $9.95 per night for Internet access. Hilton reports that 62 percent of its business guests arrive with laptops and gladly pay the Internet fee. The following table exemplifies the hotel Internet wiring rage sweeping the United States:

| Brand | No. Hotels in Chain | Hotels Year 1999 | Wired Year 2000 | Web-site Address | Mission Statement Given on Web |
|---|---|---|---|---|---|
| Marriott | 684 | 20 | 100+ | www.marriott.com | No |
| Hilton | 275 | 25 | 50 | www.hilton.com | Yes |
| Holiday Inn | 1,105 | NA | NA | www.holidayinn.com | No |
| Hyatt | 111 | 16 | 20 | www.hyatt.com | No |
| Radisson | 228 | NA | 100 | NA | NA |
| Westin | 56 | 5 | 11 | NA | NA |
| Sheraton | 170 | 17 | 34 | www.sheraton.com | No |

*USA Today* recently rated the Web sites of national hotels in terms of quality and reported Marriott, Hilton, Hyatt, and Sheraton to be best, with Radisson second tier, Holiday Inn third tier, and Westin with no Web site.

Adapted from: Chris Woodyard, "Hotels Fired Up to Get Wired Up," *USA Today* (September 2, 1999): p. B1. Also, Salina Khan, "Checking Out Web Sites of National Hotel Chains," *USA Today* (September 27, 1999): p. 3B.

wealth and things into goods. What a business thinks it produces is not of first importance, especially not to the future of the business and to its success. What the customer thinks he/she is buying, what he/she considers value, is decisive—it determines what a business is, what it produces, and whether it will prosper. And what the customer buys and considers value is never a product. It is always utility, meaning what a product or service does for him or her. The customer is the foundation of a business and keeps it in existence.[14]

## A Declaration of Social Policy

The words *social policy* embrace managerial philosophy and thinking at the highest levels of an organization. For this reason, social policy affects the development of a business mission statement. Social issues mandate that strategists consider not only what the organization owes its various stakeholders but also what responsibilities the firm has to consumers, environmentalists, minorities, communities, and other groups. After decades of debate on the topic of social responsibility, many firms still struggle to determine appropriate social policies.

The issue of social responsibility arises when a company establishes its business mission. The impact of society on business and vice versa is becoming more pronounced each year. Social policies directly affect a firm's customers, products and services, markets, technology, profitability, self-concept, and public image. An organization's social policy should be integrated into all strategic-management activities, including the development of a mission statement. Corporate social policy should be designed and articulated during strategy formulation, set and administered during strategy implementation, and reaffirmed or changed during strategy evaluation.[15] The emerging view of social responsibility holds that social issues should be attended to both directly and indirectly in determining strategies. The year 1998 was good for charity with Americans donating a record $180 billion. The following table provides a breakdown $contributions in 1998.[16]

| Category | Amount (% Change from 1997) |
| --- | --- |
| Religion | $76 (+5%) |
| Education | $25 (+11%) |
| Health | $17 (+20%) |
| Foundations | $17 (+16%) |
| Human Services | $16 (+27%) |
| Arts/Humanities | $11 (−1%) |
| Public/Social Benefit | $11 (+30%) |
| Environment/Wildlife | $ 5 (+28%) |
| World Affairs | $ 2 (+9%) |

Firms should strive to engage in social activities that have economic benefits. For example, Merck & Company recently developed the drug ivermectin for treating river blindness, a disease caused by a fly-borne parasitic worm endemic in poor, tropical areas of Africa, the Middle East, and Latin America. In an unprecedented gesture that reflected its corporate commitment to social responsibility, Merck then made ivermectin available at no cost to medical personnel throughout the world. Merck's action highlights the dilemma of orphan drugs, which offer pharmaceutical companies no economic incentive for development and distribution.

Despite differences in approaches, most American companies try to assure outsiders that they conduct business in a socially responsible way. The mission statement is an effective instrument for conveying this message.

## COMPONENTS OF A MISSION STATEMENT

Mission statements can and do vary in length, content, format, and specificity. Most practitioners and academicians of strategic management consider an effective statement to exhibit nine characteristics or components. Because a mission statement is often the most visible and public part of the strategic-management process, it is important that it includes all of these essential components. Components and corresponding questions that a mission statement should answer are given here.

1. *Customers:* Who are the firm's customers?

2. *Products or services:* What are the firm's major products or services?

3. *Markets:* Geographically, where does the firm compete?

4. *Technology:* Is the firm technologically current?

5. *Concern for survival, growth, and profitability:* Is the firm committed to growth and financial soundness?

6. *Philosophy:* What are the basic beliefs, values, aspirations, and ethical priorities of the firm?

7. *Self-concept:* What is the firm's distinctive competence or major competitive advantage?

8. *Concern for public image:* Is the firm responsive to social, community, and environmental concerns?

9. *Concern for employees:* Are employees a valuable asset of the firm?

Excerpts from the mission statements of different organizations are provided in Table 2–2 to exemplify the nine essential components.

## WRITING AND EVALUATING MISSION STATEMENTS

Perhaps the best way to develop a skill for writing and evaluating mission statements is to study actual company missions. Therefore eight mission statements are presented in Table 2–3. These statements are then evaluated in Table 2–4 based on the nine criteria presented above.

There is no one best mission statement for a particular organization, so good judgment is required in evaluating mission statements. In Table 2–4, a *Yes* indicates that the given mission statement answers satisfactorily the question posed in Table 2–2 for the respective evaluative criteria. Some persons are more demanding than others in rating mission statements in this manner. For example, if a statement includes the word "employees" or "customer" is that alone sufficient for the respective component? Some companies answer this question in the affirmative and some in the negative. You may ask yourself this question: "If I worked for this company, would I have done better in regards to including a particular component in their mission statement." Perhaps the important issue here is that mission statements include each of the nine components in some manner.

As indicated in Table 2–4, the Genentech mission statement was rated to be best among the eight statements evaluated. Note, however, that the Genentech statement lacks inclusion of the "Market" and the "Technology" components. The PepsiCo and Pressure Systems International mission statements are evaluated worst with inclusion of only three of the nine components. Note that none of these eight statements included the "Technology" component in their document.

TABLE 2-2    **Examples of the Nine Essential Components of a Mission Statement**

1.  CUSTOMERS

We believe our first responsibility is to the doctors, nurses, and patients, to mothers and all others who use our products and services. (Johnson & Johnson)

2.  PRODUCTS OR SERVICES

AMAX's principal products are molybdenum, coal, iron ore, copper, lead, zinc, petroleum and natural gas, potash, phosphates, nickel, tungsten, silver, gold, and magnesium. (AMAX)

Standard Oil Company (Indiana) is in business to find and produce crude oil, natural gas and natural gas liquids; to manufacture high-quality products useful to society from these raw materials; and to distribute and market those products and to provide dependable related services to the consuming public at reasonable prices. (Standard Oil Company)

3.  MARKETS

We are dedicated to the total success of Corning Glass Works as a worldwide competitor. (Corning Glass Works)

Our emphasis is on North American markets, although global opportunities will be explored. (Blockway)

4.  TECHNOLOGY

Control Data is in the business of applying micro-electronics and computer technology in two general areas: computer-related hardware; and computing-enhancing services, which include computation, information, education, and finance. (Control Data)

The common technology in these areas is discrete particle coatings. (Nashua)

5.  CONCERN FOR SURVIVAL, GROWTH, AND PROFITABILITY

In this respect, the company will conduct its operations prudently, and will provide the profits and growth which will assure Hoover's ultimate success. (Hoover Universal)

To serve the worldwide need for knowledge at a fair profit by adhering, evaluating, producing, and distributing valuable information in a way that benefits our customers, employees, other investors, and our society. (McGraw-Hill)

6.  PHILOSOPHY

We believe human development to be the worthiest of the goals of civilization and independence to be the superior condition for nurturing growth in the capabilities of people. (Sun Company)

It's all part of the Mary Kay philosophy—a philosophy based on the golden rule. A spirit of sharing and caring where people give cheerfully of their time, knowledge, and experience. (Mary Kay Cosmetics)

7.  SELF-CONCEPT

Crown Zellerbach is committed to leapfrogging ongoing competition within 1,000 days by unleashing the constructive and creative abilities and energies of each of its employees. (Crown Zellerbach)

8.  CONCERN FOR PUBLIC IMAGE

To share the world's obligation for the protection of the environment. (Dow Chemical)

To contribute to the economic strength of society and function as a good corporate citizen on a local, state, and national basis in all countries in which we do business. (Pfizer)

9.  CONCERN FOR EMPLOYEES

To recruit, develop, motivate, reward, and retain personnel of exceptional ability, character, and dedication by providing good working conditions, superior leadership, compensation on the basis of performance, an attractive benefit program, opportunity for growth, and a high degree of employment security. (The Wachovia Corporation)

To compensate its employees with remuneration and fringe benefits competitive with other employment opportunities in its geographical area and commensurate with their contributions toward efficient corporate operations. (Public Service Electric and Gas Company)

TABLE 2-3     **Mission Statements of Seven Organizations**

PepsiCo's mission is to increase the value of our shareholders' investment. We do this through sales growth, cost controls, and wise investment resources. We believe our commercial success depends upon offering quality and value to our consumers and customers; providing products that are safe, wholesome, economically efficient and environmentally sound; and providing a fair return to our investors while adhering to the highest standards of integrity.

Ben & Jerry's mission is to make, distribute and sell the finest quality all-natural ice cream and related products in a wide variety of innovative flavors made from Vermont dairy products. To operate the Company on a sound financial basis of profitable growth, increasing value for our shareholders, and creating career opportunities and financial rewards for our employees. To operate the Company in a way that actively recognizes the central role that business plays in the structure of society by initiating innovative ways to improve the quality of life of a broad community—local, national, and international.

The Mission of the Institute of Management Accountants (IMA) is to provide to members personal and professional development opportunities through education, association with business professionals, and certification in management accounting and financial management skills. The IMA is globally recognized by the financial community as a respected institution influencing the concepts and ethical practices of management accounting and financial management.

The Mission of Pressure Systems International (PSI) is to provide automatic tire inflation systems to our customers along with customer-valued services and tire maintenance-related solutions that best meet the needs and exceeds the expectations of our customers while meeting the growth and financial objectives of our investors/owners.

The Mission of Genentech, Inc. is to be the leading biotechnology company, using human genetic information to develop, manufacture and market pharmaceuticals that address significant unmet medical needs. We commit ourselves to high standards of integrity in contributing to the best interests of patients, the medical profession, and our employees, and to seeking significant returns to our stockholders based on the continued pursuit of excellent science.

The Mission of the California Department of Fish and Game is to manage California's diverse fish, wildlife, and plant resources, and the habitats upon which they depend, for their ecological values and for their use and enjoyment by the public.

The Mission of Barrett Memorial Hospital is to operate a high-quality health care facility providing an appropriate mix of services to the residents of Beaverhead County and surrounding areas. Service is given with ultimate concern for patients, medical staff, hospital staff, and the community. Barrett Memorial Hospital assumes a strong leadership role in the coordination and development of health-related resources within the community.

TABLE 2-4   **An Evaluation Matrix of Mission Statements**

COMPONENTS

| Organization | Customers | Products/ Services | Markets | Concern for Survival, Growth, Profitability | Technology |
|---|---|---|---|---|---|
| PepsiCo | Yes | No | No | Yes | No |
| Ben & Jerry's | No | Yes | Yes | Yes | No |
| National Pawnbrokers Association | Yes | No | No | No | No |
| Institute of Management Accountants | Yes | Yes | Yes | No | No |
| Pressure Systems International | Yes | Yes | No | Yes | No |
| Genentech, Inc. | Yes | Yes | No | Yes | No |
| California Department of Fish and Game | Yes | Yes | Yes | No | No |
| Barrett Memorial Hospital | Yes | Yes | Yes | No | No |

| Organization | Philosophy | Self-Concept | Concern for Public Image | Concern for Employees |
|---|---|---|---|---|
| PepsiCo | Yes | No | No | No |
| Ben & Jerry's | No | Yes | Yes | Yes |
| National Pawnbrokers Association | Yes | Yes | Yes | No |
| Institute of Management Accountants | Yes | Yes | Yes | No |
| Pressure Systems International | No | No | No | No |
| Genentech, Inc. | Yes | Yes | Yes | Yes |
| California Department of Fish and Game | No | Yes | No | No |
| Barrett Memorial Hospital | No | Yes | Yes | Yes |

# CONCLUSION

Every organization has a unique purpose and reason for being. This uniqueness should be reflected in vision and mission statements. The nature of a business vision and mission can represent either a competitive advantage or disadvantage for the firm. An organization achieves a heightened sense of purpose when strategists, managers, and employees develop and communicate a clear business vision and mission. Drucker says developing a clear business vision and mission is the "first responsibility of strategists."

A good mission statement reveals an organization's customers, products or services, markets, technology, concern for survival, philosophy, self-concept, concern for public image, and concern for employees. These nine basic components serve as a practical framework for evaluating and writing mission statements. As the first step in strategic management, the vision and mission statement provides direction for all planning activities.

A well-designed vision and mission statement is essential for formulating, implementing, and evaluating strategy. Developing and communicating a clear business vision and mission is one of the most commonly overlooked tasks in strategic management. Without clear statements of vision and mission, a firm's short-term actions can be counterproductive to long-term interests. A vision and mission statement always should be subject to revision but, if carefully prepared, they will require major changes only infrequently. Organizations usually reexamine their vision and mission statements annually. Effective mission statements stand the test of time.

A vision and mission statement are essential tools for strategists, a fact illustrated in a short story told by Porsche CEO Peter Schultz:

Three people were at work on a construction site. All were doing the same job, but when each was asked what his job was, the answers varied. "Breaking rocks," the first replied, "Earning a living," responded the second. "Helping to build a cathedral," said the third. Few of us can build cathedrals. But to the extent we can see the cathedral in whatever cause we are following, the job seems more worthwhile. Good strategists and a clear mission help us find those cathedrals in what otherwise could be dismal issues and empty causes.[17]

We invite you to visit the DAVID page on the Prentice Hall Web site at **www.prenhall.com/davidsm** for this chapter's World Wide Web exercise.

## KEY TERMS AND CONCEPTS

Concern for Employees  (p. 65)

Concern for Public Image  (p. 65)

Concern for Survival, Growth, and Profitability  (p. 65)

Creed Statement  (p. 55)

Customers  (p. 62)

Markets  (p. 65)

Mission Statement  (p. 55)

Mission Statement Components  (p. 65)

Philosophy  (p. 65)

Products or Services  (p. 52)

Self-Concept  (p. 65)

Social Policy  (p. 63)

Stakeholders  (p. 60)

Technology  (p. 65)

Vision Statement  (p. 56)

## ISSUES FOR REVIEW AND DISCUSSION

1. Compare and contrast vision statements with mission statements in terms of composition and importance.
2. Do local service stations need to have written vision and mission statements? Why or why not?
3. Why do you think organizations that have a comprehensive mission tend to be high performers? Does having a comprehensive mission cause high performance?
4. Explain why a mission statement should not include strategies and objectives.
5. What is your college or university's self-concept? How would you state that in a mission statement?
6. Explain the principal value of a vision and a mission statement.
7. Why is it important for a mission statement to be reconciliatory?

8. In your opinion, what are the three most important components to include in writing a mission statement? Why?
9. How would the mission statements of a for-profit and a nonprofit organization differ?
10. Write a vision and mission statement for an organization of your choice.
11. Go to www.altavista.com and conduct a search by keyword "vision statement" and "mission statement." Find vision and mission statements and evaluate the documents.
12. Who are the major stakeholders of the bank that you do business with locally? What are the major claims of those stakeholders?
13. Select one of the current readings at the end of this chapter. Look up that article in your college library and give a five-minute oral report to the class summarizing the article.

## NOTES

1. PETER DRUCKER, *Management: Tasks, Responsibilities, and Practices* (New York: Harper & Row, 1974): 61.
2. FRED DAVID, "How Companies Define Their Mission," *Long Range Planning* 22, no. 1 (February 1989): 90–92. Also, see John Pearce II and Fred David, "Corporate Mission Statements: The Bottom Line," *Academy of Management Executive* 1, no. 2 (May 1987): 110.
3. JOSEPH QUIGLEY, "Vision: How Leaders Develop It, Share It and Sustain It," *Business Horizons* (September–October 1994): 39.

4. ANDREW CAMPBELL and SALLY YEUNG, "Creating a Sense of Mission," *Long Range Planning* 24, no. 4 (August 1991): 17.

5. CHARLES RARICK and JOHN VITTON, "Mission Statements Make Cents," *Journal of Business Strategy,* 16, (1995): 11. Also, Christopher Bart and Mark Baetz, "The Relationship Between Mission Statements and Firm Performance: An Exploratory Study," *Journal of Management Studies* 35, 1998, p. 823. Also, "Mission Possible," August 1999, *Business Week,* 3642, p. F12.

6. W. R. KING and D. I. CLELAND, *Strategic Planning and Policy* (New York: Van Nostrand Reinhold, 1979): 124.

7. BRIAN DUMAINE, "What the Leaders of Tomorrow See," *Fortune* (July 3, 1989): 50.

8. DRUCKER, 78, 79.

9. "How W. T. Grant Lost $175 Million Last Year," *Business Week* (February 25, 1975): 75.

10. DRUCKER, 88.

11. JOHN PEARCE II, "The Company Mission as a Strategic Tool," *Sloan Management Review* 23, no. 3 (Spring 1982): 74.

12. GEORGE STEINER, *Strategic Planning: What Every Manager Must Know* (New York: The Free Press, 1979): 160.

13. VERN McGINNIS, "The Mission Statement: A Key Step in Strategic Planning," *Business* 31, no. 6 (November–December 1981): 41.

14. DRUCKER, 61.

15. ARCHIE CARROLL and FRANK HOY, "Integrating Corporate Social Policy into Strategic Management," *Journal of Business Strategy* 4, no. 3 (Winter 1984): 57.

16. ANNE CAREY and ALEJANDRO GONZALEZ, "1998 Was Good For Charity," *USA Today* (June 29, 1999): p. 1A.

17. ROBERT WATERMAN, JR., *The Renewal Factor: How the Best Get and Keep the Competitive Edge* (New York: Bantam, 1987). Also, *Business Week* (September 14, 1987): 120.

## CURRENT READINGS

BAETZ, MARK C. and CHRISTOPHER K. BART. "Developing Mission Statements Which Work." *Long Range Planning* 29, no. 4 (August 1996): 526–533.

BARTLETT, CHRISTOPHER A. and SUMANTRA GHOSHAL. "Changing the Role of Top Management: Beyond Strategy to Purpose." *Harvard Business Review* (November–December 1994): 79–90.

BRABET, JULIENNE and MARY KLEMM. "Sharing the Vision: Company Mission Statements in Britain and France." *Long Range Planning* (February 1994): 84–94.

CIULLA, JOANNE B. "The Importance of Leadership in Shaping Business Values." *International Journal of Strategic Management* 32, no. 2 (April 1999): 166–172.

COLLINS, JAMES C. and JERRY I. PORRAS. "Building a Visionary Company." *California Management Review* 37, no. 2 (Winter 1995): 80–100.

COLLINS, JAMES C. and JERRY I. PORRAS. "Building Your Company's Vision." *Harvard Business Review* (September–October 1996): 65–78.

CUMMINGS, STEPHEN and JOHN DAVIES. "Brief Case—Mission, Vision, Fusion." *Long Range Planning* 27, no. 6 (December 1994): 147–150.

DAVIES, STUART W. and KEITH W. GLAISTER. "Business School Mission Statements—The Bland Leading the Bland?" *Long Range Planning* 30, no. 4 (August 1997): 594–604.

GRATTON, LYNDA. "Implementing a Strategic Vision—Key Factors for Success." *Long Range Planning* 29, no. 3 (June 1996): 290–303.

GRAVES, SAMUEL B. and SANDRA A. WADDOCK. "Institutional Owners and Corporate Social Performance." *Academy of Management Journal* 37, no. 4 (August 1994): 1034–1046.

HEMPHILL, THOMAS A. "Legislating Corporate Social Responsibility." *Business Horizons* 40, no. 2 (March–April 1997): 53–63.

JONES, IAN W. and MICHAEL G. POLLITT. "Putting Values into Action: Lessons from Best Practice." *International Journal of Strategic Management* 32, no. 2 (April 1999): 162–165.

LARWOOD, LAURIE, CECILIA M. FALBE, MARK P. KRIGER, and PAUL MIESING. "Structure and Meaning of Organizational Vision." *Academy of Management Journal* 38, no. 3 (June 1995): 740–769.

McTAVISH, RON. "One More Time: What Business Are You In?" *Long Range Planning* 28, no. 2 (April 1995): 49–60.

MITOFF, IAN I. and ELIZABETH A. DENTON. "A Study of Spirituality in the Workplace." *Sloan Management Review* 40, no. 4 (Summer 1999): 83–92.

OSBORNE, RICHARD L. "Strategic Values: The Corporate Performance Engine." *Business Horizons* 39, no. 5 (September–October 1996): 41–47.

OSWALD, S. L., K. W. MOSSHOLDER, and S. G. HARRIS. "Vision Salience and Strategic Involvement: Implications for Psychological Attachment to Organization and Job." *Strategic Management Journal* 15, no. 6 (July 1994): 477–490.

SNYDER, NEIL H. and MICHELLE GRAVES. "The Editor's Chair/Leadership and Vision." *Business Horizons* 37, no. 1 (January–February 1994): 1–7.

SWANSON, DIANE L. "Addressing a Theoretical Problem by Reorienting the Corporate Social Performance Model." *Academy of Management Review* 20, no. 1 (January 1995): 43–64.

SWANSON, DIANE L. "Toward an Integrative Theory of Business and Society: A Research Strategy for Corporate Social Performance." *The Academy of Management Review* 24, no. 3 (July 1999): 506–521.

# EXPERIENTIAL EXERCISES

**EXPERIENTIAL
EXERCISE 2A** ▶

Evaluating Mission
Statements

## PURPOSE

A business mission statement is an integral part of strategic management. It provides direction for formulating, implementing, and evaluating strategic activities. This exercise will give you practice evaluating mission statements, a skill that is prerequisite to writing a good mission statement.

## INSTRUCTIONS

**Step 1**  Your instructor will select some or all of the following mission statements to evaluate. On a separate sheet of paper, construct an evaluation matrix like the one presented in Table 2–4. Evaluate the mission statements based on the nine criteria presented in the chapter.

**Step 2**  Record a *yes* in appropriate cells of the evaluation matrix when the respective mission statement satisfactorily meets the desired criteria. Record a *no* in appropriate cells when the respective mission statement does not meet the stated criteria.

## MISSION STATEMENTS

*Criterion Productions, Inc.*
The mission statement of Criterion Productions, Inc. is to increase the success of all who avail themselves of our products and services by providing image enhancement, and a medium that communicates our customer's corporate identity and unique message to a targeted audience. In this, our tenth year of business, Criterion Productions, Inc. pledges to offer a distinct advantage and a superior value in all of your video production needs. We will assist our customers in their endeavors to grow and prosper through celebrity associations that are "effectively appropriate" to their industry, and/or who possess the qualities and characteristics most respected by our customers.

*Mid-America Plastics, Inc.*
"Continuous Improvement Every Day, In Everything We Do."
In order for us to accomplish our mission, every employee must be "Committed to Excellence" in everything they do by performing their job right the first time.

*Hatboro Area YMCA*
To translate the principles of the YMCA's Christian heritage into programs that nurture children, strengthen families, build strong communities, and develop healthy minds, bodies and spirits for all.

*Integrated Communications, Inc.*
Our mission is to be perceived by our customers as providing the highest quality of customer service and salesmanship, delivered with a sense of ownership, friendliness, individual pride and team spirit. We will accomplish this with the quality of our Wireless Products that supply complete solutions to our customers needs. And, through unyielding loyalty to our customers and suppliers, ICI will provide opportunities and security to our employees as well as maximizing our long-term financial growth.

*American Counseling Association (ACA)*
The Mission of ACA is to promote public confidence and trust in the counseling profession.

*Idaho Hospital Association*
The mission of the Idaho Hospital Association is to provide representation, advocacy and assistance for member hospitals, healthcare systems and the healthcare services they provide. The Association, through leadership and collaboration among healthcare providers and others, promotes quality healthcare that is adequately financed and accessible to all Idahoans.

### EXPERIENTIAL EXERCISE 2B ▶

## Writing a Vision and Mission Statement for America Online (AOL)

### *PURPOSE*

There is no one best vision or mission statement for a given organization. Analysts feel that the AOL vision statement and mission statement provided in the Cohesion Case can be improved. Writing a mission statement that includes desired components—and at the same time is inspiring and reconciliatory—requires careful thought. Mission statements should not be too lengthy; statements under two hundred words are desirable.

### *INSTRUCTIONS*

**Step 1**   Take 15 minutes to write a vision and mission statement for AOL. Scan the case for needed details as you prepare your statements.

**Step 2**   Join with three other classmates to form a group of four people. Read each other's statements silently. As a group, select the best vision statement and best mission statement from your group.

**Step 3**   Read those best statements to the class.

### EXPERIENTIAL EXERCISE 2C ▶

## Writing a Vision and Mission Statement for My University

### *PURPOSE*

Most universities have a vision and mission statement. The purpose of this exercise is to give you practice writing a vision and mission statement for a nonprofit organization such as your own university.

### *INSTRUCTIONS*

**Step 1**   Take 15 minutes to write a vision statement and mission statement for your university. Your mission statement should not exceed two hundred words.

**Step 2**   Read your vision and mission statements to the class.

**Step 3**   Determine whether your institution has a vision and/or mission statement. Look in the front of the college handbook. If your institution has a written statement, contact an appropriate administrator of the institution to inquire as to how and when the statement was prepared. Share this information with the class. Analyze your college's mission statement in light of concepts presented in this chapter.

**EXPERIENTIAL EXERCISE 2D** ▶

Conducting Mission Statement Research

*PURPOSE*

This exercise gives you the opportunity to study the nature and role of vision and mission statements in strategic management.

*INSTRUCTIONS*

Step 1    Call various organizations in your city or county to identify firms that have developed a formal vision and/or mission statement. Contact nonprofit organizations and government agencies in addition to small and large businesses. Ask to speak with the director, owner, or chief executive officer of one organization. Explain that you are studying vision and mission statements in class and are conducting research as part of a class activity.

Step 2    Ask several executives the following four questions and record their answers.

1. When did your organization first develop its vision and/or mission statement? Who was primarily responsible for its development?

2. How long have your current statements existed? When were they last modified? Why were they modified at that point in time?

3. By what process are your firm's vision and mission statement altered?

4. How are your vision and mission statements used in the firm? How do they affect the firm's strategic-planning process?

Step 3    Provide an overview of your findings to the class.

# 3

# THE EXTERNAL ASSESSMENT

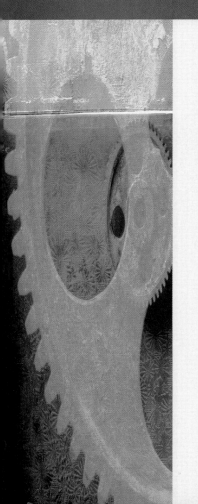

## CHAPTER OUTLINE

- The Nature of an External Audit
- Economic Forces
- Social, Cultural, Demographic, and Environmental Forces
- Political, Governmental, and Legal Forces
- Technological Forces
- Competitive Forces
- Competitive Analysis: Porter's Five-Forces Model
- Sources of External Information
- Forecasting Tools and Techniques
- The Global Challenge
- Industry Analysis: The External Factor Evaluation (EFE) Matrix
- The Competitive Profile Matrix (CPM)

**EXPERIENTIAL EXERCISE 3A**
*Developing an EFE Matrix for America Online*

**EXPERIENTIAL EXERCISE 3B**
*The Internet Search*

**EXPERIENTIAL EXERCISE 3C**
*Developing an EFE Matrix for My University*

**EXPERIENTIAL EXERCISE 3D**
*Developing a Competitive Profile Matrix for America Online*

**EXPERIENTIAL EXERCISE 3E**
*Developing a Competitive Profile Matrix for My University*

## CHAPTER OBJECTIVES

*After studying this chapter, you should be able to do the following:*

1. Describe how to conduct an external strategic-management audit.
2. Discuss ten major external forces that affect organizations: economic, social, cultural, demographic, environmental, political, governmental, legal, technological, and competitive.
3. Identify key sources of external information, including the Internet.
4. Discuss important forecasting tools used in strategic management.
5. Discuss the importance of monitoring external trends and events.
6. Explain how to develop an EFE Matrix.
7. Explain how to develop a Competitive Profile Matrix.
8. Discuss the importance of gathering competitive intelligence.
9. Describe the trend toward cooperation among competitors.
10. Discuss the political environment in Mexico, Russia, and China.
11. Discuss the global challenge facing American firms.

# NOTABLE QUOTES

If you're not faster than your competitor, you're in a tenuous position, and if you're only half as fast, you're terminal.

GEORGE SALK

The opportunities and threats existing in any situation always exceed the resources needed to exploit the opportunities or avoid the threats. Thus, strategy is essentially a problem of allocating resources. If strategy is to be successful, it must allocate superior resources against a decisive opportunity.

WILLIAM COHEN

Organizations pursue strategies that will disrupt the normal course of industry events and forge new industry conditions to the disadvantage of competitors.

IAN C. MACMILLAN

The idea is to concentrate our strength against our competitor's relative weakness.

BRUCE HENDERSON

There was a time in America when business was easier. We set the pace for the rest of the world. We were immune to serious foreign competition. Many of us were regulated therefore protected. No longer. Today's leaders must recreate themselves and their ways of doing business in order to stay on top and stay competitive.

ROBERT H. WATERMAN, JR.

This chapter examines the tools and concepts needed to conduct an external strategic-management audit (sometimes called *environmental scanning* or *industry analysis*). An *external audit* focuses on identifying and evaluating trends and events beyond the control of a single firm, such as increased foreign competition, population shifts to the Sunbelt, an aging society, information technology, and the computer revolution. An external audit reveals key opportunities and threats confronting an organization so that managers can formulate strategies to take advantage of the opportunities and avoid or reduce the impact of threats. This chapter presents a practical framework for gathering, assimilating, and analyzing external information.

# THE NATURE OF AN EXTERNAL AUDIT

The purpose of an external audit is to develop a finite list of opportunities that could benefit a firm and threats that should be avoided. As the term *finite* suggests, the external audit is not aimed at developing an exhaustive list of every possible factor that could influence the business; rather, it is aimed at identifying key variables that offer actionable responses. Firms should be able to respond either offensively or defensively to the factors by formulating strategies that take advantage of external opportunities or that minimize the impact of potential threats. Figure 3–1 illustrates how the external audit fits into the strategic-management process.

## Key External Forces

*External forces* can be divided into five broad categories: (1) economic forces; (2) social, cultural, demographic, and environmental forces; (3) political, governmental, and legal forces; (4) technological forces; and (5) competitive forces. Relationships among these forces and an organization are depicted in Figure 3–2. External trends and events significantly affect all products, services, markets, and organizations in the world.

Changes in external forces translate into changes in consumer demand for both industrial and consumer products and services. External forces affect the types of products developed, the nature of positioning and market segmentation strategies, the types of services offered, and the choice of businesses to acquire or sell. External forces directly affect both suppliers and distributors. Identifying and evaluating external opportunities and threats enables organizations to develop a clear mission, to design strategies to achieve long-term objectives, and to develop policies to achieve annual objectives.

The increasing complexity of business today is evidenced by more countries' developing the capacity and will to compete aggressively in world markets. Foreign businesses and countries are willing to learn, adapt, innovate, and invent to compete successfully in the marketplace. There are more competitive new technologies in Europe and the Far East today than ever before. American businesses can no longer beat foreign competitors with ease.

## The Process of Performing an External Audit

The process of performing an external audit must involve as many managers and employees as possible. As emphasized in earlier chapters, involvement in the strategic-management process can lead to understanding and commitment from organizational members. Individuals appreciate having the opportunity to contribute ideas and to gain a better understanding of their firm's industry, competitors, and markets.

## FIGURE 3–1

### A Comprehensive Strategic-Management Model

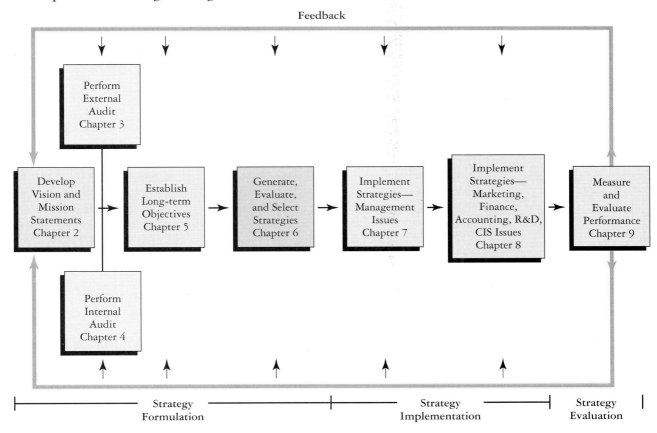

## FIGURE 3–2

### Relationships Between Key External Forces and an Organization

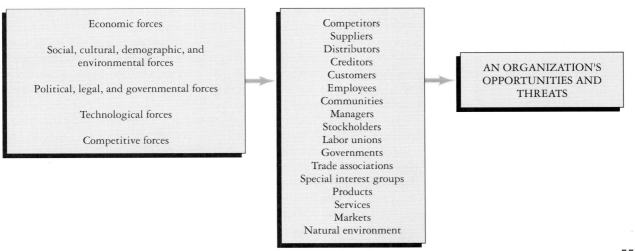

To perform an external audit, a company first must gather competitive intelligence and information about social, cultural, demographic, environmental, economic, political, legal, governmental, and technological trends. Individuals can be asked to monitor various sources of information such as key magazines, trade journals, and newspapers. These persons can submit periodic scanning reports to a committee of managers charged with performing the external audit. This approach provides a continuous stream of timely strategic information and involves many individuals in the external-audit process. The Internet provides another source for gathering strategic information, as do corporate, university, and public libraries. Suppliers, distributors, salespersons, customers, and competitors represent other sources of vital information.

Once information is gathered, it should be assimilated and evaluated. A meeting or series of meetings of managers is needed to collectively identify the most important opportunities and threats facing the firm. These key external factors should be listed on flip charts or a blackboard. A prioritized list of these factors could be obtained by requesting all managers to rank the factors identified, from 1 for the most important opportunity/threat to 20 for the least important opportunity/threat. These key external factors can vary over time and by industry. Relationships with suppliers or distributors are often a critical success factor. Other variables commonly used include market share, breadth of competing products, world economies, foreign affiliates, proprietary and key account advantages, price competitiveness, technological advancements, population shifts, interest rates, and pollution abatement.

Freund emphasized that these key external factors should be (1) important to achieving long-term and annual objectives, (2) measurable, (3) applicable to all competing firms, and (4) hierarchical in the sense that some will pertain to the overall company and others will be more narrowly focused on functional or divisional areas.[1] A final list of the most important key external factors should be communicated and distributed widely in the organization. Both opportunities and threats can be key external factors.

 ## ECONOMIC FORCES

In the 2000s, the United States is benefiting from the best economic conditions in fifty years (U.S. Department of Commerce, www.doc.gov). A balanced federal government budget coupled with low inflation, low interest rates, and low unemployment benefit companies and consumers. The robust U.S. economy is the envy of the world as gross domestic product continues its 4.3 percent annual growth. Wages are rising, consumer spending is soaring, and the U.S. stock market is outperforming every other major stock market in the world. Competitiveness of domestic companies has been higher as companies quickly adopt new technologies and new processes to gain competitive advantage.

Increasing numbers of two-income households is an economic trend in America. As affluence increases, individuals place a premium on time. Improved customer service, immediate availability, trouble-free operation of products, and dependable maintenance and repair services are becoming more important. Americans today are more willing than ever to pay for good service if it limits inconvenience.

Economic factors have a direct impact on the potential attractiveness of various strategies. For example, as interest rates rise, then funds needed for capital expansion become more costly or unavailable. Also, as interest rates rise, discretionary income declines, and the demand for discretionary goods falls. As stock prices increase, the desirability of equity as a source of capital for market development increases. Also, as the market rises, consumer and business wealth expands. A summary of economic variables that often represent opportunities and threats for organizations is provided in Table 3–1.

TABLE 3-1          Key Economic Variables to Be Monitored

| | |
|---|---|
| Shift to a service economy in the United States | Demand shifts for different categories of goods and services |
| Availability of credit | Income differences by region and consumer groups |
| Level of disposable income | |
| Propensity of people to spend | Price fluctuations |
| Interest rates | Exportation of labor and capital from the United States |
| Inflation rates | |
| Money market rates | Monetary policies |
| Federal government budget deficits | Fiscal policies |
| Gross domestic product trend | Tax rates |
| Consumption patterns | European Economic Community (ECC) policies |
| Unemployment trends | |
| Worker productivity levels | Organization of Petroleum Exporting Countries (OPEC) policies |
| Value of the dollar in world markets | |
| Stock market trends | Coalitions of Lesser Developed Countries (LDC) policies |
| Foreign countries' economic conditions | |
| Import/export factors | |

Trends in the dollar's value have significant and unequal effects on companies in different industries and in different locations. For example, the pharmaceutical, tourism, entertainment, motor vehicle, aerospace, and forest products industries benefit greatly when the dollar falls against the yen, franc, and mark. Agricultural and petroleum industries are hurt by the dollar's rise against the currencies of Mexico, Brazil, Venezuela, and Australia. Generally, a strong or high dollar makes American goods more expensive on overseas markets. This worsens America's trade deficit. When the value of the dollar falls, tourism-oriented firms benefit because Americans do not travel abroad as much when the value of the dollar is low; rather, foreigners visit and vacation more in the United States.

A low value of the dollar means lower imports and higher exports; it helps U.S. companies' competitiveness in world markets. The years 1997 through 2000 have seen the U.S. dollar gaining against virtually every other currency. One benefit of this trend is that consumers pay less for imported goods such as cars and computer memory chips. Domestic firms that manufacture extensively outside the United States also benefit from the rising value of the dollar. However in Japan, the yen's strengthening against the euro and dollar has made Japanese products more expensive overseas and cut into the profits of companies such as Sony, Honda Motor, and Canon. A surging yen could become a renewed drag on Japan's economy by driving up prices of exports, depriving Japanese firms of sales abroad. In September 1999, the dollar fell to 107.78 yen and also weakened against the European currency to 1.0544 euros. As value of the dollar decreases, prices of products the United States imports increase, which can result in higher inflation and interest rates domestically.

Every business day, thousands of American workers learn that they will lose their jobs. More than 500,000 annual employee layoffs by U.S. firms in the 1990s led to terms such as *downsizing, rightsizing,* and *decruiting* becoming common. European firms, too, are beginning to downsize. The U.S. and world economies face a sustained period of slow, low-inflationary expansion, global overcapacity, high unemployment, price wars, and increased competitiveness. Thousands of laid-off workers are being forced to become entrepreneurs to make a living. The United States is becoming more entrepreneurial every day.

Deregulation of industries worldwide is acting to restrain inflation worldwide. Deregulation in the utility and telecommunications industries for example is lowering electricity and phone prices worldwide. Energy deregulation worldwide contributes to keeping inflation in check in most industrialized countries of the world. Global cross-border mergers and alliances, too, serve to increase competitiveness within industries, which lowers prices and also lessens inflation pressures worldwide.

# SOCIAL, CULTURAL, DEMOGRAPHIC, AND ENVIRONMENTAL FORCES

Social, cultural, demographic, and environmental changes have a major impact upon virtually all products, services, markets, and customers. Small, large, for-profit and non-profit organizations in all industries are being staggered and challenged by the opportunities and threats arising from changes in social, cultural, demographic, and environmental variables. In every way, the United States is much different today than it was yesterday, and tomorrow promises even greater changes.

**e·biz**

The United States is getting older and less Caucasian, feeding generational and racial competition for jobs and government money. The gap between rich and poor is growing in the United States, as indicated in the E-Commerce Perspective. America's 76 million baby boomers plan to retire in 2011, and this has lawmakers and younger tax-payers deeply worried and concerned about who will pay their social security, Medicare, and Medicaid. Persons aged 65 and older in the United States will rise from 12.7 percent of the population to 18.5 percent between 1997 and 2025.

By the year 2075, the United States will have no racial or ethnic majority. This forecast is aggravating tensions over issues such as immigration and affirmative action. Hawaii and New Mexico already have no majority race or ethnic group and as of the year 2000, neither has California.

An increase in tourism worldwide is an opportunity for many firms. France is the destination for more tourists annually than any other country. Spain recently passed the United States as the second most common destination for tourists. Italy, Britain, China, Mexico, and Poland are fourth through eighth, respectively, in hosting the largest number of tourists annually.[2]

Population of the world passed 6 billion on October 12, 1999; the United States has less than 300 million persons. That leaves billions of persons outside the United States who may be interested in the products and services produced through domestic firms. Remaining solely domestic is increasing a risky strategy. Table 3–2 provides the percentage increase in population projected for major areas of the world between 1998 and 2050. The world population will reach 7 billion in 2013; 8 billion in 2028; and 9 billion in 2054.

Social, cultural, demographic, and environmental trends are shaping the way Americans live, work, produce, and consume. New trends are creating a different type of

TABLE 3-2    **World Population Statistics**

|  | 1998 | 2050 | % INCREASE |
|---|---|---|---|
| Asia | 3.6 billion | 5.3 billion | 47.22 |
| Africa | 749 million | 1.8 billion | 140.32 |
| Latin America/Caribbean | 504 million | 809 million | 60.52 |
| Europe | 628 million | 729 million | 16.08 |
| North America | 305 million | 392 million | 28.52 |
| Oceania | 30 million | 46 million | 53.33 |

Adapted from United Nations Population Division, World Population Prospects, 1999.

# E-COMMERCE PERSPECTIVE

### *Is the Internet Revolution Bypassing Poor, Minorities?*

YES. The U.S. Department of Commerce recently conducted a massive study that concluded the Internet revolution in America is largely bypassing the poor, minorities, rural areas, and inner cities. This fact is resulting in a widening gap between the rich and the poor in this country and a widening gap between the educated and uneducated. Some alarming facts reported in the landmark Department of Commerce study are given below:

- 42 percent of American households have a personal computer, but 80 percent of these are in households with family income above $75,000 while fewer than 16 percent are in houses in which families make less than $20,000 per year.

- Internet usage is lowest, 3 percent, among Americans who make $10,000 or less per year and live in rural areas.

- Asian Americans are twice as likely to use the Internet and three times more likely to be online than blacks and Hispanics.

- 26.7 percent of white Americans use the Internet at home, compared to 9.2 percent of blacks and 8.8 percent of Hispanics.

- 18.8 percent of white Americans use the Internet away from home, compared to 12.4 percent of blacks and 10.0 percent of Hispanics.

- College graduates are three times more likely to use the Internet than high school gradu-

ates, and eight times more likely than individuals who never completed high school.

- The five states with the lowest percent of households using the Internet are Mississippi (13.6%), Arkansas (14.7%), West Virginia (17.6%), Louisiana (17.8%), and North Carolina (19.9%).

- The five states with the highest percent of households using the Internet are Alaska (44.1%), New Hampshire (37.1%), Washington (36.6%), Utah (35.8%), and Colorado (34.5%).

Nearly 90 percent of all shares of common stock of American companies are held by the wealthiest 10 percent of Americans. The wealthiest 10 percent of Americans hold 73.2 percent of this country's net worth today, up from 68.2 percent in 1983. Stock ownership disparity between rich and poor Americans exemplifies growing separation between economic classes. Net worth (adjusted for inflation) of the wealthiest 20 percent of Americans increased from 18.3 percent from 1983 to 1997; net worth of the lowest 40 percent of Americans decreased 36.2 percent during that same time period.

Adapted from: David Lieberman, "Internet Gap Widening—Study: Revolution Bypassing Poor; Minorities," *USA Today* (July 9, 1999): 1A. Also, Jacob Schlesinger, "Wealth Gap Grows: Why Does It Matter," *The Wall Street Journal* (September 13, 1999): A1. [Alejandro Gonzalez, "Average Net Worth for U.S. Families," *USA Today* (October 12, 1999): 5A].

---

consumer and, consequently, a need for different products, different services, and different strategies. There are now more American households with people living alone or with unrelated people than there are households consisting of married couples with children. Census data suggest that Americans are not returning to traditional life styles. Church membership fell substantially during the 1980s for nearly all religious denominations, except Southern Baptists and Mormons. It is interesting to note that Protestant churches in the United States take in over $7 billion in donations annually. The eight largest U.S. church denominations are (in millions of members) Roman Catholic (60.3), Southern Baptist (15.7), National Baptist (11.7), United Methodist (8.5), Lutheran (5.2), Morman (4.7), Presbyterian (3.7), and Episcopalian (3.5).

Significant trends for the 2000's include consumers becoming more educated, the population aging, minorities becoming more influential, people looking for local rather than federal solutions to problems, and fixation on youth decreasing. The United States Census Bureau projects that the number of Hispanics will increase to 15 percent of the population by 2021, when they will become a larger minority group than African Americans in America. The percentage of African Americans in the U.S. population is expected to increase from 12 percent to 14 percent between 1999 and 2021. Many states currently have more than 500,000 Hispanics as registered voters, including California, New Mexico, Arizona, Texas, Florida, New York, Illinois, and New Jersey. The fastest-growing businesses in the United States are owned by women of color. The Hispanic population in the United States increased by 40 percent from 1990 to 1998. States with the largest percentage increase of Hispanics during that period were Arkansas (149%), Nevada (124%), North Carolina (110%), Georgia (103%), and Nebraska (96%).

During the 1990s, the number of individuals aged fifty and over increased 18.5 percent, to 76 million. In contrast, the number of Americans under age fifty grew by just 3.5 percent. The trend toward an older America is good news for restaurants, hotels, airlines, cruise lines, tours, resorts, theme parks, luxury products and services, recreational vehicles, home builders, furniture producers, computer manufacturers, travel services, pharmaceutical firms, automakers, and funeral homes. Older Americans are especially interested in health care, financial services, travel, crime prevention, and leisure. The world's longest-living people are the Japanese, with Japanese women living to 86.3 years and men living to 80.1 years on average. By 2050, the Census Bureau projects the number of Americans age one hundred and older to increase to over 834,000 from just under 100,000 centenarians in the United States in 2000. Senior citizens are also senior executives at hundreds of American companies. Examples include eighty-four-year-old William Dillard at Dillard's Department Stores, seventy-six-year-old Sumner Redstone, CEO of Viacom, sixty-eight-year-old Ellen Gordon, President of Tootsie Roll Industries, seventy-four-year-old Richard Jacobs, CEO of the Cleveland Indians, seventy-three-year-old Leslie Quick, CEO of Quick & Reilly, eighty-year-old Ralph Roberts, Chairman of Comcast, and seventy-three-year-old Alan Greenspan, Chairman of the Federal Reserve. Americans age sixty-five and over will increase from 12.6 percent of the U.S. population in 2000 to 20.0 percent by the year 2050.

The aging American population affects the strategic orientation of nearly all organizations. Apartment complexes for the elderly, with one meal a day, transportation, and utilities included in the rent, have increased nationwide. Called *lifecare facilities,* these complexes now exceed 2 million. Some well-known companies building these facilities include Avon, Marriott, and Hyatt. By the year 2005, individuals aged 65 and older in the United States will rise to 13 percent of the total population; Japan's elderly population ratio will rise to 17 percent, and Germany's to 19 percent.

Americans are on the move in a population shift to the South and West (Sun Belt) and away from the Northeast and Midwest (Frost Belt). The Internal Revenue Service provides the Census Bureau with massive computer files of demographic data. By comparing individual address changes from year to year, the Census Bureau publishes extensive information about population shifts across the country. For example, Arizona is the fastest-growing state. Nevada, New Mexico, and Florida are close behind. Wyoming is the nation's least-populated state and California the most-populated state. States incurring the greatest loss of people are North Dakota, Wyoming, Pennsylvania, Iowa, and West Virginia. This type of information can be essential for successful strategy formulation, including where to locate new plants and distribution centers and where to focus marketing efforts.

Americans are becoming less interested in fitness and exercise. Fitness participants declined in the United States by 3.5 percent annually in the 1990s. Makers of fitness products, such as Nike, Reebok International, and CML Group—which makes NordicTrack—are experiencing declines in sales growth. American Sports Data in Hartsdale, New York, reports that "the one American in five who exercises regularly is now outnumbered by three couch potatoes."

Mark Starik at George Washington University argues that with the thawing of the Cold War, no greater threat to business and society exists than the voracious, continuous decimation and degradation of our natural environment. The U.S. Clean Air Act went into effect in 1994. The U.S. Clean Water Act went into effect in 1984. As indicated in the Natural Environment Perspective, air and water pollution causes great anguish worldwide. A summary of important social, cultural, demographic, and environmental variables that represent opportunities or threats for virtually all organizations is given in Table 3–3.

## The U.S.–Mexican Border

Stretching 2,100 miles from the Pacific Ocean to the Gulf of Mexico, this 180-mile wide strip of land is North America's fastest-growing region. With 11 million people and $150 billion in output, this region is an economy larger than Poland. For the 6.1 million residents on the U.S. side, the average hourly wage plus benefits is $7.71, but for the 5.1 million residents on the Mexican side, the average is $1.36. The First and Third Worlds meet along this border, which features shantytowns just down the street from luxury residential neighborhoods.

There are now over fifteen hundred *maquiladoras,* assembly plants on the Mexican side of the border. Many analysts content that the *maquiladoras* are a vital key to continued U.S. global competitiveness. Mexico now ranks only behind China as global investors'

TABLE 3–3      **Key Social, Cultural, Demographic,
and Environmental Variables**

| | |
|---|---|
| Childbearing rates | Attitudes toward retirement |
| Number of special interest groups | Attitudes toward leisure time |
| Number of marriages | Attitudes toward product quality |
| Number of divorces | Attitudes toward customer service |
| Number of births | Pollution control |
| Number of deaths | Attitudes toward foreign peoples |
| Immigration and emigration rates | Energy conservation |
| Social security programs | Social programs |
| Life expectancy rates | Number of churches |
| Per capita income | Number of church members |
| Location of retailing, manufacturing, and service businesses | Social responsibility |
| Attitudes toward business | Attitudes toward careers |
| Lifestyles | Population changes by race, age, sex, and level of affluence |
| Traffic congestion | Attitudes toward authority |
| Inner-city environments | Population changes by city, county, state, region, and country |
| Average disposable income | Value placed on leisure time |
| Trust in government | Regional changes in tastes and preferences |
| Attitudes toward government | Number of women and minority workers |
| Attitudes toward work | Number of high school and college graduates by geographic area |
| Buying habits | |
| Ethical concerns | Recycling |
| Attitudes toward saving | Waste management |
| Sex roles | Air pollution |
| Attitudes toward investing | Water pollution |
| Racial equality | Ozone depletion |
| Use of birth control | Endangered species |
| Average level of education | |
| Government regulation | |

# NATURAL ENVIRONMENT

## *Is Your Business Polluting the Air or Water?*

### AIR

More than 1.5 billion people around the world live in urban areas with dangerous levels of air pollution. Alarmingly, cities are growing more rapidly than progress is being made to reverse this trend. Seven of the ten worst cities for sulfur dioxide and carbon monoxide are in developing countries. These and other pollutants cause acute and chronic lung disease, heart disease, lung cancer, and lead-induced neurological damage in children. Lung cancer alone killed 989,000 people in 1996, and 1.32 million new cases of lung cancer were diagnosed that year. In the European Union countries, a 33 percent increase in female lung cancer cases is predicted by 2005. There is no effective treatment for lung cancer—only 10 percent of patients are alive five years after diagnosis. Polluted air knows no city, state, country, or continent boundaries.

The Environmental Protection Agency (EPA) wants to expand air pollution regulation in the United States to cover microscopic particles as tiny as 2.5 microns, down from the current standard of 10 microns. The EPA says this will cut premature deaths in the United States by 20,000; cases of aggravated asthma by 250,000; cases of acute childhood respiratory problems by 250,000; bronchitis cases by 60,000; hospital admissions by 9,000; and cases of major breathing problems by 1.5 million. The total savings of these benefits would exceed $115 billion. Critics say the proposed new regulation will cost too much to U.S. companies and cities.

*Source:* Adapted from William Miller, "Clean-Air Contention," *Industry Week* (May 5, 1997): 14. Also, *World Health Organization Report,* 1997.

### WATER

Is your business polluting the water? Contaminated water is blamed for as much as 80 percent of all disease in developing countries. Well over one billion people in the world still are without safe water to drink, bathe, cook, and clean. Less than 2 percent of the domestic and industrial wastewater generated in developing countries receives any kind of treatment. It just runs into rivers and groundwater resources, thus poisoning populations, the environment, and the planet. Unsafe drinking water is a prime cause of diarrhea, malaria, cancer, infant deformities, and infant mortality. A few statistics reveal the severity, harshness, and effect of water pollution.

- More than 5 million babies born in developing countries die annually in the first month of life, mainly because of polluted water.
- About 4 million babies are born with deformities annually.
- Diarrhea and dysentery kill 2.5 million people annually.
- Malaria kills 2.1 million people annually.

Industrial discharge, a major water problem even in the United States, contributes significantly to the dramatic rise in cancer both here and abroad. More than 10 million new cases of cancer are diagnosed annually and about 6.5 million people die of cancer annually. More than 1.2 billion of these deaths are caused by stomach and colon cancer, two types often associated with poor water and eating habits. Besides deaths, the anguish, sickness, suffering, and expense inflicted upon people directly or indirectly because of contaminated water is immeasurably high even in the United States. Dangerous industrial chemicals are used here as fertilizers, pesticides, solvents, food additives, fuels, medicines, cosmetics, and in a wide range of manufacturing processes.

The EPA's most recent proposal for the Great Lakes would reduce by 91 percent the twenty-two toxic chemicals comprising about ninety thousand pounds being dumped each year into those waters. The chemicals include mercury, dioxin, chordane, DDT, and mirex.

*Source:* Adapted from *World Health Organization Report,* 1997. John Jones, "EPA Proposes To Limit PCBs In Great Lakes," *The Wall Street Journal* (September 27, 1999): B19G.

favorite location for establishing business in the developing world. Amidst the swelter of economic activity, deep disparities and contrasts are likely to persist. But the two sides of the border are now so interdependent that they can only move forward together.

Tijuana, fifteen minutes from San Diego, is the television-manufacturing capital of the world. Plants of Sony, Samsung, Matsushita, and others produce fourteen million units annually. Per capita income in San Diego is $25,000; in Tijuana, $3,200. Tijuana's *maquiladoras* employed 118,000 in 1996 up 28 percent from the prior year.

Cuidad Juarez, midway between the Pacific Ocean and the Gulf of Mexico and just 15 minutes from El Paso, has 235 factories employing 178,000, the largest concentration of *maquiladoras* anywhere along the border. General Motors alone has 17 auto parts plants. But explosive industrial growth and uncontrolled urban expansion have far surpassed municipal services such as sewers and street paving. Juarez and El Paso share the worst air pollution anywhere on the border.

Nuevo Laredo, fifteen minutes from Laredo, Texas, is home to the largest rail and truck crossings of the Rio Grande River from Mexico into the United States. More than four thousand loaded trucks cross the Rio Grande at Nuevo Laredo, which is home to Wal-Mart's largest distribution center.

## POLITICAL, GOVERNMENTAL, AND LEGAL FORCES

Federal, state, local, and foreign governments are major regulators, deregulators, subsidizers, employers, and customers of organizations. Political, governmental, and legal factors therefore can represent key opportunities or threats for both small and large organizations. For industries and firms that depend heavily on government contracts or subsidies, political forecasts can be the most important part of an external audit. Changes in patent laws, antitrust legislation, tax rates, and lobbying activities can affect firms significantly. The United States Justice Department offers excellent information at its Web site (www.justice2.usdoj.gov) on such topics.

In the world of biopolitics, Americans are still deeply divided over issues such as assisted suicide, genetic testing, genetic engineering, cloning, and abortion. Such political issues have great ramifications for companies in many industries ranging from pharmaceuticals to computers.

The increasing global interdependence among economies, markets, governments, and organizations makes it imperative that firms consider the possible impact of political variables on the formulation and implementation of competitive strategies. A number of nationally known firms forecast political, governmental, and legal variables. Some of the best Web sites for finding legal help on the Internet are listed below:[3]

www.findlaw.com
www.lawguru.com
www.freeadvice.com
www.nolo.com
www.lectlaw.com
www.abanet.org

Political forecasting can be especially critical and complex for multinational firms that depend on foreign countries for natural resources, facilities, distribution of products, special assistance, or customers. Strategists today must possess skills to deal more legalistically and politically than previous strategists, whose attention was directed more to economic and technical affairs of the firm. Strategists today are spending more time anticipating and influencing public policy actions. They spend more time meeting with government officials, attending hearings and government-sponsored conferences, giving public speeches, and meeting with trade groups, industry associations, and government agency directors. Before entering or expanding international operations, strategists need a good understanding of the political and decision-making processes in countries where their firm may conduct business. For example, republics that made up the former Soviet Union differ greatly in wealth, resources, language, and lifestyle.

Nearly fifty European and Latin American heads of state recently signed the sixty-nine-point Declaration of Rio, a sweeping agreement liberalizing trade between countries on both continents. Tariffs and non-tariff trade barriers between the two continents are being reduced in the new era of political cooperation. The Declaration of Rio of 1999 enhanced economic development and trade between those continents as well as the United States.

Increasing global competition accents the need for accurate political, governmental, and legal forecasts. Many strategists will have to become familiar with political systems in Europe and Asia and with trading currency futures. East Asian countries already have become world leaders in labor-intensive industries. A world market has emerged from what previously was a multitude of distinct national markets, and the climate for international business today would be much more favorable than yesterday. Mass communication and high technology are creating similar patterns of consumption in diverse cultures worldwide! This means that many companies may find it difficult to survive by relying solely on domestic markets.

> It is no exaggeration that in an industry that is, or is rapidly becoming, global, the riskiest possible posture is to remain a domestic competitor. The domestic competitor will watch as more aggressive companies use this growth to capture economies of scale and learning. The domestic competitor will then be faced with an attack on domestic markets using different (and possibly superior) technology, product design, manufacturing, marketing approaches, and economies of scale. A few examples suggest how extensive the phenomenon of world markets has already become. Hewlett-Packard's manufacturing chain reaches halfway around the globe, from well-paid, skilled engineers in California to low-wage assembly workers in Malaysia. General Electric has survived as a manufacturer of inexpensive audio products by centralizing its world production in Singapore.[4]

Local, state, and federal laws, regulatory agencies, and special interest groups can have a major impact on the strategies of small, large, for-profit, and nonprofit organizations. Many companies have altered or abandoned strategies in the past because of political or governmental actions. For example, many nuclear power projects have been halted and many steel plants shut down because of pressure from the Environmental Protection Agency (EPA). Other federal regulatory agencies include the Food and Drug Administration (FDA), the National Highway Traffic and Safety Administration (NHTSA), the Occupational Safety and Health Administration (OSHA), the Consumer Product Safety Commission (CPSC), the Federal Trade Commission (FTC), the Securities Exchange Commission (SEC), the Equal Employment Opportunity Commission (EEOC), the Federal Communications Commission (FCC), the Federal Maritime Commission (FMC), the Interstate Commerce Commission (ICC), the Federal Energy Regulatory Commission (FERC), the National Labor Relations Board (NLRB), and the Civil Aeronautics Board (CAB). A summary of political, governmental, and legal variables that can represent key opportunities or threats to organizations is provided in Table 3–4.

TABLE 3-4    Some Political, Governmental, and Legal Variables

| | |
|---|---|
| Government regulations or deregulations | Sino-American relationships |
| Changes in tax laws | Russian-American relationships |
| Special tariffs | European-American relationships |
| Political action committees | African-American relationships |
| Voter participation rates | Import-export regulations |
| Number, severity, and location of government protests | Government fiscal and monetary policy changes |
| Number of patents | Political conditions in foreign countries |
| Changes in patent laws | Special local, state, and federal laws |
| Environmental protection laws | Lobbying activities |
| Level of defense expenditures | Size of government budgets |
| Legislation on equal employment | World oil, currency, and labor markets |
| Level of government subsidies | Location and severity of terrorist activities |
| Antitrust legislation | Local, state, and national elections |

## Politics in Mexico

Mexico is a much better place for doing business today than yesterday. President Zedillo and his government have made significant political, social, and economic progress in Mexico. He has basically reinvented Mexico's economic model with a focus on export-led growth, higher savings rates, and careful management of finances. Direct foreign investment into Mexico is nearly $12 billion annually. The Mexican economy is growing nicely at about 4 percent in 1999 and 5 percent in 2000. This growth beats regional growth for Latin America, which was flat in 1999 and about 3 percent in 2000. The Mexican peso has appreciated nicely against the U.S. dollar, making it cheaper for companies to repay their dollar-denominated debt. A boom in manufactured exports and better oil prices has allowed Mexico to lower its inflation rate to 12 percent in 1999 and to 10 percent in 2000. President Ernesto Zedillo's government has cut Mexico's fiscal deficit from 1.25 percent of gross domestic product in 1999 to 1 percent in 2000. Mr. Zedillo, unlike his predecessors, is determined to leave office in 2000 with the Mexican economy prospering. Zedillo's $800 million annual program called Progresa makes cash payments to poverty-stricken mothers in rural areas and is successful. This program is in sharp contrast to previous Mexican welfare programs historically aimed at urban poverty for the primary purpose of garnering political votes. In late 1999, Mexico and the European Union reached a free-trade deal that ends all tariffs on their bilateral trade in industrial goods by 2007.

The pro-business, center-right National Action Party (PAN) and the left-leaning Party of the Democratic Revolution (PRD) are gearing up for the year 2000 Mexican presidential elections. Currently the Institutional Revolutionary Party (PRI) with Mr. Zedillo holds the presidential office. PRI's two candidates for the presidency are former Interior Minister Francisco Labastida and Roberto Madrazo, governor of Tabasco state. Madrazo recently blasted Zedillo for privatizing public companies and opening domestic markets to foreign competition, making the rich richer and the poor poorer. Labastida is Zedillo's favorite candidate. PRI has enjoyed a seventy-year hold on the Mexican presidency. Mexico City's Mayor Cuauhtemoc Cardenas is PRD's candidate while Vicente Fox, former governor of Guanajuato state, is the PAN candidate. Cardenas advocates greater state control over the economy and opposed the North American Free Trade Agreement (NAFTA). Vicente Fox once headed Coca-Cola's Mexican operations. PAN is pro-business and favors privatizing two state-owned electricity companies, while PRD steadfastly opposes further privatization. There is talk of a PRD/PAN Alliance to defeat PRI in 2000, but this has not been consumated.

Passage of the North American Free Trade Agreement (NAFTA) and the resultant lower tariffs have spurred trade between the United States and Mexico. NAFTA enabled Mexico to export its way out of the severe 1994 peso crisis. Mexico recently passed Japan as the second-largest market for U.S. products, trailing only Canada. Passage of NAFTA did not, as Ross Perot predicted, "create a giant sucking sound as U.S. jobs move south." U.S. unemployment rates remain low.

President Zedillo has done a good job fighting the drug trade, privatizing industry, reducing corruption, promoting democracy, and improving the natural environment. Zedillo is good for Mexico and offers hope. But his government has much work to do before he runs for reelection in the year 2000. Nearly 80 percent of Mexico's wealth rests with thirty families. About 20 percent of the population lives on roughly a dollar per day income. About 60 percent of Mexican workers take home less than $140 per month. The minimum wage is still 80 cents per hour. Unemployment rates and interest rates are high. Banks are reluctant to make loans because consumer and business delinquency rates are high.

Shipment of illegal drugs to the United States via Mexico has climbed every year and now exceeds $120 billion per year. This level is more than twice the value of Mexico's legal exports. Over 20 percent of the Mexican population in rural areas is actually employed by drug traffickers, who have built schools and hospitals for their workers and invested in local banks. The U.S. Drug Enforcement Administration estimates that 75 percent of all drugs entering the United States from South America now come through Mexico, up from 25 percent in the 1980s. Pornography, prostitution, drug addiction, drug trafficking, illegal immigration, and pollution still are severe problems for business and society.

### Politics in Russia

*Economy*    The Russian economy is in shambles. Most companies are bankrupt and out of cash but keep operating. Most employees are not paid in cash but keep working. Most companies do not pay their electricity bills yet rarely face power cutoffs. *Business Week* magazine calls the Russian economy bizarre because real money, goods, and output play such a small role.[5] Most business between companies and individuals is done through IOUs known as *veksels* and barter. Noncash forms of payment now make up 45 percent of most companies' and cities' budget. Many companies rely totally on barter such as Velta Company, a bicycle factory on Perm's outskirts, which pays its employees in bicycles. Velta swaps bicycles for raw materials and electric power. Overall, the Russian economy plunged 5 percent in 1998 and another 6 percent in 1999. Newly elected President Vladimir Putin plans to revive the Russian economy which has a Gross Domestic Product (GDP) of $190 billion, one-fiftieth the size of the U.S.'s.

The Russian government has failed at one of its primary responsibilities—collecting taxes. The government has no money to send to regional governments for social services, the military, or to pay government employees. It has no money to run the judicial system or to enforce federal laws. The Russian people have lost all trust in their government, their banking system, their legal system, and their currency. Law and order itself is in jeopardy in Russia as a result of a crippled economy. The Yeltsin administration's mismanagement of the economy and corruption so severely discredited democracy in the eyes of ordinary Russian people that communist and organized crime approaches to government are the rule rather than the exception. Age 47, President Putin promises to crack down on organized crime, revamp the Russian tax code, strengthen the judiciary, and maintain democratic freedoms.

*Trade*    The major barriers to increased U.S. exports to Russia are a substantial value-added tax, high import duties, and onerous Russian excise levies. In addition, the government has imposed strict quality and safety standards on the majority of goods entering Russia. However, Russian standards authorities have permitted only a tightly circumscribed number of groups to perform this testing in the United States. The customs clearance process at Russian borders points is frequently cumbersome and unpredictable. Local transportation problems also complicate the process of getting goods to the Russian market.

*Corruption*    In recent years, Russia privatized nearly 200,000 businesses that employed 70 percent of the nation's workforce. Privatizing simply meant giving the firm to its workers. Being untrained and unorganized, these workers most often, in turn, gave the firm to the top directors, who have largely become rich barons. Nearly 90 percent of Russian employees still live below the poverty level. "Imagine if Lee Iacocca had thought about nothing all day but how to steal from Chrysler," says Mikhail Harshan. "This is the situation in 99 percent of Russian businesses." Many Russians eat cabbage, bread, and potatoes at nearly every meal; most live in crowded apartments sharing bedrooms and bathrooms with other families.

The climate for business in Russia continues to worsen because of further director stealing, continued devaluation of the ruble, high unemployment, organized crime, high inflation, and skyrocketing taxes. Russian tax laws are among the world's most punitive and confusing, so firms keep business off the books to avoid paying out about 90 percent of profits to the government. Tax receipts by the Russian government are far lower than expected or needed to run the country.

It is almost impossible today to run a business in Russia legally. Racketeering, money laundering, financial scams, and organized criminal activity plague business. Former President Boris Yeltsin's greatest failure was the state's forced criminalization of the economy. More than five hundred businesspeople are murdered annually. Over forty thousand Russian enterprises are connected in some way to organized crime. Ten of Russia's twenty-five largest banks are operated by organized crime bosses. There are daily reports of business disputes being settled fatally.

The Russian government acknowledges that 40 percent of the nation's economy and businesses and half of its banking assets are controlled by organized crime.[6] Russian organized crime lords charge thousands of Russian businesses various amounts of money for "protection." More than 80 percent of Moscow businesses pay protection money. Russian organized crime operations have been so successful within the country that they now aggressively infiltrate governments and businesses worldwide. Frank Cilluffo of the Center for Strategic & International Studies says "Crime is the fastest-growing industry in Russia today." The Center has found Russian organized crime operations in 58 countries. Howard Abadinsky at St. Xavier College says, "Russian organized crime chiefs are an international threat to the United States. They are able to find all the weak links in American capitalism."

In 1999 and 2000, the 182-nation International Monetary Fund which loaned Russia more than $48 billion since 1992 discovered that much of this money was stolen by organized crime figures in Russia. Germany alone contributed more than $18 billion to Russia while the United States contributed over $7 billion. Monetary Fund loans were illegally diverted by Kremlin officials and organized crime groups through U.S., British, Swiss, and Austrian banks. The money was laundered (stolen) through banks such as Bank of New York. Barclays PLC, a large British bank, is withdrawing all its business with Russia, as is National Westminster Bank PLC and many other banks.

The risk of business investments in Russia decreases from south to north and west to east. Thus, investments in Siberia and along the Pacific coast are more stable and much less corrupt than those near Moscow or the Russian areas bordering Europe. Because the ruble is virtually of no value in Russia, companies need to pay their workers with something besides money, such as apartments, health care, and medical and food products. Bartering is an excellent way to motivate Russian workers.

Russia's economic problems are evidenced in the fact that the number of domestic airline passengers plunged for the ninth straight year in 1999, from a peak in 1990. U.S. companies investing in Russia today speak of getting a toehold there, not a foothold. It is just too risky. President Putin promises reform and change.

## Politics in China

After growth eight years in a row, the Chinese economy significantly retracted in 1999 to the extent that many analysts feel a devaluation of their currency, the yuan, will be necessary in 2000. Exports, which make up 20 percent of the Chinese economy, are dramatically slowing while unemployment has risen sharply to about 15 percent. There are more and more worker protests. Economic growth in China slowed from 8 percent in 1998 to 4.5 percent in 1999. Chinese manufacturers are dealing with serious overcapacity as inventories have swelled to over $500 billion or half the total economy in 1999.[7] Deflation pressure is huge in the economy. Housing privatization has stalled and consumers in China have stopped consuming. They worry that their jobs at state-run companies will be eliminated along with their health care and housing, so they save 40 percent of what money they make. State factories still manufacture billions of dollars of unwanted goods. China ran a surplus of $19.4 billion for 1999 through September, even though imports rose 19.3 percent to $117 billion while exports rose just 2.1 percent to $137 billion.

Foreign firms are either withdrawing from China altogether or scaling back their investment and lending. Foreign investment in China dropped from $40 billion in 1998 to less than $27 billion in 1999. Chinese banks are strapped with mostly bad loans and foreign companies already doing business are getting tired of continually losing money in that country. DaimlerChrysler AG is pulling out of its truck joint venture in Shanghai, Royal Ahold NV is exiting from China, Whirlpool Corporation and Caterpillar Inc. have recently pulled out of joint ventures in China. China has made illegal any foreign capital for Internet start-up businesses, which greatly slows that country's Internet development. No foreign investor is allowed to operate telecommunication networks or services in China. There are of course numerous companies, such as General Motors and Motorola, that continue to hold out hope of ever earning back their investment in China.[8] And some new companies invest in China as evidenced by foreign firms spending $29.2 billion in China during the first nine months of 1999; this amount was a 6.8 percent decline from the same period in 1998 however.

China continues to take steps to become admitted to the World Trade Organization. For example, rules on lending by Chinese banks to foreign companies were relaxed in 1999 and duty-free imports of technology equipment were established. Foreign companies transferring technology to China are now exempt from income and sales taxes. China has established new free-trade zones to encourage foreign investment into the heart of the country. Finally, foreign companies can now list shares on China's domestic stock markets. Total trade between the U.S. and China amounted to $84.7 billion in 1998 and this would increase 10 percent annually if China is admitted to the World Trade Organization. Joining the WTO would benefit Chinese consumers and force numerous Chinese companies to become more competitive but could devastate many inefficient government-owned businesses.

The taboo against private ownership of large industrial enterprises, has been abandoned in China. President Jiang Zemin encourages all types of state- and locally owned companies to issue shares of stock to diversify their ownership. State-owned enterprises accounted for 62 percent of industrial production in 1986 but today account for only 35 percent. China today is powered by small private businesses, foreign-owned companies, joint ventures, agricultural collectives, and profitable village- and township-owned businesses.

The year 1999 did not bode well for China politically. The country was accused of illegal spending to influence a U.S. election, pilfering secrets from U.S. nuclear labs, exporting materials used to make weapons of mass destruction, and menacing the island government of Taiwan.[9] China cracked down on its citizens' religious and political expression. Relations between the United States and China were further strained in 1999 by the accidental bombing of the Chinese Embassy in Yugoslavia. The U.S. Cox Report in 1999 concluded that China pilfered and continues to steal secret design information from U.S. national labs on every American nuclear weapon including neutron-bomb secrets and anti-satellite technology.

Under the leadership of President Jiang Zemin, China is making rapid progress toward becoming a stable, economic trading partner in Asia. China is moving forward quickly with privatization, deregulation, reform through stock issuances to workers, stock listings, divestitures, mergers, bankruptcies, and sale of the country's 370,000 state-run enterprises. More than half of these enterprises are losing money, which undermines the health of state banks and overall reform. About half of the 113 million workers employed by these enterprises are not needed and do not work, yet still receive full benefits.

China still has more than 120 television manufacturers, 700 beer companies, and 30,000 rubber belt makers. But the state is encouraging merger and consolidation, which is transforming the economic landscape. Jiang's plan is to create large, private, efficient, Chinese companies that can compete effectively and globally.

Jiang is also focusing on improving health care, pensions, education, unemployment, and poverty relief by strengthening the rule of law, promoting greater separation of government and business, and guaranteeing human rights. China has extended direct elections from villages to townships. Jiang has cut the number of specialized economic departments to ease bureaucratic meddling in business.

Jiang, however, is tightening control over the press and publishing and upholds the ruling role of the Communist Party. The Chinese government will retain control over only about one thousand enterprises, including all those involved in infrastructure, telecommunications, certain raw materials, and the military. Beijing has evolved a policy of engaging protesters in dialogue and trying to mediate.

China still only takes in about 12 percent of gross domestic product in taxes, about one-third the level of most developed countries. This leaves the country strapped for cash in providing even the most basic social needs. China spends only 3.8 percent of its GDP on health care, compared with about 10 percent in developed countries. China is releasing state companies from the burden of providing health care, pensions, and housing by setting up national health and retirement systems.

Jiang Zemin's reform agenda consists of five key strategies:

1. Restructure state enterprises. Convert state enterprises into corporations owned by shareholders.

2. Strengthen financial markets. Expand capital markets by authorizing hundreds of new stock listings annually.

3. Sell state assets. Require all but 1,000 of China's 305,000 state enterprises to sell to shareholders or go bankrupt.

4. Build social services. Build low-cost housing, set up pension programs, and retrain workers to relieve burdens on state enterprises.

5. Reduce Tariffs. Reduce tariffs from 17 percent in 1997 to 15 percent in 2000 as part of a bid to join the World Trade Organization.[10]

# TECHNOLOGICAL FORCES

Revolutionary technological changes and discoveries such as superconductivity, computer engineering, thinking computers, robotics, unstaffed factories, miracle drugs, space communications, space manufacturing, lasers, cloning, satellite networks, fiber optics, biometrics, and electronic funds transfer are having a dramatic impact on organizations. Superconductivity advancements alone, which increase the power of electrical products by lowering resistance to current, are revolutionizing business operations, especially in the transportation, utility, health care, electrical, and computer industries.

The Internet is acting as a national and even global economic engine that is spurring productivity, a critical factor in a country's ability to improve living standards. The Internet is saving companies billions of dollars in distribution and transaction costs from direct sales to self-service systems. For example, the familiar Hypertext Markup Language (HTML) is being replaced by Extensible Markup Language (XML). XML is a programming language based on "tags" whereby a number represents a price, an invoice, a date, a zip code, or whatever. XML is forcing companies to make a major strategic decision in terms of whether to open their information to the world in the form of catalogs, inventories, prices and specifications, or attempt to hold their data closely to preserve some perceived advantage.[11] XML is reshaping industries, reducing prices, accelerating global trade, and revolutionizing all commerce. Microsoft has reoriented most of its software development around XML, replacing HTML.

Ultra-wideband (UWB) wireless communications that sends information on tiny wave pulses may soon replace continuous radio waves, allowing ever-smaller devices to do vastly more powerful wireless communications. The Federal Communications Commission (FCC) is slow to approve UWB in fear of its disrupting existing wireless communication, but UWB technology pioneered by Time Domain of Huntsville, Alabama, has the potential to permanently change the way all individuals and businesses communicate worldwide.

The Internet is changing the very nature of opportunities and threats by altering the life cycles of products, increasing the speed of distribution, creating new products and services, erasing limitations of traditional geographic markets, and changing the historical trade-off between production standardization and flexibility. The Internet is altering economies of scale, changing entry barriers, and redefining the relationship between industries and various suppliers, creditors, customers, and competitors.

To effectively capitalize on information technology, a number of organizations are establishing two new positions in their firms: *chief information officer (CIO)* and *chief technology officer (CTO)*. This trend reflects the growing importance of *information technology* in strategic management. A CIO and CTO work together to ensure that information needed to formulate, implement, and evaluate strategies is available where and when it is needed. These persons are responsible for developing, maintaining, and updating a company's information database. The CIO is more a manager, managing the overall external-audit process; the CTO is more a technician, focusing on technical issues such as data acquisition, data processing, decision support systems, and software and hardware acquisition.

Technological forces represent major opportunities and threats that must be considered in formulating strategies. Technological advancements dramatically can affect organizations' products, services, markets, suppliers, distributors, competitors, customers, manufacturing processes, marketing practices, and competitive position. Technological advancements can create new markets, result in a proliferation of new and improved products, change the relative competitive cost positions in an industry, and render existing products and services obsolete. Technological changes can reduce or eliminate cost barriers between businesses, create shorter production runs, create shortages in technical skills, and result in changing values and expectations of employees, managers, and customers. Technological advancements can create new *competitive advantages* that are more powerful than existing advantages. No company or industry today is insulated against emerging technological developments. In high-tech industries identification and evaluation of key technological opportunities and threats can be the most important part of the external strategic-management audit.

Organizations that traditionally have limited technology expenditures to what they can fund after meeting marketing and financial requirements urgently need a reversal in thinking. The pace of technological change is increasing and literally wiping out businesses every day. An emerging consensus holds that technology management is one of the key responsibilities of strategists. Firms should pursue strategies that take advantage of technological opportunities to achieve sustainable, competitive advantages in the marketplace.

> Technology-based issues will underlie nearly every important decision that strategists make. Crucial to those decisions will be the ability to approach technology planning analytically and strategically. . . . technology can be planned and managed using formal techniques similar to those used in business and capital investment planning. An effective technology strategy is built on a penetrating analysis of technology opportunities and threats, and an assessment of the relative importance of these factors to overall corporate strategy.[12]

In practice, critical decisions about technology too often are delegated to lower organizational levels or are made without an understanding of their strategic implications. Many strategists spend countless hours determining market share, positioning products in terms of features and price, forecasting sales and market size, and monitoring distributors; yet too often technology does not receive the same respect:

> The impact of this oversight is devastating. Firms not managing technology to ensure their futures may eventually find their futures managed by technology. Technology's impact reaches far beyond the "high-tech" companies. Although some industries may appear to be relatively technology-insensitive in terms of products and market requirements, they are not immune from the impact of technology; companies in smokestack as well as service industries must carefully monitor emerging technological opportunities and threats.[13]

Not all sectors of the economy are affected equally by technological developments. The communications, electronics, aeronautics, and pharmaceutical industries are much more volatile than the textile, forestry, and metals industries. For strategists in industries affected by rapid technological change, identifying and evaluating technological opportunities and threats can represent the most important part of an external audit.

Some technological advancements expected soon in the computer and medical industry are computers that recognize handwriting; voice-controlled computers; gesture-controlled computers; picture phones; and defeat of heart disease, AIDS, rheumatoid arthritis, multiple sclerosis, leukemia, and lung cancer. New technological advancements in the computer industry alone are revolutionizing the way businesses operate today. As indicated in the Global Perspective, cell phone and wireless Internet access are becoming common, with Finland leading all countries in this new technology. Estimates

# GLOBAL PERSPECTIVE

### *What Country Is the Most Wireless Nation?*

The answer is Finland. Despite its small size and Arctic location, Finland leads the world in Web site and cell phone usage. Most new homeowners in Finland never bother ordering fixed-line telephone service because the wireless mentality has engulfed the nation. Sixty percent of Finns own mobile phones, compared with about 25 percent of Americans. The Finnish company Nokia recently passed Motorola as the leading supplier of mobile handsets with 37.4 million sold in 1998. "Finland will hit 100 percent penetration of cell phones by late 2000," predicts Christian Kern. "For the average person, having a mobile phone will mean not having to carry an ATM card and will be your cash and your access to the Internet."

Americans are coming to realize like the Finns that a phone number is something that should follow them around rather than being at a particular location. The number of wireless subscribers in the United States is expected to double from 72 million in mid-1999 to nearly 150 million in the early 2000's. Sprint PCS chief Andy Sukawaty says, "The whole concept behind personal computers is that the wireless phone becomes your primary communications device." A wireless phone makes special sense for some persons, such as single people who can take the phone from their residence without inconveniencing others and for college students who do not want to share a phone bill.

In Finland, 31 percent of individuals regularly use the Internet compared to 28 percent in the United States. Across all of Europe, 9 percent of households use the Internet compared to 37 percent of households in the United States. The following table provides a breakdown of European countries in terms of percentage of households on the Internet.

| Country | % of Households on the Net |
| --- | --- |
| Finland | 23 |
| Sweden | 18 |
| Denmark | 15 |
| United Kingdom | 14 |
| Switzerland | 13 |
| Norway | 13 |
| Germany | 11 |
| Portugal | 03 |
| Spain | 03 |
| Italy | 03 |
| Belgium | 04 |
| Austria | 05 |
| France | 05 |
| Ireland | 06 |

Adapted from: Marco della Cava, "Wireless Nation—Finland Pushes Cell Phone to High-Tech Limit," *USA Today* (August 25, 1999): 1A. Also, Steve Rosenbush, "More Using Cell Instead of Home Phones," *USA Today* (July 2, 1999): A1. Also, David Lynch, "Fishing for Customers," *USA Today,* (July 16, 1999): 2B.

are that there will be 48 million smart phone (cell phones equipped with microbrowsers) users worldwide by 2002 and a whopping 204 million by 2005.[14] About 28 million Americans will be using smart phones by 2002.

## COMPETITIVE FORCES

The top five U.S. competitors in four different industries are identified in Table 3–5. An important part of an external audit is identifying rival firms and determining their strengths, weaknesses, capabilities, opportunities, threats, objectives, and strategies.

Collecting and evaluating information on competitors is essential for successful strategy formulation. Identifying major competitors is not always easy because many firms have divisions that compete in different industries. Most multidivisional firms generally do not provide sales and profit information on a divisional basis for competitive reasons. Also, privately held firms do not publish any financial or marketing information.

TABLE 3-5     The Top Five U.S. Competitors in Four Different Industries in 1999

| | 1999 SALES IN $ MILLIONS | PERCENTAGE CHANGE FROM 1998 | 1999 PROFITS IN $ MILLIONS | PERCENTAGE CHANGE FROM 1998 |
|---|---|---|---|---|
| AEROSPACE | | | | |
| Boeing | 57,993 | +3 | 2,309 | +106 |
| Lockheed Martin | 25,530 | −3 | 737 | −26 |
| United Technologies | 24,127 | +6 | 841 | −27 |
| Northrop Grumman | 8,995 | +1 | 483 | +149 |
| General Dynamics | 8,959 | +21 | 880 | +49 |
| FOREST PRODUCTS | | | | |
| International Paper | 24,600 | +3 | 199 | −19 |
| Georgia-Pacific | 17,790 | +35 | 716 | +545 |
| Kimberly-Clark | 13,006 | +6 | 1,668 | +50 |
| Boise Cascade | 6,952 | +13 | 200 | NM |
| Fort James | 6,827 | +0 | 350 | −29 |
| COMPUTERS | | | | |
| IBM | 87,548 | +7 | 7,712 | +22 |
| Hewlett-Packard | 43,808 | +10 | 3,016 | +8 |
| Compaq Computer | 38,525 | +24 | 569 | NM |
| Dell Computer | 25,265 | +38 | 1,666 | +14 |
| Xerox | 19,228 | −1 | 1,424 | +143 |
| PUBLISHING | | | | |
| Time Warner | 27,333 | +87 | 1,960 | +1067 |
| CBS | 7,373 | +8 | 157 | NM |
| Gannett | 5,260 | +8 | 919 | −5 |
| McGraw-Hill | 3,992 | +7 | 426 | +25 |
| Knight-Ridder | 3,228 | +4 | 340 | +11 |

*Source:* Adapted from Corporate Scoreboard, *Business Week* (March 27, 2000): 167–192.
NM: Not Measurable

Despite the problems mentioned above, information on leading competitors in particular industries can be found in publications such as *Moody's Manuals, Standard Corporation Descriptions, Value Line Investment Surveys, Ward's Business Directory, Dun's Business Rankings, Standard & Poor's Industry Surveys, Industry Week, Forbes, Fortune, Business Week,* and *Inc.* In addition, the *Million Dollar Directory* lists key personnel, products, divisions, and SIC codes for over 160,000 U.S. public and private companies whose revenues exceed $500,000. *Standard & Poor's Register of Corporate Directors and Executives* and the *Directory of Corporate Affiliations* are other excellent sources of competitive information. However, many businesses use the Internet to obtain most of their information on competitors. The Internet is fast, thorough, accurate, and increasingly indispensable in this regard. Questions about competitors such as those presented in Table 3–6 are important to address in performing an external audit.

Competition in virtually all industries can be described as intense, and sometimes cutthroat. For example, when United Parcel Service (UPS) employees were on strike in 1997, competitors such as Federal Express, Greyhound, Roadway, and United Airlines lowered prices, doubled advertising efforts, and locked new customers into annual contracts in efforts to leave UPS customer-less when the strike ended. If a firm detects weakness in a competitor, no mercy at all is shown in capitalizing on its problems.

TABLE 3-6        **Key Questions About Competitors**

1. What are the major competitors' strengths?
2. What are the major competitors' weaknesses?
3. What are the major competitors' objectives and strategies?
4. How will the major competitors most likely respond to current economic, social, cultural, demographic, environmental, political, governmental, legal, technological, and competitive trends affecting our industry?
5. How vulnerable are the major competitors to our alternative company strategies?
6. How vulnerable are our alternative strategies to successful counterattack by our major competitors?
7. How are our products or services positioned relative to major competitors?
8. To what extent are new firms entering and old firms leaving this industry?
9. What key factors have resulted in our present competitive position in this industry?
10. How have the sales and profit rankings of major competitors in the industry changed over recent years? Why have these rankings changed that way?
11. What is the nature of supplier and distributor relationships in this industry?
12. To what extent could substitute products or services be a threat to competitors in this industry?

America Online and Microsoft are currently locked in a schoolyard brawl over free instant messaging service. Instant messaging has more users than chat rooms, but less users than e-mail. America Online contends that Microsoft's MSN Messenger makes unauthorized use of its network and the two firms are at loggerheads over the issue.[15] MSN Messenger, which asks for your AOL username and password, was developed by reverse engineering AOL software.

Seven characteristics describe the most competitive companies in America: (1) Market share matters; the 90th share point isn't as important as the 91st, and nothing is more dangerous than falling to 89; (2) Understand and remember precisely what business you are in; (3) Whether it's broke or not, fix it—make it better; not just products, but the whole company if necessary; (4) Innovate or evaporate; particularly in technology-driven businesses, nothing quite recedes like success; (5) Acquisition is essential to growth; the most successful purchases are in niches that add a technology or a related market; (6) People make a difference; tired of hearing it? Too bad; (7) There is no substitute for quality and no greater threat than failing to be cost-competitive on a global basis; these are complementary concepts, not mutually exclusive ones.[16]

## Competitive Intelligence Programs

France, Germany, Japan, and South Korea are our military and political partners since the end of World War II. Unfortunately, this is not only a list of America's trustworthy friends, it is a list of governments that have systematically practiced economic espionage against American companies in the past—and continue to do so to this day. France openly admits that it operates a special department devoted to obtaining confidential information about U.S. companies. Good competitive intelligence in business, as in the military, is one of the keys to success. The more information and knowledge a firm can obtain about its competitors, the more likely it can formulate and implement effective strategies. Major competitors' weaknesses can represent external opportunities; major competitors' strengths may represent key threats.

What is competitive intelligence? Competitive intelligence, as formally defined by the Society of Competitive Intelligence Professionals (SCIP), is a systematic and ethical process for gathering and analyzing information about the competition's activities and general business trends to further a business' own goals (SCIP Web site).

Unfortunately, the majority of U.S. executives grew up in times when American firms dominated foreign competitors so much that gathering competitive intelligence seemed not worth the effort. Too many of these executives still cling to these attitudes, to the detriment of their organizations today. Even most MBA programs do not offer a course in competitive and business intelligence, thus reinforcing this attitude. As a consequence, three strong misperceptions about business intelligence prevail among American executives today:

1. Running an intelligence program requires lots of people, computers, and other resources.
2. Collecting intelligence about competitors violates antitrust laws; business intelligence equals espionage.
3. Intelligence gathering is an unethical business practice.[17]

All three of these perceptions are totally misguided. Any discussions with a competitor about price, market, or geography intentions could violate antitrust statutes, but this fact must not lure a firm into underestimating the need for and benefits of systematically collecting information about competitors for the purpose of enhancing a firm's effectiveness. The Internet has become an excellent medium for gathering competitive intelligence. Information gathering from employees, managers, suppliers, distributors, customers, creditors, and consultants also can make the difference between having superior or just average intelligence and overall competitiveness.

Firms need an effective *competitive intelligence (CI)* program. The three basic missions of a CI program are (1) to provide a general understanding of an industry and its competitors, (2) to identify areas in which competitors are vulnerable and to assess the impact strategic actions would have on competitors, and (3) to identify potential moves that a competitor might make that would endanger a firm's position in the market.[18] Competitive information is equally applicable for strategy formulation, implementation, and evaluation decisions. An effective CI program allows all areas of a firm to access consistent and verifiable information in making decisions. All members of an organization, from the chief executive officer to custodians, are valuable intelligence agents and should feel a part of the CI process. Special characteristics of a successful CI program include flexibility, usefulness, timeliness, and cross-functional cooperation.

The increasing emphasis on *competitive analysis* in the United States is evidenced by corporations putting this function on their organizational charts under job titles such as Director of Competitive Analysis, Competitive Strategy Manager, Director of Information Services, or Associate Director of Competitive Assessment. The responsibilities of a *director of competitive analysis* include planning, collecting data, analyzing data, facilitating the process of gathering and analyzing data, disseminating intelligence on a timely basis, researching special issues, and recognizing what information is important and who needs to know. Competitive intelligence is not corporate espionage because 95 percent of the information a company needs to make strategic decisions is available and accessible to the public. Sources of competitive information include trade journals, want ads, newspaper articles, and government filings, as well as customers, suppliers, distributors, and competitors themselves.

Unethical tactics such as bribery, wire tapping, and computer break-ins should never be used to obtain information. Marriott and Motorola—two American companies that do a particularly good job of gathering competitive intelligence—agree that all the information you could wish for can be collected without resorting to unethical tactics. They keep their intelligence staffs small, usually under five people, and spend less than $200,000 per year on gathering competitive intelligence.

## Cooperation Among Competitors

Strategies that stress cooperation among competitors are being used more. For example, Lockheed recently teamed up with British Aerospace PLC to compete against Boeing Company to develop the next-generation U.S. fighter jet. Lockheed's cooperative strategy with a profitable partner in the Airbus Industrie consortium encourages broader Lockheed-European collaboration as Europe's defense industry consolidates. The British firm offers Lockheed special expertise in the areas of short takeoff and vertical landing technologies, systems integration, and low-cost design and manufacturing.

Cooperative agreements even between competitors are becoming popular. For example, Canon supplies photocopies to Kodak, France's Thomson and Japan's FVC manufacture videocassette recorders, Siemens and Fujitsu work together, and General Motors and Toyota assemble automobiles. Italian automaker Piat SpA and Russia's Gorky Automobile Factory recently formed a joint venture to produce 150,000 cars annually for the Russian market. Gorky is Russia's largest and most successful automaker. For collaboration between competitors to succeed, both firms must contribute something distinctive, such as technology, distribution, basic research, or manufacturing capacity. But a major risk is that unintended transfers of important skills or technology may occur at organizational levels below where the deal was signed.[19] Information not covered in the formal agreement often gets traded in day-to-day interactions and dealings of engineers, marketers, and product developers. Firms often give away too much information to rival firms when operating under cooperative agreements! Tighter formal agreements are needed.

Microsoft, Dell Computer, Lycos, and Excite At Home have all teamed up against eBay Inc. to form a new online auction business. Cooperation among these competitors was deemed necessary to gain market share from eBay which dominates the online auction industry with more than four million auction listings. Ebay's online auction business dwarfs even well-know rivals like Yahoo! Inc. and Amazon.com Inc.

The idea of joining forces with a competitor is not easily accepted by Americans, who often view cooperation and partnerships with skepticism and suspicion. Indeed, joint ventures and cooperative arrangements among competitors demand a certain amount of trust to combat paranoia about whether one firm will injure the other. However, multinational firms are becoming more globally cooperative, and increasing numbers of domestic firms are joining forces with competitive foreign firms to reap mutual benefits. Kathryn Harrigan at Columbia University says, "Within a decade, most companies will be members of teams that compete against each other."

British Telecommunications PLC and AT&T Corporation recently formed an alliance to sell mobile-phone service around the world. These two competitors formed the alliance to compete with the newly merged Vodafone PLC/AirTouch Communications firm. BT PLC and AT&T are creating a single mobile phone that will work in the United States and Europe.

American companies often enter alliances primarily to avoid investments, being more interested in reducing the costs and risks of entering new businesses or markets than in acquiring new skills. In contrast, *learning from the partner* is a major reason why Asian and European firms enter into cooperative agreements. American firms, too, should place learning high on the list of reasons to cooperate with competitors. American companies often form alliances with Asian firms to gain an understanding of their manufacturing excellence, but Asian competence in this area is not easily transferable. Manufacturing excellence is a complex system that includes employee training and involvement, integration with suppliers, statistical process controls, value engineering, and design. In contrast, American know-how in technology and related areas more easily can be imitated. American firms thus need to be careful not to give away more intelligence than they receive in cooperative agreements with rival Asian firms.

## COMPETITIVE ANALYSIS: PORTER'S FIVE-FORCES MODEL

As illustrated in Figure 3–3, *Porter's Five-Forces Model* of competitive analysis is a widely used approach for developing strategies in many industries. The intensity of competition among firms varies widely across industries. Table 3–7 reveals the average return on equity for firms in twenty-four different industries in 1999. Intensity of competition is highest in lower-return industries. According to Porter, the nature of competitiveness in a given industry can be viewed as a composite of five forces:

1. Rivalry among competitive firms
2. Potential entry of new competitors
3. Potential development of substitute products
4. Bargaining power of suppliers
5. Bargaining power of consumers

### Rivalry Among Competing Firms

Rivalry among competing firms is usually the most powerful of the five competitive forces. The strategies pursued by one firm can be successful only to the extent that they provide competitive advantage over the strategies pursued by rival firms. Changes in strategy by one firm may be met with retaliatory countermoves, such as lowering prices, enhancing quality, adding features, providing services, extending warranties, and increasing advertising. For example, Pepsi recently filed a complaint against Coca-Cola for "illegally trying to force competitors out of the European market." The complaint to the European Union resulted in government raids at Coca-Cola offices in four European countries seizing documents relating to the issue. Coca-Cola denied any wrongdoing.

In the Internet world, competitiveness is fierce. Amazon.com watches in dismay as customers use their site's easy-to-use format, in-depth reviews, expert recommendations, and then bypass the cash register as they click their way over to deep-discounted sites such as Buy.com to make their purchase. Buy.com CEO says, "The Internet is going to shrink retailers' margins to the point where they will not survive." Price-comparison Web sites allow consumers to efficiently find the lowest-priced seller on the Internet. Kate Delhagen of Forrester Research says, "If you're a consumer and you're thinking about any kind of researched purchase, you're leaving thousands of dollars on the table if you don't at least look online."[20] The costs of setting up a great e-commerce site are nothing compared to with the cost of acquiring real estate for building retail stores, or even printing and mailing catalogs.

**e·biz**

Free-flowing information on the Internet is driving down prices and inflation worldwide. Japan is in a downright deflation. The Internet, coupled with the common currency in Europe, enables consumers to easily make price comparisons across countries. Just for a moment consider the implications for car dealers who used to know everything about a new car's pricing while you the consumer knew very little. You could bargain, but being in the dark you rarely could win. Now you can go to Web sites such as CarPoint or Edmunds.com and know more about new car prices than the car salesperson, and you can even shop online in a few hours at every dealership within five hundred miles to find the best price and terms. So you the consumer can win. This is true in many if not most business-to-consumer and business-to-business sales transactions today.

The intensity of rivalry among competing firms tends to increase as the number of competitors increases, as competitors become more equal in size and capability, as demand

## FIGURE 3–3

**The Five-Forces Model of Competition**

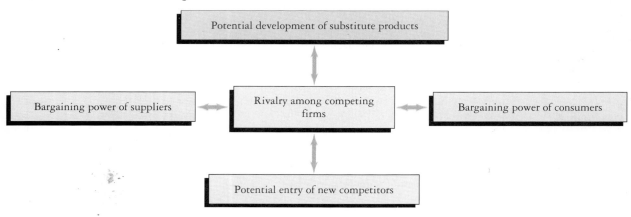

TABLE 3-7    **Intensity of Competition Among Firms in Different Industries—1999 Results Provided**

| RANK | INDUSTRY | 1999 AVERAGE RETURN ON EQUITY/ AVERAGE EARNINGS PER SHARE |
|------|----------|----------------------------------------------------------|
| 1 | Consumer Products | 26.5/1.76 |
| 2 | Automotive | 25.6/4.78 |
| 3 | Health Care | 25.2/1.37 |
| 4 | Conglomerates | 23.9/1.86 |
| 5 | Food | 23.6/1.41 |
| 6 | Housing and Real Estate | 22.2/3.08 |
| 7 | Office Equipment and Computers | 21.4/1.42 |
| 8 | Banks | 18.7/2.92 |
| 9 | Discount and Fashion Retailing | 17.8/1.56 |
| 10 | Nonbank Financial | 17.3/3.13 |
| 11 | Service Industries | 16.6/0.36 |
| 12 | Publishing and Broadcasting | 15.0/2.50 |
| 13 | Manufacturing | 14.5/2.36 |
| 14 | Electrical and Electronics | 14.3/1.38 |
| 15 | Fuel | 13.4/1.61 |
| 16 | Aerospace and Defense | 13.3/2.89 |
| 17 | Paper and Forest Products | 12.3/2.32 |
| 18 | Telecommunications | 12.2/1.10 |
| 19 | Leisure Time Industries | 11.7/1.32 |
| 20 | Transportation | 11.5/2.60 |
| 21 | Utilities and Power | 11.1/2.46 |
| 22 | Chemicals | 10.1/1.90 |
| 23 | Containers and Packaging | 09.5/2.14 |
| 24 | Metals and Mining | 05.9/0.57 |

*Source:* Adapted from "Corporate Scoreboard," *Business Week* (March 27, 2000): 167–192. Also, "Corporate Scoreboard," *Business Week* (March 2, 1998): 113–136.

for the industry's products declines, and as price cutting becomes common. Rivalry also increases when consumers can switch brands easily; when barriers to leaving the market are high; when fixed costs are high; when the product is perishable; when rival firms are diverse in strategies, origins, and culture; and when mergers and acquisitions are common in the industry. As rivalry among competing firms intensifies, industry profits decline, in some cases to the point where an industry becomes inherently unattractive.

## Potential Entry of New Competitors

Whenever new firms can easily enter a particular industry, the intensity of competitiveness among firms increases. Barriers to entry, however, can include the need to gain economies of scale quickly, the need to gain technology and specialized know-how, the lack of experience, strong customer loyalty, strong brand preferences, large capital requirements, lack of adequate distribution channels, government regulatory policies, tariffs, lack of access to raw materials, possession of patents, undesirable locations, counterattack by entrenched firms, and potential saturation of the market.

Despite numerous barriers to entry, new firms sometimes enter industries with higher-quality products, lower prices, and substantial marketing resources. The strategist's job, therefore, is to identify potential new firms entering the market, to monitor the new rival firms' strategies, to counterattack as needed, and to capitalize on existing strengths and opportunities.

## Potential Development of Substitute Products

In many industries, firms are in close competition with producers of substitute products in other industries. Examples are plastic container producers competing with glass, paperboard, and aluminum can producers, and acetaminophen manufacturers competing with other manufacturers of pain and headache remedies. The presence of substitute products puts a ceiling on the price that can be charged before the consumers will switch to the substitute product.

Competitive pressures arising from substitute products increase as the relative price of substitute products declines and as consumers' switching costs decrease. The competitive strength of substitute products is best measured by the inroads into market share those products obtain, as well as those firms' plans for increased capacity and market penetration.

## Bargaining Power of Suppliers

The bargaining power of suppliers affects the intensity of competition in an industry, especially when there is a large number of suppliers, when there are only a few good substitute raw materials, or when the cost of switching raw materials is especially costly. It often is in the best interest of both suppliers and producers to assist each other with reasonable prices, improved quality, development of new services, just-in-time deliveries, and reduced inventory costs, thus enhancing long-term profitability for all concerned.

Firms may pursue a backward integration strategy to gain control or ownership of suppliers. This strategy is especially effective when suppliers are unreliable, too costly, or not capable of meeting a firm's needs on a consistent basis. Firms generally can negotiate more favorable terms with suppliers when backward integration is a commonly used strategy among rival firms in an industry.

## Bargaining Power of Consumers

When customers are concentrated or large, or buy in volume, their bargaining power represents a major force affecting intensity of competition in an industry. Rival firms may offer extended warranties or special services to gain customer loyalty whenever the bargaining power of consumers is substantial. Bargaining power of consumers also is higher when the products being purchased are standard or undifferentiated. When this is the case, consumers often can negotiate selling price, warranty coverage, and accessory packages to a greater extent. Wal-Mart is the offline retailing champ. However, Wal-Mart today is scrambling to improve its wal-mart.com Web site which looks prehistoric compared to many new competitors hungry to seize retailing market share through online entry into the industry. Even for a huge company such as Wal-Mart, the drastic increase in bargaining power of consumers caused by Internet usage is a major external threat.

## SOURCES OF EXTERNAL INFORMATION

A wealth of strategic information is available to organizations from both published and unpublished sources. Unpublished sources include customer surveys, market research, speeches at professional and shareholders' meetings, television programs, interviews, and conversations with stakeholders. Published sources of strategic information include periodicals, journals, reports, government documents, abstracts, books, directories, newspapers, and manuals. Computerization and the Internet have made it easier today for firms to gather, assimilate, and evaluate information.

### Internet

Millions of people today use online services for both business and personal purposes. *America Online* and *EarthLink* are leading commercial online services. These companies are expanding their menu of available services to include everything from online access to most major television networks, newspapers, and magazines to online interviewing of celebrities, and they offer access to the furthermost boundaries of the Internet. These companies harness the power of multimedia, combining sound, video, and graphics with text. Excellent sources of strategic management and case research information on the *World Wide Web* are provided in Table 3–8. Table 3–9 provides selected academic and consulting strategic planning Web sites.

TABLE 3-8     **Excellent Internet Sources of Information**

**I. INVESTMENT RESEARCH**

Strategic Management Club Online→www.strategyclub.com
American Stock Exchange→www.amex.com
DBC Online→www.dbc.com
Hoover's Online→www.hoovers.com
InvestorGuide→www.investorguide.com
Wall Street Research Net→www.wsrn.com
Market Guide→www.marketguide.com
Money Search – Find It!→www.moneysearch.com
NASDAQ→www.nasdaq.com
New York Stock Exchange→www.nyse.com/public/home.html
PC Financial Network→www.dljdirect.com
Quote.Com→www.quote.com
Stock Smart→www.stocksmart.com
Wright Investors' Service on the World Wide Web→www.wisi.com
Zacks Investment Research→www.zacks.com/docs/Bob/hotlinks.htm

*continued*

TABLE 3-8    **Excellent Internet Sources of Information** *(continued)*

## II. SEARCH ENGINES

Alta Vista→www.altavista.digital.com
Deja News→www.dejanews.com
DogPile→www.dogpile.com
Excite→www.excite.com
HotBot→www.hotbot.com
InfoSeek→www.infoseek.com
Lycos→www.lycos.com
Magellan Internet Guide→www.mckinley.com
Metacrawler→www.metacrawler.com
Starting Point→www.stpt.com
WebCrawler→www.webcrawler.com
Yahoo!→www.yahoo.com

## III. DIRECTORIES

Argus Clearinghouse→www.clearinghouse.net
BigBook→www.bigbook.com
ComFind→www.comfind.com
U.S. Business Advisor→www.business.gov/business.html
Thomas Publishing Co.→www.thomaspublishing.com
Competitive Intelligence Guide→www.fuld.com

## IV. NEWS, MAGAZINES, AND NEWSPAPERS

PR Newswire→www.prnewswire.com
*American Demographics*→www.marketingtools.com
*Barron's Magazine*→www.barrons.com
*Business Week*→www.businessweek.com
*CNNfn*→www.cnnfn.com/search
*Financial Times*→www.usa.ft.com
*Forbes Magazine* On-line→www.forbes.com
*Fortune Magazine*→www.fortune.com
*USA Today*→www.usatoday.com
*Wall Street Journal*→www.wsj.com
*Washington Post* Online→www.washingtonpost.com

## V. U.S. GOVERNMENT

Better Business Bureau→www.bbb.org
Census Bureau→www.census.gov
Federal Trade Commission→www.ftc.gov
FreeEDGAR→www.freeedgar.com
Edgar-Online→www.edgar-online.com
General Printing Office→www.gpo.gov
Internal Revenue Service→www.irs.ustreas.gov
Library of Congress→www.loc.gov
SEC's Edgar Database→www.sec.gov/edgarhp.htm
Small Business Administration→www.sba.gov
U.S. Department of Commerce→www.doc.gov
U.S. Department of the Treasury→www.ustreas.gov
Environmental Protection Agency→www.epa.gov
National Aeronautics and Space Administration→www.hq.nasa.gov

TABLE 3-9    Important Strategic Planning Web Sites

### I. ACADEMIC

*1. NEW MEXICO STATE UNIVERSITY—www.nmsu.edu/strategic/*
This site provides a full description of the strategic planning process at New Mexico State University, including a chart, reading material on strategic planning, and guidelines about how to do strategic planning. A great site for seeing strategic planning in action.

*2. STRATEGIC MANAGEMENT SOCIETY—www.virtual-indiana.com/sms/*
This is a not-for-profit professional society composed of nearly two thousand academic, business, and consulting members from forty-five countries. This group publishes the *Strategic Management Journal* and offers annual meetings and conferences. The Web site is well designed and outlines the society's services and resources.

*3. AMERICAN MANAGEMENT ASSOCIATION—www.amanet.org*
AMA provides educational forums worldwide for businesses to learn practical business skills. This Web site is comprehensive in providing access to all AMA seminars, videos, and courses worldwide, including strategic planning products. AMA publishes *Management Review.*

*4. ACADEMY OF MANAGEMENT ONLINE—www.aom.pace.edu*
This not-for-profit organization is the leading professional association for management research and education in the United States. Almost ten thousand members from businesses and universities around the world participate. About twenty-five hundred of these members specify Business Policy and Strategy as their primary interest. This site provides a search engine to locate and contact all these members. Many links and personal Web pages are provided. This organization publishes *Academy of Management Executive, Academy of Management Review,* and *Academy of Management Journal.*

*5. STRATEGIC LEADERSHIP FORUM—www.slfnet.org*
This is an international organization of executives focusing on strategic management and planning. The Web site is outstanding. Many excellent strategic planning links are provided. The Forum publishes *Strategy and Leadership* (formerly *Planning Review*).

### II. CONSULTANTS

*1. STRATEGIC PLANNING SYSTEMS—www.checkmateplan.com*
This site provides CheckMATE, the industry leader in strategic planning software worldwide. This software is Windows-based and easy to use. Twenty-three different industry versions are available. Also provided on this site is a strategic planning video and workbook, as well as free links to scores for other good sites for gathering strategic planning information.

*2. MIND TOOLS—www.mindtools.com/planpage.html*
This is an excellent Web site for providing strategic planning information. More than thirty pages of narrative about how and why to do strategic planning are provided. Planning templates are provided.

*3. PERFORMANCE STRATEGIES, INC.—www.perfstrat.com/articles/ptp.htm*
This Web site offers about twenty pages of excellent narrative about how and why to do strategic planning. A model of the planning process is provided, as well as excellent discussion of mission, benefits of planning, objectives, priorities, and timing.

*4. PALO ALTO SOFTWARE—www.bizplans.com*
This Web site offers a model of the business planning process with excellent narrative as well as seven example business plans from real firms. This is one of the two best sites available for business planning information. (The other is the Small Business Administration Web site.)

*continued*

TABLE 3-9        **Important Strategic Planning Web Sites** *(continued)*

5. *CENTER FOR STRATEGIC MANAGEMENT—www.csmweb.com*
   This Web site describes strategic management training, seminars, and facilitation services. The site also provides excellent links to other strategic planning academic and government sites.
6. *BOSTON CONSULTING GROUP—www.bcg.com*
   This perhaps is the best-known strategic planning consulting firm. The Web site offers some nice discussion of strategic planning but focuses mostly on getting a job with BCG rather than on strategic planning information.
7. *FULD & COMPANY—www.fuld.com*
   This Web site specializes in competitive intelligence. Nice links are provided regarding the importance of gathering information about competitors. This site offers audio answers to key questions about intelligence systems.

The Internet offers consumers and businesses a widening range of services and information resources from all over the world. Interactive services offer users not only access to information worldwide but also the ability to communicate with the person or company that created the information. Historical barriers to personal and business success—time zones and diverse cultures—are being eliminated. The Internet is poised to become as important to our society by the end of this decade as television and newspapers.

Internet hubs are a key to providing fast, inexpensive access to the Internet, yet some states—West Virginia, Montana, South Dakota, North Dakota, Maine, and Vermont—have no Internet hubs. Households and businesses in these states connect to the Internet through "daisy chaining" which is slower, more expensive, and has more interruptions.[21] States with the most high-speed Internet hubs are California (177), Texas (90), New York (58), Florida (58), Ohio (56), and Illinois (44).

A recent study reveals why people use the Internet. The top six reasons Americans use the Internet are for research (49%), to gather information about products and services (43%), to use e-mail (37%), to purchase goods and services (24%), to surf for new sites (16%), to check for news, weather updates (15%).[22]

# FORECASTING TOOLS AND TECHNIQUES

Forecasts are educated assumptions about future trends and events. Forecasting is a complex activity because of factors such as technological innovation, cultural changes, new products, improved services, stronger competitors, shifts in government priorities, changing social values, unstable economic conditions, and unforeseen events. Managers often must rely upon published forecasts to identify key external opportunities and threats effectively.

A sense of the future permeates all action and underlies every decision a person makes. People eat expecting to be satisfied and nourished—in the future. People sleep assuming that in the future they will feel rested. They invest energy, money, and time because they believe their efforts will be rewarded in the future. They build highways assuming that automobiles and trucks will need them in the future. Parents educate children on the basis of forecasts that they will need certain skills, attitudes, and knowledge when they grow up. The truth is we all make implicit forecasts throughout our daily lives. The question, therefore, is not whether we should forecast but rather how can we best forecast to enable us to move beyond our ordinarily unarticulated assumptions about the future. Can we obtain information and then make educated assumptions (forecasts) to better guide our current decisions to achieve a more desirable future state of affairs. We should go into the future with our eyes and our minds open, rather than stumbling into the future with our eyes closed.[23]

Many publications and sources on the Internet forecast external variables. Several published examples include *Industry Week's* "Trends and Forecasts," *Business Week's* "Investment Outlook," and Standard & Poor's *Industry Survey.* The reputation and continued success of these publications depend partly on accurate forecasts, so published sources of information can offer excellent projections.

Sometimes organizations must develop their own projections. Most organizations forecast (project) their own revenues and profits annually. Organizations sometimes forecast market share or customer loyalty in local areas. Because forecasting is so important in strategic management and because the ability to forecast (in contrast to the ability to use a forecast) is essential, selected forecasting tools are examined further here.

Forecasting tools can be broadly categorized into two groups: quantitative techniques and qualitative techniques. Quantitative forecasts are most appropriate when historical data are available and when the relationships among key variables are expected to remain the same in the future. The three basic types of quantitative forecasting techniques are econometric models, regression, and *trend extrapolation. Econometric models* are based on simultaneous systems of regression equations that forecast variables such as interest rates and money supply. With the advent of sophisticated computer software, econometric models have become the most widely used approach for forecasting economic variables.

All quantitative forecasts, regardless of statistical sophistication and complexity, are based on historical relationships among key variables. *Linear regression,* for example, is based on the assumption that the future will be just like the past—which, of course, it never is. As historical relationships become less stable, quantitative forecasts becomes less accurate.

The six basic qualitative approaches to forecasting are (1) sales force estimates, (2) juries of executive opinion, (3) anticipatory surveys or market research, (4) scenario forecasts, (5) delphi forecasts, and (6) brainstorming. Qualitative or judgmental forecasts are particularly useful when historical data are not available or when constituent variables are expected to change significantly in the future.

Due to advancements in computer technology, quantitative forecasting techniques are usually cheaper and faster than qualitative methods. Quantitative techniques such as multiple regression can generate measures of error that allow a manager to estimate the degree of confidence associated with a given forecast. Forecasting tools must be used carefully or the results can be more misleading than helpful, but qualitative techniques require more intuitive judgment than do quantitative ones. Managers sometimes erroneously forecast what they would like to occur.

No forecast is perfect, and some forecasts are even wildly inaccurate. This fact accents the need for strategists to devote sufficient time and effort to study the underlying bases for published forecasts and to develop internal forecasts of their own. Key external opportunities and threats can be effectively identified only through good forecasts. Accurate forecasts can provide major competitive advantages for organizations. Forecasts are vital to the strategic-management process and to the success of organizations.

## Making Assumptions

Planning would be impossible without assumptions. McConkey defines assumptions as "best present estimates of the impact of major external factors, over which the manager has little if any control, but which may exert a significant impact on performance or the ability to achieve desired results.[24] Strategists are faced with countless variables and imponderables that can be neither controlled nor predicted with 100 percent accuracy.

By identifying future occurrences that could have a major effect on the firm and making reasonable assumptions about those factors, strategists can carry the strategic-management process forward. Assumptions are needed only for future trends and events that are most likely to have a significant effect on the company's business. Based on the best information at the time, assumptions serve as checkpoints on the validity of strategies. If future occurrences deviate significantly from assumptions, strategists know that corrective actions may be needed. Without reasonable assumptions, the strategy-formulation process could not proceed effectively. Firms that have the best information generally make the most accurate assumptions, which can lead to major competitive advantages.

## THE GLOBAL CHALLENGE

Foreign competitors are battering U.S. firms in many industries. In its simplest sense, the international challenge faced by U.S. business is twofold: (1) how to gain and maintain exports to other nations and (2) how to defend domestic markets against imported goods. Few companies can afford to ignore the presence of international competition. Firms that seem insulated and comfortable today may be vulnerable tomorrow; for example, foreign banks do not yet compete or operate in most of the United States.

America's economy is becoming much less American. A world economy and monetary system is emerging. Corporations in every corner of the globe are taking advantage of the opportunity to share in the benefits of worldwide economic development. Markets are shifting rapidly and in many cases converging in tastes, trends, and prices. Innovative transport systems are accelerating the transfer of technology, and shifts in the nature and location of production systems are reducing the response time to changing market conditions.

More and more countries around the world are welcoming foreign investment and capital. As a result, labor markets have steadily become more international. East Asian countries have become market leaders in labor-intensive industries, Brazil offers abundant natural resources and rapidly developing markets, and Germany offers skilled labor and technology. The drive to improve the efficiency of global business operations is leading to greater functional specialization. This is not limited to a search for the familiar low-cost labor in Latin America or Asia. Other considerations include the cost of energy, availability of resources, inflation rates, existing tax rates, and the nature of trade regulations. Yang Shangkun insists that China's door is still open to foreign capital and technology, despite the continued strength of the Communist Party.

The ability to identify and evaluate strategic opportunities and threats in an international environment is a prerequisite competency for strategists. The nuances of competing in international markets are seemingly infinite. Language, culture, politics, attitudes, and economies differ significantly across countries. The availability, depth, and reliability of economic and marketing information in different countries vary extensively, as do industrial structures, business practices, and the number and nature of regional organizations. Differences between domestic and multinational operations that affect strategic management are summarized in Table 3–10.

### The Impact of Diverse Industrial Policies

Some *industrial policies* include providing government subsidies, promoting exports, restructuring industries, nationalizing businesses, imposing regulations, changing tax laws, instituting pollution standards, and establishing import quotas. The vicissitudes of foreign affairs make identifying and selecting among alternative strategies more challenging for multinational corporations (MNCs) than for their domestic counterparts.

TABLE 3-10   **Differences Between U.S. and Multinational Operations That Affect Strategic Management**

| FACTOR | U.S. OPERATIONS | INTERNATIONAL OPERATIONS |
|---|---|---|
| Language | English used almost universally | Local language must be used in many situations |
| Culture | Relatively homogeneous | Quite diverse, both between countries and within a country |
| Politics | Stable and relatively unimportant | Often volatile and of decisive importance |
| Economy | Relatively uniform | Wide variations among countries and between regions within countries |
| Government interference | Minimal and reasonably predictable | Extensive and subject to rapid change |
| Labor | Skilled labor available | Skilled labor often scarce, requiring training or redesign of production methods |
| Financing | Well-developed financial markets | Poorly developed financial markets Capital flows subject to government control |
| Market research | Data easy to collect | Data difficult and expensive to collect |
| Advertising | Many media available; few restrictions | Media limited; many restrictions; low literacy rates rule out print media in some countries |
| Money | U.S. dollar used | Must change from one currency to another; changing exchange rates and government restrictions are problems |
| Transportation/ Communication | Among the best in the world | Often inadequate |
| Control | Always a problem; centralized control will work | A worse problem. Centralized control won't work. Must walk a tightrope between overcentralizing and losing control through too much decentralizing |
| Contracts | Once signed, are binding on both parties, even if one party makes a bad deal | Can be voided and renegotiated if one party becomes dissatisfied |
| Labor relations | Collective bargaining; can lay off workers easily | Often cannot lay off workers; may have mandatory worker participation in management; workers may seek change through political process rather than collective bargaining |
| Trade barriers | Nonexistent | Extensive and very important |

*Source:* R. G. Murdick, R. C. Moor, R. H. Eckhouse, and T. W. Zimmerer, *Business Policy: A Framework for Analysis,* 4th ed. (Columbus, Ohio: Grid Publishing Company, 1984): 275.

Strategic management has proven to be a valuable tool in the successful firm's repertoire. Firms traveling on the path of international business face more risks than their domestic counterparts, but also may reap greater rewards. Properly done, strategic management offers these firms a map to guide them on their journey through the perilous paths of international business.[25]

Multinational business strategists can contribute to the solution of economic trade problems and improve their firms' competitive positions by maintaining and strengthening communication channels with domestic and foreign governments. Strategists are commonly on the front line of trade and financial crises around the world, so they often have direct knowledge of the gravity and interrelated nature of particular problems. Strategists should relay this knowledge and experience to political leaders. A steady stream of counsel and advice from international business strategists to policymakers and lawmakers is needed.

## FIGURE 3–4

### The Typical Evolution of an MNC

| *Begin Export Operations* | *Conduct Licensing Activities* | *Add Foreign Sales Representatives* | *Build Foreign Manufacturing Facilities* | *Establish a Foreign Division of the Firm* | *Establish Several Foreign Business Units* | *An MNC* |
| --- | --- | --- | --- | --- | --- | --- |

*Source:* Adapted from C. A. Bartlett, "How Multinational Organizations Evolve," *Journal of Business Strategy* (Summer 1982): 20–32. Also, D. Shanks, "Strategic Planning for Global Competition," *Journal of Business Strategy* (Winter 1985): 83.

Multinational corporations face unique and diverse risks such as expropriation of assets, currency losses through exchange rate fluctuations, unfavorable foreign court interpretations of contracts and agreements, social/political disturbances, import/export restrictions, tariffs, and trade barriers. Strategists in MNCs are often confronted with the need to be globally competitive and nationally responsive at the same time. With the rise in world commerce, government and regulatory bodies are more closely monitoring foreign business practices. The United States Foreign Corrupt Practices Act, for example, defines corrupt practices in many areas of business. A sensitive issue is that some MNCs sometimes violate legal and ethical standards of the home country, but not of the host country.

Before entering international markets, firms should scan relevant journals and patent reports, seek the advice of academic and research organizations, participate in international trade fairs, form partnerships, and conduct extensive research to broaden their contacts and diminish the risk of doing business in new markets. Firms can also reduce the risks of doing business internationally by obtaining insurance from the United States government's Overseas Private Investment Corporation (OPIC).

## Globalization

Globalization is a process of worldwide integration of strategy formulation, implementation, and evaluation activities. Strategic decisions are made based on their impact upon global profitability of the firm, rather than on just domestic or other individual country considerations. A global strategy seeks to meet the needs of customers worldwide with the highest value at the lowest cost. This may mean locating production in countries with the lowest labor costs or abundant natural resources, locating research and complex engineering centers where skilled scientists and engineers can be found, and locating marketing activities close to the markets to be served. A global strategy includes designing, producing, and marketing products with global needs in mind, instead of considering individual countries alone. A global strategy integrates actions against competitors into a worldwide plan.

Globalization of industries is occurring for many reasons, including a worldwide trend toward similar consumption patterns, the emergence of global buyers and sellers, e-commerce and instant transmission of money and information across continents. The European Economic Community (EEC), religions, the Olympics, the World Bank, world trade centers, the Red Cross, the Internet, environmental conferences, telecommunications, and economic summits all contribute to global interdependencies and the emerging global marketplace. The typical evolution of a domestic firm into a multinational corporation is illustrated in Figure 3–4.

e·biz

It is clear that different industries become global for different reasons. The need to amortize massive R&D investments over many markets is a major reason why the aircraft manufacturing industry became global. Monitoring globalization in one's industry is an important strategic-management activity. Knowing how to use that information for one's competitive advantage is even more important. For example, firms may look around the world for the best technology and select one that has the most promise for the largest number of markets. When firms design a product, they design it to be marketable in as many countries as possible. When firms manufacture a product, they select the lowest cost source, which may be Japan for semiconductors, Sri Lanka for textiles, Malaysia for simple electronics, and Europe for precision machinery. MNCs design manufacturing systems to accommodate world markets. One of the riskiest strategies for a domestic firm is to remain solely a domestic firm in an industry that is rapidly becoming global.

## China: Opportunities and Threats

U.S. firms increasingly are doing business in China as market reforms create a more businesslike arena daily. Foreign direct investment in China is about $50 billion annually. This places China second behind the United States.

In an effort to appease opponents of China entering the World Trade Organization (WTO), China reduced its average tariff rates by 26 percent, from 23 percent to 17 percent, on forty-eight hundred items shipped in and out of the country. These cuts have accelerated national economic growth even more. If China is admitted soon, as expected, into the WTO, this should further accelerate economic development and trade. The major reason why the United States has historically not supported China's acceptance into WTO has been that country's human rights violations.

China is modernizing its stock and bond markets so that companies can depend less on banks for financing. There is immense opportunity in China for private-sector entrepreneurs. In Shanghai, the number of private enterprises now exceeds eleven thousand. The vibrant, efficient private sector explains why Chinese growth continues despite huge losses at state factories. By 2005, more than 60 percent of the Chinese economy will be in private hands and employ some 75 percent of China's workforce.[26] Private enterprise is gaining the legal standing it has long lacked in China as evidenced by the country's constitution being amended in 1999 to provide legal rights for private-property ownership. New laws delineate the rights and responsibilities of private businessmen.

China is still a communist-run country whose legal system is stacked overwhelmingly in favor of the prosecution. Acquittals are rare in China. A recent report put the conviction rate at 99.7 percent.[27] Government officials have historically had total leeway to do whatever they think necessary to punish suspects. Suspects may today request an attorney who may make arguments in court, but severe limitations exist. For example, defense attorneys cannot cross-examine witnesses and testimony is delivered only in writing. Defense attorneys face surprise witnesses with no chance to cross-examine. In the United States, there are 1 million lawyers among the population of 274 million; in China there are 110,000 lawyers among the population of 1.2 billion, so oftentimes a defense lawyer is not available. Defense attorneys in China make little money and enjoy low prestige and low social standing. China is under pressure by foreign companies and countries to change their legal system to be fair rather than dominated by unpredictable, unconstrained government officials.

## Hong Kong

Evidence of the success of China's market reforms is the government's attitude toward Hong Kong. As promised, China is operating Hong Kong as a separate democratic state with freedom of religion, press, and speech, and a fair legal system. Hong Kong is the

**FIGURE 3–5**

**Hong Kong's Strategic Location**

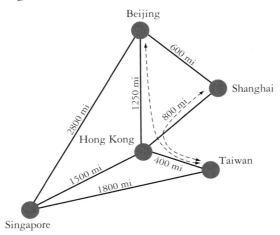

centerpiece of China's efforts to reform, privatize, and expand imports and exports worldwide. The map in Figure 3–5 illustrates Hong Kong's strategic location for China. With its 6.3 million people, magnificent harbor, financial wealth, 500 banks from 43 countries, the world's eighth-largest stock market, and minimum taxation, Hong Kong serves as the gateway to fast-growing China. U.S. companies alone have 178 regional headquarters in Hong Kong and $10.5 billion in direct investment.

As the twenty-first century begins, Hong Kong is still an attractive city/nation to establish business operations, but China is moving Hong Kong more towards regulation, government control, and China-like. For example, schools now must adopt Chinese as the main language of instruction whereas English proficiency previously was required at schools. The Hong Kong government recently awarded various companies rights to develop government land without public bids which previously was the accepted democratic way to do business. The government previously was a regulator of the Hong Kong stock market but now is its biggest investor and controller. The government is making decisions that trample longstanding principles of free markets and consistent rule of law. The Heritage Foundation has lowered Hong Kong's rating as a free economy to one notch below that of Singapore "unless it sees the error of its ways and reverses course."[28]

## Taiwan

Fifty years of separation between China and Taiwan has pushed the two countries so far apart politically, socially, and culturally that it is hard to even imagine them ever being part of the same whole. In recent research, 46 percent of Taiwan residents consider themselves as strictly Taiwanese, up from 37 percent a year earlier; those identifying themselves as only Chinese dropped to 11.4 percent from 12.7 percent.[29] Taiwan's 22 million people enjoy a vibrant democracy whereas China's 1.5 billion people are communist ruled. Taipei, Taiwan's capital, is crowded with cars and motorcycles where Beijing, China's capital, has mostly bicycles for transportation. The value of trade between China and Taiwan is about $25 billion a year. Taiwan has rejected China's "one China" policy of unifying the two countries and desires independence from the mainland, but China adamantly rejects that proposal and threatens hostilities.

China and the Philippines argue more these days about the Spratly Islands, which the Philippines claim, in the South China Sea. Singapore worries a lot now about a spread of anti-ethnic Chinese violence from Malaysia and Indonesia.[30]

Risks that still restrain firms from initiating business with China include the following:

- Poor infrastructure
- Disregard for the natural environment
- Absence of a legal system
- Rampant corruption
- Lack of freedom of press, speech, and religion
- Severe human rights violations
- Little respect for patents, copyrights, brands, and logos
- Counterfeiting, fraud, and pirating of products
- Little respect for legal contracts
- No generally accepted accounting principles

McDonald's, for instance, was recently evicted from its site in Beijing after operating its largest store in the world for only two of twenty years on its lease agreement. DuPont's herbicide Londax that kills weeds in rice fields was recently pirated and manufactured extensively in China. Scores of U.S. firms such as BellSouth have lost millions of dollars in China due to "illegal business actions." You can walk into any store in Beijing and buy a pirated copy of Microsoft's Windows 95 software.

At least 20 percent of credit loans in China are nonperforming; China's banking system is in shambles. Fully 75 percent of domestic credit goes to ailing state-run businesses that generate only 1 percent of industrial production. Managers of state-run enterprises are not very ethical either, often stealing money from the business.

Technological research is almost nonexistent in China. China's factories operate with ancient equipment, old-fashioned production methods, and little regard for the needs of the marketplace. Quality control is poor, and there basically are no books or records. Ninety percent of people in China live below the poverty level; 10 percent are very rich. Urban unemployment has grown to 15 percent, but may be even higher if idle farmers and furloughed workers are included. A major reason for falling prices is increased competition, but this is putting many state-run enterprises out of business. Exports from China are rising rapidly but imports into China are falling. Private factories in China are now laying off workers faster than even the state-owned companies. State-owned enterprises have fired or drastically cut the pay of more than ten million workers annually in recent years.

The minimum wage in China is twelve cents per hour but many firms pay even less. Chinese workers usually have no health care and no compensation for injury. Few factories have fire extinguishers. Bribes are often paid to officials to avoid fines and shutdowns. Labor unions are illegal and nonexistent in China. Child labor is commonplace. Political and religious oppression and imprisonment occur. Levi Strauss has pulled all its business operations out of China in protest to its human rights violations.

*Business Week* offers the following formula for success in doing business with China:

Pick partners wisely. Avoid forming ventures with inefficient state-owned enterprises. Search for entrepreneurial companies owned by local governments, or go it alone. Insist on management control.

Focus on fundamentals. Capitalize on China rapidly becoming a market economy by executing the basics, such as marketing, distribution, and service.

Guard know-how. Do not hand over state-of-the-art technology just to get an agreement. Aggressively fight theft of intellectual property because China wants to shed its bad reputation in this regard.

Fly low. Begin with a series of small ventures rather than big, costly, high-profile projects that often get snarled in bureaucratic red tape and politics.[31]

Thousands of American companies over the last few decades have embarked on establishing operations in China. More than one billion people live in China. Success has come to some American firms but not to many. *Fortune* magazine recently conducted research to determine the American companies most successful in doing business with China. For example, McDonald's now operates 250 restaurants in 40 Chinese cities and is adding 90 new restaurants annually. McDonald's treats each Chinese city as a different country because there are so many diverse dialects, local governments, and infrastructure considerations. American International Group was the first insurance company to win a license to sell insurance in China and now has 9,700 agents in China. Boeing has 70 percent market share of the commercial aircraft industry in China.

The following list of companies in rank order are the winners in conducting business successfully in China. Note that Coca-Cola is considered the most successful of all American firms doing business in China. New companies considering doing business in China would be well served to study the tactics and approach of the ten firms listed below:

1. Coca-Cola
2. McDonald's
3. Motorola
4. General Electric
5. American International Group
6. Boeing
7. Procter & Gamble
8. IBM
9. Volkswagen
10. Microsoft[32]

# INDUSTRY ANALYSIS: THE EXTERNAL FACTOR EVALUATION (EFE) MATRIX

An *External Factor Evaluation (EFE) Matrix* allows strategists to summarize and evaluate economic, social, cultural, demographic, environmental, political, governmental, legal, technological, and competitive information. Illustrated in Table 3–11, the EFE Matrix can be developed in five steps:

1. List key external factors as identified in the external-audit process. Include a total of from ten to twenty factors, including both opportunities and threats affecting the firm and its industry. List the opportunities first and then the threats. Be as specific as possible, using percentages, ratios, and comparative numbers whenever possible.

2. Assign to each factor a weight that ranges from 0.0 (not important) to 1.0 (very important). The weight indicates the relative importance of that factor to being successful in the firm's industry. Opportunities often receive higher weights than

TABLE 3-11    An Example External Factor Evaluation Matrix
for UST, Inc.

| KEY EXTERNAL FACTORS | WEIGHT | RATING | WEIGHTED SCORE |
|---|---|---|---|
| *Opportunities* | | | |
| 1. Global markets are practically untapped by smokeless tobacco market | .15 | 1 | .15 |
| 2. Increased demand caused by public banning of smoking | .05 | 3 | .15 |
| 3. Astronomical Internet advertising growth | .05 | 1 | .05 |
| 4. Pinkerton is leader in discount tobacco market | .15 | 4 | .60 |
| 5. More social pressure to quit smoking, thus leading users to switch to alternatives | .10 | 3 | .30 |
| *Threats* | | | |
| 1. Legislation against the tobacco industry | .10 | 2 | .20 |
| 2. Production limits on tobacco increases competition for production | .05 | 3 | .15 |
| 3. Smokeless tobacco market is concentrated in southeast region of United States | .05 | 2 | .10 |
| 4. Bad media exposure from the FDA | .10 | 2 | .20 |
| 5. Clinton Administration | .20 | 1 | .20 |
| TOTAL | 1.00 | | 2.10 |

threats, but threats too can receive high weights if they are especially severe or threatening. Appropriate weights can be determined by comparing successful with unsuccessful competitors or by discussing the factor and reaching a group consensus. The sum of all weights assigned to the factors must equal 1.0.

3. Assign a 1-to-4 rating to each key external factor to indicate how effectively the firm's current strategies respond to the factor, where 4 = *the response is superior,* 3 = *the response is above average,* 2 = *the response is average,* and 1 = *the response is poor.* Ratings are based on effectiveness of the firm's strategies. Ratings are thus company-based, whereas the weights in Step 2 are industry-based. It is important to note that both threats and opportunities can receive a 1, 2, 3, or 4.

4. Multiply each factor's weight by its rating to determine a weighted score.

5. Sum the weighted scores for each variable to determine the total weighted score for the organization.

Regardless of the number of key opportunities and threats included in an EFE Matrix, the highest possible total weighted score for an organization is 4.0 and the lowest possible total weighted score is 1.0. The average total weighted score is 2.5. A total weighted score of 4.0 indicates that an organization is responding in an outstanding way to existing opportunities and threats in its industry. In other words, the firm's strategies

TABLE 3-12    A Competitive Profile Matrix

| CRITICAL SUCCESS FACTORS | WEIGHT | AVON | | L'OREAL | | PROCTER & GAMBLE | |
|---|---|---|---|---|---|---|---|
| | | RATING | SCORE | RATING | SCORE | RATING | SCORE |
| Advertising | 0.20 | 1 | 0.20 | 4 | 0.80 | 3 | 0.60 |
| Product Quality | 0.10 | 4 | 0.40 | 4 | 0.40 | 3 | 0.30 |
| Price Competitiveness | 0.10 | 3 | 0.30 | 3 | 0.30 | 4 | 0.40 |
| Management | 0.10 | 4 | 0.40 | 3 | 0.30 | 3 | 0.30 |
| Financial Position | 0.15 | 4 | 0.60 | 3 | 0.45 | 3 | 0.45 |
| Customer Loyalty | 0.10 | 4 | 0.40 | 4 | 0.40 | 2 | 0.20 |
| Global Expansion | 0.20 | 4 | 0.80 | 2 | 0.40 | 2 | 0.40 |
| Market Share | 0.05 | 1 | 0.05 | 4 | 0.20 | 3 | 0.15 |
| TOTAL | 1.00 | | 3.15 | | 3.25 | | 2.80 |

*Note:* (1) The ratings values are as follows: 1 = major weakness, 2 = minor weakness, 3 = minor strength, 4 = major strength. (2) As indicated by the total weighted score of 2.8, Competitor 3 is weakest. (3) Only eight critical success factors are included for simplicity; this is too few in actuality.

effectively take advantage of existing opportunities and minimize the potential adverse effect of external threats. A total score of 1.0 indicates that the firm's strategies are not capitalizing on opportunities or avoiding external threats.

An example of an EFE Matrix is provided in Table 3–11 for UST, Inc., the manufacturer of Skoal and Copenhagen smokeless tobacco. Note that the Clinton Administration was considered to be the most important factor affecting this industry, as indicated by the weight of 0.20. UST was not pursuing strategies that effectively capitalize on this opportunity, as indicated by the rating of 1.01. The total weighted score of 2.10 indicates that UST is below average in its effort to pursue strategies that capitalize on external opportunities and avoid threats. It is important to note here that a thorough understanding of the factors being used in the EFE Matrix is more important than the actual weights and ratings assigned.

## THE COMPETITIVE PROFILE MATRIX (CPM)

The *Competitive Profile Matrix (CPM)* identifies a firm's major competitors and their particular strengths and weaknesses in relation to a sample firm's strategic position. The weights and total weighted scores in both a CPM and EFE have the same meaning. However, the factors in a CPM include both internal and external issues; therefore, the ratings refer to strengths and weaknesses, where 4 = major strength, 3 = minor strength, 2 = minor weakness, and 1 = major weakness. There are some important differences between the EFE and CPM. First of all, the critical success factors in a CPM are broader; they do not include specific or factual data and even may focus on internal issues. The critical success factors in a CPM also are not grouped into opportunities and threats as they are in an EFE. In a CPM the ratings and total weighted scores for rival firms can be compared to the sample firm. This comparative analysis provides important internal strategic information.

A sample Competitive Profile Matrix is provided in Table 3–12. In this example, advertising and global expansion are the most important critical success factors, as indicated by a weight of 0.20. Avon's and L'Oreal's product quality are superior, as evidenced

**e·biz**

by a rating of 4; L'Oreal's "financial position" is good, as indicated by a rating of 3; Procter & Gamble is the weakest firm overall, as indicated by a total weighted score of 2.80.

Other than the critical success factors listed in the example CPM, other factors often included in this analysis include breadth of product line, effectiveness of sales distribution, proprietary or patent advantages, location of facilities, production capacity and efficiency, experience, union relations, technological advantages, and e-commerce expertise.

A word on interpretation: Just because one firm receives a 3.2 rating and another receives a 2.8 rating in a Competitive Profile Matrix, it does not follow that the first firm is 20 percent better than the second. Numbers reveal the relative strength of firms, but their implied precision is an illusion. Numbers are not magic. The aim is not to arrive at a single number, but rather to assimilate and evaluate information in a meaningful way that aids in decision making.

## CONCLUSION

Increasing turbulence in markets and industries around the world means the external audit has become an explicit and vital part of the strategic-management process. This chapter provides a framework for collecting and evaluating economic, social, cultural, demographic, environmental, political, governmental, legal, technological, and competitive information. Firms that do not mobilize and empower their managers and employees to identify, monitor, forecast, and evaluate key external forces may fail to anticipate emerging opportunities and threats and, consequently, may pursue ineffective strategies, miss opportunities, and invite organizational demise. Firms not taking advantage of the Internet are falling behind technologically.

A major responsibility of strategists is to ensure development of an effective external-audit system. This includes using information technology to devise a competitive intelligence system that works. The external-audit approach described in this chapter can be used effectively by any size or type of organization. Typically, the external-audit process is more informal in small firms, but the need to understand key trends and events is no less important for these firms. The EFE Matrix and five-forces model can help strategists evaluate the market and industry, but these tools must be accompanied by good intuitive judgment. Multinational firms especially need a systematic and effective external-audit system because external forces among foreign countries vary so greatly.

We invite you to visit the DAVID page on the Prentice Hall Web site at **www.prenhall.com/davidsm** for this chapter's World Wide Web exercises.

## KEY TERMS AND CONCEPTS

America Online  (p. 102)

Chief Information Officer (CIO) (p. 92)

Chief Technology Officer (CTO) (p. 92)

Competitive Advantages  (p. 93)

Competitive Analysis  (p. 97)

Competitive Intelligence (CI) (p. 97)

Competitive Profile Matrix (CPM) (p. 115)

Critical Success Factors  (p. 115)

Decruiting  (p. 79)

Director of Competitive Analysis (p. 97)

Downsizing  (p. 79)

Econometric Models  (p. 106)

Environmental Scanning  (p. 76)

External Audit  (p. 76)

External Factor Evaluation (EFE) Matrix  (p. 113)

External Forces  (p. 76)

Industry Analysis  (p. 76)

Industrial Policies  (p. 107)

Information Technology (IT)  (p. 92)

Internet  (p. 102)

Learning from the Partner  (p. 98)

Linear Regression  (p. 106)   Porter's Five-Forces Model  (p. 99)   Trend Extrapolation  (p. 106)
Lifecare Facilities  (p. 82)   Rightsizing  (p. 79)   World Wide Web  (p. 102)

## ISSUES FOR REVIEW AND DISCUSSION

1. Explain how to conduct an external strategic-management audit.
2. Identify a recent economic, social, political, or technological trend that significantly affects financial institutions.
3. Discuss the following statement: Major opportunities and threats usually result from an interaction among key environmental trends rather than from a single external event or factor.
4. Identify two industries experiencing rapid technological changes and three industries that are experiencing little technological change. How does the need for technological forecasting differ in these industries? Why?
5. Use Porter's five-forces model to evaluate competitiveness within the U.S. banking industry.
6. What major forecasting techniques would you use to identify (1) economic opportunities and threats and (2) demographic opportunities and threats? Why are these techniques most appropriate?
7. How does the external audit affect other components of the strategic-management process?
8. As the owner of a small business, explain how you would organize a strategic-information scanning system. How would you organize such a system in a large organization?
9. Construct an EFE Matrix for an organization of your choice.
10. Make an appointment with a librarian at your university to learn how to use online databases. Report your findings in class.
11. Give some advantages and disadvantages of cooperative versus competitive strategies.
12. As strategist for a local bank, explain when you would use qualitative versus quantitative forecasts.
13. What is your forecast for interest rates and the stock market in the next several months? As the stock market moves up, do interest rates always move down? Why? What are the strategic implications of these trends?
14. Explain how information technology affects strategies of the organization where you worked most recently.
15. Let's say your boss develops an EFE Matrix that includes sixty-two factors. How would you suggest reducing the number of factors to twenty?
16. Select one of the current readings at the end of this chapter. Prepare a one-page written summary that includes your personal opinion of the article.
17. Discuss the ethics of gathering competitive intelligence.
18. Discuss the ethics of cooperating with rival firms.
19. Visit the SEC Web site at www.sec.gov and discuss the benefits of using information provided there.
20. What are the major differences between U.S. and multinational operations that affect strategic management?
21. Why is globalization of industries a common factor today?
22. Discuss the opportunities and threats a firm faces in doing business in China.

## NOTES

1. YORK FREUND, "Critical Success Factors," *Planning Review* 16, no. 4 (July–August 1988): 20.
2. ANNE CAREY and SUZY PARKER, "Where Tourists Flock," *USA Today* (July 8, 1999): A1.
3. SUSAN DECKER, "Where to Find Legal Help On the Net," *USA Today* (October 18, 1999): 8B.
4. FREDERICK GLUCK, "Global Competition in the 1990s," *Journal of Business Strategy* (Spring 1983): 22, 24.
5. EMILY THORTON, "Russia—What Happens When Markets Fail," *Business Week* (April 26, 1999): 50–52.
6. JAMES KIM, "Allegations Help Topple Once-Elite Russian Bank," *USA Today* (September 24, 1999): 2B.

7. DEXTER ROBERTS, "How Long Can Beijing Hang Tough?" *Business Week* (February 8, 1999): 38.

8. CRAIG SMITH, "Foreign Firms Reassess Chinese Joint Ventures," *The Wall Street Journal* (October 26,1999): A18.

9. JESSICA LEE, "House Oks China's Trade Status," *USA Today* (July 28, 1999): A1.

10. MARK CLIFFORD, "Can China Reform Its Economy?" *Business Week* (September 29, 1997): 117–124.

11. DAVID BANK, "Internet Learns New Lingo, XML, and the Hype Is On," *The Wall Street Journal* (September 16, 1999): A10.

12. JOHN HARRIS, ROBERT SHAW, JR., and WILLIAM SOMMERS, "The Strategic Management of Technology," *Planning Review* 11, no. 1 1 (January–February 1983): 28, 35.

13. SUSAN LEVINE and MICHAEL YALOWITZ, "Managing Technology: The Key to Successful Business Growth," *Management Review* 72, no. 9 (September 1983): 44.

14. CHRISTIAN HILL, "First Voice, Now Data," *The Wall Street Journal* (September 20, 1999): R4.

15. PAUL DAVIDSON, "Instant Messaging Ignites Turf War," *USA Today* (July 27, 1999): 3B.

16. BILL SAPORITO, "Companies That Compete Best," *Fortune* (May 22, 1989): 36.

17. KENNETH SAWKA, "Demystifying Business Intelligence," *Management Review,* (October 1996): 49.

18. JOHN PRESCOTT and DANIEL SMITH, "The Largest Survey of 'Leading-Edge' Competitor Intelligence Managers," *Planning Review* 17, no. 3 (May–June 1989): 6–13.

19. GARY HAMEL, YVES DOZ, and C. K. PRAHALAD, "Collaborate with Your Competitors—and Win," *Harvard Business Review* 67, no. 1 (January–February 1989):133.

20. DAVID BANK, "A Site-Eat-Site World," *The Wall Street Journal* (July 12, 1999): R8.

21. DAVID LIEBERMAN, "Net Hubs Lacking In Rural Pockets," *USA Today* (July 27, 1999): B1.

22. JAMES ABUNDIS and KEVIN RECHIN, "Why People Surf the Web," *USA Today* (August 30, 1999): 1A.

23. http://horizon.unc.edu/projects/seminars/futures research/rationale.asp

24. DALE McCONKEY, "Planning in a Changing Environment," *Business Horizons* 31, no. 5 (September–October 1988): 67.

25. ELLEN FINGERHUT and DARYL HATANO, "Principles of Strategic Planning Applied to International Corporations," *Managerial Planning* 31, no. 5 (September–October 1983): 4–14. Also, Narendra Sethi, "Strategic Planning Systems for Multinational Companies," *Long Range Planning* 15, no. 3 (June 1982): 80–89.

26. DEXTER ROBERTS, SHERI PORASSO, and MARK CLIFFORD, "China's New Revolution," *Business Week* (September 27, 1999): 74.

27. PAUL WISEMAN, "China's Defense Lawyers in a Court with No Mercy," *USA Today* (November 3, 1999): 21A.

28. ERIK GUYOT, "Reined In: For Years, Hong Kong was the Poster Child for Laissez-faire Economics. No Longer," *The Wall Street Journal* (September 27, 1999): R20.

29. JULIE SCHMIT, "Despite Unification Dreams, Taiwan, China Worlds Apart" *USA Today* (August 26, 1999): 10A.

30. STAN CROCK, "Asia is Whispering: Yankee Come Back," *Business Week* (August 9, 1999): 53.

31. "How You Can Win in China?:" *Business Week* (May 26, 1997): 65.

32. Adapted from JEREMY KAHN, "The world's Most Admired Companies," *Fortune* (October 11, 1999): 282.

# CURRENT READINGS

AREND, R. J. "Emergence of Entrepreneurs Following Exogenous Technological Change." *Strategic Management Journal* 20, no. 1 (January 1999): 31–48.

COOL, K., L.-H. ROLLER, and B. LELEUX. "The Relative Impact of Actual and Potential Rivalry on Firm Profitability in the Pharmaceutical Industry." *Strategic Management Journal* 20, no. 1 (January 1999): 1–14.

GEROSKI, PAUL A. "Early Warning of New Rivals." *Sloan Management Review* 40, no. 3 (Spring 1999): 107–116.

GIMENO, J. "Reciprocal Threats in Multimarket Rivalry: Staking Out 'Spheres of Influences' in the U.S. Airline Industry." *Strategic Management Journal* 20, no. 2 (February 1999): 101–128.

GLAZER, RASHI. "Winning in Smart Markets." *Sloan Management Review* 40, no. 4 (Summer 1999): 59–70.

GRIFFITH, DAVID A. and JONATHAN W. PALMER. "Leveraging the Web for Corporate Success." *Business Horizons* 42, (January–February 1999): 3–10.

HARRISON, JEFFERY S. and R. EDWARD FREEMAN. "Stakeholders, Social Responsibility, and Performance: Empirical Evidence and Theoretical Perspectives." *The Academy of Management Journal* 42, no. 5 (October 1999): 479–487.

HERBERT, THEODORE T. "Multinational Strategic Planning: Matching Central Expectations to Local Realities." *International Journal of Strategic Management* 32, no. 1 (February 1999): 81–87.

KIM, CHAN W. and RENEE MAUBORGNE. "Strategy, Value Innovation, and the Knowledge Economy." *Sloan Management Review* 40, vol. 3 (Spring 1999): 65–72.

MILLER, DANNY and JAMAL SHAMSIE. "Strategic Responses to Three Kinds of Uncertainty: Product Line Simplicity at the Hollywood Film Studios." *Journal of Management* 25, no. 1 (1999): 97–112.

MITROFF, IAN I. and ELIZABETH A. DENTON. "A Study of Spirituality in the Workplace." *Sloan Management Review* 40, no. 4 (Summer 1999): 83–91.

PUFFER, SHEILA M. Academy Speech and Interview. "Global Executive: Intel's Andrew Grove on Competitiveness." *The Academy of Management Executive* 13, no. 1 (February 1999): 15–24.

RINDOVA, V. P. and C. J. FOMBRUN. "Constructing Competitive Advantage: The Role of Firm-Constituent Interactions." *Strategic Management Journal* 20, no. 8 (August 1999): 691–710.

SIMONIN, B. L. "Ambiguity and the Process of Knowledge Transfer in Strategic Alliances." *Strategic Management Journal* 20 no. 7 (July 1999): 595–624.

ZAHRA, SHAKER A. Guest Editor. "The Changing Rules of Global Competitiveness in the 21st Century." *The Academy of Management Executive* 13, no. 1 (February 1999): 36–42.

# EXPERIENTIAL EXERCISES

**EXPERIENTIAL EXERCISE 3A** ▶

Developing an EFE Matrix for America Online

## PURPOSE

This exercise will give you practice developing an EFE Matrix. An EFE Matrix summarizes the results of an external audit. This is an important tool widely used by strategists.

## INSTRUCTIONS

**Step 1**    Join with two other students in class and jointly prepare an EFE Matrix for AOL. Refer back to the Cohesion Case and to Experiential Exercise 1A if needed to identify external opportunities and threats.

**Step 2**    All three-person teams participating in this exercise should record their EFE total weighted scores on the board. Put your initials after your score to identify it as your team's.

**Step 3**    Compare the total weighted scores. Which team's score came closest to the instructor's answer? Discuss reasons for variation in the scores reported on the board.

**EXPERIENTIAL EXERCISE 3B** ▶

The Internet Search

## PURPOSE

This exercise will help you become familiar with important sources of external information available in your college library. A key part of preparing an external audit is searching the Internet, and examining published sources of information for relevant economic, social, cultural, demographic, environmental, political, governmental, legal, technological, and competitive trends and events. External opportunities and threats must be identified and evaluated before strategies can be formulated effectively.

## INSTRUCTIONS

**Step 1**    Select a company or business. Conduct an external audit for this company. Find opportunities and threats in recent issues of newspapers and magazines. Search for information using the Internet.

**Step 2**    On a separate sheet of paper, list ten opportunities and ten threats that face this company. Be specific in stating each factor.

**Step 3**    Include a bibliography to reveal where you found the information.

**Step 4**    Share your information with a manager of that company. Ask for his or her comments and additions.

**Step 5**    Write a three-page summary of your findings and submit it to your teacher.

**EXPERIENTIAL EXERCISE 3C** ▶

Developing an EFE Matrix for My University

## PURPOSE

More colleges and universities are embarking upon the strategic-management process. Institutions are consciously and systematically identifying and evaluating external opportunities and threats facing higher education in your state, the nation, and the world.

## INSTRUCTIONS

**Step 1**    Join with two other individuals in class and jointly prepare an EFE Matrix for your institution.

**Step 2**   Go to the board and record your total weighted score in a column that includes the scores by all three-person teams participating. Put your initials after your score to identify it as your team's.

**Step 3**   Which team viewed your college's strategies most positively; which team viewed your college's strategies most negatively? Discuss the nature of the differences.

**EXPERIENTIAL EXERCISE 3D** ▶

Developing a Competitive Profile Matrix for America Online

## PURPOSE

Monitoring competitors' performance and strategies is a key aspect of an external audit. This exercise is designed to give you practice evaluating the competitive position of organizations in a given industry and assimilating that information in the form of a Competitive Profile Matrix.

## INSTRUCTIONS

**Step 1**   Turn back to the Cohesion Case and review the section on competitors.

**Step 2**   On a separate sheet of paper, prepare a Competitive Profile Matrix that includes America Online and Microsoft.

**Step 3**   Turn in your Competitive Profile Matrix for a classwork grade.

**EXPERIENTIAL EXERCISE 3E** ▶

Developing a Competitive Profile Matrix for My University

## PURPOSE

Your college or university competes with all other educational institutions in the world, especially those in your own state. State funds, students, faculty, staff, endowments, gifts, and federal funds are areas of competitiveness. The purpose of this exercise is to give you practice thinking competitively about the business of education in your state.

## INSTRUCTIONS

**Step 1**   Identify two colleges or universities in your state that compete directly with your institution for students. Interview several persons who are aware of particular strengths and weaknesses of those universities. Record information about the two competing universities.

**Step 2**   Prepare a Competitive Profile Matrix that includes your institution and the two competing institutions. Include the following factors in your analysis:

  1.  Tuition costs
  2.  Quality of faculty
  3.  Academic reputation
  4.  Average class size
  5.  Campus landscaping
  6.  Athletic programs
  7.  Quality of students
  8.  Graduate programs
  9.  Location of campus
  10. Campus culture

**Step 3**   Submit your Competitive Profile Matrix to your instructor for evaluation.

# THE INTERNAL ASSESSMENT

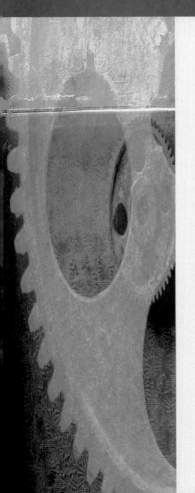

## CHAPTER OUTLINE

# CHAPTER OBJECTIVES

*After studying this chapter, you should be able to do the following:*

1. Describe how to perform an internal strategic-management audit.
2. Discuss key interrelationships among the functional areas of business.
3. Compare and contrast culture in America versus other countries.
4. Identify the basic functions or activities that make up management, marketing, finance/accounting, production/operations, research and development, and computer information systems.
5. Explain how to determine and prioritize a firm's internal strengths and weaknesses.
6. Explain the importance of financial ratio analysis.
7. Discuss the nature and role of computer information systems in strategic management.
8. Develop an Internal Factor Evaluation (IFE) Matrix.

# NOTABLE QUOTES

Like a product or service, the planning process itself must be managed and shaped, if it is to serve executives as a vehicle for strategic decision-making.

ROBERT LENZ

The difference between now and five years ago is that information systems had limited function. You weren't betting your company on it. Now you are.

WILLIAM GRUBER

Weak leadership can wreck the soundest strategy.

SUN ZI

A firm that continues to employ a previously successful strategy eventually and inevitably falls victim to a competitor.

WILLIAM COHEN

An organization should approach all tasks with the idea that they can be accomplished in a superior fashion.

THOMAS WATSON, JR.

By 2010, managers will have to handle greater cultural diversity. Managers will have to understand that employees don't think alike about such basics as "handling confrontation" or even what it means "to do a good day's work."

JEFFREY SONNENFELD

Sad but true, U.S. businesspeople have the lowest foreign language proficiency of any major trading nation. U.S. business schools do not emphasize foreign languages, and students traditionally avoid them.

RONALD DULEK

This chapter focuses on identifying and evaluating a firm's strengths and weaknesses in the functional areas of business, including management, marketing, finance/accounting, production/operations, research and development, and computer information systems. Relationships among these areas of business are examined. Strategic implications of important functional area concepts are examined. The process of performing an internal audit is described.

 ## THE NATURE OF AN INTERNAL AUDIT

All organizations have strengths and weaknesses in the functional areas of business. No enterprise is equally strong or weak in all areas. Maytag, for example, is known for excellent production and product design, whereas Procter & Gamble is known for superb marketing. Internal strengths/weaknesses, coupled with external opportunities/threats and a clear statement of mission, provide the basis for establishing objectives and strategies. Objectives and strategies are established with the intention of capitalizing upon internal strengths and overcoming weaknesses! The internal-audit part of the strategic-management process is illustrated in Figure 4–1.

**FIGURE 4–1**

**A Comprehensive Strategic-Management Model**

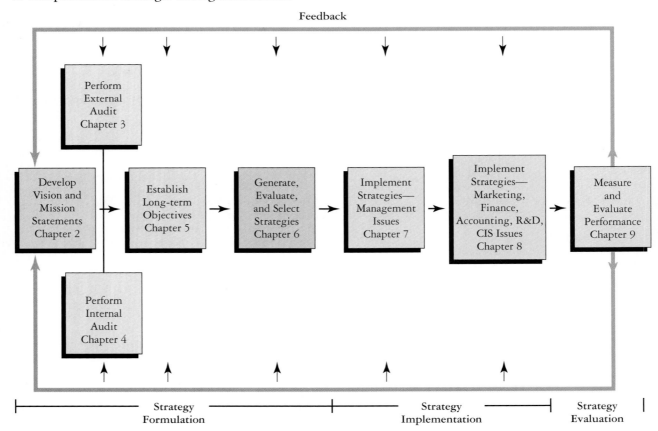

## Key Internal Forces

It is not possible in a business policy text to review in depth all the material presented in courses such as marketing, finance, accounting, management, computer information systems, and production/operations; there are many subareas within these functions, such as customer service, warranties, advertising, packaging, and pricing under marketing.

For different types of organizations, such as hospitals, universities, and government agencies, the functional business areas, of course, differ. In a hospital, for example, functional areas may include cardiology, hematology, nursing, maintenance, physician support, and receivables. Functional areas of a university can include athletic programs, placement services, housing, fund raising, academic research, counseling, and intramural programs. Within large organizations, each division has certain strengths and weaknesses. For example, AT&T is strong in communications and weak in computers.

A firm's strengths that cannot be easily matched or imitated by competitors are called *distinctive competencies*. Building competitive advantages involves taking advantage of distinctive competencies. For example, 3M exploits its distinctive competence in research and development by producing a wide range of innovative products. Strategies are designed in part to improve on a firm's weaknesses, turning them into strengths, and maybe even into distinctive competencies.

Some researchers emphasize the importance of the internal audit part of the strategic-management process by comparing it to the external audit. Robert Grant concluded that the internal audit is more important, saying:

> In a world where customer preferences are volatile, the identity of customers is changing, and the technologies for serving customer requirements are continually evolving, an externally focused orientation does not provide a secure foundation for formulating long-term strategy. When the external environment is in a state of flux, the firm's own resources and capabilities may be a much more stable basis on which to define its identity. Hence, a definition of a business in terms of what it is capable of doing may offer a more durable basis for strategy than a definition based upon the needs which the business seeks to satisfy.[1]

## The Process of Performing an Internal Audit

The process of performing an *internal audit* closely parallels the process of performing an external audit. Representative managers and employees from throughout the firm need to be involved in determining a firm's strengths and weaknesses. The internal audit requires gathering and assimilating information about the firm's management, marketing, finance/accounting, production/operations, research and development (R&D), and computer information systems operations. Key factors should be prioritized as described in Chapter 3 so that the firm's most important strengths and weaknesses can be determined collectively.

Compared to the external audit, the process of performing an internal audit provides more opportunity for participants to understand how their jobs, departments, and divisions fit into the whole organization. This is a great benefit because managers and employees perform better when they understand how their work affects other areas and activities of the firm. For example, when marketing and manufacturing managers jointly discuss issues related to internal strengths and weaknesses, they gain a better appreciation of issues, problems, concerns, and needs in all the functional areas. In organizations that do not use strategic management, marketing, finance, and manufacturing managers often do not interact with each other in significant ways. Performing an internal audit thus is an excellent vehicle or forum for improving the process of communication in the organization. "Communication" may be the most important word in management.

Performing an internal audit requires gathering, assimilating, and evaluating information about the firm's operations. Critical success factors, consisting of both strengths and weaknesses, can be identified and prioritized in the manner discussed in Chapter 3. According to William King, a task force of managers from different units of the organization, supported by staff, should be charged with determining the ten to twenty most important strengths and weaknesses that should influence the future of the organization:

> The development of conclusions on the 10 to 20 most important organizational strengths and weaknesses can be, as any experienced manager knows, a difficult task, when it involves managers representing various organizational interests and points of view. Developing a 20-page list of strengths and weaknesses could be accomplished relatively easily, but a list of the 10 to 15 most important ones involves significant analysis and negotiation. This is true because of the judgments that are required and the impact which such a list will inevitably have as it is used in the formulation, implementation, and evaluation of strategies.[2]

Strategic management is a highly interactive process that requires effective coordination among management, marketing, finance/accounting, production/operations, R&D, and computer information systems managers. Although the strategic-management process is overseen by strategists, success requires that managers and employees from all functional areas work together to provide ideas and information. Financial managers, for example, may need to restrict the number of feasible options available to operations managers, or R&D managers may develop such good products that marketing managers need to set higher objectives. A key to organizational success is effective coordination and understanding among managers from all functional business areas! Through involvement in performing an internal strategic-management audit, managers from different departments and divisions of the firm come to understand the nature and effect of decisions in other functional business areas in their firm. Knowledge of these relationships is critical for effectively establishing objectives and strategies.

A failure to recognize and understand relationships among the functional areas of business can be detrimental to strategic management, and the number of those relationships that must be managed increases dramatically with a firm's size, diversity, geographic dispersion, and the number of products or services offered. Governmental and nonprofit enterprises traditionally have not placed sufficient emphasis on relationships among the business functions. For example, some state governments, utilities, universities, and hospitals only recently have begun to establish marketing objectives and policies that are consistent with their financial capabilities and limitations. Some firms place too great an emphasis on one function at the expense of others. Ansoff explained:

> During the first fifty years, successful firms focused their energies on optimizing the performance of one of the principal functions: production/operations, R&D, or marketing. Today, due to the growing complexity and dynamism of the environment, success increasingly depends on a judicious combination of several functional influences. This transition from a single function focus to a multifunction focus is essential for successful strategic management.[3]

*Financial ratio analysis* exemplifies the complexity of relationships among the functional areas of business. A declining return on investment or profit margin ratio could be the result of ineffective marketing, poor management policies, research and development errors, or a weak computer information system. The effectiveness of strategy formulation, implementation, and evaluation activities hinges upon a clear understanding of how major business functions affect one another. For strategies to succeed, a coordinated effort among all the functional areas of business is needed. In the case of planning, George wrote:

> We may conceptually separate planning for the purpose of theoretical discussion and analysis, but in practice, neither is it a distinct entity nor is it capable of being separated. The planning function is mixed with all other business functions and, like ink once mixed with water, it cannot be set apart. It is spread throughout and is a part of the whole of managing an organization.[4]

# INTEGRATING STRATEGY AND CULTURE

Relationships among a firm's functional business activities perhaps can be exemplified best by focusing on organizational culture, an internal phenomenon that permeates all departments and divisions of an organization. *Organizational culture* can be defined as "a pattern of behavior developed by an organization as it learns to cope with its problem of external adaptation and internal integration, that has worked well enough to be considered valid and to be taught to new members as the correct way to perceive, think, and feel."[5] This definition emphasizes the importance of matching external with internal factors in making strategic decisions.

Organizational culture captures the subtle, elusive, and largely unconscious forces that shape a workplace. Remarkably resistant to change, culture can represent a major strength or weakness for the firm. It can be an underlying reason for strengths or weaknesses in any of the major business functions.

Defined in Table 4–1, *cultural products* include values, beliefs, rites, rituals, ceremonies, myths, stories, legends, sagas, language, metaphors, symbols, heroes, and heroines. These products or dimensions are levers that strategists can use to influence and direct strategy formulation, implementation, and evaluation activities. An organization's culture compares to an individual's personality in the sense that no organization has the same culture and no individual has the same personality. Both culture and personality are fairly enduring and can be warm, aggressive, friendly, open, innovative, conservative, liberal, harsh, or likable.

As indicated in the Global Perspective on page 129, women have historically been treated harshly in Japanese business culture, but this is changing.

Dimensions of organizational culture permeate all the functional areas of business. It is something of an art to uncover the basic values and beliefs that are buried deeply in an organization's rich collection of stories, language, heroes, and rituals, but cultural products can represent important strengths and weaknesses. Culture is an aspect of organizations that no longer can be taken for granted in performing an internal strategic-management audit because culture and strategy must work together.

The strategic-management process takes place largely within a particular organization's culture. Lorsch found that executives in successful companies are emotionally committed to the firm's culture, but he concluded that culture can inhibit strategic management in two basic ways. First, managers frequently miss the significance of changing external conditions because they are blinded by strongly held beliefs. Second, when a particular culture has been effective in the past, the natural response is to stick with it in the future, even during times of major strategic change.[6] An organization's culture must support the collective commitment of its people to a common purpose. It must foster competence and enthusiasm among managers and employees.

Organizational culture significantly affects business decisions and thus must be evaluated during an internal strategic-management audit. If strategies can capitalize on

TABLE 4-1    **Cultural Products and Associated Definitions**

| | |
|---|---|
| Rites | Relatively elaborate, dramatic, planned sets of activities that consolidate various forms of cultural expressions into one event, carried out through social interactions, usually for the benefit of an audience |
| Ceremonial | A system of several rites connected with a single occasion or event |
| Ritual | A standardized, detailed set of techniques and behaviors that manage anxieties, but seldom produce intended, technical consequences of practical importance |
| Myth | A dramatic narrative of imagined events, usually used to explain origins or transformations of something. Also, an unquestioned belief about the practical benefits of certain techniques and behaviors that is not supported by facts |
| Saga | An historical narrative describing the unique accomplishments of a group and its leaders, usually in heroic terms |
| Legend | A handed-down narrative of some wonderful event that is based on history but has been embellished with fictional details |
| Story | A narrative based on true events, sometimes a combination of truth and fiction |
| Folktale | A completely fictional narrative |
| Symbol | Any object, act, event, quality, or relation that serves as a vehicle for conveying meaning, usually by representing another thing |
| Language | A particular form or manner in which members of a group use sounds and written signs to convey meanings to each other |
| Metaphors | Shorthand words used to capture a vision or to reinforce old or new values |
| Values | Life-directing attitudes that serve as behavioral guidelines |
| Belief | An understanding of a particular phenomenon |
| Heroes/Heroines | Individuals whom the organization has legitimized to model behavior for others |

*Source:* Adapted from H.M. Trice and J.M. Beyer, "Studying Organizational Cultures through Rites and Ceremonials," *Academy of Management Review* 9, no. 4 (October 1984): 655.

cultural strengths, such as a strong work ethic or highly ethical beliefs, then management often can implement changes swiftly and easily. However, if the firm's culture is not supportive, strategic changes may be ineffective or even counterproductive. A firm's culture can become antagonistic to new strategies, with the result being confusion and disorientation. An organization's culture should infuse individuals with enthusiasm for implementing strategies. Allarie and Firsirotu emphasized the need to understand culture:

> Culture provides an explanation for the insuperable difficulties a firm encounters when it attempts to shift its strategic direction. Not only has the "right" culture become the essence and foundation of corporate excellence, it is also claimed that success or failure of reforms hinges on management's sagacity and ability to change the firm's driving culture in time and in tune with required changes in strategies.[7]

The potential value of organizational culture has not been realized fully in the study of strategic management. Ignoring the effect that culture can have on relationships among the functional areas of business can result in barriers to communication, lack of

## GLOBAL PERSPECTIVE

### Changing Role of Women in Japan

Japan's population is projected to decline by nearly half by the end of the twenty-first century, while the aging population puts a huge burden on working people. Consequently, the conservative and male-dominated Japanese legislature is reconsidering gender equality. In 1999, the Japanese legislature passed a sweeping "basic law" to promote equal participation in society by men and women. This law covers everything from equal hiring and promotion in business and government to common practices such as listing boys' names ahead of girls' names on class rosters in public schools. Also in 1999, the legislature passed a new law that bans sexual discrimination in the workplace. The law also bans child pornography and sex with minors. Further in 1999, Japan became the last member of the United Nations to approve relatively safe, low-dose birth control pills. These are all legislative victories for Japanese women who now feel more comfortable having children or joining the work force if they desire. New Japanese law also encourages men to join in helping women in child rearing and housework. Currently Japanese men do only 6 percent of the housework and 11 percent of the work caring for children or elders.

Any national culture that prohibits or discourages women from working outside the home disadvantages firms in that particular country as they strive to compete with firms in other countries that capitalize on the proven capability of women to perform equally with men in nearly all jobs. Certainly it will take years to change this type of business culture, but Japan got started in 1999. This business culture shift should enhance Japan's business competitiveness worldwide.

Adapted from: Steven Butler, "In Japan, Finally the Women Catch a Break," *U.S. News & World Report,* (July 5, 1999): 41.

coordination, and an inability to adapt to changing conditions. Some tension between culture and a firm's strategy is inevitable, but the tension should be monitored so that it does not reach a point at which relationships are severed and the culture becomes antagonistic. The resulting disarray among members of the organization would disrupt strategy formulation, implementation, and evaluation. On the other hand, a supportive organizational culture can make managing much easier.

Internal strengths and weaknesses associated with a firm's culture sometimes are overlooked because of the interfunctional nature of this phenomenon. It is important, therefore, for strategists to understand their firm as a sociocultural system. Success is often determined by linkages between a firm's culture and strategies. The challenge of strategic management today is to bring about the changes in organizational culture and individual mind-sets necessary to support the formulation, implementation, and evaluation of strategies.

### American Versus Foreign Cultures

To successfully compete in world markets, U.S. managers must obtain a better knowledge of historical, cultural, and religious forces that motivate and drive people in other countries. In Japan, for example, business relations operate within the context of *Wa,* which stresses group harmony and social cohesion. In China, business behavior revolves around *guanxi,* or personal relations. In Korea, activities involve concern for *inhwa,* or harmony based on respect of hierarchical relationships, including obedience to authority.[8]

In Europe, it is generally true that the farther north on the continent, the more participatory the management style. Most European workers are unionized and enjoy more frequent vacations and holidays than U.S. workers. A ninety-minute lunch break plus twenty-minute morning and afternoon breaks are common in European firms. Guaranteed permanent employment is commonly a part of employment contracts in Europe. In socialist countries such as France, Belgium, and the United Kingdom, the only ground for immediate dismissal from work is a criminal offense. A six-month trial period at the beginning of employment is usually part of the contract with a European firm. Many Europeans resent pay-for-performance, commission salaries, and objective measurement and reward systems. This is true especially of workers in southern Europe. Many Europeans also find the notion of team spirit difficult to grasp because the unionized environment has dichotomized worker-management relations throughout Europe.

A weakness that U.S. firms have in competing with Pacific Rim firms is a lack of understanding of Far Eastern cultures, including how Asians think and behave. Spoken Chinese, for example, has more in common with spoken English than with spoken Japanese or Korean. Managers around the world face the responsibility of having to exert authority while at the same time trying to be liked by subordinates. U.S. managers consistently put more weight on being friendly and liked, whereas Asian and European managers exercise authority often without this concern. Americans tend to use first names instantly in business dealings with foreigners, but foreigners find this presumptuous. In Japan, for example, first names are used only among family members and intimate friends; even long-time business associates and coworkers shy away from the use of first names. Other cultural differences or pitfalls that U.S. managers need to know are given in Table 4–2.

U.S. managers have a low tolerance for silence, whereas Asian managers view extended periods of silence as important for organizing and evaluating one's thoughts. U.S. managers are much more action-oriented than their counterparts around the world; they rush to appointments, conferences, and meetings, and then feel the day has been productive. But for foreign managers, resting, listening, meditating, and thinking is considered productive. Sitting through a conference without talking is unproductive in the United States, but it is viewed as positive in Japan if one's silence helps preserve unity.

U.S. managers also put greater emphasis on short-term results than foreign managers. In marketing, for example, Japanese managers strive to achieve "everlasting customers," whereas many Americans strive to make a one-time sale. Marketing managers in Japan see making a sale as the beginning, not the end, of the selling process. This is an

## TABLE 4-2    Cultural Pitfalls That You Need to Know

Waving is a serious insult in Greece and Nigeria, particularly if the hand is near someone's face.

Making a "good-bye" wave in Europe can mean "no," but means "come here" in Peru.

In China, last names are written first.

A man named Carlos Lopez-Garcia should be addressed as Mr. Lopez in Latin America, but as Mr. Garcia in Brazil.

Breakfast meetings are considered uncivilized in most foreign countries.

Latin Americans average being twenty minutes late to business appointments.

Direct eye contact is impolite in Japan.

Don't cross your legs in Arab or many Asian countries—it's rude to show the sole of your shoe.

In Brazil, touching your thumb and first finger—an American "OK" sign—is the equivalent of raising your middle finger.

Nodding or tossing your head back in southern Italy, Malta, Greece, and Tunisia means "no." In India, this body motions means "yes."

Snapping your fingers is vulgar in France and Belgium.

Folding your arms across your chest is a sign of annoyance in Finland.

In China, leave some food on your plate to show that your host was so generous that you couldn't finish.

Do not eat with your left hand when dining with clients from Malaysia or India.

One form of communication works the same worldwide. It's the smile, so take that along wherever you go.

important distinction. Japanese managers often criticize U.S. managers for worrying more about shareholders, whom they do not know, than employees, whom they do know. Americans refer to "hourly employees," whereas Japanese refer to "lifetime employees."

Rose Knotts recently summarized some important cultural differences between U.S. and foreign managers:[9]

1. Americans place an exceptionally high priority on time, viewing time as an asset. Many foreigners place more worth on relationships. This difference results in foreign managers often viewing U.S. managers as "more interested in business than people."

2. Personal touching and distance norms differ around the world. Americans generally stand about three feet from each other in carrying on business conversations, but Arabs and Africans stand about one foot apart. Touching another person with the left hand in business dealings is taboo in some countries. American managers need to learn the personal space rules of foreign managers with whom they interact in business.

3. People in some cultures do not place the same significance on material wealth as American managers often do. Lists of the "largest corporations" and "highest-paid" executives abound in the United States. "More is better" and "bigger is better" in the United States, but not everywhere. This can be a consideration in trying to motivate individuals in other countries.

4. Family roles and relationships vary in different countries. For example, males are valued more than females in some cultures, and peer pressure, work situations, and business interactions reinforce this phenomenon.

5. Language differs dramatically across countries, even countries where people speak the same language. Words and expressions commonly used in one country may be greedy or disrespectful in another.

6. Business and daily life in some societies is governed by religious factors. Prayer times, holidays, daily events, and dietary restrictions, for example, need to be respected by American managers not familiar with these practices in some countries.

7. Time spent with the family and quality of relationships are more important in some cultures than the personal achievement and accomplishments espoused by the traditional American manager. For example, where a person is in the hierarchy of a firm's organizational structure, how large the firm is, and where the firm is located are much more important factors to American managers than to many foreign managers.

8. Many cultures around the world value modesty, team spirit, collectivity, and patience much more than the competitiveness and individualism which are so important in America.

9. Punctuality is a valued personal trait when conducting business in America, but it is not revered in many of the world's societies. Eating habits also differ dramatically across cultures. For example, belching is acceptable in many countries as evidence of satisfaction with the food that has been prepared. Chinese cultures consider it good manners to sample a portion of each food served.

10. To prevent social blunders when meeting with managers from other lands, one must learn and respect the rules of etiquette of others. Sitting on a toilet seat is viewed as unsanitary in most countries, but not the United States. Leaving food or drink after dining is considered impolite in some countries. Bowing instead of shaking hands is customary in many countries. Many cultures view Americans as

unsanitary for locating toilet and bathing facilities in the same area, while Americans view people of some cultures as unsanitary for not taking a bath or shower every day.

11. Americans often do business with individuals they do not know, but this practice is not accepted in many other cultures. In Mexico and Japan, for example, an amicable relationship is often mandatory before conducting business.

In many countries, effective managers are those who are best at negotiating with government bureaucrats rather than those who inspire workers. Many U.S. managers are uncomfortable with nepotism and bribery, which are common in many countries. In almost every country except the United States, bribery is tax-deductible.

The United States has gained a reputation for defending women from sexual harassment and minorities from discrimination, but not all countries embrace the same values. For example, in the Czech Republic, it is considered a compliment when the boss openly flirts with his female secretary and invites her to dinner. U.S. managers in the Czech Republic who do not flirt seem cold and uncaring to some employees.

American managers in China have to be careful about how they arrange office furniture because Chinese workers believe in *feng shui,* the practice of harnessing natural forces. American managers in Japan have to be careful about *nemaswashio* whereby Japanese workers expect supervisors to alert them privately of changes rather than informing them in a meeting. Japanese managers have little appreciation for versatility, expecting all managers to be the same. In Japan, "If a nail sticks out, you hit it into the wall," says Brad Lashbrook, an international consultant for Wilson Learning.

Probably the biggest obstacle to the effectiveness of U.S. managers, or managers from any country working in another, is the fact that it is almost impossible to change the attitude of a foreign workforce. "The system drives you; you cannot fight the system or culture," says Bill Parker, president of Phillips Petroleum in Norway.

 ## MANAGEMENT

The *functions of management* consist of five basic activities: planning, organizing, motivating, staffing, and controlling. An overview of these activities is provided in Table 4–3.

### Planning

The only thing certain about the future of any organization is change, and *planning* is the essential bridge between the present and the future that increases the likelihood of achieving desired results. Planning is the process by which one determines whether to attempt a task, works out the most effective way of reaching desired objectives, and prepares to overcome unexpected difficulties with adequate resources. Planning is the start of the process by which an individual or business may turn empty dreams into achievements. Planning enables one to avoid the trap of working extremely hard but achieving little.

Planning is an up-front investment in success. Planning helps a firm achieve maximum effect from a given effort. Planning enables a firm to take into account relevant factors and focus on the critical ones. Planning helps ensure that the firm can be prepared for all reasonable eventualities and for all changes that will be needed. Planning enables a firm to gather the resources needed and carry out tasks in the most efficient way possible. Planning enables a firm to conserve its own resources, avoid wasting ecological resources, make a fair profit, and be seen as an effective, useful firm. Planning enables a

TABLE 4-3    The Basic Functions of Management

| FUNCTION | DESCRIPTION | STAGE OF STRATEGIC-MANAGEMENT PROCESS WHEN MOST IMPORTANT |
|---|---|---|
| Planning | Planning consists of all those managerial activities related to preparing for the future. Specific tasks include forecasting, establishing objectives, devising strategies, developing policies, and setting goals. | Strategy Formulation |
| Organizing | Organizing includes all those managerial activities that result in a structure of task and authority relationships. Specific areas include organizational design, job specialization, job descriptions, job specifications, span of the control, unity of command, coordination, job design, and job analysis. | Strategy Implementation |
| Motivating | Motivating involves efforts directed toward shaping human behavior. Specific topics include leadership, communication, work groups, behavior modification, delegation of authority, job enrichment, job satisfaction, needs fulfillment, organizational change, employee morale, and managerial morale. | Strategy Implementation |
| Staffing | Staffing activities are centered on personnel or human resource management. Included are wage and salary administration, employee benefits, interviewing, hiring, firing, training, management development, employee safety, affirmative action, equal employment opportunity, union relations, career development, personnel research, discipline policies, grievance procedures, and public relations. | Strategy Implementation |
| Controlling | Controlling refers to all those managerial activities directed toward ensuring that actual results are consistent with planned results. Key areas of concern include quality control, financial control, sales control, inventory control, expense control, analysis of variances, rewards, and sanctions. | Strategy Evaluation |

firm to identify precisely what is to be achieved and to detail precisely the who, what, when, where, and why needed to achieve desired objectives. Planning enables a firm to assess whether the effort, costs and implications associated with achieving desired objectives are warranted.[10] Planning is the cornerstone of effective strategy formulation. But even though it is considered the foundation of management, it is commonly the task that managers neglect most. Planning is essential for successful strategy implementation and strategy evaluation, largely because organizing, motivating, staffing, and controlling activities depend upon good planning.

The process of planning must involve managers and employees throughout an organization. The time horizon for planning decreases from two to five years for top-level to less than six months for lower-level managers. The important point is that all managers do planning and should involve subordinates in the process to facilitate employee understanding and commitment.

Planning can have a positive impact on organizational and individual performance. Planning allows an organization to identify and take advantage of external opportunities and minimize the impact of external threats. Planning is more than extrapolating from the past and present into the future. It also includes developing a mission, forecasting future events and trends, establishing objectives, and choosing strategies to pursue.

An organization can develop synergy through planning. *Synergy* exists when everyone pulls together as a team that knows what it wants to achieve; synergy is the $2 + 2 = 5$ effect.

By establishing and communicating clear objectives, employees and managers can work together toward desired results. Synergy can result in powerful competitive advantages. The strategic-management process itself is aimed at creating synergy in an organization.

Planning allows a firm to adapt to changing markets and thus shape its own destiny. Strategic management can be viewed as a formal planning process that allows an organization to pursue proactive rather than reactive strategies. Successful organizations strive to control their own futures rather than merely react to external forces and events as they occur. Historically, organisms and organizations that have not adapted to changing conditions have become extinct. Swift adaptation is needed today more than ever before because changes in markets, economies, and competitors worldwide are accelerating.

## Organizing

The purpose of *organizing* is to achieve coordinated effort by defining task and authority relationships. Organizing means determining who does what and who reports to whom. There are countless examples in history of well-organized enterprises successfully competing against, and in some cases defeating, much stronger but less-organized firms. A well-organized firm generally has motivated managers and employees who are committed to seeing the organization succeed. Resources are allocated more effectively and used more efficiently in a well-organized firm than in a disorganized firm.

The organizing function of management can be viewed as consisting of three sequential activities: breaking tasks down into jobs (work specialization), combining jobs to form departments (departmentalization), and delegating authority. Breaking tasks down into jobs requires development of job descriptions and job specifications. These tools clarify for both managers and employees what particular jobs entail. In *Wealth of Nations* published in 1776, Adam Smith cited the advantages of work specialization in the manufacture of pins:

> One man draws the wire, another straightens it, a third cuts it, a fourth points it, a fifth grinds it at the top for receiving the head. Ten men working in this manner can produce 48,000 pins in a single day, but if they had all wrought separately and independently, each might at best produce twenty pins in a day.[11]

Combining jobs to form departments results in an organizational structure, span of control, and a chain of command. Changes in strategy often require changes in structure because new positions may be created, deleted, or merged. Organizational structure dictates how resources are allocated and how objectives are established in a firm. Allocating resources and establishing objectives geographically, for example, is much different from doing so by product or customer.

The most common forms of departmentalization are functional, divisional, strategic business unit, and matrix. These types of structure are discussed further in Chapter 7.

Delegating authority is an important organizing activity, as evidenced in the old saying "You can tell how good a manager is by observing how his or her department functions when he or she isn't there." Employees today are more educated and more capable of participating in organizational decision making than ever before. In most cases, they expect to be delegated authority and responsibility, and to be held accountable for results. Delegation of authority is embedded in the strategic-management process.

## Motivating

*Motivating* can be defined as the process of influencing people to accomplish specific objectives.[12] Motivation explains why some people work hard and others do not. Objectives, strategies, and policies have little chance of succeeding if employees and managers are not motivated to implement strategies once they are formulated. The motivating function of management includes at least four major components: leadership, group dynamics, communication, and organizational change.

When managers and employees of a firm strive to achieve high levels of productivity, this indicates that the firm's strategists are good leaders. Good leaders establish rapport with subordinates, empathize with their needs and concerns, set a good example, and are trustworthy and fair. Leadership includes developing a vision of the firm's future and inspiring people to work hard to achieve that vision. Kirkpatrick and Locke reported that certain traits also characterize effective leaders: knowledge of the business, cognitive ability, self-confidence, honesty, integrity, and drive.[13]

Research suggests that democratic behavior on the part of leaders results in more positive attitudes toward change and higher productivity than does autocratic behavior. Drucker said:

> Leadership is not a magnetic personality. That can just as well be demagoguery. It is not "making friends and influencing people." That is flattery. Leadership is the lifting of a person's vision to higher sights, the raising of a person's performance to a higher standard, the building of a person's personality beyond its normal limitations.[14]

Group dynamics play a major role in employee morale and satisfaction. Informal groups or coalitions form in every organization. The norms of coalitions can range from being very positive to very negative toward management. It is important, therefore, that strategists identify the composition and nature of informal groups in an organization to facilitate strategy formulation, implementation, and evaluation. Leaders of informal groups are especially important in formulating and implementing strategy changes.

*Communication,* perhaps the most important word in management, is a major component in motivation. An organization's system of communication determines whether strategies can be implemented successfully. Good two-way communication is vital for gaining support for departmental and divisional objectives and policies. Top-down communication can encourage bottom-up communication. The strategic-management process becomes a lot easier when subordinates are encouraged to discuss their concerns, reveal their problems, provide recommendations, and give suggestions. A primary reason for instituting strategic management is to build and support effective communication networks throughout the firm.

> The manager of tomorrow must be able to get his people to commit themselves to the business, whether they are machine operators or junior vice-presidents. Ah, you say, participative management. Have a cigar. But just because most managers tug a forelock at the P word doesn't mean they know how to make it work. In the 1990s, throwing together a few quality circles won't suffice. The key issue will be empowerment, a term whose strength suggests the need to get beyond merely sharing a little information and a bit of decision making.[15]

## Staffing

The management function of *staffing,* also called *personnel management* or *human resource management,* includes activities such as recruiting, interviewing, testing, selecting, orienting, training, developing, caring for, evaluating, rewarding, disciplining, promoting, transferring, demoting, and dismissing employees, and managing union relations.

Staffing activities play a major role in strategy-implementation efforts, and for this reason human resource managers are becoming more actively involved in the strategic-management process. Strengths and weaknesses in the staffing area are important to identify.

The complexity and importance of human resource activities have increased to such a degree that all but the smallest organizations now need a full-time human resource manager. Numerous court cases that directly affect staffing activities are decided each day. Organizations and individuals can be penalized severely for not following federal, state, and local laws and guidelines related to staffing. Line managers simply cannot stay abreast of all the legal developments and requirements regarding staffing. The human resources department coordinates staffing decisions in the firm so that an organization as a whole meets legal requirements. This department also provides needed consistency in administering company rules, wages, and policies.

Human resources management is particularly challenging for international companies. For example, the inability of spouses and children to adapt to new surroundings has become a major staffing problem in overseas transfers. The problems include premature returns, job performance slumps, resignations, discharges, low morale, marital discord, and general discontent. Firms such as Ford Motor and Exxon have begun screening and interviewing spouses and children before assigning persons to overseas positions. 3M Corporation introduces children to peers in the target country and offers spouses educational benefits.

Strategists are becoming increasingly aware of how important human resources are to effective strategic management. Human resource managers are becoming more involved and more proactive in formulating and implementing strategies. They provide leadership for organizations that are restructuring or allowing employees to work at home.

Waterman described staffing activities among successful companies:

> Successful (renewing) companies are busy taking out layers of management, cutting staff, and pushing decisions down. Nucor Corporation runs a successful, near billion-dollar steel enterprise from a headquarters office and complement of seven people in a Charlotte, N.C., shopping mall. At Dana Corporation, President Woody Morcott and others take extraordinary pride in the fact that today there are only five layers between the chief executive's office and the person on the factory floor. In the mid-1970s there were 14. . . Leaner organizations set the stage for success (renewal). They make each one of us more important. They empower the individual.[16]

## Controlling

The *controlling* function of management includes all those activities undertaken to ensure that actual operations conform to planned operations. All managers in an organization have controlling responsibilities, such as conducting performance evaluations and taking necessary action to minimize inefficiencies. The controlling function of management is particularly important for effective strategy evaluation. Controlling consists of four basic steps:

1. Establishing performance standards
2. Measuring individual and organizational performance
3. Comparing actual performance to planned performance standards
4. Taking corrective actions

Measuring individual performance is often conducted ineffectively or not at all in organizations. Some reasons for this shortcoming are that evaluation can create confrontations that most managers prefer to avoid, can take more time than most managers are willing to give, and can require skills that many managers lack. No single approach to measuring individual performance is without limitations. For this reason, an organization should examine various methods, such as the graphic rating scale, the behaviorally anchored rating scale, and the critical incident method, and then develop or select a performance appraisal approach that best suits the firm's needs. Increasingly, firms are striving to link organizational performance with managers' and employees' pay. This topic is discussed further in Chapter 7.

## Management Audit Checklist of Questions

The checklists of questions provided below can help determine specific strengths and weaknesses in the functional area of business. An answer of *no* to any question could indicate a potential weakness, although the strategic significance and implications of negative answers, of course, will vary by organization, industry, and severity of the weakness. Positive or *yes* answers to the checklist questions suggest potential areas of strength.

1. Does the firm use strategic-management concepts?
2. Are company objectives and goals measurable and well communicated?
3. Do managers at all hierarchical levels plan effectively?
4. Do managers delegate authority well?
5. Is the organization's structure appropriate?
6. Are job descriptions and job specifications clear?
7. Is employee morale high?
8. Are employee turnover and absenteeism low?
9. Are organizational reward and control mechanisms effective?

 ## MARKETING

Marketing can be described as the process of defining, anticipating, creating, and fulfilling customers' needs and wants for products and services. There are seven basic *functions of marketing:* (1) customer analysis, (2) selling products/services, (3) product and service planning, (4) pricing, (5) distribution, (6) marketing research, and (7) opportunity analysis.[17] Understanding these functions helps strategists identify and evaluate marketing strengths and weaknesses.

### Customer Analysis

*Customer analysis*—the examination and evaluation of consumer needs, desires, and wants—involves administering customer surveys, analyzing consumer information, evaluating market positioning strategies, developing customer profiles, and determining optimal market segmentation strategies. The information generated by customer analysis can be essential in developing an effective mission statement. Customer profiles can reveal the demographic characteristics of an organization's customers. Buyers, sellers, distributors, salespeople, managers, wholesalers, retailers, suppliers, and creditors can all participate in gathering information to identify customers' needs and wants successfully. Successful organizations continually monitor present and potential customers' buying patterns.

### Selling Products/Services

Successful strategy implementation generally rests upon the ability of an organization to sell some product or service. *Selling* includes many marketing activities such as advertising, sales promotion, publicity, personal selling, sales force management, customer relations, and dealer relations. These activities are especially critical when a firm pursues a market penetration strategy. The effectiveness of various selling tools for consumer and industrial products varies. Personal selling is most important for industrial goods companies, and advertising is most important for consumer goods companies. Determining organizational strengths and weaknesses in the selling function of marketing is an important part of performing an internal strategic-management audit.

**e·biz**

With regard to advertising products and services on the Internet, a new trend is to base advertising rates exclusively on sale rates. This new accountability contrasts sharply with traditional broadcast and print advertising that bases rates on the number of persons expected to see a given advertisement. The new cost-per-sale on-line advertising rates are possible because any Web site can monitor which user clicks on which advertisement and then can record whether that consumer actually buys the product. If there are no sales, then the advertisement is free.

Some mass retailers such as Amazon Books and CUC International are paying millions of dollars in sales commissions and advertising fees in exchange for prominent placement on high-traffic Web sites, search engines, and home pages of online service providers such as America Online. Advertising spending on the Web is projected to explode from $2.8 billion in 1999 to $22 billion in 2004. Performance-based pricing, whether it's cost per click, cost per sale, or cost per lead, is rapidly replacing cost per thousand impressions (CPMs) as the industry standard for pricing the cost of an advertisement.[18] The most popular type of Internet advertisement is the banner. However, many people just ignore online banner advertisements. More than half of online consumers have never clicked on a banner ad, according to a recent report from Forrester Research, Inc.[19]

Procter & Gamble (P&G) recently joined Colgate-Palmolive, Campbell Soup, AT&T, Sears Roebuck, Kraft Foods, and Ford Motor in changing the way it compensates its advertising agencies. These companies are now paying advertising agencies based on a particular product's sales growth or decline. Several P&G products being advertised on a performance-based system include Vidal Sassoon, Bounty, and Nyquil, with more than two hundred P&G products under this system by mid-2000.[20]

Overall advertising expenditures in the United States increased from $213.95 billion in 1999 to $230 billion in 2000, a 7 percent increase. This increase was down slightly from 7.5 percent the prior year.

### Product and Service Planning

*Product and service planning* includes activities such as test marketing; product and brand positioning; devising warranties; packaging; determining product options, product features, product style, and product quality; deleting old products; and providing for customer service. Product and service planning is particularly important when a company is pursuing product development or diversification.

One of the most effective product and service planning techniques is *test marketing*. Test markets allow an organization to test alternative marketing plans and to forecast future sales of new products. In conducting a test market project, an organization must decide how many cities to include, which cities to include, how long to run the test, what information to collect during the test, and what action to take after the test has been completed. Test marketing is used more frequently by consumer goods companies than by industrial goods companies. Test marketing can allow an organization to avoid substantial losses by revealing weak products and ineffective marketing approaches before large-scale production begins.

### Pricing

Five major stakeholders affect *pricing* decisions: consumers, governments, suppliers, distributors, and competitors. Sometimes an organization will pursue a forward integration strategy primarily to gain better control over prices charged to consumers. Governments can impose constraints on price fixing, price discrimination, minimum prices, unit pricing, price advertising, and price controls. For example, the Robinson-Patman Act prohibits manufacturers and wholesalers from discriminating in price among channel member purchasers (suppliers and distributors) if competition is injured.

Competing organizations must be careful not to coordinate discounts, credit terms, or condition of sale; not to discuss prices, markups, and costs at trade association meetings; and not to arrange to issue new price lists on the same date, to rotate low bids on contracts, or to uniformly restrict production to maintain high prices. Strategists should view price from both a short-run and a long-run perspective, because competitors can copy price changes with relative ease. Often a dominant firm will aggressively match all price cuts by competitors.

With regard to pricing, as the value of the dollar increases, which it has been doing steadily, U.S. multinational companies have a choice. They can raise prices in the local currency of a foreign country or risk losing sales and market share. Alternatively, multinational firms can keep prices steady and face reduced profit when their export revenue is reported in the United States in dollars.

## Distribution

*Distribution* includes warehousing, distribution channels, distribution coverage, retail site locations, sales territories, inventory levels and location, transportation carriers, wholesaling, and retailing. Most producers today do not sell their goods directly to consumers. Various marketing entities act as intermediaries; they bear a variety of names such as wholesalers, retailers, brokers, facilitators, agents, middlemen, vendors, or simply distributors.

Major cargo carriers in the United States, including trains, trucks, ships, and planes, are being swamped with business in the late 1990s. Union Pacific, the nation's largest railroad, has such a monumental backlog that the firm now ships goods by sea, through the Panama Canal. Freight in the United States has piled up at rail terminals, ship docks, and trucking centers. Trucks move 80 percent of consumer goods in the United States. There is a widespread shortage of both truck drivers and trucks in this country.

Distribution becomes especially important when a firm is striving to implement a market development or forward integration strategy. Some of the most complex and challenging decisions facing a firm concern product distribution. Intermediaries flourish in our economy because many producers lack the financial resources and expertise to carry out direct marketing. Manufacturers who could afford to sell directly to the public often can gain greater returns by expanding and improving their manufacturing operations. Even General Motors would find it very difficult to buy out its more than eighteen thousand independent dealers.

Successful organizations identify and evaluate alternative ways to reach their ultimate market. Possible approaches vary from direct selling to using just one or many wholesalers and retailers. Strengths and weaknesses of each channel alternative should be determined according to economic, control, and adaptive criteria. Organizations should consider the costs and benefits of various wholesaling and retailing options. They must consider the need to motivate and control channel members and the need to adapt to changes in the future. Once a marketing channel is chosen, an organization usually must adhere to it for an extended period of time.

But as indicated in the E-Commerce Perspective, furniture manufacturers are now selling direct to consumers to the dismay of their brick-and-mortar distributors.

**e·biz**

## Marketing Research

*Marketing research* is the systematic gathering, recording, and analyzing of data about problems relating to the marketing of goods and services. Marketing research can uncover critical strengths and weaknesses, and marketing researchers employ numerous scales, instruments, procedures, concepts, and techniques to gather information. Marketing research activities support all of the major business functions of an organization.

# E-COMMERCE PERSPECTIVE

## E-Stores Replacing Brick Stores

Like many industries, retail furniture stores nationwide are intensely debating whether the Internet will destroy their business or simply add another small sales channel. Furniture retailers nationwide are demanding assurance from furniture suppliers (manufacturers) that discount Internet retailers will not be supplied with their same furniture brands. The furniture industry is crazed over this subject. Some analysts contend that all furniture stores in the United States will disappear, and some say Internet furniture sales will actually spur retail furniture sales. The furniture manufacturer, Stanley Furniture Company in Stanleytown, Virginia decided to sell its products on the Internet but after a month of loud protests from their retail distributors, Stanley banned all online sales of its products. But two other big furniture makers, Ethan Allan Interiors in Danbury, Connecticut, and La-Z-Boy Inc. in Monroe, Michigan, both plan to distribute their products online in "cooperation" with their retailers. The nation's largest furniture manufacturer with 9 percent of the market, Furniture Brands in St. Louis, contends that people will want to "see and touch" before purchasing furniture. However an increasing number of discount online furniture companies such as Benchmark Industries in Olathe, Kansas, and J.C. Penney of Plano, Texas, now offer furniture online. Online furniture sales are expected to increase to nearly $4 billion by 2004 from $0.5 billion in 2000, representing a market share increase from 0.75 to 5.0.

Gone are the days when furniture stores had a geographically captive customer, when merchants had the advantage of being the only store within driving distance, and when only the merchants knew actual costs of their brands being sold. Using the Internet, the next furniture store is only seconds away for customers, and it is open twenty-four hours a day. Cybershoppers research furniture brands and prices from any computer, anywhere, and make their purchase(s) with the click of a mouse. Various Web sites now do the furniture research for the customer. This approach is garnering an ever-increasing number of furniture customers. Traditional brick-and-mortar furniture stores must offer superior customer service, low prices, and more to have a chance to compete in this market.

Adapted from: James Hagerty, "Furniture Brands May Have to Rethink Its Web Policy," *The Wall Street Journal* (September 14, 1999): B4.

Organizations that possess excellent marketing research skills have a definite strength in pursuing generic strategies.

> The President of PepsiCo says, "Looking at the competition is the company's best form of market research. The majority of our strategic successes are ideas that we borrow from the marketplace, usually from a small regional or local competitor. In each case, we spot a promising new idea, improve on it, and then out-execute our competitor."[21]

About twenty thousand new products are introduced by U.S. companies annually, but 85 percent of these fail within three years. Many CEOs continue to trust their own best judgment over market research; this mind-set can be detrimental to a business. For example, the Greyhound Bus Company first pursued the African American market by placing advertising on African American radio stations. However, instead of creating a new commercial, Greyhound used its popular Country & Western music ad, which later was considered to have failed in that market.

## Opportunity Analysis

The eighth function of marketing is *opportunity analysis,* which involves assessing the costs, benefits, and risks associated with marketing decisions. Three steps are required to perform a *cost/benefit analysis:* (1) compute the total costs associated with a decision,

(2) estimate the total benefits from the decision, and (3) compare the total costs with the total benefits. As expected benefits exceed total costs, an opportunity becomes more attractive. Sometimes the variables included in a cost/benefit analysis cannot be quantified or even measured, but usually reasonable estimates can be made to allow the analysis to be performed. One key factor to be considered is risk. Cost/benefit analyses should also be performed when a company is evaluating alternative ways to be socially responsible.

## Marketing Audit Checklist of Questions

Similarly as provided earlier for management, the following questions about marketing are pertinent:

1. Are markets segmented effectively?
2. Is the organization positioned well among competitors?
3. Has the firm's market share been increasing?
4. Are present channels of distribution reliable and cost-effective?
5. Does the firm have an effective sales organization?
6. Does the firm conduct market research?
7. Are product quality and customer service good?
8. Are the firm's products and services priced appropriately?
9. Does the firm have an effective promotion, advertising, and publicity strategy?
10. Are marketing planning and budgeting effective?
11. Do the firm's marketing managers have adequate experience and training?

 ## FINANCE/ACCOUNTING

Financial condition is often considered the single best measure of a firm's competitive position and overall attractiveness to investors. Determining an organization's financial strengths and weaknesses is essential to formulating strategies effectively. A firm's liquidity, leverage, working capital, profitability, asset utilization, cash flow, and equity can eliminate some strategies as being feasible alternatives. Financial factors often alter existing strategies and change implementation plans.

## Finance/Accounting Functions

According to James Van Horne, the *functions of finance/accounting* comprise three decisions: the investment decision, the financing decision, and the dividend decision.[22] Financial ratio analysis is the most widely used method for determining an organization's strengths and weaknesses in the investment, financing, and dividend areas. Because the functional areas of business are so closely related, financial ratios can signal strengths or weaknesses in management, marketing, production, research and development, and computer information systems activities.

The *investment decision*, also called *capital budgeting*, is the allocation and reallocation of capital and resources to projects, products, assets, and divisions of an organization. Once strategies are formulated, capital budgeting decisions are required to implement strategies successfully. The *financing decision* concerns determining the best capital structure for the firm and includes examining various methods by which the firm can raise capital (for example, by issuing stock, increasing debt, selling assets, or using a combination of these approaches). The financing decision must consider both short-term and long-term needs for working capital. Two key financial ratios that indicate whether a firm's financing decisions have been effective are the debt-to-equity ratio and the debt-to-total-assets ratio.

*Dividend decisions* concern issues such as the percentage of earnings paid to stockholders, the stability of dividends paid over time, and the repurchase or issuance of stock. Dividend decisions determine the amount of funds that are retained in a firm compared to the amount paid out to stockholders. Three financial ratios that are helpful in evaluating a firm's dividend decisions are the earnings-per-share ratio, the dividends-per-share ratio, and the price-earnings ratio. The benefits of paying dividends to investors must be balanced against the benefits of retaining funds internally, and there is no set formula on how to balance this trade-off. For the reasons listed here, dividends are sometimes paid out even when funds could be better reinvested in the business or when the firm has to obtain outside sources of capital:

1. Paying cash dividends is customary. Failure to do so could be thought of as a stigma. A dividend change is considered a signal about the future.
2. Dividends represent a sales point for investment bankers. Some institutional investors can buy only dividend-paying stocks.
3. Shareholders often demand dividends, even in companies with great opportunities for reinvesting all available funds.
4. A myth exists that paying dividends will result in a higher stock price.

## Basic Types of Financial Ratios

Financial ratios are computed from an organization's income statement and balance sheet. Computing financial ratios is like taking a picture because the results reflect a situation at just one point in time. Comparing ratios over time and to industry averages is more likely to result in meaningful statistics that can be used to identify and evaluate strengths and weaknesses. Trend analysis, illustrated in Figure 4–2, is a useful technique that incorporates both the time and industry average dimensions of financial ratios. Note that the dotted lines reveal projected ratios. Some Web sites such as Wall Street Research Net at www.wsrn.com calculate financial ratios and provide data with charts. Four major sources of industry-average financial ratios follow:

1. Dun & Bradstreet's *Industry Norms and Key Business Ratios*—Fourteen different ratios are calculated in an industry-average format for eight hundred different types of businesses. The ratios are presented by Standard Industrial Classification (SIC) number and are grouped by annual sales into three size categories.
2. Robert Morris Associates' *Annual Statement Studies*—Sixteen different ratios are calculated in an industry-average format. Industries are referenced by SIC numbers published by the Bureau of the Census. The ratios are presented in four size categories by annual sales for all firms in the industry.
3. *Almanac of Business & Industrial Financial Ratios*—Twenty-two financial ratios and percentages are provided in an industry-average format for all major industries. The ratios and percentages are given for twelve different company-size categories for all firms in a given industry.
4. Federal Trade Commission Reports—The FTC publishes quarterly financial data, including ratios on manufacturing companies. FTC reports include analyses by industry group and asset size.

Table 4–4 provides a summary of key financial ratios showing how each ratio is calculated and what each ratio measures. However, all the ratios are not significant for all industries and companies. For example, accounts receivable turnover and average collec-

**FIGURE 4–2**

**A Financial Ratio Trend Analysis**

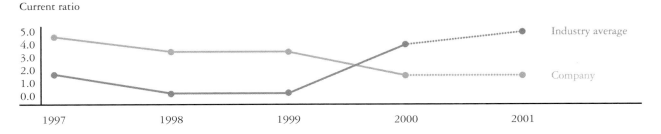

Current ratio

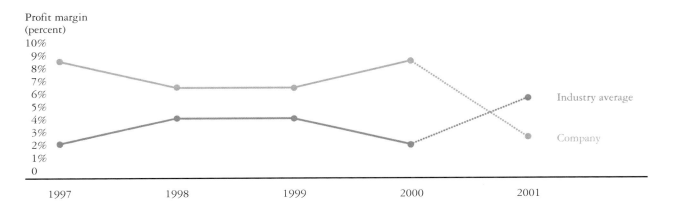

tion period are not very meaningful to a company that does primarily a cash receipts business. Key financial ratios can be classified into the following five types:

1. *Liquidity ratios* measure a firm's ability to meet maturing short-term obligations.
   Current ratio
   Quick (or acid-test) ratio

2. *Leverage ratios* measure the extent to which a firm has been financed by debt.
   Debt-to-total-assets ratio
   Debt-to-equity ratio
   Long-term debt-to-equity ratio
   Times-interest-earned (or coverage) ratio

3. *Activity ratios* measure how effectively a firm is using its resources.
   Inventory-turnover
   Fixed assets turnover
   Total assets turnover
   Accounts receivable turnover
   Average collection period

4. *Profitability ratios* measure management's overall effectiveness as shown by the returns generated on sales and investment.
   Gross profit margin
   Operating profit margin
   Net profit margin
   Return on total assets (ROA)

## TABLE 4-4   A Summary of Key Financial Ratios

| RATIO | HOW CALCULATED | WHAT IT MEASURES |
|---|---|---|
| **Liquidity Ratios** | | |
| Current Ratio | $\dfrac{\text{Current assets}}{\text{Current liabilities}}$ | The extent to which a firm can meet its short-term obligations |
| Quick Ratio | $\dfrac{\text{Current assets minus inventory}}{\text{Current liabilities}}$ | The extent to which a firm can meet its short-term obligations without relying upon the sale of its inventories |
| **Leverage Ratios** | | |
| Debt-to-Total-Assets Ratio | $\dfrac{\text{Total debt}}{\text{Total assets}}$ | The percentage of total funds that are provided by creditors |
| Debt-to-Equity Ratio | $\dfrac{\text{Total debt}}{\text{Total stockholders' equity}}$ | The percentage of total funds provided by creditors versus by owners |
| Long-Term Debt-to-Equity Ratio | $\dfrac{\text{Long-term debt}}{\text{Total stockholders' equity}}$ | The balance between debt and equity in a firm's long-term capital structure |
| Times-Interest-Earned Ratio | $\dfrac{\text{Profits before interest and taxes}}{\text{Total interest charges}}$ | The extent to which earnings can decline without the firm becoming unable to meet its annual interest costs |
| **Activity Ratios** | | |
| Inventory Turnover | $\dfrac{\text{Sales}}{\text{Inventory of finished goods}}$ | Whether a firm holds excessive stocks of inventories and whether a firm is selling its inventories slowly compared to the industry average |
| Fixed Assets Turnover | $\dfrac{\text{Sales}}{\text{Fixed assets}}$ | Sales productivity and plant and equipment utilization |
| Total Assets Turnover | $\dfrac{\text{Sales}}{\text{Total assets}}$ | Whether a firm is generating a sufficient volume of business for the size of its asset investment |
| Accounts Receivable Turnover | $\dfrac{\text{Annual credit sales}}{\text{Accounts receivable}}$ | The average length of time it takes a firm to collect credit sales (in percentage terms) |
| Average Collection Period | $\dfrac{\text{Accounts receivable}}{\text{Total credit sales/365 days}}$ | The average length of time it takes a firm to collect on credit sales (in days) |
| **Profitability Ratios** | | |
| Gross Profit Margin | $\dfrac{\text{Sales minus cost of goods sold}}{\text{Sales}}$ | The total margin available to cover operating expenses and yield a profit |
| Operating Profit Margin | $\dfrac{\text{Earnings before interest and taxes (EBIT)}}{\text{Sales}}$ | Profitability without concern for taxes and interest |
| Net Profit Margin | $\dfrac{\text{Net income}}{\text{Sales}}$ | After-tax profits per dollar of sales |
| Return on Total Assets (ROA) | $\dfrac{\text{Net income}}{\text{Total assets}}$ | After-tax profits per dollar of assets; this ratio is also called return on investment (ROI) |
| Return on Stockholders' Equity (ROE) | $\dfrac{\text{Net income}}{\text{Total stockholders' equity}}$ | After-tax profits per dollar of stockholders' investment in the firm |
| Earning Per Share (EPS) | $\dfrac{\text{Net income}}{\text{Number of shares of common stock outstanding}}$ | Earnings available to the owners of common stock |
| Price-earning Ratio | $\dfrac{\text{Market price per share}}{\text{Earnings per share}}$ | Attractiveness of firm on equity markets. |
| **Growth Ratios** | | |
| Sales | Annual percentage growth in total sales | Firm's growth rate in sales |
| Income | Annual percentage growth in profits | Firm's growth rate in profits |
| Earnings Per Share | Annual percentage growth in EPS | Firm's growth rate in EPS |
| Dividends Per Share | Annual percentage growth in dividends per share | Firm's growth rate in dividends per share |

Return on stockholders' equity (ROE)
Earnings per share
Price-earnings ratio

5. *Growth ratios* measure the firm's ability to maintain its economic position in the growth of the economy and industry.

Sales
Net income
Earnings per share
Dividends per share

Financial ratio analysis is not without some limitations. First of all, financial ratios are based on accounting data, and firms differ in their treatment of such items as depreciation, inventory valuation, research and development expenditures, pension plan costs, mergers, and taxes. Also, seasonal factors can influence comparative ratios. Therefore, conformity to industry composite ratios does not establish with certainty that a firm is performing normally or that it is well managed. Likewise, departures from industry averages do not always indicate that a firm is doing especially well or badly. For example, a high inventory turnover ratio could indicate efficient inventory management and a strong working capital position, but it also could indicate a serious inventory shortage and a weak working capital position.

It is important to recognize that a firm's financial condition depends not only on the functions of finance, but also on many other factors that include (1) management, marketing, production/operations, research and development, and computer information systems decisions; (2) actions by competitors, suppliers, distributors, creditors, customers, and shareholders; and (3) economic, social, cultural, demographic, environmental, political, governmental, legal, and technological trends. Even natural environment liabilities can affect financial ratios, as indicated in the Natural Environment Perspective. So financial ratio analysis, like all other analytical tools, should be used wisely.

# NATURAL ENVIRONMENT

### *Environmental Liability on the Balance Sheet*

Environmental liability may be the largest recognized or unrecognized liability on a company's balance sheet. More American firms are finding themselves liable for cleanup costs and damages stemming from waste disposal practices of the past, in some cases going back 100 years. Environmental liabilities associated with air and water pollution, habitat destruction, deforestation, and medical problems can be immense. For this reason, many financial institutions now inquire about environmental liabilities as part of their commercial lending procedures. Firms such as American Insurance Company specialize in providing environmental liability insurance to companies.

Environmental Protection Agency (EPA) regulations take up more than 11,000 pages; they vary with location and size of firm and are added to daily. The complexity of these regulations can translate into liabilities for the environmentally reactive firm. Proactive firms, on the other hand, are adding a "green executive" and department to oversee management of environmental policies and practices of the firm. The responsibility of green executives includes thinking through environmental regulations, marketing needs, public attitudes, consumer demands, and potential problems. Ideally, green executives should promote development of a corporate culture in which all managers and employees become "green," or environmentally sensitive. Such a culture would represent an internal strength to the firm.

### Finance/Accounting Audit Checklist of Questions

Similarly as provided earlier, the following finance/accounting questions should be examined:

1. Where is the firm financially strong and weak as indicated by financial ratio analyses?
2. Can the firm raise needed short-term capital?
3. Can the firm raise needed long-term capital through debt and/or equity?
4. Does the firm have sufficient working capital?
5. Are capital budgeting procedures effective?
6. Are dividend payout policies reasonable?
7. Does the firm have good relations with its investors and stockholders?
8. Are the firm's financial managers experienced and well trained?

 ## PRODUCTION/OPERATIONS

The *production/operations function* of a business consists of all those activities that transform inputs into goods and services. Production/operations management deals with inputs, transformations, and outputs that vary across industries and markets. A manufacturing operation transforms or converts inputs such as raw materials, labor, capital, machines, and facilities into finished goods and services. As indicated in Table 4–5, Roger Schroeder suggested that production/operations management comprises five functions or decision areas: process, capacity, inventory, workforce, and quality.

Most automakers require a thirty-day notice to build vehicles, but Toyota Motor recently announced it will fill a buyer's new car order in just five days. Honda Motor was

**TABLE 4–5      The Basic Functions of Production Management**

| FUNCTION | DESCRIPTION |
|---|---|
| 1. Process | Process decisions concern the design of the physical production system. Specific decisions include choice of technology, facility layout, process flow analysis, facility location, line balancing, process control, and transportation analysis. |
| 2. Capacity | Capacity decisions concern determination of optimal output levels for the organization—not too much and not too little. Specific decisions include forecasting, facilities planning, aggregate planning, scheduling, capacity planning, and queuing analysis. |
| 3. Inventory | Inventory decisions involve managing the level of raw materials, work in process, and finished goods. Specific decisions include what to order, when to order, how much to order, and materials handling. |
| 4. Workforce | Workforce decisions are concerned with managing the skilled, unskilled, clerical, and managerial employees. Specific decisions include job design, work measurement, job enrichment, work standards, and motivation techniques. |
| 5. Quality | Quality decisions are aimed at ensuring that high-quality goods and services are produced. Specific decisions include quality control, sampling, testing, quality assurance, and cost control. |

*Source:* Adapted from R. Schroeder, *Operations Management* (New York: McGraw-Hill Book Co., 1981): 12.

considered the industry's fastest producer, filling orders in fifteen days. Automakers have for years operated under just-in-time inventory systems, but Toyota's 360 suppliers are linked to the company via computer on a virtual assembly line. The new Toyota production system was developed in the company's Cambridge, Ontario, plant and now applies to its Solara, Camry, Corolla, and Tacoma vehicles.

Production/operations activities often represent the largest part of an organization's human and capital assets. In most industries, the major costs of producing a product or service are incurred within operations, so production/operations can have great value as a competitive weapon in a company's overall strategy. Strengths and weaknesses in the five functions of production can mean the success or failure of an enterprise.

Many production/operations managers are finding that cross-training of employees can help their firms respond to changing markets faster. Cross-training of workers can increase efficiency, quality, productivity, and job satisfaction. For example, at General Motors's Detroit Gear & Axle plant, costs related to product defects were reduced 400 percent in two years as a result of cross-training workers. A shortage of qualified labor in America is another reason cross-training is becoming a common management practice.

Singapore today rivals Hong Kong as an attractive site for locating production facilities in Southeast Asia. Singapore is a city-state near Malaysia that has bounced back from Asia's financial turmoil of 1998 in grand fashion. An island nation of about four million persons, Singapore is changing from an economy built on trade and services to one built upon information technology. A large-scale program in computer education for older (over twenty-six year old) residents called Coach has trained more than 225,000 persons since 1997. Singapore children receive outstanding computer training in schools. All government services are computerized nicely. Singapore lures multinational businesses with great tax breaks, world-class infrastructure, excellent courts that handle business disputes efficiently, exceptionally low tariffs, large land giveaways, impressive industrial parks, excellent port facilities, and a government very receptive to and cooperative with foreign businesses. Foreign firms now account for 70 percent of manufacturing output in Singapore. Singapore's economic growth averages about 5 percent per year in 1999 to 2000.

The World Economic Forum in Basel, Switzerland now ranks Singapore as the world's most competitive and attractive economy. A recent study of four thousand business executives ranked Singapore number-one among fifty-nine countries in the following categories:

- Overall infrastructure
- Trust in politicians' honesty
- Government subsidies
- Government economic policies
- High savings rate
- Labor/employee relations[23]

There is much reason for concern that many organizations have not taken sufficient account of the capabilities and limitations of the production/operations function in formulating strategies. Scholars contend that this neglect has had unfavorable consequences on corporate performance in America. As shown in Table 4–6, James Dilworth outlined several types of strategic decisions that a company might make with production/operations implications of those decisions. Production capabilities and policies can also greatly affect strategies:

> Given today's decision-making environment with shortages, inflation, technological booms, and government intervention, a company's production/operations capabilities and policies may not be able to fulfill the demands dictated by

## TABLE 4-6 Impact of Strategy Elements on Production Management

| POSSIBLE ELEMENTS OF STRATEGY | CONCOMITANT CONDITIONS THAT MAY AFFECT THE OPERATIONS FUNCTION AND ADVANTAGES AND DISADVANTAGES |
|---|---|
| 1. Compete as low-cost provider of goods or services | Discourages competition<br>Broadens market<br>Requires longer production runs and fewer product changes<br>Requires special-purpose equipment and facilities |
| 2. Compete as high-quality provider | Often possible to obtain more profit per unit, and perhaps more total profit from a smaller volume of sales<br>Requires more quality-assurance effort and higher operating cost<br>Requires more precise equipment, which is more expensive<br>Requires highly skilled workers, necessitating higher wages and greater training efforts |
| 3. Stress customer service | Requires broader development of servicepeople and service parts and equipment<br>Requires rapid response to customer needs or changes in customer tastes, rapid and accurate information system, careful coordination<br>Requires a higher inventory investment |
| 4. Provide rapid and frequent introduction of new products | Requires versatile equipment and people<br>Has higher research and development costs<br>Has high retraining costs and high tooling and changeover in manufacturing<br>Provides lower volumes for each product and fewer opportunities for improvements due to the learning curve |
| 5. Strive for absolute growth | Requires accepting some projects or products with lower marginal value, which reduces ROI<br>Diverts talents to areas of weakness instead of concentrating on strengths |
| 6. Seek vertical integration | Enables company to control more of the process<br>May not have economies of scale at some stages of process<br>May require high capital investment as well as technology and skills beyond those currently available within the organization |
| 7. Maintain reserve capacity for flexibility | Provides ability to meet peak demands and quickly implement some contingency plans if forecasts are too low<br>Requires capital investment in idle capacity<br>Provides capability to grow during the lead time normally required for expansion |
| 8. Consolidate processing (Centralize) | Can result in economies of scale<br>Can locate near one major customer or supplier<br>Vulnerability: one strike, fire, or flood can halt the entire operation |
| 9. Disperse processing of service (Decentralize) | Can be near several market territories<br>Requires more complex coordination network: perhaps expensive data transmission and duplication of some personnel and equipment at each location<br>If each location produces one product in the line, then other products still must be transported to be available at all locations<br>If each location specializes in a type of component for all products, the company is vulnerable to strike, fire, flood, etc.<br>If each location provides total product line, then economies of scale may not be realized |
| 10. Stress the use of mechanization, automation, robots | Requires high capital investment<br>Reduces flexibility<br>May affect labor relations<br>Makes maintenance more crucial |
| 11. Stress stability of employment | Serves the security needs of employees and may develop employee loyalty<br>Helps to attract and retain highly skilled employees<br>May require revisions of make-or-buy decisions, use of idle time, inventory, and subcontractors as demand fluctuates |

*Source: Production and Operations Management: Manufacturing and Nonmanufacturing,* Second Edition, by J. Dilworth. Copyright © 1983 by Random House, Inc. Reprinted by permission of Random House, Inc.

strategies. In fact, they may dictate corporate strategies. It is hard to imagine that an organization can formulate strategies today without first considering the constraints and limitations imposed by its existing production/operations structure.[24]

### Production/Operations Audit Checklist of Questions

Questions such as the following should be examined:

1. Are suppliers of raw materials, parts, and subassemblies reliable and reasonable?
2. Are facilities, equipment, machinery, and offices in good condition?
3. Are inventory-control policies and procedures effective?
4. Are quality-control policies and procedures effective?
5. Are facilities, resources, and markets strategically located?
6. Does the firm have technological competencies?

# RESEARCH AND DEVELOPMENT

The fifth major area of internal operations that should be examined for specific strengths and weaknesses is research and development (R&D). Many firms today conduct no R&D, and yet many other companies depend on successful R&D activities for survival. Firms pursuing a product development strategy especially need to have a strong R&D orientation.

Organizations invest in R&D because they believe that such investment will lead to superior product or services and give them competitive advantages. Research and development expenditures are directed at developing new products before competitors do, improving product quality, or improving manufacturing processes to reduce costs.

One article on planning emphasized that effective management of the R&D function requires a strategic and operational partnership between R&D and the other vital business functions. A spirit of partnership and mutual trust between general and R&D managers is evident in the best-managed firms today. Managers in these firms jointly explore; assess; and decide the what, when, why, and how much of R&D. Priorities, costs, benefits, risks, and rewards associated with R&D activities are discussed openly and shared. The overall mission of R&D thus has become broad-based, including supporting existing businesses, helping launch new businesses, developing new products, improving product quality, improving manufacturing efficiency, and deepening or broadening the company's technological capabilities.[25]

The best-managed firms today seek to organize R&D activities in a way that breaks the isolation of R&D from the rest of the company and promotes a spirit of partnership between R&D managers and other managers in the firm. R&D decisions and plans must be integrated and coordinated across departments and divisions by sharing experiences and information. The strategic-management process facilitates this new cross-functional approach to managing the R&D function.

### Internal and External R&D

Cost distributions among R&D activities vary by company and industry, but total R&D costs generally do not exceed manufacturing and marketing start-up costs. Four approaches to determining R&D budget allocations commonly are used: (1) financing as many project proposals as possible, (2) using a percentage-of-sales method, (3) budgeting about the same amount that competitors spend for R&D, or (4) deciding how many successful new products are needed and working backward to estimate the required R&D investment.

R&D in organizations can take two basic forms: (1) internal R&D, in which an organization operates its own R&D department, and/or (2) contract R&D, in which a firm hires independent researchers or independent agencies to develop specific products. Many companies use both approaches to develop new products. A widely used approach for obtaining outside R&D assistance is to pursue a joint venture with another firm. R&D strengths (capabilities) and weaknesses (limitations) play a major role in strategy formulation and strategy implementation.

Most firms have no choice but to continually develop new and improved products because of changing consumer needs and tastes, new technologies, shortened product life cycles, and increased domestic and foreign competition. A shortage of ideas for new products, increased global competition, increased market segmentation, strong special-interest groups, and increased government regulation are several factors making the successful development of new products more and more difficult, costly, and risky. In the pharmaceutical industry, for example, only one out of every ten thousand drugs created in the laboratory ends up on pharmacists' shelves. Scarpello, Boulton, and Hofer emphasized that different strategies require different R&D capabilities:

> The focus of R&D efforts can vary greatly depending on a firm's competitive strategy. Some corporations attempt to be market leaders and innovators of new products, while others are satisfied to be market followers and developers of currently available products. The basic skills required to support these strategies will vary, depending on whether R&D becomes the driving force behind competitive strategy. In cases where new product introduction is the driving force for strategy, R&D activities must be extensive. The R&D unit must then be able to advance scientific and technological knowledge, exploit that knowledge, and manage the risks associated with ideas, products, services, and production requirements.[26]

### Research and Development Audit Checklist of Questions

Questions such as follows should be asked in performing an R&D audit:

1. Does the firm have R&D facilities? Are they adequate?
2. If outside R&D firms are used, are they cost-effective?
3. Are the organization's R&D personnel well qualified?
4. Are R&D resources allocated effectively?
5. Are management information and computer systems adequate?
6. Is communication between R&D and other organizational units effective?
7. Are present products technologically competitive?

# COMPUTER INFORMATION SYSTEMS

Information ties all business functions together and provides the basis for all managerial decisions. It is the cornerstone of all organizations. Information represents a major source of competitive advantage or disadvantage. Assessing a firm's internal strengths and weaknesses in information systems is a critical dimension of performing an internal audit. The company motto of Mitsui, a large Japanese trading company, is "Information is the lifeblood of the company." A satellite network connects Mitsui's 200 worldwide offices.

A computer information system's purpose is to improve the performance of an enterprise by improving the quality of managerial decisions. An effective information system thus collects, codes, stores, synthesizes, and presents information in such a manner that it answers important operating and strategic questions. The heart of an information system is a database containing the kinds of records and data important to managers.

A *computer information system* receives raw material from both the external and internal evaluation of an organization. It gathers data about marketing, finance, production, and personnel matters internally, and social, cultural, demographic, environmental, economic, political, government, legal, technological, and competitive factors externally. Data is integrated in ways needed to support managerial decision making.

There is a logical flow of material in a computer information system, whereby data is input to the system and transformed into output. Outputs include computer printouts, written reports, tables, charts, graphs, checks, purchase orders, invoices, inventory records, payroll accounts, and a variety of other documents. Payoffs from alternative strategies can be calculated and estimated. *Data* becomes *information* only when it is evaluated, filtered, condensed, analyzed, and organized for a specific purpose, problem, individual, or time.

An effective computer information system utilizes computer hardware, software, models for analysis, and a database. Some people equate information systems with the advent of the computer, but historians have traced recordkeeping and noncomputer data processing to Babylonian merchants living in 3500 B.C. Benefits of an effective information system include an improved understanding of business functions, improved communications, more informed decision making, analysis of problems, and improved control.

Because organizations are becoming more complex, decentralized, and globally dispersed, the function of information systems is growing in importance. Spurring this advance is the falling cost and increasing power of computers. There are costs and benefits associated with obtaining and evaluating information, just as with equipment and land. Like equipment, information can become obsolete and may need to be purged from the system. An effective information system is like a library, collecting, categorizing, and filing data for use by managers throughout the organization. Information systems are a major strategic resource, monitoring environment changes, identifying competitive threats, and assisting in the implementation, evaluation, and control of strategy.

We are truly in an information age. Firms whose information-system skills are weak are at a competitive disadvantage. On the other hand, strengths in information systems allow firms to establish distinctive competencies in other areas. Low-cost manufacturing and good customer service, for example, can depend on a good information system.

A good executive information system provides graphic, tabular, and textual information. Graphic capabilities are needed so current conditions and trends can be examined quickly; tables provide greater detail and enable variance analyses; textual information adds insight and interpretation to data.

## Strategic Planning Software

The computer revolution today is being compared in magnitude to the industrial revolution. Computers are now common at the desks of almost every professional and administrative employee of industry, government, and academia. The proliferation of computers has aided strategic management because software products can be designed to enhance participation and to provide integration, uniformity, analysis, and economy. Strategic planning software can allow firms to tap the knowledge base of everyone in the firm. There are a number of commercially available software products designed to train and assist managers in strategic planning, including *Business Advantage, Business Simulator, SUCCESS, ANS-PLAN-A, Strategy!, CheckMATE, EXCEL, STRATPAC, SIMPLAN, REVEAL, COSMOS, and BASICS P-C.*

Some strategic decision support systems, however, are too sophisticated, expensive, or restrictive to be used easily by managers in a firm. This is unfortunate because the strategic-management process must be a people process to be successful. People make the difference! Strategic planning software thus should be simple and unsophisticated. Simplicity allows wide participation among managers in a firm and participation is essential for effective strategy implementation.

One strategic planning software product that parallels this text and offers managers and executives a simple yet effective approach for developing organizational strategies is *CheckMATE*. This IBM-compatible, personal computer software performs planning analyses and generates strategies a firm could pursue. *CheckMATE*, a Windows-based program, incorporates the most modern strategic planning techniques. No previous experience with computers or knowledge of strategic planning is required of the user. *CheckMATE* thus promotes communication, understanding, creativity, and forward thinking among users.

*CheckMATE* is not a spreadsheet program or database; it is an expert system that carries a firm through strategy formulation and implementation. A major strength of the new *CheckMATE* strategic-planning software is its simplicity and participative approach. The user is asked appropriate questions, responses are recorded, information is assimilated, and results are printed. Individuals can work through the software independently and then meet to develop joint recommendations for the firm.

The *CheckMATE* software utilizes the most modern strategic-planning analytical matrices to generate alternative strategies firms could pursue. Specific analytical procedures included in the *CheckMATE* program are Strategic Position and Action Evaluation (SPACE) analysis, Threats-Opportunities-Weaknesses-Strengths (TOWS) analysis, Internal-External (IE) analysis, and Grand Strategy Matrix analysis. These widely used strategic-planning analyses are described in Chapter 6.

Twenty-three customized industry applications of *CheckMATE* are available in a new Windows format. An individual license costs $195. More information about *CheckMATE* can be obtained at www.checkmateplan.com or 843-669-6960 (phone).

## Computer Information Systems Audit Checklist of Questions

Questions such as the following should be asked in conducting this audit:

1. Do all managers in the firm use the information system to make decisions?
2. Is there a chief information officer or director of information systems position in the firm?
3. Are data in the information system updated regularly?
4. Do managers from all functional areas of the firm contribute input to the information system?
5. Are there effective passwords for entry into the firm's information system?
6. Are strategists of the firm familiar with the information systems of rival firms?
7. Is the information system user-friendly?
8. Do all users of the information system understand the competitive advantages that information can provide firms?
9. Are computer training workshops provided for users of the information system?
10. Is the firm's information system continually being improved in content and user-friendliness?

# THE INTERNAL FACTOR EVALUATION (IFE) MATRIX

A summary step in conducting an internal strategic-management audit is to construct an *Internal Factor Evaluation (IFE) Matrix.* This strategy-formulation tool summarizes and evaluates the major strengths and weaknesses in the functional areas of a business, and it also provides a basis for identifying and evaluating relationships among those areas. Intuitive judgments are required in developing an IFE Matrix, so the appearance of a scientific approach should not be interpreted to mean this is an all-powerful technique. A thorough understanding of the factors included is more important than the actual numbers. Similar to the EFE Matrix and Competitive Profile Matrix described in Chapter 3, an IFE Matrix can be developed in five steps:

1. List key internal factors as identified in the internal-audit process. Use a total of from ten to twenty internal factors, including both strengths and weaknesses. List strengths first and then weaknesses. Be as specific as possible, using percentages, ratios, and comparative numbers.

2. Assign a weight that ranges from 0.0 (not important) to 1.0 (all-important) to each factor. The weight assigned to a given factor indicates the relative importance of the factor to being successful in the firm's industry. Regardless of whether a key factor is an internal strength or weakness, factors considered to have the greatest effect on organizational performance should be assigned the highest weights. The sum of all weights must equal 1.0.

3. Assign a 1-to-4 rating to each factor to indicate whether that factor represents a major weakness (rating = 1), a minor weakness (rating = 2), a minor strength (rating = 3), or a major strength (rating = 4). Note that strengths must receive a 4 or 3 rating and weaknesses must receive a 1 or 2 rating. Ratings are thus company-based, whereas the weights in Step 2 are industry-based.

4. Multiply each factor's weight by its rating to determine a weighted score for each variable.

5. Sum the weighted scores for each variable to determine the total weighted score for the organization.

Regardless of how many factors are included in an IFE Matrix, the total weighted score can range from a low of 1.0 to a high of 4.0, with the average score being 2.5. Total weighted scores well below 2.5 characterize organizations that are weak internally, whereas scores significantly above 2.5 indicate a strong internal position. Like the EFE Matrix, an IFE Matrix should include from 10 to 20 key factors. The number of factors has no effect upon the range of total weighted scores because the weights always sum to 1.0.

When a key internal factor is both a strength and a weakness, the factor should be included twice in the IFE Matrix, and a weight and rating should be assigned to each statement. For example, the Playboy logo both helps and hurts Playboy Enterprises; the logo attracts customers to the *Playboy* magazine, but it keeps the Playboy cable channel out of many markets.

An example of an IFE Matrix for Circus Circus Enterprises is provided in Table 4–7. Note that the firm's major strengths are its size, occupancy rates, property, and long-range planning as indicated by the rating of 4. The major weaknesses are locations and recent joint venture. The total weighted score of 2.75 indicates that the firm is above average in its overall internal strength.

TABLE 4–7    **A Sample Internal Factor Evaluation Matrix for Mandalay Resort Group**

| KEY INTERNAL FACTORS | WEIGHT | RATING | WEIGHTED SCORE |
|---|---|---|---|
| *Internal Strengths* | | | |
| 1.  Largest casino company in the United States | .05 | 4 | .20 |
| 2.  Room occupancy rates over 95% in Las Vegas | .10 | 4 | .40 |
| 3.  Increasing free cash flows | .05 | 3 | .15 |
| 4.  Owns one mile on Las Vegas Strip | .15 | 4 | .60 |
| 5.  Strong management team | .05 | 3 | .15 |
| 6.  Buffets at most facilities | .05 | 3 | .15 |
| 7.  Minimal comps provided | .05 | 3 | .15 |
| 8.  Long-range planning | .05 | 4 | .20 |
| 9.  Reputation as family-friendly | .05 | 3 | .15 |
| 10. Financial ratios | .05 | 3 | .15 |
| *Internal Weaknesses* | | | |
| 1.  Most properties are located in Las Vegas | .05 | 1 | .05 |
| 2.  Little diversification | .05 | 2 | .10 |
| 3.  Family reputation, not high rollers | .05 | 2 | .10 |
| 4.  Laughlin properties | .10 | 1 | .10 |
| 5.  Recent loss of joint ventures | .10 | 1 | .10 |
| TOTAL | 1.00 | | 2.75 |

In multidivisional firms, each autonomous division or strategic business unit should construct an IFE Matrix. Divisional matrices then can be integrated to develop an overall corporate IFE Matrix.

# CONCLUSION

Management, marketing, finance/accounting, production/operations, research and development, and computer information systems represent the core operations of most businesses. A strategic-management audit of a firm's internal operations is vital to organizational health. Many companies still prefer to be judged solely on their bottom-line performance. However, an increasing number of successful organizations are using the internal audit to gain competitive advantages over rival firms.

Systematic methodologies for performing strength-weakness assessments are not well developed in the strategic-management literature, but it is clear that strategists must identify and evaluate internal strengths and weaknesses in order to formulate and choose among alternative strategies effectively. The EFE Matrix, Competitive Profile Matrix, IFE Matrix, and clear statements of vision and mission provide the basic information needed to formulate competitive strategies successfully. The process of performing an internal audit represents an opportunity for managers and employees throughout the organization to participate in determining the future of the firm. Involvement in the process can energize and mobilize managers and employees.

We invite you to visit the DAVID page on the Prentice Hall Web site at **www.prenhall.com/davidsm** for this chapter's World Wide Web exercises.

## KEY TERMS AND CONCEPTS

Activity Ratios  (p. 143)

Capital Budgeting  (p. 141)

Communication  (p. 135)

Computer Information
  Systems  (p. 151)

Controlling  (p. 136)

Cost/Benefit Analysis  (p. 140)

Cultural Products  (p. 127)

Customer Analysis  (p. 137)

Distinctive Competencies  (p. 125)

Distribution  (p. 139)

Dividend Decision  (p. 142)

Financial Ratio Analysis  (p. 126)

Financing Decision  (p. 141)

Functions of Finance/
  Accounting  (p. 141)

Functions of Management  (p. 132)

Functions of Marketing  (p. 137)

Functions of Production/
  Operations  (p. 146)

Growth Ratio  (p. 145)

Human Resource Management
  (p. 135)

Internal Audit  (p. 125)

Internal Factor Evaluation (IFE)
  Matrix  (p. 153)

Investment Decision  (p. 141)

Leverage Ratios  (p. 143)

Liquidity Ratios  (p. 143)

Marketing Research  (p. 139)

Motivating  (p. 134)

Opportunity Analysis  (p. 140)

Organizational Culture  (p. 127)

Organizing  (p. 134)

Personnel Management  (p. 135)

Planning  (p. 132)

Pricing  (p. 138)

Product and Service
  Planning  (p. 138)

Production/Operations
  Function  (p. 146)

Profitability Ratios  (p. 143)

Research and Development  (p. 149)

Selling  (p. 137)

Staffing  (p. 135)

Synergy  (p. 133)

Test Marketing  (p. 138)

## ISSUES FOR REVIEW AND DISCUSSION

1. Explain why prioritizing the relative importance of strengths and weaknesses to include in an IFE Matrix is an important strategic-management activity.

2. How can delegation of authority contribute to effective strategic management?

3. Diagram a formal organizational chart that reflects the following positions: a president, two executive officers, four middle managers, and eighteen lower-level managers. Now, diagram three overlapping and hypothetical informal group structures. How can this information be helpful to a strategist in formulating and implementing strategy?

4. How could a strategist's attitude toward social responsibility affect a firm's strategy? What is your attitude toward social responsibility?

5. Which of the three basic functions of finance/accounting do you feel is most important in a small electronics manufacturing concern? Justify your position.

6. Do you think aggregate R&D expenditures for American firms will increase or decrease next year? Why?

7. Explain how you would motivate managers and employees to implement a major new strategy.

8. Why do you think production/operations managers often are not directly involved in strategy-formulation activities? Why can this be a major organizational weakness?

9. Give two examples of staffing strengths and two examples of staffing weaknesses of an organization with which you are familiar.

10. Would you ever pay out dividends when your firm's annual net profit is negative? Why? What effect could this have on a firm's strategies?

11. If a firm has zero debt in its capital structure, is that always an organizational strength? Why or why not?

12. Describe the production/operations system in a police department.

13. After conducting an internal audit, a firm discovers a total of 100 strengths and 100 weaknesses. What procedures then could be used to determine the most important of these? Why is it important to reduce the total number of key factors?

14. Select one of the suggested readings at the end of this chapter. Look up that article and give a five-minute oral report to the class summarizing the article and your views on the topic.

15. Why do you believe cultural products affect all the functions of business?

16. Do you think cultural products affect strategy formulation, implementation, or evaluation the most? Why?

17. Identify cultural products at your college or university. Do these products, viewed collectively or separately, represent a strength or weakness for the organization?

18. Describe the computer information system at your college or university.

19. Explain the difference between data and information in terms of each being useful to strategists.

20. What are the most important characteristics of an effective computer information system?

## NOTES

1. Robert Grant, "The Resource-Based Theory of Competitive Advantage: Implications for Strategy Formulation," *California Management Review* (Spring 1991): 116.

2. Reprinted by permission of the publisher from "Integrating Strength-Weakness Analysis into Strategic Planning," by William King, *Journal of Business Research II*, no. 4: p. 481. Copyright 1983 by Elsevier Science Publishing Co., Inc.

3. Igor Ansoff, "Strategic Management of Technology," *Journal of Business Strategy* 7, no. 3 (Winter 1987): 38.

4. Claude George, Jr., *The History of Management Thought,* 2nd ed. (Englewood Cliffs, N.J.: Prentice-Hall, 1972): 174.

5. Edgar Schein, *Organizational Culture and Leadership* (San Francisco: Jossey-Bass, 1985): 9.

6. John Lorsch, "Managing Culture: The Invisible Barrier to Strategic Change," *California Management Review* 28, no. 2 (1986): 95–109.

7. Y. Allarie and M. Firsirotu, "How to Implement Radical Strategies in Large Organizations," *Sloan Management Review* (Spring 1985): 19.

8. Jon Alston, "Wa, Guanxi, and Inhwa: Managerial Principles in Japan, China and Korea," *Business Horizons* 32, no. 2 (March–April 1989): 26.

9. Rose Knotts, "Cross-Cultural Management: Transformations and Adaptations," *Business Horizons* (January–February 1989): 29–33.

10. http://www.mindtools.com/plfailpl.html

11. Adam Smith, *Wealth of Nations* (New York: Modern Library, 1937): 3–4.

12. Richard Daft, *Management,* 3rd ed. (Orlando, Fla.: Dryden Press, 1993): 512.

13. Shelley Kirkpatrick and Edwin Locke, "Leadership: Do Traits Matter?" *Academy of Management Executive* 5, no. 2 (May 1991): 48.

14. Peter Drucker, *Management Tasks, Responsibilities, and Practice* (New York: Harper & Row, 1973): 463.

15. Brian Dumaine, "What the Leaders of Tomorrow See," *Fortune* (July 3, 1989): 51.

16. Robert Waterman, Jr., "The Renewal Factor," *Business Week* (September 14, 1987): 104.

17. J. Evans and B. Bergman, *Marketing* (New York: Macmillan, 1982): 17.

18. Greg Farrell, "Ad Rates on Web May Be Pay-Per-View," *USA Today* (September 1, 1999): B1.

19. Katherine Yung, "Internet's Banner Ads Just Don't Click," *Wilmington Morning Star* (July 4, 1999): 5E.

20. Kathryn Kranhold, "P&G Expands Its Program to Tie Agency Pay to Brand Performance," *The Wall Street Journal* (September 16, 1999): B12.

21. Quoted in Robert Waterman, Jr., "The Renewal Factor," *Business Week* (September 14, 1987): 108.

22. J. Van Horne, *Financial Management and Policy* (Englewood Cliffs, N.J.: Prentice-Hall, 1974): 10.

23. Jon Hilsenrath, "Time to Ease Up," *The Wall Street Journal* (September 27, 1999): B6. Also, Michelle Levander, "Singapore Turns People Into E-Citizens," *The Wall Street Journal* (October 27, 1999): A14.

24. W. Boulton and B. Saladin, "Let's Make Production-Operations Management Top Priority for Strategic Planning in the 1980s," *Managerial Planning* 32, no. 1 (July–August 1983): 19.

25. Philip Rouseel, Kamal Saad, and Tamara Erickson, "The Evolution of Third Generation R&D," *Planning Review* 19, no. 2 (March–April 1991): 18–26.

26. Vida Scarpello, William Boulton, and Charles Hofer, "Reintegrating R&D into Business Strategy," *Journal of Business Strategy* 6, no. 4 (Spring 1986): 50, 51.

## CURRENT READINGS

Anderson, Ralph E., Alan J. Dubinsky, and Rajiv Mehta. "Sales Managers: Marketing's Best Example of the Peter Principle?" *Business Horizons* 42, no. 1 (January–February 1999): 19–26.

Biecher, Elisa, Paul N. Keaton, and A. William Pollnan. "Casual Dress at Work." *Advanced Management Journal* 64, no. 1 (Winter 1999): 17–28.

BOWMAN, EDWARD H., HARBIR SINGH, MICHAEL USEEM, and RAJA BHADURY. "When Does Restructuring Improve Economic Performance?" *California Management Review,* 41, no. 2 (Winter 1999): 33–43.

BROUTHERS, LANCE ELIOT, JOHN P. McCRAY, and TIMOTHY J. WILKINSON. "Maquiladoras: Entrepreneurial Experimentation to Global Competitiveness." *Business Horizons* 42, no. 2 (March–April 1999): 37–44.

CHATTOPADHYAY, P., W. H. GLICK, C. C. MILLER, and G. P. HUBER. "Determinates of Executive Beliefs: Comparing Functional Conditioning and Social Influence." *Strategic Management Journal* 20, no. 8 (August 1999): 763–777.

CHI, P. S. K. "Financial Performance and Survival of Multinational Corporations in China." *Strategic Management Journal* 20, no. 4 (April 1999): 359–374.

DASS, PARSHOTAM and BARBARA PARKER. "Strategies for Managing Human Resource Diversity: From Resistance to Learning." *The Academy of Management Executive* 13, no. 2 (May 1999): 68–80.

DOOLEY, ROBERT S. and GERALD E. FRYXELL. "Attaining Decision Quality and Commitment from Dissent: The Moderating Effects of Loyalty and Competence in Strategic Decision Making Teams." *The Academy of Management Journal* 42, no. 4 (August 1999): 389–402.

EARL, MICHAEL J. and IAN J. SCOTT. "Opinion: What is a Chief Knowledge Officer?" *Sloan Management Review* 40, no. 2 (Winter 1999): 29–38.

FLEMING, MARY M. K. "When Customer Service Goes Bad . . ." *Business Horizons* 42, no. 4 (July–August 1999): 43–52.

HANSEN, MORTEN T., NITIN NOHRIA, and THOMAS TIERNEY. "What's Your Strategy for Managing Knowledge?" *Harvard Business Review* (March–April 1999): 106–116.

HARRIS, LLOYD C. "Initiating Planning: The Problem of Entrenched Cultural Values." *International Journal of Strategic Management* 32, no. 1 (February 1999): 117–126.

JOHNSON, BRUCE, WALTER W. WOOLFOLK, and PETER LIGEZINSKI. "Counterintuitive Management of Information Technology." *Business Horizons* 42, no. 2 (March–April 1999): 29–36.

LI, ZHAN G. and DIANA E. EADINGTON. "Marketing Agricultural Products to China." *Business Horizons* 42, no. 2 (March–April 1999): 45–51.

PETRICK, JOSEPH A., ROBERT F. SCHERER, JAMES D. BRODZINSKI, JOHN F. QUINN, and M. FALL AININA. "Global Leadership Skills and Reputational Capital: Intangible Resources for Sustainable Competitive Advantage." *The Academy of Management Executive* 13, no. 1 (February 1999): 58–69.

PRAHALAD, C. K. and M. S. KRISHNAN. "The New Meaning of Quality in the Information Age." *Harvard Business Review* 77, no. 5 (September–October 1999): 109–122.

RESEARCH BRIEFS. "Building Organizational Capabilities in the Canadian Energy Sector." *The Academy of Management Executive* 13, no. 2 (May 1999): 88.

# EXPERIENTIAL EXERCISES

## PURPOSE

Financial ratio analysis is one of the best techniques for identifying and evaluating internal strengths and weaknesses. Potential investors and current shareholders look closely at firms' financial ratios, making detailed comparisons to industry averages and to previous periods of time. Financial ratio analyses provide vital input information for developing an IFE Matrix.

## INSTRUCTIONS

Step 1    On a separate sheet of paper, number from 1 to 20. Referring to AOL's income statement and balance sheet (pp. 40–44), calculate 20 financial ratios for 1999 for the company. Use Table 4–4 as a reference.

Step 2    Go to your college library and find industry average financial ratios for the confectionery industry. Record the industry average values in a second column on your paper.

Step 3    In a third column, indicate whether you consider each ratio to be a strength, a weakness, or a neutral factor for AOL.

## PURPOSE

This exercise will give you experience developing an IFE Matrix. Identifying and prioritizing factors to include in an IFE Matrix fosters communication among functional and divisional managers. Preparing an IFE Matrix allows human resource, marketing, production/operations, finance/accounting, R&D, and computer information systems managers to vocalize their concerns and thoughts regarding the business condition of the firm. This results in an improved collective understanding of the business.

## INSTRUCTIONS

Step 1    Join with two other individuals to form a three-person team. Develop a team IFE Matrix for AOL.

Step 2    Compare your team's IFE Matrix to other teams' IFE Matrices. Discuss any major differences.

Step 3    What strategies do you think would allow AOL to capitalize on its major strengths? What strategies would allow AOL to improve upon its major weaknesses?

## PURPOSE

This exercise gives you the opportunity to evaluate your university's major strengths and weaknesses. As will become clearer in the next chapter, an organization's strategies are largely based upon striving to take advantage of strengths and improving upon weaknesses.

### INSTRUCTIONS

Step 1    Join with two other individuals to form a three-person team. Develop a team IFE Matrix for your university. You may use the strengths/weaknesses determined in Experiential Exercise 1D.

Step 2    Go to the board and diagram your team's IFE Matrix.

Step 3    Compare your team's IFE Matrix to other teams' IFE Matrices. Discuss any major differences.

Step 4    What strategies do you think would allow your university to capitalize on its major strengths? What strategies would allow your university to improve upon its major weaknesses?

# 5 STRATEGIES IN ACTION

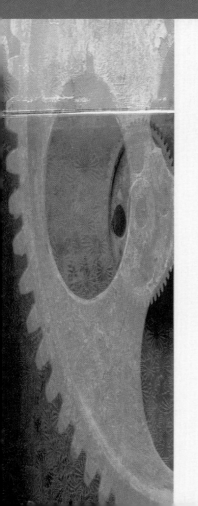

## CHAPTER OUTLINE

## CHAPTER OBJECTIVES

*After studying this chapter, you should be able to do the following:*

1. Discuss the value of establishing long-term objectives.
2. Identify sixteen types of business strategies.
3. Identify numerous examples of organizations pursuing different types of strategies.
4. Discuss guidelines when particular strategies are most appropriate to pursue.
5. Discuss Porter's generic strategies.
6. Describe strategic management in nonprofit, governmental, and small organizations.
7. Discuss joint ventures as a way to enter the Russian market.

# NOTABLE QUOTES

Alice said, "Would you please tell me which way to go from here?" The cat said, "That depends on where you want to get to."

LEWIS CARROLL

Tomorrow always arrives. It is always different. And even the mightiest company is in trouble if it has not worked on the future. Being surprised by what happens is a risk that even the largest and richest company cannot afford, and even the smallest business need not run.

PETER DRUCKER

Planning. Doing things today to make us better tomorrow. Because the future belongs to those who make the hard decisions today.

EATON CORPORATION

By taking over companies and breaking them up, corporate raiders thrive on failed corporate strategies. Fueled by junk bond financing and growing acceptability, raiders can expose any company to takeover, no matter how large or blue chip.

MICHAEL PORTER

One big problem with American business is that when it gets into trouble, it redoubles its effort. It's like digging for gold. If you dig down twenty feet and haven't found it, one of the strategies you could use is to dig twice as deep. But if the gold is twenty feet to the side, you could dig a long time and not find it.

EDWARD DE BONO

If you don't invest for the long term, there is no short term.

GEORGE DAVID

Innovate or evaporate. Particularly in technology-driven businesses, nothing quite recedes like success.

BILL SAPORITO

Hundreds of companies today, including Sears, IBM, Searle, and Hewlett-Packard, have embraced strategic planning fully in their quest for higher revenues and profits. Kent Nelson, chair of UPS, explains why his company has created a new strategic planning department: "Because we're making bigger bets on investments in technology, we can't afford to spend a whole lot of money in one direction and then find out 5 years later it was the wrong direction."[1]

This chapter brings strategic management to life with many contemporary examples. Sixteen types of strategies are defined and exemplified, including Michael Porter's generic strategies: cost leadership, differentiation, and focus. Guidelines are presented for determining when different types of strategies are most appropriate to pursue. An overview of strategic management in nonprofit organizations, governmental agencies, and small firms is provided.

 # LONG-TERM OBJECTIVES

*Long-term objectives* represent the results expected from pursuing certain strategies. Strategies represent the actions to be taken to accomplish long-term objectives. The time frame for objectives and strategies should be consistent, usually from two to five years.

## The Nature of Long-Term Objectives

Objectives should be quantitative, measurable, realistic, understandable, challenging, hierarchical, obtainable, and congruent among organizational units. Each objective should also be associated with a time line. Objectives are commonly stated in terms such as growth in assets, growth in sales, profitability, market share, degree and nature of diversification, degree and nature of vertical integration, earnings per share, and social responsibility. Clearly established objectives offer many benefits. They provide direction, allow synergy, aid in evaluation, establish priorities, reduce uncertainty, minimize conflicts, stimulate exertion, and aid in both the allocation of resources and the design of jobs.

Long-term objectives are needed at the corporate, divisional, and functional levels in an organization. They are an important measure of managerial performance. Many practitioners and academicians attribute a significant part of U.S. industry's competitive decline to the short-term, rather than long-term, strategy orientation of managers in the United States. Arthur D. Little argues that bonuses or merit pay for managers today must be based to a greater extent on long-term objectives and strategies. A general framework for relating objectives to performance evaluation is provided in Table 5–1. A particular organization could tailor these guidelines to meet its own needs, but incentives should be attached to both long-term and annual objectives.

TABLE 5-1    **Varying Performance Measures by Organizational Level**

| ORGANIZATIONAL LEVEL | BASIS FOR ANNUAL BONUS OR MERIT PAY |
|---|---|
| Corporate | 75% based on long-term objectives |
|  | 25% based on annual objectives |
| Division | 50% based on long-term objectives |
|  | 50% based on annual objectives |
| Function | 25% based on long-term objectives |
|  | 75% based on annual objectives |

Clearly stated and communicated objectives are vital to success for many reasons. First, objectives help stakeholders understand their role in an organization's future. They also provide a basis for consistent decision making by managers whose values and attitudes differ. By reaching a consensus on objectives during strategy-formulation activities, an organization can minimize potential conflicts later during implementation. Objectives set forth organizational priorities and stimulate exertion and accomplishment. They serve as standards by which individuals, groups, departments, divisions, and entire organizations can be evaluated. Objectives provide the basis for designing jobs and organizing activities to be performed in an organization. They also provide direction and allow for organizational synergy.

Without long-term objectives, an organization would drift aimlessly toward some unknown end! It is hard to imagine an organization or individual being successful without clear objectives. Success only rarely occurs by accident; rather, it is the result of hard work directed toward achieving certain objectives.

## Not Managing by Objectives

An unknown educator once said, "If you think education is expensive, try ignorance." The idea behind this saying also applies to establishing objectives. Strategists should avoid the following alternative ways to "not managing by objectives."

- Managing by Extrapolation—adheres to the principle "If it ain't broke, don't fix it." The idea is to keep on doing about the same things in the same ways because things are going well.

- Managing by Crisis—based on the belief that the true measure of a really good strategist is the ability to solve problems. Because there are plenty of crises and problems to go around for every person and every organization, strategists ought to bring their time and creative energy to bear on solving the most pressing problems of the day. Managing by crisis is actually a form of reacting rather than acting and of letting events dictate the whats and whens of management decisions.

- Managing by Subjectives—built on the idea that there is no general plan for which way to go and what to do; just do the best you can to accomplish what you think should be done. In short, "Do your own thing, the best way you know how" (sometimes referred to as *the mystery approach to decision making* because subordinates are left to figure out what is happening and why).

- Managing by Hope—based on the fact that the future is laden with great uncertainty, and that if we try and do not succeed, then we hope our second (or third) attempt will succeed. Decisions are predicted on the hope that they will work and the good times are just around the corner, especially if luck and good fortune are on our side![2]

 ## TYPES OF STRATEGIES

The model illustrated in Figure 5–1 provides a conceptual basis for applying strategic management. Defined and exemplified in Table 5–2, alternative strategies that an enterprise could pursue can be categorized into thirteen actions—forward integration, backward integration, horizontal integration, market penetration, market development, product development, concentric diversification, conglomerate diversification, horizontal diversification, joint venture, retrenchment, divestiture, and liquidation—and a combination strategy. Each alternative strategy has countless variations. For example, market penetration can include adding salespersons, increasing advertising expenditures, couponing, and using similar actions to increase market share in a given geographic area.

**FIGURE 5–1**

**A Comprehensive Strategic-Management Model**

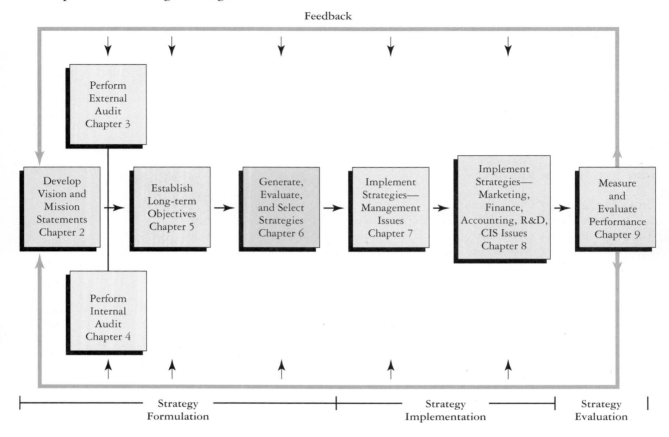

 INTEGRATION STRATEGIES

Forward integration, backward integration, and horizontal integration are sometimes collectively referred to as *vertical integration* strategies. Vertical integration strategies allow a firm to gain control over distributors, suppliers, and/or competitors.

### Forward Integration

*Forward integration* involves gaining ownership or increased control over distributors or retailers. Increasing numbers of manufacturers (suppliers) today are pursuing a forward integration strategy by establishing Web sites to sell products directly to consumers. This strategy is causing turmoil in some industries. For example, Home Depot recently warned its suppliers not to compete with them in selling products online. Many manufacturers are reluctant to offend their distributors (retailers) by selling online, but low relative costs in selling online versus retail stores makes forward integration a very tempting strategy for many suppliers. Manufacturer Joe Boxer sells underwear on Macy's Web site, but this degree of cooperation between supplier and distributor is the exception rather than the rule. Online sales are projected to increase from $18 billion in 1999 to $108 billion by 2003.[3]

**e·biz**

TABLE 5-2    Alternative Strategies Defined and Exemplified

| STRATEGY | DEFINITION | EXAMPLE |
|---|---|---|
| Forward Integration | Gaining ownership or increased control over distributors or retailers | General Motors is acquiring 10 percent of its dealers. |
| Backward Integration | Seeking ownership or increased control of a firm's suppliers | Motel-8 acquired a furniture manufacturer. |
| Horizontal Integration | Seeking ownership or increased control over competitors | Hilton recently acquired Promus. |
| Market Penetration | Seeking increased market share for present products or services in present markets through greater marketing efforts | Ameritrade, the online broker, tripled its annual advertising expenditures to $200 million to convince people they can make their own investment decisions. |
| Market Development | Introducing present products or services into new geographic area | Britain's leading supplier of buses, Henlys PLC, acquires Blue Bird Corp., North America's leading school bus maker. |
| Product Development | Seeking increased sales by improving present products or services or developing new ones | Apple developed the G4 chip that runs at 500 megahertz. |
| Concentric Diversification | Adding new, but related, products or services | National Westminister Bank PLC in Britain buys the leading British insurance company, Legal & General Group PLC. |
| Conglomerate Diversification | Adding new, unrelated products or services | H&R Block, the top tax preparation agency, said it will buy discount stock brokerage Olde Financial for $850 million in cash. |
| Horizontal Diversification | Adding new, unrelated products or services for present customers | The New York Yankees baseball team is merging with the New Jersey Nets basketball team. |
| Joint Venture | Two or more sponsoring firms forming a separate organization for cooperative purposes | Lucent Technologies and Philips Electronics NV formed Philips Consumer Communications to make and sell telephones. |
| Retrenchment | Regrouping through cost and asset reduction to reverse declining sales and profit | Singer, the sewing machine maker, declared bankruptcy. |
| Divestiture | Selling a division or part of an organization | Harcourt General, the large U.S. publisher, selling its Neiman Marcus division. |
| Liquidation | Selling all of a company's assets, in parts, for their tangible worth | Ribol sold all its assets and ceases business. |

The external threat of online sales, perhaps from suppliers, eroding its catalog market share is a primary reason why L.L. Bean recently opened its first full-line retail store in eighty-seven years. The store is located in McLean, Virginia. L.L. Bean is pursuing forward integration out of concern that online stores opening up by the nanosecond will further erode catalog sales, which are slowing. Other catalog retailers such as Delia's and J. Jill also are opening retail stores for the first time in their history.

Brick-and-mortar retailers such as Wal-Mart, Sharper Image, and The Right Start are rapidly combating the purely online retailers by mobilizing a multi-channel attack selling via stores and the Internet. Many traditional retailers are adding catalogs too and offering auctions to further enhance their distribution network. www.Wal-Mart.com is aimed at becoming the leading Internet discounter. Even Amway in 1999 launched a new online division named Quixtar to sell its and other companies' products. "We're looking at the biggest change in forty years," said Amway executive Ken McDonald.

**e·biz**

Amway's sales force continues to sell products to friends and family but now also has the option to sell products online for Quixtar. As indicated in the E-Commerce Perspective, online sales are tax-free; note this is a highly controversial topic in business today.

IBM recently halted distribution of its desktop computers through retailers because it loses money on every desktop it sells through retailers. Now CompUSA, Best Buy, and Circuit City stores for example no longer carry the IBM desktops. IBM plans to replace this distribution outlet with its own online distribution system.

An effective means of implementing forward integration is *franchising*. Approximately two thousand companies in about fifty different industries in the United States use franchising to distribute their products or services. Businesses can expand rapidly by franchising because costs and opportunities are spread among many individuals. Total sales by franchises in the United States are about $1 trillion annually.

Six guidelines when forward integration may be an especially effective strategy are:[4]

- When an organization's present distributors are especially expensive, or unreliable, or incapable of meeting the firm's distribution needs
- When the availability of quality distributors is so limited as to offer a competitive advantage to those firms that integrate forward
- When an organization competes in an industry that is growing and is expected to continue to grow markedly; this is a factor because forward integration reduces an organization's ability to diversify if its basic industry falters
- When an organization has both the capital and human resources needed to manage the new business of distributing its own products
- When the advantages of stable production are particularly high; this is a consideration because an organization can increase the predictability of the demand for its output through forward integration
- When present distributors or retailers have high profit margins; this situation suggests that a company profitably could distribute its own products and price them more competitively by integrating forward

## Backward Integration

Both manufacturers and retailers purchase needed materials from suppliers. *Backward integration* is a strategy of seeking ownership or increased control of a firm's suppliers. This strategy can be especially appropriate when a firm's current suppliers are unreliable, too costly, or cannot meet the firm's needs.

When you buy a box of Pampers diapers at Wal-Mart, a scanner at the store's checkout counter instantly zaps an order to Procter & Gamble Company. In contrast, in most hospitals, reordering supplies is a logistics nightmare. Inefficiency caused by lack of control of suppliers in the health-care industry is, however, rapidly changing as many giant health-care purchasers, such as the Defense Department and Columbia/HCA Healthcare Corporation, move to require electronic bar codes on every supply item purchased. This allows instant tracking and reordering without invoices and paperwork. Of the estimated $83 billion spent annually on hospital supplies, industry reports indicate that $11 billion can be eliminated through more effective backward integration.

Some industries in the United States (such as the automotive and aluminum industries) are reducing their historical pursuit of backward integration. Instead of owning their suppliers, companies negotiate with several outside suppliers. Ford and Chrysler buy over half of their components parts from outside suppliers such as TRW, Eaton, General Electric, and Johnson Controls. Deintegration makes sense in industries that have global sources of supply. *Outsourcing,* whereby companies use outside suppliers, shop around, play one seller against another, and go with the best deal, is becoming widely practiced. Small steel manufacturers such as Arrowhead Steel Company and Worthington Steel Company

## E-COMMERCE PERSPECTIVE

### *Should Internet Sales Remain Tax Free?*

Currently nobody pays sales taxes when they buy books, clothing, cars, or anything else on the Internet. The average sales tax nationwide is 6.3 percent, so lack of any tax on Internet sales means that state and local governments are giving E-business a huge subsidy. Currently about 49 percent of all state tax revenues are from sales taxes, more than individual and corporate taxes combined. Those revenues are used for schools, law enforcement, highway repair, and other work of governments. Traditional retail stores argue that it will soon be impossible for them to compete with E-tailers if Internet sales remain tax free.

A thorny question thus looms on the horizon in terms of whether to tax Internet sales. With online sales rising 300 percent a year and topping $200 billion in 2000 and $1 trillion in 2003, advocates pro and con debate whether those sales taxes should go uncollected. The national moratorium on new Internet taxes expires in October 2001. Grover Norquist, president of Americans for Tax Reform, says, "Any business guy stupid enough to participate in leading the charge to tax the Internet is going to find that tax named after him or his company." And surely no state or federal legislator wants an Internet tax named for them.

Some considerations and contentions regarding taxing Internet sales are as follows:

- Keeping Internet sales tax-free will help the economy grow faster.
- Traditional merchants contend that online shopping with no sales tax robs them of customers.
- Local and state governments contend those sales tax dollars are needed for schools and public safety.
- Americans may buy from foreign companies if sales taxes are imposed on Internet shopping.
- Consumers in other countries may bypass U.S. products if sales taxes are imposed.
- Imposing a sales tax on Internet shopping will slow growth of Internet shopping, thus hurting online businesses.
- Neither state nor federal legislators want to be responsible for tax increases.
- Currently there are over sixty-six hundred sales tax jurisdictions in the United States; taxing Internet sales could logistically be a nightmare for interstate retailers who would have to calculate these rates.
- Research concludes that online spending would drop by 30 percent or more if taxes were suddenly imposed. This would cripple many marginal Internet businesses.

*Source:* Adapted from: Mike France, "A Web Sales Tax: Not If, But When," *Business Week* (June 21, 1999): 104–106. Also, Richard Wolf, "Taxes on Internet Sales Opposed," *USA Today* (September 14, 1999): 6A.

---

are pursuing backward integration today through use of the Internet. Owners of most small steel firms now click on Web sites such as MetalSite LP, based in Pittsburgh, or e-Steel Corporation, based in New York, to find the lowest-priced supplier of scrap steel that they need. These two sites give buyers and sellers of steel the opportunity to trade, buy, and sell metal from a variety of companies. Many steel companies now have Web sites to capitalize on backward integration opportunities in the industry, but the largest steel producer in the United States, USX-U.S. Steel Group, does not have a Web site and does not use sites such as MetalSite or e-Steel. Historically the steel industry has been notoriously slow to embrace change, but its rush into cyberspace has been remarkable.[5]

Global competition also is spurring firms to reduce their number of suppliers and to demand higher levels of service and quality from those they keep. Although traditionally relying on many suppliers to ensure uninterrupted supplies and low prices, American firms now are following the lead of Japanese firms, which have far fewer suppliers and closer, long-term relationships with those few. "Keeping track of so many suppliers is onerous," says Mark Shimelonis of Xerox.

Seven guidelines when backward integration may be an especially effective strategy are:[6]

- When an organization's present suppliers are especially expensive, or unreliable, or incapable of meeting the firm's needs for parts, components, assemblies, or raw materials
- When the number of suppliers is small and the number of competitors is large
- When an organization competes in an industry that is growing rapidly; this is a factor because integrative-type strategies (forward, backward, and horizontal) reduce an organization's ability to diversify in a declining industry
- When an organization has both capital and human resources to manage the new business of supplying its own raw materials
- When the advantages of stable prices are particularly important; this is a factor because an organization can stabilize the cost of its raw materials and the associated price of its product through backward integration
- When present supplies have high profit margins, which suggests that the business of supplying products or services in the given industry is a worthwhile venture
- When an organization needs to acquire a needed resource quickly

### Horizontal Integration

*Horizontal integration* refers to a strategy of seeking ownership of or increased control over a firm's competitors. One of the most significant trends in strategic management today is the increased use of horizontal integration as a growth strategy. Mergers, acquisitions, and takeovers among competitors allow for increased economies of scale and enhanced transfer of resources and competencies. Kenneth Davidson makes the following observation about horizontal integration:

> The trend towards horizontal integration seems to reflect strategists' misgivings about their ability to operate many unrelated businesses. Mergers between direct competitors are more likely to create efficiencies than mergers between unrelated businesses, both because there is a greater potential for eliminating duplicate facilities and because the management of the acquiring firm is more likely to understand the business of the target.[7]

**e·biz**

Horizontal integration has become the most favored growth strategy in many industries. For example, explosive growth in e-commerce has telecommunications firms worldwide frantically merging, pursuing horizontal integration to gain competitiveness. Telecommunications mergers occur almost weekly. The largest 1999/1998 telecommunications mergers are as follows: MCI WorldCom purchased Sprint for $127.27 billion, SBC Communications purchased Ameritech for $72.36 billion, Bell Atlantic purchased GTE for $71.32 billion, Vodafone Group purchased AirTouch Communications for $65.90 billion, Qwest Communications purchased US West for $48.48 billion, Olivetti purchased Telecom Italia for $34.76 billion, and Mannesmann purchased Orange for $30 billion.

Five guidelines when horizontal integration may be an especially effective strategy are:[8]

- When an organization can gain monopolistic characteristics in a particular area or region without being challenged by the federal government for "tending substantially" to reduce competition
- When an organization competes in a growing industry
- When increased economies of scale provide major competitive advantages
- When an organization has both the capital and human talent needed to successfully manage an expanded organization

- When competitors are faltering due to a lack of managerial expertise or a need for particular resources that an organization possesses; note that horizontal integration would not be appropriate if competitors are doing poorly because overall industry sales are declining

#  INTENSIVE STRATEGIES

Market penetration, market development, and product development are sometimes referred to as *intensive strategies* because they require intensive efforts to improve a firm's competitive position with existing products.

## Market Penetration

A *market-penetration* strategy seeks to increase market share for present products or services in present markets through greater marketing efforts. This strategy is widely used alone and in combination with other strategies. Market penetration includes increasing the number of salespersons, increasing advertising expenditures, offering extensive sales promotion items, or increasing publicity efforts. Five guidelines when market penetration may be an especially effective strategy are:[9]

- When current markets are not saturated with a particular product or service
- When the usage rate of present customers could be increased significantly
- When the market shares of major competitors have been declining while total industry sales have been increasing
- When the correlation between dollar sales and dollar marketing expenditures historically has been high
- When increased economies of scale provide major competitive advantages

## Market Development

*Market development* involves introducing present products or services into new geographic areas. The climate for international market development is becoming more favorable. In many industries, such as airlines, it is going to be hard to maintain a competitive edge by staying close to home.

Carolina Power & Light recently purchased Florida Progress, moving into the fast-growing Florida market for the first time. The acquisition doubled the size of CP&L, which now is the nation's ninth-largest energy utility company.

Swedish retailer Hennes & Mauritz AB recently entered the U.S. market by opening two store locations in Manhattan. Hennes & Mauritz operates 120 department stores in Sweden and 400 more elsewhere in Europe. The company sells discount "hip and fashionable" clothing and plans to open more stores in U.S. malls.

Marks & Spencer PLC, Britain's biggest retailer, is expanding its Brooks Brothers clothing chain internationally into the rest of Europe. There are currently 225 Brooks Brothers stores in the Britain, the United States, Japan, Hong Kong, and Taiwan. Brooks Brothers stores mainly sell formal clothing, although casual clothes now are being offered given the trend worldwide towards a more casual look at work.

Walt Disney Company is building a new theme park in Hong Kong valued at over $3 billion. The new park, a "scaled-down" version of Disney's classic Magic Kingdom park complete with Main Street and Cinderella's castle, is being built on Lantau Island near Hong Kong's new international airport.

Federal Express Corporation is expanding throughout Europe in much greater force than previously through a new delivery service called Euro One. The company is adding many more cargo flights to European cities, approaching two hundred daily by the year 2000. All of these strategies, from CP&L to Fed Ex, are market-development strategies.

Six guidelines when market development may be an especially effective strategy are:[10]

- When new channels of distribution are available that are reliable, inexpensive, and of good quality
- When an organization is very successful at what it does
- When new untapped or unsaturated markets exist
- When an organization has the needed capital and human resources to manage expanded operations
- When an organization has excess production capacity
- When an organization's basic industry rapidly is becoming global in scope

### Product Development

*Product development* is a strategy that seeks increased sales by improving or modifying present products or services. Product development usually entails large research and development expenditures. The U.S. Postal Service now offers stamps and postage via the Internet, which represents a product development strategy. Called PC Postage, stamps can now be obtained online from various Web sites such as www.stamps.com and then printed on an ordinary laser or inkjet printer. E-Stamp Corporation, Neopost, and Pitney Bowes, too, are actively pursuing product development by creating their own versions of digital stamps.

**e·biz**

Volkswagen is developing a pickup truck to compete in this fast-growing market. Volkswagen is on a roll in the United States, with 1999 first half sales up 44.6 percent over a year ago. Volkswagen's CEO Ferdinand Piech says VW will strive for "the comfort of a passenger car in a pickup truck that allows a high payload."

Five guidelines when product development may be an especially effective strategy to pursue are:[11]

- When an organization has successful products that are in the maturity stage of the product life cycle; the idea here is to attract satisfied customers to try new (improved) products as a result of their positive experience with the organization's present products or services
- When an organization competes in an industry that is characterized by rapid technological developments
- When major competitors offer better-quality products at comparable prices
- When an organization competes in a high-growth industry
- When an organization has especially strong research and development capabilities

As indicated in the Natural Environment Perspective, a decreasing number of firms appear to be actively developing green products—in response to an alarming decline in consumer interest in such efforts.

 ## DIVERSIFICATION STRATEGIES

There are three general types of *diversification strategies:* concentric, horizontal, and conglomerate. Overall, diversification strategies are becoming less popular as organizations are finding it more difficult to manage diverse business activities. In the 1960s and

# NATURAL ENVIRONMENT

### *Is Consumer Concern for Environmental Matters Declining?*

Americans are not as vigilant about environmentally driven purchases as they used to be, partly because they feel businesses are making changes. There is a declining willingness among consumers to spend extra money on green products. The only natural environment activity that has gained support in recent years has been recycling, but even this activity may be waning as supply/demand/price relationships hinder company and community efforts.

The national recycling rate for all products in the United States reached 27 percent in 1995, up from only 7 percent in 1970. Many states such as Indiana, California, Colorado, and New York have a goal to recycle 5 percent of their trash by the year 2000. Many communities find costs four times as much to collect and process recyclables as it does to dump trash in landfills. More trucks and more sorting plants also add to pollution. Professors at Carnegie Mellon University recently concluded that recycling benefits the environment, but at too high a cost.

Other environmental activities such as avoiding restaurants using Styrofoam, avoiding ecologically irresponsible companies, buying refillable packages, buying products made of recycled materials, using biodegradable soaps, avoiding aerosol and reading labels for environmental impacts have less support today than in 1990. The percentage of American adults who care nothing at all about the natural environment has risen from 20 percent in 1990 to 37 percent today. Research suggests that consumers' buying habits are increasingly determined by past experience, price, brand recognition, others' recommendations, and convenience rather than environmental impact. Although Americans do not shop with environmental purpose as they once did, they have internalized deep concerns for the welfare of earth's living plants and animals. Indirect, displaced, and often hidden costs, such as pain and suffering associated with pollution, far exceed direct costs such as cleanup and equipment.

*Source:* Adapted from Tibbett Speer, "Growing the Green Market," *American Demographics,* (August 1997): 45–50; and Laura Litvan, "Has Recycling Reached Its Limit?" *Investors Business Daily* (August 1997): 1.

1970s, the trend was to diversify so as not to be dependent on any single industry, but the 1980s saw a general reversal of that thinking. Diversification is now on the retreat. Michael Porter of the Harvard Business School says, "Management found they couldn't manage the beast." Hence, businesses are selling, or closing, less profitable divisions in order to focus on core businesses.

There are, however, a few companies today that pride themselves on being a conglomerate, from small firms such as Pentair Inc. and Blount International to huge companies such as Textron, Allied Signal, Emerson Electric, General Electric, and Viacom. Viacom's recent acquisition of CBS for $36 billion has turned Viacom into an $80 billion company with diverse assets in broadcast and cable television, movies, radio, theme parks, Internet sites, home video, publishing, and billboards. Similarly, Textron, through numerous diverse acquisitions, now produces and sells Cessna airplanes, Bell helicopters, Jacobsen lawn mowers, golf products, transmissions, consumer loans, and telescopic machinery. Conglomerates prove that focus and diversity are not always mutually exclusive.

Peters and Waterman's advice to firms is to "stick to the knitting" and not to stray too far from the firm's basic areas of competence. However, diversification is still an appropriate and successful strategy sometimes. Hamish Maxwell, Philip Morris's CEO, says, "We want to become a consumer-products company." Diversification makes sense for Philip Morris because cigarette consumption is declining, product liability suits are a risk, and some investors reject tobacco stocks on principle. In a diversification move, Philip Morris spent $12.9 billion in a hostile takeover of Kraft General Foods, the world's second-largest food producer behind Nestlé.

## Concentric Diversification

Adding new, but related, products or services is widely called *concentric diversification.* An example of this strategy is AT&T recently spending $120 billion acquiring cable television companies in order to wire America with fast Internet service over cable rather than telephone lines. AT&T's concentric diversification strategy has led the firm into talks with American Online (AOL) about a possible joint venture or merger to provide AOL customers cable access to the Internet.

Walt Disney recently used concentric diversification when it acquired the Internet search engine Infoseek. About the acquisition, Disney CEO Michael Eisner said, "Our products, our movies, sports and news all have to be delivered to the home and will be delivered via broadband lines from cable, TV or satellite. We want to be in control of our destinations. We want to control our films, products, and entertainment."[12]

The Ritz Carlton Hotel Company is entering the timeshare industry by building two resorts in the Virgin Islands and near Aspen, Colorado. Named Ritz Carlton Clubs, this concentric diversification strategy targets buyers with incomes of $150,000 and above. Ritz Carlton is based in Atlanta and is owned by Marriott International.

Six guidelines when concentric diversification may be an effective strategy are provided below:[13]

- When an organization competes in a no-growth or a slow-growth industry
- When adding new, but related, products significantly would enhance the sales of current products
- When new, but related, products could be offered at highly competitive prices
- When new, but related, products have seasonal sales levels that counterbalance an organization's existing peaks and valleys
- When an organization's products are currently in the decline stage of the product life cycle
- When an organization has a strong management team

## Horizontal Diversification

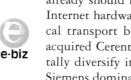

Adding new, unrelated products or services for present customers is called *horizontal diversification.* This strategy is not as risky as conglomerate diversification because a firm already should be familiar with its present customers. For example, Cisco Systems, an Internet hardware company, is pursuing horizontal diversification by entering the optical transport business, which is moving data over fiber-optic lines. Cisco recently acquired Cerent for $6.9 billion and Monterey Networks for $500 million to horizontally diversify itself. Major competitors such as Lucent, Nortel Networks, Alcatel, and Siemens dominate the optical transport business. At the time Cisco purchased Cerent in mid-1999, Cerent had been in business only 2.5 years, had posted only $10 million in sales, and never had made a profit.

Amazon, the huge online bookstore, is pursuing horizontal diversification with an aggressive entry into the toys and consumer electronics business. You may now purchase camcorders, cameras, DVD players, televisions, and toys from three hundred manufacturers from the amazon.com Web site. Unlike its policy with books, Amazon will reimburse shipping and handling costs on returned toy and electronics items.

Dutch publisher, VNU, recently horizontally diversified by acquiring the United States' number-one television ratings service, Nielsen Media Research for $2.5 billion. VNU owns magazines such as *The Hollywood Reporter, ADWeek, Mediaweek,* and *Billboard.* With this acquisition, VNU now owns NetRatings, which is a leading collector and disseminator of information about television and Internet viewing habits.

Four guidelines when horizontal diversification may be an especially effective strategy are:[14]

- When revenues derived from an organization's current products or services would increase significantly by adding the new, unrelated products
- When an organization competes in a highly competitive and/or a no-growth industry, as indicated by low industry profit margins and returns
- When an organization's present channels of distribution can be used to market the new products to current customers
- When the new products have countercyclical sales patterns compared to an organization's present products

## Conglomerate Diversification

Adding new, unrelated products or services is called *conglomerate diversification*. Some firms pursue conglomerate diversification based in part on an expectation of profits from breaking up acquired firms and selling divisions piecemeal. Richard West, dean of New York University's School of Business, says, "The stock market is rewarding deconglomerations, saying company assets are worth more separately than together. There is a kind of antisynergy, the whole being worth less than the parts."

Electric utilities across the United States are diversifying into a broad range of unrelated businesses that include plumbing, heating and air-conditioning repair, telephone service, home-security services, and natural gas.[15] Historically low margins coupled with the trend towards residential and commercial customers purchasing their own free-standing power source has spurred this diversification. Between 1995 and 2000, there were more than twenty-five acquisitions of natural-gas companies by electric utilities in the United States with a total value of over $30 billion.

Reader's Digest is pursuing conglomerate diversification by launching a gift-selling business on the Internet. This is the company's first foray into electronic commerce and offers such brands as Burberry clothing and Lenox china at the Web site www.gifts.com. This new business faces tough competition from Amazon.com, CDNow, and other established online gift-sellers.

**e·biz**

Federated Department Stores, which operates Macy's and Bloomingdale's, as well as Nordstrom, each have a conglomerate diversification strategic plan to convert their credit card subsidiaries into full-fledged banks.

The National Basketball Association (NBA) recently launched its own twenty-four-hour television network called NBA.com TV. This diversification strategy is the first time a major sports league has created a television channel successfully. Viewers can get access to about forty NBA games per week and more for about $150 per season. The television network is designed to supplement the NBA's existing coverage on broadcast and cable channels for the most ardent basketball fans.

Six guidelines when conglomerate diversification may be an especially effective strategy to pursue are listed below:[16]

- When an organization's basic industry is experiencing declining annual sales and profits
- When an organization has the capital and managerial talent needed to compete successfully in a new industry
- When an organization has the opportunity to purchase an unrelated business that is an attractive investment opportunity
- When there exists financial synergy between the acquired and acquiring firm; note that a key difference between concentric and conglomerate diversification is that the former should be based on some commonality in markets, products, or technology, whereas the latter should be based more on profit considerations
- When existing markets for an organization's present products are saturated
- When antitrust action could be charged against an organization that historically has concentrated on a single industry

General Electric is a classic firm that is highly diversified. GE makes locomotives, lightbulbs, power plants, and refrigerators; GE manages more credit cards than American Express; GE owns more commercial aircraft than American Airlines.

## DEFENSIVE STRATEGIES

In addition to integrative, intensive, and diversification strategies, organizations also could pursue retrenchment, divestiture, or liquidation.

### Retrenchment

*Retrenchment* occurs when an organization regroups through cost and asset reduction to reverse declining sales and profits. Sometimes called a turnaround or reorganizational strategy, retrenchment is designed to fortify an organization's basic distinctive competence. During retrenchment, strategists work with limited resources and face pressure from shareholders, employees, and the media. Retrenchment can entail selling off land and buildings to raise needed cash, pruning product lines, closing marginal businesses, closing obsolete factories, automating processes, reducing the number of employees, and instituting expense control systems.

United Technologies' Pratt & Whitney aircraft-engine division is an example company using a retrenchment today by cutting its workforce 6.8 percent including fifteen hundred employees. Pratt & Whitney is moving much of its West Palm Beach, Florida, and North Haven, Connecticut, operations to other locations. By the end of 2000, Pratt & Whitney plans to cut its total floor space from fifteen to twelve million square feet and to offer transfers to thousands of employees.

Glaxo Wellcome, the world's second-largest drugmaker, is cutting thirty-four hundred jobs amounting to 6 percent of its global workforce in 2000 to retrench and streamline.

The U.S. Postal Service expects to close many of its thirty-eight thousand post offices nationwide or reduce hours over the next decade as online transactions for sending and paying bills is expected to reduce first class mail dramatically beginning in 2003.[17] First-class mail volume will peak in 2002 and then decline at an annual rate of 2.5 percent from 2003 to 2008. Advertisers shifting their business to the Internet from bulk mailings also contributes to the Postal Service considering a retrenchment strategy for the future.

In some cases, *bankruptcy* can be an effective type of retrenchment strategy. Bankruptcy can allow a firm to avoid major debt obligations and to void union contracts. There are five major types of bankruptcy: Chapter 7, Chapter 9, Chapter 11, Chapter 12, and Chapter 13.

*Chapter 7 bankruptcy* is a liquidation procedure used only when a corporation sees no hope of being able to operate successfully or to obtain the necessary creditor agreement. All the organization's assets are sold in parts for their tangible worth.

*Chapter 9 bankruptcy* applies to municipalities. The most recent municipality successfully declaring bankruptcy is Camden, New Jersey, the state's poorest city and the fifth-poorest city in the United States. A crime-ridden city of eighty-seven thousand, Camden received $62.5 million in state aid and has withdrawn its bankruptcy petition. Between 1980 and 2000, only eighteen U.S. cities declared bankruptcy. Some states do not allow municipalities to declare bankruptcy.

*Chapter 11 bankruptcy* allows organizations to reorganize and come back after filing a petition for protection. Filene Basement Corporation in Massachusetts and Loehmann's

Inc. of New York were among numerous discount retailers that recently declared Chapter 11 bankruptcy. Suppliers of clothing to discount retailers are increasingly opening their own outlets which, coupled with competition from large discount retailers such as Wal-Mart, are squeezing smaller discount retailers.

Vencor recently declared bankruptcy. Vencor is the largest long-term health-care company in the United States operating three hundred nursing homes and more than sixty long-term care hospitals.

London Fog Industries recently filed for Chapter 11 bankruptcy, too, and will lay-off four hundred employees. London Fog's late 1990s strategy to build retail stores in competition with its traditional distributors failed.

*Chapter 12 bankruptcy* was created by the Family Farmer Bankruptcy Act of 1986. This law became effective in 1987 and provides special relief to family farmers with debt equal to or less than $1.5 million.

*Chapter 13 bankruptcy* is a reorganization plan similar to Chapter 11 but available only to small businesses owned by individuals with unsecured debts of less than $100,000 and secured debts of less than $350,000. The Chapter 13 debtor is allowed to operate the business while a plan is being developed to provide for the successful operation of the business in the future.

Five guidelines when retrenchment may be an especially effective strategy to pursue are as follows:[18]

- When an organization has a clearly distinctive competence, but has failed to meet its objectives and goals consistently over time
- When an organization is one of the weaker competitors in a given industry
- When an organization is plagued by inefficiency, low profitability, poor employee morale, and pressure from stockholders to improve performance
- When an organization has failed to capitalize on external opportunities, minimize external threats, take advantage of internal strengths, and overcome internal weaknesses over time; that is, when the organization's strategic managers have failed (and possibly will be replaced by more competent individuals)
- When an organization has grown so large so quickly that major internal reorganization is needed

## Divestiture

Selling a division or part of an organization is called *divestiture.* Divestiture often is used to raise capital for further strategic acquisitions or investments. Divestiture can be part of an overall retrenchment strategy to rid an organization of businesses that are unprofitable, that require too much capital, or that do not fit well with the firm's other activities. An example company using divestiture as a primary strategy is Walt Disney which recently divested its Fairchild Publications division that publishes *Women's Wear Daily, Jane,* and *W.* Disney also is actively trying to divest of its Anaheim Angels baseball team and its Anaheim Mighty Ducks hockey franchises. Other Walt Disney divisions rumored to soon be divested include Disney Stores, ESPN Zone, Disney Quest, and Club Disneys.

AutoNation, the nation's largest auto dealership chain, plans to divest National Car Rental, Alamo Rent-A-Car, and CarTemps USA. AutoNation had originally acquired the rental car companies to help its used-car superstore chain get a steady supply of vehicles, but this strategy was not working well.

The Burlington, Ontario, company Laidlaw, Inc. is divesting its waste-management operations, including Safety-Kleen in Columbia, South Carolina. Laidlaw is also divesting its ambulance operations, including its EmCare division, which manages U.S. hospital emergency rooms.

Microsoft recently divested its Internet travel division, Expedia. Expedia had a $20 million loss in fiscal 1999 and today operates as a free-standing company. Kellogg Company recently divested Lender's Bagels.

Divestiture has become a very popular strategy as firms try to focus on their core strengths, lessening their level of diversification. For example retailer Venator Group, formerly Woolworth, in 1999 divested eight divisions in order to become solely an athletic footwear and apparel company. The eight divisions were: Music Box, Randy River, Foot Locker Outlets, Colorado U.S., Team Edition, Going to the Game, Weekend Edition, and Burger King. Venator several years ago was a $4.6 billion conglomerate before CEO Farah divested thirty-five of Venator's forty-two divisions, including all Woolworth and Kinney Shoe stores. A few divestitures consummated in 2000 are given in Table 5–3.

Six guidelines when divestiture may be an especially effective strategy to pursue are listed below[19]:

- When an organization has pursued a retrenchment strategy and it failed to accomplish needed improvements
- When a division needs more resources to be competitive than the company can provide
- When a division is responsible for an organization's overall poor performance
- When a division is a misfit with the rest of an organization; this can result from radically different markets, customers, managers, employees, values, or needs

### TABLE 5–3     Recent Divestitures

| PARENT COMPANY | DIVESTED COMPANY |
| --- | --- |
| Microsoft | Sidewalk Entertainment |
| AlliedSignal | Laminate-Systems |
| Monsanto | NutraSweet |
| Compaq Computer Corp. | AltaVista |
| Dupont | Conoco |
| Mead Corp. | Northwood, Inc. |
| IBM | Networking Technology |
| Kohlberg Kravis Roberts | Gillette |
| Borg-Warner Automotive | Kuhlman Electric |
| De La Rue PLC | Smart Cards |
| Walt Disney | Anaheim Angels |
| Walt Disney | Anaheim Might Ducks |
| Walt Disney | Fairchild Publications |
| Harcourt General | Neiman Marcus |
| 3Com | Palm Computing |
| North American Van Lines | Allied Van Lines |
| Harvard Industries, Inc. | Kingston-Warren |
| Cendant Corp. | Entertainment Publications |
| Marks & Spencer PLC | Kings Supermarket |
| U.S. Industries, Inc. | USI Diversified |
| Silicon Graphics, Inc. | Cray Supercomputer |
| Eastman Kodak Co. | Image Bank |
| Microsoft | Expedia |
| Kellogg Company | Lender's Bagels |
| Sabre Holdings | Travelocity.com |

- When a large amount of cash is needed quickly and cannot be obtained reasonably from other sources
- When government antitrust action threatens an organization

## Liquidation

Selling all of a company's assets, in parts, for their tangible worth is called *liquidation.* Liquidation is a recognition of defeat and consequently can be an emotionally difficult strategy. However, it may be better to cease operating than to continue losing large sums of money.

For example, American Retail Group recently liquidated its chain of seventy-five Uptons department stores located in the Southeast, eliminating more than four thousand jobs. A spokesman for the company said it was too expensive to keep Uptons running. For another example, Hechinger, a home-improvement retailer based in Largo, Maryland, liquidated in late 1999 after earlier that year declaring Chapter 11 bankruptcy. Hechinger had been slowly strangled by number-one Home Depot with 11 percent of the home improvement market and number-two Lowes with 5 percent of the market, as well as Menard and HomeBase, two other strong rival firms. The penalty of ineffective strategies for any type or size of organization can be cruelly severe.

Thousands of small businesses in the United States liquidate annually without ever making the news. It is tough to start and successfully operate a small business. In China and Russia, thousands of government-owned businesses liquidate annually as those countries try to privatize and consolidate industries.

Three guidelines when liquidation may be an especially effective strategy to pursue are:[20]

- When an organization has pursued both a retrenchment strategy and a divestiture strategy, and neither has been successful
- When an organization's only alternative is bankruptcy; liquidation represents an orderly and planned means of obtaining the greatest possible cash for an organization's assets. A company can legally declare bankruptcy first and then liquidate various divisions to raise needed capital
- When the stockholders of a firm can minimize their losses by selling the organization's assets

# JOINT VENTURE AND COMBINATION STRATEGIES

## Joint Venture

*Joint venture* is a popular strategy that occurs when two or more companies form a temporary partnership or consortium for the purpose of capitalizing on some opportunity. Often, the two or more sponsoring firms form a separate organization and have shared equity ownership in the new entity. Other types of *cooperative arrangements* include research and development partnerships, cross-distribution agreements, cross-licensing agreements, cross-manufacturing agreements, and joint-bidding consortia.

Joint ventures and cooperative arrangements are being used increasingly because they allow companies to improve communications and networking, to globalize operations, and to minimize risk. Kathryn Rudie Harrigan, professor of strategic management at Columbia University, summarizes the trend toward increased joint venturing:

> In today's global business environment of scarce resources, rapid rates of techno-
> logical change, and rising capital requirements, the important question is no

longer "Shall we form a joint venture?" Now the question is "Which joint ventures and cooperative arrangements are most appropriate for our needs and expectations?" followed by "How do we manage these ventures most effectively?"[21]

**e·biz**

Ford Motor Company and Microsoft Corporation recently formed a joint venture that enables Ford to build cars to online orders. The venture underscores how e-commerce is challenging traditional ways of doing business, pushing the high technology and manufacturing industries closer together. Ford wants technology allies to revamp its distribution system, cut costs and inventory, and gain broad access to Internet car consumers. Microsoft wants to bolster its car-buying Web site, CarPoint, and promote the MSN Internet portal. Ford also gains access to information about how shoppers search for cars online and what kind of cars they actually want. General Motors and Sun Microsystems recently created a similar joint venture to sell cars online. An excellent Web site to purchase a car online is www.carsdirect.com which sells more than three thousand cars per month in the United States.

America Online and German media company Bertelsmann AG recently established a joint venture named AOL Europe that is today battling European firms in providing Internet access. Freeserve is the largest Internet provider in Britain while Deutsche Telekom leads in Germany, although AOL Europe has targeted both countries with a new service called Netscape Online.

Two rival firms, *The Wall Street Journal* and the *Financial Times,* entered into a joint venture recently with Independent Media, the Dutch-owned publisher of the *Moscow Times*, to launch *Vedomosti,* a Russian-language newspaper. *Vedomosti* is unique because most newspapers in Russia are run by rich bankers or government entities that use their paper to promote their personal interests. *Vedomosti* challenges *Kommersant,* Russia's main business newspaper. *Vedomosti* hopes to reach a circulation goal of over 60,000 by 2001; *Kommersant* already has 117,000 readers.

Nestlé and Pillsbury recently formed a joint venture named Ice Cream Partners USA based in northern California. The new company primarily sells superpremium ice cream which is high in fat—and price. Superpremium ice cream sales were up nearly 13 percent in 1998. Ice cream makers in the United States introduced 124 new products in 1999, and most of these were superpremium brands. "The consumer today is leaning more towards indulgence," says Joe Weller, CEO of Nestlé USA.[22]

Six guidelines when joint venture may be an especially effective strategy to purse are:[23]

- When a privately owned organization is forming a joint venture with a publicly owned organization; there are some advantages of being privately held, such as close ownership; there are some advantages of being publicly held, such as access to stock issuances as a source of capital. Sometimes, the unique advantages of being privately and publicly held can be synergistically combined in a joint venture

- When a domestic organization is forming a joint venture with a foreign company; a joint venture can provide a domestic company with the opportunity for obtaining local management in a foreign coutnry, thereby reducing risks such as expropriation and harassment by host country officials

- When the distinct competencies of two or more firms complement each other especially well

- When some project is potentially very profitable, but requires overwhelming resources and risks; the Alaskan pipeline is an example

- When two or more smaller firms have trouble competing with a large firm

- When there exists a need to introduce a new technology quickly

TABLE 5-4    Some Recent Example Joint Ventures

| PARENT COMPANY #1 | PARENT COMPANY #2 | NEWLY CREATED COMPANY |
|---|---|---|
| AOL | Bertelsmann AG | AOL Europe |
| Walt Disney | Infoseek | Go Network |
| Nestlé | Pillsbury | Ice Cream Partners USA |
| Dow Jones | Pearson | Vedomosti |
| Volkswagen AG | Porsche | Sport Utility Vehicle |
| Pacific Century Group | DaimlerChrysler Aerospace AG | Pacific Century Matrix |
| Microsoft | Ford Motor Company | CarPoint |
| EBay | Microsoft | FairMarket |
| Excite At Home | TeleColumbus Gmblt | At Home Deutschland |

*Joint Ventures into Russia*    A joint venture strategy offers a possible way to enter the Russian market. Joint ventures create a mechanism to generate hard currency, which is important because of problems valuing the ruble. Russia's joint venture law has been revised to allow foreigners to own up to 99 percent of the venture and to allow a foreigner to serve as chief executive officer.

The list of U.S. companies that have active joint ventures with Russia include Archer-Daniels-Midland, Chevron, Combustion Engineering, Dresser Industries, Hewlett-Packard, Honeywell, Johnson & Johnson, MCI, Marriott, McDonald's, Ogilvy & Mather, Radisson, RJR/Nabisco, and Young & Rubicam. In the aerospace industry, Russian firms are cooperating with Germany's Messerschmitt Company; in computers, with IBM; in manufacturing, with Combustion Engineering, Honeywell, and Siemens; in nuclear power, with Asea-Brown Boveri, and Siemens; and in telecommunications, with Nokia. PepsiCo, Inc., recently formed a joint venture with Moscow Metropolitan to sell PepsiCo food products in Moscow's subway stations.

Some analysts believe Russia will become a market that many U.S. firms will want to enter. Those firms that start mastering the complexities early and keep informed about the latest developments may likely gain the biggest rewards. Thousands of businesses in Russia have been given financial independence and broad management autonomy. Poor telecommunications equipment, however, often isolates foreign managers in Russia from the parent company. Russia's telephone system is comparable to the U.S. phone system of the 1930s.

The following guidelines are appropriate when considering a joint venture into Russia. First, avoid regions with ethnic conflicts and violence. Also, make sure the potential partner has a proper charter that has been amended to permit joint venture participation. Be aware that businesspeople in these lands have little knowledge of marketing, contract law, corporate law, fax machines, voice mail, and other business practices that Westerners take for granted.

Business contracts with Russian firms should address natural environment issues because Westerners often get the blame for air and water pollution problems and habitat destruction. Work out a clear means of converting rubles to dollars before entering a proposed joint venture because neither Russian banks nor authorities can be counted on to facilitate foreign firms' getting dollar profits out of a business. Recognize that chronic shortages of raw materials hamper business in Russia, so make sure an adequate supply of competitively priced, good-quality raw materials is reliably available. Finally, make sure the business contract limits the circumstances in which expropriation would be legal. Specify a lump sum in dollars if expropriation should occur unexpectedly, and obtain expropriation insurance before signing the agreement.

A number of organizations in Russia assist foreign companies interested in initiating, continuing, or expanding business operations there. Some of these organizations are Amtorg, the Consultation Center of the Chamber of Commerce and Industry, Inpred, Interfact, and the U.S. Commercial Office (USCO). Inpred, for example, is a consulting firm in Russia that helps Western managers operate within regulations. Inpred also helps foreign firms locate partners in the republics and develop contracts, and contacts officials to set up meetings between Russian and foreign businesspersons. USCO annually sponsors about twenty-five trade fairs and exhibitions that introduce foreign companies and individuals to the new Russian markets, customers, buyers, and sellers.

## Combination

Many, if not most, organizations pursue a combination of two or more strategies simultaneously, but a *combination strategy* can be exceptionally risky if carried too far. No organization can afford to pursue all the strategies that might benefit the firm. Difficult decisions must be made. Priority must be established. Organizations, like individuals, have limited resources. Both organizations and individuals must choose among alternative strategies and avoid excessive indebtedness.

Organizations cannot do too many things well because resources and talents get spread thin and competitors gain advantage. In large diversified companies, a combination strategy is commonly employed when different divisions pursue different strategies. Also, organizations struggling to survive may employ a combination of several defensive strategies, such as divestiture, liquidation, and retrenchment, simultaneously.

Wal-Mart Stores is an example company pursuing a combination of many strategies. Wal-Mart is opening Computer Doctor centers in its stores to repair computers and install software. This is horizontal diversification and is aimed directly at Radio Shack and CompUSA that dominate the market for helping consumers with their computer problems. Wal-Mart is planning to open coffee bars and bath shops in the front of its stores, which is considered product development. Wal-Mart's planned entry into the banking business by acquiring Federal BankCentre of Broken Arrow, Oklahoma, and opening branch banks in Wal-Mart stores in several states is horizontal diversification. Regulators have yet to approve this acquisition plan but Wal-Mart is aggressively pursuing this diversification strategy. Wal-Mart already leases space in 450 of its stores to banks. In addition to horizontal diversification, Wal-Mart is adding 305 Wal-Mart and supercenter stores worldwide in 2000 along with 25 new Sam's Clubs Stores, and 10 Neighborhood Market full-line grocery stores. The market development strategy brings the number of Wal-Mart stores to 1,861, supercenters to 815, and Sam's Clubs to 478 in the United States, while international stores rise to 1,074 in 2000.

# MICHAEL PORTER'S GENERIC STRATEGIES

Probably the three most widely read books on competitive analysis in the 1980s were Michael Porter's (www.hbs.edu/bios/mporter) *Competitive Strategy* (Free Press, 1980), *Competitive Advantage* (Free Press, 1985), and *Competitive Advantage of Nations* (Free Press, 1989). According to Porter, strategies allow organizations to gain competitive advantage from three different bases: cost leadership, differentiation, and focus. Porter calls these bases *generic strategies*. *Cost leadership* emphasizes producing standardized products at very low per-unit cost for consumers who are price-sensitive. *Differentiation* is a strategy aimed at producing products and services considered unique industrywide and directed at consumers who are relatively price-insensitive. *Focus* means producing products and services that fulfill the needs of small groups of consumers.

Porter's strategies imply different organizational arrangements, control procedures, and incentive systems. Larger firms with greater access to resources typically compete on a cost leadership and/or differentiation basis, whereas smaller firms often compete on a focus basis.

Porter stresses the need for strategists to perform cost-benefit analyses to evaluate "sharing opportunities" among a firm's existing and potential business units. Sharing activities and resources enhances competitive advantage by lowering costs or raising differentiation. In addition to prompting sharing, Porter stresses the need for firms to "transfer" skills and expertise among autonomous business units effectively in order to gain competitive advantage. Depending upon factors such as type of industry, size of firm, and nature of competition, various strategies could yield advantages in cost leadership, differentiation, and focus.

## Cost Leadership Strategies

A primary reason for pursuing forward, backward, and horizontal integration strategies is to gain cost leadership benefits. But cost leadership generally must be pursued in conjunction with differentiation. A number of cost elements affect the relative attractiveness of generic strategies, including economies or diseconomies of scale achieved, learning and experience curve effects, the percentage of capacity utilization achieved, and linkages with suppliers and distributors. Other cost elements to consider in choosing among alternative strategies include the potential for sharing costs and knowledge within the organization, R&D costs associated with new product development or modification of existing products, labor costs, tax rates, energy costs, and shipping costs.

Striving to be the low-cost producer in an industry can be especially effective when the market is composed of many price-sensitive buyers, when there are few ways to achieve product differentiation, when buyers do not care much about differences from brand to brand, or when there are a large number of buyers with significant bargaining power. The basic idea is to underprice competitors and thereby gain market share and sales, driving some competitors out of the market entirely.

A successful cost leadership strategy usually permeates the entire firm, as evidenced by high efficiency, low overhead, limited perks, intolerance of waste, intensive screening of budget requests, wide spans of control, rewards linked to cost containment, and broad employee participation in cost control efforts. Some risks of pursuing cost leadership are that competitors may imitate the strategy, thus driving overall industry profits down; technological breakthroughs in the industry may make the strategy ineffective; or buyer interest may swing to other differentiating features besides price. Several example firms that are well known for their low-cost leadership strategies are Wal-Mart, BIC, McDonald's, Black and Decker, Lincoln Electric, and Briggs and Stratton.

## Differentiation Strategies

Different strategies offer different degrees of differentiation. Differentiation does not guarantee competitive advantage, especially if standard products sufficiently meet customer needs or if rapid imitation by competitors is possible. Durable products protected by barriers to quick copying by competitors are best. Successful differentiation can mean greater product flexibility, greater compatibility, lower costs, improved service, less maintenance, greater convenience, or more features. Product development is an example of a strategy that offers the advantages of differentiation.

A differentiation strategy should be pursued only after careful study of buyers' needs and preferences to determine the feasibility of incorporating one or more differentiating features into a unique product that features the desired attributes. A successful differentiation strategy allows a firm to charge a higher price for its product and to gain customer loyalty because consumers may become strongly attached to the differentiation features.

Special features to differentiate one's product can include superior service, spare parts availability, engineering design, product performance, useful life, gas mileage, or ease of use.

A risk of pursuing a differentiation strategy is that the unique product may not be valued highly enough by customers to justify the higher price. When this happens, a cost leadership strategy easily will defeat a differentiation strategy. Another risk of pursuing a differentiation strategy is that competitors may develop ways to copy the differentiating features quickly. Firms thus must find durable sources of uniqueness that cannot be imitated quickly or cheaply by rival firms.

Common organizational requirements for a successful differentiation strategy include strong coordination among the R&D and marketing functions and substantial amenities to attract scientists and creative people. Firms pursuing a differentiation strategy include Dr. Pepper, Jenn-Air, The Limited, BMW, Grady-White, Ralph Lauren, Maytag, and Cross.

### Focus Strategies

A successful focus strategy depends upon an industry segment that is of sufficient size, has good growth potential, and is not crucial to the success of other major competitors. Strategies such as market penetration and market development offer substantial focusing advantages. Midsize and large firms effectively can pursue focus-based strategies only in conjunction with differentiation or cost leadership–based strategies. All firms in essence follow a differentiated strategy. Because only one firm can differentiate itself with the lowest cost, the remaining firms in the industry must find other ways to differentiate their products.

Focus strategies are most effective when consumers have distinctive preferences or requirements and when rival firms are not attempting to specialize in the same target segment. Firms pursuing a focus strategy include Midas, Red Lobster, Federal Express, Sprint, MCI, Coors, and Schwinn. Federal-Mogul Corporation recently divested its lighting, wiper-blade, and fuel-components divisions to focus on its core businesses, which are brake systems, powertrain, and sealing operations. Based in Southfield, Michigan, Federal-Mogul has about fifty-five thousand employees and annual sales of $4.5 billion.

Risks of pursuing a focus strategy include the possibility that numerous competitors recognize the successful focus strategy and copy the strategy, or that consumer preferences drift toward the product attributes desired by the market as a whole. An organization using a focus strategy may concentrate on a particular group of customers, geographic markets, or product line segments in order to serve a well-defined but narrow market better than competitors who serve a broader market.

### The Value Chain

According to Porter, the business of a firm can best be described as a *value chain* in which total revenues minus total costs of all activities undertaken to develop and market a product or service yields value. All firms in a given industry have a similar value chain, which includes activities such as obtaining raw materials, designing products, building manufacturing facilities, developing cooperative agreements, and providing customer service. A firm will be profitable as long as total revenues exceed the total costs incurred in creating and delivering the product or service. Firms should strive to understand not only their own value chain operations, but also their competitors', suppliers', and distributors' value chains.

 # MERGERS

Acquisition and merger are two commonly used ways to pursue strategies. An *acquisition* occurs when a large organization purchases (acquires) a smaller firm, or vice versa. A *merger* occurs when two organizations of about equal size unite to form one enterprise. When an acquisition or merger is not desired by both parties, it can be called a *takeover* or *hostile takeover*. There are numerous and powerful driving forces driving once-fierce rivals to merge around the world. Some of these forces are deregulation, technological change, excess capacity, inability to boost profits through price increases, a robust stock market, and the need to gain economies of scale.

Phone giants US West and Qwest for example merged in 1999 in a $36.5 billion deal. Prior to the merger, Qwest aimed to "takeover" the larger US West. Qwest later compromised to a "merger of equals" in which the two chief executive officers, Joe Nacchio of Qwest and Philip Anschutz of US West, serve as co-chairmen of the combined firm. Mr. Nacchio is the CEO.

Two huge takeover bids were launched and completed in Milan, Italy, recently when Olivetti SpA won its battle to take over the much larger Telecom Italia SpA, and when Assicurazioni Generali SpA won its battle to take over Istituto Nazionale delle Assicurazioni SpA. These are very large insurance and banking firms.

Dow Chemical plans to buy Union Carbide for $8.5 billion creating the world's second-largest chemical maker. The combined company would overtake Germany's BASF in size and rank, behind only DuPont. Shareholders of both companies as well as regulators must approve the merger.

Veba AG and Viag AG, large Germany utilities, recently merged to form the third-largest industrial group in Germany. Veba-Viag plans now to make numerous acquisitions across Europe which has deregulated the utility industry spurring consolidation.

Reynolds Metals recently gave in to Alcoa Inc.'s unsolicited takeover offer by agreeing to be acquired for $4.35 billion creating the world's largest aluminum maker. The global aluminum industry is consolidating as evidenced by a recent three-way merger between Canada's Alcan Aluminum Ltd, France's Pechiney SA, and Switzerland's Alusuisse Lonza AG.

Volkswagen AG in the last two years has purchased Rolls-Royce, Bentley, Lamborghini, Cosworth, and Bugatti. Sales of Volkswagen's Audi brand was up nearly 40 percent in 1999, while its Passat beat Toyota's Camry as *Consumer Reports'* best family sedan.

Not all mergers are effective and successful as evidenced by Compaq's recent acquisition of Digital Equipment resulting in severe demise for Compaq. PricewaterhouseCoopers LLP recently researched mergers and found that the average acquirer's stock was 3.7 percent lower than its industry peer group a year later. *BusinessWeek* and *The Wall Street Journal* studied mergers and concluded that about half produced negative returns to shareholders; for the first nine months of 1999, the stock price of an acquiring firm fell 0.25 percent upon announcement of a merger—in 1994 in comparison, the stock price rose 1.86 percent.[24] Warren Buffett once said in a speech that, "A too-high purchase price for the stock of an excellent company can undo the effects of a subsequent decade of favorable business developments." So, merger between two firms can yield great benefits, but the price and reasoning must be right.

The volume of mergers continues to spiral upwards and exceeded $2.7 billion in 1998. The top-ten highest-price mergers ever all occurred in 1998 and 1999, led by the MCI WorldCom acquisition of Sprint for $115 billion in 1999 and the Exxon acquisition of Mobil for $78.9 billion in 1998. Regarding merger-mania restructuring, *Business Week* offered the following conclusion:

It is clear now that restructurings are driven by a lot more than tax considerations, low stock prices, raiders' desire for a quick buck, and aggressive merger merchants on Wall Street. . . . Restructuring continues because U.S. industry needs it. Deregulation in industries from financial services to energy, from communications to transportation, has exposed managerial complacency and inefficient practices caused by years of shelter from market forces. . . . Plenty of companies have simply recognized that if they want to compete globally, they must slim down, toughen up, and focus on a narrower range of businesses.[25]

Among mergers, acquisitions, and takeovers in recent years, same-industry combinations have predominated. A general market consolidation is occurring in many industries, especially banking, insurance, defense, and health care, but also pharmaceuticals, food, airlines, accounting, publishing, computers, retailing, financial services, and biotechnology. For example, three large Japanese banks, Dai-Ichi Kangyo Bank Ltd., Fuji Bank Ltd., and Industrial Bank of Japan merged in October 2000 to form the world's largest financial holding company. The huge merged firm now competes with other large global banks such as number-two Deutsche Bank AG, number-three Citigroup, and number-four Bank of America. The DKB-Fuji-IBJ merger comes amid major deregulation by the Japanese government to encourage industry consolidation.

From January through May, 1999, American and European companies announced 140 mergers and acquisitions of Asian companies worth a total of $29 billion. This compares to 86 deals worth $9 billion announced the same time period in 1998.[26] Whenever a rival firm moves into a new geographic area, other firms in the industry often feel compelled to do the same to compete. Table 5–5 shows some mergers and acquisitions completed in 2000. There are many reasons for mergers and acquisitions, including the following:

- To provide improved capacity utilization
- To make better use of existing sales force
- To reduce managerial staff
- To gain economies of scale
- To smooth out seasonal trends in sales
- To gain access to new suppliers, distributors, customers, products, and creditors
- To gain new technology
- To reduce tax obligations

The volume of mergers completed annually worldwide is growing dramatically and exceeds $1 trillion annually. There are more than ten thousand mergers annually in the United States that total more than $700 billion. For the first six months of 1999, the value of digital media deals alone in North America skyrocketed nearly 700 percent to $36.5 billion.[27] More than 165 Web properties were bought during these six months for an average price of $200 million. During this time, Yahoo acquired five firms for a total of $10.5 billion while America Online acquired ten firms for $4.4 billion.

e-biz

The proliferation of mergers is fueled by companies' drive for market share, efficiency, and pricing power as well as by globalization, the need for greater economies of scale, reduced regulation and antitrust concerns, the Internet, e-commerce, and the stock market rewarding merger activity with higher stock prices.

Mergers do not always give quick results. For example, Waste Management merged with USA Waste in 1998 creating the world's largest trash hauler. However, in 1999, Waste Management was in turmoil and disarray. The company released its top managers including CEO Drury and President Proto and divested all international and some domestic businesses to pay down debt. The company's stock price plunged from the mid-50s in 1998 to the low 20s in 1999. Similarly, a major reason for Compaq Computers dramatic demise in 1998/1999 was their ineffective acquisition of Digital Computer Corporation.

## Leveraged Buyouts (LBOs)

A *leveraged buyout* (LBO) occurs when a corporation's shareholders are bought (hence *buyout*) by the company's management and other private investors using borrowed funds

TABLE 5-5     **Some Recent Example Mergers**

| ACQUIRING FIRM | ACQUIRED FIRM |
| --- | --- |
| AOL | MovieFone |
| Amazon.com | Exchange.com |
| EBay, Inc. | Butterfield & Butterfield |
| Lycos | Sonique |
| Jefferson-Pilot Corp. | Guarantee Life Cos. |
| Qwest | US West |
| Royal Numico | General Nutrition Co. (GNC) |
| Healtheon | WebMD |
| Hilton | Promus |
| Viacom | CBS |
| Fleet Financial | BankBoston |
| BP | Amoco |
| TotalFina | Elf |
| Grupo Sanborns SA | CompUSA, Inc. |
| Heinz | Bestfoods |
| Motorola | General Instrument |
| Estee Lauder | Stila |
| Excite | At Home Corp. |
| Yahoo | GeoCities |
| Lycos | E-stamps |
| SBC | Ameritech |
| H&R Block | McGladrey & Pullen |
| Nortel | Periphonics |
| Dupont | Herberts |
| American Airlines | Reno Air |
| NCR | Gasper Corp. |
| Masco | Inrecon |

(hence *leverage*).[28] Besides trying to avoid a hostile takeover, other reasons for initiating an LBO are senior management decisions that particular divisions do not fit into an overall corporate strategy or must be sold to raise cash, or receipt of an attractive offering price. An LBO takes a corporation private.

## STRATEGIC MANAGEMENT IN NONPROFIT AND GOVERNMENTAL ORGANIZATIONS

The strategic-management process is being used effectively by countless nonprofit and governmental organizations, such as the Girl Scouts and Boy Scouts, the Red Cross, chambers of commerce, educational institutions, medical institutions, public utilities, libraries, government agencies, and churches. The nonprofit sector, surprisingly, is by far America's largest employer. Many nonprofit and governmental organizations outperform private firms and corporations on innovativeness, motivation, productivity, and strategic management. For many nonprofit examples of strategic planning in practice, click on Strategic Planning Links found at the www.strategyclub.com Web site.

Compared to for-profit firms, nonprofit and governmental organizations often function as a monopoly, produce a product or service that offers little or no measurability of performance, and are totally dependent on outside financing. Especially for these organizations, strategic management provides an excellent vehicle for developing and justifying requests for needed financial support.

## Educational Institutions

Educational institutions are using strategic-management techniques and concepts more frequently. Richard Cyert, president of Carnegie-Mellon University, says, "I believe we do a far better job of strategic management than any company I know." Population shifts nationally from the Northeast and Midwest to the Southeast and West are but one factor causing trauma for educational institutions that have not planned for changing enrollments. Ivy League schools in the Northeast are recruiting more heavily in the Southeast and West. This trend represents a significant change in the competitive climate for attracting the best high school graduates each year.

The first all-Internet law school, Concord University School of Law, boasts nearly two hundred students who can access lectures anytime and chat at fixed times with professors. Online college degrees are becoming common and represent a threat to traditional colleges and universities. "You can put the kids to bed and go to law school," says Andrew Rosen, chief operating officer of Kaplan Education Centers, a subsidiary of the Washington Post Company, that owns Concord. Annual tuition for the four-year law program at Concord is a reasonable forty-two hundred dollars. Concord is not accredited by the American Bar Association which prohibits study by correspondence and requires more than one thousand hours of classroom time.

For a list of college strategic plans, click on strategic-planning links found at the www.strategyclub.com Web site and scroll down through the academic sites.

## Medical Organizations

The $200 billion American hospital industry is experiencing declining margins, excess capacity, bureaucratic overburdening, poorly planned and executed diversification strategies, soaring health care costs, reduced federal support, and high administrator turnover. The seriousness of this problem is accented by a 20 percent annual decline in inpatient use nationwide. Declining occupancy rates, deregulation, and accelerating growth of health maintenance organizations, preferred provider organizations, urgent care centers, outpatient surgery centers, diagnostic centers, specialized clinics, and group practices are other major threats facing hospitals today. Many private and state-supported medical institutions are in financial trouble as a result of traditionally taking a reactive rather than a proactive approach in dealing with their industry.

Hospitals—originally intended to be warehouses for people dying of tuberculosis, smallpox, cancer, pneumonia, and infectious diseases—are creating new strategies today as advances in the diagnosis and treatment of chronic diseases are undercutting that earlier mission. Hospitals are beginning to bring services to the patient as much as bringing the patient to the hospital; in twenty years, health care will be concentrated in the home and in the residential community, not on the hospital campus. Chronic care will require day-treatment facilities, electronic monitoring at home, user-friendly ambulatory services, decentralized service networks, and laboratory testing. A successful hospital strategy for the future will require renewed and deepened collaboration with physicians, who are central to hospitals' well-being, and a reallocation of resources from acute to chronic care in home and community settings.

Current strategies being pursued by many hospitals include creating home health services, establishing nursing homes, and forming rehabilitation centers. Backward integration strategies that some hospitals are pursuing include acquiring ambulance services, waste disposal services, and diagnostic services. During 1999, more than thirty-three million persons researched medical ailments online which is causing a dramatic shift in the balance of power between doctor, patient, and hospitals.[29] This number of persons using the Internet to obtain medical information will skyrocket in 2000 and 2001. A motivated patient using the Internet can gain knowledge on a particular subject far beyond their doctor's knowledge, because no person can keep up with the results and implications of billions of dollars of medical research reported weekly. Patients today often walk into the doctor's office with a file folder of the latest articles detailing research and treatment options for their ailment. On Web sites such as America's Doctor (www.americasdoctor.com), consumers can consult with a physician in an online chat room twenty-four hours a day. Excellent consumer health Web sites are proliferating, boosted by investments from such firms at Microsoft, America Online, Reader's Digest, and CBS. Drug companies such as Glaxo Wellcome are getting involved as are hospitals. The whole strategic landscape of health-care is changing because of the Internet. Intel recently began offering a new secure medical service whereby doctors and patients can conduct sensitive business on the Internet, such as sharing results of medical tests and prescribing medicine. The ten most successful hospital strategies today are providing free-standing outpatient surgery centers, freestanding outpatient diagnostic centers, physical rehabilitation centers, home health services, cardiac rehabilitation centers, preferred provider services, industrial medicine services, women's medicine services, skilled nursing units, and psychiatric services.[30]

**e·biz**

### Governmental Agencies and Departments

Federal, state, county, and municipal agencies and departments, such as police departments, chambers of commerce, forestry associations, and health departments, are responsible for formulating, implementing, and evaluating strategies that use taxpayers' dollars in the most cost-effective way to provide services and programs. Strategic-management concepts increasingly are being used to enable governmental organizations to be more effective and efficient. For a list of government agency strategic plans, click on strategic-planning links found at the www.strategyclub.com Web site and scroll down through the government sites.

**e·biz**

But strategists in governmental organizations operate with less strategic autonomy than their counterparts in private firms. Public enterprises generally cannot diversify into unrelated businesses or merge with other firms. Governmental strategists usually enjoy little freedom in altering the organizations' missions or redirecting objectives. Legislators and politicians often have direct or indirect control over major decisions and resources. Strategic issues get discussed and debated in the media and legislatures. Issues become politicized, resulting in fewer strategic choice alternatives. There is more predictability in the management of public sector enterprises.

Government agencies and departments are finding that their employees get excited about the opportunity to participate in the strategic-management process and thereby have an effect on the organization's mission, objectives, strategies, and policies. In addition, government agencies are using a strategic-management approach to develop and substantiate formal requests for additional funding.

## STRATEGIC MANAGEMENT IN SMALL FIRMS

Strategic management is vital for large firms' success, but what about small firms? The strategic-management process is just as vital for small companies. From their inception, all organizations have a strategy, even if the strategy just evolves from day-to-day operations. Even if conducted informally or by a single owner/entrepreneur, the strategic-management process significantly can enhance small firms' growth and prosperity. Recent data clearly show that an ever-increasing number of men and women in the United States are starting their own businesses. This means more individuals are becom-

# GLOBAL PERSPECTIVE

### *Does the United States Lead in Small Business Start-Ups Globally?*

The answer is YES. The London Business School and Babson College which recently completed one of the most comprehensive studies of global entrepreneurs ever undertaken concluded that North America remains way ahead of European countries in the percentage of adults starting new businesses. The results show that one in twelve Americans is trying to start a new business today, compared to just one in thirty Britons, one in forty-five Germans, and one in sixty-seven Finns. Since there is a strong link between new business start-ups and growth in gross domestic product, the implications of these results for European countries is dismal. Why are there so few entrepreneurs in Europe compared to America? The answer primarily is the social pressure to conform as well as fear of failure, but attitudes towards entrepreneurs are changing. Most Germans, in contrast to Britons, now show a relatively high regard for people involved in starting a new business. And young Italian adults show a relatively high level of entrepreneurial activity, third behind the United States and Canada. The following table reveals the percentage of the adult population starting a new business at any given time in eight countries:

| Country | Percentage of Adults Starting a New Business |
| --- | --- |
| United States | 8.5% |
| Canada | 6.8 |
| Italy | 3.4 |
| Britain | 3.3 |
| Germany | 2.2 |
| Denmark | 2.0 |
| France | 1.8 |
| Finland | 1.4 |

In Japan, new business ventures are becoming common. Entrepreneurs are changing the way young Japanese think about work as evidenced by national erosion of devotion to large corporations and increasing value being placed on originality. Small business start-ups in Japan accounted for an increase in that country's gross domestic product in early 1999, the first increase in several years. Fiachra MacCanna says, "Japanese small companies are the single most efficient and productive part of the Japanese economy." About 25 percent of new Japanese small businesses are Internet or service-related.

*Source:* Adapted from: Julia Flynn, "Gap Exists Between Entrepreneurship in Europe, North America, Study Shows," *The Wall Street Journal* (July 2, 1999): A10. Also, Peter Hadfield, "Young, Small Companies Energize Japan's Economy," *USA Today* (July 7, 1999): 2B.

ing strategists. Widespread corporate layoffs have contributed to an explosion in small businesses and new ideas.

Numerous magazine and journal articles have focused on applying strategic-management concepts to small businesses.[31] A major conclusion of these articles is that a lack of strategic-management knowledge is a serious obstacle for many small business owners. Other problems often encountered in applying strategic-management concepts to small businesses are a lack of both sufficient capital to exploit external opportunities and a day-to-day cognitive frame of reference. Research also indicates that strategic management in small firms is more informal than in large firms, but small firms that engage in strategic management outperform those that do not. The *CheckMATE* strategic planning software at www.checkmateplan.com offers a version especially for small businesses.

More than 2.1 million small businesses now have their own home page, up from 1.2 million last year.[32]

**e·biz**

It is vitally important for the U.S. economy that small businesspersons utilize strategic planning to enhance performance, as evidenced by the following statistics:

- From 1994 through 1998, small businesses with 20 or fewer employees generated nearly 9 million jobs—about 80 percent of the total created in the USA.

- Small businesses with one hundred or fewer employees spend $2.2 trillion annually, just a bit less than all big companies, which spend $2.6 trillion.
- Women own 9.1 million small businesses which represents 38 percent of all firms in the United States.
- Small companies with 500 or fewer employees account for about 51 percent of the U.S. private gross domestic product.[33]

As indicated in the Global Perspective on page 188, 8.5 percent of Americans today are trying to start their own small business.

## CONCLUSION

The main appeal of any managerial approach is the expectation that it will enhance organizational performance. This is especially true of strategic management. Through involvement in strategic-management activities, managers and employees achieve a better understanding of an organization's priorities and operations. Strategic management allows organizations to be efficient, but more importantly, it allows them to be effective. Although strategic management does not guarantee organizational success, the process allows proactive rather than reactive decision making. Strategic management may represent a radical change in philosophy for some organizations, so strategists must be trained to anticipate and constructively respond to questions and issues as they arise. The sixteen strategies discussed in this chapter can represent a new beginning for many firms, especially if managers and employees in the organization understand and support the plan for action.

We invite you to visit the DAVID page on the Prentice Hall Web site at **www.prenhall.com/davidsm** for this chapter's World Wide Web exercise.

## KEY TERMS AND CONCEPTS

Acquisition (p. 182)

Backward Integration (p. 166)

Bankruptcy (p. 174)

Combination Strategy (p. 180)

Concentric Diversification (p. 172)

Conglomerate Diversification (p. 173)

Cooperative Arrangements (p. 177)

Cost Leadership (p. 180)

Differentiation (p. 180)

Diversification Strategies (p. 170)

Divestiture (p. 175)

Focus (p. 180)

Forward Integration (p. 164)

Franchising (p. 166)

Generic Strategies (p. 180)

Horizontal Diversification (p. 172)

Horizontal Integration (p. 168)

Integration Strategies (p. 164)

Intensive Strategies (p. 169)

Joint Venture (p. 177)

Leveraged Buyout (p. 184)

Liquidation (p. 177)

Long-Term Objectives (p. 162)

Market Development (p. 169)

Market Penetration (p. 169)

Merger (p. 183)

Outsourcing (p. 166)

Product Development (p. 170)

Retrenchment (174)

Takeover (p. 183)

Vertical Integration (p. 164)

## ISSUES FOR REVIEW AND DISCUSSION

1. How does strategy formulation differ for a small versus a large organization? for a for-profit versus a nonprofit organization?
2. Give recent examples of market penetration, market development, and product development.
3. Give recent examples of forward integration, backward integration, and horizontal integration.
4. Give recent examples of concentric diversification, horizontal diversification, and conglomerate diversification.
5. Give recent examples of joint venture, retrenchment, divestiture, and liquidation.
6. Read one of the suggested readings at the end of this chapter. Prepare a five-minute oral report on the topic.
7. Do you think hostile takeovers are unethical? Why or why not?
8. What are the major advantages and disadvantages of diversification?
9. What are the major advantages and disadvantages of an integrative strategy?
10. How does strategic management differ in profit and nonprofit organizations?
11. Why is it not advisable to pursue too many strategies at once?
12. Consumers can purchase tennis shoes, food, cars, boats, and insurance on the Internet. Are there any products today than cannot be purchased online? What is the implication for traditional retailers?
13. Do you feel Internet sales should remain tax free? What are the pro's and con's of Internet commerce remaining a tax-free haven?
14. What are the pro's and con's of a firm merging with a rival firm?
15. Does the United States lead in small business start-ups globally?
16. Visit the *CheckMATE* Strategic Planning software Web site at www.checkmateplan.com and discuss the benefits offered.

## NOTES

1. JOHN BYRNE, "Strategic Planning—It's Back," *Business Week* (August 26, 1996): 46.
2. STEVEN C. BRANDT, *Strategic Planning in Emerging Companies* (Reading, Massachusetts: Addison-Wesley, 1981). Reprinted with permission of the publisher.
3. SARA NATHAN, Defining the Seller in On-line Market," *USA Today* (August 26, 1999): 3B.
4. Adapted from F. R. DAVID, "How Do We Choose Among Alternative Growth Strategies?" *Managerial Planning* 33, no. 4 (January–February 1985): 14–17, 22.
5. ROBERT MATTHEWS, "Web Sites Made of Steel," *The Wall Street Journal* (September 16, 1999): B1, B4.
6. Adapted from F. R. DAVID, "How Do We Choose Among Alternative Growth Strategies?" *Managerial Planning* 33, no. 4 (January–February 1985): 14–17, 22.
7. KENNETH DAVIDSON, "Do Megamergers Make Sense?" *Journal of Business Strategy* 7, no. 3 (Winter 1987): 45.
8. Adapted from F. R. DAVID, "How Do We Choose Among Alternative Growth Strategies?" *Managerial Planning* 33, no. 4 (January–February 1985): 14–17, 22.
9. Ibid.
10. Ibid.
11. Ibid.
12. KEITH ALEXANDER, "Disney Adds Infoseek to Net Assets," *USA Today* (July 13, 1999): 3B.

13. Adapted from F. R. DAVID, "How Do We Choose Among Alternative Growth Strategies?" *Managerial Planning* 33, no. 4 (January–February 1985): 14–17, 22.
14. Ibid.
15. J. C. CONKLIN, "Extension Cords," *The Wall Street Journal* (September 13, 1999): R13.
16. Adapted from F. R. DAVID, "How Do We Choose Among Alternative Growth Strategies?" *Managerial Planning* 33, no. 4 (January–February 1985): 14–17, 22.
17. MIKE SNIDER, "E-mail Use May Force Postal Service Cuts," *USA Today* (October 20, 1999): 1A.
18. Adapted from F. R. DAVID, "How Do We Choose Among Alternative Growth Strategies?" *Managerial Planning* 33, no. 4 (January–February 1985): 14–17, 22.
19. Ibid.
20. Ibid.
21. KATHRYN RUDIE HARRIGAN, "Joint Ventures: Linking for a Leap Forward," *Planning Review* 14, no. 4 (July–August 1986): 10.
22. SHELLY BRANCH, "Double Dip: Merger Creates A New Emperor of Ice Cream," *The Wall Street Journal* (August 20, 1999): 99, B1.
23. STEVEN RATTNER, "Mergers: Windfalls or Pitfalls?" *The Wall Street Journal* (October 11, 1999): A22. Also, NIKHIL DEOGUN, "Merger Wave Spurs More Stock Wipeouts," *The Wall Street Journal* (November 29, 1999): C1.

24. "Why Nothing Seems to Make a Dent in Dealmaking," *Business Week* (July 20, 1987): 75.
25. JULIE SCHMIT, "Climate Is Right For Mergers In Asia," *USA Today* (July 7, 1999:) B1.
26. THOR VALDMANIS, "Internet Frenzy Extends to M&As," *USA Today* (July 28, 1999): B1.
27. DAN DALTON, "The Ubiquitous Leveraged Buyout (LBO): Management Buyout or Management Sellout?" *Business Horizons* 32, no. 4 (July–August 1989): 36.
28. ROBERT DAVIS, "Net Empowering Patients," *USA Today* (July 14, 1999): 1A.
29. *Hospital,* May 5, 1991: 16.
30. Some recent articles are KEITH D. BROUTHERS, FLORIS ANDRIESSEN, and IGOR NICOLAES, "Driving Blind: Strategic Decision-Making in Small Companies," *Long Range Planning* 31 (1998): 130–138; KARGAR, JAVAD, "Strategic Planning System Characteristics and Planning Effectiveness in Small Mature Firms," *Mid-Atlantic Journal of Business* 32, no. 1 (1996): 19–35; PEEL, MICHAEL J. and JOHN BRIDGE, "How Planning and Capital Budgeting Improve SME Performance," *Long Range Planning* 31, no. 6 (1998): 848–856; SMELTZER, LARRY R., GAIL L. FANN, and V. NEAL NIKOLAISEN, "Environmental Scanning Practices in Small Business," *Journal of Small Business Management* 26, no. 3 (1988): 55–63; STEINER, MICHAEL P. and OLAF SOLEM, "Factors for Success in Small Manufacturing Firms," *Journal of Small Business Management* 26, no. 1 (1988): 51–57.
31. ANNE CAREY and GRANT JERDING, "Internet's Reach on Campus," *USA Today* (August 26,1999): A1. Also, BILL MEYERS, "It's a Small-Business World," *USA Today* (July 30,1999): B1-2.
32. BILL MEYERS, "It's a Small-Business World," *USA Today* (July 30,1999): p. B1-2.

# CURRENT READINGS

ABELL, DEREK F. "Competing Today While Preparing for Tomorrow." *Sloan Management Review* 40, no. 3 (Spring 1999): 73–82.

AFUAH, ANIL. "Strategies to Turn Adversity into Profits." *Sloan Management Review* 40, no. 2 (Winter 1999): 99–108.

ARNOLD DAVID J. and JOHN A. QUELCH. "New Strategies in Emerging Markets." *Sloan Management Review* 40, no. 1 (Fall 1998): 7–20.

BARRINGER, B. R. and A. C. BLUEDORN. "The Relationship Between Corporate Entrepreneurship and Strategic Management." *Strategic Management Journal* 20, no. 5 (May 1999): 421–444.

BIRKINSHAW, JULIAN. "Acquiring Intellect: Managing the Integration of Knowledge-Intensive Acquisitions." *Business Horizons* 42, no. 3 (May–June 1999): 33–40.

COOPER, ROBIN and REGINE SLAGMULDER. "Develop Profitable New Products with Target Costing." *Sloan Management Review* 40, no. 4 (Summer 1999): 23–34.

DAWAR, NIRAJ and TONY FROST. "Competing With Giants: Survival Strategies for Local Companies in Emerging Markets." *Harvard Business Review* (March–April 1999): 119–129.

HENNART, J. F., T. ROEHL, and D. S. ZIETLOW. 'Trojan Horse' or 'Workhorse'? The Evolution of U.S.–Japanese Joint Ventures in the United States." *Strategic Management Journal* 20, no. 1 (January 1999): 15–30.

HOMBURG, C., H. KROHMER, and J. P. WORKMAN, JR. "Strategic Consensus and Performance: The Role of Strategy Type and Market-Related Dynamism." *Strategic Management Journal* 20, no. 4 (April 1999): 339–349.

LUBATKIN, MICHAEL, DAVID SCHWEIGER, and YAAKOV WEBER. "Top Management Turnover in Related M&A's: An Additional Test of the Theory of Relative Standing." *Journal of Management* 25, no. 1 (1999): 55–74.

MILLER, DANNY AND JOHN O. WHITNEY. "Beyond Strategy: Configuration as a Pillar of Competitive Advantage." *Business Horizons* 42, no. 3 (May–June 1999): 5–17.

MUNSON, CHARLES L., MEIR J. ROSENBLATT, and ZEHAVA ROSENBLATT. "The Use and Abuse of Power in Supply Chains." *Business Horizons* 42, no. 1 (January–February 1999): 55–65.

QUINN, JAMES BRIAN. "Strategic Outsourcing: Leveraging Knowledge Capabilities." *Sloan Management Review* 40, no. 4 (Summer 1999): 9–22.

RYAN, WILLIAM P. "The New Landscape for Nonprofits." *Harvard Business Review* (January–February 1999): 127–137.

SCOTT, GEORGE M. "Top Priority Management Concerns About New Product Development." *The Academy of Management Executive* 13, no. 3 (August 1999): 77–84.

SI, STEVEN X. AND GARRY D. BRUTON. "Knowledge Transfer in International Joint Ventures in Transitional Economies: The China Experience."*The Academy of Management Executive* 13, no. 1 (February 1999): 83–90.

WONG, YIM YU, THOMAS E. MAHER, RICHARD A. JENNER, ALLEN L. APPELL, and LEN G. HEBERT. "Are Joint Ventures Losing Their Appeal in China?" *Advanced Management Journal* 64, no. 1 (Winter 1999): 4–12.

# EXPERIENTIAL EXERCISES

## PURPOSE

In performing business policy case analysis, you will need to find epilogue information about the respective companies to determine what strategies actually were
employed since the time of the case. Comparing *what actually happened* with *what you
would have recommended and expected to happen* is an important part of business policy
case analysis. Do not recommend what the firm actually did, unless in-depth analysis
of the situation at the time reveals those strategies to have been best among all feasible alternatives. This exercise gives you experience conducting library research to
determine what strategies AOL, Yahoo, and Microsoft pursued in 2000.

## INSTRUCTIONS

**Step 1**   Look up AOL, Yahoo, and Microsoft on the Internet. Find some recent arti-
cles about firms in the confectionery industry. Scan Moody's, Dun &
Bradstreet, and Standard & Poor's publications for information. Check the
Edgar files at www.sec.gov and Hoover's online at www.hoovers.com.

**Step 2**   Summarize your findings in a three-page report titled "Strategies of AOL in
2000." Include information about Yahoo and Microsoft. Also include your
personal reaction to AOL's strategies in terms of their attractiveness.

## PURPOSE

Strategy articles can be found weekly in journals, magazines, and newspapers. By
reading and studying strategy articles, you can gain a better understanding of the
strategic-management process. Several of the best journals in which to find corporate
strategy articles are *Planning Review, Long Range Planning, Journal of Business Strategy,*
and *Strategic Management Journal.* These journals are devoted to reporting the results
of empirical research in strategic management. They apply strategic-management
concepts to specific organizations and industries. They introduce new strategic-
management techniques and provide short case studies on selected firms.

Other good journals in which to find strategic-management articles are *Harvard
Business Review, Sloan Management Review, Business Horizons, California Management
Review, Academy of Management Review, Academy of Management Journal, Academy of
Management Executive, Journal of Management,* and *Journal of Small Business Management.*

In addition to journals, many magazines regularly publish articles that focus on
business strategies. Several of the best magazines in which to find applied strategy
articles are *Dun's Business Month, Fortune, Forbes, Business Week, Inc. Magazine,* and
*Industry Week.* Newspapers such as *USA Today, The Wall Street Journal, The New York
Times,* and *Barrons* cover strategy events when they occur—for example, a joint venture announcement, a bankruptcy declaration, a new advertising campaign start,
acquisition of a company, divestiture of a division, a chief executive officer's hiring or
firing, or a hostile takeover attempt.

In combination, journal, magazine, and newspaper articles can make the business policy course more exciting. They allow current strategies of profit and nonprofit
organizations to be identified and studied.

## INSTRUCTIONS

**Step 1**    Go to your college library and find a recent journal article that focuses on a strategic-management topic. Select your article from one of the journals listed above, not from a magazine. Copy the article and bring it to class.

**Step 2**    Give a three-minute oral report summarizing the most important information in your article. Include comments giving your personal reaction to the article. Pass your article around in class.

**EXPERIENTIAL EXERCISE 5C** ▶

**Classifying Some Year 2000 Strategies**

## PURPOSE

This exercise can improve your understanding of various strategies by giving you experience classifying strategies. This skill will help you use the strategy-formulation tools presented later. Consider the following year 2000 strategies by various firms:

1. Philip Morris, the world's-largest tobacco company, is spending $100 million in 2000 on advertising to remake its corporate image.
2. 3Com and Nokia teamed up to produce a palm-size smart-phone that allows phoning, paging, e-mail, and net surfing.
3. Advanced Micro Devices is selling its communications-chip business to raise funds to compete better with its primary rival, Intel.
4. Hoffmann-La Roche is spending heavily on advertising its new prescription diet pill Xenical.
5. Nissan introduced its SULEV (Super-ultra low-emission vehicle) in February 2000 into its first market—California.
6. SBC Communications, the huge phone company, recently acquired 43 percent of Prodigy, the Internet Service Provider.
7. Exxon and Mobil are selling 15 percent of their gas stations (1,700) as part of their $1.026 billion merger.
8. BB&T Corporation, the large North Carolina bank, acquired First Liberty Financial, the Georgia-based bank.
9. Pfizer, the giant drug company, proposed to acquire Warner-Lambert, a major competitor, for $72 billion.
10. Nickelodeon formed an alliance with Gateway, Inc., for Gateway computers to be preloaded with Nickelodeon's sounds and screen savers.
11. Trans World Airlines (TWA) announced plans to end service to Rome, Madrid, and Barcelona.
12. General Electric is trying to sell its NBC television division.
13. Marriott is adding one thousand new hotels between 1998 and 2003 worldwide.
14. The German postal monopoly, Deutsche Pot, acquired the largest U.S. air-freight forwarder, Air Express International.

## INSTRUCTIONS

**Step 1**    On a separate sheet of paper, number from 1 to 14. These numbers correspond to the strategies described above.

**Step 2**    What type of strategy best describes the 14 actions cited above? Indicate your answers.

**Step 3**    Exchange papers with a classmate and grade each other's paper as your instructor gives the right answers.

Strategic
Management at the
Dynamic Computer
Company

## PURPOSE

This exercise can give you experience choosing among alternative growth strategies for a specific company. Remember that organizations cannot pursue all the strategies that potentially may benefit the firm. Difficult decisions have to be made to eliminate some options. Use the guidelines given in Chapter 5 to complete this exercise.

## BACKGROUND

Dynamic Computer, Inc. (DCI) is a highly regarded personal computer manufacturer based in central California. DCI designs, develops, produces, markets, and services personal computer systems for individuals' needs in business, education, science, engineering, and the home. The company's main product is the Dynamic II personal computer system, complete with optional accessories and software. The company recently announced a new system, the Dynamic III, that is aimed at large business firms. It is much more expensive than the Dynamic II. Dynamic's computer systems are distributed in the United States and Canada by 1,000 independent retail stores and internationally through 21 independent distributors, who resell to 850 foreign retail outlets. Approximately 700 of the retail outlets in the United States and Canada are authorized service centers for Dynamic products, but none of the outlets sell Dynamic products exclusively. Many of these outlets are not marketing Dynamic's products effectively.

The American computer industry grew at an inflation-adjusted, compound annual rate of about 20 percent during the 1990s. The outlook for personal computers continues to be positive. However, this market is highly competitive and is characterized by rapid technological advances in both hardware and software. Margins on software are nearly double operating margins on hardware. New firms are entering the industry at an increasing rate, and this has resulted in a decline in Dynamic's sales, earnings, and market share in recent years. Many computer companies expect software sales and services to represent 50 percent of their total revenues by 2002. Dynamic is concerned about its future direction and competitiveness. Selected financial information for Dynamic is given in Table 5D–1.

## INSTRUCTIONS

The owners of DCI have indicated a willingness to explore a number of alternative growth strategies for the future. They have hired you as a consultant to assist them in making strategic decisions regarding the future allocation of resources. The feeling is that to sustain growth, the company must make some critical decisions. Dynamic is financially capable of investing in several projects. The owners wish to use their

TABLE 5D–1     Selected Financial Information for DCI

|              | 1999 | 2000 | 2001 |
|--------------|------|------|------|
| Sales        | $13,000,000 | $12,000,000 | $10,000,000 |
| New Income   | 3,000,000 | 1,000,000 | 500,000 |
| Total Assets | 180,000,000 | 200,000,000 | 250,000,000 |
| Market Share | 15% | 12% | 10% |

resources wisely to produce the highest possible return on investment in the future. They are considering five alternative strategies:

1. Market penetration—establish a nationwide sales force to market Dynamic products to large firms that do not buy through independent retailers.
2. Product development—develop an easier-to-use computer for small business firms.
3. Forward integration—offer major new incentives to distributors who sell and service Dynamic products.
4. Backward integration—purchase a major outside supplier of software.
5. Conglomerate diversification—acquire Toys Unlimited, a large and successful toy manufacturer.

Based on the strategy guidelines given in Chapter 5, your task is to offer specific recommendations to the strategists of DCI. Follow these steps:

**Step 1**   Across the top of a separate sheet of paper, set up five columns, with the following headings:

| Individual Percentage Allocations | Group Percentage Allocations | Expert Percentage Allocations | The Absolute Difference Between Columns 1 and 3 | The Absolute Difference Between Columns 2 and 3 |
|---|---|---|---|---|

Down the left side of your paper, number from 1 to 5. These numbers correspond to the five strategies listed above.

**Step 2**   Take ten minutes to determine how you would allocate DCI's resources among the five alternative strategies. Record your answers by placing individual percentage values for strategies 1 through 5 under column 1. Your only constraint is that the total resources allocated must equal 100 percent. Distribute resources in the manner you think will offer the greatest future return on investment and profitability.

**Step 3**   Join with two other students in class. Develop a set of group percentage allocations and record these values for strategies 1 through 5 under column 2. Do not change your individual percentage allocations once discussion begins in your group.

**Step 4**   As your teacher reveals the right answer and supporting rationale, record these values for strategies 1 through 5 under column 3.

**Step 5**   For each row, subtract column 3 values from column 1 values and record the absolute difference (ignore negatives) in column 4. Then, sum the column 4 values.

**Step 6**   For each row, subtract column 3 values from column 2 values and record the absolute difference (ignore negatives) in column 5. Then, sum the column 5 values.

**Step 7**   If the sum of column 4 values exceeds the sum of column 5 values, then your group allocation of DCI's resources was better than your individual allocation. However, if the sum of column 4 values is less than the sum of column 5 values, you were a better strategist than your group on this exercise.

Strategic-management research indicates that group strategic decisions are almost always better than individual strategic decisions. Did you do better than your group?

**EXPERIENTIAL
EXERCISE 5E** ▶

How Risky Are
Various Alternative
Strategies?

## PURPOSE

This exercise focuses on how risky various alternative strategies are for organizations to pursue. Different degrees of risk are based largely on varying degrees of *externality,* defined as movement away from present business into new markets and products. In general, the greater the degree of externality, the greater the probability of loss resulting from unexpected events. High-risk strategies generally are less attractive than low-risk strategies.

## INSTRUCTIONS

**Step 1**   On a separate sheet of paper, number vertically from 1 to 10. Think of 1 as "most risky," 2 as "next most risky," and so forth to 10, "least risky."

**Step 2**   Write the following strategies beside the appropriate number to indicate how risky you believe the strategy is to pursue: horizontal integration, horizontal diversification, liquidation, forward integration, backward integration, product development, market development, market penetration, joint venture, and conglomerate diversification.

**Step 3**   Grade your paper as your teacher gives you the right answers and supporting rationale. Each correct answer is worth 10 points.

**EXPERIENTIAL
EXERCISE 5F** ▶

Developing
Alternative Strategies
for My University

## PURPOSE

It is important for representatives from all areas of a college or university to identify and discuss alternative strategies that could benefit faculty, students, alumni, staff, and other constituencies. As you complete this exercise, notice the learning and understanding that occurs as people express differences of opinions. Recall that *the process of planning is more important than the document.*

## INSTRUCTIONS

**Step 1**   Recall or locate the external opportunity/threat and internal strength/weakness factors that you identified as part of Experiential Exercise 1D. If you did not do that exercise, discuss now as a class important external and internal factors facing your college or university.

**Step 2**   Identify and put on the chalkboard alternative strategies that you feel could benefit your college or university. Your proposed actions should allow the institution to capitalize on particular strengths, improve upon certain weaknesses, avoid external threats, and/or take advantage of particular external opportunities. List at least twenty possible strategies on the board. Number the strategies as they are written on the board.

**Step 3**   On a separate sheet of paper, number from 1 to the total number of strategies listed on the board. Everyone in class individually should rate the strategies identified, using a 1 to 3 scale, where 1 = *I do not support implementation,* 2 = *I am neutral about implementation,* and 3 = *I strongly support implementation.* In rating the strategies, recognize that your institution cannot do everything desired or potentially beneficial.

**Step 4**   Go to the board and record your ratings in a row beside the respective strategies. Everyone in class should do this, going to the board perhaps by rows in the class.

Step 5   Sum the ratings for each strategy so that a prioritized list of recommended strategies is obtained. This prioritized list reflects the collective wisdom of your class. Strategies with the highest score are deemed best.

Step 6   Discuss how this process could enable organizations to achieve understanding and commitment from individuals.

Step 7   Share your class results with a university administrator and ask for comments regarding the process and top strategies recommended.

**EXPERIENTIAL EXERCISE 5G** ▶

Lessons in Doing Business Globally

### PURPOSE

The purpose of this exercise is to discover some important lessons learned by local businesses who do business internationally.

### INSTRUCTIONS

Contact several local business leaders by phone. Find at least three firms that engage in international or export operations. Ask the businessperson to give you several important lessons his or her firm has learned in doing business globally. Record the lessons on paper and report your findings to the class.

# 6

# STRATEGY ANALYSIS AND CHOICE

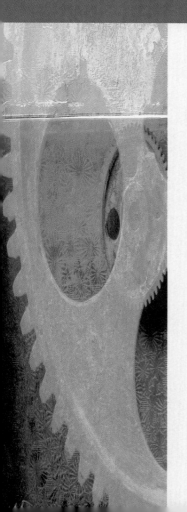

## CHAPTER OUTLINE

- The Nature of Strategy Analysis and Choice
- A Comprehensive Strategy-Formulation Framework
- The Input Stage
- The Matching Stage
- The Decision Stage
- Cultural Aspects of Strategy Choice
- The Politics of Strategy Choice
- The Role of a Board of Directors

**EXPERIENTIAL EXERCISE 6A**
*Developing a TOWS Matrix for America Online (AOL)*

**EXPERIENTIAL EXERCISE 6B**
*Developing a SPACE Matrix for America Online (AOL)*

**EXPERIENTIAL EXERCISE 6C**
*Developing a BCG Matrix for America Online (AOL)*

**EXPERIENTIAL EXERCISE 6D**
*Developing a QSPM for America Online (AOL)*

**EXPERIENTIAL EXERCISE 6E**
*Formulating Individual Strategies*

**EXPERIENTIAL EXERCISE 6F**
*The Mach Test*

**EXPERIENTIAL EXERCISE 6G**
*Developing a BCG Matrix for My University*

**EXPERIENTIAL EXERCISE 6H**
*The Role of Boards of Directors*

**EXPERIENTIAL EXERCISE 6I**
*Locating Companies in a Grand Strategy Matrix*

## CHAPTER OBJECTIVES

*After studying this chapter, you should be able to do the following:*

1. Describe a three-stage framework for choosing among alternative strategies.

2. Explain how to develop a TOWS Matrix, SPACE Matrix, BCG Matrix, IE Matrix, and QSPM.

3. Identify important behavioral, political, ethical, and social responsibility considerations in strategy analysis and choice.

4. Discuss the role of intuition in strategic analysis and choice.

5. Discuss the role of organizational culture in strategic analysis and choice.

6. Discuss the role of a board of directors in choosing among alternative strategies.

# NOTABLE QUOTES

Strategic management is not a box of tricks or a bundle of techniques. It is analytical thinking and commitment of resources to action. But quantification alone is not planning. Some of the most important issues in strategic management cannot be quantified at all.

PETER DRUCKER

Objectives are not commands; they are commitments. They do not determine the future; they are the means to mobilize resources and energies of an organization for the making of the future.

PETER DRUCKER

Life is full of lousy options.

GENERAL P. X. KELLEY

When a crisis forces choosing among alternatives, most people will choose the worse possible one.

RUDIN'S LAW

Strategy isn't something you can nail together in slap-dash fashion by sitting around a conference table.

TERRY HALLER

Planning is often doomed before it ever starts, either because too much is expected of it or because not enough is put into it.

T. J. CARTWRIGHT

To acquire or not to acquire, that is the question.

ROBERT J. TERRY

Corporate boards need to work to stay away from the traps that force every member to go along with the majority. Devil's advocates represent one easy-to-implement solution.

CHARLES SCHWENK

Whether it's broke or not, fix it—make it better. Not just products, but the whole company if necessary.

BILL SAPORITO

Strategic analysis and choice largely involves making subjective decisions based on objective information. This chapter introduces important concepts that can help strategists generate feasible alternatives, evaluate those alternatives, and choose a specific course of action. Behavioral aspects of strategy formulation are described, including politics, culture, ethics, and social responsibility considerations. Modern tools for formulating strategies are described, and the appropriate role of a board of directors is discussed.

# THE NATURE OF STRATEGY ANALYSIS AND CHOICE

As indicated by Figure 6–1, this chapter focuses on establishing long-term objectives, generating alternative strategies, and selecting strategies to pursue. Strategy analysis and choice seeks to determine alternative courses of action that could best enable the firm to achieve its mission and objectives. The firm's present strategies, objectives, and mission, coupled with the external and internal audit information, provide a basis for generating and evaluating feasible alternative strategies.

Unless a desperate situation faces the firm, alternative strategies will likely represent incremental steps to move the firm from its present position to a desired future position. Alternative strategies do not come out of the wild blue yonder; they are derived

**FIGURE 6–1**

**A Comprehensive Strategic-Management Model**

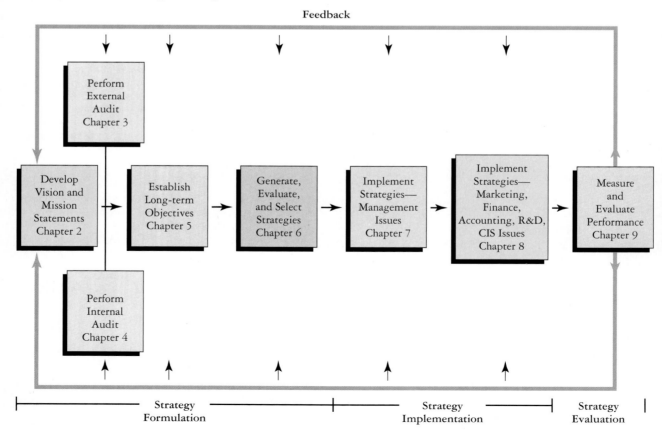

from the firm's mission, objectives, external audit, and internal audit; they are consistent with, or build upon, past strategies that have worked well!

## The Process of Generating and Selecting Strategies

Strategists never consider all feasible alternatives that could benefit the firm, because there are an infinite number of possible actions and an infinite number of ways to implement those actions. Therefore, a manageable set of the most attractive alternative strategies must be developed. The advantages, disadvantages, trade-offs, costs, and benefits of these strategies should be determined. This section discusses the process that many firms use to determine an appropriate set of alternative strategies.

Identifying and evaluating alternative strategies should involve many of the managers and employees who earlier assembled the organizational mission statement, performed the external audit, and conducted the internal audit. Representatives from each department and division of the firm should be included in this process, as was the case in previous strategy-formulation activities. Recall that involvement provides the best opportunity for managers and employees to gain an understanding of what the firm is doing and why, and to become committed to helping the firm accomplish its objectives.

All participants in the strategy analysis and choice activity should have the firm's external and internal audit information by their sides. This information, coupled with the firm's mission statement, will help participants crystallize in their own minds particular strategies that they believe could benefit the firm most. Creativity should be encouraged in this thought process.

Alternative strategies proposed by participants should be considered and discussed in a meeting or series of meetings. Proposed strategies should be listed in writing. When all feasible strategies identified by participants are given and understood, the strategies should be ranked in order of attractiveness by all participants, with 1 = *should not be implemented, 2 = possibly should be implemented, 3 = probably should be implemented,* and 4 = *definitely should be implemented.* This process will result in a prioritized list of best strategies that reflects the collective wisdom of the group.

## A COMPREHENSIVE STRATEGY-FORMULATION FRAMEWORK

Important strategy-formulation techniques can be integrated into a three-stage decision-making framework, as shown in Figure 6–2. The tools presented in this framework are applicable to all sizes and types of organizations and can help strategists identify, evaluate, and select strategies.

Stage 1 of the formulation framework consists of the EFE Matrix, the IFE Matrix, and the Competitive Profile Matrix. Called the *Input Stage,* Stage 1 summarizes the basic input information needed to formulate strategies. Stage 2, called the *Matching Stage,* focuses upon generating feasible alternative strategies by aligning key external and internal factors. Stage 2 techniques include the Threats-Opportunities-Weaknesses-Strengths (TOWS) Matrix, the Strategic Position and Action Evaluation (SPACE) Matrix, the Boston Consulting Group (BCG) Matrix, the Internal-External (IE) Matrix, and the Grand Strategy Matrix. Stage 3, called the *Decision Stage,* involves a single technique, the Quantitative Strategic Planning Matrix (QSPM). A QSPM uses input information from Stage 1 to objectively evaluate feasible alternative strategies identified in Stage 2. A QSPM reveals the relative attractiveness of alternative strategies and thus provides an objective basis for selecting specific strategies.

All nine techniques included in the *strategy-formulation framework* require integration of intuition and analysis. Autonomous divisions in an organization commonly use

# NATURAL ENVIRONMENT

## Formulating Strategies Based on Environmental Attitudes

Americans can be grouped into categories based on their attitudes, actions, and concern toward natural environment deterioration and preservation. Note in the table that persons most concerned about the natural environment tend to be female, have higher household income, and live in the Midwest or Northeast. These persons especially engage in activities such as not purchasing products from companies that are environmentally irresponsible, avoiding purchasing aerosol products, recycling paper and bottles, using biodegradable products, and contributing money to environmental groups. This information can be helpful to companies in formulating strategies such as market development (where to locate new facilities), product development (manufacturing new equipment or developing green products), and market penetration (whom to focus advertising efforts upon).

*Source:* Adapted from the Roper Organization, 205 East 42nd Street, New York, NY 10017. Also from Joe Schwartz and Thomas Miller, "The Earth's Best Friends," *American Demographics* (February 1991): 28.

| CHARACTERISTICS | HIGH CONCERN FOR THE NATURAL ENVIRONMENT | LOW CONCERN FOR THE NATURAL ENVIRONMENT |
|---|---|---|
| **Sex** | | |
| Male | 34% | 55% |
| Female | 66 | 45 |
| **Education** | | |
| Less than High School | 11 | 30 |
| High School Graduate | 39 | 39 |
| Some College | 22 | 20 |
| College Graduate Or More | 28 | 11 |
| **Occupation** | | |
| Executive/Professional | 25 | 11 |
| White Collar | 18 | 15 |
| Blue Collar | 19 | 36 |
| **Marital Status** | | |
| Married | 69 | 59 |
| Not Married | 30 | 41 |
| **Political/Social Ideology** | | |
| Conservative | 43 | 36 |
| Middle of the Road | 26 | 41 |
| Liberal | 28 | 16 |
| **Region** | | |
| Northeast | 31 | 17 |
| Midwest | 27 | 22 |
| South | 18 | 48 |
| West | 24 | 13 |
| *Median Income* (in thousands) | $32.1 | $21.2 |

strategy-formulation techniques to develop strategies and objectives. Divisional analyses provide a basis for identifying, evaluating, and selecting among alternative corporate-level strategies.

Strategists themselves, not analytic tools, are always responsible and accountable for strategic decisions. Lenz emphasized that the shift from a words-oriented to a numbers-oriented planning process can give rise to a false sense of certainty; it can reduce dialogue, discussion, and argument as a means to explore understandings, test assumptions and foster organizational learning.[1] Strategists therefore must be wary of this possibility and use analytical tools to facilitate, rather than diminish, communication. Without objective information and analysis, personal biases, politics, emotions, personalities, and *halo error* (the tendency to put too much weight on a single factor) unfortunately may play a dominant role in the strategy-formulation process.

**FIGURE 6–2**

**The Strategy-Formulation Analytical Framework**

| STAGE 1: THE INPUT STAGE | | |
|---|---|---|
| External Factor Evaluation (EFE) Matrix | Competitive Profile Matrix | Internal Factor Evaluation (IFE) Matrix |

| STAGE 2: THE MATCHING STAGE | | | | |
|---|---|---|---|---|
| Threats-Opportunities-Weaknesses-Strengths (TOWS) Matrix | Strategic Position and Action Evaluation (SPACE) Matrix | Boston Consulting Group (BCG) Matrix | Internal-External (IE) Matrix | Grand Strategy Matrix |

| STAGE 3: THE DECISION STAGE |
|---|
| Quantitative Strategic Planning Matrix (QSPM) |

## THE INPUT STAGE

Procedures for developing an EFE Matrix, an IFE Matrix, and a Competitive Profile Matrix were presented in the previous two chapters. The information derived from these three matrices provides basic input information for the matching and decision stage matrices described later in this chapter.

The input tools require strategists to quantify subjectivity during early stages of the strategy-formulation process. Making small decisions in the input matrices regarding the relative importance of external and internal factors allows strategists to generate and evaluate alternative strategies more effectively. Good intuitive judgment is always needed in determining appropriate weights and ratings.

## THE MATCHING STAGE

Strategy is sometimes defined as the match an organization makes between its internal resources and skills and the opportunities and risks created by its external factors.[2] The matching stage of the strategy-formulation framework consists of five techniques that can be used in any sequence: the TOWS Matrix, the SPACE Matrix, the BCG Matrix, the IE Matrix, and the Grand Strategy Matrix. These tools rely upon information derived from the input stage to match external opportunities and threats with internal strengths and weaknesses. *Matching* external and internal critical success factors is the key to effectively generating feasible alternative strategies! For example, a firm with excess working capital (an internal strength) could take advantage of the cablevision industry's 20 percent annual growth rate (an external opportunity) by acquiring a firm in the cablevision industry. This example portrays simple one-to-one matching. In most situations, external and internal relationships are more complex, and the matching requires multiple alignments for each strategy generated. The basic concept of matching is illustrated in Table 6–1.

TABLE 6-1    **Matching Key External and Internal Factors to Formulate Alternative Strategies**

| KEY INTERNAL FACTOR | | KEY EXTERNAL FACTOR | | RESULTANT STRATEGY |
|---|---|---|---|---|
| Excess working capacity (an internal strength) | + | 20% annual growth in the cablevision industry (an external opportunity) | = | Acquire Visioncable, Inc. |
| Insufficient capacity (an internal weakness) | + | Exit of two major foreign competitors from the industry (an external opportunity) | = | Pursue horizontal integration by buying competitors' facilities |
| Strong R & D expertise (an internal strength) | + | Decreasing numbers of young adults (an external threat) | = | Develop new products for older adults |
| Poor employee morale (an internal weakness) | + | Strong union activity (an external threat) | = | Develop a new employee benefits package |

e·biz

Any organization, whether military, product-oriented, service-oriented, governmental, or even athletic, must develop and execute good strategies to win. A good offense without a good defense, or vice versa, usually leads to defeat. Developing strategies that use strengths to capitalize on opportunities could be considered an offense, whereas strategies designed to improve upon weaknesses while avoiding threats could be termed defensive. Every organization has some external opportunities and threats and internal strengths and weaknesses that can be aligned to formulate feasible alternative strategies. As indicated in the E-Commerce Perspective, the Internet itself creates significant opportunities and threats for firms.

### The Threats-Opportunities-Weaknesses-Strengths (TOWS) Matrix

The *Threats-Opportunities-Weaknesses-Strengths (TOWS) Matrix* is an important matching tool that helps managers develop four types of strategies: SO Strategies, WO Strategies, ST Strategies, and WT Strategies.[3] Matching key external and internal factors is the most difficult part of developing a TOWS Matrix and requires good judgment, and there is no one best set of matches. Note in Table 6–1 that the first, second, third, and fourth strategies are SO, WO, ST, and WT Strategies, respectively.

*SO Strategies* use a firm's internal strengths to take advantage of external opportunities. All managers would like their organizations to be in a position where internal strengths can be used to take advantage of external trends and events. Organizations generally will pursue WO, ST, or WT Strategies in order to get into a situation where they can apply SO Strategies. When a firm has major weaknesses, it will strive to overcome them and make them strengths. When an organization faces major threats, it will seek to avoid them in order to concentrate on opportunities.

*WO Strategies* aim at improving internal weaknesses by taking advantage of external opportunities. Sometimes key external opportunities exist, but a firm has internal weaknesses that prevent it from exploiting those opportunities. For example, there may be a high demand for electronic devices to control the amount and timing of fuel injection in automobile engines (opportunity), but a certain auto parts manufacturer may lack the technology required for producing these devices (weakness). One possible WO Strategy would be to acquire this technology by forming a joint venture with a firm having competency in this area. An alternative WO Strategy would be to hire and train people with the required technical capabilities.

*ST Strategies* use a firm's strengths to avoid or reduce the impact of external threats. This does not mean that a strong organization should always meet threats in the external environment head-on. A recent example of ST Strategy occurred when Texas Instruments used an excellent legal department (a strength) to collect nearly $700 million in damages and royalties from nine Japanese and Korean firms that infringed on patents for semi-

## E-COMMERCE PERSPECTIVE

**e·biz**   *What Industries Are Most Affected by Online Sales?*

Nearly all industries are today affected by online sales, as indicated by the large "Other" category in the table below. Business-to-business e-commerce exploded from $43.1 billion in 1998 to $109.3 billion in 1999 and is expected to be $1.3 trillion and ten times e-commerce sales by 2003. Online sales by product category (in millions) in some industries are provided below. Note dramatic increases from 1999 to 2002.

*Source:* Adapted from: George Anders "Buying Frenzy," *The Wall Street Journal* (July 12, 1999): R6.

### A. BUSINESS TO CONSUMER

| Product Category | 1997 | 1999 | 2002 |
|---|---|---|---|
| Travel | $911.3 | $3,933.5 | $11,699.4 |
| PC hardware | 985.5 | 3,106.0 | 6,434.4 |
| Books | 151.9 | 1,138.8 | 3,661.0 |
| Apparel and accessories | 103.1 | 641.5 | 2,844.5 |
| PC software | 84.5 | 507.4 | 2,379.1 |
| Grocery | 63.3 | 350.3 | 3,529.2 |
| Specialty gifts | 99.9 | 336.3 | 1,356.5 |
| Music | 36.6 | 280.6 | 1,590.6 |
| Tickets | 51.8 | 104.5 | 575.2 |
| Videos | 15.0 | 104.5 | 575.2 |
| Consumer electronics | 15.0 | 77.9 | 792.5 |
| Health & beauty | 2.0 | 65.5 | 1,182.9 |
| Toys | 2.0 | 52.6 | 555.3 |
| Other | 484.7 | 1,086.9 | 2,688.7 |

### B. BUSINESS TO BUSINESS

| | 1999 | 2001 | 2003 |
|---|---|---|---|
| Computing and electronics | $50,379 | $229,108 | $395,302 |
| Utilities | 15,406 | 62,896 | 169,545 |
| Petrochemicals | 10,327 | 48,001 | 178,311 |
| Motor vehicles | 9,254 | 53,219 | 212,925 |
| Aerospace and defense | 6,553 | 25,633 | 38,205 |
| Paper products and office equip. | 2,859 | 14,269 | 65,192 |
| Consumer goods | 2,946 | 12,722 | 51,915 |

conductor memory chips (threat). Rival firms that copy ideas, innovations, and patented products are a major threat in many industries. This is a major problem for U.S. firms selling products in China.

*WT Strategies* are defensive tactics directed at reducing internal weaknesses and avoiding environmental threats. An organization faced with numerous external threats and internal weaknesses may indeed be in a precarious position. In fact, such a firm may have to fight for its survival, merge, retrench, declare bankruptcy, or choose liquidation.

A schematic representation of the TOWS Matrix is provided in Figure 6–3. Note that a TOWS Matrix is composed of nine cells. As shown, there are four key factor cells, four strategy cells, and one cell that is always left blank (the upper-left cell). The four strategy cells, labeled *SO, WO, ST,* and *WT,* are developed after completing four key factor cells, labeled *S, W, O,* and *T.* There are eight steps involved in constructing a TOWS Matrix:

1. List the firm's key external opportunities.
2. List the firm's key external threats.
3. List the firm's key internal strengths.
4. List the firm's key internal weaknesses.
5. Match internal strengths with external opportunities and record the resultant SO Strategies in the appropriate cell.

**FIGURE 6–3**

**The TOWS Matrix**

| Always leave blank | STRENGTHS—S<br>1.<br>2.<br>3.<br>4.<br>5.<br>6.<br>7.<br>8.<br>9.<br>10.<br><br>List strengths | WEAKNESSES—W<br>1.<br>2.<br>3.<br>4.<br>5.<br>6.<br>7.<br>8.<br>9.<br>10.<br><br>List weaknesses |
|---|---|---|
| OPPORTUNITIES—O<br>1.<br>2.<br>3.<br>4.<br>5.<br>6.<br>7.<br>8.<br>9.<br>10.<br><br>List opportunities | SO STRATEGIES<br>1.<br>2.<br>3.<br>4.<br>5.<br>6.<br>7.<br>8.<br>9.<br>10.<br><br>Use strengths to take advantage of opportunities | WO STRATEGIES<br>1.<br>2.<br>3.<br>4.<br>5.<br>6.<br>7.<br>8.<br>9.<br>10.<br><br>Overcome weaknesses by taking advantage of opportunities |
| THREATS—T<br>1.<br>2.<br>3.<br>4.<br>5.<br>6.<br>7.<br>8.<br>9.<br>10.<br><br>List threats | ST STRATEGIES<br>1.<br>2.<br>3.<br>4.<br>5.<br>6.<br>7.<br>8.<br>9.<br>10.<br><br>Use strengths to avoid threats | WT STRATEGIES<br>1.<br>2.<br>3.<br>4.<br>5.<br>6.<br>7.<br>8.<br>9.<br>10.<br><br>Minimize weaknesses and avoid threats |

6. Match internal weaknesses with external opportunities and record the resultant WO Strategies.

7. Match internal strengths with external threats and record the resultant ST Strategies.

8. Match internal weaknesses with external threats and record the resultant WT Strategies.

The purpose of each Stage 2 matching tool is to generate feasible alternative strategies, not to select or determine which strategies are best! Not all of the strategies developed in the TOWS Matrix, therefore, will be selected for implementation. A sample TOWS Matrix for Cineplex Odeon, the large cinema company, is provided in Figure 6–4.

The strategy-formulation guidelines provided in Chapter 5 can enhance the process of matching key external and internal factors. For example, when an organization has both the capital and human resources needed to distribute its own products (internal

**FIGURE 6–4**

**Cineplex Odeon TOWS Matrix**

|  | STRENGTHS—S | WEAKNESSES—W |
|---|---|---|
|  | 1. Located in large population centers | 1. Poor labor relations |
|  | 2. Positive cash flow 3 years running | 2. Current ratio of 0.25 |
|  | 3. Double the industry concession sales rate | 3. Flat operating cost through falling revenue |
|  | 4. Many cost-cutting measures in place | 4. Triple the G&A expenses of Carmike |
|  | 5. Upgraded audio in many places | 5. Significant losses in the United States |
|  | 6. Profitable in Canada | 6. Management concentrating on market share |
|  |  | 7. Restrictive covenants set by lenders |
| **OPPORTUNITIES—O** | **SO STRATEGIES** | **WO STRATEGIES** |
| 1. Approached by most major chains for potential merger | 1. Open theaters in Eastern Europe (S1, O2, O5) | 1. Pursue merger with American Cinemas (O1, O2, W3, W4, W5, W6) |
| 2. Opening economies in Eastern Europe |  |  |
| 3. Rebounding attendance (up 6.4%) |  |  |
| 4. Videotape industry worth estimated $18 billion vs. $6.4 billion for movie theaters |  |  |
| 5. Foreign per capita income growth outpacing the United States |  |  |
| **THREATS—T** | **ST STRATEGIES** | **WT STRATEGIES** |
| 1. 80% of all households own VCRs | 1. Open 50 video rental stores in 10 markets (S1, S6, T1, T3, T5) | 1. Reduce corporate overhead (W3, W4, T3, T5, T6) |
| 2. Aging population | 2. Construct 20 multidimensional entertainment complexes (S1, T3, T5, T6) | 2. Divest U.S. operations (W2, W3, W4, W5, W6, T6) |
| 3. Dependence on successful movies |  |  |
| 4. Switch from bid to allocation for licenses |  |  |
| 5. Seasonality for movie releases |  |  |
| 6. Increased competition in exhibition |  |  |

strength) and distributors are unreliable, costly, or incapable of meeting the firm's needs (external threat), then forward integration can be an attractive ST Strategy. When a firm has excess production capacity (internal weakness) and its basic industry is experiencing declining annual sales and profits (external threat), then concentric diversification can be an effective WT Strategy. It is important to use specific, rather than general, strategy terms when developing a TOWS Matrix. In addition, it is important to include the "S1,O2"-type notation after each strategy in the TOWS Matrix. This notation reveals the rationale for each alternative strategy.

**FIGURE 6–5**

**The SPACE Matrix**

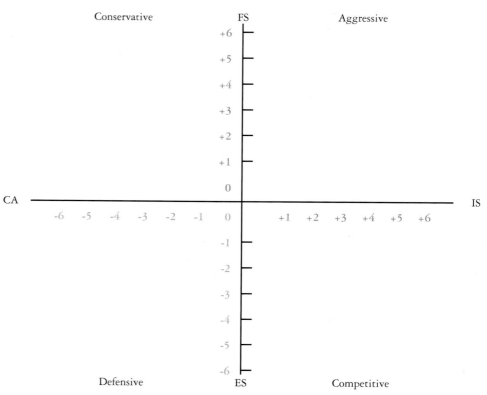

Source: H. Rowe, R. Mason, and K. Dickel, *Strategic Management and Business Policy: A Methodological Approach* (Reading, Massachusetts: Addison-Wesley Publishing Co. Inc., © 1982): 155. Reprinted with permission of the publisher.

## The Strategic Position and Action Evaluation (SPACE) Matrix

*The Strategic Position and Action Evaluation (SPACE) Matrix,* another important Stage 2 *matching* tool, is illustrated in Figure 6–5. Its four-quadrant framework indicates whether aggressive, conservative, defensive, or competitive strategies are most appropriate for a given organization. The axes of the SPACE Matrix represent two internal dimensions (*financial strength* [FS] and *competitive advantage* [CA]) and two external dimensions (*environmental stability* [ES] and *industry strength* [IS]). These four factors are the most important determinants of an organization's overall strategic position.[4]

Depending upon the type of organization, numerous variables could make up each of the dimensions represented on the axes of the SPACE Matrix. Factors earlier included in the firm's EFE and IFE matrices should be considered in developing a SPACE Matrix. Other variables commonly included are given in Table 6–2. For example, return on investment, leverage, liquidity, working capital, and cash flow commonly are considered determining factors of an organization's financial strength. Like the TOWS Matrix, the SPACE Matrix should be tailored to the particular organization being studied and based on factual information as much as possible.

The steps required to develop a SPACE Matrix are as follows:

1. Select a set of variables to define financial strength (FS), competitive advantage (CA), environmental stability (ES), and industry strength (IS).

TABLE 6-2        **Example Factors That Make Up the SPACE**
                 **Matrix Axes**

| INTERNAL STRATEGIC POSITION | EXTERNAL STRATEGIC POSITION |
|---|---|
| *Financial Strength (FS)* | *Environmental Stability (ES)* |
| Return on investment | Technological changes |
| Leverage | Rate of inflation |
| Liquidity | Demand variability |
| Working capital | Price range of competing products |
| Cash flow | Barriers to entry into market |
| Ease of exit from market | Competitive pressure |
| Risk involved in business | Price elasticity of demand |
| *Competitive Advantage (CA)* | *Industry Strength (IS)* |
| Market share | Growth potential |
| Product quality | Profit potential |
| Product life cycle | Financial stability |
| Customer loyalty | Technological know-how |
| Competition's capacity utilization | Resource utilization |
| Technological know-how | Capital intensity |
| Control over suppliers and distributors | Ease of entry into market |
| | Productivity, capacity utilization |

*Source:* H. Rowe, R. Mason, and K. Dickel, *Strategic Management and Business Policy: A Methodological Approach* (Reading, Massachusetts: Addison-Wesley Publishing Co. Inc., © 1982): 155–156. Reprinted with permission of the publisher.

2. Assign a numerical value ranging from +1 (worst) to +6 (best) to each of the variables that make up the FS and IS dimensions. Assign a numerical value ranging from −1 (best) to −6 (worst) to each of the variables that make up the ES and CA dimensions.

3. Compute an average score for FS, CA, IS, and ES by summing the values given to the variables of each dimension and dividing by the number of variables included in the respective dimension.

4. Plot the average scores for FS, IS, ES, and CA on the appropriate axis in the SPACE Matrix.

5. Add the two scores on the *x*-axis and plot the resultant point on X. Add the two scores on the *y*-axis and plot the resultant point on Y. Plot the intersection of the new *xy* point.

6. Draw a *directional vector* from the origin of the SPACE Matrix through the new intersection point. This vector reveals the type of strategies recommended for the organization: aggressive, competitive, defensive, or conservative.

Some examples of strategy profiles that can emerge from a SPACE analysis are shown in Figure 6–6. The directional vector associated with each profile suggests the type of strategies to pursue: aggressive, conservative, defensive, or competitive. When a firm's directional vector is located in the *aggressive quadrant* (upper-right quadrant) of the SPACE Matrix, an organization is in an excellent position to use its internal strengths to (1) take advantage of external opportunities, (2) overcome internal weaknesses, and (3) avoid external threats. Therefore, market penetration, market development, product development, backward integration, forward integration, horizontal integration, conglomerate

# FIGURE 6–6

## Example Strategy Profiles

Aggressive Profiles

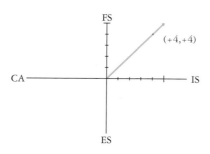

A financially strong firm that has achieved
major competitive advantages in a growing
and stable industry

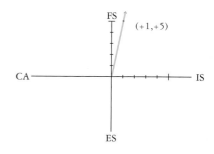

A firm whose financial strength is a
dominating factor in the industry

Conservative Profiles

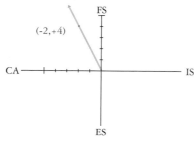

A firm that has achieved financial strength
in a stable industry that is not growing; the
firm has no major competitive advantages

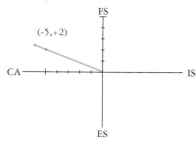

A firm that suffers from major competitive
disadvantages in an industry that is
technologically stable but declining in sales

Competitive Profiles

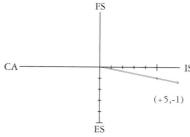

A firm with major competitive advantages
in a high-growth industry

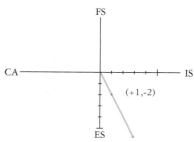

An organization that is competing fairly
well in an unstable industry

Defensive Profiles

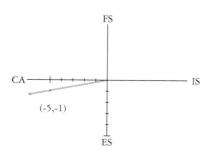

A firm that has a very weak competitive
position in a negative growth, stable industry

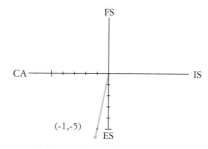

A financially troubled firm in a very
unstable industry

*Source:* H. Rowe, R. Mason, and K. Dickel, *Strategic Management and Business Policy: A Methodological Approach* (Reading, Massachusetts: Addison-Wesley Publishing Co. Inc. © 1982): 155. Reprinted with permission of the publisher.

diversification, concentric diversification, horizontal diversification, or a combination strategy all can be feasible, depending on the specific circumstances that face the firm.

The directional vector may appear in the *conservative quadrant* (upper-left quadrant) of the SPACE Matrix, which implies staying close to the firm's basic competencies and not taking excessive risks. Conservative strategies most often include market penetration, market development, product development, and concentric diversification. The directional vector may be located in the lower-left or *defensive quadrant* of the SPACE Matrix, which suggests that the firm should focus on rectifying internal weaknesses and avoiding external threats. Defensive strategies include retrenchment, divestiture, liquidation, and concentric diversification. Finally, the directional vector may be located in the lower-right or *competitive quadrant* of the SPACE Matrix, indicating competitive strategies. Competitive strategies include backward, forward, and horizontal integration; market penetration; market development; product development; and joint venture.

SPACE Matrix analysis for a bank is provided in Table 6–3. Note that the competitive strategies are recommended.

## TABLE 6-3    A SPACE Matrix for a Bank

| FINANCIAL STRENGTH | RATINGS |
|---|---|
| The bank's primary capital ratio is 7.23 percent, which is 1.23 percentage points over the generally required ratio of 6 percent. | 1.0 |
| The bank's return on assets is negative 0.77, compared to a bank industry average ratio of positive 0.70. | 1.0 |
| The bank's net income was $183 million, down 9 percent from a year earlier. | 3.0 |
| The bank's revenues increased 7 percent to $3.46 billion. | 4.0 |
|  | 9.0 |

| INDUSTRY STRENGTH | |
|---|---|
| Deregulation provides geographic and product freedom. | 4.0 |
| Deregulation increases competition in the banking industry. | 2.0 |
| Pennsylvania's interstate banking law allows the bank to acquire other banks in New Jersey, Ohio, Kentucky, the District of Columbia, and West Virginia. | 4.0 |
|  | 10.0 |

| ENVIRONMENTAL STABILITY | |
|---|---|
| Less-developed countries are experiencing high inflation and political instability. | −4.0 |
| Headquartered in Pittsburgh, the bank historically has been heavily dependent on the steel, oil, and gas industries. These industries are depressed. | −5.0 |
| Banking deregulation has created instability throughout the industry. | −4.0 |
|  | −13.0 |

| COMPETITIVE ADVANTAGE | |
|---|---|
| The bank provides data processing services for more than 450 institutions in 38 states. | −2.0 |
| Superregional banks, international banks, and nonbanks are becoming increasingly competitive. | −5.0 |
| The bank has a large customer base. | −2.0 |
|  | −9.0 |

### CONCLUSION

ES Average is  −13.0 ÷ 3 = −4.33  IS Average is + 10.0 ÷ 3 = 3.33
CA Average is  −9.0 ÷ 3 = −3.00  FS Average is  + 9.0 ÷ 4 = 2.25
Directional Vector Coordinates: x-axis: −3.00 + (+3.33) = +0.33
                                         y-axis: −4.33 + (+2.25) = −2.08
The bank should pursue Competitive Strategies.

### The Boston Consulting Group (BCG) Matrix

Autonomous divisions (or profit centers) of an organization make up what is called a *business portfolio.* When a firm's divisions compete in different industries, a separate strategy often must be developed for each business. The *Boston Consulting Group (BCG) Matrix* and the *Internal-External (IE) Matrix* are designed specifically to enhance a multidivisional firm's efforts to formulate strategies.

The BCG Matrix graphically portrays differences among divisions in terms of relative market share position and industry growth rate. The BCG Matrix allows a multidivisional organization to manage its portfolio of businesses by examining the relative market share position and the industry growth rate of each division relative to all other divisions in the organization. *Relative market share position* is defined as the ratio of a division's own market share in a particular industry to the market share held by the largest rival firm in that industry. For example, in Table 6–4, the relative market share of Ocean Spray premium noncarbonated beverage is 14.7/40.5 = 0.36 and Sony's market share in the music industry is 16/27 = 0.59, and the new Hilton-Promus hotel company's market share is 290,000/528,896 = 0.55.

**TABLE 6–4**   **A. Market Share of Premium Noncarbonated Beverages**

| BRAND | MARKET SHARE IN 1999 | % CHANGE IN SHARE FROM 1998 |
|---|---|---|
| Snapple | 40.5% | 3.7% |
| Ocean Spray | 14.7 | −2.9 |
| AriZona | 13.7 | −2.3 |
| Lipton | 10.8 | −1.3 |
| SoBe | 9.3 | 6.9 |
| Mistic | 5.0 | −3.2 |
| Nestea | 4.7 | −0.9 |
| Nantucket Nectars | 1.4 | −0.1 |

**B. Market Share of the World's Largest Music Companies**

| COMPANY | MARKET SHARE IN 1999 | MARKET SHARE IN 1998 |
|---|---|---|
| Universal Music Group | 27% | 23% |
| Time Warner Music | 17 | 22 |
| Sony | 16 | NA |
| Bertelsmann's BMG | 14 | 12 |
| EMI | 10 | NA |
| Independents | 17 | NA |

**C. Market Share of the World's Largest Hotel Companies in 1999**

| COMPANY | # OF ROOMS |
|---|---|
| 1. Cendant | 528,896 |
| 2. Bass | 461,434 |
| 3. Marriott | 328,300 |
| 4. Choice | 305,171 |
| 5. Best Western | 301,899 |
| 6. Accor | 291,770 |
| 7. Hilton-Promus | 290,000 |

*Source:* Adapted from: Paul Georgis, "Market Share for Premium Noncarbonated Beverages," *USA Today* (August 3,1999): 2B. Also, Keith Alexander, "Music Sales Hitting Sour Note," *USA Today* (August 25, 1999): 2B. Also, Chris Woodyard, "Hilton to Buy Promus in $3B Deal," *USA Today,* (October 12, 1999): p. 2B.

Relative market share position is given on the *x*-axis of the BCG Matrix. The midpoint on the *x*-axis usually is set at .50, corresponding to a division that has half the market share of the leading firm in the industry. The *y*-axis represents the industry growth rate in sales, measured in percentage terms. The growth rate percentages on the *y*-axis could range from −20 to +20 percent, with 0.0 being the midpoint. These numerical ranges on the *x*- and *y*- axes often are used, but other numerical values could be established as deemed appropriate for particular organizations.

An example of a BCG Matrix appears in Figure 6–7. Each circle represents a separate division. The size of the circle corresponds to the proportion of corporate revenue generated by that business unit, and the pie slice indicates the proportion of corporate profits generated by that division. Divisions located in Quadrant I of the BCG Matrix are called Question Marks, those located in Quadrant II are called Stars, those located in Quadrant III are called Cash Cows, and those divisions located in Quadrant IV are called Dogs. As indicated in the Global Perspective, European firms are becoming Stars through consolidation, which represents a threat to many American firms.

- Question Marks—Divisions in Quadrant I have a low relative market share position, yet compete in a high-growth industry. Generally these firms' cash needs are high and their cash generation is low. These businesses are called *Question Marks* because the organization must decide whether to strengthen them by pursuing an intensive strategy (market penetration, market development, or product development) or to sell them.

- Stars—Quadrant II businesses (often called *Stars*) represent the organization's best long-run opportunities for growth and profitability. Divisions with a high relative market share and a high industry growth rate should receive substantial investment to maintain or strengthen their dominant positions. Forward, backward, and horizontal integration; market penetration; market development; product development; and joint ventures are appropriate strategies for these divisions to consider.

## FIGURE 6–7
## The BCG Matrix

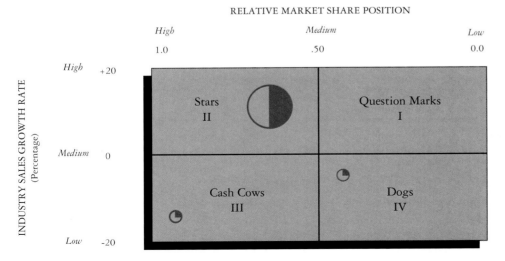

*Source:* Adapted from Boston Consulting Group, *Perspectives on Experience* (Boston, MA: The Boston Consulting Group, 1974).

# GLOBAL PERSPECTIVE

## *Merger Mania in Europe*

Hostile mergers were once considered declasse in Europe, but the corporate consolidation frenzy ongoing in Europe today is making hostile takeovers commonplace. Throughout the 1980s and 1990s, Europe shunned mergers and shunned hostile takeovers, but today the Continent rivals the United States in both quantity and volume of merger activity. More than $1 trillion in mergers were consummated in Europe in 1999, and many were hostile as opposed to the "historical quiet merger agreements among members of a clubby business elite." For example, LVMH and Pinault Printemps Redoute engaged in a takeover battle over Gucci, and Banque Nationale de Paris gained hostile control over Paribas and Societe Generale.

European companies are restructuring, reengineering, globalizing, and consolidating to become more competitive, basically playing catch-up with American firms that have employed these strategies for years. There were more leveraged buyouts in Europe in 1999 than in the United States. The single currency and the Internet has spurred the merger frenzy in Europe. European firms are acquiring not only other European firms but also American and other foreign firms. American buyout companies such as Kohlberg Kravis Roberts are opening new offices and beefing up existing offices in Europe.

A few recent example acquisitions by European firms are listed below:

| *Acquiring Company* | *Acquired Company* |
| --- | --- |
| BP Amoco PLC | Atlantic Richfield |
| BNP | Paribas |
| Carrefour | Promodes |
| Scottish & Newcastle PLC | Greenalls Group PLC |
| Rolls-Royce PLC | Vickers PLC |
| Veba AG | Viag AG |
| British Telecommunications PLC | Yellow book USA |
| Dyckerhoff AG | Lone Star Industries |
| Vodafone | Airtouch |
| Vodafone | CommNet Cellular |
| UniCredito Italiano | BCI |
| San Paolo-IMI | Banca di Roma |
| Olivetti | Telecom Italia |

*Source:* Adapted from: John Rossant, "Deal Mania," *Business Week* (April 5, 1999): 50–54.

- Cash Cows—Divisions positioned in Quadrant III have a high relative market share position but compete in a low-growth industry. Called *Cash Cows* because they generate cash in excess of their needs, they often are milked. Many of today's Cash Cows were yesterday's Stars. Cash Cow divisions should be managed to maintain their strong position for as long as possible. Product development or concentric diversification may be attractive strategies for strong Cash Cows. However, as a Cash Cow division becomes weak, retrenchment or divestiture can become more appropriate.

- Dogs—Quadrant IV divisions of the organization have a low relative market share position and compete in a slow- or no-market-growth industry; they are *Dogs* in the firm's portfolio. Because of their weak internal and external position, these businesses often are liquidated, divested, or trimmed down through retrenchment. When a division first becomes a Dog, retrenchment can be the best strategy to pursue because many Dogs have bounced back, after strenuous asset and cost reduction, to become viable, profitable divisions.

The major benefit of the BCG Matrix is that it draws attention to the cash flow, investment characteristics, and needs of an organization's various divisions. The divisions of many firms evolve over time: Dogs become Question Marks, Question Marks become Stars, Stars become Cash Cows, and Cash Cows become Dogs in an ongoing counterclockwise motion. Less frequently, Stars become Question Marks, Question Marks become Dogs, Dogs become Cash Cows, and Cash Cows become Stars (in a clockwise

**FIGURE 6–8**

**An Example BCG Matrix**

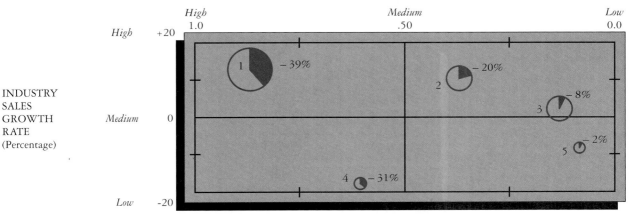

| Division | Revenues | Percent Revenues | Profits | Percent Profits | Percent Market Share | Percent Growth Rate |
|---|---|---|---|---|---|---|
| 1 | $60,000 | 37 | $10,000 | 39 | 80 | +15 |
| 2 | 40,000 | 24 | 5,000 | 20 | 40 | +10 |
| 3 | 40,000 | 24 | 2,000 | 8 | 10 | 1 |
| 4 | 20,000 | 12 | 8,000 | 31 | 60 | -20 |
| 5 | 5,000 | 3 | 500 | 2 | 5 | -10 |
| Total | $165,000 | 100 | $25,500 | 100 | | |

motion). In some organizations, no cyclical motion is apparent. Over time, organizations should strive to achieve a portfolio of divisions that are Stars.

One example of a BCG Matrix is provided in Figure 6–8, which illustrates an organization composed of five divisions with annual sales ranging from $5,000 to $60,000. Division I has the greatest sales volume, so the circle representing that division is the largest one in the matrix. The circle corresponding to Division 5 is the smallest because its sales volume ($5,000) is least among all the divisions. The pie slices within the circles reveal the percent of corporate profits contributed by each division. As shown, Division 1 contributes the highest profit percentage, 39 percent. Notice in the diagram that Division 1 is considered a Star, Division 2 is a Question Mark, Division 3 also is a Question Mark, Division 4 is a Cash Cow, and Division 5 is a Dog.

The BCG Matrix, like all analytical techniques, has some limitations. For example, viewing every business as either a Star, Cash Cow, Dog, or Question Mark is an oversimplification; many businesses fall right in the middle of the BCG Matrix and thus are not easily classified. Furthermore, the BCG Matrix does not reflect whether or not various divisions or their industries are growing over time; that is, the matrix has no temporal qualities, but rather is a snapshot of an organization at a given point in time. Finally, other variables besides relative market share position and industry growth rate in sales, such as size of the market and competitive advantages, are important in making strategic decisions about various divisions.

## The Internal-External (IE) Matrix

The *Internal-External (IE) Matrix* positions an organization's various divisions in a nine-cell display illustrated in Figure 6–9. The IE Matrix is similar to the BCG Matrix in that both tools involve plotting organization divisions in a schematic diagram; this is why

**FIGURE 6–9**

**The Internal-External (IE) Matrix**

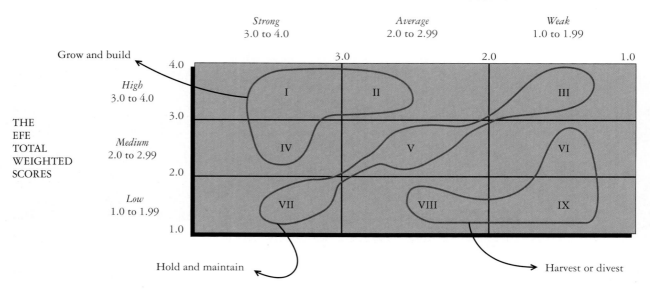

Note: The IE Matrix was developed from the General Electric (GE) Business Screen Matrix. For a description of the GE Matrix, see Michael Allen, "Diagramming GE's Planning for What's WATT" in *Corporate Planning: Techniques and Applications,* eds. R. Allio and M. Pennington (New York: AMA-COM, 1979).

they are both called portfolio matrices. Also, the size of each circle represents the percentage sales contribution of each division, and pie slices reveal the percentage profit contribution of each division in both the BCG and IE Matrix.

But there are some important differences between the BCG Matrix and IE Matrix. First, the axes are different. Also, the IE Matrix requires more information about the divisions than the BCG Matrix. Further, the strategic implications of each matrix are different. For these reasons, strategists in multidivisional firms often develop both the BCG Matrix and the IE Matrix in formulating alternative strategies. A common practice is to develop a BCG Matrix and an IE Matrix for the present and then develop projected matrices to reflect expectations of the future. This before-and-after analysis forecasts the expected effect of strategic decisions on an organization's portfolio of divisions.

The IE Matrix is based on two key dimensions: the IFE total weighted scores on the *x*-axis and the EFE total weighted scores on the *y*-axis. Recall that each division of an organization should construct an IFE Matrix and an EFE Matrix for its part of the organization. The total weighted scores derived from the divisions allow construction of the corporate-level IE Matrix. On the *x*-axis of the IE Matrix, an IFE total weighted score of 1.0 to 1.99 represents a weak internal position; a score of 2.0 to 2.99 is considered average; and a score of 3.0 to 4.0 is strong. Similarly, on the *y*-axis, an EFE total weighted score of 1.0 to 1.99 is considered low; a score of 2.0 to 2.99 is medium; and a score of 3.0 to 4.0 is high.

The IE Matrix can be divided into three major regions that have different strategy implications. First, the prescription for divisions that fall into cells I, II, or IV can be described as *grow and build.* Intensive (market penetration, market development, and product development) or integrative (backward integration, forward integration, and horizontal integration) strategies can be most appropriate for these divisions. Second, divisions that fall into cells III, V, or VII can be managed best with *hold and maintain* strategies; market penetration and product development are two commonly employed

**FIGURE 6–10**

**An Example IE Matrix**

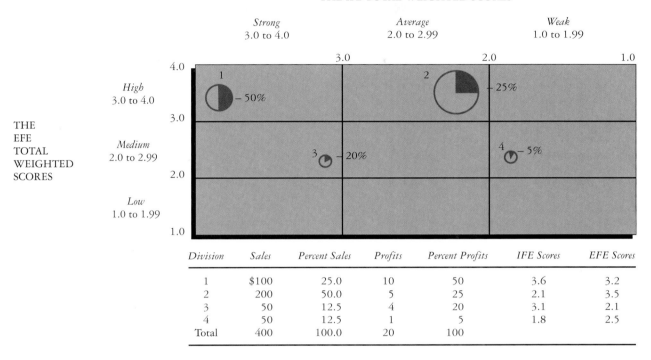

| Division | Sales | Percent Sales | Profits | Percent Profits | IFE Scores | EFE Scores |
|----------|-------|---------------|---------|-----------------|------------|------------|
| 1 | $100 | 25.0 | 10 | 50 | 3.6 | 3.2 |
| 2 | 200 | 50.0 | 5 | 25 | 2.1 | 3.5 |
| 3 | 50 | 12.5 | 4 | 20 | 3.1 | 2.1 |
| 4 | 50 | 12.5 | 1 | 5 | 1.8 | 2.5 |
| Total | 400 | 100.0 | 20 | 100 | | |

strategies for these types of divisions. Third, a common prescription for divisions that fall into cells VI, VIII, or IX is *harvest or divest.* Successful organizations are able to achieve a portfolio of businesses positioned in or around cell I in the IE Matrix.

An example of a completed IE Matrix is given in Figure 6–10, which depicts an organization composed of four divisions. As indicated by the positioning of the circles, *grow and build* strategies are appropriate for Division 1, Division 2, and Division 3. Division 4 is a candidate for *harvest or divest.* Division 2 contributes the greatest percentage of company sales and thus is represented by the largest circle. Division 1 contributes the greatest proportion of total profits; it has the largest-percentage pie slice.

## The Grand Strategy Matrix

In addition to the TOWS Matrix, SPACE Matrix, BCG Matrix, and IE Matrix, the *Grand Strategy Matrix* has become a popular tool for formulating alternative strategies. All organizations can be positioned in one of the Grand Strategy Matrix's four strategy quadrants. A firm's divisions likewise could be positioned. As illustrated in Figure 6–11, the Grand Strategy Matrix is based on two evaluative dimensions: competitive position and market growth. Appropriate strategies for an organization to consider are listed in sequential order of attractiveness in each quadrant of the matrix.

Firms located in Quadrant I of the Grand Strategy Matrix are in an excellent strategic position. For these firms, continued concentration on current markets (market penetration and market development) and products (product development) are appropriate strategies. It is unwise for a Quadrant I firm to shift notably from its established competitive advantages. When a Quadrant I organization has excessive resources, then

**FIGURE 6–11**

**The Grand Strategy Matrix**

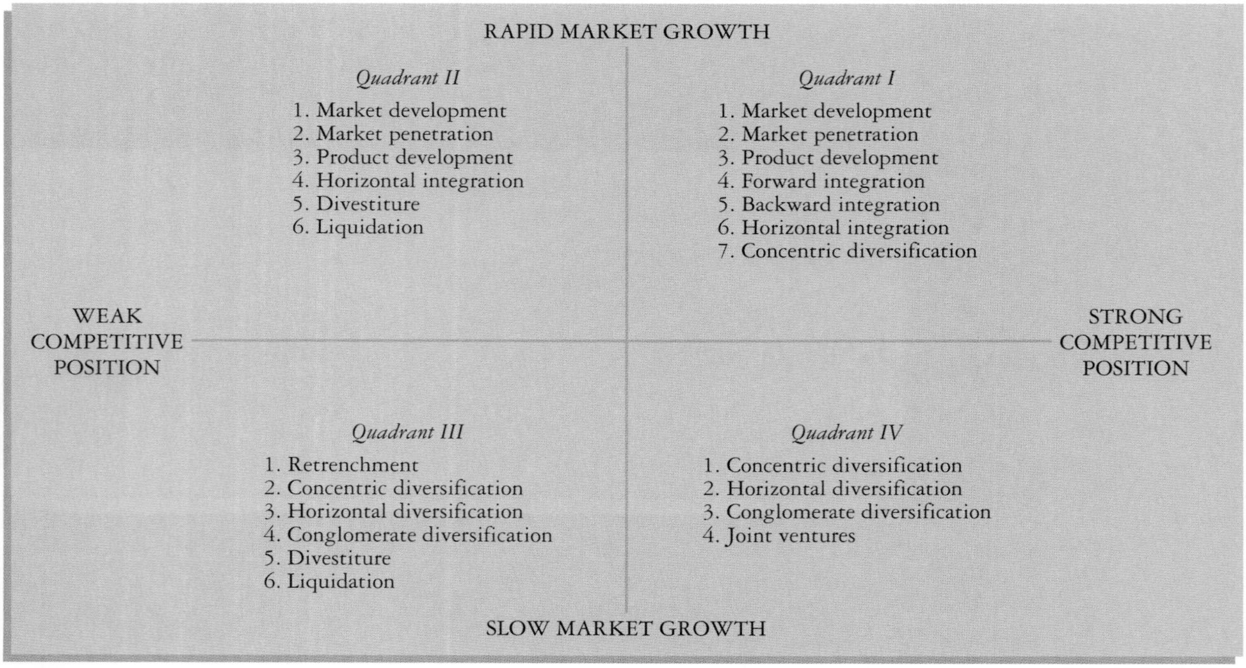

RAPID MARKET GROWTH

*Quadrant II*
1. Market development
2. Market penetration
3. Product development
4. Horizontal integration
5. Divestiture
6. Liquidation

*Quadrant I*
1. Market development
2. Market penetration
3. Product development
4. Forward integration
5. Backward integration
6. Horizontal integration
7. Concentric diversification

WEAK
COMPETITIVE
POSITION

STRONG
COMPETITIVE
POSITION

*Quadrant III*
1. Retrenchment
2. Concentric diversification
3. Horizontal diversification
4. Conglomerate diversification
5. Divestiture
6. Liquidation

*Quadrant IV*
1. Concentric diversification
2. Horizontal diversification
3. Conglomerate diversification
4. Joint ventures

SLOW MARKET GROWTH

*Source:* Adapted from Roland Christensen, Norman Berg, and Malcolm Salter, *Policy Formulation and Administration* (Homewood, Ill.: Richard D. Irwin, 1976): 16–18.

backward, forward, or horizontal integration may be effective strategies. When a Quadrant I firm is too heavily committed to a single product, then concentric diversification may reduce the risks associated with a narrow product line. Quadrant I firms can afford to take advantage of external opportunities in several areas: they can take risks aggressively when necessary.

Firms positioned in Quadrant II need to evaluate their present approach to the marketplace seriously. Although their industry is growing, they are unable to compete effectively, and they need to determine why the firm's current approach is ineffectual and how the company can best change to improve its competitiveness. Because Quadrant II firms are in a rapid-market-growth industry, an intensive strategy (as opposed to integrative or diversification) is usually the first option that should be considered. However, if the firm is lacking a distinctive competence or competitive advantage, then horizontal integration is often a desirable alternative. As a last result, divestiture or liquidation should be considered. Divestiture can provide funds needed to acquire other businesses or buy back shares of stock.

Quadrant III organizations compete in slow-growth industries and have weak competitive positions. These firms must make some drastic changes quickly to avoid further demise and possible liquidation. Extensive cost and asset reduction (retrenchment) should be pursued first. An alternative strategy is to shift resources away from the current business into different areas. If all else fails, the final options for Quadrant III businesses are divestiture or liquidation.

Finally, Quadrant IV businesses have a strong competitive position but are in a slow-growth industry. These firms have the strength to launch diversified programs into more promising growth areas. Quadrant IV firms have characteristically high cash flow levels and limited internal growth needs and often can pursue concentric, horizontal, or conglomerate diversification successfully. Quadrant IV firms also may pursue joint ventures.

# THE DECISION STAGE

Analysis and intuition provide a basis for making strategy-formulation decisions. The matching techniques just discussed reveal feasible alternative strategies. Many of these strategies will likely have been proposed by managers and employees participating in the strategy analysis and choice activity. Any additional strategies resulting from the matching analyses could be discussed and added to the list of feasible alternative options. As indicated earlier in this chapter, participants could rate these strategies on a 1 to 4 scale so that a prioritized list of the best strategies could be achieved.

## The Quantitative Strategic Planning Matrix (QSPM)

Other than ranking strategies to achieve the prioritized list, there is only one analytical technique in the literature designed to determine the relative attractiveness of feasible alternative actions. This technique is the *Quantitative Strategic Planning Matrix (QSPM)*, which comprises Stage 3 of the strategy-formulation analytical framework.[5] This technique objectively indicates which alternative strategies are best. The QSPM uses input from Stage 1 analyses and matching results from Stage 2 analyses to decide objectively among alternative strategies. That is, the EFE Matrix, IFE Matrix, and Competitive Profile Matrix that make up Stage 1, coupled with the TOWS Matrix, SPACE Analysis, BCG Matrix, IE Matrix, and Grand Strategy Matrix that make up Stage 2, provide the needed information for setting up the QSPM (Stage 3). The QSPM is a tool that allows strategists to evaluate alternative strategies objectively, based on previously identified external and internal critical success factors. Like other strategy-formulation analytical tools, the QSPM requires good intuitive judgment.

The basic format of the QSPM is illustrated in Table 6–5. Note that the left column of a QSPM consists of key external and internal factors (from Stage 1), and the top

**T A B L E  6 – 5      The Quantitative Strategic Planning Matrix—QSPM**

| Key Factors | Weight | STRATEGIC ALTERNATIVES | | |
| --- | --- | --- | --- | --- |
| | | Strategy 1 | Strategy 2 | Strategy 3 |
| **Key External Factors** | | | | |
| Economy | | | | |
| Political/Legal/Governmental | | | | |
| Social/Cultural/Demographic/Environmental | | | | |
| Technological | | | | |
| Competitive | | | | |
| **Key Internal Factors** | | | | |
| Management | | | | |
| Marketing | | | | |
| Finance/Accounting | | | | |
| Production/Operations | | | | |
| Research and Development | | | | |
| Computer Information Systems | | | | |

row consists of feasible alternative strategies (from Stage 2). Specifically, the left column of a QSPM consists of information obtained directly from the EFE Matrix and IFE Matrix. In a column adjacent to the critical success factors, the respective weights received by each factor in the EFE Matrix and the IFE Matrix are recorded.

The top row of a QSPM consists of alternative strategies derived from the TOWS Matrix, SPACE Matrix, BCG Matrix, IE Matrix, and Grand Strategy Matrix. These matching tools usually generate similar feasible alternatives. However, not every strategy suggested by the matching techniques has to be evaluated in a QSPM. Strategists should use good intuitive judgment in selecting strategies to include in a QSPM.

Conceptually, the QSPM determines the relative attractiveness of various strategies based on the extent to which key external and internal critical success factors are capitalized upon or improved. The relative attractiveness of each strategy within a set of alternatives is computed by determining the cumulative impact of each external and internal critical success factor. Any number of sets of alternative strategies can be included in the QSPM, and any number of strategies can make up a given set, but only strategies within a given set are evaluated relative to each other. For example, one set of strategies may include concentric, horizontal, and conglomerate diversification, whereas another set may include issuing stock and selling a division to raise needed capital. These two sets of strategies are totally different, and the QSPM evaluates strategies only within sets. Note in Table 6–6 that three strategies are included and they make up just one set.

A QSPM for a food company is provided in Table 6–6. This example illustrates all the components of the QSPM: Key Factors, Strategic Alternatives, Weights, Attractiveness Scores, Total Attractiveness Scores, and the Sum Total Attractiveness Score. The three new terms just introduced—(1) Attractiveness Scores, (2) Total Attractiveness Scores, and (3) the Sum Total Attractiveness Score—are defined and explained below as the six steps required to develop a QSPM are discussed.

**Step 1**  **Make a list of the firm's key external opportunities/threats and internal strengths/weaknesses in the left column of the QSPM.** This information should be taken directly from the EFE Matrix and IFE Matrix. A minimum of 10 external critical success factors and 10 internal critical success factors should be included in the QSPM.

**Step 2**  **Assign weights to each key external and internal factor.** These weights are identical to those in the EFE Matrix and the IFE Matrix. The weights are presented in a straight column just to the right of the external and internal critical success factors.

**Step 3**  **Examine the Stage 2 (matching) matrices and identify alternative strategies that the organization should consider implementing.** Record these strategies in the top row of the QSPM. Group the strategies into mutually exclusive sets if possible.

**Step 4**  **Determine the Attractiveness Scores (AS),** defined as numerical values that indicate the relative attractiveness of each strategy in a given set of alternatives. *Attractiveness Scores* are determined by examining each key external or internal factor, one at a time, and asking the question, "Does this factor affect the choice of strategies being made?" If the answer to this question is *yes,* then the strategies should be compared relative to that key factor. Specifically, Attractiveness Scores should be assigned to each strategy to indicate the relative attractiveness of one strategy over others, considering the particular factor. The range for Attractiveness Scores is 1 = *not attractive,* 2 = *somewhat attractive,* 3 = *reasonably attractive,* and 4 = *highly attractive.* If the answer to the above question is *no,* indicating that the respective key factor has no effect upon the specific choice being made, then do not assign Attractiveness Scores to the strategies in that

TABLE 6-6      A QSPM for Campbell Soup Company

| | | STRATEGIC ALTERNATIVES | | | |
| --- | --- | --- | --- | --- | --- |
| | | Joint Venture in Europe | | Joint Venture in Asia | |
| Key Factors | Weight | AS | TAS | AS | TAS |
| *Opportunities* | | | | | |
| 1. One European currency—Euro | .10 | 4 | .40 | 2 | .20 |
| 2. Rising health consciousness in selecting foods | .15 | 4 | .60 | 3 | .45 |
| 3. Free market economies arising in Asia | .10 | 2 | .20 | 4 | .40 |
| 4. Demand for soups increasing 10 percent annually | .15 | 3 | .45 | 4 | .60 |
| 5. NAFTA | .05 | – | – | – | – |
| *Threats* | | | | | |
| 1. Food revenues increasing only 1 percent annually | .10 | 3 | .30 | 4 | .40 |
| 2. ConAgra's Banquet TV Dinners lead market with 27.4 percent share | .05 | – | – | – | – |
| 3. Unstable economies in Asia | .10 | 4 | .40 | 1 | .10 |
| 4. Tin cans are not biodegradable | .05 | – | – | – | – |
| 5. Low value of the dollar | .15 | 4 | .60 | 2 | .30 |
| | 1.0 | | | | |
| *Strengths* | | | | | |
| 1. Profits rose 30 percent | .10 | 4 | .40 | 2 | .20 |
| 2. New North American division | .10 | – | – | – | – |
| 3. New health-conscious soups are successful | .10 | 4 | .40 | 2 | .20 |
| 4. Swanson TV dinners' market share has increased to 25.1 percent | .05 | 4 | .20 | 3 | .15 |
| 5. One-fifth of all managers' bonuses is based on overall corporate performance | .05 | – | – | – | – |
| 6. Capacity utilization increased from 60 percent to 80 percent | .15 | 3 | .45 | 4 | .60 |
| *Weaknesses* | | | | | |
| 1. Pepperidge Farm sales have declined 7 percent | .05 | – | – | – | – |
| 2. Restructuring cost $302 million | .05 | – | – | – | – |
| 3. The company's European operation is losing money | 1.5 | 2 | .30 | 4 | .60 |
| 4. The company is slow in globalizing | .15 | 4 | .60 | 3 | .45 |
| 5. Pretax profit margin of 8.4 percent is only one-half industry average | .05 | – | – | – | – |
| *Sum Total Attractiveness Score* | 1.0 | | 5.30 | | 4.65 |

AS = Attractiveness Score; TAS = Total Attractiveness Score
Attractiveness Score: 1 = not acceptable; 2 = possibly acceptable; 3 = probably acceptable; 4 = most acceptable.

set. Use a dash to indicate that the key factor does not affect the choice being made. Note: If you assign an AS score to one strategy, then assign AS score(s) to the other. In other words, if one strategy receives a dash, then all others must receive a dash in a given row.

**Step 5**   **Compute the Total Attractiveness Scores.** *Total Attractiveness Scores* are defined as the product of multiplying the weights (Step 2) by the Attractiveness Scores (Step 4) in each row. The Total Attractiveness Scores indicate the relative attractiveness of each alternative strategy, considering only the impact of the adjacent external or internal critical success factor. The higher the Total Attractiveness Score, the more attractive the strategic alternative (considering only the adjacent critical success factor).

**Step 6**   **Compute the Sum Total Attractiveness Score.** Add Total Attractiveness Scores in each strategy column of the QSPM. The *Sum Total Attractiveness Scores* reveal which strategy is most attractive in each set of alternatives. Higher scores indicate more attractive strategies, considering all the relevant external and internal factors that could affect the strategic decisions. The magnitude of the difference between the Sum Total Attractiveness Scores in a given set of strategic alternatives indicates the relative desirability of one strategy over another.

In Table 6–6, two alternative strategies—establishing a joint venture in Europe and establishing a joint venture in Asia—are being considered by Campbell Soup.

Note that NAFTA has no impact on the choice being made between the two strategies, so a dash (–) appears several times across that row. Several other factors also have no effect on the choice being made, so dashes are recorded in those rows as well. If a particular factor affects one strategy but not the other, it affects the choice being made, so attractiveness scores should be recorded. The sum total attractiveness score of 5.30 in Table 6–6 indicates that the joint venture in Europe is a more attractive strategy when compared to the joint venture in Asia.

You should have a rationale for each AS score assigned. In Table 6–6, the rationale for the AS scores in the first row is that the unification of Western Europe creates more stable business conditions in Europe than in Asia. The AS score of 4 for the joint venture in Europe and 2 for the joint venture in Asia indicates that the European venture is most acceptable and the Asian venture is possibly acceptable, considering only the first critical success factor. AS scores, therefore, are not mere guesses; they should be rational, defensible, and reasonable. Avoid giving each strategy the same AS score. Note in Table 6–6 that dashes are inserted all the way across the row when used. Also note that never are double 4's, or double 3's, or double 2's, or double 1's in a given row. These are important guidelines to follow in constructing a QSPM.

## Positive Features and Limitations of the QSPM

A positive feature of the QSPM is that sets of strategies can be examined sequentially or simultaneously. For example, corporate-level strategies could be evaluated first, followed by division-level strategies, and then function-level strategies. There is no limit to the number of strategies that can be evaluated or the number of sets of strategies that can be examined at once using the QSPM.

Another positive feature of the QSPM is that it requires strategists to integrate pertinent external and internal factors into the decision process. Developing a QSPM makes it less likely that key factors will be overlooked or weighted inappropriately. A QSPM draws attention to important relationships that affect strategy decisions. Although developing a QSPM requires a number of subjective decisions, making small decisions along the way enhances the probability that the final strategic decisions will be best for the organization. A QSPM can be adapted for use by small and large for-profit and nonprofit organizations and can be applied to virtually any type of organization. A QSPM especially can enhance strategic choice in multinational firms because many key factors and strategies can be considered at once. It also has been applied successfully by a number of small businesses.[6]

The QSPM is not without some limitations. First, it always requires intuitive judgments and educated assumptions. The ratings and attractiveness scores require judgmental decisions, even though they should be based on objective information. Discussion among strategists, managers, and employees throughout the strategy-formulation process, including development of a QSPM, is constructive and improves strategic decisions. Constructive discussion during strategy analysis and choice may arise because of genuine differences of interpretation of information and varying opinions. Another limitation of the QSPM is that it can be only as good as the prerequisite information and matching analyses upon which it is based.

## CULTURAL ASPECTS OF STRATEGY CHOICE

All organizations have a culture. *Culture* includes the set of shared values, beliefs, attitudes, customs, norms, personalities, heroes, and heroines that describe a firm. Culture is the unique way an organization does business. It is the human dimension that creates solidarity and meaning, and inspires commitment and productivity in an organization when strategy changes are made. All human beings have a basic need to make sense of their world, to feel in control, and to make meaning. When events threaten meaning, individuals react defensively. Managers and employees even may sabotage new strategies in an effort to recapture the status quo.

It is beneficial to view strategic management from a cultural perspective because success often rests upon the degree of support that strategies receive from a firm's culture. If a firm's strategies are supported by cultural products such as values, beliefs, rites, rituals, ceremonies, stories, symbols, language, heroes, and heroines then managers often can implement changes swiftly and easily. However, if a supportive culture does not exist and is not cultivated, then strategy changes may be ineffective or even counterproductive. A firm's culture can become antagonistic to new strategies, and the result of that antagonism may be confusion and disarray.

Strategies that require fewer cultural changes may be more attractive because extensive changes can take considerable time and effort. Whenever two firms merge, culture-strategy linkages become especially important to evaluate and consider. For example, the recently approved AOL and Time Warner merger unites two quite diverse cultures.

Culture provides an explanation for the difficulties a firm encounters when it attempts to shift its strategic direction, as the following statement explains:

> Not only has the "right" corporate culture become the essence and foundation
> of corporate excellence, but success or failure of needed corporate reforms
> hinges on management's sagacity and ability to change the firm's driving culture in time and in tune with required changes in strategies.[7]

## THE POLITICS OF STRATEGY CHOICE

All organizations are political. Unless managed, political maneuvering consumes valuable time, subverts organizational objectives, diverts human energy, and results in the loss of some valuable employees. Sometimes political biases and personal preferences get unduly embedded in strategy choice decisions. Internal politics affect the choice of strategies in all organizations. The hierarchy of command in an organization, combined with the career aspirations of different people and the need to allocate scarce resources, guarantees the formation of coalitions of individuals who strive to take care of themselves first and the organization second, third, or fourth. Coalitions of individuals often form around key strategy issues that face an enterprise. A major responsibility of strategists is to guide the development of coalitions, to nurture an overall team concept, and to gain the support of key individuals and groups of individuals.

In the absence of objective analyses, strategy decisions too often are based on the politics of the moment. With development of improved strategy-formation tools, political factors become less important in making strategic decisions. In the absence of objectivity, political factors sometimes dictate strategies, and this is unfortunate. Managing political relationships is an integral part of building enthusiasm and esprit de corps in an organization.

A classic study of strategic management in nine large corporations examined the political tactics of successful and unsuccessful strategists.[8] Successful strategists were found to let weakly supported ideas and proposals die through inaction and to establish additional hurdles or tests for strongly supported ideas considered unacceptable but not openly opposed. Successful strategists kept a low political profile on unacceptable proposals and strived to let most negative decisions come from subordinates or a group consensus, thereby reserving their personal vetoes for big issues and crucial moments. Successful strategists did a lot of chatting and informal questioning to stay abreast of how things were progressing and to know when to intervene. They led strategy but did not dictate it. They gave few orders, announced few decisions, depended heavily on informal questioning, and sought to probe and clarify until a consensus emerged.

Successful strategists generously and visibly rewarded key thrusts that succeeded. They assigned responsibility for major new thrusts to *champions*, the individuals most strongly identified with the idea or product and whose futures were linked to its success. They stayed alert to the symbolic impact of their own actions and statements so as not to send false signals that could stimulate movements in unwanted directions.

Successful strategists ensured that all major power bases within an organization were represented in, or had access to, top management. They interjected new faces and new views into considerations of major changes. (This is important because new employees and managers generally have more enthusiasm and drive than employees who have been with the firm a long time. New employees do not see the world the same old way nor act as screens against changes.) Successful strategists minimized their own political exposure on highly controversial issues and in circumstances where major opposition from key power centers was likely. In combination, these findings provide a basis for managing political relationships in an organization.

Because strategies must be effective in the marketplace and capable of gaining internal commitment, the following tactics used by politicians for centuries can aid strategists:

- *Equifinality:* It is often possible to achieve similar results using different means or paths. Strategists should recognize that achieving a successful outcome is more important than imposing the method of achieving it. It may be possible to generate new alternatives that give equal results but with far greater potential for gaining commitment.

- *Satisfying:* Achieving satisfactory results with an acceptable strategy is far better than failing to achieve optimal results with an unpopular strategy.

- *Generalization:* Shifting focus from specific issues to more general ones may increase strategists' options for gaining organizational commitment.

- *Focus on Higher-Order Issues:* By raising an issue to a higher level, many short-term interests can be postponed in favor of long-term interests. For instance, by focusing on issues of survival, the auto and steel industries were able to persuade unions to make concessions on wage increases.

- *Provide Political Access on Important Issues:* Strategy and policy decisions with significant negative consequences for middle managers will motivate intervention behavior from them. If middle managers do not have an opportunity to take a position on such decisions in appropriate political forums, they are capable of successfully resisting the decisions after they are made. Providing such political access provides strategists with information that otherwise might not be available and that could be useful in managing intervention behavior.[9]

# THE ROLE OF A BOARD OF DIRECTORS

A "director" according to *Webster's Dictionary* is "one of a group of persons entrusted with the overall direction of a corporate enterprise." A "board of directors" is a group of persons elected by the ownership of a corporation to have oversight and guidance over management and who look out for shareholders' interests. The act of oversight and direction is referred to as *"governance."* The National Association of Corporate Directors defines governance as: The characteristic of ensuring that long-term strategic objectives and plans are established and that the proper management structure is in place to achieve those objectives, while at the same time making sure that the structure functions to maintain the corporation's integrity, reputation, and responsibility to its various constituencies. This broad scope of responsibility for the board shows how boards are being held accountable for the entire performance of the firm. The roles and duties of a board of directors can be divided into four broad categories, as indicated in Table 6–7.

## TABLE 6-7   Board of Director Duties and Responsibilities

### 1. CONTROL AND OVERSIGHT OVER MANAGEMENT
   a. Select the Chief Executive Officer
   b. Sanction the CEO's team
   c. Provide the CEO with a forum
   d. Assure managerial competency
   e. Evaluate management's performance
   f. Set management's salary levels, including fringe benefits
   g. Guarantee managerial integrity through continuous auditing
   h. Chart the corporate course
   i. Devise and revise policies to be implemented by management

### 2. ADHERENCE TO LEGAL PRESCRIPTIONS
   a. Keep abreast of new laws
   b. Ensure the entire organization fulfills legal prescriptions
   c. Pass bylaws and related resolutions
   d. Select new directors
   e. Approve capital budgets
   f. Authorize borrowing, new stock issues, bonds, etc.

### 3. CONSIDERATION OF STAKEHOLDERS' INTERESTS
   a. Monitor product quality
   b. Facilitate upward progression in employee quality of work life
   c. Review labor policies and practices
   d. Improve the customer climate
   e. Keep community relations at the highest level
   f. Use influence to better governmental professional association, and educational contacts
   g. Maintain good public image

### 4. ADVANCEMENT OF STOCKHOLDERS' RIGHTS
   a. Preserve stockholders' equity
   b. Stimulate corporate growth so that the firm will survive and flourish
   c. Guard against equity dilution
   d. Assure equitable stockholder representation
   e. Inform stockholders through letters, reports, and meetings
   f. Declare proper dividends
   g. Guarantee corporate survival

The widespread lack of involvement by *boards of directors* in the strategic-management process is changing in America. Historically, boards of directors mostly have been insiders who would not second-guess top executives on strategic issues. It generally has been understood that strategists are responsible and accountable for implementing strategy, so they, not board members, should formulate strategy. Consequently, chief executive officers usually avoided discussions of overall strategy with directors because the results of those discussions often restricted their freedom of action. The judgments of board members seldom were used on acquisitions, divestitures, large capital investments, and other strategic matters. Often, the board would meet only annually to fulfill its minimum legal requirements; in many organizations, boards served merely a traditional legitimizing role.

Today, boards of directors are composed mostly of outsiders who are becoming more involved in organizations' strategic management. The trend in America is toward smaller boards, now averaging twelve members rather than eighteen as they did a few years ago. Smaller boards can discuss issues more easily; individuals in small groups take responsibility more personally.

Just as directors are beginning to place more emphasis on staying informed about an organization's health and operations, they also are taking a more active role in ensuring that publicly issued documents are accurate representations of a firm's status. It is becoming widely recognized that a board of directors has legal responsibilities to stockholders and society for all company activities, for corporate performance, and for ensuring that a firm has an effective strategy. Failure to accept responsibility for auditing or evaluating a firm's strategy is considered a serious breach of a director's duties. Stockholders, government agencies, and customers are filing legal suits against directors for fraud, omissions, inaccurate disclosures, lack of due diligence, and culpable ignorance about a firm's operations with increasing frequency. Liability insurance for directors has become exceptionally expensive and has caused numerous directors to resign.

Boards of directors in corporate America today seriously are evaluating strategic plans, evaluating the top management team, and assuming responsibility for management succession. TIAA-CREF, the nation's largest pension fund, now regularly evaluates governance practices at more than fifteen hundred companies in which it owns a stake. *Business Week*'s annual board of director's evaluation[10] posited that good boards of directors actively perform the following responsibilities:

- Evaluate the CEO annually.
- Link the CEO's pay to specific goals.
- Evaluate long-range strategy.
- Evaluate board members' performance through a governance committee.
- Compensate board members only in company stock.
- Require each director to own a large amount of company stock.
- Ensure no more than two board members are insiders (work for the company).
- Require directors to retire at age seventy.
- Place the entire board up for election every year.
- Limit the number of other boards a member can serve on.
- Ban directors who draw consulting fees or other monies from the company.
- Ban interlocking directorships.

Two rulings particularly affected the role of boards of directors in the strategy-formulation process. First, the Supreme Court of Delaware ruled that the directors of the Trans Union Corporation violated the interests of shareholders when they hastily accepted a takeover bid from the Marmon Group; that ruling eroded the so-called business judgment rule, which protects directors from liability as long as their decisions represent a good-faith effort to serve the best interests of the corporation. One clear signal from the Trans Union case is that haste can be costly for board members.

In another landmark ruling that illustrates how boards of directors increasingly are being held responsible for the overall performance of organizations, the Federal Deposit Insurance Corporation forced Continental Illinois to accept the resignations of ten of the troubled bank's outside directors. The impact of increasing legal pressures on board members is that directors are demanding greater and more regular access to financial performance information.

Some boardroom reforms that are lessening the likelihood of lawsuits today include increasing the percentage of outsiders on the board, separating the positions of CEO and chairperson, requiring directors to hold substantial amounts of stock in the firm, and decreasing the board size. Outsiders now outnumber insiders at 90 percent of all American firms' boards, and the average number of outsiders is three times that of insiders.

A direct response of increased pressure on directors to stay informed and execute their responsibilities is that audit committees are becoming commonplace. A board of directors should conduct an annual strategy audit in much the same fashion that it reviews the annual financial audit. In performing such an audit, a board could work jointly with operating management and/or seek outside counsel.

The trend among corporations toward decreased diversification, increased takeover activity, increased legal pressures, multidivisional structures, and multinational operations augments the problem of keeping directors informed. Boards should play a role beyond that of performing a strategic audit. They should provide greater input and advice in the strategy-formulation process to ensure that strategists are providing for the long-term needs of the firm. This is being done through the formation of three particular board committees: nominating committees to propose candidates for the board and senior officers of the firm; compensation committees to evaluate the performance of top executives and determine the terms and conditions of their employment; and public policy committees to give board-level attention to company policies and performance on subjects of concern such as business ethics, consumer affairs, and political activities.

A board of directors' mission statement outlines the purpose and intent of the board and defines to whom, or for what, the board is held accountable. A board mission statement also indicates company expectations about the quality of preparation for and the process for conducting board meetings. Overall, the mission of boards of directors must be expanded. Companies should assign managers to join directors on board committees, rather than limit the board's contact with only a few top managers. Directors must assume a more activist stance in management development, rather than just react to management initiatives.

Powerful boards of directors are associated with high organizational performance. Powerful boards participate in corporate decisions more fully, share their experiences with the CEO regarding certain strategies, and are actively involved in industry analysis. Firms can develop more powerful boards by regularly reviewing board committee activities, evaluating board meetings, and involving the board more extensively in strategic issues. More companies are paying board members partly or totally in stock, which gives outside directors more reason to identify with the shareholders they represent rather than with the CEO they oversee.

Church boards have historically been made up of parishioners only, but an increasing number of churches are placing outsiders (non-members) on their board.[11] These outsiders include influential persons in the community who have financial planning, fund-raising, trust management, and other desired skills. Churches desire to create endowments and capitalize on older members' growing estates.

## CONCLUSION

The essence of strategy formulation is an assessment of whether an organization is doing the right things and how it can be more effective in what it does. Every organization should be wary of becoming a prisoner of its own strategy, because even the best strategies become obsolete sooner or later. Regular reappraisal of strategy helps management avoid complacency. Objectives and strategies should be consciously developed and coordinated and should not merely evolve out of day-to-day operating decisions.

An organization with no sense of direction and no coherent strategy precipitates its own demise. When an organization does not know where it wants to go, it usually ends up some place it does not want to be! Every organization needs to consciously establish and communicate clear objectives and strategies.

Modern strategy-formulation tools and concepts are described in this chapter and integrated into a practical three-stage framework. Tools such as the TOWS Matrix, SPACE Matrix, BCG Matrix, IE Matrix, and QSPM can enhance significantly the quality of strategic decisions, but they should never be used to dictate the choice of strategies. Behavioral, cultural, and political aspects of strategy generation and selection are always important to consider and manage. Because of increased legal pressure from outside groups, boards of directors are assuming a more active role in strategy analysis and choice. This is a positive trend for organizations.

We invite you to visit the DAVID page on the Prentice Hall Web site at **www.prenhall.com/** for this chapter's World Wide Web exercise.

## KEY TERMS AND CONCEPTS

Aggressive Quadrant  (p. 209)

Attractiveness Scores (AS)  (p. 220)

Boards of Directors  (p. 226)

Boston Consulting Group (BCG)
    Matrix  (p. 212)

Business Portfolio  (p. 212)

Cash Cows  (p. 214)

Champions  (p. 224)

Competitive Advantage
    (CA)  (p. 208)

Competitive Quadrant  (p. 211)

Conservative Quadrant  (p. 211)

Culture  (p. 223)

Decision Stage  (p. 201)

Defensive Quadrant  (p. 211)

Directional Vector  (p. 209)

Dogs  (p. 214)

Environmental Stability
    (ES)  (p. 208)

Financial Strength (FS)  (p. 208)

Governance  (p. 225)

Grand Strategy Matrix  (p. 217)

Halo Error  (p. 202)

Industry Strength (IS)  (p. 208)

Input Stage  (p. 201)

Internal-External (IE)
    Matrix  (p. 212)

Matching  (p. 208)

Matching Stage  (p. 201)

Quantitative Strategic Planning
    Matrix (QSPM)  (p. 219)

Question Marks  (p. 213)

Relative Market Share
    Position  (p. 212)

SO Strategies  (p. 204)

ST Strategies  (p. 204)

Stars  (p. 213)

Strategic Position and Action
    Evaluation (SPACE)
    Matrix  (p. 208)

Strategy-Formulation
    Framework  (p. 201)

Sum Total Attractiveness
    Scores  (p. 221)

Threats-Opportunities-
    Weaknesses-Strengths (TOWS)
    Matrix  (p. 204)

Total Attractiveness Scores
    (TAS)  (p. 221)

WO Strategies  (p. 204)

WT Strategies  (p. 205)

## ISSUES FOR REVIEW AND DISCUSSION

1. How would application of the strategy-formulation framework differ from a small to a large organization?

2. What types of strategies would you recommend for an organization that achieves total weighted scores of 3.6 on the IFE and 1.2 on the EFE Matrix?

3. Given the following information, develop a SPACE Matrix for the XYZ Corporation: FS = +2; ES = −6; CA = −2; IS = +4.

4. Given the information in the table below, develop a BCG Matrix and an IE Matrix:

| Divisions | 1 | 2 | 3 |
| --- | --- | --- | --- |
| Profits | $10 | $15 | $25 |
| Sales | $100 | $50 | $100 |
| Relative Market Share | 0.2 | 0.5 | 0.8 |
| Industry Growth Rate | +.20 | +.10 | −.10 |
| IFE Total Weighted Scores | 1.6 | 3.1 | 2.2 |
| EFE Total Weighted Scores | 2.5 | 1.8 | 3.3 |

5. Explain the steps involved in developing a QSPM.

6. How would you develop a set of objectives for your school of business?

7. What do you think is the appropriate role of a board of directors in strategic management? Why?

8. Discuss the limitations of various strategy-formulation analytical techniques.

9. Explain why cultural factors should be an important consideration in analyzing and choosing among alternative strategies.

10. How are the TOWS Matrix, SPACE Matrix, BCG Matrix, IE Matrix, and Grand Strategy Matrix similar? How are they different?

11. How would profit and nonprofit organizations differ in their applications of the strategy-formulation framework?

12. Select an article from the suggested readings at the end of this chapter and prepare a report on that article for your class.

13. Calculate the Relative Market Share Position of Hardee's given the following 1998 year-end sales figures (in $billions) of the seven largest hamburger chains: McDonald's ($18.1), Burger King ($8.2), Wendy's ($5.0), Hardee's ($2.4), Dairy Queen ($2.0), Jack in the Box ($1.4), Sonic Drive-In ($1.3).

## NOTES

1. R. T. LENZ, "Managing the Evolution of the Strategic Planning Process," *Business Horizons* 30, no. 1 (January–February 1987): 37.

2. ROBERT GRANT, "The Resource-Based Theory of Competitive Advantage: Implications for Strategy Formulation," *California Management Review* (Spring 1991): 114.

3. HEINZ WEIHRICH, "The TOWS Matrix: A Tool for Situational Analysis," *Long Range Planning* 15, no. 2 (April 1982): 61.

4. H. ROWE, R. MASON, and K. DICKEL, *Strategic Management and Business Policy: A Methodological Approach* (Reading, Massachusetts: Addison-Wesley Publishing Co. Inc., 1982): 155–156. Reprinted with permission of the publisher.

5. FRED DAVID, "The Strategic Planning Matrix—A Quantitative Approach," *Long Range Planning* 19, no. 5 (October 1986): 102. ANDRE GIB and ROBERT MARGULIES, "Making Competitive Intelligence Relevant to the User," *Planning Review* 19, no. 3 (May/June 1991): 21.

6. FRED DAVID, "Computer-Assisted Strategic Planning in Small Businesses," *Journal of Systems Management* 36, no. 7 (July 1985): 24–34.

7. Y. ALLARIE and M. FIRSIROTU, "How to Implement Radical Strategies in Large Organizations," *Sloan Management Review* 26, no. 3 (Spring 1985): 19. Another excellent article is P. Shrivastava, "Integrating Strategy Formulation with Organizational Culture," *Journal of Business Strategy* 5, no. 3 (Winter 1985): 103–111.

8. JAMES BRIAN QUINN, *Strategies for Change: Logical Incrementalism* (Homewood, Ill.: Richard D. Irwin, 1980): 128–145. These political tactics are listed in A. Thompson and A. Strickland, *Strategic Management: Concepts and Cases* (Plano, Texas: Business Publications, 1984): 261.

9. WILLIAM GUTH and IAN MACMILLAN, "Strategy Implementation Versus Middle Management Self-Interest," *Strategic Management Journal* 7, no. 4 (July–August 1986): 321.

10. "Best and Worst Corporate Boards of Directors," *Business Week* (November 25, 1996): 82–98.

11. LISA MILLER, "Seeking Cash and Connections, Churches Revamp Boards," *The Wall Street Journal* (September 23, 1999): B1.

## CURRENT READINGS

BENSAOU, M. "Portfolios of Buyer-Supplier Relationships." *Sloan Management Review* 40, no. 4 (Summer 1999): 35–44.

CADBURY, ADRIAN. "What Are the Trends in Corporate Governance? How Will They Impact Your Company." *International Journal of Strategic Management* 32, no. 1 (February 1999): 12–19.

CHARAN, RAM. "Boards at Work: How Corporate Boards Create Competitive Advantage." Reviewed by Joseph Ryan. *Human Resource Management* 38, no. 1 (Spring 1999): 87–97.

DAILY, CATHERINE M. and DAN R. DALTON. "Executive Briefing/Corporate Governance Digest." *Business Horizons* 42, no. 3 (May–June 1999): 2–4.

DAILY, C. M., S. T. CERTO, and D. R. DALTON. "A Decade of Corporate Women: Some Progress in the Boardroom, *None* in the Executive Suite." Research Notes and Communications. *Strategic Management Journal* 20, no. 1 (January 1999): 93–102.

DEEPHOUSE, D. L. "To Be Different, or To Be the Same? It's a Question (and Theory) of Strategic Balance." *Strategic Management Journal* 20, no. 2 (February 1999); 147–166.

FORBES, DANIEL P. and FRANCES J. MILLIKEN. "Cognition and Corporate Governance: Understanding Boards of Directors As Strategic Decision-Making Groups." *The Academy of Management Review* 24, no. 3 (July 1999): 489–505.

FORNEY, NATHAN A. "Rommel in the Boardroom." *Business Horizons* 42, no. 4 (July–August 1999): 37–42.

GARRETT, BOB. "Developing Effective Directors and Building Dynamic Boards." *International Journal of Strategic Management* 32, no. 1 (February 1999): 28–35.

HEMPHILL, THOMAS A. "Corporate Governance, Strategic Philanthropy, and Public Policy." *Business Horizons* 42, no. 3 (May–June 1999): 57–62.

HILLMAN, A. J., A. ZARDKOOHI, and L. BIERMAN. "Corporate Political Strategies and Firm Performance: Indications of Firm-Specific Benefits from Personal Service in the U.S. Government." *Strategic Management Journal* 20, no. 1 (January 1999): 67–82.

JOHNSON, RICHARD A. and DANIEL W. GREENING. "The Effects of Corporate Governance and Institutional Influences on Board Composition and Structure." *The Academy of Management Journal* 42, no. 5 (October 1999): 553–563.

LEE, JENNY S. Y. "Organizational Learning in China." *Business Horizons* 42, no. 1 (January–February 1999): 37–44.

LORSCH, JAY W. and RAKESH KHURANA. "Changing Leaders: The Board's Role in CEO Succession." A Roundtable With Philip Caldwell, George D. Kennedy, G. G. Michelson, Henry Wendt, and Alfred M. Zeien. *Harvard Business Review* 77, no. 4 (May–June 1999): 96–106.

LUOMA, PATRICE and JERRY GOODSTEIN. "Stakeholders and Corporate Boards: Institutional Influences on Board Composition and Structure." *The Academy of Management Journal* 42, no. 5 (October 1999): 564–580.

PRAHALAD, C. K. and JAN P. OOSTERVELD. "Transforming Internal Governance: The Challenge of Multinationals." *Sloan Management* 40, no. 3 (Spring 1999): 31–40.

THOMAS, HOWARD, TIMOTHY POLLOCK, and PHILLIP GORMAN. "Global Strategic Analyses: Frameworks and Approaches." *The Academy of Management Executive* 13, no. 1 (February 1999): 70–82.

WESTPHAL, JAMES D. "Collaboration in the Boardroom: Behavioral and Performance Consequences of CEO-Board Social Ties." *The Academy of Management Journal* 42, no. 1 (February 1999): 7–24.

# EXPERIENTIAL EXERCISES

**EXPERIENTIAL EXERCISE 6A** ▶

Developing a TOWS Matrix for America Online (AOL)

## PURPOSE

The most widely used strategy-formulation technique among American firms is the TOWS Matrix. This exercise requires development of a TOWS Matrix for America Online. Matching key external and internal factors in a TOWS Matrix requires good intuitive and conceptual skills. You will improve with practice in developing a TOWS Matrix.

## INSTRUCTIONS

Recall from Experiential Exercise 1A that you already may have determined AOL's external opportunities/threats and internal strengths/weaknesses. This information could be used in completing this exercise. Follow the steps outlined below:

**Step 1** On a separate sheet of paper, construct a large nine-cell diagram that will represent your TOWS Matrix. Label the cells appropriately.

**Step 2** Record AOL's opportunities/threats and strengths/weaknesses appropriately in your diagram.

**Step 3** Match external and internal factors to generate feasible alternative strategies for AOL. Record SO, WO, ST, and WT Strategies in appropriate cells of the TOWS Matrix. Use the proper notation to indicate the rationale for the strategies. You do not necessarily have to have strategies in all four strategy cells.

**Step 4** Compare your TOWS Matrix to another student's TOWS Matrix. Discuss any major differences.

**EXPERIENTIAL EXERCISE 6B** ▶

Developing a SPACE Matrix for America Online (AOL)

## PURPOSE

Should AOL pursue aggressive, conservative, competitive, or defensive strategies? Develop a SPACE Matrix for AOL to answer this question. Elaborate on the strategic implications of your directional vector. Be specific in terms of strategies that could benefit AOL.

## INSTRUCTIONS

**Step 1** Join with two other persons in class and develop a joint SPACE Matrix for AOL.

**Step 2** Diagram your SPACE Matrix on the board. Compare your matrix with other teams' matrices.

**Step 3** Discuss the implications of your SPACE Matrix.

**EXPERIENTIAL EXERCISE 6C** ▶

Developing a BCG Matrix for America Online (AOL)

## PURPOSE

Portfolio matrices are widely used by multidivisional organizations to help identify and select strategies to pursue. A BCG analysis identifies particular divisions that should receive fewer resources than others. It may identify some divisions to be divested. This exercise can give you practice developing a BCG Matrix.

## INSTRUCTIONS

**Step 1** Place the following five column headings at the top of a separate sheet of paper: Divisions, Revenues, Profits, Relative Market Share Position, Industry Growth Rate.

Step 2    Complete a BCG Matrix for AOL.

Step 3    Compare your BCG Matrix to other students' matrices. Discuss any major differences.

## PURPOSE

This exercise can give you practice developing a Quantitative Strategic Planning Matrix to determine the relative attractiveness of various strategic alternatives.

## INSTRUCTIONS

Step 1    Join with two other students in class to develop a joint QSPM for AOL.

Step 2    Go to the blackboard and record your strategies and their Sum Total Attractiveness Scores. Compare your team's strategies and sum total attractiveness scores to those of other teams. Be sure not to assign the same AS score in a given row. Recall that dashes should be inserted all the way across a given row when used.

Step 3    Discuss any major differences.

## PURPOSE

Individuals and organizations are alike in many ways. Each has competitors and each should plan for the future. Every individual and organization faces some external opportunities and threats and has some internal strengths and weaknesses. Both individuals and organizations establish objectives and allocate resources. These and other similarities make it possible for individuals to use many strategic-management concepts and tools. This exercise is designed to demonstrate how the TOWS Matrix can be used by individuals to plan their futures. As one nears completion of a college degree and begins interviewing for jobs, planning can be particularly important.

## INSTRUCTIONS

On a separate sheet of paper, construct a TOWS Matrix. Include what you consider to be your major external opportunities, your major external threats, your major strengths, and your major weaknesses. An internal weakness may be a low grade point average. An external opportunity may be that your university offers a graduate program that interests you. Match key external and internal factors by recording in the appropriate cell of the matrix alternative strategies or actions that would allow you to capitalize upon your strengths, overcome your weaknesses, take advantage of your external opportunities, and minimize the impact of external threats. Be sure to use the appropriate matching notation in the strategy cells of the matrix. Because every individual (and organization) is unique, there is no one right answer to this exercise.

## PURPOSE

The purpose of this exercise is to enhance your understanding and awareness of the impact that behavioral and political factors can have on strategy analysis and choice.

## INSTRUCTIONS

Step 1    On a separate sheet of paper, number from 1 to 10. For each of the 10 statements given below, record a *1, 2, 3, 4,* or *5* to indicate your attitude, where

1 = I disagree a lot.

2 = I disagree a little.

3 = My attitude is neutral.

4 = I agree a little.

5 = I agree a lot.

1. The best way to handle people is to tell them what they want to hear.
2. When you ask someone to do something for you, it is best to give the real reason for wanting it, rather than a reason that might carry more weight.
3. Anyone who completely trusts anyone else is asking for trouble.
4. It is hard to get ahead without cutting corners here and there.
5. It is safest to assume that all people have a vicious streak, and it will come out when they are given a chance.
6. One should take action only when it is morally right.
7. Most people are basically good and kind.
8. There is no excuse for lying to someone else.
9. Most people forget more easily the death of their father than the loss of their property.
10. Generally speaking, people won't work hard unless they're forced to do so.

**Step 2**   Add up the numbers you recorded beside statements 1, 3, 4, 5, 9, and 10. This sum is Subtotal One. For the other four statements, reverse the numbers you recorded, so a *5* becomes a *1*, *4* becomes *2*, *2* becomes *4*, *1* becomes *5*, and *3* remains *3*. Then add those four numbers to get Subtotal Two. Finally, add Subtotal One and Subtotal Two to get your Final Score.

### *YOUR FINAL SCORE*

Your Final Score is your Machiavellian Score. Machiavellian principles are defined in a dictionary as "manipulative, dishonest, deceiving, and favoring political expediency over morality." These tactics are not desirable, are not ethical, and are not recommended in the strategic-management process! You may, however, encounter some highly Machiavellian individuals in your career, so beware. It is important for strategists not to manipulate others in the pursuit of organizational objectives. Individuals today recognize and resent manipulative tactics more than ever before. J. R. Ewing (on a television show in the 1980s, "Dallas") was a good example of someone who was a high Mach (score over 30). The National Opinion Research Center used this short quiz in a random sample of American adults and found the national average Final Score to be 25.[1] The higher your score, the more Machiavellian (manipulative) you tend to be. The following scale is descriptive of individual scores on this test:

- Below 16:     Never uses manipulation as a tool.
- 16 to 20:     Rarely uses manipulation as a tool.
- 21 to 25:     Sometimes uses manipulation as a tool.
- 26 to 30:     Often uses manipulation as a tool.
- Over 30:      Always uses manipulation as a tool.

### *TEST DEVELOPMENT*

The Mach (Machiavellian) test was developed by Dr. Richard Christie, whose research suggests the following tendencies:

1. Men generally are more Machiavellian than women.
2. There is no significant difference between high Machs and low Machs on measures of intelligence or ability.

3. Although high Machs are detached from others, they are detached in a pathological sense.

4. Machiavellian Scores are not statistically related to authoritarian values.

5. High Machs tend to be in professions that emphasize the control and manipulation of individuals; for example, law, psychiatry, and behavioral science.

6. Machiavellianism is not significantly related to major demographic characteristics such as educational level or marital status.

7. High Machs tend to come from a city or have urban backgrounds.

8. Older adults tend to have lower Mach scores than younger adults.[2]

A classic book on power relationships, *The Prince,* was written by Niccolo Machiavelli. Several excerpts from *The Prince* are given below:

Men must either be cajoled or crushed, for they will revenge themselves for slight wrongs, while for grave ones they cannot. The injury therefore that you do to a man should be such that you need not fear his revenge.

We must bear in mind . . . that there is nothing more difficult and dangerous, or more doubtful of success, than an attempt to introduce a new order of things in any state. The innovator has for enemies all those who derived advantages from the old order of things, while those who expect to be benefitted by the new institution will be but lukewarm defenders.

A wise prince, therefore, will steadily pursue such a course that the citizens of his state will always and under all circumstances feel the need for his authority, and will therefore always prove faithful to him.

A prince should seem to be merciful, faithful, humane, religious, and upright, and should even be so in reality; but he should have his mind so trained that, when occasion requires it, he may know how to change to the opposite.[3]

## NOTES

1. RICHARD CHRISTIE and FLORENCE GEIS, *Studies in Machiavellianism* (Orlando, Florida: Academic Press, 1970). Material in this exercise adapted with permission of the authors and the Academic Press.
2. Ibid., 82–83.
3. NICCOLO MACHIAVELLI, *The Prince* (New York: The Washington Press, 1963).

**EXPERIENTIAL EXERCISE 6G** ▶

Developing a BCG Matrix for My University

### PURPOSE

A BCG Matrix is useful to develop for many nonprofit organizations, including colleges and universities. Of course, there are no profits for each division or department and in some cases no revenues. However, you can be creative in performing a BCG Matrix. For example, the pie slice in the circles can represent the number of majors receiving jobs upon graduation, or the number of faculty teaching in that area, or some other variable that you believe is important to consider. The size of the circles can represent the number of students majoring in particular departments or areas.

### INSTRUCTIONS

Step 1   On a separate sheet of paper, develop a BCG Matrix for your university. Include all academic schools, departments, or colleges.

Step 2   Diagram your BCG Matrix on the blackboard.

Step 3   Discuss differences among the BCG Matrices on the board.

**EXPERIENTIAL
EXERCISE 6H** ▶

The Role of Boards
of Directors

### PURPOSE

This exercise will give you a better understanding of the role of boards of directors in formulating, implementing, and evaluating strategies.

### INSTRUCTIONS

Identify a person in your community who serves on a board of directors. Make an appointment to interview that person and seek answers to the questions given below. Summarize your findings in a five-minute oral report to the class.

On what board are you a member?

How often does the board meet?

How long have you served on the board?

What role does the board play in this company?

How has the role of the board changed in recent years?

What changes would you like to see in the role of the board?

To what extent do you prepare for the board meeting?

To what extent are you involved in strategic management of the firm?

**EXPERIENTIAL
EXERCISE 6I** ▶

Locating Companies
in a Grand Strategy
Matrix

### PURPOSE

The Grand Strategy Matrix is a popular tool for formulating alternative strategies. All organizations can be positioned in one of the Grand Strategy Matrix's four strategy quadrants. The divisions of a firm likewise could be positioned. The Grand Strategy Matrix is based on two evaluative dimensions: competitive position and market growth. Appropriate strategies for an organization to consider are listed in sequential order of attractiveness in each quadrant of the matrix. This exercise gives you experience using a Grand Strategy Matrix.

### INSTRUCTIONS

Using the year-end 1999 financial information given below, prepare a Grand Strategy Matrix on a separate sheet of paper. Write the respective company names in the appropriate quadrant of the matrix. Based on this analysis, what strategies are recommended for each company?

| COMPANY | COMPANY SALES/PROFIT GROWTH (%) | INDUSTRY | INDUSTRY SALES/PROFITS GROWTH (%) |
|---|---|---|---|
| DuPont | +9/−87 | Chemical | +9/−18 |
| J.C. Penney | +7/−43 | Retailing | +14/+14 |
| Intel | +12/+21 | Electrical | +14/+101 |
| Quaker Oats | −2/+60 | Food | +4/+1 |
| Biogen | +42/+59 | Health Care | +14/+12 |
| Mattel | −2/+0 | Leisure Time | +7/+4 |
| Nucor | −3/−7 | Metals | −2/−2 |
| Oracle | +17/+33 | Computers | +14/+63 |

*Source:* Adapted from "Industry Rankings," *Business Week* (March 27, 2000): 167–195.

■ PART 3

*Strategy Implementation*

# 7 IMPLEMENTING STRATEGIES: MANAGEMENT ISSUES

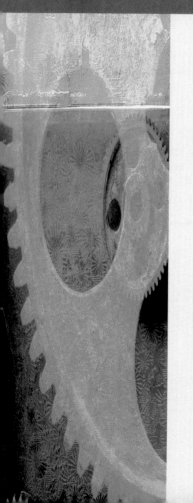

## CHAPTER OUTLINE

- The Nature of Strategy Implementation
- Annual Objectives
- Policies
- Resource Allocation
- Managing Conflict
- Matching Structure with Strategy
- Restructuring, Reengineering, and E-Engineering
- Linking Performance and Pay to Strategies
- Managing Resistance to Change
- Managing the Natural Environment
- Creating a Strategy-Supportive Culture
- Production/Operations Concerns When Implementing Strategies
- Human Resource Concerns When Implementing Strategies

## CHAPTER OBJECTIVES

*After studying this chapter, you should be able to do the following:*

1. Explain why strategy implementation is more difficult than strategy formulation.
2. Discuss the importance of annual objectives and policies in achieving organizational commitment for strategies to be implemented.
3. Explain why organizational structure is so important in strategy implementation.
4. Compare and contrast restructuring and reengineering.
5. Describe the relationships between production/operations and strategy implementation.
6. Explain how a firm can effectively link performance and pay to strategies.
7. Discuss employee stock ownership plans (ESOPs) as a strategic-management concept.
8. Describe how to modify an organizational culture to support new strategies.
9. Discuss the culture in Mexico, Russia, and Japan.
10. Describe the glass ceiling in the United States.

# NOTABLE QUOTES

You want your people to run the business as if it were their own.

WILLIAM FULMER

The ideal organizational structure is a place where ideas filter up as well as down, where the merit of ideas carries more weight than their source, and where participation and shared objectives are valued more than executive orders.

EDSON SPENCER

A management truism says structure follows strategy. However, this truism is often ignored. Too many organizations attempt to carry out a new strategy with an old structure.

DALE MCCONKEY

Poor Ike; when he was a general, he gave an order and it was carried out. Now, he's going to sit in that office and give an order and not a damn thing is going to happen.

HARRY TRUMAN

Changing your pay plan is a big risk, but not changing it could be a bigger one.

NANCY PERRY

Objectives can be compared to a compass bearing by which a ship navigates. A compass bearing is firm, but in actual navigation, a ship may veer off its course for many miles. Without a compass bearing, a ship would neither find its port nor be able to estimate the time required to get there.

PETER DRUCKER

The best game plan in the world never blocked or tackled anybody.

VINCE LOMBARDI

In most organizations, the top performers are paid too little and the worst performers too much.

CASS BETTINGER

The strategic-management process does not end when the firm decides what strategy or strategies to pursue. There must be a translation of strategic thought into strategic action. This translation is much easier if managers and employees of the firm understand the business, feel a part of the company, and through involvement in strategy-formulation activities have become committed to helping the organization succeed. Without understanding and commitment, strategy-implementation efforts face major problems.

Implementing strategy affects an organization from top to bottom; it impacts all the functional and divisional areas of a business. It is beyond the purpose and scope of this text to examine all the business administration concepts and tools important in strategy implementation. This chapter focuses on management issues most central to implementing strategies in the year 2001, and Chapter 8 focuses on marketing, finance/accounting, R&D, and computer information systems issues.

> Even the most technically perfect strategic plan will serve little purpose if it is not implemented. Many organizations tend to spend an inordinate amount of time, money, and effort on developing the strategic plan, treating the means and circumstances under which it will be implemented as afterthoughts! Change comes through implementation and evaluation, not through the plan. A technically imperfect plan that is implemented well will achieve more than the perfect plan that never gets off the paper on which it is typed.[1]

# THE NATURE OF STRATEGY IMPLEMENTATION

The strategy-implementation stage of strategic management is revealed in Figure 7–1. Successful strategy formulation does not guarantee successful strategy implementation. It is always more difficult to do something (strategy implementation) than to say you are going to do it (strategy formulation)! Although inextricably linked, strategy implementation is fundamentally different from strategy formulation. Strategy formulation and implementation can be contrasted in the following ways:

- Strategy formulation is positioning forces before the action.
- Strategy implementation is managing forces during the action.
- Strategy formulation focuses on effectiveness.
- Strategy implementation focuses on efficiency.
- Strategy formulation is primarily an intellectual process.
- Strategy implementation is primarily an operational process.
- Strategy formulation requires good intuitive and analytical skills.
- Strategy implementation requires special motivation and leadership skills.
- Strategy formulation requires coordination among a few individuals.
- Strategy implementation requires coordination among many persons.

Strategy-formulation concepts and tools do not differ greatly for small, large, for-profit, or nonprofit organizations. However, strategy implementation varies substantially among different types and sizes of organizations. Implementing strategies requires such actions as altering sales territories, adding new departments, closing facilities, hiring new employees, changing an organization's pricing strategy, developing financial budgets, developing new employee benefits, establishing cost-control procedures, changing advertising strategies, building new facilities, training new employees, transferring managers among divisions, and building a better computer information system. These types of activities obviously differ greatly between manufacturing, service, and governmental organizations.

**FIGURE 7–1**

**A Comprehensive Strategic-Management Model**

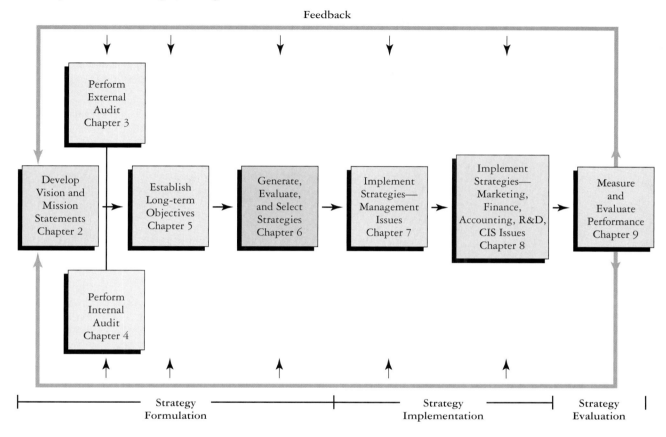

**Management Perspectives**

In all but the smallest organizations, the transition from strategy formulation to strategy implementation requires a shift in responsibility from strategists to divisional and functional managers. Implementation problems can arise because of this shift in responsibility, especially if strategy-formulation decisions come as a surprise to middle- and lower-level managers. Managers and employees are motivated more by perceived self-interests than by organizational interests, unless the two coincide. Therefore, it is essential that divisional and functional managers be involved as much as possible in strategy-formulation activities. Of equal importance, strategists should be involved as much as possible in strategy-implementation activities.

Management issues central to strategy implementation include establishing annual objectives, devising policies, allocating resources, altering an existing organizational structure, restructuring and reengineering, revising reward and incentive plans, minimizing resistance to change, matching managers with strategy, developing a strategy-supportive culture, adapting production/operations processes, developing an effective human resource function and, if necessary, downsizing. Management changes are necessarily more extensive when strategies to be implemented move a firm in a major new direction.

Managers and employees throughout an organization should participate early and directly in strategy-implementation decisions. Their role in strategy implementation should build upon prior involvement in strategy-formulation activities. Strategists' genuine personal commitment to implementation is a necessary and powerful motivational force for managers and employees. Too often, strategists are too busy to actively support strategy-implementation efforts, and their lack of interest can be detrimental to organizational success. The rationale for objectives and strategies should be understood and clearly communicated throughout an organization. Major competitors' accomplishments, products, plans, actions, and performance should be apparent to all organizational members. Major external opportunities and threats should be clear, and managers' and employees' questions should be answered. Top-down flow of communication is essential for developing bottom-up support.

Firms need to develop a competitor focus at all hierarchical levels by gathering and widely distributing competitive intelligence; every employee should be able to benchmark her or his efforts against best-in-class competitors so that the challenge becomes personal. This is a challenge for strategists of the firm. Firms should provide training for both managers and employees to ensure they have and maintain the skills necessary to be world-class performers.

 ## ANNUAL OBJECTIVES

*Establishing annual objectives* is a decentralized activity that directly involves all managers in an organization. Active participation in establishing annual objectives can lead to acceptance and commitment. *Annual objectives* are essential for strategy implementation because they (1) represent the basis for allocating resources; (2) are a primary mechanism for evaluating managers; (3) are the major instrument for monitoring progress toward achieving long-term objectives; and (4) establish organizational, divisional, and departmental priorities. Considerable time and effort should be devoted to ensuring that annual objectives are well conceived, consistent with long-term objectives, and supportive of strategies to be implemented. Approving, revising, or rejecting annual objectives is much more than a rubber-stamp activity. The purpose of annual objectives can be summarized as follows:

> Annual objectives serve as guidelines for action, directing and channeling efforts and activities of organization members. They provide a source of legitimacy in an enterprise by justifying activities to stakeholders. They serve as standards of performance. They serve as an important source of employee motivation and identification. They give incentives for managers and employees to perform. They provide a basis for organizational design.[2]

Clearly stated and communicated objectives are critical to success in all types and sizes of firms. Annual objectives, stated in terms of profitability, growth, and market share by business segment, geographic area, customer groups, and product are common in organizations. Figure 7–2 illustrates how the Stamus Company could establish annual objectives based on long-term objectives. Table 7–1 reveals associated revenue figures that correspond to the objectives outlined in Figure 7–2. Note that, according to plan, the Stamus Company will slightly exceed its long-term objective of doubling company revenues between 2001 and the year 2003.

Figure 7–2 also reflects how a hierarchy of annual objectives can be established based on an organization's structure. Objectives should be consistent across hierarchical levels and form a network of supportive aims. *Horizontal consistency of objectives* is as important as *vertical consistency.* For instance, it would not be effective for manufacturing to achieve more than its annual objective of units produced if marketing could not sell the additional units.

**FIGURE 7–2**

The Stamus Company's Hierarchy of Aims

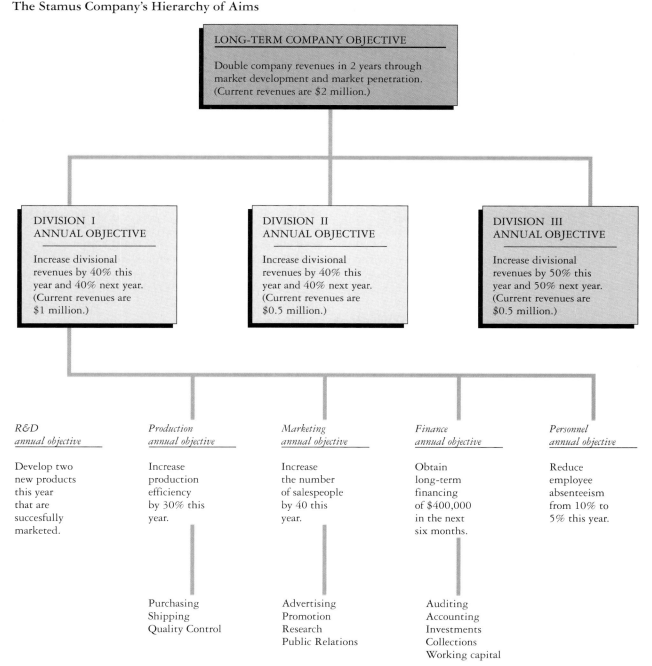

Annual objectives should be measurable, consistent, reasonable, challenging, clear, communicated throughout the organization, characterized by an appropriate time dimension, and accompanied by commensurate rewards and sanctions. Too often, objectives are stated in generalities, with little operational usefulness. Annual objectives such as "to improve communication" or "to improve performance" are not clear, specific, or measurable.

TABLE 7-1     The Stamus Company's Revenue Expectations
              (in millions of dollars)

|                         | 2001 | 2002  | 2003  |
|-------------------------|------|-------|-------|
| Division I Revenues     | 1.0  | 1.400 | 1.960 |
| Division II Revenues    | 0.5  | 0.700 | 0.980 |
| Division III Revenues   | 0.5  | 0.750 | 1.125 |
| Total Company Revenues  | 2.0  | 2.850 | 4.065 |

Objectives should state quantity, quality, cost, and time and also be verifiable. Terms such as "maximize," "minimize," "as soon as possible," and "adequate" should be avoided.

Annual objectives should be compatible with employees' and managers' values and should be supported by clearly stated policies. More of something is not always better! Improved quality or reduced cost may, for example, be more important than quantity. It is important to tie rewards and sanctions to annual objectives so that employees and managers understand that achieving objectives is critical to successful strategy implementation. Clear annual objectives do not guarantee successful strategy implementation but they do increase the likelihood that personal and organizational aims can be accomplished. Overemphasis on achieving objectives can result in undesirable conduct, such as faking the numbers, distorting the records, and letting objectives become ends in themselves. Managers must be alert to these potential problems.

 POLICIES

Changes in a firm's strategic direction do not occur automatically. On a day-to-day basis, policies are needed to make a strategy work. Policies facilitate solving recurring problems and guide the implementation of strategy. Broadly defined, *policy* refers to specific guidelines, methods, procedures, rules, forms, and administrative practices established to support and encourage work toward stated goals. Policies are instruments for strategy implementation. Policies set boundaries, constraints, and limits on the kinds of administrative actions that can be taken to reward and sanction behavior; they clarify what can and cannot be done in pursuit of an organization's objectives. For example, Carnival's new *Paradise* ship has a no-smoking policy anywhere, anytime aboard ship. It is the first cruise ship to comprehensively ban smoking. Another example of corporate policy relates to surfing the Web while at work. About 40 percent of companies today do not have a formal policy preventing employees from surfing the Internet, but software is being marketed now that allows firms to monitor how, when, where, and how long various employees use the Internet at work.

Policies let both employees and managers know what is expected of them, thereby increasing the likelihood that strategies will be implemented successfully. They provide a basis for management control, allow coordination across organizational units, and reduce the amount of time managers spend making decisions. Policies also clarify what work is to be done by whom. They promote delegation of decision making to appropriate managerial levels where various problems usually arise. Many organizations have a policy manual that serves to guide and direct behavior.

Policies can apply to all divisions and departments (for example, "We are an equal opportunity employer"). Some policies apply to a single department ("Employees in this department must take at least one training and development course each year").

TABLE 7-2      **A Hierarchy of Policies**

**Company Strategy:** Acquire a chain of retail stores to meet our sales growth and profitability objectives.
**Supporting policies:**
1. "All stores will be open from 8 A.M. to 8 P.M. Monday through Saturday." (This policy could increase retail sales if stores currently are open only 40 hours a week.)
2. "All stores must submit a Monthly Control Data Report." (This policy could reduce expense-to-sales ratios.)
3. "All stores must support company advertising by contributing 5 percent of their total monthly revenues for this purpose." (This policy could allow the company to establish a national reputation.)
4. "All stores must adhere to the uniform pricing guidelines set forth in the Company Handbook." (This policy could help assure customers that the company offers a consistent product in terms of price and quality in all its stores.)

**Divisional Objective:** Increase the division's revenues from $10 million in 2000 to $15 million in 2002.
**Supporting policies:**
1. "Beginning in January 2001, this division's salespersons must file a weekly activity report that includes the number of calls made, the number of miles traveled, the number of units sold, the dollar volume sold, and the number of new accounts opened." (This policy could ensure that salespersons do not place too great an emphasis in certain areas.)
2. "Beginning in January 2001, this division will return to its employees 5 percent of its gross revenues in the form of a Christmas bonus." (This policy could increase employee productivity.)
3. "Beginning in January 2001, inventory levels carried in warehouses will be decreased by 30 percent in accordance with a Just-in-Time manufacturing approach." (This policy could reduce production expenses and thus free funds for increased marketing efforts.)

**Production Department Objective:** Increase production from 20,000 units in 2000 to 30,000 units in 2002.
**Supporting policies:**
1. "Beginning in January 2001, employees will have the option of working up to 20 hours of overtime per week." (This policy could minimize the need to hire additional employees.)
2. "Beginning in January 2001, perfect attendance awards in the amount of $100 will be given to all employees who do not miss a workday in a given year." (This policy could decrease absenteeism and increase productivity.)
3. "Beginning in January 2001, new equipment must be leased rather than purchased." (This policy could reduce tax liabilities and thus allow more funds to be invested in modernizing production processes.)

Whatever their scope and form, policies serve as a mechanism for implementing strategies and obtaining objectives. Policies should be stated in writing whenever possible. They represent the means for carrying out strategic decisions. Examples of policies that support a company strategy, a divisional objective, and a departmental objective are given in Table 7–2.

Some example issues that may require a management policy are as follows:

- To offer extensive or limited management development workshops and seminars
- To centralize or decentralize employee-training activities
- To recruit through employment agencies, college campuses, and/or newspapers
- To promote from within or hire from the outside
- To promote on the basis of merit or on the basis of seniority
- To tie executive compensation to long-term and/or annual objectives
- To offer numerous or few employee benefits
- To negotiate directly or indirectly with labor unions
- To delegate authority for large expenditures or to retain this authority centrally
- To allow much, some, or no overtime work
- To establish a high- or low-safety stock of inventory
- To use one or more suppliers
- To buy, lease, or rent new production equipment
- To stress quality control greatly or not

- To establish many or only a few production standards
- To operate one, two, or three shifts
- To discourage using insider information for personal gain
- To discourage sexual harassment
- To discourage smoking at work
- To discourage insider trading
- To discourage moonlighting

# RESOURCE ALLOCATION

*Resource allocation* is a central management activity that allows for strategy execution. In organizations that do not use a strategic-management approach to decision making, resource allocation is often based on political or personal factors. Strategic management enables resources to be allocated according to priorities established by annual objectives. Nothing could be more detrimental to strategic management and to organizational success than for resources to be allocated in ways not consistent with priorities indicated by approved annual objectives.

All organizations have at least four types of resources that can be used to achieve desired objectives: financial resources, physical resources, human resources, and technological resources. Allocating resources to particular divisions and departments does not mean that strategies will be successfully implemented. A number of factors commonly prohibit effective resource allocation, including an overprotection of resources, too great an emphasis on short-run financial criteria, organizational politics, vague strategy targets, a reluctance to take risks, and a lack of sufficient knowledge.

Below the corporate level, there often exists an absence of systematic thinking about resources allocated and strategies of the firm. Yavitz and Newman explained why:

> Managers normally have many more tasks than they can do. Managers must allocate time and resources among these tasks. Pressure builds up. Expenses are too high. The CEO wants a good financial report for the third quarter. Strategy formulation and implementation activities often get deferred. Today's problems soak up available energies and resources. Scrambled accounts and budgets fail to reveal the shift in allocation away from strategic needs to currently squeaking wheels.[3]

The real value of any resource allocation program lies in the resulting accomplishment of an organization's objectives. Effective resource allocation does not guarantee successful strategy implementation because programs, personnel, controls, and commitment must breathe life into the resources provided. Strategic management itself is sometimes referred to as a "resource allocation process."

# MANAGING CONFLICT

Interdependency of objectives and competition for limited resources often leads to conflict. *Conflict* can be defined as a disagreement between two or more parties on one or more issues. Establishing annual objectives can lead to conflict because individuals have different expectations and perceptions, schedules create pressure, personalities are incompatible, and misunderstandings between line and staff occur. For example, a collection manager's objective of reducing bad debts by 50 percent in a given year may conflict with a divisional objective to increase sales by 20 percent.

Establishing objectives can lead to conflict because managers and strategists must make trade-offs, such as whether to emphasize short-term profits or long-term growth, profit margin or market share, market penetration or market development, growth or stability, high risk or low risk, and social responsiveness or profit maximization. Conflict is unavoidable in organizations, so it is important that conflict be managed and resolved before dysfunctional consequences affect organizational performance. Conflict is not always bad. An absence of conflict can signal indifference and apathy. Conflict can serve to energize opposing groups into action and may help managers identify problems.

Various approaches for managing and resolving conflict can be classified into three categories: avoidance, defusion, and confrontation. *Avoidance* includes such actions as ignoring the problem in hopes that the conflict will resolve itself or physically separating the conflicting individuals (or groups). *Defusion* can include playing down differences between conflicting parties while accentuating similarities and common interests, compromising so that there is neither a clear winner nor loser, resorting to majority rule, appealing to a higher authority, or redesigning present positions. *Confrontation* is exemplified by exchanging members of conflicting parties so that each can gain an appreciation of the other's point of view, or holding a meeting at which conflicting parties present their views and work through their differences.

##  MATCHING STRUCTURE WITH STRATEGY

Changes in strategy often require changes in the way an organization is structured for two major reasons. First, structure largely dictates how objectives and policies will be established. For example, objectives and policies established under a geographic organizational structure are couched in geographic terms. Objectives and policies are stated largely in terms of products in an organization whose structure is based on product groups. The structural format for developing objectives and policies can significantly impact all other strategy-implementation activities.

The second major reason why changes in strategy often require changes in structure is that structure dictates how resources will be allocated. If an organization is structured based on customer groups, then resources will be allocated in that manner. Similarly, if an organization's structure is set up along functional business lines, then resources are allocated by functional areas. Unless new or revised strategies place emphasis in the same areas as old strategies, structural reorientation commonly becomes a part of strategy implementation.

Changes in strategy lead to changes in organizational structure. Structure should be designed to facilitate the strategic pursuit of a firm and, therefore, follows strategy. Without a strategy or reasons for being (mission), designing an effective structure is difficult. Chandler found a particular structure sequence to be often repeated as organizations grow and change strategy over time; this sequence is depicted in Figure 7–3.

There is no one optimal organizational design or structure for a given strategy or type of organization. What is appropriate for one organization may not be appropriate for a similar firm, although successful firms in a given industry do tend to organize themselves in a similar way. For example, consumer goods companies tend to emulate the divisional structure-by-product form of organization. Small firms tend to be functionally structured (centralized). Medium-size firms tend to be divisionally structured (decentralized). Large firms tend to use an SBU (strategic business unit) or matrix structure. As

**FIGURE 7–3**

**Chandler's Strategy-Structure Relationship**

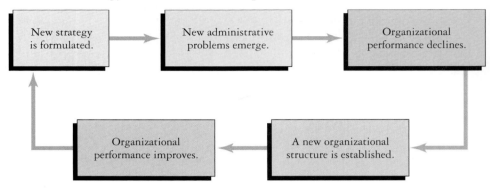

*Source:* Adapted from Alfred Chandler, *Strategy and Structure* (Cambridge, Massachusetts: MIT Press, 1962).

organizations grow, their structures generally change from simple to complex as a result of concatenation, or the linking together of several basic strategies.

Numerous external and internal forces affect an organization; no firm could change its structure in response to every one of these forces, because to do so would lead to chaos. However, when a firm changes its strategy, the existing organizational structure may become ineffective. Symptoms of an ineffective organizational structure include too many levels of management, too many meetings attended by too many people, too much attention being directed toward solving interdepartmental conflicts, too large a span of control, and too many unachieved objectives. Changes in structure can facilitate strategy-implementation efforts, but changes in structure should not be expected to make a bad strategy good, to make bad managers good, or to make bad products sell.

Structure undeniably can and does influence strategy. Strategies formulated must be workable, so if a certain new strategy required massive structural changes it would not be an attractive choice. In this way, structure can shape the choice of strategies. But a more important concern is determining what types of structural changes are needed to implement new strategies and how these changes can best be accomplished. We examine this issue by focusing on seven basic types of organizational structure: functional, divisional by geographic area, divisional by product, divisional by customer, divisional by process, strategic business unit (SBU), and matrix.

## The Functional Structure

The most widely used structure is the functional or centralized type because this structure is the simplest and least expensive of the seven alternatives. A *functional structure* groups tasks and activities by business function such as production/operations, marketing, finance/accounting, research and development, and computer information systems. A university may structure its activities by major functions that include academic affairs, student services, alumni relations, athletics, maintenance, and accounting. Besides being simple and inexpensive, a functional structure also promotes specialization of labor, encourages efficiency, minimizes the need for an elaborate control system, and allows rapid decision making. Some disadvantages of a functional structure are that it forces accountability to the top, minimizes career development opportunities, and is sometimes characterized by low employee morale, line/staff conflicts, poor delegation of authority, and inadequate planning for products and markets.

The 1980s and 1990s witnessed most large companies abandoning the functional structure in favor of decentralization and improved accountability.

## The Divisional Structure

The *divisional* or *decentralized structure* is the second most common type used by American businesses. As a small organization grows, it has more difficulty managing different products and services in different markets. Some form of divisional structure generally becomes necessary to motivate employees, control operations, and compete successfully in diverse locations. The divisional structure can be organized in one of four ways: by geographic area, by product or service, by customer, or by process. With a divisional structure, functional activities are performed both centrally and in each separate division.

Walt Disney recently created a new Internet division named Toysmart.com to compete in the online toy market, which is dominated by eToys and Amazon.com online. Toys R Us and Wal-Mart, leaders on off-line toy sales, are floundering for an online toy strategy. Similarly, Nordstrom, the upscale department store chain, has made its Internet business a separate division of the company. Nordstrom's site is designed to boost both online and catalog sales.

A divisional structure has some clear advantages. First and perhaps foremost, account-ability is clear. That is, divisional managers can be held responsible for sales and profit lev-els. Because a divisional structure is based on extensive delegation of authority, managers and employees can easily see the results of their good or bad performances. As a result, employee morale is generally higher in a divisional structure than it is in a centralized struc-ture. Other advantages of the divisional design are that it creates career development oppor-tunities for managers, allows local control of local situations, leads to a competitive climate within an organization, and allows new businesses and products to be added easily.

Bank One recently created a new division named Wingspan, a new bank that is accessible only on the Internet at wingspanbank.com. Wingspan competes directly with Bank One and all other banks, offers higher certificate of deposit interest rates than Bank One, and thus is a break from Bank One's traditional strategy of offering the same prod-ucts through numerous divisions. Bank One CEO John McCoy says, "All of the sudden now, there are ways you can go and get customers without having the full brick and mor-tar. I'm not about ready to sit here and let somebody else take my business.[4]

Visa USA Inc., the largest credit card association in the United States, recently formed a separate Internet division named e-Visa. This new division employs thirty-five people and is headed by Michael Beindorff. BellSouth Corporation is reorganizing into five divisions in order to flatten its organizational structure. The new divisions are customer markets; network services; wireless services; international; and advertising and publishing.

The divisional design is not without some limitations, however. Perhaps the most important limitation is that a divisional structure is costly, for a number of reasons. First, each division requires functional specialists who must be paid. Second, there exists some duplication of staff services, facilities, and personnel; for instance, functional specialists are also needed centrally (at headquarters) to coordinate divisional activities. Third, managers must be well qualified because the divisional design forces delegation of authority; better-qualified individuals require higher salaries. A divisional structure can also be costly because it requires an elaborate, headquarters-driven control system. Finally, certain regions, products, or customers may sometimes receive special treatment, and it may be difficult to maintain consistent, companywide practices. Nonetheless, for most large organizations and many small firms, the advantages of a divisional structure more than offset the potential limitations.

A *divisional structure by geographic area* is appropriate for organizations whose strate-gies need to be tailored to fit the particular needs and characteristics of customers in dif-ferent geographic areas. This type of structure can be most appropriate for organizations that have similar branch facilities located in widely dispersed areas. A divisional struc-ture by geographic area allows local participation in decision making and improved coor-dination within a region.

The *divisional structure by product* is most effective for implementing strategies when specific products or services need special emphasis. Also, this type of structure is widely used when an organization offers only a few products or services, or when an organization's products or services differ substantially. The divisional structure allows strict control and attention to product lines, but it may also require a more skilled management force and reduced top management control. General Motors, DuPont, and Procter & Gamble use a divisional structure by product to implement strategies. Huffy, the largest bicycle company in the world, is another firm that is highly decentralized based on a divisional-by-product structure. Based in Ohio, Huffy's divisions are the Bicycle division, the Gerry Baby Products division, the Huffy Sports division, YLC Enterprises, and Washington Inventory Service. Harry Shaw, Huffy's chairman, believes decentralization is one of the keys to Huffy's success.

When a few major customers are of paramount importance and many different services are provided to these customers, then a *divisional structure by customer* can be the most effective way to implement strategies. This structure allows an organization to cater effectively to the requirements of clearly defined customer groups. For example, book publishing companies often organize their activities around customer groups such as colleges, secondary schools, and private commercial schools. Some airline companies have two major customer divisions: passengers and freight or cargo services. Merrill Lynch is organized into separate divisions that cater to different groups of customers, including wealthy individuals, institutional investors, and small corporations.

A *divisional structure by process* is similar to a functional structure, because activities are organized according to the way work is actually performed. However, a key difference between these two designs is that functional departments are not accountable for profits or revenues, whereas divisional process departments are evaluated on these criteria. An example of a divisional structure by process is a manufacturing business organized into six divisions: electrical work, glass cutting, welding, grinding, painting, and foundry work. In this case, all operations related to these specific processes would be grouped under the separate divisions. Each process (division) would be responsible for generating revenues and profits. The divisional structure by process can be particularly effective in achieving objectives when distinct production processes represent the thrust of competitiveness in an industry.

## The Strategic Business Unit (SBU) Structure

As the number, size, and diversity of divisions in an organization increase, controlling and evaluating divisional operations become increasingly difficult for strategists. Increases in sales often are not accompanied by similar increases in profitability. The span of control becomes too large at top levels of the firm. For example, in a large conglomerate organization composed of 90 divisions, the chief executive officer could have difficulty even remembering the first names of divisional presidents. In multidivisional organizations an SBU structure can greatly facilitate strategy-implementation efforts.

The *SBU structure* groups similar divisions into strategic business units and delegates authority and responsibility for each unit to a senior executive who reports directly to the chief executive officer. This change in structure can facilitate strategy implementation by improving coordination between similar divisions and channeling accountability to distinct business units. In the ninety-division conglomerate just mentioned, the ninety divisions could perhaps be regrouped into ten SBUs according to certain common characteristics such as competing in the same industry, being located in the same area, or having the same customers.

Two disadvantages of an SBU structure are that it requires an additional layer of management, which increases salary expenses, and the role of the group vice-president is often ambiguous. However, these limitations often do not outweigh the advantages of improved coordination and accountability. Atlantic Richfield and Fairchild Industries are examples of firms that successfully use an SBU-type structure.

Lockheed Martin Corporation uses a strategic-business-unit-type organizational structure. The company currently is restructuring by reducing its five strategic business units to four. The four surviving groups are: military aircraft, space systems, systems integration, and technology services. Within those four strategic business units, twenty-seven divisions are being condensed to seventeen.

### The Matrix Structure

A *matrix structure* is the most complex of all designs because it depends upon both vertical and horizontal flows of authority and communication (hence the term *matrix*). In contrast, functional and divisional structures depend primarily on vertical flows of authority and communication. A matrix structure can result in higher overhead because it creates more management positions. Other characteristics of a matrix structure that contribute to overall complexity include dual lines of budget authority (a violation of the unity-of-command principle), dual sources of reward and punishment, shared authority, dual reporting channels, and a need for an extensive and effective communication system.

Despite its complexity, the matrix structure is widely used in many industries, including construction, healthcare, research, and defense. Some advantages of a matrix structure are that project objectives are clear, there are many channels of communication, workers can see visible results of their work, and shutting down a project can be accomplished relatively easily.

In order for a matrix structure to be effective, organizations need participative planning, training, clear mutual understanding of roles and responsibilities, excellent internal communication, and mutual trust and confidence. The matrix structure is being used more frequently by American businesses because firms are pursuing strategies that add new products, customer groups, and technology to their range of activities. Out of these changes are coming product managers, functional managers, and geographic-area managers, all of whom have important strategic responsibilities. When several variables, such as product, customer, technology, geography, functional area, and line of business, have roughly equal strategic priorities, a matrix organization can be an effective structural form.

## RESTRUCTURING, REENGINEERING, AND E-ENGINEERING

Restructuring and reengineering are becoming commonplace on the corporate landscape across the United States and Europe. *Restructuring*—also called *downsizing, rightsizing,* or *delayering*—involves reducing the size of the firm in terms of number of employees, number of divisions or units, and number of hierarchical levels in the firm's organizational structure. This reduction in size is intended to improve both efficiency and effectiveness. Restructuring is concerned primarily with shareholder well-being rather than employee well-being.

The Internet is ushering in a new wave of business transformation. No longer is it enough for companies to put up simple Web sites for customers and employees. To take full advantage of the Internet, companies need to change the way they distribute goods, deal with suppliers, attract customers, and serve customers. The Internet eliminates the geographic protection/monopoly of local businesses. Basically companies need to reinvent the way they do business to take full advantage of the Internet. This whole process is being called E-engineering.[5] Dow Corning Corporation and many others have recently appointed an e-commerce top executive.

**e·biz**

Unforgiving competition from leaner U.S. firms is forcing many European companies to downsize, laying off managers and employees. This was almost unheard of prior to the mid-1990s because European labor unions and laws required lengthy negotiations or huge severance checks before workers could be terminated. Unlike in the United States, labor union executives sit on most boards of directors of large European firms.

Job security in European companies is slowly moving toward a U.S. scenario in which firms lay off almost at will. From banks in Milan to factories in Mannhelm, European employers are starting to show people the door in an effort to streamline operations, increase efficiency, and compete against already slim and trim U.S. firms. Massive U.S.-style layoffs are still rare in Europe, but unemployment rates throughout the continent are rising quite rapidly. European firms still prefer to downsize by attrition and retirement rather than by blanket layoffs because of culture, laws, and unions. As indicated in the Global Perspective, all eyes are on Nissan in Japan which is restructuring in a manner untraditional to accepted business practices in that nation.

In contrast, *reengineering* is concerned more with employee and customer well-being than shareholder well-being. Reengineering—also called process management, process innovation, or process redesign—involves reconfiguring or redesigning work, jobs, and processes for the purpose of improving cost, quality, service, and speed. Reengineering does not usually affect the organizational structure or chart, nor does it imply job loss or employee layoffs. Whereas restructuring is concerned with eliminating

# GLOBAL PERSPECTIVE

## *Restructuring at Nissan Changes a Country*

All Japanese eyes these days are on Nissan, a highly respected company that is using American-style restructuring to reverse two years of dismal performance. Between 2000 and 2003, Nissan plans to close five plants, layoff 14 percent of the company workforce, eliminate 21,500 jobs, reduce debt from 1.4 trillion yen to less than half that amount, reduce the number of suppliers from 1,145 to 600, and reduce manufacturing capacity from 2.4 million cars to 1.65 million annually. Called the Nissan Revival Plan, this strategy runs fully against many long-time Japanese business traditions—as noted below. If Nissan succeeds, then many other Japanese companies may employ restructuring to become more competitive.

- By laying off thousands of workers, the Nissan Revival Plan disregards the "lifetime employment practice" for which Japanese firms are well-known.
- The Nissan Revival Plan violates *keiretsu,* the Japanese business custom that links manufacturers to suppliers through shareholdings, exchanges of key managers, and long-term relationships.

- The Nissan Revival Plan changes the pay and promotion of managers from seniority to performance. This ends the widespread Japanese custom at Nissan whereby managers are promoted up the corporate ladder merely by sticking around.
- The Nissan Revival Plan dissolves the company's shareholding stake in most of its 1,394 affiliated companies. This Japanese system marries business interests when divorce might be healthier.
- The Nissan Revival Plan calls for a single worldwide advertising agency to keep the company message consistent worldwide.

Following Nissan's lead, Nippon Telegraph & Telephone (NTT) has announced plans to lay off twenty thousand employees by 2003. NTT historically has had a monopoly on phone service in Japan, but now faces stiff competition.

*Source:* Adapted from: Norihiko Shirouzu, "Nissan Ambitious Restructuring Plan Delivers a Blow to Japan's Longstanding System of Corporate Families," *The Wall Street Journal* (October 20, 1999): A4. James Healey, "Retooling Nissan," *USA Today* (October 19, 1999): 2B.

or establishing, shrinking or enlarging, and moving organizational departments and divisions, the focus of reengineering is changing the way work is actually carried out.

Reengineering is characterized by many tactical (short-term, business function–specific) decisions, whereas restructuring is characterized by strategic (long-term, affecting all business functions) decisions.

## Restructuring

Firms often employ restructuring when various ratios appear out of line with competitors as determined through benchmarking exercises. *Benchmarking* simply involves comparing a firm against the best firms in the industry on a wide variety of performance-related criteria. Some benchmarking ratios commonly used in rationalizing the need for restructuring are headcount-to-sales-volume, or corporate-staff-to-operating-employees, or span-of-control figures.

The primary benefit sought from restructuring is cost reduction. For some highly bureaucratic firms, restructuring can actually rescue the firm from global competition and demise. But the downside of restructuring can be reduced employee commitment, creativity, and innovation that accompanies the uncertainty and trauma associated with pending and actual employee layoffs.

Another downside of restructuring is that many people today do not aspire to become managers, and many present-day managers are trying to get off the management track.[6] Sentiment against joining management ranks is higher today than ever. About 80 percent of employees say they want nothing to do with management, a major shift from just a decade ago when 60 to 70 percent hoped to become managers. Managing others historically led to enhanced career mobility, financial rewards, and executive perks; but in today's global, more competitive, restructured arena, managerial jobs demand more hours and headaches with fewer financial rewards. Managers today manage more people spread over different locations, travel more, manage diverse functions, and are change agents even when they have nothing to do with the creation of the plan or even disagree with its approach. Employers today are looking for people who can do things, not for people who make other people do things. Restructuring in many firms has made a manager's job an invisible, thankless role. More workers today are self-managed, entrepreneurs, intrepreneurs, or team-managed. Managers today need to be counselors, motivators, financial advisors, and psychologists. They also run the risk of becoming technologically behind in their areas of expertise. "Dilbert" cartoons commonly portray managers as enemies or as morons.

An example company undergoing major restructuring is South Korea's second-largest conglomerate, Daewoo Group. South Korea's powerful conglomerates, called *chaebols,* are being dismantled nationwide as President Kim Dae Jung's drives to reform that country's economy. All but six Daewoo divisions are being divested; the six remaining divisions, all automobile-related, are being renamed and reorganized, with General Motors becoming actively involved in their management.

## Reengineering

The argument for a firm engaging in reengineering usually goes as follows: Many companies historically have been organized vertically by business function. This arrangement has led over time to managers' and employees' mind-sets being defined by their particular functions rather than by overall customer service, product quality, or corporate performance. The logic is that all firms tend to bureaucratize over time. As routines become entrenched, turf becomes delineated and defended, and politics takes precedence over performance. Walls that exist in the physical workplace can be reflections of "mental" walls.

In reengineering, a firm uses information technology to break down functional barriers and create a work system based on business processes, products, or outputs rather than on functions or inputs. Cornerstones of reengineering are decentralization, reciprocal interdependence, and information sharing. A firm that exemplifies complete information sharing is Springfield ReManufacturing Corporation, which provides to all employees a weekly income statement of the firm, as well as extensive information on other companies' performances.

There are numerous examples of firms that benefited in the 1990s from reengineering—including Union Carbide, which reduced its fixed costs by $400 million; Taco Bell, which raised its restaurant peak capacity from $400 per hour to $1,500 per hour; and AT&T which created a new business telephone system called PBX.

A benefit of reengineering is that it offers employees the opportunity to see more clearly how their particular jobs impact the final product or service being marketed by the firm. However, reengineering also can raise manager and employee anxiety which, unless calmed, can lead to corporate trauma.

 ## LINKING PERFORMANCE AND PAY TO STRATEGIES

Most companies today are practicing some form of pay-for-performance for employees and managers other than top executives. The average employee performance bonus is 6.8 percent of pay for individual performance, 5.5 percent of pay for group productivity, and 6.4 percent of pay for companywide profitability.

Staff control of pay systems often prevents line managers from using financial compensation as a strategic tool. Flexibility regarding managerial and employee compensation is needed to allow short-term shifts in compensation that can stimulate efforts to achieve long-term objectives. NBC recently unveiled a new method for paying its affiliated stations. The compensation formula is 50 percent based on audience viewing of shows from 4 P.M. to 8 P.M. and 50 percent based on how many adults aged 25 to 54 watch NBC over the course of a day.

How can an organization's reward system be more closely linked to strategic performance? How can decisions on salary increases, promotions, merit pay, and bonuses be more closely aligned to support the long-term strategic objectives of the organization? There are no widely accepted answers to these questions, but a dual bonus system based on both annual objectives and long-term objectives is becoming common. The percentage of a manager's annual bonus attributable to short-term versus long-term results should vary by hierarchical level in the organization. A chief executive officer's annual bonus could, for example, be determined on a 75 percent short-term and 25 percent long-term basis. It is important that bonuses not be based solely on short-term results because such a system ignores long-term company strategies and objectives.

DuPont Canada has a 16 percent return-on-equity objective. If this objective is met, the company's four thousand employees receive a "performance sharing cash award" equal to 4 percent of pay. If return-on-equity falls below 11 percent, employees get nothing. If return-on-equity exceeds 28 percent, workers receive a 10 percent bonus.

In an effort to cut costs and increase productivity, more and more Japanese companies are switching from seniority-based pay to performance-based approaches. Toyota Motor switched in mid-1999 to a full merit system for twenty thousand of its seventy thousand white-collar workers. Fujitsu, Sony, Matsushita Electric Industrial, and Kao also have switched to merit pay systems. Nearly 30 percent of all Japanese companies have switched to merit pay from seniority pay.[7] This switching is hurting morale at some Japanese companies which have trained workers for decades to cooperate rather than to compete and to work in groups rather than individually.

Richard Brown, the new CEO of Electronic Data Systems recently removed the bottom 20 percent of EDS's sales force and said, "You have to start with an appraisal system that gives genuine feedback and differentiates performance. Some call it ranking people. That seems a little harsh. But you can't have a manager checking a box that says you're either stupendous, magnificent, very good, good or average. Concise, constructive feedback is the fuel workers use to get better. A company that doesn't differentiate performance risks losing its best people."[8]

*Profit sharing* is another widely used form of incentive compensation. More than 30 percent of American companies have profit sharing plans, but critics emphasize that too many factors affect profits for this to be a good criterion. Taxes, pricing, or an acquisition would wipe out profits, for example. Also, firms try to minimize profits in a sense to reduce taxes.

Still another criterion widely used to link performance and pay to strategies is gain sharing. *Gain sharing* requires employees or departments to establish performance targets; if actual results exceed objectives, all members get bonuses. More than 26 percent of American companies use some form of gain sharing; about 75 percent of gain sharing plans have been adopted since 1980. Carrier, a subsidiary of United Technologies, has had excellent success with gain sharing in its six plants in Syracuse, New York; Firestone's tire plant in Wilson, North Carolina, has experienced similar success with gain sharing.

Criteria such as sales, profit, production efficiency, quality, and safety could also serve as bases for an effective *bonus system.* If an organization meets certain understood, agreed-upon profit objectives, every member of the enterprise should share in the harvest. A bonus system can be an effective tool for motivating individuals to support strategy-implementation efforts. BankAmerica, for example, recently overhauled its incentive system to link pay to sales of the bank's most profitable products and services. Branch managers receive a base salary plus a bonus based on the number of new customers and on sales of bank products. Every employee in each branch is also eligible for a bonus if the branch exceeds its goals. Thomas Peterson, a top BankAmerica executive, says, "We want to make people responsible for meeting their goals, so we pay incentives on sales, not on controlling costs or on being sure the parking lot is swept."

Five tests are often used to determine whether a performance-pay plan will benefit an organization:

1. *Does the plan capture attention?* Are people talking more about their activities and taking pride in early successes under the plan?
2. *Do employees understand the plan?* Can participants explain how it works and what they need to do to earn the incentive?
3. *Is the plan improving communications?* Do employees know more than they used to about the company's mission, plans, and objectives?
4. *Does the plan pay out when it should?* Are incentives being paid for desired results—and being withheld when objectives are not met?
5. *Is the company or unit performing better?* Are profits up? Has market share grown? Have gains resulted in part from the incentives?[9]

In addition to a dual bonus system, a combination of reward strategy incentives such as salary raises, stock options, fringe benefits, promotions, praise, recognition, criticism, fear, increased job autonomy, and awards can be used to encourage managers and employees to push hard for successful strategic implementation. The range of options for getting people, departments, and divisions to actively support strategy-implementation activities in a particular organization is almost limitless. Merck, for example, recently gave each of its thirty-seven thousand employees a ten-year option to buy one hundred shares of Merck stock at a set price of $127. Steven Darien, Merck's vice-president of human resources, says, "We needed to find ways to get everyone in the workforce on board in terms of our goals and objectives. Company executives will begin meeting with all Merck workers to explore ways in which employees can contribute more."

Increasing criticism aimed at chief executive officers for their high pay has resulted in executive compensation being linked to performance of their firm more closely than ever before. Although the linkage between CEO pay and corporate performance is getting closer, CEO pay in the United States still can be astronomical.

CEO pay in 1998 for the largest 365 companies in the United States rose 36 percent in 1998, while earnings for those companies fell 1.4 percent.[10] The average salary of these CEO's in 1998 was $2.1 million. The 36 percent compares to a 2.7 percent increase for the average blue-collar worker and 3.9 percent increase for the average white-collar worker. The four CEOs who received the highest salary in 1998 were Jack Welch at General Electric ($10.1 million), Sanford Weill at Citigroup ($7.4 million), Michael Eisner at Walt Disney ($5.7 million), and Mel Karmazin at CBS ($4.0 million). But these amounts do not include stock options exercised, which for many CEOs were gigantic. For example, Michael Eisner's total 1998 compensation from Walt Disney was $569.8 million.

 ## MANAGING RESISTANCE TO CHANGE

No organization or individual can escape change. But the thought of change raises anxieties because people fear economic loss, inconvenience, uncertainty, and a break in normal social patterns. Almost any change in structure, technology, people, or strategies has the potential to disrupt comfortable interaction patterns. For this reason, people resist change. The strategic-management process itself can impose major changes on individuals and processes. Reorienting an organization to get people to think and act strategically is not an easy task.

*Resistance to change* can be considered the single greatest threat to successful strategy implementation. Resistance in the form of sabotaging production machines, absenteeism, filing unfounded grievances, and an unwillingness to cooperate regularly occurs in organizations. People often resist strategy implementation because they do not understand what is happening or why changes are taking place. In that case, employees may simply need accurate information. Successful strategy implementation hinges upon managers' ability to develop an organizational climate conducive to change. Change must be viewed as an opportunity rather than as a threat by managers and employees.

Resistance to change can emerge at any stage or level of the strategy-implementation process. Although there are various approaches for implementing changes, three commonly used strategies are a force change strategy, an educative change strategy, and a rational or self-interest change strategy. A *force change strategy* involves giving orders and enforcing those orders; this strategy has the advantage of being fast, but it is plagued by low commitment and high resistance. The *educative change strategy* is one that presents information to convince people of the need for change; the disadvantage of an educative change strategy is that implementation becomes slow and difficult. However, this type of strategy evokes greater commitment and less resistance than does the force strategy. Finally, a *rational* or *self-interest change strategy* is one that attempts to convince individuals that the change is to their personal advantage. When this appeal is successful, strategy implementation can be relatively easy. However, implementation changes are seldom to everyone's advantage.

The rational change strategy is the most desirable, so this approach is examined a bit further. Managers can improve the likelihood of successfully implementing change by carefully designing change efforts. Jack Duncan described a rational or self-interest change strategy as consisting of four steps. First, employees are invited to participate in the process of change and the details of transition; participation allows everyone to give opinions, to feel a part of the change process, and to identify their own self-interests regarding the recommended change. Second, some motivation or incentive to change is required; self-interest can be the most important motivator. Third, communication is needed so that people can understand the purpose for the changes. Giving and receiving feedback is the fourth step; everyone enjoys knowing how things are going and how much progress is being made.[11]

Igor Ansoff summarized the need for strategists to manage resistance to change as follows:

> Observation of the historical transitions from one orientation to another shows that, if left unmanaged, the process becomes conflict-laden, prolonged, and costly in both human and financial terms. Management of resistance involves anticipating the focus of resistance and its intensity. Second, it involves eliminating unnecessary resistance caused by misperceptions and insecurities. Third, it involves mustering the power base necessary to assure support for the change. Fourth, it involves planning the process of change. Finally, it involves monitoring and controlling resistance during the process of change. . . .[12]

Because of diverse external and internal forces, change is a fact of life in organizations. The rate, speed, magnitude, and direction of changes vary over time by industry and organization. Strategists should strive to create a work environment in which change is recognized as necessary and beneficial so that individuals can adapt to change more easily. Adopting a strategic-management approach to decision making can itself require major changes in the philosophy and operations of a firm.

Strategists can take a number of positive actions to minimize managers' and employees' resistance to change. For example, individuals who will be affected by a change should be involved in the decision to make the change and in decisions about how to implement change. Strategists should anticipate changes and develop and offer training and development workshops so managers and employees can adapt to those changes. They also need to communicate the need for changes effectively. The strategic-management process can be described as a process of managing change. Robert Waterman describes how successful organizations involve individuals to facilitate change:

> Implementation starts with, not after, the decision. When Ford Motor Company embarked on the program to build the highly successful Taurus, management gave up the usual, sequential design process. Instead they showed the tentative design to the workforce and asked their help in devising a car that would be easy to build. Team Taurus came up with no less than 1,401 items suggested by Ford employees. What a contrast from the secrecy that characterized the industry before! When people are treated as the main engine rather than interchangeable parts, motivation, creativity, quality, and commitment to implementation go up.[13]

## MANAGING THE NATURAL ENVIRONMENT

All business functions are affected by natural environment considerations or striving to make a profit. However, both employees and consumers are expecially resentful of firms that take from more than they give to the natural envrironment; likewise, people today are especially appreciative of firms that conduct operations in a way that mends rather than harms the environment.

The U.S. Justice Department recently issued new guidelines for companies to uncover environmental wrongdoing among their managers and employees without exposing themselves to poetntial criminal liability. The new guidelines give nine hypothetical examples to illustrate the new legal requirements. The examples include Company A, which regularly conducts a comprehensive environmental audit, goes straight to the government as soon as something wrong is turned up, disciplines the responsible people in the company, and gives their names as well as all relevant documentation to the government. The Justice Department will prosecute but be lenient in this case. The extreme example is Company K, which tries to cover up an environmental violation and does not cooperate with the government or provide names. Its audit is narrow, and its compliance program is "no more than a collection of paper." No leniency is likely for this firm.

Monsanto, a large U.S. chemical company, is an excellent example of a firm that protects the natural environment. Monsanto's motto is "Zero Spills, Zero Releases, Zero Incidents, and Zero Excuses." As indicated in the Natural Environment Perspective, there needs to be more Monsanto-type companies in Asia, a continent that became more polluted in the 1990s.

The 1990s may well be remembered as the decade of the environment. Earth itself has become a stakeholder for all business firms. Consumer interest in businesses' preserving nature's ecological balance and fostering a clean, healthy environment is high. As indicated in the Natural Environment Perspective, an increasing number of businesses today are purchasing their own independent, non-polluting power source. This strategy is in contrast to continuing to purchase electricity from large polluting, coal burning utilities.

The ecological challenge facing all organizations requires managers to formulate strategies that preserve and conserve natural resources and control pollution. Special natural environmental issues include ozone depletion, global warming, depletion of rain forests, destruction of animal habitats, protecting endangered species, developing biodegradable products and packages, waste management, clean air, clean water, erosion, destruction of natural resources, and pollution control. Firms increasingly are developing green product lines that are biodegradable and/or are made from recycled products. Green products sell well.

The Environmental Protection Agency recently reported that U.S. citizens and organizations spend more than about $200 billion annually on pollution abatement. Environmental concerns touch all aspects of a business's operations, including workplace risk exposures, packaging, waste reduction, energy use, alternative fuels, environmental cost accounting, and recycling practices.

Managing as if the earth matters requires an understanding of how international trade, competitiveness, and global resources are connected. Managing environmental affairs can no longer be simply a technical function performed by specialists in a firm; more emphasis must be placed on developing an environmental perspective among all employees and managers of the firm. Many companies are moving environmental affairs from the staff side of the organization to the line side, to make the corporate environmental group report directly to the chief operating officer.

Societies have been plagued by environmental disasters to such an extent recently that firms failing to recognize the importance of environmental issues and challenges could suffer severe consequences. Managing environmental affairs can no longer be an incidental or secondary function of company operations. Product design, manufacturing, and ultimate disposal should not merely reflect environmental considerations, but be driven by them. Firms that manage environmental affairs will enhance relations with consumers, regulators, vendors, and other industry players—substantially improving their prospects of success.

# NATURAL ENVIRONMENT

### *Does Your Business Generate Its Own Electricity?*

If no, perhaps it should. A new era of power production generators are rapidly selling into homes and businesses. Personal power is poised to explode into everyday life just like personal computers in 1984 and cellular phones more recently. Even the New York City Central park police station has pulled the plug on their public utility. Companies such as Plug Power LLC of Latham, New York, are selling dishwashers-size fuel cells for the home for less than four thousand dollars. These new systems which run on propane or natural gas, not diesel, are exceptionally efficient and non-polluting. In a fossil fuel plant, only 29 percent of the original energy in that coal or oil remains when it arrives at a home or business. "The era of big central power plants is certainly over," says Chuck Linderman of Edison Electric Institute. Some businesses such as First National Bank in Omaha have purchased a personal power system because "being down for one hour would cost the bank about $6 million." Storms often result in big power plants cutting off power to homes and businesses, which is so costly to some businesses, personal systems are in great demand. Some large companies leading the way in using personal power systems include McDonald's, Rogan Corporation,

Heinemann Bakeries, and Citigroup. Some manufacturers of personal power plants include Caterpillar Inc., Ingersoll-Rand Company, and General Electric.

More than one hundred companies have already entered the personal power business, which goes by the name "distributed generation." All public utilities are worried about exponential growth in personal power. Some large utilities in the United States try to make it impossible for homes to switch to personal power, but this is a losing battle. If personal power becomes the standard business practice by 2010 as expected, then the United States can meet the stringent reductions in carbon dioxide emissions agreed to in the international global warming treaty. Global warming isn't just a fear, it's a fact and carbon dioxide from large power plants is a major culprit. $CO_2$ is the most common air pollution worldwide and the United States emits over six million tons of it annually, by far the most among all countries.

*Source:* Adapted from: Ann Keeton, "Future Generations—Small Businesses May Soon Be Producing Much of Their Own Power On-site," *The Wall Street Journal* (September 13, 1999): p. R8. Also, Seth Borenstein, "New Devices May Let Homes Generate Own Electricity," *Wilmington Morning Star* (July 7, 1999): 1A.

Firms should formulate and implement strategies from an environmental perspective. Environmental strategies could include developing or acquiring green businesses, divesting or altering environment-damaging businesses, striving to become a low-cost producer through waste minimization and energy conservation, and pursuing a differentiation strategy through green product features. In addition to creating strategies, firms could include an environmental representative on the board of directors, conduct regular environmental audits, implement bonuses for favorable environmental results, become involved in environmental issues and programs, incorporate environmental values in mission statements, establish environmentally oriented objectives, acquire environmental skills, and provide environmental training programs for company employees and managers.

California reimburses companies that buy natural gas trucks rather than cheaper diesel ones because diesel exhaust from big trucks and buses account up to 70 percent of the soot in USA air.[14] Diesel trucks can emit 100 times more soot than cars. Researchers have found that diesel fumes pose a higher cancer risk than all other air pollution combined.

Northeast Utilities recently agreed to pay a record $10 million in penalties and plead guilty to 25 felony counts recently for polluting water near Waterford, Connecticut, and discharging chlorine into Long Island Sound while concealing those actions. This company previously had discharged hydrazine, a highly toxic chemical used to clean out industrial piping, into area waters without a permit.

# CREATING A STRATEGY-SUPPORTIVE CULTURE

Strategists should strive to preserve, emphasize, and build upon aspects of an existing *culture* that support proposed new strategies. Aspects of an existing culture that are antagonistic to a proposed strategy should be identified and changed. Substantial research indicates that new strategies are often market-driven and dictated by competitive forces. For this reason, changing a firm's culture to fit a new strategy is usually more effective than changing a strategy to fit an existing culture. Numerous techniques are available to alter an organization's culture, including recruitment, training, transfer, promotion, restructure of an organization's design, role modeling, and positive reinforcement.

Jack Duncan described *triangulation* as an effective, multi-method technique for studying and altering a firm's culture.[15] Triangulation includes the combined use of obtrusive observation, self-administered questionnaires, and personal interviews to determine the nature of a firm's culture. The process of triangulation reveals needed changes in a firm's culture that could benefit strategy.

Schein indicated that the following elements are most useful in linking culture to strategy:

1. Formal statements of organizational philosophy, charters, creeds, materials used for recruitment and selection, and socialization
2. Designing of physical spaces, facades, buildings
3. Deliberate role modeling, teaching, and coaching by leaders
4. Explicit reward and status system, promotion criteria
5. Stories, legends, myths, and parables about key people and events
6. What leaders pay attention to, measure, and control
7. Leader reactions to critical incidents and organizational crises
8. How the organization is designed and structured
9. Organizational systems and procedures
10. Criteria used for recruitment, selection, promotion, leveling off, retirement, and "excommunication" of people.[16]

In the personal and religious side of life, the impact of loss and change is easy to see.[17] Memories of loss and change often haunt individuals and organizations for years. Ibsen wrote, "Rob the average man of his life illusion and you rob him of his happiness at the same stroke."[18] When attachments to a culture are severed in an organization's attempt to change direction, employees and managers often experience deep feelings of grief. This phenomenon commonly occurs when external conditions dictate the need for a new strategy. Managers and employees often struggle to find meaning in a situation that changed many years before. Some people find comfort in memories; others find solace in the present. Weak linkages between strategic management and organizational culture can jeopardize performance and success. Deal and Kennedy emphasized that making strategic changes in an organization always threatens a culture:

> . . . people form strong attachments to heroes, legends, the rituals of daily life, the hoopla of extravaganza and ceremonies, and all the symbols of the workplace. Change strips relationships and leaves employees confused, insecure, and often angry. Unless something can be done to provide support for transitions from old to new, the force of a culture can neutralize and emasculate strategy changes.[19]

The old corporate culture at AT&T consisted of lifetime careers, intense loyalty to the company, up-from-the-ranks management succession, dedication to the service ethos, and management by consensus. As AT&T moved from a regulated monopoly to a highly competitive environment in the 1980s, the company made numerous changes to create a culture that supported the new strategy; it redesigned its organizational structure, articulated its value system explicitly, provided management training to modify behavior in support of new values, revised recruiting aims and practices, and modified old symbols. AT&T abandoned its familiar logo, a bell with a circle, and adopted a new logo, a globe encircled by electronic communications, that symbolizes its new strategies to compete with Sprint and MCI.

## The Mexican Culture

Mexico always has been and still is an authoritarian society in terms of schools, churches, businesses, and families. Employers seek workers who are agreeable, respectful, and obedient, rather than innovative, creative, and independent. Mexican workers tend to be activity-oriented rather than problem solvers. When visitors walk into a Mexican business, they are impressed by the cordial friendly atmosphere. This is almost always true because Mexicans desire harmony rather than conflict; desire for harmony is an overriding social fabric in worker-manager relations. There is a much lower tolerance for adversarial relations or friction at work in Mexico as compared to the United States.

Mexican employers are paternalistic, providing workers with more than a paycheck, but in return, they expect allegiance. Weekly food baskets, free meals, free bus service, and free day care are often a part of compensation. The ideal working conditions for a Mexican worker is the family model, with everyone working together, doing their share, according to their designated roles. Mexican workers do not expect or desire a work environment where self-expression and initiative are encouraged. Whereas U.S. business embodies individualism, achievement, competition, curiosity, pragmatism, informality, spontaneity, and doing more than expected on the job, Mexican businesses stress collectivism, continuity, cooperation, belongingness, formality, and doing exactly what you're told.

# E-COMMERCE PERSPECTIVE

## *CEO More and More Acting as Chief E-Commerce Officer*

An increasing number of CEOs are acting as the chief e-commerce officer in organizations. Percentages reported in the following table reveal answers to the question: Who is in charge of Internet initiatives at your firm?

| | 3rd Quarter of 1998 | 3rd Quarter of 1999 |
|---|---|---|
| Information Technology Executives | 54% | 48% |
| Chief Executive Officer | 15% | 26% |
| Marketing Executives | 21% | 12& |
| Sales Executives | 04% | 05% |
| Others | 06% | 09% |

Zona Research Inc. of Redwood City, California conducted this study. Companies have traditionally used technology to make existing business practices run faster, better, and cheaper. A Chief Information Officer (CIO) or Chief Technology Officer (CTO) has typically handled this work. However, a similar approach is ineffective in regards to e-commerce decisions because these are more strategic and critical to business success. Current research indicates that CEO's more and more recognize the importance of e-commerce, even to the extent of handling major Internet decisions themselves.

*Source:* Adapted from: George Anders, "Better, Faster, Prettier," *The Wall Street Journal* (November 22, 1999): R6.

In Mexico, business associates only rarely entertain at their home, a place reserved exclusively for close friends and family. Business meetings and entertaining are nearly always done at a restaurant. Preserving one's honor, saving face, and looking important is also exceptionally important in Mexico. This is why Mexicans do not accept criticism and change easily; many find it humiliating to acknowledge having made a mistake. A meeting among employees and managers in a business located in Mexico is a forum for giving orders and directions rather than for discussing problems or participating in decision making. Mexican workers desire to be closely supervised, cared for, and corrected in a civil manner. Opinions expressed by employees are often regarded as back talk in Mexico. Mexican supervisors are viewed as weak if they explain the rationale for their orders to workers.

Mexicans do not feel compelled to follow rules that are not associated with a particular person in authority they know well or work for. Thus, signs to wear ear plugs or safety glasses, or attendance or seniority policies, and even one-way street signs are often ignored. Whereas Americans follow the rules, Mexicans often do not.

Life is slower in Mexico than in the United States. People do not wear watches. The first priority is often assigned to the last request, rather than the first. Telephone systems break down. Banks may suddenly not have pesos. Phone repair can take months. Electricity for an entire plant or town can be down for hours or even days. Business and government offices open and close at different hours. Buses and taxis may be hours off schedule. Meeting times for appointments are not rigid. Tardiness is common everywhere. Doing business effectively in Mexico requires knowledge of the Mexican way of life, culture, beliefs, and customs.

As noted, Mexican minimum wage is 80 cents per hour. Easier access to Mexico's abundant, low-cost, high-quality labor has spurred U.S. firms to locate manufacturing facilities in Mexico. Jerry Perlman, former president and chairman of Zenith Electronics Corporation, said, "If we didn't have support operations in Mexico, our annual operating costs would be $350 million to $400 million higher, and we'd be out of business." Despite low wages in Mexico, Mexicans are acquiring a global reputation for quality work, as evidenced by Ford Motor Company's $1 billion Hermosillo plant, which recently tied the Daimler-Benz plant in Germany for the auto industry's first-place award for lowest production defects.

## The Russian Culture

In America, unsuccessful business entrepreneurs are viewed negatively as failures, whereas successful small business owners enjoy high esteem and respect. In Russia, however, there is substantial social pressure against becoming a successful entrepreneur. Being a winner in Russia makes you the object of envy and resentment, a member of the elite rather than of the masses. Personal ambition and success are often met with vindictiveness and derision. Initiative is met with indifference at best and punishment at worst. In the face of public ridicule and organized crime, however, thousands of Russians, particularly young persons, are opening all kinds of businesses. Public scorn and their own guilt from violating the values they were raised with do not deter many. Because Russian society scorns success, publicizing achievements, material possessions, awards, or privileges earned by Russian workers is not an effective motivation tool for those workers.

The Russian people are best known for their drive, boundless energy, tenacity, hard work, and perseverance in spite of immense obstacles. This is as true today as ever. The notion that the average Russian is stupid or lazy is nonsense; Russians on average are more educated than their American counterparts and bounce up more readily from failure.

In the United States, business ethics and personal ethics are essentially the same. Deception is deception and a lie is a lie whether in business or personal affairs in America. However, in Russia, business and personal ethics are separate. To deceive someone, bribe someone, or lie to someone to promote a business transaction is ethical in

Russia, but to deceive a friend or trusted colleague is unethical. There are countless examples of foreign firms being cheated by Russian business partners. The implication of this fact for American businesses is to forge strong personal relationships with their Russian business partners whenever possible; spend time with the Russians eating, relaxing, and exercising; and in the absence of a personal relationship, be exceptionally cautious with agreements, partnerships, payments, and granting credit.

The Russian people have great faith, confidence, and respect for American products and services. Russians generally have low self-confidence. American ideas, technology, and production practices are viewed by Russians as a panacea that can save them from a gloomy existence. For example, their squeaky telephone system and lack of fax machines make them feel deprived. This mind-set presents great opportunity in Russia for American products of all kinds.

Russia has historically been an autocratic state. This cultural factor is evident in business; Russian managers generally exercise power without ever being challenged by subordinates. Delegation of authority and responsibility is difficult and often nonexistent in Russian businesses. The American participative management style is not well received in Russia.

A crackdown on religion is underway in Russia. The government recognizes only Russian Orthodoxy, Judaism, Islam, and Buddhism as indigenous religions. All other faiths and churches, including all other Christian denominations, have to apply each year for permission to practice in Russia. Permission may not be granted. President Putin opposes the antireligion movement and new law but is losing the battle to prevent religious persecution—especially directed at Christians—throughout the country. The lower house of Russia's parliament, the State Duma, is dominated by Communists who favor antireligion and resist further economic reforms.

The Russian republic of Ingushetia in July 1999 passed a decree legalizing the practice of polygyny whereby men can have multiple wives, even a harem. The new law is a direct challenge to the Russian government which has jurisdiction over eighty-nine republics. The Russian Constitution prohibits polygyny, but the criminal code does not provide for any penalty. Ingushetian men take more than one wife especially when the first wife does not have a son, despite the scientific discovery in 1959 that the father's contribution alone in procreation determines a child's sex.

## The Japanese Culture

The Japanese place great importance upon group loyalty and consensus, a concept called *Wa*. Nearly all corporate activities in Japan encourage Wa among managers and employees. Wa requires that all members of a group agree and cooperate; this results in constant discussion and compromise. Japanese managers evaluate the potential attractiveness of alternative business decisions in terms of the long-term effect on the group's Wa. This is why silence, used for pondering alternatives, can be a plus in a formal Japanese meeting. Discussions potentially disruptive to Wa are generally conducted in very informal settings, such as at a bar, so as to minimize harm to the group's Wa. Entertaining is an important business activity in Japan because it strengthens Wa. Formal meetings are often conducted in informal settings. When confronted with disturbing questions or opinions, Japanese managers tend to remain silent, whereas Americans tend to respond directly, defending themselves through explanation and argument.

Most Japanese managers are reserved, quiet, distant, introspective, and other-oriented, whereas most U.S. managers are talkative, insensitive, impulsive, direct, and individual-oriented. Americans often perceive Japanese managers as wasting time and carrying on pointless conversations, whereas U.S. managers often use blunt criticism, ask prying questions, and make quick decisions. These kinds of cultural differences have disrupted many potentially productive Japanese-American business endeavors. Viewing the

Japanese communication style as a prototype for all Asian and Oriental cultures is a related stereotype that must be avoided.

Americans have more freedom to control their own fate than do the Japanese. Life is much different in the United States than in Japan; the United States offers more upward mobility to its people. This is a great strength of the United States. Sherman explained:

> America is not like Japan and can never be. America's strength is the opposite: It opens its doors and brings the world's disorder in. It tolerates social change that would tear most other societies apart. This openness encourages Americans to adapt as individuals rather than as a group. Americans go west to California to get a new start; they move east to Manhattan to try to make the big time; they move to Vermont or to a farm to get close to the soil. They break away from their parents' religions or values or class; they rediscover their ethnicity. They go to night school; they change their names.[20]

# PRODUCTION/OPERATIONS CONCERNS WHEN IMPLEMENTING STRATEGIES

Production/operations capabilities, limitations, and policies can significantly enhance or inhibit attainment of objectives. Production processes typically constitute more than 70 percent of a firm's total assets. A major part of the strategy-implementation process takes place at the production site. Production-related decisions on plant size, plant location, product design, choice of equipment, kind of tooling, size of inventory, inventory control, quality control, cost control, use of standards, job specialization, employee training, equipment and resource utilization, shipping and packaging, and technological innovation can have a dramatic impact on the success or failure of strategy-implementation efforts.

Examples of adjustments in production systems that could be required to implement various strategies are provided in Table 7–3 for both for-profit and nonprofit organizations. For instance, note that when a bank formulates and selects a strategy to add ten new branches, a production-related implementation concern is site location. The largest bicycle company in the United States, Huffy, recently ended its own production of bikes and now contracts out those services to Asian and Mexican manufacturers. Huffy focuses instead on design, marketing, and distribution of bikes, but no longer produces bikes itself. The Dayton, Ohio, company closed its plants in Ohio, Missouri, and Mississippi.

*Just in Time (JIT)* production approaches have withstood the test of time. JIT significantly reduces the costs of implementing strategies. With JIT, parts and materials are

TABLE 7-3    **Production Management and Strategy Implementation**

| TYPE OF ORGANIZATION | STRATEGY BEING IMPLEMENTED | PRODUCTION SYSTEM ADJUSTMENTS |
| --- | --- | --- |
| Hospital | Adding a cancer center (Product Development) | Purchase specialized equipment and add specialized people. |
| Bank | Adding ten new branches (Market Development) | Perform site location analysis. |
| Beer brewery | Purchasing a barley farm operation (Backward Integration) | Revise the inventory control system. |
| Steel manufacturer | Acquiring a fast-food chain (Conglomerate Diversification) | Improve the quality control system. |
| Computer company | Purchasing a retail distribution chain (Forward Integration) | Alter the shipping, packaging, and transportation systems. |

delivered to a production site just as they are needed, rather than being stockpiled as a hedge against later deliveries. Harley-Davidson reports that at one plant alone, JIT freed $22 million previously tied up in inventory and greatly reduced reorder lead time.

Factors that should be studied before locating production facilities include the availability of major resources, the prevailing wage rates in the area, transportation costs related to shipping and receiving, the location of major markets, political risks in the area or country, and the availability of trainable employees.

For high-technology companies, production costs may not be as important as production flexibility because major product changes can be needed often. Industries such as biogenetics and plastics rely on production systems that must be flexible enough to allow frequent changes and rapid introduction of new products. An article in *Harvard Business Review* explained why some organizations get into trouble:

> They too slowly realize that a change in product strategy alters the tasks of a production system. These tasks, which can be stated in terms of requirements for cost, product flexibility, volume flexibility, product performance, and product consistency, determine which manufacturing policies are appropriate. As strategies shift over time, so must production policies covering the location and scale of manufacturing facilities, the choice of manufacturing process, the degree of vertical integration of each manufacturing facility, the use of R&D units, the control of the production system, and the licensing of technology.[21]

A common management practice, cross-training of employees, can facilitate strategy implementation and can yield many benefits. Employees gain a better understanding of the whole business and can contribute better ideas in planning sessions. Production/operations managers need to realize, however, that cross-training employees can create problems related to the following issues:

1. It can thrust managers into roles that emphasize counseling and coaching over directing and enforcing.
2. It can necessitate substantial investments in training and incentives.
3. It can be very time-consuming.
4. Skilled workers may resent unskilled workers who learn their jobs.
5. Older employees may not want to learn new skills.

## HUMAN RESOURCE CONCERNS WHEN IMPLEMENTING STRATEGIES

The job of human resource manager is changing rapidly as companies downsize and reorganize in the 1990s. Strategic responsibilities of the human resource manager include assessing the staffing needs and costs for alternative strategies proposed during strategy formulation and developing a staffing plan for effectively implementing strategies. This plan must consider how best to manage spiraling health care insurance costs. Employers' health coverage expenses consume an average 26 percent of firms' net profits, even though most companies now require employees to pay part of their health insurance premiums. The plan must also include how to motivate employees and managers during a time when layoffs are common and workloads are high.

The human resource department must develop performance incentives that clearly link performance and pay to strategies. The process of empowering managers and employees through involvement in strategic-management activities yields the greatest benefits when all organizational members understand clearly how they will benefit personally if the firm does well. Linking company and personal benefits is a major new strategic responsibility of human resource managers. Other new responsibilities for human resource managers may include establishing and administering an *employee stock ownership plan (ESOP)*, instituting an effective child care policy, and providing leadership for managers and employees to balance work and family.

A well-designed strategic-management system can fail if insufficient attention is given to the human resource dimension. Human resource problems that arise when businesses implement strategies can usually be traced to one of three causes: (1) disruption of social and political structures, (2) failure to match individuals' aptitudes with implementation tasks, and (3) inadequate top management support for implementation activities.[22]

Strategy implementation poses a threat to many managers and employees in an organization. New power and status relationships are anticipated and realized. New formal and informal groups' values, beliefs, and priorities may be largely unknown. Managers and employees may become engaged in resistance behavior as their roles, prerogatives, and power in the firm change. Disruption of social and political structures that accompany strategy execution must be anticipated and considered during strategy formulation and managed during strategy implementation.

A concern in matching managers with strategy is that jobs have specific and relatively static responsibilities, although people are dynamic in their personal development. Commonly used methods that match managers with strategies to be implemented include transferring managers, developing leadership workshops, offering career development activities, promotions, job enlargement, and job enrichment.

A number of other guidelines can help ensure that human relationships facilitate rather than disrupt strategy-implementation efforts. Specifically, managers should do a lot of chatting and informal questioning to stay abreast of how things are progressing and to know when to intervene. Managers can build support for strategy-implementation efforts by giving few orders, announcing few decisions, depending heavily on informal questioning, and seeking to probe and clarify until a consensus emerges. Key thrusts that succeed should be rewarded generously and visibly.

It is surprising that so often during strategy formulation, individual values, skills, and abilities needed for successful strategy implementation are not considered. It is rare that a firm selecting new strategies or significantly altering existing strategies possesses the right line and staff personnel in the right positions for successful strategy implementation. The need to match individual aptitudes with strategy-implementation tasks should be considered in strategy choice.

Inadequate support from strategists for implementation activities often undermines organizational success. Chief executive officers, small business owners, and government agency heads must be personally committed to strategy implementation and express this commitment in highly visible ways. Strategists' formal statements about the importance of strategic management must be consistent with actual support and rewards given for activities completed and objectives reached. Otherwise, stress created by inconsistency can cause uncertainty among managers and employees at all levels.

Perhaps the best method for preventing and overcoming human resource problems in strategic management is to actively involve as many managers and employees as possible in the process. Although time-consuming, this approach builds understanding, trust, commitment, and ownership and reduces resentment and hostility. The true potential of strategy formulation and implementation resides in people.

## Employee Stock Ownership Plans (ESOPs)

An ESOP is a tax-qualified, defined-contribution, employee-benefit plan whereby employees purchase stock of the company through borrowed money or cash contributions. ESOPs empower employees to work as owners; this is a primary reason why the number of ESOPs grew dramatically throughout the 1980s and 1990s to more than ten thousand plans covering more than fifteen million employees. ESOPs now control more than $80 billion in corporate stock in the United States.

Besides reducing worker alienation and stimulating productivity, ESOPs allow firms other benefits, such as substantial tax savings. Principal, interest, and dividend payments on ESOP-funded debt are tax-deductible. Banks lend money to ESOPs at interest rates below prime. This money can be repaid in pretax dollars, lowering the debt service as much as 30 percent in some cases.

If an ESOP owns more than 50 percent of the firm, those who lend money to the ESOP are taxed on only 50 percent of the income received on the loans. ESOPs are not for every firm, however, because the initial legal, accounting, actuarial, and appraisal fees to set up an ESOP are about $50,000 for a small or mid-sized firm, with annual administration expenses of about $15,000. Analysts say ESOPs also do not work well in firms that have fluctuating payrolls and profits. Human resource managers in many firms conduct preliminary research to determine the desirability of an ESOP, and then facilitate its establishment and administration if benefits outweigh the costs.

To establish an ESOP, a firm sets up a trust fund and purchases shares of its stock, which are allocated to individual employee accounts. All full-time employees over age twenty-one usually participate in the plan. Allocations of stock to the trust are made on the basis of relative pay, seniority, or some other formula. When an ESOP borrows money to purchase stock, the debt is guaranteed by the company and thus appears on the firm's balance sheet. On average, ESOP employees get $1,300 worth of stock per year, but cannot take physical possession of the shares until they quit, retire, or die. The median level of employee ownership in ESOP plans is 30 to 40 percent, although the range is from about 10 to 100 percent.

Research confirms that ESOPs can have a dramatic positive effect on employee motivation and corporate performance, especially if ownership is coupled with expanded employee participation and involvement in decision making. Market surveys indicate that customers prefer to do business with firms that are employee-owned.

Many companies are following the lead of Polaroid, which established an ESOP as a tactic for preventing a hostile takeover. Polaroid's CEO MacAllister Booth says, "Twenty years from now we'll find that employees have a sizable stake in every major American corporation." (It is interesting to note here that Polaroid is chartered in the state of Delaware, which requires corporate suitors to acquire 85 percent of a target company's shares to complete a merger; over 50 percent of all American corporations are incorporated in Delaware for this reason.) Wyatt Cafeterias, a Southwestern U.S. operator of 120 cafeterias, also adopted the ESOP concept to prevent a hostile takeover. Employee productivity at Wyatt greatly increased since the ESOP began, as illustrated in the following quote:

> The key employee in our entire organization is the person serving the customer on the cafeteria line. In the past, because of high employee turnover and entry-level wages for many line jobs, these employees received far less attention and recognition than managers. We now tell the tea cart server, "You own the place. Don't wait for the manager to tell you how to do your job better or how to provide better service. You take care of it." Sure, we're looking for productivity increases, but since we began pushing decisions down to the level of people who deal directly with customers, we've discovered an awesome side effect—suddenly the work crews have this "happy to be here" attitude that the customers really love.[23]

Companies such as Avis, Procter & Gamble, BellSouth, ITT, Xerox, Delta, Austin Industries, Health Trust, The Parsons Corporation, Dyncorp, and Charter Medical have established ESOPs to assist strategists in divesting divisions, going private, and consummating leveraged buyouts. ESOPs can be found today in all kinds of firms, from small retailers to large manufacturers. Employees can own any amount from 1 percent to 100 percent of the company. Nearly all ESOPs are established in health firms, not failing firms.

## Balancing Work Life and Home Life

Work/family strategies have become so popular among companies in the 1990s that the strategies now represent a competitive advantage for those firms that offer such benefits as elder care assistance, flexible scheduling, job sharing, adoption benefits, an on-site summer camp, employee help lines, pet care, and even lawn service referrals. New corporate titles such as Work/Life Coordinator and Director of Diversity are becoming common. *Business Week* and the Center on Work and Family at Boston University have for the first time begun rating companies on their family-friendly strategies. The ten U.S. companies that received the highest ratings for providing work-family benefits are given below in rank order:

|     | 1996 | 1997 |
| --- | --- | --- |
| 1. | DuPont | MBNA America Bank |
| 2. | Eddie Bauer | Motorola |
| 3. | Eli Lilly | Barnett Banks |
| 4. | First Tennessee Bank | Hewlett-Packard |
| 5. | Hewlett-Packard | Unum Life Insurance |
| 6. | Marriott International | Lincoln National |
| 7. | MBNA America Bank | Merrill Lynch |
| 8. | Merrill Lynch | DuPont |
| 9. | Motorola | TRW |
| 10. | Unum Life Insurance | Cigna |

Human resource managers need to foster more effective balancing of professional and private lives because nearly sixty million people in the United States are now part of two-career families. A corporate objective to become more lean and mean must today include consideration for the fact that a good home life contributes immensely to a good work life.

The work/family issue is no longer just a women's problem. Some specific measures that firms are taking to address this issue are providing spouse relocation assistance as an employee benefit, providing company resources for family recreational and educational use, establishing employee country clubs such as those at IBM and Bethlehem Steel, and creating family/work interaction opportunities. A recent study by Joseph Pleck of Wheaton College found that in companies that do not offer paternity leave for fathers as a benefit, most men take short informal paternity leaves anyway by combining vacation time and sick days.

Some organizations have developed family days, when family members are invited into the workplace, taken on plant or office tours, dined by management, and given a chance to see exactly what other family members do each day. Family days are inexpensive and increase the employee's pride in working for the organization. Flexible working hours during the week are another human resource response to the need for individuals to balance work life and home life. The work/family topic is being made part of the agenda at meetings and thus is becoming discussable in many organizations.

Research indicates that employees who are dissatisfied with child care arrangements are most likely to be absent or unproductive.[24] Lack of adequate child care in a community can be a deterrent in recruiting and retaining good managers and employees. Some benefits of on-site child care facilities are improved employee relations, reduced absenteeism and turnover, increased productivity, enhanced recruitment, and improved community relations.

A recent survey of women managers revealed that one-third would leave their present employer for another employer offering child care assistance. The Conference Board recently reported that more than five hundred firms in the United States had created on-site or near-site child care centers for their employees, including Merck, Campbell Soup, Hoffman-La Roche, Stride-Rite, Johnson Wax, CIGNA, Champion International, Walt Disney World, and Playboy Resorts.

Other common child care service arrangements include employer-sponsored day care, child care information, and referral services. IBM, Steelcase, Honeywell, Citibank, 3M, and Southland have established contracts with third-party child care information and referral services.

Most of the sixty-four million women in the U.S. labor force are employed in what the Department of Labor calls "nontraditional occupations"—areas of employment in which women now comprise 25 percent or less of the workforce. This list includes pilots, truck drivers, funeral directors, dentists, architects, bellhops, barbers, meter readers, and construction workers. Women in the United States now head one in every four households with children under age eighteen. Women must and should therefore get their fair share of these jobs for our society to progress. More women in the United States are employed as teachers, secretaries, and cashiers than work in any other jobs. Among the jobs in which less than 5 percent of those employed are women include fishermen (4.6%), pest control (4.1%), airplane pilots and navigators (4.1%), firefighting and fire prevention (2.5%), construction (2.0%), and tool and die makers (0.2%).[25]

It is encouraging to note that talented women in technology are more and more being promoted to top-level managerial positions in the United States. Carleton Fiorina recently became CEO of Hewlett-Packard and Andrea Jung became CEO of Avon—by far the largest companies ever run by a woman. Thirteen percent of Texas Instruments' top executives are women, up from only 2 percent in 1994. Top executives who run divisions at Electronic Data Systems (EDS) rose from 8 percent in 1998 to 13 percent in 1999. Motorola today has eleven female vice presidents who are Black, Hispanic, or Asian, up from only one in 1991. Fiorina is only the third woman CEO of a Fortune 500 company however, the others being Barad at Mattel and Sandler at Golden West Financial. Among the Fortune 1000 companies, there are only seven female CEOs, so the *glass ceiling* in America still exists and needs to be broken. Only 11.1 percent of all company executives are female among Fortune 500 companies. In the automobile industry, only 8 percent of executives at Ford, DaimlerChrysler, and General Motors are female. However, women buy more than half the vehicles sold in the United States and take part in more than 80 percent of all purchases.[26]

## Corporate Fitness Programs

At least ten thousand U.S. employers now offer programs to improve or maintain their employees' health, such as programs to stop smoking, reduce cholesterol, promote regular exercise, and control high blood pressure. Another one thousand American firms offer on-site, fully equipped fitness centers to promote good employee health. Perhaps the leader in this area is Johnson & Johnson, which provides an eleven thousand square-foot fitness center, aerobics and other exercise classes, seminars on AIDS and alcohol abuse, and an indoor track. J & J's program is called Live for Life.

## CONCLUSION

Successful strategy formulation does not at all guarantee successful strategy implementation. Although inextricably interdependent, strategy formulation and strategy implementation are characteristically different. In a single word, strategy implementation means *change*. It is widely agreed that "the real work begins after strategies are formulated." Successful strategy implementation requires support, discipline, motivation, and hard work from all managers and employees. It is sometimes frightening to think that a single individual can sabotage strategy-implementation efforts irreparably.

Formulating the right strategies is not enough, because managers and employees must be motivated to implement those strategies. Management issues considered central to strategy implementation include matching organizational structure with strategy, linking performance and pay to strategies, creating an organizational climate conducive to change, managing political relationships, creating a strategy-supportive culture, adapting production/operations processes, and managing human resources. Establishing annual objectives, devising policies, and allocating resources are central strategy-implementation activities common to all organizations. Depending on the size and type of organization, other management issues could be equally important to successful strategy implementation.

We invite you to visit the DAVID page on the Prentice Hall Web site at **www.prenhall.com/davidsm** for this chapter's World Wide Web exercises.

## KEY TERMS AND CONCEPTS

Annual Objectives (p. 240)

Avoidance (p. 245)

Benchmarking (p. 251)

Bonus System (p. 253)

Conflict (p. 244)

Confrontation (p. 245)

Culture (p. 258)

Defusion (p. 245)

Delayering (p. 249)

Decentralized Structure (p. 247)

Divisional Structure by Geographic Area, Product, Customer, or Process (pp. 247, 248)

Downsizing (p. 249)

Educative Change Strategy (p. 254)

Employee Stock Ownership Plan (ESOP) (p. 264)

Establishing Annual Objectives (p. 240)

Force Change Strategy (p. 254)

Functional Structure (p. 246)

Gain Sharing (p. 253)

Glass Ceiling (p. 267)

Horizontal Consistency of Objectives (p. 240)

Just in Time (p. 262)

Matrix Structure (p. 249)

Policy (p. 242)

Profit Sharing (p. 253)

Rational Change Strategy (p. 254)

Reengineering (p. 250)

Resistance to Change (p. 254)

Resource Allocation (p. 244)

Restructuring (p. 251)

Rightsizing (p. 249)

Self-Interest Change Strategy (p. 254)

Strategic Business Unit (SBU) Structure (p. 248)

Triangulation (p. 258)

Vertical Consistency of Objectives (p. 240)

## ISSUES FOR REVIEW AND DISCUSSION

1. Allocating resources can be a political and an ad hoc activity in firms that do not use strategic management. Why is this true? Does adopting strategic management ensure easy resource allocation? Why?

2. Compare strategy formulation with strategy implementation in terms of each being an art or a science.

3. Describe the relationship between annual objectives and policies.
4. Identify a long-term objective and two supporting annual objectives for a familiar organization.
5. Identify and discuss three policies that apply to your present business policy class.
6. Explain the following statement: Horizontal consistency of goals is as important as vertical consistency.
7. Describe several reasons why conflict may occur during objective-setting activities.
8. In your opinion, what approaches to conflict resolution would be best for resolving a disagreement between a personnel manager and a sales manager over the firing of a particular salesperson? Why?
9. Describe the organizational culture of your college or university.
10. Explain why organizational structure is so important in strategy implementation.
11. In your opinion, how many separate divisions could an organization reasonably have without using an SBU-type organizational structure? Why?
12. Would you recommend a divisional structure by geographic area, product, customer, or process for a medium-sized bank in your local area? Why?
13. What are the advantages and disadvantages of decentralizing the wage and salary function of an organization? How could this be accomplished?
14. Consider a college organization with which you are familiar. How did management issues affect strategy implementation in that organization?
15. As production manager of a local newspaper, what problems would you anticipate in implementing a strategy to increase the average number of pages in the paper by 40 percent?
16. Read an article from the suggested readings at the end of this chapter and give a summary report to the class revealing your thoughts on the topic.
17. Do you believe expenditures for child care or fitness facilities are warranted from a cost/benefit perspective? Why or why not?
18. Explain why successful strategy implementation often hinges on whether the strategy-formulation process empowers managers and employees.
19. Compare and contrast the culture in Mexico, Russia, and Japan.
20. Discuss the glass ceiling in the United States, giving your ideas and suggestions.

# NOTES

1. DALE MCCONKEY, "Planning in a Changing Environment," *Business Horizons* (September–October 1988): 66.
2. A. G. BEDEIAN and W. F. GLUECK, *Management,* 3rd ed. (Chicago: The Dryden Press, 1983): 212.
3. BORIS YAVITS and WILLIAM NEWMAN, *Strategy in Action: The Execution, Politics, and Payoff of Business Planning* (New York: The Free Press, 1982): 195.
4. RICK BROOKS, "Bank One's Strategy As Competition Grows: New, Online Institution," *USA Today* (August 25, 1999): A1.
5. STEVE HAMM and MARCIA STEPANEK, "From Reengineering to E-engineering," *Business Week* (March 22, 1999): EB15.
6. "Want to Be a Manager? Many People Say No, Calling Job Miserable," *The Wall Street Journal* (April 4, 1997): 1. Also, STEPHANIE ARMOUR, "Management Loses Its Allure," *USA Today* (October 10, 1997): 1B.
7. JULIE SCHMIT, "Japan Shifts to Merit Pay," *USA Today* (July 23, 1999): 5B.
8. RICHARD BROWN, "Outsider CEO: Inspiring Change With Force and Grace," *USA Today* (July 19, 1999): 3B.
9. YAVITS and NEWMAN, 58.
10. JOHN RAY, "Executive Pay," *Business Week* (April 19, 1999): 74.
11. JACK DUNCAN, *Management* (New York: Random House, 1983): 381–390.
12. H. IGOR ANSOFF, "Strategic Management of Technology," *Journal of Business Strategy* 7, no. 3 (Winter 1987): 38.
13. ROBERT WATERMAN, JR., "How the Best Get Better," *Business Week* (September 14, 1987): 104.
14. TRACI WATSON, "Pollution From Trucks Targeted," *USA Today* (July 7, 1999): 4A.
15. JACK DUNCAN, "Organizational Culture: Getting a Fix on an Elusive Concept," *Academy of Management Executive,* no. 3 (August 1989): 229.
16. E. H. SCHEIN, "The Role of the Founder in Creating Organizational Culture," *Organizational Dynamics* (Summer 1983): 13–28.
17. T. DEAL and A. KENNEDY, "Culture: A New Look Through Old Lenses," *Journal of Applied Behavioral Science* 19, no. 4 (1983): 498–504.
18. H. IBSEN, "The Wild Duck," in O. G. Brochett and L. Brochett (eds.), *Plays for the Theater* (New York: Holt, Rinehart & Winston, 1967). Also, R. Pascale, "The Paradox of 'Corporate Culture': Reconciling Ourselves to Socialization," *California Management Review* 28, 2 (1985): 26, 37–40.
19. T. DEAL and A. KENNEDY, *Corporate Cultures: The Rites and Rituals of Corporate Life* (Reading, Massachusetts: Addison-Wesley, 1982).

20. STRATFORD SHERMAN, "How to Beat the Japanese," *Fortune* (April 10, 1989): 145.

21. ROBERT STOBAUGH and PIERO TELESIO, "Match Manufacturing Policies and Product Strategy ," *Harvard Business Review* 61, no. 2 (March–April 1983): 113.

22. R. T. LENZ and MARJORIE LYLES, "Managing Human Resource Problems in Strategy Planning Systems," *Journal of Business Strategy* 60, no. 4 (Spring 1986): 58.

23. J. WARREN HENRY, "ESOPs with Productivity Payoffs," *Journal of Business Strategy* (July–August 1989): 33.

24. RICHARD LEVINE, "Childcare: Inching up the Corporate Agenda," *Management Review* 78, no. 1 (January 1989): 43.

25. DEWAYNE WICKHAM, "Women Still Fighting for Job Equality," *USA Today* (August 31, 1999): 15A.

26. MICHELINE MAYNARD, "Practically Alone at the Top," *USA Today* (September 7, 1999): B1.

# CURRENT READINGS

AVOLIO, BRUCE J., JANE M. HOWELL, and JOHN J. SOSIK. "A Funny Thing Happened on the Way to the Bottom Line: Humor as a Moderator of Leadership Style Effects." *The Academy of Management Journal* 42, no. 2 (April 1999): 219–229.

BOLINO, MARK C. "Citizenship and Impression Management: Good Soldiers or Good Actors?" *The Academy of Management Review* 24, no. 1 (January 1999): 82–98.

BUTLER, TIMOTHY and JAMES WALDROP. "Job Sculpting: The Art of Retaining Your Best People." *Harvard Business Review* 77, no. 5 (September–October 1999): 144–154.

DANNA, KAREN and RICKY W. GRIFFIN. "Health and Wellbeing in the Workplace: A Review and Synthesis of Literature." *Journal of Management* 25, no. 3 (1999): 417–456.

DECKOP, JOHN R., ROBERT MANGEL, and CAROL C. CIRKA. "Getting More Than You Pay for: Organizational Citizenship Behavior and Pay-for-Performance Plans." *The Academy of Management Journal* 42, no. 4 (August 1999): 420–428.

ECCLES, ROBERT G., KERSTEN L. LANES, and THOMAS C. WILSON. "Are You Paying Too Much For That Acquisition?" *Harvard Business Review* 77, no. 4 (July–August 1999): 136–148.

GERWIN, DONALD. "Team Empowerment in New Product Development." *Business Horizons* 42, no. 4 (July–August 1999): 29–36.

GRATTON, LYNDA, VERONICA HOPE-HAILEY, PHILIP STILES, and CATHERINE TRUSS. "Linking Individual Performance to Business Strategy: The People Process Model." *Human Resource Management* 38, no. 1 (Spring 1999): 17–27.

GREGERSEN, HAL B., ALLEN J. MORRISON, and J. STEWART BLACK. "Developing Leaders for the Global Frontier." *Sloan Management Review* 40, no. 1 (Fall 1999): 21–32.

IRELAND, R. DUANE and MICHAEL A. HITT. "Achieving and Maintaining Strategic Competitiveness in the 21st Century: The Role of Strategic Leadership." *The Academy of Management Executive* 13, no. 1 (February 1999): 43–57.

JUNG, DONG I. and BRUCE J. AVOLIO. "Effects of Leadership Style and Followers' Cultural Orientation on Performance in Group and Individual Task Conditions." *The Academy of Management Journal* 42, no. 2 (April 1999): 208–218.

KHANNA, TARUN and KRISHNA PALEPU. "The Right Way To Restructure Conglomerates in Emerging Markets." *Harvard Business Review* 77, no. 4 (July–August 1999): 125–135.

KIRKLAND, BRADLEY L. and BENSON ROSEN. "Beyond Self-Management: Antecedents and Consequences of Team Empowerment." *The Academy of Management Journal* 42, no. 1 (February 1999): 58–75.

LUTHANS, FRED and ALEXANDER D. STAJKOVIC. "Reinforce for Performance: The Need to Go Beyond Pay and Even Rewards." *The Academy of Management Executive* 13, no. 2 (May 1999): 49–57.

MCDERMOTT, CHRISTOPHER and KENNETH K. BOYER. "Strategic Consensus: Marching to the Beat of a Different Drummer?" *Business Horizons* 42, no. 4 (July–August 1999): 21–28.

MEEK, CHRISTOPHER B. "Ganbatte: Understanding the Japanese Employee." *Business Horizons* 42, no. 1 (January–February 1999): 27–36.

RAPPAORT, ALFRED. "New Thinking on How to Link Executive Pay with Performance." *Harvard Business Review* (March–April 1999): 91–101.

REINHARDT, FOREST L. "Bringing the Environment Down to Earth." *Harvard Business Review* 77, no. 4 (July–August 1999): 149–159.

STARBUCK, WILLIAM H. "Presidential Address: Our Shrinking Earth." *The Academy of Management Review* 24, no. 2 (April 1999): 187–190.

WERTHER, WILLIAM B., JR. "Structure-Driven Strategy and Virtual Organization Design." *Business Horizons* 42, no. 2 (March–April 1999): 13–18.

# EXPERIENTIAL EXERCISES

**EXPERIENTIAL EXERCISE 7A** ▶

**Revising America Online's Organizational Chart**

## PURPOSE

Developing and altering organizational charts is an important skill for strategists to possess. This exercise can improve your skill in altering an organization's hierarchical structure in response to new strategies being formulated.

## INSTRUCTIONS

**Step 1**   Turn back to the America Online Cohesion Case (p. 30). On a separate sheet of paper, diagram an organizational chart that you believe would best suit AOL's needs if the company decided to form a divisional structure by product.

**Step 2**   Provide as much detail in your chart as possible, including the names of individuals and the titles of positions.

**EXPERIENTIAL EXERCISE 7B** ▶

**Matching Managers with Strategy**

## PURPOSE

For many years, strategists believed that good managers could adapt to handle any situation. Consequently, strategists rarely replaced or transferred managers as the need arose to implement new strategies. Today, this situation is changing. Research supports the notion that certain management characteristics are needed for certain strategic situations.[1] Chase Manhattan Bank, Heublein, Texas Instruments, Corning Glass, and General Electric are examples of companies that match managers to strategic requirements.

This exercise can improve your awareness and understanding of particular managerial characteristics that have been found to be most desirable for implementing certain types of strategies. Having the right managers in the right jobs can determine the success or failure of strategy-implementation efforts. This exercise is based on a framework that has proved to be useful in "matching managers to strategy."[2]

## INSTRUCTIONS

Your task is to match specific managerial characteristics with particular generic strategies. Four broad types of strategies are examined:

1. Retrenchment/Turnaround
2. Intensive (market penetration, market development, and product development)
3. Liquidation/Divestiture
4. Integration (backward, forward, and horizontal)

Five managerial characteristics have been found to be associated with each of these strategies. On a separate sheet of paper, list the four types of strategies. Beside each strategy, record the appropriate letter of the five managerial characteristics that you believe are most needed to successfully implement those strategies. Each of the managerial characteristics in the following list should be used only once in completing this exercise.

A. Is technically knowledgeable—"knows the business"

B. Is "callous"—tough-minded, determined, willing to be the bad guy

C. Is "take charge"—oriented—strong leader

D. Is a good negotiator

E. Wants to be respected, not necessarily liked

F. Has good analytical ability

G. Is low glory-seeking—willing to do dirty jobs; does not want glamour

H. Has excellent staffing skills

I. Handles pressure well

J. Is a risk taker

K. Has good relationship-building skills

L. Has good organizational and team-building skills

M. Is oriented to getting out the most efficiency, not growth

N. Anticipates problems—"problem finder"

O. Has strong analytical and diagnostic skills, especially financial

P. Is an excellent business strategist

Q. Has good communication skills

R. Has personal magnetism

S. Is highly analytical—focuses on costs/benefits, does not easily accept current ways of doing things

T. Has good interpersonal influence

## NOTES

1. MARC GERSTEIN and HEATHER REISMAN, "Strategic Selection: Matching Executives to Business Conditions," *Sloan Management Review* 24, no. 2 (Winter 1983): 33–47.
2. Ibid., 37.

### PURPOSE

Objectives provide direction, allow synergy, aid in evaluation, establish priorities, reduce uncertainty, minimize conflicts, stimulate exertion, and aid in both the allocation of resources and the design of jobs. This exercise will enhance your understanding of how organizations use or misuse objectives.

### INSTRUCTIONS

Step 1 Join with one other person in class to form a two-person team.

Step 2 Contact by telephone the owner or manager of an organization in your city or town. Request a thirty-minute personal interview or meeting with that person for the purpose of discussing "business objectives." During your meeting, seek answers to the following questions:

1. Do you believe it is important for a business to establish and clearly communicate long-term and annual objectives? Why or why not?

2. Does your organization establish objectives? If yes, what type and how many? How are the objectives communicated to individuals? Are your firm's objectives in written form or simply communicated orally?

3. To what extent are managers and employees involved in the process of establishing objectives?

4. How often are your business objectives revised and by what process?

**Step 3**  Take good notes during the interview. Let one person be the note taker and one person do most of the talking. Have your notes typed up and ready to turn in to your professor.

**Step 4**  Prepare a five-minute oral presentation for the class, reporting the results of your interview. Turn in your typed report.

**EXPERIENTIAL EXERCISE 7D** ▶

Understanding My University's Culture

## PURPOSE

It is something of an art to uncover the basic values and beliefs that are buried deeply in an organization's rich collection of stories, language, heroes, heroines, and rituals, yet culture can be the most important factor in implementing strategies.

## INSTRUCTIONS

**Step 1**  On a separate sheet of paper, list the following terms: hero/heroine, belief, metaphor, language, value, symbol, story, legend, saga, folktale, myth, ceremonial, rite, and ritual.

**Step 2**  For your college or university, give examples of each term. If necessary, speak with faculty, staff, alumni, administration, or fellow students of the institution to identify examples of each term.

**Step 3**  Report your findings to the class. Tell the class how you feel regarding cultural products being consciously used to help implement strategies.

# IMPLEMENTING STRATEGIES: MARKETING, FINANCE/ACCOUNTING, R&D, AND CIS ISSUES

**8**

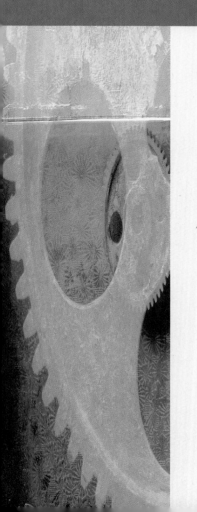

## CHAPTER OUTLINE

- The Nature of Strategy Implementation
- Marketing Issues
- Finance/Accounting Issues
- Research and Development (R&D) Issues
- Computer Information Systems (CIS) Issues

**EXPERIENTIAL EXERCISE 8A**
*Developing a Product-Positioning Map for America Online (AOL)*

**EXPERIENTIAL EXERCISE 8B**
*Performing an EPS/EBIT Analysis for America Online (AOL)*

**EXPERIENTIAL EXERCISE 8C**
*Preparing Pro Forma Financial Statements for America Online (AOL)*

**EXPERIENTIAL EXERCISE 8D**
*Determining the Cash Value of America Online (AOL)*

**EXPERIENTIAL EXERCISE 8E**
*Developing a Product-Positioning Map for My University*

**EXPERIENTIAL EXERCISE 8F**
*Do Banks Require Pro Forma Statements?*

# CHAPTER OBJECTIVES

*After studying this chapter, you should be able to do the following:*

1. Explain market segmentation and product positioning as strategy-implementation tools.
2. Discuss procedures for determining the worth of a business.
3. Explain why pro forma financial analysis is a central strategy-implementation tool.
4. Explain how to evaluate the attractiveness of debt versus stock as a source of capital to implement strategies.
5. Discuss the nature and role of research and development in strategy implementation.
6. Explain how computer information systems can determine the success of strategy-implementation efforts.

# NOTABLE QUOTES

The greatest strategy is doomed if it's implemented badly.

BERNARD REIMANN

There is no "perfect" strategic decision. One always has to pay a price. One always has to balance conflicting objectives, conflicting opinions, and conflicting priorities. The best strategic decision is only an approximation—and a risk.

PETER DRUCKER

The real question isn't how well you're doing today against your own history, but how you're doing against your competitors.

DONALD KRESS

As market windows open and close more quickly, it is important that R&D be tied more closely to corporate strategy.

WILLIAM SPENSER

Most of the time, strategists should not be formulating strategy at all; they should be getting on with implementing strategies they already have.

HENRY MINTZBERG

Strategies have no chance of being implemented successfully in organizations that do not market goods and services well, in firms that cannot raise needed working capital, in firms that produce technologically inferior products, or in firms that have a weak information system. This chapter examines marketing, finance/accounting, R&D, and computer information systems (CIS) issues that are central to effective strategy implementation. Special topics include market segmentation, market positioning, evaluating the worth of a business, determining to what extent debt and/or stock should be used as a source of capital, developing pro forma financial statements, contracting R&D outside the firm, and creating an information support system. Manager and employee involvement and participation are essential for success in marketing, finance/accounting, R&D, and CIS activities.

 ## THE NATURE OF STRATEGY IMPLEMENTATION

The quarterback can call the best play possible in the huddle, but that does not mean the play will go for a touchdown. The team may even lose yardage unless the play is executed (implemented) well. Less than 10 percent of strategies formulated are successfully implemented! There are many reasons for this low success rate, including failing to segment markets appropriately, paying too much for a new acquisition, falling behind competitors in R&D, and not recognizing the benefit of computers in managing information.

Strategy implementation directly affects the lives of plant managers, division managers, department managers, sales managers, product managers, project managers, personnel managers, staff managers, supervisors, and all employees. In some situations, individuals may not have participated in the strategy-formulation process at all and may not appreciate, understand, or even accept the work and thought that went into strategy formulation. There may even be foot dragging or resistance on their part. Managers and employees who do not understand the business and are not committed to the business may attempt to sabotage strategy-implementation efforts in hopes that the organization will return to its old ways. The strategy-implementation stage of the strategic-management process is emphasized in Figure 8–1.

 ## MARKETING ISSUES

Countless marketing variables affect the success or failure of strategy implementation, and the scope of this text does not allow addressing all those issues. Some examples of marketing decisions that may require policies are as follows:

1. To use exclusive dealerships or multiple channels of distribution
2. To use heavy, light, or no TV advertising
3. To limit (or not) the share of business done with a single customer
4. To be a price leader or a price follower
5. To offer a complete or limited warranty
6. To reward salespeople based on straight salary, straight commission, or a combination salary/commission
7. To advertise online or not.

**FIGURE 8–1**

**A Comprehensive Strategic-Management Model**

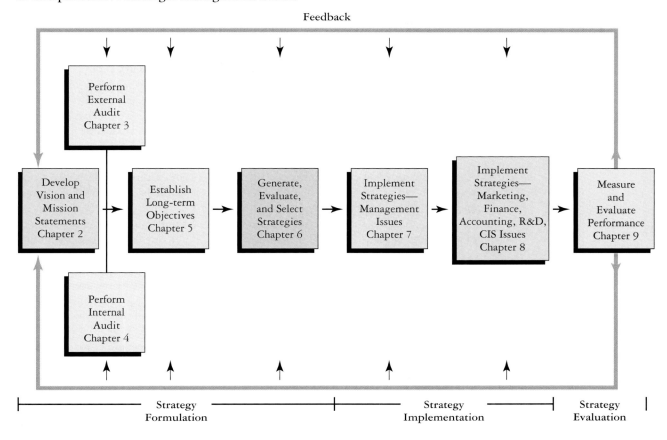

A marketing issue of increasing concern to consumers today is the extent to which companies can track individuals movements on the Internet, and even be able to identify the individual by name and email address. Individuals' wanderings on the Internet are no longer anonymous as many persons believe. Marketing companies such as Doubleclick, Flycast, AdKnowledge, AdForce, and Real Media have sophisticated methods to identify who you are and your particular interests.[1] If you are especially concerned about being tracked, visit the www.networkadvertising.org Web site that gives details about how marketers today are identifying you and your buying habits.

Recently completed research reveals that Web advertising dollars spent by businesses will increase to 27 percent of total advertising expenditures by 2002, up from 17 percent in 1999. Web advertising's market share increase will come at the expense of all other media. Newspapers, radio, magazine, television, and Yellow Pages have long worried about online rivals siphoning off advertising dollars. This worry now totals about $500 billion in business advertising expenditures annually being diverted to online media. Among total nonbroadcast advertising dollars spent annually, Yellow Pages still has 25 percent, newspapers 17 percent, direct mail 11 percent, and magazines 9 percent, but Web advertising now commands a robust 7 percent of the advertising pie.[2]

Two variables are of central importance to strategy implementation: *market segmentation* and *product positioning.* Market segmentation and product positioning rank as marketing's most important contributions to strategic management.

## Market Segmentation

Market segmentation is widely used in implementing strategies, especially for small and specialized firms. Market segmentation can be defined as the subdividing of a market into distinct subsets of customers according to needs and buying habits.

Market segmentation is an important variable in strategy implementation for at least three major reasons. First, strategies such as market development, product development, market penetration, and diversification require increased sales through new markets and products. To implement these strategies successfully, new or improved market-segmentation approaches are required. Second, market segmentation allows a firm to operate with limited resources because mass production, mass distribution, and mass advertising are not required. Market segmentation can enable a small firm to compete successfully with a large firm by maximizing per-unit profits and per-segment sales. Finally, market segmentation decisions directly affect *marketing mix variables:* product, place, promotion, and price, as indicated in Table 8–1. For example, SnackWells, a pioneer in reduced-fat snacks, has shifted its advertising emphasis from low-fat to great taste as part of its new market-segmentation strategy.

Perhaps the most dramatic new market-segmentation strategy is the targeting of regional tastes. Firms from McDonald's to General Motors are increasingly modifying their products to meet different regional preferences within the United States. Campbell's has a spicier version of its nacho cheese soup for the Southwest, and Burger King offers breakfast burritos in New Mexico but not in South Carolina. When Viacom recently acquired CBS, Dennis McAlpine said, "Viacom delivers mostly to a young audience and CBS delivers mostly to older persons. It's going to be tough to make that work."[3]

Geographic and demographic bases for segmenting markets are the most commonly employed, as illustrated in Table 8–2. Beer producers, for example, have generally divided the light beer market into three segments:

> The light beer market can be meaningfully separated into three motivation segments: those who are calorie-conscious, those who prefer less alcohol, and those who prefer a lighter taste. In fact, it is possible for one person to consume light beer on three separate occasions for three different reasons. The situation may therefore dictate the segment the consumer falls into.[4]

Evaluating potential market segments requires strategists to determine the characteristics and needs of consumers, analyze consumer similarities and differences, and develop consumer group profiles. Segmenting consumer markets is generally much simpler and

TABLE 8-1    **The Marketing Mix Component Factors**

| PRODUCT | PLACE | PROMOTION | PRICE |
|---|---|---|---|
| Quality | Distribution channels | Advertising | Level |
| Features and options | Distribution coverage | Personal selling | Discounts and |
| Style | Outlet location | Sales promotion | allowances |
| Brand name | Sales territories | Publicity | Payment terms |
| Packaging | Inventory levels | | |
| Product line | and locations | | |
| Warranty | Transportation carriers | | |
| Service level | | | |
| Other services | | | |

*Source:* E. Jerome McCarthy, *Basic Marketing: A Managerial Approach,* 9th ed. (Homewood, Illinois: Richard D. Irwin, Inc., 1987): 37–44.

easier than segmenting industrial markets, because industrial products, such as electronic circuits and forklifts, have multiple applications and appeal to diverse customer groups.

A market segment of increasing importance today is online purchasers. Of the 22 million Internet users ages five to eighteen, 67 percent make purchases on the Internet. Children aged thirteen to eighteen spent $274 million on line in 2000, up from $125 million in 1999.[5] However, there is increasing evidence that Internet shoppers are being short-changed according to recent studies reporting that 10 percent of items purchased never arrive, 50 percent of orders arrive without receipts, and the wait for refunds often is months.[6]

Another important market segment for companies are Americans who are Asian and Pacific Islanders. This group in the United States grew by 47 percent from 1990 to

**TABLE 8-2    Alternative Bases for Market Segmentation**

| VARIABLE | TYPICAL BREAKDOWNS |
| --- | --- |
| **GEOGRAPHIC** | |
| Region | Pacific, Mountain, West North Central, West South Central, East North Cental, East South Central, South Atlantic, Middle Atlantic, New England |
| County Size | A, B, C, D |
| City Size | Under 5,000; 5,000–20,000; 20,000–50,000; 50,000–100,000; 100,000–250,000; 250,000–500,000; 500,000–1,000,000; 1,000,000–4,000,000; 4,000,000 or over |
| Density | Urban, suburban, rural |
| Climate | Northern, southern |
| **DEMOGRAPHIC** | |
| Age | Under 6, 6–11, 12–19, 20–34, 35–49, 50–64, 65+ |
| Sex | Male, female |
| Family Size | 1–2, 3–4, 5+ |
| Family Life Cycle | Young, single; young, married, no children; young, married, youngest child under 6; young, married, youngest child 6 or over; older, married, with children; older, married, no children under 18; older, single; other |
| Income | Under $10,000; $10,001–$15,000; $15,001–$20,000; $20,001–$30,000; $30,001–$50,000; $50,001–$70,000; $70,001–$100,000; over $100,000 |
| Occupation | Professional and technical; managers, officials, and proprietors; clerical, sales; craftsmen, foremen; operatives; farmers; retired; students; housewives; unemployed |
| Education | Grade school or less; some high school; high school graduate; some college; college graduate |
| Religion | Catholic, Protestant, Jewish, other |
| Race | White, Asian, Hispanic, African American |
| Nationality | American, British, French, German, Scandinavian, Italian, Latin American, Middle Eastern, Japanese |
| **PSYCHOGRAPHIC** | |
| Social Class | Lower lowers, upper lowers, lower middles, upper middles, lower uppers, upper uppers |
| Personality | Compulsive, gregarious, authoritarian, ambitious |
| **BEHAVIORAL** | |
| Use Occasion | Regular occasion, special occasion |
| Benefits Sought | Quality, service, economy |
| User Status | Nonuser, ex-user, potential user, first-time user, regular user |
| Usage Rate | Light user, medium user, heavy user |
| Loyalty Status | None, medium, strong, absolute |
| Readiness Stage | Unaware, aware, informed, interested, desirous, intending to buy |
| Attitude Toward Product | Enthusiastic, positive, indifferent, negative, hostile |

*Source:* Adapted from Philip Kotler, *Marketing Management: Analysis, Planning and Control,* © 1984; 256. Adapted by permission of Prentice-Hall, Inc., Englewood Cliffs, New Jersey.

**FIGURE 8–2**

Tools for Segmenting the Lawn Fertilizer Market

| | | |
|---|---|---|
| **Heavy users** | High income | Central city |
| | | Suburban |
| | | Rural |
| | Low income | Central city |
| | | Suburban |
| | | Rural |
| **Light users** | High income | Central city |
| | | Suburban |
| | | Rural |
| | Low income | Central city |
| | | Suburban |
| | | Rural |
| **Nonusers** | High income | Central city |
| | | Suburban |
| | | Rural |
| | Low income | Central city |
| | | Suburban |
| | | Rural |

*Source:* Fred Winter, "Market Segmentation: A Tactical Approach," *Business Horizons* (January–February 1984): 60, 61.

1998.[7] States with the largest percentage increase of Asian and Pacific Islanders during that time period were Nevada (106%), Georgia (95%), North Carolina (87%), Florida (73%), and Nebraska (73%).

Market segmentation matrices and decision trees can facilitate implementing strategies effectively. An example of a matrix for segmenting the lawn fertilizer market is provided in Figure 8–2. Similar matrices could be developed for almost any market, product, or service.

Segmentation is a key to matching supply and demand, which is one of the thorniest problems in customer service. Segmentation often reveals that large, random fluctuations in demand actually consist of several small, predictable, and manageable patterns. Matching supply and demand allows factories to produce desirable levels without extra shifts, overtime, and subcontracting. Matching supply and demand also minimizes the number and severity of stockouts. The demand for hotel rooms, for example, can be dependent on foreign tourists, businesspersons, and vacationers. Focusing on these three market segments separately, however, can allow hotel firms to predict overall supply and demand more effectively.

Banks now are segmenting markets to increase effectiveness. "You're dead in the water if you aren't segmenting the market," says Anne Moore, president of a bank consulting firm in Atlanta. As indicated in the E-Commerce Perspective, the Internet makes market segmentation easier today because consumers naturally form "communities" on the Web.

e·biz

### Product Positioning

After segmenting markets so that the firm can target particular customer groups, the next step is to find out what customers want and expect. This takes analysis and research. A severe mistake is to assume the firm knows what customers want and expect.

# E-COMMERCE PERSPECTIVE

**e·biz**

### *Does the Internet Make Market Segmentation Easier?*

Yes. The segments of people that marketers desire to reach online are much more precisely defined than the segments of people reached through traditional forms of media such as television, radio, and magazines. For example, the NetNoir and MSBET.com are Web sites greatly visited by Blacks online, Asian Avenue is widely visited by Asian-Americans, and Quepasa.com is widely visited by Hispanics. Marketers aiming to reach college students, who are notoriously difficult to reach via traditional media, focus on sites such as collegeclub.com and studentadvantage.com. The gay and lesbian population, which is estimated to comprise about 5 percent of the United States, has always been difficult to reach via traditional media but now can be focused upon in sites such as gay.com. Marketers can reach persons interested in specific topics such as travel or fishing by placing banners on related Web sites.

People all over the world are congregating into virtual communities on the Web by becoming members/customers/visitors of Web sites that focus on an endless range of topics. People in essence segment themselves by nature of the Web sites that comprise their "favorite places" and many of these Web sites sell information regarding their "visitors." Businesses and groups of individuals all over the world pool their purchasing power in Web sites to get volume discounts.

Toby Lenk, founder of eToys, Inc. and Jeff Bezos, founder of Amazon.com, are betting their company's future on totally different Internet strategies. Theirs is an old debate—niche versus mass market. EToys is tightly focused on one category, children's goods, whereas Amazon is a big and varied superstore. Thousands of businesses today wrestle with this dilemma of mass versus niche marketing.

Toby believes in niche marketing, focusing eToys on one product segment—toys—offering the best toys at the lowest prices in the world. Jeff believes in mass marketing, focusing Amazon on everything from modems to toys to clothes to books. Amazon now offers more than eighteen thousand different items on its Web site. Jeff says being an all-purpose Internet department store can offer enormous variety without building huge showrooms. Toby says focusing on toys alone allows his company to be child-sensitive and get all the details of that market perfect. For example, eToys has removed its name from the return addresses on boxes so children will not be tempted to open boxes prematurely. EToys wraps toys and ships them wrapped if requested. So far less than 10 percent of Amazon's sales come from toys.

Internet niche stores such as eToys often obtain exclusive rights to some upscale goods. For example, Brio Corporation sells its wooden train sets through eToys but will not use Amazon. Brio feels eToys can showcase their products better than Amazon. Specialty Internet stores such as eToys feel they can offer better convenience, pricing, and selection than Internet superstores such as Amazon that try to be everything to everybody.

For the year 1999, Amazon's profits were negative $720 million. Amazon profits for the first quarter of 2000 were negative $308 million. Amazon sales are rising but with negative profits.

*Source:* Adapted from: George Anders, "Amazon, EToys Make Big Opposing Bets: Which One Is Right?" *The Wall Street Journal* (November 2, 1999): A1, A14. Also, Greg Farrell, "Web Opens Hard-To-Reach Markets To Advertisers," *USA Today* (August 6, 1999): 12B.

---

Countless research studies reveal large differences between how customers define service and rank the importance of different service activities and how producers view services. Many firms have become successful by filling the gap between what customers and producers see as good service. What the customer believes is good service is paramount, not what the producer believes service should be.

Identifying target customers upon whom to focus marketing efforts sets the stage for deciding how to meet the needs and wants of particular consumer groups. Product positioning is widely used for this purpose. Positioning entails developing schematic representations that reflect how your products or services compare to competitors' on dimensions most important to success in the industry. The following steps are required in product positioning:

1. Select key criteria that effectively differentiate products or services in the industry.
2. Diagram a two-dimensional product-positioning map with specified criteria on each axis.
3. Plot major competitors' products or services in the resultant four-quadrant matrix.
4. Identify areas in the positioning map where the company's products or services could be most competitive in the given target market. Look for vacant areas (niches).
5. Develop a marketing plan to position the company's products or services appropriately.

Because just two criteria can be examined on a single product-positioning map, multiple maps are often developed to assess various approaches to strategy implementation. Multidimensional scaling could be used to examine three or more criteria simultaneously, but this technique requires computer assistance and is beyond the scope of this text. Some examples of product-positioning maps are illustrated in Figure 8–3.

Some rules of thumb for using product positioning as a strategy-implementation tool are the following:

1. Look for the hole or *vacant niche.* The best strategic opportunity might be an unserved segment.
2. Don't squat between segments. Any advantage from squatting (such as a larger target market) is offset by a failure to satisfy one segment. In decision-theory terms, the intent here is to avoid suboptimization by trying to serve more than one objective function.
3. Don't serve two segments with the same strategy. Usually, a strategy successful with one segment cannot be directly transferred to another segment.
4. Don't position yourself in the middle of the map. The middle usually means a strategy that is not clearly perceived to have any distinguishing characteristics. This rule can vary with the number of competitors. For example, when there are only two competitors, as in U.S. presidential elections, the middle becomes the preferred strategic position.[8]

An effective product-positioning strategy meets two criteria: (1) it uniquely distinguishes a company from the competition, and (2) it leads customers to expect slightly less service than a company can deliver. Firms should not create expectations that exceed the service the firm can or will deliver. Network Equipment Technology is an example of a company that keeps customer expectations slightly below perceived performance. This is a constant challenge for marketers. Firms need to inform customers about what to expect and then exceed the promise. Underpromise and then overdeliver!

 ## FINANCE/ACCOUNTING ISSUES

In this section, we examine several finance/accounting concepts considered to be central to strategy implementation: acquiring needed capital, developing pro forma financial statements, preparing financial budgets, and evaluating the worth of a business. Some examples of decisions that may require finance/accounting policies are:

**FIGURE 8–3**

**Examples of Product-Positioning Maps**

A.  A PRODUCT-POSITIONING MAP
    FOR BANKS

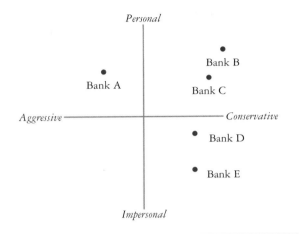

B.  A PRODUCT-POSITIONING MAP
    FOR PERSONAL COMPUTERS

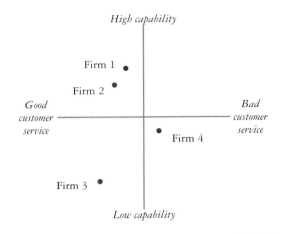

C.  A PRODUCT-POSITIONING MAP FOR
    MENSWEAR RETAIL STORES

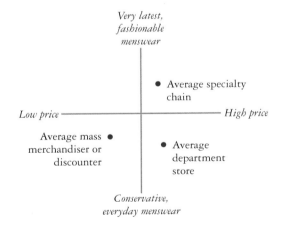

D.  A PRODUCT-POSITIONING MAP
    FOR THE RENTAL CAR MARKET

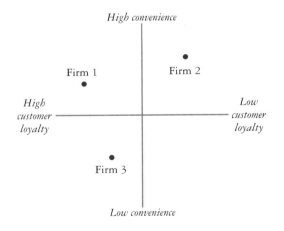

1. To raise capital with short-term debt, long-term debt, preferred stock, or common stock.

2. To lease or buy fixed assets.

3. To determine an appropriate dividend payout ratio.

4. To use LIFO, FIFO, or a market-value accounting approach.

5. To extend the time of accounts receivable.

6. To establish a certain percentage discount on accounts within a specified period of time.

7. To determine the amount of cash that should be kept on hand.

## Acquiring Capital to Implement Strategies

Successful strategy implementation often requires additional capital. Besides net profit from operations and the sale of assets, two basic sources of capital for an organization are debt and equity. Determining an appropriate mix of debt and equity in a firm's capital structure can be vital to successful strategy implementation. An *Earnings Per Share/Earnings Before Interest and Taxes (EPS/EBIT) analysis* is the most widely used technique for determining whether debt, stock, or a combination of debt and stock is the best alternative for raising capital to implement strategies. This technique involves an examination of the impact that debt versus stock financing has on earnings per share under various assumptions as to EBIT.

Theoretically, an enterprise should have enough debt in its capital structure to boost its return on investment by applying debt to products and projects earning more than the cost of the debt. In low earning periods, too much debt in the capital structure of an organization can endanger stockholders' return and jeopardize company survival. Fixed debt obligations generally must be met, regardless of circumstances. This does not mean that stock issuances are always better than debt for raising capital. Some special concerns with stock issuances are dilution of ownership, effect on stock price, and the need to share future earnings with all new shareholders.

Without going into detail on other institutional and legal issues related to the debt versus stock decision, EPS/EBIT may be best explained by working through an example. Let's say the Brown Company needs to raise $1 million to finance implementation of a market-development strategy. The company's common stock currently sells for $50 per share, and 100,000 shares are outstanding. The prime interest rate is 10 percent and the company's tax rate is 50 percent. The company's earnings before interest and taxes next year are expected to be $2 million if a recession occurs, $4 million if the economy stays as is, and $8 million if the economy significantly improves. EPS/EBIT analysis can be used to determine if all stock, all debt, or some combination of stock and debt is the best capital financing alternative. The EPS/EBIT analysis for this example is provided as shown in Table 8–3.

As indicated by the EPS values of 9.5, 19.50, and 39.50 in Table 8–3, debt is the best financing alternative for the Brown Company if a recession, boom, or normal year is expected. An EPS/EBIT chart can be constructed to determine the break-even point, where one financing alternative becomes more attractive than another. Figure 8–4 indi-

## TABLE 8–3  EPS/EBIT Analysis for the Brown Company (in millions)

|  | COMMON STOCK FINANCING | | | DEBT FINANCING | | | COMBINATION FINANCING | | |
|---|---|---|---|---|---|---|---|---|---|
|  | *Recession* | *Normal* | *Boom* | *Recession* | *Normal* | *Boom* | *Recession* | *Normal* | *Boom* |
| EBIT | $2.0 | $ 4.0 | $ 8.0 | $2.0 | $ 4.0 | $ 8.0 | $2.0 | $ 4.0 | $ 8.0 |
| Interest[a] | 0 | 0 | 0 | .10 | .10 | .10 | .05 | .05 | .05 |
| EBT | 2.0 | 4.0 | 8.0 | 1.9 | 3.9 | 7.9 | 1.95 | 3.95 | 7.95 |
| Taxes | 1.0 | 2.0 | 4.0 | .95 | 1.95 | 3.95 | .975 | 1.975 | 3.975 |
| EAT | 1.0 | 2.0 | 4.0 | .95 | 1.95 | 3.95 | .975 | 1.975 | 3.975 |
| #Shares[b] | .12 | .12 | .12 | .10 | .10 | .10 | .11 | .11 | .11 |
| EPS[c] | 8.33 | 16.66 | 33.33 | 9.5 | 19.50 | 39.50 | 8.86 | 17.95 | 36.14 |

[a]The annual interest charge on $1 million at 10% is $100,000 and on $0.5 million is $50,000. This row is in $, not %.
[b]To raise all of the needed $1 million with stock, 20,000 new shares must be issued, raising the total to 120,000 shares outstanding. To raise one-half of the needed $1 million with stock, 10,000 new shares must be issued, raising the total to 110,000 shares outstanding.
[c]EPS = Earnings After Taxes (EAT) divided by shares (number of shares outstanding).

cates that issuing common stock is the least attractive financing alternative for the Brown Company.

EPS/EBIT analysis is a valuable tool for making capital financing decisions needed to implement strategies, but several considerations should be made whenever using this technique. First, profit levels may be higher for stock or debt alternatives when EPS levels are lower. For example, looking only at the earnings after taxes (EAT) values in Table 8–3, the common stock option is the best alternative, regardless of economic conditions. If the Brown Company's mission includes strict profit maximization, as opposed to the maximization of stockholders' wealth or some other criterion, then stock rather than debt is the best choice of financing.

Another consideration when using EPS/EBIT analysis is flexibility. As an organization's capital structure changes, so does its flexibility for considering future capital needs. Using all debt or all stock to raise capital in the present may impose fixed obligations, restrictive covenants, or other constraints that could severely reduce a firm's ability to raise additional capital in the future. Control is also a concern. When additional stock is issued to finance strategy implementation, ownership and control of the enterprise are diluted. This can be a serious concern in today's business environment of hostile takeovers, mergers, and acquisitions. For example, Aetna, Inc., headquartered in Hartford, Connecticut, is buying back $1 billion of its own common stock during 2000 to avoid a takeover and because top management believes the stock is undervalued.

Dilution of ownership can be an overriding concern in closely held corporations where stock issuances affect the decision-making power of majority stockholders. For example, the Smucker family owns 30 percent of the stock in Smucker's, a well-known jam and jelly company. When Smucker's acquired Dickson Family, Inc., the company used mostly debt rather than stock in order not to dilute the family ownership.

When using EPS/EBIT analysis, timing in relation to movements of stock prices, interest rates, and bond prices becomes important. In times of depressed stock prices, debt may prove to be the most suitable alternative from both a cost and a demand standpoint. However, when cost of capital (interest rates) is high, stock issuances become more attractive. In fact, even when interest rates are low, as in 1998, stock issuances can be very popular. The explosion of new mergers and acquisitions in the 1990s was fueled by equity at a time when stock prices were high. Using stock for acquisitions rather than

**FIGURE 8–4**

**An EPS/EBIT Chart for the Brown Company**

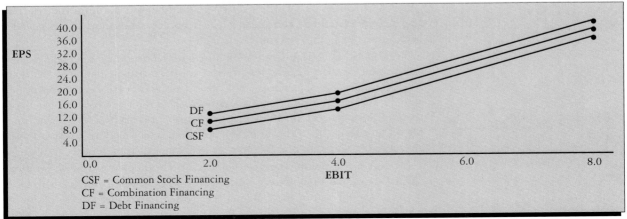

CSF = Common Stock Financing
CF = Combination Financing
DF = Debt Financing

debt enhances a firm's reported earnings because, unlike debt acquirers, stock acquirers do not have to deduct goodwill from their earnings for years to come.

## Pro Forma Financial Statements

*Pro forma (projected) financial statement analysis* is a central strategy-implementation technique because it allows an organization to examine the expected results of various actions and approaches. This type of analysis can be used to forecast the impact of various implementation decisions (for example, to increase promotion expenditures by 50 percent to support a market-development strategy, to increase salaries by 25 percent to support a market-penetration strategy, to increase research and development expenditures by 70 percent to support product development, or to sell $1 million of common stock to raise capital for diversification). Nearly all financial institutions require at least three years of projected financial statements whenever a business seeks capital. A pro forma income statement and balance sheet allow an organization to compute projected financial ratios under various strategy-implementation scenarios. When compared to prior years and to industry averages, financial ratios provide valuable insights into the feasibility of various strategy-implementation approaches.

A 2002 pro forma income statement and balance sheet for the Litten Company are provided in Table 8–4. The pro forma statements for Litten are based on five assumptions: (1) The company needs to raise $45 million to finance expansion into foreign markets; (2) $30 million of this total will be raised through increased debt and $15 million through common stock; (3) sales are expected to increase 50 percent; (4) three new facilities, costing a total of $30 million, will be constructed in foreign markets; and (5) land for the new facilities is already owned by the company. Note in Table 8–4 that Litten's strategies and their implementation are expected to result in a sales increase from $100 million to $150 million and in a net increase in income from $6 million to $9.75 million, in the forecasted year.

There are six steps in performing pro forma financial analysis:

1. Prepare the pro forma income statement before the balance sheet. Start by forecasting sales as accurately as possible.

2. Use the percentage-of-sales method to project cost of goods sold (CGS) and the expense items in the income statement. For example, if CGS is 70 percent of sales in the prior year (as it is in Table 8–4), then use that same percentage to calculate CGS in the future year—unless there is a reason to use a different percentage. Items such as interest, dividends, and taxes must be treated independently and cannot be forecasted using the percentage-of-sales method.

3. Calculate the projected net income.

4. Subtract from the net income any dividends to be paid and add the remaining net income to Retained Earnings. Reflect the Retained Earnings total on both the income statement and balance sheet because this item is the key link between the two projected statements.

5. Project the balance sheet items, beginning with retained earnings and then forecasting stockholders' equity, long-term liabilities, current liabilities, total liabilities, total assets, fixed assets, and current assets (in that order). Use the cash account as the plug figure; that is, use the cash account to make the assets total the liabilities and net worth. Then, make appropriate adjustments. For example, if the cash needed to balance the statements is too small (or too large), make appropriate changes to borrow more (or less) money than planned.

6. List comments (remarks) on the projected statements. Any time a significant change is made in an item from a prior year to the projected year, an explanation (remark) should be provided. Remarks are essential because otherwise pro formas are meaningless.

TABLE 8-4    **A Pro Forma Income Statement and Balance Sheet for the Litten Company (in millions)**

| | PRIOR YEAR 2001 | PROJECTED YEAR 2002 | REMARKS |
|---|---|---|---|
| **PRO FORMA INCOME STATEMENT** | | | |
| Sales | 100 | 150.00 | 50% increase |
| Cost of Goods Sold | 70 | 105.00 | 70% of sales |
| Gross Margin | 30 | 45.00 | |
| Selling Expense | 10 | 15.00 | 10% of sales |
| Administrative Expense | 5 | 7.50 | 5% of sales |
| Earnings Before Interest and Taxes | 15 | 22.50 | |
| Interest | 3 | 3.00 | |
| Earnings Before Taxes | 12 | 19.50 | |
| Taxes | 6 | 9.75 | 50% rate |
| Net Income | 6 | 9.75 | |
| Dividends | 2 | 5.00 | |
| Retained Earnings | 4 | 4.75 | |
| **PRO FORMA BALANCE SHEET** | | | |
| Assets | | | |
| Cash | 5 | 7.75 | Plug figure |
| Accounts Receivable | 2 | 4.00 | Incr. 100% |
| Inventory | 20 | 45.00 | |
| Total Current Assets | 27 | 56.75 | |
| Land | 15 | 15.00 | |
| Plant and Equipment | 50 | 80.00 | Add 3 new plants at $10 million each |
| Less Depreciation | 10 | 20.00 | |
| Net Plant and Equipment | 40 | 60.00 | |
| Total Fixed Assets | 55 | 75.00 | |
| Total Assets | 82 | 131.75 | |
| Liabilities | | | |
| Accounts Payable | 10 | 10.00 | |
| Notes Payable | 10 | 10.00 | |
| Total Current Liabilities | 20 | 20.00 | |
| Long-term Debt | 40 | 70.00 | Borrowed $30 million |
| Additional Paid-in-Capital | 20 | 35.00 | Issued 100,000 shares at $150 each |
| Retained Earnings | 2 | 6.75 | 2 + 4.75 |
| Total Liabilities and Net Worth | 82 | 131.75 | |

## Financial Budgets

A *financial budget* is a document that details how funds will be obtained and spent for a specified period of time. Annual budgets are most common, although the period of time for a budget can range from one day to more than ten years. Fundamentally, financial budgeting is a method for specifying what must be done to complete strategy implementation successfully. Financial budgeting should not be thought of as a tool for limiting expenditures but rather as a method for obtaining the most productive and profitable use of an organization's resources. Financial budgets can be viewed as the planned allocation of a firm's resources based on forecasts of the future.

There are almost as many different types of financial budgets as there are types of organizations. Some common types of budgets include cash budgets, operating budgets, sales budgets, profit budgets, factory budgets, capital budgets, expense budgets, divisional budgets, variable budgets, flexible budgets, and fixed budgets. When an organization is experiencing financial difficulties, budgets are especially important in guiding strategy implementation.

Perhaps the most common type of financial budget is the *cash budget*. The Financial Accounting Standards Board has mandated that every publicly held company in the United States must issue an annual cash-flow statement in addition to the usual financial reports. The statement includes all receipts and disbursements of cash in operations, investments, and financing. It supplements the Statement on Changes in Financial Position formerly included in the annual reports of all publicly held companies. A cash budget for the year 2000 for the Toddler Toy Company is provided in Table 8–5. Note that Toddler is not expecting to have surplus cash until November of 2002.

Financial budgets have some limitations. First, budgetary programs can become so detailed that they are cumbersome and overly expensive. Overbudgeting or underbudgeting can cause problems. Second, financial budgets can become a substitute for objectives. A budget is a tool and not an end in itself. Third, budgets can hide inefficiencies if based solely on precedent rather than periodic evaluation of circumstances and standards. Finally, budgets are sometimes used as instruments of tyranny that result in frustration, resentment, absenteeism, and high turnover. To minimize the effect of this last concern, managers should increase the participation of subordinates in preparing budgets.

### Evaluating the Worth of a Business

Evaluating the worth of a business is central to strategy implementation because integrative, intensive, and diversification strategies are often implemented by acquiring other firms. Other strategies, such as retrenchment and divestiture, may result in the sale of a division of an organization or of the firm itself. Approximately twenty thousand transactions occur each year in which businesses are bought or sold in the United States.

TABLE 8–5    **A Six-Month Cash Budget for the Toddler Toy Company in 2002**

| CASH BUDGET (IN THOUSANDS) | JULY | AUG. | SEPT. | OCT. | NOV. | DEC. | JAN. |
|---|---|---|---|---|---|---|---|
| Receipts | | | | | | | |
| Collections | $12,000 | $21,000 | $31,000 | $35,000 | $22,000 | $18,000 | $11,000 |
| Payments | | | | | | | |
| Purchases | 14,000 | 21,000 | 28,000 | 14,000 | 14,000 | 7,000 | |
| Wages and Salaries | 1,500 | 2,000 | 2,500 | 1,500 | 1,500 | 1,000 | |
| Rent | 500 | 500 | 500 | 500 | 500 | 500 | |
| Other Expenses | 200 | 300 | 400 | 200 | 200 | 100 | |
| Taxes | — | 8,000 | — | — | — | — | |
| Payment on Machine | — | — | 10,000 | — | — | — | |
| Total Payments | $16,200 | $31,800 | $41,400 | $16,200 | $16,000 | $8,600 | |
| Net Cash Gain (Loss) During Month | −4,200 | −10,800 | −10,400 | 18,800 | 5,800 | 9,400 | |
| Cash at Start of Month If No Borrowing Is Done | 6,000 | 1,800 | −9,000 | −19,400 | −600 | 5,200 | |
| Cumulative Cash (Cash at start plus gains or minus losses) | 1,800 | −9,000 | −19,400 | −600 | 5,200 | 14,600 | |
| Less Desired Level of Cash | −5,000 | −5,000 | −5,000 | −5,000 | −5,000 | −5,000 | |
| Total Loans Outstanding to Maintain $5,000 Cash Balance | $3,200 | $14,000 | $24,400 | $5,600 | — | — | |
| Surplus Cash | — | — | — | — | $200 | $9,600 | |

In all these cases, it is necessary to establish the financial worth or cash value of a business to successfully implement strategies.

All the various methods for determining a business's worth can be grouped into three main approaches: what a firm owns, what a firm earns, or what a firm will bring in the market. But it is important to realize that valuation is not an exact science. The valuation of a firm's worth is based on financial facts, but common sense and intuitive judgment must enter into the process. It is difficult to assign a monetary value to factors—such as a loyal customer base, a history of growth, legal suits pending, dedicated employees, a favorable lease, a bad credit rating, or good patents—that may not be reflected in a firm's financial statements. Also, different valuation methods will yield different totals for a firm's worth, and no prescribed approach is best for a certain situation. Evaluating the worth of a business truly requires both qualitative and quantitative skills.

The first approach in evaluating the worth of a business is determining its net worth or stockholders' equity. Net worth represents the sum of common stock, additional paid-in capital, and retained earnings. After calculating net worth, add or subtract an appropriate amount for goodwill (such as high customer loyalty) and overvalued or undervalued assets. This total provides a reasonable estimate of a firm's monetary value. If a firm has goodwill, it will be listed on the balance sheet, perhaps as "intangibles."

The second approach to measuring the value of a firm grows out of the belief that the worth of any business should be based largely on the future benefits its owners may derive through net profits. A conservative rule of thumb is to establish a business's worth as five times the firm's current annual profit. A five-year average profit level could also be used. When using this approach, remember that firms normally suppress earnings in their financial statements to minimize taxes.

The third approach, letting the market determine a business's worth, involves three methods. First, base the firm's worth on the selling price of a similar company. A potential problem, however, is that sometimes comparable figures are not easy to locate, even though substantial information on firms that buy or sell to other firms is available in major libraries. The second approach is called the *price-earnings ratio method.* To use this method, divide the market price of the firm's common stock by the annual earnings per share and multiply this number by the firm's average net income for the past five years. The third approach can be called the *outstanding shares method.* To use this method, simply multiply the number of shares outstanding by the market price per share and add a premium. The premium is simply a per share dollar amount that a person or firm is willing to pay to control (acquire) the other company. As indicated in the Global Perspective, European firms aggressively are acquiring American firms, using these and perhaps other methods for evaluating the worth of their target companies.

Business evaluations are becoming routine in many situations. Businesses have many strategy-implementation reasons for determining their worth in addition to preparing to be sold or to buy other companies. Employee plans, taxes, retirement, mergers, acquisitions, expansion plans, banking relationships, death of a principal, divorce, partnership agreements, and IRS audits are other reasons for a periodic valuation. It is just good business to have a reasonable understanding of what your firm is worth. This knowledge protects the interests of all parties involved.

The Financial Accounting Standards Board (FASB) recently prohibited the "pooling of interests" accounting method for recording mergers on financial statements, leaving the purchase method as the only way companies can book their merger deals. Under the purchase method, companies must write off goodwill against earnings for up to twenty years.

# GLOBAL PERSPECTIVE

## *Europe Is Acquiring the United States*

European companies are acquiring American companies in record numbers. During the first nine months of 1999, European companies purchased $256 billion worth of American companies, compared to U.S. firms purchasing $121.9 billion worth of European companies. American investment firms are leading advisers to European firms making acquisitions. For example, Goldman Sachs led all investment bankers during the first nine months of 1999, closing twenty-seven European acquisitions of U.S. firms worth $161.15 billion. Morgan Stanley Dean Witter was close behind at thirty-two deals worth $150.74 billion. A distant third was Salomon Smith Barney closing seventeen deals worth $67.31 billion. The largest European acquisitions of American firms in 1998 and 1999 are listed below:

| Target | Acquirer (Country) | Date | Value (billions) |
|---|---|---|---|
| AirTouch Communications | Vodafone (U.K.) | Jan. 99 | $65.90 |
| Amoco | British Petroleum (U.K.) | Aug. 98 | 55.04 |
| Chrysler | Daimler-Benz (Germany) | May 98 | 40.47 |
| ARCO | BP Amoco (U.K.) | April 99 | 33.70 |
| PacifiCorp | Scottish Power (U.K.) | Dec. 98 | 12.59 |
| TransAmerica | Aegon (Netherlands) | Feb. 99 | 10.81 |
| Bankers Trust | Deutsche Bank (Germany) | Nov. 98 | 9.08 |
| SmithKline Beckman | Beecham Group (U.K.) | March 99 | 8.90 |

*Source:* Adapted from: Nikhil Deogun, "Made in U.S.A.: Deals From Europe Hit Record," *The Wall Street Journal*, (October 25, 1999): C1.

### Deciding Whether to Go Public

Going public means selling off a percentage of your company to others in order to raise capital; consequently, it dilutes the owners' control of the firm. Going public is not recommended for companies with less than $10 million in sales because the initial costs can be too high for the firm to generate sufficient cash flow to make going public worthwhile. One dollar in four is the average total cost paid to lawyers, accountants, and underwriters when an initial stock issuance is under $1 million; one dollar in twenty will go to cover these costs for issuances over $20 million.

In addition to initial costs involved with a stock offering, there are costs and obligations associated with reporting and management in a publicly held firm. For firms with more than $10 million in sales, going public can provide major advantages: It can allow the firm to raise capital to develop new products, build plants, expand, grow, and market products and services more effectively.

Before going public, a firm must have quality management with a proven track record for achieving quality earnings and positive cash flow. The company also should enjoy growing demand for its products. Sales growth of about 5 or 6 percent a year is good for a private firm, but shareholders expect public companies to grow around 10 to 15 percent per year.

Both the New York Stock Exchange and the Nasdaq Stock Exchange have unveiled plans to go public in order to raise capital needed for technological improvements. Each exchange also desires to acquire rival exchanges. Cheaper and faster electronic trading systems are pushing exchanges worldwide to either cooperate, compete, merge, or acquire in what many analysts consider an industry way too fragmented. The Australian and Swedish exchanges went public in 1998. The Chicago Board of Trade, Chicago Board of Options Exchange, and the London Stock Exchange are considering going public.

United Parcel Service (UPS), the world's largest express delivery firm, went public in 1999 after ninety-two years as a private company. Based in Atlanta, Georgia, UPS had earnings of $1.7 billion in 1998 on revenues of $24.8 billion. The boom in Internet sales has boosted UPS's revenues dramatically since all merchandise bought over the Internet must be shipped.

Even the New York Yankees are moving forward with a plan to go public as soon as their merger with the New Jersey Nets of the National Basketball Association (NBA) is completed. The merged teams desire capital to entice a National Football League team to join them. The merged teams also are considering launching their own cable channel. The Cleveland Indians baseball team and the Boston Celtics basketball team are already listed on the Nasdaq and New York Stock Exchanges, respectively.

Small businesses today are increasingly offering Direct Public Offerings (DPOs) as a way for ordinary investors to get stock before a company formally goes public. With a DPO, a small firm sells shares for $5 to $10 per share without an underwriter and without listing on any exchange. The initial costs are much less. For 1998, 321 companies in the United States filed DPOs, up from 273 in 1997. For example, Internet Ventures raised $3.8 million recently via a DPO.[9]

During the first half of 1999, there were 66 Internet companies that went public in the United States, up from 40 in all of 1998. Internet public offerings comprise about 25 percent of the more than $20 billion raised annually in domestic public offerings.

**e·biz**

## RESEARCH AND DEVELOPMENT (R&D) ISSUES

*Research and development* (R&D) personnel can play an integral part in strategy implementation. These individuals are generally charged with developing new products and improving old products in a way that will allow effective strategy implementation. R&D employees and managers perform tasks that include transferring complex technology, adjusting processes to local raw materials, adapting processes to local markets, and altering products to particular tastes and specifications. Strategies such as product development, market penetration, and concentric diversification require that new products be successfully developed and that old products be significantly improved. But the level of management support for R&D is often constrained by resource availability:

> If U.S. business is to maintain its position in the global business environment, then R&D support will have to become a major U.S. commitment. U.S. managers cannot continue to ignore it or take funds away from it for short-term profits and still have long-term strategic options. If one runs away from more aggressive product and process strategies, one should not be surprised by the fact that competitive advantages are lost to foreign competitors.[10]

Technological improvements that affect consumer and industrial products and services shorten product life cycles. Companies in virtually every industry are relying on the development of new products and services to fuel profitability and growth.

Surveys suggest that the most successful organizations use an R&D strategy that ties external opportunities to internal strength and is linked with objectives. Well-formulated R&D policies match market opportunities with internal capabilities and provide an initial screen to all ideas generated. R&D policies can enhance strategy-implementation efforts to:

1. Emphasize product or process improvements.
2. Stress basic or applied research.

3. Be leaders or followers in R&D.
4. Develop robotics or manual-type processes.
5. Spend a high, average, or low amount of money on R&D.
6. Perform R&D within the firm or to contract R&D to outside firms.
7. Use university researchers or private sector researchers.

There must be effective interactions between R&D departments and other functional departments in implementing different types of generic business strategies. Conflicts between marketing, finance/accounting, R&D, and information systems departments can be minimized with clear policies and objectives. Table 8–6 gives some examples of R&D activities that could be required for successful implementation of various strategies. Many American utility, energy, and automotive companies are employing their research and development departments to determine how the firm can effectively reduce its greenhouse gas emissions.

Many firms wrestle with the decision to acquire R&D expertise from external firms or to develop R&D expertise internally. The following guidelines can be used to help make this decision:

1. If the rate of technical progress is slow, the rate of market growth is moderate, and there are significant barriers to possible new entrants, then in-house R&D is the preferred solution. The reason is that R&D, if successful, will result in a temporary product or process monopoly that the company can exploit.
2. If technology is changing rapidly and the market is growing slowly, then a major effort in R&D may be very risky, because it may lead to development of an ultimately obsolete technology or one for which there is no market.
3. If technology is changing slowly but the market is growing fast, there generally is not enough time for in-house development. The prescribed approach is to obtain R&D expertise on an exclusive or nonexclusive basis from an outside firm.
4. If both technical progress and market growth are fast, R&D expertise should be obtained through acquisition of a well-established firm in the industry.[11]

There are at least three major R&D approaches for implementing strategies. The first strategy is to be the first firm to market new technological products. This is a glamorous and exciting strategy but also a dangerous one. Firms such as 3M, Polaroid, and General Electric have been successful with this approach, but many other pioneering firms have fallen, with rival firms seizing the initiative.

## TABLE 8–6    Research and Development Involvement in Selected Strategy-Implementation Situations

| TYPE OF ORGANIZATION | STRATEGY BEING IMPLEMENTED | R&D ACTIVITY |
| --- | --- | --- |
| Pharmaceutical company | Product development | Develop a procedure for testing the effects of a new drug on different subgroups. |
| Boat manufacturer | Concentric diversification | Develop a procedure to test the performance of various keel designs under various conditions. |
| Plastic container manufacturer | Market penetration | Develop a biodegradable container. |
| Electronics company | Market development | Develop a telecommunications system in a foreign country. |

A second R&D approach is to be an innovative imitator of successful products, thus minimizing the risks and costs of start-up. This approach entails allowing a pioneer firm to develop the first version of the new product and to demonstrate that a market exists. Then, laggard firms develop a similar product. This strategy requires excellent R&D personnel and an excellent marketing department.

A third R&D strategy is to be a low-cost producer by mass-producing products similar to but less expensive than products recently introduced. Far Eastern countries used this approach effectively during the 1980s to crush the $8 billion U.S. consumer electronics industry. As a new product is accepted by customers, price becomes increasingly important in the buying decision. Also, mass marketing replaces personal selling as the dominant selling strategy. This R&D strategy requires substantial investment in plant and equipment, but fewer expenditures in R&D than the two approaches described earlier.

R&D activities among American firms need to be more closely aligned to business objectives. There needs to be expanded communication between R&D managers and strategists. Corporations are experimenting with various methods to achieve this improved communication climate, including different roles and reporting arrangements for managers and new methods to reduce the time it takes research ideas to become reality.

Perhaps the most current trend in R&D management has been lifting the veil of secrecy whereby firms, even major competitors, are joining forces to develop new products.

# NATURAL ENVIRONMENT PERSPECTIVE

### *Business Reaction to Global Warming*

More and larger companies are accepting the scientific theory that manmade carbon-dioxide emissions are warming the earth. Recent research reveals that half of the fifty largest American companies are in some phase of assessing or reducing their greenhouse gases. The Kyoto Protocol, recently ratified by the U.S. Congress, requires nations to cut worldwide emissions by 5.2 percent below 1990 levels by 2012. Consider the following facts:

- BP Amoco PLC managers in 1999 for the first time were evaluated on how well they cut emissions.

- American Electric Power, the nation's second-largest producer of coal-powered electricity, is spending $5.5 million on a Bolivian reforestation project—to offset the carbon dioxide it releases in the United States.

- Royal Dutch/Shell Group and other European firms lead in support of the Kyoto Protocol. Shell has promised to reduce its greenhouse gases by 10 percent below the 1990 baseline by 2002.

- David Peyser Sportswear, Inc. President Fredric Stollmack says, "We have changed the entire complexion of our company and our product line because of the global warming trend. For example, all of our heavy jackets now come with zip-out linings."

- Most coal-industry firms, automakers, and oil companies in the United States oppose the Kyoto Protocol and actively lobby against ratification by the Congress.

- Two of General Motors' most fuel-efficient models, the Chevy Metro and the EV1 electric car, have sold poorly. Car and truck exhaust is a major environmental problem worldwide.

- Scientists cannot agree whether rising temperatures, which are undisputed worldwide, will make the world wetter or drier. If wetter, many diseases such as malaria will prosper. If drier, agricultural products will suffer. There are many more implications.

- U.S. emissions of greenhouse gases today are 10 percent more than in 1990, so the U.S. Congress must step in with strict regulation to have a chance in meeting the Kyoto agreement.

*Source:* Adapted from: Steve Liesman, "Inside the Race to Profit From Global Warming," *The Wall Street Journal* (October 19, 1999): B1.

Collaboration is on the rise due to new competitive pressures, rising research costs, increasing regulatory issues, and accelerated product development schedules. Companies not only are working more closely with each other on R&D, but they are also turning to consortia at universities for their R&D needs. More than 600 research consortia are now in operation in the United States. Lifting of R&D secrecy among many firms through collaboration has allowed marketing of new technologies and products even before they are available for sale.

## COMPUTER INFORMATION SYSTEMS (CIS) ISSUES

Although no firm would use the same marketing or management approach for twenty years, many companies have twenty-year-old *computer information systems* that threaten their very existence. Developing new user applications often takes a backseat to keeping an old system running. Countless firms still do not use the Internet. This unfortunate situation is happening at a time when the quantity and quality of information available to firms and their competitors is increasing exponentially.

Firms that gather, assimilate, and evaluate external and internal information most effectively are gaining competitive advantages over other firms. Recognizing the importance of having an effective computer information system will not be an option in the future; it will be a requirement. Information is the basis for understanding in a firm. Robert Kavner, president of AT&T Data Systems Group, says, "Modern corporations are organizing around information flow. With the growth of communications networks such as the Internet, the barriers of time and place have been breached. By mirroring people's work needs and habits, networked computing systems have made new modes of work possible."

It is estimated that the quantity of human knowledge is doubling every decade. In many industries, information is becoming the most important factor differentiating successful and unsuccessful firms. The process of strategic management is facilitated immensely in firms that have an effective information system. Many companies are establishing a new approach to information systems, one that blends the technical knowledge of the computer experts with the vision of senior management.

Information collection, retrieval, and storage can be used to create competitive advantages in ways such as cross-selling to customers, monitoring suppliers, keeping managers and employees informed, coordinating activities among divisions, and managing funds. Like inventory and human resources, information is becoming recognized as a valuable organizational asset that can be controlled and managed. Firms that implement strategies using the best information will reap competitive advantages in the twenty-first century. John Young, president and CEO of Hewlett-Packard, says, "There really isn't any right amount to spend on information systems. Many management teams spend too much time thinking about how to beat down the information system's cost, instead of thinking about how to get more value out of the information they could have available and how to link that to strategic goals of the company."

A good information system can allow a firm to reduce costs. For example, online orders from salespersons to production facilities can shorten materials ordering time and reduce inventory costs. Direct communications between suppliers, manufacturers, marketers, and customers can link elements of the value chain together as though they were one organization. Improved quality and service often result from an improved information system.

Firms must increasingly be concerned about computer hackers and take specific measures to secure and safeguard corporate communications, files, orders, and business conducted over the Internet.

The Gap, Playboy Enterprises, Hitachi America, PeopleSoft, and Twentieth Century Fox average over thirty computer intrusion attempts daily. Thousands of companies today are plagued by computer hackers who include disgruntled employees, competitors, bored teens, sociopaths, thieves, spies, and hired agents. Computer vulnerability is a giant, expensive headache. Over 40 percent of U.S. corporations reported severe computer break-ins in 1996 and spent over $6 billion that year to safeguard their computers. These firms lost more than $10 billion due to computer hackers.

The FBI reports that 95 percent of computer break-ins go undetected and fewer than 15 percent are reported to law enforcement agencies. The FBI's senior expert on computer crime, Dennis Hughes, says "Hackers are driving us nuts. Everyone is getting hacked into. It's out of control." Hackers can download computer break-in programs free off the Internet, and hacker magazines provide easy, step-by-step tips. Hackers can read a computer screen from over a mile away, can intercept all passwords and e-mail messages, steal trade secrets and patents, and read all confidential messages such as bids on projects and new strategy initiatives.

To minimize the hacker threat, companies today must purchase expensive encryption software to scramble the traffic that flows through their computer networks; companies must teach all employees to be security conscious; companies must construct several, not just one, complex computer firewalls to deter hackers. Hacker technology is getting exotic and developing faster than safeguards. Companies naive to the computer hacker threat are grossly negligent and vulnerable.

Even the U.S. federal government is becoming more worried about cyberterror. Research costs on cyberspace security related to the federal government are expected to reach $1 billion per year by 2004. Thomas Marsh, chair of President Clinton's Commission on Critical Infrastructure Protection, says, "Vulnerability is serious and increasing." Former senator Sam Nunn, also on the commission, says, "The only issue of equal or greater concern today is nuclear, chemical, or biological weapon proliferation."[12]

Dun & Bradstreet is an example of a company that has an excellent information system. Every D & B customer and client in the world has a separate nine-digit number. The database of information associated with each number has become so widely used that it is like a business social security number. D & B reaps great competitive advantages from its information system.

In many firms information technology is doing away with the workplace and allowing employees to work at home or anywhere, anytime. The number of work-at-home employees and managers is expected to exceed 18 million by 2001 in the United States. "There is nothing I can do in an office that I can't do at home," says William Holtz, vice-president for global enterprise services with Northern Telecom. From his home in Philadelphia, Holtz supervises a staff of 1,000 in Nashville, Tennessee. Managers are moving away from the mindset of having to see their employees and watch them work.

The mobile concept of work allows employees to work the traditional 9-5 workday across any of the 24 time zones around the globe. Affordable desktop videoconferencing software developed by AT&T, Lotus, or Vivo Software allows employees to beam in whenever needed. Any manager or employee that travels a lot away from the office is a good candidate for working at home rather than in an office provided by the firm. Salespersons or consultants are good examples, but any person whose job largely involves talking to others or handling information could easily operate at home with the proper computer system and software. The accounting firm Ernst & Young has reduced its office space requirements by 2 million square feet over the past three years by allowing employees to work at home.

Many people see the officeless office trend as leading to resurgence of family togetherness in American society. Even the design of homes may change form having large open areas to having more private small areas conducive to getting work done.[13]

## CONCLUSION

Successful strategy implementation depends upon cooperation among all functional and divisional managers in an organization. Marketing departments are commonly charged with implementing strategies that require significant increases in sales revenues in new areas and with new or improved products. Finance and accounting managers must devise effective strategy-implementation approaches at low cost and minimum risk to that firm. R&D managers have to transfer complex technologies or develop new technologies to successfully implement strategies. Information systems managers are being called upon more and more to provide leadership and training for all individuals in the firm. The nature and role of marketing, finance/accounting, R&D, and computer information systems activities, coupled with management activities described in Chapter 7, largely determine organizational success.

We invite you to visit the DAVID page on the Prentice Hall Web site at **www.prenhall.com/davidsm** for this chapter's World Wide Web exercises.

## KEY TERMS AND CONCEPTS

Cash Budget (p. 288)

Computer Information Systems (p. 294)

Direct Public Offerings (DPO) (p. 291)

EPS/EBIT Analysis (p. 284)

Financial Budget (p. 287)

Market Segmentation (p. 277)

Marketing Mix Variables (p. 278)

Outstanding Shares Method (p. 289)

Price-Earnings Ratio Method (p. 289)

Pro Forma Financial Statement Analysis (p. 286)

Product Positioning (p. 277)

Research and Development (p. 291)

Vacant Niche (p. 282)

## ISSUES FOR REVIEW AND DISCUSSION

1. Suppose your company has just acquired a firm that produces battery-operated lawn mowers, and strategists want to implement a market-penetration strategy. How would you segment the market for this product? Justify your answer.
2. Explain how you would estimate the total worth of a business.
3. Diagram and label clearly a product-positioning map that includes six fast-food restaurant chains.
4. Explain why EPS/EBIT analysis is a central strategy-implementation technique.
5. How would the R&D role in strategy implementation differ in small versus large organizations?
6. Discuss the limitations of EPS/EBIT analysis.
7. Explain how marketing, finance/accounting, R&D, and computer information systems managers' involvement in strategy formulation can enhance strategy implementation.

8. Consider the following statement: "Retained earnings on the balance sheet are not monies available to finance strategy implementation." Is it true or false? Explain.
9. Explain why pro forma financial statement analysis is considered both a strategy-formulation and a strategy-implementation tool.
10. Describe some marketing, finance/accounting, R&D, and computer information systems activities that a small restaurant chain might undertake to expand into a neighboring state.
11. Select one of the suggested readings at the end of this chapter, find that article in your college library, and summarize it in a five-minute oral report for the class.
12. Discuss the computer information systems at your college or university.
13. What effect is e-commerce having on firms' efforts to segment markets?

# NOTES

1. LESLIE MILLER and ELIZABETH WEISE, "E-Privacy—FTC Studies 'Profiling' by Web Sites," *USA Today* (November 8, 1999): 1A, 2A.

2. Adapted from: JANET KORNBLUM, "Web Snags Ads From Newspapers, Phone Books," *USA Today* (June 28, 1999): B1.

3. DAVID LIEBERMAN, "CBS to Join Viacom Empire," *USA Today* (September 8, 1999): 1A.

4. FRED WINTER, "Market Segmentation: A Tactical Approach," *Business Horizons* 27, no. 1 (January–February 1984): 59.

5. JESSICA SUPINSKI and SUZY PARKER, "Kids Shopping On-line," *USA Today* (August 25, 1999): B1.

6. SARA NATHAN, "Internet Shopping," *USA Today* (September 7, 1999): B1.

7. KEN THURSTON, "Asian Population Growth," *USA Today* (October 4, 1999): A1.

8. RALPH BIGGADIKE, "The Contributions of Marketing to Strategic Management," *Academy of Management Review* 6, no. 4 (October 1981): 627.

9. JAMES KIM, "Net Breathes New Life Into Old Concept," *USA Today* (July 20, 1999): B1.

10. VIDA SCARPELLO, WILLIAM BOULTON, and CHARLES HOFER, "Reintegrating R&D into Business Strategy," *Journal of Business Strategy* 6, no. 4 (Spring 1986): 55.

11. PIER ABETTI, "Technology: A Key Strategic Resource," *Management Review* 78, no. 2 (February 1989): 38.

12. Adapted from RICHARD BEHAR, "Who's Reading Your E-Mail?" *Fortune* (February 3, 1997): 57–70. Also M.J. Zuckerman, "Clinton to get Cyberterror Plan," *USA Today* (October 9, 1997): 1A.

13. Adapted from EDWARD BAIG, "Welcome to the Officeless Office," *Business Week* (June 26, 1995).

# CURRENT READINGS

ALDEN, DANA L., JAN-BENEDICT, E. M., STEENKAMP, J., and RAJEEV, BATRA. "Brand Positioning Through Advertising in Asia, North America, and Europe: The Role of Global Consumer Culture." *Journal of Marketing* 63, no. 1 (January 1999): 75–85.

AMRAM, MARTHA and NALIN KULATILAKA. "Disciplined Decisions: Aligning Strategy with the Financial Markets." *Harvard Business Review* (January–February 1999): 95–105.

BENSAOU, M., M. COYNE, and N. VENKATRAMAN. "Testing Metric Equivalence in Cross-National Strategy Research: An Empirical Test Across the United States and Japan." *Strategic Management Journal* 20, no. 7 (July 1999): 671–692.

BERTHON, PIERRE, JAMES M. HULBERT, and LEYLAND F. PITT. "Brand Management Prognostications." *Sloan Management Review* 40, no. 2 (Winter 1999): 53–66.

BROUTHERS, KEITH D. and FRANS A. ROOZEN. "Is It Time to Start Thinking About Strategic Accounting?" *Internal Journal of Strategic Management* 32, no. 3 (June 1999): 311–320.

BROWNLIE, DOUGLAS. "Benchmarking Your Marketing Process." *International Journal of Strategic Planning* 32, no. 1 (February 1999): 88–95.

CHAN, RICKY Y. K. "At the Crossroads of Distribution Reform: China's Recent Ban on Direct Selling." *Business Horizons* 42, no. 5 (September-October 1999): 41–46.

CHAUDHURI, SAIKAT and BEHNAM TABRIZI. "Capturing the Real Value in High-Tech Acquisitions." *Harvard Business Review* 77, no. 5 (September-October 1999): 123–132.

GOTTSCHALK, PETTER. "Implementation of Formal Plans: The Case of Information Technology Strategy." *International Journal of Strategic Management* 32, no. 3 (June 1999): 362–372.

KHURANA, ANIL. "Managing Complex Production Processes." *Sloan Management Review* 40, no. 1 (Fall 1999): 85–98.

KROLL, M., P. WRIGHT and R. A. HEIENS. "The Contribution of Product Quality to Competitive Advantage: Impacts on Systematic Variance and Unexplained Variance in

Returns." Research Notes and Communications. *Strategic Management Journal* 20, no. 4 (April 1999): 375–384.

MARKIDES, CONSTANTINOS C. "A Dynamic View of Strategy." *Sloan Management Review* 40, no. 3 (Spring 1999): 55–64.

MEYER, MARC H. and ARTHUR DETORE. "Product Development for Services." *The Academy of Management Executive* 13, no. 3 (August 1999): 64–76.

PEPPERS, DON, MARTHA ROGERS, and BOB DORF. Manager's Tool Kit. "Is Your Company Ready for One-to-One Marketing?" *Harvard Business Review* (January–February 1999): 151–161.

PITT, LEYLAND, PIERRE BERTHON, and JEAN-PAUL BERTHON. "Changing Channels: The Impact of the Internet on Distribution Strategy." *Business Horizons* 42, no. 2 (March–April 1999): 19–28.

PITT, LEYLAND, PIERRE BERTHON, and RICHARD T. WATSON. "Cyberservice: Taming Service Marketing Problems with the World Wide Web." *Business Horizons* 42, no. 1 (January–February 1999): 11–18.

RUEFLI, T. W., J. M. COLLINS, and J. R. LACUGNA. "Risk Measures in Strategic Management Research: Auld Lang Syne?" *Strategic Management Journal* 20, no. 2 (February 1999): 167–194.

SAMU, SRIDHAR, H. SHANKER KRISHNAN, and ROBERT E. SMITH. "Using Advertising Alliances for New Product Introduction: Interactions Between Product Complementarity and Promotional Strategies." *Journal of Marketing* 63, no. 1 (January 1999): 57–67.

THOMAS III, L. G., and G. WARING. "Competing Capitalisms: Capital Investment in American, German and Japanese Firms." *Strategic Management Journal* 20, no. 8 (August 1999): 729–748.

VAKRATSAS, DEMETRIOS and TIM AMBLER. "How Advertising Works: What Do We Really Know." *Journal of Marketing* 63, no. 1 (January 1999): 26–36.

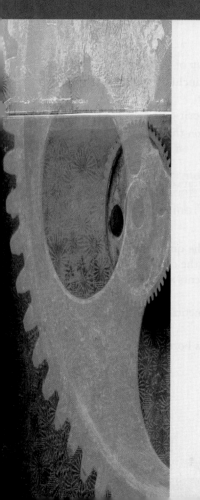

# 9

# STRATEGY REVIEW, EVALUATION, AND CONTROL

## CHAPTER OUTLINE

- The Nature of Strategy Evaluation
- A Strategy-Evaluation Framework
- Published Sources of Strategy-Evaluation Information
- Characteristics of an Effective Evaluation System
- Contingency Planning
- Auditing
- Using Computers to Evaluate Strategies

**EXPERIENTIAL EXERCISE 9A**
*Preparing a Strategy-Evaluation Report for America Online (AOL)*

**EXPERIENTIAL EXERCISE 9B**
*Evaluating My University's Strategies*

**EXPERIENTIAL EXERCISE 9C**
*Who Prepares an Environmental Audit?*

# CHAPTER OBJECTIVES

*After studying this chapter, you should be able to do the following:*

1. Describe a practical framework for evaluating strategies.
2. Explain why strategy evaluation is complex, sensitive, and yet essential for organizational success.
3. Discuss the importance of contingency planning in strategy evaluation.
4. Discuss the role of auditing in strategy evaluation.
5. Explain how computers can aid in evaluating strategies.

# NOTABLE QUOTES

Complicated controls do not work. They confuse. They misdirect attention from what is to be controlled to the mechanics and methodology of the control.

SEYMOUR TILLES

Although Plan A may be selected as the most realistic . . . the other major alternatives should not be forgotten. They may well serve as contingency plans.

DALE McCONKEY

Organizations are most vulnerable when they are at the peak of their success.

R. T. LENZ

As spans of control widen, computers will become even more necessary.

BRIAN DUMAINE

Strategy evaluation must make it as easy as possible for managers to revise their plans and reach quick agreement on the changes.

DALE McCONKEY

While strategy is a word that is usually associated with the future, its link to the past is no less central. Life is lived forward but understood backward. Managers may live strategy in the future, but they understand it through the past.

HENRY MINTZBERG

Unless strategy evaluation is performed seriously and systematically, and unless strategists are willing to act on the results, energy will be used up defending yesterday. No one will have the time, resources, or will to work on exploiting today, let alone to work on making tomorrow.

PETER DRUCKER

The best-formulated and -implemented strategies become obsolete as a firm's external and internal environments change. It is essential, therefore, that strategists systematically review, evaluate, and control the execution of strategies. This chapter presents a framework that can guide managers' efforts to evaluate strategic-management activities, to make sure they are working, and to make timely changes. Computer information systems being used to evaluate strategies are discussed. Guidelines are presented for formulating, implementing, and evaluating strategies.

## THE NATURE OF STRATEGY EVALUATION

The strategic-management process results in decisions that can have significant, long-lasting consequences. Erroneous strategic decisions can inflict severe penalties and can be exceedingly difficult, if not impossible, to reverse. Most strategists agree, therefore, that strategy evaluation is vital to an organization's well-being; timely evaluations can alert management to problems or potential problems before a situation becomes critical. Strategy evaluation includes three basic activities: (1) examining the underlying bases of a firm's strategy, (2) comparing expected results with actual results, and (3) taking corrective actions to ensure that performance conforms to plans. The strategy-evaluation stage of the strategic-management process is illustrated in Figure 9–1.

**FIGURE 9–1**

**A Comprehensive Strategic-Management Model**

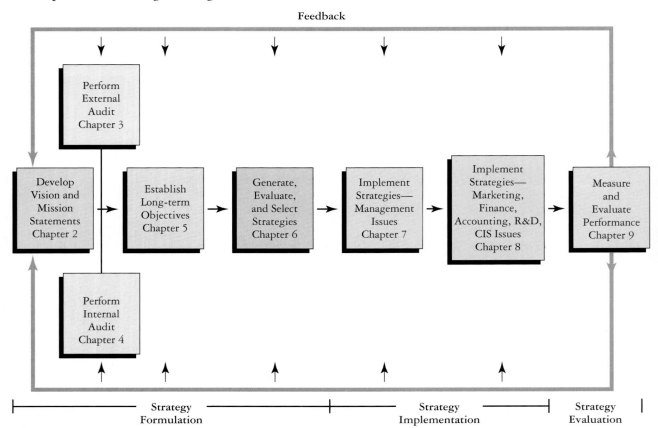

Adequate and timely feedback is the cornerstone of effective strategy evaluation. Strategy evaluation can be no better than the information on which it operates. Too much pressure from top managers may result in lower managers contriving numbers they think will be satisfactory.

Strategy evaluation can be a complex and sensitive undertaking. Too much emphasis on evaluating strategies may be expensive and counterproductive. No one likes to be evaluated too closely! The more managers attempt to evaluate the behavior of others, the less control they have. Yet, too little or no evaluation can create even worse problems. Strategy evaluation is essential to ensure that stated objectives are being achieved.

In many organizations, strategy evaluation is simply an appraisal of how well an organization has performed. Have the firm's assets increased? Has there been an increase in profitability? Have sales increased? Have productivity levels increased? Have profit margin, return on investment, and earnings-per-share ratios increased? Some firms argue that their strategy must have been correct if the answers to these types of questions are affirmative. Well, the strategy or strategies may have been correct, but this type of reasoning can be misleading, because strategy evaluation must have both a long-run and short-run focus. Strategies often do not affect short-term operating results until it is too late to make needed changes.

It is impossible to demonstrate conclusively that a particular strategy is optimal or even to guarantee that it will work. One can, however, evaluate it for critical flaws. Richard Rumelt offered four criteria that could be used to evaluate a strategy: consistency, consonance, feasibility, and advantage. Described in Table 9–1, *consonance* and *advantage* are mostly based on a firm's external assessment, whereas *consistency* and *feasibility* are largely based on an internal assessment.

Strategy evaluation is important because organizations face dynamic environments in which key external and internal factors often change quickly and dramatically. Success today is no guarantee for success tomorrow! An organization should never be lulled into complacency with success. Countless firms have thrived one year only to struggle for survival the following year. Organizational trouble can come swiftly, as further evidenced by the examples described in Table 9–2.

Strategy evaluation is becoming increasingly difficult with the passage of time, for many reasons. Domestic and world economies were more stable in years past, product life cycles were longer, product development cycles were longer, technological advancement was slower, change occurred less often, there were fewer competitors, foreign companies were weak, and there were more regulated industries. Other reasons why strategy evaluation is more difficult today include the following trends:

1. A dramatic increase in the environment's complexity
2. The increasing difficulty of predicting the future with accuracy
3. The increasing number of variables
4. The rapid rate of obsolescence of even the best plans
5. The increase in the number of both domestic and world events affecting organizations
6. The decreasing time span for which planning can be done with any degree of certainty[1]

A fundamental problem facing managers today is how to effectively control employees in light of modern organizational demands for greater flexibility, innovation, creativity, and initiative from employees.[2] How can managers today ensure that empowered employees acting in an entrepreneurial manner do not put the well-being of the business at risk? Recall that Kidder, Peabody, & Company lost $350 million when one of their traders allegedly booked fictitious profits; Sears, Roebuck and Company took a

TABLE 9-1    Rumelt's Criteria for Evaluating Strategies

### CONSISTENCY

A strategy should not present inconsistent goals and policies. Organizational conflict and interdepartmental bickering are often symptoms of a managerial disorder, but these problems may also be a sign of strategic inconsistency. There are three guidelines to help determine if organizational problems are due to inconsistencies in strategy:

- If managerial problems continue despite changes in personnel and if they tend to be issue-based rather than people-based, then strategies may be inconsistent.
- If success for one organizational department means, or is interpreted to mean, failure for another department, then strategies may be inconsistent.
- If policy problems and issues continue to be brought to the top for resolution, then strategies may be inconsistent.

### CONSONANCE

Consonance refers to the need for strategists to examine *sets of trends* as well as individual trends in evaluating strategies. A strategy must represent an adaptive response to the external environment and to the critical changes occurring within it. One difficulty in matching a firm's key internal and external factors in the formulation of strategy is that most trends are the result of interactions among other trends. For example, the day care explosion came about as a combined result of many trends that included a rise in the average level of education, increased inflation, and an increase in women in the workforce. Although single economic or demographic trends might appear steady for many years, there are waves of change going on at the interaction level.

### FEASIBILITY

A strategy must neither overtax available resources nor create unsolvable subproblems. The final broad test of strategy is its feasibility; that is, can the strategy be attempted within the physical, human, and financial resources of the enterprise? The financial resources of a business are the easiest to quantify and are normally the first limitation against which strategy is evaluated. It is sometimes forgotten, however, that innovative approaches to financing are often possible. Devices such as captive subsidiaries, sale-leaseback arrangements, and tying plant mortgages to long-term contracts have all been used effectively to help win key positions in suddenly expanding industries. A less quantifiable, but actually more rigid, limitation on strategic choice is that imposed by individual and organizational capabilities. In evaluating a strategy, it is important to examine whether an organization has demonstrated in the past that it possesses the abilities, competencies, skills, and talents needed to carry out a given strategy.

### ADVANTAGE

A strategy must provide for the creation and/or maintenance of a competitive advantage in a selected area of activity. Competitive advantages normally are the result of superiority in one of three areas: 1) resources, 2) skills, or 3) position. The idea that the positioning of one's resources can enhance their combined effectiveness is familiar to military theorists, chess players, and diplomats. Position can also play a crucial role in an organization's strategy. Once gained, a good position is defensible—meaning that it is so costly to capture that rivals are deterred from full-scale attacks. Positional advantage tends to be self-sustaining as long as the key internal and environmental factors that underlie it remain stable. This is why entrenched firms can be almost impossible to unseat, even if their raw skill levels are only average. Although not all positional advantages are associated with size, it is true that larger organizations tend to operate in markets and use procedures that turn their size into advantage, while smaller firms seek product/market positions that exploit other types of advantage. The principal characteristic of good position is that it permits the firm to obtain advantage from policies that would not similarly benefit rivals without the same position. Therefore, in evaluating strategy, organizations should examine the nature of positional advantages associated with a given strategy.

*Source:* Adapted from Richard Rumelt, "The Evaluation of Business Strategy," in W. F. Glueck, ed., *Business Policy and Strategic Management* (New York: McGraw-Hill, 1980): 359–367.

$60 million charge against earnings after admitting that its automobile service businesses were performing unnecessary repairs. The costs to companies such as these in terms of damaged reputations, fines, missed opportunities, and diversion of management's attention are enormous.

When empowered employees are held accountable for and pressured to achieve specific goals and are given wide latitude in their actions to achieve them, there can be dysfunctional behavior. For example, Nordstrom, the upscale fashion retailer known for

TABLE 9-2    **Examples of Organizational Trouble**

A few large Fortune 500 companies that experienced more than a 15 percent decline in revenues for 1999 are:

| | |
|---|---|
| Archer Daniels Midland | McDermott International |
| Schlumberger | Reynolds Metals |
| Baker Hughes | USX |
| Rowan | Deluxe |
| Transocean Sedco Forex | |

These large companies experienced more than a 50 percent decline in profits in 1999:

| | |
|---|---|
| St. Jude Medical | Reebok International |
| C.R. Bard | Limited |
| Albertson's | Brunswick |
| B.F. Goodrich | Deere |
| Ford Motor | Newell Rubbermaid |
| Goodyear Tire & Rubber | USX |
| DuPont | Autodesk |
| Eastman Chemical | Fluor |
| Perkinelmer | Norfolk Southern |
| Seagram | PG&E |
| Coca-Cola Enterprises | |

outstanding customer services, recently was subjected to lawsuits and fines when employees underreported hours worked in order to increase their sales per hour—the company's primary performance criterion. Nordstrom's customer service and earnings were enhanced until the misconduct was reported, at which time severe penalties were levied against the firm.

## The Process of Evaluating Strategies

Strategy evaluation is necessary for all sizes and kinds of organizations. Strategy evaluation should initiate managerial questioning of expectations and assumptions, should trigger a review of objectives and values, and should stimulate creativity in generating alternatives and formulating criteria of evaluation.[3] Regardless of the size of the organization, a certain amount of *management by wandering around* at all levels is essential to effective strategy evaluation. Strategy-evaluation activities should be performed on a continuing basis, rather than at the end of specified periods of time or just after problems occur. Waiting until the end of the year, for example, could result in a firm closing the barn door after the horses have already escaped.

Evaluating strategies on a continuous rather than a periodic basis allows benchmarks of progress to be established and more effectively monitored. Some strategies take years to implement; consequently, associated results may not become apparent for years. Successful strategists combine patience with a willingness to take corrective actions promptly when necessary. There always comes a time when corrective actions are needed in an organization! Centuries ago, a writer (perhaps Solomon) made the following observations about change:

> There is a time for everything,
> A time to be born and a time to die,
> A time to plant and a time to uproot,
> A time to kill and a time to heal,
> A time to tear down and a time to build,
> A time to weep and a time to laugh,
> A time to mourn and a time to dance,

A time to scatter stones and a time to gather them,

A time to embrace and a time to refrain,

A time to search and a time to give up,

A time to keep and a time to throw away,

A time to tear and a time to mend,

A time to be silent and a time to speak,

A time to love and a time to hate,

A time for war and a time for peace.[4]

Managers and employees of the firm should be continually aware of progress being made toward achieving the firm's objectives. As critical success factors change, organizational members should be involved in determining appropriate corrective actions. If assumptions and expectations deviate significantly from forecasts, then the firm should renew strategy-formulation activities, perhaps sooner than planned. In strategy evaluation, like strategy formulation and strategy implementation, people make the difference. Through involvement in the process of evaluating strategies, managers and employees become committed to keeping the firm moving steadily toward achieving objectives.

# A STRATEGY-EVALUATION FRAMEWORK

Table 9–3 summarizes strategy-evaluation activities in terms of key questions that should be addressed, alternative answers to those questions, and appropriate actions for an organization to take. Notice that corrective actions are almost always needed except when (1) external and internal factors have not significantly changed and (2) the firm is progressing satisfactorily toward achieving stated objectives. Relationships among strategy-evaluation activities are illustrated in Figure 9–2.

## Reviewing Bases of Strategy

As shown in Figure 9–2, *reviewing the underlying bases of an organization's strategy* could be approached by developing a revised EFE Matrix and IFE Matrix. A *revised IFE Matrix* should focus on changes in the organization's management, marketing, finance/accounting, production/operations, R&D, and computer information systems strengths and weaknesses.

TABLE 9–3     **A Strategy-Evaluation Assessment Matrix**

| HAVE MAJOR CHANGES OCCURRED IN THE FIRM'S INTERNAL STRATEGIC POSITION? | HAVE MAJOR CHANGES OCCURRED IN THE FIRMS'S EXTERNAL STRATEGIC POSITION? | HAS THE FIRM PROGRESSED SATISFACTORILY TOWARD ACHEIVING ITS STATED OBJECTIVES? | RESULT |
|---|---|---|---|
| No | No | No | Take corrective actions |
| Yes | Yes | Yes | Take corrective actions |
| Yes | Yes | No | Take corrective actions |
| Yes | No | Yes | Take corrective actions |
| Yes | No | No | Take corrective actions |
| No | Yes | Yes | Take corrective actions |
| No | Yes | No | Take corrective actions |
| No | No | Yes | Continue present strategic course |

**FIGURE 9–2**

**A Strategy-Evaluation Framework**

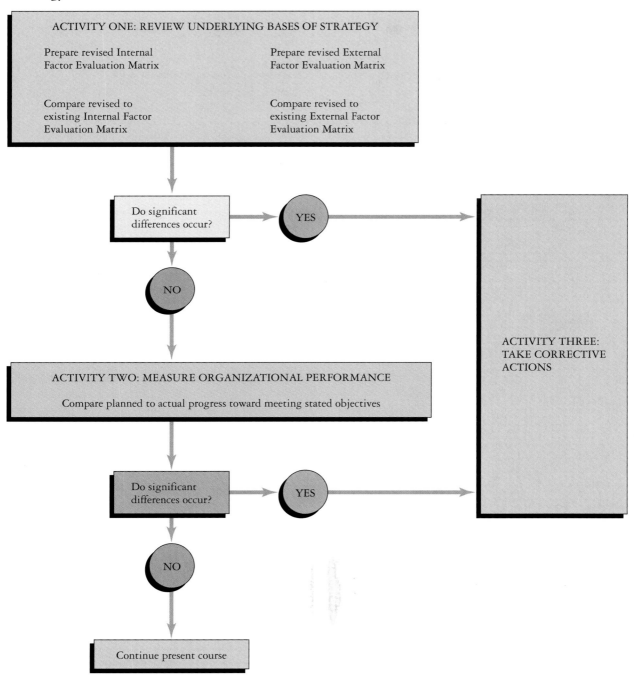

A *revised EFE Matrix* should indicate how effective a firm's strategies have been in response to key opportunities and threats. This analysis could also address such questions as the following:

1. How have competitors reacted to our strategies?
2. How have competitors' strategies changed?
3. Have major competitors' strengths and weaknesses changed?
4. Why are competitors making certain strategic changes?
5. Why are some competitors' strategies more successful than others?
6. How satisfied are our competitors with their present market positions and profitability?
7. How far can our major competitors be pushed before retaliating?
8. How could we more effectively cooperate with our competitors?

Numerous external and internal factors can prohibit firms from achieving long-term and annual objectives. Externally, actions by competitors, changes in demand, changes in technology, economic changes, demographic shifts, and governmental actions may prohibit objectives from being accomplished. Internally, ineffective strategies may have been chosen or implementation activities may have been poor. Objectives may have been too optimistic. Thus, failure to achieve objectives may not be the result of unsatisfactory work by managers and employees. All organizational members need to know this to encourage their support for strategy-evaluation activities. Organizations desperately need to know as soon as possible when their strategies are not effective. Sometimes managers and employees on the front line discover this well before strategists.

External opportunities and threats and internal strengths and weaknesses that represent the bases of current strategies should continually be monitored for change. It is not really a question of whether these factors will change, but rather when they will change and in what ways. Some key questions to address in evaluating strategies are given here.

1. Are our internal strengths still strengths?
2. Have we added other internal strengths? If so, what are they?
3. Are our internal weaknesses still weaknesses?
4. Do we now have other internal weaknesses? If so, what are they?
5. Are our external opportunities still opportunities?
6. Are there now other external opportunities? If so, what are they?
7. Are our external threats still threats?
8. Are there now other external threats? If so, what are they?
9. Are we vulnerable to a hostile takeover?

## Measuring Organizational Performance

Another important strategy-evaluation activity is *measuring organizational performance.* This activity includes comparing expected results to actual results, investigating deviations from plans, evaluating individual performance, and examining progress being made toward meeting stated objectives. Both long-term and annual objectives are commonly used in this process. Criteria for evaluating strategies should be measurable and easily verifiable. Criteria that predict results may be more important than those that reveal what already has happened. For example, rather than simply being informed that sales last quarter were 20 percent under what was expected, strategists need to know that sales next quarter may be 20 percent below standard unless some action is taken to counter the trend. Really effective control requires accurate forecasting.

Failure to make satisfactory progress toward accomplishing long-term or annual objectives signals a need for corrective actions. Many factors, such as unreasonable policies, unexpected turns in the economy, unreliable suppliers or distributors, or ineffective strategies, can result in unsatisfactory progress toward meeting objectives. Problems can result from ineffectiveness (not doing the right things) or inefficiency (doing the right things poorly).

Determining which objectives are most important in the evaluation of strategies can be difficult. Strategy evaluation is based on both quantitative and qualitative criteria. Selecting the exact set of criteria for evaluating strategies depends on a particular organization's size, industry, strategies, and management philosophy. An organization pursuing a retrenchment strategy, for example, could have an entirely different set of evaluative criteria from an organization pursuing a market-development strategy. Quantitative criteria commonly used to evaluate strategies are financial ratios, which strategists use to make three critical comparisons: (1) comparing the firm's performance over different time periods, (2) comparing the firm's performance to competitors', and (3) comparing the firm's performance to industry averages. Some key financial ratios that are particularly useful as criteria for strategy evaluation are as follows:

1. Return on investment
2. Return on equity
3. Profit margin
4. Market share
5. Debt to equity
6. Earnings per share
7. Sales growth
8. Asset growth

But there are some potential problems associated with using quantitative criteria for evaluating strategies. First, most quantitative criteria are geared to annual objectives rather than long-term objectives. Also, different accounting methods can provide different results on many quantitative criteria. Third, intuitive judgments are almost always involved in deriving quantitative criteria. For these and other reasons, qualitative criteria are also important in evaluating strategies. Human factors such as high absenteeism and turnover rates, poor production quality and quantity rates, or low employee satisfaction can be underlying causes of declining performance. Marketing, finance/accounting, R&D, or computer information systems factors can also cause financial problems. Seymour Tilles identified six qualitative questions that are useful in evaluating strategies:

1. Is the strategy internally consistent?
2. Is the strategy consistent with the environment?
3. Is the strategy appropriate in view of available resources?
4. Does the strategy involve an acceptable degree of risk?
5. Does the strategy have an appropriate time framework?
6. Is the strategy workable?[5]

Some additional key questions that reveal the need for qualitative or intuitive judgments in strategy evaluation are as follows:

1. How good is the firm's balance of investments between high-risk and low-risk projects?
2. How good is the firm's balance of investments between long-term and short-term projects?

3. How good is the firm's balance of investments between slow-growing markets and fast-growing markets?

4. How good is the firm's balance of investments among different divisions?

5. To what extent are the firm's alternative strategies socially responsible?

6. What are the relationships among the firm's key internal and external strategic factors?

7. How are major competitors likely to respond to particular strategies?

## Taking Corrective Actions

The final strategy-evaluation activity, *taking corrective actions,* requires making changes to reposition a firm competitively for the future. Examples of changes that may be needed are altering an organization's structure, replacing one or more key individuals, selling a division, or revising a business mission. Other changes could include establishing or revising objectives, devising new policies, issuing stock to raise capital, adding additional salespersons, allocating resources differently, or developing new performance incentives. Taking corrective actions does not necessarily mean that existing strategies will be abandoned or even that new strategies must be formulated.

> The probabilities and possibilities for incorrect or inappropriate actions increase geometrically with an arithmetic increase in personnel. Any person directing an overall undertaking must check on the actions of the participants as well as the results, that they have achieved. If either the actions or results do not comply with preconceived or planned achievements, then corrective actions are needed.[6]

No organization can survive as an island; no organization can escape change. Taking corrective actions is necessary to keep an organization on track toward achieving stated objectives. In his thought-provoking books, *Future Shock* and *The Third Wave,* Alvin Toffler argued that business environments are becoming so dynamic and complex that they threaten people and organizations with *future shock,* which occurs when the nature, types, and speed of changes overpower an individual's or organization's ability and capacity to adapt. Strategy evaluation enhances an organization's ability to adapt successfully to changing circumstances. Brown and Agnew referred to this notion as *corporate agility.*[7]

Taking corrective actions raises employees' and managers' anxieties. Research suggests that participation in strategy-evaluation activities is one of the best ways to overcome individuals' resistance to change. According to Erez and Kanfer, individuals accept change best when they have a cognitive understanding of the changes, a sense of control over the situation, and an awareness that necessary actions are going to be taken to implement the changes.[8]

Strategy evaluation can lead to strategy-formulation changes, strategy-implementation changes, both formulation and implementation changes, or no changes at all. Strategists cannot escape having to revise strategies and implementation approaches sooner or later. Hussey and Langham offered the following insight on taking corrective actions:

> Resistance to change is often emotionally based and not easily overcome by rational argument. Resistance may be based on such feelings as loss of status, implied criticism of present competence, fear of failure in the new situation, annoyance at not being consulted, lack of understanding of the need for change, or insecurity in changing from well-known and fixed methods. It is necessary, therefore, to overcome such resistance by creating situations of participation and full explanation when changes are envisaged.[9]

Corrective actions should place an organization in a better position to capitalize upon internal strengths; to take advantage of key external opportunities; to avoid,

# NATURAL ENVIRONMENT

## *How Much Carbon Dioxide Is Your Firm Emitting?*

Global warming isn't just a fear. It's a fact. Carbon dioxide is the major culprit and the most common air pollutant. Plants, of course, breathe in carbon dioxide, which is the reason why widespread cutting of trees and rain forests as well as clearing of land and harvesting kelp in the oceans are so detrimental to the natural environment. The following statistics reveal annual carbon-dioxide emissions for various countries worldwide. Note that the United States is guiltiest.

| | TOTAL TONS (MILLIONS) | TONS PER CAPITA |
|---|---|---|
| United States | 5,475 | 20.52 |
| China | 3,196 | 2.68 |
| Russia | 1,820 | 12.26 |
| Japan | 1,126 | 9.03 |
| India | 910 | 0.90 |
| Germany | 833 | 10.24 |
| United Kingdom | 539 | 9.29 |
| Ukraine | 437 | 8.48 |
| Canada | 433 | 14.83 |
| Italy | 411 | 7.19 |
| South Korea | 370 | 8.33 |
| Mexico | 359 | 3.93 |

Continents and countries' relative share of harmful $CO_2$ emissions is given below:

| | |
|---|---|
| Eastern Europe and former Soviet Union | 27% |
| United States | 22% |
| Western Europe | 17% |
| Other Asian countries | 13% |
| China | 11% |
| Latin America | 4% |
| Africa | 3% |

*Source:* Adapted from "Clear Skies Are Goal as Pollution Is Turning into a Commodity," *The Wall Street Journal* (October 3, 1997): A4.

reduce, or mitigate external threats; and to improve internal weaknesses. Corrective actions should have a proper time horizon and an appropriate amount of risk. They should be internally consistent and socially responsible. Perhaps most importantly, corrective actions strengthen an organization's competitive position in its basic industry. Continuous strategy evaluation keeps strategists close to the pulse of an organization and provides information needed for an effective strategic-management system. Carter Bayles described the benefits of strategy evaluation as follows:

> Evaluation activities may renew confidence in the current business strategy or point to the need for actions to correct some weaknesses, such as erosion of product superiority or technological edge. In many cases, the benefits of strategy evaluation are much more far-reaching, for the outcome of the process may be a fundamentally new strategy that will lead, even in a business that is already turning a respectable profit, to substantially increased earnings. It is this possibility that justifies strategy evaluation, for the payoff can be very large.[10]

# PUBLISHED SOURCES OF STRATEGY-EVALUATION INFORMATION

A number of publications are helpful in evaluating a firm's strategies. For example, *Fortune* annually identifies and evaluates the Fortune 1,000 (the largest manufacturers) and the Fortune 50 (the largest retailers, transportation companies, utilities, banks, insurance companies, and diversified financial corporations in the United States). *Fortune*

TABLE 9-4    *Fortune*'s 1999 Top Industry Performers

| INDUSTRY | COMPANY |
|---|---|
| Aerospace | United Technologies |
| Airlines | Southwest Airlines |
| Beverages | Coca-Cola |
| Chemicals | Du Pont |
| Commercial Banks | J.P. Morgan |
| Computers | Intel |
| Electronics | General Electric |
| Entertainment | Time Warner |
| Farm and Industrial Equipment | Caterpillar |
| Food | Nestlé |
| Food Services | McDonald's |
| Imaging and Office Equipment | Xerox |
| Insurance: Life, Health | Northwestern Mutual Life |
| Insurance: Property, Casualty | Berkshire Hathaway |
| Mail, Pkg. And Freight Delivery | United Parcel Service |
| Metals, Metal Products | Fortune Brands |
| Motor Vehicles | Ford Motor |
| Petroleum Refining | Exxon |
| Pharmaceuticals | Merck |
| Publishing | Tribune |
| Retailers: Specialists | Home Depot |
| Securities, Diversified Financials | American Express |
| Soap, Cosmetics | Procter & Gamble |
| Telecommunications | SBC Communications |

*Source:* Adapted from Jeremy Kahn, "The World's Most Admired Companies," *Fortune,* (October 11, 1999): 267–280.

ranks the best and worst performers on various factors such as return on investment, sales volume, and profitability. In its March issue each year, *Fortune* publishes its strategy evaluation research in an article titled "America's Most Admired Companies." Nine key attributes serve as evaluative criteria: quality of management; innovativeness; quality of products or services; long-term investment value; financial soundness; community and environmental responsibility; ability to attract, develop, and keep talented people; and use of corporate assets: international acumen. In October of each year, *Fortune* publishes additional strategy evaluation research in an article titled "The World's Most Admired Companies."[11] The Global Perspective reveals the best managed companies in Britain, France, Germany, and elsewhere in Europe. *Fortune's* 1999 evaluation in Table 9–4 reveals the firms considered best in their respective industries.

Another excellent evaluation of corporations in America, "The Annual Report on American Industry," is published annually in the January issue of *Forbes.* It provides a detailed and comprehensive evaluation of hundreds of American companies in many different industries. *Business Week, Industry Week,* and *Dun's Business Month* also periodically publish detailed evaluations of American businesses and industries. Although published sources of strategy-evaluation information focus primarily on large, publicly held businesses, the comparative ratios and related information are widely used to evaluate small businesses and privately owned firms as well.

## GLOBAL PERSPECTIVE

### *What Are the Best Companies in Britain, France, Germany, and Europe (other)?*

*Fortune* annually evaluates companies within particular countries. The evaluative criteria are management, products/services, innovativeness, long-term investment value, financial soundness, getting/keeping talent, social/environmental responsibility/wise use of assets, and international acumen. In 1999, the best companies in Britain, France, Germany, and Europe (other) based on these criteria are listed below in rank order:

| Company | Industry | Company | Industry |
|---|---|---|---|
| **Britain** | | **Germany** | |
| BP Amoco | Petroleum refining | Bertelsmann | Publishing |
| Royal Dutch/Shell Group | Petroleum refining | Mannesmann | Industrial & farm |
| Unilever | Food | | equipment |
| British Airways | Airlines | Lufthansa Group | Airlines |
| Reuters Group | Publishing | Bayer | Chemicals |
| | | DaimlerChrysler | Motor vehicles |
| **France** | | **Europe (Other)** | |
| L'Oreal | Soaps, cosmetics | Nestlé (Switzerland) | Food |
| AXA | Insurance: Life and health | ABB Asea Brown Boveri | Electronics |
| Groupe Danone | Food | (Switzerland) | |
| Total Fina | Petroleum refining | L.M. Ericsson (Sweden) | Electronics |
| Groupe Pinault-Printemps | Retailers: General | Sairgroup (Switzerland) | Airlines |
| | | Novartis (Switzerland) | Pharmaceuticals |

*Source:* Adapted from Jeremy Kahn, "The World's Most Admired Companies," *Fortune* (October 11, 1999): 272.

## CHARACTERISTICS OF AN EFFECTIVE EVALUATION SYSTEM

Strategy evaluation must meet several basic requirements to be effective. First, strategy-evaluation activities must be economical; too much information can be just as bad as too little information; and too many controls can do more harm than good. Strategy-evaluation activities also should be meaningful; they should specifically relate to a firm's objectives. They should provide managers with useful information about tasks over which they have control and influence. Strategy-evaluation activities should provide timely information; on occasion and in some areas, managers may need information daily. For example, when a firm has diversified by acquiring another firm, evaluative information may be needed frequently. However, in an R&D department, daily or even weekly evaluative information could be dysfunctional. Approximate information that is timely is generally more desirable as a basis for strategy evaluation than accurate information that does not depict the present. Frequent measurement and rapid reporting may frustrate control rather than give better control. The time dimension of control must coincide with the time span of the event being measured.

Strategy evaluation should be designed to provide a true picture of what is happening. For example, in a severe economic downturn, productivity and profitability ratios may drop alarmingly, although employees and managers are actually working harder. Strategy evaluations should portray this type of situation fairly. Information derived from the strategy-evaluation process should facilitate action and should be directed to those individuals in the organization who need to take action based on it. Managers commonly ignore evaluative reports that are provided for informational purposes only; not all managers need to receive all reports. Controls need to be action-oriented rather than information-oriented.

The strategy-evaluation process should not dominate decisions; it should foster mutual understanding, trust, and common sense! No department should fail to cooperate with another in evaluating strategies. Strategy evaluations should be simple, not too cumbersome, and not too restrictive. Complex strategy-evaluation systems often confuse people and accomplish little. The test of an effective evaluation system is its usefulness, not its complexity.

Large organizations require a more elaborate and detailed strategy-evaluation system because it is more difficult to coordinate efforts among different divisions and functional areas. Managers in small companies often communicate with each other and their employees daily and do not need extensive evaluative reporting systems. Familiarity with local environments usually makes gathering and evaluating information much easier for small organizations than for large businesses. But the key to an effective strategy-evaluation system may be the ability to convince participants that failure to accomplish certain objectives within a prescribed time is not necessarily a reflection of their performance.

There is no one ideal strategy-evaluation system. The unique characteristics of an organization, including its size, management style, purpose, problems, and strengths, can determine a strategy-evaluation and control system's final design. Robert Waterman offered the following observation about successful organizations' strategy-evaluation and control systems:

> Successful companies treat facts as friends and controls as liberating. Morgan Guaranty and Wells Fargo not only survive but thrive in the troubled waters of bank deregulation, because their strategy evaluation and control systems are sound, their risk is contained, and they know themselves and the competitive situation so well. Successful companies have a voracious hunger for facts. They see information where others see only data. They love comparisons, rankings, anything that removes decision-making from the realm of mere opinion. Successful companies maintain tight, accurate financial controls. Their people don't regard controls as an imposition of autocracy, but as the benign checks and balances that allow them to be creative and free.[12]

 ## CONTINGENCY PLANNING

A basic premise of good strategic management is that firms plan ways to deal with unfavorable and favorable events before they occur. Too many organizations prepare contingency plans just for unfavorable events; this is a mistake, because both minimizing threats and capitalizing on opportunities can improve a firm's competitive position.

Regardless of how carefully strategies are formulated, implemented, and evaluated, unforeseen events such as strikes, boycotts, natural disasters, arrival of foreign competitors, and government actions can make a strategy obsolete. To minimize the impact of potential threats, organizations should develop contingency plans as part of the strategy-evaluation process. *Contingency plans* can be defined as alternative plans that can be put into effect if certain key events do not occur as expected. Only high-priority areas require the insurance of contingency plans. Strategists cannot and should not try to cover all bases by planning for all possible contingencies. But in any case, contingency plans should be as simple as possible.

Some contingency plans commonly established by firms include the following:

1. If a major competitor withdraws from particular markets as intelligence reports indicate, what actions should our firm take?
2. If our sales objectives are not reached, what actions should our firm take to avoid profit losses?
3. If demand for our new product exceeds plans, what actions should our firm take to meet the higher demand?
4. If certain disasters occur—such as loss of computer capabilities; a hostile takeover attempt; loss of patent protection; or destruction of manufacturing facilities because of earthquakes, tornados, or hurricanes—what actions should our firm take?
5. If a new technological advancement makes our new product obsolete sooner than expected, what actions should our firm take?

Too many organizations discard alternative strategies not selected for implementation although the work devoted to analyzing these options would render valuable information. Alternative strategies not selected for implementation can serve as contingency plans in case the strategy or strategies selected do not work.

When strategy-evaluation activities reveal the need for a major change quickly, an appropriate contingency plan can be executed in a timely way. Contingency plans can promote a strategist's ability to respond quickly to key changes in the internal and external bases of an organization's current strategy. For example, if underlying assumptions about the economy turn out to be wrong and contingency plans are ready, then managers can make appropriate changes promptly.

In some cases, external or internal conditions present unexpected opportunities. When such opportunities occur, contingency plans could allow an organization to capitalize on them quickly. Linneman and Chandran reported that contingency planning gave users such as DuPont, Dow Chemical, Consolidated Foods, and Emerson Electric three major benefits: It permitted quick response to change, it prevented panic in crisis situations, and it made managers more adaptable by encouraging them to appreciate just how variable the future can be. They suggested that effective contingency planning involves a seven-step process as follows:

1. Identify both beneficial and unfavorable events that could possibly derail the strategy or strategies.
2. Specify trigger points. Calculate about when contingent events are likely to occur.
3. Assess the impact of each contingent event. Estimate the potential benefit or harm of each contingent event.
4. Develop contingency plans. Be sure that contingency plans are compatible with current strategy and are economically feasible.
5. Assess the counterimpact of each contingency plan. That is, estimate how much each contingency plan will capitalize on or cancel out its associated contingent event. Doing this will quantify the potential value of each contingency plan.
6. Determine early warning signals for key contingent events. Monitor the early warning signals.
7. For contingent events with reliable early warning signals, develop advance action plans to take advantage of the available lead time.[13]

AUDITING

A frequently used tool in strategy evaluation is the audit. *Auditing* is defined by the American Accounting Association (AAA) as "a systematic process of objectively obtaining and evaluating evidence regarding assertions about economic actions and events to ascertain the degree of correspondence between those assertions and established criteria, and communicating the results to interested users."[14] People who perform audits can be divided into three groups: independent auditors, government auditors, and internal auditors. Independent auditors basically are certified public accountants (CPAs) who provide their services to organizations for a fee; they examine the financial statements of an organization to determine whether they have been prepared according to generally accepted accounting principles (GAAP) and whether they fairly represent the activities of the firm. Independent auditors use a set of standards called generally accepted auditing standards (GAAS). Public accounting firms often have a consulting arm that provides strategy-evaluation services.

Two government agencies—the General Accounting Office (GAO) and the Internal Revenue Service (IRS)—employ government auditors responsible for making sure that organizations comply with federal laws, statutes, and policies. GAO and IRS auditors can audit any public or private organization. The third group of auditors are employees within an organization who are responsible for safeguarding company assets, for assessing the efficiency of company operations, and for ensuring that generally accepted business procedures are practiced. To evaluate the effectiveness of an organization's strategic-management system, internal auditors often seek answers to the questions posed in Table 9–5.

TABLE 9–5     **Key Strategy-Evaluation Questions**

1. Do you feel that the strategic-management system exists to provide service to you in your day-to-day work? How has it helped you in this respect?
2. Has the strategic-management system provided the service that you feel was promised at the start of its design and implementation? In which areas has it failed and exceeded, in your opinion?
3. Do you consider that the strategic-management system has been implemented with due regard to costs and benefits? Are there any areas in which you consider the costs to be excessive?
4. Do you feel comfortable using the system? Could more attention have been paid to matching the output of the system to your needs and, if so, in what areas?
5. Is the system flexible enough in your opinion? If not, where should changes be made?
6. Do you still keep a personal store of information in a notebook or elsewhere? If so, will you share that information with the system? Do you see any benefits in so doing?
7. Is the strategic-management system still evolving? Can you influence this evolution and, if not, why not?
8. Does the system provide timely, relevant, and accurate information? Are there any areas of deficiency?
9. Do you think that the strategic-management system makes too much use of complex procedures and models? Can you suggest areas in which less complicated techniques might be used to advantage?
10. Do you consider that there has been sufficient attention paid to the confidentiality and security of the information in the system? Can you suggest areas for improvement of these aspects of its operation?

*Source:* Adapted from K. J. Radford, *Information Systems for Strategic Decisions.* © 1978: 220–221. Adapted by permission of Prentice-Hall, Inc., Englewood Cliffs, New Jersey. Also, Lloyd Byars, *Strategic Management* (New York: Harper & Row, 1984): 237.

## The Environmental Audit

For an increasing number of firms, overseeing environmental affairs is no longer a technical function performed by specialists; it rather has become an important strategic-management concern. Product design, manufacturing, transportation, customer use, packaging, product disposal, and corporate rewards and sanctions should reflect environmental considerations. Firms that effectively manage environmental affairs are benefiting from constructive relations with employees, consumers, suppliers, and distributors.

Shimell emphasized the need for organizations to conduct environmental audits of their operations and to develop a Corporate Environmental Policy (CEP).[15] Shimell contended that an environmental audit should be as rigorous as a financial audit and should include training workshops in which staff can help design and implement the policy. The CEP should be budgeted and requisite funds allocated to ensure that it is not a public relations facade. A Statement of Environmental Policy should be published periodically to inform shareholders and the public of environmental actions taken by the firm.

Instituting an environmental audit can include moving environmental affairs from the staff side of the organization to the line side. Some firms are also introducing environmental criteria and objectives in their performance appraisal instruments and systems. Conoco, for example, ties compensation of all its top managers to environmental action plans. Occidental Chemical includes environmental responsibilities in all its job descriptions for positions.

## USING COMPUTERS TO EVALUATE STRATEGIES

When properly designed, installed, and operated, a computer network can efficiently acquire information promptly and accurately. Networks can allow diverse strategy-evaluation reports to be generated for—and responded to by—different levels and types of managers. For example, strategists will want reports concerned with whether the mission, objectives, and strategies of the enterprise are being achieved. Middle managers could require strategy-implementation information such as whether construction of a new facility is on schedule or a product's development is proceeding as expected. Lower-level managers could need evaluation reports that focus on operational concerns such as absenteeism and turnover rates, productivity rates, and the number and nature of grievances. As indicated in the E-Commerce Perspective, Virtual Close is a Cisco Systems software product that promises to revolutionize the strategy-evaluation process. Virtual Close allows strategists to close the financial books for the company on a daily or even hourly basis, rather than on a quarterly or annual basis.

Business today has become so competitive that strategists are being forced to extend planning horizons and to make decisions under greater degrees of uncertainty. As a result, more information has to be obtained and assimilated to formulate, implement, and evaluate strategic decisions. In any competitive situation, the side with the best intelligence (information) usually wins; computers enable managers to evaluate vast amounts of information quickly and accurately. Use of the Internet, World Wide Web, e-mail, and search engines can make the difference today between a firm that is up-to-date or out-of-date in the currentness of information the firm uses to make strategic decisions.

A limitation of computer-based systems to evaluate and monitor strategy execution is that personal values, attitudes, morals, preferences, politics, personalities, and emotions are not programmable. This limitation accents the need to view computers as tools, rather than as actual decision-making devices. Computers can significantly

**e·biz**

# E-COMMERCE PERSPECTIVE

## *Can Virtual Close Revolutionize Strategy Evaluation?*

Virtual Close is a Cisco Systems strategy-evaluation and control software product that allows a company to close its financial books with a one-hour notice rather than quarterly or annually. Virtual Close is an electronic infrastructure via intranet that almost instantly shares all information. Cisco CEO John Chambers says Virtual Close allows the firm to spot problems and opportunities quickly so the firm can be more proactive. Close recommends a firm empower employees by giving them access to the information, so decision making can be pushed lower down in the organization. Chambers says, "It's better to get a 10 percent increase in productivity from 20,000 employees than a 10 percent increase in productivity from the

CEO." Chambers emphasizes the importance of creating a corporate culture where risk taking and problem reporting is encouraged, where change is promoted and the firm does not punish people who report problems and take risks. Virtual Close allows managers to control everything from the supply of components all the way to shipment, while making the information available any hour to customers, employees, and top managers. Chambers says any firm not using Virtual Close for strategy evaluation within a few years will be greatly disadvantaged in competitive industries.

*Source:* Adapted from Darr Beiser, "Cisco Chief: Virtual Close to Big Hit," *USA Today* (October 12, 1999): 3B.

enhance the process of effectively integrating intuition and analysis in strategy evaluation. The General Accounting Office of the U.S. Government offered the following conclusions regarding the appropriate role of computers in strategy evaluation:

> The aim is to enhance and extend judgment. Computers should be looked upon not as a provider of solutions, but rather as a framework which permits science and judgment to be brought together and made explicit. It is the explicitness of this structure, the decision-maker's ability to probe, modify, and examine "What if?" alternatives, that is of value in extending judgment.[16]

## CONCLUSION

This chapter presents a strategy-evaluation framework that can facilitate accomplishment of annual and long-term objectives. Effective strategy evaluation allows an organization to capitalize on internal strengths as they develop, to exploit external opportunities as they emerge, to recognize and defend against threats, and to mitigate internal weaknesses before they become detrimental.

Strategists in successful organizations take the time to formulate, implement, and then evaluate strategies deliberately and systematically. Good strategists move their organization forward with purpose and direction, continually evaluating and improving the firm's external and internal strategic position. Strategy evaluation allows an organization to shape its own future rather than allowing it to be constantly shaped by remote forces that have little or no vested interest in the well-being of the enterprise.

Although not a guarantee for success, strategic management allows organizations to make effective long-term decisions, to execute those decisions efficiently, and to take corrective actions as needed to ensure success. Computer networks and the Internet help to coordinate strategic-management activities and to ensure that decisions are based on good information. A key to effective strategy evaluation and to successful strategic management is an integration of intuition and analysis.

A potentially fatal problem is the tendency for analytical and intuitive issues to polarize. This polarization leads to strategy evaluation that is dominated by either analysis or intuition, or to strategy evaluation that is discontinuous, with a lack of coordination among analytical and intuitive issues.[17]

Strategists in successful organizations realize that strategic management is first and foremost a people process. It is an excellent vehicle for fostering organizational communication. People are what make the difference in organizations.

The real key to effective strategic management is to accept the premise that the planning process is more important than the written plan, that the manager is continuously planning and does not stop planning when the written plan is finished. The written plan is only a snapshot as of the moment it is approved. If the manager is not planning on a continuous basis—planning, measuring, and revising—the written plan can become obsolete the day it is finished. This obsolescence becomes more of a certainty as the increasingly rapid rate of change makes the business environment more uncertain.[18]

We invite you to visit the DAVID page on the Prentice Hall Web site at **www.prenhall.com/davidsm** for this chapter's World Wide Web exercises.

## KEY TERMS AND CONCEPTS

Advantage  (p. 303)

Auditing  (p. 319)

Consistency  (p. 303)

Consonance  (p. 303)

Contingency Plans  (p. 314)

Corporate Agility  (p. 310)

Feasibility  (p. 303)

Future Shock  (p. 310)

Management by Wandering Around  (p. 305)

Measuring Organizational Performance  (p. 308)

Planning Process Audit  (p. 316)

Reviewing the Underlying Bases of an Organization's Strategy  (p. 306)

Revised EFE Matrix  (p. 308)

Revised IFE Matrix  (p. 306)

Taking Corrective Actions  (p. 310)

## ISSUES FOR REVIEW AND DISCUSSION

1. Why has strategy evaluation become so important in business today?

2. BellSouth Services is considering putting divisional EFE and IFE matrices online for continual updating. How would this affect strategy evaluation?

3. What types of quantitative and qualitative criteria do you think David Glass, CEO of Wal-Mart, uses to evaluate the company's strategy?

4. As owner of a local, independent supermarket, explain how you would evaluate the firm's strategy.

5. Under what conditions are corrective actions not required in the strategy-evaluation process?

6. Identify types of organizations that may need to evaluate strategy more frequently than others. Justify your choices.

7. As executive director of the state forestry commission, in what way and how frequently would you evaluate the organization's strategies?

8. Identify some key financial ratios that would be important in evaluating a bank's strategy.

9. As owner of a chain of hardware stores, describe how you would approach contingency planning.

10. Strategy evaluation allows an organization to take a proactive stance toward shaping its own future. Discuss the meaning of this statement.

# NOTES

1. DALE McCONKEY, "Planning in a Changing Environment," *Business Horizons* (September–October 1988): 64.
2. ROBERT SIMONS, "Control in an Age of Empowerment," *Harvard Business Review* (March–April 1995): 80.
3. DALE ZAND, "Reviewing the Policy Process," *California Management Review* 21, no. 1 (Fall 1978): 37.
4. ECCLES. 3: 1–8.
5. SEYMOUR TILLES, "How to Evaluate Corporate Strategy," *Harvard Business Review* 41 (July–August 1963): 111–21.
6. CLAUDE GEORGE, JR., *The History of Management Thought* (Englewood Cliffs, New Jersey: Prentice-Hall, 1968), 165–66.
7. JOHN BROWN and NEIL AGNEW, "Corporate Agility," *Business Horizons* 25, no. 2 (March–April 1982): 29.
8. M. EREZ and F. KANFER, "The Role of Goal Acceptance in Goal Setting and Task Performance," *Academy of Management Review* 8, no. 3 (July 1983): 457.
9. D. HUSSEY and M. LANGHAM, *Corporate Planning: The Human Factor* (Oxford, England: Pergamon Press, 1979): 138.
10. CARTER BAYLES, "Strategic Control: The President's Paradox," *Business Horizons* 20, no. 4 (August 1977): 18.
11. JEREMY KAHN, "The World's Most Admired Companies," *Fortune* (October 11, 1999): 267–80.
12. ROBERT WATERMAN, JR., "How the Best Get Better," *Business Week* (September 14, 1987): 105.
13. ROBERT LINNEMAN and RAJAN CHANDRAN, "Contingency Planning: A Key to Swift Managerial Action in the Uncertain Tomorrow," *Managerial Planning* 29, no. 4 (January–February 1981): 23–27.
14. American Accounting Association, *Report of Committee on Basic Auditing Concepts* (1971): 15–74.
15. PAMELA SHIMELL, "Corporate Environmental Policy in Practice," *Long Range Planning* 24, no. 3 (June 1991): 10.
16. GAO *Report* PAD—80–21, 17.
17. MICHAEL McGINNIS, "The Key to Strategic Planning: Integrating Analysis and Intuition," *Sloan Management Review* 26, no. 1 (Fall 1984): 49.
18. McCONKEY, 72.

# CURRENT READINGS

AVENI, RICHARD A. "Strategic Supremacy Through Disruption and Dominance." *Sloan Management* 40, no. 3 (Spring 1999): 127–136.
GUPTA, A. K., V. GOVINDARAJAN, and A. MALHOTRA. "Feedback-Seeking Behavior Within Multinational Corporations." *Strategic Management Journal* 20, no. 3 (March 1999): 205–222.
MURALIDHARAN, RAMAN and ROBERT D. HAMILTON III. "Aligning Multinational Control Systems." *International Journal of Strategic Management* 32, no. 3 (June 1999): 352–361.
WEAVER, GARY R., LINDA KLEBE TREVIÑO, and PHILIP L. COCHRAN. "Corporate Ethics Programs as Control Systems: Influences of Executive Commitment and Environmental Factors." *The Academy of Management Journal* 42, no. 1 (February 1999): 41–57.

# EXPERIENTIAL EXERCISES

## EXPERIENTIAL EXERCISE 9A ▶

### Preparing a Strategy-Evaluation Report for America Online (AOL)

### PURPOSE

This exercise can give you experience locating strategy-evaluation information. Use of the Internet coupled with published sources of information can significantly enhance the strategy-evaluation process. Performance information on competitors, for example, can help put into perspective a firm's own performance.

### INSTRUCTIONS

**Step 1**   Use *F & S Index of Corporations and Industries, Business Periodicals Index, The Wall Street Journal Index* and the Internet to locate strategy-evaluation information on AOL's competitors. Read five to ten articles written in the last six months that discuss the Internet Service Provider (ISP) industry.

**Step 2**   Summarize your research findings by preparing a strategy-evaluation report for your instructor. Include in your report a summary of AOL's strategies and performance in 1998 and a summary of your conclusions regarding the effectiveness of AOL strategies.

**Step 3**   Based on your analysis, do you feel AOL is pursuing effective strategies? What recommendations would you offer to AOL's chief executive officer?

## EXPERIENTIAL EXERCISE 9B ▶

### Evaluating My University's Strategies

### PURPOSE

An important part of evaluating strategies is determining the nature and extent of changes in an organization's external opportunities/threats and internal strengths/weaknesses. Changes in these underlying critical success factors can indicate a need to change or modify the firm's strategies.

### INSTRUCTIONS

As a class, discuss positive and negative changes in your university's external and internal factors during your college career. Begin by listing on the board new or emerging opportunities and threats. Then identify strengths and weaknesses that have changed significantly during your college career. In light of the external and internal changes identified, discuss whether your university's strategies need modifying. Are there any new strategies that you would recommend? Make a list to recommend to your department chair, dean, or chancellor.

## EXPERIENTIAL EXERCISE 9C ▶

### Who Prepares an Environmental Audit?

### PURPOSE

The purpose of this activity is to determine the nature and prevalence of environmental audits among companies in your state.

### INSTRUCTIONS

Contact by phone at least five different plant managers or owners of large businesses in your area. Seek answers to the questions listed below. Present your findings in a written report to your instructor.

1. Does your company conduct an environmental audit? If yes, please describe the nature and scope of the audit.

2. Are environmental criteria included in the performance evaluation of managers? If yes, please specify the criteria.

3. Are environmental affairs more a technical function or a management function in your company?

4. Does your firm offer any environmental workshops for employees? If yes, please describe them.

# NAME INDEX

# SUBJECT INDEX

*Note:* Page numbers followed by *f* indicate figures; page numbers followed by *t* indicate tables.

# COMPANY INDEX

*Note:* Page numbers followed by *t* indicate tables.

# STRATEGIC
# MANAGEMENT
## CASES

# E*TRADE, INC.—2000

Phillip Lynn
Francis Marion University

**EGRP**

www.etrade.com

Why does it cost $140.00 to trade 100 shares of stock through a broker when those shares can be traded for $19.95 through E*Trade? E*Trade offers such services as free stock quotes, free market reports and even free checking. What does all this mean for the securities industry? The days of the $100,000 broker are coming to an end because customers perceive that commissions are too high, brokers are overpaid, and information is available at no charge.

E*Trade is an online securities broker that specializes in efficient and economical trading by using the Internet and touch-tone dialing. E*Trade offers fast trade execution, good customer service, reasonably priced commissions and a rich and detailed Web site. E*Trade also offers an extensive line of trading tools and services that allows the most inexperienced online trader to participate with confidence. E*Trade can be reached online at www.etrade.com or phoned at 1-800-786-2575.

E*Trade is located in Palo Alto, California, in the Silicon Valley among many other Internet start-ups and high-tech firms. Thanks to continuous improvements to tools and services, E*trade is leading the way in the online securities industry with over one million active accounts. E*Trade's total customer assets have grown to $30 billion, representing 14 percent of the total market share, placing E*Trade a distant second to Charles Schwab.

E*Trade was the first online Internet company to actually make money, but it lost $54,438,000 in 1999 with a $13,200,000 loss in the first quarter of fiscal 1999. E*Trade accounts more than doubled in 1998 to 676,000 and increased 78 percent in value during the first half of 1999. By the year 2003, close to one million E*Trade households worldwide will manage more than three trillion in customer assets in over 21 million active accounts.

E*Trade now offers direct international trades to exchanges around the world during trading hours and, for some, after-hours trading. Australians on their lunch break can purchase stock listed on the Tokyo Stock Exchange; a fisherman off the coast of Costa Rica can short South African mining companies; a herdsman in Botswana can hedge against forecastable conditions with El Niño by purchasing call options on European grain stocks. E*Trade continues aggressive marketing in the United States by actively promoting its Web site with what looks like the Oscar-Meyer Wienermobile. With day trading and transaction volumes at an all-time high, coupled with younger affluent traders, E*Trade plans to get its share of the rapidly growing market.

## HISTORY

E*Trade was founded in 1982 by visionary and physician Bill Porter as a service bureau to Fidelity, Charles Schwab, and Quick & Riley. On July 11, 1983, the first transaction using E*Trade occurred. Today, E*Trade customers are found in all 50 U.S. states and, worldwide, from Aruba to Zambia. E*Trade started out providing online quotes and trading services to Fidelity, Charles Schwab, and Quick & Riley. Bill Porter pondered why, as an individual investor, he had to pay hundreds of dollars to a broker in order to place a transaction. He anticipated the day that everyone in the world would own a personal computer and be able to invest with E*Trade online via the Internet. Porter's vision became a reality in 1992 when E*Trade began to offer online investing through such carriers as America Online and CompuServe. Only in 1996, following the introduction of www.etrade.com, did Porter's dream become reality with the birth of direct online trading.

In 1996, Bill Porter appointed Christos Cotsakos CEO and President of E*Trade. Cotsakos brought 20 years of senior management experience from Federal Express and A. C. Nielson. E*Trade, in 1999, was named the best online investing site in the world by Lafferty Information and Research Group for the second consecutive year. As of September 1999, E*Trade ranked first overall in the Gomez Advisors Internet Brokers Scorecard 4 out of the past 5 quarters. This scorecard is based on a rigorous review of the nation's top 53 online brokerages across 10 major categories and 150 different criteria. E*Trade's common stock is publicly traded on the NASDAQ National Market under the ticker EGRP.

## EXTERNAL FACTORS

E*Trade and the investment banking and brokerage industry have experienced increasing demand and volatility since their inception. Trading volumes are at an all-time high with the stock market closing daily with well over 10,000 trades. Increasing trade volumes lead to higher commissions, revenues, and profits for online securities industry firms, such as E*Trade, Ameritrade, TD Waterhouse, and Fidelity.

As indicated in Exhibit 1, E*Trade's major competitors are Charles Schwab, TD Waterhouse, Datek, Fidelity, Ameritrade, and DJL Direct.

### Charles Schwab

Based in San Francisco, Charles Schwab is the largest broker in the industry as indicated in Exhibit 1. Charles Schwab offers securities brokerage and related financial services. For the first nine months of 1999, Charles Schwab had a net income of $418.4 million and $2.82 billion in total revenues.

EXHIBIT 1    Industry Comparison of Major Competitors in 1998

| Broker | Market Share | Customer Accts. | Client Assets | Revenues (in thousands) | Net Income (in thousands) |
|---|---|---|---|---|---|
| Charles Schwab | 27.50% | 2,500,000 | $215,000,000,000 | $43,139,000 | $348,642 |
| E*Trade | 12.90 | 909,000 | 25,000,000,000 | 335,575 | 2,973 |
| TD Waterhouse | 11.60 | 615,000 | 32,000,000,000 | 484,133 | 76,421 |
| Datek | 10.00 | 205,000 | 5,000,000,000 | N/A | N/A |
| Fidelity | 9.30 | 2,300,000 | 152,000,000,000 | N/A | N/A |
| Ameritrade | 8.40 | 428,000 | 2,400,000,000 | 15,534,909 | 210,438 |
| DLJ Direct | 3.60 | 580,000 | 10,000,000,000 | 540,704 | 370,800 |
| Others | 21.40 | 552,000 | 32,000,000,000 | — | — |

*Source:* "Industry report," *Market Guide;* www.marketguide.com and individual companies annual reports and 10Ks, 1998; www.freeedgar.com
* Fidelity and Datek are privately held entities.

## TD Waterhouse

Based in New York, TD Waterhouse has operations in the United States, Canada, Australia, United Kingdom, and Hong Kong. TD Waterhouse is a provider of online investing services and related financial products to individual retail investors. For the first nine months of 1999, total revenues rose 59 percent to $707 million while net income totaled $76.4 million, up 24 percent from the same period in 1998.

## Ameritrade

Located in Omaha, Nebraska, Ameritrade provides discounted brokerage services and related financial services. Ameritrade offers online trading through the Internet or touch-tone telephone along with market data and research. For the first nine months of 1999, Ameritrade increased revenues 95 percent to $226 million and profits of $20.7 million. Ameritrade has increased its profit margin by decreasing advertising and promotional expenditures by 14 percent and increasing securities transactions and interest revenues.

## DLJ Direct

Donaldson, Lufkin, and Jenrette's (DLJ Direct) online brokerage unit is located in New York. The discount brokerage firm offers online trading via the Internet and touch-tone phone with information and research capabilities. For the first three months of 1999, profits and revenues totaled $7.2 million and $47.2 million, respectively. Revenues increased 96 percent after a loss of $2.3 million from the prior year. Revenues and profits grew through an increase in customer trading.

## INDUSTRY OUTLOOK

Due to the increased Internet usage per household (170 million people worldwide) and increased accessibility and affordability of Internet providers, online trading is expected to increase in the future. Favorable demographic trends also play a major role in the increase of investors. The average online trader is thirty-nine years old as opposed to the average age of brick-and-mortar brokerage trader (fifty-nine years). Brick-and-mortar brokers such as Merrill Lynch, Schwab, and Lehman Brothers profit from the fact that only 20 percent of the total investing population is currently online. Social trends and the growing enthusiasm for online trading are expected to boost revenues for the online broker. Today, there are more affluent and younger investors than ever willing to trade online.

Recent negative publicity about system responsiveness and crashes has plagued the online sector. Most online brokers have established alliances with such providers as AOL, AT&T, CompuServe, Intuit, Microsoft, Prodigy, USA Today, YAHOO and Smartnet, to avoid steep increases in charges. Economic fluctuations, such as another recession, could significantly hamper the industry.

## INTERNAL CONDITIONS

*Key Executives*

| | |
|---|---|
| Christos M. Cotsakos | CEO and president |
| Judy Balint | CEO and president |
| Debra Chrapaty | Senior vice president and CIO |
| Leonard C. Purkis | Executive vice president and CFO |

EXHIBIT 2    E*Trade Five-Year Summary of Revenues and Profits

| Y/E Sept. 31 | Revenues (in thousands) | Net Income (in thousands) |
|---|---|---|
| 1999 | $621,402 | $(54,438) |
| 1998 | 335,756 | 2,972 |
| 1997 | 234,128 | 19,913 |
| 1996 | 141,803 | 4,166 |
| 1995 | 108,961 | 7,333 |

*Source:* E*Trade Group Inc., Annual Report and 10K, 1995–1999; www.freeedgar.com.

As indicated in Exhibit 2, E*Trade's revenues increased 126 percent in 1999, aided by a significant increase in active accounts and a 168 percent increase in customer transactions in the second quarter of 1999. Although online growth seems to be slowing down, E*Trade enjoys the first-mover advantage of being the brand name for online investing by offering a rich array of products and services. By offering so many different user-friendly tools, E*Trade has become the "learning center" for new online investors.

E*Trade is implementing an aggressive marketing effort for the year 1999: Advertising expenditures now exceed 47 percent of sales or $292,058,000. In comparison, Procter & Gamble spends about 27 percent of sales on marketing. These expenses are a major reason why E*Trade posted a $132,402 million operating loss and a $54,438 million net loss of income in 1999 as indicated in Exhibit 2. It is expected that E*Trade will take yet another, not as significant, loss in 2000. As indicated by Exhibit 1, E*Trade's advertising efforts have paid off by allowing them 12.90 percent of market share overall behind Charles Schwab (27.50 percent). As E*Trade invests billions in the years to come on ongoing improvements in products and services, along with acquiring an online bank and financial news site, additional value will be brought to the customer.

As indicated in Exhibit 1, except for Charles Schwab, E*Trade has the greatest market share and customer accounts followed by TD Waterhouse, Datek, Fidelity, Ameritrade and DLJ Direct. Charles Schwab is not a part of this group because Schwab is a brick-and-mortar discount broker rather than an exclusive online broker. Charles Schwab is, however, discussed in this case in order to represent the investment sector as a whole. Charles Schwab offers walk-in visits with agents twice a year as a free service for their online clients, and total revenues from their online segment are approximately 30 percent of gross revenues. As indicated in Exhibit 1, E*Trade has less client assets than several of its competitors even though it obtain the greatest market share of all exclusive online securities brokers. Client assets are overstated for Ameritrade and DLJ Direct because security trades are not their only source of revenue. Fidelity and TD Waterhouse consist of client accounts ranging from insurance policies to securities, thereby inflating their client assets. E*Trade obtained the lowest revenues of $335 million in the industry for exclusively online brokers as of year-end 1998, according to Exhibit 1. Revenues are derived from commissions charged per transaction based on the first 1,000 shares traded. As indicated by Exhibit 3, E*Trade's commissions per trade are $14.95 per 1,000 shares, lower than those of DLJ Direct and Charles Schwab. Ameritrade offers the lowest commissions of $8.00 per 1,000 shares traded and obtained the highest revenues of $15,534 million as of year-end 1998. Datek offers $9.99 per trade but, because it is privately held, like Fidelity, financial information is not available to the public. Low transaction

EXHIBIT 3    Commission Comparison of Leading Brokerage Firms

| Company | Commission per 1,000 Shares 1999 |
| --- | --- |
| Ameritrade | $ 8.00 |
| Datek | 9.99 |
| E*Trade | 14.95 |
| DLJ Direct | 20.00 |
| Charles Schwab | 29.95 |

*Source:* "Investment Brokerage Industry Report," *Market Guide;* www.marketguide.com

costs are the primary attraction for current online investors. Second to low commission costs is technical quality (minimal interruptions and 95 percent–100 percent availability) of the Web page. Low commission costs, coupled with the expensive ongoing technical improvements, lead to declining profit margins for E*Trade, Ameritrade, DLJ Direct, and the others.

## CONCLUSION

E*Trade intends to keep its focus domestic and in Japan, Korea, Finland, Sweden, Mexico, and Canada. The online securities industry is rapidly becoming a commodity, and competition is at its height. E*Trade is exploring market penetration and product development as optimal strategies to maintain its position in the market. E*Trade is pursuing all advertising media: business journals, sporting events, television commercials, and online Web sites, in order to attract every investor not yet online. E*Trade plans an advertising and marketing campaign on its own Web site as well as other online sites, direct one-on-one marketing, public relations and co-marketing programs. E*trade's advertising focus is on building awareness of the company and its products, and services. By implementing this aggressive marketing campaign, E*Trade wants to establish itself with the individual investor as a better way of handling security transactions, accessing financial and market data, and managing portfolios.

E*Trade's strategy to obtain its position in the market should be supported by the following activities: E*Trade should increase expenditures on advertising and marketing to 51 percent of sales or $171,143,250, based on 1998 gross revenues. It should consider television commercials, sporting-event sponsorships, business publications, and newspapers. E*Trade needs to target its advertising to everyone who is eighteen and older. The largest target markets consist of baby boomers and senior citizens, who represent the 80 percent of investors not yet online. E*Trade should continue its product development and continuous improvements to its customer and technical services. E*Trade should structure funding by issuing stock to raise the $150 million needed for future improvements and advancements. Although E*Trade has not yet incurred any debt as of year-end 1999, the issuance of additional stock will be beneficial. Additional issuance of stock will increase earnings per share, thereby increasing the attractiveness of their stock to investors, while increasing the net worth of the company. The sum of $150 million should be sufficient for advancements and improvements needed to attract both the investors not yet online and investors already online.

## REFERENCES

AMERITRADE, INC., *Annual Report and 10K* (1998); www.freeedgar.com

CHARLES SCHWAB, INC., *Annual Report and 10K* (1998); www.freeedgar.com

DATEK, INC., *Annual Report and 10K* (1998); www.freeedgar.com

DLJ DIRECT, INC., *Annual Report and 10K* (1998); www.freeedgar.com

E*TRADE GROUP, INC., *Annual Report and 10K* (1995–1999); www.freeedgar.com

FIDELITY, INC., *Annual Report and 10K* (1998); www.freeedgar.com

"INVESTMENT BANKING AND BROKERAGE INDUSTRY." *Standard and Poor's Industry Survey* (September 25, 1999).

"INVESTMENT BROKERAGE INDUSTRY REPORT", *Market Guide;* www.marketguide.com

TD WATERHOUSE, INC., *Annual Report and 10K* (1998); www.freeedgar.com

EXHIBIT 4     E*Trade's Organizational Chart

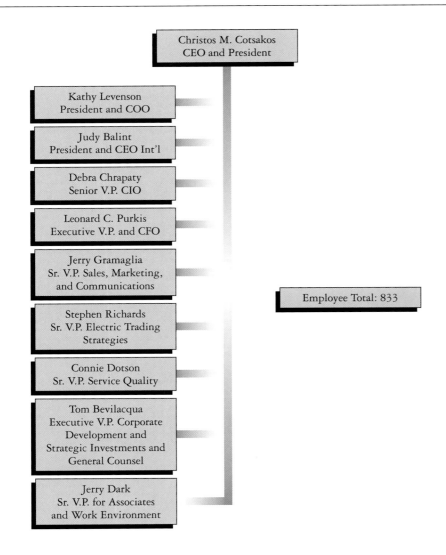

EXHIBIT 5     **E\*Trade**

**Consolidated Income Statement (in thousands)**

|  | 1999 | 1998 | 1997 |
|---|---|---|---|
| Revenues: | | | |
| Transaction revenues | $355,830 | $162,097 | $109,659 |
| Global and institutional | 110,959 | 95,829 | 80,128 |
| Interest—net of interest expense (A) | 122,308 | 56,701 | 25,739 |
| Other | 32,305 | 21,129 | 18,602 |
| Net revenues | 621,402 | 335,756 | 234,128 |
| Cost of services | 283,869 | 138,942 | 95,933 |
| Operating expenses: | | | |
| Selling and marketing | 301,658 | 117,283 | 67,281 |
| Technology development | 76,878 | 33,699 | 13,547 |
| General and administrative | 85,095 | 41,752 | 27,098 |
| Merger-related expenses | 6,304 | 1,167 | — |
| Total operating expenses | 469,935 | 193,901 | 107,926 |
| Total cost of services and operating expenses | 753,804 | 332,843 | 203,859 |
| Operating income (loss) | (132,402) | 2,913 | 30,269 |
| Nonoperating income (expense): | | | |
| Gain on sale of investments | 49,957 | — | — |
| Equity in losses of investments | (9,103) | — | — |
| Gain (loss) on foreign exchange | 12 | (762) | (946) |
| Total nonoperating income (expense) | 40,866 | (762) | (946) |
| Pre-tax income (loss) | (91,536) | 2,151 | 29,323 |
| Income tax expense (benefit) | (37,098) | 224 | 10,130 |
| Net income (loss) | (54,438) | 1,927 | 19,193 |
| Preferred stock dividends | 222 | 240 | 240 |
| Income (loss) applicable to common stock | $ (54,660) | $ 1,687 | $ 18,953 |
| Income (loss) per share: | | | |
| Basic | $ (0.23) | $ 0.01 | $ 0.14 |
| Diluted | $ (0.23) | $ 0.01 | $ 0.13 |
| Shares used in computation of income (loss) per share: | | | |
| Basic | 235,926 | 173,906 | 133,572 |
| Diluted | 235,926 | 185,479 | 147,833 |

EXHIBIT 6    E*Trade Group, Inc. and Subsidiaries
Consolidated Balance Sheets
(in thousands, except share amounts)

| | September 30, 1999 | September 30, 1998 |
|---|---|---|
| **Assets** | | |
| Current assets: | | |
| Cash and equivalents | $ 85,734 | $ 47,776 |
| Cash and investments required to be segregated under federal or other regulations | 103,500 | 5,000 |
| Investment securities | 189,145 | 502,534 |
| Brokerage receivables—net | 2,912,581 | 1,365,247 |
| Other assets | 41,987 | 24,287 |
| Total current assets | 3,332,947 | 1,944,844 |
| Property and equipment—net | 155,785 | 50,555 |
| Investments | 424,293 | 59,276 |
| Related party receivable | — | 3,719 |
| Other assets | 13,955 | 7,892 |
| Total assets | $3,926,980 | $2,066,286 |
| **Liabilities and Shareowners' Equity** | | |
| Liabilities: | | |
| Brokerage payables | $2,824,212 | $1,244,513 |
| Deferred income taxes | 23,256 | 704 |
| Accounts payable, accrued and other liabilities | 165,845 | 83,659 |
| Total liabilities | 3,013,313 | 1,328,876 |
| Mandatorily redeemable preferred securities | — | 3,000 |
| Commitments and contingencies (Notes 13, 14, 15 and 19) | | |
| Shareowners' equity: | | |
| Common stock, $.01 par: shares authorized, 600,000,000; shares issued and outstanding: 1999, 239,822, 663; 1998, 231,270,400 | 2,398 | 2,313 |
| Additional paid-in capital | 763,958 | 685,553 |
| Retained earnings (deficit) | (20,874) | 33,786 |
| Accumulated other comprehensive income | 168,185 | 12,758 |
| Total shareowners' equity | 913,667 | 734,410 |
| Total liabilities and shareowners' equity | $3,926,980 | $2,066,286 |

# eBAY INC.—2000

**Stephen M. Giordano**
**Francis Marion University**

## eBAY

www.ebay.com

The thrill of the chase, the art of the deal—Americans are always looking for a bargain, and eBay gives them the opportunity to test their skills and resolve at striking the best deal possible. From Beanie Babies to coins and other collectibles, sports memorabilia, and even adult items, eBay allows anyone to shop and to bargain for over one million items in over one thousand categories. eBay is currently the world's largest person-to-person trading community on the Internet, based on the number of items for sale, the number of registered users, and the minutes of usage logged each month on the eBay site.

eBay has established an Internet-based community of buyers and sellers that get together in an auction format to buy and sell items ranging from antiques to electronics, collectibles, and many types of memorabilia. Because the service is completely automated, it operates 24 hours a day, seven days a week.

## HISTORY

eBay was started in September 1995 by Pierre Omidyar. Omidyar, born in France and raised in the United States, moved to the West Coast after graduating from college with a degree in computer programming. The business was started in his apartment so that his girlfriend, an avid dispenser collector, could contact others who shared her interest in Pez dispensers. She had previously complained that it was difficult to locate others to buy from and to sell to. Omidyar's creation allowed her and other individuals to use the Internet for their trading needs.

In the beginning, the original site, called "Auction Web," made no promises or guarantees. Individuals logged on, bid for items, and made transactions. At that time there were no fees, no registrations, no security, few items, and little business until Mr. Omidyar made one very positive marketing decision. He listed his trading site on the National Center for Supercomputing Applications' "What's Cool" list, and the rest is history. After the listing, business started to pick up, and in March 1996 the business turned a profit.

The business continued to grow, and in 1998 the company, now renamed eBay, went public. Revenues continue to grow, and today eBay is the largest Internet auction site with revenues growing from $47 million in 1998 to $224 million in 1999.

## HOW IT WORKS

Anyone can visit eBay and browse through the items listed for sale. However, if you wish to bid on items or list items for sale, you must register. The registration process is simple and quick, it takes less then five minutes, and once registered, you can immediately bid or list items for sale. All buyers and sellers must be eighteen years old to bid or list items. The registration form is honor system based; it asks if the registrant is eighteen or older, but there seems to be no way for eBay to verify if the registrant is the legal age.

Once registered, bidders can immediately search for specific items by category and subcategory and click on individual items for detailed descriptions. The entire database can be queried by entering keywords that describe a desired item. eBay's search engine will locate all relevant items for sale and link the bidder to detailed descriptions of them. Each auction has a unique identifier that allows bidders to easily locate specific items. In addition, bidders can search and find individual sellers who have a particular history of items for sale.

eBay also provides highlights that alert bidders to certain types of auctions. For example, auctions that have started within the past 24 hours are highlighted with "New Today," auctions that are ending on that day are highlighted with "Ending Today," and those ending within three hours are highlighted under "Going Going Gone."

When the bidding on a particular auction has ended, eBay will determine if a bid exceeds the minimum asking price and the reserve price if a reserve has been set. A seller can set a reserve price, the minimum that the seller will accept, which is usually higher than the minimum asking price. eBay will then notify both buyer and seller via e-mail, and the buyer and seller consummate the transaction independently of eBay. The buyer and seller agree upon and arrange for shipment and payment. eBay has no power to force the buyer and seller to complete the transaction, but it can ban the offending party from trading on eBay in the future.

Today eBay's core business model remains person-to-person selling, and most revenue is generated in this method.

## REVENUE

There is no charge for buyers to shop on eBay and to bid on items. Bidding is free, and revenue is derived from fees sellers are charged for listing and selling items. Sellers pay a small placement fee to list items for sale, and placement fee rates are as follows:

| Fee | Auction Starting Price |
| --- | --- |
| $ .25 | Less than $10.00 |
| .50 | $10.00 to $24.99 |
| 1.00 | $25.00 to $49.99 |
| 2.00 | $50.00 and greater |

Additional revenue from listings can come in a variety of ways. eBay offers sellers many ways to enhance listings to attract bidders, such as by paying additional incremental fees for various highlights. Available highlights and fee schedule are as follows:

| Fee | Highlight |
| --- | --- |
| $ .25 | Place photos in the Gallery section |
| 1.00 | Place seasonal icons next to listings (Hearts on Valentine's Day) |
| 2.00 | Use a boldface font for heading |
| 14.95 | Choose "category-featured auction," featured within an eBay category |
| 19.95 | Feature the item in the Gallery section |
| 99.95 | Choose a "featured auction" that allows the item to be rotated on the eBay homepage |

Finally, the seller pays eBay a commission if the items are sold. At the time of notification of a winning bid, eBay charges the seller a fee based on the purchase price.

| *Success Fee* | *Purchase Price* |
|---------------|------------------|
| 5% | First $25.00 of the purchase price |
| 2.5 | Portion of the purchase price from $25.01 to $1,000.00 |
| 1.25 | Portion of the purchase price over $1000.00 |

In the event that buyer and seller cannot complete the transaction, the seller can notify eBay to credit the fee. All invoices for placement fees, highlight fees, and selling fees are sent to sellers via e-mail on a monthly basis. Many sellers maintain a credit with eBay, and the account is charged shortly after an invoice is sent. At no time does eBay take possession of the merchandise or hold the receivable for the item.

Unlike other Internet firms, the company does not receive revenue from advertisements. eBay sells no ad space on its site.

## THE eBAY COMMUNITY

In providing a place for trading of various items, eBay attempts to foster a sense of community among its users. CEO and President Meg Whitman has stated that eBay began with commerce but quickly grew into a very large community. eBay users believe that this sense of community is what separates it from other Internet auction and retail sites, and eBay invests heavily in the programs that make users feel that their transactions and information are safe from Internet thieves and fraudulent users.

One method used to establish the reputations of users is eBay's Feedback Forum, which encourages users to record comments, both favorable and unfavorable, about their trading partners. Comments can be about specific trading transactions or general in nature, and the Forum allows comments to be differentiated between transaction-specific comments and general feedback. All this feedback information is recorded and creates in a feedback rating for a specific person. Naturally, too many negative comments will likely cause users to avoid transactions with the individual in question.

eBay users with favorable reputations will have a star next to their user identification. This star is color coded and indicates the amount of positive versus negative feedback that the user has received. Users may review a person's feedback profile prior to doing business with that person.

The Feedback Forum is a self-regulating system: The users police themselves. However, some users may be tempted to manipulate the system in order to discredit other users or enhance their own reputations. eBay has several policies in place to prevent this, and the system has several automated features to detect and to prevent various forms of abuse. In order to prevent users from registering on eBay for the sole purpose of delivering excessive positive or negative feedback, the user must be registered for five days in order to leave feedback.

Dealing with unknown individuals over the Internet can cause concern for some and may cause many others to shy away from eBay. In order to ease users' fears, eBay has instituted their Safe Harbor program; which provides trading guidelines and rules, provides information to help resolve disputes among users, and addresses and responds to misuse of the eBay system. Safe Harbor is composed of approximately 28 persons, a group that includes regular eBay employees and contract employees. These individuals investigate possible misuse of the system and will take appropriate action, which may include suspension from buying or selling on the site. Safe Harbor provides users with information to assist with disputes over quality of goods and possible fraudulent activities. If fraudulent activities occur, eBay will usually suspend the offending party from further activity.

Because community plays such an important part in the eBay experience, the company has focused resources on establishing a community experience. The company believes that the eBay community is one of the strongest on the Internet. eBay offers a wide array of features that support the community, and these solidify the eBay community and insure its continued growth and loyalty. The company uses e-mail to provide users with category-specific chat rooms, the eBay café (a chat room for the entire community), a bulletin board for feedback on new features, announcements that cover new features and other eBay news, customer support bulletin boards, and an "items wanted" listing where users can post their desire for specific items.

Also available is My eBay, which gives users a report of their recent activity. Users who have their own Web pages can post links to their homepage, and those without a Web site can use About Me to create a homepage free of charge. eBay has recently begun publishing a news magazine about eBay and its community of users.

The company recently announced an insurance program for users. To qualify, a user must be a buyer in good standing or a seller with a Feedback rating of zero or above. The insurance program provides coverage on qualified transactions if a winning bidder sends money to a seller and either does not receive the item or does not receive the item described on the site.

In addition, in June 1998, the company donated over 300,000 shares (over $42 million at October 19, 1999 price) of common stock to the Community Foundation of Silicon Valley, a tax-exempt public charity. It established a fund called the "eBay Foundation" and solicits input from users for worthwhile charities.

## MARKETING

Historically, eBay has relied on word of mouth to promote its Web site and occasionally has utilized links and sponsorships with other Web sites. Today eBay has expanded its marketing to include purchases of some online advertising in sites in which it believes it can reach its target customer. The company also uses traditional media such as print media, trade shows and other events.

In October 1998, eBay kicked off a national advertising campaign in traditional media and online to promote its product and attract new users. In August 1998, the company entered into a three-year marketing agreement with AOL, whereby eBay is featured as the preferred site of Internet person-to-person auction services. The company will also benefit from placement on AOL.com, Digital Cities, ICQ, Compuserve, and Netscape. eBay will pay $75 million for the four-year contract. It will develop a co-branded version of its auction format for each AOL site, and each site will feature each party's brand and AOL will receive all advertising from the co-branded site.

The company also uses its site for brand advertising by offering a variety of eBay-branded merchandize that can be purchased through its own online "eBay Store."

Strategic personnel were added to increase marketing and further solidify the business. Prior to 1998, eBay had a loose coalition of independent sellers who listed their wares on the Internet. In February 1998, the company recruited Meg Whitman as president and CEO. Whitman's Harvard MBA and experience with Stride-Rite, Disney, Procter & Gamble and as CEO of FTD Florists gave the company a badly needed marketing management boost. Almost immediately, Whitman recruited Brian Swette, then head of marketing at Pepsi. Mr. Swette's responsibilities were to build and oversee eBay's marketing group. One result of the new emphasis on marketing was replacement of the gray and white face on the online site with one with bright colors.

## OPERATIONS PLATFORM

The eBay site operates on a software platform that was internally developed. This platform handles all aspects of the trading cycle including e-mail notifications of when a bid is successful and when a bidder is outbid. The system sends daily reports to all active sellers and bidders on the status of their auctions. In addition, the system also stores registration information, billing information, and credit card information for traders who use an open account balance. The software system is also the platform for all eBay chat room and bulletin board information.

With the exception of once-per-week maintenance that takes a few hours, the system operates 24 hours per day, seven days per week. The eBay platform consists of Sun database servers running Oracle relational database management software. The company uses an outside load-balancing system and uses its own servers as backup to reduce faults and outages. Outages do occasionally occur and are caused by a number of factors, including problems from third-party hardware and software providers. At present, eBay does not have a fully redundant system or other providers of hosting services that would eliminate or minimize operational interruptions.

The company's systems are vulnerable to attack from unauthorized persons, and eBay has experienced a break-in by a hacker who stated that he/she can cause future damage. An independent computer programmer says that he has developed a code that can collect the identity and passwords of bidders, allowing hackers to create fake listings, fake auctions, and change user information.

From June 10 to June 15, 1999 the company's Web site experienced numerous outages and downtime. One outage lasted almost 24 hours, and eBay issued users $3.9 million in credits. That outage resulted in approximately $5 million in lost revenue and a $4 billion reduction in market value. The problem seems to stem from problems with software, servers, and the fact that eBay may not have properly backed up its operating system and database. During this outage, all eBay competitors reported an increase in bidding volume on their sites.

The use rate of the eBay site has increased substantially during the past few years, and, in fact, the increase has not been linear but exponential. As a result, the company is constantly adding to its infrastructure of software, hardware, and engineers. Because the entire eBay system operates on this platform, integrity and uptime are of the utmost importance. Any unscheduled or unanticipated downtime could severely harm current revenues and cause a ripple effect that could make users switch to competitive sites and thus affect long-term revenue.

## GROWTH

Growth, as measured by several factors, has increased exponentially over the past three years. As measured by registered users, merchandise sales, number of items listed, number of log-on's and number of minutes on the site per user, the company is one of the most popular sites on the Web. By all measures, eBay is one of the most active and widely visited Internet sites. eBay usage almost approaches a drug-induced addiction, with many members spending over 130 minutes per month on the site, a rate that is much higher than time spent on rival site Amazon.

The number of registered users has increased from 41,000 in 1996 to over 2.1 million at the end of 1998, and eBay is currently adding 200,000 new users per day. Current registration rates resulted in the number of users exceeding 3.8 million at year-end 1999.

Gross merchandise sales, that is, the dollar value of transactions between buyers and sellers increased from $7,279 million in 1996 to $745,395 million at the end of

1998. The number of items listed on the eBay site increased from 289,000 in 1996 to 33,688 million at the end of 1998.

Gross revenue, gross profits, and net income all increased substantially from 1996 to 1998. Revenues have increased for 18 consecutive quarters and grew from $372,000 in 1996 to over $47,352 million in 1999. Gross profits increased from $358,000 in 1996 to $167 million in 1998, and net income grew from $148,000 in 1996 to $2,398 million at the end of 1998. Net income for 1999 was $10.82 million.

eBay is one of the few Internet companies to return a profit. From the years 1996 to 1999, when the company went public, cash, working capital, total assets, and total stockholders' equity have all increased substantially. Acting as a facilitator and broker for individual traders keeps the company's business model a very profitable one.

## COMPETITION

The market for Internet person-to-person trading is new and increasing rapidly, and the potential market value may not be known at this time. Auction trading via e-commerce now exceeds $2.0 billion annually. Unlike the demand for cars, refrigerators, and other products sold via bricks-and-mortar establishments, online trading demand is, at this time, difficult to measure. As demand increases, eBay expects competition to grow and intensify. The barriers to entry are somewhat low, and current Internet companies that engage in online commerce can easily add or convert to auction trading.

Competitors include Yahoo!, Onsale, Excite, Auction Universe, and smaller specialty services such as CityAuction. Currently Yahoo! is one of eBay's strongest competitors. Yahoo! has over 300,000 listings, approximately 18 percent of eBay's total. Some of these competitors' auction services are free to both buyers and sellers.

In addition to companies offering person-to-person auctions, eBay also competes with companies like Onsale, First Auction, uBid, and others offering business to consumer online auctions. Other indirect competitors include QVC and USA Network.

Perhaps the biggest long-term threat to eBay's dominance in Internet auction commerce is the giant Amazon.com. With over 16 million items for sale, it is the world's biggest store, according to Chief Executive Jeffery Bezos. Amazon boasts more than 8.4 million customers, which is double the number of eBay's, and it had revenues of $1.639 billion in 1999. The Amazon brand is a widely recognized name, and it enjoys the best brand recognition in the e-commerce world, while eBay has the third best.

In April 1999, Amazon announced plans to acquire LiveBid.com, an Internet auction site, a clear indication that Amazon wanted to enter the auction format to supplement its successful fixed-price format. Amazon invented one-click shopping with software that remembers past purchases and suggests new purchases. All of this has resulted in a loyal customer base: Repeat purchasers account for up to 66 percent of current sales.

Amazon has an excellent team and, in its quest to provide the best customer service, has hired several executives from Wal-Mart. It has quickly dominated every aspect of Internet commerce that it has entered. For example, after Amazon's first quarter in the music business, it became the Internet's largest CD seller, and Amazon competitors worry about "getting Amazoned."

Other formidable competition will likely come from the newly announced alliance of Microsoft, Dell, Lycos, and Excite. On September 17, 1999, these four companies joined forces to form an Internet auction-trading forum. This new forum allows items to be shared across the different company formats. Someone listing a product on Excite will cause the product to appear on the other three sites. A user logging on to Lycos will see the listing but will have no knowledge that the listing came from another site. The cross listings will be transparent to the user. The company that is coordinating the pooling of these auctions is FairMarket, Inc., a Massachusetts-based company that sets up and runs auction sites for companies. Policies and operating procedures have not been announced so it is difficult to determine how this alliance will affect eBay, but the potential competition that these four powerful Internet companies can provide cannot be underestimated.

As a result, eBay constantly monitors the activities of all competitors and adjusts its services to counter competitive activity. Aggressive action resulted in new categories of products and a Personal Shopper program, and eBay will launch a new national marketing program ahead of schedule. The entrance of competitors into auction selling has made eBay develop new marketing programs faster.

## INTERNET FRAUD AND NEGATIVE PUBLICITY

Current laws regarding liability issues for online service providers remain vague and are still evolving. Although eBay only provides the platform in which individuals trade their merchandise, the company realizes that it may face potential liability for certain user conduct on its site. eBay understands that items such as alcohol, tobacco, firearms, and adult material are subject to local, state, and federal guidelines. The company also understands that it may be unable to prevent unlawful activity on its site and may be subject to penalties for the conduct of some of its users.

The company realizes that Internet fraud can severely damage its community atmosphere. Users will quickly abandon a community that is rife with fraud and dishonesty, and eBay has taken steps to prevent fraud and unlawful activity by implementing certain checks and balances during the registration process. The Safe Harbor program, customer service department, and Feedback Forum have been put in place to foster the sense of community that eBay holds as important to successful trading. eBay is counting on the community at large to hold fraudulent and illegal activity to a minimum.

According to eBay, fewer than 30 auctions per million generate a possible fraud complaint, but the company wants to lower the number of complaints and eliminate the potential for an unhappy experience. In response to fraud concerns, the company has established a simpler escrow system, new rules preventing sellers from bidding on their own items, tougher ID checks, penalties if bidders do not complete transactions, and free buyer's insurance. The company's reputation could be severely damaged, or it could be held liable for any illegal of fraudulent activity that occurs on its Web site. Even if found innocent, the costs of litigation could cause financial harm. In January 1999, eBay was asked to produce records and information regarding possibly illegal transactions on its site. The company is cooperating with the government investigation but admits that any civil or criminal charges would be damaging, causing negative publicity and diversion of management attention away from normal operations, not to mention the direct adverse financial effect.

Complaints of alleged fraudulent activity prompted the New York Consumer Affairs Department to investigate the situation. The company fully cooperated and, as a result, instituted additional measures to insure a safe trading environment. A California man had posted fake listings with eBay and collected over $37,000 from bidders. This individual contacted the winning bidders for payment but never delivered the merchandise.

In addition to outright fraud, negative publicity from deceptive or publicity-seeking sellers can also harm the company's reputation, sense of community, and revenue. A teenager ran up millions of dollars of transactions of his parent's account. In an effort to gain employment, an engineer in California placed himself up for bid. And although selling one's own organs is illegal under federal law, in one widely published incident, an individual attempted to auction his kidney. The auction hit $5.7 million before eBay discovered it and shut down the auction.

The company has recently decided to discontinue the listings for firearms and ammunition on its site. Because firearm laws are difficult to impossible to enforce over the Internet, eBay has decided to eliminate the potential for liability and bad publicity that could result from firearms being traded to an irresponsible individual.

## Government Regulation

Because eBay does not take possession of any of the items sold on its site or hold any receivable for merchandise sold, the company does not collect sales taxes associated with the transactions. Any tax requirements resulting from transactions must be conducted by the individual seller. At present, sellers are not likely to collect and administer sales taxes. In the future, federal, state, and local governments may force the issue of sales tax collection and require compensation for such taxes. At that time, because eBay provides the platform for operation, the government may press eBay into some type of assistant or administrative role. This could conceivably increase the costs of operations without adding revenues.

Today very few laws govern Internet sales. However, because Internet commerce is becoming more popular, it is very likely that within a few years laws will be enacted to address user contracts, privacy, price structures, freedom of expression, security, and other areas. Additional costs may result from compliance.

## Legal Proceedings

The company has been sued by Network Engineering Software, Inc., in U.S. District Court for the Northern District of California for willful and deliberate violation of patent. The lawsuit requests an unspecified amount of monetary compensation and an injunction against eBay's operations. eBay believes it is innocent of any and all charges and is vigorously defending its position. However, the company does state that if it were required to pay expenses due to an unfavorable judgement, its business would be harmed.

In January 1999, eBay received a request from the federal government to produce documents relating to an investigation into possible illegal transactions on its site. The company is fully cooperating with the investigation, and the federal court has ordered that no additional public disclosures can be made with respect to this investigation.

Also, the company has been investigated by the New York City Department of Consumer Affairs after receiving complaints from users regarding some transactions on the site. The company produced all the requested information and has made changes to its operations and policies to minimize future complaints.

## ACQUISITIONS AND JOINT VENTURES

The company acquired all the outstanding shares of Jump Inc., an online trading service that operates in an auction format and derives revenues from advertising. It exchanged $260 million in eBay stock for the San Francisco auction house Butterfield & Butterfield. With its average auction closing at $1,400, Butterfield & Butterfield brings high-end auctions under the eBay umbrella.

eBay has also acquired Germany's leading online person-to-person trading company, Alando.deAG., Germany's largest online trading company with more than 500 categories. It has over 80,000 items listed and over 500,000 registered users. Alando.deAG will transition to a new Web address and give German users access to the eBay site.

The company also entered into a joint venture with Kruse International, one of the world's most respected organizations in the rare and collector automobile market. This venture will allow eBay to introduce a new automotive category that will include subcategories for parts, recreational vehicles, motorcycles, and trucks.

In an effort to assist its traders with shipping products as well as winning bidders, the company has entered into a joint venture with Mail Boxes Etc. and iShip.com. Mail Boxes Etc. will provide central shipping points for customers to give traders a location at which their item can be professionally packed and shipped. The iShip.com software enables traders to calculate shipping costs.

## FINANCIAL STATEMENTS

eBay's income statements, and balance sheets provided reveal the company to be one of a few online Internet companies to enjoy positive net income for the past three years. Overall, eBay's financials look strong, and projected revenues for 2000 are expected to be as strong as those of the past several years.

## CONCLUSION

Currently, eBay seems to be at a crossroads. It has established a very profitable Internet business model. This feat is something that many other Internet businesses have failed to accomplish. It is the market leader in Internet auction selling and operates in a rapidly expanding market. Its success has been noticed, and competition from Net heavyweights like Amazon and the new alliance coordinated by FairMarket Inc. will provide substantial competition.

Most of the company's revenue is from a single product that services a single market. Their operating system, although good, needs to be fortified, and foreign markets seem to be untapped. eBay operates in the wide-open Net environment with little government intervention and low barriers to entry. Entry barriers for new competitors are low, and the costs of switching services and loyalties by users are also low.

The questions facing eBay are how to use its profitable position to fend off competition and continue to gain share and whether to move out of its core competence and into other areas of e-commerce.

---

## REFERENCES

"December 31, 1998 Form 10K," eBay Inc.
"December 31, 1999 Annual Report," eBay Inc.

# EXHIBIT 1    eBAY INC. Annual Income Statement
## (in millions except EPS data)

| | Fiscal Year End for eBAY Inc. (eBAY) falls in the month of December | | | |
| --- | --- | --- | --- | --- |
| | 12/31/99 | 12/31/98 | 12/31/97 | 12/31/96 |
| Sales | $224.72 | $ 47.35 | $ 5.74 | $0.37 |
| Cost of Goods | 57.58 | 6.85 | 0.74 | 0.01 |
| Gross Profit | 167.13 | 40.49 | 4.99 | 0.35 |
| Selling & Administrative & Depr. & Amort. Expenses | 163.53 | 34.32 | 3.51 | 0.09 |
| Income after Depreciation & Amortization | 3.61 | 6.18 | 1.49 | 0.27 |
| Non-Operating Income | 16.62 | 0.90 | 0.05 | 0.00 |
| Interest Expense | N/A | 0.03 | 0.00 | 0.00 |
| Pretax Income | 20.21 | 7.03 | 1.54 | 0.25 |
| Income Taxes | 9.38 | 4.63 | 0.66 | 0.10 |
| Minority Interest | N/A | 0.00 | 0.00 | 0.00 |
| Investment Gains/Losses(+) | N/A | 0.00 | 0.00 | 0.00 |
| Other Income/Charges | N/A | 0.00 | 0.00 | 0.00 |
| Income from Cont. Operations | N/A | N/A | N/A | N/A |
| Extras & Discontinued Operations | 0.00 | 0.00 | 0.00 | 0.00 |
| Net Income | $ 10.82 | $ 2.39 | $ 0.87 | $0.14 |

## Depreciation Footnote

| | | | | |
| --- | --- | --- | --- | --- |
| Income before Depreciation & Amortization | $ 4.75 | $ 6.98 | $ 1.58 | $0.27 |
| Depreciation & Amortization (Cash Flow) | 1.14 | 0.80 | 0.09 | 0.00 |
| Income after Depreciation & Amortization | $ 3.61 | $ 6.18 | $ 1.49 | $0.27 |

## Earnings Per Share Data

| | | | | |
| --- | --- | --- | --- | --- |
| Average of Shares | $135.91 | $114.59 | $82.66 | N/A |
| Diluted EPS Before Non-Recurring Items | 0.14 | 0.07 | 0.01 | N/A |
| Diluted Net EPS | $ 0.08 | $ 0.02 | $ 0.01 | N/A |

*Source:* www.freeedgar.com

# EXHIBIT 2    eBAY INC. Annual Balance Sheet
## (in millions, except book value per share)

|  | Fiscal Year End for eBAY INC. (eBAY) falls in the month of December | | | |
|---|---|---|---|---|
|  | 12/31/99 | 12/31/98 | 12/31/97 | 12/31/96 |

### Assets

|  | 12/31/99 | 12/31/98 | 12/31/97 | 12/31/96 |
|---|---|---|---|---|
| Cash & Equivalents | $400.75 | $72.19 | $3.72 | $0.10 |
| Receivables | 36.53 | 6.36 | 1.02 | 0.16 |
| Notes Receivable | N/A | 0.00 | 0.00 | 0.00 |
| Inventories | N/A | 0.00 | 0.00 | 0.00 |
| Other Current Assets | 22.53 | 4.82 | 0.22 | 0.01 |
| **Total Current Assets** | 459.83 | 83.38 | 4.96 | 0.28 |
| Net Property & Equipment | 111.80 | 7.83 | 0.65 | 0.02 |
| Investments & Advances | 373.98 | 0.00 | 0.00 | 0.00 |
| Other Non-Current Assets | N/A | 0.00 | 0.00 | 0.00 |
| Deferred Charges | 5.63 | 0.00 | 0.00 | 0.00 |
| Intangibles | 12.67 | 1.26 | 0.00 | 0.00 |
| Deposits & Other Assets | N/A | 0.00 | 0.00 | 0.00 |
| **Total Assets** | $963.94 | $92.48 | $5.61 | $0.30 |

### Liabilities & Shareholders' Equity

|  | 12/31/99 | 12/31/98 | 12/31/97 | 12/31/96 |
|---|---|---|---|---|
| Notes Payable | N/A | 0.00 | 0.00 | 0.00 |
| Accounts Payable | $ 31.53 | 1.38 | 0.25 | 0.02 |
| Current Portion Long Term Debt | 12.28 | 0.00 | 0.25 | 0.00 |
| Current Portion Capital Leases | N/A | 0.00 | 0.00 | 0.00 |
| Accrued Expenses | 32.55 | 0.00 | 0.00 | 0.00 |
| Income Taxes Payable | 6.45 | 1.68 | 0.16 | 0.05 |
| Other Current Liabilities | 5.99 | 4.97 | 0.44 | 0.01 |
| **Total Current Liabilities** | 88.82 | 8.03 | 1.12 | 0.09 |
| Mortgages | N/A | 0.00 | 0.00 | 0.00 |
| Deferred Taxes/Income | N/A | 0.00 | 0.15 | 0.05 |
| Convertible Debt | N/A | 0.00 | 0.00 | 0.00 |
| Long Term Debt | 15.01 | 0.00 | 0.30 | 0.00 |
| Non-Current Capital Leases | N/A | 0.00 | 0.00 | 0.00 |
| Other Non-Current Liabilities | 7.63 | 0.00 | 0.00 | 0.00 |
| Minority Interest (Liabilities) | N/A | 0.00 | 0.00 | 0.00 |
| **Total Liabilities** | $111.47 | $8.03 | $4.60 | $0.14 |

### Shareholders' Equity

|  | 12/31/99 | 12/31/98 | 12/31/97 | 12/31/96 |
|---|---|---|---|---|
| Preferred Stock | N/A | 0.00 | 3.01 | 0.00 |
| Common Stock (Par) | N/A | 0.12 | 0.02 | 0.02 |
| Capital Surplus | N/A | 86.26 | 1.48 | 0.05 |
| Retained Earnings | N/A | 3.32 | 0.97 | 0.14 |
| Other Equity | N/A | (5.26) | (1.46) | (0.06) |
| Treasury Stock | N/A | 0.00 | 0.00 | 0.00 |
| Total Shareholders' Equity | $852.46 | 84.44 | 1.01 | 0.16 |
| **Total Liabilities & Shareholders' Equity** | 963.94 | 92.48 | 5.61 | 0.30 |
| Total Common Equity | 852.46 | 84.44 | (2.00) | $0.16 |
| Average of Shares | 135.91 | 114.59 | 82.66 | N/A |
| Book Value Per Share | $ 6.81 | $ 0.70 | $(0.02) | N/A |

*Source:* www.freeedgar.com

# AMAZON.COM, INC.—2000

**Phillip Bartlett and Fred David**
**Francis Marion University**

## AMZN

www.amazon.com

Have you ever thought about going into business for yourself? Did your vision include picking the perfect location? Was it in cyberspace? That is exactly where businesses today are clamoring to build. A prime example is Amazon.com, Inc.

Amazon.com, Inc. is an Internet-based company located in Seattle, Washington. The founder of the company as well as the president, CEO, and chairman of the board is Jeff Bezos. While working as a senior vice president for D.E. Shaw & Company in 1994, Bezos was assigned to find good Internet companies in which to invest. Upon "Web surfing" for the first time, a site showing the number of Internet users growing by 2,300 percent per month was found. Bezos began thinking of products and services that could be sold efficiently on the Web and developed a list of around twenty items. Within two months, Jeff set off with his wife, Mackenzie, across America. While Mackenzie drove the Chevy Blazer, Jeff constructed a business plan on a laptop and contacted potential investors by cellular phone. Book sales was chosen as the market to pursue because no clear powerhouse was visible. The largest competitor was Barnes & Noble, Inc., which had only 15 percent of that market in 1994.

Initially Bezos wanted to call the company Cadabra, but after an acquaintance thought the name was "Cadaver," the search for a name continued. The company was eventually named after the mightiest river in the world, the Amazon. The company's 1999 net income was negative $719.97 million on revenues of $1.6 billion.

## HISTORY

In 1994, Amazon.com, Inc. was incorporated first in the State of Washington, then in 1996 in Delaware. Seattle was chosen as Amazon's headquarters because of the proximity to Ingram Book Group's warehouse and the population's noted computer expertise. In 1995, operating out of a rented 45,000-square-foot facility and using doors laid across sawhorses for desks, Amazon started selling books exclusively online.

Amazon immediately enjoyed astounding growth rates. Sales for 1995, 1996, 1997, 1998, and 1999 were $0.5, $16, $147, $610 and $1,640 million, respectively. Amazon's 1999 financial statements are shown in Exhibits 1 and 2. Amazon's customer base increased from 180,000 in 100 countries in 1996 to 12 million in 160 countries by mid-1999. The repeat purchase rate of existing customers rose from 44 percent in 1996 to 70 percent in 1999. The number of titles available to consumers increased from 1 million in 1995 to 4.5 million by 1998. Amazon went public in 1997 and is traded on the NASDAQ exchange under the symbol AMZN.

In 1998, Amazon began expanding. Music and videos were added to the product mix. Within two months of the initial offering of these products, Amazon became the number-one seller of books, music, and videos online. Further expansion followed in

EXHIBIT 1    Amazon.com, Inc. Annual Income Statement
             (in millions except EPS data)

| | *Fiscal Year End for AMAZON.COM INC (AMZN) falls in the month of December.* | | | |
| | 12/31/99 | 12/31/98 | 12/31/97 | 12/31/96 |
|---|---|---|---|---|
| Sales | $1,639.84 | $ 609.99 | $147.76 | $ 15.75 |
| Cost of Goods | 1,349.19 | 476.11 | 118.94 | 12.29 |
| **Gross Profit** | 290.65 | 133.88 | 28.81 | 3.46 |
| Selling & Administrative & Depr. & Amort. Expenses | N/A | 195.62 | 58.02 | 9.44 |
| **Income after Depreciation & Amortization** | 290.65 | (61.74) | (29.21) | (5.98) |
| Non-Operating Income | N/A | (36.15) | 1.90 | 0.20 |
| Interest Expense | 84.57 | 26.63 | 0.28 | 0.00 |
| **Pretax Income** | (719.97) | (124.54) | (27.59) | (5.78) |
| Income Taxes | N/A | 0.00 | 0.00 | 0.00 |
| Minority Interest | N/A | 0.00 | 0.00 | 0.00 |
| Investment Gains/Losses (+) | N/A | 0.00 | 0.00 | 0.00 |
| Other Income/Charges | N/A | 0.00 | 0.00 | 0.00 |
| **Income from Cont. Operations** | N/A | N/A | N/A | N/A |
| Extras & Discontinued Operations | 0.00 | 0.00 | 0.00 | 0.00 |
| **Net Income** | $ (719.97) | $(124.54) | $(27.59) | $ (5.78) |

**Depreciation Footnote**

| | | | | |
|---|---|---|---|---|
| Income before Depreciation & Amortization | $ 290.65 | $ (49.67) | $(24.47) | $ (5.69) |
| Depreciation & Amortization (Cash Flow) | N/A | 12.07 | 4.74 | 0.29 |
| **Income after Depreciation & Amortization** | $ 290.65 | $ (61.74) | $(29.21) | $ (5.98) |

**Earnings Per Share Data**

| | | | | |
|---|---|---|---|---|
| **Average of Shares** | $ 326.75 | $ 296.34 | $260.68 | $271.86 |
| Diluted EPS Before Non-Recurring Items | (1.19) | (0.25) | (0.10) | (0.02) |
| **Diluted Net EPS** | $ (2.20) | $ (0.42) | $ (0.10) | $ (0.02) |

*Source:* www.freeedgar.com

1999. The company now also offers electronics and software, toys and video games, home improvements, electronic greeting cards, online auctions, DVDs, and a virtual mall called zShops. In addition, Amazon has purchased two Internet sites in Europe, one in Germany and the other in the United Kingdom. Domestically, Amazon now owns a significant minority interest in a drugstore, a pet shop, a sport shop, and a grocer. All of these businesses operate in cyberspace. Also, Amazon has acquired businesses to produce e-commerce software and to establish a database to track customer demographic and online buying habits.

**EXTERNAL ASSESSMENT**

The number of Internet users is continuing to rise. The totals for 1996, 1998, and the projections for 2002 are 61, 147 and 300 million worldwide users, respectively. In 1999, Internet traffic doubled every 100 days. By 2002, predictions suggest that the U.S. mar-

# EXHIBIT 2   Amazon.com, Inc. Annual Balance Sheet
## (in millions, except book value per share)

| | Fiscal Year End for AMAZON.COM INC (AMZN) falls in the month of December | | | |
|---|---|---|---|---|
| | 12/31/99 | 12/31/98 | 12/31/97 | 12/31/96 |
| **Assets** | | | | |
| Cash & Equivalents | $ 706.19 | $373.44 | $125.07 | $6.25 |
| Receivables | N/A | 0.00 | 0.00 | 0.00 |
| Notes Receivable | N/A | 0.00 | 0.00 | 0.00 |
| Inventories | 220.65 | 29.50 | 8.97 | 0.57 |
| Other Current Assets | N/A | 21.30 | 3.30 | 0.32 |
| **Total Current Assets** | 1,012.18 | 424.25 | 137.34 | 7.14 |
| Net Property & Equipment | 317.61 | 29.79 | 9.27 | 0.99 |
| Investments & Advances | N/A | 0.00 | 0.00 | 0.00 |
| Other Non-Current Assets | N/A | 0.00 | 0.00 | 0.00 |
| Deferred Charges | N/A | 7.41 | 2.24 | 0.00 |
| Intangibles | N/A | 186.37 | 0.00 | 0.00 |
| Deposits & Other Assets | N/A | 0.62 | 0.17 | 0.15 |
| **Total Assets** | $2,471.55 | $648.46 | $149.01 | $8.27 |
| **Liabilities & Shareholders' Equity** | | | | |
| Notes Payable | N/A | 0.00 | 0.00 | 0.00 |
| Accounts Payable | N/A | 113.27 | 32.70 | 2.85 |
| Current Portion Long Term Debt | N/A | 0.68 | 1.50 | 0.00 |
| Current Portion Capital Leases | N/A | 0.00 | 0.00 | 0.00 |
| Accrued Expenses | N/A | 47.61 | 3.45 | 1.10 |
| Income Taxes Payable | N/A | 0.00 | 0.00 | 0.00 |
| Other Current Liabilities | N/A | 0.00 | 6.17 | 0.92 |
| **Total Current Liabilities** | 738.94 | 161.57 | 43.82 | 4.87 |
| Mortgages | N/A | 0.00 | 0.00 | 0.00 |
| Deferred Taxes/Income | N/A | 0.00 | 0.00 | 0.00 |
| Convertible Debt | N/A | 0.00 | 0.00 | 0.00 |
| Long Term Debt | 1,466.34 | 348.07 | 76.52 | 0.00 |
| Non-Current Capital Leases | N/A | 0.06 | 0.18 | 0.00 |
| Other Non-Current Liabilities | N/A | 0.00 | 0.00 | 0.00 |
| Minority Interest (Liabilities) | N/A | 0.00 | 0.00 | 0.00 |
| **Total Liabilities** | N/A | $509.71 | $120.52 | $4.87 |
| **Shareholders' Equity** | | | | |
| Preferred Stock | N/A | 0.00 | 0.00 | 0.01 |
| Common Stock (Par) | 3.45 | 1.59 | 0.24 | 0.16 |
| Capital Surplus | N/A | 300.13 | 63.79 | 9.87 |
| Retained Earnings | N/A | (162.06) | (33.62) | (6.03) |
| Other Equity | N/A | (0.91) | (1.93) | (0.61) |
| Treasury Stock | N/A | 0.00 | 0.00 | 0.00 |
| Total Shareholder's Equity | 266.28 | 138.74 | 28.49 | 3.40 |
| **Total Liabilities & Shareholders' Equity** | 2,471.55 | 648.46 | 149.01 | 8.27 |
| Total Common Equity | 266.28 | 138.74 | 28.49 | 3.39 |
| Average of Shares | 326.75 | 296.34 | 260.68 | $271.86 |
| Book Value Per Share | $ 0.79 | $ 0.44 | $ 0.10 | N/A |

Source: www.freeedgar.com

ket will be saturated, and most of the growth will come from Asia and Western Europe. Although once predominately male, Internet users are now almost equally divided between males and females. Internet users are more educated than the general population, with over 80 percent having at least some college experience. This percentage is falling as more people are acquiring access to the Net via inexpensive computers and public access points, such as libraries and schools.

The number of Web sites on the World Wide Web is also increasing. Of the 3.6 million total sites in 1999, 2.2 million are public access sites. In 1997, there were only 800 thousand public access sites. The 25,000 largest public sites contain approximately half of all Web pages. English is the predominant language on Web sites. It is the main language of Australia, Canada, Ireland, New Zealand, South Africa, the United Kingdom, and the United States. The combined population and gross domestic product of these countries are 322 million and $10.8 trillion, respectively.

Over 29 million people in the United States speak Spanish. That number is expected to grow to 40 million by 2010. Presently, the U.S. Hispanic market is estimated at $325 billion. Worldwide, 800 million people speak Spanish. Hispanics, both domestically and abroad, demonstrate high levels of brand loyalty.

E-commerce can be broken into four segments: (1) business to business (B2B); (2) business to consumer (B2C); (3) business to administration; and (4) customer to administration. The two most familiar are business-to-business and business-to-consumer commerce, during which products and services are exchanged via electronic networking systems instead of via person to person. For example, at a new checkout counter, an item is scanned. That information is relayed to a computer system, which, when the appropriate level has been sold, will order new supplies via an Electronic Data Interchange (EDI). This form of business-to-business commerce that has been around since the 1960s. The U.S. Commerce Department projects that e-commerce will be the primary economic growth engine of the United States for the next 100 years. The number of Internet-related jobs has increased from 1.6 million to 2.3 million from the first quarter of 1998 to the first quarter of 1999.

The business-to-customer e-commerce segment is now experiencing rapid growth. As more people become Internet users and become comfortable with ordering products online, businesses make more profit. Online B2C sales for 1996, 1997, 1998, and the projected volume for 2000 and 2002 are $0.324, $3, $9, $30, and $42 billion, respectively.

Although over 90 percent of all e-commerce is generated through U.S.-based Web sites, other countries are also experiencing growth. For example, Western Europe's sales are projected to increase from US$775 million in 1999 to US$8.6 billion by 2003. Germany, France, and Britain sales exceeded US$290, US$85, and $170 million in 1999, respectively. E-commerce is also expanding in Asia. Excluding Japan, Asia sales exceeded US$2 billion in 1999, and sales should increase by 400 percent to over US$32 billion by 2003. Japan's business-to-consumer commerce is expected to surpass 1 trillion yen by 2003 but still remain below 1 percent of total household sales. According to the Boston Consulting Group, online retail spending in Latin America was estimated at $77 million in 1999 and could reach $3.8 billion by 2003. But as previously hinted at, consumers as a whole are still not comfortable ordering online.

Internet companies, including Amazon, are having problems as people visit and browse but do not buy. Web sites are being used to gather information about products, which is then used to purchase the product at local businesses or other Web sites. The major reason that people refuse to purchase online is fear of the theft of private financial information. To combat this security issue, companies such as Amazon are using encryption methods to encode transmitted data. In fact, encryption is more secure than calling a business and giving a credit card number over ordinary phone lines.

Another issue facing online companies is the purchase-return stigma of the 1998 holiday season. As reported by major media sources, many customers experienced great difficulty in returning merchandise. Amazon has improved the company's return policy. Now, a package pickup agent is sent to collect and return products, all done to keep the customer happy.

As potential profits increase, more businesses are now coming online. To paraphrase a commercial, "If you are not online, then you are not really in business." In today's business environment, three basic business-to-consumer structures exist: (1) traditional brick and mortar, (2) completely online, or (3) a combination of (1) and (2). Amazon and E-bay, Inc., are completely online, but Barnes & Noble, Inc., Wal-Mart Stores, Inc., and Toys-R-Us, Inc., are combinations of brick-and-mortar and virtual companies. Each offers products or services to the Internet user. Although Amazon is often considered the "800-lb. gorilla" of e-commerce, the Internet business market is still fragmented. Amazon has only captured 3 percent of the book-selling market, and e-commerce is only about 1 percent of total commerce. Even with its large and growing revenue and customer base, Amazon must recognize that Wal-Mart, the world's largest retailer, is just starting to expand online and that companies such as Barnes & Noble are developing excellent Web sites, new software, and new technology to attract and track new customers.

## INTERNAL ASSESSMENT

Amazon is committed to customer satisfaction. Bezos claims that the key to keeping customers is to give them what they want. Amazon has designed a system that is not only easy to use but also efficient. Amazon copyrighted the one-click approach to online shopping. A customer can now shop in several areas throughout Amazon's entire domain without having to reregister or change virtual shopping carts. In addition, the company tracks customer purchases and preferences to personalize the shopping experience. Also, the customer is allowed to participate in the review of some products. Thus, in the end, the customers feel as if they were members of a community than just customers.

Amazon is also effective and resourceful with its promotions and advertisements. One of the company's first moves was to initiate an "associates program" to establish exclusive contracts with owners of valuable cyberspace real estate. In return, Amazon may pay an up-front fee and up to 8 percent for every referral that produces a sale. Accumulating 800 sites in 1996, the program included over 260,000 associates by the third quarter of 1999. Also linked with the marketing effort is the push to build name brand recognition. By advertising and promoting on many Internet sites and through print, radio, and TV ads, the name Amazon.com is recognized by 25 percent of all Americans.

Amazon has hired several well-established people from several major companies. These new employees' expertise ranges from software development, to international distribution, to brand name-building. Wal-Mart filed a lawsuit to restrain Amazon from approaching Wal-Mart employees. Amazon countersued, and an out-of-court agreement was reached. Amazon cannot approach Wal-Mart employees directly but can hire them if the employees approach Amazon themselves.

Amazon is increasing the number of its distribution centers. In 1995, the company had one in Seattle, Washington. In 1997, a second center in New Castle, Delaware was added. By the fourth quarter of 1999, the company is expected to have five more in Campbellsville and Lexington, Kentucky; Atlanta, Georgia; Coffeyville, Kansas; and Fernley, Nevada. The goal is to ship 95 percent of all orders on the same day they are received. By having more distribution centers, the company can hold more accessible inventory. Some criticism has been leveled against Amazon's management for not focusing on making a profit. Management's response is that the focus is on the long term, not the short, and that a strong infrastructure is necessary in today's ever-changing marketplace.

Amazon has demonstrated the ability to raise capital resources effectively and efficiently. Several small firms have been acquired using the company's professional reputation and the use of stock swaps. Through a 1999 junk bond offering, $1.25 billion at a 4.75 percent interest rate was easily raised. This bond can be converted to common stock in around three years at $150. In addition, the stock price has risen from its initial offing of $18 to around $200. Amazon's stock has split several times.

Supporting the company's financial position are its low building and maintenance costs. Unlike brick-and-mortar retailers, Amazon does not have the overhead associated with setting up storefronts for multiple target markets. The distribution centers are located to cover and service vast regions. Also, Amazon, unlike mail-order houses, does not have printing and phone operator costs.

However, the whole Amazon.com site operates on a single computer system and has experienced several periods of extended downtime. Amazon does not have a redundant computer system. If a disaster happened at the Seattle location, the company could lose its ability to service customers.

In 1996, Ingram supplied 60 percent of all books bought by Amazon. Although it only supplied 40 percent in 1999, Ingram is still the largest single supplier. In 1998 Barnes & Noble, Inc., tried unsuccessfully to acquire Ingram Books for $500 million. The acquisition of a major supplier could cause higher prices for inventory and reduce profit margins.

With the opening and expansion of distribution centers and product types, Amazon's workforce is expanding rapidly. In 1994, the company started with seven employees. Through 1995–1999, the number of employees increased to 4,500. In addition, about 2,000 more persons may be hired in 2000 to operate new and expanding distribution centers.

At this time, Amazon does not have an official mission statement. The company's stated goal is to put customer satisfaction first by using the Internet to transform book buying into the fastest, easiest, and most enjoyable shopping experience possible. At the same time, another universally accepted goal of Amazon's is to sell anything that can be sold on the Web. These are not mission statements but could be considered vision statements.

## COMPETITORS

Amazon faces stiff and growing competition from Internet companies. Barnes & Noble, Inc., has always been a classic comparative competitor for Amazon. Barnes & Noble, Inc., is incorporated in the State of Delaware and headquartered on Fifth Avenue in New York. The company operates 1,009 bookstores under several names: Barnes & Noble Booksellers, Bookstop, Bookstar, B. Dalton Booksellers, Doubleday Bookshops, and Scribner's Bookstore. Touted as the world's largest bookseller, the company's share of the consumer book market was approximately 15 percent in 1998. The company's principal business is the retail sale of trade books, mass market paperbacks, children's books, off-price bargain books and magazines. Best sellers only account for 3 percent of Barnes & Noble sales. Sales of $2.797 and $3.006 billion were recorded for 1997 and 1998, respectively. With stores in high-traffic areas with convenient access to major commercial thoroughfares and ample parking, Barnes & Noble was the first bookseller to utilize the "superstore" concept. The company has a Web site, http//www.barnesandnoble.com, and is the exclusive bookseller on America Online. In January of 1999, Barnes & Noble started offering music with 50,000 titles in classical music, opera, jazz, blues, and pop rock.

Wal-Mart Stores, Inc., is a Delaware corporation with headquarters in Bentonville, Arkansas. With net sales over $137 billion for the fiscal year that ended January 31, 1999, the company is billed as the world's largest retailer. The founder was Sam M. Walton. Wal-Mart operates 1,869 discount stores, 564 Supercenters, and 451 SAM's Clubs domestically. The company has operating units in Argentina, Brazil, Canada, Germany, Mexico, and Korea. Wal-Mart is principally engaged in the operation of mass merchandising stores. A typical store is generally organized with 40 departments and offers a wide variety of merchandise. Each store carries electronics, home furnishings, small appliances, automotive accessories, horticulture equipment, sporting goods, toys, pet food and accessories, cameras and supplies, health and beauty aids, pharmaceuticals, and jewelry. Also, Supercenters offer meat, produce, deli, bakery, dairy, frozen foods, and dry groceries. Wal-Mart utilizes a national sales campaign that accounts for a majority of sales in the stores. The Company has several brands, including but not limited to "Sam's American Choice," "One Source," and "Great Value."

General U.S. operating hours range from 7:00 A.M. to 11:00 P.M., six days a week and from 10:00 A.M. to 8:00 P.M. on Sunday for discount stores and Supercenters. However, an increasing number of Wal-Mart discount stores and almost all of the Supercenters are now open 24 hours each day.

Wal-Mart's Web site, http//www.wal-mart.com, was launched in late 1999. Wal-Mart has the second largest database in the world to track and predict customer purchases. Amazon is concerned about Wal-Mart's e-commerce plans.

## CONCLUSION

Amazon is a pioneer in the emerging business-to-consumer e-commerce market. By recognizing and taking advantage of the growing number of Internet users, the company has led the way in defining B2C e-commerce. But many opportunities and threats still lie ahead. Can Amazon use its strengths to capitalize on the opportunities, mitigate the treats, and improve on its weaknesses?

Amazon might buy Ingram Book Group to lower costs and expand distribution. Or should Amazon acquire a major Internet company such as Yahoo!? Perhaps Amazon should establish a back-up computer system or expand its distribution network internationally. How can Amazon reach the increasing Hispanic population?

Develop a three-year strategic plan for CEO Jeff Bezos.

*Note:*
*This Amazon case was used for the student Case Competition at the Society for the Advancement of Management (SAM) meeting in St. Augustine, Florida in March 2000. The following colleges and students were winners:*

*Undergraduate Division*

| | |
|---|---|
| *1st Place - Bentley College* | *(Tatiana Finkelsteyn, Bilal Kazmi, Nancy Novak, Timothy Williams, Hala Zeine)* |
| *2nd Place - Campbell University* | *(Rayford Dunning, Jr., William Taylor)* |
| *3rd Place - Harding University* | *(Brian Alldredge, John Cox, Christy Graham)* |

*Open Division*

| | |
|---|---|
| *1st Place - East Carolina University* | *(Javier Castillo, Jr., Melinda Griffin, Geoffrey Hodges, and John Wiley, Jr.)* |
| *2nd Place - Radford University* | *(Michelle Clore, Dolly King, and Jason Shinn)* |
| *3rd Place - Wright State University* | *(Charlotte Jackson, Tracy Poreter, Gail Thieman)* |

# THE LIMITED, INC.—2000

**M. Jill Austin**
**Middle Tennessee State University**

## LTD
www.limited.com

The Limited, Inc., headquartered in Columbus, Ohio, is the largest women's apparel specialty store and mail-order retailer in the United States. For over thirty years, Wexner's Limited stores have achieved success by "breaking the rules" in the specialty retailing industry. Instead of offering a wide variety of types of clothing, the stores offer a limited assortment of sportswear in large quantities and a variety of colors. The company emphasizes rapid turnover of inventory so only the newest fashion is in the stores at all times. In the mid-1990s, The Limited, Inc., made a strategic decision to develop strong brand associations for its stores. Net sales from 1998 to 1999 increased 4 percent to $9.723 billion. Operating income however declined from $2.424 billion in 1998 to $920 thousand in 1999, while net income declined 77 percent to $460 thousand. Stores now number 5,023 in 1999, down from 5,382 in 1998.

In 1996, Wexner's Limited saw its vulnerabilities. In response to the significant sales problems at Express, Wexner says, "we are fundamentally reinventing the business: sweeping change, greater discipline, more centralization, and a plan to build brands, not just business." This transition required each division to clearly define its fashion, advertising, price, and market position and required cooperation, not competition, among the division leaders. Leslie Wexner, chairman of The Limited, believes that future retailing success will be based on brand development. According to Wexner, "Better brands. Best brands. I don't believe bigger is better. I believe better is better."

## HISTORY

Leslie Wexner's parents both worked in retailing. His father worked for the Miller Wall specialty chain, and his mother was a buyer for Lazarus. When Wexner was fourteen, his parents opened their own specialty apparel store in Columbus, Ohio. After college and one year in law school, Wexner worked in his parents' store until he decided what he wanted to do with his life. He assumed that his work in retail would be temporary, but he "got hooked."

In 1963 Leslie Wexner borrowed $10,000 from an aunt and a bank to open The Limited's first store. During its first year of operation, this store achieved sales of $157,000. His strategy was to provide a "limited" assortment of quality, fashionable sportswear at medium prices. The concept worked well, and by the late 1970s, Wexner began a twofold strategy of market development and product development. New stores were opened and acquired to appeal to women of different ages, sizes, and budget limits.

In the 1980s, Wexner attempted to acquire department store chains such as Federated Department Stores, R. H. Macy, and Carter Hawley Hale (CHH). Probably his greatest disappointment was Wexner's failure to acquire CHH. Wexner submitted an offer to buy CHH for $1.1 billion. At the time of the offer, CHH consisted of 124 department stores, 117 specialty stores, and 841 book stores. Some of the store names associated with CHH at the time included Thalhimers, Neiman-Marcus, Broadway, and Bergdorf Goodman. The Limited acquired about 700,000 shares of CHH stock at the time of its offer. In response to The Limited's takeover attempt, General Cinema acquired $300 million of CHH stock, and CHH began buying its own stock. The Securities and Exchange Commission stepped in to stop both The Limited and CHH from unfairly attempting to control the takeover situation. These legal developments stalled Wexner's takeover attempt. After the CHH takeover attempt failed in 1986, Wexner began thinking more about internal growth than about new acquisitions. After CHH filed for Chapter 11 bankruptcy, Wexner said, "we wouldn't take it for free."

Throughout the 1980s, Wexner acquired a variety of businesses including Lane Bryant, Victoria's Secret, Sizes Unlimited, Lerner New York, Henri Bendel, and Abercrombie & Fitch. Each of these stores was in financial trouble when acquired by Wexner. Wexner also started several store divisions during the 1980s. These include Express, Structure, Limited Too, and Cacique. Penhaligon's was acquired in 1990 and Galyan's Trading Company was acquired in 1995. Bath & Body Works was started by The Limited, Inc., in 1990. In May 1998, the company's Abercrombie & Fitch stores became independent. Cacique stores closed in 1998, and Penhaligon's stores were sold in 1997.

## PRESENT CONDITIONS

The Limited, Inc., continues to expand and make dramatic change in its brands. Victoria's Secret began selling online through http://www.VictoriasSecret.com in 1998, and the Intimate Brands, Inc., group started the White Barn Candle Company at the end of 1999. In August 1999, the name of Limited Too stores was changed to "Too, Inc.," and the company was made a fully independent public company. The growth of The Limited, Inc., is shown in Exhibit 1.

The Limited, Inc., continues to be successful in spite of significant problems in its apparel division. Apparel division sales in 1998 were $5.045 billion, but the division had an operating loss of $11 million. According to Wexner,

> The strategic business plan that we set in motion in 1995, a plan that essentially reinvented our core businesses and operations, is working. It's having an impact at nearly every level, within the operating businesses and in the support group.

Almost all of the business divisions showed good financial results in 1996, but the year was so bad for Express that performance at that division negated the gains made in the other divisions. By 1998, Express had dramatically improved its performance with sales of $1.356 billion. However, the apparel stores Structure, Lerner, and Limited showed decreases in sales in 1998. In January 1999, the company formed the Intimate Beauty Corporation, which will develop distinct beauty businesses.

## BUSINESS STRUCTURE

The Limited, Inc., operates as four separate business groups: Apparel, Intimate Brands, Inc. (85 percent owned by The Limited, Inc.), Other Retail Brands (Henri Bendel and Galyan's), and Center Functions. Stores and operations in each business group and net sales for each are shown in Exhibit 2.

EXHIBIT 1    The Limited's Stores

|  | | End of Year | |
|---|---|---|---|
|  | Plan 2000 | 1999 | 1998 |
| Express Stores | 680 | 688 | 702 |
| Retail selling square ft. | 4,377,000 | 4,429,000 | 4,511,000 |
| Lerner New York Stores | 578 | 594 | 643 |
| Retail selling square ft. | 4,392,000 | 4,592,000 | 5,000,000 |
| Lane Bryant Stores | 698 | 688 | 730 |
| Retail selling square ft. | 3,392,000 | 3,343,000 | 3,517,000 |
| Limited Stores | 415 | 443 | 551 |
| Retail selling square ft. | 2,546,000 | 2,749,000 | 3,371,000 |
| Structure Stores | 487 | 499 | 532 |
| Retail selling square ft. | 1,936,000 | 1,978,000 | 2,118,000 |
| Total Apparel Businesses Stores | 2,858 | 2,912 | 3,158 |
| Retail selling square ft. | 16,643,000 | 17,091,000 | 18,517,000 |
| Victoria's Secret Stores | 971 | 896 | 829 |
| Retail selling square ft. | 4,270,000 | 3,976,000 | 3,702,000 |
| Both & Body Works Stores | 1,386 | 1,214 | 1,061 |
| Retail selling square ft. | 2,993,000 | 2,490,000 | 2,092,000 |
| Total Intimate Brands Stores | 2,357 | 2,110 | 1,890 |
| Retail selling square ft. | 7,263,000 | 6,466,000 | 5,794,000 |
| Henri Bendel Stores | 1 | 1 | 1 |
| Retail selling square ft. | 35,000 | 35,000 | 35,000 |
| Galyan's Stores | — | — | 14 |
| Retail selling square ft. | — | — | 964,000 |
| TOO Stores | — | — | 319 |
| Retail selling square ft. | — | — | 1,006,000 |
| Total Retail Businesses Stores | 5,216 | 5,023 | 5,382 |
| Retail selling square ft. | 23,941,000 | 23,592,000 | 26,316,000 |

Source: The Limited, Inc. Annual Report, 1999, p. 29–30.

## Apparel Division

### Limited Stores

This is the flagship division of the organization. Originally, merchandise in these stores was targeted to women between the ages of sixteen and twenty-five, but management changed that orientation to women in their thirties and forties several years ago. Limited Stores recently shifted the orientation to twenty-something women who want "casual American fashion." These stores sell medium-priced fashion clothing and accessories. Most of the 551 Limited stores are located in regional shopping centers or malls across the United States.

### Express

The Express was redesigned in the early 1990s for a more sophisticated, European image instead of the neon-lit high-tech store of the mid-1980s. The company now describes its Express stores as providing "hot new fashion to young women in their early twenties." Merchandise includes "young and spirited fashions of good taste and quality." Express added a lingerie department in 1999. The 702 Express stores are located mostly in shopping malls.

# EXHIBIT 2    Financial Data by Segment for the Limited (in millions)

| Net Sales | 1999 | 1998 | 1997 | % Ch 1999–98 |
|---|---|---|---|---|
| Express | $1,399 | $1,356 | $1,189 | 3% |
| Lerner New York | 1,013 | 940 | 946 | 8% |
| Lane Bryant | 934 | 933 | 907 | 0% |
| Limited Stores | 715 | 757 | 776 | (6%) |
| Structure | 617 | 610 | 660 | 1% |
| Other (principally Mast) | 107 | 72 | 6 | n/m |
| Total apparel businesses | $4,785 | $4,668 | $4,484 | 3% |
| Victoria's Secret Stores | 2,138 | 1,829 | 1,702 | 17% |
| Bath & Body Works | 1,550 | 1,272 | 1,057 | 22% |
| Victoria's Secret Catalogue | 799 | 759 | 734 | 5% |
| Other (principally Gryphon) | 24 | 26 | #125 | n/m |
| Total Intimate Brands | $4,511 | $3,886 | $3,618 | 16% |
| Henri Bendel | 39 | @40 | 83 | (3%) |
| Galyan's (through August 31, 1999) | 165 | 220 | 160 | n/m |
| TOO (through August 23, 1999) | 223 | 377 | 322 | n/m |
| A&F (through May 19, 1998) | — | 156 | 522 | n/m |
| Total net sales | $9,723 | $9,347 | $9,189 | 4% |
| **Operating Income** | | | | |
| Apparel businesses | $132 | $(45) | $34 | 393% |
| Intimate Brands | 794 | 671 | 563 | 18% |
| Other | (29) | 58 | 98 | n/m |
| Subtotal | 897 | 684 | 695 | 31% |
| Special and nonrecurring items | +24 | 1,740 | *(226) | |
| Total operating income | $921 | $2,424 | $469 | |

Source: Annual Report, 1999, p. 16–17.

## Lerner New York

This division sells fashionable women's sportswear for "value minded customers." The store created a brand called NY and Company. Presently there are 643 Lerner stores in operation in malls and shopping centers across the United States.

## Lane Bryant

Lane Bryant had been in operation for 80 years and was actually larger than The Limited, Inc., when The Limited bought it in 1982. Lane Bryant's market is primarily women between thirty and fifty. The store specializes in medium-priced clothing, intimate apparel, and accessories for the "special-sized woman" (sizes 14 and up). Nearly all Lane Bryant stores were originally located in regional shopping centers, but Wexner has shifted them to mall locations near the other Limited stores. Much growth is expected for Lane Bryant because about 40 percent of American women are size 14 or larger. There are presently 730 Lane Bryant stores.

### Structure

The Limited, Inc., began testing the market for men's fashions by offering "Express for Men" in Express stores beginning in 1987. Sixty-nine Structure stores were opened in 1989, and by the end of 1998, there were 532 stores. Structure stocks good-quality, affordable clothing in the latest styles. The target customer is in his mid-twenties and "urban, active, young, and creative." Structure stores generally open into Express stores so that customers can shop in both stores without having to exit to the mall area.

### Limited, Too

The market for girls' clothing (sizes 6–14) was tested by The Limited in the late 1980s when the Limited Too brand was offered in The Limited's flagship stores. Sixty-two stores opened in 1989, and by the end of 1998, there were 319 Limited Too stores. This division was established as an independent public company in 1999.

### Mast Industries

This division arranges for the manufacture and import of women's clothing from around the world and sells this merchandise wholesale to The Limited's stores and to other companies. This division delivers more than 100 million garments to The Limited, Inc., each year.

## Intimate Brands, Inc. (IBI)

### Victoria's Secret Stores

Victoria's Secret stores are the dominant intimate apparel stores in the world, presently selling more lingerie than their competitors Vanity Fair and Maidenform. Victoria's Secret is consumers' second most-recognized fashion brand in the United States. The stores were redecorated in the early 1990s in a "Victorian Parlor" style. Victoria's Secret bath and fragrance products are an increasingly important portion of store sales. Currently, Victoria's Secret Beauty Stores are located in Victoria's Secret stores. There are 820 Victoria's Secret stores in the United States.

### Victoria's Secret Catalogue

This division is one of the fastest growing mail-order operations in the United States. Since its purchase by The Limited in 1982, the catalogue has steadily increased its operations. Now Victoria's Secret Catalogue is the dominant catalogue for lingerie in the world. In 1996, the division established a phone center in Japan to establish this market for mail-order sales. At the end of 1998 the company launched a Web site (http://www.VictoriasSecret.com) so consumers worldwide can shop online.

### Bath & Body Works

In response to demand by consumers for natural personal care products, The Limited opened six Bath & Body Works stores in 1990. These stores have a natural market atmosphere and sell a variety of personal care products. There are 1,061 Bath & Body Works stores. The company mailed its first catalogue in 1998 and plans more catalogues in the future.

### White Barn Candle Company

This division offers an assortment of home fragrance products. In 1999, 50 Bath & Body Works stores were converted to White Barn Candle Company stores. Fifty more store openings are planned for 2000. The company's Web site is http://www.whitebarncandlecompany.com.

### Gryphon Development L.P.

This division, acquired by The Limited in 1992, develops and supplies fragrances for IBI stores. More than one thousand different products have been developed by this division. In 1998, the division delivered 300 million units of more than 1,500 different products.

## Other Retail Businesses

### Henri Bendel

In 1985, The Limited purchased this upscale fashion store. The store offers the best in clothing and accessories from international designers. Prices are designed for "today's modern woman in her mid-thirties in a higher income household." This is the only upscale store owned by The Limited and was expanded to six stores in 1996. However, the company closed five Henri Bendel stores in 1998.

### Galyan's Trading Company

In 1995, The Limited, Inc. acquired six Galyan's sporting goods stores for $18 million in cash and stock. The company had a total of 14 stores at the end of 1998. In 1999, The Limited, Inc. sold 60 percent of its interest in Galyan's.

## Center Functions

### Limited Distribution Services

The Limited's distribution center is in Columbus, Ohio. The Center now has seven buildings and about 4.2 million square feet. This includes a 760,000-square-foot fulfillment center and office complex for Victoria's Secret Catalogue that was completed in 1992. The Limited also owns a mail-order center of approximately 750,000 square feet in Indianapolis, Indiana.

### Limited Store Planning

This division is responsible for designing store layout and developing merchandising techniques for all of The Limited's retail store divisions.

### Limited Real Estate

This division handles store leases for the retail divisions. By the end of 1996, the total selling space of Limited Stores was 28.4 million square feet. Selling space decreased to 26.3 million square feet by the end of 1998.

### Limited Design Services

This division manages the design of apparel and merchandise for the retail stores.

### Limited Brand and Creative Services

The division works with the individual businesses and Wexner to create brands that have a distinctive character.

### Limited Technology Services

This division handles the telecommunications and computing needs for the company.

## COMPETITION

The retail sale of women's clothing is a very competitive business. Competitors of The Limited, Inc., include nationally, regionally, and locally owned department stores, specialty stores, and mail-order catalogue businesses. Some of The Limited's major competitors are The Gap, Casual Corner, Federated Department Stores, Dayton-Hudson, Dillard's, May Department Stores, Charming Shoppes, Nordstrom, TJX, Intimate Brands, Sears, and J. C. Penney.

Two of The Limited's major competitors are The Gap, Inc., and TJX Companies.

### The Gap, Inc.

At the end of July 1999, The Gap, Inc., had 2,611 U.S. apparel stores in operation. The Gap has several divisions that compete directly with The Limited stores. The Gap sells casual sportswear items for both men and women (1,163 stores). GapKids (699 stores) sells children's sportswear. Banana Republic (307 stores) sells upscale casual wear. Old Navy Clothing Company, the company's fastest-growing division (442 stores), sells budget-priced casual clothing. The Gap, Inc., also operates 331 GapKids, Gap, and Banana Republic stores primarily in Canada, the United Kingdom, and France. Financial information for The Gap, Inc. is shown in Exhibit 3.

The Gap, Inc., changed its merchandise mix in the mid-1990s and began offering more women's clothing and accessories and allotting less store space to casual wear such as jeans. In addition, more clothing in the stores is gender specific; fewer items are unisex sizes and styles. The Gap also has worked to define the target market of its stores as The Limited has done, and CEO Mickey Drexler also talks in terms of identifying Gap stores as "brands."

The company added more than 400 stores in 1999 with the largest percent being Old Navy stores. The Gap now has a catalogue business and sells its merchandise online at http://www.gap.com. GapBody Stores that sell underwear, sleepwear, and personal care products were opened in 1999.

### TJX Companies

TJX Companies is the largest off-price apparel chain in the United States. At the end of July 1999, TJX Companies had 1,288 apparel stores in operation. The apparel division includes: T. J. Maxx (617 stores), Marshalls (487 stores), Winners Apparel Ltd. (91 stores), Home Goods (39 stores), A. J. Wright (11 stores), and T. K. Maxx (43 stores). T. K. Maxx is an off-price apparel store in the United Kingdom. The company acquired Marshalls in 1995. Financial information for TJX Companies is shown in Exhibit 4.

EXHIBIT 3    Financial Information for the Gap, Inc.
(in millions except per-share amount)

|  | 1996 | 1997 | 1998 |
|---|---|---|---|
| Gross revenue | $5284.4 | $6507.8 | $9054.5 |
| Net income | 452.9 | 533.9 | 824.5 |
| Long-term debt | — | 496.0 | 496.5 |
| Net worth | 1654.5 | 1584.0 | 1573.7 |
| Earnings per share | $    .47 | $    .58 | $    .91 |

EXHIBIT 4    Financial Information for TJX Companies
(in millions except per-share amount)

|  | 1996 | 1997 | 1998 |
|---|---|---|---|
| Gross revenue | $6689.4 | $7389.1 | $7949.1 |
| Net income | 213.8 | 306.6 | 433.2 |
| Long-term debt | 244.4 | 221.0 | 220.3 |
| Net worth | 1127.2 | 1164.1 | 120.7 |
| Earnings per share | .59 | .88 | 1.29 |

Target customers for TJX include middle-income women between the ages of twenty-five and fifty. Most TJX stores are located in strip shopping centers.

## DEMOGRAPHIC AND SOCIETAL TRENDS

Some analysts suggest that retailers and manufacturers of women's apparel have not provided for the needs of baby boomers in their fifties. This large market group for women's apparel has found only youthful fashions and fads available for purchase. As a result, large numbers of customers began staying away from the stores entirely or purchasing fewer clothing items. There is a trend toward wearing more casual clothing in the workplace that has women and men of all ages demanding more selection in retail stores.

Currently, there is a "mini-baby boom" and many of these parents are older and have more disposable income than new parents did in the past. Also, the grandparents of these children are more likely to be affluent. Even though these trends would ordinarily indicate a good future for apparel retailing, there is a strong simultaneous trend away from the conspicuous consumption of the 1980s. In addition, many "baby boomers" have placed retirement savings, college tuition, and mortgages at a higher priority than spending for apparel. As more companies sell through the Internet, retail stores will have to learn how to contend with these competitors. Retailers in the apparel industry are likely to struggle.

## ECONOMIC CONDITIONS

The U.S. economy remains strong; employment levels are high; income levels are increasing, and inflation is under control. However, consumer debt is high, and personal bankruptcies are high. Consumers are likely to change their purchasing habits for items such as clothing in order to pay off credit card debt. The gap between rich and poor also continues to increase. In 2000, it is estimated that the number of households with annual incomes of $15,000 or less (in 1984 dollars) will increase to about 36 percent of U.S. families or about 40 million families. The number of "downscale" shoppers is increasing. Because many adults carry significant debt for cars and homes and are unable to spend much money for apparel, they often purchase clothing at outlet malls or discount stores. Occasionally, however, the "downscale" shopper may want to indulge him- or herself by purchasing fashion items from specialty stores. However, many women in the baby boom group spend their disposable income on items for their children and not clothing for themselves.

Apparel retailers are worried. Several major retail chains have filed for reorganization under Chapter 11 bankruptcy, and many others have not been profitable for years. It is difficult for retail chains to predict consumer spending patterns. In the past 50 years, apparel retailers have seen about 16 economic cycles. The longest cycle was six years, and the shortest was about a year. These cycles corresponded with the business cycle 60 percent of the time, so apparel sales are likely to stay strong when the economy is good.

Specialty retailers may have to take more gambles to gain a competitive advantage in this volatile industry. Specialty retailers have done this in the past by guessing a fashion trend early and purchasing inventory to provide that trend to customers. If a specialty retailer purchases inventory for a fashion trend but cannot turn over the inventory, the store loses profit and cannot afford to take more risks. However, if one does not gamble by trying to keep up with fashion trends, it is impossible to make a profit when the economy turns around because the merchandise will be out of date.

## INTERNAL FACTORS FOR THE LIMITED, INC.

### Marketing

Wexner believes that his company is "reinventing the specialty store business." Because The Limited retail store divisions sell different price ranges and styles of clothing and related goods, Wexner has created the impact of a department store in many malls by locating the stores in close proximity. Wexner has begun to think of his stores as a collection of brands rather than a group of stores. He says, "When you think of yourself as a brand, you think more broadly. You think of the efficacy of the brand, the reputation, the integrity, the channels of distribution, whether that be in a store, a catalogue, on television, or overseas." Brand building includes defining each store's image, fashion, advertising, price, and market position. In the past, Limited divisions copied each other's designs so that the only difference in some divisions was the price of the items. Design teams are now assigned to each business, and the fashions are designed around narrowly defined brand positions for each division. Leslie Wexner believes this is "good for now. Even better for the long run."

The Limited spent very little on advertising campaigns in its first twenty years. Instead, the company relied on walk-in traffic in malls to sell their products. The company launched its first national advertising campaign in November 1989. The $10 million campaign included advertisements in *Vogue, Vanity Fair,* and other women's magazines in an attempt to increase brand recognition for the company's private labels. Wexner's approach to advertising has changed dramatically in recent years. Currently, the only brands that are advertised heavily are Victoria's Secret and Lane Bryant. Victoria's Secret launched a Web site in December 1998. The television announcements during the Super Bowl in January 1999 of a live online fashion show generated one million hits to the Web site. Lane Bryant started its Web site in 1999 by advertising Venezia jeans with spokesperson Camryn Manheim (actress on "The Practice"). Lane Bryant's ad with Manheim also appeared in the *Wall Street Journal, USA Today,* and *The New York Times.* Another approach to advertising was selected by Express; their clothing is worn by actors on shows such as "Ally McBeal" and "Party of Five." In 1999 the company created Limited Brands and Creative Services, a department that serves as an in-house advertising agency for The Limited's businesses. Approximately $80 million was spent on advertising in 1999, and the budget is expected to increase to $200 million by 2002.

The Limited's distribution center is in Columbus, Ohio. Over 60 percent of the U.S. population is located within a 500-mile radius of Columbus, so Wexner feels it is an ideal location for a distribution center. Another advantage of the Columbus location is its proximity to New York, where incoming merchandise produced in foreign countries is received by Mast Industries. All merchandise arriving in New York is shipped directly to the distribution center for allocation among The Limited's stores. A computerized distribution system helps distributors select each store's inventory. This system allows The

Limited to monitor inventory levels, merchandise mix, and sales pattern at each store so that appropriate adjustments can be made as needed. A new $42.1 million Bath & Body Works distribution center was opened in July 1997. The company recently created an intranet computer system called Limited, Inc. Freight Tracking System (LIFTS) that tracks purchase orders from overseas plants to their delivery point. The company plans to upgrade the system so that orders can be tracked through the entire production process.

## Production

The Limited, Inc. does not produce its own clothing, but it does have a division that contracts for the manufacture of clothing. Mast Industries specializes in contracting for production of high-quality, low-cost products. Much of the merchandise imported by Mast is marked with one of The Limited's own labels: The Limited, Compagnie Internationale, Structure, Victoria's Secret, and NY & Co. Leslie Wexner believes that having private-label brands allows The Limited to keep merchandise inventory current and unique.

The Limited can also maintain control over its clothing supply through Mast Industries. Company managers try to maintain a 1,000-hour turnaround time between recognizing a new style and delivering the merchandise to stores. Mast can send high-resolution computer images of clothing designs by satellite to Far Eastern manufacturers. In addition, computer information collected from all individual stores is used to determine what needs to be produced in the Far East the next day. In a few days, the newly produced items arrive at the Columbus distribution center and are sent to the stores.

In 1998, Mast purchased merchandise from approximately 4,700 different suppliers, but no more than 5 percent of The Limited's inventory was purchased from any single manufacturer. About half of the inventory is produced outside the United States. The coordination of work with so many factories makes it difficult to ensure consistent quality. Two changes were made in 1995 in an effort to make sure the company's products were of consistent quality: presidents of the store divisions were given the responsibility for ensuring quality in their division, and individual store managers were no longer allowed to make significant sourcing decisions on their own. The Limited flagship store was the pilot for another new approach to production in 1996. The Limited Stores reduced the number of its major manufacturers from 60 to 20, and quality control was rigidly monitored. It is expected that other store divisions will adopt this strategy.

## Management

Leslie Wexner has been a guiding force for the company since its beginning. His risk-taking style has concerned some investors, but his new marketing concepts have made The Limited, Inc., the envy of other specialty retailers. Some critics suggest that Wexner is great at starting businesses but has not been effective as a day-to-day leader of the established businesses. His tendency was to micromanage store divisions, and as recently as 1992, Wexner had 24 people reporting directly to him.

Wexner now leads a centralized process for planning. This approach to leadership allows Wexner to remain involved in each store division, without his involvement in every detail of division operations. After the company began to consider store divisions as brands, Wexner started meeting with the top managers (president, marketing director, chief financial officer, head merchant, and head designer) of each store division on a monthly basis to make sure there is "agreement and alignment around core elements of the brand."

EXHIBIT 5     Income Statements for The Limited, Inc.
(in millions except per-share amount)

|  | 1996 | 1997 | 1998 | 1999 |
|---|---|---|---|---|
| Net sales | $8,644.8 | $9,188.8 | $9,346.9 | $9723.3 |
| Cost of goods sold, occupancy and buying costs | 6,148.2 | 6,370.8 | 6,348.9 | 6365.8 |
| Gross income | 2,496.6 | 2,818.0 | 2,998.0 | 3357.4 |
| General, administrative, and store operating expenses | 1,848.5 | 2124.7 | 2,300.5 | 2460.3 |
| Special and Nonrecurring items, net | 12.0 | 213.2 | 1,740.0 | 23.5 |
| Operating income | 636.1 | 480.1 | 2,437.5 | 920.6 |
| Interest expense | 75.4 | 68.7 | 68.5 | 78.2 |
| Other income (expense), net | 41.9 | 36.9 | 59.2 | 51.0 |
| Minority interest | 45.6 | 56.5 | 64.6 | 72.6 |
| Gain on sale of subsidiary stock | 118.2 | 8.6 | — | 11.0 |
| Income before taxes | 675.2 | 400.4 | 2363.6 | 831.7 |
| Provision for income taxes | 241.0 | 183 | 310.0 | 371.0 |
| Net income | 434.2 | 217.4 | 2,053.6 | 460.7 |
| Net income per share | $   1.54 | $     .79 | $     8.32 | $     2.10 |

*Source:* The Limited, Inc. 1992, 1994, 1996, 1998, 1999 *Annual Reports.*

## Financial Condition

The Limited's income statements and balance sheets are provided in Exhibit 5 and Exhibit 6, respectively. These statements reveal significant changes in levels for sales, income, assets, and shareholder's equity.

## FUTURE OUTLOOK

Wexner says he is "determined to build a company of powerful, differentiated retail brands that maintain and strengthen our position as the world's dominant specialty retailer." His position is that if a division does not have potential to earn at least $1 billion in sales in the United States, The Limited, Inc. should get out of that business. If a new concept works, Wexner is aggressive. He says, "Invent the concept. Prove it. Move forward fast." Some critics suggest that Wexner has the talent to identify unserved markets and create a marketing concept around those markets but that he has not yet demonstrated the skill at reinventing mature businesses. Wexner responds, "My view is that whether you are turning around a business—that is reconceptualizing it—or whether you are starting from scratch, your vision of what you are driving toward is the same."

The company's plans for growth include the following:

1. Sales will increase annually by 10 percent to 12 percent through 2004.
2. Selling space will increase 10 percent to 12 percent each year through 2004.
3. Approximately $450 million will be spent for capital expenditures in 1999, with $350 million for new stores and remodeling of existing stores.
4. During 1999 the company expects to close as many as 200 underperforming stores and open 340 stores so that selling space will increase to 132,000 selling square feet.
5. The company leaders will continue to refocus the company through brand building.

## EXHIBIT 6     Balance Sheet for The Limited, Inc. (in millions)

|  | 1996 | 1997 | 1998 | 1999 |
|---|---|---|---|---|
| **Assets** | | | | |
| Current assets | | | | |
|   Cash and equivalents | $ 312.8 | $ 746.4 | $ 870.3 | $ 817.2 |
|   Accounts receivable | 69.3 | 83.4 | 77.7 | 108.7 |
|   Inventories | 1007.3 | 1002.7 | 1119.7 | 1050.9 |
|   Store supplies | 90.4 | 99.2 | 98.8 | 99.9 |
|   Other | 65.3 | 99.5 | 151.7 | 169.3 |
| Total current assets | 1545.1 | 2031.2 | 2318.2 | 2246.2 |
| Property and equipment | 1828.9 | 1415.9 | 1361.8 | 1229.6 |
| Restricted cash | 351.6 | 351.6 | 351.6 | — |
| Deferred income taxes | — | 56.6 | 48.7 | 125.1 |
| Other assets | 394.4 | 445.5 | 469.4 | 486.6 |
| Total assets | $4120.0 | $4300.8 | $4549.7 | $4087.6 |
| **Liabilities and Shareholders' Equity** | | | | |
| Current liabilities | | | | |
|   Accounts payable | $ 307.8 | $ 300.7 | $ 289.9 | $ 256.3 |
| Current portion of long-term debt | | — | 100.00 | 250.0 |
|   Accrued expenses | 481.8 | 676.7 | 681.5 | 579.4 |
|   Certificates of deposit | — | — | — | — |
|   Income taxes payable | 117.3 | 116.0 | 176.5 | 152.4 |
| Total current liabilities | 906.9 | 1093.4 | 1247.9 | 1238.1 |
| Long-term debt | 650.0 | 650.0 | 550.0 | 400.0 |
| Deferred income taxes | 169.9 | — | — | — |
| Other long-term liabilities | 51.7 | 58.7 | 56.0 | 183.3 |
| Minority interest | 67.3 | 102.1 | 110.9 | 119.0 |
| Contingent stock redemption | | | | |
|   agreement | 351.6 | 351.6 | 351.6 | — |
| Shareholders' equity | | | | |
| Common stock | 180.3 | 180.4 | 180.4 | 189.7 |
| Paid-in capital | 142.9 | 148.0 | 157.2 | 178.3 |
| Retained earnings | 3526.2 | 3613.2 | 5537.0 | 6109.3 |
| Less treasury stock, at cost | (1926.9) | (1896.6) | (3641.3) | (4330.3) |
| Total shareholders' equity | 1922.6 | 2045.0 | 2233.3 | 2147.0 |
| Total liabilities and shareholders' | | | | |
|   equity | $4120.0 | $4300.8 | $4549.7 | $4087.4 |

*Source:* The Limited, Inc. 1992, 1994, 1996, 1998, 1999 *Annual Reports.*

Additional strategies include improving the merchandise mix and quality of products in the stores, continuing to take advantage of company name recognition and the supplier advantages provided by Mast Industries, and building new retailing concepts. Wexner hopes these plans will allow The Limited, Inc., to continue improving its position in the specialty retailing industry.

However, the potential for serious problems exists. Some of these include: (1) the possibility of downturns in the growth-oriented lingerie and personal care divisions, (2) another downturn in the women's apparel industry, (3) a saturation of Limited stores in U.S. malls, (4) difficulty in finding reliable foreign suppliers and (5) failure of the company's new cosmetics and skin care businesses.

Wexner is aggressive regarding The Limited's ability to compete in the specialty apparel industry of the future. His new campaign to motivate workers is called WAR (Winning At Retail). Wexner says, "It is a war, and in wars people really do live and people do die." Wexner hopes this program will help the company overcome its uninspiring performance of the past ten years.

The following list presents some of the questions that Wexner—and you—might consider:

1. Is The Limited expanding too rapidly and becoming too diversified?
2. Will the branding concept help The Limited to improve its market segmentation strategies?
3. Is locating stores in close proximity in malls a good idea for The Limited? Should the company locate some of its stores in strip shopping centers?
4. Is The Limited's strategy of spending more money on print and television advertising a good one?
5. What is the likelihood of another downturn in the women's apparel industry?
6. Will Wexner be able to turn around the Structure, Lerner, and Limited stores? What approach should he take in addition to concentrating on branding?
7. How serious are the potential problems The Limited could face in the future?
8. Should the company continue its strategy of developing a company and splitting it off as a separate company?

## REFERENCES

CAMINITI, SUSAN. "Can the Limited Fix Itself?" *Fortune.* October 17, 1994.

D'INNOCENZIO, ANNE. "Turnaround at Express Attributed to Faster Pickup on Hot Trends." *Women's Wear Daily.* July 14, 1999.

EDELSON, SHARON. "Sisman: An Aggressive Plan for Advertising by Limited." *Women's Wear Daily.* June 2, 1999.

GILL, PENNY. "Les Wexner: Unlimited Success Story." *Stores.* January 1993.

http://www.intimatebrands.com

http://www.limited.com

http://www.VictoriasSecret.com

JAFFE, THOMAS. "One Last Throw." *Forbes.* December 18, 1995.

JAFFE, THOMAS, AND ESTHER W. BOOK. "A Thin Coat of Whitewash?" *Forbes.* April 8, 1996.

"Intimate Brands, Inc." *Happi-Household & Personal Products Industry.* July 1999.

The Limited, Inc. *Annual Reports.* 1990, 1992, 1994, 1996, 1998, 1999.

LIPPE, DAN (with news from Alice Cuneo). "The Ltd. Casts a Wider Net." *Advertising Age.* June 14, 1999.

MACHAN, DYAN. "Knowing Your Limits." *Forbes.* June 5, 1995.

QUICK, REBECCA. "Retail, Like War, Is Hell at The Limited." *The Wall Street Journal.* April 21, 1999.

SHEIN, ESTHER. "Intranet Logistics Goes High Fashion." *PC Week.* September 8, 1997.

"State of the Industry: Apparel Stores: New Merchandising and Marketing Strategies Account for Growth." *Chain Store Age: State of the Industry Supplement.* August 1999.

Top 1000 Specialty Stores. *Stores.* August 1998.

# WAL-MART STORES, INC.—2001

Amit Shah and Tyra Phipps
Frostburg State University

**WMT**

www.wal-mart.com

Headquartered in Bentonville, Arkansas, Wal-Mart's sales rose from $137.6 billion in fiscal 1999 to $165 billion in fiscal 2000. Net income rose from $4.4 billion to $5.3 billion during that period. For more than a decade, Wal-Mart has been on a rollercoaster ride, growing by leaps and bounds, rolling over large competitors such as Kmart and thousands of small businesses. Financial statements are shown in Exhibits 1 and 2.

In 1995, Wal-Mart ended a five-year battle with local leaders of Bennington, Vermont, to open its first store in that state and, thereby, lay claim to having stores in all 50 states (see Exhibit 3). The Bennington store was Wal-Mart's 2,158th store. To get approval for this store, Wal-Mart abandoned its usual 200,000-square-foot store near a major highway exit and located in a downtown building of just 50,000 square feet. Environmentalists in Vermont say the rural character of the state is endangered by "sprawl-mart development." Other chains such as Ames and Kmart have operated in Vermont for years, so some residents are mystified by current controversy. Wal-Mart had four stores in Vermont by the end of fiscal 2000.

In 1998, another Wal-Mart entrance has dramatically impacted a Los Angeles community, Panorama City, in a positive way. The area's major employer had been a General Motors plant until it closed in 1992 affecting the surrounding businesses. The community was deteriorating and traffic declined immensely. Wal-Mart's arrival has brought retail excitement and bustling crowds back to the area.

Wal-Mart does not have a formal mission statement. When asked about Wal-Mart's lack of a mission, Public Relations Coordinator Kim Ellis recently replied, "We believe that our customers are most interested in other aspects of our business, and we are focused on meeting their basic consumer needs. If in fact we did have a formal mission statement, it would be something like this: 'To provide quality products at an everyday low price and with extended customer service . . . always.' "

## HISTORY

No word better describes Wal-Mart than "growth." In 1945, Sam Walton opened his first Ben Franklin franchise in Newport, Arkansas. Based in rural Bentonville, Arkansas, Walton, his wife Helen, and his brother Bud operated the nation's most successful Ben Franklin franchises. "We were a small chain," said Walton of his 16-store operation. "Things were running so smoothly we even had time for our families." What more could a man want? A great deal, as it turned out.

Sam and Bud Walton could see that the variety store was gradually dying as supermarkets and discounters developed. Far from being secure, Walton knew that he was under siege. He decided to counterattack. He first tried to convince the top management

EXHIBIT 1   Wal-Mart's Consolidated Statement of Income
            (Amounts in millions except per-share data)

| Fiscal years ended January 31, | 2000 | 1999 | 1998 | 1997 |
|---|---|---|---|---|
| **Revenues:** | | | | |
| Net sales | $165,013 | $137,634 | $117,958 | $104,859 |
| Other income-net | 1,796 | 1,574 | 1,341 | 1,319 |
| | 166,809 | 139,208 | 119,299 | 106,178 |
| **Costs and expenses:** | | | | |
| Cost of sales | 129,664 | 108,725 | 93,438 | 83,510 |
| Operating, selling and general and administrative expenses | 27,040 | 22,363 | 19,358 | 16,946 |
| **Interest costs:** | | | | |
| Debt | 756 | 529 | 555 | 629 |
| Capital leases | 266 | 268 | 229 | 216 |
| | $157,726 | $131,885 | $113,580 | $101,301 |
| **Income before income taxes, minority interest and equity in unconsolidated subsidiaries** | 9,083 | 7,323 | 5,719 | 4,877 |
| **Provision for income taxes** | | | | |
| Current | 3,476 | 3,380 | 2,095 | 1,974 |
| Deferred | (138) | (640) | 20 | (180) |
| | 3,338 | 2,740 | 2,115 | 1,794 |
| **Income before minority interest and equity in unconsolidated subsidiaries** | 5,745 | 4,583 | 3,604 | 3,083 |
| **Minority interest and equity in unconsolidated subsidiaries** | (170) | (153) | (78) | (27) |
| **Net income** | $ 5,575 | $ 4,430 | $ 3,526 | $ 3,056 |
| **Net income per share—basic and dilutive** | $ 1.25 | $ 0.99 | $ 0.78 | $ 0.67 |
| **Average number of common shares:** | | | | |
| Basic | 4,451 | 4,464 | 4,516 | 4,585 |
| Dilutive | 4,474 | 4,485 | 4,533 | 4,592 |

*Source:* www.freeedgar.com

of Ben Franklin to enter discounting. After their refusal, Sam Walton made a quick trip around the country in search of ideas. He then began opening his own discount stores in small Arkansas towns like Bentonville and Rogers.

The company opened its first discount department store (Wal-Mart) in November 1962. The early stores had bare tile floors and pipe racks. Wal-Mart did not begin to revamp its image significantly until the mid-1970s, and growth in the early years was slow. However, once the company went public in 1970, sales began to increase rapidly. When it first went public, 100 shares of Wal-Mart stock cost $1,650. Now those 100 shares are worth $11,264,000. Wal-Mart's stock was up 106 percent in 1999 and was named the number one stock on the Dow.

Such retailers as Target, Venture, and Kmart provided the examples that Wal-Mart sought to emulate in its growth. The old Wal-Mart store colors, dark blue and white (too harsh), were dumped in favor of a three-tone combination of light beige, soft blue, and burnt orange. Carpeting, which had long been discarded on apparel sales floors, was put back. New racks were installed that displayed the entire garment instead of only an outer edge.

## EXHIBIT 2    Wal-Mart's Consolidated Balance Sheet
### (Amounts in millions)

| January 31, | 2000 | 1999 | 1998 |
|---|---|---|---|
| **Assets** | | | |
| Current assets: | | | |
| Cash and cash equivalents | $ 1,856 | $ 1,879 | $ 1,447 |
| Receivables | 1,341 | 1,118 | 976 |
| Inventories | | | |
| At replacement cost | 20,171 | 17,549 | 16,845 |
| Less LIFO reserve | 378 | 473 | 348 |
| Inventories at LIFO cost | 19,793 | 17,076 | 16,497 |
| Prepaid expenses and other | 1,366 | 1,059 | 432 |
| Total current assets | 24,356 | 21,132 | 19,352 |
| *Property, plant and equipment, at cost:* | | | |
| Land | 8,785 | 5,219 | 4,691 |
| Building and improvements | 21,169 | 16,061 | 14,646 |
| Fixtures and equipment | 10,362 | 9,296 | 7,636 |
| Transportation equipment | 747 | 553 | 403 |
| | 41,063 | 31,129 | 27,376 |
| Less accumulated depreciation | 8,224 | 7,455 | 5,907 |
| Net property, plant and equipment | 32,839 | 23,674 | 21,469 |
| *Property under capital lease:* | | | |
| Property under capital lease | 4,285 | 3,335 | 3,040 |
| Less accumulated amortization | 1,155 | 1,036 | 903 |
| Net property under capital leases | 3,130 | 2,299 | 2,137 |
| Goodwill | 9,392 | 0 | 0 |
| Other assets and deferred charges | 632 | 2,891 | 2,426 |
| Total assets | $70,349 | $49,996 | $45,384 |
| **Liabilities and shareholders' equity** | | | |
| *Current liabilities:* | | | |
| Commercial paper | $ 3,323 | 0 | 0 |
| Accounts payable | 13,105 | 10,257 | 9,126 |
| Accrued liabilities | 6,161 | 4,998 | 3,628 |
| Accrued income taxes | 1,129 | 501 | 565 |
| Long-term debt due within one year | 1,964 | 900 | 1,039 |
| Obligations under capital leases due within one year | 121 | 106 | 102 |
| Total current liabilities | 25,803 | 16,762 | 14,460 |
| *Long-term debt* | 13,672 | 6,908 | 7,191 |
| *Long-term obligations under capital leases* | 3,002 | 2,699 | 2,483 |
| *Deferred income taxes and other* | 759 | 716 | 809 |
| *Minority interest* | 1,279 | 1,799 | 1,938 |
| *Shareholders' equity* | | | |
| Preferred stock ($.10 par value; 100 shares authorized, none issued) | | | |
| Common stock ($.10 par value; 5,500 shares authorized, 4,457 and 4,448 issued and outstanding in 2000 and 1999, respectively) | 446 | 445 | 224 |
| Capital in excess of par value | 714 | 435 | 585 |
| Retained earnings | 25,129 | 20,741 | 18,167 |
| Other accumulated comprehensive income | (455) | (509) | (473) |
| Total shareholders' equity | 25,834 | 21,112 | 18,503 |
| Total liabilities and shareholders' equity | $70,349 | $49,996 | $45,384 |

EXHIBIT 3     Wal-Mart Stores, Inc.
              Fiscal 2000 End-of-Year Store Count

| State | Discount Stores | Supercenters | SAM's Clubs |
|---|---|---|---|
| Alabama | 43 | 38 | 8 |
| Alaska | 4 | 0 | 3 |
| Arizona | 31 | 5 | 9 |
| Arkansas | 44 | 33 | 4 |
| California | 113 | 0 | 25 |
| Colorado | 23 | 16 | 12 |
| Connecticut | 14 | 0 | 3 |
| Delaware | 3 | 1 | 1 |
| Florida | 89 | 50 | 35 |
| Georgia | 59 | 35 | 16 |
| Hawaii | 5 | 0 | 1 |
| Idaho | 9 | 0 | 1 |
| Illinois | 85 | 22 | 26 |
| Indiana | 56 | 24 | 14 |
| Iowa | 36 | 11 | 7 |
| Kansas | 37 | 11 | 5 |
| Kentucky | 39 | 33 | 5 |
| Louisiana | 48 | 29 | 10 |
| Maine | 17 | 3 | 3 |
| Maryland | 25 | 1 | 11 |
| Massachusetts | 32 | 1 | 3 |
| Michigan | 52 | 1 | 21 |
| Minnesota | 35 | 1 | 9 |
| Mississippi | 34 | 25 | 4 |
| Missouri | 69 | 43 | 12 |
| Montana | 9 | 0 | 1 |
| Nebraska | 13 | 6 | 3 |
| Nevada | 13 | 0 | 2 |
| New Hampshire | 18 | 3 | 4 |
| New Jersey | 22 | 0 | 6 |
| New Mexico | 9 | 13 | 3 |
| New York | 52 | 9 | 18 |
| North Carolina | 66 | 26 | 16 |
| North Dakota | 8 | 0 | 2 |
| Ohio | 75 | 11 | 24 |
| Oklahoma | 52 | 27 | 6 |
| Oregon | 24 | 0 | 0 |
| Pennsylvania | 49 | 27 | 18 |
| Rhode Island | 7 | 0 | 1 |
| South Carolina | 32 | 25 | 9 |
| South Dakota | 8 | 0 | 2 |
| Tennessee | 49 | 38 | 14 |
| Texas | 154 | 94 | 53 |
| Utah | 14 | 0 | 5 |
| Vermont | 4 | 0 | 0 |
| Virginia | 26 | 37 | 10 |
| Washington | 24 | 0 | 2 |
| West Virginia | 8 | 18 | 3 |
| Wisconsin | 54 | 4 | 11 |
| Wyoming | 9 | 0 | 2 |
| U.S. Total | 1801 | 721 | 463 |

EXHIBIT 3    Wal-Mart Stores, Inc.
             Fiscal 2000 End-of-Year Store Count *(cont.)*

| Country | Discount Stores | Supercenters | SAM's Clubs |
|---|---|---|---|
| Argentina | 0 | 10 | 3 |
| Brazil | 0 | 9 | 5 |
| Canada | 166 | 0 | 0 |
| China | 0 | 5 | 1 |
| Germany | 0 | 95 | 0 |
| Korea | 0 | 5 | 0 |
| Mexico | 397 | 27 | 34 |
| Puerto Rico | 9 | 0 | 6 |
| United Kingdom | 0 | 232 | 0 |
| INT'L Total | 572 | 383 | 49 |
| Worldwide Grand Total | 2373 | 1104 | 512 |

*Source:* Wal-Mart's 2000 *Annual Report,* pages 20 and 21.

In 1987, Wal-Mart implemented two new concepts: (1) Hypermarkets—200,000-square-foot stores that sell everything including food, and (2) Super-centers—scaled-down supermarkets. Also in 1987, Walton named David Glass as the new CEO, while he remained chairman of the board. Mr. Glass is president and CEO today. (Exhibit 4 shows Wal-Mart's organizational structure).

In 1990, Wal-Mart completed the acquisition of 14 centers of McLane Company, a national distribution system in 11 states providing over 12,500 types of grocery and nongrocery products. Also in 1990, Wal-Mart sold its 14 Dot Discount Drug Stores. SAM's Clubs that year integrated the 28 wholesale clubs of The Whole Club, Inc., of Indianapolis, Indiana, into its operations.

Wal-Mart unveiled in mid-1993 its first environmental demonstration store, a 121,294-square-foot facility in Lawrence, Kansas. This store is designed so that a second floor could be added to allow conversion to apartments if Wal-Mart vacates the space. The store is exceptionally energy efficient but costs 20 percent more than the average Wal-Mart store, which costs about $2.4 million or $20 a square foot. The environmental store features on-site recycling, native plants as landscaping, and solar-powered lights. Planning for this store began in 1990 when Hillary Rodham Clinton served on Wal-Mart's board of directors. Wal-Mart is presently constructing in Moore, Oklahoma, a second environmental demonstration store. Companywide, Wal-Mart recycles over 700,000 tons of cardboard, paper and plastic each year.

Sam Walton died in 1992, and Bud Walton died in 1995. Wal-Mart's 1995 *Annual Report* is dedicated to Bud. Sam Walton once said about Bud: "Of course, my number-one retail partner has been my brother Bud. Bud's wise counsel and guidance kept us from many a mistake. Often, Bud would advise taking a different direction or maybe changing the timing. I soon learned to listen to him because he has exceptional judgment and a great deal of common sense."

## DIVISIONS

### Wal-Mart Stores

Most Wal-Mart stores are located in towns of 5,000 to 25,000. On occasion, smaller stores are built in communities of fewer than 5,000 people. As indicated in Exhibit 5,

**EXHIBIT 4   Wal-Mart's Organizational Chart**

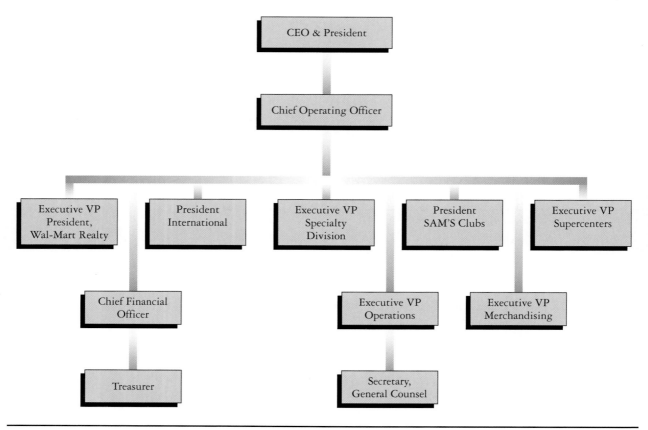

*Source:* www.freeedgar.com

Wal-Mart opened 29 Wal-Mart stores, 157 Supercenters, and 12 SAM's Clubs in fiscal 2000. Most of Wal-Mart's fiscal 2000 sales came from Wal-Mart stores and Supercenters. International sales grew to approximately 9 percent of the total sales in fiscal 1999, up from 6 percent in fiscal 1998. Exhibit 6 provides financial information for Wal-Mart's divisions, and Exhibit 7 shows Wal-Mart sales data by category in 2000.

Wal-Mart grouped its smaller discount stores such as the one in Bennington, Vermont, into a new Hometown U.S.A. program, which allows the company to give special attention to customers in smaller markets in rural America. Hometown USA consists of the stores that are smaller than 50,000 square feet and under one regional manager. The idea is to enable these stores to develop locally and with a different mix from the large prototypes. Although these stores represent Wal-Mart's heritage, they had become lost in the shuffle as the company opened 120,000- to 150,000-square-foot stores.

Wal-Mart stores generally have 40 departments and offer a wide variety of merchandise, including apparel for women, girls, men, boys, and infants. Each store also carries curtains, fabrics and notions, shoes, housewares, hardware, electronics, home supplies, sporting goods, toys, cameras and supplies, health and beauty aids, pharmaceuticals, and jewelry. Nationally advertised merchandise accounts for a majority of sales of the stores. Wal-Mart has begun marketing limited lines of merchandise under the brand

# EXHIBIT 5  Wal-Mart Stores Segment Store Count and Net Square-Footage Growth
## (Years Ended January 31, 1994 Through 2000)

## Store Count

| Fiscal Year Ended Jan 31, | Wal-Mart Discount Stores | | | | Wal-Mart Supercenters | | Total | | | SAM's Clubs | | |
|---|---|---|---|---|---|---|---|---|---|---|---|---|
| | Opened | Closed | Conversions[a] | Total | Opened[b] | Total | Opened[b] | Closed | Ending Balance | Opened | Closed | Total |
| Balance Forward | | | | 1,848 | | 34 | | | 1,882 | | | 256 |
| 1994 | 141 | 2 | 37 | 1,950 | 38 | 72 | 142 | 2 | 2,022 | 162[a] | 1 | 417 |
| 1995 | 109 | 5 | 69 | 1,985 | 75 | 147 | 115 | 5 | 2,132 | 21 | 12 | 426 |
| 1996 | 92 | 2 | 80 | 1,995 | 92 | 239 | 104 | 2 | 2,234 | 9 | 2 | 433 |
| 1997 | 59 | 2 | 92 | 1,960 | 105 | 344 | 72 | 2 | 2,304 | 9 | 6 | 436 |
| 1998 | 37 | 1 | 75 | 1,921 | 97 | 441 | 59 | 1 | 2,362 | 8 | 1 | 443 |
| 1999 | 37 | 1 | 88 | 1,869 | 123 | 564 | 72 | 1 | 2,433 | 8 | 0 | 451 |
| 2000 | 29 | 1 | 96 | 1,801 | 157 | 721 | 90 | 1 | 2,522 | 12 | 0 | 463 |

## Net Square Footage

| Fiscal Year Ended Jan 31, | Wal-Mart Discount Stores | | Wal-Mart Supercenters | | Total | | SAM's Clubs | |
|---|---|---|---|---|---|---|---|---|
| | Net Additions | Total | Net Additions | Total | Net Additions | Square Footage | Net Additions | Total |
| Balance Forward | | 147,366,428 | | 5,951,739 | | 153,318,167 | | 30,703,878 |
| 1994 | 16,185,442 | 163,551,870 | 6,762,080 | 12,713,819 | 22,947,522 | 176,265,689 | 19,670,804 | 50,374,682 |
| 1995 | 10,109,978 | 173,661,848 | 14,087,725 | 26,801,544 | 24,197,703 | 200,463,392 | 1,335,742 | 51,710,424 |
| 1996 | 8,188,223 | 181,850,071 | 16,791,559 | 43,593,103 | 24,979,782 | 225,443,174 | 825,020 | 52,535,444 |
| 1997 | (103,486) | 181,746,585 | 19,661,948 | 63,255,051 | 19,558,462 | 245,001,636 | 298,692 | 52,834,136 |
| 1998 | (2,411,149) | 179,335,436 | 17,076,582 | 80,331,633 | 14,665,433 | 259,667,069 | 716,150 | 53,550,286 |
| 1999 | (3,062,418) | 176,273,018 | 21,892,838 | 102,224,471 | 18,830,420 | 278,497,489 | 1,099,144 | 54,649,430 |
| 2000 | (5,486,901) | 170,786,117 | 28,488,737 | 130,713,208 | 23,001,836 | 301,499,325 | 1,701,478 | 56,350,908 |

*Source:* Wal-Mart 2000 *Annual Report*, page 9.
[a] Wal-Mart discount store locations relocated or expanded as Wal-Mart Supercenters.
[b] Total opened net of conversions of Wal-Mart discount stores to Wal-Mart Supercenters.

EXHIBIT 6    Wal-Mart's Divisions Financial Data

| Fiscal year ended January 31, 2000 | Wal-Mart Stores | SAM's Club | International | Other |
|---|---|---|---|---|
| Revenues from external customers | $108,721 | $24,801 | $22,728 | $ 8,763 |
| Intercompany real estate charge (income) | 1,542 | 366 | | (1,908) |
| Depreciation and amortization | 812 | 124 | 402 | 1,037 |
| Operating income | 8,419 | 759 | 817 | 110 |
| Interest expense | | | | |
| Income before income taxes, minority interest, equity in unconsolidated subsidiaries and cumulative effect of accounting change | | | | |
| Total assets | $ 18,213 | $ 3,586 | $25,330 | $23,220 |

Source: Wal-Mart 2000 Annual Report, p. 50.

EXHIBIT 7    Wal-Mart Sales Data for Fiscal Year Ended January 31, 1999

| | Percentage of Sales | |
|---|---|---|
| Category | 1999 | 2000 |
| Hardgoods | 22 | 22 |
| Softgoods/domestics | 21 | 20 |
| Grocery, candy, and tobacco | 16 | 18 |
| Pharmaceuticals | 9 | 10 |
| Electronics | 9 | 8 |
| Sporting goods and toys | 7 | 7 |
| Health and beauty aids | 7 | 7 |
| Stationery | 4 | 3 |
| Shoes | 2 | 2 |
| Jewelry | 2 | 2 |
| One-hour photo | 1 | 1 |
| | 100% | 100% |

Source: Wal-Mart 2000 Annual Report, page 5.

name SAM's American Choice. The merchandise is carefully selected to ensure quality and must be made in the United States. Wal-Mart has also developed new apparel lines such as the Kathie Lee career sportswear and dress collection, Basic Equipment sportswear, and McKids children's clothing.

Except for extended hours during certain holiday seasons, most Wal-Mart stores are open from 9:00 A.M. to 9:00 P.M. six days a week, and from 12:30 P.M. to 5:30 P.M. on Sundays (some stores are closed on Sunday). Some Wal-Mart stores and most of the Super-center stores are open 24 hours each day. Wal-Mart tries to meet or undersell local competition but maintains uniform prices except when lower prices are necessary to meet local competition. Wal-Mart stores maintain a "satisfaction guaranteed" program to promote customer goodwill and acceptance.

## McLane's

McLane's is the nation's largest distributor of food and merchandise to convenience stores, offering a wide variety of grocery and nongrocery products, both perishable and nonperishable items. The nongrocery products consist primarily of tobacco products, hard goods, health and beauty aids, toys, and stationery. McLane's is a wholesale distributor that sells merchandise to a variety of retailers, including the Wal-Mart stores, SAM's Clubs, and Supercenters.

## SAM's Clubs

SAM's Clubs are membership-only, cash-and-carry operations. A financial service credit-card program (Discover Card) is available in all clubs. Qualified members include businesses and individuals who are members of certain qualifying organizations, such as government and state employees and credit union members. Both business and individual members pay an annual membership fee of $25 for the primary membership card. In addition, two individuals of the same household who don't qualify for the membership can establish an Advantage membership for $35 annually, and additional names can be added to this membership for $15 each.

SAM's offers bulk displays of name-brand hard goods, some soft goods, and institutional-size grocery items. Each SAM's also carries jewelry, sporting goods, toys, tires, stationery, and books. Most clubs have fresh-food departments such as bakery, meat, and produce.

SAM's is a $23 billion business that is starting to grow again. The clubs were never designed to sell merchandise categories but rather items, and because the number of items is limited to about 2,000 for the wholesale part of the business (60 percent to 65 percent of sales) and to 1,000–1,500 for personal and individual use, those items must be appropriate for the location. The items have to come and go seasonally, so continuity by category is not appropriate. Thus, there is a problem for buyers, who have to be item merchants and compete for space in the clubs.

Operating hours vary among SAM's Clubs but generally are Monday through Friday from 10:00 A.M. to 8:30 P.M. Most SAM's Clubs are open on the weekend from 9:30 A.M. to 7:00 P.M. on Saturday and 12:00 P.M. to 6:00 P.M. on Sunday. SAM's attempts to maximize sales volume and inventory turnover while minimizing expenses.

During fiscal 1999, Wal-Mart opened 8 new SAM's Clubs and 12 more in fiscal 2000. This division of Wal-Mart lags behind other divisions in financial performance, but the company feels the warehouse club business has promise.

## Supercenters

Wal-Mart's supercenters combine groceries with general merchandise for one-stop shopping. Wal-Mart opened 157 Supercenters during 2000, bringing the total of Supercenters to over 721 in the United States as shown in Exhibit 5.

Supercenters constitute the company's fastest-growing division, and management is extremely pleased with them. Currently, the limitation is distribution, and Wal-Mart is working hard to expand its captive food distribution capabilities. Most of the supercenters are replacements of Wal-Mart stores, so they had a jumpstart on the general merchandise side of the store, although food has tended to build slowly. However, the company has gained market share faster than planned. Wal-Mart likes to locate Supercenters near the strongest food retailers so their facility will "either get better or be run out of town."

The Wal-Mart Supercenter is the most important retail concept on the landscape at this time. As with the discount stores, their real competitive impact does not come the year they open but in the third year, because the maturation curve resembles that of a Wal-Mart store rather than a food store. Also, the one-stop convenience aspect of the stores has such broad appeal that it is drawing a larger customer audience on a regular basis. Supercenters are continuing to get better in many categories and are attracting a higher-income audience in addition to traditional customers. Supercenters provide mart carts and are all on one floor, making the stores accessible to the handicapped. The company's broad assortments and everyday low prices are very compelling; extensive advertising is not needed. This represents an enormous advantage over the competition. Furthermore, as Supercenters move more into food distribution, they gain a major cost advantage over Super Kmart and Super Target.

### International Stores

In 1994, Wal-Mart acquired 122 Canadian Woolco stores. Wal-Mart immediately revamped these stores in less than a year. Wal-Mart Canada has already become that nation's No. 1 discount chain and is on the verge of becoming Canada's largest retailer of any sort. As indicated in Exhibit 3, the company today has 166 Wal-Mart stores in Canada, 397 in Mexico, and 9 in Puerto Rico. Note that Wal-Mart also operates 383 Supercenters and 49 SAM's clubs outside the United States as fiscal 2000 ended. The world's largest Wal-Mart is in Mexico City.

Wal-Mart has also reached a new market in Korea. Now there are five Supercenters open in Korea. With more than 815,000 associates in the United States and over 600 locations outside the United States, Wal-Mart is already serving some 75 million customers every week.

Wal-Mart has recently bought the United Kingdom's third-largest supermarket, Asda, for 6.7 billion ($11.19 billion) and is looking to grow Asda in the United Kingdom and expand further in continental Europe, including France. The U.K. market leader, Tesco, is trying to expand internationally and recently revealed plans to have around 200 Hypermarkets overseas by 2004, with more than 10 billion pounds in annual sales from outside the United Kingdom.

Global positioning puts a great emphasis on strategic competitive focus for Wal-Mart. According to Bob L. Martin, president of the International Division, "We are a global brand name. To customers everywhere it means low cost, best value, and greatest selection of quality merchandise and highest standards of customer service. But the fact that International has grown to more than $12 billion in sales in less than seven years gives us an idea of how great the potential is."

Community involvement, responsiveness to local needs and merchandise preferences, and buying locally are all hallmarks of the international Wal-Marts, just as they are in the United States.

### Distribution Centers

Wal-Mart has 43 distribution centers nationwide, nine of which are grocery distribution centers, and two of which are import distribution centers. Wal-Mart's distribution operations are highly automated. A typical Wal-Mart discount store has more than 70,000 standard items in stock; Supercenters carry more than 20,000 additional grocery items, many of which are perishable and must be ordered frequently. Associates use hand-held computers, linked by radio-frequency network to area stores. To place orders, each store wires merchandise requests to warehouses, which, in turn, either ship immediately or reorder. Wal-Mart computers are linked directly with over 200 vendors, so deliveries are faster. Wal-Mart has one of the world's largest private satellite communication systems to control distribution. In addition, Wal-Mart has installed point-of-sale bar-code scanning in all of its stores.

Wal-Mart owns a fleet of tractor trailers that can deliver goods to any store in 38 to 48 hours from the time the order is placed. After trucks drop off merchandise, they frequently pick up merchandise from manufacturers on the way back to the distribution center. This back-haul rate averages over 60 percent, which means trucks are 60 percent full on return trips to the distribution center, and is yet another way Wal-Mart cuts costs.

With an information systems staff of 1,200 people and system links with about 5,000 manufacturers, Wal-Mart leads the industry in information technology. This means Wal-Mart is dedicated to providing its associates with the technological tools to work smarter every day. "With this technology, we're getting better, quicker, and more accurate information to manage and control every aspect of our business," said Randy Mott, senior vice president and CIO.

## OPERATIONS

Wal-Mart's expense structure, measured as a percentage of sales, continues to be among the lowest in the industry. Although Walton watched expenses, he rewarded sales managers handsomely. Sales figures are available to every employee. Monthly figures for each department are ranked and made available throughout the organization. Employees who do better than average get rewarded with raises, bonuses, and a pat on the back. Poor performers are only rarely fired although demotions are possible.

All employees (called "associates") have a stake in the financial performance of the company. Store managers earn as much as $100,000 to $150,000 per year. Even part-time clerks qualify for profit-sharing and stock-purchase plans. Millionaires among Wal-Mart's middle managers are not uncommon. Executives frequently solicit ideas for improving the organization from employees and often put them into use.

With Wal-Mart stock now selling at 45 to 50 times earnings—an almost incredible price—Walton presided over a sizable fortune before his death. The Walton family holds 39 percent of Wal-Mart stock. Family holdings are worth nearly $16 billion.

Continuing a Walton tradition, Wal-Mart invites more than 100 analysts and institutional investors to the fieldhouse at the University of Arkansas for its annual meeting in mid-June. During the day-and-a-half session, investors meet top executives, as well as Wal-Mart district managers, buyers, and 200,000 hourly salespeople. Investors see a give-and-take meeting between buyers and district managers.

### Employee Benefits

Wal-Mart management takes pride in the ongoing development of its people. Training is seen as critical to outstanding performance, and new programs are often implemented in all areas of the company. The combination of grass-roots meetings, the open-door policy, videos, printed material, classroom and home study, year-end management meetings, and on-the-job training enables employees to prepare themselves for advancement and added responsibilities.

Wal-Mart managers stay current with new developments and needed changes. Executives spend one week per year in hourly jobs in various stores. Walton himself once traveled at least three days per week, visiting competitors' stores and attending the opening of new stores, leading the Wal-Mart cheer, "Give me a W, give me a A! . . . ."

Wal-Mart encourages employee stock purchases; about 8 percent of Wal-Mart stock is owned by employees. Under the stock purchase plan, stock may be bought by two different methods. First, an amount is deducted from each employee's check to a maximum amount of $62.50 per check. An additional 15 percent of the amount deducted is contributed by Wal-Mart (up to $1,800 of annual stock purchases). Second, a lump-sum purchase is allowed in April of up to $1,500, with an additional 15 percent added by the company. Wal-Mart also offers an associate stock ownership plan with approximately 4,000 management associates having stock options. Over 400,000 associates have chosen to take part in the stock purchase plan, and another 200,000 have enrolled in a direct purchase plan.

Wal-Mart has a corporate profit-sharing plan. The purpose of the profit-sharing plan is to furnish an incentive for increased efficiency, to provide progressive recognition of service, and to encourage careers with the company by Wal-Mart associates. This is a trustee-administered plan, which means the company's contributions are made only out of net profits and are held by a trustee. The company from time to time contributes 10 percent of net profits to the trust.

Company contributions can be withdrawn only on termination. If employment with the company is terminated because of retirement, death, or permanent disability, the company contribution is fully vested (meaning the entire amount is nonforfeitable). If employment is terminated for any other reason, the nonforfeitable amount depends on the number of years of service with the company. After completion of the third year of service with the company, 20 percent of each participant's account is nonforfeitable for each subsequent year of service. After seven years of service, a participant's account is 100 percent vested.

## Predatory Pricing

Three independent pharmacies in Conway, Arkansas, recently filed a suit claiming Wal-Mart was deliberately pricing products below cost to kill competition. Wal-Mart argued that it priced products below cost not to harm competitors but to meet or beat rivals' prices. Chancery Court Judge David L. Reynolds on October 11, 1996, found Wal-Mart guilty of predatory pricing and ordered the company to pay the pharmacies $286,407 in damages. The judge also forbid Wal-Mart from selling products below cost in Conway in the future.

Wal-Mart appealed the ruling to the Arkansas Supreme Court, which reversed the decision and dismissed the case. Wal-Mart's policy requires that store managers monitor the retail prices charged by competitors in their respective market area and lower prices for highly competitive merchandise without regard to the cost of individual items. This price is frequently below Wal-Mart's cost of acquiring some of these products in highly competitive markets. The stated purpose of Wal-Mart's pricing policy is to "meet or beat" the retail prices of competitors for highly competitive, price-sensitive merchandise; to maintain "low-price leadership" in the local marketplace; and to "attract a disproportionate number of customers into a store to increase traffic."

The store's pricing practices with regard to specific articles did not show violation of Arkansas Unfair Practices Act section prohibiting vendor from selling at below its cost. The mere proof of below-cost sales was not sufficient to prove violation of the Act absent intent to destroy competition. There was no demonstration of exactly which individual items were sold below cost, the frequency of those sales, the duration of the sales, and to what extent the sales existed.

## Diversity Among Employees

Sam Walton was admittedly old-fashioned in many respects. Wal-Mart store policies reflect many of his values. For example, store policies forbid employees from dating other employees without prior approval of the executive committee. Also, women are rare in management positions. Annual manager meetings include sessions for wives to speak out on the problems of living with a Wal-Mart manager. No women are among the ranks of Wal-Mart's top management. Walton resisted placing women on the board of directors; however, there are two women on the board at this time. Wal-Mart is an EEOC/AA employer but has managed to get away with apparently discriminatory policies.

Wal-Mart has instituted several initiatives to increase the recruitment and promotion of women and minorities, including:

- A mentoring program encompassing more than 750 women and minority managers
- A women's leadership group, in partnership with Herman Miller and ServiceMaster, to develop opportunities for high-potential female managers
- Store internships during the summer for college students between their junior and senior years, with 70 percent being women or minorities

## Philanthropy

Education is a primary beneficiary of Wal-Mart charitable giving. Examples include the following:

- Each store awards a $1,000 college scholarship to a qualifying high school senior. More than $11 million in scholarships have been awarded since the program's inception.
- A major commitment has been made to the United Negro College Fund. Wal-Mart pledged $1,000,000 to UNCF over a 4-year period.
- The company sponsors the Competitive Edge Scholarship Fund. In 1993, Wal-Mart teamed up with participating vendor-partners to start the fund, which makes four-year scholarships—each worth $20,000—available to students pursuing technology-related college degrees.
- Since 1993, Wal-Mart and SAM's Club associates have raised more than $80 million in support of local United Way agencies.
- Wal-Mart Stores, Inc., is the primary sponsor for the Children's Miracle Network Telethon. Associates from all U.S. divisions of the company have helped raise more than $131 million for CMN since 1988. In calendar year 1998, Wal-Mart donated $27 million to CMN of charitable contributions for that year.
- In 1999, Community Matching Grants totaled more than $42 million from the Wal-Mart Foundation.

## Marketing

The discount retailing business is seasonal to a certain extent. Generally, the highest volume of sales and net income occurs in the fourth fiscal quarter, and the lowest volume occurs during the first fiscal quarter. Wal-Mart draws customers into the store by radio and television advertising, monthly circulars, and weekly newspaper ads. Television advertising is used to convey an image of everyday low prices and quality merchandise. Radio is used to a lesser degree to promote specific products that are usually in high demand. Newspaper and monthly circulars emphasize deeply discounted items and are effective at luring customers into the store.

Efforts are also made to discount corporate overhead. Visitors often mistake corporate headquarters for a warehouse because of its minimal decorating and "show." Wal-Mart executives share hotel rooms when traveling to reduce expenses. The company avoids spending money on consultants and marketing experts. Instead, decisions are made based on the intuitive judgments of managers and employees and on the assessment of the strategies of other retail chains.

Wal-Mart censors some products. The company has banned recordings and removed magazines based on what it found to be offensive lyrics and graphics and has stopped marketing teen rock magazines. Wal-Mart advertises a "Buy American" policy in an effort to keep production at home. Consequently, Wal-Mart buyers are constantly seeking vendors in grass-roots America. In Tulsa, Zebco responded to Wal-Mart's challenge by bucking the trend toward overseas fishing tackle manufacturing. Zebco created more than 200 U.S. jobs to assemble rods and manufacture bait-and-cast reels. The company's bait-and-cast reels are the first to be manufactured in the United States in 30 years.

### Innovations

Wal-Mart's Innovation Network (WIN) is one of two related services that provide entrepreneurs with a point of entry into Wal-Mart's mammoth distribution system. "The key to our approach is our use of consistent standards and open criteria," explains Gerald Udell, a professor at Southwest Missouri State University and the executive director of its Center for Business and Economic Development. Professor Udell conceived, designed, and now administers the two Wal-Mart entrepreneurial support efforts, WIN and the Support American Made program. These programs have already helped over 3,000 inventors and entrepreneurs by evaluating products and prototypes for possible distribution by the chain.

For a $175 fee, entrepreneurs can submit their products and detailed company information to a team of analysts. Within two months, applicants receive a detailed evaluation of their company and products. These programs are intended to explain why Wal-Mart does business with some and not with others. Instead of a simple no, it explains how to get a yes.

In conjunction with Chase Manhattan Bank, Wal-Mart introduced its Wal-Mart Mastercard. There is no annual fee and a low 14.48 percent APR fixed rate for purchases. On transferred balances the APR rate is 9.9 percent.

### Internet Presence

Wal-Mart is in the retail business, which now includes Internet e-tailing. The Internet has interesting aspects and will definitely serve a growing market. Profits are not easily made over the Internet, and issues of cost of delivery, merchandise returns, and data security are top concerns when building business over the Internet. Wal-Mart has been selling from the Web site since 1997 and will continue to invest in development and learning. Wal-Mart looks at the Internet retailing as another store with great possibility but without walls. Wal-Mart is distributing the online merchandise by relying on Fingerhut to handle the fulfillment for its Web store.

Wal-Mart is expected to launch its redesigned Internet shopping site in the winter/spring 2000. The site will include more products and eventually a travel service, pharmacy, photography center, and aids to help customers with their shopping. Internet sales per quarter are expected to triple to almost $10 billion. As Internet retailing is a growing competitor to Wal-Mart, there is still quite a competitive advantage associated with Wal-Mart's $137.6 billion annually, more than 10 times the forecast for all fourth quarter Internet retail sales.

## COMPETITORS

Kmart is the second-largest U.S. retailer. However, when compared to Wal-Mart, the scope of Kmart's problem becomes evident. Even though each company operates roughly the same number of stores, Wal-Mart's sales are approximately four times Kmart's sales of almost $36.3 billion. Wal-Mart's discount stores are larger than Kmart's and produce sales of about $385 per square foot, or twice the amount of Kmart's.

Should Wal-Mart, the price leader in discounting, choose to sacrifice $0.10 to $0.15 of its estimated earnings per share, it virtually could ensure that Kmart would not operate above the breakeven point. Kmart is in a capital-intensive battle with Wal-Mart, whose 1999 capital expenditures were nearly four times that of Kmart's. Kmart's capital resources for this battle are limited, and if its earnings fail to improve, it cannot stay in this capital-intensive race for long. When Kmart recently cut its dividend rate in half, management took a step in the right direction toward conserving its financial resources. The CEO's recommendation regarding the dividend payout will be a litmus test of the urgency with which management intends to apply the company's assets toward turning around the Kmart discount stores.

Kmart had slowed its rollout of its Super Kmart Centers to allow more time to develop the staff and skills needed for these stores to achieve an adequate return. As the rollout reaccelerates, Wal-Mart is operating over 700 Supercenters, and retailing has changed greatly.

On a positive note, Kmart's board has been strengthened by new appointments and is steering the company; new management provides a fresh perspective for the company; new strategies are being implemented; same-store sales are strong; expenses are being reduced; and earnings should rise.

JCPenney and Sears responded to the reality of retail competition several years ago by offering consumers better values than they previously had. They have succeeded in lifting their sales, in both dollars and units. Kmart planned to take market share from them but was blocked. As this escape route from direct competition with Wal-Mart closes, Kmart must protect itself and fight an uneven battle with Wal-Mart and another strong firm, Target. Target operates nearly 900 stores in 44 states.

## FUTURE STRATEGIES

What strategies would you recommend to CEO David Glass? How can Wal-Mart benefit from Internet retailing? How aggressively should Wal-Mart expand internationally and where? Should Wal-Mart get a foothold in Europe before competitors seize the initiative? Should Wal-Mart expand further in Mexico, the United States, or Canada? Should Wal-Mart make further acquisitions like their Woolco acquisition in Canada? Is Wal-Mart's rate of growth for Supercenters too fast? What can Wal-Mart do to improve its SAM's Club operations?

# TARGET CORPORATION—2000

Henry H. Beam
**Western Michigan University**

**DH**

www.dhc.com

Target Corporation, previously Dayton Hudson Corporation, is the country's fourth-largest general merchandise retailer, behind Wal-Mart, Kmart, and Sears Roebuck. Company revenues were $33.7 billion in 1999 while earnings were $1.1 billion. Headquartered in Minneapolis, Minnesota, it caters to all income groups through three operating divisions: Mervyn's, the Department Store Division (DSD), and Target. Target's department stores are strong in the upper Midwest, controlling significant shares of the market in Detroit (Hudson's), Chicago (Marshall Field's), and Minneapolis (Dayton's). Target's upscale general merchandise discount stores are spread across the country and account for three quarters of the company's sales and profits. Mervyn's, with stores primarily in California and the Midwest, caters to lower- to middle-income shoppers but has not been doing well in recent years.

Almost all the department stores and half of the Mervyn's stores are located in major malls. In contrast, Target stores are located in shopping centers. Sometimes a Target store will be located near a Mervyn's or a Dayton Hudson department store, or both. In Kalamazoo, Michigan, the largest mall has a Hudson's and a Mervyn's, and less than a mile away a Target store is in a shopping center. Despite such proximity, the company has made little attempt to associate the divisions with each other in the eyes of consumers, many of whom aren't aware the three divisions are part of the same corporation.

In 1999, Target acquired Rivertown Trading Company to provide expertise in direct marketing and to support its Internet retailing efforts. It contributed less than 1 percent of company sales and earnings in 1999.

## HISTORY

The Panic of 1873 left young Joseph Hudson bankrupt. After he had paid his debts off at 60 cents on the dollar, he saved enough to open a men's clothing store 18 years later in Detroit. Among his merchandising innovations were return privileges and price marking in place of bargaining. By 1891, Hudson's was the largest retailer of men's clothing in America. Remarkably, Hudson looked up all his creditors from 1873 and repaid them in full with interest. When Hudson died in 1928, his four nephews took over and expanded the business. In 1928, Hudson's built a new building on Woodward Avenue in downtown Detroit. It eventually grew to 25 stories with 49 acres of floor space and high-quality appointments. The Woodward Avenue store was closed in 1982 as a result of the steady economic decline in downtown Detroit since the late 1950s. It was demolished in October 1998 to make room for a downtown redevelopment project. The Woodward name can still be found in Hudson's stores. The Woodward Shops department in larger Hudson's stores sells finer women's apparel.

In 1903, George Dayton, a former banker, opened his Dayton Dry Goods store in Minneapolis, where there was high foot traffic. Like Hudson, Dayton offered return privileges and liberal credit. His store became a full-line department store 12 stories tall. After World War II, both companies saw that the future of retailing lay in the suburbs. In 1954, Hudson's built Northland at the northwest edge of Detroit, then the largest shopping center in the United States. Dayton's built the world's first fully enclosed shopping mall, Southdale, in Minneapolis in 1956. In an attempt to diversify, Dayton's opened its first Target discount store in 1962. Dayton's went public in 1966, and in 1969 it bought the family-owned Hudson's for stock, forming Dayton Hudson Corporation. In 1978, the company bought the California-based Mervyn's retail chain of 47 stores started by Mervyn Morris in 1949.

The company bought Marshall Field's department stores in 1990, assuming a billion dollars of debt in the process. Marshall Field's grew out of a dry-goods business started in Chicago in 1852 by Potter Palmer. Marshall Field bought the store in 1865, the last year of the Civil War, and built it into one of Chicago's biggest retailers. His motto, "Give the lady what she wants," was a precursor of customer-oriented retailing. The original Marshall Field's store on State Street in downtown Chicago was remodeled in 1992. It is the company's largest store and a major tourist attraction for visitors to Chicago.

Target's executive office provides leadership for all divisions and establishes the values under which those divisions operate. Each of the three operating divisions has its own CEO and president and operates independently. Though their organizations are separate and their strategies are distinct, the divisions are encouraged to share advances in technology and management approaches in order to achieve efficiencies, referred to as "The Power of One," that can be gained by coordinating or combining activities. Reflecting the corporate emphasis on service, all divisions refer to their customers as "guests."

## DIVISIONS

### Target

At the end of 1999, the Target division consisted of 912 stores in 41 states from coast to coast. Target is an upscale discount store that provides good quality, family-oriented merchandise at attractive prices in a clean, spacious, and customer-friendly environment. (See Exhibit 1) Its motto is, "Expect more, pay less." A 1999 *Fortune* article on Target commented, "Going to Target is a cool experience, and everybody now considers it cool to save money. On the other hand, is it cool to save at Kmart, at Wal-Mart? I don't think so." Its stores are generally located in small, freestanding malls. Eight regional distribution centers process 90 percent of all freight for the stores and aim to provide next-day service to all locations. Target's performance has been strong and consistent across most merchandise categories and geographical regions during the past several years. Target invites evaluation from its "guests" on evaluation forms titled "Be Our Guest Commentator" available at checkout counters.

Target's micromarketing program helped improve its merchandise assortments on a store-by-store basis. Micromarketing is Target's system for tailoring merchandise assortments to customers' needs in individual stores or markets based on regional, climatic, demographic, and ethnic factors. This permits stores as close as 15 miles apart to offer different merchandise mixes. The typical Target customer is twenty-five to forty-four years old, married with children, and is part of a two-wage-earner family with a household income of $50,000. Over 80 percent of Target's customers have attended or graduated from college. Target advertises through multipage inserts in local newspapers and television advertisements featuring the familiar red circular "target" symbol.

EXHIBIT 1    Selected Data for Target Division
(in millions)

|  | 1999 | 1998 | 1997 | 1996 | 1995 | 1994 |
|---|---|---|---|---|---|---|
| Revenues | $ 26,080 | $23,056 | $20,368 | $17,853 | $15,807 | $13,600 |
| Operating profit | 2,022 | 1,578 | 1,287 | 1,042 | 719 | 732 |
| Stores | 912 | 851 | 796 | 736 | 670 | 611 |
| Square feet (000s) | 102,945 | 94,553 | 87,158 | 79,360 | 71,108 | 64,446 |

*Source:* Target Corporation, *Annual Report* (1994, 1995, 1996, 1997, 1998, 1999).

Target plans to continue opening stores in the mid-Atlantic markets such as New York, Philadelphia, Baltimore, and Washington, D.C., and plans new entries in the Boston and Pittsburgh markets. Target's growth will continue to be in adjacent territories to minimize transportation costs and to obtain maximum benefit from advertising. These areas will continue to be a primary focus for the division's short-term growth. Although the cost of a store site in these densely populated regions is generally higher, so is the sales potential. Over the past five years, Target's square footage has grown at a compound annual rate of 10 percent and is expected to continue to grow at that rate for the next few years.

In 1995, Target opened its first two super center stores (SuperTargets) in the Plains States. The stores are about 180,000 square feet in size, with a fourth of the space devoted to grocery items. Certain categories, such as health and beauty aids and paper products, link the grocery and general merchandise areas and facilitate crossover shopping. At Target's 1999 Annual Meeting, the company announced that it would accelerate the expansion of the SuperTarget format and that it planned to operate 200 or more SuperTarget stores in ten years. According to CEO Robert Ulrich, SuperTargets bring "fashion to food" and offer "a store that is attractive to our guests and as differentiated from our competition as are our discount stores."

## Mervyn's

At the end of 1999, Mervyn's consisted of 267 stores located primarily in the Northwest, West, and Southwest. Mervyn's is a moderately-priced family department store chain emphasizing brand-name and private-label casual apparel and home fashions. Its motto is "Big brands, small prices." Mervyn's typical customer is twenty-five to forty-nine years old, female, married with children, and working outside the home. Half its stores are located in regional malls, and the rest are free standing or in neighborhood shopping centers (see Exhibit 2).

Performance in recent years has been disappointing. The economy in California, where nearly half of Mervyn's stores are located, has been weak. The division instituted an aggressive effort to upgrade the merchandising to its core customers, women. In 1995, Mervyn's embarked on a new strategy that included holding more promotions, increasing the focus on national brands sold at promotional prices, refining merchandise assortments, and using a California theme with its merchandise and advertising. Like Target, Mervyn's advertises through weekly multi-page inserts in local newspapers.

## Department Store

The Department Store Division (DSD) consisted of 20 Dayton's, 20 Hudson's (all based in Michigan), and 24 Marshall Field's stores in eight Midwestern states at the end of

EXHIBIT 2    Selected Data for Mervyn's Division
(in millions)

|  | 1999 | 1998 | 1997 | 1996 | 1995 | 1994 |
|---|---|---|---|---|---|---|
| Revenues | $ 4,099 | $ 4,176 | $ 4,227 | $ 4,369 | $ 4,516 | $ 4,561 |
| Operating profit | 205 | 240 | 280 | 153 | 100 | 206 |
| Stores | 267 | 268 | 269 | 300 | 295 | 286 |
| Square feet (000s) | 21,635 | 21,729 | 21,810 | 24,518 | 24,113 | 23,130 |

*Source:* Target Corporation, *Annual Report* (1994, 1995, 1996, 1997, 1998, 1999).

EXHIBIT 3    Selected Data for the Department Store Division
(in millions)

|  | 1999 | 1998 | 1997 | 1996 | 1995 | 1994 |
|---|---|---|---|---|---|---|
| Revenues | $ 3,074 | $ 3,285 | $ 3,161 | $ 3,149 | $ 3,193 | $ 3,150 |
| Operating profit | 296 | 279 | 240 | 108 | 184 | 270 |
| Stores | 64 | 63 | 65 | 64 | 63 | 63 |
| Square feet (000s) | 14,060 | 13,890 | 14,090 | 14,111 | 13,870 | 13,824 |

*Source:* Target Corporation, *Annual Report* (1994, 1995, 1996, 1997, 1998, 1999).

1999. About half of the department stores are located in the major markets of Chicago, Detroit, and Minneapolis/St. Paul (See Exhibit 3). Historically, they have emphasized fashion leadership, quality merchandise, and superior customer service. Today, the stores offer strong national brands with competitive prices in men's and women's apparel, accessories, and home furnishings. The typical customer is married, female, has a median age of forty-three, and a median family income of $50,000. Over half of them have earned a college degree and two thirds hold white-collar positions.

The DSD had been a primary force behind the successful Workday Casual program, which consisted of seminars, mannequins, signs, advertising, and direct mail that illustrated appropriate apparel for the new dress-down work environment suggested for one or two days of the week at many companies. According to a study commissioned by Levi Strauss & Company, a major maker of casual wear, casual dress is now the norm at least one day a week for 90 percent of U.S. office workers. Employees say casual dress encourages a more collegial working environment, reduces status differentials between managers and workers, and saves money on dry cleaning. Reflecting the current interest in golf, the department stores feature The Players Shop, a department designed to outfit golfers.

In 1996, forty-five-year-old Linda Ahlers became chairman and CEO of the DSD, making her one of the highest-ranking female executives in the United States. Ahlers previously held top merchandising positions at Target, where she started her career in 1977. Under Ahlers, the division has emphasized selling more upscale merchandise, improving the look of the stores, and boosting customer service. In 1996, Hudson's opened a new 300,000-square-foot store in the Somerset North Mall located north of Detroit. In addition to building new stores in selected locations, the division is also starting to renovate some of its older stores in such locations as Toledo, Ohio and Fort Wayne, Indiana.

## RIVERTOWN TRADING COMPANY

Target acquired Rivertown Trading in 1998. A direct marketing firm based in St. Paul, Minnesota, it was started in 1981 as part of Minnesota Public Radio to offer products related to the popular radio show, "A Prairie Home Companion," hosted by Garrison Keillor. It incorporated as a separate, for-profit company in 1987. It produces niche marketing consumer catalogs including *Wireless, Signals, Seasons, The Daily Planet, Well & Good,* and *Circa.* Its two largest catalogs are *Wireless* and *Signals. Wireless* offers an eclectic assortment of gifts and entertainment merchandise. *Signals* was originally created to appeal to the public television audience. It offers a broad selection of gifts including videos, art prints, distinctive jewelry, and creative toys.

## COMPETITION

Because its three divisions, taken together, compete across all major merchandising categories, Target Corporation faces a wide range of competitors. The largest division, Target, competes directly with "the marts," Kmart and Wal-Mart. Like Target, Kmart and Wal-Mart began their discount store operations in 1962.

### Kmart

Kmart is the nation's second largest retailer, behind Wal-Mart. It traces its roots to the S.S. Kresge Company, incorporated in 1912, which was originally a Michigan-based dime store chain. By the 1950s, Kresge had become one of the largest general retailers in the nation with stores primarily in urban locations. The first Kmart was opened in a suburb of Detroit after an extensive study of changes in retailing made in 1958 by its future CEO, Harry B. Cunningham. The Kmart large-store format was so successful that the company concentrated on it, rapidly opening Kmarts from coast to coast and closing dime stores as they became unprofitable. In 1977, when 95 percent of its sales came from Kmart stores, the company changed its name to Kmart.

Kmart passed Sears in retail revenue in 1990 to briefly become the nation's largest retailer. Both were overtaken the next year by rapidly growing Wal-Mart. Kmart's stores were generally perceived as older, smaller, and less attractive than those of Wal-Mart and Target. Kmart's diversification into specialty retailing in the 1980s brought it close to bankruptcy in 1995. Since then, Kmart has divested itself of all its major acquisitions (Walden Books, Builder's Square, PayLess Drug Stores Northwest, Sports Authority, Office Max, and PACE warehouse clubs) in order to concentrate on its original discount business. It also closed all of its international stores in 1997. It has recently begun a program to convert some of its existing stores into Big Kmarts that feature a grocery section, brighter decor, and an expanded selection of merchandise. It features the popular Martha Stewart line of women's apparel and home furnishings. Kmart started offering online shopping in 1996.

### Wal-Mart

Wal-Mart is one of the best-known success stories in America. Sam Walton opened his first Wal-Mart store in Rogers, Arkansas, in 1962. Growth was slow at first. By the time Wal-Mart went public in 1970, it only had 18 stores, all in small towns in the South, and sales of $44 million. Growth accelerated during the 1970s. Wal-Mart established highly automated distribution centers to reduce shipping time and implemented an advanced computer system to track inventory and speed up checkout and reordering. Wal-Mart's motto is displayed on each of its stores, "We sell for less, satisfaction guaranteed." Wal-Mart has a liberal return policy and matches the price in competitors' advertisements.

In 1983, Wal-Mart entered the warehouse business with its SAM's Clubs. By 1996, Wal-Mart was the industry leader in the United States with 470 SAM's Clubs, which had sales of $19 billion. Its only significant competitor in warehouse clubs is Costco Companies. At the end of 1998, SAM's Clubs had sales of $23 billion, and Costco had sales of $24 billion.

At the end of 1998, Wal-Mart was the world's largest retailer, operating 1,869 Wal-Mart discount stores, 564 super centers, and 451 SAM's Clubs in the United States. The average community served has about 15,000 people. Wal-Mart has also expanded abroad. At the end of 1998, it had over 600 foreign stores, mostly discount stores in Canada and Mexico, where it is the largest retailer. It has acquired or built stores in China, Great Britain, Germany, Korea, and South America in the past few years. It also operates a store on the Internet.

Wal-Mart plans to open about 150 new super centers in the United States over the next few years. Super centers carry a full line of groceries as well as a moderate selection of soft and hard goods. They accounted for almost all of Wal-Mart's expansion in 1998. At an average size of about 180,000 square feet, these stores are more than twice as large as the company's traditional discount stores and are significantly more profitable.

Target, Mervyn's and the Department Store Division also compete to some extent with large national retailers, such as Penney's, Sears, and Montgomery Ward, and with regional department store chains such as Kohl's in the Midwest, Dillard Department Stores in the South, and May Department Stores in the East.

## FINANCIAL ASPECTS

Financial data on Target Corporation is given in Exhibits 4, 5, and 6. Advertising costs, which are included in selling, publicity, and administrative expenses, were $634 million, $679 million, and $745 million for 1996, 1997, and 1998, respectively. Capital expenditures for 1998 were $1.66 billion, up from $1.35 billion in 1997. Of this, 82 percent went to Target, 10 percent to Mervyn's, and 8 percent to the DSD. About two thirds of the capital expenditures went to open new stores. During 1998, Target opened 55 new stores; Mervyn's closed one store, and the DSD closed two stores.

Each division has its own credit card. The transactions are handled through the company's wholly owned Retailer's National Bank, chartered in 1994. The divisions will also take other credit cards, such as VISA and MasterCard. The Target credit card, called the Target Guest Card, has been very successful. By 1999, Target had over 12 million guest card accounts and expects to have 20 million cardholders by 2001.

Earnings per share increased 25 percent in 1998 largely because of a 26 percent increase in pretax profit at Target and lower promotional markdowns at the DSD. In 1999, Target Corporation announced a $1 billion share repurchase program that it expects to complete in two years.

## CORPORATE SOCIAL RESPONSIBILITY

Target Corporation is considered a model corporate citizen by consumer groups. It has contributed 5 percent of its pretax profits to philanthropic purposes every year since 1946. (By contrast, most large corporations in the United States contribute about 1 percent.) In 1999, the three operating divisions and the Dayton Hudson Foundation (funded by the corporation) gave more than $57 million to arts, education, and social action causes across the United States. Major contributions were made to programs and projects that strengthen families, promote the economic independence of individuals, or help neighborhoods respond to key social and economic concerns. Since 1997, Target will donate 1 percent of purchases made on the Target Guest Card to the school of the

EXHIBIT 4    Target Corporation's Income Statement
             (in millions, except per share data)

|  | 1999 | 1998 | 1997 | 1996 |
|---|---|---|---|---|
| Revenues | $33,702 | $30,951 | $27,757 | $25,371 |
| Costs and expenses | | | | |
| Cost of retail sales, buying, and occupancy | 23,029 | 22,634 | 20,320 | 18.628 |
| Selling, publicity and administrative | 7,490 | 5,077 | 4,532 | 4,289 |
| Depreciation and amortization | 854 | 780 | 693 | 650 |
| Interest expense | 393 | 398 | 416 | 442 |
| Taxes other than income taxes | 0 | 506 | 470 | 445 |
| Real estate repositioning | 0 | — | — | 134 |
| Total costs and expenses | 31,766 | 29,395 | 26,431 | 24,588 |
| Earnings before income taxes and extraordinary charges | 1,936 | 1,556 | 1,326 | 783 |
| Provision for income taxes | 751 | 594 | 524 | 309 |
| Net earnings before extraordinary charges | 1,185 | 962 | 802 | 474 |
| Extraordinary charges from purchase and redemption of debt, net of tax | 41 | 27 | 51 | 11 |
| Net earnings | $1,144 | $935 | $751 | $463 |
| Basic earnings per share | | | | |
| Earnings before extraordinary charges | $2.55 | $2.14 | $1.80 | $1.05 |
| Extraordinary charges | (.09) | (.06) | (.12) | (.03) |
| Basic earnings per share | $2.45 | $2.08 | $1.68 | $1.02 |
| Diluted earnings per share | | | | |
| Earnings before extraordinary charges | $2.54 | $2.04 | $1.70 | $1.00 |
| Extraordinary charges | (.09) | (.06) | (.11) | (.03) |
| Diluted earnings per share | $2.45 | $1.98 | $1.59 | $.97 |
| Weighted average common shares outstanding (millions) | | | | |
| Basic | 441.3 | 440.0 | 436.1 | 433.3 |
| Diluted | 465.7 | 467.3 | 463.7 | 460.9 |

*Source:* Target Corporation's *Annual Report,* 1999, p. 23.

guest's choice. Dayton Hudson was included in the 1993 edition of *The 100 Best Companies to Work for in America* (Currency/Doubleday).

## STORE MANAGEMENT

College graduates have long considered jobs in retailing inferior to jobs in manufacturing or the professions and seldom gave them serious consideration for anything more than part-time work. But opportunities have shifted as high-paying union jobs have decreased rapidly in the past decade. Jobs in retailing, at which a person can become a store manager and make $75,000 or more after five years, are becoming much more attractive to young people. Further, given the explosive growth of the discounters, thousands of new managers must be hired or promoted each year to run the new stores. However, the work is hard and lacks glamour. Given the high turnover among part-time workers and the constant promotion of assistant managers to other stores, store managers must spend long hours interviewing and training new workers. Work weeks average 60 hours, and relocations are frequent. Nevertheless, the discounters offer some of today's best chances for rapid advancement and high salaries.

## EXHIBIT 5    Target Corporation's Balance Sheet (in millions)

| | January 29, 2000 | January 30, 1999 | January 31, 1998 |
|---|---|---|---|
| **Assets** | | | |
| **Current assets** | | | |
| Cash and cash equivalents | $ 220 | $ 255 | $ 211 |
| Retained securitized receivables | 1,837 | 1,656 | 1,555 |
| Merchandise inventories | 3,798 | 3,475 | 3,251 |
| Other | 628 | 619 | 544 |
| Total current assets | 6,483 | 6,005 | 5,561 |
| **Property and equipment** | | | |
| Land | 2,069 | 1,868 | 1,712 |
| Building and improvements | 7,807 | 7,217 | 6,497 |
| Fixtures and equipment | 3,422 | 3,274 | 2,915 |
| Construction-in-progress | 526 | 378 | 389 |
| Accumulated depreciation | (3,925) | (3,768) | (3,388) |
| Property and equipment, net | 9,899 | 8,969 | 8,125 |
| **Other** | 761 | 692 | 505 |
| **Total assets** | $17,143 | $15,666 | $14,191 |
| **Liabilities and shareholders' investment** | | | |
| **Current liabilities** | | | |
| Accounts payable | $ 3,514 | $ 3,150 | $ 2,727 |
| Accrued liabilities | 1,520 | 1,444 | 1,346 |
| Income taxes payable | 318 | 207 | 210 |
| Current portion of long-term debt and notes payable | 498 | 256 | 273 |
| Total current liabilities | 5,850 | 5,057 | 4,556 |
| **Long-term debt** | 4,521 | 4,452 | 4,425 |
| **Deferred income taxes and other** | 910 | 822 | 720 |
| **Convertible preferred stock, net** | — | 24 | 30 |
| **Shareholders' investment** | | | |
| Convertible preferred stock | — | 268 | 280 |
| Common stock | 76 | 74 | 73 |
| Additional paid-in-capital | 730 | 286 | 196 |
| Retained earnings | 5,056 | 4,683 | 3,930 |
| Loan to ESOP | — | — | (19) |
| Total shareholders' investment | 5,862 | 5,311 | 4,460 |
| **Total liabilities and shareholders' investment** | $17,143 | $15,666 | $14,191 |

*Source:* Target Corporation's 1999 *Annual Report,* p. 26.

## ROBERT ULRICH, CHAIR AND CEO

Robert Ulrich, chair and CEO of Dayton Hudson since 1994, received a B.A. from the University of Michigan and completed the Stanford Executive Program at the Stanford University Graduate School of Business. He started as a merchandise trainee at Dayton's Department Store Company in 1967 and was named executive vice-president of Dayton's in 1981. In May 1984, he became president of the combined Dayton Hudson

---

EXHIBIT 6    **Target Financial Data**

*Revenues per Square Foot*

|  | 1999 | 1998 | 1997 |
|---|---|---|---|
| Target | $264 | $253 | $243 |
| Mervyn's | 189 | 191 | 187 |
| Department Stores | 220 | 219 | 211 |

*Profit Margin per Square Foot*

|  | 1999 | 1998 | 1997 |
|---|---|---|---|
| Target | 7.8% | 6.9% | — |
| Mervyn's | 5.0 | 5.8 | — |
| Department Stores | 9.6 | 9.1 | — |

*Source:* Target's 1999 *Annual Report,* p. 25.

---

EXHIBIT 7    Target Corporation's Organizational Chart

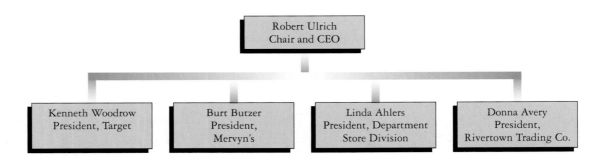

Department Store Company and was promoted to Target president in 1984. In 1987, he was promoted to Target chairman and was named to the Dayton Hudson board in 1994. He retained his position as Target's CEO and president when he became chairman of the corporation. Ulrich is a devotee of the arts and serves on the board of the Minneapolis Institute of Arts. The corporation's directors and officers are shown in Exhibit 7.

In his first year as chairman, Ulrich embarked on a program of stripping out layers of management, such as vice chairmanships, and tightening lines of control and communications. He eliminated the position of group vice president of the corporation and fired two senior vice presidents. He kept his office at Target rather than move to corporate headquarters, affirming Target's central role in the corporate hierarchy.

Ulrich's first letter to shareholders as chairman set forth the philosophy he would use to manage the corporation:

> During 1994, we began to leverage the size and strength of the entire corporation against the operating objectives of each of our three retail operations. We're doing this by creating a "boundaryless" organization where "speed is life." What is powerful about the approach is its simplicity. It means taking all the tools we have across the corporation and concentrating them on our primary purpose—serving guests by providing them with the merchandise they

want. It means sharing resources and expertise between divisions. It means taking advantage of the natural increase in speed that comes from eliminating organizational boundaries and layers. It means looking at every idea that works in one of our divisions to see if it would work just as well in another.

Robert Ulrich was named Discounter of the Year at the 1995 Supplier Performance Awards by Retail Category for his achievements as chairman of Target and its parent company, Dayton Hudson. Ulrich had been named Discounter of the Year twice before.

## THE FUTURE

The first page of the 1994 *Annual Report* stated what Dayton Hudson expected to accomplish in the future:

> We are committed to serving our guests better than the competition with trend-right, high-quality merchandise at very competitive prices. We are committed to being a low-cost, high-quality distributor of merchandise through "boundaryless" functioning—through leverage resources, expertise and economies across divisions. Our primary objective is to maximize shareholder value over time. We believe we will achieve a compound annual fully diluted earnings per share growth of 15 percent over time, while maintaining a prudent and flexible capital structure.

Dayton Hudson has maintained this philosophy of management during Robert Ulrich's tenure as CEO. Wall Street obviously liked what it saw: The price of Target's stock, adjusted for splits, has risen by a factor of 5 over this period, largely due to accelerating growth in sales and earnings at the Target division. Nevertheless, some analysts think Target's performance would be even better if it divested itself of its underperforming Mervyn's unit. Yet CEO Ulrich remains as committed as ever to keeping Mervyn's, stating in the 1998 *Annual Report*, "The financial contribution from Mervyn's and our Department Stores is a key factor in our ability to achieve 15 percent or more annual earnings per share growth over time."

## QUESTIONS

Should Target Corporation sell Mervyn's?

Should Target Corporation sell its Department Stores Division?

How should Target Corporation go about paying down its large amount of long-term debt?

Is Target Corporation's policy of donating 5 percent of pretax earnings to worthwhile social causes consistent with its primary goal of maximizing shareholder value over time?

How will Internet shopping affect Target Corporation? Was the acquisition of Rivertown Trading a good strategic move for Target Corporation?

## REFERENCES

BRANCH, SHELLY. "How Target Got Hot." *Fortune,* May 24, 1999: 168–174.

HELLIKER, KEVIN. "Sold on the Job: Retail Chains Offer a Lot of Opportunity, Young Managers Find." *The Wall Street Journal,* August 25, 1995: A1.

LEVERING, ROBERT, AND MILTON MOSKOWITZ. *The 100 Best Companies to Work for in America.* New York: Currency/Doubleday, 1993.

MAHONEY, TOM, AND LEONARD SLOANE. *The Great Merchants.* New York: Harper & Row, 1966.

# MANDALAY RESORT GROUP—2000

**John K. Ross, III, Mike Keeffe, and Bill Middlebrook**
**Southwest Texas State University**

**MBG**

www.mandalayresortgroup.com

> Circus intends to be a leading force in major gaming markets. Currently, the markets offering the most promising opportunities are Las Vegas, Detroit, Mississippi and Atlantic City. By our estimate, most of the growth in publicly traded companies' casino revenues will derive from these four venues over the next five years.
>
> Las Vegas will be central to our growth prospects. We control the largest development parcel in this key destination. In an industry where growth in earnings is typically linked to new-unit expansion (meaning rooms or casino capacity), Circus is positioned to develop more new units than any other competitor in the city. Importantly, share valuations in our industry have tended to favor companies that have a substantial and successful presence on the Las Vegas Strip.
> Annual Report, *1998*

Big projects, hot markets, and a focus on the Las Vegas Strip—these are the forces underlying the success of Mandalay Resort Group (formerly Circus Circus Enterprises). And successful it has been, with huge pink and white striped concrete circus tents, a 600-foot-long riverboat replica, a giant castle, and a great pyramid. The latest project, Mandalay Bay, is a tropical paradise in the middle of the desert and includes a 3,700-room hotel/casino, an 11-acre aquatic environment with beaches, a snorkeling reef, and a swim-up shark exhibit.

Mandalay Resort Group (hereafter Mandalay) describes itself as being in the business of entertainment and has been one of the innovators in the theme resort concept popular in casino gaming. The areas of operation are the glitzy vacation and convention meccas of Las Vegas, Reno, and Laughlin, Nevada, as well as other locations in the United States and abroad. Historically, Mandalay's marketing of its products has been called "right out of the bargain basement" and has catered to "low rollers." Mandalay has broadened its market and now aims more at the middle-income gambler and family-oriented vacationers as well as the more upscale traveler and player.

Mandalay began in 1974 when partners William G. Bennett, an aggressive cost-cutter who ran furniture stores before entering the gaming industry in 1965, and William N. Pennington bought a small and unprofitable casino operation for $50,000 (see Exhibit 1 for the board of directors and top managers). The partners were able to rejuvenate Mandalay (then Circus Circus) with fresh marketing, went public with a stock offering in October 1983, and experienced rapid growth and high profitability. Within the five-year period 1993–1997, the average return on invested capital was 16.5 percent, and Mandalay had generated over $1 billion in free cash flow. Today, Mandalay is one of the major players in the Las Vegas, Laughlin, and Reno markets in terms of square footage of casino space and number of hotel rooms despite the incredible growth in both markets. In 1997, for the first time in company history, casino gaming operations provided slightly less than one half of total revenues, and that trend continued into 1999 (see Exhibit 2). On January 31, 2000, Mandalay reported a net income of $42.1 million on revenues of $2.05 billion. Net income the prior fiscal year was $85.1 million.

## EXHIBIT 1    Directors and Officers

### Mandalay Enterprises, Inc.

| Name | Age | Title |
|------|-----|-------|
| Michael S. Ensign | 61 | Chairman of the Board, CEO, and COO Mandalay Resort Group |
| Glenn Schaeffer | 45 | President, CFO, Mandalay Resort Group |
| William A. Richardson | 52 | Vice Chairman of the Board and Executive Vice President Mandalay Resort Group |
| Arthur H. Bilger | 46 | Former President and COO New World Communications Group International |
| Rose Mckinney-James | 47 | President and CEO of the Corporation for Solar Technology and Renewable Resources |
| William E. Bannen, M.D. | 49 | Vice President/Chief Medical Officer, Blue Cross Blue Shield of Nevada |
| Donna B. More | 41 | Partner, Law Firm of Freeborn & Peters |
| Michael D. McKee | 53 | Executive Vice President, The Irving Company |

### Mandalay Resorts, Inc.

| | |
|---|---|
| Michael S. Ensign | Chairman of the Board, Chief Executive Officer and Chief Operating Officer |
| Glenn Schaeffer | President, Chief Financial Officer and Treasurer |
| William A. Richardson | Vice Chairman of the Board and Executive Vice President |
| Yvett Landau | Vice President, General Counsel and Secretary |
| Les Martin | Vice President and Chief Accounting Officer |

*Source:* Mandalay's *Annual Report 1999: Proxy Statement,* May 3, 1999.

## EXHIBIT 2    Mandalay Enterprises, Inc.
### Sources of Revenues as a Percentage of Net Revenues

| | 2000 | 1999 | 1998 | 1997 | 1996 | 1995 |
|---|------|------|------|------|------|------|
| Casinos | 46.4% | 48.0% | 46.7% | 49.2% | 51.2% | 52.3% |
| Food and Beverage | 16.9 | 16.7 | 15.9 | 15.8 | 15.5 | 16.2 |
| Rooms | 26.0 | 24.0 | 24.4 | 22.0 | 21.4 | 19.9 |
| Other | 12.3 | 11.5 | 10.5 | 11.0 | 12.2 | 14.2 |
| Unconsolidated | 4.8 | 5.7 | 7.3 | 6.5 | 3.5 | .5 |
| Less: Complimentary Allowances | 6.4 | 5.9 | 4.8 | 4.5 | 3.8 | 3.1 |

*Source:* Mandalay's 1999 *Annual Report.*

## OPERATIONS

Mandalay defines entertainment as pure play and fun, and it goes out of the way to see that customers have plenty of opportunities for both. Each Mandalay location has a distinctive personality. The largest hotel/casino, the crowning jewel in the Mandalay group, is "Mandalay Bay," which was completed in the first quarter of 1999 and opened on March 2 at an estimated cost of $950 million (excluding land). Circus owns a contiguous mile of the southern end of the Las Vegas Strip, the "Masterplan Mile," which currently contains Mandalay Bay, Excalibur, and Luxor resorts. All three "theme" hotel/casinos are connected by an elevated monorail system. Located next to the Luxor, Mandalay Bay aims for the upscale traveler and player and is styled as a South Seas adventure. A Four Seasons Hotel with some 424 rooms will complement Mandalay Bay and strive for the high-roller gamblers. Mandalay anticipates that the remainder of the Masterplan Mile will eventually be comprised of at least one additional casino resort and a number of stand-alone hotels and amusement centers.

Circus Circus—Las Vegas, is the world of the Big Top, where live circus acts perform free every 30 minutes. Kids may cluster around video games while the adults migrate to nickel slot machines and dollar game tables. Located at the north end of the Vegas strip, Circus Circus—Las Vegas, sits on 69 acres of land with 3,744 hotel rooms, shopping areas, two specialty restaurants, a buffet with seating for 1,200, fast food shops, cocktail lounges, video arcades, 109,000 square feet of casino space, and includes the Grand Slam Canyon, a five-acre glass enclosed theme park including a four-loop roller coaster. Approximately 384 guests may also stay at nearby Circusland RV Park. For the year ending January 31, 1997, $126.7 million was invested in this property for new rooms and remodeling, with another $35.2 million in fiscal year 1998.

Luxor, an Egyptian-theme hotel and casino complex, opened on October 15, 1993, when 10,000 people entered to play the 2,245 slot and video poker games and 110 table games in the 120,000-square-foot casino in the hotel atrium (reported to be the world's largest). By the end of the opening weekend 40,000 people per day were visiting the 30-story bronze pyramid that encases the hotel and entertainment facilities.

Luxor features a 30-story pyramid and two new 22-story hotel towers including 492 suites and is connected to Excalibur by a climate-controlled skyway with moving walkways. Situated at the south end of the Las Vegas Strip on a 64-acre site adjacent to Excalibur, Luxor features a food and entertainment area on three different levels beneath the hotel atrium. The pyramid's hotel rooms can be reached from the four corners of the building by state-of-the-art "inclinators" that travel at a 39-degree angle. Parking is available for nearly 3,200 vehicles, a covered garage contains approximately 1,800 spaces.

The Luxor underwent major renovations costing $323.3 million during fiscal 1997 and another $116.5 million in fiscal 1998. The resulting complex contains 4,425 hotel rooms, extensively renovated casino space, an additional 20,000 square feet of convention area, an 800-seat buffet, a series of IMAX attractions, five theme restaurants, seven cocktail lounges, and a variety of specialty shops. Mandalay expects to draw significant walk-in traffic to the newly refurbished Luxor, one of the principal components of the Masterplan Mile.

Located next to the Luxor, Excalibur is one of the first sights travelers see as they exit interstate highway 15 (management was confident that the sight of a giant colorful medieval castle would make a lasting impression on mainstream tourists and vacationing families arriving in Las Vegas). Guests cross a drawbridge, over a moat onto a cobblestone walkway with multicolored spires, turrets, and battlements. The castle walls are four 28-story hotel towers containing a total of 4,008 rooms. Inside is a medieval world complete with a Fantasy Fair inhabited by strolling jugglers, fire-eaters, and acrobats as well as a Royal Village complete with peasants, serfs, and ladies-in-waiting around medieval theme shops. The 110,000-square-foot casino encompasses 2,442 slot machines, more than 89 game tables, a sports betting area, and a poker and keno area. There are twelve restaurants, capable of feeding more than 20,000 people daily, and a 1000-seat amphitheater. Excalibur, which opened in June 1990, was built for $294 million and primarily financed with internally generated funds. In the year ending January 31, 1997, Excalibur contributed 23 percent of the organization's revenues, down from 33 percent in 1993. Yet 1997 was a record year, generating the company's highest margins and over $100 million in operating cash flow. In fiscal 1998 Excalibur underwent $25.1 million in renovations and was connected to the Luxor by enclosed, moving walkways.

Situated between the two anchors on the Las Vegas strip are two smaller casinos owned and operated by Mandalay. The Silver City Casino and Slots-a-Fun primarily depend on the foot traffic along the strip for their gambling patrons. Combined, they offer more than 1,202 slot machines and 46 gaming tables on 34,900 square feet of casino floor.

Mandalay owns and operates 11 properties in Nevada, one in Mississippi, and has a 50 percent ownership in three others (see Exhibit 3).

All of Mandalay's operations do well in the city of Las Vegas; they have a combined hotel room occupancy rates that has (until recently) remained above 90 percent. This has been due, in part, to low room rates ($29 to $59 at Circus Circus—Las Vegas) and popular buffets. Each of the major properties provide large, inexpensive buffets that management believes make staying with Mandalay more attractive. Yet, recent results show a room occupancy rate of 87.5 percent due to the building boom in Las Vegas and higher room rates at some locations ($89 to $299 at Mandalay Bay).

The company's second Big-Top facility is Circus Circus—Reno. With the addition of Skyway Tower in 1985, this facility now offers a total of 1,605 hotel rooms, 60,600 square feet of casino, a buffet that can seat 700 people, shops, video arcades, cocktail lounges, midway games, and circus acts. Circus Circus—Reno had several marginal years but has become one of the leaders in the Reno market. Mandalay anticipates that a recent remodeling, at a cost of $25.6 million, will increase this property's revenue-generating potential.

The Colorado Belle and The Edgewater Hotel are located in Laughlin, Nevada, on the banks of the Colorado River, 90 miles south of Las Vegas. The Colorado Belle, opened in 1987, features a huge paddle-wheel riverboat replica, buffet, cocktail lounges, and shops. The Edgewater, acquired in 1983, has a southwestern motif, a 57,000-square-foot casino, a bowling center, and buffet and cocktail lounges. Combined, these two properties contain 2,700 rooms and over 120,000 square feet of casino. These two operations contributed 12 percent of the company's revenues in the years that ended January 31, 1997 and 1998 and 11 percent in 1999, down from 21 percent in 1994. The extensive proliferation of casinos throughout the region, primarily on Indian land, and the development of megaresorts in Las Vegas have seriously eroded outlying markets such as Laughlin.

Three properties purchased in 1995 and located in Jean and Henderson, Nevada, represent continuing investments by Mandalay in outlying markets. The Gold Strike and Nevada Landing service the I-15 market between Las Vegas and southern California. These properties have over 73,000 square feet of casino space, 2,140 slot machines, and 42 gaming tables combined. Each has limited hotel space (1,116 rooms total), and depends heavily on I-15 traffic. The Railroad Pass is considered a local casino and is dependent on Henderson residents as its market. This smaller casino contains only 395 slot machines and 11 gaming tables.

EXHIBIT 3    Mandalay's EBITDA and Number of Rooms
by Property

A. Companies frequently refer to operating cash flow, or EBITDA, as a benchmark of earning power.
The following table shows the amounts of EBITDA (earnings before interest, taxes, depreciation
and amortization) for Mandalay's wholly owned properties and its joint venture properties.

| | Year ended January 31, | |
| --- | --- | --- |
| | 2000 | 1999 |
| *EBITDA by property (in millions):* | | |
| Luxor | $104.1 | $97.6 |
| Mandalay Bay | 86.3 | — |
| Excalibur | 83.8 | 74.2 |
| Circus Circus-Las Vegas/Slots-A-Fun/Silver City | 62.7 | 55.9 |
| Gold Strike-Tunica | 34.6 | 26.0 |
| Colorado Belle/Edgewater | 29.4 | 29.1 |
| Circus Circus-Reno | 25.7 | 24.3 |
| Gold Strike/Nevada Landing/Railroad Pass | 22.6 | 19.2 |
| Grand Victoria | 104.1 | 76.9 |
| Monte Carlo | 87.1 | 83.5 |
| Silver Legacy | 49.5 | 47.1 |
| MotorCity Casino | 7.7 | — |

B.

| Location/Property | Guest Rooms | Approximate Casino Square Footage | Slots (1) |
| --- | --- | --- | --- |
| Las Vegas, Nevada | | | |
| Mandalay Bay | 3,700 | 135,000 | 2,287 |
| Luxor | 4,404 | 120,000 | 2,031 |
| Excalibur | 4,008 | 110,000 | 2,436 |
| Circus Circus | 3,744 | 109,000 | 2,249 |
| Monte Carlo (50% Owned) | 3,002 | 90,000 | 2,073 |
| Slots-a-Fun | — | 16,700 | 526 |
| Reno, Nevada | | | |
| Circus Circus | 1,572 | 60,000 | 1,724 |
| Silver Legacy (50% Owned) | 1,711 | 85,000 | 2,186 |
| Laughlin, Nevada | | | |
| Colorado Belle | 1,226 | 64,000 | 1,269 |
| Edgewater | 1,450 | 44,000 | 1,315 |
| Jean, Nevada | | | |
| Gold Strike | 812 | 37,000 | 1,020 |
| Nevada Landing | 303 | 36,000 | 1,020 |
| Henderson, Nevada | | | |
| Railroad Pass | 120 | 21,000 | 368 |
| Tunica County, Mississippi | | | |
| Gold Strike | 1,066 | 48,000 | 1,482 |
| Detroit, Michigan | | | |
| MotorCity Casino (53.5% Owned) | — | 75,000 | 2,600 |
| Elgin, Illinois | | | |
| Grand Victoria (50% Owned) | — | 36,000 | 994 |
| Total | 27,118 | 1,086,700 | 25,580 |

*Source:* Mandalay's 1999 *Annual Report,* p. 23.

Gold Strike—Tunica (formally Circus Circus—Tunica), a dockside casino located in Tunica, Mississippi, opened in 1994 on 24 acres of land along the Mississippi River, approximately 20 miles south of Memphis. In 1997 operating income declined by more than 50 percent as a result of the increase in competition and lack of hotel rooms. Mandalay decided to renovate this property and add a 1,200-room tower hotel. Total cost for the remodeling was $119.8 million.

## Joint Ventures

In Las Vegas, Mandalay joined with Mirage Resorts to build and operate the Monte Carlo, a hotel/casino with 3,002 rooms designed along the lines of the grand casinos of the Mediterranean. It is located on 46 acres (with 600 feet on the Las Vegas strip) between the New York—New York casino and the Bellagio; all three casinos will be connected by monorail. The Monte Carlo features a 90,000-square-foot casino containing 2,221 slot machines and 95 gaming tables along with a 550-seat bingo parlor, high-tech arcade rides, restaurants, and buffets, a microbrewery, approximately 15,000 square feet of meeting and convention space and a 1,200-seat theater. Opened on June 21, 1996, the Monte Carlo generated $14.6 million as Mandalay's share in operating income for the first seven months of operation.

In Elgin, Illinois, Mandalay is in a 50 percent partnership with Hyatt Development Corporation in The Grand Victoria. Styled to resemble a Victorian riverboat, this floating casino and land-based entertainment complex includes some 36,000 square feet of casino space, containing 977 slot machines and 56 gaming tables. The adjacent land-based complex contains two movie theaters, a 240-seat buffet, restaurants and parking for approximately 2,000 vehicles. Built for a total of $112 million, Mandalay recuperated all of its initial investment in The Grand Victoria by June of 1996 with a year-end return of $44 million in operating income in 1996.

The third joint venture is a 50 percent partnership with Eldorado Limited in the Silver Legacy. Opened in 1995, this casino is located between Circus Circus—Reno and the Eldorado Hotel and Casino on two city blocks in downtown Reno, Nevada. The Silver Legacy has 1,711 hotel rooms, 85,000 square feet of casino, 2,275 slot machines, and 89 gaming tables. Management seems to believe that the Silver Legacy holds promise; however, the Reno market is suffering, and the opening of the Silver Legacy has cannibalized the Circus Circus—Reno market.

Mandalay engaged in a fourth joint venture to penetrate the Canadian market. However, on January 23, 1997, it announced it had been bought out by Hilton Hotels Corporation, one of three partners in the venture.

Mandalay has achieved success through an aggressive growth strategy and a renovated corporate structure designed to enhance that growth. A strong cash position, innovative ideas, and attention to cost control have allowed Mandalay to satisfy the bottom line during a period when competitors were typically taking on large debt obligations to finance new projects (see Exhibits 4, 5, 6, and 7). Yet the market is changing. Gambling of all kinds has spread across the country; no longer does the average individual need to go to Las Vegas or New Jersey. Instead, gambling can be found in the local market (lottery), the bingo hall, many Indian reservations, the Mississippi River, and other sites. There are now almost 300 casinos in Las Vegas alone, 60 in Colorado, and 160 in California. In order to maintain a competitive edge, Mandalay has continued to invest heavily in renovation of existing properties (a strategy common to the entertainment and amusement industry) and continues to develop new projects.

EXHIBIT 4    Selected Financial Information

|  | *FY00* | *FY99* | *FY98* | *FY97* | *FY96* | *FY95* | *FY94* | *FY93* | *FY92* | *FY91* |
|---|---|---|---|---|---|---|---|---|---|---|
| Earnings per share | .70 | .90 | 0.95 | 0.99 | 1.33 | 1.59 | 1.34 | 2.05 | 1.84 | 1.39 |
| Current ratio | 1.15 | .70 | .85 | 1.17 | 1.30 | 1.35 | .95 | .90 | 1.14 | .88 |
| Total liabilities/Total assets | .73 | .70 | .65 | .62 | .44 | .54 | .57 | .48 | .58 | .77 |
| Operating profit margin | 13.3% | 16.4% | 17.4% | 17% | 19% | 22% | 21% | 24.4% | 24.9% | 22.9% |

*Source:* Mandalay's *Annual Reports and 10Ks,* 1991–1999.

EXHIBIT 5    Twelve-Year Summary

|  | Revenues (in 000) | Net Income |
|---|---|---|
| FY00 | $2,050,898 | $ 42,163 |
| FY99 | 1,479,780 | 85,198 |
| FY98 | 1,354,487 | 89,908 |
| FY97 | 1,334,250 | 100,733 |
| FY96 | 1,299,596 | 128,898 |
| FY95 | 1,170,182 | 136,286 |
| FY94 | 954,923 | 116,189 |
| FY93 | 843,025 | 117,322 |
| FY92 | 806,023 | 103,348 |
| FY91 | 692,052 | 76,292 |
| FY90 | 522,376 | 76,064 |
| FY89 | 511,960 | 81,714 |
| FY88 | 458,856 | 55,900 |
| FY87 | 373,967 | 28,198 |
| FY86 | 306,993 | 37,375 |

*Source:* Mandalay's *Annual Reports and 10Ks,* 1986–1999.

### New Ventures

Mandalay plans three other casino projects in addition to expanding the Masterplan Mile, provided all the necessary licenses and agreements can be obtained. In Detroit, Michigan, Mandalay has combined with the Atwater Casino Group in a joint venture to build a $600 million project. Negotiations with the city to develop the project have been completed; however, the remainder of the appropriate licenses will need to be obtained before construction begins.

Along the Mississippi Gulf, at the north end of the Bay of St. Louis, Mandalay plans to construct a casino resort containing 1,500 rooms at an estimated cost of $225 million. Mandalay has received all necessary permits to begin construction, however these approvals have been challenged in court, delaying the project.

In Atlantic City, Mandalay has entered into an agreement with Mirage Resorts to develop a 181-acre site in the Marina District. Land title has been transferred to Mirage, however, Mirage has purported to cancel its agreement with Mandalay. Mandalay has filed suit against Mirage seeking to enforce the contract, but other interests have filed suit to stop all development in the area.

Most of Mandalay's projects are being tailored to attract mainstream tourists and family vacationers. However the addition of several joint ventures and the completion of the Masterplan Mile will also attract the more upscale customer.

EXHIBIT 6    **Mandalay Resort Group and Subsidiaries**
**Consolidated Statements of Income**

| *Year ended January 31,* *(in thousands, except share data)* | *2000* | *1999* | *1998* |
|---|---|---|---|
| Revenues | | | |
| Casino | $ 951,492 | $ 709,909 | $ 632,122 |
| Rooms | 534,132 | 355,635 | 330,644 |
| Food and beverage | 346,647 | 246,622 | 215,584 |
| Other | 251,509 | 170,701 | 142,407 |
| Earnings of unconsolidated affiliates | 98,627 | 83,967 | 98,977 |
| | 2,182,407 | 1,566,834 | 1,419,734 |
| Less-complimentary allowances | (131,509) | (87,054) | (65,247) |
| | 2,050,898 | 1,479,780 | 1,354,487 |
| Costs and expenses | | | |
| Casino | 510,794 | 367,449 | 316,902 |
| Rooms | 189,419 | 128,622 | 122,934 |
| Food and beverage | 276,261 | 207,663 | 199,955 |
| Other operating expenses | 179,907 | 113,864 | 99,460 |
| General and administrative | 339,455 | 253,138 | 223,263 |
| Depreciation and amortization | 169,226 | 133,801 | 117,474 |
| Operating lease rent | 25,994 | — | — |
| Preopening expenses | 49,134 | — | 3,447 |
| Abandonment loss | 5,433 | — | — |
| | 1,745,623 | 1,204,537 | 1,083,435 |
| Operating profit before corporate expense | 305,275 | 275,243 | 271,052 |
| Corporate expense | 31,539 | 32,464 | 34,552 |
| Income from operations | 273,736 | 242,779 | 236,500 |
| Other income (expense) | | | |
| Interest, dividends and other income | 3,652 | 2,730 | 9,779 |
| Interest income and guarantee fees from unconsolidated affiliate | 2,775 | 3,122 | 6,041 |
| Interest expense | (165,670) | (95,541) | (88,847) |
| Interest expense from unconsolidated affiliates | (11,085) | (12,275) | (15,551) |
| | (170,328) | (101,964) | (88,578) |
| Minority interest | (292) | — | — |
| Income before provision for income tax | 103,116 | 140,815 | 147,922 |
| Provision for income tax | 38,959 | 55,617 | 58,014 |
| Income before cumulative effect of change in accounting principle | 64,157 | 85,198 | 89,908 |
| Cumulative effect of change in accounting principle for pre-opening expenses, net of tax benefit of $11,843 | (21,994) | — | — |
| Net income | $ 42,163 | $ 85,198 | $ 89,908 |

*Source:* Mandalay's 1999 *Annual Report,* p. 96.

## EXHIBIT 7    Mandalay Resort Group and Subsidiaries
### Consolidated Balance Sheets

| January 31, (in thousands, except share data) | 2000 | 1999 |
|---|---|---|
| **Assets** | | |
| Current assets | | |
| Cash and cash equivalents | $ 116,617 | $ 81,389 |
| Accounts receivable | 53,071 | 26,136 |
| Income tax receivable | 9,096 | — |
| Inventories | 28,499 | 24,270 |
| Prepaid expenses | 47,807 | 21,451 |
| Deferred income tax | 26,449 | 8,032 |
| Total current assets | 281,539 | 161,278 |
| Property, equipment and leasehold interests, at cost, net | 3,335,071 | 3,000,822 |
| Other assets | | |
| Excess of purchase price over fair market value of net assets acquired, net | 396,433 | 367,076 |
| Notes receivable | 1,605 | 10,895 |
| Investments in unconsolidated affiliates | 264,995 | 271,707 |
| Deferred charges and other assets | 49,833 | 57,929 |
| Total other assets | 712,866 | 707,607 |
| Total assets | $4,329,476 | $3,869,707 |
| **Liabilities and Stockholders' Equity** | | |
| Current liabilities | | |
| Current portion of long-term debt | $ 13,022 | $ 3,481 |
| Accounts and contracts payable | | |
| Trade | 40,395 | 23,745 |
| Construction | 33,415 | 75,030 |
| Accrued liabilities | | |
| Salaries, wages and vacations | 46,897 | 40,006 |
| Progressive jackpots | 11,417 | 8,889 |
| Advance room deposits | 11,005 | 8,195 |
| Interest payable | 19,395 | 27,767 |
| Other | 69,073 | 44,460 |
| Total current liabilities | 244,619 | 231,573 |
| Long-term debt | 2,691,292 | 2,259,149 |
| Other liabilities | | |
| Deferred income tax | 210,689 | 200,376 |
| Other long-term liabilities | 20,192 | 20,981 |
| Total other liabilities | 230,881 | 221,357 |
| Total liabilities | 3,166,792 | 2,712,079 |
| Commitments and contingent liabilities | | |
| Minority interest | (25,096) | — |
| Stockholders' equity | | |
| Common stock $.01-2/3 par value | | |
| Authorized—450,000,000 shares | | |
| Issued—113,634,013 and 113,622,508 shares | 1,894 | 1,894 |
| Preferred stock $.01 par value | | |
| Authorized—75,000,000 shares | — | — |
| Additional paid-in capital | 565,925 | 558,935 |
| Retained earnings | 1,201,632 | 1,159,469 |
| Treasury stock (23,764,216 and 22,959,425 shares), at cost | (581,671) | (562,670) |
| Total stockholders' equity | 1,187,780 | 1,157,628 |
| Total liabilities and stockholders' equity | $4,329,476 | $3,869,707 |

*Source:* Mandalay's 1999 *Annual Report,* p. 34.

## THE GAMING INDUSTRY

By 1999 the gaming industry had captured a large amount of the vacation and leisure time dollars spent in the United States. Gamblers lost over $50.8 billion on legal wagering in 1997 (up from $29.9 billion in 1992), including wagers at racetracks, bingo parlors, lotteries, and casinos. This figure does not include dollars spent on lodging, food, transportation, and other related expenditures associated with visits to gaming facilities. Casino gambling accounts for 73.8 percent of all legal gambling expenditures, far ahead of second-place Indian reservation gambling at 12.5 percent and lotteries at 7.2 percent. The popularity of casino gambling may be credited to more frequent and somewhat higher pay-outs as compared to lotteries and racetracks; however, as winnings are recycled, the multiplier effect restores a high return to casino operators.

Geographic expansion has slowed considerably, because no additional states have approved casino-type gambling since 1993. Growth has occurred in developed locations, with Las Vegas and Atlantic City leading the way.

Las Vegas remains the largest U.S. gaming market and one of the largest convention markets, with more than 120,000 hotel rooms hosting more than 25.3 million visitors as of September 1999, up 10.8 percent over the same period in 1998. Casino operators are building to take advantage of this continued growth. Recent projects include the Monte Carlo ($350 million), New York—New York ($350 million), Bellagio ($1.4 billion), Hilton Hotels ($750 million), Mandalay Bay (950 million), Venetian (1.4 billion), and Paris—Las Vegas (760 million). Las Vegas hotel and casino capacity is expected to continue to expand with some 12,300 rooms having opened in 1999 with another 3,549 planned for 2000. According to the Las Vegas Convention and Visitor Authority, Las Vegas is a destination market, with most visitors planning their trip more than a week in advance (81 percent), arriving by car (47 percent) or airplane (42 percent), and staying in a hotel (72 percent). Gamblers are typically return visitors (77 percent), averaging 2.2 trips per year, who like playing the slots (65 percent).

For Atlantic City, besides the geographical separation, the primary differences in the two markets reflect the different types of consumers that frequent these markets. Las Vegas attracts overnight resort-seeking vacationers, but Atlantic City's clientele are predominantly day-trippers traveling by automobile or bus. Gaming revenues grew to $4.15 billion in 1999, up some 2% over 1998, split between 10 casino/hotels currently operating. Growth in the Atlantic City area will be concentrated in the Marina section of town, where Mirage Resorts has entered into an agreement with the city to develop 150 acres of the Marina as a destination resort. This development will include a resort wholly owned by Mirage, a casino/hotel developed by Mandalay, and a complex developed by a joint venture with Mirage and Boyd Corp. Currently in Atlantic City, Donald Trump's gaming empire holds the largest market share with Trump Marina, Trump Plaza, and the Trump Taj Mahal (total market share is 29 percent). The next closest in market share are Bally's (11.3 percent), Caesar's (10.5 percent), Tropicana (9.7 percent), and Showboat (8.9 percent).

There remain a number of smaller markets around the United States, primarily in Mississippi, Louisiana, Illinois, Missouri, and Indiana. Each state has imposed various restrictions on the development of casino operations within their states. For example, in Illinois, where there are only 10 gaming licenses available, growth opportunities and revenues have been severely restricted. In Mississippi and Louisiana, revenues are up 7 percent and 6 percent, respectively, in riverboat operations. Native American casinos continue to be developed on federally controlled land. These casinos are not publicly held but do tend to be managed by publicly held corporations. Overall these other locations present a mix of opportunities and generally constitute only a small portion of overall gaming revenues.

## MAJOR INDUSTRY PLAYERS

Over the past several years mergers and acquisitions have reshaped the gaming industry. As of year-end 1999, the industry was a combination of corporations, ranging from those engaged solely in gaming to multinational conglomerates. The largest competitors, in terms of revenues, combined multiple industries to generate both large revenues and substantial profits (see Exhibit 8). However, those engaged primarily in gaming could also be extremely profitable.

In 1996 Hilton began a hostile acquisition attempt of ITT Corporation. As a result of this attempt, ITT merged with Starwood Lodging Corporation and Starwood Lodging Trust. The resulting corporation is one of the world's largest hotel and gaming corporations, owning the Sheraton, Westin, The Luxury Collection, the Four Points Hotels, and Caesar's as well as communications and educational services. As a result of purchase and merger activity, Starwood owned, leased, managed, or franchised approximately 650 hotels with over 212,500 rooms in 70 countries. Gaming operations are located in Las Vegas, Atlantic City, Halifax and Sydney (Nova Scotia), Lake Tahoe, Tunica (Mississippi), Lima (Peru), Cairo (Egypt), Canada, and Australia. Expansion has dramatically increased revenue and profits and has resulted in a diversified strategic market base.

Park Place was founded from the separation of the lodging and gaming operations of Hilton Hotels in December 1998. Park Place then merged with the Mississippi gaming operations of Grand Casinos and now consists of twelve U.S. casinos, two in Australia and one in Uruguay. Their latest venture is the Paris Casino/Resort located next to Bally's in Las Vegas. The Paris features a 50-story replica of the Eiffel Tower, 85,000 square feet of casino space, 13 restaurants, and 130,000 square feet of convention space.

Harrah's Entertainment, Inc., is primarily engaged in the gaming industry with casino/hotels in Reno, Lake Tahoe, Las Vegas, and Laughlin, Nevada; Atlantic City, New Jersey; riverboats in Joliet, Illinois; and Vicksburg and Tunica, Mississippi; Shreveport, Louisiana; Kansas City, Kansas, two Native American casinos and one in Auckland, New Zealand. In June of 1998 Harrah's purchased the assets of Showboat and its operations in Atlantic City and Las Vegas, and in January 1999 they merged with Rio Hotel and Casino, Inc. The resulting company now has a total of over 1,120,000 square feet of casino space, 30,162 slot machines, and 11,658 hotel rooms. Harrah's attempts to target

EXHIBIT 8   Major U.S. Gaming, Lottery, and Pari-mutuel Companies
Revenues and Net Income (in millions)

| | 1998 Revenues | 1998 Income | 1997 Revenue | 1997 Income | 1996 Revenues | 1996 Net Income |
|---|---|---|---|---|---|---|
| Starwood/ITT | $4,710.0 | $141.0 | $2,974.0 | $(270.0) | $2,931.0 | $226.0 |
| Park Place Entertainment | 2,305.0 | 109.0 | 2,153.0 | 67.0 | NA | NA |
| Harrah's Entertainment | 2,004.0 | 102.0 | 1619.0 | 99.3 | 1586.0 | 98.9 |
| Mirage Resorts | 1,676.9 | 81.7 | 1546.0 | 207 | 1358.3 | 206.0 |
| Circus Circus | 1,479.7 | 85.1 | 1354.4 | 89.9 | 1247.0 | 100.7 |
| Trump Hotel and Casino | 979.0 | (11.0) | 982.2 | (14.0) | 976.3 | (4.9) |
| MGM Grand | 840.0 | 68.9 | 827.5 | 111.0 | 804.8 | 74.5 |
| Aztar | 806.1 | 10.1 | 782.3 | 4.4 | 777.5 | 20.6 |
| International Game Technology | 824.1 | 152.4 | 743.9 | 137.2 | 733.5 | 118.0 |

*Source:* Individual companies' *Annual Reports and 10Ks,* 1996–1999.

the experienced gambler who likes to play in multiple markets by establishing strong brand names of consistent high quality.

Mirage Resorts, Inc. owns and operates the Bellagio in Las Vegas ($1.6 billion purchase cost), the Beau Rivage in Biloxi, Mississippi ($600 million purchase cost), the Golden Nugget—Downtown, Las Vegas, the Mirage on the Strip in Las Vegas, Treasure Island, Holiday Inn—Boardwalk, and the Golden Nugget—Laughlin. Additionally it is a 50 percent owner of the Monte Carlo with Mandalay. By 1999 additions include the development of the Marina area in Atlantic City, New Jersey, and a partnership with Boyd Gaming.

MGM Grand Inc. includes the properties of the MGM Hotel and Casino, MGM Grand Australia, MGM Grand Detroit. The MGM Las Vegas is located on approximately 116 acres at the northeast corner of Las Vegas Boulevard across the street from New York—New York Hotel and Casino. The casino is approximately 171,500 square feet in size, and is one of the largest casinos in the world with 3,669 slot machines and 157 gaming tables. Current plans call for continued development of the master plan for the Las Vegas property. Through a wholly-owned subsidiary, MGM owns and operates the MGM Grand Diamond Beach Hotel and a hotel/casino resort in Darwin, Australia. In March 1999 MGM and Primadonna Resorts, Inc., merged resulting in ownership of New York—New York Hotel and Casino and three hotel/casinos on the California-Nevada border. MGM also intends to construct and operate a destination resort hotel/casino, entertainment and retail facility in Atlantic City on approximately 35 acres of land on the boardwalk.

## THE LEGAL ENVIRONMENT

Within the gaming industry all current operators must consider compliance with extensive gaming regulations a primary concern. Each state or country has its own regulations and regulatory boards, requiring extensive reporting and licensing requirements. For example, in Las Vegas, Nevada, gambling operations are subject to regulatory control by the Nevada State Gaming Control Board, the Clark County Nevada Gaming and Liquor Licensing Board, and by city government regulations. The laws, regulations, and supervisory procedures of virtually all gaming authorities are based upon public policy primarily concerned with the prevention of unsavory or unsuitable persons from having a direct or indirect involvement with gaming at any time or in any capacity and the establishment and maintenance of responsible accounting practices and procedures.

Additional regulations typically cover the maintenance of effective controls over the financial practices of licensees, including the establishment of minimum procedures for internal fiscal affairs and the safeguarding of assets and revenues, providing reliable recordkeeping and requiring the filing of periodic reports, preventing cheating and fraudulent practices, and providing a source of state and local revenues through taxation and licensing fees. Changes in such laws, regulations, and procedures could have an adverse effect on any gaming operations. All gaming companies must submit detailed operating and financial reports to authorities. Nearly all financial transactions, including loans, leases, and the sale of securities must be reported. Some financial activities are subject to approval by regulatory agencies. As Mandalay moves into other locations outside of Nevada, it will need to adhere to local regulations.

## FUTURE CONSIDERATIONS

Mandalay states that "Strategic eminence in our industry depends on owning large, hard-to-duplicate positions in the major markets, where profitable growth seems the most achievable." (Mandalay's 1999 *Annual Report*). Mandalay was one of the innovators of the gaming resort concept and has continued to be a leader in that field. However the mega-entertainment-resort industry operates differently than the traditional casino gaming industry. In the past consumers would visit a casino to experience the thrill of gambling. Now they not only gamble but also expect to be dazzled by enormous entertainment complexes that cost in the billions of dollars to build. The competition has continued to increase even as growth rates have been slowing.

For years analysts have questioned the ability of the gaming industry to continue high growth in established markets as the industry matures. Through the 1970s and 80s the gaming industry experienced rapid growth. Through the 1990s the industry began to experience a shakeout of marginal competitors and a consolidation phase. Mandalay has been successful through this turmoil but now faces the task of maintaining high growth in a more mature industry.

---

# REFERENCES

Aztar Corp. *1997, 1998, and 1999, 10K,* retrieved from EDGAR Database, http://www.sec.gov/Archives/edgar/ data/.

"Casinos Move into New Areas," *Standard and Poors Industry Surveys,* March 11, 1993, pp. L35–L41.

"Circus Circus Announces Promotion," *PR Newswire,* June 10, 1997.

Circus Circus Enterprises, Inc., *Annual Report to Shareholders,* January 31, 1989, January 31, 1990, January 31, 1993, January 31, 1994, January 31, 1995, January 31, 1996, January 31, 1997, January 31, 1998, January 31, 1999.

CORNING, BLAIR, "Luxor: Egypt Opens in Vegas," *San Antonio Express News,* October 24, 1993.

"Economic Impacts of Casino Gaming in the United States," by Arthur Andersen for the American Gaming Association, May 1997.

HARRAH'S ENTERTAINMENT, INC. *1997, 1998, and 1999 10K,* retrieved from EDGAR Database, http://www.sec.gov/Archives/edgar/data/.

"Harrah's Survey of Casino Entertainment," Harrah's Entertainment, Inc., 1996.

HILTON HOTELS CORP. *1997, 1998, and 1999 10K,* retrieved from EDGAR Database, http://www.sec.gov/Archives/ edgar/data/.

Industry Surveys—Lodging and Gaming, *Standard and Poors Industry Surveys,* June 19, 1997.

"ITT Board Rejects Hilton's Offer as Inadequate, Reaffirms Belief That ITT's Comprehensive Plan Is in the Best Interest of ITT Shareholders," Press release, August 14, 1997.

ITT Corp. *1997 10K,* retrieved from EDGAR Database, http://www.sec.gov/Archives/edgar/data/.

LALLI, SERGIO, "Excalibur Awaiteth," *Hotel and Motel Management,* June 11, 1990.

MGM Grand, Inc. *1997, 1998, and 1999 10K,* retrieved from EDGAR Database, http://www.sec.gov/Archives/edgar/data/.

Mirage Resorts, Inc. *1997, 1998, and 1999 10K,* retrieved from EDGAR Database, http://www.sec.gov/Archives/edgar/data/.

# HARRAH'S ENTERTAINMENT, INC.—2000

**Mary R. Dittman**
**Francis Marion University**

## HET

www.harrahs.com

Harrah's Entertainment, Inc., is a $3 billion-per-year gaming company that owns prop-
erties in Arizona, Illinois, Indiana, Kansas, Louisiana, Mississippi, Missouri, Nevada,
New Jersey, North Carolina, and Sydney, Australia. Harrah's is headquartered in Las
Vegas, Nevada (Harrah's had been headquartered in Memphis, Tennessee) and employs
approximately 35,000 people (53.3 percent are female; 41.5 percent are ethnic minorities) across the United States. Harrah's net income for 1999 increased 104.3 percent to
$208.4 million.

## HISTORY

William F. Harrah founded Harrah's as a bingo parlor in 1937 in Reno, Nevada. Over
the next 30-odd years, Harrah's grew into one of the nation's premier gaming establishments.

In 1973, Harrah's became the first casino to be listed on the NYSE. In 1980,
Holiday Inns, Inc., acquired Harrah's. In 1989, Holiday Inn announced the creation of a
new spin-off company, The Promus Companies, Inc. In June 1995, Promus spun off its
Embassy Suites, Hampton Inn, and Homewood Suites brands; the remaining Harrah's
brand, renamed "Harrah's Entertainment, Inc.," included Harrah's hotels and casinos,
Harrah's assets, and a majority of the Promus headquarters and employees.

In 1997 and 1998, Harrah's joined with the Cherokee Indians and the Prairie Band
of the Potawatomi Nation, respectively, to open tribal-run casinos in North Carolina and
Kansas.

Harrah's recent acquisitions include its 1998 purchase of Showboat, Inc., which
includes four properties in Atlantic City, East Chicago, Las Vegas, and Sydney, Australia,
and its 1999 merger with the Rio Hotel & Casino, a true destination resort in Las Vegas.

## EXTERNAL FACTORS

### Gaming Industry

Gaming revenues in the United States were approximately $30 billion in 1998 accord-
ing to a growth-rate-based estimate. This estimate includes gaming activity in Native
American casinos, cruise ship casinos, and some noncasino slot machines (revenues from
these activities were more than $9 billion in 1995 according to Arthur Andersen
Consulting Group, 1996). The year 1996 was the first that revenues in new markets
(cruise ships, Native American casinos, etc.) exceeded revenues in traditional (Nevada

and New Jersey) markets. The Nevada market comprises 23.3 percent of the gaming industry's volume, and New Jersey represents 20.6 percent of the volume.

The commercial casino industry employs more than 325,000 people with total wages of $8.7 billion. The American Gaming Association (1999) has disclosed that the industry is an important part of the economies of the 10 states in which casinos are located.

According to a survey by the American Gaming Association (1999):

> The casino industry work force also brought other less tangible social benefits to its communities. Nationwide, these employees contribute more than $58 million to charitable organizations annually and donate 884,000 hours of volunteer time every month. In the four states that track minority employment (Indiana, Louisiana, Missouri, and New Jersey), 45 percent of the work force is made up of minorities. In the three states that track female employment (Louisiana, Missouri, and New Jersey), the total work force of 75,289 employees includes 31,539 women. The disabled make up nearly 10 percent of the work force in New Jersey.

In 1996, the casino gaming industry employed more people than the soft drink, cellular phone services, videocassette sales and rentals, and cable television services industries. With respect to revenues, the casino gaming industry is half the size of the soft drink industry, and it is as large as the other previously mentioned industries (Arthur Anderson Consulting Group, 1996).

The gaming industry is also active in bringing attention to problem gambling. Much like alcohol companies that encourage consumers to drink responsibly, many casinos post the phone number for Gamblers Anonymous at every cashier's cage; many also offer free literature with information on problem gambling and how to get help. In the same spirit of involvement, the gaming industry is active against underage gambling; most casinos will not permit minors to even stand in the gaming areas.

### Demographics

According to a 1996 Harrah's Entertainment, Inc./NFO Research, Inc./U.S. Census Survey, the profile of the typical casino customer has remained consistent over the past several years.

The following factors seem to characterize the casino player market:

- Casino players have a household income that is higher than 28 percent of the U.S. population.
- There are slightly more male and slightly fewer female casino players as compared to the proportions in the U.S. population.
- Casino players are slightly better educated.
- Casino players are more likely to be white-collar workers.

Exhibit 1 summarizes the differences between traditional destination (Nevada and New Jersey) players and new destination (riverboat casinos, Native American reservation casinos, cruise ship casinos) players and compares those players to the U.S. population (Harrah's Entertainment, Inc., 1997).

### Competition

The gaming industry boasts six major players (in descending order by 1998 reported revenues): Starwood Hotels & Resorts, Park Place Entertainment Corporation, Harrah's Entertainment, Mirage Resorts Inc., Trump Hotels and Casino Resorts, and Mandalay

EXHIBIT 1    A Comparison of Traditional and
New Destination Players

| Characteristic | Traditional Destination Player Profile | New Destination Player Profile | United States Population |
|---|---|---|---|
| Median household income | $44,000 | $39,000 | $32,000 |
| Male/female ratio | 52/48 | 50/50 | 49/51 |
| Median age | 49 | 47 | 48 |
| **Education** | | | |
| No college | 48% | 50% | 51% |
| Some college | 23 | 22 | 22 |
| College graduate | 19 | 18 | 17 |
| Postgraduate | 10 | 9 | 10 |
| **Employment** | | | |
| White collar | 43% | 41% | 41% |
| Blue collar | 27 | 29 | 28 |
| Retired | 16 | 16 | 16 |
| Other | 14 | 14 | 15 |

EXHIBIT 2    Six Major Gaming Industry Companies

| Company | 1998 Revenue (Dollars) | 1998 Net Income (Dollars) | 1998 Estimated Market Share | Number of Rooms | Square Feet of Casino Space |
|---|---|---|---|---|---|
| Starwood | $4,710,000,000 | $1,200,000,000 | 15.7% | 223,000 | 120,000* |
| Park Place | 2,900,000,000 | 139,000,000 | 9.7 | 23,000 | 1,400,000 |
| Harrah's | 2,004,000,000 | 102,000,000 | 6.7 | 11,685 | 1,119,635 |
| Mirage | 1,676,900,000 | 81,700,000 | 5.6 | Not available | Not available |
| Trump | 1,573,202,000 | (1,921,000) | 5.2 | 3,682 | 399,000 |
| Mandalay | 1,354,487,000 | 89,908,000 | 4.5 | 23,418 | 894,700 |

*Starwood only reported the casino space of the Caesar's brands.

Resort Group. Exhibit 2 summarizes each competitor's 1998 revenues, net income, number of hotel rooms, and square feet of casino space.

### Starwood Hotels & Resorts

Starwood Hotels & Resorts resulted from the merger of Starwood with ITT Corporation (holder of Sheraton Hotels). Starwood also owns the Westin brand and Caesar's brand, which has casinos in Las Vegas, Indiana, Atlantic City, Lake Tahoe, Delaware, and several international locations.

Starwood focuses on upscale full-service lodging as well as gaming. It is the largest hotel company, and it uses its size to lower operating costs through purchasing economies in the areas of insurance, telecommunications, employee benefits, food, and fixture supplies.

Starwood's primary business objective is "to maximize earnings and cash flow by increasing the profitability of the Company's existing portfolio . . . and increasing the number of the Company's hotel management contracts and franchise agreements (Starwood Hotels & Resorts Home page)."

### Park Place Entertainment Corporation

Park Place Entertainment Corporation owns the Hilton Hotel (including the Las Vegas Hilton and Flamingo Hilton) chain, Grand Casinos, the Bally's brand, and the Paris Hotel & Casino, which opened in 1999. Park Place is the world's largest gaming company in terms of casino square footage and gaming-only revenues.

### Harrah's Entertainment

Harrah's owns the Harrah's, Showboat, and Rio brand names and is ranked third in market share. Harrah's actively concentrates on targeting particular portions of the market, providing excellent service, maintaining clear brand positioning, and building brand loyalty.

### Mirage Resorts Inc.

Mirage Resorts owns the Mirage, Bellagio, Beau Rivage, Treasure Island, and Golden Nugget brands, and it holds 50 percent ownership in the Monte Carlo (Las Vegas) with the Mandalay Resort Group. In 1998, Mirage Resorts was negatively affected by turmoil in the Asian and Middle East markets, which hurt its high-end gaming business. Its successful simultaneous opening of two major properties (Bellagio and Beau Rivage), although a difficult undertaking, signaled Mirage Resorts' ability to grow and expand; Bellagio and Beau Rivage doubled the size of Mirage Resorts.

### Trump Hotels and Casino Resorts

Trump Hotels and Casino Resorts owns three properties in Atlantic City: the Trump Taj Mahal Casino Resort, the Trump Plaza Hotel & Casino, and the Trump Marina Hotel Casino. A fourth property, the Trump Hotel Casino, is located in Buffington Harbor, Indiana.

In 1998, Trump launched an extensive television, newspaper, billboard, and direct mail campaign and succeeded in drawing both return customers and new customers to its hotel and casino properties. The company focused in 1999 on spending promotional dollars qualitatively rather than quantitatively and reducing debt.

### Mandalay Resort Group

Mandalay Resort Group holds the Mandalay Bay, Luxor, Excalibur, and Circus Circus brands as well as a 50% ownership of the Monte Carlo with Mirage Resorts. Mandalay Resort Group was founded in 1974 as Circus Circus Enterprises. It holds properties in Nevada, Mississippi, and Illinois.

### Other Competition

The six companies profiled make up slightly less than 50 percent of the gaming industry. Many other, smaller competitors both domestically and internationally make up the other half of the market.

Because gaming could be considered part of the vast entertainment industry, hotel/casinos compete with the myriad of other entertainment venues: theme parks, resorts, theaters, cruise ships, etc.

One potential source for intense gaming competition is the Internet. Both state and federal governments have actively worked to regulate and even ban Internet gaming. Internet gaming became a $10 billion-per-year industry in 1999; however, according to Andrea Lessani (1998), there are four major concerns with this type of gaming:

1. The potential for fraud over the Internet.
2. Children's access to gambling sites.
3. An increase in gambling addictions.
4. The need to preserve state revenues generated from legally enforced and state-run gambling operations.

Although the federal government does not yet ban Internet gaming, many states have passed laws regulating its use. For example, Nevada has become the first state to pass a law that specifically prohibits its residents from placing or accepting bets over the Internet (Andrea Lessani, 1998).

## Technology

Three major developments affect the gaming industry: player cards, slot technology and linked jackpots, and the Internet. The Internet was examined in the previous section; the following discussion focuses on player cards and slot technology/linked jackpots.

### Player Cards

Most casinos offer a player card, which is similar to an airline's frequent flier card. The card is inserted into the slot machine prior to begin play, or it is run through a scanner at certain table games (usually with a $25 betting minimum). The card tracks player demographics and playing habits. Each casino's card is valid at that casino's locations.

Players can earn cash, prizes, and complimentary meals, rooms, and other amenities by racking up points on their player cards.

### Slot Technology/Linked Jackpots

Gaming industry suppliers (such as International Game Technology) have been developing new types of slot-like games with such themes as Wheel of Fortune, the Addams Family, the Richard Petty Driving Experience, and I Dream of Jeannie. The goal of such suppliers is to keep players excited and satisfied.

Other than the traditional spinning-reel slot machines, there are a variety of new games on the market: video-based games, multigame machines (where the player can select from a variety of games), and interactive games.

Linked jackpots (like the Megabucks jackpot) pool revenues from around a gaming area (like Megabucks, which pools revenues from all over Nevada) and then pay out millions in winnings. It is conceivable that a player who wins a linked jackpot could win millions of dollars just by spending one dollar in a slot machine.

## Economic and Government Concerns

Casino gaming has created thousands of jobs, a high percentage of which are held by minorities and women. The hundreds of millions of dollars in tax revenues that casinos pay to cities and states each year help lower taxes and pay for many basic civic needs. Casinos also lead to growth in other areas: retail, housing construction, restaurants, and other tourism venues (Arthur Andersen Consulting Group, 1996).

For these reasons, many states support gaming. In fact, Nevada residents pay no state income tax, and sales taxes are relatively low, thanks to the taxes paid by the gaming industry.

Economically, four points relating to gaming must be addressed (Arthur Andersen Consulting Group, 1996):

1. Gaming has grown because consumers' discretionary recreational income has grown.
2. Recreation expenditures are growing faster than any other major component of the economy because when incomes increase (as they have been), spending shifts from necessities to recreation.
3. Casino gaming's growth only represents a small portion (less than 7 percent) of total spending on recreation—people are not spending on gaming at the expense of spending on other forms of recreation.
4. Other areas of discretionary spending generate more revenues than gaming.

Although some gaming opponents argue that gaming simply causes people to "rob from Peter to pay Paul" (that is, people simply transfer their spending from other forms of recreation to gaming), the economic data indicate that gaming stands as its own industry and will continue to grow as the economy and people's incomes grow.

## INTERNAL CONDITION

### Divisions

Harrah's revenues can be classified into four different categories:

- Riverboat casinos (Central Region)
- Atlantic City (Eastern Region)
- Southern and Northern Nevada (Western Region)
- Other land-based casino (including managed casinos with Tribal Nations)

### *Riverboat Casinos (Central Region)*

Riverboat casinos accounted for $970.9 million in 1999 (32.10 percent of Harrah's total revenue). Due to increased competition in the riverboat casino market, profit margins have decreased. Higher gaming taxes in some areas have also caused declines in margins.

| (In millions) | 1999 | 1998 | 1997 | 1996 | Percentage Increase/Decrease | |
|---|---|---|---|---|---|---|
| | | | | | 1999 vs 1998 | 1998 vs 1997 |
| Casino revenues | $ 970.9 | $661.9 | $614.8 | $596 | 46.7% | 7.7% |
| Total revenues | 1,020.1 | 702.7 | 656.2 | 629.1 | 45.2% | 7.1% |
| Operating profit | 201.8 | 121 | 124.2 | 141.2 | 66.8% | (2.6)% |
| Operating margin | 19.8% | 17.20% | 18.90% | 22.40% | 2.6 pts | (1.7) pts |

### *Atlantic City (Eastern Region)*

Harrah's Atlantic City operation's revenues and operating profit have increased over the past three years, mostly due to the acquisition of Showboat Atlantic City. Atlantic City accounts for approximately 23.92 percent of Harrah's total revenue.

| (In millions) | 1999 | 1998 | 1997 | 1996 | Percentage Increase/Decrease | |
| --- | --- | --- | --- | --- | --- | --- |
| | | | | | 1999 vs 1998 | 1998 vs 1997 |
| Casino revenues | $723.3% | $540.8 | $314.9 | $310.1 | 33.7% | 71.7% |
| Total revenues | 775.6 | 590.8 | 349.5 | 338.6 | 31.3 | 69.0 |
| Operating profit | 173.8 | 129.2 | 73.3 | 75 | 34.5 | 76.3 |
| Operating margin | 22.4% | 21.90% | 21.00% | 22.20% | 0.5 pts | 0.9 pts |

## Western Region

Revenues in Nevada are primarily from Harrah's on the Las Vegas Strip and operations in Reno and Lake Tahoe.

| (In millions) | 1999 | 1998 | 1997 | Percentage Increase/Decrease | |
| --- | --- | --- | --- | --- | --- |
| | | | | 1999 vs 1998 | 1998 vs 1997 |
| Casino revenues | $ 730.1 | $457.6 | $408.3 | 59.5% | 12.1% |
| Total revenues | 1,147.9 | 624.6 | 576.0 | 78.6 | 11.6 |
| Operating profit | 182.4 | 94.3 | 88.3 | 93.4 | 6.8 |
| Operating margin | 15.9% | 14.7% | 15.3% | 1.2 pts | (0.6) pts |

## Vision and Mission

Harrah's Vision is, "To offer exciting environments and to be legendary at creating smiles, laughter and lasting memories with every guest we entertain." The Mission Statement reads, "To build lasting relationships and create 'A Great Time, Every Time . . . Guaranteed,' by delivering comfort, action, shot to win and hospitality (C.A.S.H.)-to-the-MAX through enthusiastic, highly trained, friendly, attentive and empowered employees who have pledged to provide unsurpassed entertainment and service to every guest."

## Management

Harrah's management structure is fairly traditional. Philip Satre has been the president and CEO of Harrah's Entertainment since 1995 and president and CEO of Promus since 1994. In January 1997, he also assumed the duties of chairman of the board. In December 1998, *Casino Journal* named Satre "Gaming Executive of the Year." In 1995, he was selected best chief executive in the casino and hotel industries by *The Wall Street Transcript.*

Satre shares the office of the president with the chief financial officer and chief operating officer. Together, this triumvirate of managers charts the financial, marketing, operating, and development strategies for Harrah's Entertainment.

The management reports to a talented board of directors, which includes principals from the Gannett Newspaper Group, Mutual of New York, Saks Incorporated, the Graduate School of Business of Harvard University, and a host of other business leaders and private investors.

One of Harrah's top management strengths is the company's approach to strategic management and its focus on its objectives. According to the 1998 *Annual Report,*

To understand Harrah's Entertainment, you need to understand our concept of Focus. In every industry there are basically two kinds of companies: those companies that try to be all things to all people, and those who focus on a select audience and then build their products, services, knowledge and identity with them in mind. It is much more difficult to have the discipline of focus; however, we believe it is also the path that leads to the greatest opportunity. We intend to be that kind of company.

### Financial Data

All financial information are contained in Exhibits 3, 4, and 5.

### Marketing

Harrah's has an incredibly strong focus on marketing. The casino industry is highly competitive; there are billions of dollars at stake. Because Harrah's competes in the entertainment industry, its customers are purchasing "a good time." Therefore, service is of the utmost importance.

#### Product

Harrah's product is "A Great Time, Every Time . . . Guaranteed." Although this is an intangible product at best, Harrah's has targeted a segment of the overall casino market; this segmentation allows Harrah's to better identify what "a great time" is to a particular segment of the market. Perhaps it is a resort destination vacation (complete with spa, salon, and golf); perhaps it is multimillion dollar slot tournaments; perhaps it is a comfortable stay, good food, and great service. Harrah's has successfully created a tangible product.

#### Price

It is difficult to place a price on the product offered by the casino industry. In terms of room, food, and amenity pricing, Harrah's is competitive with, and in some cases, slightly below, competitive pricing. For example, a room at Bellagio in Las Vegas starts around $300 per night; a full-size suite at the Rio is well under $200 per night.

One area of "price" that is of interest to gaming customers is the probability of winning. Harrah's (Las Vegas and Reno) hosts annual multimillion-dollar slot tournaments. These tournaments are easy to compete in and take no skill. In November 1998, a thirty-three-year-old office worker from Sacramento won $1 million in Harrah's (Reno) slot tournament; her win was pure luck. This type of tournament appeals to the customer's sense of "maybe that can happen to me, too" and helps to generate traffic onto the casino floor. The slot machines are the major revenue generator at a casino, so generating more slot business usually means more revenue for the casino. The reputation of having "loose slots" draws more people in.

#### Place

Harrah's has 18 locations. There are eight land-based properties:

- Harrah's Reno
- Harrah's Lake Tahoe
- Harrah's Las Vegas
- Harrah's Atlantic City
- Atlantic City Showboat
- Bill's Casino Lake Tahoe
- Harrah's Laughlin (Nevada)
- Rio Hotel & Casino (Las Vegas)

EXHIBIT 3    Consolidated Balance Sheet (in millions)

| | December 31 | | |
| | 1999 | 1998 | 1997 |
|---|---|---|---|
| **Assets** | | | |
| Current assets | | | |
| Cash and cash equivalents | $    233,581 | $    158,995 | $    116,443 |
| Receivables | 121,186 | 55,043 | 43,767 |
| Deferred income taxes | 33,208 | 22,478 | 17,436 |
| Prepayments and other | 68,028 | 27,521 | 21,653 |
| Inventories | 30,666 | 15,306 | 13,011 |
| Total current assets | 486,669 | 279,343 | 212,310 |
| Land, buildings, riverboats, and equipment | | | |
| Land and land improvements | 653,101 | 323,692 | 218,703 |
| Buildings, riverboats, and improvements | 2,510,070 | 1,624,346 | 1,334,279 |
| Furniture, fixtures, and equipment | 820,583 | 711,966 | 600,358 |
| | 3,983,754 | 2,660,004 | 2,153,340 |
| Less: accumulated depreciation | (922,524) | (789,847) | (675,286) |
| | 3,061,230 | 1,870,157 | 1,478,054 |
| Excess of purchase price over net assets of businesses acquired, net of amortization | 505,217 | 383,450 | 43,363 |
| Investments in and advances to nonconsolidated affiliates | 168,511 | 273,508 | 152,401 |
| Deferred costs and other | 545,220 | 479,874 | 119,378 |
| | $4,766,847 | $3,286,332 | $2,005,506 |
| **Liabilities and stockholders' equity** | | | |
| Current liabilities | | | |
| Accounts payable | $      81,200 | $      57,864 | $      45,233 |
| Construction payables | — | 629 | 7,186 |
| Accrued expenses | 287,494 | 172,021 | 156,694 |
| Current portion of long-term debt | 2,877 | 2,332 | 1,837 |
| Total current liabilities | 371,571 | 232,846 | 210,950 |
| Long-term debt | 2,540,268 | 1,999,354 | 924,397 |
| Deferred credits and other | 120,827 | 112,362 | 98,177 |
| Deferred income taxes | 228,955 | 75,457 | 22,361 |
| | 3,261,621 | 2,420,019 | 1,255,885 |
| Minority Interests | $      18,949 | $      14,906 | $      14,118 |
| **Commitments and contingencies** | | | |
| Stockholders' equity | | | |
| Common stock, $0.10 par value, authorized 360,000,000 shares, outstanding—102,188,018 and 101,035,898 shares | $      12,438 | $      10,219 | $      10,104 |
| Capital surplus | 987,322 | 407,691 | 388,925 |
| Retained earnings | 512,539 | 451,410 | 349,386 |
| Accumulated other comprehensive income | (493) | 6,567 | 2,884 |
| Deferred compensation related to restricted stock | (25,529) | (24,480) | (15,796) |
| | 1,486,277 | 851,407 | 735,503 |
| | $4,766,847 | $3,286,332 | $2,005,506 |

*Source:* www.freeedgar.com

EXHIBIT 4    Harrah's Consolidated Income Statements (000 omitted)

| | 1999 | 1998 | 1997 |
|---|---|---|---|
| Revenues | | | |
| Casino | $2,424,237 | $1,660,313 | $1,338,003 |
| Food and beverage | 425,808 | 231,568 | 196,765 |
| Rooms | 253,629 | 153,538 | 128,354 |
| Management fees | 75,890 | 64,753 | 24,566 |
| Other | 131,403 | 78,320 | 78,954 |
| Less: casino promotional allowances | (286,539) | (184,477) | (147,432) |
| Total revenues | 3,024,428 | 2,004,015 | 1,619,210 |
| Operating expenses | | | |
| Direct | | | |
| Casino | 1,254,557 | 868,622 | 685,942 |
| Food and beverage | 218,580 | 116,641 | 103,604 |
| Rooms | 66,818 | 41,871 | 39,719 |
| Depreciation of buildings, riverboats and equipment | 188,199 | 130,128 | 103,670 |
| Development costs | 6,538 | 8,989 | 10,524 |
| Write-downs, reserves and recoveries | 2,235 | 7,474 | 13,806 |
| Project opening costs | 2,276 | 8,103 | 17,631 |
| Other | 690,404 | 467,999 | 383,791 |
| Total operating expenses | 2,429,607 | 1,649,827 | 1,358,687 |
| Operating profit | 594,821 | 354,188 | 260,523 |
| Corporate expense | (42,748) | (37,890) | (27,155) |
| Headquarters relocation and reorganization costs | (10,274) | — | — |
| Equity in losses of nonconsolidated affiliates | (43,467) | (14,989) | (11,053) |
| Venture restructuring costs | 322 | (6,013) | (6,944) |
| Amortization of goodwill and trademarks | (17,617) | (7,450) | (1,839) |
| Income from operations | 481,037 | 287,846 | 213,532 |
| Interest expense, net of interest capitalized | (193,407) | (117,270) | (79,071) |
| Gains on sales of equity interests in nonconsolidated affiliates | 59,824 | 13,155 | 37,388 |
| Other income, including interest income | 12,129 | 19,575 | 11,799 |
| Income before income taxes and minority interests | 359,583 | 203,306 | 183,648 |
| Provision for income taxes | (128,914) | (74,600) | (68,746) |
| Minority interests | (11,166) | (6,989) | (7,380) |
| Income before extraordinary losses | 219,503 | 121,717 | 107,522 |
| Extraordinary losses, net of tax benefit of $5,990, $10,522 and $4,477 | (11,033) | (19,693) | (8,134) |
| Net income | $ 208,470 | $ 102,024 | $ 99,388 |
| Earnings (loss) per share-basic | | | |
| Before extraordinary losses | $ 1.74 | $ 1.21 | 1.07 |
| Extraordinary losses, net | (0.09) | (0.19) | (0.08) |
| Net income | $ 1.65 | $ 1.02 | $ 0.99 |
| Earnings (loss) per share-diluted | | | |
| Before extraordinary losses | $ 1.71 | $ 1.19 | $ 1.06 |
| Extraordinary losses, net | (0.09) | (0.19) | (0.08) |
| Net income | $ 1.62 | $ 1.00 | $ 0.98 |
| Weighted average common shares outstanding | 126,072 | 100,231 | 100,618 |
| Diluted effect of stock compensation programs | 2,676 | 1,289 | 636 |
| Weighted average common and common equivalent Shares outstanding | 128,748 | 101,520 | 101,254 |

*Source:* www.freeedgar.com

# EXHIBIT 5    Harrah's Entertainment Statements of Cash Flows (in thousands)

| Year Ended December 31, | 1999 | 1998 | 1997 |
|---|---|---|---|
| Cash flows from operating activities | | | |
| Net income | $208,470 | $102,024 | $ 99,388 |
| Adjustments to reconcile net income to cash flows from operating activities | | | |
| Extraordinary losses, before income taxes | 17,023 | 29,491 | 12,611 |
| Depreciation and amortization | 218,299 | 159,183 | 122,396 |
| Write-downs, reserves and recoveries | 1,570 | 6,535 | 13,806 |
| Other noncash items | 86,976 | 28,835 | 27,712 |
| Minority interests' share of net income | 11,166 | 6,989 | 7,380 |
| Equity in losses of nonconsolidated affiliates | 43,467 | 14,989 | 11,053 |
| Realized gains from sales of equity interests in nonconsolidated affiliates | (59,824) | (13,155) | (37,388) |
| Net losses (gains) from asset sales | 878 | (6,536) | (4,117) |
| Net change in long-term accounts | 56,542 | 17,260 | (1,452) |
| Net change in working capital accounts | (70,161) | (45,244) | 3,713 |
| Cash flows provided by operating activities | 514,406 | 300,371 | 255,102 |
| Cash flows from investing activities | | | |
| Land, buildings, riverboats and equipment additions | (340,468) | (140,386) | (229,529) |
| Increase (decrease) in construction payables | 1,871 | (6,557) | (10,789) |
| Investments in and advances to nonconsolidated affiliates | (70,181) | (76,052) | (54,477) |
| Purchase of minority interest in subsidiary | (26,000) | — | — |
| Proceeds from sales of equity interests in subsidiaries | 172,576 | 17,000 | 53,755 |
| Proceeds from other asset sales | 26,359 | 12,728 | 26,570 |
| Cash acquired in acquisitions | 50,226 | — | — |
| Payment for purchase of Showboat, Inc., net of cash acquired | — | (475,334) | — |
| Purchase of marketable equity securities for defeasance of debt | — | (65,898) | — |
| Other | 1,253 | (28,739) | (6,483) |
| Cash flows used in investing activities | (184,364) | (763,238) | (220,953) |
| Cash flows from financing activities | | | |
| Net borrowings under Bank Facility, net of financing $4,556 | 1,105,444 | — | — |
| Net (repayments) borrowings under Retired Facility, net of financing costs of $9,332 in 1998 | (1,086,000) | 362,262 | 239,500 |
| Proceeds from issuance of senior notes, net of discount and issue costs of $5,980 | 494,020 | — | — |
| Proceeds from issuance of senior subordinated notes, net of issue costs of $12,552 | — | 737,448 | — |
| Other debt proceeds | 21,000 | — | — |
| Debt retirements | (625,568) | (563,522) | (202,115) |
| Purchases of treasury stock | (147,952) | — | (41,022) |
| Minority interests' distributions, net of contributions | (7,122) | (6,200) | (9,952) |
| Premiums paid on early extinguishments of debt | (9,278) | (24,569) | (9,666) |
| Other | — | — | (45) |
| Cash flows (used in) provided by financing activities | (255,456) | 505,419 | (23,300) |
| Net increase in cash and cash equivalents | 74,586 | 42,552 | 10,849 |
| Cash and cash equivalents, beginning of year | 158,995 | 116,443 | 105,594 |
| Cash and cash equivalents, end of year | $233,581 | $158,995 | $116,443 |

*Source:* www.freeedgar.com

There are seven riverboats:

- Harrah's Joliet (Illinois)
- Harrah's Vicksburg (Mississippi)
- Harrah's Tunica (Mississippi)
- Harrah's Shreveport (Louisiana)
- Harrah's North Kansas City (Missouri)
- Harrah's St. Louis—Riverport (Missouri)
- Showboat Mardi Gras (East Chicago)

Three Native American gaming properties:

- Harrah's Phoenix Ak-Chin Casino (Arizona)
- Harrah's Cherokee Smoky Mountains (North Carolina)
- Harrah's Prairie Band (Kansas)

These many locations allow Harrah's to attract many different people into the casinos. This diversification also means that Harrah's is not dependent on any one region for its customers, nor is it dependent on one area's economy.

Harrah's has also invested in National Airlines, a Las Vegas-based airline that offers nonstop flights between Las Vegas and major markets (such as Los Angeles). There are National Airlines check-in counters at Harrah's and the Rio in Las Vegas, and customers can purchase complete travel packages from Harrah's that now include airfare.

Harrah's has also joined the travel agents' Global Distribution System, which makes it easier for travel agents and customers using the Internet to book hotel reservations and access information about Harrah's hotels and casinos.

### Promotion

Harrah's is a master of promotion. From slot tournaments to Internet Web sites; from art exhibits (Treasures of Russia at the Rio was replaced by the *Titanic* exhibit featuring artifacts recovered from the famed ship's resting place) to world-class entertainers (Rod Stewart performed at the Rio on December 31, 1999), Harrah's has a complete marketing program. Using the Total Gold program, Harrah's has 15 million customer names in its database. It uses these names and the corresponding demographic information to customize programs.

In 1998, Harrah's launched its largest-ever brand image advertising campaign complete with TV, radio, newspaper, and magazine ads, and billboards. The campaign, titled, "Harrah's, Your Biggest Nights Happen Here," is based on extensive research conducted by Harrah's. Harrah's found that their players are also movie lovers, so the company aired a 30-second TV spot during the Academy Awards.

Harrah's has mastered target marketing. Not only does it talk to its customers, the company faithfully observes play patterns and conducts formal research. In fact, Harrah's surveys have formed the basis for research conducted by the Arthur Andersen Group for the American Gaming Association.

Harrah's Total Gold system, the company's player card, was introduced in 1997. The technology is patented, and it is the number-one player card in Las Vegas and Atlantic City. The customer database generated by the Total Gold system allows Harrah's to focus on serving its market.

Nineteen percent of Harrah's Total Gold play comes from multimarket play: players who use their cards in more than one Harrah's casino. Harrah's can use the Total Gold system to determine how much an Atlantic City customer plays in Las Vegas. Using this information, Harrah's placed a bank of the most popular slot machines from the Atlantic City property in the middle of Harrah's Las Vegas.

Harrah's focuses on four main strategies to grow its business:

1. More distribution
2. Quality products
3. Patented technology
4. Great service

## Distribution

Harrah's has focused on acquiring and building properties in key gaming markets. The addition of the Rio allows Harrah's to compete in the Las Vegas resort market, because the Rio is classified as a full-service resort (featuring a golf course, full-service spa and salon, meeting and convention facilities, and a museum that features the *Titanic* exhibit.

## High-Quality Products

Although none of Harrah's properties are alike, they strive for consistency in high-quality food, service, gaming, and accommodation. In 1998, Harrah's Atlantic City won 15 first-place and 8 second- and third-place awards in *Casino Player* magazine's annual "Best of" customer ratings issue. The Las Vegas property scored 7 first- and 8 second-place awards. Showboat Atlantic City took 10 top-three awards, and Rio won 13 first-place awards.

## Patented Technology

Harrah's has received patents for its Total Gold system, which allows it to keep its customer database from its competitors. Harrah's uses the database to customize marketing plans and programs and create brand loyalty to the Harrah's, Showboat, and Rio brand names.

Since the launch of the Total Gold program, Harrah's has seen solid same-store sales growth and increases in cross-market play. Rio and Showboat have their own player cards, which have been merged into the Harrah's system, meaning that a Rio player may use his Play Rio card at Harrah's and Showboat, with the rewards system between the three casinos being standardized and equal.

## Great Service

Harrah's recognizes that it is competing in a service industry. The company has a three-tiered service strategy:

1. A regular employee opinion poll that measures employee attitudes and expectations
2. Spotlight on Success—a type of mystery shopper program designed to reward excellent service and correct substandard service
3. The Target Player Satisfaction Survey, which surveys the experiences of target customers

## CONCLUSION

With the addition of the Showboat and Rio properties, Harrah's employs more than 35,000 people. The company instills in each employee its focus: to become the undisputed leader in the casino entertainment industry. In the first quarter of 1998, Harrah's was the first casino to launch a national brand image advertising campaign, with TV spots that aired during the Academy Awards.

Harrah's has become one of the gaming industry's top competitors. Although ranked third in market share in 1998, the company is poised to grow sales and increase revenues and market share.

# REFERENCES

"AGA Releases First Annual Survey of Casino Entertainment." Press release from American Gaming Association. September 14, 1999. www.americangaming.org

"Biography: Philip G. Satre." Harrah's Entertainment, Inc. April 1999.

"Company Information." Starwood Hotels & Resorts Home Page, www.starwoodlodging.com.

"Creating a Successful Brand Strategy." *1997 Annual Report.* Harrah's Entertainment, Inc.

DAVID, FRED R. *Strategic Management Concepts and Cases.* Seventh edition. Upper Saddle River, NJ: Prentice Hall, 1999.

"Economic Impacts of Casino Gaming in the United States." *Section: Casino Gaming Compared to Other Industries.* Prepared by Arthur Andersen Consulting Group for the American Gaming Association, May 1997. www.americangaming.org.

"Economic Impacts of Casino Gaming in the United States." *Section: Overall Conclusions.* Prepared by Arthur Andersen Consulting Group for the American Gaming Association, May 1997. www.americangaming.org.

"Economic Impacts of Casino Gaming in the United States." *Section: Macroeconomic Impacts of the Casino Gaming Industry.* Prepared by Arthur Andersen Consulting Group for the American Gaming Association, May 1997. www.americangaming.org.

"Harrah's Entertainment Continues Its Leadership in Information Technology." Press Release. November 6, 1998. www.prnewswire.com.

"Harrah's Entertainment, Inc. Fact Sheet." Harrah's Entertainment Inc. March 1999.

"Harrah's Launches First-Ever Brand Image Campaign." Press Release. March 23, 1998. www.prnewswire.com.

"Harrah's Survey: U.S. Casino Industry Revenue." Harrah's Entertainment, Inc., 1997. www.harrahs.com, page 4.

"How Much Do You Want to Bet That the Internet Gambling Prohibition Act of 1997 Is Not the Most Effective Way to Tackle the Problems of Online Gambling?" Andrea Lessani. May 1998. The UCLA Online Institute for Cyberspace Law and Policy. http://www.gseis.ucla.edu/iclp/hp.html, pages 1 and 2.

"If You Think You Know Harrah's, Think Again!" 1998 Annual Report, Harrah's Entertainment Company, page 15.

LESSANI, ANDREA M. "How Much Do You Want to Bet That the Internet Gambling Prohibition Act of 1997 Is Not the Most Effective Way to Tackle the Problems of Online Gambling?" The UCLA Online Institute for Cyberspace Law and Policy. May 1998. www.gseis.ucla.edu/iclp/hp.html

*Mandalay Resort Group 1998 Annual Report.* www.mandalayresortgroup.com.

*Mirage Resorts Annual Report 1998.* www.mirageresorts.com.

"New Survey Finds Churchgoing Americans Support Casino Gaming." Press Release. June 29, 1999. www.americangaming.org.

"Park Place Entertainment Corporation Reports Fourth Quarter and Year End 1998 Results." Park Place Entertainment. www.parkplace.com.

"Starwood Announces 1998 Fourth Quarter, Full Year Results 1998." Starwood Hotels & Resorts. www.starwoodlodging. com.

"Trump Hotels & Casino Resorts." www.trump.com.

# FIRST UNION CORPORATION—2000

Brian E. Williamson
Francis Marion University

FTU

www.firstunion.com

In 1999, the $520 billion U.S. banking industry had 9,000 commercial banks and approximately 2,000 thrifts. The 1994 Riegle–Neal Act that allowed single-charter interstate banking opened the floodgates for bank mergers, acquisitions, and consolidations. The year 1998 saw the merger of NationsBank and BankAmerica to form a new entity larger than Chase Manhattan (a product of Chase Manhattan and Chemical Bank), leaving Citicorp the largest in the industry with $667,400 million in assets and $5,807 million in net income. With the $16.6 billion purchase of CoreStates Financial in 1998, First Union made headlines with the largest banking merger in history at that time, including more than 500 East Coast branches. Easing of the Glass–Steagall Act, which prohibited banks from underwriting securities, yielded another wave of mergers with banks and security firms. First Union's net income for 1999 increased 6.7 percent to $2.891 billion.

## HISTORY

First Union was founded in 1908 when H. M. Victor sold 1,000 shares of stock at $100 each to form Union Bank in Charlotte, North Carolina (current corporate headquarters for First Union Corporation). Union Bank made its first merger in 1958 with National Bank and Trust Company of Asheville, North Carolina, and formed First Union National Bank of North Carolina. Over the next forty years, First Union completed approximately 200 acquisitions and mergers with institutions ranging from local thrifts, savings and loans, brokerage houses, mergers and acquisitions advisory firms, leasing companies, home equity firms, and super regional banks. Its local rivalry with hometown NationsBank was one of the major impetuses that prompted First Union to pursue growth in the manner in which they have. In the past ten years, the company has purchased 51 institutions. More recently, since 1997 First Union has purchased eight institutions, two in 1997 and six in 1998, including: Boca Raton First National Bank, Florida; Signet Bancorporation, Virginia; Covenant Bank, Inc., New Jersey; Wheat First Butcher Singer, Inc., Virginia; CoreStates Financial Corp., Pennsylvania; Bowles Hollowell Conner & Co., North Carolina; The Money Store, New Jersey; Analytic-TSA International, Inc., England (asset-leasing firm).

When First Union acquires a new institution, the new company is given First Union's business plan and model to follow. This method of standardization has caused First Union some problems recently. With the Money Store acquisition in 1998, First Union eliminated some of the higher-risk lending that the Money Store was accustomed to, a concept consistent with First Union's business plan. Shortly after the acquisition and adaptation of the new business plan, The Money Store began to have financial problems. First Union learned that by eliminating some high-risk lending, they removed The Money Store from a profitable niche market that had been developed. As a result, First

Union eased up on some of the policies and allowed The Money Store to return to servicing a large portion of the company's niche market. Because of timely changes, The Money Store is on its way to a financial recovery.

A similar situation occurred with the acquisition of CoreStates Financial. Once again, First Union gave CoreStates its business plan and model, but the two organizations cultures were so different that problems quickly followed. First Union found itself having to decide which branches to keep because in some areas CoreStates branches were directly across the street from First Union branches. Because both companies would be falling under the First Union name, branch closings began. At the present, First Union appears to have gained control of the situation, and the merger should ultimately be successful.

Due to the problems with CoreStates and The Money Store, First Union is not currently looking for additional acquisitions. Instead, the company is focusing on streamlining operations and gaining greater organizational control. This comes as a result of depressed stock prices due to lower-than-forecasted earnings resulting from the CoreStates and The Money Store acquisitions.

## OPERATIONAL OVERVIEW

As indicated in Exhibit 1, First Union has the nation's third largest branch network with about 2,400 locations in 12 states, Washington, DC, and the number-one deposit share on the East Coast. Note that First Union has more than 10 percent of the banking market share in Florida, Pennsylvania, New Jersey, North Carolina, and Virginia. The company services 16 million customers and is the sixth largest banking institution in the United States. The largest financial institution by assets is Citigroup as shown in Exhibit 2. First Union is one of the most technologically advanced competitors in its industry and was the first to design and implement a standardized data processing system across all of its holdings. As firms are acquired, they are converted almost instantaneously to First Union's common system. The CoreStates conversion was completed in less than seven months. This system, Emerald, has enabled First Union to be on the leading edge of the banking industry with new product and service offerings. First Union has

EXHIBIT 1    First Union's Geographic Dispersion (1998)

| State | Number of Branches | Number of ATM's | Market Share | Ranking |
|-------|------|------|------|------|
| Florida | 666 | 735 | 16.91% | 2 |
| Pennsylvania | 378 | 565 | 15.88 | 1 |
| New Jersey | 375 | 613 | 13.90 | 2 |
| North Carolina | 235 | 341 | 13.98 | 3 |
| Virginia | 188 | 279 | 13.17 | 3 |
| Georgia | 135 | 359 | 9.35 | 4 |
| Connecticut | 96 | 114 | 6.84 | 4 |
| Maryland | 87 | 120 | 7.88 | 5 |
| South Carolina | 59 | 82 | 6.84 | 4 |
| New York | 55 | 72 | 2.00 | 13 |
| Tennessee | 46 | 61 | 2.75 | 7 |
| Washington, DC | 29 | 61 | 17.00 | 3 |
| Delaware | 22 | 58 | 1.85 | 8 |

Source: First Union's 1999 Annual Report, p. 70–75.

EXHIBIT 2    **Ranking of U.S. Financial Institutions by Assets (1998)**

| Rank | Institution | Assets | Percent Checking | Deposits | Net Income | Percent Checking |
|------|-------------|--------|------------------|----------|------------|------------------|
| 1 | Citigroup | $667 billion | 114.2 | $229 billion | $5,807 million | 61.7 |
| 2 | BankAmerica | 618 billion | 134.4 | 357 billion | 3,441 million | 7.2 |
| 3 | Chase Manhattan | 366 billion | 0.1 | 212 billion | 3,782 million | 2.0 |
| 4 | Bank One | 262 billion | 125.6 | 162 billion | 3,108 million | 138.0 |
| 5 | JP Morgan | 261 billion | −0.4 | 55 billion | 963 million | −34.3 |
| 6 | First Union | 237 billion | 50.9 | 142 billion | 2,891 million | 52.5 |
| 7 | Wells Fargo | 202 billion | 107.8 | 137 billion | 1,950 million | 68.8 |
| 8 | Bankers Trust | 133 billion | −5.0 | 37 billion | 6 million | −99.3 |
| 9 | Fleet Financial | 104 billion | 22.0 | 70 billion | 1,532 million | 17.6 |
| 10 | SunTrust Banks | 93 billion | 60.7 | 59 billion | 971 million | 45.5 |

*Source:* First Union's 1999 *Annual Report,* p. 70–75.

rapidly developed Internet-based banking options and made them available to its customers. However, the bank is not forcefully pushing customers to this service. Instead, First Union is allowing time and convenience to move customers to the services. Planning in advance with technology has allowed First Union to cash in with one of the lowest Y2K remediation costs in the banking industry at $65 million.

First Union's goal is to divide their area of operation to 50 percent conventional banking activities and 50 percent securities, brokerage, leasing, insurance, consulting, and related financial activities. As of the year that ended December 31, 1998, 49.9 percent of First Union's revenues was from noninterest sources compared to the industry average of 30.0 percent.

First Union is currently divided into five business segments. The description of the business segments follows, and the segment summary information is provided in Exhibit 3. The complete 1998 and 1999 income statements for each segment are shown in Exhibits 4 and 5. Note the consumer bank is the largest contributor to profitability at 34 percent. However all banking activities, consumer and commercial, only account for 53 (34+19) percent of total profits.

*Consumer Bank:*    Acts as the primary deposit-taking segment and is the conduit for offering the consumer financial products including but not limited to secured/unsecured consumer loans, first and second mortgages, installment loans, credit cards, auto loans, leases, and student loans. The integrated systems utilized by First Union make the retail bank an excellent point of sale for the products offered by the Capital Management segment.

*Capital Management:*    This segment is the tie between traditional banking and investing for retail customers. It includes the 18th largest mutual fund manager and 28th largest annuity provider. The products offered by this division are marketed through three channels—First Union brokerage, Wheat First Union, and First Union Capital Markets Corp along with all full retail banking centers.

*Commercial Bank:*    Focuses on financial solutions for the corporate, commercial, and small business customer. Separated by gross revenues of $50 million to $2 billion, $10 million to $50 million and to $10 million, respectively. Again the integrated systems allow First Union to market the financial and insurance products of other segments readily.

EXHIBIT 3    **Business Segment Contributions to Profitability—Net Income (1999)**

| | |
|---|---|
| Capital Markets | 30% |
| Consumer | 22 |
| Capital Management | 17 |
| Commercial | 16 |
| Treasury Nonbank | 15 |

## Capital Markets
Contributions to Group Profitability

| | |
|---|---|
| Investment Banking | 44% |
| Commercial Leasing and Rail | 20 |
| Traditional Banking | 20 |
| International | 9 |
| Real Estate Finance | 7 |

## Capital Management
Contributions to Group Profitability

| | |
|---|---|
| Trust Services and Mutual Funds | 46% |
| Retail Brokerage and Insurance Services | 24 |
| CAP Account | 20 |
| Private Client Banking | 10 |

## Consumer
Contributions to Group Profitability

| | |
|---|---|
| Retail Branch Products | 72% |
| Credit Cards | 14 |
| First Union Mortgage | 11 |
| Home Equity and The Money Store | 3 |

## Commercial
Contributions to Group Profitability

| | |
|---|---|
| Cash Management and Deposit Services | 80% |
| Real Estate Banking | 10 |
| Lending | 5 |
| Small Business Banking | 5 |

*Source:* First Union's 1999 *Annual Report,* p. 70–75.

| | |
|---|---|
| *Capital Markets:* | This segment focused on the corporate and institutional customer, providing them with a comprehensive array of investment and banking products. The products are made available through the integrated systems and are a continuum of the commercial bank. |
| *Treasury/Nonbank:* | This segment is somewhat of a catch-all, including goodwill amortization gains on securities and all nonclassifiable by segment miscellaneous income and expenses. |

## EXHIBIT 4    Business Segments 1999 Income Statements (in millions)

|  | Investment Banking | Real Estate Finance | Traditional Banking |
|---|---|---|---|
| **Capital Markets** | | | |
| Income statement data | | | |
| Net interest income | $ 141 | $ 77 | $ 702 |
| Provision for loan losses | 7 | — | 213 |
| Trading account profits | 286 | 60 | — |
| Fee and other income | 1,035 | 95 | 40 |
| Noninterest expense | 715 | 123 | 191 |
| Income tax expense | 279 | 37 | 129 |
| Net income | 461 | 72 | 209 |
| Performance and other data | | | |
| Return on average attributed stockholders' equity | 45.11% | 34.00% | 7.72% |
| Average loans, net | 3,439 | 2,102 | 21,334 |
| Average deposits | 2,835 | 784 | 3,231 |
| Average attributed stockholders' equity | 1,021 | 211 | 2,718 |

|  | Retail Brokerage & Insurance Services | Trust Services | Mutual Funds |
|---|---|---|---|
| **Capital Management** | | | |
| Income statement data | | | |
| Net interest income | $ 96 | $ 51 | — |
| Provision for loan losses | — | — | — |
| Fee and other income | 1,136 | 678 | 460 |
| Noninterest expense | 1,009 | 431 | 232 |
| Income tax expense | 85 | 114 | 87 |
| Net income | 138 | 184 | 141 |
| Performance and other data | | | |
| Return on average attributed stockholders' equity | 34.75% | 77.83% | 64.12% |
| Average loans, net | — | 140 | — |
| Average deposits | — | 2,658 | — |
| Average attributed stockholders' equity | 396 | 236 | 160 |

|  | First Union Mortgage |
|---|---|
| **Consumer** | |
| Income statement data | |
| Net interest income | $ 76 |
| Provision for loan losses | 1 |
| Fee and other income | 317 |
| Noninterest expense | 253 |
| Income tax expense | 53 |
| Net income | $ 86 |

|  | *First Union Mortgage* |
|---|---|

## Consumer *(cont.)*

| Performance and other data | |
|---|---|
| Return on average attributed stockholders' equity | 75.23% |
| Average loans, net | $1,542 |
| Average deposits | 1,196 |
| Average attributed stockholders' equity | 114 |

|  | *Small Business Banking* |
|---|---|

## Commercial

| Income statement data | |
|---|---|
| Net interest income | $   85 |
| Provision for loan losses | 4 |
| Fee and other income | — |
| Noninterest expense | 41 |
| Income tax expense | 15 |
| Net income | 25 |
| Performance and other data | |
| Return on average attributed stockholders' equity | 13.44% |
| Average loans, net | 2,749 |
| Average deposits | — |
| Average attributed stockholders' equity | 183 |

|  | *Capital Markets* | *Capital Mgt.* | *First Union Securities* |
|---|---|---|---|

## Consolidated

| Income statement data | | | |
|---|---|---|---|
| Net interest income | $ 1,327 | $   526 | $ 1,853 |
| Provision for loan losses | 225 | — | 225 |
| Trading account profits | 346 | — | 346 |
| Fee and other income | 1,393 | 2,316 | 3,709 |
| Noninterest expense | 1,349 | 1,898 | 3,247 |
| Income tax expense | 448 | 360 | 808 |
| Net income after merger-related and restructuring charges | 1,044 | 584 | 1,628 |
| After-tax merger-related and restructuring charges | — | — | — |
| Net income before merger-related and restructuring charges | 1,044 | 584 | 1,628 |
| Performance and other data | | | |
| Return on average attributed stockholders' equity | 21.93% | 49.32% | 27.38% |
| Average loans, net | 36,807 | 3,785 | 40,592 |
| Average deposits | 11,436 | 19,979 | 31,415 |
| Average attributed stockholders' equity | 4,766 | 1,181 | 5,947 |

EXHIBIT 5   Business Segments 1998 (Year Ended December 31, 1998) Income Statements (in millions)

| | First Union Mortgage | Home Equity and The Money Store | Card Products | Retail Branch Products | Total |
|---|---|---|---|---|---|
| **Consumer Bank** | | | | | |
| Income statement data | | | | | |
| Net interest income | $ 103 | $ 273 | $ 352 | $ 3,114 | $ 3,842 |
| Provision for loan losses | 2 | 9 | 211 | 176 | 398 |
| Noninterest income | 433 | 199 | 520 | 950 | 2,102 |
| Noninterest expense | 397 | 392 | 371 | 2,368 | 3,528 |
| Income tax expense | 52 | 27 | 111 | 581 | 771 |
| Net income | $ 85 | $ 44 | $ 179 | $ 939 | $ 1,247 |
| Performance and other data | | | | | |
| Return on average attributed stockholders' equity (a) | 52.06% | 7.86% | 38.73% | 36.42% | 33.12% |
| Average loans, net | 2,203 | 5,762 | 3,461 | 46,514 | 57,940 |
| Average deposits | 1,339 | — | 21 | 76,400 | 77,760 |
| Average attributed stockholders' equity | 162 | 562 | 462 | 2,577 | 3,763 |

| | Trust | Mutual Funds | Private Client Banking | CAP Account | Retail Brokerage and Insurance Services | Other | Total |
|---|---|---|---|---|---|---|---|
| **Capital Management** | | | | | | | |
| Income statement data | | | | | | | |
| Net interest income | $60 | $ (1) | $ 166 | $ 168 | $ 64 | $ (2) | $ 455 |
| Provision for loan losses | — | — | 4 | — | — | — | 4 |
| Noninterest income | 612 | 412 | 12 | 77 | 763 | (85) | 1,791 |
| Noninterest expense | 415 | 210 | 86 | 113 | 679 | — | 1,503 |
| Income tax expense | 98 | 77 | 34 | 51 | 57 | (33) | 284 |
| Net income | $159 | $ 124 | $ 54 | $ 81 | $ 91 | $(54) | $ 455 |
| Performance and other data | | | | | | | |
| Return on average attributed stockholders' equity (a) | 66.82% | 59.92% | 22.39% | 72.26% | 31.94% | — | 45.81% |
| Average loans, net | 113 | — | 3,523 | — | 1,177 | — | 4,813 |
| Average deposits | 2,316 | — | 2,712 | 11,663 | — | — | 16,691 |
| Average attributed stockholders' equity | 238 | 146 | 243 | 113 | 286 | (28) | 998 |

EXHIBIT 5    Business Segments 1998 (Year Ended December 31, 1998) Income Statements (in millions) *(continued)*

| | *Small Business Banking* | *Lending* | *Real Estate Banking* | *Cash Management and Deposit Services* | *Total* |
|---|---|---|---|---|---|
| **Commercial Bank** | | | | | |
| Income statement data | | | | | |
| Net interest income | $91 | $549 | $232 | $1,093 | $1,965 |
| Provision for loan losses | 4 | 68 | 19 | — | 91 |
| Noninterest income | — | — | — | 520 | 520 |
| Noninterest expense | 39 | 311 | 63 | 843 | 1,256 |
| Income tax expense | 19 | 65 | 58 | 295 | 437 |
| Net income | $29 | $105 | $ 92 | $ 475 | $ 701 |
| Performance and other data | | | | | |
| Return on average attributed stockholders' equity (a) | 14.92% | 5.99% | 12.44% | 61.95% | 20.31% |
| Average loans, net | 2,603 | 24,728 | 9,432 | — | 36,763 |
| Average deposits | — | — | — | 25,682 | 25,682 |
| Average attributed stockholders' equity | 201 | 1,747 | 748 | 768 | 3,464 |

| | *Investment Banking* | *Real Estate Finance* | *Risk Management* | *Traditional Banking* | *Commercial Leasing and Rail* | *Total* |
|---|---|---|---|---|---|---|
| **Capital Markets** | | | | | | |
| Income statement data | | | | | | |
| Net interest income | $123 | $76 | $(2) | $867 | $160 | $1,224 |
| Provision for loan losses | — | 1 | — | 124 | 6 | 131 |
| Trading account profit (loss) | 62 | (104) | 163 | — | — | 121 |
| Noninterest income | 540 | 95 | 9 | 307 | 183 | 1,134 |
| Noninterest expense | 445 | 141 | 89 | 370 | 117 | 1,162 |
| Income tax expense | 107 | (28) | 31 | 260 | 84 | 454 |
| Net income | $173 | $(47) | $50 | $420 | $136 | $ 732 |
| Performance and other data | | | | | | |
| Return on average attributed stockholders' equity (a) | 21.55% | (12.95)% | 52.53% | 16.81% | 86.47% | 18.76% |
| Average loans, net | 3,024 | 1,871 | — | 24,261 | 3,930 | 33,086 |
| Average deposits | 2,019 | 656 | 246 | 7,972 | 16 | 10,909 |
| Average attributed stockholders' equity | 803 | 353 | 95 | 2,500 | 157 | 3,908 |

*Continued*

EXHIBIT 5    Business Segments 1998 (Year Ended December 31, 1998) Income Statements (in millions) *(continued)*

| | *Consumer Bank* | *Capital Management* | *Commercial Bank* | *Capital Markets* | *Treasury/ Nonbank* | *Total* |
|---|---|---|---|---|---|---|
| **Consolidated** | | | | | | |
| Income statement data | | | | | | |
| Net interest income | $3,842 | $   455 | $1,965 | $1,224 | $(209) | $7,277 |
| Provision for loan losses | 398 | 4 | 91 | 131 | 67 | 691 |
| Trading account profits | — | — | — | 121 | 2 | 123 |
| Noninterest income | 2,102 | 1,791 | 520 | 1,134 | 885 | 6,432 |
| Noninterest expense | 3,528 | 1,503 | 1,256 | 1,162 | 1,727 | 9,176 |
| Income tax expense | 771 | 284 | 437 | 454 | (872) | 1,074 |
| Net income after merger-related and restructuring charges | 1,247 | 455 | 701 | 732 | (244) | 2,891 |
| After-tax merger-related and restructuring charges | — | — | — | — | 805 | 805 |
| Net incomes before merger-related and restructuring charges | $1,247 | $   455 | $   701 | $   732 | $561 | $3,696 |
| Performance and other data | | | | | | |
| Return on average attributed stockholders' equity (a) | 33.12% | 45.81% | 20.31% | 18.76% | 14.01% | 22.81% |
| Average loans, net | 57,940 | 4,813 | 36,763 | 33,086 | 633 | 133,235 |
| Average deposits | 77,760 | 16,691 | 25,682 | 10,909 | 5,288 | 136,330 |
| Average attributed stockholders' equity | 3,763 | 998 | 3,464 | 3,908 | 4,004 | 16,137 |

*Source:* www.freeedgar.com

As indicated in Exhibit 6, at the helm of First Union is Edward E. Crutchfield, chairman of the board and CEO, with John R. Georgius president and COO. The company is organized in a divisional (decentralized) manner as illustrated by the (probable) organizational chart in Exhibit 8. Notice the co-vice chairman positions and the lack of divisional presidents except for Malcolm Everett. A divisional organizational structure by product segment or by geographic region could be more effective for First Union.

**EXTERNAL FACTORS**

Mergers and acquisitions are expected to be the trend in the U.S. banking industry. With continued low and relatively stable interest rates and associated growing economy, the banking industry is prospering. At present, credit card usage is setting new highs quarterly. First Union is a large issuer of VISA and MasterCard, but the company is not capitalizing in a comprehensive manner on this strength. First Union is not even in the top ten of the 50 largest credit card issuers in the United States in managed card loans. MBNA, on the other hand, categorically a "nonbank" (existing primarily to issue credit cards), is the nation's third largest issuer of VISA and MasterCard and is capitalizing on this growing market. MBNA has $62,144 million in managed card loans, Exhibit 7 reveals the top ten U.S. credit card issuers. Note that the sum of the total outstanding balances of the top ten exceeds $350,000 million.

First Union is the sixth largest bank in the United States with $237,363 million in assets, a 50.9 percent increase over 1997. The company also had a net income of $2,891

EXHIBIT 6    First Union's Assumed Organizational Chart (1998)

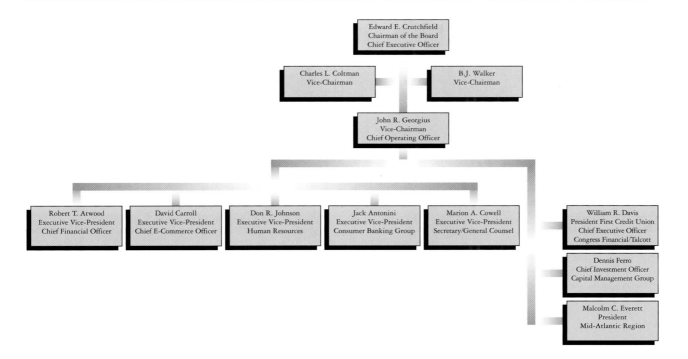

EXHIBIT 7    Ranking of U.S. Credit Card Issuers by Outstanding
Balances (1998)

| Ranking | Institution | Card Loans |
|---------|-------------|------------|
| 1 | Citigroup Inc. | $70,568 million |
| 2 | Banc One Corp. | 68,364 million |
| 3 | MBNA Corp. | 62,144 million |
| 4 | Chase Manhattan Corp. | 33,604 million |
| 5 | Morgan Stanley Dean Witter Discover & Co. | 32,134 million |
| 6 | American Express Co. | 20,800 million |
| 7 | Bank of America Corp. | 20,282 million |
| 8 | Fleet Financial Group, Inc. | 17,342 million |
| 9 | Capital One Financial Corp. | 16,472 million |
| 10 | Household International | 13,400 million |

in 1998, a 52.5 percent increase over 1997. Exhibit 2 shows a breakdown of the top 10 American banks. Note that First Union's net income as a percent of assets of 1.2 is greater than that of the top three institutions which are .87, .56, and 1.0 respectively.

With 28 million American Internet users and a projected 25 percent annual growth rate, e-commerce is causing industries to redefine the business that they are in and the way that business is conducted. The company has made a significant investment in developing their Internet banking facility to provide online services for customers. To date, this product is not generating notable revenues for the company. Instead First

Union is anticipating this service will reduce cost as more customers begin using it. The company is well poised technologically to exploit the opportunities the Internet provides. Technology changes rapidly, and First Union must strive to stay on the cutting edge of changes as they happen.

A condition that has the potential to change is the federal government's view of merger and megamerger activity. At present, they have been very gracious and agreeable to mergers and acquisitions in the banking industry, due in part to the importance of the industry to the U.S. economy and the recent failures of financial institutions. Although conditions are favorable, First Union needs to capitalize on as many strategic acquisitions as financially possible.

A national trend in the banking industry is to outsource many backroom operations and administrative functions related to data processing. Currently, several domestic companies are capitalizing on this trend and developing industries around this activity. The opportunity exists for banks to pursue such firms and integrate them into their operation (backward integration), allowing them to control costs as well as providing the same services to outside institutions.

All is not rosy for the banking industry though. With the United States currently experiencing the longest sustained period of economic expansion in history, interest rates began rising in early 2000. An economic backslide can have excessively adverse impacts on the banking industry as people and companies begin to feel the credit crunch and upward pressure is placed on interest rates. A likely next event would be an increase in the amount of bad debt experienced by creditors. This trend would be further compounded by the current trend of negative savings by Americans meaning more disparity in the consumer segment of the banking industry.

## INTERNAL CONDITIONS

There are old sayings about doing business in your own backyard and the home court advantage. First Union has both a large backyard and a significant home court. Ranking number one in deposit share in the Connecticut to Florida marketplace, First Union is a considerable force on the East Coast. Possessing the third-largest branch network enables the company to actively pursue market penetration and development at a lower cost than competitors with a less physical presence. Further expanding the company's competitive advantage is its Automated Teller Machine card (ATM) issuance network, which is the sixth largest in the nation. As consumers continue to convert to currencyless transactions and ATM surcharges, ATMs will have a growing impact on banks. Exhibit 8 gives ATM details for the top ten U.S. institutions. Note that the top institution, Banc One, has almost two and one half the number of ATMs as First Union.

First Union is not one of the leanest banks as far as personnel are concerned. As more and more mergers and acquisitions are consummated, tasks and processes have become redundant and costly. The company's current workforce of 44,333 could perhaps, be reduced by more than 15 percent or approximately 6,650 employees. Exhibit 9 gives employment statistics for the top ten U.S. banks. Notice that Citigroup is the largest U.S. financial institution employer with approximately four times the number of employees of First Union.

First Union's Mutual Fund division of the capital management segment nearly doubled its net income from 1997 to 1998. The Retail Brokerage and Insurance Services division more than doubled its net income in the same time period (the financial details for all segments are shown in Exhibits 4 through 7). Low interest rates and acquisitions and mergers have enabled First Union's Mortgage division of the Consumer Bank segment to increase net income sevenfold to $85 million from $12

EXHIBIT 8    Ranking of U.S. Financial Institutions
Based on Number of ATMs (1998)

| Rank | Institution | Number of ATMs |
|------|-------------|----------------|
| 1 | Banc One | 8,432 |
| 2 | BankAmerica | 7,850 |
| 3 | NationsBank | 6,938 |
| 4 | US Bancorp | 4,874 |
| 5 | Wells Fargo | 4,427 |
| 6 | First Union | 3,613 |
| 7 | PNC Bank | 2,593 |
| 8 | KeyCorp | 2,511 |
| 9 | Fleet Financial | 2,498 |
| 10 | National City | 2,048 |

EXHIBIT 9    Ranking of U.S. Financial Institutions
Based on Number of Employees (1998)

| Rank | Institution | Employees |
|------|-------------|-----------|
| 1 | Citigroup | 173,700 |
| 2 | BankAmerica | 170,975 |
| 3 | Chase Manhattan | 72,683 |
| 4 | Banc One | 59,986 |
| 5 | JP Morgan | 15,764 |
| 6 | First Union | 44,333 |
| 7 | Wells Fargo | 92,178 |
| 8 | Bankers Trust | 18,286 |
| 9 | Fleet Financial | 35,612 |
| 10 | SunTrust Banks | 21,227 |

million in 1997. Take notice of the great differences in the ROE between the total segments in Exhibits 4 and 5, ranging from 18.8 percent (capital markets) to 45.8 percent (capital management).

By diversifying operations away from conventional banking activities, First Union has been able to reduce the company's overall risk by generating revenues from more than one area. The consumer bank and capital management segments had ROE greater than the company average. Combined, these two segments contribute 46 percent of the company's total profit. First Union acknowledged the importance of these two segments in 1998 by spending $223 million in advertising, the majority of which targets these two segments. The company's complete income statement and balance sheet are shown in Exhibits 10 and 11.

### EXHIBIT 10   Consolidated Summaries of Income, per Common Share, Balance Sheet and Other Data

| (in millions, except per share and other data) | 1999 | 1998 |
|---|---|---|
| **Summaries of Income** | | |
| Interest income | $ 15,151 | $ 14,988 |
| Interest income | 15,269 | 15,105 |
| Interest expense | 7,699 | 7,711 |
| Net interest income | 7,570 | 7,394 |
| Provision for loan losses | 692 | 691 |
| Net interest income after provision for loan losses | 6,878 | 6,703 |
| Securities transactions—portfolio | (62) | 357 |
| Fee and other income | 6,995 | 6,078 |
| Merger-related and restructuring charges | 404 | 1,212 |
| Other noninterest expense | 8,458 | 7,844 |
| Income before income taxes | 4,949 | 4,082 |
| Income taxes | 1,608 | 1,074 |
| Tax-equivalent adjustment | 118 | 117 |
| Net income | 3,223 | 2,891 |
| Dividends on preferred stock | — | — |
| Net income applicable to common stockholders before redemption premium | 3,223 | 2,891 |
| Redemption premium on preferred stock | — | — |
| Net income applicable to common stockholders after redemption premium | $   3,223 | $   2,891 |
| **Per Common Share Data** | | |
| Basic | $   3.35 | $   2.98 |
| Diluted | 3.33 | 2.95 |
| Cash dividends | 1.88 | 1.58 |
| Average shares—Basic (In Thousands) | 959,390 | 969,131 |
| Average shares—Diluted (In Thousands) | 966,863 | 980,112 |
| Average common stockholders' equity | 15,932 | 15,878 |
| Book value | 16.91 | 17.20 |
| Common stock price | | |
| High | 65⅛ | 65¹¹⁄₁₆ |
| Low | 32⅞ | 44¹¹⁄₁₆ |
| Year-end | 32¹³⁄₁₆ | 60¹³⁄₁₆ |
| To earnings ratio | 9.89X | 20.61X |
| To book value | 195% | 353% |
| **Balance Sheet Data** | | |
| Assets | $253,024 | $237,087 |
| Long-term debt | 31,975 | 22,949 |
| **Other Data** | | |
| ATMs | $   3,778 | $   3,690 |
| Employees | 71,659 | 71,486 |
| Common stockholders | 168,989 | 146,775 |

# EXHIBIT 11　First Union CP Annual Balance Sheet

### (in millions, except book value per share)

| | 12/31/99 | 12/31/98 | 12/31/97 | 12/31/96 |
|---|---|---|---|---|
| **Assets** | | | | |
| Cash & Equivalents | $ 39,381.00 | $ 40,421.00 | $ 20,352.00 | $ 17,783.00 |
| Receivables | 135,566.00 | 133,577.00 | 95,661.00 | 94,493.00 |
| Notes Receivable | 0.00 | 0.00 | 0.00 | 0.00 |
| Inventories | 0.00 | 0.00 | 0.00 | 0.00 |
| Other Current Assets | 995.00 | 1,248.00 | 854.00 | 763.00 |
| **Total Current Assets** | 175,942.00 | 175,246.00 | 116,867.00 | 113,039.00 |
| Net Property & Equipment | 5,180.00 | 5,067.00 | 4,233.00 | 4,073.00 |
| Investments & Advances | 51,277.00 | 37,434.00 | 23,590.00 | 16,683.00 |
| Other Non-Current Assets | 0.00 | 0.00 | 0.00 | 0.00 |
| Deferred Charges | 0.00 | 0.00 | 0.00 | 0.00 |
| Intangibles | 5,626.00 | 5,036.00 | 2,674.00 | 2,849.00 |
| Deposits & Other Assets | 14,999.00 | 14,580.00 | 9,910.00 | 3,483.00 |
| **Total Assets** | **$253,024.00** | **$237,363.00** | **$157,274.00** | **$140,127.00** |
| **Liabilities & Shareholders' Equity** | | | | |
| Notes Payable | $ 51,102.00 | $ 41,438.00 | $ 27,357.00 | $ 23,024.00 |
| Account Payable | 141,047.00 | 142,467.00 | 102,889.00 | 94,815.00 |
| Current Portion Long Term Debt | 0.00 | 0.00 | 0.00 | 0.00 |
| Current Portion Capital Leases | 0.00 | 0.00 | 0.00 | 0.00 |
| Accrued Expenses | 0.00 | 0.00 | 0.00 | 0.00 |
| Income Taxes Payable | 0.00 | 0.00 | 0.00 | 0.00 |
| Other Current Liabilities | 12,191.00 | 1,281.00 | 855.00 | 764.00 |
| **Total Current Liabilities** | 204,340.00 | 185,186.00 | 131,101.00 | 118,603.00 |
| Mortgages | 0.00 | 0.00 | 0.00 | 0.00 |
| Deferred Taxes/Income | 0.00 | 0.00 | 0.00 | 0.00 |
| Convertible Debt | 0.00 | 0.00 | 0.00 | 0.00 |
| Long Term Debt | 31,975.00 | 22.949.00 | 8,042.00 | 7,660.00 |
| Non-Current Capital Leases | 0.00 | 0.00 | 0.00 | 0.00 |
| Other Non-Current Liabilities | 0.00 | 12,055.00 | 5,108.00 | 3,361.00 |
| Minority Interest (Liabilities) | 0.00 | 0.00 | 991.00 | 495.00 |
| **Total Liabilities** | **$236,315.00** | **$220,190.00** | **$145,242.00** | **$130,119.00** |
| **Shareholders' Equity** | | | | |
| Preferred Stock | $　　0.00 | $　　0.00 | $　　0.00 | $　　0.00 |
| Common stock (Par) | 3,294.00 | 3,274.00 | 2,121.00 | 958.00 |
| Capital Surplus | 5,980.00 | 4,305.00 | 1,384.00 | 2,336.00 |
| Retained Earnings | 8,365.00 | 9,187.00 | 8,273.00 | 6,727.00 |
| Other Equity | (930.00) | 407.00 | 254.00 | (13.00) |
| Treasury Stock | 0.00 | 0.00 | 0.00 | 0.00 |
| Total Shareholders' Equity | 16,709.00 | 17,173.00 | 12,032.00 | 10,008.00 |
| **Total Liabilities & Shareholders' Equity** | **$253,024.00** | **$237,363.00** | **$157,274.00** | **$140,127.00** |
| Total Common Equity | 16,709.00 | 17,173.00 | 12,032.00 | 10,008.00 |
| Average Shares | 966.86 | 980.11 | 633.77 | 625.22 |
| Book Value Per Share | 16.92 | 17.33 | 21.16 | 18.26 |

*Source:* www.freeedgar.com

## CONCLUSION

What is around the corner for First Union? One can be certain that more mergers and acquisitions will be commonplace in the banking industry. Considering the difficulties that the company had merging the cultures of CoreStates Financial and The Money Store, First Union may be reluctant to make further acquisitions. However, the credit card market is one that the company should not overlook. Perhaps the company should consider MBNA as a potential future acquisition. The purchase of MBNA would put First Union in the top three for credit issuers, allowing the bank to capitalize on this growing industry.

If First Union does not pursue strategic mergers and acquisitions in the near future, competitors will outgrow them. The seventh largest bank, Wells Fargo, is only 18 percent smaller than First Union, with assets of $237 billion as revealed in Exhibit 2. SunTrust Banks, the tenth largest U.S. bank, with $93 billion in assets might be a potential acquisition and merger candidate for First Union. This merger would make First Union the fourth largest U.S. bank with assets of $330 billion, still less than half the size of Citigroup.

Considering its track record of paying dividends every year since its inception in 1908 and 21 consecutive years of at least annual dividend increases, First Union's shareholders expect continued growth and prosperity.

# WACHOVIA CORPORATION—2000

Jule Eldridge, III
Francis Marion University

**WB**

**www.wachovia.com**

Do you know how many checks are written each year in the United States?
Do you know how many banks are located in the United States?
Do you know how many banks have failed in recent years?
Do you know the National Savings rate for Americans?
Answers to these banking questions can be found in Exhibit 1.

Each of these questions is important to executives, bank regulators, and shareholders of banks around the country. Banking is still regarded as one of the most prestigious and time-honored industries in America. A member of the New York Stock Exchange and a Fortune 500 Company, Wachovia Corporation, is a well-known bank headquartered in Winston-Salem, North Carolina. The company's annual net income passed the $1 billion mark for the first time in 1999.

## THE CORPORATION

Wachovia Corporation is a bank holding company that provides financial services to corporations, small businesses, and consumers. Wachovia covers a five-state area that includes North Carolina, South Carolina, Virginia, Georgia, and Florida. Compared to other large commercial banks, Wachovia ranks 16th among major banks. Market capitalization is about $16 billion, and assets are about $67 billion. Wachovia has a second dual headquarters in Atlanta, Georgia. Wachovia has more than 17,000 employees.

Wachovia has relationships with over 3.5 million households and 200,000 small businesses in the five-state franchise area. Wachovia also services corporate customers and has 28,000 large- and middle-market corporate relationships in its home markets and internationally. Corporate customers are defined as companies with sales greater than 2 million dollars.

Wachovia's market area is outpacing the United States in population and household income growth, providing fertile ground for customer acquisition. Operating as a separate subsidiary, Wachovia Bankcard Services is the 11th largest credit card issuer among banks. Wachovia's extensive branch system enables local bankers to cross-sell credit cards to existing banking customers to attract customers throughout the nation.

## KEY INITIATIVES

Increasing the number of customers served by Wachovia is an important aspect of the growth plan for the company. Some of these initiatives include the Wachovia to Work program, an innovative work site marketing strategy that combines the convenience of on-site banking with a packaged product line. The package includes discount checking

---

EXHIBIT 1    Answers to Questions at Beginning of Case
www.aba.com

---

*How many checks do Americans write each year?*

In 1996 approximately 64 billion checks were written with a total value of $75 trillion. (Board of Governors of the Federal Reserve System—*http://www.federalreserve.gov*)

*How many banks are there in the United States of America?*

As of the first quarter of 1999, there were 8,721 FDIC-insured commercial banks in the United States (FDIC Quarterly Banking Profile—*http://www.fdic.gov*)

*Have any banks failed lately?*

One bank failed in the first quarter of 1999, and 3 FDIC-insured commercial banks failed in 1998. For earlier years: one bank failed in 1997, five in 1996, six in 1995, eleven in 1994, forty-two in 1993. (FDIC Quarterly Banking Profile—*http://www.fdic.gov*)

*What is the national savings rate?*

The personal savings rate as a percentage of disposable personal income for the United States was .7 percent at the end of the first quarter of 1999, down from 2.1 percent in 1997. (U.S. Department of Commerce, Survey of Current Business—*http://www.bea.doc.gov/bea/pubs.htm*)

---

accounts, discounted credit cards, and free checks. This strategy is a cost-effective method to acquire new customers who tend to stay with Wachovia longer and buy more products over time. The Wachovia to Work program has also helped in cementing several large corporate relationships, because the corporation can pass along an additional benefit to their employees. Other growth initiatives include programs targeted to college students and Wachovia Access Now Account, which offers services such as electronic banking and PC Access, the online banking and bill payment business unit of the bank. The intent is to attract students at an early age and retain them as customers for life.

## CORPORATE STRUCTURE OF THE BANK

Wachovia's financial statements provided in Exhibit 2 reveal a severe decrease in net income for the fiscal year 1997. Total revenues increased significantly from the previous year, but merger-related expenses in connection with the Virginia Bank acquisitions of Jefferson Bankshares and Central Fidelity Bank diminished net income for the year. These expenses included but are not limited to higher severance pay for employees and loan losses. Expenses leveled out during the 1998 year, and loan losses continued to be at .67 percent of outstanding loans. Revenue from interest income slowed to a 9 percent growth rate, which is less than the 11.2 percent five-year compound growth rate for previous years. Return on assets rose in 1998 to 1.37, and some of this growth can be attributed to the sale of several offices within the five-state area.

Changes in the balance sheet from 1997 to 1998 reflect the increase in deposits, liabilities, and loan assets from the Virginia Bank purchase. Note in Exhibit 3 that the allowance for loan losses increased 3 percent from $520,000,000 to $535,000,000.

# EXHIBIT 2    Consolidated Statements of Income (thousands, except per share)

| | Year Ended December 31 | | | |
| | 1999 | 1998 | 1997 | 1996 |
|---|---|---|---|---|
| **Interest Income** | | | | |
| Loans, including fees | $4,000,541 | $3,873,404 | $3,455,296 | $3,109,698 |
| Securities available for sale | 504,870 | 597,557 | 625,139 | 684,134 |
| Securities held to maturity: | | | | |
| State and municipal | 11,693 | 15,044 | 16,452 | 21,039 |
| Other investments | 79,919 | 95,952 | 87,632 | 96,508 |
| Interest-bearing bank balances | 7,390 | 12,988 | 5,230 | 33,284 |
| Federal funds sold and securities purchased under | | | | |
| resale agreements | 30,696 | 25,803 | 22,319 | 15,411 |
| Trading accounts assets | 32,131 | 44,497 | 50,317 | 49,434 |
| Total interest income | 4,666,820 | 4,665,245 | 4,262,385 | 4,009,508 |
| **Interest Expense** | | | | |
| Deposits: | | | | |
| Domestic offices | 1,156,113 | 1,224,046 | 1,216,229 | 1,148,797 |
| Foreign offices | 109,082 | 135,659 | 87,320 | 54,942 |
| Total interest on deposits | 1,265,195 | 1,359,705 | 1,303,549 | 1,203,739 |
| Short-term borrowed funds | 457,161 | 563,846 | 478,162 | 482,236 |
| Long-term debt | 474,378 | 390,662 | 387,107 | 399,796 |
| Total interest expense | 2,196,734 | 2,314,213 | 2,168,818 | 2,085,771 |
| **Net Interest Income** | 2,470,086 | 2,351,032 | 2,093,567 | 1,923,737 |
| Provision for loan losses | 298,105 | 299,480 | 264,949 | 193,776 |
| Net interest income after provision for loan losses | 2,171,981 | 2,051,552 | 1,828,618 | 1,729,961 |
| **Other Income** | | | | |
| Service charges on deposit accounts | 369,646 | 334,980 | 306,231 | 280,670 |
| Fees for trust services | 216,392 | 199,949 | 175,549 | 154,621 |
| Credit card income | 255,243 | 171,127 | 162,234 | 143,382 |
| Capital markets income | 235,350 | 130,083 | 49,522 | 44,212 |
| Electronic banking | 170,771 | 74,257 | 64,640 | 56,226 |
| Investment fees | 88,626 | 44,619 | 36,251 | 30,820 |
| Mortgage fees | 33,213 | 44,929 | 23,544 | 21,371 |
| Other operating income | 240,882 | 228,175 | 187,797 | 143,430 |
| Total other operating revenue | 1,610,123 | 1,228,119 | 1,005,768 | 874,732 |
| Securities gains | 10,894 | 20,442 | 1,454 | 4,588 |
| Total other income | 1,621,017 | 1,248,561 | 1,007,222 | 879,320 |
| **Other Expense** | | | | |
| Salaries | 1,020,384 | 874,750 | 742,106 | 655,065 |
| Employee benefits | 199,902 | 180,603 | 163,051 | 141,867 |
| Total personnel expense | 1,220,286 | 1,055,353 | 905,157 | 796,932 |
| Net occupancy expense | 151,282 | 138,636 | 116,654 | 114,001 |
| Equipment expense | 198,062 | 156,203 | 142,227 | 132,775 |
| Personal computer impairment charge | — | — | 67,202 | — |
| Merger-related charges | 19,309 | 85,312 | 220,330 | — |
| Other operating expense | 661,686 | 560,828 | 515,151 | 465,265 |
| Total other expense | 2,250,625 | 1,996,332 | 1,966,721 | 1,508,973 |
| Income before income tax expense | 1,542,373 | 1,303,781 | 869,119 | 1,100,308 |
| Income tax expense | 531,152 | 429,611 | 276,313 | 343,049 |
| **Net Income** | $1,011,221 | $ 874,170 | $ 592,806 | $ 757,259 |
| Net income per common share: | | | | |
| Basic | 4.99 | 4.26 | 2.99 | 3.70 |
| Diluted | 4.90 | 4.18 | 2.94 | 3.65 |
| Average shares outstanding: | | | | |
| Basic | 202,795 | 205,058 | 198,290 | 204,889 |
| Diluted | 206,192 | 209,153 | 201,901 | 207,432 |

*Source:* www.freeedqar.com

# EXHIBIT 3    Consolidated Statements of Condition (in thousands)

| | December 31 1999 | December 31 1998 | December 31 1997 |
|---|---|---|---|
| **Assets** | | | |
| Cash and due from banks | $ 3,475,004 | $ 3,800,265 | $ 4,221,818 |
| Interest-bearing bank balances | 184,904 | 109,983 | 133,191 |
| Federal funds sold and securities purchased under resale agreements | 761,962 | 675,470 | 1,589,234 |
| Trading account assets | 870,304 | 664,812 | 999,122 |
| Securities available for sale | 7,095,790 | 7,983,648 | 8,909,537 |
| Securities held to maturity (fair value of $1,061,150 in 1999 and $1,442,126 in 1998) | 1,048,724 | 1,383,607 | 1,509,339 |
| Loans, net of unearned income | 49,621,225 | 45,719,222 | 44,194,382 |
| Less allowance for loan losses | 554,810 | 547,992 | 544,723 |
| Net loans | 49,066,415 | 45,171,230 | 43,649,659 |
| Premises and equipment | 953,832 | 901,681 | 810,155 |
| Due from customers on acceptances | 111,684 | 348,955 | 628,398 |
| Other assets | 3,783,918 | 3,083,191 | 2,946,616 |
| Total assets | $67,352,537 | $64,122,842 | $65,397,069 |
| **Liabilities** | | | |
| Deposits in domestic offices: | | | |
| Demand | $ 8,730,673 | $ 8,768,271 | $ 8,598,055 |
| Interest-bearing demand | 4,527,711 | 4,980,715 | 4,654,172 |
| Savings and money market savings | 13,760,479 | 12,641,766 | 11,679,432 |
| Savings certificates | 8,701,074 | 8,982,396 | 10,934,720 |
| Large denomination certificates | 3,154,754 | 3,344,553 | 2,284,068 |
| Total deposits in domestic offices | 38,874,691 | 38,717,701 | 38,150,447 |
| Interest-bearing deposits in foreign offices | 2,911,727 | 2,277,028 | 4,503,396 |
| Total deposits | 41,786,418 | 40,994,729 | 42,653,843 |
| Federal funds purchased and securities sold under repurchase agreements | 5,372,493 | 5,463,418 | 8,322,716 |
| Commercial paper | 1,658,988 | 1,359,382 | 1,034,024 |
| Other short-term borrowed funds | 3,071,493 | 1,912,262 | 752,874 |
| Long-term debt | 7,814,263 | 7,596,727 | 5,934,133 |
| Acceptances outstanding | 111,684 | 348,955 | 628,398 |
| Other liabilities | 1,878,741 | 1,109,137 | 896,780 |
| Total liabilities | $61,694,080 | $58,784,610 | $60,222,768 |
| Off-balance sheet items, commitments and contingent liabilities— Notes J, K and M | | | |
| **Shareholder's Equity** | | | |
| Preferred stock, par value $5 per share: Authorized 50,000,000 shares; none outstanding | — | — | — |
| Common stock, par value $5 per share: Authorized 1,000,000,000 shares in 1998 and 500,000,000 shares in 1997; issued and outstanding 202,986,100 shares in 1998 and 205,926,632 shares in 1997 | $ 1,009,061 | $ 1,014,931 | $ 1,029,633 |
| Capital surplus | 598,149 | 669,244 | 974,803 |
| Retained earnings | 4,125,524 | 3,571,617 | 3,098,767 |
| Accumulated other comprehensive income | (74,277) | 82,440 | 71,098 |
| Total shareholders' equity | 5,658,457 | 5,338,232 | 5,174,301 |
| Total liabilities and shareholders' equity | $67,352,537 | $64,122,842 | $65,397,069 |

Wachovia Bank is segmented into four primary areas of operation: (1) The consumer bank, (2) The corporate bank, (3) credit cards, and (4) treasury administration. The consumer bank consists of 752 branches and 1,372 ATMs and primarily handles personal checking accounts and loans of individual consumers. Exhibit 4 reveals that revenues from the consumer bank rose 17.4 percent from 1997 to 1998. A large portion of the increase came from an increase in net interest margin and other income. Other income is derived from service charges on checking accounts, ATM fees, and loan origination fees.

## EXHIBIT 4    Divisional Highlights

| Year Ended December 31, 1999 | Consumer | Administration | Eliminations | Total |
|---|---|---|---|---|
| External net interest margin | $ (153,647) | $ (461,128) | $ (40,486) | $ 2,470,086 |
| Internal funding (charge) credit | 1,085,423 | 405,099 | (63,105) | — |
| Net interest margin | 931,776 | (56,029) | (103,591) | 2,470,086 |
| Provision for loan losses | 15,079 | (32,873) | — | 298,105 |
| Total other income | 424,577 | 137,424 | — | 1,621,017 |
| Total expenses | 895,946 | 70,466 | (63,105) | 2,250,625 |
| Income before income tax expense | 445,328 | 43,802 | (40,486) | 1,542,373 |
| Income tax expense | 161,785 | 15,416 | (40,486) | 531,152 |
| Net income | 283,543 | 28,386 | — | 1,011,221 |
| Average total assets | $9,779,241 | $11,946,693 | $   — | $65,420,258 |

| Year Ended December 31, 1999 | Management | Corporate | Credit Card |
|---|---|---|---|
| External net interest margin | $  109,806 | $ 2,162,749 | $  852,792 |
| Internal funding (charge) credit | 33,551 | (1,144,429) | (316,539) |
| Net interest margin | 143,357 | 1,018,320 | 536,253 |
| Provision for loan losses | 790 | 58,511 | 256,598 |
| Total other income | 485,554 | 404,680 | 168,782 |
| Total expenses | 495,634 | 639,462 | 212,222 |
| Income before income tax expense | 132,487 | 725,027 | 236,215 |
| Income tax expense | 50,277 | 258,018 | 86,142 |
| Net income | 82,210 | 467,009 | 150,073 |
| Average total assets | $2,928,541 | $34,482,234 | $6,283,549 |

| Year Ended December 31, 1998 | Consumer | Corporate | Card | Treasury and Administration | Eliminations | Total |
|---|---|---|---|---|---|---|
| External net interest margin | $  336,495 | $ 1,543,168 | $  767,469 | $ (249,226) | $  (46,874) | $ 2,351,032 |
| Internal funding (charge) credit | 855,317 | −831,502 | −306,909 | 351,196 | −68,102 | — |
| Net interest margin | 1,191,812 | 711,666 | 460,560 | 101,970 | −114,976 | 2,351,032 |
| Provision for loan loss | 34,328 | 1,114 | 257,799 | 6,239 | — | 299,480 |
| Total other income | 598,208 | 396,308 | 174,410 | 79,635 | — | 1,248,561 |
| Total expenses | 1,189,175 | 542,045 | 208,381 | 124,833 | −68,102 | 1,996,332 |
| Income before income tax expense | 566,517 | 564,815 | 168,790 | 50,533 | −46,874 | 1,303,781 |
| Income tax expense | 199,675 | 199,074 | 59,491 | 18,245 | −46,874 | 429,611 |
| Net income | 366,842 | 365,741 | 109,299 | 32,288 | — | 874,170 |
| Average total assets | $16,955,302 | $26,677,485 | $6,697,455 | $13,618,293 | $   — | $63,948,535 |

*Continued*

EXHIBIT 4    Divisional Highlights *(continued)*

| Year Ended December 31, 1997 | Consumer | Corporate | Card | Treasury and Administration | Eliminations | Total |
|---|---|---|---|---|---|---|
| External net interest margin | $ 303,409 | $ 1,340,043 | $ 723,006 | $ (214,997) | $ (57,894) | $ 2,093,567 |
| Internal funding (charge) credit | 781,842 | −780,345 | −314,041 | 362,940 | −50,396 | — |
| Net interest margin | 1,085,251 | 559,698 | 408,965 | 147,943 | −108,290 | 2,093,567 |
| Provision for loan loss | 44,534 | 825 | 218,538 | 1,052 | — | 264,949 |
| Total other income | 518,409 | 298,727 | 165,992 | 24,094 | — | 1,007,222 |
| Total expenses | 1,031,469 | 466,933 | 191,143 | 327,572 | −50,396 | 1,966,721 |
| Income before income tax expense | 527,657 | 390,667 | 165,276 | −156,587 | −57,894 | 869,119 |
| Income tax expense (benefit) | 184,446 | 136,560 | 57,773 | −44,572 | −57,894 | 276,313 |
| Net income (loss) | 343,211 | 254,107 | 107,503 | (112,015) | — | 592,806 |
| Average total assets | $14,680,571 | $23,208,642 | $6,261,114 | $13,456,748 | $ — | $57,607,075 |

*Source:* www.freeedgar.com

The corporate banking division has banking relationships with companies that have sales greater than $2,000,000. This includes business banking, corporate banking, and several specialty areas. Net income rose $7,300,000 or the equivalent of 3 percent during 1998.

Credit card services yields high profit levels but also incurs a high level of risk associated with the unsecured credit product. There is little maintenance and servicing, and block units of credit cards are often bought and sold throughout the year. Credit card income experienced a small 2 percent positive change during the 1998 year. A portion of the increase was a result of higher fees charged for late charges and other miscellaneous charges.

As noted on the balance sheet in Exhibit 3, total deposits decreased from $42,654,000 in 1997 to $40,995,000 in 1998. On the other side of the balance sheet, two categories also saw downward movement. Total direct retail loans declined by 4 percent from the previous year, and total savings certificates declined by 4 percent. A portion of this decline can be attributed to the healthy returns from the stock market, and individuals who desire the much higher returns that the market can return versus the return on an individual savings account.

## GROWTH RATES AND COMPETITION

The financial services industry is facing a time when margins are diminishing. Banks hold deposits for customers and compensate them for use of their money. Banks then lend out these deposits in the form of loans and collect interest on these loans. The spread between deposits and loans accounts for much of the bank's profit. Because of an increase in competition, these margins are getting slimmer.

Wachovia faces direct and indirect competition within its geographical territory and new threats from companies operating outside its geographic territory. Direct competition arises from three sources. The first source can be classified as national banks and includes competitors such as Bank of America and First Union. A second source is superregional banks such as BB&T and Southtrust Bank. A third direct competitor that varies with each market is local community banks. Local community banks have a niche in each market and serve a particular group of customers within that geographic territory.

EXHIBIT 5    Market-Share Data
FDIC Insured Commercial Banks as of June 1998

| South Carolina Market | Rank 1997 | Percentage of Market | Rank 1998 | Percentage of Market |
|---|---|---|---|---|
| Wachovia Bank | 1 | 17.09 | 1 | 16.37 |
| BB&T | 3 | 9.47 | 3 | 10.30 |
| Bank of America | 2 | 13.99 | 2 | 13.72 |

| North Carolina Market | Rank 1997 | Percentage of Market | Rank 1998 | Percentage of Market |
|---|---|---|---|---|
| Wachovia Bank | 1 | 16.82 | 4 | 13.18 |
| BB&T | 3 | 14.45 | 2 | 16.25 |
| Bank of America | 5 | 8.02 | 1 | 20.49 |

| Virginia Market | Rank 1997 | Percentage of Market | Rank 1998 | Percentage of Market |
|---|---|---|---|---|
| Wachovia Bank | N/A | | 4 | 11.42 |
| BB&T | 13 | .85 | 6 | 2.09 |
| Bank of America | 2 | 13.19 | 2 | 14.55 |

| Georgia Market | Rank 1997 | Percentage of Market | Rank 1998 | Percentage of Market |
|---|---|---|---|---|
| Wachovia Bank | 2 | 10.54 | 2 | 10.37 |
| BB&T | N/A | | | |
| Bank of America | 1 | 16.84 | 1 | 15.00 |

*Source:* Wachovia Internal Report, 1999.

Indirect competitors on the other hand are beginning to emerge and include banks such as Netbank and Wingspan.com, online banks that have no brick-and-mortar expenses. The advent of direct deposit, electronic bill payment, and ATMs makes it possible for consumers to avoid setting foot in the bank to make a deposit, withdraw money, and review activity on their account. Internet banks enjoy great economies of scale over traditional banks and operate on a very low-cost basis. All correspondence with these banks is handled by e-mail, Web sites, toll-free telephone numbers, and U.S. mail.

Exhibit 5 reveals that Wachovia's net income and assets increased nicely in 1999. The market-share position enjoyed by Wachovia is favorable in each state except Florida, where market share is very small. Wachovia's market-share position has remained stable in South Carolina. During 1998, a slight portion of deposits were lost in South Carolina, but the position at the top was protected. BB&T has ranked third in South Carolina each year and did experience good deposit growth in 1998.

The State of North Carolina saw a drastic change in market-share leadership from 1997–1998. Wachovia lost the top share position to Bank of America, which saw its deposits soar from 8 percent to 20.49 percent of the market. BB&T also moved up a notch in its home state and captured the second-largest deposit base.

Wachovia's entry into Virginia with the acquisition of Central Fidelity and Jefferson Bancshares gave the bank the number-four spot in 1998 with 11.42 percent of the market. Bank of America has consistently held the second spot and increased its deposits during 1998. BB&T has a relatively low market share in Virginia.

The Georgia market plays host to a number of corporate banking relationships due to the city of Atlanta being home to a number of large companies. Bank of America and Wachovia have large corporate banking divisions and hold the number one and two market-share positions. BB&T does not have a presence in Georgia.

A. G. Edwards (stock symbol AGE) has been serving brokerage customers since 1887 and currently has 639 offices and 13,953 full-time employees throughout the United States. Revenues for A. G. Edwards are derived from commissions on stock trades, investment banking fees, and service fees for investment advice and planning. The company services approximately 2,340,000 customers through its affiliations with each of the major stock exchanges. A. G. Edwards also offers a full line of insurance products through its branch network.

Suntrust Banks, Inc. (stock symbol STI) is a bank holding company headquartered in Atlanta. Suntrust has a presence in Alabama, Florida, Georgia, Maryland, Tennessee, and Virginia and is the eighth-largest bank in the country with $92,755,000,000 in assets. The geographical territory that Suntrust operates in is the fast-growing southeastern portion of the country, and this has been a fertile ground for great growth for the company in the last three years. Suntrust offers consumer and commercial banking services as well as investment advising services.

## BRAND ADVERTISING

A recent unveiling of Wachovia's new brand campaign has played a central role in helping all Wachovians promote the common theme of "We are here; Let's get started." Recent quantitative research scored the campaign as more memorable, relevant, and likeable than those of key competitors. This strong brand image helps create an identity in financial services that will become more important as individuals and businesses are confronted with a bewildering array of financial choices. Wachovia is committed to delivering the brand promise at every point of contact and wants to be known as a quality provider of all financial services.

## CONCLUSION

The Financial Services Modernization Act of 1999 made it possible for banks to easily move into the brokerage and insurance industry. Wachovia might consider integrating two powerful organizations in the brokerage business (A. G. Edwards), and a large bank with a presence in Florida (Suntrust). Propose a three-year strategic plan for Wachovia Corporation, that enables the bank to take advantage of this new legislation and build market share and profitability in the brokerage, banking, and insurance industries.

# THE AUDUBON INSTITUTE—2000

Caroline Fisher
Loyola University New Orleans
Claire J. Anderson
Old Dominion University*

www.auduboninstitute.org

The Audubon Institute, Inc. is a non-profit organization that manages and operates the Audubon Park Commission (the "Commission") facilities located at the Audubon Zoo and Park, the Aquarium of the Americas, the Species Survival Center and the Louisiana Nature Center. The facilities had combined operating revenues of $22,313,000 for the year ended December 31, 1999 and combined total assets of $136,554,000 at December 31, 1999.

The Audubon Park Zoo expanded in the 1970s from 14 to 58 acres. The zoo was laid out in geographic sections: the Asian Domain, World of Primates, World's Grasslands, Savannah, North American Prairie, South American Pampas, and Louisiana Swamp according to the zoo master plan developed by the Bureau of Governmental Research. Additional exhibits included the Wisner Discovery Zoo, the sea lion exhibit, and the Flight Cage. Exhibit 1 is a map of the new zoo.

## Purpose of the Zoo

The main outward purpose of the Audubon Park Zoo is entertainment. Many of its promotional efforts are aimed at creating an image of the zoo as an entertaining place to go. Behind the scenes, the zoo preserves and breeds many animal species, conducts research, and educates the public. The mission statement of the Audubon Institute, the parent organization of the zoo, is given in Exhibit 2.

## OPERATIONS

### Audubon Institute

The Audubon Institute (until 1988 the Friends of the Zoo) was formed in 1974 and incorporated in 1975 with 400 original members. Its stated purpose was to increase support and awareness of the Audubon Park Zoo. Initially, the Institute tried to increase interest and commitment to the zoo, but its activities increased dramatically over the following years until it was involved in funding, operating, and governing the zoo.

The Institute has a 24-member governing board. Yearly elections are held for six members of the board who serve four-year terms. The board oversees policies of the zoo and sets guidelines for memberships, concessions, fundraising and marketing. However, actual policy-making and operations are controlled by the Audubon Park Commission, which sets zoo hours, admission prices, etc.

*The authors wish to thank Forest Bankston for his help in updating this case.

**EXHIBIT 1     A Map of the Audubon Park Zoo**

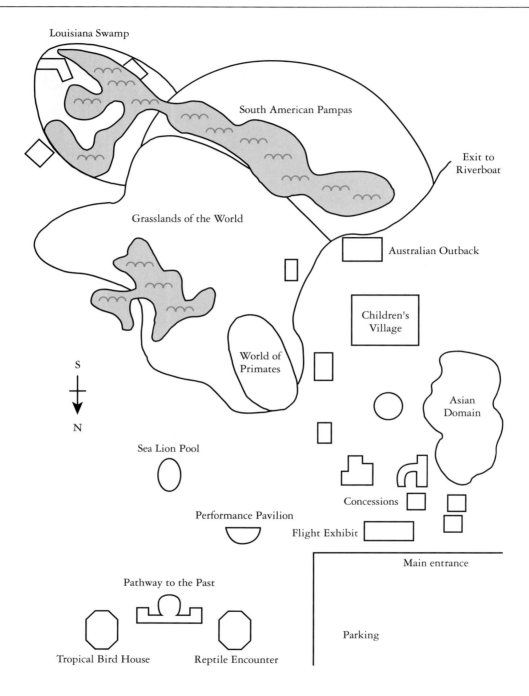

Through its volunteer programs, the Institute staffs many of the zoo's programs. Volunteers from members of the Audubon Institute serve as "edZOOcators," education volunteers who are specially trained to conduct interpretive education programs, and "zoo area patrollers," who provide general information about a geographic area of the zoo and help with crowd control. Other volunteers assist in the commissary, animal health

## EXHIBIT 2    Audubon Institute Purpose

The Audubon Institute's purpose is to celebrate life through nature.

### Audubon Institute Vision

The Audubon Institute's vision is to create a family of museums and parks dedicated to nature.

### Audubon Institute Mission Statement

The Audubon Institute's purpose of celebrating life through nature guides its mission to:
- Provide a guest experience of outstanding quality
- Exhibit the diversity of wildlife
- Preserve native Louisiana habitats
- Educate our diverse audience about the natural world
- Enhance the care and survival of wildlife through research and conservation
- Provide opportunities for recreation in natural settings
- Operate a financially self-sufficient collection of facilities
- Weave quality entertainment through the guest experiences

*Source:* The Audubon Institute Internal Report.

## EXHIBIT 3    Membership Fees and Membership

| Year | Family Membership Fees | Individual Membership Fees | Number of Memberships |
|------|------------------------|----------------------------|------------------------|
| 1992 | 49 | 30 | 28,422 |
| 1993 | 55 | 35 | 30,208 |
| 1994 | 59 | 39 | 22,507 |
| 1995 | 59 | 39 | 25,402 |
| 1996 | 59 | 39 | 25,569 |
| 1997 | 59 | 39 | 26,449 |
| 1998 | 59 | 39 | 24,413 |

*Source:* The Audubon Institute Internal Report.

care center, and wild bird rehabilitation center or help with membership, public relations, graphics, clerical work, research, or horticulture.

### Fund-Raising

The Audubon Park Zoo and the Audubon Institute raise funds through five major types of activities: the Audubon Institute membership, concessions, Adopt-an-Animal, Zoo-to-Do, and capital fund drives. Zoo managers from around the country come to the Audubon Park Zoo for tips on fund-raising.

### Membership

Membership in the Audubon Institute is open to anyone. The membership fees have increased over the years as summarized in Exhibit 3. The number of members increased steadily, from the original 400 members in 1974 to 24,413 members in 1998, but declined 7 percent from 1997 to 1998.

**EXHIBIT 4    Audubon Zoo Visitor Survey**

| | 1998 | | 1999 | |
|---|---|---|---|---|
| | Number | Percent | Number | Percent |
| First visit to Zoo | 74 | 31 | 136 | 45 |
| Number of visits in last year | | | | |
|    No visits | 32 | 22 | 37 | 23 |
|    1 visit | 29 | 20 | 36 | 22 |
|    2 visits | 20 | 14 | 27 | 17 |
|    3 or more visits | 66 | 45 | 63 | 39 |
| Average number of visits | 6.1 | | 4.7 | |
| When decided to visit | | | | |
|    Today or yesterday | 99 | 41 | 94 | 31 |
|    Within the past week | 77 | 32 | 144 | 48 |
|    Two weeks to one month ago | 37 | 15 | 45 | 15 |
|    More than one month ago | 27 | 11 | 18 | 6 |
| Reasons for visiting | | | | |
|    Interest in animals | 145 | 61 | 109 | 36 |
|    Bring children | 107 | 45 | 141 | 47 |
|    Entertainment | 101 | 42 | 103 | 34 |
|    Sightseeing | 79 | 33 | 116 | 39 |
|    Education | 71 | 30 | 70 | 23 |
| Number of persons in group | | | | |
|    Adults | 2.3 | | 2.1 | |
|    Children | 1.1 | | 1.3 | |
|    Adults (adults only) | | | | |
|      1 | 13 | 14 | 15 | 14 |
|      2 | 72 | 79 | 71 | 68 |
|      3 or more | 6 | 6 | 19 | 19 |
|    Percent of total groups | | 39 | | 36 |
|    Average group size | 1.9 | | 2.2 | |
|    Average adult age | 39.6 | | 40.4 | |
|    Number of children (groups with children) | | | | |
|      1 | 68 | 48 | 66 | 36 |
|      2 | 47 | 33 | 68 | 37 |
|      3 | 16 | 11 | 32 | 17 |
|      4 or more | 11 | 8 | 17 | 9 |
|    Percent of total groups | | 61 | | 64 |
|    Average group size | | | | |
|      Children | 1.8 | | 2.1 | |
|      Adults | 2.5 | | 2.0 | |
|    Average child age | 6.0 | | 6.5 | |
| Respondent's education | | | | |
|    Some high school or less | 4 | 2 | 19 | 6 |
|    High school graduate | 37 | 16 | 66 | 22 |
|    Some college | 69 | 30 | 70 | 23 |
|    College degree | 82 | 36 | 94 | 31 |
|    Graduate degree | 37 | 16 | 52 | 17 |
| Respondent's household family income | | | | |
|    Less than $25,000 | 31 | 14 | 47 | 16 |
|    $25,000–39,999 | 47 | 21 | 68 | 23 |
|    $40,000–54,999 | 55 | 25 | 55 | 18 |
|    $55,000–74,999 | 40 | 18 | 62 | 21 |
|    $75,000–149,999 | 42 | 19 | 59 | 20 |
|    $150,000 or more | 4 | 2 | 10 | 3 |

EXHIBIT 4    Audubon Zoo Visitor Survey (*continued*)

|  | 1998 | | 1999 | |
|---|---|---|---|---|
|  | Number | Percent | Number | Percent |
| Respondent's race |  |  |  |  |
| Caucasian | 188 | 82 | 212 | 71 |
| African American | 25 | 11 | 69 | 23 |
| Hispanic | 8 | 3 | 7 | 2 |
| Asian | 2 | 1 | 10 | 3 |
| Native American | 4 | 2 | 0 | 0 |
| Other | 3 | 1 | 1 | 0 |
| Respondent's gender |  |  |  |  |
| Female | 137 | 62 | 179 | 61 |
| Male | 84 | 38 | 116 | 39 |

*Source:* The Audubon Institute Internal Report.

Membership allows free entry to the Audubon Park Zoo and to many other zoos around the United States. Participation in Zoobilation (annual members-only evenings at the Zoo) and the many volunteer programs mentioned are other benefits of membership.

Increasing membership requires a special approach to marketing. Chip Weigand, Director of Marketing, stated,

> [I]n marketing memberships we try to encourage repeat visitations, the feeling that one can visit as often as one wants, the idea that the Zoo changes from visit to visit and that there are good reasons to make one large payment or donation for a membership card, rather than paying for each visit. . . .[T]he overwhelming factor is a good zoo that people want to visit often, so that a membership makes good economical sense.

Results of a survey of visitors to the zoo are contained in Exhibit 4. The percentage of new visitors rose from 1998 to 1999, and the average number of visits during the prior year decreased. Although bringing children was the most frequent reason for visiting, the percentage of people who were sightseeing increased in 1999.

The zoo has a membership designed for businesses, the Audubon Zoo Curator Club, with four categories of membership: Bronze ($250); Silver ($500); Gold ($1000); and Platinum ($2500 and over).

## Concessions

The Audubon Institute operates the Audubon Park Zoo concessions for refreshments and gifts. Volunteer members of the Institute run the concessions, and all profits go directly to the Zoo. Today, McDonald's and several other name-brand concessionaires operate on Zoo grounds.

## Adopt-an-Animal

Zoo Parents pay a fee to "adopt" an animal, the fee varying with the animal chosen. Zoo Parents' names are listed on a large sign inside the zoo. They also have their own celebration, Zoo Parents Day, held at the zoo yearly.

## Zoo-to-Do

Zoo-to-Do is a black-tie fundraiser held annually with live music, food and drink, and original, high-quality souvenirs such as posters or ceramic necklaces. Admission tickets,

EXHIBIT 5    1999 Marketing Budget

| | |
|---|---:|
| Administrative | $150,000 |
| Sales | 268,000 |
| Public relations | 64,000 |
| Advertising | 250,000 |
| Special events | 150,000 |
| Total | 882,000 |
| Sponsorship revenues | 160,000 |
| Net budget | $722,000 |

*Source:* The Audubon Institute Internal Report.

limited to 3,000 annually, are priced starting at $150 per person. A raffle is conducted in conjunction with the Zoo-to-Do, with raffle items varying from an opportunity to be zoo curator for the day to use of a Mercedes-Benz for a year. Despite the rather stiff price, the Zoo-to-Do is a popular sellout every year. Local restaurants and other businesses donate most of the necessary supplies, decreasing the cost of the affair. In 1985 the Zoo-to-Do raised almost $500,000 in one night, more money than any other nonmedical fundraiser in the country. The Zoo-to-Do continues to sell out annually and remains a major fundraiser as well as a great public relations event for the zoo.

### Advertising

In 1999, Audubon Zoo's marketing budget was over $722,000, including advertising and special events. Not included in this budget was developmental fundraising or membership. The marketing budget can be found in Exhibit 5.

The American Association of Zoological Parks and Aquariums reported that most zoos find the majority of their visitors live within a single population center in close proximity to the park. Thus, in order to sustain attendance over the years, zoos must attract the same visitors repeatedly. A large number of the Audubon's promotional programs and special events are aimed at just that.

### Promotional Programs

The Audubon Park Zoo and the Institute conduct a multitude of successful promotional programs. The effect is that continual parties and celebrations are going on, attracting a variety of people to the zoo (and raising additional revenue). Exhibit 6 lists the major annual promotional programs conducted by the Zoo.

In addition to these annual promotions, the zoo schedules concerts of musicians (such as Irma Thomas, Pete Fountain, The Monkees, and Manhattan Transfer) and other special events throughout the year. As a result, a variety of events occur each month.

Many educational activities are conducted all year long. These included (1) a Junior Zoo Keeper program for seventh and eighth graders, (2) a student-intern program for high school and college students, and (3) a ZOOmobile that takes live animals to such locations as special education classes, hospitals, and retirement homes. Learning adventures for adults, children, and families are creatively designed and titled, for example, Twilight Treks, Love After Hours, Families Great and Small, Critter Care, and Investigating Inverts.

### Attracting More Tourists and Other Visitors

A riverboat ride on the romantic paddle-wheeled *Cotton Blossom* takes visitors from downtown to the zoo. Originally, the trip began at a dock in the French Quarter, but it

EXHIBIT 6    Selected Audubon Park Zoo Promotional Programs

| Month | Activity |
|---|---|
| March | Earth Fest. The environment and our planet are the focus of this fun-filled and educational event. Recycling, conservation displays, and puppet shows. |
| April | Zoo-to-Do for Kids. At this "pint-sized" version of the Zoo-to-Do, fun and games abound for kids. |
| May | Zoo-to-Do. Annual black-tie fundraiser featuring over 100 of New Orleans' finest restaurants and three music stages. |
| May | Irma Thomas Mother's Day Concert. The annual celebration of Mother's Day with a buffet. |
| October | Louisiana Swamp Festival. Cajun food, music, and crafts highlight this four-day salute to Louisiana's bayou country; features hands-on contact with live swamp animals. |
| October | Boo at the Zoo. This annual Halloween extravaganza features games, special entertainment, trick or treat, a haunted house, and the zoo's Spook Train. |

*Source:* The Audubon Institute Internal Report.

was later moved to a dock immediately adjacent to the Hilton Hotel and the Riverwalk Shopping Center. Not only is the riverboat ride great fun, it also lures tourists and conventioneers from the downtown attractions of the French Quarter and the Riverwalk to the zoo, some six miles upstream. A further allure of the riverboat ride is a return trip to downtown on the New Orleans streetcar, one of the few remaining trolley cars in the United States. The Zoo Cruise not only draws more visitors but generates additional revenue through landing fees paid by the New Orleans Steamboat company and keeps traffic out of uptown New Orleans, a mostly residential neighborhood.

## Financial Statements

A comparison of the 1998 and 1999 income statement and balance sheet for the Audubon Institute is presented in Exhibits 7 and 8.

## A SHIFT IN ATTITUDE

A visitor to the new Audubon Zoo could quickly see why New Orleanians were so proud of their zoo. In a city that was called among the dirtiest in the nation, the zoo is virtually spotless as a result of adequate staffing and the clear pride of both those who worked at and those who visited the zoo. One of the first points made by volunteers guiding school groups is that anyone who sees a piece of trash on the ground must pick it up.

In 1988, the name of the Friends of the Zoo was changed to the Audubon Institute to reflect its growing interest in activities beyond the zoo. The organizational chart provided in Exhibit 9 shows the relationship between the Audubon Commission, the Audubon Institute, and zoo management. The Audubon Institute planned to promote the development of the following facilities other than the zoo and manage these facilities once they were a reality.

### Freeport-McMoRan Audubon Species Survival Center

The Institute designated the Westbank of New Orleans as the most appropriate site for their preservation projects. The Freeport-McMoRan Audubon Species Survival Center was established to provide endangered animals a refuge where they could breed and

EXHIBIT 7    The Audubon Institute, Inc. Income Statements

|  | 1999 | 1998 |
|---|---|---|
| **Revenue and Other Support:** | | |
| Government grants | $ 748,242 | $ 555,636 |
| Gifts, exhibit/program sponsorships | 4,912,989 | 1,952,166 |
| Gains on securities | (38,180) | 2,039,018 |
| Investment income | 900,920 | 740,242 |
| Imputed interest on pledges | 315,472 | 589,856 |
| Fundraising activities | 823,595 | 780,605 |
| Total revenue and other support | 7,663,038 | 6,657,523 |
| **Functional Expenses:** | | |
| Development and fundraising activities | 1,454,896 | 945,308 |
| Termite education grant | 90,609 | 27,149 |
| Interest | 37,826 | 28,928 |
| Investment expenses | 130,654 | 100,142 |
| Other expenses | 100,576 | — |
| Write down of project design costs | 750,614 | — |
| Total expenses | 2,565,175 | 1,101,527 |
| **Excess of Support and Revenue Over Expenses Before Transfers** | 5,097,863 | 5,555,996 |
| Specific grants to Audubon Commission for operations support, education programs, and capital projects (Note 6) | (3,785,136) | (1,677,032) |
| Endowment income transferred to Audubon Commission funds (Note 5) | (1,150,921) | (1,076,400) |
| **Change in Net Assets for the Period** | 161,806 | 2,802,564 |
| Net assets, beginning | 32,376,914 | 29,574,350 |
| Net assets, ending | $32,538,720 | $32,376,914 |

*Source:* The Audubon Institute Internal Report, 1999.

eventually boost their numbers. Located on 1,200-acre site, the Center initially housed such animals as the Mississippi sandhill crane and the Baird's tapir, and more species arrived as the Center expanded.

## Audubon Center for Research of Endangered Species

The Audubon Institute next constructed the Audubon Center for Research of Endangered Species. The research center was to study advanced breeding techniques, animal behavior, and nutrition. The Institute includes labs for reproduction, molecular genetics, cryogenics, and veterinary care. Senator J. Bennett Johnston secured $19 million in federal funds for the research center, the first breeding center of its kind. The third leg of the Westbank-based project was the Audubon Wilderness Park that featured an orientation center, hiking trails, and wetland facts.

## Louisiana Nature and Science Center

The Institute reaffirmed its commitment to education and entertainment with the acquisition of the Louisiana Nature and Science Center. The Audubon Institute merged with the Society for Environmental Education in 1994 and assumed control of the 86-acre site. The stated purpose of the Center was to provide ecological and environmental science programs to the entire community.

EXHIBIT 8    The Audubon Institute, Inc. Balance Sheets

|  | 1999 | 1998 |
|---|---|---|
| **Assets:** | | |
| Cash | $ 1,250,817 | $    736,270 |
| Accounts and Grants receivable | 435,531 | 258,855 |
| Investments (Note 2) | 22,924,724 | 22,477,567 |
| Accrued interest receivable | 64,863 | 52,726 |
| Pledges receivable (Note 3) | 8,295,372 | 8,470,381 |
| Due from Audubon Commission (Note 6) | — | 132,256 |
| Prepaids and other assets | 2,770 | 1,873 |
| Project design costs (Note 6) | 196,668 | 809,053 |
| Equipment less accumulated depreciation of $34,000 | | |
| and $181,000 | 95,950 | 90,597 |
| Total assets | $33,266,695 | $33,029,578 |
| **Liabilities:** | | |
| Accounts payable | $       35,946 | $      41,710 |
| Accrued salaries | 22,377 | 11,241 |
| Accrued sick and vacation | 9,275 | 10,800 |
| Other | 20,457 | 18,913 |
| Bank lines of credit (Note 8) | — | 570,000 |
| Due to Audubon Commission | 639,919 | — |
| Total liabilities | $     727,974 | $     652,664 |
| **Net Assets:** | | |
| Unrestricted | 308,882 | 646,238 |
| Board designated | 8,485,644 | 8,904,224 |
| Temporarily restricted (Note 4) | 8,617,475 | 8,110,538 |
| Permanently restricted (Note 5) | 15,126,719 | 14,715,914 |
| Total net assets | 32,538,720 | 32,376,914 |
| Total liabilities and net assets | $33,266,694 | $33,029,578 |

*Source:* The Audubon Institute Internal Report, 1999.

## Parks

Over the years, the Audubon Institute acquired control over three park areas. Its original park, Audubon Park, was located in the heart of uptown New Orleans, running from St. Charles Avenue to the Mississippi River. This 400-acre park includes over 4,000 live oak trees, gardens, lagoons, recreation areas, and a golf course.

The Woldenberg Riverfront Park is located on the Mississippi River in the French Quarter. The Aquarium of the Americas and the IMAX Theatre are located in this park. The park's 17 acres are landscaped with abundant green space and brick pathways. Its Hibernia Pavilion is used for frequent open-air concerts, and festivals are frequently held on the park's Great Lawn.

The last addition to Audubon Institute's parks was the Wilderness Park, the third leg of the Westbank-based project that included the Freeport-McMoRan Audubon

EXHIBIT 9    Audubon Institute Organizational Chart

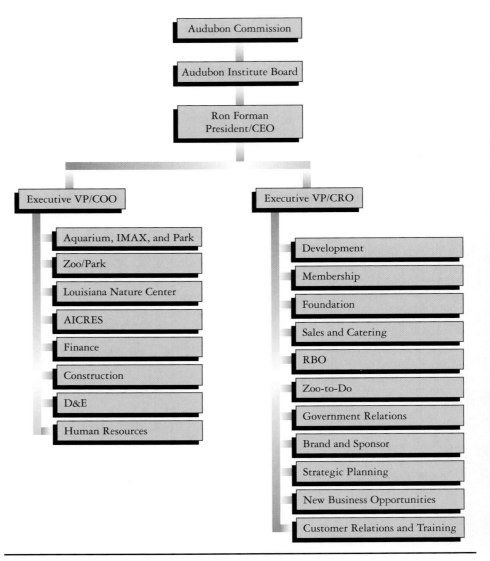

*Source:* Audubon Institute Internal Report.

Species Survival Center and the Audubon Center for Research of Endangered Species. Wilderness Park's 129 acres feature an orientation center, hiking trails, and picnic areas, open to groups by advance booking. An interpretive center and naturalists are used to facilitate Audubon Institute's educational goals by helping visitors learn about South Louisiana's unique environment.

Riverfront 2000, proposed by Ron Forman in the late 1980s, was nearly complete with the acquisition and construction of the above-mentioned projects and facilities.

However, Riverfront 2000 has presented further plans to construct an insectarium and a natural history museum.

## THE FUTURE OF THE INSTITUTE

Although the Institute has initiated many new and successful projects, the zoo is by no means relegated to the "backburner." The zoo has its own plans for the future. A new animal hospital on zoo grounds was dedicated in 1996. Forman and his staff continue to upgrade and create new exhibits. Construction in the late 1990s included a Mezoamerica exhibit, a Diefenthal earth lab, and a new elephant exhibit. The Institute operates in a city in which many attractions compete for the leisure dollar of natives and tourists. It has to vie with the French Quarter, Dixieland jazz, casinos, the Superdome, and the greatest attraction of all, Mardi Gras. Forman believes his once-weak and now over-whelmingly powerful Audubon Institute possesses the necessary message and facilities to forge successfully into the next millennium. Forman sums up the present and future of the zoo and the Institute by stating, "All of our exhibits are on the leading edge of what is being done; we believe the best way to educate people is through fun."

From 1996 to 1998, the zoo spent nearly $6 million to upgrade or create new animal exhibits, including a Komodo Dragon habitat, a Jaguar jungle exhibit, and a renovated Louisiana Swamp exhibit. In 1999, the zoo turned its attention and funds to enhancing facilities for humans. In early 1999, the expanded and reconfigured Louisiana Swamp Exhibit was opened with a new Cajun Dance Hall as its centerpiece. Features like fishing equipment invoked the feel of a 1930s bayou village. The Hall includes an animal nursery, a gift shop, and tanks for the Zoo's prize possessions, a pair of white alligators. For six months, musical events are regularly scheduled in this new facility, drawing locals to it and the zoo in general. Beginning in November 1999, the Dance Hall became a rental facility. Holding up to 1,000 people, it could be rented for $1,750, plus $500 for the outdoor porch overlooking the external exhibits. A new 10,000-square-foot Audubon Tea Room was built at the edge of the zoo for $3 million; it will be rented out for weddings, receptions, debutante parties, birthday parties, and corporate functions. Officials expect the building to become a significant revenue generator.

Late in 1999, a $4.8 million contract was awarded for a new entrance complex including a ticket office, gift shop, restrooms, and concessions area. The new entry will have an animated sign and moving animal sculptures coordinated with a clock in a new clock tower. It will be more appealing and fun than the current entrance. Future work will add a second roadway into the zoo from Magazine Street and a new entrance sign to make access more easily recognizable for first-time visitors.

The Audubon Zoo received several accolades during 1999. It was named the number-one family-friendly zoo in the Southeast in a readers' poll conducted by *FamilyFun* magazine, a nationally distributed product of Disney Publishing Worldwide. Audubon was also ranked among the top ten zoos in America by *Travel and Leisure Family Magazine.* The listing, published in the magazine's spring/summer 1999 edition, highlighted the zoo's new Louisiana Swamp exhibit. Finally, *Southern Living* magazine's survey ranked Audubon as the best zoo in the South.

Prepare a three-year plan for the Audubon Zoo to continue its success in the new millennium.

## REFERENCES

Audubon Institute, Inc. Annual Report, page 1.

EXHIBIT 10    Audubon Institute Employees and Volunteers, 1998

| Location | Employees | Volunteers | Volunteer Hours |
|---|---|---|---|
| ACRES and FMASSC | 33 | 34 | 667 |
| Aquarium | 208 | 351 | 54,737 |
| Nature Center | 23 | 132 | 14,634 |
| Zoo | 434 | 507 | 51,810 |
| Total | 698 | 1024 | 121,848 |

*Source:* The Audubon Institute Internal Report.

EXHIBIT 11    Zoo Admissions

| Year | Number of Paid Admissions | Number of Member Admissions | Per-Visitor Spending |
|---|---|---|---|
| 1994 | 637,007 | 182,903 | $6.92 |
| 1995 | 820,597 | 175,412 | 6.84 |
| 1996 | 782,804 | 167,764 | 6.95 |
| 1997 | 836,127 | 191,832 | 6.45 |
| 1998 | 782,269 | 178,209 | 6.28 |

## Admission Charges

| Year | Adult | Child/Senior |
|---|---|---|
| 1993 | 7.50 | 3.50 |
| 1994 | 7.75 | 3.75 |
| 1998 | 8.75 | 4.50 |

*Source:* The Audubon Institute Internal Report.

## EXHIBIT 12    A Few Facts About the New Orleans Area

| | |
|---|---|
| Population | 1,307,758 |
| Per-capita personal income | $23,148 |
| Unemployment rate | 2.6% |
| Average temperature | 70 degrees Fahrenheit |
| Average annual rainfall | 63 inches |
| Average Elevation | 5 feet below sea level |
| Area | 363.5 square miles |
| | 199.4 square miles of land |

### Major Economic Activities

Tourism (5 million visitors per year)
Oil and gas industry
The Port of New Orleans (170 million tons of cargo per year)

### Taxes

| | |
|---|---|
| State sales tax | 4.0% |
| Parish (county) Sales Tax | 5.0% (Orleans) |
| | 4.0% (Jefferson) |
| State income tax | 2.1–2.6% on first $20,000 |
| | 3.0–3.5% on next $30,000 |
| | 6.0% on $51,000 & over |

Parish property tax of 167.34 mills (Orleans) is based on 10% of appraised value over $75,000 homestead exemption.

*Sources:* U.S. Bureau of the Census, *State and Metropolitan Data Book,* 1997-98, Table B-1.
U.S. Department of Commerce, Bureau of Economic Analysis Web site,
http://www.bea.doc.gov/bea/regional/reis/scb/svy_mas.htm
U.S. Bureau of Labor Statistics, *Employment & Earnings,* March 1998.

## EXHIBIT 13    Audubon Zoo Nonvisitor Survey of Why Respondent Did Not Visit the Zoo (in %)

| Reason (Close Ended) | Pleasure | Business |
|---|---|---|
| No time | 47% | 66% |
| Too hot | 12 | 15 |
| Other plans | 12 | 14 |
| No interest | 11 | 4 |
| Been before | 10 | 4 |

*Source:* The Audubon Institute Internal Report.

# RIVERBANKS ZOOLOGICAL PARK AND BOTANICAL GARDEN—2000[*]

Carolyn R. Stokes and Eugene M. Bland
Francis Marion University

## www.riverbanks.org

The Riverbanks Zoo and Botanical Garden, a 170-acre park located on the Lower Saluda River in Columbia, the capital of South Carolina, celebrated its 25th anniversary in 1999. The complex is comprised of the Riverbanks Zoo, with over 2,000 animals in natural habitats, and the Riverbanks Botanical Garden on a 70-acre park devoted to woodlands, gardens, historic ruins, plant collections, and visitor facilities. The Riverbanks Zoo and Botanical Garden is a major attraction of the Columbia metropolitan area, South Carolina, and the Southeast.

Riverbanks, one of 185 accredited institutional members of the American Zoo and Aquarium Association (AZA), is recognized as one of the best zoos in America in regard to conservation efforts and recreational activities and has received numerous awards. Riverbanks is recognized as one of the top five zoos in North America with respect to support for AZA programs. The Aquarium Reptile Complex was named one of the top three new exhibits in the country by AZA in 1990. The zoo has received recognition for its captive breeding accomplishments. It received the prestigious Governor's Cup Award from the South Carolina Chamber of Commerce in 1989 as South Carolina's leading attraction and in 1989 and 1993 was named the outstanding travel attraction of the year by the Southeast Tourism Association. In 1990, with over one million people visiting the zoo, Riverbanks was recognized as one of the 20 most visited zoos in the United States. Riverbanks in the 1990s had approximately 850,000 visitors annually (Exhibit 1), with 25 percent coming from outside of the state.

Its executive director, Palmer Krantz, continues to move Riverbanks into the future. The 25th anniversary marked the launching of Zoo 2002, the largest expansion and renovation of the zoo since its opening. In the zoo, new animals are taking residence, and some current residents are receiving renovated, refurbished, or new habitats. Projects will recreate nearly 50 percent of the zoo's core exhibit space as well as create a new entrance into the botanical garden. Featured will be a new elephant exhibit, a gorilla compound Lemur Island, a bird pavilion, and the recently completed Bird Conservation Center (a research and breeding center that allows visitors to view bird conservation operations). The new bird pavilion, featuring savanna exhibits from South America and Africa and a state-of-the-art penguin facility, will replace the old Bird House that had been home to the groundbreaking research and conservation efforts that helped secure Riverbanks' reputation. All of these developments are in keeping with the mission of the Riverbanks Zoological Park and Botanical Garden, "to foster an appreciation and concern for all living things."

---

[*]This is a small nonprofit organization. Please do not contact them for case information.

EXHIBIT 1   Riverbanks Zoo Attendance Analysis

| Fiscal Year ending | June 30, 1999 | June 30, 1998 | June 30, 1997 |
|---|---|---|---|
| Paid attendance: | | | |
| Regular | 338,576 | 323,350 | 355,186 |
| Group | 115,458 | 132,704 | 137,938 |
| Total paid | 454,034 | 456,054 | 493,124 |
| Free attendance | | | |
| Lexington/Richland school groups | 31,631 | 33,543 | 35,297 |
| Riverbanks Society | 228,779 | 214,064 | 209,603 |
| Prepaid and complimentary | 18,445 | 19,119 | 30,931 |
| Promotional-Free Friday's | 47,855 | 40,498 | 31,283 |
| Children under three | 55,964 | 49,582 | 55,561 |
| Total free | 382,674 | 356,806 | 362,675 |
| Total attendance | 836,708 | 812,860 | 855,799 |

*Source:* Internal documents (financial statements for the fiscal year ended June 30, 1998, page 2 and financial statements for the fiscal year ended June 30, 1999, page 2).

In the garden, new species are being planted, and some current species are having their environments enhanced. The Saluda Factory Interpretive Center, a log cabin built on the site of the ruins of a textile mill burned by Sherman's troops as they stormed Columbia, was completed in 1999. Construction is scheduled to begin on a new West Columbia entrance. This new entrance is expected to increase attendance by substantially reducing travel time for Lexington County residents. The garden will include a new, elaborately landscaped parking lot large enough for 250 cars and a boardwalk/bridge leading over the 35-foot ravine to the garden. Attractions like the "Jewels of the Sky" (a butterfly exhibit) have been added, and special events like the "Lights Before Christmas" are being expanded.

This new construction effort is expected to cost in the neighborhood of $19 million. It is being funded with a $15 million bond referendum that was approved by the Richland and Lexington county governments, with the remaining $4 million being raised by the zoo itself. The zoo has centered its fund-raising efforts on the selling of personalized bricks that will form a 515-foot snake that will stretch from the main entrance to the Kenya Cafe Restaurant.

## DEVELOPMENT OF RIVERBANKS

For many years, citizens in Richland and Lexington Counties expressed the need for a zoo in the community. In 1969 the General Assembly of South Carolina created Riverbanks and a Riverbanks Park Commission. Individuals, businesses, and local governments recognized the need and provided the necessary financial support and work for the establishment of Riverbanks. With government and private sectors working together, the zoo opened its gates to the public on April 25, 1974, with Happy the tiger as its first official resident. It was named the most outstanding tax-supported attraction by the South Carolina Chamber of Commerce. In 1976 the private sector established the Riverbanks Society, a nonprofit organization dedicated to the support of Riverbanks and the preservation of the earth's flora and fauna. In 1981 Riverbanks was designated as a recipient of country tax millage from Richland and Lexington Counties, further solidifying the financial governmental support base.

In 1983 the Education Center opened to facilitate zoo educational programs to further directly fulfill the mission of Riverbanks by assisting in the understanding of and appreciation for animals. In 1988 a farm was added to allow visitors to see and learn more about farm animals. In 1988 the Kenya Cafe and the Elephant's Trunk Gift Shop were built to allow visitors better opportunities for refreshment and zoo-related gift purchases. In 1989 the award-winning Aquarium Reptile Complex was opened. In 1992 the African Plains underwent major renovation. The following year Riverbanks Animal Health Center opened to fulfill the mission of Riverbanks by providing a high level of health care. The Animal Health Center has facilities, equipment, and staff for varying levels of care including surgery.

In 1993, construction began on the botanical garden on property joined to the zoo grounds by a new bridge over the Lower Saluda River. The new botanical garden on the left bank of the Saluda opened on June 10, 1995, and its name was changed to the Riverbanks Zoological Park and Botanical Garden.

Riverbanks is governed by the Riverbanks Parks Commission, supported by the Riverbanks Society, and managed by the Riverbanks staff under the leadership of Palmer E. Krantz, III, the executive director. Riverbank is accredited by the American Association of Zoological Parks and Aquariums and is a member of the American Association of Botanical Gardens and Arboreta. With about 122 employees and over $6.1 million in total annual revenues (see Exhibit 2) Riverbanks Zoological Park and Botanical Garden is now one of the leading zoos in the country.

## RIVERBANKS ZOO

The zoo uses a modern approach to exhibit design by housing wild animals in natural settings that are more pleasant for both animal residents and human visitors. The natural settings at Riverbanks enable animals to exist almost as if they were in the wild and allow visitors to see the animals in a more realistic environment than formerly when many animals were warehoused in cages. At the farm some domesticated animals are exhibited in a barn and related settings so visitors can view them as they would on a working farm. The zoo is home to more than 2,000 animals, in addition to 300 birds, 300 reptiles and amphibians, and 1,300 fish and invertebrates.

Major zoo attractions include an award-winning Aquarium Reptile Complex, an African Plains section, a large-mammal area, and bird exhibits. The Aquarium Reptile Complex (ARC), with a 55,000-gallon aquarium, has four galleries featuring animals from South Carolina, the desert, the tropics, and the Pacific Ocean. The complex is a unique blending of a reptile habitat with an aquarium.

The African Plains section features giraffes, rhinoceroses, zebras, and ostriches in a savanna setting complete with moats. The large—mammal area features elephants, tigers, lions, and polar bears.

Riverbanks Farm features a barn and barnyards with a goat, cow, pig, chickens, horse, and honey bees. Here visitors can view chickens hatching from eggs and Riverbanks staff milking a cow. Visitors can also view the feeding of many animals in all sections of the zoo.

In line with the mission of the Riverbanks, the zoo actively participates in the Species Survival Plans (SSPs) of the AZA for endangered species. Many zoos participate in the program. For example, in Texas, the Houston Zoological Gardens hatched two critically endangered species, the prairie chicken and the Hawaiian thrush. Riverbanks focuses on 23 endangered species including the golden lion tamarin, Siberian tiger, palm cockatoo, Chinese alligator, and Bali mynah. Riverbanks has received awards for successfully breeding black howlers and the white-faced sakis. Riverbanks has the honor of being the first zoo to breed in captivity two rare birds, the toco toucan and the crimson

EXHIBIT 2    Riverbanks Park Commission—General Fund
Statement of Revenues and Expenditures

|  | FY 1999 | FY 1998 | FY 1997 |
|---|---|---|---|
| *Revenues* | | | |
| Earned revenues: | | | |
|    Admissions net revenue | $2,092,540 | $1,961,157 | $2,065,285 |
|    Concession fees | 613,368 | 586,902 | 598,710 |
|    Promotional/sponsorship | 72,283 | 101,395 | 73,500 |
|    Intergovernmental | 1,928,589 | 1,852,142 | 1,623,996 |
|    Riverbanks Society contribution | 705,533 | 841,288 | 432,760 |
|    Facility rental | 73,613 | 80,329 | 96,455 |
|    Sale of surplus property | 47,500 | 0 | 0 |
|    Other revenues | 377,566 | 322,738 | 259,908 |
|      Total revenues | 5,910,992 | 5,745,951 | 5,150,614 |
| *Expenditures* | | | |
|    Animal care | 1,791,659 | 1,687,978 | 1,605,212 |
|    Botanical care | 622,224 | 572,621 | 836,924 |
|    Facility management | 717,701 | 307,029 | 866,666 |
|    Utilities | 496,241 | 515,804 | 560,874 |
|    Administrative | 816,665 | 708,329 | 784,482 |
|    Education | 217,084 | 205,035 | 202,315 |
|    Marketing | 1,081,703 | 1,044,096 | 653,192 |
|    Capital outlay | 0 | 989,487 | 0 |
|    Principal retirement | 0 | 116,915 | 0 |
|    Interest and fiscal charges | 0 | 34,348 | 0 |
| *Total expenditures* | 5,743,277 | 6,181,642 | 5,509,665 |
| Excess (deficit) of revenue over expenditures | 167,715 | (435,691) | (359,051) |
| Other sources—loan proceeds | 0 | 441,700 | 165,600 |
| Fund equity—beginning of period | 0 | 496,135 | 689,586 |
| Fund equity—end of period | 0 | $502,144 | $496,135 |

*Source:* www.freeedgar.com

seedcracker, and is the first zoo in the Western Hemisphere to breed milky eagle owls, blue-billed weavers, and cinereous vultures. Riverbanks has the only pair of cinereous vultures that are raising their own young. In 1998, Riverbanks once again received the Edward H. Bean Award for its long-term success with captive breeding of *Ramphastidae* (e.g., toucans, toucanets, aracaris, etc.).

In 1996–1997 Riverbanks established a research department and added a reproductive physiologist. Riverbanks' new Conservation Research Program (CORE) is generating reproductive databases of rare species to be used internationally in zoological and scientific communities. Riverbanks' serious interest in conservation research is demonstrated by its decision to host the first Southeastern Conservation Research Consortium. The June 1998 conference provided a forum to foster conservation-oriented collaborations among zoological institutions, wildlife agencies, and academic institutions. It included 47 paper presentations, panel discussions, tours, and special activities designed to promote conservation research. Riverbanks' research department continues to fulfill its mission by leading several AZA-based conservation programs including North

American regional studbooks and population management plans (PMPs) for the Rodrigues fruit bat, African lion, Nile hippo, hawk-headed parrot, golden-breasted starling, king cobra, Leaf-tailed gecko, and False gharial.

It also maintains international studbooks for fishing cats, rare leopards, and black howler monkeys and species survival plans (SPS) for the Bali mynah and the cinereous vulture.

## THE BOTANICAL GARDEN

The botanical garden envisioned during the Riverbanks planning stages became feasible in the early 1990s. In 1993, following successful fund-raising programs, construction on the west bank of the Lower Saluda River began. On June 10, 1995, the Riverbanks Botanical Garden opened to the public. Visitors pass through the main entrance, proceed through a portion of the zoo, and then walk or ride a tram across a bridge over the Saluda River and up to the botanical garden. They enter through the Visitors Center, which has a gift shop featuring garden-related products, a terrace cafe, a gallery, and multipurpose spaces for functions. Guests exit through the rear of the Visitors Center into a walled garden with cascades and pinwheel fountains, and find seasonal exotic annuals, perennials, and bulbs complementing shrubbery and trees.

Beside the garden is a terraced amphitheater that is grass carpeted for seating with a large domed stage for cultural events such as a zoo ballet and educational programs. At the rear of the garden is the entrance to the walking trail. Here, visitors enjoy scenic river views and the Saluda Factory Interpretive Center. The trail provides visitors with a close view of many of the trees, plants, flowers, and animals indigenous to the upper and lower parts of the state. The scenic trail was featured on a 1966 episode of "Nature Scene," a nationally broadcast series originating at the educational television station in South Carolina.

The Saluda Factory Interpretive Center is a woodland log cabin. This rough-hewn cabin located near the mill ruins features exhibits that describe the mill ruins and the flora and fauna of the area. There is also an outdoor classroom for educational programs.

The garden is a leading source of horticultural and botanical information in the area. Through a cooperative effort with Clemson Extension Service, the public can access information by talking with an extension agent or by using the Internet in the Visitors Center. The garden also provides facilities for related activities. For example, the bonsai show, held in the Visitors Center, permitted guests to see miniature trees and learn how to grow them. Further, they have been selected again to host a Southern Living gardening school.

Construction of the new entrance to the garden is expected to begin in the spring of 2000. This second entrance to the Riverbanks Zoological Park and Botanical Garden on the Lexington County side should facilitate entrance to and, thus, increase the attendance of Riverbanks.

## SPECIAL ATTRACTION

In 1987 Riverbanks began an event, "Lights Before Christmas," with the lighting of about 25 percent of the zoo. Now 80 percent of the zoo is beautified in December with colorful lights along walkways, in trees, on shrubbery, and in other locations. At the entrance, visitors are greeted with lighted trees containing large stars and the sound of Christmas music. There are colorful lighted images of animals including a bear, lion, horse, deer, frog, rhino, pig, and fox. Some of the animals appear to be in motion. For example, an elephant seems to be spraying water over his back and an ostrich looks as if it is running through the woods. Visitors on their way to the bridge pass under an arch artfully decorated with colorful lights and view numerous decorated trees and shrubs as well as a group of frogs that appear to be playing. The bridge is decorated with images of fish and other sealife.

Riverbanks is one of a number of zoos that are presenting attractions of this kind. The Assiniboine Park Zoo in Winnipeg, Canada, one of the coldest zoos in the world, features the "The Lights of the Wild" and reindeer sleigh rides. The Fort Worth Zoo presents a "Zoobilee of Lights," which increased its December attendance from 10,000–12,000 visitors to over 75,000 visitors.

In 1998 Riverbanks' "Lights Before Christmas" attracted a new record of over 90,000 visitors during the 28 evenings of the lights. Winter attractions are especially important to Riverbanks because two thirds of the 850,000 annual visitors arrive from April to August. Attendance at the 1999 "Lights Before Christmas" exceeded 100,000 visitors. This event also generates revenue from concessions, carousel rides, and additional memberships purchased.

With a million lights designed to depict animal and garden scenes, the "Lights Before Christmas" has been named one of the Top 20 Events in the Southeast by the Southeast Tourism Society and one of the Top 100 Events in North America by the American Bus Association in 1997.

## RIVERBANKS EDUCATION DEPARTMENT

The education department, established in 1993, works to interpret animal exhibits and plants and assist in learning about animal and plant worlds. Its primary facility is the Education Center, which has two classrooms, an auditorium, and a library. Other facilities available for education programs include a classroom in the Aquarium Reptile Complex, another in the Riverbanks farm, an outdoor classroom at the Saluda Factory Interpretive Center, and the amphitheater adjacent to the botanical garden.

During the week, Riverbanks offers classes to groups ranging from preschool age to college (see Exhibit 3). On weekends and in the summer, Riverbanks offers classes and special programs for students, scouts, teachers, and family members. Special programs include the "Zoo Camp" for overnight programs, a one-week day camp for kindergarten children, and "Wildlife in the Zoo" for gifted classes. Annually over 40,000 people participate in the educational programs.

## FINANCING

Individuals, businesses, and government agencies have funded the original construction, major renovations and expansions, and the annual operating budget. The Riverbanks Zoological Park and Botanical Garden has an annual operating budget of over $5 million. Revenues from admissions and concession fees provide approximately 60 percent of the resources; funds from Richland and Lexington Counties, the state of South Carolina, and federal and city grants provide approximately 30 percent, and the Riverbanks Society provides approximately 10 percent. Nationally, governments provide approximately 54 percent of the support for zoos.

Riverbank, a nonprofit organization, uses fund accounting to report its financial position and results of operations. The balance sheets for the years ending June 30, 1997, to 1999 can be seen in Exhibit 4.

Admission revenues are impacted by weather conditions because most of the attractions are outdoors. Riverbanks earns admissions revenue directly from visitors who pay per visit or indirectly from Riverbanks Society members who pay per year for one of several different memberships. (Riverbanks Society membership information will be presented later.) General admission fees are small. A single admission is $6.25 for adults and

## EXHIBIT 3    Examples of Riverbanks Education Programs

### Single-Grade Programs

*Preschool and Kindergarten*

"M" is for Mammal
Varmint's Garments
No-See-Ums

*Grade 1*

Survival Senses
Whooo's There

*Grade 2*

Hedgerows to Mole Holes
Dinosaur Detectives

*Grade 3*

Trunks, Tails, Spots and Scales
Look out Below

*Grade 4*

Faunal Fun Facts
Good Buddies

*Grade 5*

Nature's Cycles and Chains
The Living Sea

*Grade 6*

Species on the Brink
Sea of Uncertainty

### Multi-Grade Programs

*All Grades*

Animal Encounters "Special Education Program"

*Grades K–2*

Ocean Odyssey

*Grades K–6*

Animal Kingdom

*Grades 4–6*

Herpetology
Ornithology

*Grades 3–6*

Wildlife in the Zoo

*Grades 4–12*

Zoo Camp

*Grades 7–12*

The World of Animals and Zoos

### College-Level Programs

History and Philosophy of Zoos
Animal Management and Captive Breeding Programs
Zoo Conservation Programs
Dynamics and Genetics of Zoo Populations
Zoo Education
Zoo Planning and Exhibit Design
Primatology
Zoos and Society
Botanical Garden Tour

*Source:* http://www.riverbanks.org/html/edu_school.html

EXHIBIT 4    **Riverbanks Park Commission—General Fund Comparative Balance Sheet**

|  | June 30, 1999 | June 30, 1998 | June 30, 1997 |
|---|---|---|---|
| **Assets** | | | |
| Cash on hand, on deposit and invested in REPO | $   800,028 | $525,626 | $432,935 |
| Accounts receivable—general | 118,918 | 140,643 | 154,215 |
| Accounts receivable—other governments | 24,250 | 0 | 58,000 |
| Accounts receivable—ticket sales | 4,313 | 4,797 | 8,819 |
| Accounts receivable—Riverbanks Society | 46,797 | 25,191 | 27,189 |
| Due from capital fund | 282,142 | 82,317 | 151,636 |
| Inventories—general supplies and animal feed | 24,017 | 23,866 | 25,941 |
| *Total assets* | $1,300,465 | $802,440 | $858,735 |
| **Liabilities and fund equity** | | | |
| *Current liabilities* | | | |
| Accounts payable | $   403,655 | $151,756 | $126,318 |
| Accrued salaries payable | 142,326 | 123,951 | 108,249 |
| Payroll taxes accrued and withheld | 972 | 912 | 841 |
| Admissions, sales and use taxes payable | 9,884 | 10,268 | 11,339 |
| State Retirement Contribution—employer and employee | 26,949 | 24,660 | 0 |
| Deferred revenue—consign, tickets and market | 77,593 | 31,121 | 92,346 |
| *Total liabilities* | 661,379 | 342,668 | 339,093 |
| *Fund equity* | | | |
| Reserved for: | | | |
| Inventories—general supplies and feed | 24,017 | 23,866 | 25,941 |
| Operating cushion | 400,000 | 400,000 | 400,000 |
| Major repairs and renovation | 0 | 11,605 | 64,824 |
| Endowment fund—Phelps | 31,028 | 33,306 | 0 |
| Unreserved, undesignated (deficit) | 184,042 | (9,003) | 28,877 |
| *Total fund equity* | 639,087 | 459,774 | 519,642 |
| *Total liabilities and fund equity* | $1,300,466 | $802,442 | $858,735 |

*Source:* Internal documents (Financial statements for the fiscal year ended June 30, 1998, page 3, and financial statements for the fiscal year ended June 30, 1999, page 3.)

$3.75 for children ages three to twelve. Discounts are available for groups, special activities, or special days. Free classes are provided for Lexington and Richland County schools. Charges for special activities vary.

Additional information concerning zoo and aquarium industry financing is available at the AZA Web site, www.aza.org.

## RIVERBANKS SOCIETY

The Riverbanks Society, which started with 200 members in 1976 grew to over 28,000 members by 1999, making it one of the largest zoo societies per capita in the United States. The society, which grew out of the private sector, provided much of the needed support prior to the opening of Riverbanks and plays a major role in its support. It provides funds for operations, construction and renovations, new exhibits, and special activities.

Many of the exhibits and portions of the gardens were provided by individual donations. For example, the Old Rose Garden recently established in the botanical garden, and the Galapagos tortoise exhibit in the zoo were fully funded by private contributions as were other projects in previous years. A new endangered species carousel, funded by a local business, is the focal point of Flamingo Plaza. The carousel has figures of 22 endangered species that children can ride and a scenic mural of other endangered species in their natural habitats.

The Riverbanks Society offers reasonable membership fees that allow admission for individuals or family members for one year. The society offers a variety of memberships for individuals and families, ranging from $25 to $100 for a standard membership and from $250 to $1,000 for Gold Card membership. Types of memberships and associated benefits are shown in Exhibit 5, but members also enjoy additional benefits such as a bimonthly newsletter and a quarterly magazine. Riverbanks arranges tours led by its staff for members to Africa, the Galapagos Islands, South America, and other places across the globe.

## EXHIBIT 5   Riverbanks Society Memberships

### Standard Memberships

Individual—$25
> Free admission for one adult named on card plus 4 guest passes

Dual—$32
> Free admission for two adults from the same household named on card, or Free admission for one adult named on card and one guest at any time, plus four guest passes

Family/grandparent—$42
> Free admission for two adults from the same household named on card and all children eighteen and under living in same household, or grandchildren eighteen and under living anywhere, plus ten guest passes

Family Plus—$56
> Free admission for four adults from the same household named on card and all children eighteen and under living in same household, or grandchildren eighteen and under living anywhere, plus ten guest passes

Patron—$100
> Free admission for four adults named on card and all children eighteen and under living in the same household, or grandchildren eighteen and under living anywhere, plus 15 guest passes

### Gold Card Memberships

Curators' Circle—$250
> Free admission for four adults named on the card and all children eighteen and under living in the same household, or grandchildren eighteen and under living anywhere, and 15 guest passes. Special added benefits: limited access to the garden through the West Gate entrance; curators' tour with society director; invitation to an annual Gold Card reception; Gold Card previews

Director's Circle—$500
> Same benefits as Curators' Circle and 20 passes. Special added benefits: duplicate Gold Card memberships; Riverbanks gift

Benefactor—$1,000
> Same benefits as Director's Circle and 25 guest passes. Special added benefits: VIP zoo and garden tour; invitation to benefactors' events.

*Source:* Riverbanks Zoo Internal Report.
http://www.riverbanks.org/html/society_membership.html

## THE FUTURE

Riverbanks Zoological Park and Botanical Garden, an institution offering many opportunities for recreation and education, should have a bright future. Riverbanks, which has a high-quality staff, continues to receive support from the public and private sectors. The Research Consortium held in 1998 enhanced Riverbanks' reputation and research programs. The Education Center should continue to grow, with more possible avenues in the garden. The botanical garden should attract more visitors as it develops and as the West Columbia entrance on the garden side of the park is completed. By the end of 2002, the zoo's renovation should be complete, and visitors should be enjoying the new bird pavilion, lemur island, gorilla compound, and elephant exhibit.

# THE CLASSIC CAR CLUB OF AMERICA, INC.—2000

**Matthew C. Sonfield**
**Hofstra University**

www.classiccarclub.org

The Classic Car Club of America, Inc. (CCCA) was formed in 1952 by a small group of enthusiasts interested in the luxury cars of the late 1920s and 1930s. CCCA ran a deficit financially in 1999 for the first time in many years. A listing of certain high-priced, high-quality, and limited-production cars were designated as "Classic Cars," and the period of 1925 to 1942 was chosen as the "Classic Era." It was felt that cars built prior to 1925 had not yet reached technical maturity, and that after World War II, the quality of most so-called luxury cars had succumbed to the economic pressures of mass production. Some pictures of Classic Cars are provided in Exhibit 1.

Over the years, the list of CCCA-recognized Classic Cars was modified and expanded, and the time period was extended to 1948 to include certain pre-WWII models that continued in production for a few years after the war. All cars included in the list were of considerably higher price and quality than the mass-production cars of this era, and most had original prices in the $2,000 to $5,000 range. (This was a considerable

---

EXHIBIT 1    **Classic Cars**

1926 Duesenberg (above); 1934 Rolls Royce (top right); 1941 Packard (right).
*Source:* The Classic Car Club of America, Inc.

EXHIBIT 2    **CCCA-Recognized Classic Cars**

| | | |
|---|---|---|
| A.C. | Excelsior* | Minerva* |
| Adler* | Farman* | N.A.G.* |
| Alfa Romeo | Fiat* | Nash* |
| Alvis* | FN* | Packard* |
| Amilcar* | Franklin* | Peerless |
| Armstrong-Siddeley* | Frazier-Nash* | Peugot* |
| Aston Martin* | Hispano-Suiza* | Pierce-Arrow |
| Auburn* | Horch | Railton* |
| Austro-Daimler | Hotchkiss* | Raymond Mays* |
| Ballot* | Hudson* | Renault* |
| Bentley* | Humber* | Reo* |
| Benz* | Invicta | Revere |
| Blackhawk | Isotta-Fraschini | Riley* |
| B.M.W.* | Itala | Roamer* |
| Brewster* | Jaguar* | Rochet Schneider* |
| Brough Superior* | Jensen* | Rohr* |
| Bucciali* | Jordan* | Rolls-Royce |
| Bugatti | Julian* | Ruxton |
| Buick* | Kissell* | Squire |
| Cadillac* | Lagonda* | S.S. and S.S. Jaguar* |
| Chenard-Walcker* | Lanchester* | Stearns-Knight |
| Chrysler* | Lancia* | Stevens-Duryea |
| Cord | La Salle* | Steyr* |
| Cunningham | Lincoln* | Studebaker* |
| Dagmar* | Lincoln Continental | Stutz |
| Daimler* | Locomobile* | Sunbeam* |
| Darracq* | Marmon* | Talbot* |
| Delage* | Maserati* | Talbot-Lago* |
| Delahaye* | Maybach | Tatra* |
| Delaunay Belleville* | McFarlan | Triumph* |
| Doble | Mercedes | Vauxhall* |
| Dorris | Mercedes-Benz* | Voisin |
| Duesenberg | Mercer | Wills St. Claire |
| Du Pont | M.G.* | Willys-Knight* |

*Indicates that only certain models of this make are considered Classic. Some other 1925–1948 custom-bodied cars not listed above may be approved as Classic upon individual application.
*Source:* The Classic Car Club of America, Inc.

amount of money at that time; in 1930 a new Ford Model A [*not* a Classic Car] sold for about $450.) Some of the most luxurious Classic Cars, such as the American Duesenberg, the English Rolls-Royce, the French Hispano-Suiza, and the Italian Isotta-Fraschini, sold when new in the $10,000–$20,000 range! Exhibit 2 lists those cars recognized as Classic Cars by the CCCA in 2000.

## THE COLLECTOR CAR HOBBY

The collector car hobby in the United States is a broad and wide-reaching activity involving a large number of Americans. Basically, a collector car is any automobile owned for purposes other than normal transportation. The most widely-read collector car hobby magazine, *Hemmings Motor News,* had a circulation of about 260,000 in January 2000. Another magazine, *Car Collector,* estimates that nearly one million Americans are interested in old cars. However, a figure of 500,000 would probably be a more conservative estimate of the number of Americans engaged in this hobby.

"Collector car" is a loose term, ranging from turn-of-the-century horseless carriages to modern limited-production cars, such as Italian super-sports cars. Naturally, owners of collector cars enjoy the company of other persons with similar interests, and thus a wide variety of car clubs exist to suit almost any particular segment of this vast hobby. The largest of these clubs, the Antique Automobile Club of America, caters to owners of virtually all cars 25 years old or older and has more than 55,000 members. In contrast, the CCCA has a much narrower collector car focus and, thus, far fewer members.

## CCCA ORGANIZATION AND ACTIVITIES

When the CCCA's 1999 fiscal year ended on December 31, 1999, the club had 5,502 members, as indicated below. Note in Exhibit 3 the drop in membership for 1999.

| | |
|---|---:|
| Active (annual regular membership—2000 dues—$40) | 4,138 |
| Associate (annual, for spouses, no publications—$7) | 1,078 |
| Life (after ten years, one-time fee—$800) | 213 |
| Life Associate (for spouses—$80) | 70 |
| Honorary (famous car designers, etc.) | 3 |
| | 5,502 |

CCCA members receive a variety of benefits. A magazine, *The Classic Car,* is published four times a year. High in quality and well respected by automotive historians, it features 48 pages or more of articles and photos of Classic Cars. A CCCA *Bulletin* is also published eight times a year that contains club and hobby news, technical columns, and members' and commercial ads for Classic Cars, parts, and related items. A further publication is the club's *Handbook and Directory,* published annually. It contains a current listing of members and their Classic Cars, so that club members can locate other members who own similar cars or who live nearby. Commercial car-related advertisements are solicited for this *Handbook and Directory,* and its cost is fully paid for by these advertisements. Advertisements also cover some of the costs of the magazine and bulletin.

The CCCA also sponsors three types of national events each year. The annual meeting in January includes business meetings and a car judging meet and is held in a different location in the United States each year. In April and again in July a series of "Grand Classic" judging meets are held simultaneously in 10 to 12 locations around the country,

EXHIBIT 3    Selected CCCA Membership Data
(At End of Fiscal Year)

| | 1999 | 1998 | 1997 | 1996 | 1995 | 1994 |
|---|---:|---:|---:|---:|---:|---:|
| Active members | 4,138 | 4,182 | 4,164 | 4,307 | 4,310 | 4,333 |
| Associate members | 1,078 | 1,077 | 996 | 1,068 | 1,035 | 1,046 |
| Life members | 213 | 207 | 205 | 201 | 197 | 198 |
| Life associate members | 70 | 69 | 66 | 66 | 63 | 59 |
| Honorary members | 3 | 3 | 5 | 5 | 5 | 5 |
| Total | 5,502 | 5,538 | 5,436 | 5,647 | 5,610 | 5,641 |

*Source:* The Classic Car Club of America, Inc.

with a total of 400 to 600 Classic Cars being exhibited and judged. At CCCA judging meets, cars are rated by a point system that takes into account the quality and authenticity of restoration and the general condition of the car, both mechanically and cosmetically. Judging meets are not usually publicized to the general public, and access to the cars is generally restricted to club members and their guests.

Each year the club sponsors several "Classic CARavans" in various parts of the United States and Canada. The CARavan is a tour in which members in as many as 100 Classic Cars join together in a week-long (occasionally longer) planned itinerary.

The annual meeting, Grand Classics meets, and CARavans are designed to be financially self-supporting; attending members pay fees that cover the costs of the events.

The CCCA also has members who have volunteered to be technical advisors to other members. Furthermore, the club sells to members certain club-related products, such as hats, ties, shirts, and umbrellas with a Classic Car design. In still another member-oriented venture, the CCCA in 1990 commissioned its publications editor to edit a 750-page hardcover book with members' photos and stories of their Classic Cars. This book was sold to members and, through bookstores, to the general public and has brought in additional revenue to the CCCA.

The club is managed by a 15-member board of directors, with a president, vice presidents, treasurer, secretary, etc. All officers are club member volunteers (from all over the United States) who have shown a willingness and ability to help run the CCCA and have been elected by the total membership to three-year terms of office. They are not reimbursed for their expenses, which include attending eight board meetings each year, most of which are held at club headquarters in a club-owned office condominium in Des Plaines, Illinois (a site chosen because of its central location within the United States and its close proximity to Chicago's airports). Another member volunteers as "executive administrator" and oversees the club's employees and its daily operations. The only paid employees are a full-time office secretary, a part-time clerical worker, and the publications editor, who is a freelance automotive writer and editor. An organization chart of the CCCA is shown in Exhibit 4.

In addition to belonging to the national CCCA, the majority of members also pay dues to a local chapter. In 2000 there were 26 regional offices throughout the United States (see Exhibit 5). Each region sponsors a variety of local activities for members and their Classic Cars and publishes its own magazine or newsletter. Many of the regions also derive revenues from the sale of Classic Car replacement parts or service items that are offered to all members of the national club.

Legally separate from the CCCA and its regional offices, a Classic Car Club of America Museum also exists. It is part of a larger old car museum in Hickory Corners, Michigan, and displays a variety of Classic cars that have been donated to it. The CCCA Museum, unlike the CCCA itself, is eligible to receive tax-deductible gifts of money and property (such as cars). Although the CCCA has granted the museum the right to use the CCCA name, the museum has a separate board of trustees and is run independently of the club. Thus, the club's directors do not have the authority to make strategic decisions for the museum, nor can the museum's performance and finances directly benefit the club.

## SOME CURRENT CONCERNS THAT FACE THE CCCA

Although the officers and directors of the CCCA believe the club to be strong, both financially and in its value to its members, a variety of concerns about the future exist.

One concern involves the use of the word "Classic" as it refers to collector cars. The CCCA uses this term to denote the specific listing of 1925–1948 luxury cars that the

**EXHIBIT 4** **2000 CCCA Organization Chart**

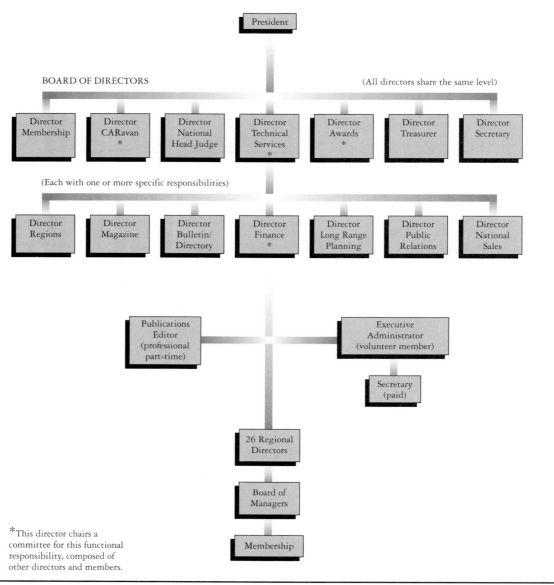

club has designated as "Classic Cars," many other car hobbyists use the term more loosely to refer to any collector car that they see as special. Thus, one can find the word "Classic" used to describe 1928 Fords and 1955 Chevrolets. Although the CCCA cannot legally protect and limit the hobby's use of "Classic," the club is in the process of registering the terms "Full Classic" (a CCCA-designated Classic Car with its original body and motor) and "Modified Classic" (a Classic Car chassis with a replica body or historically incorrect motor). It is hoped that this trademark registration will help to protect the term "Classic" as used by the club.

EXHIBIT 5    Boundaries of Regions of Classic Car Club of America

*Source:* The Classic Car Club of America, Inc.

Another concern is the effect of rising costs upon the club's ability to maintain its current level of services and benefits to the membership. In particular, the cost of publications and headquarters office administration have risen considerably over the years. The board of directors has responded by both watching costs carefully and by raising annual dues several times (from $10 in the 1960s to the current $40 per year), but it recognizes that certain cost increases are unavoidable and that raising dues too high may result in a loss of members. (Financial statements are provided in Exhibits 6 and 7.)

One way to overcome this problem is to increase the number of members and thus create greater revenues. The number of members who pay full dues has remained about the same over the years (see Exhibit 3). The directors know that many Classic Car owners do not belong to the CCCA. Although CCCA members owned about 8000 Classic Cars in 2000, no one really knows how many Classic Car owners are not in the club. Club efforts in recent years to increase membership have been targeted at these Classic Car-owning non-CCCA members. Letters have been sent to persons who failed to renew their CCCA membership (about 5 percent–10 percent each year); regional officers have contacted local non-CCCA members known to own Classic Cars; mailings have been sent to Classic Car-owning persons in directories of other old car clubs; articles about CCCA activities as well as a few paid advertisements have been placed in various old car hobby magazines, and membership ads have been placed in single-marque car clubs (such as the

EXHIBIT 6    CCCA Statements of Receipts and Disbursements (Cash Flow Basis)

| | FY1999 | FY1998 | FY1997 | FY1996 |
|---|---|---|---|---|
| **Receipts** | | | | |
| Active Membership Dues (dues received for current FY) | $ 17,302 | $ 17,367 | $ 44,104 | $ 55,033 |
| Prepaid Active Dues (dues received for next FY) | 152,440 | 148,694 | 151,266 | 85,134 |
| Associate Membership Dues | 712 | 788 | 1,891 | 2,280 |
| Prepaid Associate Dues | 6,830 | 6,733 | 6,746 | 3,395 |
| Life Memberships | 6,400 | 4,000 | 5,433 | 0 |
| Life Associate Memberships | 240 | 555 | 80 | 0 |
| Publications Sales | 2,912 | 1,499 | 1,821 | 1,726 |
| Awards Income (member registration fees for meets, etc.) | 10,831 | 9,360 | 11,992 | 9,883 |
| Caravan Income | 14,500 | 22,600 | 33,700 | 33,676 |
| National Sales Items | 6,253 | 4,920 | 6,499 | 4,850 |
| Insurance Income (from regions) | 3,540 | 3,618 | 3,490 | 4,420 |
| Book Income | 988 | 7,503 | 15,909 | 18,403 |
| Advertising Income-Bulletin | 28,205 | 21,385 | 22,465 | 23,236 |
| Advertising Income-Magazine | 1,465 | 1,500 | 1,500 | 2,300 |
| Advertising Income-Directory | 16,550 | 20,350 | 22,100 | 14,200 |
| Interest Income | 11,902 | 8,127 | 19,973 | 11,539 |
| Miscellaneous Income | 10,852 | 8,224 | 4,157 | 1,563 |
| **Total Receipts** | $291,922 | $287,223 | $353,126 | $271,638 |
| **Disbursements** | | | | |
| Membership Expense (recruitment) | $ 13,059 | $ 6,721 | $ 899 | $ 2,760 |
| Annual Meeting Expense | 2,015 | 3,459 | 2,575 | 5,938 |
| Awards Expense (meets, etc.) | 23,085 | 23,866 | 13,927 | 4,970 |
| Caravan Expense | 7,895 | 15,747 | 21,720 | 15,979 |
| National Sales Items | 1,725 | 10,052 | 2,160 | 781 |
| Book Expense | 11,061 | 3,073 | 0 | 70 |
| Bulletin Editor Fee | 13,537 | 13,392 | 15,311 | 12,276 |
| Bulletin Printing | 35,922 | 40,258 | 44,291 | 43,372 |
| Magazine Editor Fee | 10,700 | 14,641 | 12,240 | 12,135 |
| Magazine Printing | 81,004 | 51,631 | 53,139 | 49,464 |
| Directory Printing | 15,045 | 15,439 | 16,397 | 15,675 |
| General Administration supplies, (postage telephone etc.) | 29,755 | 19,424 | 25,331 | 24,483 |
| Office (wages, condo expense) | 36,106 | 45,523 | 31,486 | 34,238 |
| Insurance | 8,366 | 7,859 | 6,584 | 4,832 |
| Professional Services | 5,445 | 5,650 | 6,996 | 2,670 |
| Miscellaneous Expenses | 7,727 | 3,976 | 10,204 | 5,977 |
| **Total Expenses** | 302,447 | 280,771 | 263,260 | 235,620 |
| **Excess Receipts Over Disbursements (Deficit)** | $ (10,525) | $ 6,452 | $ 89,866 | $ 36,018 |

*Note:* Certain unusual one-time receipts and disbursements omitted.
*Source:* The Classic Car Club of America, Inc., 1999.

EXHIBIT 7    CCCA Balance Sheets

|  | FY1999 | FY1998 | FY1997 | FY1996 |
|---|---|---|---|---|
| **Assets** | | | | |
| Bank balance | $ 25,550 | $ 30,957 | $  8,685 | $ 28,970 |
| Investments (at cost) | | | | |
|   (money market funds, govt. notes, etc.) | | | | |
|   (includes life membership fund) | 322,992 | 293,019 | 385,700 | 256,743 |
| Office condominium | 151,968 | 154,698 | 84,968 | 84,968 |
| Total Assets | $500,510 | $478,674 | $479,353 | $370,681 |
| **Liabilities** | 0 | 0 | 0 | 0 |
| **Owners' Equity** | $500,510 | $478,674 | $479,353 | $370,681 |

*Source:* The Classic Car Club of America, Inc., 1999.

Packard Club) in return for allowing those clubs to place their membership ads in the CCCA's publications.

Furthermore, even though some CCCA members do not own Classic Cars, most do, since much of the pleasure of belonging to the club comes from participating in various activities with a Classic Car. Thus, Classic enthusiasts who do not own a Classic Car might be appropriate targets for CCCA new membership recruitment efforts, but the primary focus has been on persons currently owning a Classic Car.

The club's membership recruitment efforts have only been moderately successful. New members have offset the annual 5 percent to 10 percent attrition rate, but total membership has risen only slightly in recent years. Yet, unless the listing of recognized Classic Cars is expanded, the number of Classic Cars in existence is fixed, and with it, by and large, is the number of Classic Car owners.

There are varying opinions within the CCCA with regard to expanding the current listing of Classic Cars, and there are two directions for such an expansion. One way is to include further makes and models within the current 1925–1948 limits. Another way is to include those cars built before 1925 or after 1948.

Several times in recent years, the board of directors has voted to add additional models of existing Classic makes to the CCCA's 1925–1948 listing (for example, by adding a Packard model line that was slightly lower in original price to already-listed model lines of the same year). No new makes of cars have been added in recent years. Any additions have drawn a mixed reaction from the membership. Some members feel that such additions dilute the meaning of "Classic Car," but most other members either seem to support the directors' decisions or have no strong opinion.

More controversial is the issue of expanding the listing to before 1925 or after 1948. Some members support a pre-1925 listing, but more members seem to favor a post-1948 expansion. They say that high-quality cars built after 1948 should also be considered "Classic." Furthermore, they argue that the club is currently not attracting young members (only 13 percent of CCCA members are under forty-five) because younger people are less able to afford the cost of a Classic and are unable to "identify" with a 1925–1948 car as they might with a car of the 1950s or 1960s. Although current prices of Classic Cars vary greatly, depending upon the make, condition, and type of body, all prices rose significantly in the 1970s and 1980s (but leveled off or dropped a little in the 1990s). Also, many current CCCA members own Classic Cars out of nostalgia for the cars of their youth.

On the other hand, most members of the board of directors, argue against the expansion of the list of Classic Cars beyond 1948. The primary argument is that a Classic Car is more than just a high-quality luxury car. Rather, it is the product of a "Classic Era," when the truly wealthy lived a lifestyle separate from the rest of the population, and an elite group of auto makers and custom body craftsmen were willing and able to produce cars for this upper-class lifestyle. By the end of World War II, it is argued, social upheavals ended this lifestyle, and economic pressures closed down the custom body builders and most of the independent luxury car makers, with the remaining luxury cars generally becoming simply bigger, heavier, and better-appointed versions of other cars made by multiline manufacturers. Thus, expanding beyond 1948 would alter the basic focus, purpose, and "philosophy" of the club, and it is this narrow focus that differentiates the CCCA from other clubs and thus makes it so attractive and important to its members. Furthermore, it is argued, although a few truly special car models were made after 1948, the quantities produced were very small, and the addition of these cars to the CCCA listing would bring in very few new members to the club.

Beyond the Board's concerns about the meaning and usage of the term "Classic Car" and the future financial strength of the club, there is also a concern about the use of members' Classic Cars and the nature of CCCA activities. As previously mentioned, the prices of Classic Cars have risen significantly over the years. In 1952, when the club was founded, most people viewed Classic Cars as simply "old cars," which could generally be bought for a few hundred to a few thousand dollars. Today, many view Classic Cars as major investment items, and professional dealers and auctions are a significant factor in the market place. Although some less exotic and unrestored Classic Car models can be found for under $15,000, most sell for $20,000–$75,000, and the most desirable Classic Cars (convertible models with custom bodies, 12- and 16-cylinder engines, etc.) can sell for $100,000 and more. (A very small number of especially exotic and desirable Classic Cars have sold in the $250,000–$1,000,000 range, and a 1929 Bugatti Royale reportedly sold in 1987 for over $9.8 million!) Furthermore, judging meets have become very serious events, with high scores adding significantly to a Classic Car's sales value. Thus, many highly desirable or top-scoring Classic Cars are now hardly driven at all and are transported in enclosed trailers to and from judging meets. Most Classic Car owners still enjoy driving their cars, and the CCCA CARavans continue to be highly popular among club members, but some members yearn for the "old days" when there was less emphasis on judging and on a car's value and when CCCA members would drive and park their Classic Cars anywhere.

Still another concern of some members involves the possibility of a greater stress in the future on gasoline conservation in this country. If the country did focus more seriously on its high consumption of gasoline, how would the public view Classic Cars and the collector car hobby in general? Would the ownership and driving of cars for non-transportation purposes be considered unpatriotic or wasteful?

## MEMBERSHIP SURVEY

In response to these various concerns, the CCCA Board of Directors established a long-range planning committee to study issues about the future of the club and to make recommendations to the Board. In 1983 and again in 1991, a questionnaire was sent to all members along with their membership renewal material. The response rate was excellent. Exhibit 8 presents the 1991 questionnaire and a tabulation of quantifiable responses, along with a comparison to the 1983 survey responses.

EXHIBIT 8  **Classic Car Club of America 1991 Questionnaire Response Survey, with 1983 Comparative Responses as Available and Applicable (all percents based on those answering)**

1. I have been a member of the CCC:

   | | | | |
   |---|---|---|---|
   | 1991 | 8% less than 2 years | 19% 2–5 years | 20% 5–10 years | 53% more than 10 years |
   | (1983) | 11% less than 2 years | 20% 2–5 years | 18% 5–10 years | 51% more than 10 years |

2. My age is:

   | | | | | | |
   |---|---|---|---|---|---|
   | 1991 | 0% under 25 | 3% 25–34 | 10% 35–44 | 24% 45–54 | 32% 55–64 | 31% 65 or over |
   | (1983) | 1% under 25 | 3% 25–24 | 17% 35–44 | 30% 45–54 | 28% 55–64 | 22% 65 or over |

3. My age when joining CCCA was:

   | | | | | | |
   |---|---|---|---|---|---|
   | 1991 | 7% under 25 | 19% 25–34 | 25% 35–44 | 26% 45–54 | 17% 55–64 | 5% 65 or over |
   | (1983) | not asked | | | | | |

4. I live in the _____ Region. (Not tabulated in this summary.)

5. I am a member of a CCCA region:

   | | | |
   |---|---|---|
   | 1991 | 76% yes | 24% no |
   | (1983) | 69% yes | 31% no |

   If yes, which region: 15% Michigan, 13% So. Cal., 6.4% Pac. NW, others less than 6%.

   If not, why not? Of those responding here (54% of those who answered "no"): 30% indicated distance, 21% no time, 13% no Classic or not running, 8% not invited or didn't kow about it, 9% not interested, 3% lack of activities, and 16% miscellaneous of less than 2% each.

6. I have attended:

   | 1991 | (1983) | |
   |---|---|---|
   | 74% | (64%) | One or more Grand Classics |
   | 27% | (19%) | One or more National CCCA CARavans |
   | 34% | (24%) | One or more Annual Meetings |
   | 65% | (52%) | One or more Regional events |
   | 13% | — | None of the above |

7. I belong to how many other car clubs:

   | | Average | 0 | 1 | 2 | 3 | 4 | 5 | 6–9 | 10 or more |
   |---|---|---|---|---|---|---|---|---|---|
   | 1991 | 3 | 8% | 18% | 22% | 19% | 12% | 9% | 11% | 2% |
   | (1983) | 3 | 9% | 19% | 23% | 17% | 12% | 7% | 11% | 2% |

   I am more active in some of these clubs than I am in CCCA:

   | | | |
   |---|---|---|
   | 1991 | 42% yes | 58% no |
   | (1983) | 44% yes | 56% no |

   If yes, why? Of those responding here (84% of those who answered "yes"): 22% prefer a one-marque club, 21% indicated distance, 16% interested in other clubs, 10% also interested in nonclassics, 10% want more activities, 8% don't own Classic or not running, and 13% miscellaneous of 3% or less.

8. Compared to other clubs, the CCCA is:

   | | | | | |
   |---|---|---|---|---|
   | 1991 | 32% the best | 47% better than most | 20% average | 1% poor |
   | (1983) | 31% the best | 47% better than most | 21% average | 1% poor |

9. Compared to other clubs, the value I receive for my CCCA dues is:

   | | | | | |
   |---|---|---|---|---|
   | 1991 | 29% the best | 42% better than most | 28% average | 1% poor |
   | (1983) | 27% the best | 40% better than most | 31% average | 3% poor |

10. Overall, I rate *The Classic Car Magazine*:

    | | | | | |
    |---|---|---|---|---|
    | 1991 | 74% excellent | 23% good | 3% fair | 0% poor |
    | (1983) | 74% excellent | 24% good | 1% fair | 0% poor |

11. Overall, I rate the *CCCA Bulletin*:

    | | | | | |
    |---|---|---|---|---|
    | 1991 | 55% excellent | 39% good | 6% fair | 0% poor |
    | (1983) | 35% excellent | 51% good | 13% fair | 1% poor |

*Continued*

EXHIBIT 8 **Classic Car Club of America 1991 Questionnaire Response Survey,**
**with 1983 Comparative Responses as Available and Applicable**
**(all percents based on those answering)** *(continued)*

12. With regard to the CCCA listing of recognized Classic cars:

| 1991 | (1983) | |
|------|--------|---|
| 63% | (69%) | I basically think the current listing is good. |
| 32% | (28%) | I think the listing should be expanded. |
| 5% | (3%) | I think the listing should be reduced. |

Of those commenting (31%) and desiring change: 26% accept newer cars, 18% accept others in Classic era, 7% accept older cars, 11% eliminate some current Classics, 7% 1925–1948 year span, and 31% other of less than 5% each.

13. With regard to the scoring currently used and at Grand Classics and Annual Meetings:

| 1991 | (1983) | |
|------|--------|---|
| 82% | (85%) | I basically think the current system is good. |
| 18% | (14%) | I think the system could be improved. If so, how? |

Of those commenting (only 10%): 19% judging/scoring, 10% more points, 10% drive cars before judging, 8% recognize original cars, 11% better judges, etc., and 42% misc. of 5% or less.

14. Overall I would rate the Grand Classics as:

| 1991 | 46% excellent | 32% good | 3% fair | 1% poor | 18% don't know |
|------|---------------|----------|---------|---------|----------------|
| (1983) | 50% excellent | 30% good | 2% fair | 1% poor | 17% don't know |

or 100% basis without "don't know"

| 1991 | 56% excellent | 39% good | 4% fair | 1% poor | _____ |
|------|---------------|----------|---------|---------|-----------|
| (1983) | 61% excellent | 36% good | 2% fair | 1% poor | _____ |

15. Overall I would rate the Annual Meetings as:

| 1991 | 21% excellent | 23% good | 2% fair | 0% poor | 54% don't know |
|------|---------------|----------|---------|---------|----------------|
| (1983) | 15% excellent | 22% good | 5% fair | 0% poor | 59% don't know |

or 100% basis without "don't know"

| 1991 | 46% excellent | 50% good | 4% fair | 0% poor | _____ |
|------|---------------|----------|---------|---------|-----------|
| (1983) | 35% excellent | 53% good | 12% fair | 0% poor | _____ |

16. Overall I would rate the CARavans as:

| 1991 | 32% excellent | 11% good | 1% fair | 0% poor | 56% don't know |
|------|---------------|----------|---------|---------|----------------|
| (1983) | 28% excellent | 16% good | 2% fair | 0% poor | 54% don't know |

or 100% basis without "don't know"

| 1991 | 73% excellent | 25% good | 2% fair | 0% poor | _____ |
|------|---------------|----------|---------|---------|-----------|
| (1983) | 61% excellent | 35% good | 3% fair | 1% poor | _____ |

17. The CCCA has not associated itself with automobile auctions. How do you feel about this policy?

| [1991] | 62% strongly agree | 21% agree | 4% disagree | 3% strongly disagree | 9% don't know |
|--------|--------------------|-----------|-------------|----------------------|---------------|

or 100% basis without "don't know"

| [1991] | 69% strongly agree | 23% agree | 4% disagree | 3% strongly disagree |
|--------|--------------------|-----------|-------------|----------------------|

This question was not asked in 1983.

18. I completed the previous CCCA questionnaire sent to members in 1983:

23% yes      37% no      40% don't know

or 100% basis without "don't know"

38% yes      62% no

19. If there is one thing I'd recommend the CCCA *not change,* it would be:
Of those commenting (24%): 26% 1925–1948 year span, 20% publications, 9% quality of cars considered Classic, 8% CARavans, 6% happy with club, 5% Grand Classics, 4% judging/scoring, and 22% other of 3% or less.

20. If there is one thing I'd recommend the CCCA change, it would be:
Of those commenting (25%): 13% accept newer cars, 7% judging/scoring, 6% accept other cars in the Classic era, 4% encourage younger people, 4% CARavans, and 66% miscellaneous 3% or less.

EXHIBIT 8  Classic Car Club of America 1991 Questionnaire Response Survey,
with 1983 Comparative Responses as Available and Applicable
(all percents based on those answering) *(continued)*

21. I think the CCCA could be improved by: (only 15% commenting)
An emphasis on encouraging younger members. A desire to see newer cars accepted, and general happiness with the Club. Many miscellaneous comments too numerous to list.

22. Other comments (only 18% responding)
Principally a general satisfaction with the Club.
Encourage younger people.
Many miscellaneous comments too numerous to list.

*Source:* The Classic Car Club of America, Inc. Used with permission.

## FUTURE DIRECTION OF THE CCCA

As the club's 2000 fiscal year progressed, the CCCA board of directors studied these and other issues. Some issues seemed more important than others and deserved their more immediate attention. And although the 1991 survey clarified some of the opinions of the membership, the Board did not view this survey as a directive that obligated the Board to follow the majority preference in every disputed area.

Beyond the specific concerns discussed above, the officers and directors of the club simply wanted to do a good job. Their fellow members had elected them to keep the club strong and to improve it. They wanted to be proactive as well as reactive; they wanted to be imaginative in their strategic management activities as well as to respond to concerns and issues already raised.

At their regular Board of Directors meeting, the 15 officers and directors of the CCCA asked themselves the following questions:

1. What are the various criteria we should consider when making strategic decisions for the club? How do we balance financial objectives and nonfinancial objectives? Which are primary and which are secondary?

2. How important are, and how should we deal with, rising costs to the club?

3. If we are forced to choose between raising dues or lowering the services provided to the members, which takes priority?

4. Is expansion of the listing of recognized Classic Cars desirable?

5. Which is preferable: adding cars within the 1925–1948 time period or adding cars of earlier or later years? What are the pro's and con's of these alternatives?

6. How important is it to increase the number of members? What are some alternative ways to increase membership?

7. How can younger people be attracted to the CCCA? How important is this? What are some specific strategies to accomplish this?

8. Are there other possible sources of revenue to the club? What might some be?

9. How important is protecting the term "Classic Car"? What else can the CCCA do to further such protection?

10. Were important questions missing in the previous membership surveys? Should they be included in a future survey?

11. Are there other long-range issues or concerns that the club has not yet addressed?

# M. D. ANDERSON BIOMEDICAL SERVICES DEPARTMENT—2000

Paul Reed, Dana Swenson, Ronald Earl, and Joseph Kavanaugh
Sam Houston State University

## HISTORY

www.mdanderson.org

The University of Texas M. D. Anderson Cancer Center is a leading international cancer center and as such provides cutting-edge services in eliminating cancer and allied diseases as significant health problems throughout Texas, the nation, and the world. Developing and maintaining integrated quality programs in patient care, research, education, and prevention helps carries out its mission.

Clinical, inpatient, research, and support centers are all highly specialized and operate under a decentralized organizational structure with regard to biomedical technology management. Each department has the opportunity to manage equipment maintenance programs through contracting with the biomedical services department (BSD), obtaining original equipment manufacturer contracts, or purchasing services from an outside (third-party) service organization. These contracted services are for the repair and maintenance of medical equipment used in the provision of services to the patient population. What is typically not included in such a contract is a program that manages the explosion of technology as new equipment is developed and released for diagnosis and treatment of cancer patients.

Without a centralized technology management program, there has been no coordination of technology decisions. As a result opportunities have been missed to consolidate service contracts, disjointed servicing of technology, duplicate and incomplete equipment control systems, and increased overall maintenance costs. In addition, advancing technology results in increased operator training requirements, greater operational costs, and decreased operational efficiencies.

The biomedical services department of the University of Texas M. D. Anderson Cancer Center is required to function as a business within the institution. Individual departments budget for the use of the biomedical services department and transfer budgeted funds as services are incurred.

For many years, while operating as a competitive service organization within M. D. Anderson, the BSD often developed poor relationships with many of the clinical and research departments. Many customers viewed the services as unresponsive, inappropriate, and potentially unsafe repair practices. Customers thought that the goals of the BSD were not compatible with those of the clinical and research departments.

Individual departments can choose outside services, and in the past several departments, notably surgery and anesthesiology, have done this. Currently these departments are using the in-house service, but the potential for future outside moves exists.

The BSD has undergone significant changes during the past three years in an attempt to remain financially viable while developing a high level of service. A new technology manager was hired 18 months ago, and his influence on the employees and his credibility with the customers have helped to change most of the negative perceptions regarding the BSD. Some actions taken by the technology manager included:

> Development of accurate medical equipment inventory
>
> Integration of quantifiable performance indicators in employee evaluations
>
> Y2K preparations for medical equipment
>
> Specialists assigned to key customer areas (operating rooms and pharmacy)
>
> Development of a risk-based equipment maintenance program to increase efficacy and address the probability of an equipment problem causing an adverse outcome, the severity of the resultant harm to the individuals, the population affected, and any other conditions of use
>
> Participation in new equipment analysis and acquisition
>
> Successful participation and performance in the Joint Commission for the Accreditation of Healthcare Organizations (JCAHO) survey. Successful accreditation is required by the Health Care Finance Administration for Medicare reimbursements.

## STAFFING

Staff for the BSD consists of the technology manager, two clinical engineers (but one of these positions has been vacant since 1995), eleven biomedical equipment technicians, a television technician, a departmental secretary, and a data-entry clerk. Special projects such as updating the serviced equipment inventory for accuracy and the developing good database management practices were completed through the services of summer student externs. In addition, special situations—new operating rooms and electromagnetic interference between pieces of equipment within the rooms—have required expertise and special equipment from other hospitals' biomedical services departments.

## THE EXTERNAL ENVIRONMENT

### The Medical Center Site

University of Texas M. D. Anderson Cancer Center is located within the Texas Medical Center area of Houston. The Texas Medical Center campus is comprised of 42 nonprofit member institutions occupying more than 100 buildings on 675 acres. Together these institutions constitute the world's largest medical and healthcare center for patient care, research, and education. Over 100,000 patients and visitors move through the Medical Center on a daily basis. In addition to M. D. Anderson Cancer Center, the major medical centers within the Medical Center are:

- The Methodist Hospital—one of the largest hospitals in the United States
- Texas Children's Hospital—home to one of the most respected biomedical and telemedicine programs in the world
- St. Luke's Episcopal Hospital—home to the Texas Heart Institute—joint users of the Texas Children's Hospital biomedical services program
- Hermann Hospital and the adjoining University of Texas Medical School
- The Institution of Rehabilitation and Research
- Ben Taub General Hospital

## The Market Area

The market area for the BSD is currently within the M. D. Anderson Cancer Center. Existing customers are broken down as a percentage of total revenues.

| | |
|---|---|
| Pharmacy | 30.6% |
| Surgery | 19.7 |
| Division of nursing | 18.0 |
| Combined clinics | 11.9 |
| Central service | 6.3 |
| Respiratory care | 6.0 |
| Laboratory areas | 4.4 |
| Anesthesia | 3.2 |

Services provided to these areas consist of the repairs and maintenance of 15,602 pieces of equipment in a 437-bed hospital and outpatient clinical facility on a 3.1 million-square-foot campus. All parts and labor (fully loaded to include benefits) are included in the total fiscal year 1998 contract price of $753,856. Normal BSD hours of operation are 7:00 A.M. to 11:00 P.M. and after-hours service is provided through a call-in program. Individual patient care departments in 1998 either used in-house personnel in departments other than biomedical services or contracted outside services, or time and material charges totaling $1,275,844. Research department expenditures are estimated to be approximately $100,000. In addition, the diagnostic imaging department has a contractual arrangement of approximately $2.0 million with General Electric Medical Systems to provide services on computed tomography (a process whereby linked x-ray sensors are connected to a computer, and three-dimensional images assembled from the transmitted data), x-ray, flouroscopy, diagnostic ultrasound, nuclear medicine, and magnetic resonance imaging systems.

## Competitors

Competitors of the BSD are primarily outsourcing companies that provide service functions for a single contract price. Typically the existing in-house service structure is eliminated, and the existing employees are absorbed into the outsourcing company. General Electric Support Services, ServiceMaster, Core, and Premier are but a few of these competing companies. Several competitors have either bought into or developed these business lines within the past three to five years.

In many instances, outsourcing companies approach the hospital CEO, COO, or CFO and offer to evaluate the existing program and develop a proposal to provide the same services. The evaluation of the existing program typically asks for the full disclosure of budgeting information including the in-house biomedical services.

Nationally many biomedical services departments—regardless of whether they charge other departments for their services or are part of hospital operating costs—do not have a good grasp of their costs per service, or they do not market their actual costs well to the institutional top-level financial decision-makers. This lack of knowledge or communication provides fertile ground for competing companies to come into an organization and offer a competitive pricing proposal—often 10 percent to 20 percent lower than the current in-house costs.

The BSD at M. D. Anderson Cancer Center has recognized that the department functions within a competitive market. As such it has required competing companies to develop their proposals based on the amount of equipment serviced and the customers' expectations regarding service coverage and without knowing the actual in-house costs. This philosophy is based on the recognition that any company can underbid a proposal if the competition's price is known. Although the BSD compares with and competes with outsourcing companies on an ongoing basis, the department has not developed a marketing plan that will keep the financial decision-makers informed of the qualitative and quantitative cost-to-benefit ratios.

Competitive companies providing service programs provide more than just cost savings. Most competitors are large national companies, offering equipment maintenance and repairs while offering:

- Expertise through comprehensive company training programs
- Extended tracking of equipment problems and solutions from multiple clients
- Experience of being involved with national organizations
- Flexibility, the ability to provide all or only some of the services required by an institution
- Internal support resources through collaborative technical libraries, training facilities, and equipment specialists
- National equipment evaluation and comparison programs, matching features to needs and best quality to dollar ratios
- A consolidated contracting service in which individual departments do not separately contract with vendors or manufacturers but pay a single annual contract charge
- Buying power through economies of scale; making large purchases on the national level to keep new equipment prices and repair costs down
- Software to maintain equipment inventory, maintenance history, and associated service reports to the customer departments
- Guaranteed maximum contract cost with cost incentive cash rebates if incurred costs go below certain percentages of the total contract cost

## Suppliers

M. D. Anderson participates in a group-purchasing program that keeps equipment and supply costs at reasonable levels. Group purchasing is done at a national level, and economies of scale are enjoyed by the member groups. The BSD is able to take advantage of this program when purchasing parts and supplies.

## Customers

The current customer base for the BSD consists of the clinical and inpatient departments of M. D. Anderson. There is also the potential for joint ventures both internally and external to the BSD. Internally, there are two large customers for a joint venture approach. The diagnostic imaging department, in addition to a large outside service contract, has a small maintenance staff with a separate software tracking system. The BSD is working with the Diagnostic imaging staff to develop a joint equipment inventory and an integrated software system. The unique inventory and software system are in keeping with the JCAHO requirements for medical equipment management—a key item in the accreditation process.

The radiation therapy department also has a small maintenance staff and makes some outside contract arrangements for the repairs, maintenance, and upkeep of radiation equipment—primarily linear accelerators for radiation treatment of cancerous cells. Like the diagnostic imaging department, the radiation therapy department will be approached by the BSD to address collaborative activities.

There is significant potential for either a joint venture or a cooperative arrangement between the biomedical services departments and several healthcare organizations.

Preliminary discussions between the M. D. Anderson biomedical services department and the Texas Children's Hospital biomedical services department are currently taking place. This type of joint venture will capitalize on the equipment expertise in the institutions. In addition, greater economies of scale will exist through the evaluation and joint purchasing of equipment and supplies.

### Labor Pool

The unemployment rate in Houston is very low. Biomedical equipment technicians are not transferring between institutions, and the BSD has been unable to fill two positions for over a year. In addition, the availability of biomedical equipment technicians is very limited on the national level, and it is difficult to convince these skilled individuals to relocate to the Houston area.

Many undergraduate programs and technical colleges are dropping biomedical technician programs and focusing instead on computer and information systems programs, making it difficult for hospitals to recruit new employees. In addition, BSD has found that existing programs often produce weak or poorly trained candidates. One of the best sources for new employees is the military. The military programs are combining training centers, which has resulted in smaller class sizes and, thus, a smaller pool of qualified potential candidates. In order to attract potential employees, BSD's competition is willing to pay a premium price for biomedical technicians. Their pay ranges from 10%–29% more and often includes perks such as vehicles. Many biomedical technicians view employment by BSD's competition negatively because of potential relocation requirements, and they do not feel as if they belong to the healthcare organization. The result is a smaller pool of qualified candidates.

The information services industry is now drawing from the same pool of qualified individuals, further increasing the healthcare competitiveness for the labor pool. Salary differentials of $10,000 per year for inexperienced new hires are not uncommon.

### Regulatory Agencies

Three primary regulatory agencies oversee BSD's area of operations. In order to receive Medicare reimbursement, BSD must be accredited and qualified by JCAHO. To do this, BSD and all healthcare organizations undergo a JCAHO survey process at least once every three years. Compliance with the JCAHO standards is expected on an ongoing basis, and random surveys are possible within the three-year period between scheduled surveys. The mission of the Joint Commission is to improve the quality of healthcare for the public by providing accreditation and related services that support performance improvement in healthcare organizations. The Joint Commission evaluates and accredits more than 18,000 healthcare organizations in the United States, including hospitals, healthcare networks, managed care organizations, and healthcare organizations that provide home care, long-term care, behavioral health care, laboratory, and ambulatory-care services. The Joint Commission is an independent, not-for-profit organization, the nation's oldest and largest standards-setting and healthcare accrediting body.[1]

Laboratories are typically inspected separately under the College of American Pathologists program to improve the quality of laboratory medicine. The scope of these programs, which are critical to the operation of laboratories throughout the United States, is unparalleled. The College has continually remained in the forefront of leading-edge proficiency testing of products and procedural development. The contributions of highly qualified scientific committees ensure the development and introduction of prac-

---

[1]http://www.jcaho.org/pro_idx.htm

tical testing and analytic procedures. And, because committee members are active, practicing pathologists, the College is able to identify emerging technologies and practices and quickly respond with appropriate quality challenges.[2]

The Food and Drug Administration (FDA) is the controlling agency for the Safe Medical Devices Act. Any incident or event that results from either actual or potential failure or misuse of medical equipment is reported to and tracked by the FDA. In addition, the FDA monitors and distributes the medical equipment recall program. The FDA's Center for Devices and Radiological Health is responsible for ensuring the safety and effectiveness of medical devices and eliminating unnecessary human exposure to man-made radiation from medical, occupational, and consumer products. There are thousands of medical devices, from heart pacemakers to contact lenses. Radiation-emitting products regulated by FDA include microwave ovens, video display terminals, and medical ultrasound and x-ray machines. The center accomplishes its mission by

- Reviewing requests to research or market medical devices
- Collecting, analyzing, and acting on information about injuries and other experiences in the use of medical devices and radiation-emitting electronic products
- Setting and enforcing good manufacturing practice regulations and performance standards for radiation-emitting electronic products and medical devices
- Monitoring compliance and surveillance programs for medical devices and radiation-emitting electronic products
- Providing technical and other nonfinancial assistance to small manufacturers of medical devices.[3]

Liability and responsibility issues surrounding any of the regulatory agency findings rest with the healthcare organization regardless of whether the medical equipment services are provided by an in-house or an outside service contract or who owns the equipment. Ownership questions create issues with doctor-owned, leased, rented, or under-evaluation programs.

## THE INTERNAL ENVIRONMENT

### Management

#### *Goals and Objectives*

The BSD's goals and objectives for the past three years include

- Writing and editing the Institutional Safety Policy and Procedures for the Institutional Safety Working Committee to align the BSD's goals and objectives with the facilities mission and vision statements. In addition the writing and editing are expanding upon the JCAHO "Environment of Care" concept—providing a patient-care environment that is safe, clean, and comfortable—at both the department and the facility level, particularly in regard to the medical equipment management program.
- Active participation on institutional steering committees as a medical equipment management resource. These steering committees include the activation team for a new 832,000-square-foot, state-of-the-art, inpatient treatment building; telecommunications, information systems, and nurse call systems; patient physiological monitoring and patient-care information programs; the FDA recall program; and the Y2K equipment management program.

---

[2]http://www.cap.org/html/lip.html

[3]http://www.fda.gov/cdrh/overview.html

- Establishing a "zero-based budget" for the BSD support operations based upon worked hours and parts incurred.
- Increased the effective utilization of computer resources within the BSD and a local area network-based operation.
- Define and initiate a plan to establish and correct the medical equipment software database management system to reach the goal of a viable medical equipment support program (all master databases defined and fully established for the first time in over seven years while adhering to sound database management practices).
- Initiate and activate a quality improvement plan for the University of Texas M. D. Anderson Cancer Center system and, specifically, the medical equipment support program as it pertains to the "Environment of Care" JCAHO accreditation program.
- Initiate and provide an accountability of the BSD equipment support program to the internal customers of the system.

All of these goals were actively in process or nearing completion in 1999. In particular, the BSD was reviewed in a JCAHO survey in October 1998 and received no negative comments; the quality improvement project were highlighted as an institutional example, and the Y2K preparations were applauded by the total University of Texas system.

### Organizational Change

In 1995 the parent organization of the BSD—the M. D. Anderson facilities management division—completed a major engineering redesign. The resultant organization aims for product delivery that is faster, better and less costly than that of any other healthcare facilities management division.

The BSD was not included in the reengineering process, but the BSD board of directors changed effectively. As a result of the noninclusion and the new corporate leadership, the BSD operated in an indeterminate state for over two years—one year as a result of the divisional redesign process, and then another year passed before the technology manager was hired. Many of the employees have been waiting for the other shoe to drop.

The workforce at BSD has been fairly stable. Five individuals have been hired within the past four years, but the remainder of the department has been in place for at least eight years, with four of the employees having 16 or more years of seniority. Overall, including the more recent hires, the BSD staff have an average of 9.3 years of experience with the same company. As one administrative client expresses it, the BSD may provide, ". . . [a] haven for nonproducers who can't make it in [a] competitive environment."

The recruitment of the technology manager was a major step forward for the BSD. This individual had an undergraduate education and a work background in electronic engineering and business administration. He, although well grounded in the development of successful biomedical programs at two other large hospitals, also has worked as an outside support service vendor. As a result, he knows both the workings of a hospital and the competition.

In a recent survey of the BSD, employees were asked specific questions regarding the management, marketing, and production of the company. To provide a basis for comparison, the management team members, the technology manager and an M. D. Anderson customer services manager, were asked the same questions. Recognizing that measures of this type are relative, a Likert scale was used to measure the feelings of these individuals. The composite score for each group is indicated in Exhibit 1.

Note that management's perception of the company's strengths and weaknesses is, in most cases, more accurate than that of the employee. Of particular note are the feelings regarding the organizational structure, the BSD location, and adequate staffing (see

# EXHIBIT 1    Employee Survey

Respondents' were asked to circle the number that most closely matches their feelings from the following scale:

| | Strongly Disagree | Disagree | Neither Agree or Disagree | Agree | Strongly Agree |
|---|---|---|---|---|---|
| | 1 | 2 | 3 | 4 | 5 |
| **Management** | | Employees' Response | Managers' Response | | + (−) |
| 1. Objectives and goals of the biomedical department are measurable and communicated. | | 3.75 | 4.00 | | 0.25 |
| 2. Biomedical managers delegate authority well. | | 3.75 | 4.00 | | 0.25 |
| 3. The department's organizational structure is appropriate. | | 3.12 | 4.50 | | 1.38 |
| 4. Job descriptions and job specifications are clear. | | 3.25 | 4.00 | | 0.75 |
| 5. Employee morale is high. | | 2.5 | 2.00 | | (0.50) |
| 6. Employee turnover and absenteeism are low. | | 2.62 | 3.50 | | 0.88 |
| 7. Employee pay is competitive in the current job market. | | 2.88 | 2.50 | | (0.33) |
| **Marketing** | | | | | |
| 8. The department is positioned well against competitors. | | 3.14 | 3.50 | | 0.36 |
| 9. Product quality and customer service are good. | | 3.88 | 3.50 | | (0.33) |
| 10. Products and services are priced appropriately. | | 4.29 | 4.00 | | (0.29) |
| 11. The customer base has been increasing. | | 4.00 | 3.50 | | (0.50) |
| **Production** | | Employees' Response | Managers' Response | | − |
| 12. The biomedical workspace, equipment, machinery, and offices are in good condition. | | 3.33 | 4.00 | | 0.67 |
| 13. Inventory control policies and procedures are effective. | | 3.00 | 3.50 | | 0.50 |
| 14. Quality control policies and procedures are effective. | | 3.00 | 4.00 | | 1.00 |
| 15. The biomedical facilities, resources, and the customer base are strategically located. | | 2.60 | 4.50 | | 1.90 |
| 16. Biomedical services are adequately staffed for the required services. | | 1.83 | 4.00 | | 2.17 |
| 17. The biomedical department has technological competencies for information systems/telecommunication interfaces. | | 3.00 | 3.00 | | 0.00 |
| 18. The biomedical department has technological competencies for biomedical equipment. | | 3.33 | 3.50 | | 0.17 |

*Source:* M. D. Anderson, Internal Document, 1999

questions 3, 15, and 16). This is an indication that management thinks some areas are proceeding much better than the employees think. However, the employees rate the areas of pay, morale, and an increasing customer base higher than the managers—an indication that the employees are more optimistic than management in some areas (see questions 5, 7, and 11).

The organizational chart (Exhibit 2) of the BSD does not indicate its three vacancies—one clinical engineer and two biomedical technicians. Vacancies were created

EXHIBIT 2    Organizational Structure

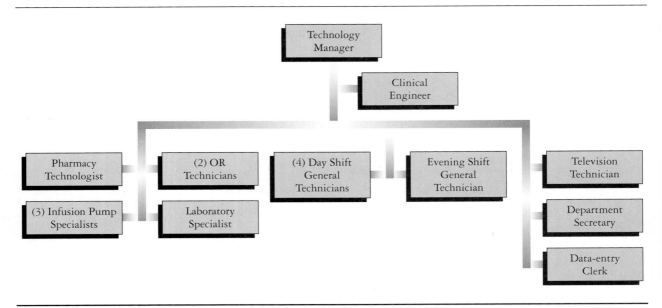

*Source:* M. D. Anderson International Document, 1999.

through attrition and as a result of a disciplinary action. The department has addressed the reduction through increased productivity and efficiency.

### Computer Information Systems

The BSD computer system keeps track of 15,602 individual pieces of biomedical equipment at M. D. Anderson Cancer Center. Each piece of equipment has a unique identifier, and the software is used to manage preventative maintenance on the devices as well as a repair and maintenance history for the equipment.

Equipment history is important for several reasons. First, should any incident involving a patient and a piece of biomedical equipment occur, both M. D. Anderson and the regulatory agencies will want to review the history of the equipment. Next, a risk-based program based on probability of an incident and the impact of the incident uses the database to measure the probability portion of the equation. Finally, life-cycle costs for equipment and timing for equipment replacement are tracked with the BSD computer system.

### Current Events

The efforts to keep the BSD financially viable and the provider of choice for medical equipment repairs and maintenance have recently focused on several key areas.

- Workspace for the BSD was consolidated from several smaller sites in a newly designed and equipped area in 1996. The new space is centralized within the major hospital and clinics facility. In addition, space in the pharmacy has been provided for a technician to work closely with the users, and the new OR suite includes a workroom for critical equipment repairs and maintenance.

- The technology manager clearly defines BSD goals and objectives; he has matched job descriptions and quantifiable performance requirements to the goals and objec-

EXHIBIT 3    Biomedical Services Statement of Operations

|  | FY98-99 | FY97-98 | FY96-97 | FY95-96 |
|---|---|---|---|---|
| **Revenues** | | | | |
| Charges for Services | $ 797,984 | $ 753,856 | $735,824 | $580,595 |
| Maint. & OP. Supplement | 260,864 | 256,531 | 247,861 | 240,641 |
| Gross Sales | $1,058,848 | $1,010,387 | $983,685 | $821,236 |
| **Expenses** | | | | |
| *Payroll Expenses* | | | | |
| Maint. & Op. Payroll | $208,691 | $205,229 | $198,289 | $192,513 |
| Maint. & Op. Benefits | 52,173 | 51,302 | 49,572 | 48,128 |
| Recharge Payroll | 379,894 | 412,346 | 437,696 | 280,950 |
| Overtime | 17,968 | 7,119 | 11,154 | 9,730 |
| Benefits | 94,903 | 108,608 | 118,392 | 61,957 |
| Total Payroll Expense | $753,629 | $784,604 | $815,103 | $593,278 |
| *Maint. & Op. Expenses* | | | | |
| Maintenance and Repairs | 138,752 | 44,372 | 192,267 | 109,712 |
| Non-capital Purchases | 7,800 | 39,016 | 93,879 | 26,957 |
| Hardware/Office Supplies | 13,223 | 1,269 | 5,535 | 3,276 |
| Travel Expense | 364 | 0 | 623 | 0 |
| Services | 13,103 | 1,455 | 106,251 | 197 |
| Medical Supplies | 161 | 0 | 25 | 58 |
| Other Consumables | 8 | 27 | 743 | 8 |
| Telecommunications | 0 | 0 | (774) | 1,479 |
| Total M&O Expenses | $173,411 | $ 86,139 | $ 398,549 | $141,687 |
| Total Expenses | $927,040 | $870,743 | $1,213,652 | $734,965 |
| **Net Income (Loss)** | $131,808 | $139,644 | $ (229,967) | $ 86,271 |

*Source:* M. D. Anderson Internal Document, 1999.

tives and communicates this information to the employees on an ongoing basis. He also delegates the necessary authority to and provides training for employees to meet these goals and objectives. This area alone has played a significant role in increasing customer service and customers' convictions that they are receiving a quality product.

- Product prices and service prices are reviewed on an ongoing basis and compared with the current prices in the marketplace. In addition, the various prices and formulas are reviewed with the customers at least annually.

The BSD has begun a strategic management process and the development of a strategic plan for the future. Customer groups have been asked to provide input to the plan through an open-ended questionnaire. The opinions of the customer base can best be summarized by the response of an anesthesiology physician.

> . . . Biomedical Engineering is undergoing a radical change. In the past, Biomedical Engineering has [sic] the responsibility for maintaining all equipment in the hospital. This was adequate in the early days of medicine where the equipment was fairly simple. It could be repaired quite easily.

With medical equipment based on microprocessors, this function of Biomedical Engineering is becoming more difficult to achieve. New regulations affect reporting and occupy a significant amount of time of the Biomedical Department. My vision of Biomedical Engineering is . . . that Biomedical Engineering is no longer for the actual maintenance of the equipment but is responsible to insure that the maintenance is done and adequately documented. The role is more of a consultative role. . . .

With respect to maintenance, it is my opinion that the Biomedical Engineering Department should do initial diagnostics and troubleshooting of equipment. When it comes to repair of the life support equipment the Biomedical Engineering Department should rely on original equipment manufacturer for maintenance. . . .

In summary, my vision of Biomedical Engineering at M. D. Anderson Cancer Center is twofold. On the higher end, Biomedical Engineering is a consultant to help plan capital equipment purchases and to evaluate the life expectancy of capital equipment. They are there to insure that OEM maintenance is performed, adequately documented, and document all the new requirements for equipment maintenance and testing. They should be responsible for the repair of "small items" that are not life support and under single-fault condition cannot result in patient injury.

As a precursor to strategic planning, the BSD technology manager and members of the M. D. Anderson administrative team have had some cooperative discussions with the biomedical departments of other Texas Medical Center organizations. At this time the discussions have focused on the definition, scope, and functions of a cooperative. The idea is very much in the initial stage, with support limited to only one or two other organizations outside of M. D. Anderson.

Finally, M. D. Anderson administration has recently been contacted by an outside vendor with an offer to provide technology management. The offer includes the standard competitor's benefits to the organization, provides for the maintenance and repair of medical devices in patient care areas, takes over the coordination of all outside contracts for medical devices (original equipment manufacturer and third party), and shifts the current BSD employees to the vendor's payroll.

The total fee for this service is $2,411,500, and the benefit to the organization is broken down as

| | |
|---|---|
| The Vendor's Estimate of BSD's Current Time and Materials Expenses[1] | $1,660,810 |
| The Vendor's Estimate of BSD's Cost of 17 FTE's | 877,307 |
| The Vendor's Estimate of Other MDACC Expenses[2] | 381,271 |
| The Vendor's Estimate of Total Annual Expenses | 2,919,388 |
| Vendor's Fee | 2,411,500 |
| Estimated Savings to M. D. Anderson | $  507,888 |

[1]Miscellaneous parts and time and material charges based on BSD charges and outside contract charges of $906,954.
[2]This number is a vendor estimate based on national averages for ventilators, anesthesia equipment, sterilizers, surgical tables, laminar flow hoods, patient beds, and two-way radios. This does not include research, diagnostic imaging, or radiation therapy.

Considering the external environment, the internal environment, and the customers' vision of the biomedical services department, should M. D. Anderson accept the proposal and divest itself of the in-house service, continue with BSD in its current form, or pursue some other form of medical equipment technology management?

# QUORUM HEALTH GROUP, INC.—2000

Teresa DeWitt Dullaghan
Francis Marion University

**QHGI**

www.quorumhealth.com

As the public demands more accountability, healthcare providers must continuously research consumers' needs, preferences, and practices to keep pace with trends of the future. Beginning in 1977 as a hospital management contract company, Quorum Health Group, Inc., has a competitive advantage because of its strong reputation for implementing marketed-oriented strategies and efficient management of healthcare costs. Quorum's size advantages contribute to purchase contracts at lower cost, creating economies of scales.

Headquartered in Brentwood, Tenn, Quorum Health Group, Inc. is one of the top ten leading providers in the United States, and its subsidiary Quorum Health Resources, LLC, is the nation's largest healthcare manager of not-for-profit hospitals. Note, in Exhibit 1, that Quorum's net operating revenues from 1998 to 1999 increased 5.1 percent to $1.65 billion, whereas net income decreased 55 percent to $38.9 million in 1999. Quorum's net operating expenses from 1998 to 1999 increased 10.9 percent to $1.39 billion.

In fiscal 1999 and fiscal 1998, Quorum Health Group, acquired six hospitals. In addition to the acquisitions, a majority-owned subsidiary of Quorum Health Group, Inc., and a subsidiary of Columbia/HCA formed a joint venture in a hospital contributed by Columbia/HCA in Vicksburg, Mississippi and one by Quorum. As manager of River Region Health System, Quorum Health Group, Inc., and subsidiaries have a majority equity interest in the joint venture.

EXHIBIT 1    Quorum's Financial Performance

(in millions, except per-share amount)

|  | 1999 | 1998 | 1997 | 1996 |
|---|---|---|---|---|
| Net operating revenues | $1652.6 | $1572.4 | $1413.9 | $1098.5 |
| Income before extraordinary item | 38.9 | 86.7 | 84.1 | 69.2 |
| Net income | $ 38.9 | $ 86.7 | $ 75.9 | $ 69.2 |
| EPS | −52.8% | 1.1% | 1.0% | — |
| **GROWTH RATES IN PERCENT** |  |  |  |  |
| Total operating revenues | 5.10% | 11.20% | 2.87% | 29.22% |
| Net income | −55.17 | 14.23 | 9.61 | 23.73 |
| Expense | 10.77 | 10.85 | 29.52 | 28.30 |

*Source:* Quorum's 1999 Annual Report.

Quorum owns 21 acute care hospitals, manages more than 220 hospitals, and has 100 consulting contracts. Quorum is also a partner in joint ventures comprised of four hospitals in Macon, Georgia, and three hospitals in Las Vegas, Nevada. Quorum operates in more than 40 states and the District of Columbia. The Quorum Health Group's corporate mission statement and values are as follows:

> Quorum owns and manages healthcare systems and is committed to meeting the needs of consumers and providers through innovative services that enhance the delivery of quality healthcare.
> We operate with personal and business integrity.
> We demonstrate respect for all people.
> We believe in developing the potential for our associates.
> We are committed to our customers.
> We believe in continued improvement and learning.
> We have a responsibility to our shareholders.
> (Quorum Health Group, Inc., 1999 *Annual Report,* p. 1).

## QUORUM HISTORY

As indicated in Exhibit 2, HCA Management Company (now Quorum Health Resources, LLC, a subsidiary of Quorum Health Group, Inc.) was formed in 1977. Hospital Corporation of America (HCA) provided efficient management services to healthcare service organizations; however, after 12 years, the investment firm of Welsh, Carson, Anderson & Stowe, senior management, and employees led a buy-out in 1989. The result of the 1989 HCA spin-off was the formation of Quorum Health Group, Inc. (QHGI). The company spin-off from HCA is known today as its subsidiary, Quorum Health Resources, LLC, the largest for-profit management company in the nation. Ultimately, in 1993, HCA was acquired by the largest for-profit health service organization known today as Columbia/HCA. Columbia/HCA is also headquartered in Brentwood, Tennessee. Columbia/HCA Healthcare Corp., Quorum's competitor and partner in three joint ventures, is the largest healthcare corporation in the United States.

EXHIBIT 2    **History of Quorum Health Group, Inc.**

| Year | Event |
| --- | --- |
| 1977 | Formation of HCA Management Company (now Quorum Health Resources, LLC) |
| 1989 | Welsh, Carson, Anderson & Stowe and management-led buyout |
| 1990 | Acquisition of Park View Regional Medical Center in Vicksburg, Mississippi |
| 1992 | Placement of $100 million senior subordinated notes due 2002 |
| 1993 | Acquisition of 10 Charter Medical Corporation acute care Hospitals; $300 million bank credit facility |
| 1994 | Initial public offering of 7.2 million shares at $15 per share |
| 1995 | Placement of $150 million senior subordinated notes due 2005 and $600 million bank credit facility |
| 1996 | Revenues exceed $1 billion |
| 1997 | $850 million unsecured bank credit facility; tender offer for 11 7/8 percent senior subordinated notes; three-for-two stock split; added $150 leasing facility |
| 1998 | Board authorization of stock repurchase program to buy back up to 8 million shares |
| 1999 | Completion of the newly constructed, $98 million, state-of-the art medical facility known as Carolinas Hospital System in Florence, South Carolina; $150 million of convertible subordinated debentures sold to Welsh, Carson, Anderson & Stowe. |

*Source:* www.quorumhealth.com

## EXHIBIT 3    Selected Operating Data

|  | 1999 | 1998 | 1997 |
|---|---|---|---|
| Payor Mix |  |  |  |
| Private and other | 48.1% | 45.3% | 44.9% |
| Medicare | 45.9 | 47.2 | 47.5 |
| Medicaid | 8.0 | 7.5 | 7.6 |
| Occupancy |  |  |  |
| Number of owned hospitals | 21 | 17 | 19 |
| Number of licensed beds | 4,551 | 3,968 | 4,205 |
| Admissions | 136,058 | 128,235 | 119,551 |
| Patient days | 764,184 | 713,906 | 666,353 |

*Source:* Quorum Health Group, Inc. *Annual Report,* p. 12.

Quorum's expertise in management and consulting gave this new organization the competitive advantage in creating Quorum Health Group, Inc. As indicated in Exhibit 3, Quorum Health Group, acquired its first hospital, ParkView Regional Medical Center in Vicksburg, Mississippi, in 1990. Since 1990, Quorum's growth strategies have remained consistent over the ten years of the company's history.

## EXTERNAL FACTORS

### The U.S. Healthcare Industry

In the past 20 years, American healthcare has been increasingly isolated from market forces that have pressured other industries to become more efficient and provide excellent customer services. However, market forces have now been present for more than ten years in the form of managed care, government program payment reductions, escalating national healthcare costs, payor-required pre-admission authorization, and competition. Healthcare spending is expected to rise as a share of gross domestic product from about 14 percent in 1999 to an estimated 16.6 percent by year 2007 (Health Care Financing Administration, Bureau of Economic Analysis).

Continuing cost containment measures imposed by Medicare and Medicaid programs and private payors over the last couple of years have placed enormous economic strains on many health service organizations as they have attempted to operate in an increasingly competitive environment. Despite aging of the baby boomers in the United States, hospital admission rates are predicted to continue to decline. Medicare and Medicaid patients make up approximately 30 percent to 50 percent or more of most hospitals' payor mix. As healthcare costs rise, Medicare and Medicaid diagnosis-related group reimbursement rates are declining more rapidly than the cost of goods and services is increasing. HSOs are threatened by escalating costs of healthcare and the low diagnosis-related group reimbursement rates for inpatient services.

### Evolution of Government Intervention to Manage Healthcare Costs

Many regulatory controls have been implemented to slow the rapid rate of inflation of healthcare costs. The Health Care Financing Administration is responsible for administering Medicare and Medicaid. It establishes a flat fixed rate each year for each Medicare and Medicaid inpatient admission based on his or her diagnosis.

Before the initiation of this provider payment system in 1983, providers' reimbursements for patients were based on costs, and there were few incentives for hospital efficiency. Upon implementation of the provider payment system by the Health Care Financing Administration in 1983, hospitals had to be certain their average costs per diagnosis-related group did not exceed the Administration's rates. Cost containment and efficiency within the hospital became the focus for health service organizations. Their managers and physicians began focusing more on improving quality in order to eliminate unnecessary testing and procedures and shorten the patient's length of stay.

## The Future of the Healthcare Industry

Congress is continuously trying to reduce Medicare costs, primarily by reducing diagnosis-related group payments to health service organizations. Initiated in 1997, the Balanced Budget Act of 1997 is mandating lower payment reimbursements from Medicare and Medicaid and will continue to contribute additional cost reduction pressures on health service organizations and has implemented reductions in home health services' payments and the transition of these services to a provider payment system since October 1, 1999. Implementation of an Medicare outpatient provider payment system is projected for June 2000. This implementation will create an enormous negative impact on outpatient revenues. In addition to the reductions listed above, numerous declining reimbursement mandates will continue to be implemented over the next couple of years.

Diagnosis-related group reimbursement rates are adjusted annually in October. In 1997 these rates increased 2 percent; in 1998, they did not change, and in 1999, they increased only by 0.5 percent and had created a devastating effect on for-profit as well as not-for-profit healthcare organizations. A 1.1 percent diagnosis-related group reimbursement rate increase is expected for 2000. Declining reimbursement rates and other federal interventions to manage healthcare costs are creating tremendous uncertainties for the healthcare industry. As indicated by the industry and Medicare payment structures in Exhibit 3, acute care hospital margins peaked in 1998 and are expected to decline for the next several years.

## Hospital Licensing

To sustain and improve quality in healthcare, hospitals are subject to periodic inspections by federal, state, and local authorities to determine their compliance with applicable regulations and standards. Compliance must be demonstrated in order to maintain licensure and to participate as a certified healthcare provider in the Medicare and Medicaid programs. All of Quorum's hospitals are licensed under appropriate states laws and are certified.

EXHIBIT 4    **Top Competitors Among Acute Healthcare For-Profit Service Organizations**

| Symbol | Company Name | Market Cap ($000) |
|--------|--------------|-------------------|
| COL | Columbia/HCA Healthcare Corp. | $1,276,885 |
| THC | Tenet Healthcare | 6,249,557 |
| HMA | Health Management Assoc. | 1,916,012 |
| UHS | Universal Health Services | 781,754 |
| QHGI | Quorum Health Group, Inc. | 483,970 |
| TRIH | Triad HOSP, Inc. | 385,271 |
| LPNT | Lifepoint HOSP, Inc. | 242,078 |
| PRHC | Providence Healthcare Corp. | 182,838 |
| PLS | Paracelsus Healthcare Corp. | 37,894 |

*Source:* www.quicken.com

## Competition

Quorum ranks fifth among the leaders in market capitalization for acute healthcare for-profit service organizations as indicated in Exhibit 4. Exhibit 5 summarizes the financial performances of Quorum's competitors. Health Management Associates (HMA) appears to be closest in size to QHGI. Note in Exhibit 6, that HMA has the lowest debt ratio. Note in Exhibit 6, that Quorum's total debt-to-equity ratio of 1.40 is higher in comparison to HMA, Universal Health Services (UHS), Columbia/HCA (COL), and Tenet Healthcare (THC). Quorum's higher debt is a result of its aggressive long-term growth strategies of acquiring at least two healthcare systems each year.

### EXHIBIT 5    Financial Comparisons ($ in millions)

| Competitors | Quorum Health Group, Inc. | Health Management Associates | Universal Health Services | Columbia/HCA | Tenet Healthcare |
|---|---|---|---|---|---|
| Net income | $ 38.0 | $ 136.8 | $ 79.6 | $ 379.0 | $ 249.0 |
| | (06/1999) | (09/1998) | (12/1998) | (12/1998) | (05/1999) |
| 1-Yr income growth | −55.1% | 16.1% | 15.5% | N/E | −39.9% |
| Last ann. revenue | $1,652.6 | $1,138.8 | $1,874.4 | $18,681.0 | $10,880.0 |
| 1-Yr revenue growth | 51.0% | 21.7% | 16.1% | −4.6% | 10.7% |
| 3-Yr revenue growth | 14.2 | 21.6 | 19.7 | −2.0 | 19.1 |
| 5-Yr revenue growth | 21.6 | 24.5 | 20.9 | 8.5 | 32.1 |
| Quarterly total return | 25.6 | −7.7 | 10.4 | 20.5 | −28.8 |
| 12-month total return | −52.6 | −49.6 | −18.2 | −21.5 | −32.0 |
| Fiscal total return | −52.6 | 29.7 | 3.0 | −16.2 | −30.0 |
| Current stock price | $ 6.63 | $ 7.56 | $ 24.69 | $ 22.63 | $ 20.13 |
| EPS | $ 0.52 | $ 0.54 | $ 2.39 | $ 0.59 | $ 0.79 |
| 1-Yr EPS growth | −53.6% | 15.7% | 17.3% | N/E | −39.8% |
| 3-Yr EPS growth | −15.9 | 19.9 | 17.4 | N/C | N/C |
| 5-Yr EPS growth | −0.9 | 27.9 | 21.4 | N/C | N/C |
| Total debt/equity | 1.40 | 0.19 | 0.67 | 0.89 | 1.66 |
| LT debt/equity | 1.40 | 0.18 | 0.67 | 0.75 | 1.65 |
| LT debt/assets | 0.48 | 0.12 | 0.29 | 0.29 | 0.46 |
| Current total debt | $ 873.10 | $ 318.30 | $ 410.40 | $6,660.00 | $6,436.00 |
| Current long-term debt | $ 872.20 | $ 308.10 | $ 406.10 | $5,718.00 | $6,391.00 |
| Current ratio | 2.1 | 2.1 | 2 | 1.1 | 2 |
| Quick ratio | 1.7 | 1.7 | 1.6 | 0.7 | 1.2 |
| Current inventory turnover | 13.2 | 9.7 | 20.9 | 20.7 | 17.8 |
| Current rec. turnover | 5.5 | 4.9 | 7.1 | 8.1 | 5.4 |
| ROA | 2.1% | 12.3% | 5.5% | 2.0% | 18.0% |
| 3-Yr avg. ROA | 48.0 | 13.8 | 5.6 | 2.7 | 1.0 |
| 5-Yr avg. ROA | 57.0 | 13.5 | 5.4 | 3.9 | 2.0 |
| Revenue/Emp. (in thousands) | $ 79.00 | $ 86.00 | $ 103.00 | $ 90.00 | $ 89.00 |
| ROE | 62.0% | 18.1% | 12.7% | 5.0% | 6.4% |
| 3-Yr ROE | 12.1 | 19.2 | 12.2 | 6.4 | 3.5 |
| 5-Yr ROE | 13.6 | 19.4 | 11.9 | 9.8 | 7.0 |
| Income/Emp. (in thousands) | $ 2.00 | $ 10.00 | $ 5.00 | $ 3.00 | $ 2.00 |
| Annual Op CF/Share | $ 134.30 | $ 187.20 | $ 185.00 | $1,779.00 | $ 805.00 |
| 1-Yr Op CF growth | −22.7% | 19.6% | 16.6% | 79.0% | −3.9% |
| 3-Yr Op CF growth | 2.7 | 23.1 | 19.4 | −11.5 | 12.2 |
| 5-Yr Op CF growth | 17.7 | 26.9 | 23.5 | 2.1 | 15.2 |
| Market cap. (millions) | 485.16 | 1916 | 781.75 | 12833.75 | 6266 |
| Shares O/S | 73,232 | 253,357 | 31,666.00 | 567,238 | 311,341 |

*Source:* Quorum Internal Report, 1999.

EXHIBIT 6    Quorum-Owned Hospitals and Number of
             Hospital Beds

| State | City | Hospital Name | Licensed | In Service |
|-------|------|---------------|----------|------------|
| Alabama | Enterprise | Medical Center Enterprise | 135 | 117 |
| | Dothan | Flowers Hospital | 400 | 400 |
| | Gadsden | Gadsden Regional Hospital | 346 | 257 |
| | Jacksonville | Jacksonville Hospital | 89 | 56 |
| Arkansas | Bentonville | Northwest Health System | 63 | 54 |
| | Springdale | Northwest Health System | 222 | 217 |
| Indiana | Fort Wayne | Lutheran Hospital of Indiana | 437 | 432 |
| | Fort Wayne | St. Joseph Medical Center | 191 | 191 |
| | Frankfort | Clinton County Hospital | 88 | 53 |
| | Warsaw | Kosciusko Community Hospital | 72 | 72 |
| Louisiana | Baton Rouge | Summit Hospital | 227 | 166 |
| Mississippi | Hattiesburg | Wesley Medical Center | 211 | 182 |
| | Vicksburg | Park View Regional Medical Center | 231 | 193 |
| | Vicksburg | Vicksburg Medical Center | 154 | 92 |
| North Dakota | Kenmore | Unimed Medical Center | 42 | 42 |
| | Minot | Unimed Medical Center | 185 | 165 |
| Ohio | Barberton | Barberton Citizens Hospital | 347 | 245 |
| | Massillon | Doctors Hospital of Stark County | 166 | 166 |
| South Carolina | Florence | Carolinas Hospital—Florence | 424 | 368 |
| | Kingstree | Carolinas Hospital—Kingstree | 78 | 42 |
| | Lake City | Carolinas Hospital—Lake City | 48 | 40 |
| | Spartanburg | Mary Black Memorial Hospital | 235 | 222 |
| Texas | Abilene | Abilene Regional Medical Center | 160 | 160 |
| | | Total | 4551 | 3932 |
| | | Percent beds in service | | 86% |

*Source:* Quorum Health Group, Inc., *Annual Report,* 1999, p. 11

Note in Exhibit 5, that QHGI has an ROA of 2.1 percent and ROE of 6.2 percent, and HMA has an ROA of 12.3 percent and an ROE of 18.1 percent. Its management effectiveness ratios indicate that HMA is much more effective than Quorum in managing costs. Quorum has a current inventory ratio of 13.2 percent and a current receivable ratio of 5.5 percent, and HMA has a current inventory ratio of 9.7 percent and a current receivable ratio of 4.9 percent. The tight turnover ratios indicate that HMA operates more efficiently than Quorum; however, Quorum's turnover ratios are lower than the industry average.

### Health Management Associates (HMA)

As CEO of HMA since 1986, William Schoen, known as healthcare's Sam Walton, pulled HMA out of cities like Houston and Atlanta and focused instead on small cities like Gadsden, Alabama (pop. 50,000). Leaving COL and THC to fight over the big cities and Quorum Health Group and UHS to fight over the suburbs, HMA's innovative strategies have paid off—32 hospitals in 11 southeastern and southwestern states, with

15,000 employees and a lean corporate staff of 60 (*Forbes Company of the Year,* January 11, 1999, p. 182).

## INTERNAL CONDITIONS

### Quorum-Owned Hospitals

Quorum owns 21 hospitals in mid-size markets with populations of 50,000 to 500,000 people. Quorum operates in more than 40 states and the District of Columbia. Revenues from Quorum's hospitals make up approximately 91 percent of Quorum's total net operating revenues. Quorum prefers the mid-size markets because it believes these markets to be more attractive for long-term growth. As indicated in Exhibit 6, Quorum's hospitals are granted a certain number of licensed beds by state regulatory agencies. Quorum prefers mid-sized markets because they are small enough to allow them, with the ownership of one or two hospitals, to be significant providers of health care services within these markets.

A board of trustees governs each Quorum-owned hospital. The board of trustees includes members of the hospital's medical staff and actively participates in establishing policies and procedures concerning medical, professional, and ethical practices. Each board of trustees is ultimately responsible for ensuring that these policies and practices conform to the legal standards. Quality-assurance programs support and monitor quality of care standards and meet accreditation and regulatory requirements.

Managed-care contracts at Quorum are increasing. Managed care includes employer plans that pay less than total charges for services, health maintenance organizations, preferred providers organizations, indemnity insurance, and various other types of managed care. Increasing payors and aggressively seeking negotiation rates for services that are lower than the hospitals' standard rate are creating strains for Quorum's hospitals. Quorum has responded to this trend by employing managed-care experts to help the management teams evaluate and negotiate contracts. The trend towards managed care has limited Quorum's net operating revenues and operating margins.

James E. Dalton has been president and CEO of Quorum since 1990 and COO since the retirement of Eugene Fleming in June 1999. As indicated in Exhibit 7, Quorum Health Group, Inc., is decentralized; therefore, a divisionally structured organizational chart is most appropriate. The three presidents of the regional healthcare service organizations represent geographic areas. Quorum's subsidiaries—Quorum Health Resources, LLC, and The Learning Institute—are organized by their services.

### Impact of Acquisitions, Joint Ventures, and Divestitures

During fiscal 1999, Quorum acquired four hospitals and affiliated healthcare entities, entered a joint venture in Vicksburg, Mississippi, and sold Park Medical Center in Columbus, Ohio. As a result, operations from acquired entities did not perform as well as Quorum expected, and Quorum had difficulties integrating some of the acquisitions into Quorum's operations.

During fiscal 1998, Quorum acquired two hospitals and affiliated healthcare entities and contributed three hospitals and cash for equity interests in joint ventures with UHS in Las Vegas, Nevada, and Macon, Georgia.

During fiscal 1997, Quorum acquired five hospitals and affiliated healthcare entities, sold minority interest in an acute care hospital in Paillion, Nebraska, while awaiting approval to sell its remaining interests in 1998 (Quorum Health Group, Inc. 1999, *Annual Report,* p. 13).

EXHIBIT 7    QHGI Organizational Chart

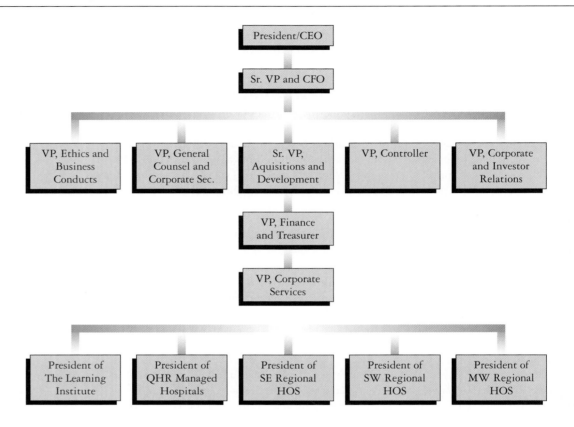

## Results of Operations

Quorum's net operating revenue increased from $1,572.3 million in 1998 to $1,652.6 million in 1999. The increase in revenues of $80.3 million is attributed to the acquisition of six hospitals, a joint venture with Columbia HCA, and a 2.2 percent increase in revenue from hospital management services during 1998 and 1999. These increasing revenues were offset by the decreasing revenues from the sale of their Columbus hospital in 1999 and the sale of the Nebraska hospital in 1998, the joint ventures of three hospitals in which Quorum has minority interest, decreased payments to healthcare facilities due to the Balanced Budget Act of 1997, increased discounts to insurance and managed care companies and increased charity care as well as decreased final settlements from the government under Medicare and Medicaid programs and from insurance and managed care companies. Quorum Health Group, Inc.'s, consolidated statement of income is provided in Exhibit 8. Note that net operating income declined from $86,680 in 1998 to $38,858 in 1999.

Exhibit 9 reveals that Quorum-owned hospitals' net revenues increased from $1.4 billion in 1998, 90.8 percent of total operating revenue, to $1.51 billion in 1999, 91.1 percent of total operating revenue. Quorum's earnings before interest, minority interest, income taxes, depreciation and amortization expense, write-down of assets and investigation and litigation-related costs (EBDITA), decreased (2.8 percent) from

EXHIBIT 8    Quorum Health Group, Inc., Income Statement
(in thousands, except where noted)

| | YE 6/30/99 | YE 6/30/98 | YE 6/30/67 |
|---|---|---|---|
| Revenue: | | | |
| Net patient service revenue | $1,505,027 | $1,427,969 | $1,274,498 |
| Hospital management/professional services | 82,698 | 79,537 | 78,708 |
| Reimbursable expenses | 64,859 | 64,846 | 60,740 |
| Net operating revenue | 1,652,584 | 1,572,352 | 1,413,946 |
| Salaries and benefits | 687,090 | 628,090 | 561,327 |
| Reimbursable expenses | 64,859 | 64,846 | 60,740 |
| Supplies | 231,299 | 210,056 | 198,469 |
| Fees | 156,885 | 140,859 | 125,720 |
| Other operating expenses | 121,948 | 102,959 | 94,629 |
| Provision for doubtful accounts | 126,525 | 106,733 | 89,919 |
| Equity in earnings of affiliates | (22,348) | (6,993) | — |
| Leases and rentals | 34,192 | 26,679 | 22,227 |
| Depreciation and amortization | 95,427 | 87,020 | 75,134 |
| Interest | 53,683 | 40,606 | 45,601 |
| Write-down of assets and investigation and litigation-related costs | 35,173 | 22,850 | — |
| Minority interest | (4,501) | 3,118 | 741 |
| Income before income taxes and extraordinary item | 72,352 | 145,529 | 139,439 |
| Provision for income taxes | 33,494 | 58,849 | 55,357 |
| Income before extraordinary item | 38,858 | 86,680 | 84,082 |
| Extraordinary charges from retirement of debt | — | — | (8,197) |
| Net income | $    38,858 | $    86,680 | $    75,885 |
| Basic earnings per share: | | | |
| Income before extraordinary item | $    0.53 | $    1.16 | $    1.14 |
| Extraordinary charges from retirement of debt | — | — | (0.11) |
| Net income | $    0.53 | $    1.16 | $    1.03 |
| Diluted earnings per share: | | | |
| Income before extraordinary item | $    0.52 | $    1.12 | $    1.11 |
| Extraordinary charges from retirement of debt | — | — | (0.11) |
| Net income | $    0.52 | $    1.12 | $    1.00 |
| Weighted average shares outstanding: | | | |
| Basic | 73,500 | 74,733 | 73,442 |
| Common stock equivalents | 930 | 2,434 | 2,235 |
| Diluted | 74,430 | 77,167 | 75,677 |

*Source:* www.freeedgar.com

$264.6 million in 1998 to $215.7 million in 1999. Quorum Health Resources, LLC, management revenues increased from $144.4 million in 1998 to $147.6 million in 1999.

Note in Exhibit 9, that total operating expenses increased from $1.426 billion in 1998, to $1.580 billion in 1999. As indicated in Exhibits 10 and 11, total assets increased 22 percent in 1999, and liabilities increased 22.9 percent in 1999 (Quorum Health Group, Inc., 1999 *Annual Report,* p. 13).

EXHIBIT 9   Quorum Health Group, Inc.—Sources of Revenues as a
Percentage of Net Revenues ($ in thousands)

|  | 1999 | 1999 | 1998 | 1998 | 1997 | 1997 |
|---|---|---|---|---|---|---|
| Net revenues: | | | | | | |
| Owned hospitals | $1,505,027 | 91.1% | $1,427,969 | 90.8% | $1,274,498 | 90.1% |
| Management services | 147,557 | 8.9 | 144,383 | 9.2 | 139,448 | 9.9 |
|  | $1,652,584 | 100.0% | $1,572,352 | 100.0% | $1,413,946 | 100.0% |
| EBITDA: | | | | | | |
| Owned hospitals | $ 215,707 | 85.6% | $ 264,568 | 88.4% | $ 229,198 | 87.8% |
| Management services | 36,427 | 14.4 | 34,555 | 11.6 | 31,717 | 12.2 |
|  | $ 252,134 | 100.0% | $ 299,123 | 100.0% | $ 260,915 | 100.0% |
| Assets: | | | | | | |
| Owned hospitals | $1,789,908 | 97.7% | $1,451,008 | 97.3% | $1,239,673 | 96.9% |
| Management services | 42,040 | 2.3 | 39,945 | 2.7 | 39,318 | 3.1 |
|  | $1,831,948 | 100.0% | $1,490,953 | 100.0% | $1,278,991 | 100.0% |

*Source:* www.freeedgar.com

EXHIBIT 10   Balance Sheet Assets Quorum Health Group, Inc.
(in thousands, except where noted)

|  | FY Ended 6/30/99 | FY Ended 6/30/98 | FY Ended 6/30/1997 |
|---|---|---|---|
| **Assets** | | | |
| Current assets: | | | |
| Cash | $ 22,258 | $ 17,549 | $ 19,008 |
| Accounts receivable, less allowance for doubtful accounts of $83,896 at June 30, 1999 and $65,561 at June 30, 1998 | 332,312 | 273,376 | 248,732 |
| Supplies | 39,003 | 29,336 | 31,622 |
| Other | 46,838 | 34,245 | 31,739 |
| **Total current assets** | 440,411 | 354,506 | 331,101 |
| Property, plant and equipment, at cost: | | | |
| Land | 88,157 | 66,424 | 62,109 |
| Buildings and improvements | 435,525 | 291,258 | 324,450 |
| Equipment | 584,017 | 464,577 | 462,726 |
| Construction in progress | 24,875 | 72,676 | 21,192 |
|  | 1,132,574 | 894,935 | 870,477 |
| Less accumulated depreciation | 297,454 | 216,229 | 183,705 |
|  | 835,120 | 678,706 | 686,772 |
| Cost in excess of net assets acquired, net | 226,038 | 144,315 | 185,932 |
| Investments in unconsolidated entities | 259,709 | 245,551 | 9,751 |
| Other | 70,670 | 67,875 | 65,435 |
| **Total assets** | $1,831,948 | $1,490,953 | $1,278,991 |

*Source:* www.freeedgar.com

# EXHIBIT 11    Balance Sheet Liabilities Quorum Health Group, Inc.
## (in thousands, except where noted)

| | FY Ended 6/30/99 | FY Ended 6/30/98 | FY Ended 6/30/97 |
|---|---|---|---|
| **LIABILITIES AND STOCKHOLDERS' EQUITY** | | | |
| Current liabilities: | | | |
| Accounts payable and accrued expenses | $ 96,904 | $ 70,483 | $ 77,225 |
| Accrued salaries and benefits | 72,558 | 64,196 | 61,936 |
| Other current liabilities | 34,841 | 27,533 | 9,589 |
| Current maturities of long-term debt | 913 | 1,273 | 1,869 |
| Total current liabilities | 205,216 | 163,485 | 150,619 |
| Long-term debt, less current maturities | 872,213 | 617,377 | 519,940 |
| Deferred income taxes | 33,422 | 29,470 | 38,249 |
| Professional liability risks and other liabilities and deferrals | 36,456 | 30,882 | 25,450 |
| Minority interests in consolidated entities | 59,975 | 27,473 | 26,618 |
| Commitments and contingencies | | | |
| Stockholders' equity: | | | |
| Common stock, $.01 par value; 300,000 shares authorized; 73,166 issued and outstanding at June 30, 1999 and 75,478 at June 30, 1998 | 732 | 755 | 741 |
| Additional paid-in capital | 253,714 | 290,149 | 272,692 |
| Retained earnings | 370,220 | 331,362 | 244,682 |
| | 624,666 | 622,266 | 518,115 |
| Total liabilities and stockholders' equity | $1,831,948 | $1,490,953 | $1,278,991 |
| | | | |
| Total liabilities | 1,207,282 | 868,687 | 760,876 |
| Total stockholders' equity | 624,666 | 622,266 | 518,115 |
| Total liabilities and stockholders' equity | $1,831,948 | $1,490,953 | $1,278,991 |

*Source:* www.freeedgar.com

## Sources of Revenues—Quorum Health Group, Inc.

Quorum received from the Medicare and Medicaid programs approximately 46%, 47%, and 48% of gross patient service revenue for the years ended June 30, 1999, 1998, and 1997, respectively.

| | Year Ended June 30 | | |
|---|---|---|---|
| | 1999 | 1998 | 1997 |
| Medicare | 45.9% | 47.2% | 47.5% |
| Medicaid | 8.0 | 7.5 | 7.6 |
| Other sources | 46.1 | 45.3 | 44.9 |
| Total | 100% | 100% | 100% |

*Source:* Quorum Health Group, Inc., 1999 *Annual Report,* p. 14.

### Business Strategy

Quorum's business strategy is to provide high-quality health care services and grow through expanding and enhancing the scope of services provided by its hospitals. Quorum believes that expansion and enhancement of outpatient and inpatient services will attract more patients and permit Quorum to continue to grow and increase its profitability. As a result of new technology and increased efforts to contain costs, many services that in the past required a patient to be admitted to a hospital are being performed on an outpatient basis. Quorum actively recruits primary care and specialty physicians and other medical personnel to maintain quality.

Currently, Quorum is focused on three strategies:

1. Completing two to four suitable acquisitions per year
2. Improving the financial performance and the scope and quality of healthcare services in its hospitals
3. Capitalizing on relationships with the not-for-profit hospital sector through Quorum's management services division (Quorum Health Group, Inc. 1999 *Annual Report,* p. 14).

### Quorum Health Resources, LLC

Quorum Heath Resources, LLC, a subsidiary of Quorum Health Group, Inc., is the leading provider of management services to acute-care hospitals, providing management services to more than 230 hospitals. The second-ranked hospital management organization managed 51 hospitals, and the third-ranked hospital management organization managed 19 hospitals. Quorum's industry reputation and leading market position provides the competitive advantage in seeking additional management contracts. Note in Exhibit 10, that in 1999, Quorum's management services accounted for 8.9 percent of net operating revenue compared to 9.2 percent in 1998 and 9.9 percent in 1997.

### The Learning Institute

The Learning Institute was founded in support of Quorum's belief in continuous learning. Located at the corporate headquarters in Brentwood, Tennessee, the Learning Institute offers more than 100 educational and training opportunities designed to meet the needs of healthcare leaders by providing customized cost-effectiveness programs. The educational facility includes three fully equipped meeting rooms, a computer-training center, a resource library, and a multimedia center. This central campus is extended through regional satellite programs and the presentation of courses at individual healthcare facilities around the country. The Learning Institute employs more than 100 operations leaders and consultants with a variety of clinical and academic credentials (Quorum Health Group, Inc. 1998, Educational Offerings Catalog, p. 4).

### CONCLUSION

The healthcare industry is highly regulated, making it difficult for large corporations to make a profit. Numerous cost factors should be analyzed thoroughly before making future acquisition decisions. Quorum is spending a lot of money to increase its market share; however, profits are not rising enough to justify operating expenses. Quorum needs a revised strategic plan and mission statement. Quorum should focus on expanding the profitable services provided and improving or eliminating the nonprofitable services in its hospitals.

Quorum has opportunities to increase their revenues; however, it should evaluate potential market segments intensively before implementing future hospital and health-care system acquisition strategies. Quorum should narrow its marketing segmentation strategies by targeting rural communities in states with higher consumer demands. Quorum should look for vacant niches in southwestern and southeastern regions with greater consumer demands for healthcare. Rural communities, in states such as Mississippi, Louisiana, Arkansas, and South Carolina, ranked 50, 49, 48, and 42, respectively, are ideal, because they have greater consumer demands for healthcare.

In pursuit of additional growth strategies, Quorum should begin a strict cost reduction plan with respect to employee staffing and volume purchasing in preparation for seeking future merger partnerships with other corporations. Health Management Associates, Inc., would be an ideal choice because of its low debt structure. The two companies' mirroring images of similar geographic acquisition growth strategies and experienced hospital management leadership would enhance a smooth transition.

Cooperation with competitors will be increasingly important as healthcare reforms evolve. Currently, the future for healthcare is uncertain. The only certainty is, healthcare regulations and cost reductions will continue. As a result of this, Quorum must use its strengths to reduce the threat of healthcare reforms in order to remain profitable. Quorum's success will depend upon how well it responds.

# GREYHOUND LINES, INC.—2000

James Harbin
Texas A&M University—Texarkana

## LDW

**www.greyhound.com also www.laidlaw.com**

Headquartered in Dallas, Texas, Greyhound is the only nationwide provider of scheduled intercity bus transportation services in the United States. The company's primary business consists of scheduled passenger service, package express service, charter, and food service at certain terminals, which accounted for 86 percent, 4 percent, and 10 percent, respectively, of the company's total operating revenues of approximately $923 million in 1999. The company transports over 20 million passengers in the United States, Canada, and Mexico. With a fleet of approximately 2,400 buses, it provided over 18,000 daily departures to 2,600 destinations. Greyhound ended 1999 with a net income of negative $16.3 million. This followed a gain of $35.2 million in 1998.

In March 1999, Greyhound merged with and became a wholly owned subsidiary of Laidlaw Inc., Burlington, Ontario. Laidlaw is North America's largest operator of school buses and ambulances. By buying Greyhound, "Laidlaw becomes the largest intercity passenger carrier and gains an otherwise unattainable platform and brand recognition for the expansion of the tourism and coach business in North America," said James Bullock, Laidlaw's CEO.

Carl Lentzsch, CEO of Greyhound since 1994, continued in that role following the merger. "Although these are very uncertain times, with Laidlaw's financial strength and access to capital markets, Greyhound will be able to make the investments we need to continue our growth while providing superior customer service," Mr. Lentzsch said just prior to the merger.

Even if Greyhound can provide that desperately needed superior customer service, the future of the bus industry remains very uncertain for a variety of reasons. In the 1960s nearly 30 percent of all interstate travel was by bus. By the early 1990s, less than 6 percent of interstate travel was by bus. Obviously not a trend line for a mature industry, much less a growing one. Can that trend be turned around? Is there still a profit to be made in a declining industry? These are indeed difficult times for a company that barely survived two near-death situations in the last decade.

## GREYHOUND'S HISTORY: 1914–1991

For generations of Americans, the Greyhound bus has been much more than a motor vehicle. It has symbolized safe, reliable, affordable travel. Passengers even flocked to the bus line to share the excitement and glamour that the 1934 Academy Award-winning movie portrayed in *It Happened One Night* starring Clark Gable and Claudette Colbert.

It all started in 1914 when Carl Wickman, a Swedish immigrant, founded Greyhound. He began transporting miners between two cities in Minnesota, for 15 cents one way or 25 cents roundtrip on a seven-seat Hupmobile. In 1926, Wickman and Orville Caesar, now owners of several small lines, acquired additional bus lines and united them under the name Motor Transit Corporation.

Frank Fageol was also running a bus line during the early 1920s from Muskegon, Michigan. Fageol's buses were so trim and graceful compared to the others of the day that someone dubbed them "greyhounds." The name stuck.

Following multiple mergers and a growing network of regional bus routes, the Motor Transit Corporation became the Greyhound Corporation in 1930. The "running dog," also referred to as "Lady Greyhound," became the famous icon shortly thereafter.

After the Great Depression, Americans were ready for the travel and glamour afforded by the luxury of reclining seats, interior lights, a smooth ride, and a view of the American countryside. After World War II, more than half the people who traveled between American cities did so by bus. With the development of air-conditioning and diesel engines, bus travel became more comfortable and economical than any other method of transportation.

By the 1960s, dozens of bus companies operated across the country, but Greyhound was the only one with a nationwide route system. The external environment changed dramatically during the 1970s and 1980s though. The interstate highway system had been completed, and almost every family owned at least one automobile. Deregulation of the airline industry and the subsequent emergence of discount airlines further undermined the bus industry.

The 1970s and 80s were decades of declining bus travel. A shakeout of the industry was taking its toll. In 1987, Greyhound purchased its last remaining direct competitor, Trailways, for $86 million. Greyhound was forced to sell it for $5.25 million four years later to reduce the company's bank debt. A bitter labor strike in 1990, combined with even larger passenger declines, forced Greyhound to file for bankruptcy in early 1991.

## REENGINEERING OR DIGGING A DEEPER HOLE?

Frank Schmieder, a former investment banker who had worked for Greyhound for two years, took over as CEO in 1991 just before the company declared bankruptcy. The creditors who had appointed him CEO were impressed by his cost-cutting fever. That fever was shared by his lieutenant, M. Michael Doyle, who came to Greyhound in 1987 from a finance post at Philips Petroleum Company.

Although neither man had much transportation experience, they hammered together a reorganization plan that called for relentless cutting of workers, routes, services, and buses. The bus fleet was reduced from 3,700 to 2,400. All that cutting, combined with a plan to computerize everything from passenger reservations to fleet scheduling, won Wall Street's approval. Within a month of Greyhound's emergence from Chapter 11, its newly issued stock was trading at $13.50 a share, compared with the $4.00 to $7.50 expected by its own advisers.

Meanwhile, at the local level, employee turnover approached 100 percent at some terminals; 30 percent was not unusual. In survey after survey, customers listed discourtesy as a major problem. Some terminal workers were observed making fun of customers or ignoring them. Under the new cost-cutting policy of not handling customers' baggage, bags were often piled up and left unprotected.

In April 1993, management unveiled a revolutionary reservation system called TRIPS. Promising that TRIPS would be the key to Greyhound's turnaround, the company rolled out a prospectus for a $90 million stock offering. The prospectus pledged that TRIPS would improve customer service, make ticket buying convenient, and allow customers to reserve space on specific trips. Doyle, as chief financial officer, and several other top Greyhound executives heavily promoted the offering.

There were some serious reservations within the company concerning this computerized reservation system. Even the vice-president in charge of developing TRIPS,

Thomas Thompson, tried to warn Doyle of anticipated problems through written reports at one particular meeting. His objections, as he recalls, were quickly rejected by Doyle, who declared, "We made these commitments, and, by God, we're going to live up to them" and ruled out any further discussion.

Some Greyhound executives were incredulous; their passengers were accustomed to arriving at a terminal, buying a ticket, and catching a bus. Some wondered how many of low-income passengers would have credit cards or even telephones to use the system. But their concerns were drowned out by financial necessity and the perception, one former executive says, "that the messenger got shot."

By June 1993, Greyhound stock was more than $20 a share. It had been about $12 at the beginning of that year. In late July 1993, the company fully activated both the telephone information service and TRIPS. The combination of terminal agents and more than 400 telephone operators taking reservations were far more than the TRIPS computers could handle. "It was like turning on a spigot to get a drink and getting a fire hose," Thompson recalled.

Historically, Greyhound's phone calls averaged 60,000 a day. The toll-free TRIPS line received an estimated 800,000 calls. At the same time, a new discount fare was introduced. The TRIPS computers were backed up so badly that on some days it took 45 seconds to respond to a single keystroke and five minutes to print a ticket. TRIPS crashed so often in some locations that agents were writing tickets manually. Lines of frustrated customers snaked around bus terminals.

Although volume was a major culprit, the inadequate training (40 hours per employee), undereducation, and low morale of TRIPS's Greyhound employees also contributed to problems as did the sheer complexity of TRIPS. Greyhound technicians estimated that they would need a system capable of managing as many as 1,800 vehicle stops a day. Greyhound had given the 40-odd people developing the system a $6 million start-up budget and little more than a year to complete it. By comparison, American Airlines, with a small army of technicians, spent three decades and several hundred million dollars perfecting its Sabre reservation system.

During this period of 1991 to 1994, while Greyhound progressed toward its goals of (1) reducing the annual operating budget by $100 million, (2) reducing the bus fleet by half, (3) reducing the workforce by a fifth, and (4) replacing many full-time positions with part-timers, Schmieder's salary rose 57 percent to $526,000 and Doyle's rose nearly 65 percent to $265,000. Greyhound first-line employees earned about $6 an hour with no chance of promotion, and the average Greyhound customer earned less than $17,000 a year.

With its stock trading at $21.75 on August 4, 1993 (largely on the promise of TRIPS and the reengineering), Doyle sold 15,000 shares that he had purchased two months earlier for $9.81. In June, he had exercised options to buy and sell 22,642 Greyhound shares on similar terms. In the first 2 weeks of August 1993, Schmieder exercised options and sold 13,600 shares for an indicated profit of $155,000. During the same period, two other Greyhound executives sold a total of 21,300 shares at similar profits.

On September 23, nearly two months after the TRIPS trouble began, Greyhound stunned Wall Street by announcing that ridership had plunged 12 percent in August and that 1993 earnings would trail expectations. Greyhound stock tumbled 24 percent, to $11.75 a share, in a single day. That same day, the company released a press report blaming the ridership fall on an uncertain economy. There was no mention of TRIPS.

Under pressure from Greyhound's board of directors, Schmieder resigned in midsummer 1994. Doyle resigned shortly after that.

## THE TURNAROUND STRATEGY

Craig Lentzch, a former Greyhound executive, was appointed president and CEO in November 1994. Lentzsch, a forty-eight-year-old Wharton Business school graduate, was known for his grasp of the technical side of the industry. He had worked for Greyhound as vice-chairman in the late 1980s and, prior to that, had worked in strategic planning for then-rival Trailways Lines, Inc.

A key to Greyhound's turnaround involved a "back-to-basics" strategy. Lentzsch noted one of the very first things Greyhound did: "We started answering the damn telephone." Before his arrival, a potential bus customer had to call four or five times before getting through to a sales representative. "The prior management had cut costs so deeply that they didn't have enough people answering the telephone," Lentzsch said. "And if you did get through, you often were told the bus was full. How much of that misery are you going to put up with?"

The previous management team had decided that a bus line should be run the way an airline was. That decision lead to the introduction of TRIPS, which meant that customers needed to make reservations weeks in advance, and buses were supposed to roll out full or close to it. The problem with this approach was not so much that bus customers didn't make reservations—some did—but that they didn't then show up and get on the bus.

"Over 80 percent of those who made reservations were no-shows," said Jack Haugsland, COO. "About 75 percent of our customers buy tickets with cash three hours before the bus leaves the station." Because of the large percentage of no-shows, many walk-up customers without reservations were turned away. It was a classic example, said Greyhound's new chief financial officer, of a company not understanding its customers. "Our customer base is last-minute buyers," he said.

One of the first things management did was dismantle the airline model that relied on reservations. It was replaced with a much simpler one: If you want to travel by bus, you show up at the terminal, and, within a reasonable period of time, you will get a seat on the bus at an affordable price.

Another new strategy was the switch from a capacity-constrained system such as the airlines use to a capacity-flexible system. For example, if a bus scheduled to leave at 10 A.M. is full, an additional bus will be rolled out. Because buses are a lot cheaper than planes, a bus company can afford to have extra buses in the wings, especially for peak travel periods in the summer months and for the Thanksgiving and Christmas holidays.

A third new strategy was revamping the pricing structure. Previous management had raised the prices of the walk-in tickets as high as possible and lowered those of the advance-purchase tickets, thereby pricing many of their core customers, last-minute walk-ins, out of the market. Greyhound dropped its prices significantly, turning to an "everyday low pricing," year-round strategy in an attempt to make bus travel more affordable. Greyhound also reopened several hundred rural stops, thereby offering service that other forms of transportation no longer provided.

Greyhound exploited opportunities as alliance partners with air, rail, and other regional bus lines in providing reliable mixed-mode transportation. With the NAFTA agreement in place, research studies estimated that the Mexican market is worth approximately $200 million a year and growing at 20 percent annually. Therefore, opportunities existed for partnerships with Mexican bus lines. In the summer of 1997 Greyhound bus began servicing a 800-mile route between Los Angeles and Ciudad Obregon, a city in the border state of Sonora.

By obtaining a new credit line, convincing bondholders to trade for equity, and raising $35 million for a 1994 rights offering that priced shares at $2.15, Greyhound was able to buy several hundred new buses (reducing the average age of their fleet from

9.5 years in 1993 to 6 years in 1996) and build several new terminals in better areas of cities. During the first half of 1998, Greyhound purchased 163 new buses.

Previous management did not think that package express was worth much effort, but the new team believed the potential was there for increased business. At one time, this portion of the business was lucrative, generating revenue in the $90 million range, about 15 percent of total revenue. Because Greyhound puts packages on buses that are already carrying passengers, that's mostly gravy.

The company also generated additional revenue by selling advertising on the outside and inside of their buses. Certain niche opportunities such as casino trips and college markets were also pursued.

### RESULTS: 1998–1999

Greyhound reported net income before preferred dividends of $35.2 million, or 50 cents a share, for 1998 and negative $16.3 million for 1999 (Exhibit 1). 1998 was the first full-year profit realized since 1993. Exhibit 2 reveals Greyhound's balance sheets. Note the 1999 decrease in total assets and increase in long-term debt.

### EXHIBIT 1    Greyhound's Recent Income Statements

|  | Years Ended December 31, | | |
|  | 1999 | 1998 | 1997 |
|---|---|---|---|
| Operating Revenues | | | |
| Transportation services | | | |
| Passenger services | $783,299 | $727,786 | $658,396 |
| Package express | 39,051 | 33,790 | 35,676 |
| Food services | 39,124 | 31,127 | 29,611 |
| Other operating revenues | 62,057 | 53,293 | 47,439 |
| Total Operating Revenues | 923,531 | 845,996 | 771,122 |
| Operating Expenses | | | |
| Maintenance | 90,999 | 83,444 | 77,022 |
| Transportation | 220,477 | 201,190 | 187,311 |
| Agents' commissions and station costs | 173,091 | 155,799 | 141,100 |
| Marketing, advertising and traffic | 31,325 | 27,349 | 26,860 |
| Insurance and safety | 51,178 | 49,748 | 45,860 |
| General and administrative | 119,396 | 99,836 | 91,307 |
| Depreciation and amortization | 44,396 | 36,332 | 31,259 |
| Operating taxes and licenses | 59,818 | 56,703 | 51,511 |
| Operating rents | 78,222 | 65,756 | 59,105 |
| Cost of goods sold—Food services | 26,045 | 20,656 | 19,631 |
| Other operating expenses | 3,054 | 2,352 | 3,050 |
| Total Operating Expenses | 898,001 | 799,165 | 734,016 |
| Operating Income | 25,530 | 46,831 | 37,106 |
| Settlement of Stock Options | 21,294 | — | |
| Interest Expense | 21,993 | 27,899 | 27,657 |
| Net Income (Loss) Before Income Taxes | (17,757) | 18,932 | 9,449 |
| Income Tax Provision (Benefit) | (4,612) | (16,856) | 1,051 |
| Minority Interests | 1,278 | 556 | |
| Net Income (Loss) Before Extraordinary Items | (14,423) | 35,232 | 8,398 |
| Extraordinary Items (net of a tax benefit of $1,021 and $0) | 1,897 | — | 25,323 |
| Net Income (Loss) | $ (16,320) | $ 35,232 | $ (16,925) |

# EXHIBIT 2    Greyhound's Recent Balance Sheets (000 omitted)

| | December 31 | |
|---|---|---|
| | 1999 | 1998 |
| **CURRENT ASSETS** | | |
| Cash and cash equivalents | $ 8,295 | $ 4,736 |
| Accounts receivable, less allowance for doubtful accounts of $402 and $198 | 46,830 | 40,774 |
| Inventories, less allowance for shrinkage of $226 and $205 | 7,494 | 5,705 |
| Prepaid expenses | 5,694 | 5,170 |
| Assets held for sale | 4,545 | 3,029 |
| Current portion of deferred tax assets | 12,864 | 24,053 |
| Other current assets | 1,851 | 9,907 |
| Total Current Assets | 87,573 | 93,374 |
| Prepaid Pension Plans | 29,983 | 27,917 |
| Property, Plant and Equipment, net of accumulated depreciation of $173,273 and $151,468 | 397,077 | 362,417 |
| Investments in Unconsolidated Affiliates | 16,028 | 13,560 |
| Deferred Income Taxes | 14,711 | 8,988 |
| Insurance and Security Deposits | 22,220 | 67,908 |
| Goodwill, net of accumulated amortization of $3,523 and $1,755 | 45,384 | 39,510 |
| Intangible Assets, net of accumulated amortization of $31,825 and $28,503 | 25,821 | 29,704 |
| Total Assets | $638,797 | $643,378 |
| **CURRENT LIABILITIES** | | |
| Accounts payable | $ 23,824 | $ 27,724 |
| Due to Laidlaw | 42,560 | — |
| Accrued liabilities | 76,367 | 64,819 |
| Unredeemed tickets | 11,956 | 12,143 |
| Current portion of reserve for injuries and damages | 1,473 | 22,967 |
| Current maturities of long-term debt | 5,671 | 7,970 |
| Total Current Liabilities | 161,851 | 135,623 |
| Reserve for Injuries and Damages | 5,840 | 37,392 |
| Long-Term Debt, net | 174,581 | 225,688 |
| Minority Interests | 4,233 | 3,058 |
| Other Liabilities | 22,432 | 23,604 |
| Total Liabilities | 368,937 | 425,365 |
| Redeemable Preferred Stock (2,400,000 shares authorized and 1,678,150 shares issued as of December 31, 1999) | 41,954 | — |
| Commitments and Contingencies | | |
| Stockholders' Equity | | |
| Preferred Stock (10,000,000 shares authorized as of December 31, 1998; par value $.01) | | |
| 8 1/2% Convertible Exchangeable Preferred Stock (2,760,000 shares authorized and 2,400,000 shares issued as of December 31,1998) | — | 60,000 |
| Series A Junior Preferred Stock (1,500,000 shares authorized as of December 31, 1998; par value $.01; none issued) | — | — |
| Common Stock (100,000,000 shares authorized; 58,743,069 and 60,255,117 shares issued as of December 31, 1999 and 1998, respectively; par value $.01) | 587 | 603 |
| Treasury Stock, at cost (109,192 shares as of December 31, 1998) | — | (1,038) |
| Capital in Excess of Par Value | 322,026 | 237,441 |
| Accumulated Other Comprehensive Loss, net of tax benefit of $1,360 and $3,181. | (2,525) | (7,232) |
| Retained Deficit | (92,182) | (71,761) |
| Total Stockholders' Equity | 227,906 | 218,013 |
| Total Liabilities and Stockholders' Equity | $638,797 | $643,378 |

*Source:* www.freeedgar.com

EXHIBIT 3    Greyhound Consolidated Traffic Statistics (in thousands except as noted)

|  | 1999 | 1998 | 1997 | 1996 | 1995 |
|---|---|---|---|---|---|
| Passenger miles | 8,739,219 | 7,820,225 | 7,049,637 | 6,243,262 | 6,033,780 |
| Load factor (percentage) | 52.9% | 52.3% | 52.6% | 51.2% | 51.1% |
| Passengers carried | 24,698 | 22,552 | 19,893 | 18,348 | 17,548 |
| Regular service miles operated | 339,752 | 316,045 | 285,689 | 265,259 | 256,683 |
| Yield (passenger revenue per passenger mile) (cents) | — | 9.31 | 9.34 | 9.57 | 9.29 |
| Average trip length (miles) | — | 347 | 354 | 340 | 344 |

*Source:* www.freeedgar.com

In the fourth quarter of 1998, Greyhound formed joint ventures with several Mexican bus carriers to create Autobuses Americanos and Autobuses Amigos. The two new companies operate under Greyhound's subsidiary Sistema Internacional Trensporte de Autobuses, Inc., and enable the company to provide cross-border service at all major gateways between the United States and Mexico.

In February 1999, Greyhound acquired On Time Delivery, a Minnesota-based courier. In June of 1999, they acquired Larson Express, a Chicago-area courier. Both of these acquisitions allow Greyhound to grow their delivery business through pickup and delivery services. Note in Exhibit 3 that Greyhound carried almost a million more passengers in 1999 than 1998.

## LAIDLAW MERGER: 1999

In October 1998, Greyhound announced it had entered into an agreement and plan of merger with Laidlaw, Inc., which would acquire all outstanding Greyhound common and convertible preferred shares. At the time there were approximately 60 million common shares, plus 2.4 million convertible preferred shares, which represented 12.3 million equivalent common shares. Exhibit 4 provides financial highlights for Laidlaw.

Under the terms of the merger plan, Greyhound stockholders would receive $6.50 per common, or equivalent share. At Laidlaw's option, up to $4.00 of the consideration could be satisfied with Laidlaw common shares.

Some were unhappy with the terms of the merger. Alan Snyder, president of a money-management firm holding 20 percent of Greyhound's common and preferred shares commented, "It's not a high premium for the turn-around Greyhound management has accomplished."

However, Laidlaw's CEO Bullock, and Lentzsch, who will continue as Greyhound's CEO, were both glowing with their support of the merger. Lentzsch believed that the transaction would benefit both the company's customers and employees because Laidlaw was committed to growth in the intercity bus business. "This merger with a new owner, coming in our 85th year, will serve the best interests of everyone who cares about Greyhound Lines."

## GREYHOUND'S FUTURE: A LIGHT OR A TRAIN (OR PLANE) AT THE END OF THE TUNNEL?

### The Case for "a Light"

There are several reasons for guarded optimism at Greyhound. Internally, it now has a CEO with industry and Greyhound experience. Additionally, with the merger it has access to financial resources not previously available.

EXHIBIT 4    Laidlaw Financial Highlights
(in millions, except per-share, dividends and ratios)

| | 9 months 1999 31 May | 1998 31 Aug | 1997 31 Aug | 1996 31 Aug |
|---|---|---|---|---|
| Revenue | $2,823 | $3,690 | $3,031 | $2,296 |
| Operating expenses | 2,089 | 2,722 | 2,214 | 1,720 |
| Income from operations | 351 | 422 | (36) | 233 |
| Income before tax | (101) | 419 | (110) | 147 |
| Net income | (124) | 346 | 610 | 162 |
| **Assets** | | | | |
| Cash | 230 | 268 | 241 | 226 |
| Noncash | 885 | 649 | 866 | 548 |
| Total current | 1,116 | 917 | 1,107 | 774 |
| Noncurrent | 6,089 | 5,268 | 5,010 | 4,158 |
| Total assets | 7,204 | 6,185 | 6,117 | 4,932 |
| **Liabilities** | | | | |
| Current | 846 | 631 | 624 | 480 |
| Noncurrent | 3,427 | 2,464 | 2,699 | 2,324 |
| Total liabilities | 4,273 | 3,095 | 3,323 | 2,804 |
| **Equity** | | | | |
| Shareholders' equity | 2,932 | 3,090 | 2,794 | 2,128 |
| Total liabilities and equity | $7,204 | $6,185 | $6,117 | $4,932 |
| **Earnings per share** | | | | |
| Weighted average number of shares (millions) | 330.2 | 329.8 | 317.1 | 293.2 |
| Continuing operations | (0.38) | 1.05 | 0.14 | 0.40 |
| Discontinued operations | | | 1.78 | 0.15 |
| Total | (0.38) | 1.05 | 1.92 | 0.55 |
| **Dividends per share ($)** | | | | |
| Common shares | 0.21 | 0.26 | 0.20 | 0.19 |
| Preference shares | 0.75 | 1.00 | 1.00 | 1.00 |
| **Ratios** | | | | |
| Gross margin | 26.0% | 26.2% | 26.9% | 25.1% |
| Debt to equity | 1.06:1 | 0.74:1 | 0.78:1 | 0.90:1 |
| Return on equity | | 8.9% | 7.8% | 8.5% |
| Percent of revenue from United States | | 90.3 | 90.3 | 90.1 |
| Percent of profit from United States | | 89.8 | 87.6 | 89.4 |
| Number of employees | | 85,000 | 79,500 | 66,000 |

*Source:* http://www.laidlaw.com/laidlaw/investor/his_three.html

Greyhound serves a diverse customer base, consisting primarily of low- to middle-income passengers from a wide variety of ethnic backgrounds. Management believes that the demographic groups that make up the core of the company's customer base are growing at rates faster than those of the U.S. population as a whole. Greyhound believes that it is uniquely positioned to serve this broad and growing market because (1) its operating costs, which are lower on an available-seat-mile basis than other modes of intercity transportation, enable it to offer passengers everyday low prices; (2) it offers the only means of regularly scheduled intercity transportation in many of its markets, and (3) it provides additional capacity during peak travel periods to accommodate passengers who lack the flexibility to shift their travel to off-peak periods.

First and foremost, Greyhound must convince more travelers to take the bus. The company is regaining lost ridership with its return to its "Take the bus and leave the driving to us" strategy. Pricing its services more realistically certainly will help to entice riders.

Greyhound's strong brand name is synonymous with bus travel. Its icon of a running greyhound may be one of the United States' most recognizable, at least for older generations of Americans.

Its national network may yet prevail against discount airlines. As excess capacity is taken out of service, airlines may have to increase their prices. Bus travel should benefit if fewer people can afford to fly. Amtrak cutbacks and concerns about commuter airline safety also should place more passengers on buses. Congress has mandated that Amtrack operate in the black by 2003, or it will lose governmental subsidies.

Analysts estimate that there is a pool of about four million people who ride the bus nationwide. As baby boomers age and new Asian and Mexican immigrants enter the United States and disperse, the pool will grow to about 6 million riders over the next three to five years.

In 1999, Mexico announced plans for hefty deposits on all cars driven into Mexico. Even though these deposits are refundable upon exiting, this policy creates tremendous hardships on many people, who may then decide that bus travel is a better option.

A large number of companies in the United States do well serving less-affluent Americans. There are 20 to 25 million households in the United States (representing 60 to 70 million people) that do not have bank accounts. Ever wonder why in the front of nearly every phone book there are instructions and locations for telephone customers to pay their bills in person? It is to serve a growing group, composed mostly of low-wage blue-collar workers, the unemployed, recent immigrants, and retirees. These are some of Greyhound's prime target markets.

### The Case for "a Train (or Plane) at the End of the Tunnel"

On the other hand, the future for Greyhound looks anything but bright. Is the glass half-full or half-empty? Increased automobile ownership and discount airlines have reduced the bus industry's share of interstate travel to an estimated 6 percent, down from 30 percent in 1960. The entire industry carries only about 35 million passengers annually. This is compared to more than 430 million air travelers. These trends do not bode well for Greyhound.

Bus ridership suffers from an image problem. Many assume that only the poor board buses. The poor do ride the bus, but more than 50 percent of Greyhound's revenue comes from middle-income America.

Many Americans see little glamour or rationale for riding a bus and passing through dismal terminals. Many travelers no more think of taking a bus than taking a horse. Unlike generations of Americans in the 1930s, 1940s, and 1950s, many people have never been on a bus, not counting school buses. When it's time to travel, they either drive or fly.

# CARNIVAL CORPORATION—2000

Mike Keefe, John Ross, and Bill Middlebrook
Southwest Texas State University

**CCL**
www.carnival.com

Carnival Corporation, in terms of passengers carried, revenues generated, and available capacity, is the largest cruise line in the world and considered the leader and innovator in the cruise travel industry. Carnival has grown from two converted ocean liners to an organization with two cruise divisions and a chain of Alaskan hotels and tour coaches. Corporate revenues for fiscal 1999 reached $3.49 billion, with net income from operations of $1.027 billion. Carnival has several "firsts" in the cruise industry—over one million passengers carried in a single year and five million total passengers by fiscal 1994. Currently, its market share of the cruise travel industry stands at approximately 34 percent overall.

Carnival Corporation CEO and chairman, Micky Arison, and Carnival Cruise Lines president, Bob Dickinson, are prepared to maintain their reputation as leaders and innovators in the industry. They have assembled one of the newest fleets catering to travelers with the introduction of several superliners built specifically for the Caribbean and Alaskan cruise markets, and expect to invest over $3.0 billion in new ships by the year 2002. Additionally, the company has expanded its Holland American Lines fleet to cater to more established travelers and plans to add three of the new ships to their fleet in the premium cruise segment. Strategically, Carnival Corporation seems to have made the right moves at the right time, sometimes in direct contradiction to industry analysts and trends.

Cruise Lines International Association (CLIA), an industry trade group, has tracked the growth of the cruise industry for over 25 years. In 1970, approximately 500,000 passengers took cruises for three consecutive nights or more, reaching a peak of 5.9 million passengers in 1998, an average annual compound growth rate of approximately 8.9 percent. The growth rate had declined to approximately 2 percent per year over the period from 1991 to 1995 but increased to 7.8 percent growth in 1998. By the end of 1998, CLIA estimates there were 145 ships with 140,000-berth capacity, with utilization at a record 91.6 percent. The number of cruise passengers increased 8.6 percent in 1999 and reached the 6 million-passenger mark in early 2000. Through new ships to be delivered and others to be "stretched," the North American market will increase capacity by the end of 2000, 2001, 2002, and 2003 to 156, 168, 176, and 181 vessels respectively.

Carnival passenger capacity in 1991 was 17,973 berths and increased to 43,810 by the end of fiscal 1999. Additional capacity will be added with the delivery of several new cruise ships already on order. By the Summer of 2002, the company expects to have some 56,858 passenger capacity, a 44.1 percent growth over 1998.

Even with the growth in the cruise industry, the company believes that cruises represent only 2 percent of the North American vacation market, defined as persons who travel for leisure purposes on trips of three nights or longer, involving at least one night's stay in a hotel. Carnival Corporation believes that only 9 percent of the North American population has ever cruised. Various cruise operators, including Carnival Corporation, have based their expansion and capital spending programs on the possibility of capturing part of the 93 percent to 95 percent of the North American population who have yet to take a cruise vacation.

## The Evolution of Cruising

With the replacement of ocean liners by aircraft in the 1960s as the primary means of transoceanic travel, the opportunity for developing the modern cruise industry was created. Ships no longer required to ferry passengers from destination to destination became available to investors with visions of a new vacation alternative to complement the increasing affluence of Americans. Cruising, once the purview of the rich and leisure class, was targeted to the middle class, with service and amenities similar to the grand days of first-class ocean travel.

According to Robert Meyers, editor and publisher of *Cruise Travel* magazine, the increasing popularity of cruise vacations can be traced to two serendipitously timed events. First, television's "Love Boat" series dispelled many myths associated with cruising and depicted people of all ages and backgrounds enjoying the cruise experience. This show was among the top ten shows on television for many years according to Nielsen ratings and provided extensive publicity for cruise operators. Second, the increasing affluence of Americans and the increased participation of women in the workforce gave couples and families more disposable income for discretionary purposes, especially vacations. As the myths were dispelled and disposable income grew, younger couples and families "turned on" to the benefits of cruising as a vacation alternative, creating a large new target market for the cruise product that accelerated the growth in the number of Americans taking cruises as a vacation.

## CARNIVAL HISTORY

In 1972 Ted Arison, backed by American Travel Services, Inc. (AITS), purchased an aging ocean liner from Canadian Pacific Empress Lines for $6.5 million. The new AITS subsidiary, Carnival Cruise Line, refurbished the vessel from bow to stern and renamed it the *Mardi Gras* to capture the party spirit. (Also included in the deal was another ship that was later renamed the *Carnivale.*) The company start was not promising, however, as on the first voyage the *Mardi Gras,* with over 300 invited travel agents aboard, ran aground in Miami Harbor. The ship was slow and guzzled expensive fuel, limiting the number of ports of call and lengthening the minimum stay of passengers on the ship to the break-even point. Arison then bought another older vessel from Union Castle Lines to complement the *Mardi Gras* and the *Carnivale* and named it the *Festivale.* To attract customers, Arison began adding diversions on board such as planned activities, a casino, nightclubs, discos, and other forms of entertainment designed to enhance the shipboard experience.

Carnival lost money for the next two years, and in late 1974 Ted Arison bought out the Carnival Cruise subsidiary of AITS, Inc., for $1 cash and the assumption of $5 million in debt. One month later, the *Mardi Gras* began showing a profit and, through the remainder of 1975, operated at more than 100% capacity. (Normal ship capacity is determined by the number of fixed berths available. Ships, like hotels, can operate beyond this fixed capacity by using rollaway beds, pullmans, and upper bunks.) Ted Arison (then chairman), along with Bob Dickinson (then vice president of sales and marketing) and his son Micky Arison (then president of Carnival), began to alter

Americans' approach to cruise vacations. Carnival went after first-time and younger travelers with a moderately priced vacation package that included airfare to the port of embarkation and home after the cruise. Per-diem rates were very competitive with other vacation packages, and Carnival offered passage to multiple exotic Caribbean ports, several meals served daily with premier restaurant service, and all forms of entertainment and activities included in the base fare. The only items not included in the fare were of a personal nature, liquor purchases, gambling, and tips for the cabin steward, table waiter, and busboy. Carnival continued to add to the shipboard experience with a greater variety of activities, nightclubs, and other forms of entertainment and varied ports of call to increase its attractiveness. It was the first modern cruise operator to use multimedia advertising promotions and established the theme of "Fun Ship" cruises, primarily promoting the ship as the destination and ports of call as secondary. Carnival told the public that it was throwing a shipboard party and everyone was invited. Today, the "Fun Ship" theme still permeates all Carnival Cruise ships.

The 1993 to 1995 period saw the addition of the superliner *Imagination* to Carnival Cruise Lines and the *Ryndam* to Holland America Lines. In 1994, the company discontinued operations of Fiestamarina Lines, which had attempted to serve Spanish-speaking clientele. Fiestamarina was beset with marketing and operational problems and never achieved continuous operations. Many industry analysts and observers were surprised at the failure of Carnival to successfully develop this market. In 1995 Carnival sold a 49 percent interest in the Epirotiki Line, a Greek cruise operation, for $25 million and purchased $101 million (face amount) of senior secured notes of Kloster Cruise Limited, the parent of competitor Norwegian Cruise Lines, for $81 million.

Carnival Corporation is expanding through internally generated growth as evidenced by the number of new ships on order (see Exhibit 1). Additionally, Carnival seems to be willing to continue with its external expansion through acquisitions if the right opportunity arises.

## EXHIBIT 1    Carnival and Holland America Ships under Construction

| Vessel | Expected Delivery | Shipyard | Passenger Capacity* | Cost (millions) |
|---|---|---|---|---|
| Carnival Cruise Lines | | | | |
| *Carnival Victory* | 09/00 | Fincantieri | 2,758 | $   440 |
| *Carnival Spirit* | 4/01 | Masa-Yards | 2,112 | 375 |
| *Carnival Pride* | 1/02 | Masa-Yards | 2,112 | 375 |
| *Carnival Conquest* | 12/02 | Fincantieri | 2,758 | 450 |
| *Carnival Glory* | 8/03 | Fincantieri | 2,758 | 450 |
| Total Carnival Cruise Lines | | | 112,498 | $2,090 |
| Holland America Line | | | | |
| *Volendam* | 11/99 | Fincantieri | 1,440 | 300 |
| *Zaandam* | 4/00 | Fincantieri | 1,440 | 300 |
| *Amsterdam* | 11/00 | Fincantieri | 1,380 | 300 |
| Total Holland America Line | | | 4,260 | $   900 |
| Total all Vessel's | | | 16,758 | $2,990 |

*In accordance with industry practice all capacities indicated within this document are calculated based on two passengers per cabin even though some cabins can accommodate three or four passengers. Form 10Q-10/9/99.

In June 1997, Royal Caribbean made a bid to buy Celebrity Cruise Lines for $500 million and assumption of $800 million in debt. Within a week, Carnival had responded by submitting a counteroffer to Celebrity for $510 million and the assumption of debt, then two days later raised the bid to $525 million. However, Royal Caribbean seems to have had the inside track and announced on June 30, 1997, the final merger arrangements with Celebrity. The resulting company will have 17 ships with approximately 30,000 berths.

Not to be thwarted in their attempts at continued expansion, Carnival announced in June 1997 the purchase of Costa, an Italian cruise company and the largest European cruise line, for $141 million. External expansion continued when on May 28, 1998, Carnival announced the acquisition of Cunard Line for $500 million from Kvaerner ASA. Canard then merged with Seabourn Cruise Line (50 percent owned by Carnival), with Carnival owning 68 percent of the resulting Cunard Line Limited. In an attempt at further expansion, Carnival announced on December 2, 1999, a hostile bid for NCL Holding ASA, the parent company of Norwegian Cruise Lines. If successful, Carnival could end up owning some 44 percent of the cruise market.

## THE CRUISE PRODUCT

Ted and Mickey Arison envisioned the classical cruise elegance along with modern convenience at a price comparable to land-based vacation packages sold by travel agents. Carnival's all-inclusive package, when compared to resorts or a theme park such as Walt Disney World, often is priced below these destinations, especially when the array of activities, entertainment, and meals are considered.

A typical vacation on a Carnival cruise ship starts when luggage is tagged for the ship at the airport. Upon arriving at the port of embarkation, passengers are ferried by air-conditioned buses to the ship for boarding, and luggage is delivered by the cruise ship staff to the passenger's cabin. Waiters dot the ship, offering tropical drinks to the backdrop of a Caribbean rhythm, while the cruise staff orients passengers to the various decks, cabins, and public rooms. In a few hours (most ships sail in the early evening), dinner is served in the main dining rooms, in which the wine selection rivals that of the finest restaurants, and the variety of main dishes are designed to suit every palate. Diners can always order double portions if they decide not to save room for the variety of desserts and after-dinner specialties.

After dinner, cruisers can choose between many forms of entertainment, including live music, dancing, nightclubs, and a selection of movies, or they can sleep through the midnight buffet until breakfast. (Most ships have five or more distinct nightclubs.) During the night, a daily program of activities arrives at the passengers' cabins. The biggest decisions to be made for the duration of the vacation will be what to do (or not to do), what to eat and when (usually eight separate serving times not including the 24-hour room service), and when to sleep. Service in all areas from dining to housekeeping is upscale and immediate. The service is so good that a common shipboard joke says that if you leave your bed during the night to visit the head (sea talk for bathroom), your cabin steward will have made the bed and placed chocolates on the pillow by the time you return.

After the cruise, passengers are transported back to the airport in air-conditioned busses for the flight home. Representatives of the cruise line are on hand at the airport to help cruisers in meeting their scheduled flights. When all amenities are considered, most vacation packages would be hard pressed to match Carnival's per-diem prices that range from $112 to $250 per person per day, depending on accommodations. (Holland America and Seabourn are higher, ranging from $157 to $624 per person per day.) Occasional specials allow for even lower prices, and special suite accommodations can be had for an additional payment.

## CARNIVAL OPERATIONS

Carnival Corporation, headquartered in Miami, is composed of Carnival Cruise Lines, Holland America Lines (which includes Windstar Sail Cruises as a subsidiary), Holland America Westours, Westmark Hotels, Airtours, Costa, Seabourn, Gay Line of Alaska and Seattle, and the newly created Cunard Line Limited. Carnival Cruise Lines, Inc., is a Panamanian corporation, and its subsidiaries are incorporated in Panama, the Netherlands, Antilles, the British Virgin Islands, Liberia, and the Bahamas. The ships are subject to inspection by the U.S. Coast Guard for compliance with the Convention for the Safety of Life at Sea, which requires specific structural requirements for safety of passengers at sea, and by the U.S. Public Health Service for sanitary standards. The company is also regulated in some aspects by the Federal Maritime Commission.

At its helm, Carnival Corporation is led by CEO and chairman of the board Micky Arison and Carnival Cruise Lines president and COO Bob Dickinson. A. Kirk Lanterman is the president and CEO of the Holland America cruise division, which includes Holland America Westours and Windstar Sail Cruises. A listing of corporate officers is presented in Exhibit 2.

The company's product positioning stems from its belief that the cruise market is actually comprised of three primary segments with different passenger demographics, passenger characteristics, and growth requirements. The three segments are the contemporary, premium, and luxury segments. The contemporary segment is served by Carnival ships for cruises that are seven days or shorter in length and feature a casual ambiance. The premium segment, served by Holland America, serves the seven-day and longer market and appeals to more affluent consumers. The luxury segment, although considerably smaller than the other segments, caters to experienced cruisers for seven-day and longer sailings and is served by Seabourn. Specialty sailing cruises are provided by Windstar Sail Cruises, a subsidiary of Holland America.

Corporate structure is built around the profit-center concept and is updated periodically when needed for control and coordination purposes. The cruise subsidiaries of Carnival give the corporation a presence in most of the major cruise segments and provides for worldwide operations.

Carnival has always placed a high priority on marketing in an attempt to promote cruises as alternatives to land-based vacations. It wants customers to know that the ship itself is the destination, and the ports of call are important, but secondary, to the cruise experience. Education and the creation of awareness are critical to corporate marketing

---

EXHIBIT 2    **Corporate Officers of Carnival Corporation**

| | |
|---|---|
| Micky Arison | Howard S. Frank |
| Chairman of the Board and Chief Executive Officer | Vice chairman and chief operating officer |
| Gerald R. Cahill | Ian Gaunt |
| Senior vice president finance and CFO | Senior vice president—international |
| Lowell Zemnick | Kenneth D. Dubbin |
| Vice president and treasurer | Vice president—corporate development |
| Robert H. Dickinson | A. Kirk Lanterman |
| President and COO Carnival Cruise Lines | Chairman of the Board and CEO Holland America Lines |

*Source:* Carnival Corporation, 1999 *Annual Report.*

efforts. Carnival was the first cruise line to successfully break away from traditional print media and use television to reach a broader market. Even though other lines have followed Carnival's lead in selecting promotional media and are near in total advertising expenditures, the organization still leads all cruise competitors in advertising and marketing expenditures.

Carnival wants to remain the leader and innovator in the cruise industry and intends to do this with sophisticated promotional efforts and by gaining loyalty from former cruisers, by refurbishing ships, varying activities and ports of call, and being innovative in all aspects of ship operations. Management intends to build on the theme of the ship as a destination, given their historical success with this promotional effort. The company capitalizes and amortizes direct-response advertising and expenses other advertising costs as incurred. Advertising expense totaled $142 million in 1998, $112 million in 1997, $109 million in 1996, $98 million in 1995, and $85 million in 1994.

## FINANCIAL PERFORMANCE

The consolidated financial statements for Carnival Cruise Lines, Inc., are shown in Exhibits 3 and 4, and selected financial data are presented in Exhibit 5.

EXHIBIT 3    Carnival Corp. Annual Income Statement (in millions except EPS data)

|  | 11/30/99 | 11/30/98 | 11/30/97 | 11/30/96 |
|---|---|---|---|---|
| Sales | $3,497.47 | $3,009.30 | $2,447.47 | $2,212.57 |
| Cost of goods | 1,862.63 | 1,619.37 | 1,322.67 | 1,241.27 |
| Gross profit | 1,634.83 | 1,389.92 | 1,124.80 | 971.30 |
| Selling and administrative and depr. and amort. expenses | 690.88 | 570.12 | 463.84 | 419.84 |
| Income after depreciation and amortization | 943.96 | 819.81 | 660.96 | 551.46 |
| Nonoperating income | 147.04 | 77.68 | 60.99 | 87.98 |
| Interest expense | 46.95 | 57.77 | 55.90 | 64.09 |
| Pretax income | 1,044.03 | 839.70 | 666.05 | 575.35 |
| Income taxes | 2.77 | 3.81 | 0 | 9.05 |
| Minority interest | 14.01 | 0 | 0 | 0 |
| Investment gains/losses (+) | 0 | 0 | 0 | 0 |
| Other income/charges | 0 | 0 | 0 | 0 |
| Income from continued operations | N/A | N/A | N/A | N/A |
| Extras and discontinued operations | 0 | 0 | 0 | 0 |
| Net income | $1,027.24 | $ 835.88 | $ 666.05 | $ 566.30 |

*Depreciation footnote*

|  | | | | |
|---|---|---|---|---|
| Income before depreciation and amortization | $1,187.61 | $1,020.47 | $ 838.25 | $ 696.45 |
| Depreciation and amortization (cash flow) | 243.65 | 200.66 | 167.29 | 144.99 |
| Income after depreciation and amortization | $ 943.96 | $ 819.81 | $ 660.96 | $ 551.46 |

*Earnings per-share data*

|  | | | | |
|---|---|---|---|---|
| Average shares | $ 616.00 | $ 598.40 | $ 596.40 | $ 580.40 |
| Diluted earnings per share before nonrecurring items | 1.66 | 1.41 | 1.13 | 0.95 |
| Diluted net earnings per share | $   1.66 | $   1.40 | $   1.12 | $   0.98 |

*Source:* www.freeedgar.com

EXHIBIT 4    Carnival Corp. Annual Balance Sheet
             (in millions, except book value per share)

| | 11/30/99 | 11/30/98 | 11/30/97 | 11/30/96 |
|---|---|---|---|---|
| **Assets** | | | | |
| Cash and equivalents | $   544.57 | $   143.22 | $   149.73 | $   124.11 |
| Receivables | 62.88 | 60.83 | 57.09 | 38.11 |
| Notes receivable | 0 | 0 | 0 | 0 |
| Inventories | 84.01 | 75.44 | 54.97 | 53.28 |
| Other Current Assets | 100.15 | 90.76 | 74.24 | 75.43 |
| Total current assets | 791.63 | 370.27 | 366.02 | 290.93 |
| Net property and equipment | 6,410.52 | 5,768.11 | 4,327.41 | 4,099.04 |
| Investments and advances | 586.92 | 546.69 | 479.33 | 430.33 |
| Other noncurrent assets | 0 | 0 | 0 | 0 |
| Deferred charges | 0 | 0 | 0 | 0 |
| Intangibles | 462.34 | 437.46 | 212.61 | 219.59 |
| Deposits and other assets | 34.93 | 56.77 | 71.40 | 62.00 |
| Total assets | $8,286.35 | $7,179.32 | $5,426.77 | $5,101.89 |
| **Liabilities & shareholders' equity** | | | | |
| Notes payable | 0 | 0 | 0 | 0 |
| Accounts payable | $   195.87 | $   168.54 | $   106.78 | $     84.75 |
| Current portion long-term debt | 206.26 | 67.62 | 59.62 | 66.37 |
| Current portion capital leases | 0 | 0 | 0 | 0 |
| Accrued expenses | 262.17 | 206.96 | 154.25 | 126.51 |
| Income taxes payable | 0 | 0 | 0 | 0 |
| Other current liabilities | 740.59 | 691.97 | 465.49 | 385.11 |
| Total current liabilities | 1,404.91 | 1,135.11 | 786.14 | 662.74 |
| Mortgages | 0 | 0 | 0 | 0 |
| Deferred taxes/income | 82.68 | 63.03 | 20.24 | 91.63 |
| Convertible debt | 0 | 0 | 0 | 39.10 |
| Long-term debt | 867.51 | 1,563.01 | 1,015.29 | 1,277.53 |
| Noncurrent capital leases | 0 | 0 | 0 | 0 |
| Other noncurrent liabilities | 0 | 0 | 0 | 0 |
| Minority interest (liabilities) | 0 | 132.68 | 0 | 0 |
| Total liabilities | $2,355.10 | $2,893.84 | $1,821.68 | $2,071.00 |
| **Shareholders' equity** | | | | |
| Preferred stock | 0 | 0 | 0 | 0 |
| Common stock (par) | $       6.17 | $       5.95 | $       2.97 | $       2.95 |
| Capital surplus | 1,757.40 | 880.48 | 866.10 | 819.61 |
| Retained earnings | 4,176.49 | 3,379.62 | 2,731.21 | 2,207.78 |
| Other equity | (8.82) | 19.40 | 4.82 | 0.55 |
| Treasury stock | 0 | 0 | 0 | 0 |
| Total shareholders' equity | 5,931.24 | 4,285.47 | 3,605.10 | 3,030.88 |
| Total liabilities and shareholders' equity | 8,286.35 | 7,179.32 | 5,426.77 | 5,101.89 |
| Total common equity | 5,931.24 | 4,285.47 | 3,605.10 | 3,030.88 |
| Average shares | 616.00 | 598.40 | 596.40 | 580.40 |
| Book value per share | $       9.66 | $       7.21 | $       6.05 | $       5.20 |

*Source:* www.freeedgar.com

## EXHIBIT 5   Carnival Financial Data by Segment

### A. Product Data

| | Revenues | Operating Income (Loss) | Depreciation and Amortization | Capital Expenditures | Segment Assets |
|---|---|---|---|---|---|
| **1999** | | | | | |
| Cruise | $3,286,701 | $ 947,452 | $ 232,942 | $ 836,351 | $6,938,411 |
| Tour | 271,828 | 10,403 | 10,716 | 25,191 | 185,591 |
| Affiliate operations | | 75,758 | | | 586,922 |
| Reconciling items | (61,059) | (13,914) | | 11,442 | 575,431 |
| | 3,497,470 | 1,019,699 | 243,658 | 872,984 | 8,286,355 |
| **1998** | | | | | |
| Cruise | 2,797,856 | 822,242 | 189,345 | 1,113,191 | 6,327,599 |
| Tour | 274,491 | 9,248 | 9,491 | 28,480 | 174,140 |
| Affiliate operations | | 76,732 | | | 546,693 |
| Reconciling items | (63,041) | (11,698) | 1,832 | 8,742 | 130,891 |
| | 3,009,306 | 896,524 | 200,668 | 1,150,413 | 7,179,323 |
| **1997** | | | | | |
| Cruise | 2,257,567 | 656,009 | 157,454 | 414,963 | 4,617,583 |
| Tour | 242,646 | 13,262 | 8,862 | 42,507 | 163,941 |
| Affiliate operations | | 53,091 | | | 479,329 |
| Reconciling items | (52,745) | (8,292) | 971 | 40,187 | 165,922 |
| | 2,447,468 | 714,070 | 167,287 | 497,657 | 5,426,775 |

### B. Geographic Data

| | 1999 | 1998 | 1997 |
|---|---|---|---|
| **Revenues** | | | |
| Domestic | $3,077,499 | $2,667,289 | $2,234,063 |
| Foreign | 419,971 | 342,017 | 213,405 |
| | $3,497,470 | $3,009,306 | $2,447,468 |
| **Assets** | | | |
| Domestic | $1,249,798 | $ 801,759 | $ 762,994 |
| Foreign | 7,036,557 | 6,377,564 | 4,663,781 |
| | $8,296,355 | $7,179,323 | $5,426,775 |

Customer cruise deposits, which represent unearned revenue, are included in the balance sheet when received and recognized as cruise revenues on completion of the voyage. Customers also are required to pay the full cruise fare (minus deposit) 60 days in advance, with the fares being recognized as cruise revenue on completion of the voyage.

Property and equipment on the financial statements are stated at cost. Depreciation and amortization are calculated using the straight-line method over the following estimated useful lives: vessels, 25–30 years; buildings, 20–40 years; equipment, 2–20 years; and leasehold improvements at the shorter of the term of lease or related asset life. During 1995, Carnival received $40 million from the settlement of litigation with Metra Oy, the former parent company of Wartsila Marine Industries, related to losses suffered in connection with the construction of three cruise ships. (Wartsila declared bankruptcy in late 1994.) Of this amount, $14.4 million was recorded as "other income," with the remainder used to pay legal fees and reduce the cost basis of the three ships.

On June 25, 1996, Carnival reached an agreement with the trustees of Wartsila and creditors for the bankruptcy that resulted in a cash payment of approximately $80 million. Of the $80 million received, $5 million was used to pay certain costs; $32 million was recorded as other income, and $43 million was used to reduce the cost basis of certain ships that had been affected by the bankruptcy.

By August 31, 1999, Carnival had outstanding long-term debt of $1.18 billion with the current portion being $33.6 million. According to the Internal Revenue Code of 1986, Carnival is considered a controlled foreign corporation because 50 percent of its stock is held by residents of foreign countries and its countries of incorporation exempt shipping operations of U.S. persons from income tax. Because of this status, Carnival expects that all of its income (with the exception of U.S. source income from the transportation, hotel, and tour businesses of Holland America) will be exempt from U.S. federal income taxes at the corporate level.

The primary financial consideration of importance to Carnival management involves the control of costs, both fixed and variable, for the maintenance of a healthy profit margin. Carnival has the lowest break-even point of any organization in the cruise industry (ships break even at approximately 60 percent of capacity) due to operational experience and economies of scale. Unfortunately, fixed costs, including depreciation, fuel, insurance, port charges, and crew costs, which represent more than 33 percent of the company's operating expenses, cannot be significantly reduced in relation to decreases in passenger loads and aggregate passenger ticket revenue. Major expense items are air fares (25 percent–30 percent), travel agent fees (10 percent), and labor (13 percent–15 percent). Increases in these costs could negatively affect the profitability of the organization.

## PRINCIPAL SUBSIDIARIES

### Carnival Cruise Line

At the end of fiscal 1999, Carnival operated 14 ships with a total berth capacity of 24,404. Carnival operates principally in the Caribbean and has an assortment of ships and ports of call serving the three-, four-, and seven-day cruise markets (See Exhibit 6).

Each ship is a floating resort with a full maritime staff, shopkeepers and casino operators, entertainers, and complete hotel staff. Approximately 14 percent of corporate revenue is generated from shipboard activities such as casino operations, liquor sales, and gift shop items. At various ports of call, passengers can also take advantage of tours, shore excursions, and duty-free shopping at their own expense.

Shipboard operations are designed to provide maximum entertainment, activities, and service. The size of the company and the similarity in design of the new cruise ships have allowed Carnival to achieve various economies of scale, and management is very cost conscious.

Although the Carnival Cruise Lines division is increasing its presence in the shorter cruise markets, their general marketing strategy is to use three-, four-, or seven-day moderately priced cruises to fit the time and budget constraints of the middle class. Shorter cruises can cost less than $500 per person (depending on accommodations) up to roughly $3,000 per person in a luxury suite on a seven-day cruise, including port charges. (Per-diem rates for shorter cruises are slightly higher, on average, than per-diem rates for seven-day cruises.) Average rates per day are approximately $180, excluding gambling, liquor and soft drinks, and items of a personal nature. Guests are expected to tip their cabin steward and waiter (at a suggested rate of $3 per person per day) and the bus boy (at $1.50 per person per day).

Some 99 percent of all Carnival cruises are sold through travel agents who receive a standard commission of 10 percent (15 percent in Florida). Carnival works extensively

## EXHIBIT 6    The Ships of Carnival Corporation

| Name | Built | Service Cap | Gross Tons | Areas of Operation |
|------|-------|-------------|------------|--------------------|
| **Carnival Cruise Lines** | | | | |
| *Triumph* | 1999 | 2,758 | 102,000 | East Coast, Caribbean |
| *Paradise* | 1998 | 2,040 | 70,367 | Caribbean |
| *Elation* | 1998 | 2,040 | 70,367 | Mexican Riviera |
| *Destiny* | 1996 | 2,642 | 101,000 | Caribbean |
| *Inspiration* | 1996 | 2,040 | 70,367 | Caribbean |
| *Imagination* | 1995 | 2,040 | 70,367 | Caribbean |
| *Fascination* | 1994 | 2,040 | 70,367 | Caribbean |
| *Sensation* | 1993 | 2,040 | 70,367 | Caribbean |
| *Ecstasy* | 1991 | 2,040 | 70,367 | Caribbean |
| *Fantasy* | 1990 | 2,044 | 70,367 | Bahamas |
| *Celebration* | 1987 | 1,486 | 47,262 | Caribbean |
| *Jubilee* | 1986 | 1,486 | 47,262 | Mexican Riviera |
| *Holiday* | 1985 | 1,452 | 46,052 | Mexican Riviera |
| *Tropicale* | 1982 | 1,022 | 36,674 | Alaska, Caribbean |
| Total Carnival Ships Capacity | | 24,404 | | |
| **Holland America Line** | | | | |
| *Rotterdam* | 1997 | 1,316 | 62,000 | Europe, Worldwide |
| *Veendam* | 1996 | 1,266 | 55,451 | Alaska, Caribbean |
| *Ryndam* | 1994 | 1,266 | 55,451 | Alaska, Caribbean |
| *Maasdam* | 1993 | 1,266 | 55,451 | Europe, Caribbean |
| *Statendam* | 1993 | 1,266 | 55,451 | Alaska, Caribbean |
| *Westerdam* | 1986 | 1,494 | 53,872 | Canada, Caribbean |
| *Noordam* | 1984 | 1,214 | 33,930 | Alaska, Caribbean |
| *Nieuw Amsterdam* | 1983 | 1,214 | 33,930 | Alaska, Caribbean |
| Total HAL Ships Capacity | | 10,302 | | |
| *Windstar Cruises* | | | | |
| *Wind Surf* | 1990 | 312 | 17,745 | Caribbean |
| *Wind Spirit* | 1988 | 148 | 5,736 | Caribbean, Mediterranean |
| *Wind Song* | 1987 | 148 | 5,703 | Costa Rica, Tahiti |
| *Wind Star* | 1986 | 148 | 5,703 | Caribbean, Mediterranean |
| Total Windstar Ships Capacity | | 758 | | |
| **Cunard** | | | | |
| *Royal Viking Sun* | 1988 | 758 | 37,845 | Worldwide |
| *Sea Goddess II* | 1985 | 116 | 4,253 | Asia |
| *Sea Goddess I* | 1984 | 116 | 4,253 | Caribbean |
| *Vistafjord* | 1973 | 675 | 24,492 | Worldwide |
| *Queen Elizabeth 2* | 1969 | 1,715 | 70,327 | Worldwide |
| Total Cunard Ship Capacity | | 3,380 | | |
| *Seabourn* | | | | |
| *Seabourn Legend* | 1992 | 208 | 9,975 | Pacific |
| *Seabourn Spirit* | 1989 | 208 | 9,975 | Asia |
| *Seabourn Pride* | 1988 | 208 | 9,975 | South America |
| Total Seabourn Ships Capacity | | 624 | | |
| Total Capacity | | 39,466 | | |

with travel agents to help promote cruises as an alternative to a Disney or European vacation. In addition to training travel agents from nonaffiliated travel or vacation firms to sell cruises, a special group of employees regularly visit travel agents in order to pose as prospective clients. If the agent recommends a cruise before another vacation option, he or she receives $100. If the travel agent specifies a Carnival cruise before other options, they receive $1,000 on the spot. During fiscal 1995, Carnival took reservations from about 29,000 of the approximately 45,000 travel agencies in the United States and Canada, and no one travel agency accounted for more than 2 percent of Carnival's revenues.

On-board service is labor intensive, employing help from some 51 nations—mostly Third World countries—with reasonable returns to employees. For example, waiters on the *Jubilee* can earn approximately $18,000 to $27,000 per year (base salary and tips), significantly more than could be earned in their home country for similar employment. Waiters typically work ten hours per day with approximately one day off per week for a specified contract period (usually three to nine months). Carnival records show that employees remain with the company for approximately eight years and that applicants exceed demand for all cruise positions. Nonetheless, the American Maritime Union has cited Carnival (and other cruise operators) several times for exploitation of its crew.

## Holland America Lines

On January 17, 1989, Carnival acquired all the outstanding stock of HAL Antillen N.V. from Holland America Lines N.V. for $625 million in cash. Carnival financed the purchase through $250 million in retained earnings (cash account) and borrowed the other $375 million from banks at .25 percent over the prime rate. Carnival received the assets and operations of the Holland America Lines, Westours, Westmark Hotels, and Windstar Sail Cruises. Holland America currently has eight cruise ships with a capacity of 10,302 berths, with new ships to be delivered in the future.

Founded in 1873, Holland America Lines is an upscale (its cruises cost an average of 25 percent more than similar Carnival cruises) line. The principal destinations are Alaska during the summer months and the Caribbean during the fall and winter, with some worldwide cruises of up to 98 days. Holland America targets an older, more sophisticated traveler with fewer youth-oriented activities. On Holland America ships, passengers can dance to the sounds of the Big Band era instead of the discos of Carnival ships. Passengers on Holland America ships enjoy better service (a higher staff-to-passenger ratio than Carnival) and have more cabin and public space per person and a no-tipping shipboard policy. Holland America has not enjoyed the spectacular growth of Carnival cruise ships but sustained constant growth over the 1980s and early 1990s with high occupancy. The operation of these ships and the structure of the crew are similar to those of the Carnival cruise ship model, and the acquisition of the line gave the Carnival Corporation a presence in the Alaskan market that it had previously lacked.

Holland America Westours is the largest tour operator in Alaska and the Canadian Rockies and provides vacation synergy with Holland America cruises. The transportation division of Westours includes over 290 motor coaches comprised of the Gray Line of Alaska, the Gray Line of Seattle, Westours motorcoaches, the McKinley Explorer railroad coaches, and three-day boats for tours to glaciers and other points of interest. Carnival management believes that Alaskan cruises and tours should increase in the future due to a number of factors. These include the fact that the aging population wants relaxing vacations with scenic beauty and that Alaska is a United States destination.

Westmark Hotels consist of 16 hotels in Alaska and the Yukon territories that provide synergy with cruise operations and Westours. Westmark is the largest group of hotels in the region to provide moderately priced rooms for the vacationer.

Windstar Sail Cruises was acquired by Holland America Lines in 1988 and consists of three computer-controlled sailing vessels with a berth capacity of 444. Windstar is very upscale and offers an alternative to traditional cruise liners by providing a more intimate, activity-oriented cruise. The ships operate primarily in the Mediterranean and the South Pacific, visiting ports not accessible to large cruise ships. Although it caters to a small segment of the cruise vacation industry, Windstar augments Carnival's commitment to participate in all segments of the cruise industry.

### Seabourn Cruise Lines

In April 1992, the company acquired 25 percent of the capital stock of Seabourn. As part of the transaction, the company also made a subordinated secured ten-year loan of $15 million and a $10 million convertible loan to Seabourn. In December 1995, it converted the $10 million convertible loan into an additional 25 percent equity interest in Seabourn.

Seabourn targets the luxury market with three vessels and provides 200 passengers per ship with all-suite accommodations. Seabourn is considered the Rolls-Royce of the cruise industry and in 1992 was named the "World's Best Cruise Line" by the prestigious Condé Nast Traveler's Fifth Annual Readers Choice poll. Seabourn cruises the Americas, Europe, Scandinavia, the Mediterranean, and the Far East.

### Airtours

In April 1996, the Company acquired a 29.5 percent interest in Airtours for approximately $307 million. Airtours and its subsidiaries form the largest air-inclusive tour operator in the world and is publicly traded on the London Stock Exchange. Airtours provides air-inclusive packaged holidays to the British, Scandinavian, and North American markets. Airtours provides holidays to approximately 5 million people per year and owns or operates 32 hotels, 2 cruise ships, and 31 aircraft.

Airtours owns or operates 32 hotels (6,500 rooms), which provide rooms to Airtours' tour operators principally in the Mediterranean and the Canary Islands. In addition, Airtours has a 50 percent interest in Tenerife Sol, a joint venture with Sol Hotels Group of Spain, which owns and operates three additional hotels in the Canary Islands that supply 1,300 rooms.

Through its subsidiary Sun Cruises, Airtours owns and operates two cruise ships. Both the 800-berth *Seawing* and the 1,062-berth *Carousel* commenced operations in 1995. Recently, Airtours acquired a third ship, the *Sundream,* the sister ship of the *Carousel.* The *Sundream* is expected to commence operations in May 1997. The ships operate in the Mediterranean, the Caribbean, and around the Canary Islands and are booked exclusively by Airtours' tour operators.

### Costa Crociere S.p.A.

In June 1997, Carnival and Airtours purchased the equity securities of Costa from the Costa family at a cost of approximately $141 million. Costa is headquartered in Italy and is considered Europe's largest cruise line with seven ships and 7,710-passenger capacity. Costa operates primarily in the Mediterranean, Northern Europe, the Caribbean, and South America. The major market for Costa is southern Europe—mainly Italy, Spain and France. In January 1998, Costa signed an agreement to construct an eighth ship with a capacity of approximately 2,100 passengers.

## Cunard Line

Carnival's most recent acquisition has been the Cunard Line, announced on May 28, 1998. Comprised of five ships, the Cunard Line is considered a luxury line with strong brand-name recognition. Carnival purchased 50 percent of Cunard for an estimated $255 million; the other 50 percent is owned by Atle Brynestad. Cunard was immediately merged with Seabourn, and the resulting Cunard Cruise Line Limited (68 percent owned by Carnival) with its eight ships is headed by the former president of Seabourn, Larry Pimentel.

## Joint Venture with Hyundai Merchant Marine Co. Ltd.

In September 1996, the Carnival and Hyundai Merchant Marine Co. Ltd. signed an agreement to form a 50/50 joint venture to develop the Asian cruise vacation market. Each have contributed $4.8 million as the initial capital of the joint venture. In addition, in November 1996, Carnival sold the cruise ship *Tropicale* to the joint venture for approximately $95.5 million cash. Carnival then chartered the vessel from the joint venture until the joint venture began cruise operations in the Asian market in the Spring of 1998. The joint venture borrowed the $95.5 million purchase price from a financial institution, and Carnival and HMM each guaranteed 50 percent of the borrowed funds. This arrangement was, however, short lived as in September 1997, the joint venture was dissolved, and the company repurchased the *Tropicale* for $93 million.

## FUTURE CONSIDERATIONS

Carnival's management will have to continue to monitor several strategic factors and issues for the next few years. The industry itself should see further consolidation through mergers and buyouts, and the expansion of the industry could negatively affect the profitability of various cruise operators. Another factor of concern to management is how to reach the large North American market, of which only 5 percent to 7 percent has ever taken a cruise.

With the industry maturing, cruise competitors have become more sophisticated in their marketing efforts, and price competition is the norm in most cruise segments. (For a partial listing of major industry competitors, see Exhibit 7.) Royal Caribbean Cruise Lines has also instituted a major shipbuilding program and is successfully challenging Carnival Cruise Lines in the contemporary segment. The announcement that the Walt Disney Company was entering the cruise market with two 80,000-ton cruise liners in 1998 could significantly impact the family cruise vacation segment.

With competition intensifying, industry observers believe the failures, mergers, buyouts, and strategic alliances will increase. Regency Cruises ceased operations on October 29, 1995, and filed for Chapter 11 bankruptcy. American Family Cruises, a spin-off from Costa Cruise Lines, failed to reach the family market, and Carnival's Fiestamarina failed to reach the Spanish-speaking market. EffJohn International sold its Commodore Cruise subsidiary to a group of Miami-based investors, which then chartered one of its two ships to World Explorer Cruises/Semester at Sea. Sun Cruise Lines merged with Epirotiki Cruise Line under the name of Royal Olympic Cruises, and Cunard bought the Royal Viking Line and its name from Kloster Cruise Ltd., with one ship of its fleet being transferred to Kloster's Royal Cruise Line. All of these failures, mergers, and buyouts occurred in 1995, which was not an unusual year for changes in the cruise line industry.

EXHIBIT 7    Major Industry Competitors

**Celebrity Cruises,** 5200 Blue Lagoon Drive, Miami, FL 33126

Celebrity Cruises operates six modern cruise ships on four-, seven- and ten-day cruises to Bermuda, the Caribbean, the Panama Canal, and Alaska. Celebrity attracts first-time as well as seasoned travelers. Purchased by Royal Caribbean on July 30, 1997.

**Norwegian Cruise Lines,** 95 Merrick Way, Coral Gables, FL 33134

Norwegian Cruise Lines, formally Norwegian Caribbean Lines, was the first to base a modern fleet of cruise ships in the Port of Miami. It operates nine modern cruise liners on three-, four-, and seven-day eastern and western Caribbean cruises and cruises to Bermuda. A wide variety of activities and entertainment attracts a diverse array of customers. Norwegian Cruise Lines has just completed reconstruction of two ships and its newest ship, the *Norwegian Sky,* a 2,000-passenger ship, was delivered in the summer of 1999.

**Disney Cruise Line,** 500 South Buena Vista Street, Burbank, CA 91521

Disney has just recently entered the cruise market with the introduction of the *Disney Magic* and *Disney Wonder.* Both ships will cater to both children and adults and will feature 875 staterooms. Each cruise will include a visit to Disney's private island, Castaway Cay. Although Disney currently has only two ships, and the cruise portion of Disney is small, its potential for future growth is substantial, with over $22 billion in revenues and $1.9 billion net profits in 1997.

**Princess Cruises,** 10100 Santa Monica Boulevard, Los Angeles, CA 90067

Princess Cruises, with its fleet of nine "Love Boats," offers seven-day and extended cruises to the Caribbean, Alaska, Canada, Africa, the Far East, South America, and Europe. Princess's primary market is the upscale 50-plus experienced traveler, according to Mike Hannan, senior vice president for marketing services. Princess ships have an ambiance best described as casual elegance and are famous for their Italian-style dining rooms and onboard entertainment.

**Royal Caribbean Cruise Lines,** 1050 Caribbean Way, Miami, FL 33132

Royal Caribbean's nine ships have consistently been given high marks by passengers and travel agents over the past 21 years. Royal Caribbean's ships are built for the contemporary market, are large and modern, and offer three-, four-, and seven-day as well as extended cruises. The cruise line prides itself on service and exceptional cuisine. With the purchase of *Celebrity,* Royal Caribbean becomes the largest cruise line in the world with 17 ships and a passenger capacity of over 31,100. Plans include the introduction of six additional ships by the year 2002. In 1997 this cruise line had net income of $175 million on revenues of $1.93 billion.

**Other Industry Competitors (Partial List)**

| | |
|---|---|
| American Hawaii Cruises | (2 ships—Hawaiian Islands) |
| Club Med | (2 ships—Europe, Caribbean) |
| Commodore Cruise Line | (1 ship—Caribbean) |
| Dolphin Cruise Line | (3 ships—Caribbean, Bermuda) |
| Radisson Seven Seas Cruises | (3 ships—worldwide) |
| Royal Olympic Cruises | (6 ships—Caribbean, worldwide) |
| Royal Cruise Line | (4 ships—Caribbean, Alaska, worldwide) |

*Source:* Cruise Line International Association, 1996 and company 10Ks and annual reports.

The increasing industry capacity is also a source of concern to cruise operators. The slow growth in industry demand is occurring during a period when industry berth capacity continues to grow. The entry of Disney and the ships already on order by current operators will increase industry berth capacity by over 10,000 per year for the next three years, a significant increase. (See Exhibit 8 for new ships under construction.) The danger lies in cruise operators using the "price" weapon in their marketing campaigns to fill cabins. If cruise operators cannot make a reasonable return on investment, operating costs will have to be reduced (affecting quality of services) to remain profitable. This will

EXHIBIT 8    New Carnival Ships Under Construction

| Vessel | Expected Service Date | Shipyard | Capacity | Gross Tons | Estimated Costs (in millions) |
|---|---|---|---|---|---|
| **Carnival** | | | | | |
| Carnival Victory | 9/00 | Fincantieri | 2,758 | 101,000 | $   450 |
| Carnival Spirit | 4/01 | Masa-Yards | 2,120 | 84,000 | 375 |
| Carnival Pride | 1/02 | Masa-Yards | 2,120 | 84,000 | 375 |
| Carnival Legend | 8/02 | Masa-Yards | 2,120 | 84,000 | 375 |
| Carnival Conquest | 12/02 | Fincantieri | 2,758 | 101,000 | 450 |
| Carnival Glory | 8/03 | Fincantieri | 2,758 | 101,000 | 450 |
| Total Carnival Ships | | | 14,634 | | 2,475 |
| **Holland America** | | | | | |
| Zaandam | 5/00 | Fincantieri | 1,440 | 63,000 | 300 |
| Amsterdam | 11/00 | Fincantieri | 1,380 | 62,000 | 300 |
| Newbuild | 10/02 | Fincantieri | 1,820 | 84,000 | 400 |
| Newbuild | 8/03 | Fincantieri | 1,820 | 84,000 | 400 |
| Newbuild | 1/04 | Fincantieri | 1,820 | 84,000 | 400 |
| Newbuild | 9/04 | Fincantieri | 1,820 | 84,000 | 400 |
| Total Holland America Ships | | | 10,100 | | 2,200 |
| Total | | | 24,734 | | $4,675 |

*Source:* Carnival's 1999 *Annual Report,* p. 9.

increase the likelihood of further industry acquisitions, mergers, and consolidations. A worst-case scenario would be the financial failure of weaker lines.

Still, Carnival's management believes that demand should increase well into the 2000s. Considering that only 5 percent to 7 percent of the North American market has taken a cruise vacation, reaching more of the North American target market would improve industry profitability. Industry analysts state the problem is that an "assessment of market potential" is only an "educated guess"; and wonder if the current demand figures are reflective of the future?

# SOUTHWEST AIRLINES CO.—2000

Amit Shah and Charles R. Sterrett
Frostburg State University

## LUV
www.iflyswa.com also www.southwest.com

For nine consecutive years (1991 through 1999), the Department of Transportation (DOT) *Air Travel Consumer Report* listed Southwest Airlines as having the best on-time performance, best baggage handling, and fewest customer complaints of all the major carriers. In a highly competitive industry, all carriers continually strive for the first place listing in any of the categories of the DOT report; Southwest is the only airline to ever hold the Triple Crown for its annual performance. No other airline has even earned the Triple Crown for even one month. In addition to this honor, Southwest is consistently among *Fortune* magazine's most admired companies (sixth in 1998) and on the magazine's list of the 100 best companies to work for. In September 1999, the *Wall Street Journal* also ranked Southwest among the top 30 companies on the basis of reputation—the only airline to make the cut. In addition to these achievements, Southwest continues to operate profitably; it made $474.3 million in net income on $4.7 billion in 1999 revenues. In an industry that historically has been awash in red ink, in which airlines continually go in and out of bankruptcy or fail, Southwest has an enviable record of over 27 consecutive years of operating at a profit. How has it accomplished this?

In their best-selling book *Nuts,* Kevin and Jackie Freiburg point to a company of people who are committed to working hard and having fun and who avoid following industry trends. The Freiburgs note that Southwest, based in Dallas, Texas, is a company that likes to keep prices at rock bottom; believes the customer comes first; runs recruiting ads that say, "Work at a place where wearing pants is optional"; paints its $30 million assets to look like killer whales and state flags; avoids trendy management programs; avoids formal, documented strategic planning; spends more time planning parties than writing policies; and once settled a legal dispute by arm wrestling.

## HISTORY AND GROWTH OF SOUTHWEST AIRLINES

According to Southwest folklore, the airline was conceived in 1967 on a napkin when Rollin King, an investment advisor, met with his lawyer, Herb Kelleher, to discuss his idea for a low-fare, no-frills airline to fly between three of the major cities in Texas. At that time, King ran an unprofitable air charter service between small Texas cities. One day, his banker, John Parker, suggested that King concentrate on flying between the three biggest cities in the state. Parker suggested that the market was open for exploitation because he could never get a seat on the airlines currently flying between those cities, and besides, the fares were too high. King knew he couldn't compete, so he decided to start a bigger airline. He put together a plan and a feasibility study and went to see Kelleher. In that meeting, King scribbled three lines on a cocktail napkin; labeled the points Houston, Dallas, and San Antonio, and muttered, "Herb, let's start our own airline." Kelleher loosened his tie and knitted his brow before replying: "Rollin, you're crazy. Let's do it!" Kelleher completed the necessary paperwork to create Air Southwest Co. (later Southwest Airlines). Then, the two filed for approval, and on February 20, 1968, the Texas Aeronautical Commission approved their plans to fly between the three cities.

The very next day, the upstart airline ran into stiff opposition from several of the major carriers then doing business in Texas. On February 21, 1968, these carriers— Braniff, Texas International, and Continental—blocked approval with a temporary restraining order. They argued that Texas didn't need another carrier. For the next three years, Southwest was unable to proceed while it fought legal battles with these airlines over the right to offer flights between the three cities. In 1971, however, Southwest won the right to fly and began to offer service with a total of four planes and about 200 employees. The efforts to quash the airline led to the unbridled enthusiasm by King, Kelleher, and the other employees that became an important part of Southwest's culture.

The outlook for Southwest remained bleak, however. The legal battles left the airline flat broke and deep in debt. In its first year of operation, it lost $3.7 million, and it did not earn a profit for the next year and a half. But in 1973, it turned its first profit and never looked back. By 1978, it was one of the most profitable airlines in the country.

In its early years, Southwest faced other legal battles. For example, in 1974 a new airport opened to serve the greater Dallas–Fort Worth area; but it was further from downtown Dallas than Love Field. Southwest was using Love Field and wanted to continue to do so, but competitors wanted Southwest to move to the new airport to share in the costs and began to pressure Congress to pass a law barring flights from Love Field to any airport outside of Texas. Southwest was able to negotiate a compromise, known as the Wright amendment, that allowed flights to airports (including Love Field) in the four states bordering on Texas. The Wright amendment forced Southwest into a key part of its strategy—to become an interstate carrier.

Southwest grew steadily and by 1975 had expanded its operations to eight more cities in Texas. By the end of the 1970s, it dominated the Texas market. Its major appeal was to passengers who wanted low prices and frequent departures. In the 1980s and 1990s, Southwest continued to expand, and by 1993, it was serving 34 cities in 15 states. Southwest slowly, but methodically, moved across the Southwestern states into California, the Midwest, and the Northwest. It added new destinations in Florida and the East Coast. With its low prices and no-frills approach, it quickly dominated whatever markets it entered. In some markets, after Southwest entered, competitors soon withdrew, allowing the airline to expand even faster than projected. For example, when Southwest entered the California market in 1990, it quickly became the second-largest player, with over 20 percent of the intrastate market. Several competitors soon abandoned the Los Angeles–San Francisco route when they were unable to match Southwest's $59 one-way fare. Before Southwest entered this market, fares had been as high as $186 one way.

The California route offers a good example of the real dilemma facing competing carriers, who often referred to Southwest as a "500-pound cockroach, too big to stamp out." While airfares were dropping, passenger traffic increased dramatically. But competitors such as American and US Air were losing money on several key route segments, even though they cut service drastically. In late 1994, United began to fight back by launching a low-cost, high-frequency shuttle service on the West Coast, but it found that even a shuttle could not win against Southwest in a head-to-head battle. So United repositioned its shuttle away from Southwest's routes and even abandoned some routes altogether. According to the DOT, eight airlines surrendered West Coast routes to

Southwest while one-way fares fell by over 30 percent to an average of $60, and traffic increased by almost 60 percent. The major problem for the larger airlines was the fact that many of these West Coast routes were critical for feeding traffic into their highly profitable transcontinental and transpacific routes, and Southwest was cutting into that market.

Southwest is currently the fourth-largest domestic carrier in terms of customers boarded. The airline has transformed itself from a regional carrier operating out of Dallas into a truly national carrier. As of July 1999, the airline serves 55 cities in 29 states and operates more than 2,450 flights a day with its fleet of 296 Boeing 737s. In 1998, Southwest flew 31.4 billion revenue passenger miles (RPMs) compared with 28.4 billion RPMs in 1997. But most remarkable is 27 years in a row of profitable operations, with total revenue in 1999 being $4.7 billion—an increase of 13 percent over 1998. Operating income in 1999 rose by 14 percent over 1998. Net income rose by 9 percent from $433.4 million in 1998 to $474.3 million in 1999. Financial statements are shown in Exhibit 1 and 2.

EXHIBIT 1    Southwest Airlines Co. Consolidated Income Statement (in thousands except per-share amounts)

|  | Years Ended December 31, | |
|  | 1999 | 1998 |
| --- | --- | --- |
| **Operating Revenues:** | | |
| Passenger | $4,499,360 | $3,963,781 |
| Freight | 102, 990 | 98,500 |
| Other | 133,237 | 101,699 |
| Total operating revenues | 4,735,587 | 4,163,980 |
| **Operating Expenses:** | | |
| Salaries, wages, and benefits | 1,455,237 | 1,285,942 |
| Fuel and oil | 492,415 | 388,348 |
| Maintenance materials and repairs | 367,606 | 302,431 |
| Agency commissions | 156,419 | 157,766 |
| Aircraft rentals | 199,740 | 202,160 |
| Landing fees and other rentals | 242,002 | 214,907 |
| Depreciation | 248,660 | 225,212 |
| Other operating expenses | 791,932 | 703,603 |
| Total operating expenses | 3,954,011 | 3,480,369 |
| Operating Income | 781,576 | 683,611 |
| **Other expenses (income):** | | |
| Interest expense | 54,145 | 56,276 |
| Capitalized interest | (31,262) | (25,588) |
| Interest income | (25,200) | (31,083) |
| Other (gains) losses, net | 10,282 | (21,106) |
| Total other expenses (income) | 7,965 | (21,501) |
| Income before income taxes | 773,611 | 705,112 |
| Provision for income taxes | 299,233 | 271,681 |
| Net income | $ 474,378 | $ 433,431 |

*Source:* www.freeedgar.com

EXHIBIT 2    Southwest Airlines Co. Consolidated Balance Sheet
(in thousands except per-share amounts)

| | December 31, | |
| | 1999 | 1998 |
|---|---|---|
| **Assets** | | |
| Current assets: | | |
| Cash and cash equivalents | $ 418,819 | $ 389,511 |
| Accounts receivable | 73,448 | 88,799 |
| Inventories of parts and supplies, at cost | 65,152 | 50,035 |
| Deferred income taxes | 20,929 | 20,734 |
| Prepaid expenses and other current assets | 52,657 | 36,076 |
| Total current assets | 631,005 | 574,155 |
| Property and equipment, at cost | | |
| Flight equipment | 5,768,506 | 4,709,059 |
| Ground property and equipment | 742,230 | 720,604 |
| Deposits on flight equipment purchase contracts | 338,229 | 309,356 |
| | 6,848,965 | 5,739,019 |
| Less allowance for depreciation | 1,840,799 | 1,601,409 |
| | 5,008,166 | 4,137,610 |
| Other assets | 12,942 | 4,231 |
| | $5,652,113 | $4,715,996 |
| **Liabilities and stockholders' equity** | | |
| Current liabilities: | | |
| Accounts payable | $ 156,755 | $ 157,415 |
| Accrued liabilities | 535,024 | 477,448 |
| Air traffic liability | 256,942 | 200,078 |
| Current maturities of long-term debt | 7,873 | 11,996 |
| Other current liabilities | 3,872 | 3,716 |
| Total current liabilities | 960,466 | 850,653 |
| Long-term debt less current maturities | 871,717 | 623,309 |
| Deferred income taxes | 692,342 | 549,207 |
| Deferred gains from sale and leaseback of aircraft | 222,700 | 238,412 |
| Other deferred liabilities | 69,100 | 56,497 |
| Commitments and contingencies | | |
| Stockholders' equity | | |
| Common stock, $1.00 par value: 1,300,000 shares authorized; 505,005 and 335,904 shares issued in 1999 and 1998, respectively | 505,005 | 335,904 |
| Capital in excess of par value | 35,436 | 89,820 |
| Retained earnings | 2,385,854 | 2,044,975 |
| Treasury stock, at cost: 5,579 and 5,402 shares in 1999 and 1998, respectively | (90,507) | (72,781) |
| Total stockholders' equity | 2,835,788 | 2,397,918 |
| Total liabilities and stockholders' equity | $5,652,113 | $4,715,996 |

*Source:* www.freeedgar.com

## MANAGEMENT

While Southwest was going through its traumatic beginnings, King and Kelleher realized they needed someone to run the company. King hired Lamar Muse, an executive who had airline experience, as CEO. Muse raised funding to keep the airline going and hired an experienced management team as company officers. He was able to purchase three brand new Boeing 737s at bargain-basement prices because Boeing had overproduced in a period when airlines were in a slump. Muse led the airline in its climb to profitability, but, after a dispute with the board, he was ousted in 1978. With Muse out, Kelleher moved into the top position and has run the airline ever since. Exhibit 3 shows the organizational chart of the company.

Kelleher is well known for his zany antics and his fun-loving, seemingly carefree style of management. For example, in 1992 he made headlines with an event called "Malice in Dallas," which was the result of a dispute over Southwest's "Just Plane Smart" slogan. Stevens Aviation, a small airline sales company in South Carolina, had been using the slogan "Plane Smart" and claimed Southwest was infringing on its territory. Rather than go to court over the trademark, Stevens' chairman suggested an arm-wrestling match. Kelleher readily agreed, lost amid much fanfare, and was carried out on a stretcher while a "trainer" fed him shots of whiskey. Stevens let him use the slogan anyway, and both companies benefited by the bonanza of publicity surrounding the event. Kelleher is the guy who has dressed up as the Easter Bunny, Elvis, and other costumed characters for some of the company's many parties, but he is also the shrewd businessperson who has led the airline to 26 profitable years. His skills have made him one of America's most admired CEOs. If Herb Kelleher is crazy, as some claim, perhaps the CEO of Southwest is crazy like a fox.

EXHIBIT 3    Southwest organizational chart

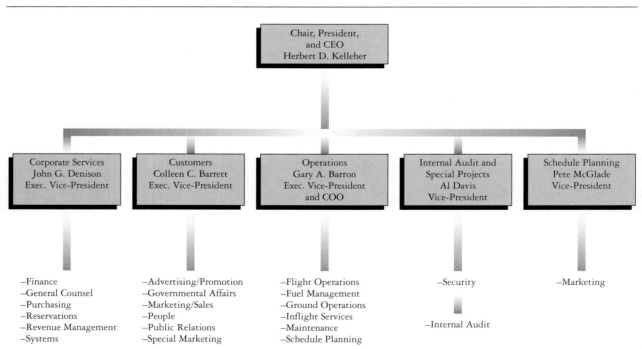

*Source:* Southwest Airlines Co., Feb. 1998.

Even though the airline has grown to over 28,000 employees, Southwest's management team drives home the feeling that all of its people are part of one big family. Southwest's Culture Committee is headed by Colleen Barrett, Kelleher's former legal secretary and now an executive vice-president, who is the highest-ranking woman in the airline industry. Barrett regularly visits each of the company's stations to reiterate the airline's history and motivate employees. As keeper of the company's culture, Barrett has devised unique ways to preserve Southwest's underdog background and can-do spirit. She constantly reinforces the company's message that employees should be treated like customers and continually celebrates workers who go above and beyond the call of duty. Barrett also commemorates all employee birthdays and special events with cards signed "Herb and Colleen." Employees know the culture and expect others to live up to it.

## STRATEGY

Southwest's operation under Herb Kelleher has a number of characteristics that seem to contribute to its success. It has always been able to seize quickly a strategic opportunity whenever it arises. Other key factors are its conservative growth pattern, cost-containment policy, and the commitment of its employees.

Kelleher has always resisted attempts to expand too rapidly. His philosophy has been to expand only when there were resources available to go into a new location with 10 to 12 flights per day—not just one or two. For years he also resisted the temptation to begin transcontinental operations or to get into a head-to-head battle with the major carriers on long-distance routes. But even with a conservative approach, Southwest expanded at a vigorous pace. Its debt has remained the lowest among U.S. carriers, and, with an A-rating, Southwest has the highest Standard and Poor's credit rating in the industry.

Southwest has made its mark by concentrating on flying large numbers of passengers on high-frequency, short hops (usually one hour or less) at bargain fares. Southwest avoided the hub-and-spoke operations of its larger rivals, taking its passengers directly from city to city. Southwest also tends to avoid the more congested major airports in favor of smaller satellite fields. Kelleher revealed the niche strategy of Southwest in noting that when other airlines set up hub-and-spoke systems in which passengers were shunted to a few major hubs from which they were transferred to other planes to their destinations, "we wound up with a unique market niche: We are the world's only short-haul, high-frequency, low-fare, point-to-point carrier. . . . We wound up with a market segment that is peculiarly ours, and everything about the airline has been adapted to serving that market segment in the most efficient and economical way possible."

However, this strategy may be changing. Southwest is beginning to introduce longer, nonstop trips on such routes as Baltimore, Maryland, to Las Vegas, Nevada, (2,099 miles) and Austin, Texas, to Los Angeles, California, (1,234 miles). Even one-stop trips are being added through central cities such as Nashville and Kansas City for coast-to-coast travel. The prospect of Southwest going long-haul on a grand scale is "the genie [rivals] always hoped would not come out of the bottle," says analyst Kevin C. Murphy of Morgan Stanley Dean Witter. He believes Southwest will continue its expansion and that it "will really rewrite the economics of the airline industry." This shifting strategy is downplayed by the fact that about 80 percent of Southwest's flights are still shorter than 750 miles. "We're built for the short-haul markets, and we know that," says CFO Gary C. Kelly. Kelleher explains the jump into routes that are 1,000-plus miles as a way to deal with the changes in the federal ticket tax in 1997 that was pushed by the bigger carriers. The new tax system replaces a percentage tax with a tax that includes a flat, per-segment fee that hits low-fare carriers harder.

Competitors believe that Southwest would have moved strongly into the long-haul flights despite the altered tax requirements. "They've dug all the shallow holes," says

Rona J. Dutta, senior vice-president for planning at United Airlines Inc. He also notes that the majors' low-fare units are increasing the competition in Southwest's core markets. Short-haul lines such as US Airways' MetroJet, Shuttle by United, and Delta Express may affect Southwest's profitability, but analysts say that with its lower costs and impressive balance sheet, Southwest should prevail.

Southwest continues to be the least expensive airline in its markets. Even when they tried to match Southwest's cut-rate fares, the larger carriers could not do so without incurring substantial losses. Southwest's operating costs per available seat mile (the number of seats multiplied by the distance flown) average 15 percent to 25 percent below its rivals. One of the major factors in this enviable record is that all its planes used to be of a single type—Boeing 737s—which dramatically lowered the company's cost of training, maintenance, and inventory. Because all Southwest crews know the 737 inside and out, they can substitute personnel rapidly from one flight to another in an emergency. In addition, Southwest has recognized that planes only earn you money while they are in the air, so the company has worked hard to achieve a faster turnaround time on the ground. Most airlines take up to one hour to unload passengers, clean and service the plane, and board new passengers. Southwest has a turnaround time for most flights of 20 minutes or less. Thorough knowledge of the 737 has helped in this achievement.

Southwest also has cut costs in the customer service area as well. Because its flights are usually one hour or less, it does not offer meals—only peanuts and drinks. Boarding passes are reusable plastic cards, and boarding time is less because there is no assigned seating. The airline does not subscribe to any centralized reservation service. It will not even transfer baggage to other carriers: That is the passenger's responsibility. Even with this frugality, passengers do not seem to object because the price is right.

Southwest has achieved a team spirit that others can only envy. One of the reasons for this is that the company truly believes that employees come first, not the customers. Southwest is known for providing the employees with tremendous amounts of information that will enable them to better understand the company, its mission, its customers, and its competition. Southwest believes that information is power. It is the resource that enables employees to do their jobs better and serve the customer better, and customers who deal with Southwest rarely get the runaround.

Even though unionized, Southwest has been able to negotiate flexible work rules that enabled it to meet the rapid turnaround schedules. It's not unusual for pilots to help flight attendants clean the airplanes or help the ground crew load baggage. Consequently, employee productivity is very high, and the airline is able to maintain a lean staff. In good times, Kelleher resisted the temptation to overhire and so avoided layoffs during lean times. Southwest has only laid off three people in 25 years, and it immediately hired them back. This employee retention policy has contributed to employees' feelings of security and a fierce sense of loyalty. The people of Southwest see themselves as crusaders whose mission is to give ordinary people the opportunity to fly.

Maximizing profitability is a major goal at Southwest. This leads to a drive to keep costs low and quality high. The airline's ideal products are safe, frequent, low-cost flights that get passengers to their destination on time—and often closer to their final destination than the major airlines that use the larger airports further from the cities. Southwest uses Dallas's Love Field, Houston's Hobby Airport, and Chicago's Midway, which are closer to their respective downtowns, are less congested, and are, therefore, more convenient for the business traveler. This also helps their on-time performance.

In its marketing approach, Southwest always tries to set itself apart from the rest of the industry. It also played up its fun-loving, rebel reputation. In the early years when the big airlines were trying to run Southwest out of business by undercutting its low fares, Southwest made its customers an unprecedented offer. In response to a Braniff ad offering a $13 fare between Houston and Dallas, Southwest placed an ad that read,

"Nobody's going to shoot Southwest Airlines out of the sky for a lousy $13." It then offered passengers the opportunity to purchase a ticket from Southwest for the same price, which was half the normal fare, or buy a full-fare ticket for $26 and receive a bottle of premium whiskey along with it. The response was also unprecedented. Southwest's planes were full, and, for a short time, Southwest was one of the top liquor distributors in the state of Texas.

Southwest's ads always try to convince the customer that what the airline offers is of real value to them. Southwest also believe they are in the business of making flying fun. With its ads, they want customers to know that when they fly Southwest, they'll have an experience unlike any other. Southwest promises safe, reliable, frequent, low-cost air transportation topped off with outstanding service. By keeping its promises, Southwest has earned extremely high credibility in every market it serves.

Southwest has also been aggressively marketing its products on the Internet. When *Fortune* magazine asked the experts which businesses have e-plays that work, the answer they got was: not many. However, Southwest was one of ten cited as a business that is doing it right. In the Internet travel race, many observers think Southwest has lost the battle to a subsidiary of American Airlines, Travelocity. Yet, although American has been getting the attention, Southwest has been getting the business. According to Nielsen/NetRatings' August 1999 survey, 13.8 percent of people who visited Southwest's site booked a flight. The company's "look-to-book" ratio is twice that of Travelocity and higher than that of any traditional retailer on the Web. Southwest, it seems, has been a success in turning browsers into buyers.

## COMPETITORS

Three of Southwest's major competitors are United Airlines, Delta Air Lines, and America West Airlines. United, with over 90,000 employees, is one of Southwest's most formidable competitors. United, the number-two U.S. airline, flies over 500 aircraft to about 140 locations in the United States and overseas. In addition, it operates the United Express, which feeds passengers from regional carriers into the United system, and its United shuttle provides over 450 short-haul flights between 20 cities in the western states. The latter service is one that has often put them into direct competition with Southwest.

Delta, the third-largest U.S. carrier, has over 63,000 employees and fiscal 1999 sales of $14.7 billion. Delta flies to about 225 U.S. and foreign locations and is particularly strong throughout much of the southern tier of the U.S., where two of its major hubs—Atlanta and Dallas–Fort Worth—are located. Delta has also built up a low-fare regional carrier service and has acquired a minority stake in three regional airlines that can feed passengers into its several hubs. Delta has begun to focus much of its attention on its transatlantic operations but remains a strong U.S. competitor and is intent on attracting more business traffic.

America West, the smallest of Southwest's competitors, has about 11,000 employees. The airline serves 144 cities in the United States and seven foreign locations in Mexico and Canada. America West has strong positions in its hubs, Phoenix and Las Vegas. However, many of its locations put it into direct competition with Southwest. With Continental and Mesa Airlines, which have small stakes in America West, America West has formed alliances that give it access to another 35 destinations.

All of the competitors have come into head-to-head competition with Southwest on several occasions. Southwest always welcomed competition and firmly believes it can come out ahead in any of those situations. Kelleher, when asked about his thoughts on facing a competitor such as the United shuttle head on, stated: "I think it's good to have some real competitive activity that gets your people stirred up and renews their vigor and their energy and their desire to win. I think the United's Shuttle assault on Southwest Airlines, which was a very direct assault, drew our people closer together and made them better as a consequence."

Long-haul success for Southwest will build pressure on profits realized by its bigger competitors. The cost advantage for Southwest is a result of the rapid 20-minute gate turnarounds; an efficient all-Boeing 737 fleet, including new 737-700s that can fly cross country nonstop; and a more productive workforce. Even if longer flights increase the costs, Southwest still realizes a significant competitive advantage. Roberts, Roach & Associates Inc., an airline consultant in Hayward, Calif., says Southwest has at least a 59 percent cost advantage over bigger rivals in flights of 500 miles, and 35 percent lead for flights at 1,500 miles. "It's a huge threat," says a rival airline executive. These long-haul flights will be a new focus for Southwest's higher-cost rivals. Already, nonstop flights longer than 1,000 miles account for more than 16 percent of Southwest's capacity, estimates analyst Samuel C. Buttrick from Paine Webber, Inc.

## THE FUTURE

Today, Southwest provides service to only 55 cities, so there are tremendous opportunities for expansion. The problem: Where to go next? Over 100 cities have asked the airline to begin service in their communities because of the positive impact the company has when it begins operations in a new location. The introduction of Southwest's low fares and frequent flights opens more market and gives more people the freedom to fly.

Southwest continues to forge ahead in other ways as well. The airline introduced a new aircraft to the fleet in 1997: the Boeing 737-700. Southwest was the launch customer for this aircraft, which is able to fly high, fast, and far and still be fuel efficient. Southwest has purchased 60 of these aircraft, which require less maintenance time than the traditional 737s, and purchased 32 more in 1999.

Southwest Airlines has a 24-hour emergency medical service for its customers for in-flight medical emergencies. The airline now has emergency room physicians on call 24 hours a day through a service called MedLink. MedLink can put a physician in contact with Southwest's flight attendants during a medical emergency. The physician can make diagnoses, advise treatment, and issue medical recommendations, including whether an emergency landing should be made. Southwest is the first major airline to make medical service accessible by in-flight telephone.

Throughout its history, Southwest consistently had a clearly defined purpose and a well-thought-out strategy: to make a profit, achieve job security for every employee, and make flying affordable for more people. Can Southwest continue to maintain this strategy? Will its position remain unassailable by competitors? What are the implications of expanding to longer-haul operations? Will Southwest begin to lose the characteristics that were the hallmarks of its success? And how about international routes, especially to Canada or Mexico? Southwest has certainly come a long way from the little company with three aircraft that began operations in 1971. What's next?

# CENTRAL UNITED METHODIST CHURCH—2000

Robert T. Barrett
Francis Marion University

www.centralumcsc.web.com

As the end of his ten-year service came to a close in spring 1999, the minister of the Central Methodist Church, in the heart of downtown Florence, South Carolina, was happy to report that the church's drive to fund a physical plant expansion had reached a level that would allow the start of the project. Of the $2.5 million pledged, a full $1.8 million had been given. This minister could retire with the sense that the Lord had placed a final blessing of approval on his ministry in Florence. However, the church has had to overcome numerous challenges (and several more remain) in order to be able to initiate its building plans. An actual incident illustrates what had been a long-standing problem.

> A family came into the Fellowship Hall for the church's Wednesday night supper program and found an excited mass of people. The group of four waited in line to receive their food, picked up drinks, and moved on to look for places to sit. All places were either taken or "reserved" by regulars at the dinner. The family of four ate their food while standing in the hallway, left before the programs began, and decided to join another church.

Central United Methodist Church is a vibrant and growing church. The Wednesday night supper program, centered around family ministries, is so popular that it has exceeded the capacity of the Fellowship Hall. The ministerial staff, church leaders, and other church members are concerned and do not want to lose one more potential member just because of inadequate space.

## CENTRAL UNITED METHODIST CHURCH—PAST AND PRESENT

Central United Methodist Church was established in the late 1800s and moved to its present site at the corner of Irby and Cheves Streets in 1913, near the "n" in Florence on the map in Exhibit 1. Through a variety of land and property acquisitions since 1913, Central's main campus has grown to include approximately 200 feet of frontage on Irby Street and 300 feet of frontage on Cheves Street. Even in this downtown location, a limited number of acquisition possibilities remain available to Central. In the mid-1900s, Central had the opportunity to purchase a house that was adjacent to church property for a cost of $30,000. The church turned down this opportunity, and the owner sold the property to a group who developed a hotel and cafeteria on the property. After the hotel failed, the church was able to buy the property in 1980 for $100,000. In 1984, Central purchased a building adjacent to the property that currently serves as the primary facility for the youth ministry as well as the location of five Sunday School classes. Central continues to actively seek property for building and parking purposes.

EXHIBIT 1    Florence, South Carolina, City Map

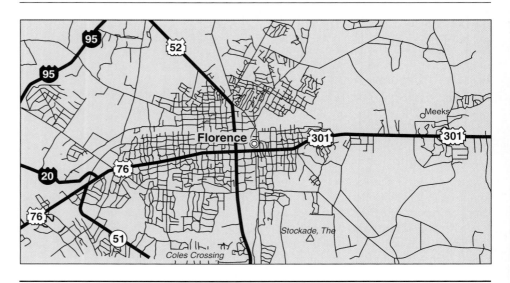

© 1997 GeoSystems Global Corp.

EXHIBIT 2    Central United Methodist Church Membership and
Attendance Levels

| Year | Church Membership | Average Attendance | Sunday School Membership | Average Attendance |
|------|-------------------|--------------------|--------------------------|--------------------|
| 1999 | 1,901 | 604 | 1,872 | 333 |
| 1998 | 1,899 | 617 | 1,757 | 443 |
| 1997 | 1,874 | 593 | 1,399 | 325 |
| 1996 | 1,863 | 589 | 1,572 | 322 |
| 1995 | 1,866 | 590 | 1,416 | 380 |
| 1994 | 1,855 | 551 | 1,376 | 331 |
| 1993 | 1,826 | 535 | 1,206 | 323 |
| 1992 | 1,801 | 522 | 1,111 | 308 |
| 1991 | 1,797 | 523 | 1,088 | 338 |
| 1990 | 1,795 | 540 | 1,091 | 336 |
| 1989 | 1,800 | 534 | 1,048 | 342 |

Exhibit 2 shows the membership levels for Central over the past ten years, along with average attendance levels for Sunday morning worship (two services) and Sunday School. Of this membership, approximately 23 percent are younger than ten years of age (note, young people on rolls prior to formally joining the church in the seventh grade are only considered "preparatory members"); approximately 12 percent are in the eleven-to-twenty-year age bracket, approximately 16 percent are in the twenty-one- to-thirty-year age bracket; approximately 14 percent in the thirty-to-forty-year age bracket; approximately 12 percent are in both the forty-one-to-fifty and fifty-one-to-sixty-year age brackets, and the remaining 11 percent are aged sixty-one or over. Note that over 60 percent of the membership are aged less than forty, with 35 percent of this

EXHIBIT 3    Central United Methodist Church Assets and Debt

| Year | Value of Church Campus Property | Parsonage and Furniture | Other Assets | Debt |
|------|-------------------------------|-------------------------|--------------|------|
| 1999 | $9,376,600 | $475,000 | $2,737,150 | $    0 |
| 1998 | 9,298,340 | 457,900 | 2,143,500 | 0 |
| 1997 | 8,880,000 | 421,000 | 918,000 | 0 |
| 1996 | 8,223,700 | 432,700 | 476,997 | 103,100 |
| 1995 | 8,223,700 | 432,700 | 476,997 | 188,000 |
| 1994 | 8,223,700 | 432,500 | 535,625 | 206,105 |
| 1993 | 6,944,000 | 213,500 | 320,000 | 388,271 |
| 1992 | 7,492,875 | 313,000 | 380,000 | 458,166 |
| 1991 | 7,492,875 | 313,000 | 380,000 | 467,532 |
| 1990 | 7,492,875 | 313,000 | 380,000 | 27,348 |
| 1989 | 6,107,068 | 314,000 | 380,000 | 526,000 |

EXHIBIT 4    Central United Methodist Church Contributions

| Year | Operating Budget | Building Fund | Building Fund Extra |
|------|------------------|---------------|---------------------|
| 1999 | $968,110.00 | $    * | $    * |
| 1998 | 868,987.00 | 614,814.00 | 104,133.72 |
| 1997 | 820,610.00 | 592,400.00 | 75,108.00 |
| 1996 | 830,009.91 | 145,231.33 | 6,464.75 |
| 1995 | 734,799.03 | 131,661.41 | 7,251.00 |
| 1994 | 691,713.08 | 133,602.07 | 26,527.24 |
| 1993 | 631,750.74 | 125,171.98 | 1,589.50 |
| 1992 | 587,278.22 | 110,831.43 | 2,204.50 |
| 1991 | 561,148.50 | 115,747.47 | 3,810.77 |
| 1990 | 518,341.80 | 120,976.75 | 8,635.50 |
| 1989 | 499,069.64 | 102,735.34 | 38,221.41 |

*Note: With a new accounting process to deal with the building program, beginning with 1999, the building fund is reported as cash on hand. This amount includes regular donations to the building fund, donations to cover pledges, memorials, and interest earned minus deductions for the costs of construction to date. As of December 31, 1999, cash on hand for the building project was $1,841,116.30

group classified as children and youth. Another interesting breakdown of church membership shows that approximately 60 percent of the members are married, with a bulk of the remaining 40 percent being children and youth. This demonstrates the commitment of the membership to strong family values. In a time of declining memberships in churches across the country, Central has been able to maintain membership and participation levels.

Exhibit 3 gives the value of property owned and debt owed by Central over the past ten years. The value of church property has grown while debt service has continued to decline.

Exhibit 4 gives information on contributions to the operating budget, the building fund and a category labeled building fund extra for gifts designated for special projects. Contributions have steadily increased over the past ten years. Prior to 1999, church budgets in excess of $800,000 have been overpledged (and collected). One problem the church has experienced since the building campaign began is that the membership has

EXHIBIT 5     Central United Methodist Church, Salary for
              Key Personnel

|  | *2000* | *1999* | *1998* |
|---|---|---|---|
| Pastor | $68,413 | $65,156 | $62,939 |
| Associate Pastor | 29,132 | 26,476 | 25,600 |
| Director of Children's Ministry | 15,662 | 14,239 | 0 |
| Director of Youth Ministries | 14,137 | 13,726 | 0 |
| Director of Adult Ministries | 15,662 | 14,239 | 0 |
| Business Manager | 24,000 | 0 | 0 |
| Church Secretary | 18,939 | 18,211 | 16,556 |
| Financial Secretary | 17,500 | 21,118 | 19,199 |
| Music Director/Organist | 43,489 | 41,419 | 39,631 |
| Building/Property Superintent | 18,287 | 18,287 | 16,625 |

committed many dollars to the building fund at the expense of the operating budget. In 1999, approximately 88% of the $928,498 operating budget was pledged. Although the amount collected in 1999 covered the budget, the low pledge amount makes for difficult planning. Total funds collected for the building fund exceeded $2 million by the end of 1999. The proposed operating budget for 2000 exceeded $1 million.

The Administrative Board approved modifications in the church office administrative structure to be effective in the 2000 fiscal year. With the new building project on the horizon, job descriptions and personnel shifts were justified. Some of the changes are apparent in the list of salaries of key church personnel given in Exhibit 5.

## FLORENCE, SOUTH CAROLINA

Founded in 1850, Florence has been and remains a railroad city. The city is located in a region of South Carolina called the "Pee Dee," after a tribe of Indians that inhabited the area. The Chamber of Commerce touts Florence as the trade, industrial, medical, transportation, cultural, financial, and educational center of the Pee Dee. Located where interstate highways I-95 and I-20 intersect, Florence sees many travelers headed north to New York, south to Florida, east to Myrtle Beach, and west to the Appalachian Mountains.

The city has more than 33,000 residents and is projected to double in size by the year 2010. Florence County has 122,000 residents and projects growth to 130,000 by 2010. Florence has churches of all denominations. Within three miles of the Central United Methodist Church are Baptist, Presbyterian, Lutheran, Episcopal, and other Methodist churches. The city of Florence contains five Methodist churches. Many other churches have chosen to locate in areas on the outskirts of town. Thus, as the population of Florence grows, there is increased "competition" for parishioners.

## CHURCH STAFF AND VOLUNTEER STRUCTURE

Central United Methodist Church is served by a staff of 23 persons. The senior pastor acts as the chief administrative officer. Other primary staff members include one associate minister, a minister of music, a part-time director of children's ministries, a part-time director of adult ministries, and a part-time director of youth ministries. Clerical and custodian assistants make up most of the remaining staff positions. The church has successfully used part-time staff. The benefits of this strategy are apparent in efficiencies and quality of service. The church can hire a person who is skilled in a particular function for the limited amount of time needed for a job.

As is true of most churches, much of the church's work is carried out by volunteers. The committee structure that helps to govern and carry out church programs is headed by the administrative board. The council on ministries, the finance committee, the trustees, and the pastor parish committee report to this board. The council on ministries is the major programming arm with some 12 councils and committees in charge of a variety of church programs. These volunteer groups include the children's council, youth council, adult council, senior adult council, family life council, recreation committee, scouting committee, outreach committee, worship committee, stewardship committee, evangelism committee, and Camp Sexton committee.

## CHURCH PROPERTY

Central United Methodist Church owns property in the downtown Florence location at Cheves and Irby Streets, a large tract of land just outside of Florence named Camp Sexton after the donor, and a Boy Scout hut a few miles from the main church property. Most church programs are held at the downtown location. A summer camp for children is held for several weeks at Camp Sexton. Camp Sexton hosts special programs during the year and a Sunday afternoon swim session for church members during the summer. The church-sponsored Boy Scout troop meets weekly in the Boy Scout hut.

The church sanctuary seats approximately 400 people. Attendance averages for the two Sunday morning services are shown for the past ten years in Exhibit 2. The sanctuary overflows for performances of the Masterworks Choir, the Christmas Eve services, Easter and Mother's Day services, and large funerals and weddings.

Every classroom on the property is filled with a Sunday School class. Classes are held in the library, the Fellowship Hall, and the youth lounge. Many of the classrooms have been deemed inadequate, particularly the small children's classrooms and nurseries. Sunday School classes for adults typically develop around age groupings. As the church grows, it will likely need to provide additional Sunday School classes.

As the example at the beginning of this case pointed out, the Fellowship Hall, the only large multipurpose space on the church campus, is not able to accommodate the larger programs of the church. Specifically, the enormous popularity of the Wednesday night supper program attracts crowds that exceed the physical capacity of the Fellowship Hall, which can comfortably seat about 250 people at the most. Other church events that require a large space include wedding receptions, Sunday School promotions, district youth rallies, and church charge conferences. Other programs, such as state conference meetings, could also utilize a larger space.

## LONG-RANGE PLANNING COMMITTEE

The Fellowship Hall capacity problem was one of a number of concerns facing Central United Methodist Church as it continued to expand its ministry. In 1991, the administrative board of the church formed the long-range planning committee to review existing programs of the church, evaluate the adequacies of the facilities to carry out these programs, evaluate staffing levels that support current programs, and project future needs. The committee consisted of church members over a wide range of ages (from youth representatives to retired members), lengths of church membership (from less than five years as a member of Central to over 50 years as a member), and vocations (housewives and mothers, teachers, engineers, and lawyers).

The committee met monthly, beginning with research of the literature on church development, discussions of church trends in U.S. society, and analysis of how these trends apply to Central Church. The committee received reports from all programs of the church and interviewed all professional and volunteer leaders responsible for programs in an effort to develop an understanding of existing programs and their projected needs. The committee made a physical inspection of all properties and facilities of the church. The Committee developed and distributed a questionnaire to obtain direct input from the congregation during the planning process. Open meetings were held to gather additional information from members of the congregation.

One of the staff reports, given by the minister of music, highlighted some needs of the sanctuary. Based on recommendations made by an expert on acoustics, the minister of music recommended some major modifications to the sanctuary to enhance the sound quality. In addition to the sound-quality issue in the sanctuary, new carpet was needed; some repair was needed in the dome ceiling, and the walls required patching and painting.

The long-range planning committee identified three levels of facility needs for the church—urgent needs, immediate needs, and future needs. In addition, the committee defined a list of general needs.

**Specific Facility Needs**
*Urgent*

- Sanctuary repair and renovation with full consideration of the recommendations of the acoustical study and to specifically include:
  - Floor and carpet repair, replacement, or refinishing
  - Upgrading of sound system, including radio broadcasting and tape-recording facilities
  - Interior painting and entrance paving
  - Chancel alterations

*Immediate*

- Four preschool classrooms in accordance with appropriate state regulations (e.g., first-floor location)
- Four classrooms for other age groups (adults, older children)
- Multiple-use social and recreational facility with adjacent kitchen (500–600 seats)
- Increased administrative office space
- Covered entrance for passenger delivery by automobile or bus
- Designated Girl Scout meeting and equipment storage area
- Medium-size meeting room (125–200 seats) with adjacent kitchen for formal functions

*Future*

- Sanctuary improvements to increase space for greeting and gathering, especially in inclement weather; improve traffic flow within and between buildings (sanctuary, nursery, classrooms); improve chancel area; and consider enlargement
- Covered walkways connecting buildings
- Improved restroom facilities for sanctuary and education building (enlarged capacity, better location and distribution for convenience, improved plumbing and appearance, and additional number)
- All-weather facility (e.g., lodge) at Camp Sexton

*General Needs*

- Long-term (10–25 years) facility development and land-use plan should be developed by professional planner or architect
- Adoption of policy to rigidly adhere to this plan when considering and authorizing renovation or construction of all facilities, including those provided as memorials and honorariums
- Development of a plan for funding construction or renovation of facilities that will rely more on establishment of a building fund before construction and less on loans

## THE BUILDING PROJECT'S STATUS

Urgent needs centered on renovations to the sanctuary. Using a generous gift from an estate of a church member, each of these needs was met in summer 1996. Other funds were used to purchase a building adjacent to the church property for office space, thus helping to satisfy one of the immediate needs.

In 1996, the administrative board approved a $5 million building project, to be carried out in two phases. Phase I of the project (which would require $3.5 million) would help to satisfy many of the immediate needs listed above. Phase II would generally address future needs. At that same meeting, the board established the building committee to oversee planning and implementation of the project. The committee was charged with the responsibilities of setting in motion a capital fund campaign, acquiring appropriate downtown property when it became available, and identifying and carrying out other actions required to move the project along. The committee was also responsible for the general needs as listed.

It was determined that at least one half of the projected cost of the project would need to be on hand before any construction could begin. Over $2.5 million was pledged during the Capital Fund Campaign. To begin Phase I construction, $1.75 million was required. Note the significant jump in building fund assets beginning in 1997 in Exhibit 4. This increase is attributed to the capital campaign.

As is noted in the introductory paragraph of this case, in 1999 the building fund reached a level above the threshold for starting the building project. With half of the needed funds on hand, a number of property additions purchased, and people excited about moving forward, several challenges still remain for Central United Methodist Church.

Some of the building related challenges include the following. The church will need to raise additional funds to complete Phase I and to move forward with Phase II of the building project. While raising these funds, the church must ensure adequate funds are available to maintain current and new property. Issues specifically tied to Phase I of the project are finalizing architectural designs, selecting a builder, demolishing some of the existing buildings on church property to make way for the new building, and developing parking facilities. Some logistical concerns during construction include temporary parking, disruption of walking and auto traffic flow, and limitations on classroom space.

Providing adequate space is indeed crucial to the growth of Central United Methodist Church. The church must, however, keep in mind the need to maintain an appropriate operating budget to support the expanded programs that come with the expanded space. Additional staffing changes may also be required to support these programs.

Develop a three year strategic plan for Central to best assure that the church fulfills its mission and obligation to all stakeholders.

# ELKINS LAKE BAPTIST CHURCH—2000

Paul Reed, Christie Haney, and Ronald Earl
Sam Housten State University

www.elbc.org

Dr. Hugghins thought back to 1990 when he first became pastor of Elkins Lake Baptist Church (ELBC) in Huntsville, Texas. The membership then consisted of 487 followers in a cramped building and has now grown to 799 members. Now, as the church begins the millennium, its pastor and its members face various questions. Is the membership willing or ready to accept newer, younger, more liberal members with different ideas? Is the pastor equipped to manage and lead a broad-based following? Will the membership be able to fund the continued growth of the physical plant as well as its membership? Will ELBC be able to continue to function without a strategic plan? Should ELBC consider restructuring?

The questions seemed to multiply quickly as plans for ELBC flowed through Dr. Hugghins's mind. No doubt, Dr. Hugghins will rely on his vast library and personal contacts to try to find some guidance or a solution for questions regarding the church. However, it will take more than one man to deal with these issues.

## EXTERNAL ENVIRONMENT

### History

Elkins Lake Baptist Church originated in the Elkins Lake Subdivision's clubhouse in 1970. Two years later, the group relocated across I-45 from the subdivision. In 1986, the members of Elkins Lake Baptist Church voted to purchase the current site in hopes of relocating the church closer to central Huntsville, Texas. The land was purchased for $225,000 by a loan from one of the local banks and by the church's building fund. The site is located on Highway 19 in Huntsville, Texas (see Exhibit 1).

In 1995, ground was broken for the building. In March of 1996, construction began. The timber sold from clearing only the necessary trees was applied toward the loan. The building was funded by a bank loan for approximately $620,000 that was backed by pledges from church members. In addition to the bank loan, the church also approached the membership about a separate bond program, securing $160,000 from its members. The members were paid back when the old church and property recently sold for $300,000. The remainder of the profit from the sale went toward paying down the current note.

In March 1997 the church opened its doors for services. It consists of 6,527 square feet of sanctuary space, 1,890 square feet of offices and library space, 7,067 square feet of classrooms, and 2,314 square feet of kitchen, bathrooms, and miscellaneous space. The interior of the church is very modern. For example, interlocking chairs are used instead of the pews that are commonly associated with Southern Baptist churches. The sanctuary space is commonly used as a multifunctional space so the chairs can be taken apart and the floor cleared. The church does not have the typical stained glass windows. The win-

EXHIBIT 1    Huntsville's Southern Baptist Church Locations

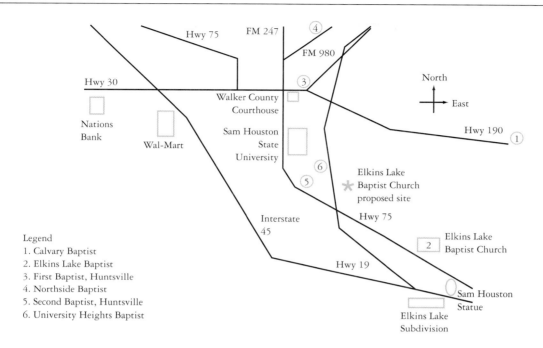

Legend
1. Calvary Baptist
2. Elkins Lake Baptist
3. First Baptist, Huntsville
4. Northside Baptist
5. Second Baptist, Huntsville
6. University Heights Baptist

dows of the sanctuary overlook the property and a creek that runs through it. New members and visitors notice that there are no altar flowers or Sunday children's sermon. Because many members of ELBC come from small towns, these nontraditional features bother some parishioners. To these more conservative members, a church just is not a Southern Baptist church without the stained glass, pews, altar flowers, and children's sermon. Conversely, a young family of four that is considering joining Elkins Lake Baptist Church might consider it a fashionable place of worship.

Temporary buildings were moved from the old church to the present site to be utilized as classroom space until the other building phases are completed. Recently, two additional temporary buildings were brought in to accommodate the growing religious educational space needs. Each of the new buildings can contain two classrooms with 20 people to a classroom. However, lack of space continues to be a problem. Classes have to be held in the sanctuary as well as in the regular classrooms. When asked about the shortage of educational space and questioned about a possible date to begin the next stage of construction, Dr. Hugghins cleverly remarked, "It is not about running an organization with a lot of amenities, it is about teaching people the word of God and that can be done in living rooms." Dr. Hugghins would feel at home giving a sermon either in a large sanctuary or in a small office or living room. However, Dr. Hugghins does have individuals looking into various loans so that the building program can continue. The next phase of the plan would be to construct educational space.

## Local Area

Huntsville is located on Interstate 45, approximately 70 miles north of Houston and 170 miles south of Dallas–Fort Worth. Besides being a typical East Texas county seat, Huntsville has Sam Houston State University, the headquarters of the Texas Department of Criminal Justice (TDCJ), and four prison units within its city limits. The population of Huntsville in 1998 was 34,592. In addition to the local citizens, the population totals include inmates housed in the prisons and all university students residing in the town. The TDCJ employs approximately 3,200 staff in the system's administrative headquarters and prisons. The university has approximately 12,000 students and 2,224 faculty and staff members. The population is supported by these institutions and by the normal small service and light industry-type firms present in the community. Fewer than 30 percent of the residents of Huntsville are members of a local church.

Huntsville, for its size, has a relatively large amount of criminal activity. In 1998, of the 1,176 misdemeanors on record, 63.6 percent were for alcohol- or drug-related offenses. Recreational and social activities are limited in number.

On the immediate west side of the city are three residential communities, the largest being the Elkins Lake Subdivision. "Elkins," as it is called, was originally developed as a retirement community for those who wished to live in a rural setting with all the amenities of a big city, such as nearby Houston. Elkins contains approximately 860 homes. During the past several years, the average age of an Elkins Lake resident has decreased as more working families with children have purchased property. Now, only half of Elkins Lake residents are retired. The remaining residents are employed and range from thirty to fifty years of age. Because Elkins Lake is where ELBC originated, the church members have also grown younger as more and more young families moved in and joined the church.

Elkins Lake Baptist Church is located on busy state Highway 19, but its position on the reverse slope of a hill covered with large pine trees causes the many passersby to miss it. The two-lane highway is not completely developed and is not used to full capacity at this time. Huntsville is expected to grow in the direction of ELBC.

## Competition

There are 76 churches of different denominations in Walker County. ELBC, which is affiliated with the Southern Baptist Convention, faces competition from five other Southern Baptist churches in Huntsville. Dr. Hugghins has served ELBC longer than any of the other pastors. Occasionally, the Baptist preachers get together for discussions, and four of the churches come together annually for Bible Study. Dr. Hugghins has an off-and-on ministerial alliance with all ministers in town, not just those of the Baptist faith. Three of the other Southern Baptist churches are located in central Huntsville, and ELBC and the other two are on the outer perimeter of town. (See Exhibit 1.) Assorted data from the Southern Baptist churches of Huntsville are presented in Exhibits 2 through 11.

EXHIBIT 2    **Walker County Southern Baptist Church Membership**

| *Church* | *1998* | *1997* | *1996* | *1995* | *1994* |
|---|---|---|---|---|---|
| Calvary Baptist | 623 | 779 | 665 | 674 | 646 |
| Elkins Lake Baptist | 799 | 776 | 719 | 708 | 651 |
| First Baptist | 2,455 | 2,481 | 2,496 | 2,468 | 2,415 |
| Northside Baptist | 1,015 | 949 | 825 | 635 | 532 |
| Second Baptist | 1,007 | N/A | 983 | 986 | 1,006 |
| University Heights Baptist | 1,650 | 1,602 | 1,554 | 1,515 | 1,677 |

*Source:* Tyron Evergreen Baptist Association.

EXHIBIT 3    Walker County Southern Baptist Church Members Lost within the Past Year

| Church | 1997 | 1996 | 1995 | 1994 |
|---|---|---|---|---|
| Calvary Baptist | 16 | 27 | 30 | 33 |
| Elkins Lake Baptist | 11 | 33 | 16 | 34 |
| First Baptist | 73 | 61 | 53 | 60 |
| Northside Baptist | 10 | 11 | 14 | 11 |
| Second Baptist | N/A | 15 | 34 | 52 |
| University Heights Baptist | 41 | 42 | 57 | 33 |

*Source:* Tyron Evergreen Baptist Association.

EXHIBIT 4    Walker County Southern Baptist Church Receipts

| Church | 1998 | 1997 | 1996 | 1995 | 1994 |
|---|---|---|---|---|---|
| Calvary Baptist | $271,988 | $210,151 | $233,732 | $248,724 | $202,314 |
| Elkins Lake Baptist | 428,806 | 544,993 | 363,556 | 323,451 | 248,589 |
| First Baptist | 833,406 | 812,551 | 788,394 | 776,039 | 672,594 |
| Northside Baptist | 356,862 | 301,737 | 249,936 | 221,000 | 181,280 |
| Second Baptist | 152,869 | N/A | 110,195 | 159,632 | 115,963 |
| University Heights Baptist | 409,942 | 915,620 | 660,947 | 453,675 | 407,454 |

*Source:* Tyron Evergreen Baptist Association.

EXHIBIT 5    Walker County Southern Baptist Church Expenditures

| Church | 1997 | 1996 | 1995 | 1994 |
|---|---|---|---|---|
| Calvary Baptist | $165,338 | $172,956 | $215,380 | $203,407 |
| Elkins Lake Bapist | 236,873 | 195,243 | 172,442 | 163,805 |
| First Baptist | 619,762 | 688,989 | 675,128 | 415,638 |
| Northside Baptist | 289,840 | 204,623 | 149,753 | 135,900 |
| Second Baptist | N/A | 104,857 | 88,293 | 76,708 |
| University Heights Baptist | 402,456 | 546,376 | 299,088 | 306,001 |

*Source:* Tyron Evergreen Baptist Association.

EXHIBIT 6    Walker County Southern Baptist Church Debt

| Church | 1998 | 1997 | 1996 | 1995 | 1994 |
|---|---|---|---|---|---|
| Calvary Baptist | $296,262 | $312,573 | $328,951 | $344,500 | $359,020 |
| Elkins Lake Baptist | 541,000 | 222,000 | 69,543 | 77,943 | 87,842 |
| First Baptist | 482,637 | 745,500 | 830,124 | 880,092 | 545,493 |
| Northside Baptist | 0 | 88,774 | 113,010 | 200,000 | 3,000 |
| Second Baptist | 0 | N/A | 0 | 0 | 0 |
| University Heights Baptist | 790,000 | 790,000 | 17,948 | 14,090 | 28,846 |

*Source:* Tyron Evergreen Baptist Association.

EXHIBIT 7    **Walker County Southern Baptist Church Salaries**

| Church | 1998 | 1997 | 1996 | 1995 | 1994 |
|---|---|---|---|---|---|
| Calvary Baptist | N/A | N/A | $ 91,420 | $ 86,529 | $ 96,376 |
| Elkins Lake Baptist | N/A | N/A | 133,523 | 126,215 | 124,446 |
| First Baptist | N/A | N/A | 218,560 | 222,756 | 235,610 |
| Northside Baptist | N/A | N/A | 41,482 | 28,529 | 23,800 |
| Second Baptist | N/A | N/A | 79,447 | 67,980 | 57,792 |
| University Heights Baptist | N/A | N/A | 234,029 | 129,611 | 210,711 |

*Source:* Tyron Evergreen Baptist Association.

EXHIBIT 8    **Walker County Southern Baptist Church Attendance at Morning Service**

| Church | 1998 | 1997 | 1996 | 1995 | 1994 |
|---|---|---|---|---|---|
| Calvary Baptist | N/A | 170 | 132 | 170 | 300 |
| Elkins Lake Baptist | 228 | 207 | 210 | 278 | 192 |
| First Baptist | 300 | 384 | 417 | 464 | 474 |
| Northside Baptist | 350 | 375 | 325 | 275 | 225 |
| Second Baptist | 135 | N/A | 84 | 80 | 95 |
| University Heights Baptist | 550 | 600 | 500 | 500 | 500 |

*Source:* Tyron Evergreen Baptist Association.

EXHIBIT 9    **Walker County Southern Baptist Church Sunday School Enrollment**

| Church | 1998 | 1997 | 1996 | 1995 | 1994 |
|---|---|---|---|---|---|
| Calvary Baptist | 251 | 213 | 223 | 297 | 351 |
| Elkins Lake Baptist | 407 | 393 | 421 | 424 | 398 |
| First Baptist | 997 | 1,034 | 1,094 | 1,139 | 1,066 |
| Northside Baptist | 292 | 290 | 292 | 260 | 176 |
| Second Baptist | 80 | N/A | 109 | 131 | 128 |
| University Heights Baptist | 979 | 942 | 940 | 942 | 1,064 |

*Source:* Tyron Evergreen Baptist Association.

EXHIBIT 10    **Walker County Southern Baptist Church Young Adult Sunday School Enrollment**

| Church | 1998 | 1997 | 1996 | 1995 | 1994 |
|---|---|---|---|---|---|
| Calvary Baptist | 35 | 34 | 57 | 47 | 42 |
| Elkins Lake Baptist | 126 | 90 | 77 | 117 | 51 |
| First Baptist | 229 | 300 | 292 | 237 | 156 |
| Northside Baptist | 34 | 49 | 57 | 56 | 12 |
| Second Baptist | 17 | N/A | 8 | 0 | 12 |
| University Heights Baptist | 347 | 275 | 143 | 155 | 119 |

*Source:* Tyron Evergreen Baptist Association.

EXHIBIT 11   **Walker County Southern Baptist Church**
**Property Value**

| Church | 1998 | 1997 | 1996 | 1995 | 1994 |
|---|---|---|---|---|---|
| Calvary Baptist | $ 650,000 | $ 650,000 | $ 650,000 | $ 650,000 | $ 650,000 |
| Elkins Lake Baptist | 1,250,000 | 1,600,000 | 800,000 | 800,000 | 800,000 |
| First Baptist | 4,473,000 | 4,472,909 | 4,600,000 | 4,600,000 | 4,472,909 |
| Northside Baptist | 1,500,000 | 1,500,000 | 1,500,000 | 1,500,000 | 265,000 |
| Second Baptist | 2,000,000 | N/A | 1,275,000 | 1,275,000 | 1,275,000 |
| University Heights Baptist | 2,800,000 | 2,800,000 | 1,700,000 | 1,700,000 | 1,700,000 |

*Source:* Tyron Evergreen Baptist Association.

## INTERNAL ENVIRONMENT

Elkins Lake Baptist Church is incorporated under the state laws of Texas and operates under a constitution and by-laws. It follows the Southern Baptist doctrine, which tends to take the Bible literally.

### Personnel and Organized Committees

Besides Dr. Hugghins, ELBC has only one other full-time staff member. Previously, there were three full-time members and eight part-time employees. At present, the church is in need of a full-time administrative assistant. Part-time employees are handling the office and trying to employ the procedures used by the past employees and continue with the daily operations of the church. The church also heavily depends on volunteers from the membership who provide services ranging from nursery care to mowing the yard to playing the piano in church.

The ELBC is currently preparing a formal personnel policy manual. However, there are no formal guidelines for committees. Dr. Hugghins feels that revisions need to be made to the constitution; for example, he wants to remove references to gender in the constitution. He also thinks that duties of the committees would not be mentioned, because he would like to emphasize more of a "here is what matters, go and do," attitude. He considers that it would be clear to the committee what is important to do, and they should, in turn, be empowered to handle what needs to be done.

The church's financial affairs are directed by the treasurer and finance and budget committee. The budget for each year is established through a process by which the various committees and pastor present their respective needs and anticipated expenditures for the coming year. Revenue projections are adjusted for attendance trends. When the budget is finalized, it is presented to the membership for vote. (Financial statements are shown in Exhibit 12.)

The pastor looks to a panel of deacons for general policy guidance, but, in fact, he is given great latitude in exercising control over the church's affairs. There are a total of 38 deacons (only 30 on active status), and they each serve a three-year term. The pastor and his deacons use a participative management style. Normally, the pastor confers with the deacons before recommending a change to the membership, who finalize the decision by vote.

### The Pastor's Outlook

When Dr. Hugghins came to Elkins Lake Baptist Church, he assumed that it was a modern church. Various facts had led him to this conclusion: the church's method of ministry

### EXHIBIT 12  Elkins Lake Baptist Church Financial Statement (as of December 31)

| | 1999 | 1998 | 1997 | 1996 | 1995 |
|---|---|---|---|---|---|
| **Summary of Accounts** | | | | | |
| Bank balance | | | | | |
| Checking | $ (1,408.00) | $ 17,193.77 | $ 30,538.53 | $ 5,000.00 | $ 10,766.98 |
| Building fund | 78,769.00 | 29,561.04 | 56,369.11 | 94,121.75 | 28,922.64 |
| Certificate of deposit | 51,275.00 | 20,378.83 | 30,000.00 | 79,709.69 | 32,500.00 |
| Special/Designation | 98,327.00 | 26,884.72 | | | |
| Total receipts year to date | 505,413.00 | 522,869.00 | 346,074.95 | 357,174.69 | 317,229.84 |
| Projected budget needs | 455,823.00 | 422,877.24 | 320,382.00 | 278,388.91 | 227,148.00 |
| Percentage of collections over expenses | 110.88% | 123.65% | 108.02% | 128.30% | 139.66% |
| **Expenditures** | | | | | |
| 100 Missions | $ 51,240.00 | $ 63,562.44 | $ 61,200.89 | $ 54,447.24 | $ 55,384.95 |
| 200 Personnel | 127,740.00 | 174,808.39 | 159,583.76 | 136,255.08 | 145,417.99 |
| 300 Music ministry | 4,805.00 | 3,278.17 | 3,564.91 | 3,205.11 | 3,902.41 |
| 400 Education ministry | 27,945.00 | 18,871.14 | 10,826.83 | 8,594.52 | 11,255.26 |
| 500 College and youth | 5,742.00 | 1,762.92 | 2,841.46 | 1,054.77 | 3,783.22 |
| 600 Church administration | 20,573.00 | 19,982.47 | 20,874.27 | 15,666.26 | 15,318.49 |
| 700 Building and equipment | 6,812.00 | 42,956.58 | 30,313.02 | 28,110.57 | 23,856.98 |
| 800 Debt retirement | 105,376.00 | 82,957.97 | 18,715.32 | 17,186.55 | 18,863.10 |
| 900 Miscellaneous | 0 | 1,402.52 | 458.02 | 227.80 | 431.83 |
| | $350,027.00 | $409,582.60 | $308,378.48 | $264,747.90 | $278,214.23 |

*Source:* Elkins Lake Baptist Church.

of music, the women on staff (education director), the well-educated pastor who preceded him, and the fact that Huntsville was a university town. Within a month of his arrival, Dr. Hugghins began to see that the membership was more conservative than his style.

Dr. Hugghins, a relatively liberal man, especially given his occupation, believes in a "modern Southern Baptist atmosphere," that is, female deacons and ministers, a less literal interpretation of the Bible, and increased pastoral authority. He is well read and regularly quotes authors of other denominations. He has been criticized for not quoting more Baptist authors in his sermons. Dr. Hugghins feels that ELBC is the most diverse Baptist church in town. He sees the "big picture" of the future growth possibilities of Huntsville, is convinced that some church needs to be different (more modern), and thinks that ELBC is in a good location. Dr. Hugghins feels that ELBC will grow when individuals bring friends to church and if he can follow up on visitors who happen to show up by chance.

Members have recently been lost to other churches, possibly because they wanted a more conservative church. One former member states that not only is Dr. Hugghins too modern, but he likes to do "things his own way." This person also stated that this is "not particularly what the members want." Several other members who were large donors to the church have gone to other churches. Some feel that Dr. Hugghins should consider changing his style, taking a more conservative approach. Dr. Hugghins is finding himself the subject of a controversy between old versus new members as well as old versus new ideas. He feels that he has not found a common element to deal with everyone, i.e., old members, new members, Elkins residents, and non-Elkins residents.

Originally, the target market for Elkins Lake Baptist Church was retired upper-middle-class individuals. At present, the target group is becoming the working middle class. One individual, who has been a member for over twenty years, feels that the target market is definitely changing although no one has stated the fact or discussed the reason. Dr. Hugghins states that a lot of young families are joining, and they are coming from all over Huntsville, not just the Elkins Lake Subdivision.

Dr. Hugghins has found that some people are resistant to new members, their ideas, and their more liberal ways. Dr. Hugghins quotes a coworker, "It's not all about you." The members should think about what is best for the membership as a whole and not what makes them "most comfortable." He also feels that all change cannot originate from the pulpit. If it had been left up to some members, ELBC would have never moved in the first place. Some of the older, more influential members seem to be resistant to change.

When asked what the "product" of the church was, Dr. Hugghins said that most would say individual salvation. However, Dr. Hugghins wants to know, "What about from then on. . . ?"

Dr. Hugghins fears that some misperceptions may occur because of the name, Elkins Lake Baptist Church. He is afraid that outsiders will assume that the church is for members of the Elkins Lake Subdivision only and only for the upper middle class of Huntsville. He has toyed with the idea of renaming the church.

## Outreach Programs

ELBC has developed several outreach programs to attract new membership, especially young families and children. Dr. Hugghins considers the active and visible ministries with leadership from the congregation a real asset for the church. A Sunday morning Bible Study is conducted at the Elkins Lake Country Club for those individuals looking for a more interactive worship session. Approximately 20 individuals of various denominations regularly attend this Bible Study.

ELBC also has a presence on the Sam Houston State University's campus. ELBC are affiliated with the Baptist Student Union (BSU) and regularly hold lunches and services in a facility on campus. ELBC also works with the Walker County Jail and the Gulf Coast Trade Center (GCTC), a facility for the rehabilitation for juvenile delinquents. The church regularly holds two classes at the GCTC to reach these troubled young people. In addition, the church supports various missions, such as the Mexican Mission in order to reach the Hispanic population in the area. The church also makes its presence known at retirement facilities to bring the word of God to elderly individuals who are immobile. It is important to mention that all of these outreach programs are staffed by volunteers of the church.

## Marketing

Dr. Hugghins is quite proud of ELBC's marketing efforts, which consist of a weekly radio broadcast of the Sunday morning service, newspaper advertisements, two 30-second radio advertisements during each Huntsville High School home football game, and seasonal radio greetings during the Christmas season. Dr. Hugghins also writes a weekly inspirational column in the local paper. The ELBC is also promoted by the Baptist Student Union at SHSU with flyers about special events and announcements concerning the activities of the church.

For the church building itself, ELBC has a textured concrete sign on one side of the two entrances that is four feet high and five feet wide. The sign is hard to read because it is all one color and cannot be read from the highway. It only contains the name of the church and the pastor. Two small blue and red "enter" signs mark each of the entrances.

EXHIBIT 13   Worship Attendance Averaged
by Month for ELBC

| Month and Year | Average Persons Attending | Number of Persons below Full Capacity |
|---|---|---|
| January 1998 | 204 | −212 |
| February 1998 | 235 | −181 |
| March 1998 | 308 | −108 |
| April 1998 | 274 | −142 |
| May 1998 | 251 | −165 |
| June 1998 | 247 | −169 |
| July 1998 | 217 | −199 |
| August 1998 | 261 | −155 |
| September 1998 | 229 | −187 |
| October 1998 | 251 | −165 |
| November 1998 | 218 | −198 |
| December 1998 | 216 | −200 |

*Source:* Elkins Lake Baptist Church newsletter *The Window.*

Also, there is a large red and blue sign that sits parallel to the trees and can only be read by drivers going in one direction down the highway. This sign contains the name of the church, an arrow pointing toward its location, and the times of service.

### Preparing for Future Growth

Southern Baptists have long held to the strategy of going to Sunday School from early childhood through adolescence. Therefore, great emphasis is usually placed in properly designing and utilizing the educational space. Two rules of thumb are normally used: (1) to provide approximately 45 square feet of floor space per person; (2) to maintain an average Sunday school attendance in less than 80 percent the church's capacity. The "80 percent rule" also stands true for worship services (see Exhibit 13).

Dr. Hugghins would like to fully utilize today's technology. He would like to have a Web site developed and fully operational for the church to serve as a forum to inform not only members but also potential members of the activities of the church and any special events. The pastor recognizes how fast things are changing and wants ELBC to keep up. "But is the church ready to follow?" he wonders.

## REFERENCES

Elkins Lake Baptist Church. *Constitution and Bylaws.* Author, n.d.

Elkins Lake Baptist Church. *The Window.* 1997 and 1998.

Huntsville–Walker County Chamber of Commerce. *Community/Economic Profile for 1998, 1999.* http://chamber.huntsville.tx.us/economy.html

Judicial District Community Supervision and Corrections Department. *Fiscal Year 1998 Annual Report.* Author, n.d.

Minutes of the Tyron Evergreen Baptist Association of Texas, 91st Annual Session, Conroe, Texas, 1994.

Minutes of the Tyron Evergreen Baptist Association of Texas, 92nd Annual Session, Conroe, Texas, 1995.

Minutes of the Tyron Evergreen Baptist Association of Texas, 93rd Annual Session, Conroe, Texas, 1996.

Minutes of the Tyron Evergreen Baptist Association of Texas, 94th Annual Session, Conroe, Texas, 1997.

Minutes of the Tyron Evergreen Baptist Association of Texas, 95th Annual Session, Conroe, Texas, 1998.

# RAILTEX, INC.—2000

Paul Reed, Ronald Earl, and Joseph Kavanaugh
Sam Houston State University

**RTEX RailTex**
www.railtex.com
**RAIL RailAmerica**
www.railamerica.com

Ron Rittenmeyer caught himself shaking his head as he thought back over the twelve months since he joined RailTex, Inc., in August 1998 as president and chief executive officer. On the surface, RailTex, the largest North American shortline railroad holding company, appeared to be running fairly smoothly. However, many things were not going as Rittenmeyer would have preferred. In June 1998, RailTex paid $14.1 million, far too much, for two nonconnecting 173 miles of track in north central and southeastern Indiana. In January 1999, a wholly-owned subsidiary began operating on 89 miles of track leased from the Union Pacific Railroad. Estimated expenses of operating this trackage were too low, resulting in operating expenses that far exceeded operating revenues. For example, during the months of June and July 1999, this operating ratio averaged 125 percent.

On the other hand, Ron had made considerable progress towards correcting other problem areas. He had restructured the organization and replaced many of his predecessor's key staff. Plus, there had been considerable turnover in the managerial ranks of the 26 railroads owned by RailTex. The financial situation had been greatly improved; revenues and net income were up; debt was reduced and the cash flow was healthy again.

The future of RailTex was far from certain, however. The railroad industry had never been as volatile as it had been during the past ten years. Mergers of major rail lines and increased competition in the short-line portion of the industry along with escalating acquisition prices would require a steady hand, Ron thought.

## INTERNAL ENVIRONMENT

### Description of the Company

RailTex, Inc., is headquartered in San Antonio, Texas, and through its subsidiaries operates 26 short-line railroads in the United States, Canada and Mexico. These lines total approximately 4,100 miles and vary in length from 14 to 527 miles. Traffic on individual railroads runs from a few thousand to approximately 100 thousand carloads annually. Total cars shipped in 1998 were 547 thousand. Traffic through June 1999 was 17 percent ahead of a similar period in the previous year.

The majority of RailTex track is maintained to support train speeds of 25 miles per hour or less. This is in keeping with the relative short distance that its trains travel and the delivery and pick-up nature of its business. On those rail lines where time is a factor, RailTex does maintain track that can support speeds up to 40 to 60 miles per hour. This flexible philosophy often enables RailTex to have lower capital expenditures for track maintenance than was the case for the previous owners. Regular track maintenance is

## EXHIBIT 1   RailAmerica's Income Statements (000 omitted)

| | 1999 | 1998 | 1997 |
|---|---|---|---|
| Operating revenue: | | | |
| Transportation—railroad | $118,910,941 | $30,303,562 | $22,023,717 |
| Other | 6,461,383 | 2,700,421 | 2,472,188 |
| Motor Carrier | — | 4,252,329 | — |
| Total operating income | 125,372,324 | 37,256,312 | 24,495,905 |
| Operating expenses: | | | |
| Transportation—railroad | 75,375,742 | 15,702,487 | 12,502,153 |
| Selling, general and administrative | 19,549,612 | 9,075,571 | 6,840,467 |
| Depreciation and amortization | 9,179,239 | 2,543,115 | 1,788,594 |
| Motor Carrier | — | 4,438,039 | — |
| Total operating expenses | 104,104,593 | 31,759,212 | 21,131,214 |
| Operating income | 21,267,731 | 5,497,100 | 3,364,691 |
| Interest and other expense | (20,490,358) | (4,944,113) | (3,641,164) |
| Other income | 6,012,072 | 232,070 | 1,000,382 |
| Minority interest in income of subsidiary | (1,550,700) | (1,671,750) | (851,243) |
| Income from continuing operations before income taxes | 5,238,745 | (886,693) | (127,334) |
| Provision for income taxes | (786,979) | (1,000,000) | (415,000) |
| Income from continuing operations | 6,025,724 | 113,307 | 287,666 |
| Discontinued operations: | | | |
| Estimated loss on disposal of discontinued segments (net of income tax benefit of $277,000) | — | — | (452,402) |
| Income from operations of discontinued segments (less applicable income tax provisions of $2,300,000, $2,500,000, and $1,200,000) | 3,895,512 | 4,287,842 | 2,103,935 |
| Net income | $ 9,921,236 | $ 4,401,149 | $ 1,939,199 |
| Net income available to common stockholders | $ 8,885,702 | $ 4,401,149 | $ 1,939,199 |
| Basic earnings per common share | | | |
| Continuing operations | $     0.45 | $     0.01 | $     0.02 |
| Discontinued operations | 0.35 | 0.45 | 0.21 |
| Net income | $     0.80 | $     0.46 | $     0.23 |
| Diluted earnings per common share | | | |
| Continuing operations | $     0.43 | $     0.01 | $     0.02 |
| Discontinued operations | 0.34 | 0.44 | 0.20 |
| Net income | $     0.77 | $     0.45 | $     0.22 |
| Weighted average common shares outstanding: | | | |
| Basic | 11,089,614 | 9,552,866 | 8,303,938 |
| Diluted | 11,664,871 | 9,777,866 | 8,586,938 |

*Source:* www.freeedgar.com

performed by RailTex employees, and major renovation is usually contracted out. Most of this labor is not unionized, and wages are, accordingly, lower.

The company owned 258 locomotives and leased 15 more as of July 1, 1999. The average age of the fleet is 30 years, and most cars have been rebuilt or overhauled within the past several years. Unit availability averaged 95 percent in 1998. RailTex personnel perform normal maintenance and mid-level overhaul, but a large part of major overhaul is contracted out. RailTex owns or leases 3,329 freight cars of various categories.

# EXHIBIT 2    RailAmerica's Balance Sheets (000 omitted)

| | 1999 | 1998 |
|---|---|---|
| **Assets** | | |
| Current assets: | | |
| Cash | $ 11,597,540 | $ 5,085,402 |
| Accounts and notes receivable | 40,856,772 | 7,733,238 |
| Inventories | 9,928,789 | 3,647,885 |
| Other current assets | 3,500,166 | 1,480,637 |
| Net assets of discontinued operation | 14,995,915 | 13,882,586 |
| Total current assets | 80,879,182 | 31,829,748 |
| Property, plant and equipment, net | 347,617,262 | 91,875,650 |
| Notes receivable, less current portion | 2,122,843 | 1,284,200 |
| Investment in affiliates | 4,666,776 | 1,938,942 |
| Other assets | 8,642,071 | 4,035,372 |
| Total assets | $443,928,134 | $130,963,912 |
| **Liabilities and Stockholders' Equity** | | |
| Current Liabilities: | | |
| Current maturities of long-term debt | $ 17,811,326 | $ 3,557,430 |
| Accounts payable | 23,731,732 | 7,004,497 |
| Accrued expenses | 15,379,461 | 2,775,962 |
| Total current liabilities | 56,922,519 | 13,337,889 |
| Long-term debt, less current maturities | 145,016,269 | 62,769,869 |
| Subordinated debt | 100,000,000 | — |
| Convertible subordinated debt | 22,448,642 | — |
| Other liabilities | 16,374,169 | 427,288 |
| Deferred income taxes | 15,382,013 | 4,848,869 |
| Minority interest | 9,488,693 | 7,937,992 |
| Commitments and contingencies | | |
| Redeemable convertible preferred stock, $0.01 par value, $25 liquidation value, 1,000,000 shares authorized; 378,400 and 300,600 outstanding, respectively | 8,829,844 | 6,881,684 |
| Stockholders' equity: | | |
| Common stock, $0.001 par value 30,000,000 shares authorized; 12,610,725 issued and 11,894,136 outstanding at December 31, 1999; 10,207,477 issued and 9,631,188 outstanding at December 31, 1998 | 12,611 | 10,207 |
| Additional paid-in capital | 52,304,578 | 28,277,533 |
| Retained earnings | 18,170,824 | 9,285,122 |
| Accumulated other comprehensive income | 3,485,717 | 470,820 |
| Treasury stock (716,589 and 576,289 shares, respectively, at cost) | (4,507,745) | (3,283,361) |
| Total stockholders' equity | 69,465,985 | 34,760,321 |
| Total liabilities and stockholders' equity | $443,928,134 | $130,963,912 |

In 1998 lumber and forest product, coal, and chemical traffic made up 45 percent of RailTex revenues. Some of its railroads have a diversified traffic mix, but others ship only one or two commodities. In time, RailTex hopes to reduce its heavy reliance on a few types of traffic by acquiring railroads that ship other commodities.

## Management Philosophy

RailTex stresses a decentralized management structure, placing a general manager (GM) in charge of each railroad who is responsible for pricing, staffing, safety, marketing, and train operations. Every railroad has a corporate-approved annual plan that is updated quarterly and reviewed monthly. General managers report to a geographically based regional general manager (RGM). The six RGMs are located at one of the railroads in their region and serve not only as supervisors but as points of contact, expediters, advisors, and mentors. Final decisions in the above areas are still under the purview of the GM.

Corporate staff support the short lines by developing policies in such functional areas as maintenance, fuel purchase, human resource, accounting, and government-regulation compliance. In addition, financial and strategic planning guidance is provided. Lastly, the corporate marketing staff assists and coordinates sales calls, provides industrial development expertise, and offers formal marketing training.

Each railroad's workforce varies in size and composition, the smallest having 4 employees and the largest 137. Some of the larger railroads have an assistant general manager (AGM). The majority of lines have a manager in charge of train operations, a marketing director, one or more clerks and, in all cases, transportation specialists (transpecs) who operate the locomotive and switch cars. Flexibility is the key on the short line, and cross training of employees is a must. Transpecs are qualified not only to operate trains but can make a minor engine or railcar repair, grab a broom or paint brush, etc. All employees are expected to pitch in when and where needed. This willingness to do the "extra" enhances teamwork and morale and eliminates the need to hire individuals to perform narrowly defined jobs as is often the case on unionized railroads.

An incentive compensation program is used for all employees. Short-line employees, except the GM, receive a quarterly bonus based upon that railroad's net income. Individual performance determines the employee's share of the bonus pool. Bonus for these employees ranges from zero to more than 20 percent. On average, short-line employees receive a yearly bonus of approximately 12 percent of their annual salary.

RGM's, GM's, and AGM's annual bonuses are based upon individual, railroad, and corporate actual performance against the target in five categories. These target cash bonuses are 25 percent of annual earnings for RGMs and 20 percent for GMs and AGMs. The actual bonus amount paid can increase (up to a maximum of 150 percent of target) or decrease (to zero) based on performance.

At corporate headquarters, employees below executive and senior management receive quarterly profit-sharing based upon a percentage of aggregate salaries for those employees. The executive incentive plan pertains to managers above RGM. From 20 percent to 40 percent of their annual compensation is at "risk," based upon goal attainment, and the remainder of their salary is fixed. In addition, stock options and other long-term incentives are available if various performance targets are met or exceeded.

## Strategy

Corporate strategy is twofold. The first goal is the creation of new business and improvement in operating performance of new and old properties. Improving service to current customers while increasing marketing efforts to attract new and former rail users adds to the revenue side of the operation. At the same time, operating efficiency, reduction in capital spent, and a flexible workforce have a positive impact on expenses. Annual increases in the number of carloads and resultant operating revenue growth have been a perennial occurrence on the vast majority of RailTex properties. Operating expenses, in general, increase along with higher operating revenues but at a slower rate. The end result is an improved bottom line.

The second goal is to make additions to and divestitures from RailTex's portfolio of short-line railroads. Acquisitions will center on properties that are in close proximity to current RailTex lines to enable the company to achieve operating, marketing, and administrative synergies by combining the operations of the new addition with the existing railroad.

Rittenmeyer believes that major railroads will continue to sell off unwanted branch lines but at a slower pace than previously. Also purchase opportunities exist among the 515 railroads that make up the short-line industry.

The divestiture of rail properties is a recent phenomenon at RailTex. Smaller railroads that are relatively isolated from the rest of the company's operations and that have reached the limit of revenues and profit growth are likely candidates. In the first six months of 1999, RailTex had sold three properties totaling 150 miles in length.

## Acquisition Technique

RailTex has a staff section that is tasked with implementing the corporate acquisition strategy. Expansion opportunities are either presented to the company by the divesting carrier or are identified through contacts throughout the rail industry.

Potential candidates are evaluated according to the railroad's geographic location, types of commodities hauled, customers served, number of connecting railroads, size, and revenues. The acquisition team conducts on-site visits, reviews historical information, interviews employees, and talks with current, former and potential new customers and local officials. Much is gained by just looking around. RailTex has bid on fewer than half of the lines it evaluated and won the bid on approximately one third of these.

Sixteen of RailTex's 26 North American rail lines are owned; three are leased; five others are both owned and leased, and two are operated under contract. Three of the four lines added in 1998 were purchased and one was leased. The only transaction during the first six months of 1999 was by lease. Normally, RailTex bids against other short-line operators for available properties. The selling railroad will make its selection based on such factors as the price it will receive from the buyer and the price per carload it will pay the new operator for interchange traffic. Other important factors for the divesting line to consider are prospective operator experience and the ability to close the financial transaction and begin immediate operations.

RailTex has a competitive advantage over many of its short-line competitors because it can finance acquisitions quickly with borrowings under a $175 million revolving line of credit (U.S. Acquisition Facility) and a $20 million Canadian revolving credit line (Canadian Acquisition Facility).

New properties are integrated into RailTex by a "Go Team" headed by the RGM and consisting of selected marketing, support, and operational personnel from headquarters and the other RailTex railroads. The Go Team arrives on site while the former owner is still operating the line. Visits with customers and familiarization with the property receive top priority. After a few days RailTex's policies and procedures are put in place, and the Go Team begins operating the line until the newly appointed GM has time to hire and train a permanent workforce. Assembling a workforce is often difficult, particularly if the divesting line's employees are unionized. Many elect to transfer to other union jobs rather than join RailTex. The Go Team usually completes its work in a few weeks, and its members then return to their former jobs. The Go Team helps the new line begin operations with minimum interruption and service delay. Some glitches are bound to occur, however, such as putting railcars in wrong sidings, missing connections, and other minor mishaps. Safety concerns are always paramount.

## Marketing

Marketing plays a key role in RailTex's combination strategies of acquisition and internal growth of the "same railroad," i.e., increased revenues on railroads owned more than one year. The company's marketing efforts are aimed at satisfying the business needs of its more than 1,100 customers. The company often increases scheduled train service or dispatches extra trains in the event of customer emergency. It also helps customers negotiate price and service levels with connecting railroads. Also, it secures various types of railcars to assist customers in their operations via equipment purchase, lease, or rental.

The GM is responsible for the railroad's marketing effort and is assisted by not only local and corporate marketing personnel but their entire staff. All employees have business cards. Transpecs, for example, are encouraged to identify and, if possible, satisfy customer needs as they pick up and deliver railcars on site. Items beyond their control are passed on to the appropriate individual for action.

Each railroad marketing director or salesman job has been restructured so as to eliminate most duties in nonmarketing areas. Now these employees can devote much of their time to making customer contacts and identifying potential customers within 50 miles of the rail line. Off-line businesses are made aware of the cost and service advantages of using a combination of rail or truck transportation. The long haul would be via RailTex and connecting rail, and the short haul would be by truck. This intermodal connection could be at a transload warehouse or an on/off ramp. Marketer compensation is now more commission based, and bonuses are tied to revenue growth. A semi-annual performance-quality survey is used to measure customer satisfaction. The response rate has increased to 90 percent and a "six" on a seven-point Likert scale is the target for this critical success factor.

### Communications

Good communications is a must for the geographically distant RailTex operations. The company utilizes a wide variety of techniques to communicate with its various constituencies. Quarterly business review meetings are held for headquarters employees, and the RGM and other corporate officials hold frequent "Town Hall Meetings" out on the rail lines. Face-to-face communications is supplemented by the HRM-slanted bi-monthly *RailTex Express* employee newsletter and the *RailTex Quarterly,* which reaches a larger audience of employees and customers. The company provides a 1-800 number for current and potential shareholders to obtain latest news releases via fax. The company also has a Web site, www.railtex.com. The company utilizes and responds to employee attitude surveys and an anonymous question-and-answer section of *RailTex Express.* In 1998 the company installed a new operating system, INFO, in the field. INFO measures revenue on a daily basis and tracks performance by commodity, customer, and property. This allows development of marketing plans and anticipation of changes far more rapidly than in the past. Although most employees have a positive attitude towards these efforts, some desire more one-on-one contact, and others wonder if they are really listened to.

*Workforce*

RailTex recognizes the importance of job security to employee morale, turnover and productivity. The use of temporary employees and contract labor serves to greatly minimize layoffs in the seasonal transportation, engineering, and mechanical areas. The company also believes in promotion from within, and movement across and up career ladders is encouraged. Short-line vacancies are often filled by qualified employees who are working on overstaffed RailTex properties. Approximately 73 percent of the workforce of 896 are white males. Black and Hispanic males are concentrated in the skilled craft areas. Women are moving into professional and management areas but are still overwhelmingly employed as clerical workers.

Turnover on RailTex appears within reasonable limits, and most losses are the result of resignation rather than termination. The company conducts exit interviews with voluntary departees to determine why they are leaving. Terminations are usually the result of chronic rule infractions. In 1995, RailTex instituted the grievance peer panel (GPP) that permits employees to challenge termination. The GPP is comprised of two employee volunteers selected by the grievant and one management volunteer selected by the company, with a majority vote deciding the case. The three panel members are not involved in the issue. These informal hearings have been well received and are an example of RailTex's belief in employee empowerment. To date, the vast majority of management discipline decisions have been upheld by the GPP.

*Unions*

Union activity has become a major issue at RailTex. Currently, 169 employees, or 18.9 percent of the company's workforce, of five U.S. properties are represented by labor unions—four by the United Transportation Union (UTU) and one by the Brotherhood of Locomotive Engineers (BLE). Two railroads have active contracts, and the remaining three are in negotiation. RailTex recently defeated an attempt by the BLE to organize its Central Oregon & Pacific Railroad (CORP). The company believes that its efforts to improve communications throughout the organization were a major factor in its victory. Twenty-six employees of one Canadian RailTex property are represented by the BLE. The company assumes that unionization efforts will continue to be a threat into the future.

## Summary of Financial Performance: 1996–1999

RailTex has continued to improve its financial condition since start-up and, particularly, since 1996. The company generated $121.1 million in operating revenues in 1996, while traffic volume was 359.7 thousand carloads. Operating revenues for 1997 were $148.8 million and traffic volume, 488.3 thousand carloads, a 22.8 percent increase in revenues and a 35.7 percent increase in carloads. Operating revenues attributable to new properties accounted for 79.9 percent of the total operating revenues increase and 85.6 percent of the carload increase while "same railroad" contributed a 5.5 percent revenue increase and 5.7 percent increase in carloads. In 1998 revenues were $161.0 and traffic volume at 549.5 thousand carloads, an 8.1 percent revenue increase and a 12.5 percent increase in carloads. Operating revenues attributable to new properties accounted for 24.3 percent of total operating revenue increase and 13.7 percent carload increase while "same railroad" contributed 5.5 and 5.7 percent, respectively. During the first six months of 1999 as compared to a similar period in 1998, operating revenue increased 16.5 percent to $90.3 million as carloads rose 17 percent to 307.2 thousand. Net income for the six-month period was $6.9 million as compared to $3.6 million for the period in 1998. See the Exhibit 3 income statement data for years 1996–1998 and RailTex's balance sheets are provided in Exhibit 4.

EXHIBIT 3     RailTex Consolidated Income Statements
(in thousands, except per share amounts)

| Years Ended December 31, | 1998 | 1997 | 1996 |
|---|---|---|---|
| Operating revenues | $161,020 | $148,791 | $121,106 |
| Operating expenses: | | | |
| Transportation | 56,852 | 54,361 | 39,006 |
| General and administrative | 26,675 | 26,367 | 20,948 |
| Equipment | 18,937 | 17,954 | 15,718 |
| Maintenance of way | 16,646 | 14,168 | 13,246 |
| Depreciation and amortization | 14,258 | 12,940 | 10,147 |
| Total operating expenses | 133,368 | 125,790 | 99,065 |
| Operating income | 27,652 | 23,001 | 22,041 |
| Interest expense | (11,236) | (10,527) | (6,893) |
| Other income, net | 4,215 | 4,198 | 1,521 |
| Income before income taxes and cumulative effect of a change in accounting principle | 20,631 | 16,672 | 16,669 |
| Income taxes | (7,853) | (6,048) | (6,708) |
| Net income before cumulative effect of a change in accounting principle | $ 12,778 | $ 10,624 | $ 9,961 |
| Cumulative effect of change in accounting principle (net of income taxes) | (1,703) | — | — |
| Net income | $ 11,075 | $ 10,624 | $ 9,961 |
| Basic earnings per share: | | | |
| Net income before cumulative effect of a change in accounting principle | $ 1.39 | $ 1.16 | $ 1.09 |
| Cumulative effect of a change in accounting principle (net of income taxes) | (0.19) | — | — |
| Net income | $ 1.20 | $ 1.16 | $ 1.09 |
| Weighted average number of shares of common stock and common stock equivalents outstanding | 9,205 | 9,153 | 9,112 |

*Source:* www.freeedgar.com

## EXTERNAL ENVIRONMENT

### Industry Background

The Surface Transportation Board classifies all common carrier railroads operating within the United States into one of three categories based primarily on annual operating revenue. The major rail freight carriers, Class I railroads, must meet an adjustable revenue threshold for a period of three continuous years. In 1998, this threshold was $259.4 million. Regional railroads operate at least 350 miles of track or earn revenue between $40 million and the Class I threshold. Local short-line railroads are all those that fall below the regional criteria and include switching and terminal railroads. RailTex, Inc., owns or leases railroads in this latter category. A comparison of these three types of railroads is shown in Exhibit 5.

# EXHIBIT 4    RailTex's Consolidated Balance Sheets
## (in thousands, except share and per-share amounts)

| December 31, | 1998 | 1997 |
|---|---|---|
| **Assets** | | |
| Current assets: | | |
| Cash and cash equivalents | $    1,243 | $     570 |
| Accounts receivable, less doubtful receivables of $844 in 1998; | | |
| $1,563 in 1997 | 33,866 | 32,171 |
| Prepaid expenses and other current assets | 4,848 | 2,527 |
| Deferred tax assets, net | 1,906 | 1,777 |
| Total current assets | 41,863 | 37,045 |
| Property and equipment, net | 291,779 | 259,444 |
| Other assets: | | |
| Investments in Brazilian railroad companies | 19,994 | 17,809 |
| Other, net | 8,709 | 5,610 |
| Total other assets | 28,703 | 23,419 |
| Total assets | $362,345 | $319,908 |
| **Liabilities and shareholders' equity** | | |
| Current liabilities: | | |
| Short-term notes payable | $     215 | $     384 |
| Current portion of long-term debt | 8,568 | 7,763 |
| Accounts payable | 20,574 | 18,829 |
| Accrued liabilities | 17,729 | 17,434 |
| Total current liabilities | 47,086 | 44,410 |
| Deferred income taxes, net | 30,294 | 20,521 |
| Long-term debt, less current portion | 122,982 | 117,893 |
| Other liabilities | 6,835 | 3,826 |
| Total liabilities | 207,197 | 186,650 |
| Commitments and contingencies | | |
| Minority interest in Brazilian investment | 11,000 | — |
| Shareholders' equity | | |
| Preferred stock; $1.00 par value; 10 million shares | | |
| authorized; no shares issued or outstanding | — | — |
| Common stock; $.10 par value; 30 million shares authorized; | | |
| issued and outstanding 1998–9, 273,936; 1997–9, 160,924 | 927 | 916 |
| Paid-in capital | 85,115 | 83,799 |
| Retained earnings | 59,976 | 48,901 |
| Deferred compensation | (948) | — |
| Accumulated other comprehensive income | (922) | (358) |
| Total shareholders' equity | 144,148 | 133,258 |
| Total liabilities and shareholders' equity | $362,345 | $319,908 |

*Source:* Company Records. www.freeedgar.com

234 PAUL REED, RONALD EARL, AND JOSEPH KAVANAUGH

---

**EXHIBIT 5**   Types of Railroads in the United States: 1998

| Type of Railroad | Number | Miles Operated | Employees | Freight Revenue (in millions) |
|---|---|---|---|---|
| Class I | 9 | 119,813 | 178,222 | $32.25 |
| Regional | 35 | 21,356 | 11,094 | 1.59 |
| Local (short line) | 515 | 28,629 | 11,590 | 1.46 |
| Total | 559 | 169,798 | 200,906 | $35.30 |

*Source:* Association of American Railroads, *Railroad Facts: 1999*, p. 3.

---

### The Short-Line Segment

Although there have been short-line railroads since the early part of the nineteenth century, their number has almost doubled since 1980. Deregulation of the U.S. and Canadian railroad industries has permitted major (Class I) North American railroads to improve profitability by downsizing both workforce and operations. Included in this has been the ability to divest (through sale or lease) marginal or unprofitable branch lines to smaller railroad operators. These short-line railroads are normally more cost effective because they are not bound by the onerous union-imposed labor cost structure and associated archaic work rules that their larger brothers are. Savings from the use of older equipment and lower capital expenditures are also an added plus for these lines. Operating over shorter distances and serving fewer customers enable these railroads to provide more responsive services than the long-haul-oriented, major railroads could. This improved service often attracts increased business from current customers and the return of former rail users. Thus, lower costs and increased business are often the outcome for both the short-line buyer and the connecting Class I seller. Obviously, the seller in these transactions carefully assesses the business experience and acumen of the buyer.

### ACQUISITIONS

Trackage will continue to become available for sale as major U.S. railroads and the two principal Canadian railroads continue downsizing. The percentage increase in trackage has slowed down in the last couple of years, however, and in some cases Class I railroads have purchased short-line trackage. In addition, the privatization of rail lines in Mexico and Latin America creates opportunities for U.S. Class I, regional, and short-line railroads. A third source of possible acquisition is the approximately 500 other small railroads owned by other railroads, nonrailroad companies, investment partnerships, and individuals.

### COMPETITION

RailTex properties are subject to competition from railroads and trucks.

#### Rail

Company rail lines are partners to their major rail connections. Good working relationships serve both parties, whereas poor performance by one carrier offsets the good actions of the other. The railroad industry has improved in rates, quality, and reliability of service in the last few years, and this has complemented RailTex's strong customer orientation.

Many regional and short-line railroads actively compete with RailTex in the short-line acquisition market. Many of these organizations are privately owned, and financial information is unavailable. Short-line holding companies and group operators portfolios vary from 1 to as many as 15 railroads. Some individual lines ship less than 200 carloads a year, and the most traveled moved over 470,000. Transtar Inc.'s seven railroads hauled over 1.1 million loads that same year. RailAmerica, Transtar, and Genesee & Wyoming are three major competitors that have significantly increased the number of railroads that they have purchased in recent years. As such, these railroads have decreased the supply of short-line railroads available and have bid up the prices of those railroads that have become available.

### Trucks

Trucks carry a greater share of intercity traffic than do railroads. Their innate flexibility, relatively low capital requirements, and huge network of tax-supported highways give them great advantage in smaller-volume and under 500-mile shipments. Railroads are very competitive in bulk shipments over long distances. Intermodal shipments (truck or container on rail flatcar) often offer the advantages of both modes to shippers. Improved rail service has increasingly moved trucks and containers off the highway and onto the rails. In many instances, customers have transferred their business to rail.

### GOVERNMENT

RailTex properties are subject to various federal, state or province, and local laws and regulations pertaining, in varying degrees, to virtually every phase of their operations.

### Federal

Government programs and policies that influence the value of the dollar, export enhancement, crop support prices, and interest rates greatly affect overall economic activity and, therefore, RailTex. Major federal agencies aimed specifically at the rail industry are

1. The Surface Transportation Board (the successor to the ICC) regulates the acquisition of new railroad properties by purchase, lease, or contract to operate. Along with the demise of the ICC came less stringent requirements in several areas, including severance pay to employees who lost their jobs as a result of the acquisition, the rail line abandonment process, and the setting of rates and tariffs.
2. Federal Railroad Administration (FRA) regulates railroad safety and equipment standards, including track maintenance, train speeds, procedures for handling hazardous shipments, locomotive and railcar inspection and repair, operating practices, and crew qualifications. FRA inspectors are regularly in the field and have, on occasion, stopped a train or, in effect, a railroad until violations were corrected.

### State and Local

State regulatory agencies no longer have the authority to engage in economic regulation of railroads that are a part of the intrastate network. State and local governments maintain jurisdiction over local rail safety matters, such as speed within city limits and the installation of grade crossings and crossing warning devices.

## Canada

The company's three railroad properties are subject to the regulations of Canada and the provinces in which they are located. Recent federal legislation has simplified the acquisition of railroads. Lines operating within one province are governed almost exclusively by the laws of that province. Each of the ten provinces in Canada has different laws with respect to rail regulation. Recent provincial legislation indicates a more favorable stance toward the operation of short lines.

## Natural Environment

RailTex operations are subject to the increasingly strict U.S. and Canadian federal, state or provincial, and local laws and regulations relating to the protection of the environment. Agencies created by these acts govern the management of hazardous wastes, the discharge of pollutants into the air and into surface and underground waters, and the disposal of certain substances. In the past, RailTex has been evaluated by environmental agencies on two of its railroads for incidents such as oil spills caused by train derailment, on-site burial of railroad ties, leaking storage tanks, and the release of diesel fuel during locomotive refueling. These incidents, however, did occur prior to the company's acquisition of these properties, and RailTex has maintained its innocence in these matters. Another train derailment that spilled 2,000 gallons of hazardous material cost RailTex $2 million for clean-up costs and related expenses. Prevention of such incidents is continually stressed at all levels of the company.

## UNCONTROLLABLE FACTORS

Approximately 30 percent of the company's carloads interchange with Union Pacific (UP). As a result, the company has been impacted by the congestion the UP is experiencing primarily through car-supply issues and increased operating expenses as a result of overtime associated with running trains on unscheduled days and delays caused by waiting for access to UP yards. Additionally, revenues have been lost to other modes of transportation as customers avoid the service problems caused by the UP congestion. To the extent that the UP problems continue or worsen, the company's results of operations could be adversely impacted.

As a result of the acquisition of Consolidated Rail Corporation (Conrail) by CSX Transportation, Inc. (CSX) and Norfolk Southern Railway Company (NS), Conrail's rail lines will be divided between CSX and NS, which may cause revenue to be diverted from the New England Central Railroad, Inc. (NECR) and the Indiana Southern Railroad, Inc. (ISRR), wholly-owned subsidiaries of RailTex. In addition, the INOH, a wholly owned subsidiary of RailTex, believes the division of rail lines between CSX and NS will cause operating inefficiencies for INOH. The company believes the effect on revenues and operating efficiencies will be minimal.

## THE FUTURE

Rittenmeyer's day soon filled with the normal business of a busy executive. He spent several hours gathering and dispersing information, making decisions, and checking on the progress of previous ones. It was late afternoon before he got back to his thoughts of the railroad's future. He ponders to what extent RailAmerica will allow RailTex to operate independently and autonomously.

On Friday October 13, 1999, the boards of directors of RailAmerica, Inc. and RailTex, Inc. agreed to a merger in which RailAmerica would acquire RailTex. On

February 1, 2000 both companies announced that their shareholders had voted over-whelmingly to approve the merger proposal. RailTex shareholders received $13.50 in cash and two-thirds of a share of RailAmerica stock in exchange for each share of RailTex stock. RailTex, which operated 25 railroads over 4,100 miles of rail lines in North America, is now a wholly-owned operating subsidiary of RailAmerica. Currently owning or having equity interest in 50 railroads operating 12,500 miles of rail lines around the globe, RailAmerica becomes the world's largest operation of short line and regional rail-roads. RailAmerica's financial statements are provided in Exhibits 1 and 2.

# HARLEY-DAVIDSON, INC.—2000

**Ricky Cox**
**Francis Marion University**

## HDI
www.harley-davidson.com

> A road-sculpted old man sat down at the counter of a one-horse-town coffee shop. His Harley was parked outside.
> "Nice bike," said the short-order.
> "Thanks."
> "Where ya headed?"
> "Everywhere. No-wheres."
>
> His coffee cup filled, the old man pointed to the Blue Plate Special and nodded his head.
> "Where ya been?" Simple question. Difficult answer.
> Without saying a word, the old man took off his jacket, revealing a right arm tattooed with every place he'd ever been. From Frankfurt to Copenhagen, Tokyo to Thailand, Quebec to Key West and on to Caracas. He'd even been to Bora Bora.
> The awesome display was followed by an awkward silence, broken when the short-order asked the old man where he called home.
> He then rolled up his sleeve, where an ancient Harley-Davidson tattoo remained uncluttered. "Show me to the nearest Harley dealer. And I'll show you home."
>
> (www.harley-davidson.com)

When was the last time you felt this strongly about anything? How many company names do you have tattooed on your body? The Harley-Davidson name is worn like a badge of honor. These lifelong customers have a passionate commitment to the experience of riding a Harley-Davidson. For motorcycle enthusiasts, even those without the tattoos, Harley-Davidson is engraved in their lifestyle. This loyalty has helped Harley to survive against fierce international competition and maintain strong financial performance.

Harley-Davidson has delivered double-digit growth in both revenue and earnings for more than a decade. As shown in Exhibit 1, Harley-Davidson's net sales totaled $2,452.9 million in 1999, an 18.8 percent increase over 1998. Net income was $267.2 million, up 25.2 percent from 1998, and diluted earnings per share for 1999 was $1.73, up 25.3 percent. The company increased its quarterly dividend payment in June 1998 from $.035 per share to $.04 per share resulting in an annual payout of $.155 per share. The price of the company's shares increased 74 percent during 1998. The company has experienced a compound annual growth rate in its stock price of over 40 percent since going public in 1986 (1998 *Annual Report*). Harley's 1999 balance sheet is provided in Exhibit 2.

EXHIBIT 1    Harley-Davidson Annual Income Statement and Balance Sheet
(in millions except earnings-per-share data)

|  | 12/31/99 | 12/31/98 | 12/31/97 | 12/31/96 |
|---|---|---|---|---|
| Sales | $2,452.93 | $2,063.95 | $1,762.57 | $1,531.23 |
| Cost of goods | 1,617.25 | 1,373.28 | 1,176.35 | 1,041.13 |
| **Gross profit** | 835.68 | 690.67 | 586.22 | 490.09 |
| Selling and administrative and department and amortization expenses | 447.51 | 377.26 | 328.57 | 269.45 |
| **Income after depreciation and amortization** | 388.17 | 313.41 | 257.65 | 220.64 |
| Nonoperating income | 32.61 | 22.82 | 18.65 | 6.98 |
| Interest expense | 0 | 0 | 0 | 0 |
| **Pretax income** | 420.79 | 336.22 | 276.30 | 227.62 |
| Income taxes | 153.59 | 122.72 | 102.23 | 84.21 |
| Minority interest | 0 | 0 | 0 | 0 |
| Investment gains/losses (+) | 0 | 0 | 0 | 0 |
| Other income/charges | 0 | 0 | 0 | 0 |
| **Income from continued operations** | N/A | N/A | N/A | N/A |
| Extras and discontinued operations | 0 | 0 | 0 | 22.62 |
| **Net income** | $  267.20 | $  213.50 | $  174.07 | $  166.03 |

## Depreciation footnote

|  | 12/31/99 | 12/31/98 | 12/31/97 | 12/31/96 |
|---|---|---|---|---|
| Income before depreciation and amortization | $  501.99 | $  400.83 | $  327.83 | $  275.03 |
| Depreciation and amortization (cash flow) | 113.82 | 87.42 | 70.18 | 55.28 |
| **Income after depreciation and amortization** | $  388.17 | $  313.41 | $  257.65 | $  220.64 |

## Earnings-per-share data

|  | 12/31/99 | 12/31/98 | 12/31/97 | 12/31/96 |
|---|---|---|---|---|
| **Average shares** | $  154.86 | $  154.70 | $  153.96 | $  150.91 |
| Diluted EPS before non-recurring items | 1.73 | 1.38 | 1.13 | 0.95 |
| **Diluted net EPS** | $    1.73 | $    1.38 | $    1.13 | $    1.10 |

## HISTORY

"Harley-Davidson began in a shed, went to war, became the symbol of American individualism and ended up 'king of the road,' all in 95 years. . . ." (1998 *Annual Report*) In the Davidson family's backyard in 1903 what was to become the legendary motorcycle company was formed. The Davidson Brothers—William D., Walter, Arthur—and William S. Harley made their first motorcycle there. In 1909, Harley-Davidson introduced its first V-Twin engine, which is the company standard to this day.

During World War I, Harley-Davidson supplied the military with 20,000 motorcycles. After the war, there were major advancements made in the design of motorcycles, and Harley was the leader. Soon after the war, the Great Depression devastated the motorcycle industry. Only Harley and Indian survived through the 1930s.

In 1941, World War II called, and Harley answered with more than 90,000 motorcycles. After the war, demand for motorcycles exploded, and Harley added additional facilities in Milwaukee in 1947. After Indian closed in 1953, Harley was the "king

# EXHIBIT 2    Harley-Davidson Annual Balance Sheet
## (in millions, except book value per share)

| | 12/31/99 | 12/31/98 | 12/31/97 | 12/31/96 |
|---|---|---|---|---|
| **Assets** | | | | |
| Cash and equivalents | $   183.41 | $   165.17 | $   147.46 | $   142.48 |
| Receivables | 542.65 | 473.75 | 102.80 | 141.32 |
| Notes receivable | 0 | 0 | 0 | 0 |
| Inventories | 168.61 | 155.61 | 117.47 | 101.39 |
| Other current assets | 54.30 | 50.41 | 336.29 | 44.14 |
| **Total current assets** | **948.99** | **844.96** | **704.02** | **429.32** |
| Net property and equipment | 681.74 | 627.75 | 528.87 | 409.43 |
| Investments and advances | 0 | 0 | 0 | 0 |
| Other noncurrent assets | 354.88 | 319.42 | 249.35 | 338.07 |
| Deferred charges | 0 | 0 | 3.00 | 24.69 |
| Intangibles | 55.40 | 51.19 | 38.71 | 40.90 |
| Deposits and other assets | 71.04 | 76.86 | 74.96 | 77.57 |
| **Total assets** | **$2,112.07** | **$1,920.20** | **$1,598.90** | **$1,319.98** |
| **Liabilities and shareholders' equity** | | | | |
| Notes payable | 0 | 0 | 0 | 2.58 |
| Accounts payable | 137.66 | 122.72 | 106.11 | 100.70 |
| Current portion long-term debt | 181.16 | 146.74 | 90.64 | 0 |
| Current portion capital leases | 0 | 0 | 0 | 0 |
| Accrued expenses | 199.33 | 199.05 | 164.94 | 160.32 |
| Income taxes payable | 0 | 0 | 0 | 0 |
| Other current liabilities | 0 | 0 | 0 | 0 |
| **Total current liabilities** | **518.15** | **468.51** | **361.69** | **263.59** |
| Mortgages | 0 | 0 | 0 | 0 |
| Deferred taxes/income | 12.03 | 2.32 | 0 | 0 |
| Convertible debt | 0 | 0 | 0 | 0 |
| Long-term debt | 345.09 | 280.00 | 280.00 | 258.07 |
| Noncurrent capital leases | 0 | 0 | 0 | 0 |
| Other noncurrent liabilities | 75.71 | 139.45 | 130.54 | 135.61 |
| Minority interest (liabilities) | 0 | 0 | 0 | 0 |
| **Total liabilities** | **$   950.99** | **$   890.29** | **$   772.23** | **$   657.27** |
| **Shareholders' equity** | | | | |
| Preferred stock | 0 | 0 | 0 | 0 |
| Common stock (par) | 1.59 | 1.58 | 1.57 | 0.78 |
| Capital surplus | 236.54 | 211.96 | 187.18 | 175.15 |
| Retained earnings | 1,113.37 | 873.17 | 683.32 | 530.78 |
| Other equity | (2.43) | 0.32 | (3.95) | (2.06) |
| Treasury stock | 187.99 | 57.13 | 41.96 | 41.93 |
| Total shareholders' equity | 1,161.08 | 1,029.91 | 826.67 | 662.72 |
| **Total liabilities and shareholders' equity** | **2,112.07** | **1,920.20** | **1,598.90** | **1,319.98** |
| Total common equity | 1,161.08 | 1,029.91 | 826.67 | 662.72 |
| Average shares | 154.86 | 154.70 | 153.95 | 150.91 |
| Book value per share | $      7.67 | $      6.74 | $      5.43 | $      4.39 |

*Source:* www.freeedgar.com

of the road." Harley ended family ownership in 1965 with a public offering. Only four years later, the company merged with the American Machine and Foundry Company (AMF).

By the early 1970s, the Japanese were importing huge numbers of lower-priced motorcycles into the United States. Japanese firms were able to capture a large portion of Harley's market share. Harley was also having quality problems as a result of expanding production so rapidly. In 1981, 13 managers purchased the business from AMF. The company convinced President Ronald Reagan, upon recommendation from the International Trade Commission (ITC), to impose additional tariffs on imported heavy-weight Japanese motorcycles for five years. Then in 1986, Harley-Davidson, Inc., became publicly held. That same year, Harley regained its place at the top of the U.S. superheavyweight market, beating out Honda. The next year, the company asked the ITC to remove the tariffs one year early. Harley's U.S. market share continued to grow. After being praised by President Reagan as an "American success story," Harley has continued to improve all parts of its operations. Worldwide demand for the company's products continues to grow.

## CORPORATE MISSION STATEMENT

Harley's mission statement as provided in their 1999 *Annual Report* is as follows:

> We fulfill dreams through the experience of motorcycling, by providing to motorcyclists and to the general public an expanding line of motorcycles and branded products and services in selected market segments.

## CORPORATE VISION STATEMENT

Harley's vision statement as provided in the 1999 *Annual Report* is as follows:

> Harley-Davidson is an action-oriented, international company, a leader in its commitment to continuously improve our mutually beneficial relationships with stakeholders (customers, suppliers, employees, shareholders, government, and society). Harley-Davidson believes the key to success is to balance stakeholders' interests through the empowerment of all employees to focus on value-added activities.

## DIVISIONS

Harley-Davidson is divided into two divisions: Motorcycles and Related Products and Financial Services. The Motorcycles segment designs, manufactures, and sells motorcycles, motorcycle parts, accessories, and general merchandise. Harley is the only major American motorcycle manufacturer.

The average U.S. Harley-Davidson purchaser is a married male in his mid-forties, with a household income of approximately $73,000. Over two thirds of the sales of Harley-Davidson motorcycles are to buyers with at least one year of higher education beyond high school, and 32 percent of the buyers have college degrees. Approximately 7 percent of Harley's U.S. retail motorcycle sales are to women.

Harley's heavyweight class of motorcycles is divided into four segments: standard, performance, touring, and custom. The standard segment emphasizes simplicity and cost, and the performance segment for Harley Davidson emphasizes handling and acceleration. The touring segment focuses on comfort for long-distance travel. Harley-Davidson pioneered this segment of the heavyweight market. Harley's custom segment gives owners the opportunity to customize their bikes. Harley-Davidson makes 24 models of Harley-Davidson touring and custom heavyweight motorcycles, with retail prices

EXHIBIT 3    Harley-Davidson Divisional Units and Sales (in millions)

| | 1999 | 1998 | 1997 | *Increase* | *% Change* |
|---|---|---|---|---|---|
| **Motorcycle** | **UNITS** | **UNITS** | **UNITS** | | |
| Harley-Davidson motorcycle units | 132,285 | 150,818 | 132,285 | 18,533 | 14.0 |
| Buell motorcycle units | 4,415 | 6,334 | 4,415 | 1,919 | 43.5 |
| Total motorcycle units | 136,700 | 157,152 | 136,700 | 20,452 | 15.0 |
| | | | | | |
| **Net sales** | **SALES** | **SALES** | **SALES** | | |
| Harley-Davidson motorcycles | — | $1,595.4 | $1,382.8 | $212.6 | 15.4 |
| Buell motorcycles | — | 53.5 | 40.3 | 13.2 | 32.8 |
| Total motorcycles | $1,762.0 | 1,648.9 | 1,423.1 | 225.8 | 15.9 |
| Motorcycle parts and accessories | — | 297.1 | 241.9 | 55.2 | 22.8 |
| General merchandise | — | 114.5 | 95.1 | 19.4 | 20.4 |
| Other | — | 3.5 | 2.5 | 1.0 | 37.8 |
| Total motorcycles and related products | $2,453.0 | $2,064.0 | $1,762.6 | $301.5 | 17.1 |

*Source:* www.freeedgar.com

ranging from $5,350 to $18,500. The performance segment of the market is served by the Buell motorcycle line, which offers sport and sport-touring models. As shown in Exhibit 3, the Buell division sold 6,334 motorcycles in 1998 but only 4,415 in 1999, a 30.2 percent decline. The prices for the high end of Harley's custom product line can be as much as 50 percent higher than its competitors' custom motorcycles. The custom segment makes up the highest number of Harleys sold, and the product continues to demand a higher price because of its features, styling, and high resale value.

The Financial Services segment consists of Harley's wholly owned subsidiary, Eaglemark Financial Services, Inc. Eaglemark provides motorcycle showroom floor planning and parts and accessories financing to the Harley-Davidson dealers in North America. In Europe, Eaglemark provides wholesale financing to dealers through a joint venture agreement with Transamerica Distribution Finance Corporation. Eaglemark also provides property and casualty insurance and extended service contracts for motorcycles through a group of unaffiliated insurance underwriters. As Harley-Davidson increases the production of motorcycles in the next few years, Eaglemark will help to provide the financing for a growing customer base.

## MARKETING AND DISTRIBUTION

Harley-Davidson has approximately 615 independently owned full-service dealerships in the United States. The marketing efforts are divided among dealer promotions, customer events, magazine and direct mail advertising, and public relations. Harley also sponsors racing activities and special promotional events and participates in all major motorcycle consumer shows and rallies. The Harley Owners Group (HOG), which was formed in 1983, currently has approximately 430,000 members worldwide and is the industry's largest company-sponsored motorcycle enthusiast organization. The Buell Riders' Adventure Group (BRAG) was also formed in recent years and has grown to approximately 8,000 members. Both HOG and BRAG sponsor events, including national rallies and rides, across the United States for motorcycle enthusiasts.

Harley-Davidson is one of the most admired and recognized companies in the world today. Recently, the company has attempted to create an increased awareness of the

Harley-Davidson brand name among the nonriding public and to provide a wide range of products for enthusiasts by licensing the name "Harley-Davidson." The company has licensed the production and sale of a wide range of items, including T-shirts, jewelry, small leather goods, toys, and other products. As can be seen in Exhibit 3, the General Merchandise part of Harley's sales went up 20.4 percent, to about $114,500,000 in 1998.

Harley has also recently formed an alliance with Ford Motor Company, and the two released a limited edition 2000 Harley-Davidson F-150 pickup truck at the 1999 Sturgis Rally and Races, which attract over 350,000 motorcyclists from around the world every year. The truck, all black with Harley orange pinstriping and chrome accessories, is the first product developed under a five-year strategic alliance announced in March 1999 between the two American legends, Ford and Harley. The alliance will also include celebrations of each company's centennial in 2003.

## INTERNATIONAL SALES

International sales were $497 million in 1998 and $537 million in 1999, which is about 24 percent of net sales of the Motorcycles segment in 1998 and 21 percent in 1999. The international heavyweight market is growing and is now larger than the U.S. heavyweight market. As shown in Exhibit 4, Harley ended 1999 with a 6.5 percent share of the European heavyweight market and a 19.6 percent share of the Japan/Australia heavyweight market. In total, there are 586 independent international Harley-Davidson dealerships in 60 countries. There are also 272 independent Buell dealerships. In Europe, there are currently 298 Harley-Davidson dealerships.

Harley-Davidson faces some unique competitive challenges in the international markets. In Europe, for instance, it must consider the various tastes of many individual countries that together represent a market larger than any other single market. Also, the European Union's motorcycle noise standards are more stringent than those of the Environmental Protection Agency and may grow more so. Research and development costs related to motorcycle noise are higher for motorcycles produced for the European market.

The standard and performance segments make up 70 percent of the European heavyweight motorcycle market. Harley has only recently started to compete in the performance market. As can be seen in Exhibit 4, The European market had 306,700 new registrations in 1999, up from 270,200 in 1998. The European market is larger than the North American market and represents the single largest motorcycle market in the world. The company's share of the 651+cc custom segment is highest in the United Kingdom, where in 1998 it grew to 49 percent. The XL883 Sportster is the best-selling bike in that country. However, the company has had difficulty gaining market share in other European countries.

In the Japan/Australia region, double-digit market growth over the past two years has made the market very attractive for Harley-Davidson. This growth, driven by a change in licensing requirements in Japan, allows for fewer restrictions. It is now easier to obtain a heavyweight motorcycle driver's license in Japan. The Harley brand is established in Japan, and over 14,000 HOG members live there.

Harley-Davidson also claims nearly 40 percent of the Australian motorcycle market. The company has been "down under" for more than 80 years, and the Harley name is widely recognized there. The independent distributor in Sweden has developed a floating store and restaurant. Spain has experienced growth as well, with motorcycle registrations up 23.2 percent in 1998. The Spanish local distributor is adding some new dealers to meet the increasing demand.

Harley has established an assembly operation in Brazil that imports U.S.-made components for final assembly in Brazil. This increases the availability of Harley's

EXHIBIT 4    Harley-Davidson International Sales and Market Share (in thousands)

|  | 1999 | 1998 | 1997 |
|---|---|---|---|
| **North America:** | | | |
| Total market new registrations | 297.9 | 246.2 | 205.4 |
| Harley-Davidson registered trademark— new registrations | 142.1 | 116.1 | 99.3 |
| Buell registered trademark—new registrations | 4.0 | 3.3 | 1.9 |
| Total company registrations | 146.1 | 119.4 | 101.2 |
| Total company market share percent | 49.0% | 48.5% | 49.3% |
| **Europe:** | | | |
| Total market—new registrations | 306.7 | 270.2 | 250.3 |
| Harley-Davidson—new registrations | 17.8 | 15.7 | 15.3 |
| Buell—new registrations | 2.1 | 1.6 | 0.8 |
| Total company registrations | 19.9 | 17.3 | 16.1 |
| Total company market share percent | 6.5% | 6.4% | 6.4% |
| **Japan/Australia:** | | | |
| Total market—new registrations | 63.1 | 69.2 | 58.9 |
| Harley-Davidson—new registrations | 11.6 | 10.3 | 9.7 |
| Buell—new registrations | 0.7 | 0.5 | 0.4 |
| Total company registrations | 12.3 | 10.8 | 10.1 |
| Total company market share percent | 19.6% | 15.6% | 17.2% |
| **Total** | | | |
| Total—new registrations | 667.17 | 585.6 | 514.6 |
| Harley-Davidson—new registrations | 171.5 | 142.1 | 124.3 |
| Buell—new registrations | 6.8 | 5.4 | 3.1 |
| Total company registrations | 178.3 | 147.5 | 127.4 |
| Total company market share percent | 26.7% | 25.2% | 24.8% |

*Source:* www.freeedgar.com

motorcycles in Brazil and reduce duties and taxes, making them more affordable to a larger group of Brazilian customers. In the past, only wealthy Brazilians could afford a Harley because of the steep import tariffs.

## COMPETITION

The U.S. and international heavyweight motorcycle markets are highly competitive. Some of Harley's major competitors have larger financial and marketing resources and are more diversified. For example, only about half of the sales for Yamaha Motor Company are of motorcycles. Yamaha also has annual sales of over $6.7 billion. Competition in the heavyweight motorcycle market is based on price, quality, reliability, styling, and customer preference. Harley-Davidson does not emphasize price in its products, one reason for this being that the resale price for a used Harley-Davidson motorcycle is generally higher than that of its competitors.

For the past 11 years, Harley has led the industry in domestic sales of heavyweight motorcycles. As shown in Exhibit 5, Harley's share of the U.S. heavyweight market was 50.2 percent in 1999. This is significantly greater than its largest competitor in the domestic market, Honda, which had a 16.4 percent market share in 1999 (see Exhibit 5). Harley now faces a new domestic competitor, Polaris. Polaris, the world's number-one

EXHIBIT 5    U.S. Motorcycle Market (in thousands)

|  | 1999 | 1998 | 1997 |
|---|---|---|---|
| **New U.S. registrations** | | | |
| Total market new registrations | 275.6 | 227.1 | 190.2 |
| Harley-Davidson new registrations | 134.5 | 109.1 | 93.5 |
| Buell new registrations | 3.9 | 3.2 | 1.9 |
| Total company new registrations | 138.4 | 112.3 | 95.4 |
| **Percentage market share:** | | | |
| Harley-Davidson motorcycles | 48.8% | 48.1% | 49.2% |
| Buell motorcycles | 1.4 | 1.4 | 1.0 |
| Total company | 50.2 | 49.5 | 50.2 |
| Honda | 16.4 | 20.3 | 18.5 |
| Suzuki | 9.4 | 10.0 | 10.1 |
| Kawasaki | 10.3 | 10.1 | 10.4 |
| Yamaha | 7.0 | 4.2 | 5.4 |
| Other | 6.7 | 5.9 | 5.4 |
| Total | 100.0% | 100.0% | 100.0% |

*Source:* www.freeedgar.com

maker of snowmobiles, introduced its first motorcycle, the Victory cruiser, in 1998. This motorcycle is priced lower than the typical heavyweight Harley. Although not yet a major player in the worldwide market for motorcycles, Polaris poses a potential threat to Harley-Davidson in the coming years. This company has the manufacturing and marketing skills necessary to compete in the motorcycle market.

## PLAN 2003

For the past several years, Harley has been executing a comprehensive motorcycle manufacturing strategy designed to increase its motorcycle production capacity. The plan will increase capacity, improve quality, and reduce costs. Harley has constructed a new assembly plant in Kansas City, Missouri, and moved into a new powertrain plant. Harley plans to continue to increase its motorcycle production in order to sustain its annual double-digit growth rate. As shown in Exhibit 3, Harley sold 157,152 motorcycles in 1998 but only 136,700 in 1999.

## THE FUTURE

Harley-Davidson has spent enormous resources in the past few years expanding production to meet the growing demand for its motorcycles. Has it spent enough? The strong economy and aging baby boomers have caused a surge in the worldwide market for motorcycles. This leaves the company with the task of increasing production while maintaining quality. The company has already doubled production in the past ten years. Harley's goal is to increase its annual output to 200,000 annually.

1. How can Harley manage the increasing threat of foreign competition?
2. Can Harley continue to survive on image?
3. What will it take to make Harley-Davidson successful in the future?
4. Evaluate the strategic plan Harley is currently pursuing, and develop or recommend a strategy for the future of the company.

EXHIBIT 6    Harley's Segment Financial Data (in thousands)

|  | 1999 | 1998 | 1997 | 1996 |
|---|---|---|---|---|
| **Revenues (Geographical)** | | | | |
| United States | $1,915,631 | $1,566,559 | $1,304,748 | $1,110,527 |
| Canada | 80,271 | 73,908 | 62,717 | 58,053 |
| Germany | 88,814 | 84,436 | 81,541 | 82,800 |
| Japan | 135,589 | 102,245 | 90,243 | 79,401 |
| Other foreign countries | 232,634 | 236,808 | 223,320 | 200,446 |
| Total revenues | $2,452,939 | $2,063,956 | $1,762,569 | $1,531,227 |
| **Revenues (Segments)** | | | | |
| Motorcycles and related products | $2,452,939 | $2,063,956 | $1,762,569 | $1,531,227 |
| Financial services | N/A | N/A | N/A | N/A |
| Total revenues | $2,452,939 | $2,063,956 | $1,762,569 | $1,531,227 |
| **Income from operations:** | | | | |
| Motorcycles and related products | $ 397,601 | $ 324,448 | $ 265,486 | $ 228,093 |
| Financial services | 27,685 | 20,211 | 12,355 | 7,801 |
| General corporate expenses | (9,427) | (11,043) | (7,838) | (7,448) |
| Total income from operations | $ 415,859 | $ 333,616 | $ 270,003 | $ 228,446 |

*Source:* www.freeedgar.com

# WINNEBAGO INDUSTRIES, INC.—2000

Eugene M. Bland
Francis Marion University
John G. Marcis
Coastal Carolina University

WGO

www.winnebagoind.com

Saving money is nice, but it is not the real reason that people travel in a motor home. "Motor homing" is just plain fun. Motor homers are an adventurous lot—they like to go, see, and do. Florida residents have replaced Californians as the most active motor home campers. New Yorkers are third on the "most on the go" list. Recreational vehicle (RV) owners say that they not only save money when camping but can avoid the bother of having to stop for restaurants and bathrooms.

Motor-home traveling is purported to be much less expensive than traveling by car or plane and staying in a motel. Motor homers stop when there is something to see and do. They often spend summers where it is cool and winters where it is warm. In fact, industry advertisements tout the RV lifestyle with the slogan "Wherever you go, you're always at home."

Winnebago Industries, Inc., is a leading manufacturer of motor homes. Company revenues increased to $667.67 million in 1999 from $525 million in 1998. Motor home shipments (Class A and Class C) during fiscal 1999 were 10,276 units, an increase of 1,505 units, or 17.2 percent. The company builds quality products with state-of-the-art computer-aided design and manufacturing systems on automotive-style assembly lines. Although Winnebago competes with Fleetwood and Coachmen, the name "Winnebago" is considered synonymous with the term "motor home."

Winnebago was founded in 1958 and has always been headquartered in Forest City, Iowa. The company's common stock is listed on the New York, Chicago, and Pacific Stock Exchanges and traded under the symbol WGO. Options for Winnebago's common stock are traded on the Chicago Board Options Exchange. Winnebago's home page can be accessed at www.winnebagoind.com, and corporate press releases are available through Company New On-Call at www.prnewswire.com/cnoc/exec/menu/105967.

Winnebago Industries is financially stable: The firm owns its land, buildings, and equipment and has no long-term debt. The firm has an enviable cash balance, which provides the company with the opportunity for future growth. In 1998 and 1999, the board of directors approved three programs to repurchase 13.1 percent of the outstanding shares of the firm's stock. The company is devoted to focusing resources on building RVs, increasing its share of the RV market, and enhancing profitability.

## EARLY MOTOR HOMING

The first motor home was built in 1915 to take people from the Atlantic Coast to San Francisco. It had wooden wheels and hard rubber tires. It was promoted as having all the comforts of an ocean cruiser. By the 1920s the house car had become a fixture in the United States and a symbol of freedom. All kinds of house cars could be seen traveling across America's dirt roads. They ranged from what looked like large moving cigars to two-story houses with porches on wheels. However, these house cars featured poor weight distribution, insulation, and economy. From the 1930s to the 1950s, they gave way in popularity to the trailer.

In the mid-1950s motor homes were called motorized trailers. They were overweight, underpowered, and poorly insulated but still a vast improvement over the house cars of the 1920s. In the 1960s motor homing became much more popular, largely as a result of the innovations of Winnebago. From Forest City, Iowa, where the company was founded in 1958, Winnebago set the pace for new development of motor homes. The Winnebago name became a household word. Buyers of motor homes were asked, "When will your Winnebago be delivered?"

## CORPORATE PROFILE

### Corporate Mission Statement

Winnebago's motto is "Quality is a Journey—Not a Destination." From the beginning, the company recognized the critical roles played by employees, customers, and dealers in the total quality process. The significance of quality to the firm is evidenced by its mission statement, which includes a statement of values, and a statement of guiding principles (Exhibit 1).

### Production Facilities

Winnebago's major production facilities are in Forest City, Iowa. Currently, it has over 20 buildings at this location, comprising over two million square feet and containing the company's manufacturing, maintenance, and service operations. There are also satellite manufacturing facilities at Hampton and Lorimor, Iowa. These two facilities add another 700,000 square feet of manufacturing space. This manufacturing space increased by another 45,000 square feet in 2000. The new development is expected to increase manufacturing capabilities by nearly 1,000 units per year and add another 200 workers to the nearly 3,400 people employed at these locations in 1999. In addition, a 16,000-square-foot addition to the customer service facility will add 14 service bays that will enhance service and training capabilities. All corporate facilities in Forest City are located on approximately 784 acres of land owned by Winnebago.

Winnebago has three 900-foot assembly lines for the final assembly of motor homes. Statistical process control is practiced at Winnebago and has enhanced the quality of its van products. As a motor home moves down the assembly line, quality control is carefully monitored. Units are taken randomly from the line for a thorough examination. The performance of every RV is tested before it is delivered to a dealer's lot. The company makes sure that all of its motor home components meet or exceed federal durability standards. Some of the tests routinely performed include lamination strength, appliance performance, chip resistance, vibration, drop, salt spray, and crash tests.

EXHIBIT 1    Winnebago Industries, Inc. Mission Statement

*Mission Statement*

Winnebago Industries, Inc., is a leading manufacturer of recreation vehicles (RVs) and related products and services. Our mission is to continually improve our products and services to meet or exceed the expectations of our customers. We emphasize employee teamwork and involvement in identifying and implementing programs to save time and lower production costs while maintaining the highest quality values. These strategies allow us to prosper as a business with a high degree of integrity and to provide a reasonable return for our shareholders, the ultimate owners of our business.

*Values*

How we accomplish our mission is as important as the mission itself. Fundamental to the success of the Company are these basic values we describe as the four P's:

**People**—Our employees are the source of our vast strength. They provide our corporate intelligence and determine our reputation and vitality. Involvement and teamwork are our core human values.

**Products**—Our products are the end result of our team's efforts, and they should be the best in meeting or exceeding our customers' expectations worldwide. As our products are viewed, so are we viewed.

**Plant**—The Company believes its plant is the most technologically advanced in the RV industry. We continue to review facility improvements that will increase the utilization of our plant capacity and enable us to build the best quality product for the investment.

**Profitability**—Profitability is the ultimate measure of how efficiently we provide our customers with the best products for their needs. Profitability is required to survive and grow. As our respect and position within the marketplace grows, so will our profit.

*Guiding Principles*

**Quality comes first**—To achieve customer satisfaction, the quality of our products and services must be our number one priority.

**Customers are central to our existence**—Our work must be done with our customers in mind, providing products and services that meet or exceed the expectations of our customers. We must not only satisfy our customers, we must also surprise and delight them.

**Continuous improvement is essential to our success**—We must strive for excellence in everything we do: in our products, in their safety and value, as well as in our services, our human relations, our competitiveness, and our profitability.

**Employee involvement is our way of life**—We are a team. We must treat each other with trust and respect.

**Dealers and suppliers are our partners**—The Company must maintain mutually beneficial relationships with dealers, suppliers, and our other business associates.

**Integrity is never compromised**—The Company must pursue conduct in a manner that is socially responsible and that commands respect for its integrity and for its positive contributions to society. Our doors are open to all men and women alike without discrimination and without regard to ethnic origin or personal beliefs.

*Source:* Winnebago Industries 1999 Annual Report p. 21.

### Research and Development

Winnebago uses computer technology to design its motor homes. The company has a state-of-the-art, computer-aided design/computer-aided manufacturing (CAD/CAM) system. This system aids in producing low-cost sheet metal parts, new paint lines for steel and aluminum parts, and modifications of assembly equipment.

One of Winnebago's product-testing facilities at Forest City houses some of the most sophisticated technology used in the RV industry (such as a high- and low-temperature chamber for subjecting parts to extreme temperatures and high stress).

### Product Line

In the second quarter of 1997, the board of directors elected Ronald D. Buckmeier as vice president of product development. The new product development team recently implemented a process to develop new products and maximize production efficiencies that involves a cross-functional approach to the design and manufacture of RVs and streamlines the production process. Nearly all of the 60 product series have either been dramatically redesigned or introduced as a completely new product since the 1997 offerings.

Winnebago manufactures three principal kinds of recreational vehicles (see Exhibit 2): Class A Motor Homes, Class B Van Campers, and Class C Motor Homes (Mini). Class A motor homes are constructed on a chassis that already has the engine and drive components. They range in length from 23 to 37 feet and in price from $32,000 to over $250,000. Class A motor homes include the Winnebago Adventurer, Brave, Chieftain, and Journey; the Itasca Suncruiser, Sunrise, Sunflyer, and Horizon; and Ultimate Advantage and Freedom (see Exhibit 3). Although the Winnebago Adventurer and Itasco Suncruiser are popular, the Winnebago Brave and Itasca Sunrise models are the company's top-selling vehicles. According to a 1999 report by Statistical Surveys, Inc., a national reporting service, RV industry motor home unit sales grew by 12.2 percent in the first seven months of 1999. Winnebago reported retail sales increased even more rapidly, growing by 13.8 percent over the same period. As of August 28, 1999, the backlog for orders for Class A and C motor homes was nearly 2,700 units (compared to only 1,700 in August of 1998).

---

EXHIBIT 2    Motor Home Product Classification

---

***Class A Motor Homes***

These are conventional motor homes constructed directly on medium-duty truck chassis which include the engine and drivetrain components. The living area of the driver's compartments are designed and produced by Winnebago Industries. Class A motor homes from Winnebago Industries include Winnebago Brave, Adventurer, Chieftain and Journey; Itasca Sunrise, Suncruiser, Sunflyer and Horizon; and Ultimate Advantage and Freedom.

***Class B Van Campers***

These are panel-type trucks to which sleeping, kitchen, and toilet facilities are added. These models also have a top extension to provide more headroom. Winnebago Industries converts the EuroVan Camper, which is distributed by Volkswagen of America and Volkswagen of Canada.

***Class C Motor Homes (Mini)***

These are mini motor homes built on a van-type chassis onto which Winnebago Industries constructs a living area with access to the driver's compartment. Class C motor homes from Winnebago Industries include Winnebago Minnie and Minnie Winnie; Itasca Spirit and Sundancer; and Rialta.

---

*Source:* Winnebago *1999 Annual Report,* page 18.

EXHIBIT 3    Winnebago Family Tree

Winnebago Industries manufactures four brands of Class A and C motor homes. Listed below are the brand names and model designations of the company's 2000 product line.

| Winnebago | Itasca | Rialta | Ultimate |
|---|---|---|---|
| –Minnie | –Spirit | –Rialta | –Ultimate Advantage |
| –Minnie Winnie | –Sundancer | | –Ultimate Freedom |
| –Brave | –Sunrise | | |
| –Adventurer | –Suncruiser | | |
| –Chieftain | –Sunflyer | | |
| –Journey | –Horizon | | |

*Other Related Products:*

**Winnebago Conversion Vehicles**—Licensed truck and van conversions manufactured and marketed by Choo Choo Customs Group, Inc.

**Winnebago Park Homes**—Licensed products manufactured and marketed by Chariot Eagle, Inc.

**Winnebago Tents**—Licensed products manufactured and marketed by Avid Outdoor.

*Source: 1999 Annual Report, page 18.*

Winnebago's Class B Van Campers are actually conventional vans manufactured by Ford, General Motors, and Chrysler that are custom tailored by Winnebago with special interiors, exteriors, windows, and vents. In many American households, van campers are replacing the family car as the vehicle of choice. These vehicles can turn a long family trip from an ordeal into a pleasant adventure. Winnebago manufacturers the Euro Van Camper conversion for Volkswagen of America and Volkswagen of Canada. Class B Van Campers are 17 feet in length.

Class C Motor Homes are constructed on a van chassis; the driver's compartment is accessible to the living area. These motor homes are compact and easy to drive. They range from 21 to 29 feet in length and have five popular floor plans. Typical options of a Class C vehicle include six feet of headroom, shower, stove, sink, refrigerator, and two double beds. Winnebago's Minnie Winnie vehicle is the most popular Class C Motor Home in the country. The company's Itasca Sundancer and Itasca Spirit also are popular.

## Marketing

Consumer research reveals that demographics for motor home buyers are undergoing change. Traditionally, buyers have been "woofies" (well-off older folks, that is, people over fifty years of age with discretionary income) with time to enjoy leisure travel and outdoor recreation. According to research, an individual in the United States is turning fifty every 7.5 seconds, contributing an additional 350,000 people per *month* to that prime target market. Available demographic information indicates that this trend will continue for the next 30 years.

The peak selling season for RVs has historically been spring and summer. Class A and Class C motor homes are marketed under the Winnebago and Itasca brand names and are sold through a network of approximately 340 dealers, up from 325 in 1994, in the United States and, to a limited extent, in Canada and other foreign countries.

### Service

Winnebago believes it has the most comprehensive service program in the RV industry. An example of its commitment to this area was its 1999 announcement that it would build a 16,000-square-foot addition to the customer service facility to add 14 service bays to enhance service and training capabilities. The service program provides the firm with a critical market advantage. With the purchase of any new Class A or Class C motor home (except the Rialta), Winnebago offers a comprehensive 12-month or 15,000-mile warranty, a 3-year or 36,000-mile warranty on sidewalls and slideout room assemblies, and a 10-year fiberglass roof warranty. Winnebago features a 2-year or 24,000-mile warranty on the Rialta. Winnebago also instituted a toll-free hotline at which experienced service advisors respond to inquiries from prospective customers and expedite and resolve warranty issues. Every owner of a new Winnebago motor home receives free roadside assistance for 12 months.

### The Winnebago Logo and Licensing

Winnebago is a recognizable name. Although licensing of the Winnebago name began in 1982, revenues to date have not been significant. There are now Winnebago bass and fishing boats, marine flotation devices, backpacks, sports bags, travel bags, slacks, shorts, shirts, vests, jackets, gloves, socks, hats, stoves, lanterns, grills, sleeping bags, air mattresses, tents, screenhouses, and suitcases. Winnebago's Scout 1 sleeping bag, Chieftain IV tent, Double Diamond air mattress, and other products have been advertised in many magazines. Winnebago has a series of recreational vehicle trading cards.

### WINNEBAGO: 1958 THROUGH 1999

Winnebago's phenomenal growth during the 1960s came to an end in 1970. That year was marked by a recession, and Winnebago's stock plunged nearly 60 percent before recovering. The OPEC oil disruptions in 1973–1974 and 1979 had disastrous effects on Winnebago because gas was either unavailable or became unaffordable to many families. The company's net income averaged less than 1 percent of sales between 1973 and 1978. From a level of $229 million in 1978, Winnebago's sales dropped to $92 million in 1979.

The board of directors called John Hanson, founder of the company, out of retirement in March 1979 and reelected him chairman of the board and president of Winnebago. To resolve Winnebago's problems, Hanson reduced the number of employees from 4,000 to 800 in less than nine months. He initiated the development of a propane conversion system for motor homes. This system allows users to power their vehicles with less costly propane, which eliminates worries about the supply and cost of gasoline. Hanson also pioneered the development of a lightweight, fuel-efficient motor home powered by a revolutionary heavy-duty diesel engine.

In 1992, Winnebago's sales increased 32 percent, but net income was a negative $10.6 million. Several new products were introduced, including the new bus-styled Vectra. The company created a new subsidiary in 1992, Winnebago Industries Europe, headquartered in Cologne, Germany, to expand operations internationally.

In June 1996, Winnebago's founder and chairman, John K. Hanson died at the age of 83. Fred G. Dohrmann, the company's CEO, added the title of chairman. Dohrmann had guided Winnebago through an industrywide slump in the late 1980s and early 1990s.

In a series of strategic moves, Winnebago refocused its core business operation by divesting itself of business and corporate assets that were not directly related to domestic production, sales, and financing of RVs. In 1996, the board of directors decided to sell Cycle-Sat, Inc. (a telecommunications service firm that used satellite, fiber-optic, and digital technologies) and voted to discontinue financial support of the buyer of its former North Iowa Electronics business. In 1997, the board approved the sale of its European division (Winnebago Industries Europe) as well as Outdoor America (a mall in Texas).

In December of 1997, Dohrmann, a 23-year employee of the firm, announced his plans to retire in April 1998. The board of directors elected Bruce D. Hertzke to the position of chairman and CEO upon Dohrmann's retirement. Hertzke had joined Winnebago in 1971 as an hourly production employee and worked in various production and engineering supervisory positions since then.

## Comments: 1998–1999

Winnebago celebrated its fortieth anniversary in 1998 with a banner year for both production and revenue. Although the motor home industry had a good year overall, Winnebago outperformed the industry by 12 percent during the first nine months of the calendar year. Revenues were a record $525.1 million for the fiscal year (compared with $438.1 million for the 1997 fiscal year). Income from continuing operations for the year reflected a near fourfold increase from the previous fiscal year. In December, Winnebago had a sales order backlog of over 3,000 units, the largest in the company's history.

Winnebago's good fortune continued through the 1999 fiscal year. Unit production increased about 27.2 percent (from $525.1 million to $667.7 million). To help ease its production backlog, the firm will have an additional 45,000 square feet of manufacturing space operational early in the year 2000.

## WINNEBAGO'S EXTERNAL ENVIRONMENT

Winnebago's motor homes can attract a low-frills buyer desiring the most stripped-down RV, the person with expensive tastes desiring the ultimate in RV luxury, and everyone in between. RVs can be purchased or rented. Many families unable to buy a mobile home rent one for a vacation. As the baby boomers age and approach retirement, many of them will consider selling their primary residence, purchasing, and moving into a motor home, and traveling to any point they desire in North America.

The motel and hotel industries have been experiencing an oversupply of available rooms, which has resulted in low room rates. The cost of owning or renting and operating an RV is about the same as staying in a motel (or perhaps a little higher). Motor home sales historically increase whenever travel, tourism, and vacationing gain in popularity. The converse is also true.

Lower fuel prices, interest rates, inflation rates, and a robust, fully employed economy generally spur motor home sales. Despite favorable economic conditions in 1997, Winnebago did not prosper. However, since 1997, Winnebago has been considerably more fortunate.

There are about 122,000 campsites in U.S. state parks, including 4,500 maintained by the U.S. Forest Service and 100 in the National Parks System. In addition, there are more than 15,000 private campgrounds and over 1,620 county parks. Winnebagos can gain access to nearly all of these sites.

## COMPETITORS

Twelve firms account for 80 percent of the RV industry's volume. Among the largest publicly held firms are Fleetwood Enterprises, Winnebago Industries, Coachman Industries, Rexhall Industries, Mallard Coach, Kit Manufacturing, Harley-Davidson, and Skyline

Corporation. Of all the competitors, Fleetwood Enterprises is first in sales, followed by Coachman and then Winnebago. The following is a list of major motor home competitors:

| Company | Headquarters Location |
| --- | --- |
| Fleetwood Enterprises, Inc. | Riverside, CA |
| Coachman Industries, Inc. | Elkhart, IN |
| Mark III Industries, Inc. | Ocala, FL |
| Jayco, Inc. | Middlebury, IN |
| Glaval Corp. | Elkhart, IN |
| Newmar Corp. | Nappanee, IN |
| Monaco Coach Corp. | Junction City, OR |
| Tiffin Motor Homes, Inc. | Red Bay, AL |

Fleetwood

Fleetwood Enterprises is the nation's largest producer of both RVs and manufactured housing. It has 30 percent of the RV market. The RV line includes conventional Class A motor homes, chopped-van Class C motor homes, travel trailers, fifth-wheel travel trailers, folding camping trailers, and truck campers. Motor homes represent 62 percent of Fleetwood's sales, and mobile home sales comprise 38 percent of revenues.

Fleetwood's folding campers sell under the name Coleman (the famous brand that it acquired in 1989); motor homes sell under the names Pace Arrow, Southwind, Cambria, Limited, Flair, Jamboree, and Tioga; and travel trailers are sold as Avion, Prowler, Terry, and Wilderness brands. For Fleetwood, the payoff is a greater presence and enhanced sales.

Fleetwood recently acquired the Germany-based luxury-priced motor home manufacturer Nielsmen and Bischoff. This acquisition paves the way for expanded distribution of Fleetwood recreational vehicles in Europe. Fleetwood is adding 20 percent more production capacity to its base of 27 plants in order to meet rising demand in both its motor homes and mobile homes.

CONCLUSION

Winnebago had the top selling Class A and Class C motor home brands in the industry in 1999. However, gas prices are rising in 2000 so demand for Winnebago products may begin falling. Prepare a three year strategic plan for Winnebago to best assure prosperity for the company.

EXHIBIT 4    Winnebago Industries, Inc. Net (dollars in thousands)
Revenues by Major Product Class (Unaudited)

| | Fiscal Year Ended [a] | | | | |
|---|---|---|---|---|---|
| | August 28, 1999 | August 29, 1998 | August 30, 1997 | August 31, 1996 | August 26, 1995 |
| Motor homes (Class A and C) | $610,987 | $468,004 | $381,191 | $432,212 | $402,435 |
| | 91.5% | 89.1% | 87.0% | 89.2% | 87.5% |
| Other recreation vehicle revenues[b] | 15,587 | 18,014 | 19,771 | 17,166 | 19,513 |
| | 2.3% | 3.5% | 4.5% | 3.5% | 4.2% |
| Other manufactured products revenues[c] | 38,081 | 37,000 | 35,750 | 34,020 | 36,961 |
| | 5.7% | 7.0% | 8.2% | 7.0% | 8.0% |
| Total manufactured products revenues | 664,655 | 523,018 | 436,712 | 483,398 | 458,909 |
| | 99.5% | 99.6% | 99.7% | 99.7% | 99.7% |
| Finance revenues[d] | 2,995 | 2,076 | 1,420 | 1,406 | 1,220 |
| | .5% | .4% | .3% | .3% | .3% |
| Total net revenues | $667,650 | $525,094 | $438,132 | $484,804 | $460,129 |
| | 100.0% | 100.0% | 100.0% | 100.0% | 100.0% |

[a]The fiscal year ended August 31, 1996, contained 53 weeks; all other fiscal years in the table contained 52 weeks. All years prior to fiscal 1998 are appropriately restated to exclude the Company's discontinued Cycle-Sat subsidiary's revenues from satellite courier and tape duplication services.
[b]Primarily recreation vehicle related parts, EuroVan Campers, and recreation vehicle service revenue.
[c]Primarily sales of extruded aluminum, commercial vehicles, and component products for other manufacturers.
[d]WAC revenues from dealer financing.
*Source:* Winnebago *1999 Annual Report,* page 41.

EXHIBIT 5    Winnebago Industries, Inc., Unit Sales
of Recreation Vehicles

| Year Ended | August 28, 1999 | August 29, 1998 | August 30, 1997 | August 26, 1995 | August 28, 1993 |
|---|---|---|---|---|---|
| Class A | 6,054 | 5,381 | 4,834 | 5,993 | 6,095 |
| Class C | 4,222 | 3,390 | 2,724 | 2,853 | 1,988 |
| Total | 10,276 | 8,771 | 7,558 | 8,843 | 8,093 |
| Class B Conversions | 600 | 978 | 1,205 | 1,014 | 0 |

*Source:* www.freeedgar.com.

EXHIBIT 6   Winnebago Consolidated Statements of Income (in thousands, except per-share data)

| | Year Ended | | |
| --- | --- | --- | --- |
| | *August 28 1999* | *August 29 1998* | *August 30 1997* |
| **Continuing operations** | | | |
| Revenues | | | |
| Manufactured products | $664,655 | $523,018 | $436,712 |
| Dealer financing | 2,995 | 2,076 | 1,420 |
| Total net revenues | 667,650 | 525,094 | 438,132 |
| Costs and expenses | | | |
| Cost of manufactured products | 557,991 | 450,934 | 385,540 |
| Selling and delivery | 23,525 | 21,197 | 27,131 |
| General and administrative | 22,152 | 19,986 | 20,313 |
| Total costs and expenses | 603,668 | 492,117 | 432,984 |
| Operating income | 63,982 | 32,977 | 5,148 |
| Financial income | 2,627 | 2,950 | 1,844 |
| Income from continuing operations before income taxes | 66,609 | 35,927 | 6,992 |
| Provision for taxes | 22,349 | 11,543 | 416 |
| Income from continuing operations | 44,260 | 24,384 | 6,576 |
| **Discontinued operations** | | | |
| Gain on sale of Cycle-Sat subsidiary (net of applicable income tax provision of $13,339) | — | — | 16,472 |
| Net income | $ 44,260 | $ 24,384 | $ 23,048 |
| Income per share | | | |
| Continuing operations: | | | |
| Basic | $ 1.99 | $ 1.01 | $ .26 |
| Diluted | 1.96 | 1.00 | .26 |
| Discontinued operations: | | | |
| Basic | — | — | .65 |
| Diluted | — | — | .64 |
| Net income per share: | | | |
| Basic | $ 1.99 | $ 1.01 | $ .91 |
| Diluted | 1.96 | 1.00 | .90 |
| Weighted average common shares outstanding (in thousands) | | | |
| Basic | 22,209 | 24,106 | 25,435 |
| Diluted | 22,537 | 24,314 | 25,550 |

*Source:* Winnebago *1999 Annual Report*, page 26.

EXHIBIT 6    Winnebago Consolidated Balance Sheets (in thousands)

|  | August 28 1999 | August 29 1998 |
|---|---|---|
| **Assets** | | |
| **Current assets** | | |
| Cash and cash equivalents | $ 48,160 | $ 54,740 |
| Receivables, less allowance for doubtful accounts ($960 and $1,582, respectively) | 33,342 | 22,025 |
| Dealer financing receivables, less allowance for doubtful accounts ($73 and $78, respectively) | 24,573 | 12,782 |
| Inventories | 87,031 | 55,433 |
| Prepaid expenses | 3,593 | 3,516 |
| Deferred income taxes | 6,982 | 6,906 |
| Total current assets | 203,681 | 155,402 |
| **Property and equipment,** at cost | | |
| Land | 1,150 | 1,158 |
| Buildings | 41,136 | 38,779 |
| Machinery and equipment | 73,839 | 69,095 |
| Transportation equipment | 5,345 | 5,047 |
|  | 121,470 | 114,079 |
| Less accumulated depreciation | 83,099 | 81,167 |
| Total property and equipment, net | 38,371 | 32,912 |
| **Long-term notes receivable,** less allowances ($262 and $973, respectively) | 787 | 4,515 |
| Investment in life insurance | 19,749 | 18,750 |
| Deferred income taxes | 18,654 | 16,071 |
| Other assets | 4,657 | 2,962 |
| Total assets | $285,889 | $230,612 |
| **Liabilities and stockholders' equity** | | |
| **Current liabilities** | | |
| Accounts payable, trade | $ 38,604 | $ 24,461 |
| Income taxes payable | 10,201 | 12,623 |
| Accured expenses: | | |
| Accured compensation | 13,204 | 9,479 |
| Product warranties | 6,407 | 5,260 |
| Insurance | 3,962 | 3,566 |
| Promotional | 2,629 | 2,236 |
| Other | 4,954 | 4,977 |
| Total current liabilities | 79,961 | 62,602 |
| Postretirement health care and deferred compensation benefits | 56,544 | 51,487 |
| Contingent liabilities and commitments | | |
| **Stockholders' equity** | | |
| Capital stock common, par value $.50; authorized 60,000,000 shares, issued 25,874,000 and 25,865,000 shares, respectively | 12,937 | 12,932 |
| Additional paid-in capital | 21,907 | 22,507 |
| Reinvested earnings | 151,482 | 111,665 |
|  | 186,326 | 147,104 |
| Less treasury stock, at cost | 36,942 | 30,581 |
| Total stockholders' equity | 149, 384 | 116,523 |
| Total liabilities and stockholders' equity | $285,889 | $230,612 |

*Source:* Winnebago *1999 Annual Report,* page 24.

EXHIBIT 7    Winnebago Industries, Inc. Business Segment
Information (in thousands)

| | Recreation Vehicles and Other Manufactured Products | Dealer Financing | General Corporate | Total |
|---|---|---|---|---|
| **1999** | | | | |
| Net revenues | $664,655 | $ 2,995 | $  — | $667,650 |
| Operating income (loss) | 60,435 | 4,085 | (538) | 63,982 |
| Identifiable assets | 181,951 | 25,439 | 78,499 | 285,889 |
| Depreciation and amortization | 5,507 | 4 | 237 | 5,748 |
| Capital expenditures | 11,463 | 18 | 96 | 11,577 |

Operating income of the dealer financing segment reflects a $1,100,000 repayment of a previously fully reserved receivable.

| | Recreation Vehicles and Other Manufactured Products | Dealer Financing | General Corporate | Total |
|---|---|---|---|---|
| **1998** | | | | |
| Net revenues | $523,018 | $ 2,076 | $  — | $525,094 |
| Operating income (loss) | 32,466 | 1,845 | (1,334) | 32,977 |
| Identifiable assets | 132,954 | 15,441 | 82,217 | 230,612 |
| Depreciation and amortization | 5,323 | 5 | 254 | 5,582 |
| Capital expenditures | 5,545 | 19 | 3 | 5,567 |
| **1997** | | | | |
| Net revenues from continuing operations | $436,712 | $ 1,420 | $  — | $438,132 |
| Operating income (loss) from continuing operations | 6,976 | 736 | (2,564) | 5,148 |
| Identifiable assets | 135,973 | 16,912 | 60,590 | 213,475 |
| Depreciation and amortization | 5,797 | 9 | 662 | 6,468 |
| Capital expenditures | 3,982 | 35 | 421 | 4,438 |

Summary information for WIE is as follows: Net Revenues—$9,655, operating loss—$(6,376). The company sold WIE during August 1997. As a result of the sale, the company recorded a capital loss for tax purposes resulting in a tax credit of approximately $3,700,000 due to this loss. These amounts are included in the Recreation Vehicles and Other Manufactured Products segment above.

*Source:* Winnebago *1999 Annual Report,* page 38.

# AVON PRODUCTS, INC.—2000

Jim Camerius
**Northern Michigan University**

AVP

www.avon.com

It has been a long day. Andrea Jung reflects on what has occurred as she sits down at her desk for the first time in her new executive office. Avon Products, Inc., announced that morning of November 4, 1999, that she had been promoted from the position of president and COO to president and chief executive officer. At forty-one years old, she is the first woman to lead Avon in that position in the company's history.

Jung expected the appointment and is aware of the awesome responsibility of the position. Avon enjoys a global reputation stemming largely from its formidable worldwide network of independent sales agents. But the effectiveness of the sales force has waned in recent years as the company grappled with how best to sell cosmetics, jewelry, and apparel to an increasingly sophisticated customer and how to compete against other mass merchandisers. Jung is particularly disappointed when she picks up a memo on her desk reminding her that Avon's profit in its fourth quarter is expected to fall short of expectations.

Jung recently worked on a strategic plan with Charles Perrin, the previous chief executive, who had retired after serving only 16 months in that position. "The strategic plan," she notes, "addresses Avon's domestic weakness with new products for 2000, including a 'renovation' of the company's major color-cosmetics brand and the introduction of haircare products, a segment that is relatively new for the company. It also includes expansion of consumer-marketing programs and calls for modernizing the direct selling system," she continues.

Earlier in the day, following the formal announcement of her appointment, Jung suggested to the press that she had "inherited a wonderful company poised for an accelerated growth story." Now in the position of CEO, she feels she must do something more to rejuvenate Avon's direct-selling model and attract new customers for what some consider an old-fashioned business.

## THE COMPANY AND ITS PRODUCTS

In 1999, Avon Products, Inc., was one of the world's largest direct-selling merchandisers of beauty and beauty-related products. From corporate offices in New York City, Avon markets product lines to women in 135 countries through 2.8 million independent sales representatives who sell primarily on a door-to-door or direct selling basis. Total sales in 1999 were $5.28 billion, up only slightly from $5.21 billion in 1998. The company's workforce of 40,500 employees at year-end 1999 staffed divisions of product management, manufacturing, and sales and service worldwide. Only 8,800 of these employees work in the United States.

Avon's product line includes skincare items, makeup, perfume fragrances for men and women, and toiletries for bath, haircare, personal care, hand and body care, and sun

## EXHIBIT 1    Avon Product Line

***Skincare Products***

    Daily Revival Line: Everyday skincare necessities
    Avon Visible Improvement Program: Problem-solving formulas
    Advanced Beauty Treatments: Items for aging skin
    Clearskin: For oily, blemish-prone skin
    Moisture Therapy: For dry skin

***Makeup***

    Advanced Foundation: Perfectors, enhancers, finishers
    Color for Cheeks: Skin blush
    Color for Eyes: Eyeshadow
    Mascara: Alternative formulae
    Eye-makeup removers: Lotion and gel
    Color for Lips: Lipsticks, pencils, and liners
    Color for Nails: Nail enamel in various colors
    Nail Solutions: For alternative nail needs

***Toiletries***

    Bath: Bubble bath, Avon bath line, shower gel, Skin-So-Soft
    Haircare: Brushes, stylers, shampoos, and conditioners
    Personal Care: Deodorant, footcare products, and hand soaps
    Hand- and Bodycare: Alternative skincare lines
    Suncare: Sun protection and tanning systems

***Jewelry*** (fashion, classic, and seasonal)

***Gift Line*** (collectibles and unusual gifts)

***Avon Home*** (bedding, linens, limited home furnishings)

*Source:* Company records.

protection. It also includes an extensive line of fashion jewelry, apparel, gifts, and collectibles. Recognizable brand names such as Anew, Skin-So-Soft, Avon Color, Far Away, and Rare Gold are featured as well as global "power" brands like Anew, Perfect Wear, and the recently introduced Women of Earth fragrance. There are approximately 600 items in the product line. The major categories and subcategories of products are shown in Exhibit 1.

    Internationally, the company's product line is marketed primarily at moderate prices. The marketing strategy emphasizes department-store quality at discount-store prices. Global marketing efforts are resulting in a number of highly successful brands in the areas of cosmetics, skincare, and fragrance.

    Avon is also the world's largest manufacturer and distributor of fashion jewelry and markets an extensive line of gifts and collectibles.

### THE EARLY YEARS

In the late 1800s, David McConnell, a door-to-door book salesman, used a common trade practice of the period to encourage women to buy his books. He gave prospective customers a gift of perfume to arouse their interest. Before long, he discovered that the perfume was more popular than the books. He formed a new firm, which he called the California Perfume Company. "I started in a space scarcely larger than an ordinary kitchen pantry," David McConnell noted in 1900. "My ambition was to manufacture a

EXHIBIT 2    The Principles That Guide Avon

1. To provide individuals an opportunity to earn in support of their well-being and happiness
2. To serve families throughout the world with products of the highest quality backed by a guarantee of satisfaction
3. To render a service to customers that is outstanding in its helpfulness and courtesy
4. To give full recognition to employees and Representatives, on whose contributions Avon depends
5. To share with others the rewards of growth and success
6. To meet fully the obligations of corporate citizenship by contributing to the well-being of society and the environment in which it functions
7. To maintain and cherish the friendly spirit of Avon

*Source: Avon Representative Success Book, 1999.*

line of goods superior to any other and take those goods through canvassing agents directly from the laboratory to the consumer." McConnell based his business upon: (1) products sold directly to the consumer, (2) an image of the company that captured the beauty and excitement of the state of California, and (3) a national network of sales agents he had organized during his years as a bookseller.

A series of corporate principles developed by McConnell provided direction and continued to influence decision making for the company throughout its history. These principles are listed in Exhibit 2.

As the firm grew, so did the product line. In 1920, the company introduced the Avon line of products that consisted of a toothbrush, cleanser, and vanity set. The Avon name was inspired by the area around the company's laboratory in Suffern, New York, which McConnell thought resembled the countryside of William Shakespeare's home, Stratford-on-Avon, England. The line became so popular that in 1929, the company officially became Avon. By 1929, the company was selling low-cost home care and beauty products door-to-door and through catalogues in all 48 states.

The 1970s presented Avon management with some of its greatest challenges. The strength of the dollar reduced the company's international profits; recession and inflation affected sales of some products; in 1975, some 25,000 Avon sales representatives quit due to decreased earning opportunities. Avon products were outpaced by offerings of retail cosmetic firms that appealed to younger women who wanted more exciting product lines. The traditional direct sales approach was nearly toppled during this period by social changes that management had not anticipated, such as the increased number of working women. Direct sales firms were hurt in two ways: fewer women were at home for door-to-door salespeople to call on, and fewer women wanted to make money in their spare time selling cosmetics to their neighbors. These trends continued throughout the 1980s and the 1990s.

Selective, relatively small acquisitions in the core direct selling and direct marketing areas of expertise were seen by management in the 1990s as one way to accelerate overall growth of the firm. A 1996 purchase of Justine Pty. Ltd., a South African direct seller of cosmetics, provided a potential entry point to other markets in subSaharan Africa.

The Avon vision statement is: "To be the company that best understands and satisfies the product, service and self-fulfillment needs of women, globally." As Perrin suggests:

We are, uniquely among major corporations, a woman's company. We sell our products to, for and through women. We understand their needs and preferences better than most. This understanding should guide our basic business and influence our choice of new business opportunities. We need to become, and are becoming, more customer-oriented and more market-driven.

I can't think of a better definition of a woman's company. And that has a lot of implications for us. If we are really going to be a preeminent company for women around the world, it requires that we have on a market by market basis, a very good understanding of where women are; what their needs, wants, and aspirations are; what the issues are; and what the trends are regarding women, segment by segment.

Each one of the 18 words in the vision statement has considerable meaning. The three most important elements, however, are the focus on women, on being global, and on the additional opportunities for Avon in self-fulfillment.

When Charles Perrin and Andrea Jung became Avon's top executives, they initiated a companywide re-engineering program and launched a new strategic plan to accelerate revenue and bolster Avon's image among consumers and sales representatives. In 1998, Avon announced a strategic plan that included expanded consumer-marketing programs to drive growth in beauty sales and a modernized direct-selling system that used the new technology.

Key elements of the strategic plan were developed in 1999. They included a "commitment to beauty leadership," which, in company terms, meant creating a consistent, "aspirational" image for the Avon Brand around the world. The company planned to increase beauty and beauty-related products as a percentage of total sales by continuing to develop first-to-market, state-of-the-art global brands that provided discernable benefits to meet women's beauty needs. As part of this program, management also intended to increase market share in the personal care category, which had been relatively untapped for the firm. The strategy also included making the direct-selling system more relevant to the contemporary woman by providing more meaningful career opportunities as well as harnessing technology to make Avon more "user friendly" for the sales representatives.

## A CHANGING, MORE COMPETITIVE ENVIRONMENT

Competition in the direct-selling industry consists of a few large, well-established firms and many small organizations that sell about every product imaginable, including toys, animal food, collectibles, plantcare products, clothing, computer software, and financial services. In addition to Avon, the dominant companies include Mary Kay (cosmetics), Amway (home maintenance products), Shaklee Corporation (vitamins and health foods), Encyclopaedia Britannica (reference books and learning systems), Tupperware (plastic dishes and food containers), Electrolux (vacuum cleaners), and Fuller (brushes and household products). Avon is substantially larger in terms of sales representatives, sales volume, and resources than Mary Kay Cosmetics, Inc., its nearest competitor in direct sales.

Several other firms, such as Procter & Gamble Co., Unilever NV, Revlon, Inc., Estée Lauder, and France's L'Oréal sell cosmetics and personal care products primarily through department stores and mass merchandisers and are major competitors. Revlon, whose image varies by product line, has built a multibillion-dollar business by buying out established lines like Max Factor, Charles of the Ritz, Germain Monte, Diane Von Furstenberg, and Almay. Some international firms, such as Shiseido, Japan's biggest cosmetics maker, are experimenting with "beauty service centers" in the United States and other countries. The centers offered free lessons on massage techniques and information on how to apply makeup. Shiseido is finding that many customers who visit such centers soon make a purchase in the department stores in which Shiseido products are sold.

The changing nature of science and technology is also identified as a strategic concern in the external environment. Orth Laboratories' Retin-A treatment for acne, which doubled as an anti-wrinkle cream, is evidence of this change. New drug applications for six to eight other retinoids were known to be underway with anti-aging claims. At the same time, greater understanding of skin physiology is enabling the development of more advanced traditional skincare products, including those that could legitimately make counterirritant claims and those that could protect users from environmental damage, such as sun damage.

Some industry analysts suggested that "beauty had gone back to basics" and is being made over by boutique companies such as Osmotics, Tony & Tina, and BeneFit that offer unusual products and appeal to younger people. Nadya Labi noted in *Time* magazine:

> In the United States's $16 billion cosmetics industry, you don't need supermodels like Cindy Crawford. You don't need to ply customers with giveaways. And with the advent of the Web and beauty boutique stores, you don't need counter space at Saks or Macy's (upscale department stores). The business of beauty, that most undemocratic phenomenon, has been made over by boutique companies. Together they capture a relatively small share of the market, but their quirky products and hip attitude influence the entire industry.

## INTERNATIONAL MARKETING AND EXPANSION

Avon's international sales in 1999 were $3.21 billion, up 2 percent from 1998, while total international profit in 1999 was $581.9 million, up 14 percent from 1998. The international operations of the company are divided into four geographic regions: (1) North America, which includes Canada, the Dominican Republic, Puerto Rico, and the United States; (2) Latin America, which includes Brazil, Mexico, Argentina, and Venezuela; (3) the Pacific, which includes the Philippines, Thailand, Japan, New Zealand, Australia, and China; and (4) Europe, which comprises the United Kingdom, Central Europe, and Russia. Avon's Latin American sales declined 3 percent in 1999 to $1.61 billion. Avon's Pacific region sales increased 16 percent in 1999 to $720 million. Avon has increased 1999 sales in Poland and the United Kingdom, but decreased sales in Russia, France, and Germany.

Avon management feels that it is time to reevaluate and map out the long-term future of the firm's beauty businesses on a global level. Senior management knows that the traditional Avon system of door-to-door house calls works "wonderfully" in developing nations. "We entered new markets, we added new products, and we saw developing nations grow to 27 percent of our sales volume," noted Perrin. Avon has entered 19 new investment markets since 1990, including Uruguay in 1998. The company has direct investments in 46 markets and through distributorships, specially appointed representatives, and licensees in 89 other countries, including a significant presence in Egypt, Greece, and Saudi Arabia.

Enormous growth opportunities exist in countries with huge populations such as China, Indonesia, and India. In Eastern Europe, management is excited about the potential in Poland, the Czech Republic, Slovakia, and Hungary. In the Pacific Rim area, countries like Vietnam, Cambodia, and Laos are targeted as market opportunities.

## EMERGING AND DEVELOPING MARKETS

In the emerging and developing markets of Latin America and the Pacific Rim, the retail infrastructure is undeveloped, especially in the interiors of those countries. The Avon representative provides consumers with an opportunity to buy a wide range of quality products at acceptable prices. In some developing markets, in which access to quality goods is particularly prized, Avon's direct selling method opens up unprecedented prospects for women. In China, for example, women are so eager for Avon products that a projected six-month inventory of lotion sold out in only two weeks. China, however, presented some extraordinary challenges in 1998. Sales and operating profit had declined because of the temporary disruption of Avon's operations. On April 28, 1998, the Chinese government ordered all direct-selling companies to cease business activities because it was concerned about unethical practices. In September, Avon received permission from the government to utilize "sales promoters" at most of its 75 branches throughout the country.

Keen demand for Avon products also presents an extraordinary earnings opportunity for sales representatives. For example, in Poland, Avon offers customers access to cosmetics and personal care items that have never before been available to them. In one corporate study, it was determined that Avon products are satisfying such a pent-up demand that Polish women are willing to spend a considerable portion of their discretionary income on Avon products. The markets of Central and Eastern Europe, excluding Russia, are considered Avon's primary opportunities for growth by management in the new millennium.

The number of people buying from Avon in markets such as the United States has been dwindling by 2 percent to 3 percent per year for about 12 years. "We applied all the tried-and-true stimuli to our direct-selling system: changes in recruiting, incentives, commissions, brochures, and more," suggests Perrin. "We had some success. But, we didn't stop the decline of customer purchasing activity." Management feels growth will come by updating the direct selling channel. Avon management considers Japan to be one of the most significant trouble spots for the firm. The sluggish Japanese economy combined with intense pricing pressure as well as operating issues have contributed to Avon Japan's disappointing performance.

## NEW GLOBAL MARKETING STRATEGIES

Satisfying the subtleties and intricacies of customer demand around the world means that the firm's business varies from country to country and market to market. In the United States, for example, Avon is testing Avon Select, a direct marketing program, to enable customers to buy Avon products in various settings. Customers can order products via any one of four methods: (1) through their Avon representative, (2) by mail through special Select catalogs, (3) by the 1-800-FOR-AVON telephone, or (4) by fax.

Similar opportunities are offered worldwide. In Taiwan, for instance, Avon products are sold by Avon representatives in some 2,000 storefront shops, where orders can be placed via fax for next-day delivery. Also in Taiwan, the company is testing the sale of products in the cosmetic aisles of outlets that are similar to American drugstores. In Malaysia, Avon has 145 franchised boutiques that provide half of the company's Malaysian sales. In all cases, new programs are designed to complement the existing network of sales representatives. The company also spends 2 percent to 3 percent of annual sales on image-enhancing advertising and promotion programs worldwide to make customers aware of Avon products and the purchase options available.

The traditional door-to-door method, with the Avon lady as the homemakers' friend and beauty consultant, has made the company the world's largest cosmetics firm and direct seller. The approach is considered expensive (the salesperson gets a 20 percent to 50 percent commission), and there are the problems associated with hiring, training, managing, and motivating the salesforce.

Retail stores offer a fixed location and a controlled environment but have the potential of conflict with direct-selling methods of distribution as a competing channel. In early 1997, in an effort to discontinue salespeople who were only working in order to buy at reduced prices for themselves, Avon eliminated deep discounts on certain promotional items. The move prompted an estimated loss of 25,000 Avon sales representatives, about 6 percent of the U.S. sales force. Avon U.S. president, Susan Kropf, said that the policy change confused many representatives, including those who were not affected by the change. "There are some lessons learned," noted Kropf. "Any major field changes we may undertake . . . will be pre-tested, very simple to understand, and communicated with painstaking care."

In addition to retail stores, Avon is continuing to test a direct-mail catalogue, so that customers can bypass the Avon representative and place orders themselves. The success of a mail-order catalogue depends greatly upon Avon's ability to manage its mailing and customer lists, to control inventory carefully, offer quality merchandise, and project a distinctive, customer-benefiting image. In a limited test of a catalogue, Avon reached a "more upscale customer" who placed an average order of $40, more than double the amount of orders placed through the regular Avon sales brochure.

Management considers upgrading the Avon global image to be extremely important. One important element of the image upgrade is the announcement of a global advertising strategy. By consolidating worldwide advertising, Avon management feels it could expand its global presence and communicate a more unified brand image throughout its international markets.

Another change in the company's image came with the opening in November 1998 of the Avon Center, a spa, salon, and retail store located in the prestigious Trump Tower on Fifth Avenue in New York City. The center showcases Avon products in an upscale environment and "encourages more women to take a fresh look at the new Avon." A similar center was developed in Brazil that included a facial clinic and beauty salon as well as a retail store counter.

In an attempt to accommodate women's changing lifestyles and needs, emphasis is placed on how and where customers buy products. In the United States, for example, the company is entering new markets through its award-winning Web site (www.avon.com). The company also opened kiosks, called Avon Beauty Centers, in about 40 high-traffic shopping malls. The centers are designed to display an upscale beauty image, showcase the company's beauty brands, and encourage customers' trials of products. The centers were modeled after similar initiatives in Malaysia, the Philippines, Taiwan, Spain, Chile, Venezuela, and Mexico.

## Corporate Responsibility

This part of the program supports the firm's vision as a company committed to responding to the needs of women globally. Developed under the slogan, "Avon Cares About Me," the program provides financial resources to increase women's health and fitness knowledge, recognize and celebrate women who inspired others, and support causes that affect women's lives.

## THE CHALLENGE

"Management succession is one of the most important responsibilities of CEOs and boards of directors," said James Preston just prior to his retirement. "If done well," he noted, "a succession plan puts in place the next generation of executives who can build on the company's past and provide visionary leadership for the future."

Andrea Jung has worked closely with Charles Perrin before he retired to execute a companywide overhaul and is openly acknowledged in the firm and in the business community as the CEO's successor. But her appointment, which has come one month after Avon announced that it would miss fourth-quarter profit targets, arrived sooner than analysts expected. The recently appointed chairman of the board, Stanley Gault, called her at home this past Wednesday morning to inform her of her new role.

Jung is aware of the deep problems that face the company. With fewer women staying at home, direct selling appears to be a less viable business model in developed markets. Important decisions have to be made about product strategy and on whether the company should sell its products through the direct sales force, via the Internet, through retail locations, or some combination of the alternatives.

EXHIBIT 3    Avon Products, Inc. Annual Income Statement
(in millions except earnings-per-share data)

|  | 12/31/99 | 12/31/98 | 12/31/97 |
|---|---|---|---|
| Sales | $5,289.10 | $5,212.70 | $5,079.40 |
| Cost of goods | 2,031.50 | 2,053.00 | 2,051.00 |
| **Gross profit** | **3,257.60** | **3,159.70** | **3,028.40** |
| Selling and administrative and depreciation and amortization expenses | 2,603.00 | 2,563.70 | 2,484.30 |
| **Income after depreciation and amortization** | **654.60** | **596.00** | **544.10** |
| Nonoperating income | (104.80) | (99.10) | 32.60 |
| Interest expense | 43.20 | 41.00 | 41.80 |
| **Pretax income** | **506.60** | **455.90** | **534.90** |
| Income taxes | 204.20 | 190.80 | 197.90 |
| Minority interest | 0 | (4.90) | (1.80) |
| Investment gains/losses (+) | 0 | 0 | 0 |
| Other income charges | 0 | 0 | 0 |
| **Income from continuous operations** | **N/A** | **N/A** | **N/A** |
| Extras and discontinued operations | 0 | 0 | 0 |
| **Net income** | **$  302.40** | **$  270.00** | **$  338.80** |

**Depreciation footnote**

|  |  |  |  |
|---|---|---|---|
| Income before depreciation and amortization | $  737.60 | $  668.00 | $  616.20 |
| Depreciation and amortization (cash flow) | 83.00 | 72.00 | 72.10 |
| **Income after depreciation and amortization** | **$  654.60** | **$  596.00** | **$  544.10** |

**Earnings-per-share data**

|  |  |  |  |
|---|---|---|---|
| **Average shares** | **$  259.37** | **$  265.95** | **$  267.00** |
| Diluted EPS before nonrecurring items | 1.64 | 1.47 | 1.21 |
| **Diluted net EPS** | **$     1.17** | **$     1.10** | **$     1.27** |

*Source:* www.freeedgar.com

# EXHIBIT 4    Avon Products, Inc. Annual Balance Sheet
### (in millions, except book value per share)

| | 12/31/99 | 12/31/98 | 12/31/97 |
|---|---|---|---|
| **Assets** | | | |
| Cash and equivalents | $ 117.40 | $ 105.60 | $ 141.90 |
| Receivables | 495.60 | 492.60 | 444.80 |
| Notes receivable | 0 | 0 | 0 |
| Inventories | 523.50 | 538.40 | 564.80 |
| Other current assets | 201.30 | 204.80 | 192.50 |
| Total current assets | 1,337.80 | 1,341.40 | 1,344.00 |
| Net property and equipment | 734.80 | 669.90 | 611.00 |
| Investments and advances | 0 | 0 | 0 |
| Other noncurrent assets | 0 | 0 | 0 |
| Deferred charges | 0 | 0 | 0 |
| Intangibles | 0 | 0 | 0 |
| Deposits and other assets | 456.00 | 422.20 | 317.90 |
| Total assets | $2,528.60 | $2,433.50 | $2,272.90 |
| **Liabilities and shareholders' equity** | | | |
| Notes payable | $ 306.00 | $ 55.30 | $ 132.10 |
| Accounts payable | 435.90 | 416.90 | 476.00 |
| Current portion long-term debt | 0 | 0 | 0 |
| Current portion capital leases | 0 | 0 | 0 |
| Accrued expenses | 684.90 | 575.70 | 481.20 |
| Income taxes payable | 286.00 | 281.60 | 266.60 |
| Other current liabilities | 0 | 0 | 0 |
| Total current liabilities | 1,712.80 | 1,329.50 | 1,355.90 |
| Mortgages | 0 | 0 | 0 |
| Deferred taxes/income | 36.70 | 36.30 | 31.20 |
| Convertible debt | 0 | 0 | 0 |
| Long-term debt | 701.40 | 201.00 | 102.20 |
| Noncurrent capital leases | 0 | 0 | 0 |
| Other noncurrent liabilities | 483.80 | 581.60 | 461.10 |
| Minority interest (liabilities) | 0 | 0 | 37.50 |
| Total liabilities | $2,934.70 | $2,148.40 | $1,987.90 |
| **Shareholders' equity** | | | |
| Preferred stock | 0 | 0 | 0 |
| Common stock (par) | $ 88.10 | $ 87.80 | $ 43.70 |
| Capital surplus | 819.40 | 780.00 | 733.10 |
| Retained earnings | 837.20 | 719.10 | 660.90 |
| Other equity | (349.70) | (301.30) | (270.30) |
| Treasury stock | 1,801.10 | 1,000.50 | 882.40 |
| Total shareholders' equity | (406.10) | 285.10 | 285.00 |
| Total liabilities and shareholders' equity | $2,528.60 | $2,433.50 | $2,272.90 |
| Total common equity | (406.10) | 285.10 | 285.00 |
| Average shares | 259.37 | 265.95 | 267.00 |
| Book value per share | $ (1.68) | $ 1.09 | $ 1.08 |

*Source:* www.freeedgar.com

EXHIBIT 5    Senior Management Organization

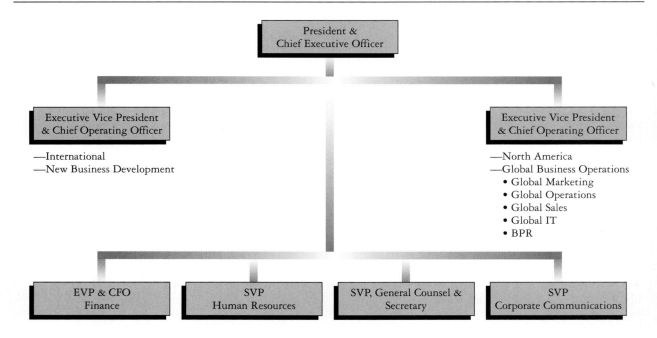

EXHIBIT 6    Avon Financial Data by Region
(in millions)

| Years ended December 31 | 1999 | | 1998 | | 1997 | |
|---|---|---|---|---|---|---|
| | Net Sales | Operating Profit | Net Sales | Operating Profit | Net Sales | Operating Profit |
| North America: | | | | | | |
| U.S. | $1,809.3 | $329.3 | $1,774.0 | $302.8 | $1,696.7 | $261.8 |
| Other | 274.0 | 44.7 | 287.6 | 40.2 | 275.4 | 35.1 |
| Total | 2,083.3 | 374.0 | 2,061.6 | 343.0 | 1,972.1 | 296.9 |
| International: | | | | | | |
| Latin America | 1,607.7 | 353.6 | 1,665.1 | 344.4 | 1,513.3 | 280.0 |
| Europe | 878.0 | 126.2 | 862.7 | 102.2 | 811.6 | 85.4 |
| Pacific | 720.1 | 102.1 | 623.3 | 62.5 | 782.4 | 67.0 |
| Total | 3,205.8 | 581.9 | 3,151.1 | 509.1 | 3,107.3 | 432.4 |
| Total from operations | $5,289.1 | 955.9 | $5,212.7 | 852.1 | $5,079.4 | 729.3 |
| Global expenses | | (255.3) | | (224.5) | | (191.5) |
| Special and non-recurring charges | | (151.2) | | (154.4) | | — |
| Operating profit | | $549.4 | | $473.2 | | $537.8 |
| Canada, Dominican Republic and Puerto Rico are included in North America—Other. | | | | | | |

Source: www.freeedgar.com

EXHIBIT 7   Avon's Sales by Product
            (in millions)

| | Years ended December 31 | | |
| --- | --- | --- | --- |
| | 1999 | 1998 | 1997 |
| Cosmetics, fragrance and toiletries | $3,226.1 | $3,176.6 | $3,093.9 |
| Beauty Plus: | | | |
|   Jewelry and accessories | 455.4 | 408.1 | 370.2 |
|   Apparel | 556.1 | 567.7 | 565.6 |
| | 1,011.5 | 975.8 | 935.8 |
| Non-core* | 1,051.5 | 1,060.3 | 1,049.7 |
| Total net sales | $5,289.1 | $5,212.7 | $5,079.4 |

*Non-core category primarily includes gift and decorative and home entertainment items.
*Source:* www.freeedgar.com

# REVLON, INC.—2000

**M. Jill Austin**
**Middle Tennessee State University**

**REV**

www.revlon.com

The vision of Revlon is to "provide glamour, excitement and innovation to consumers through high-quality products at affordable prices." According to President and CEO George Fellows, in recent years Revlon has seen a "mix of strong growth and intense challenge." Some of the company's challenges are global economic problems, increasing competition, and debt management concerns. Net sales for 1999 decreased 17 percent to $1.861 billion (compared to $2.252 billion in 1998), and operating income decreased 159 percent in 1999 to negative $371.5 million. International sales decreased by 10 percent ($93 million) from 1998 to 1999. Revlon products are sold in 175 countries around the world with sales outside the United States accounting for approximately 56 percent of sales in 1999, up from 41 percent of sales in 1998.

Product categories for the company include skincare, cosmetics, personal care, fragrance, and professional products. Some of the company's most recognized brand names include Revlon, Ultima II, ColorStay, Almay, Charlie, Flex, Mitchum, and Jean Naté. Successful products developed recently by the company include ColorStay lip color, Revlon Age Defying makeup, ColorStay eye and face makeup, Charlie White fragrance, Almay Clear Complexion makeup, and Lasting fragrance. Exhibit 1 shows the company products in each business category.

It is the long-term goal of Revlon to emerge as the dominant cosmetics and personal care firm through the twenty-first century.

## HISTORY

Revlon, Inc., was formed in 1932 by brothers Charles and Joseph Revson and Charles Lachmann with a $300 investment. Charles Lachmann was a nail-polish supplier who is most notably remembered for his contribution of the "l" in the Revlon name. Charles Revson was the primary force behind the success of Revlon until his death in 1968. In the early years, Revson developed a near-monopoly on beauty parlor sales by selling his nail polish door-to-door at salons. He expanded into the lipstick market with the slogan "Matching Lips and Fingertips." Some of the landmark advertising campaigns directed by Revson included "Fatal Apple" and "Fire and Ice." Revson was a hard taskmaster, expecting the same lifelong devotion of his workers that he gave to Revlon. He sometimes held meetings until two in the morning, called employees at home to discuss business, cursed out employees, and pretended to fall asleep during some presentations.

The company started with only one product, nail enamel. Revlon nail enamel was manufactured with pigments instead of the dyes typically used in this enamel. This approach allowed Revlon to market a large number of color options to consumers relatively quickly. It took the three company founders just six years to transform their small nail enamel company into a multimillion-dollar organization. This successful collaboration launched one of the most recognizable brands and companies in the world.

EXHIBIT 1    Revlon, Inc., Products and Business Categories

| Brand | Cosmetics | Skincare | Fragrances | Personal Care Products | Professional Products |
|---|---|---|---|---|---|
| Revlon | Revlon, ColorStay, Revlon Age Defying, Super Lustrous, MoistureStay Moon Drops, Line & Shine, New Complexion, Touch & Glow, Top Speed, Lashful, Naturally Glamorous, Custom Eyes, Timeliner, StreetWear, Revlon Implements | Moon Drops, Revlon Results, Eterna 27, Revlon Age Defying | Charlie, Charlie Red, Charlie White, Fire & Ice, Jontue, Ciara | Flex, Outrageous, Aquamarine, Mitchum, Lady Mitchum, Hi & Dri, ColorStay, Colorsilk, African Pride, Frost & Glow, Revlon Shadings, Jean Naté, Roux Fanci-full, Realistic, Creme of Nature, Herba Rich, Fabu-laxer | Revlon Professional Roux Fanci-full, Realistic, Creme of Nature, Sensor Perm, Perfect Perm, Fermodyl, Perfect Touch, Salon Perfection, Revlonissimo, Voila, Young Color, Creative Nail, Contours, American Crew, R PRO True System |
| Almay | Almay, Time-Off Amazing, One Coat, Stay Smooth, Almay Stay Clean | Sensitive Care, Oil Control, Time-Off, Moisture Balance, Moisture Renew, Almay Clear Complexion Skin Care | | Almay | |
| Ultima II | Ultima II, Beautiful Nutrient, Wonderwear, The Nakeds, Full Moisture | Glowtion, Vital Radiance, Interactives, CHR | | | |
| Significant Regional Brands | Colorama(a), Juvena(a), Jeanne Gatineau(a), Cutex(a) | Jeanne Gatineau(a), Natural Honey | Floid(a), Charlie Gold | Plusbelle(a), Bozzano(a), Juvena(a), Geniol(a), Colorama(a), Llongueras(a), Bain de Soleil(a), ZP-11 | Colomer(a) Intercosmo(a), Personal Bio Point, Natural Wonder, Llongueras(a) |

*Source:* Revlon, Inc., 1998, Form 10-K.

Originally Revlon offered its nail enamels through a limited distribution system in which professional salons carried the products. However, as the 1930s progressed, the products were distributed widely in select drugstores and department stores. As the world entered WWII, Revlon contributed to the war effort by providing first-aid kits and dye markers for the U.S. Navy. After the war, Revlon expanded its product lines with the introduction of manicure and pedicure instruments (a natural complement to the nail enamel products). Revlon management recognized global demand potential and began offering company products in a number of new markets. Stock was first offered in the company in 1955. The 1960s were associated with the "American Look" campaign designed to introduce the All-American girl to the world cosmetics market via well-known U.S. models. Further identifying with the changing role of women in the market and society, the Charlie fragrance line was introduced in the early 1970s. Sales for this extremely popular line surpassed $1 billion by 1977.

After the death of Charles Revson, Michel Bergerac took control of the company. He built up the pharmaceutical side of the business. By 1985 two thirds of Revlon's sales were healthcare products such as TUMS and Oxy acne medication, and the company was losing ground in cosmetics. Millionaire Ronald Perelman made five offers to purchase Revlon and eventually took over the company for $1.8 billion in a leveraged buyout. Perelman returned the company to its roots and sold off the healthcare products. He refocused the company to become an internationally known manufacturer and seller of cosmetics and fragrances. Perelman took the company private in 1987 by buying the stock from all of the public shareholders. A subsidiary of MacAndrews & Forbes still holds 83 percent of the outstanding shares of Revlon, and Perelman is chairman and CEO of MacAndrews & Forbes Holdings, Inc. The company was taken public in 1996 and is traded on the New York Stock Exchange (NYSE).

In September 1996 Revlon was given approval to manufacture, distribute, and market Revlon products in China, and the first manufactured goods rolled off the production line in December 1996. The company acquired Bionature S.A., a South American manufacturer of haircare and personal care products in 1997. The completion of acquisitions in South America increased distribution and manufacturing capabilities in these markets.

## PRESENT CONDITIONS

The company has struggled in recent years and has a debt of about $2 billion. Since October 1998, sales have fallen significantly in the United States and in countries such as Russia and Brazil. As a result, Revlon stock has lost half its value. In April 1999, Revlon announced it would sell all or part of the business. Unilever and Coty both expressed an interest in the company, but in October 1999, majority stockholder Perelman took the company off the market because of lack of substantial offers. Perelman sold the salon products business and some of the company's businesses in Latin America to raise $500 million. In addition, in the fourth quarter of 1999, Revlon decided not to ship $280 million worth of products in order to reduce retailer inventories.

Even with these financial difficulties, Revlon is the best-selling brand in the U.S. mass market for color cosmetics, and Almay is the fastest-growing major cosmetic brand. The company continues to launch new products. A new hair-color line for teenagers called Super Lustrous was launched in 1998. The brand African Pride was acquired in 1998, and Revlon plans to launch an African Pride men's haircare line. In 1999, the new products Age Defying Makeup and Concealer Compact, Everylash Mascara, and ColorStay Compact Makeup were introduced in the United States, and Almay introduced a lightweight foundation makeup and gel-based makeup called Almay Foundation Compact Skin Stays Clean Makeup.

## DEMOGRAPHIC AND SOCIAL TRENDS

The cosmetics and personal care industry is impacted by two major changes in U.S. demographics: the aging population and the change in proportions of racial and ethnic groups. Aging baby boomers make up a significant proportion of the adult U.S. population. The 75 million Americans born between 1946 and 1964 are a significant market for the cosmetics and personal care industry. Many baby boomers have high levels of disposable income and are brand-loyal consumers. In addition, it appears that baby boomers' consumption patterns and rates have not necessarily changed as they have aged. The number of people in the mature market (fifty-five years old and older) also continues to increase in number. Many of these consumers are wealthier and more willing to spend than ever before. Additionally, mature women now remain in the workforce for longer periods of time than in the past. The aging of the population has been coupled with a mini baby boom.

The ethnic and racial makeup of the American population is shifting. Although African Americans represent the largest minority segment (36 million as of 2000), the Hispanic-American segment is the fastest-growing segment and is projected to become the largest minority group in the United States by 2010, with approximately 40.5 million individuals. Thus, the nonHispanic white share of the U.S. population is expected to decline to 68 percent by that year. The Asian-American population is also growing rapidly.

Other social and demographic issues that may impact the industry include consumers' concerns about product safety and the use of animal testing by cosmetics companies. Increasingly, cosmetics and personal care items are not for women only; men purchase personal care products such as skin creams and haircare products and dyes, and many men are trying cosmetics in an effort to improve their appearance. The market for hair coloring has expanded with teenagers and adults wanting more vibrant coloring options. Styles have also changed from minimal makeup to a more colorful, glamorous style of makeup.

## COMPETITION

Competition is intense in the cosmetics and skincare industry. In the past, the retail cosmetics industry was dominated by sales of cosmetics in specialty stores and department stores that had beauty consultants providing service. Today large numbers of women prefer purchasing these items at drugstores, supermarkets, mass-volume retailers such as Kmart and Wal-Mart, from door-to-door sellers such as Avon, and on the Internet. Revlon's major competitors include Procter & Gamble; Avon Products; Estée Lauder Companies, Inc.; Cosmair/L'Oréal; Unilever; and Coty. Recent entrants into the color cosmetics market include Oil of Olay (Procter & Gamble) and Neutrogena (Johnson & Johnson). The cosmetics and skincare industry is expected to be a $200 billion business worldwide by 2003.

Other competitors include small companies such as Urban Decay; specialty stores such as Bath and Body Works, Bath and Body Shop and H20; and retailers selling their own brands such as Benneton, Banana Republic, and Victoria's Secret. Competition for the African-American market is also increasing with brands such as Fashion Flair and cosmetics lines launched by Iman and Patti LaBelle. A discussion of the major competitors of Revlon, Inc. follows.

### Procter & Gamble

Procter & Gamble (P&G) is a multinational company offering products in a wide range of categories including personal care, cosmetics, fragrances, haircare, and skincare. The company also deals in such unrelated areas as diapers, baking mixes, bleach, dishwashing products, juice, laundry products, oral care products, and peanut butter and operates in more than 70 countries.

Revlon faces competition from P&G in a number of product categories as P&G offers haircare products through its Pantene, Vidal Sassoon, and Ivory brands; its skincare lines include Oil of Olay, Noxzema, and Clearasil; its fragrance lines include Giorgio, Hugo Boss, Old Spice, Venezia, and Wings; and its cosmetics line includes

Cover Girl, Max Factor, and Oil of Olay. The singer Brandy was hired to promote Cover Girl products, and the company spent $100 million in 1999 to introduce new Cover Girl products. The company will spend $55 million in the initial promotion for its new Oil of Olay cosmetics.

### Cosmair, Inc. (L'Oréal/Maybelline)

L'Oréal is the world's largest cosmetics firm. Profits increased by 12 percent in 1998 to $767.7 million. L'Oréal acquired Maybelline, one of its leading competitors, in 1996 for $758 million in an attempt to strengthen its position in the U.S. market. L'Oréal previously held only a 7.5 percent share of the market, but the acquisition of Maybelline made L'Oréal the number-two cosmetics firm in the United States. L'Oréal competes with Revlon in the area of cosmetics (L'Oréal, Maybelline, and Helena Rubenstein), haircare (L'Oréal and Redken), and fragrances (Vanderbilt and Ralph Lauren perfumes). Some of the advertising spokespersons for the company are Christy Turlington, Tomiko Fraser, and Sarah Michelle Gellar. In 1998, L'Oréal acquired Soft Sheen, an ethnic haircare business and introduced a quick-dry nail polish called Jet-Set. From 1997 to 1999, Maybelline sales almost doubled ($320 million to $600 million), and sales outside the United States during these years accounted for 50 percent of total sales. Cosmair, Inc., is a privately held company.

### Coty/Benckiser

Coty is owned by a Dutch holding company called Benckiser and is controlled primarily by the Reinmann family of Germany. Coty is one of the world's largest cosmetics and fragrance companies in the world, with sales of $1.7 billion in 1999. Some Coty brands include Calgon, Jovan, Sand & Sable, Stetson, Adidas fragrances, Exclamation, L'Aimant, Sensiq, Cutex, and Dark Vanilla. The company's prestige brands are Davidoff, Chopard, Yue-Sai, and Lancaster. In 1996, Coty bid against L'Oréal for Maybelline but was not successful. In 1998, Coty opened a manufacturing plant in China. Coty managers considered making a bid to purchase Revlon, but after evaluating Revlon's financial situation and brands in 1999, Coty decided against it.

### Unilever

Unilever is an Anglo-Dutch firm that until recently has been noted as a manufacturer of soap and detergent products and food products. The company also manufactures personal care products. Some of the Unilever brands include mass skincare (Ponds, Vaseline, Pears, Hazeline), haircare (Organics, Sunsilk, Clinic, Gloria), mass perfume (Brute, Impulse, Denim, Axe/Lynx, Rexoral/Reward), and prestige fragrances (Elizabeth Arden, Calvin Klein, Elizabeth Taylor, Karl Lagerfeld, and Chloe). Unilever now markets seven of the top ten fragrance products in the United States including Obsession, White Diamonds, Passion, Black Pearls, and Eternity.

The company is a world leader in prestige fragrances and leads the hair care market in Africa, the Middle East, Latin America, and Asia and the Pacific Rim. Their skincare products lead the market in North America, Africa, Latin America, Asia and the Pacific Rim, and the Middle East.

### Avon Products, Inc.

Avon is the largest direct seller of cosmetics and beauty products in the world. The direct salesforce numbers 2.8 million people. Some brand names for Avon products include their cosmetics line Avon Color, fragrances such as Josie and Natori, and toiletries such as Skin-So-Soft. The company's products can be purchased through its Internet site www.avon.com. Avon also sells jewelry, gift items, lingerie, and casual clothing. Avon has subsidiaries in 41 countries and distributes its products in 89 additional countries. Avon posted sales of $5.2 billion dollars in 1998.

## Estée Lauder

The Estée Lauder Companies, Inc., manufactures and markets cosmetics, fragrances, and skincare products. Some of the company's cosmetics and skincare brands include Estée Lauder and Clinique. Fragrances are sold under the brand names of Beautiful and White Linen. In addition, Estée Lauder holds the worldwide license for fragrances and cosmetics with the brand names Tommy Hilfiger, Donna Karan New York, and DKNY. In 1998 the company acquired jane, a color cosmetics line targeted toward young women, and Aveda, a prestige brand of products for haircare. The company also has an investment in MAC (Make-Up Art Cosmetics, Limited). Stila Cosmetics, Inc., a Los Angeles-based company known for eco-friendly packaging, was acquired in 1999. Other Estée Lauder brands include Bobbi Brown Essentials, Aramia, Prescriptives, and Origins. Estée Lauder has sales in over 100 countries. In 1999, the company rehired model Karen Graham, known as "the face of Estée Lauder," to be in advertisements for Resilience Lift products targeted to mature women. The first DKNY fragrance was launched in 2000.

## INTERNAL FACTORS

### Organization and Management

In 1990, Chairman Levin lead the company in recruiting a strong team of experienced managers who worked to achieve leadership in the cosmetics and skincare industry. About this same time, Revlon developed its vision to "provide glamour, excitement, and innovation to consumers through high-quality products at affordable prices." The company set up the Revlon Learning Center and developed training programs to communicate its strategic principles to employees. Training helped ensure that the company's teamwork approach remained effective. In 1994, Revlon established the "Charlie Awards" to recognize employees whose accomplishments significantly impacted Revlon. A number of these awards are given to deserving employees each year.

At the core of the Revlon organization is the belief in individual values and the integrity of the firm and its actions. Revlon and its employees are active in supporting women's health programs and other community efforts. In the last decade, Revlon has spend $25 million on services and research that help women. Revlon sponsors the Revlon Run/Walk in Los Angeles, which has raised millions of dollars for the Revlon/UCLA Women's Cancer Research Center. In 1998, the company established a partnership with the National Council of Negro Women to help support wellness programs for African-American women.

In 1998, Revlon began restructuring the company by firing 720 employees. The downsizing resulted in a $42.9 million charge for severance packages and employee benefits. However, it is expected that $30 to $40 million will be saved through these restructuring efforts, with $15 to $20 million in savings in 1999. In addition to downsizing, the company recently merged its cosmetics and beauty care salesforces in an effort to build brands rather than product categories. The business is set as two units with Revlon products in one unit and Almay, Ultima II, and StreetWear lines in another unit.

### Marketing

The primary customers for Revlon products are large mass merchandisers and chain drugstores. Some of the major retail customers are Walgreens, Wal-Mart, Target, Kmart, CVS, Drug Emporium, Eckerds, Rite Aid, and JC Penney.

Advertising continues to be one of the primary areas of promotion spending by Revlon, and spokesperson Cindy Crawford is one of the most recognizable faces in the cosmetics world. In addition to Cindy Crawford, the company's television and print advertisements also feature Halle Berry, Melanie Griffith, Courtney Thorne-Smith, Shania Twain, and Cybil Sheperd. Plus-sized model Emme first appeared in Revlon print advertisements in June 1999. Revlon has two tractor-trailer trucks called "Discovery Centers" that are decorated with photos of Revlon spokespersons. These trailers are taken to outdoor festivals for promotional activities. In mid-1998, Revlon marketing managers decided to reduce advertising expenditures because of Revlon's high name recognition in the market. However, by March 1999, company managers decided that advertising is a critical activity, and new advertising campaigns were developed. The new brand-building program launched by the company includes new products and development of closer ties with retail stores. The company will provide more special programs for retailers tied in with merchandising. In addition, Revlon began providing product samples starting in April 1999 issues of fashion and beauty magazines.

### Production

Globalization of the company's manufacturing and distribution efforts has enabled the consolidation of production facilities. This consolidation and coordination of markets has provided increased operating efficiency and better use of capital assets. The number of production facilities has been reduced and centralized to cover core regions. Currently, the company has production facilities in Phoenix, Arizona (Revlon); Oxford, North Carolina (Ultima II); Vista, California (nail enamels); and Jacksonville, Florida (professional products and personal care consumer products). Production facilities are also located in China, Canada, Spain, Mexico, Ireland, Venezuela, New Zealand, Brazil, Argentina, Italy, South Africa, and France. Several of the company's plants have ISO-9002 certification signifying their commitment to high-quality manufacturing standards. Planning for long-term growth includes a focus on and utilization of top-notch production facilities and distribution systems.

The Revlon Phoenix site distribution center handles components and raw materials as well as finished stocks of cosmetics and personal care products. The distribution center maintains a 99 percent accuracy rating in both inventory accuracy and order accuracy. An automated-materials-handling system was installed at the distribution center in 1980, and several improvements have been made in the system since that time. In 1981 a change was made so that automated guided vehicles (AGVs) no longer delivered components directly to the production lines. In 1984 the company moved to a paperless receiving process, and bar coding was first used in 1988. Software enhancements were made in 1994 to increase capacity of operations. The company's emphasis on continuous improvement means that Revlon managers look for ways to provide greater efficiency in company operations on an on-going basis.

### Financial Conditions

Significant financial issues impact the company's operations. Long-term debt at the end of 1999 was $1.76 billion, a number that represents several years of debt problems for Revlon.

Revlon, Inc., income statements and balance sheets are provided in Exhibits 2 and 3, respectively. These statements reveal financial trouble.

## EXHIBIT 2    Revlon, Inc. Annual Income Statement and Balance Statement
### (in millions except EPS data and book value per share)

|  | 12/31/99 | 12/31/98 | 12/31/97 |
|---|---|---|---|
| Sales | $1,861.30 | $2,252.20 | $2,390.90 |
| Cost of goods | 686.10 | 765.70 | 832.10 |
| Gross profit | 1,175.20 | 1,486.50 | 1.558.80 |
| Selling and administrative and depreciation and amortization expenses | 1,351.90 | 1,333.90 | 1,344.60 |
| Income after depreciation and amortization | (176.70) | 152.60 | 214.20 |
| Nonoperating income | (37.80) | (37.00) | (10.10) |
| Interest expense | 147.90 | 137.90 | 136.20 |
| Pretax income | (362.40) | (22.30) | 67.90 |
| Income taxes | 9.10 | 5.00 | 9.40 |
| Minority interest | N/A | 0 | 0 |
| Investment gains/losses (+) | N/A | 0 | 0 |
| Other income/charges | N/A | 0 | 0 |
| Income from continued operations | N/A | N/A | N/A |
| Extras and discontinued operations | 0 | (115.90) | (14.90) |
| Net income | $ (371.50) | $ (143.20) | $    43.60 |

### Depreciation Footnote

|  | 12/31/99 | 12/31/98 | 12/31/97 |
|---|---|---|---|
| Income before depreciation and amortization | $ (172.40) | $  157.70 | $  220.90 |
| Depreciation and amortization (cash flow) | 4.30 | 5.10 | 6.70 |
| Income after depreciation and amortization | $ (176.70) | $  152.60 | $  214.20 |

### Earnings-per-share data

|  | 12/31/99 | 12/31/98 | 12/31/97 |
|---|---|---|---|
| Average shares | $    51.24 | $    51.22 | $    51.54 |
| Diluted EPS before nonrecurring items | (6.04) | 0.17 | 1.21 |
| Diluted net EPS | $    (7.25) | $    (2.80) | $     0.85 |

*Source:* www.freeedgar.com

## OUTLOOK FOR THE FUTURE

According to the 1998 *Annual Report,* Revlon considers adjustment to change as its fundamental strength:

> Though business conditions constantly change, the fundamental strengths of our business and the power of our brand franchises endure. The steps we have taken in 1998 will align the Company with market forces and will strengthen our solid foundation. The cornerstone of our foundation is our brands, our organization and our leadership in meeting consumer needs.

As Revlon, Inc., deals with its debt problems and tries to continue its strategy of innovation, product development, and globalization, several questions must be asked.

1. Should Revlon concentrate its efforts on international markets?
2. Should Revlon diversify its operations or develop joint ventures with other cosmetics companies?

EXHIBIT 3    Revlon, Inc. Annual Balance Sheet
(in millions, except book value per share)

|  | 12/31/99 | 12/31/98 | 12/31/97 |
|---|---|---|---|
| **Assets** | | | |
| Cash and equivalents | $ 25.40 | $ 34.70 | $ 37.40 |
| Receivables | 332.60 | 536.00 | 493.90 |
| Notes receivable | N/A | 0 | 0 |
| Inventories | 278.30 | 264.10 | 349.30 |
| Other current assets | 51.30 | 69.90 | 97.50 |
| **Total current assets** | **687.60** | **904.70** | **983.50** |
| Net property and equipment | 336.40 | 378.90 | 378.20 |
| Investments and advances | N/A | 0 | 0 |
| Other noncurrent assets | N/A | 0 | 0 |
| Deferred charges | N/A | 0 | 0 |
| Intangibles | 534.30 | 546.40 | 329.20 |
| Deposits and other assets | N/A | 0 | 143.70 |
| **Total assets** | **$ 1,558.30** | **$1,830.00** | **$1,834.60** |
| **Liabilities and shareholders' equity** | | | |
| Notes payable | $ 37.60 | $ 27.90 | $ 42.70 |
| Accounts payable | 549.50 | 524.50 | 195.50 |
| Current portion long-term debt | 10.20 | 6.00 | 5.50 |
| Current portion capital leases | N/A | 0 | 0 |
| Accrued expenses | N/A | 0 | 366.10 |
| Income taxes payable | N/A | 0 | 0 |
| Other current liabilities | N/A | 0 | 0 |
| **Total current liabilities** | **597.30** | **558.40** | **609.80** |
| Mortgages | N/A | 0 | 0 |
| Deferred taxes/income | N/A | 0 | 0 |
| Convertible debt | N/A | 0 | 0 |
| Long-term debt | 1,761.90 | 1,654.00 | 1,458.70 |
| Noncurrent capital leases | N/A | 0 | 0 |
| Other noncurrent liabilities | 214.00 | 265.60 | 224.60 |
| Minority interest (liabilities) | N/A | 0 | 0 |
| **Total liabilities** | **$ 2,573.20** | **$2,478.00** | **$2,293,10** |
| **Shareholders' equity** | | | |
| Preferred stock | N/A | 54.60 | 54.60 |
| Common stock (par) | N/A | 0.50 | 0.50 |
| Capital surplus | N/A | (228.50) | (231.10) |
| Retained earnings | N/A | (402.00) | (258.80) |
| Other equity | N/A | (72.60) | (23.70) |
| Treasury stock | N/A | 0 | 0 |
| Total shareholders' equity | (1,014.90) | (648.00) | (458.50) |
| **Total liabilities and shareholders' equity** | **1,558.30** | **1,830.00** | **1,834.60** |
| Total common equity | (1,014.90) | (702.60) | (513.10) |
| Average shares | $ 51.24 | $ 51.22 | $ 51.54 |
| Book value per share | (19.81) | (13.71) | (10.04) |

*Source:* www.freeedgar.com

3. What role does innovation play in the strategic planning of Revlon, Inc.? Which specific types of innovation might Revlon use?

4. What role should "branding" play in future growth strategies of Revlon?

5. How will competitive reactions impact Revlon's future plans?

6. What is the impact of social trends and economic trends on companies in the cosmetics and skincare industry?

7. What plans should Revlon, Inc., develop to pay off long-term debt?

EXHIBIT 4    Revlon's Net Income (Loss)
By Geographic Area
(in millions)

|  | 1999 | 1998 | 1997 |
|---|---|---|---|
| Domestic | $(289.7) | $15.3 | $82.6 |
| Foreign | (72.7) | (37.6) | (15.5) |
|  | $(362.4) | $(22.3) | $67.1 |

EXHIBIT 5    Revlon's Advertising and R&D Expenses (in millions)

|  | 1999 | 1998 | 1997 |
|---|---|---|---|
| Advertising and Promotion Expenditures | $411.8 | $422.9 | $397.4 |
| R&D Expenditures | 32.9 | 31.9 | 29.7 |

EXHIBIT 6    Revlon's Sales By Segment (in millions)

|  | 1999 | 1998 | 1997 |
|---|---|---|---|
| Net Sales |  |  |  |
| USA | $1,046.2 | $1,343.7 | $1,304.9 |
| International | 815.1 | 908.5 | 933.7 |
|  | $1,861.3 | $2,252.2 | $2,238.6 |
| Cosmetics, Skin Care, and Fragrances | $1,001.8 | $1,309.7 | $1,319.6 |
| Personal Care and Professional | 859.5 | 942.5 | 919.0 |
|  | $1,861.3 | $2,252.2 | $2,238.6 |

# REFERENCES

BENADY, DAVID. "Fading Beauty: Struggling Cosmetics Giant Is Almost Certainly up for Sale," *Marketing Week,* April 1, 1999, pp. 28–30.

"BENCKISER GEARS UP FOR BRAND DOMINANCE," *Marketing Week,* August 5, 1999, p. 19.

DAY, JULIA. "Coty Sets up International Fragrance Unit in London," *Marketing Week,* p. 6.

EDMONDSON, GAIL. "The Beauty of Global Branding," *Business Week,* June 28, 1999, pp. 70–75.

FAIRCLOUGH, GORDON. "Revlon Takes down 'for Sale' Sign, as Shares Sink 34%," *The Wall Street Journal,* October 4, 1999, p. B6.

GROSSMAN, ANDREA. "Teens, Males Boost Color Sales," *Drug Store News,* November 23, 1998, p. 53.

KLEPACKI, LAURA. "Revlon Builds Brand Foundation," *Brandmarketing,* March 1999, p. 6.

PARKER-POPE, TARA, and GREGORY ZUCKERMAN. "Revlon's Stock Gains on Perelman Plan for Refinancing $1.15 Billion in Debt," *The Wall Street Journal,* February 24, 1997, p. B7.

PARKS, LIZ. "Record and Support, Launches Drive Sales," *Drug Store News,* January 11, 1999, p. 18.

PARKS, LIZ. "Upcoming Launches to Fuel Cosmetics Sales," *Drug Store News,* June 7, 1999, p. 206.

REVLON, INC. 1996, 1998 *Annual Report.*

"REVLON RESORTS TO CUTS," *Cosmetic Insider's Report,* November 8, 1999, p. 2.

SANDLER, LINDA, and YUMIKO ONO. "Revlon's Makeup Fails to Hide Some Frowns as Investors Wonder If Perelman Will Pay Debt," *The Wall Street Journal,* December 2, 1997.

TODE, CHANTAL. "Beauty Advertising Puts on a New Face," *Brandmarketing,* May 1999, p. 66.

www.avon.com

www.pg.com

www.revlon.com

www.unilever.com

# PILGRIM'S PRIDE CORPORATION—2000

James L. Harbin
Texas A&M University—Texarkana

## CHX
### www.pilgrimspride.com

Headquartered in Pittsburg, Texas, Pilgrim's Pride Corporation is engaged in the production, processing, and marketing of fresh chicken and further processed and prepared chicken products. The company offers a broad range of over 600 value-added products, such as breast fillets, nuggets, tenders, patties, and deli foods. These products, which undergo one or more further processing steps (including deboning, cutting, forming, battering, breading, and cooking) are packaged in various quantities. Additionally, Pilgrim's develops and produces new products to meet specific customers' needs. Approximately 10 percent of Pilgrim's Pride U.S. sales were derived from newly created products annually. Pilgrims is a major supplier to Wendy's and Kentucky Fried Chicken, and in 1998 began selling to Burger King.

Under the Pilgrim's Pride brand name, the fresh retail line is sold regionally in the central, southwestern, and western United States and also in Mexico. Food service and industrial products are sold in the United States and Mexico. Pilgrim's exports approximately 12 percent of its product line internationally. At year-end 1999, Pilgrims employed 11,200 persons in the United States and 3,950 persons in Mexico.

Pilgrim's Pride is one of approximately 45 survivors out of approximately 4,000 chicken processing firms in existence a few decades ago. Lonnie ("Bo") Pilgrim, one of a family of seven children raised during the Great Depression, took his concern from a small farm-supply store 40 years ago to a corporation producing $1.35 billion in 1999 sales, up 1.9 percent from 1998. Currently, Pilgrim's is the fourth-largest chicken company in the United States and the second largest of 25 major chicken producers in Mexico. It is the 22nd-largest egg producer in the United States, with eggs representing 10.7 percent of sales. It produces more than 1.7 billion pounds of chicken and 41 million dozen eggs annually. Pilgrim's employs more than 13,000 workers and has over 1,500 contract growers. Its facilities are located in Texas, Arkansas, Oklahoma, Arizona, and Mexico. For 1999, Pilgrims' chicken sales to Mexico decreased $23.6 million to $254.5 million.

Pilgrim's remarkable growth has taken place in a commodity industry for which, every year over the past 50 years, economists have been predicting doom and gloom. Citing industry sales as an indicator, experts have also deducted that the chicken industry has finally matured. The big question facing Pilgrim's today is whether it can continue to grow through additional marketing techniques, further cost curtailment, increased integration (gaining control over supplies and distribution), improved genetics and growing techniques, and possible acquisitions while at the same time facing competitors who are larger and just as savvy.

## BO PILGRIM'S BACKGROUND AND PHILOSOPHY

Bo Pilgrim's story is a classic one of deprivation to determination and then to success. Born in northwest Texas in 1928, he was the fourth of seven children. His father died when Bo was nine, and he left home at twelve to live with his grandmother.

His entrepreneurial spirit had early roots. One of his first goals in life, he says, was "to be able to buy a soda when I wanted it. My father would on occasion give me money for a cold drink, but only after I had finished some work he wanted done for it." He learned early how to buy his own soft drinks. He bought sodas from his father's general merchandise store and sold them at a profit to the local factory workers. He later peddled newspapers, raised chickens and hogs, hauled gravel, picked peas and cotton, and sacked groceries—all before he turned eighteen.

Bo is still a tireless worker at age seventy-two. "Getting up with the chickens" would aptly describe Pilgrim's daily routines. Bo still works 12-hour days, which include a daily exercise regimen of treadmill work and swimming (he had a heart attack about 12 years ago). "People retire too early," says Pilgrim, "they should retire when they don't enjoy working anymore. I won't retire!"

He likens business to "a game, even a war." Commenting on how he spends his time, he says "I spend one third of my working days dealing with the government, one third with lawyers, and the remaining one third of my time is spent constructively."

He commented, "Today we don't appreciate how much we have and how easy it is to get things. I'm definitely hooked on the free enterprise system." He added, "In fact, when I visited with President Reagan, I reminded him that the chicken and the egg industry has never had any kind of subsidy. I also shared my belief that the government should not be in the business of protecting the inefficient."

On entrepreneurship, Pilgrim said, "It is more than just shooting from the hip. A company has four resources—people, dollars, time, and facilities. Our company's objective is to gain optimum use of these four through planning, building pride, and rewarding your employees."

Educated in a three-room school without electricity, Bo still believes in "old-fashioned Christian values" and the idea that "there is more to life than just making a dollar." He had three children with his wife of 42 years, and for more than 30 years, he has taught a Sunday School class.

When asked about his secret of success, Bo responded, "Take your abilities, season them with experience on the job and combine that with drive and motivation and you will be successful. The way to make a difference in your life is to make that *mind-boggling* decision not to be average."

Most Texans know Bo as the chicken king who wears a Pilgrim's hat in his television commercials. Visitors to corporate headquarters get parking spaces marked with a picture of a chicken and the words, "Pullet her in." First-floor lobby walls are festooned with more than 300 samples of memorabilia of Pilgrim and his company—wooden thank-you plaques, framed newspaper clippings, and photographs of him with prominent politicians. In the second-floor executive office suite, representations of chickens are everywhere—ceramic chickens, oil paintings of chickens, photographs of chickens, and stuffed chickens.

## HISTORY

Because commodity chicken downcycles has almost bankrupted Pilgrim's twice over the years, the company has increasingly emphasized value-added and branded products, including its chill-pack and further processed and prepared food lines. In the late 1980s, Pilgrim's spent $25 million on a facility for preparing chickens. Such products generate higher prices per pound, exhibit lower price volatility, and result in higher and more consistent profit margins than non-value-added products such as whole ice-pack chicken.

In order to crack the food service business with processed and prepared chicken, Pilgrim's had to price its products below those of Tyson Foods, Inc. (its chief competitor) at a loss. The company also had to spend approximately $6 million to $8 million a year on advertising, promotion, and supermarket slotting allowances to entice this business.

Pilgrim's Pride lost about $50 million over three years trying to enter the prepared chicken market. In fiscal 1988, the company lost a net $8 million on $506 million in sales. Disgruntled investors dumped the stock, which had just had an initial public offering in January 1987. The value of Bo Pilgrim's stake shrank by 76 percent to $61 million.

Pilgrim's finally turned the corner with a strategic retreat from the supermarkets and a major advance into the food service market. Retail products now account for a mere 2 percent of Pilgrim's prepared chicken sales. In food service Pilgrim's positioned itself as an alternative to Tyson, aiming at those customers leery of being too dependent on one supplier. "A lot of buyers gave us information to help us duplicate the products they were buying from Tyson," Pilgrim says. With customers such as Kraft General Foods, Wendy's, and KFC, the company now has been able to raise its prices to be in line with Tyson.

After suffering its biggest loss ($29.6 million) in the history of the company in 1992, Pilgrim's rebounded in 1993 and 1994. They lost $7.9 million in 1995 and $4.5 million in 1996. Pilgrim's achieved successive record net income levels in 1997, 1998, and 1999, of $41.0, $50.0, and $65.3 million respectively (see Exhibit 1).

## MISSION

A large group of Pilgrim employees representing all areas of the company recently met to brainstorm their direction, vision, and mission. Many in the group were fearful that rather than developing a mission, they might end up with a "mission statement." The difference, according to Monty Henderson, then president and CEO, was "that a mission statement becomes very wordy and usually winds up as a long paragraph or two that no one—not even the authors—can remember and usually winds up in a file somewhere. A mission, by contrast, is known by everyone, practiced daily by everyone, and becomes a way of life."

After much discussion about their business, their customers, and their competition, the group came to a consensus that Pilgrim's vision is "to achieve and maintain leadership in each product and service that we provide." To achieve this, the group felt that their mission was summed up as "Our job is customer satisfaction . . . every day." Because of increased emphasis in the international market, Pilgrim's later amended its vision to "To be a world class chicken company—better than the best."

## MARKETING

Pilgrim's has a consumer-oriented marker strategy. The company annually increased its marketing activities and expenditures as it developed new products and geographic markets. As a result of its marketing activities, the company has achieved significant consumer awareness for the Pilgrim's Pride brand name in southwestern and western metropolitan markets. The company believes that this brand awareness is beneficial to the introduction and acceptance of new products, such as its further-processed and prepared food lines.

The company utilizes television, radio, and newspaper advertising; point-of-sale and coupon promotions; and other marketing techniques to develop consumer awareness and brand loyalty for its products. Bo Pilgrim has been the featured spokesperson in the company's television and radio commercials, and his likeness in a pilgrim's hat appears

EXHIBIT 1    Pilgrim's Pride Annual Income Statement
(in millions except earnings-per-share data)

|  | 9/30/99 | 9/30/98 | 9/30/97 |
|---|---|---|---|
| Sales | $1,357.40 | $1,331.54 | $1,277.65 |
| Cost of goods | 1,171.69 | 1,195.44 | 1,163.15 |
| **Gross profit** | 185.70 | 136.10 | 114.50 |
| Selling and administrative and depreciation and amortization expenses | 76.20 | 58.84 | 50.60 |
| **Income after depreciation and amortization** | 109.51 | 77.26 | 63.89 |
| Nonoperating income | (0.93) | (0.58) | 2.01 |
| Interest expense | 17.66 | 20.14 | 22.08 |
| **Pretax income** | 90.90 | 56.52 | 43.82 |
| Income taxes | 25.65 | 6.51 | 2.79 |
| Minority interest | 0 | 0 | 0 |
| Investment gains/losses (+) | 0 | 0 | 0 |
| Other income/charges | 0 | 0 | 0 |
| **Income from continued operations** | N/A | N/A | N/A |
| Extras and discontinued operations | 0 | 0 | 0 |
| **Net income** | $   65.25 | $   50.01 | $   41.04 |

### Depreciation Footnote

|  |  |  |  |
|---|---|---|---|
| Income before depreciation and amortization | $ 144.04 | $ 109.85 | $  93.69 |
| Depreciation and amortization (cash flow) | 34.53 | 32.59 | 29.80 |
| **Income after depreciation and amortization** | $ 109.51 | $  77.26 | $  63.89 |

### Earnings per-share data

|  |  |  |  |
|---|---|---|---|
| **Average shares** | $   41.38 | $   41.38 | $   41.38 |
| Diluted earnings-per-share before nonrecurring items | 1.58 | 1.21 | 0.99 |
| **Diluted net earnings-per-share** | $    1.58 | $    1.21 | $    0.99 |

*Source:* www.freeedgar.com

on all the company's branded products. Advertising slogans have included "Better from the egg to the leg," "It's a mind-boggling thing," "The honest chicken from real Pilgrim's," and "Real chickens from real Pilgrim's."

The company maintains an active program to identify consumer preferences primarily by testing new product ideas, packaging designs, and methods through taste panels and focus groups located in key geographic markets. This program led to the identification and introduction of new products such as the company's whole boneless chicken, leaner chicken, and the entire further-processed and prepared foods line.

Pilgrim's has a total of seven processing facilities, three further-prepared food facilities, seven distribution centers, seven growing facilities, and two sales and marketing divisions located in Dallas and Mexico City. Their corporate office is in Pittsburg, Texas.

## COMPETITION

Pilgrim's competes with other integrated chicken companies and to a lesser extent with local and regional poultry companies that are not fully integrated. Pilgrim's has been competing for retail grocery sales of chill-pack products since 1982 and fast-food product sales of whole and precut chickens since 1965. It currently supplies over 40 of the country's largest restaurant chains such as: KFC, Church's, Wendy's, Grandy's, PepsiCo, Chili's, and Long John Silver's.

The primary competitive factors in the chicken industry include price, product line, and customer service. Although its products are competitively priced and generally supported with in-store promotions and discount programs, the company believes that product quality, brand awareness, and customer service are the primary tools with which it competes. Pilgrim's believes that it has only one competitor (Tyson) with a more complete line of value-added products.

Tyson, the number-one poultry processor with sales of about $8 billion, generates 24 percent of the U.S. poultry production. Gold Kist has 10 percent; Perdue Farms has 8 percent; and Pilgrim's and Conagra Poultry each have approximately 6 percent.

Tyson's strategy has been one of many acquisitions over the past decade. They acquired Hudson Foods, Inc., for $682 million in 1997. At that time Hudson had 5 percent of the market. There were rumors in 1988 that Tyson would acquire Pilgrim's for approximately $162 million. The deal was retracted however.

"Our marketing strategy for success is simple—segment, concentrate, dominate. We identify a promising market segment, concentrate our resources in it, and ultimately gain for Tyson Foods a dominate share of that segment," stated a recent Tyson annual report. "Our customers include all of the nation's top 50 food service distributors, 88 of the top 100 restaurant chains, 100 of the top retail supermarket chains, and every major wholesale club."

## MEXICAN STRATEGY

After only a few short years, Pilgrim's became the second-largest chicken producer in Mexico. Its business strategy for Mexico calls for using its U.S. management expertise to solidify its position as the most efficient operator in Mexico and, at the same time, to develop a strong consumer and trade franchise for the Pilgrim's Pride brand. Pilgrim's sales in Mexico rose to $278 million in 1998, an increase of 22 percent over $228 million in 1996 (see Exhibit 2). With Mexico's rising population and strengthening economy, demand for chicken is expected to continue to be strong.

EXHIBIT 2    **Pilgrim's U.S. and Mexico Sales**

|  | 1999 | 1998 | 1997 | 1996 |
|---|---|---|---|---|
| Sales: |  |  |  |  |
| United States | $1,102,903 | $1,053,458 | $1,002,652 | $ 911,181 |
| Mexico | 254,500 | 278,087 | 274,997 | 228,129 |
| Total Sales | $1,357,403 | $1,331,545 | $1,277,649 | $1,239,310 |
| Operating income (loss): |  |  |  |  |
| United States | $ 88,177 | $ 36,279 | $ 29,321 | $ 29,705 |
| Mexico | 21,327 | 40,977 | 34,573 | (8,201) |
| Total Income | $ 109,504 | $ 77,256 | $ 63,894 | $ 21,504 |
| Identifiable assets: |  |  |  |  |
| United States | — | 424,591 | 404,213 | 363,543 |
| Mexico | — | $ 176,848 | $ 174,911 | $ 173,179 |

*Source:* www.freeedgar.com

## THE BROILER INDUSTRY

The domestic integrated broiler industry encompasses the breeding, growing, processing, and marketing of chicken products. The production of poultry is one of the largest agricultural industries in the United States. Prior to World War II, the broiler industry was highly fragmented with numerous small, independent breeders, growers, and processors. The industry has experienced consolidation during the past five decades and now has a relatively small number of larger, more integrated companies. Integration of the industry led to lower profit margins at each independent production stage and enhanced the need for coordination between stages.

The broiler industry is characterized by intense price competition, resulting in an emphasis on improving genetic, nutritional, and processing technologies in an effort to minimize production costs. These factors, coupled with the feed-conversion advantages of chickens, have enabled the industry to enjoy consistently lower production costs per pound than other competing meats. As an example of the adoption of improved methods and technology, certain industry participants have moved toward product packaging at the plant level, including deep-chill processing as an alternative to ice-packing whole chickens and shipping in bulk form. Deep-chill processing rapidly lowers the temperatures of chickens to slightly above freezing and extends freshness and shelf life.

### Profitability

Industry profitability is primarily a function of consumption of chicken and competing meats and the costs of feed grains. Historically, the broiler industry operated on a fairly predictable cycle of about three years—a year of good profits, followed by a year of expanded output and declining profits, followed by a year of losses and production cuts.

The chicken companies have spent much of their energy trying to escape the commodity cycle through marketing. Frank Perdue, with his classic commercials, was the first to demonstrate that a company could charge a premium for a brand-name bird. Today the biggest producers all play the brand-loyalty game. This leaves the chicken producers in an odd situation: They are commodities concerns trying to behave like consumer products companies. As Prudential-Bache's John McMillin foretold in the 1980s, "The 1990s chicken industry will be better capitalized, more competitive, and less profitable." The prediction came true.

Industry profitability can be significantly influenced by feed costs, which are influenced by a number of factors unrelated to the broiler industry, including legislation that provides discretion to the federal government to set price and income supports for grain. Historically, feed costs have averaged approximately 50 percent of total production costs of non-value-added products and have fluctuated substantially with the price of corn, milo, and soybean meal. By comparison, feed costs typically average approximately 25 percent of total production costs of further-processed and prepared chicken products such as nuggets, fillets, and deli products and, as a result, increased emphasis on sales of such products by chicken producers reduces the sensitivity of earnings to feed cost movements.

Although feed costs may vary dramatically, the production costs of chicken are not as severely affected by changing feed ingredient prices as are the production costs of beef and pork. Chickens require approximately two pounds of dry feed to produce one pound of meat, compared to cattle and hogs, which require approximately seven to three pounds, respectively, of feed.

### Problems

Across the southeastern United States, where 85 percent of the country's chickens are processed, the poultry industry is brooding over a barrage of bad publicity. Chicken processing plants are said to be dirty; rotten meat is reaching the market; *salmonella*-tainted chickens are poisoning people; and the chicken growers who contract with the processors are being ripped off. Even Ross Perot publicly lambasted Bill Cinton's gubernatorial record by saying that the Arkansas poultry business is "not an industry of tomorrow."

Leaders of the South's largest agribusiness concede that they have a problem. In September 1993, a coalition of the Arkansas Poultry Federation, Hudson Foods, Pilgrim's Pride, and Tyson Foods ran full-page ads in several Arkansas newspapers to counter the problem. Its main caption was "Here in Arkansas, It Wasn't a Goose That Laid the Golden Egg. It Was a Chicken." It further stated that one out of twelve working Arkansans was employed by the poultry industry; poultry was a $3 billion-plus industry in Arkansas; salaries and benefits averaged more than $25,000 per employee; and the poultry industry was the largest taxpayer in Arkansas.

The industry's biggest worry may be microscopic in physical size. Chickens often live in their own dung, which, in turn, encourages the growth of bacteria such as *salmonella* and *compylobacter,* which, in turn, contaminate the meat during processing. About 6 million Americans are made ill by such bacteria every year, and about 1,300 die. Scientists at the Centers for Disease Control say chickens may be the cause in up to half of those cases.

The industry's high-tech, fast-paced production lines, which process some 200,000 birds a day at a single plant, heighten fecal contamination. Bacteria often spread from bird to bird as they speed along conveyors from hot collective baths through wet mechanical feather pickers to tanks of cold water. Partly to hold down the price of poultry, the industry has not tried to produce cleaner chickens but instead relies on consumers to cook the meat thoroughly.

Injury and illness rates for poultry workers are double the rates of manufacturing workers generally according to the Labor Department. And new technology often is used to reduce stress for chickens—to make their meat more tender—rather than for workers. "The industry has one foot in the twenty-first century when it comes to chickens, but they left one foot back in the nineteenth century when it comes to people," stated Bob Hall, research director for the Institute for Southern Studies, a labor-funded advocacy group in Durham, North Carolina.

Conditions for the production-line workers can be tough. Repetitive motion from such tasks as pulling out chicken guts can cause disabling injuries. Employees frequently spend shifts in either a freezing cooler or 95° F heat. Conditions can be so crowded that blood from a chicken that one worker handles sometimes can splash onto a coworker. The line speed—up to 90 chickens a minute—is double the rate of a decade ago.

In the past 20 years, the number of major U.S. processors decreased from more than 3000 to about 45. This consolidation resulted in a highly centralized and vertically integrated industry in which the five top players control 54 percent of American production. As a result, the country has been carved up into regional buying monopolies, and each region's dominant processor can dictate terms to the growers.

The processors provide growers with chicks and feed and then slaughter and market the birds. The growers provide chicken houses, utilities, and labor. The growers receive only short-term contracts from the processors with no formal assurances of long-term business relationships.

A recent report from the Texas Commissioner of Agriculture concluded that although "the grower makes a substantial capital investment and takes most of the risk, he or she is not sharing in the success of the industry." In some cases, growers have received as little as $579 in annual income from a 20,000-bird-capacity chicken house.

The processors defend their practices. Industry spokespeople point out that growers are guaranteed a certain price for adult chickens, typically about 3.5¢ to 4¢ a pound. Thus, the processors contend, growers are sheltered from much of the risk of the volatile chicken market. Bill Roenigk, spokesperson for the National Broiler Council, a processor trade group, says studies have shown that chicken farmers' average return on investment is 5 percent or higher than that in many other agriculture operations.

### Changing Demand and Supply

Chicken has experienced greater growth in per-capita consumption than most other major meat categories over the last 25 years. Chicken consumption has increased more than 110 percent, and beef consumption has dropped about 34 percent. The USDA estimates that chicken consumption will increase at a 3 percent compounded annual growth rate into the future.

The major factors influencing this growth are consumer awareness of the health and nutritional characteristics of chicken, the price advantage of chicken relative to red meat, and the convenience of further processed and prepared chicken products. The principal health and nutritional characteristics include lower levels of fat, cholesterol, and calories per pound for chicken relative to red meat. When compared with other meats, chicken has a significant price advantage, which has increased over time.

Recent growth in the consumption of chicken has been enhanced by new product forms and packaging that increase convenience and product versatility. A larger, more affluent, mobile population has created a demand for more convenient foods. These products typically undergo one or more further processing steps, including deboning, forming, battering, breading, and cooking. People are willing to trade dollars for time, and the industry has cashed in by providing value-added products.

Many projections show chicken consumption per person in the United States to reach 100 pounds by the year 2005. Consumption is currently 38 pounds per capita in Mexico and is projected to grow by 10 percent per year.

The poultry sector isn't solely chicken; it also includes turkey, duck, goose, and quail. But the poultry industry in America is chicken-driven. Last year, chicken nuggets accounted for about 10 percent of total U.S. broiler output and showed chicken companies what could happen if they went beyond selling what are called, in the trade, "feathers-off, guts-out birds."

Chicken, priced pound per pound, is one third the cost of beef and one half the cost of pork. Non-value-added chickens are selling for less than they did in 1923, when Wilmer Steele of Ocean View, Delaware, sold what industry historians say was the nation's first flock of commercial broilers for 62¢ a pound. Why is chicken cheaper than the competition? The answer has to do with the fact that a chicken is highly efficient at converting feed to flesh. As noted, to produce a pound of meat, a chicken consumes less than two pounds of feed, compared with six or seven pounds for a cow and three for a pig.

Also, a chicken doesn't live long. The shorter a creature's life cycle, the quicker its generations can be manipulated genetically. Chicken breeders steadily have developed birds that grow bigger on less feed in less time. Breeders may be approaching the limits of practicality on this score; modern chickens have "put on so much weight that they have some real problems mating," said Walter Becker, professor emeritus of genetics and cell biology at Washington State University.

Furthermore, chickens don't graze. Raising cattle requires an investment in land; raising chickens doesn't. Chickens used to need to run around in the sun; otherwise, they would develop a vitamin D deficiency and rickets. By the 1920s, poultry producers had solved the vitamin D problem by adding cod-liver oil to chicken feed. Since then, they have been able to raise thousands of chickens in confinement, allowing about 0.7 square feet per bird.

## THE FUTURE

During the next few years, per-capita consumption of chicken could more than double throughout the world. In 1996, poultry consumption for Russia, Japan, and China was 16, 28, and 7 pounds per person, respectively.

Russia's per-capita consumption of poultry is about equal to the rate at which Americans consumed chicken and turkey in 1910. In 1997, the United States exported $793 million of poultry to Russia. Russians prefer dark meat four times out of five, so a quarter of all American chicken legs is sent to Russia.

In the domestic market, fewer and fewer meals consumed at home are made from scratch. In 1999, Americans spent approximately $970 million a day eating out. With 70 percent of mothers working outside of the home and 40 percent of consumers not knowing what they will eat as late as four o'clock in the afternoon, meal planning and preparation take a back seat to convenience and eating out.

Overseas markets are always unpredictable. During 1996, in response to planned U.S. sanctions on textiles and electronics, China threatened to impose an additional 100 percent tariff on top of its existing 45 percent levy on U.S. poultry. Russia briefly banned U.S. chicken imports in 1996 and only recently backed off a threat to impose quotas.

Concern for healthy food may be slackening. Some say nutrition is on the back burner, with taste the big thing. One analyst recently commented, "A few years back, when everyone was concerned about health and diet, the fast-food restaurants started wringing fat from hamburgers, but sales dropped because they had less and less flavor. So restaurants took bacon and slapped slices of that on the sandwiches, and sales took off like gangbusters." The increasing size of meals served in restaurants is but another sign that fat may be back.

In June of 1998, Pilgrim's created a new stock—Pilgrim's Pride Class A common stock. It can be used either to raise capital or to make acquisitions. This may help confront Tyson's aggressive acquisition strategy.

Also in 1998, the company appointed David Van Hoose their new CEO, president, and COO. Mr. Hoose was previously Pilgrim's Pride president of Mexican Operations. "Bo" Pilgrim remains the chairman of the board. The company's stated objectives are to increase sales, profit margins, and earnings and outpace the growth of the chicken industry by focusing on growth in the prepared-food products market, by focusing on growth in the Mexico market and through greater utilization of the company's existing assets.

EXHIBIT 3    Pilgrim's Pride Annual Balance Sheet
(in millions, except book value per share)

|  | 9/30/99 | 9/30/98 | 9/30/97 | 9/30/96 |
|---|---|---|---|---|
| **Assets** | | | | |
| Cash and equivalents | $ 15.70 | $ 25.12 | $ 20.34 | $ 18.04 |
| Receivables | 84.36 | 81.81 | 77.97 | 65.89 |
| Notes receivable | 0 | 0 | 0 | 0 |
| Inventories | 168.03 | 141.68 | 146.18 | 136.87 |
| Other current assets | 10.28 | 9.91 | 6.66 | 8.47 |
| **Total current assets** | **278.39** | **258.53** | **251.15** | **229.26** |
| Net property and equipment | 363.73 | 331.14 | 309.88 | 288.64 |
| Investments and advances | 0 | 0 | 0 | 0 |
| Other noncurrent assets | 0 | 0 | 0 | 0 |
| Deferred charges | 0 | 0 | 0 | 0 |
| Intangibles | 0 | 0 | 0 | 0 |
| Deposits and other assets | 13.63 | 11.75 | 18.09 | 18.83 |
| **Total assets** | **$655.76** | **$601.43** | **$579.12** | **$536.72** |
| **Liabilities and shareholders' equity** | | | | |
| Notes payable | 0 | 0 | 0 | 27.00 |
| Accounts payable | 81.58 | 70.06 | 71.22 | 71.35 |
| Current portion long-term debt | 4.35 | 5.88 | 11.60 | 8.85 |
| Current portion capital leases | 0 | 0 | 0 | 0 |
| Accrued expenses | 38.21 | 35.53 | 34.78 | 33.60 |
| Income taxes payable | 0 | 0 | 0 | 0 |
| Other current liabilities | 0 | 0 | 0 | 0 |
| **Total current liabilities** | **124.15** | **111.49** | **117.61** | **140.80** |
| Mortgages | 0 | 0 | 0 | 0 |
| Deferred taxes/income | 52.70 | 58.40 | 53.42 | 53.61 |
| Convertible debt | 0 | 0 | 0 | 0 |
| Long-term debt | 183.75 | 199.78 | 224.74 | 198.33 |
| Noncurrent capital leases | 0 | 0 | 0 | 0 |
| Other noncurrent liabilities | 0 | 0 | 0 | 0 |
| Minority interest (liabilities) | 0.88 | 0.88 | 0.84 | 0.84 |
| **Total liabilities** | **$361.50** | **$370.56** | **$396.61** | **$393.59** |
| **Shareholders' equity** | | | | |
| Preferred stock | 0 | 0 | 0 | 0 |
| Common stock (Par) | 0.41 | 0.27 | 0.28 | 0.28 |
| Capital surplus | 79.62 | 79.76 | 79.76 | 79.76 |
| Retained earnings | 214.22 | 150.83 | 102.48 | 63.10 |
| Other equity | 0 | 0 | 0 | 0 |
| Treasury stock | 0 | 0 | 0 | 0 |
| Total shareholders' equity | 294.25 | 230.87 | 182.52 | 143.13 |
| **Total liabilities and shareholders' equity** | **655.76** | **601.43** | **579.12** | **536.72** |
| Total common equity | 294.25 | 230.87 | 182.52 | 143.13 |
| Average shares | 41.38 | 41.38 | 41.38 | 41.38 |
| Book value per share | $  7.11 | $  5.58 | $  4.41 | $  3.46 |

*Source:* www.freeedgar.com

EXHIBIT 4    Pilgrim's U.S. Sales by Segment (in thousands)

| | *Fiscal Year Ended* | | | | |
| | 1999 | 1998 | 1997 | 1996 | 1995 |
|---|---|---|---|---|---|
| U.S. Chicken Sales: | | | | | |
| Prepared Foods: | | | | | |
| Food Service | $  530,340 | $  420,396 | $  348,961 | $  305,250 | $241,594 |
| Retail | 28,254 | 46,400 | 42,289 | 43,442 | 39,071 |
| Total Prepared Foods | 558,594 | 466,796 | 391,250 | 348,692 | 280,665 |
| Fresh Chicken: | | | | | |
| Food Service | 125,395 | 145,297 | 174,103 | 145,377 | 140,433 |
| Retail | 161,180 | 162,283 | 153,554 | 141,876 | 138,950 |
| Total Fresh Chicken | 286,575 | 307,580 | 327,657 | 287,253 | 279,383 |
| Export and Other | 118,327 | 139,976 | 142,030 | 140,614 | 113,414 |
| Total U.S. Chicken | 963,496 | 914,352 | 860,937 | 776,559 | 673,462 |
| Mexico | 254,500 | 278,087 | 274,997 | 228,129 | 159,491 |
| Total Chicken Sales | 1,217,996 | 1,192,439 | 1,135,934 | 1,004,688 | 832,953 |
| Sales of Other U.S. Products | 139,407 | 139,106 | 141,715 | 134,622 | 98,853 |
| Total Net Sales | $1,357,403 | $1,331,545 | $1,277,649 | $1,139,310 | $931,806 |

*Source:* www.freeedgar.com

EXHIBIT 5    Pilgrim's U.S. Sales by Segment (in percentage)

| | *Fiscal Year Ended* | | | | |
| | 1999 | 1998 | 1997 | 1996 | 1995 |
|---|---|---|---|---|---|
| U.S. Chicken Sales: | | | | | |
| Prepared Foods: | | | | | |
| Foodservice | 55.1% | 46.0% | 40.5% | 39.3% | 35.9% |
| Retail | 2.9 | 5.1 | 4.9 | 5.6 | 5.8 |
| Total Prepared Foods | 58.0 | 51.1 | 45.4 | 44.9 | 41.7 |
| Fresh Chicken: | | | | | |
| Foodservice | 13.0 | 15.9 | 20.2 | 18.7 | 20.9 |
| Retail | 16.7 | 17.7 | 17.9 | 18.3 | 20.6 |
| Total Fresh Chicken | 29.7 | 33.6 | 38.1 | 37.0 | 41.5 |
| Export and Other | 12.3 | 15.3 | 16.5 | 18.1 | 16.8 |
| Total U.S. Chicken Sales Mix | 100.0% | 100.0% | 100.0% | 100.0% | 100.0% |

*Source:* www.freeedgar.com

# H. J. HEINZ COMPANY—2000

Henry H. Beam
Western Michigan University

## HNZ
### www.heinz.com

H. J. Heinz Company is a worldwide provider of processed food products. Headquartered in Pittsburgh, Pennsylvania, Heinz has 38,600 employees and markets 5,700 varieties of food products in more than 200 countries. It has manufacturing facilities in 21 countries. Heinz reported sales of $9.3 billion and net income of $474 million in its fiscal year ending April 28, 1999. Over the years, Heinz has expanded its core businesses and continues to grow through selected acquisitions. In addition to ketchup, its original and best-known product, Heinz's product mix includes sauces, pet food, baby food, frozen potatoes, snacks, canned tuna, other condiments, and soup. In 1999, Boston Chicken, parent company of the Boston Market restaurant chain, licensed H. J. Heinz Company to make and sell packaged food products bearing the Boston Market name. Heinz competes with many other major food companies such as Campbell Soup, ConAgra, Nabisco, Sara Lee, Quaker Oats, Kellogg, Archer Daniels, and General Mills.

## HISTORY

In 1869, Henry J. Heinz formed a partnership with his friend, L. C. Noble, to sell grated horseradish fresh from his family's garden in western Pennsylvania. The firm soon moved to Pittsburgh and continued to grow until the overextended enterprise was forced into bankruptcy by the banking panic of 1875. Heinz paid all related debts before founding a new business, F. & J. Heinz, with his cousin and brother that same year. In its first year, the company produced pickles, horseradish, and what would become a world-renowned product—bottled ketchup. By 1888 Heinz gained financial control of the company and changed its name to H. J. Heinz. Heinz put his ketchup in the familiar narrow-necked bottle to make it easier to pour and to reduce the amount of contact with air, which darkened the sauce. He deliberately used a clear bottle so consumers could see that it did not contain any impurities, a dedication to quality that Heinz has maintained ever since. In 1895, a 17-ounce "Imperial Bottle" of ketchup was introduced with a delicately embossed symmetrical shape to appeal to higher-end hotels, restaurants, and upper-income families. A succession of prepared products followed. Heinz had discovered that most people were willing to let someone else take over a share of their kitchen operations and that a pure product of superior quality will find a ready market if properly packaged and promoted.

While traveling on a New York City elevated train in 1896, Heinz saw a shoe store sign advertising "21 styles." He liked the phrase and came up with the slogan "57 varieties" to describe what his company produced. The H. J. Heinz Company already produced more than 57 varieties, but Heinz used the phrase anyway because he liked the sound of "57." Heinz then drew a streetcar ad featuring the slogan. The public latched onto the slogan, which is displayed on the Heinz label to this day. In 1910, Heinz added a small dark-green pickle on the bottom of the keystone label to further promote product recognition.

When Henry Heinz died in 1919, he was succeeded by his son, Howard, who continued to grow the business internally. The company was run by H. J. Heinz II from 1941–1966. It became a publicly held firm in 1946. By the end of the 1940s, Heinz and ketchup went together naturally. As stated in a 1949 issue of the *Saturday Evening Post,* "Heinz Ketchup, although not the first commercial ketchup, has led the American market for so long that it has determined the shape of almost all ketchup bottles because the public just naturally recognizes that shape as ketchup."

In 1958, Heinz began to make acquisitions in Europe and Mexico as well in the United States. Dr. Anthony J. F. O'Reilly became the company's fifth president and CEO in 1979. Under his guidance, Heinz became a leader in the nutrition and wellness field with the 1978 purchase of Weight Watchers and its development into a global brand. He also created major company production bases in Spain, Portugal, and New Zealand. Locations of its major facilities are given in Exhibit 1. In 1998, William R. Johnson assumed the positions of president and CEO from Dr. O'Reilly, who retained his position as chairman.

---

EXHIBIT 1    **H. J. Heinz Company and Subsidiaries:**
**World Locations as of April 28, 1999**

---

**World Headquarters**
600 Grant Street, Pittsburgh, Pennsylvania.

**The Americas**
*Heinz U.S.A.* Established 1869. Pittsburgh, Pennsylvania.
 *Portion Pac, Inc.* Acquired 1989, Mason, Ohio.

*Heinz Frozen Food Company.* Established 1998. Pittsburgh, Pennsylvania.

*Star-Kist Foods, Inc.* Acquired 1963. Newport, Kentucky.
 *Heinz Pet Products.* Established 1988. Newport, Kentucky.
 *StarKist Seafood.* Established 1988. Newport, Kentucky.
 *Star-Kist Caribe, Inc.* Acquired 1963. Mayaguez, Puerto Rico.
 *Star-Kist Samoa, Inc.* Acquired 1963. Pago Pago, American Samoa.
 *Empresa Pesquera Ecuatoriana.* Acquired 1991. Guayaquil, Ecuador.

*Weight Watchers International, Inc.* Acquired 1978. Woodbury, New York.
 *Cardio-Fitness Corporation.* Acquired 1985. New York, New York.
 *The Fitness Institute Ltd.* Acquired 1988. Willowdale, Ontario, Canada.

**The Americas (cont'd)**
*H. J. Heinz Company of Canada Ltd.* Established 1909. North York, Ontario, Canada.
 *Omstead Foods Limited.* Acquired 1991. Wheatley, Ontario, Canada.
 *Shady Maple Farm Ltd.* Acquired 1989. LaGuadeloupe, Quebec, Canada.
 *Martin Pet Foods.* Acquired 1996. Elmira, Ontario, Canada.

*Alimentos Heinz C.A.* Established 1959. Caracas, Venezuela.

**Europe and Africa**
*H. J. Heinz European Grocery.* Established 1995. Stockley Park, Middlesex, England.
 *H. J. Heinz Company Limited.* Established 1917. Stockley Park, Middlesex, England.
 *H. J. Heinz B.V.* Acquired 1958. Elst. Gelderland, The Netherlands.
 *H. J. Heinz Branch Belgium.* Established 1984. Brussels, Belgium.
 *H. J. Heinz GmbH.* Established 1970. Cologne, Germany.
 *Sonnen Bassermann.* Acquired 1998. Seesen, Germany.
 *H. J. Heinz S.A.R.L.* Established 1979. Paris, France.
 *H. J. Heinz S.A.* Established 1987. Madrid, Spain.
 *IDAL (Industrias de Alimentação, Lda).* Acquired 1965. Lisbon, Portugal.
 *COPAIS Food and Beverage Company S.A.* Acquired 1990. Athens, Greece.
 *Heinz Polska Sp. Z.O.O.* Established 1994. Warsaw, Poland.
 *Cario Food Industries SAE.* Established 1992. Cairo, Egypt.

*Continued*

## Europe and Africa (cont'd)

*H. J. Heinz European Infant Feeding.* Established 1999. Stockley Park, Middlesex, England.

*Heinz Italia S.r.l. (formerly Plasmon Dietetici Alimentari S.r.l.).* Acquired 1963. Milan, Italy.

*H. J. Heinz Company Limited.* Established 1917. Stockley Park, Middlesex, England.

*Farley's Healthcare Products.* Acquired 1994. Kendal, Cumbria, England.

*Fattoria Scaldasole S.p.A.* Acquired 1996. Monguzzo, Italy.

*H. J. Heinz Company C.I.S.* Establisheded 1994. Moscow, Russia.

*H. J. Heinz European Foodservice.* Established 1997. Stockley Park, Middlesex, England.

*Heinz Single Serve Limited.* Acquired 1995. Telford, England.

*Serv-A-Portion.* Acquired 1999. Turnhout, Belgium.

*AIAL (Arimpex Industrie Alimentari S.r.l.).* Acquired 1992. Rovereto, Italy.

*Dega S.r.l.* Acquired 1994. Rovereto, Italy.

*H. J. Heinz European Frozen and Chilled.* Established 1997. Stockley Park, Middlesex, England.

*H. J. Heinz European Frozen and Chilled Foods Limited.* Established 1993. Dundalk, Ireland.

*H. J. Heinz Company (Ireland) Limited.* Incorporated 1966. Dublin, Ireland.

*H. J. Heinz European Seafood.* Established 1997. Paris, France.

*H. J. Heinz Company Limited.* Established 1917. Stockley Park, Middlesex, England.

*John West Foods Limited.* Acquired 1997. Liverpool, England.

*Pioneer Food Cannery Ltd.* Acquired 1995. Tema, Ghana.

*Indian Ocean Tuna, Ltd.* Acquired 1995. Victoria, Republic of Seychelles.

*Ets. Paul Paulet S.A.* Acquired 1981. Douarnenez, France.

*IDAL (Industrias de Alimentação, Lda.) Fish Division.* Acquired 1988. Peniche, Portugal.

*Mareblu S.r.l.* Acquired 1996. Latina, Italy.

*H. J. Heinz Central Eastern Europe.* Established 1994.

*H. J. Heinz Company C.I.S.* Established 1994. Moscow, Russia.

*Heinz Polska Sp. Z.0.0.* Established 1994. Warsaw, Poland.

*Pudliszki S.A.* Acquired 1997. Pudliszki, Poland.

*Kecskemeti Konzervgyar Rt.* Acquired 1992. Kecskemet, Hungary.

*Heinz P.M.V.* Acquired 1995. Zabreh, Czech Republic.

*H. J. Heinz Southern Africa (Proprietary) Limited.* Established 1995. Johannesburg, South Africa.

*H. J. Heinze (Botswana) (Proprietary) Ltd.* Formed 1988. Gaborone, Botswana.

*Kgalagadi Soap Industries (PTy) Ltd.* Acquired 1988. Gaborone, Botswana.

*Refined Oil Products (Proprietary) Ltd.* Formed 1987. Gaborone, Botswana.

*Olivine Industries (Private) Limited.* Acquired 1982. Harare, Zimbabwe.

*Chegutu Canners (Pvt) Ltd.* Established 1992. Chegutu, Zimbabwe.

*Heinz South Africa (Pty) Ltd.* Established 1995. Johannesburg, South Africa.

*Pets Products (Pty) Limited.* Acquired 1997. Cape Town, South Africa.

*Heinz Frozen Foods (Pty) Ltd.* Established 1995. Klerksdorp, South Africa.

*Heinz Wellington's (Pty) Ltd.* Acquired 1997. Wellington, South Africa.

## The Pacific Rim and Southwest Asia

*H. J. Heinz Pacific Rim.* Established 1996. Auckland, New Zealand.

*H. J. Heinz Australia Ltd.* Established 1935. Doveton, Victoria, Australia.

*Heinz-Wattie Limited.* Acquired 1992. Auckland, New Zealand.

*Heinz Japan Ltd.* Established 1961. Tokyo, Japan.

*Heinz-UFE Ltd.* Established 1984. Guangzhou, People's Republic of China.

*Seoul-Heinz Ltd.* Established 1986. Inchon, South Korea.

*Heinz Win Chance Ltd.* Established 1987. Bangkok, Thailand.

*Heinz India (Private) Limited.* Acquired 1994. Mumbai, India.

*PT Heinz ABC Indonesia.* Acquired 1999. Jakarta, Indonesia.

*PT Surya Pratista Hutama.* Acquired 1997. Surabaya, Indonesia.

*Source:* H. J. Heinz *Annual Report* 1999.

## PRODUCT CATEGORIES

Heinz has organized its products into six core categories in which it seeks global leadership. Sales data for fiscal years 1997, 1998, and 1999 for each of these segments is given in Exhibit 2. Products with the leading market share position in their respective markets generate about two thirds of the company's sales.

### Foodservice

Heinz is the largest prepared food supplier to the U.S. foodservice market, which consists of restaurants, diners, cafeterias, and other away-from-home eating places. Prepared foods include ketchup, salad dressings, and frozen items such as onion rings, vegetables, and soup concentrate. Ketchup is supplied in bottles, large dispensers, and single-serve packets. Over 10 billion single-serve ketchup packets are used in the United States each year.

The foodservice industry is growing at 3 percent annually in the United States and 10 percent in Europe. Today, U.S. families spend about 50 cents of every food dollar on

---

### EXHIBIT 2    Heinz's Segment Financial Data (in thousands)

A reconciliation of total segment operating income to total consolidated income before income taxes is as follows:

|  | 1999 | 1998 | 1997 |
|---|---|---|---|
| Total operating income for reported segments | $1,109,312 | $1,520,330 | $756,271 |
| Interest income | 25,082 | 32,655 | 39,359 |
| Interest expense | 258,813 | 258,616 | 274,746 |
| Other expense, net | 40,450 | 39,388 | 41,820 |
| Consolidated income before income taxes | $  835,131 | $1,254,981 | $479,064 |

The company's revenues are generated via the sale of products in the following categories:

|  | Ketchup, Condiments and Sauces | Frozen Foods | Tuna | Soups, Beans and Pasta Meals | Infant Foods | Pet Products | Other | Total |
|---|---|---|---|---|---|---|---|---|
| Fiscal year ended April 28, 1999 | $2,230,403 | $1,399,111 | $1,084,847 | $1,117,328 | $1,039,781 | $1,287,356 | $1,140,784 | $9,299,610 |
| Fiscal year ended April 29, 1998 | 2,046,578 | 1,473,228 | 1,080,576 | 1,085,438 | 986,203 | 1,315,774 | 1,221,487 | 9,209,284 |
| Fiscal year ended April 30, 1997 | 1,958,362 | 2,023,058 | 873,610 | 1,021,615 | 1,013,826 | 1,238,109 | 1,228,427 | 9,357,007 |

The company has significant sales and long-lived assets in the following geographic areas. Sales are based on the location in which the sale originated. Long-lived assets include property, plant and equipment, goodwill, trademarks and other intangibles, net of related depreciation, and amortization.

| Fiscal Year Ended | Net External Sales | | | Long-Lived Assets | | |
|---|---|---|---|---|---|---|
|  | 1999 | 1998 | 1997 | April 28, 1999 | April 29, 1998 | April 30, 1997 |
| United States | $4,917,967 | $4,873,710 | $5,169,779 | $2,856,315 | $2,885,359 | $3,075,793 |
| United Kingdom | 1,182,690 | 1,170,935 | 967,644 | 399,669 | 491,850 | 436,709 |
| Other | 3,198,953 | 3,164,639 | 3,219,584 | 1,385,404 | 1,393,505 | 1,397,366 |
| Total | $9,299,610 | $9,209,284 | $9,357,007 | $4,641,388 | $4,770,714 | $4,909,868 |

*Source:* H. J. Heinz *Annual Report* 1999.

meals outside the home, up from about 33 cents in the 1970s. Heinz expects its foodservice business to double in Europe in the next five years. It is also seeking to increase its presence in Asia.

### Infant Foods

The Infant Foods category includes jarred baby foods, cereals, formulas, juices, and biscuits. In the United States, Heinz's market share is about 17 percent on sales of $100 million, considerably behind industry leader Gerber (a division of Swiss-based Novartis) but ahead of Beechnut (a division of Ralcorp Holdings). However, Heinz is the market leader outside the United States. It has over half of the infant food market in Australia, Canada, Italy, New Zealand, and the United Kingdom. It has also expanded its infant feeding business in Eastern Europe, Russia, India, and China. In 1995, Heinz built a $20 million baby food plant in Russia.

### Ketchup, Condiments, and Sauces

Heinz ketchup has always been the company's flagship brand. The company is the world's largest buyer of tomatoes, a key ingredient for its ketchup and related products, such as steak and barbecue sauce. Each year, it processes more than 2 million tons of tomatoes. It sells more than $1 billion of ketchup (nine billion ounces) around the world and has more than 50 percent of the domestic ketchup market and a third of the worldwide ketchup market. As U.S. fast food chains grow in popularity around the world, so will Heinz ketchup and condiments. Heinz's CEO has a goal "to make Heinz ketchup as ubiquitous as Coca-Cola. Everywhere fast food is sold—whether in Asia, Africa, Europe or the Americas—Heinz ketchup will be there, too."

After a five-year absence from television advertising, Heinz started a $50 million global advertising campaign aimed at increasing consumption of ketchup by teenagers. Children six to twelve years old are the largest consumers of ketchup, followed closely by twelve- to eighteen-year-olds. Households with children consume over twice as much ketchup as households without children. Ketchup is used in many different ways around the world. It is eaten with pasta in Sweden, with rice in Venezuela, and with fish and chips in the United Kingdom. In Eastern Europe, it is put on pizza. Heinz is building a ketchup factory in China to supply its emerging market for prepared foods. Global ketchup sales are expected to increase about 6 percent annually.

Heinz's ketchup faces challenges from salsa and private ketchup brands. Salsa was introduced to American consumers in 1947. It includes an array of sauces that include picante, enchilada, taco, and other chili-based sauces. In the 1990s, salsa outsold ketchup in some retail stores, indicating a change in American tastes. Large food retailers such as Kroger, Jewel, and Meijer's Thrifty Acres offer lower-cost, private-label ketchup which competes directly with Heinz ketchup. Private-label brands can be sold for less because there are no promotion or advertising costs associated with them.

### Pet Products

Heinz Pet Products offers a broad range of cat and dog foods. In 1995, Heinz acquired Quaker Oats' pet food business for $725 million. Its 9-Lives cat food (promoted by Morris the cat) is the market leader. Its dog food brands include Kibbles 'n Bits, Gravy Train, Cycle, and Ken-L Ration. Heinz, Ralcorp, and Nestle-Alpo each have about 20 percent of the domestic pet food business. Heinz also has about 50 percent of the fast-growing and high-margin pet treats market. Its pet treats include Pup-Peroni, Jerky Treats, and Wagwells.

## Tuna

Tuna is a high-quality, low-cost, low-fat source of protein. Heinz wants to become "the tuna supplier to the world." It operates canneries and fishing fleets in each of the oceans in which tuna swim. Heinz's Star-Kist division is the world's largest processor of canned tuna and holds 21 percent of the $5-billion worldwide retail market and 48 percent of the $1.5-billion U.S. retail market. Although the U.S. market for tuna is relatively flat, international tuna sales are growing at about 6 percent per year. In addition to its U.S. seafood business, Heinz operates modern, automated canneries in the Pacific and Indian Oceans, in Africa and in Europe. In June 1997, Heinz acquired John West Foods Limited, the United Kingdom's leading brand of canned tuna and fish. However, it did not acquire John West's operations in South Africa, New Zealand, or Australia.

## Soups, Beans, and Pasta Meals

Heinz is the country's largest producer of private-label soup, with nearly 90 percent of the private-label canned soup market. Campbell Soup Company is by far the largest producer of brand-name canned soups in the United States, with nearly 80 percent of the $2.5 billion U.S. canned soup market.

Heinz attempted to enter the brand name soup business in 1970 in the United States but didn't adequately fund national media advertising. Instead, it soon withdrew from the brand-name soup market in the United States and concentrated on its private-label business. Heinz's profitable private-label soup business in the United States complements its leadership position in branded soups in countries such as Canada, the United Kingdom, Australia, and New Zealand. Heinz is the largest seller of canned beans in the United Kingdom.

## Frozen Foods

Heinz Frozen Foods Company was created in 1999 by combining Ore-Ida Foods (Ore-Ida potatoes and onion rings, Tater Tots and Bagel Bites pizza-topped snacks) and Weight Watchers Gourmet Food Company to form a $1.4 billion business. In 1999, Heinz announced an agreement by which it would sell a frozen version of the popular food entrees found in the 850-unit Boston Market restaurant chain. Heinz will pay Boston Chicken, Boston Market's parent company, a royalty fee based on retail sales as part of a ten-year agreement. William Johnson, Heinz's president and CEO, expressed enthusiasm over the agreement. "Boston Market will be one of the biggest and most exciting new product introductions in the history of Heinz. We expect Boston Market to quickly emerge as a powerful brand for Heinz." Boston Market Home Style Meals will offer premium quality and the convenience of quick and easy preparation at home. Full meals for one person range in price from $3.89 to $4.29, about the same price as the equivalent meal at a Boston Market restaurant.

## FINANCIAL ASPECTS

Heinz has increased its dividend every year for over 20 years. Income statement and balance sheet data are given in Exhibits 3 and 4. Business segment information is given in Exhibit 5. Heinz's fiscal year ends the Wednesday closest to April 30 each year. The figures for 1997 included restructuring charges of $647 million associated with Project Millennia and capital gains of $85 million on sale of assets. The figures for 1999 included charges and implementation costs of $552.8 million associated with the implementation of Operation Excel. Project Millennia, announced in 1997, and Operation

EXHIBIT 3 Consolidated Statements of Income H. J. Heinz Company and Subsidiaries
(in thousands, except per-share data)

| Fiscal Year Ended | April 28, 1999 | April 29, 1998 | April 30, 1997 |
|---|---|---|---|
| | (52 weeks) | (52 weeks) | (52 weeks) |
| *Sales* | $9,299,610 | $9,209,284 | $9,357,007 |
| Cost of products sold | 5,944,867 | 5,711,213 | 6,385,091 |
| Gross profit | 3,354,743 | 3,498,071 | 2,971,916 |
| Selling, general and administrative expenses | 2,245,431 | 1,977,741 | 2,215,645 |
| *Operating income* | 1,109,312 | 1,520,330 | 756,271 |
| Interest income | 25,082 | 32,655 | 39,359 |
| Interest expense | 258,813 | 258,616 | 274,746 |
| Other expense, net | 40,450 | 39,388 | 41,820 |
| Income before income taxes | 835,131 | 1,254,981 | 479,064 |
| Provision for income taxes | 360,790 | 453,415 | 177,193 |
| *Net income* | $ 474,341 | $ 801,566 | $ 301,871 |
| Per Common Share Amounts: | | | |
| Net Income—diluted | $1.29 | $2.15 | $0.81 |
| Net income—basic | $1.31 | $2.19 | $0.82 |
| Cash dividends | $1.34¼ | $1.23½ | $1.13½ |
| Average common shares outstanding—diluted | 367,830,419 | 372,952,851 | 374,043,705 |
| Average common shares outstanding—basic | 361,203,539 | 365,982,290 | 367,470,850 |
| Number of employees | 38,600 | 40,500 | 44,700 |

*Source:* H. J. Heinz *Annual Report* 1999.

EXHIBIT 4 Consolidated Balance Sheets H. J. Heinz Company and Subsidiaries
(in thousands)

| | April 28, 1999 | April 29, 1998 |
|---|---|---|
| **Assets** | | |
| **Current assets:** | | |
| Cash and cash equivalents | $ 115,982 | $ 96,300 |
| Short-term investments, at cost which approximates market | 7,139 | 3,098 |
| Receivables (net of allowances: 1999—$21,633 and 1998—$17,627) | 1,163,915 | 1,071,837 |
| Inventories: | | |
| Finished goods and work-in-process | 1,064,015 | 988,322 |
| Packaging material and ingredients | 345,636 | 340,521 |
| | 1,409,651 | 1,328,843 |
| Prepaid expenses | 154,619 | 167,431 |
| Other current assets | 35,472 | 19,010 |
| Total current assets | 2,886,778 | 2,686,519 |
| **Property, plant and equipment:** | | |
| Land | 48,649 | 51,129 |
| Buildings and leasehold improvements | 798,307 | 806,299 |
| Equipment, furniture and other | 3,227,019 | 3,210,695 |
| | 4,073,975 | 4,068,123 |
| Less accumulated depreciation | 1,902,951 | 1,673,461 |
| Total property, plant and equipment, net | 2,171,024 | 2,394,662 |

EXHIBIT 4    Consolidated Balance Sheets H. J. Heinz Company and Subsidiaries
(in thousands) *(continued)*

| | *April 28, 1999* | *April 29, 1998* |
|---|---|---|
| **Assets** *(cont.)* | | |
| **Other noncurrent assets:** | | |
| Goodwill (net of amortization: 1999—$352,209 and 1998—$297,868) | $1,781,466 | $1,764,574 |
| Trademarks (net of amortization: 1999—$84,672 and 1998—$67,791) | 511,608 | 416,918 |
| Other intangibles (net of amortization: 1999—$117,038 and 1998—$112,768) | 177,290 | 194,560 |
| Other noncurrent assets | 525,468 | 566,188 |
| Total other noncurrent assets | 2,995,832 | 2,942,240 |
| Total assets | $8,053,634 | $8,023,421 |

## Liabilities and shareholders' equity

| | | |
|---|---|---|
| **Current liabilities:** | | |
| Short-term debt | $  290,841 | $  301,028 |
| Portion of long-term debt due within one year | 613,366 | 38,598 |
| Accounts payable | 945,488 | 978,365 |
| Salaries and wages | 74,098 | 66,473 |
| Accrued marketing | 182,024 | 163,405 |
| Accrued restructuring costs | 147,786 | 94,400 |
| Other accrued liabilities | 372,623 | 360,608 |
| Income taxes | 160,096 | 161,396 |
| Total current liabilities | 2,786,322 | 2,164,273 |
| **Long-term debt and other liabilities:** | | |
| Long-term debt | 2,472,206 | 2,768,277 |
| Deferred income taxes | 310,799 | 291,161 |
| Non-pension postretirement benefits | 208,102 | 209,642 |
| Other | 473,201 | 373,552 |
| Total long-term debt and other liabilities | $3,464,308 | $3,642,632 |

## Shareholders' equity:

| | | |
|---|---|---|
| **Capital stock:** | | |
| Third cumulative preferred, $1.70 first series, $10 par value | 173 | 199 |
| Common stock, 431,096,485 shares issued, $.25 par value | 107,774 | 107,774 |
| | 107,947 | 107,973 |
| Additional capital | 277,652 | 252,773 |
| Retained earnings | 4,379,742 | 4,390,248 |
| | 4,765,341 | 4,750,994 |
| **Less:** | | |
| Treasury shares, at cost (71,968 shares at April 28, 1999 and 67,678,632 shares at April 29, 1998) | 2,435,012 | 2,103,979 |
| Unearned compensation relating to the ESOP | 11,728 | 14,822 |
| Accumulated other comprehensive loss | 515,597 | 415,677 |
| Total shareholders' equity | 1,803,004 | 2,216,516 |
| Total liabilities and shareholders' equity | $8,053,634 | $8,023,421 |

*Source:* H. J. Heinz *Annual Report* 1999.

## EXHIBIT 5  Heinz Statements of Income by Segment (in thousands)

Items below the operating income line of the Consolidated Statements of Income are not presented by segment, because they are excluded from the measure of segment profitability reviewed by the company's management.
The following table presents information about the company's reportable segments.

| | North American Dry | North American Frozen | Europe | Asia/ Pacific R/M | Other Operating Entities | Non- Operating | Consolidated Totals |
|---|---|---|---|---|---|---|---|
| **Fiscal year ended April 28, 1999** | | | | | | | |
| Intersegment sales | $ 32,144 | $ 21,131 | $ 6,661 | $ 13 | $ 6,971 | $ (66,920) | — |
| Net external sales | 4,062,683 | 1,014,370 | 2,460,698 | 1,011,764 | 750,095 | — | 9,299,610 |
| Operating income (loss) | 716,979 | 80,231 | 246,187 | 89,830 | 95,715 | (119,630) | 1,109,312 |
| Operating income (loss), exlcuding restructuring related items | 834,629 | 183,409 | 467,159 | 145,654 | 121,950 | (99,792) | 1,653,009 |
| Depreciation and amortization expense | 121,363 | 39,773 | 85,408 | 20,549 | 23,278 | 11,841 | 302,212 |
| Capital expenditures | 138,081 | 35,293 | 100,569 | 25,209 | 12,757 | 4,814 | 316,723 |
| Identifiable assets | 3,418,096 | 832,226 | 2,208,208 | 998,685 | 374,852 | 221,567 | 8,053,634 |
| **Fiscal year ended April 29, 1998** | | | | | | | |
| Intersegment sales | $ 28,492 | $ 14,467 | $ 3,756 | — | $ 6,298 | $ (53,013) | — |
| Net external sales | 3,935,269 | 1,076,080 | 2,332,594 | 1,072,856 | 792,485 | — | 9,209,284 |
| Operating income (loss) | 797,191 | 258,199 | 386,874 | 136,501 | 53,677 | (112,112) | 1,520,330 |
| Operating income (loss), excluding restructuring related items | 825,981 | 170,732 | 405,425 | 142,348 | 63,586 | (100,219) | 1,507,853 |
| Depreciation and amortization expense | 117,739 | 41,855 | 84,583 | 30,406 | 28,291 | 10,748 | 313,622 |
| Capital expenditures | 121,783 | 34,244 | 90,829 | 53,856 | 40,076 | 32,966 | 373,754 |
| Identifiable assets | 3,248,068 | 918,807 | 2,230,857 | 839,176 | 564,391 | 222,122 | 8,023,421 |
| **Fiscal year ended April 30, 1997** | | | | | | | |
| Intersegment sales | $ 34,475 | $ 27,067 | $ 3,430 | — | $ 6,524 | $ (71,496) | — |
| Net external sales | 3,698,797 | 1,551,690 | 2,154,686 | 1,220,885 | 730,949 | — | 9,357,007 |
| Operating income (loss) | 442,461 | (4,698) | 316,563 | 171,577 | (64,291) | (105,341) | 756,271 |
| Operating income (loss), excluding restructuring related items | 707,861 | 130,402 | 375,218 | 136,241 | 50,209 | (81,742) | 1,318,189 |
| Depreciation and amortization expense | 128,930 | 58,030 | 81,850 | 30,684 | 30,517 | 10,479 | 340,490 |
| Capital expenditures | 118,377 | 63,682 | 107,166 | 38,415 | 48,565 | 1,252 | 377,457 |
| Identifiable assets | $3,309,675 | $1,324,293 | $2,015,296 | $1,017,875 | $571,711 | $198,937 | $8,437,787 |

*Source:* Notes to Consolidated Financial Statements

Excel, announced in 1999, are global restructuring and growth initiatives designed to increase competitiveness, reduce costs, and increase sales. Advertising costs for fiscal years ending in 1999, 1998, and 1997 were $373.9 million, $363.1 million, and $319.0 million, respectively.

Throughout the world, Heinz affiliates have contributed to the welfare of their communities. In 1999, the H. J. Heinz Company Foundation gave $6.3 million in grants to 820 organizations. In June 1999, Heinz announced that it would repurchase up to 20 million shares of its common stock. Heinz President and CEO William Johnson commented, "Because Heinz stock is a great value, this is a tangible way of sharing the benefits of our growth plan, Operation Excel, with Heinz shareholders."

## THE FOOD INDUSTRY

H. J. Heinz Company is one of the largest publicly held food companies in the United States as shown in Exhibit 6. Food companies prospered during the 1980s, aided by cost reduction efficiencies, consolidation, and inflation. In the 1990s, inflation, a major factor in sales and earnings increases in the 1980s, fell to a minimal 2 percent or 3 percent per year. Food companies typically employ two basic strategies to increase sales and earnings:

1. *Major acquisitions.* Because it is very difficult to increase market share of an established brand, some firms seek to expand by acquiring complementary brands. Heinz has periodically made purchases or acquisitions that complemented its pet food business (from Quaker Oats in 1995), its foodservice business (acquiring the Moore's and Domani brands of frozen onion rings, vegetables, and pastas in 1994), and its tuna business (acquiring John West Foods in 1997).

2. *Divestment.* Some large, multiproduct companies sought to improve overall efficiency by selling off selected businesses. Ralston Purina created separate stocks for its Ralston-Continental (breakfast foods) and Ralcorp (consumer foods) units. General Mills sold off its seafood and restaurant businesses, leaving itself primarily in the cereal and convenience food businesses. Campbell Soup has divested itself of several low-margin businesses, including pickles and its Swanson line of frozen foods, in order to concentrate on its higher-margined products such as soup. In similar fashion, Heinz sold several of its peripheral businesses, including its Italian confectionery business (1994), its Near East specialty rice business (1994), its Ore-Ida frozen foodservice business (1997), its New Zealand ice cream business (1997), and its bakery products unit (1998).

## CEO WILLIAM R. JOHNSON

In November 1998 William R. Johnson, forty-eight, became president and COO while Dr. O'Reilly retained his position as chairman of the board of directors. Johnson joined Heinz in 1982 after working for two other food-processing firms, Ralston Purina and Anderson Clayton. He made his mark at Heinz by successfully cutting costs in the tuna and pet food businesses. In those jobs, he instituted "price-based costing," whereby he determined first what consumers were willing to pay, then drove costs down to provide adequate margins at that selling price.

When William Johnson took office, Heinz had been criticized by stock market analysts for several years for not doing as much as it could to increase earnings in an environment of low inflation and annual food industry growth of about 1 percent. Sensitive to such criticisms, Johnson quickly took steps to improve Heinz's competitive position. In quick order, he created the Frozen Foods Division by merging Ore-Ida with

Weight Watchers Gourmet Foods, created a unified headquarters in Pittsburgh for Heinz's $5-billion North American food business, combined divisional sales forces in North America into a unified salesforce, and entered into the licensing agreement with Boston Market.

One of Johnson's most significant decisions was to sell the Weight Watchers International weight control meeting business that Dr. O'Reilly had acquired in 1977 and built into the world's largest weight-control service system. Each week, more than one million people attend Weight Watchers meetings. According to Johnson, Weight Watchers was sold after careful analysis because it "does not fit strategically with Heinz. The skills required to manage this retail business are not synergistic with our core competencies." Weight Watchers was profitable in Europe but had not been profitable in the United States in recent years. In September 1999, Heinz announced completion of its sale of the Weight Watchers classroom business to Artel Luxembourg, a European private investment firm, for $735 million. However, Heinz retained its Weight Watchers Smart Ones line of frozen meals, desserts, and breakfast items.

## THE FUTURE

Even with the implementation of Project Millennia and Operation Excel, investors showed little enthusiasm for Heinz stock. Both Chairman O'Reilly and President and CEO Johnson stated the reasons why investors should consider buying Heinz stock in the 1999 H. J. Heinz *Annual Report.* According to Chairman O'Reilly

> Heinz's steady, solid performance amidst change rebuts the shortsighted notion that the recent fascination with the so-called "dot com" should somehow diminish the attractiveness of investments in the food sector. A more insightful, long-range perspective is to see the two sectors as complementary, rather than competitive. The true value of today's technology revolution is its transformative effect on our global society. By shrinking the world, homogenizing its culture and speeding the conveyance of information, technology is expanding tremendously the market opportunities for a global food processor like Heinz.

Johnson added

> Heinz fundamentals are good, and we fit well in any long-term investor's portfolio. This is why there are more "buy" recommendations on our stock than at any time in recent history. Global expansion and our renewed emphasis on marketing and innovation will drive our top line. Ketchup is found in virtually every household in America but tops host foods like hot dogs, french fries and hamburgers less than 50 percent of the time. Therefore, our battle really relates to getting people to use *more ketchup.* Our mission states, "A bottle on every table, everywhere."

# HERSHEY FOODS CORPORATION—2000

Forest R. David
Francis Marion University

HSY
www.hersheys.com

## OVERVIEW

Have you ever been to Hershey, Pennsylvania, the home of Hershey Foods Corporation? Known as Chocolate Town, USA, the air in this city actually smells like chocolate. There you can walk down Chocolate Avenue, see sidewalks lit with lights in the shape of Hershey Kisses, visit the Hershey Zoo, and see the chocolate kiss tower in Hershey Park. Hershey's Chocolate World is America's most popular corporate visitor's center.

Hershey has grown from a one-product, one-plant operation in 1894 to a $3.9 billion company producing an array of quality chocolate, nonchocolate confectionary products, and grocery products. Hershey's prominent products are chocolate and nonchocolate confectionery products consisting of bar goods, bagged items, and boxed items. Hershey grocery products include baking ingredients, peanut butter, chocolate drink mixes, dessert toppings, and beverages. Hershey markets these products under more than 50 different brands such as Hershey Bar, Mr. GoodBar, Reese's, Kit Kat, Kisses and Mounds.

Hershey in 1999 sold 94 percent of its U.S. pasta business to New World Pasta for $450 million. Hershey had the largest pasta business in the United States, which had provided the company with growth and substantial cash flow. However, Hershey decided it could maximize shareholders' wealth more efficiently by concentrating solely on confectionery and related grocery products.

Hershey at year-end 1999 is in unfamiliar territory behind M&M Mars in the confectionery market. Previously the largest candy maker, Hershey has slipped below Mars in market share. Reasons for Hershey's decline stem from its poor marketing strategies and inability to meet demand during Halloween and Christmas 1999. Lack of new "seasonal" products to captivate customer interest furthered Hershey's demise. Earnings increased 35 percent in 1999, but Hershey's sales were down 10 percent.

Almost 90 percent of Hershey's sales are generated in domestic markets. Hershey remains inexperienced, ineffective, and uncommitted in markets outside the United States, Mexico, and Canada, even though the candy industry has globalized. Mars, Borden, Nestle, and other competitors all have a growing and effective presence in international markets. In contrast, Hershey recently divested its two main European businesses, Gubor in Germany and Sperlari in Italy, and its Canadian Planters business. Analysts question whether Hershey can continue to survive as a domestic producer of candy while its competitors gain economies of scale and learning in world markets. Shareholders are becoming concerned too. Hershey needs a clear strategic plan to guide future operations and decisions.

## HISTORY

Milton Hershey's love for candy making began with a childhood apprenticeship under candymaker Joe Royer of Lancaster, Pennsylvania. Hershey was eager to own a candy-making business. After numerous attempts and even bankruptcy, he finally gained success in the caramel business. Upon seeing the first chocolate-making equipment at the Chicago Exhibition in 1893, Mr. Hershey envisioned endless opportunities for the chocolate industry.

By 1901, the chocolate industry in America was growing rapidly. Hershey's sales reached $662,000 that year, creating the need for a new factory. Hershey moved his company to Derry Church, Pennsylvania, a town that was renamed Hershey in 1906. The new Hershey factory provided a means of mass-producing a single chocolate product. In 1909, the Milton Hershey School for Orphans was founded. The Hersheys were childless, and for years the Hershey Chocolate Company operated mainly to provide funds for the orphanage. Hershey's sales reached $5 million in 1911.

In 1927, the Hershey Chocolate Company was incorporated under the laws of the state of Delaware and listed on the New York Stock Exchange. That same year, 20 percent of Hershey's stock was sold to the public. Between 1930 and 1960, Hershey went through rapid growth; the name "Hershey" became a household word. The legendary Milton Hershey died in 1945.

In the 1960s, Hershey acquired the H. B. Reese Candy Company, which makes Reese's Peanut Butter Cups, Reese's Pieces, and Reese's Peanut Butter Chips. Hershey also acquired San Giorgio Macaroni and Delmonico Foods, both pasta manufacturers. In 1968, Hershey Chocolate Corporation changed its name to Hershey Foods Corporation. Between 1976 and 1984, William Dearden served as Hershey's chief executive officer. An orphan who grew up in the Milton Hershey School for Orphans, Dearden diversified the company to reduce its dependence on fluctuating cocoa and sugar prices.

Hershey purchased Nacional de Dulces and renamed this company Hershey Mexico, which today produces, imports, and markets chocolate products for the Mexican market under the Hershey brand name. In 1996, Hershey acquired Leaf North America to gain market-share leadership in North America in nonchocolate confectioneries.

Hershey Foods' mission statement in the 1980s was

> Hershey Foods Corporation's mission is to become a major diversified food company and a leading company in every aspect of our business as:
> The number-one confectionery company in North America, moving toward worldwide confectionery market share leadership.
> A respected and valued supplier of high quality, branded consumer food products in North America and selected international markets.

Hershey's mission statement today has been modified and reads as follows.

> To be a focused food company in North America and selected international markets and a leader in every aspect of our business.

Note that the current statement is shorter and backs off from aspiring to be a world leader in the confectionery industry. It also lacks a number of components generally included in a good mission statement.

## DIVISIONS

### Hershey Chocolate and Grocery North America

This division combines Hershey's Mexico, Canadian, and U.S. operations and generates about 90 percent of total company sales. Hershey's U.S. confectionery manufacturing operations are located in

Hershey, Pennsylvania
Oakdale, California
Stuarts Draft, Virginia
Lancaster, Pennsylvania
Robinson, Illinois

Hershey's Leaf facilities and Henry Heide's confectionery operations are located in the last four cities in the previous list. Canadian operations are located in Smith Falls, Ontario; Montreal, Quebec; and Dartmouth, Nova Scotia. Mexican operations are in Guadalajara, Mexico.

Hershey Chocolate and Grocery North America produces an extensive line of chocolate and nonchocolate products sold in the form of single bars, bagged goods, and boxed items. Hershey introduced its first full-line boxed chocolate, Pot of Gold, in late 1996. These products are marketed under more than fifty brand names and sold in over two million retail outlets in the United States, including grocery wholesalers, chain stores, mass merchandisers, drugstores, vending companies, wholesale clubs, convenience stores, and food distributors. Sales to Wal-Mart stores account for 15 percent of Hershey's total revenues.

The U.S. confectionery market is growing only 2 percent annually in sales volume. The nonchocolate segment, which accounts for about one third of the overall sweets market, is growing at 5 percent annually, and the chocolate segment is growing at 1 percent. Hershey has only 4 percent of the nonchocolate confectionery market, and the leader is RJR Nabisco with 18 percent. RJR's Life Savers and Gummy Life Savers compete with Hershey's Amazin' Fruit Gummy Bears.

## Hershey International

This division has been a trouble spot for Hershey. Hershey exports confectionery and grocery products to over 90 countries outside of North America. Europeans have the highest per-capita chocolate consumption rates in the world, but Hershey has no plans to overtake or even threaten Nestle or Mars in Europe. In the Far East, Hershey has signed licensing agreements with Selecta Dairy Products to manufacture Hershey's ice cream products in the Philippines and with Kuang Chuan Dairy in Taiwan to manufacture Hershey's beverages. Hershey introduced its products into Russia, the Philippines, and Taiwan. Overall in the Far East however, Hershey is not planning sustained efforts because of the perceived high political and economic risks coupled with their lack of experience.

## OPERATIONS

### Social Responsibility

Hershey Foods Corporation is committed to the values of its founder Milton S. Hershey—the highest standard of quality, honesty, fairness, integrity, and respect. The firm makes annual contributions of cash, products, and services to a variety of national and local charitable organizations. Hershey is the sole sponsor of the Hershey National Track and Field Youth Program. Hershey also makes contributions to the Children's Miracle Network, a national program benefiting children's hospitals across the United States.

Hershey operates the Milton Hershey School, whose mission is to provide full-time care and education including all costs of disadvantaged children (mainly orphans). The school currently cares for over 1,000 boys and girls in grades kindergarten through twelve. The Hershey School Trust owns over 75 percent of all Hershey Corporation's common stock.

### Employees

As of December 31, 1999, Hershey had approximately 13,900 full-time and 1,400 part-time employees, of whom approximately 6,400 were covered by collective bargaining agreements. In January 1999, a reduction of approximately 900 full-time and 30 part-time employees resulted from the completion of the sale of the pasta business.

### FINANCE

Hershey's financial statements are provided in Exhibit 1 and Exhibit 2. Note the decline in Hershey's sales in 1999.

### MARKETING

Hershey's marketing strategy is based upon the consistently superior quality of its products, mass distribution, and the best possible consumer value in terms of price and weight. The company devotes considerable resources to the identification, development, testing, manufacturing, and marketing of new products. Hershey has developed a distribution network from its manufacturing plants, distribution centers, and field warehouses strategically located throughout the United States, Canada, and Mexico.

Hershey changes the prices and weights of its products to accommodate changes in manufacturing costs, the competitive environment, and profit objectives while at the same time maintaining consumer value.

EXHIBIT 1    **Hershey Foods Corporation**
**Consolidated Statements of Income**

| For the years ended December 31, | 1999 | 1998 | 1997 |
|---|---|---|---|
| In thousands of dollars except per share amounts | | | |
| *Net Sales* | $3,970,924 | $4,435,615 | $4,302,236 |
| Costs and Expenses | | | |
| Cost of sales | 2,354,724 | 2,625,057 | 2,488,896 |
| Selling, marketing, and administrative | 1,057,840 | 1,167,895 | 1,183,130 |
| Gain on sale of business | (243,785) | — | — |
| Total costs and expenses | 3,168,779 | 3,792,952 | 3,672,026 |
| Income before Interest and Income Taxes | 802,145 | 642,663 | 630,210 |
| Interest expense, net | 74,271 | 85,657 | 76,255 |
| Income before Income Taxes | 727,874 | 557,006 | 553,955 |
| Provision for Income Taxes | 267,564 | 216,118 | 217,704 |
| Net Income | $ 460,310 | $ 340,888 | $ 336,251 |
| Net Income Per Share—Basic | $ 3.29 | $ 2.38 | $ 2.25 |
| Net Income Per Share—Diluted | $ 3.26 | $ 2.34 | $ 2.23 |
| Cash Dividends Paid Per Share: | | | |
| Common Stock | $ 1.00 | $ .920 | $ .840 |
| Class B Common Stock | .905 | .835 | .760 |

*Source:* www.freeedgar.com

## EXHIBIT 2    Hershey's Balance Sheets

| December 31, | 1999 | 1998 |
|---|---|---|
| In thousands of dollars | | |

### Assets

| | 1999 | 1998 |
|---|---|---|
| **Current Assets:** | | |
| Cash and cash equivalents | $ 118,078 | $ 39,024 |
| Accounts receivable—trade | 352,750 | 451,324 |
| Inventories | 602,202 | 493,249 |
| Deferred income taxes | 80,303 | 58,505 |
| Prepaid expenses and other | 126,647 | 91,864 |
| Total current assets | 1,279,980 | 1,133,966 |
| Property, Plant and Equipment, Net | 1,510,460 | 1,648,058 |
| Intangibles Resulting from Business Acquisitions | 450,165 | 530,464 |
| Other Assets | 106,047 | 91,610 |
| Total assets | $3,346,652 | $3,404,098 |

### Liabilities and Stockholders' Equity

| | 1999 | 1998 |
|---|---|---|
| **Current Liabilities:** | | |
| Accounts payable | $ 136,567 | $ 156,937 |
| Accrued liabilities | 292,497 | 294,415 |
| Accrued income taxes | 72,159 | 17,475 |
| Short-term debt | 209,166 | 345,908 |
| Current portion of long-term debt | 2,440 | 89 |
| Total current liabilities | 712,829 | 814,824 |
| Long-term Debt | 878,213 | 879,103 |
| Other Long-term Liabilities | 330,938 | 346,769 |
| Deferred Income Taxes | 326,045 | 321,101 |
| Total liabilities | $2,248,025 | $2,361,797 |

### Stockholders' Equity

| | 1999 | 1998 |
|---|---|---|
| Preferred Stock, shares issued: none in 1999 and 1998 | — | — |
| Common Stock, Shares issued: 149,506,964 in 1999 and 149,502,964 in 1998 | 149,507 | 149,503 |
| Class B Common Stock, shares issued: 30,443,908 in 1999 and 30,447,908 in 1998 | 30,443 | 30,447 |
| Additional paid-in capital | 30,079 | 29,995 |
| Unearned ESOP compensation | (22,354) | (25,548) |
| Retained earnings | 2,513,275 | 2,189,693 |
| Treasury—Common Stock shares, at cost: 41,491,253 in 1999 and 36,804,157 in 1998 | (1,552,708) | (1,267,422) |
| Accumulated other comprehensive loss | (49,615) | (64,367) |
| Total stockholders' equity | 1,098,627 | 1,042,301 |
| Total liabilities and stockholders' equity | $3,346,652 | $3,404,098 |

*Source:* www.freeedgar.com

EXHIBIT 3    Hershey Expense Data and Other (in thousands)

|  | 1999 | 1998 | 1997 |
| --- | --- | --- | --- |
| Advertising | $164,894 | $187,505 | $135,016 |
| Promotion | 395,849 | 469,709 | 202,408 |
| Capital additions | 115,448 | 161,328 | 172,939 |
| Full-time employees | 13,900 | 14,700 | 14,900 |
| Common stock price at year-end | 43¾ | 32½ | 24¾ |
| Sales to Wal-Mart | $605,300 | $619,100 | $529,600 |

*Source:* www.freeedgar.com

Per-capita candy sales in the United States have increased by 7.1 percent over the past five years. Americans spend over $21 billion a year on sweets. Upscale candy items such as Mars' Dove Promises are selling well. People are eating more ethnic foods today than ten years ago, which means more garlic and flavor. Breath-freshener-type candies are selling very well in response to this eating trend.

Conventional wisdom in the candy industry is that a person rarely selects the same candy bar twice in a row; consequently, product variety is crucial to success. Marketing issues relative to health, nutrition, and weight consciousness are important. The media Hershey uses most for advertising are network television, followed by syndicated television, television, magazines, and network and radio.

Confectionery sales are generally lowest during the second quarter of the year and highest during the third and fourth quarters, largely as a result of the holiday seasons. Hershey generates about 20 percent of annual sales during the second quarter and 30 percent of annual sales during the fourth quarter.

## GLOBAL ISSUES

The most significant raw material used in the production of Hershey's chocolate products is cocoa. Cocoa beans are imported principally from West African, South American, and Far Eastern equatorial regions. West Africa accounts for 70 percent of the world's crop. Cocoa beans are not uniform, and the various grades and varieties reflect the diverse agricultural practices and natural conditions in the many growing areas. Hershey buys a mix of cocoa beans to meet its manufacturing requirements. Exhibit 4 revels annual average cocoa prices as well as the highest and lowest monthly averages for 1994 through 1999.

Hershey's second most important commodity for its domestic chocolate and confectionery products is sugar. Due to import quotas and duties imposed to support the price of sugar, sugar prices paid by U.S. users are currently substantially higher than prices on the world sugar market. The average wholesale list price of refined sugar, F.O.B. Northeast, has remained relatively stable in a range of $.27 to $.35 per pound for the past ten years.

Peanut prices remained near normal levels throughout 1999 while almond prices declined to low levels due to a record crop in California. Dairy prices reached historic highs in 1999, reflecting generally poor weather, which adversely affected production and strong demand for cheese and butter.

Hershey also attempts to minimize the effect of price fluctuations on sugar, corn sweeteners, natural gas, and dairy products related to the purchase of its major raw mate-

EXHIBIT 4  **Percent Cocoa Futures Contract Prices**
**(cents per pound)**

|  | 1994 | 1995 | 1996 | 1997 | 1998 | 1999 |
|---|---|---|---|---|---|---|
| Annual Average | 59.1 | 61.2 | 62.1 | 70.0 | 72.7 | 48.8 |
| High | 66.1 | 64.1 | 64.4 | 77.2 | 78.3 | 62.7 |
| Low | 51.3 | 58.3 | 57.4 | 59.1 | 65.5 | 39.6 |

*Source:* www.freeedgar.com

rials primarily through the forward purchasing of such commodities to cover future manufacturing requirements. These periods generally cover 3 to 24 months.

The chocolate and cocoa products industry is SIC 2066, and candy/confectionery is SIC 2064. The main distribution channels for chocolate are grocery, drug, and department stores as well as vending machine operators. Almost all of these distributors are local, regional, or national; only a few are multinational. Although chocolate producers have not yet developed globally uniform marketing programs, the situation is changing. European unification extended grocery and department store channels of distribution. For example, Safeway, a U.S. grocer chain, now operates stores in Canada, Britain, Germany, and Saudi Arabia. As global channels of distribution become more available for chocolate manufacturers, global marketing uniformity will become more prevalent in the industry. Global cultural convergence is accelerating the need for more global marketing uniformity in the confectionery industry. Hershey's competitors are taking advantage of this globalization trend.

The confectionery industry is characterized by high manufacturing economies of scale. Hershey's main chocolate factory, for example, occupies more than two-million-square feet, is highly automated, and contains much heavy equipment, vats, and containers. It is the largest chocolate plant in the world. High manufacturing costs in any industry encourages global market expansion, globally standardized products, and globally centralized production.

The confectionery industry is also characterized by high transportation costs for moving milk and sugar, the primary raw materials. This fact motivates companies such as Hershey to locate near their sources of supply. Because milk can be obtained in large volumes in many countries, chocolate producers have many options in locating plants. Also, producing chocolate is not labor intensive, nor does it require highly skilled labor.

Industry analysts expect the candy industry to continue to grow. Consumption of chocolate, according to industry analysts, is closely related to national income, although the Far East is an exception to this rule. Candy consumption varies in the major markets of the developed nations. Americans consume about 22 pounds of candy annually per person, and Europeans consume about 27 pounds of candy per person.

Chocolate accounts for about 54 percent of all candy consumed. Northern Europeans consume almost twice as much chocolate per capita as Americans. Among European countries, Switzerland, Norway, and the United Kingdom citizens consume the most chocolate, and Finland, the former Yugoslavia, and Italy consume the least. The Japanese also consume very little chocolate—about 1.4 kilos per capita. Throughout Asia and Southern Europe, there is a preference for types of sweets other than chocolate, partly because of high incidence of lactose intolerance (difficulty in digesting dairy products) in such nations.

## COMPETITORS

The $10-billion U.S. confectionery industry is composed of five major competitors who control nearly 70 percent of the market: Hershey, M&M Mars, Brach & Brock, Nestle of Switzerland, and RJR Nabisco. The remaining 30 percent is divided among many local and regional candy manufacturers as shown in Exhibit 5.

Based in Switzerland, Nestle clearly has an edge internationally, being the world leader in many food categories including candy. Almost 98 percent of Nestle's revenues come from international sales. Hershey's other competitors also do much of their business outside North America. For example, Cadbury-Schweppes and Mars each obtain 50 percent of their income from international sales. Hershey's two major candy competitors are Mars and Nestle.

### Mars

Mars has a stronger presence than Hershey in Europe, Asia, Mexico, and Japan. Mars gained 12 percent of the market in Mexico after only one year of entering that market. Analysts estimate Mars' worldwide sales and profits to be over $7 billion and $1 billion, respectively. Mars was successful introducing its Bounty chocolate candy into the United States without prior test marketing. Bounty was originally a European candy. Mars, unlike Hershey, uses uniform marketing globally. For example, the company's M&M candies slogan, "It melts in your mouth, not in your hands," is used worldwide. In contrast, Hershey's successful BarNone candy, for example, is named Temptation in Canada.

Mars is controlled by the Mars family through two brothers, John and Forrest, Jr. Mars is one of the world's largest private, closely held companies. It is a secretive company, unwilling to divulge financial information and corporate strategies. Unlike Hershey, Mars has historically relied upon extensive marketing and advertising expenditures to gain market share rather than on product innovation. Mars has been repackaging, restyling, and reformulating its leading brands, including Snickers, M&M's, Milky Way, and 3 Musketeers, but that strategy is now being supplemented with extensive product development. New Mars products include Bounty, Balisto, and PB Max. It also successfully developed and marketed Snickers ice cream bars. The product was so successful that it dislodged Eskimo Pie and Original Klondike from the number-one ice cream snack slot without any assistance from promotional advertising. Mars has world-class production facilities in Hackettstown, New Jersey; from that plant it ships products worldwide. In addition, it has manufacturing plants in Mexico and in several European locations.

Mars entered Russia in 1992, and today virtually owns the chocolate market there. Hershey is trying to gain a presence in Russia and China but so far is struggling.

EXHIBIT 5    Small Competitors in Candy Industry

| Company | 1998 Sales (in millions) | Percent Change from 1997 |
| --- | --- | --- |
| Bobs Candies | $ 22.2 | −4.1% |
| R. M. Palmer | 19.3 | +5.1 |
| Russell Stover Candies | 17.6 | −12.20 |
| Spangler Candy | 11.4 | −11.1 |
| Frankford Candy/Chocolate | 8.1 | +11.6 |
| Allan Candy | 7.5 | +27.5 |
| Industry Total | $108.4 | −6.0 |

## Nestlé

With annual sales of $7.3 billion in the United States and having recently acquired Carnation, Nestlé is the largest food company in the world. Nestlé's U.S. operations are headquartered in Glendale, California. With corporate headquarters in Vevey, Switzerland, Nestlé is a major competitor in Europe, the Far East, and South America. Nestlé sells products in over 360 countries on all five continents, many of them in the Third World. It is the world's largest instant coffee manufacturer, with Nescafe as the dominant product. Nestlé also produces and markets chocolate and malt drinks and is the world's largest producer of milk powder and condensed milk.

Nestlé's chocolate and confectionery products carry some popular brand names including Callier, Crunch, and Yes. With the acquisition of Rowntree, additional notable brands were added to the product line including, Smarties, After Eight, and Quality Street. The Perugina division produces Baci. Through the RJR Nabisco acquisition, Nestlé acquired Curtiss Brand, a U.S. confectionery producer with such products as Baby Ruth and Butterfinger. Nestlé manufactures chocolate in 23 countries, particularly in Switzerland and Latin America. Each factory is highly automated, employing an average of 250 people.

## CONCLUSION

Hershey's global market share in the chocolate confectionery industry is only 10 percent, lowest among its competitors. A major strategic issue facing Hershey today is where, when, and how to best expand geographically. Perhaps Hershey should expand into the Far East because the economies of those countries are growing so rapidly. China and India are huge untapped markets. Malaysia, Indonesia, Vietnam, Thailand also are untapped. Should Hershey wait for Mars and Nestle to gain a foothold in those countries?

More and more firms are becoming environmentally proactive in their manufacturing and service delivery processes. Environmentally responsible firms market themselves and their products as "green-sensitive." Concern for the natural environment is an issue Hershey should address before competitors seize the initiative. Developing environmentally safe products and packages, reducing industrial waste, recycling, and establishing an environmental audit process are strategies that could benefit Hershey.

Some analysts contend that Hershey International as a separate division producing and selling diverse products is an ineffective structural design. Can you recommend an improved organizational design that could enhance Hershey's lackluster international operations?

Should Hershey acquire firms in other foreign countries? Analysis is needed to identify and value specific acquisition candidates. In developing an overall strategic plan, what recommendations would you present to CEO Kenneth Wolfe? Should Hershey diversify more into nonchocolate candies because that segment is growing most rapidly? Should a new manufacturing plant be built in Asia or in Europe?

Design a global marketing strategy that could enable Hershey to boost exports of chocolate. Should Hershey increase its debt or dilute ownership of their stock further to raise the capital needed to implement your recommended strategies? Develop pro-forma financial statements to fully assess and evaluate the impact of your proposed strategies.

# THE BOEING COMPANY—2000

**Carolyn R. Stokes**
**Francis Marion University**

BA

www.boeing.com

The Boeing Company, headquartered in Seattle, Washington, is the largest aerospace firm in the world as measured by total sales, the world's leading manufacturer of commercial aircraft (on average of over 60 percent of the market for the past 20 years), the world's leader in military aircraft, and the largest contractor for NASA. Boeing is one of the largest U.S. exporters, with over $26 billion in sales to foreign countries in 1999 (see Exhibit 1). Boeing acquired the Rockwell space division and McDonnell Douglas to gain a greater share of the military and space market. Boeing is organized into three major segments: Commercial Aircraft, Military Aircraft and Missiles, and Space and Communications. Jetliners currently in production include the families of the Boeing 717, 737, 747, 757, 767, and 777 models and the MD-11, MD-80, and MD-90. Boeing manufactures helicopters, military aircraft, electronic systems, and missiles; provides communication services for aerospace-related activities, and is a major contractor for the Space Station.

The late 1990's were good for most airline carriers, which are Boeing's primary customers. Better cost management, lower fuel costs, and increased passenger revenue led to substantially better financial operating profits for the airline industry.

EXHIBIT 1    The Boeing Company and Subsidiaries Sales by Geographic Area (in millions)

| Year ended December 31 | 1999 | 1998 | 1997 | 1996 |
|---|---|---|---|---|
| Asia, other than China[a] | $10,776 | $14,065 | $11,437 | $ 8,470 |
| China | 1,231 | 1,572 | 1,265 | 951 |
| Europe[b] | 9,678 | 8,646 | 7,237 | 4,198 |
| Oceania | 942 | 844 | 1,078 | 821 |
| Africa | 386 | 702 | 192 | 156 |
| Non-US Western Hemisphere | 461 | 701 | 228 | 466 |
| United States[c] | 34,519 | 29,624 | 24,363 | 20,391 |
| Total Sales | $57,993 | $56,154 | $45,800 | $34,453 |

[a]Defense sales were approximately 19%, 19%, and 22% of total sales to Non-Chinese Asia in 1998, 1997, and 1996.
[b]Military Aircraft and Missiles and Space and Communications segment combined sales were approximately 16%, 19%, and 22% of total sales to Europe in 1998, 1997, and 1996.
[c]Military Aircraft and Missiles and Space and Communications segment sales were principally to the U.S. government.
*Source:* Boeing Company, *Annual Report* (1999), p. 50.

Growth in passenger traffic averaged approximately 6.0 percent over the last five years. Over the next 20-year period, Boeing predicts an annual growth rate of 4.7 percent in passenger traffic and 6.0 percent in cargo traffic. The market for new aircraft is strengthened by this growth in the airline industry. Boeing, led by the Chairman and CEO Philip M. Condit and President and COO Harry C. Stonecipher, had revenues of $57.9 billion with deliveries of 620 commercial jet aircraft and 124 military aircraft and missile deliveries in 1999 as compared with $56.1 billion with deliveries of 559 commercial jet aircraft and 133 military aircraft and missile deliveries in 1998.

In defense and space Boeing recorded an operating profit of $1.6 billion on sales of $19.0 billion in 1999. This revenue includes $12.2 billion from Military Aircraft and Missiles and $6.8 billion from Space and Communications. Note in Exhibit 6 that all these numbers are down from 1998. Boeing is in an aerospace environment facing rising demand for some commercial aircraft and defense products and increasing revenues from additional defense and space contracts obtained in part with the acquisition of Rockwell and merger with McDonnell Douglas. The company needs a clear strategic plan for the future.

## COMMERCIAL AIRCRAFT

Airline demand for new aircraft rose over the past few years. Boeing's backlog of orders rose from $86.2 billion in 1996 to $93.8 billion in 1997 before dropping to $86.1 in 1998. Boeing worked to solve the problem by rapidly accelerating the production process. In 1996–1997 when Boeing was aiming to more than double production in 18 months, manufacturing problems at one point halted production of the 736 and 747 for a month. By the end of 1998, the increased production rate had helped to reduce the backlog of orders to $86.1 billion. Boeing continues for two decades to average over a 60 percent share of the world market for commercial jets. In 1998 customers announced orders for 656 jetcraft as compared with 568 in 1997. However, in 1999 Boeing announced only 368 orders. Even with the decline in orders from Asian markets, approximately 47 percent of Boeing's 1998 airline sales were from non-U.S. carriers, up from 42 percent in 1996. The declining economic conditions in Asian markets are expected to influence current orders and production. Boeing's recent aircraft deliveries are shown in Exhibit 2 and Exhibit 3.

Boeing production has greatly increased from the 274 jetcraft in 1997 and 269 in 1996. However, the backlogs, increases in current orders, and expected increases in demand generated by air line travel should push production levels for aircraft up to 480 jetcraft by the end of 2000.

Boeing commercial airjet segment currently produces the new 717 family together with the 737, 747, 757, 767, and 777 families and the McDonnell Douglas MD-11, MD-80, and MD-90. The MD-95 was redesigned as the new Boeing 717. Boeing commercial airjet development has focused on the 717, 777, and the 737 families.

The new 717, originally the MD-95, was delivered in 1999. This 717-200 responds to the need for a 100-seat regional jet. The MD-11, MD-80, and MD-90 are scheduled to be phased out in 2001, 1999, and 2000. Boeing had received 65 orders in 1998 and delivered 12 planes in 1999.

Boeing is pleased with the response to the Boeing 777 family. United Airlines received and put into service in May 1995 the first 777 developed to meet the need for more efficient, comfortable, and high-capacity jets. The 777-200 and 777-300 series can seat from 305 to 550 passengers and have ranges from 5,925 to 8,861 miles. A survey

EXHIBIT 2    The Boeing Company Commercial Jet
Aircraft Deliveries by Model

|              | 1999 | 1998 | 1997 | 1996 |
|--------------|------|------|------|------|
| 717          | 12   | 0    | 0    | 0    |
| 737 Classic  | 42   | 116  | 132  | 76   |
| 737 NG       | 278  | 165  | 3    | 0    |
| 747          | 47   | 53   | 39   | 26   |
| 757          | 67   | 50   | 46   | 42   |
| 767          | 44   | 47   | 41   | 42   |
| 777          | 83   | 74   | 59   | 32   |
| MD-80        | 26   | 8    | 16   | 12   |
| MD-90        | 13   | 34   | 26   | 24   |
| MD-11        | 8    | 12   | 12   | 15   |
| Total        | 620  | 559  | 374  | 269  |

Source: Boeing Company, *Annual Report* (1999), p. 27.

EXHIBIT 3    The Boeing Company Military Aircraft
and Missile Deliveries (Selected Programs)

|                 | 1999 | 1998 | 1997 | 1996 |
|-----------------|------|------|------|------|
| C-17            | 11   | 10   | 7    | 6    |
| F-15            | 35   | 39   | 19   | 11   |
| F/A-18 C/D      | 25   | 29   | 46   | 32   |
| F/A-18 C/D Kits | 0    | 0    | 20   | 9    |
| F/A-18 EF       | 13   | 1    | 0    | 0    |
| T-45TS          | 12   | 16   | 11   | 9    |
| CH-47           | 14   | 18   | 1    | 0    |
| 757/C-32A       | 0    | 4    | 0    | 0    |
| 767 AWACS       | 2    | 2    | 0    | 0    |
| Delta II        | 11   | 13   | 12   | 11   |
| Delta III       | 1    | 1    | 0    | 0    |

Source: Boeing Company, *Annual Report* (1999), p. 29.

was conducted on six airlines flying long-range flights to and from Europe. The survey showed that passengers who had flown both the Boeing 777 and the Airbus A330/A340 preferred the 777 3:1. The survey was conducted by these airlines on behalf of themselves and Boeing. Boeing delivered 83 777 jets in 1999.

The smallest member of the Boeing jetliner family is the 737, the best-selling aircraft of all time with 4,234 orders and 3,256 deliveries. The 737 family developed for short-to-medium range is designed for greater range, speed, and compliance with new noise and emission standards. The 700, 800, and 900 members of the 737 family have outsold all aircraft in their market. The 737 family includes the Boeing Business Jet, a derivative of the 700 member. Boeing delivered 278 737s in 1999.

The Boeing 757 and 767 are medium-capacity, fuel-efficient twinjets that meet FAA requirements for extended-range operations. The 757 can carry 180 to 230 passengers, depending on the configuration, as far as 4,600 nautical miles. In 1999 Boeing introduced the 757-300 which has 20 percent additional seating and 10 percent lower per-seat operating costs than the 757-200. Boeing delivered 67 757s in 1999.

The 767 is larger, carrying about 260 passengers in mixed class, with a range on some versions in excess of 6,000 nautical miles. The 767-200 can carry 210 passengers a range of 7,500 miles, and the 767-300 can carry 252 passengers. A new extended-range version of the 767 was introduced early in 1997, and a planned 767-400ERX for 300 passengers is scheduled for delivery in the year 2000. Boeing delivered 44 767s in 1999.

The flagship of the Boeing airplane family, the 747-400, can carry 568 passengers more than 8,000 nautical miles and offers airline customers the lowest seat-mile costs of any aircraft in the world. The 747-400 has both an all-cargo and a Combi model for passengers and freight. The Boeing 747 freight aircraft is in great demand at the Narita, the new Tokyo International Airport that handles more than 1.5 million tons of freight, more than any other airport in the world. Almost 80 percent of the jets using Narita are Boeing 747s. The 747-400F gives Boeing's airline customers the capability of carrying 20 tons more payload compared to 747-200 freighters or carrying the same payload 800 nautical miles farther. Boeing delivered 47 747-440Fs in 1999.

For several years Boeing has been researching the market and optimum configuration for an aircraft even larger than the current 747-400. Boeing is planning within the next two years to proceed with the development of the Boeing 747-Stretch, a super jumbo jet that will travel over 7,500 miles and seat 500. The range of the new super jumbo jetcraft will allow passengers to bypass crowded airports. The Boeing plane should be ready before the Airbus A-3XX, which will have a double-deck cabin seating up to 655 passengers.

The European Airbus consortium remains Boeing's most formidable competitor in the commercial aircraft industry. The Airbus consortium consists of Aerospatiale SA of France, British Aerospace PLC, the aircraft unit of Daimier Benz AG of Germany, and Construcciones Aeronauticas SA of Spain. However, with the acquisition of Rockwell International in 1996 and the merger with McDonnell Douglas in 1997, Airbus appears to be able to offer less competition in the aerospace industry. However, with the downturn in the Asian market, Airbus orders are increasing, and Boeing orders are on a slight decline. According to the October 14, 1999, report of Von Rumohn with SG Cowen Securities Corp., Airbus's share of the orders went from 42 percent in 1996 to 46 percent in 1998 while Boeing's orders declined from 58 percent to 54 percent. Airbus's share of backlog went from 32 percent in 1996 to 42 percent while Boeing's backlog declined from 68 percent to 58 percent. As of December 15, 1999, Airbus with 417 orders had 60 percent of the 1999 market. Orders and backlogs can change with economic conditions and customer demands. Decreases in orders result in decreased sales, production, and actual deliveries. Although Boeing orders were declining in 1998, its share of actual deliveries rose from 68 percent in 1996 to 71 percent in 1998.

With quality, service, and competitive pricing, Boeing now has 10,000 of the approximately 12,000 planes of the world fleet. On December 9, 1999, Jeff Cole in the *Wall Street Journal* revealed that Boeing won the right to launch more than 40 satellites for the Skybridge and European telecommunications operation. Boeing also became a minority stakeholder in Skybridge. On December 15 Cole reported in the *Wall Street Journal* additional Boeing orders totaling $8.5 billion, which brought the Boeing order total for 1999 up to 292. The 120-aircraft order included an order from General Electric and from other unidentified buyers. On December 14, Boeing announced a contract with Pembroke, an aircraft financing, leasing, and management group in Dublin, Ireland. Pembroke committed to an order for 15 Boeing 717s and options for 15 more. A later Boeing report brought the total orders to 368 for 1999. Boeing has changed from a policy of announcing only orders that customers have already announced to announcing all orders.

In the highly competitive market for commercial aircraft, Boeing's reputation for customer service is an effective marketing tool. Boeing is providing ready access to parts and training programs using the Web and ED-ROM technologies. Customers can access parts information via the Internet. Information availability of parts, lead time, backorders, status of orders, and exchangeability of parts is now available to small and large customers. In 1994 Boeing began performing full checks on jets at a facility near the airport in Saudi Arabia. In 1994 Boeing opened the world's largest spare center in Beijing, assigned a senior executive to be president of China operations at a new headquarters in Beijing, and in 1995 opened a new avionics service center in Singapore. Boeing opened its seventh regional parts distribution center in Dubai and plans to open the eighth facility in Amsterdam. Boeing maintains field representatives in 63 countries. Boeing can now provide technical support 24 hours a day and ship emergency spare parts in 2 hours and routine parts in 24 hours.

Boeing provides "distance learning" for customers in training for pilots, mechanics, and maintenance people using the latest technology. Boeing trains about 6,000 pilots and ground personnel annually for airline customers around the world at the Customer Service Training Center in Seattle, located approximately half way between London and Tokyo.

## MILITARY AND SPACE PRODUCTS

Boeing made a major advance in the defense and space segment by purchasing the Rockwell defense and space division and finalizing a merger with McDonnell Douglas that is greatly impacting future revenues. Following these additions, the information, defense, and space segment revenues were $19.0 billion in 1999, down from 1998. U.S. spending on defense and space is expected to remain level. However, Boeing expects a rapid expansion of the communications technologies and market demand. The Boeing defense and space business is broadly diversified, with no program accounting for more than 15 percent of total defense and space revenue. Boeing is working toward better quality and lower cost with new designs, technologies, materials, and processes. The principal defense and space programs, based on 1999 revenues, included the Military Aircraft and Missiles programs of C-17 Globemaster III, F-15 fighter-bomber, F/A-18 C/D and F/A-18 E/F Hornets, and AH-64 Apache helicopter, the E-3 and 767 AWACS (Airborne Warning and Control System), and the Space Station programs. U.S. government classified projects also continue to contribute to defense and space segment revenues.

Major development programs include the International Space Station, F/A-18 E/F, F-22 Fighter, Joint Strike Fighter, V-22 Osprey tiltrotor aircraft, the RAH-66 Comanche helicopter, and the National Missile Defense Lead System Integration. Boeing is transferring the V-22 Osprey into initial production and has received funding for initial production of the F-22 Raptor.

Boeing recently won the major portion of the Air Force's Evolved Expendable Launch Vehicle (EELV) program. The Air Force required a cost reduction of 25 percent on medium and heavy payloads in orbit, and Boeing's Delta IV launches reduce the cost by almost 50 percent. Boeing also was selected as the lead system integrator for the National Missile Defense program. Boeing is working on all of the defense systems for troops, including the Airborne Laser, third-generation Patriot, the Navy's Theater Wide System for the sea.

Boeing continues working on a $660-million contract in competition with Lockheed Martin on the building of the Joint Strike Fighter (JSF), with orders for 3,000 aircraft for the winner expected in the next century. Boeing North America, in a joint venture with Lockheed Martin, signed a six-year $7-billion contract with NASA to consolidate shuttle ground flights and ground operations. Boeing North America has a contract for up to $1.3 billion with the U.S. Airforce to produce the Navstar Global Positioning System satellites. Boeing led a team that was awarded a $1.1 billion Airborne Laser Program Definition and Risk Reduction contract for developing a high-power laser and optical steering system.

Boeing has been successful teaming with other defense and space companies. Boeing, in partnership with Lockheed Martin Corporation, continues with the development of the F-22 fighter. Boeing continues working on the V-22 Osprey helicopter with Bell Helicopter Textron program. The Bell Boeing aircraft entered the $1.38-billion low-rate production in 1996. Deliveries of the 360 V-22 designed for the Marines began in 1999. The Special Forces have 50 V-22s on order. This helicopter will meet the need for medium-lift requirements with exceptional mobility and rapid deployment. The CH-47 Chinook helicopter program consists of the remanufacture of existing helicopters and the manufacture of new Ch-47s. Contracts are mostly with foreign governments. A Boeing/Sikorsky team is developing a twenty-first-century version of the RAH-66 Comanche armed-reconnaissance helicopter and is currently flight-testing a prototype that is the centerpiece of the U.S. Army's modernization plan.

Boeing is a significant player in NASA, the prime contractor for the restructured International Space Station Alpha, and for the NASA station's living and laboratory modules. Boeing is leading the team in the largest international venture in science and space ever undertaken. The project is aided by the efforts of 15 nations. In December 1998 Space Shuttle *Endeavor* completed its first historic flight to start assembly of the International Space Station. The *Endeavor* carried the Boeing-built Unity module, which the crew attached to a Russian-built Zarya power unit. When the space station is completed in 2004, it will weigh almost a million pounds and be the length of a football field.

Boeing teamed with RSC Energia of Moscow, KB Yuzhnoye/PO Yuzhmash of Ukraine, and Kvaerner Maritime of Norway in a joint venture for a Sea Launch that uses a rocket, a launch platform, and 656-foot-long command ship. In 1999 the Sea Launch began sailing regularly to waters near the equator to launch satellites. The joint venture has 18 firm contracts through the year 2004.

## BOEING PROBLEMS IN THE NEWS

In recent years, defective parts and airline crashes have given rise to concerns over safety. The crash of an EgyptAir Boeing jet into the Atlantic in November 1999 gained wide media attention. Questions arose as to possible defects in the thrust reversers. Boeing reported that due to a manufacturing slip-up, defective insulation strips had been used in the cockpits of 757s, 767s, 777s, and 747s. Boeing said that the problem is not believed to pose an immediate safety hazard; however, it is moving to correct the problem. Federal regulators issued emergency mandatory rules for tougher maintenance requirements and operating restrictions for the Boeing 777 because of electrical problems.

The FAA is conducting a technical audit of Boeing. The audit is the result of recent media attention on issues including nonconforming drip shields and environmental control system ducts. Boeing welcomes the audit as an opportunity to validate its processes and systems to make them better. All aerospace companies and their suppliers routinely undergo evaluation to verify compliance with Federal Aviation regulations.

## CONCLUSION

As indicated in Exhibits 4–6, Boeing's net earnings increased from $1.12 billion in 1998 to $2.30 billion in 1999. Boeing still has to compete with Airbus, a major competitor

EXHIBIT 4    Boeing Company Annual Income Statement
(in millions except earnings per share data)

| | 12/31/99 | 12/31/98 | 12/31/97 | 12/31/96 |
|---|---|---|---|---|
| Sales | $57,993.00 | $56,154.00 | $45,800.00 | $22,681.00 |
| Cost of goods | 51,320.00 | 0 | 0 | 21,327.00 |
| **Gross profit** | 6,673.00 | 56,154.00 | 45,800.00 | 1,354.00 |
| Selling and administrative and depreciation and amortization expenses | 3,385.00 | 54,434.00 | 44,755.00 | 0 |
| **Income after depreciation and amortization** | 3,288.00 | 1,720.00 | 1,045.00 | 1,354.00 |
| Nonoperating income | 467.00 | 130.00 | (873.00) | 154.00 |
| Interest expense | 431.00 | 453.00 | 513.00 | 145.00 |
| **Pretax income** | 3,324.00 | 1,397.00 | (341.00) | 1,363.00 |
| Income taxes | 1,015.00 | 277.00 | (163.00) | 268.00 |
| Minority interest | 0 | 0 | 0 | 0 |
| Investment gains/losses (+) | 0 | 0 | 0 | 0 |
| Other income/charges | 0 | 0 | 0 | 0 |
| **Income from continued operations** | N/A | N/A | N/A | N/A |
| Extras and discontinued operations | 0 | 0 | 0 | 0 |
| **Net income** | $ 2,309.00 | $ 1,120.00 | $ (178.00) | $ 1,095.00 |

## Depreciation footnote

| | | | | |
|---|---|---|---|---|
| Income before depreciation and amortization | $ 4,933.00 | $ 3,342.00 | $ 2,503.00 | $ 2,345.00 |
| Depreciation and amortization (cash flow) | 1,645.00 | 1,622.00 | 1,458.00 | 991.00 |
| **Income after depreciation and amortization** | $ 3,288.00 | $ 1,720.00 | $ 1,045.00 | $ 1,354.00 |

## Earnings-per-share data

| | | | | |
|---|---|---|---|---|
| **Average shares** | $ 925.90 | $ 976.70 | $ 984.50 | $ 686.30 |
| Diluted earnings per share before nonrecurring items | 2.35 | 1.12 | 0.63 | 1.00 |
| **Diluted net earnings per share** | $ 2.49 | $ 1.15 | $ (0.18) | $ 1.00 |

*Source:* www.freeedgar.com

with commercial jetliners, Lockheed Martin, a major defense contractor, and with others in the aerospace market. Boeing also has to continue to work on coordinating the activities and reducing the costs of its many operations.

With expertise in each of the three areas, Boeing should be better able to compete with technological innovations and costs. The aerospace business environment remains uncertain, but Boeing with its extraordinary resources, magnificent record in aerospace, and an excellent strategic plan should continue to be the world leader in aerospace. In the face of the expected business environment, prepare a strategic plan for CEO Philip M. Condit and COO Harry C. Stonecipher. Keep in mind Boeing's current mission statement (from its *Annual Report*): "To be the number one aerospace company in the world and among the premier industrial concerns in terms of quality, profitability, and growth."

EXHIBIT 5    Boeing Company Annual Balance Sheet
(in millions, except book value per share)

| | 12/31/99 | 12/31/98 | 12/31/97 | 12/31/96 |
|---|---|---|---|---|
| **Assets** | | | | |
| Cash and equivalents | $ 3,454.00 | $ 2,462.00 | $ 5,149.00 | $ 5,258.00 |
| Receivables | 3,453.00 | 3,288.00 | 3,121.00 | 1,988.00 |
| Notes receivable | 0 | 0 | 0 | 150.00 |
| Inventories | 6,539.00 | 8,349.00 | 8,967.00 | 6,939.00 |
| Other current assets | 2,266.00 | 2,276.00 | 2,026.00 | 745.00 |
| Total current assets | 15,712.00 | 16,375.00 | 19,263.00 | 15,080.00 |
| Net property and equipment | 8,245.00 | 8,589.00 | 8,391.00 | 6,813.00 |
| Investments and advances | 0 | 0 | 0 | 0 |
| Other noncurrent assets | 5,205.00 | 4,930.00 | 4,339.00 | 648.00 |
| Deferred charges | 0 | 411.00 | 15.00 | 415.00 |
| Intangibles | 2,233.00 | 2,312.00 | 2,395.00 | 2,478.00 |
| Deposits and other assets | 4,752.00 | 4,055.00 | 3,621.00 | 1,820.00 |
| Total assets | $36,147.00 | $36,672.00 | $38,024.00 | $27,254.00 |
| **Liabilities and shareholders' equity** | | | | |
| Notes payable | 0 | 0 | 0 | 0 |
| Accounts payable | 11,269.00 | 10,733.00 | 11,548.00 | 7,306.00 |
| Current portion long-term debt | 752.00 | 869.00 | 731.00 | 13.00 |
| Current portion capital leases | 0 | 0 | 0 | 0 |
| Accrued Expenses | 0 | 0 | 0 | 0 |
| Income taxes payable | 420.00 | 569.00 | 298.00 | 350.00 |
| Other current liabilities | 1,215.00 | 1,251.00 | 1,575.00 | 973.00 |
| Total current liabilities | 13,656.00 | 13,422.00 | 14,152.00 | 8,420.00 |
| Mortgages | 0 | 0 | 0 | 0 |
| Deferred taxes/income | 172.00 | 0 | 0 | 0 |
| Convertible debt | 0 | 0 | 0 | 0 |
| Long-term debt | 5,980.00 | 6,103.00 | 6,123.00 | 3,980.00 |
| Noncurrent capital leases | 0 | 0 | 0 | 0 |
| Other noncurrent liabilities | 4,877.00 | 4,831.00 | 4,796.00 | 3,691.00 |
| Minority interest (liabilities) | 0 | 0 | 0 | 0 |
| Total liabilities | $24,685.00 | $24,356.00 | $25,071.00 | $16,313.00 |
| **Shareholders' Equity** | | | | |
| Preferred stock | 0 | 0 | 0 | 0 |
| Common stock (par) | 5,059.00 | 5,059.00 | 5.00 | 1,802.00 |
| Capital surplus | 1,684.00 | 1,147.00 | 1,090.00 | 1,951.00 |
| Retained earnings | 10,487.00 | 8,706.00 | 8,147.00 | 8,447.00 |
| Other equity | (1,607.00) | (1,275.00) | 3,720.00 | (1,258.00) |
| Treasury stock | 4,161.00 | 1,321.00 | 9.00 | 1.00 |
| Total shareholders' equity | 11,462.00 | 12,316.00 | 12,953.00 | 10,941.00 |
| Total liabilities and shareholders' equity | 36,147.00 | 36,672.00 | 38,024.00 | 27,254.00 |
| Total common equity | 11,462.00 | 12,316.00 | 12,953.00 | 10,941.00 |
| Average shares | 925.90 | 976.70 | 984.50 | 686.52 |
| Book value per share | $    12.26 | $    12.33 | $    12.96 | $    15.93 |

*Source:* www.freeedgar.com

# EXHIBIT 6　The Boeing Company and Subsidiaries Product Segment Information
## (in millions)

| Year ended December 31 | Net earnings (loss) | | | Revenues | | |
|---|---|---|---|---|---|---|
| | 1999 | 1998 | 1997 | 1999 | 1998 | 1997 |
| Commercial aircraft | $2,016 | $ (266) | $(1,589) | $38,409 | $36,880 | $27,479 |
| Military aircraft and missiles | 1,193 | 1,283 | — | 12,220 | 12,900 | — |
| Space and communications | 415 | 218 | — | 6,831 | 6,889 | — |
| Information, space, and defense systems | 1,608 | 1,531 | 1,317 | 19,051 | 19,879 | 18,125 |
| Customer and commercial financing and other | 492 | 367 | 381 | 837 | 730 | 746 |
| Accounting differences | (432) | 372 | (177) | (304) | (1,335) | (550) |
| Share-based plans | (209) | (153) | 99 | | | |
| Other unallocated costs | (305) | (284) | (287) | | | |
| Earnings (loss) from operations | 3,170 | 1,567 | (256) | | | |
| Other income, principally interest | 585 | 283 | 428 | | | |
| Interest and debt expense | (431) | (453) | (513) | | | |
| Earnings (loss) before taxes | 3,324 | 1,397 | (341) | | | |
| Income tax expense (benefit) | 1,015 | 277 | (163) | | | |
| | $2,309 | $1,120 | $ (178) | $57,993 | $56,154 | $45,800 |

| | Research and Development | | | Depreciation and Amortization | | |
|---|---|---|---|---|---|---|
| | 1999 | 1998 | 1997 | 1999 | 1998 | 1997 |
| Commercial aircraft | $ 585 | $1,021 | $1,208 | $ 595 | $ 628 | $ 570 |
| Military aircraft and missiles | 264 | 304 | — | 201 | 208 | — |
| Space and communications | 492 | 570 | — | 168 | 142 | — |
| Information, space, and defense systems | 756 | 874 | 716 | 369 | 350 | 365 |
| Customer and commercial financing and other | | | | 163 | 135 | 91 |
| Unallocated | | | | 518 | 509 | 432 |
| | $1,341 | $1,895 | $1,924 | $1,645 | $1,622 | $1,458 |

| | Assets at December 31 | | | Liabilities at December 31 | | |
|---|---|---|---|---|---|---|
| | 1999 | 1998 | 1997 | 1999 | 1998 | 1997 |
| Commercial aircraft | $ 8,075 | $11,003 | $11,000 | $ 6,135 | $ 6,907 | $ 7,617 |
| Military aircraft and missiles | 3,206 | 3,560 | — | 1,080 | 743 | — |
| Space and communications | 4,245 | 3,032 | — | 1,350 | 1,452 | — |
| Information, space, and defense systems | 7,451 | 6,592 | 6,597 | 2,430 | 2,195 | 2,379 |
| Customer and commercial financing and other | 6,004 | 5,751 | 4,716 | 228 | 301 | 396 |
| Unallocated | 14,617 | 13,561 | 15,980 | 15,892 | 15,850 | 14,948 |
| | $36,147 | $37,024 | $38,293 | $24,685 | $24,708 | $25,340 |

| | Capital Expenditures, Net | | | Contractual Backlog at December 31 (unaudited) | | |
|---|---|---|---|---|---|---|
| | 1999 | 1998 | 1997 | 1999 | 1998 | 1997 |
| Commercial aircraft | $ 307 | $ 754 | $ 531 | $72,972 | $ 86,057 | $ 93,788 |
| Military aircraft and missiles | 215 | 213 | — | 15,691 | 17,007 | — |
| Space and communications | 585 | 339 | — | 10,585 | 9.832 | — |
| Information, space, and defense systems | 800 | 552 | 463 | 26,276 | 26,839 | 27,852 |
| Customer and commercial financing and other | 1 | 1 | 1 | — | — | — |
| Unallocated | 128 | 358 | 396 | — | — | — |
| | $1,236 | $1,665 | $1,391 | $99,248 | $112,896 | $121,640 |

# LOCKHEED MARTIN CORPORATION—2000

Wayne Chamblee
Francis Marion University

## LMT
www.lockheedmartin.com

As the second-largest company in the defense and aerospace industry, Lockheed Martin Corporation builds many of the best-known military aircraft and rocket systems, such as the C-5A, C-130, F-16, F-22, F-117 aircraft and the Atlas, Titan, and Trident rocket systems. Lockheed Martin is currently developing the X-33, which may replace the Space Shuttle. Lockheed Martin also produces many lower-visibility high-technology products and services. Lockheed Martin handles the operation of many federal and state government data processing and communications systems, including many post office, air traffic control, and social services systems. Lockheed Martin's stated vision is "For Lockheed Martin to be the world's leading technology and systems enterprise, providing best value to our customers, growth opportunities to our employees and superior returns to our stockholders."

## HISTORY

Lockheed Aircraft Company was formed in 1926 by Allan Loughead, Malcolm Loughead, and Fred Keeler after the Loughead (pronounced Lockheed) brothers had previously had several unsuccessful forays into the aircraft-manufacturing business. The company's first aircraft, the Vega, was designed by the future founder of the Northrup Corporation, John Northrup. Amelia Earhart was flying a Vega when she became the first woman to fly solo across the Atlantic. Wiley Post flew a Lockheed Vega around the world solo.

Robert Gross, Carl Squier, and Lloyd Stearman purchased Lockheed Aircraft Corporation in 1932. The Lockheed Electra, the first successful pressurized commercial aircraft, was developed in the 1930s. Lockheed continued to produce many famous aircraft including the P-38 Lightning of WWII fame, the P-80 Shooting Star, and the F-104 Starfighter. Spy planes such as the U-2 ( 1955 ) and the SR-71 Blackbird (1964). The C5-A Galaxy, C-130 Hercules, and C-141 Starlifter military cargo aircraft as well as the L-1011 Tristar passenger airliner were also produced by Lockheed.

In the 1960s and 1970s, Lockheed suffered many financial setbacks including C-5A cost overruns, cancellation of the Cheyenne helicopter program, and cost problems associated with the L-1011 passenger jet. Additional problems arose in the 1970s when Lockheed became involved in a corporate bribery scandal that led to revisions in anti-bribery laws. Government loans were required in 1971 to save the company from bankruptcy. In 1992, Lockheed entered an agreement to provide satellites for Motorola's Iridium phone project.

Glenn Martin founded the Glenn L. Martin Aircraft Company in 1912 and merged with the company founded by the Wright Brothers in 1916. The twin-engine

Martin MB-2 was used by General Billy Mitchell to demonstrate the potential of air bombardment. In the 1930s, Martin built the M-130 Clipper flying boat, which became famous as the Pan Am Clipper. Martin produced the B-26 bomber during World War II.

Martin produced missiles, electronics, and nuclear systems during the 1950s. In an attempt to diversify in 1961, Martin merged with the chemical and construction material company American-Marietta Company to become Martin Marietta. Martin Marietta developed the Titan II rocket in the 1960s. Other Martin Marietta projects included the Viking Mars lander, the MX missile, and the external fuel tanks for the Space Shuttle. Martin Marietta was forced to sell off many of its businesses in 1982 after it acquired $1 million of debt fending off a takeover attempt from Bendix Corporation. In 1992, Martin Marietta purchased the aerospace operations of General Electric.

Lockheed Martin was formed in 1995 when Lockheed acquired Martin Marietta. These two companies seemed to an ideal match because Lockheed was a major builder of military aircraft, and Martin Marietta was a strong force in defense electronics. Lockheed Martin paid $7.6 billion in 1996 to acquire the majority of an electronics giant, the Loral Corporation. The merger of Lockheed and Martin Marietta and many of Lockheed Martin's early acquisitions allowed Lockheed Martin to achieve a high degree of vertical integration in many of its businesses. This could be seen in the way the electronics and systems integration business acquired with the purchase of Loral complemented the defense electronics business of Martin Marietta.

In 1996, Lockheed Martin sold Defense Systems and Armament Systems business to General Dynamics. In 1997 L-3 Communications was formed when Lockheed Martin spun off portions of 10 technology units not deemed to be part of the core business. Lockheed Martin offered to buy Northrop Grumman for $11.6 billion in 1997, but the deal collapsed in 1998 when the U.S. government indicated it has antitrust issues with the deal.

The overall strategy of Lockheed Martin since the company was formed has had two components. The first element was to maintain its relatively large share of the U.S. defense business while growing business activity in closely related high-technology non-defense areas such as information systems, telecommunications, and infrastructure support. Lockheed Martin has almost always chosen to grow in familiar markets with relatively familiar technology. By 1998, acquisitions and mergers had resulted in an 185 percent increase in the number of core competencies in Lockheed Martin's technology profile with only 15 percent of the competencies being duplicated as a result of acquisitions. Lockheed Martin has achieved a high degree of vertical integration in military aircraft, avionics, airframes, and space vehicles (Advani et al., 1998).

## OPERATIONS

In 1999, Lockheed Martin purchased 49 percent of the satellite network company COMSAT for $1.7 billion. The remainder of COMSAT cannot be purchased without government approval. COMSAT is an entity that acts as an interface between U.S. communications companies and INTELSAT, an international agency that controls the majority of the world's communications satellites. Lockheed Martin also purchased 30 percent of Asia Cellular Satellite in 1999 and invested $400 million in the Astrolink wireless broadband satellite system.

Because few of Lockheed Martin's businesses were relocated after acquisition, Lockheed Martin now operates approximately 440 facilities, most of them in the United States. The company has used its own information technology to generate internal networks to facilitate the sharing of information and technology. In this respect, Lockheed Martin operates as a virtual enterprise. Although some economies of scale could be achieved by relocating divisions together, Lockheed Martin believes innovation may be

EXHIBIT 1    Organizational Chart for Lockheed Martin

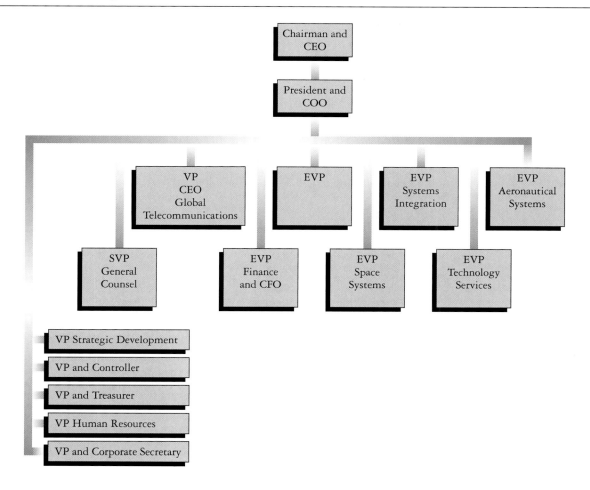

better promoted by small organizations working independently while remaining electronically connected to the rest of the organization.

Lockheed Martin has made several attempts to lower costs and improve profitability. Lockheed Martin Aeronautical Systems (LMAS) embraced the "lean" or Toyota production system in 1997 and plans to have the Toyota system fully in place in four years. This appears to be a rather ambitious goal—GE required 12 years to accomplish the same task (Kandebo, 1999).

Lockheed Martin is organized by sectors (see Exhibit 1). The five principal Lockheed Martin sectors in 1999 were Systems Integration, Space Systems, Aeronautical Systems, Technology Services, and Corporate and other. Lockheed Martin's financial statements are shown in Exhibits 2 and 3.

The data in Exhibit 4 present the sector contributions to Lockheed Martin's sales and income. The sales of the Space Systems sector decreased by 17 percent in 1999. This decrease was due to many factors including decreased Trident missile sales associated with the end of the Cold War and reduced Atlas and Proton commercial satellite launching activities. The Systems Integration sector posted both increased sales and profits for 1999. Postal systems equipment, surface ship systems, and control equipment accounted

EXHIBIT 2    Lockheed Martin Annual Income Statement
             (in millions except earnings per share data)

|  | 12/31/99 | 12/31/98 | 12/31/97 |
|---|---|---|---|
| Sales | $25,530.00 | $26,266.00 | $28,069.00 |
| Cost of goods | 23,865.00 | 23,914.00 | 25,772.00 |
| **Gross profit** | **1,665.00** | **2,352.00** | **2,297.00** |
| Selling and administrative and depreciation and amortization expenses | 0 | 0 | 0 |
| **Income after depreciation and amortization** | **1,665.00** | **2,352.00** | **2,297.00** |
| Nonoperating income | 344.00 | 170.00 | 482.00 |
| Interest expense | 809.00 | 861.00 | 842.00 |
| **Pretax income** | **1,200.00** | **1,661.00** | **1,937.00** |
| Income taxes | 463.00 | 660.00 | 637.00 |
| Minority interest | 0 | 0 | 0 |
| Investment gains/losses (+) | 0 | 0 | 0 |
| Other income/charges | 0 | 0 | 0 |
| **Income for continued operations** | **N/A** | **N/A** | **N/A** |
| Extras and discontinued operations | (355.00) | 0 | 0 |
| **Net income** | **$   382.00** | **$ 1,001.00** | **$ 1,300.00** |

### Depreciation footnote

|  | 12/31/99 | 12/31/98 | 12/31/97 |
|---|---|---|---|
| Income before depreciation and amortization | $ 2,634.00 | $ 3,357.00 | $ 3,349.00 |
| Depreciation and amortization (cash flow) | 969.00 | 1,005.00 | 1,052.00 |
| **Income after depreciation and amortization** | **$ 1,665.00** | **$ 2,352.00** | **$ 2,297.00** |

### Earnings per-share data

|  | 12/31/99 | 12/31/98 | 12/31/97 |
|---|---|---|---|
| Average shares | $   384.10 | $   381.10 | $   427.00 |
| Diluted earnings per share before Nonrecurring items | 1.50 | 3.11 | 3.03 |
| **Diluted net earnings per share** | **$     0.99** | **$     2.63** | **$     3.08** |

*Source:* www.freeedgar.com

for much of the increased sales in this sector. Improved margins for electronic defense systems helped this sector. Sales for the Aeronautical Systems sector increased slightly in 1999. Sales of older technology F-16 and C-130 aircraft continue to be the main source of revenue for this sector.

In 1999 Lockheed Martin initiated operations of a new wholly owned subsidiary providing broadband satellite technology and operating as Lockheed Martin Global Communications. In addition to portions of Lockheed Martin Missiles and Space, Lockheed Martin Management & Data Systems, and Lockheed Martin Western Development Labs, Lockheed Martin Global Communications will include Lockheed Martin's joint venture activities with Americon Asia Pacific and AceS International Limited. Eventually the Global Communications unit is scheduled to merge with COMSAT.

It should be noted that most current aerospace products are developed and constructed from products produced by numerous defense and aerospace companies. As an example, an Apache helicopter has a Boeing airframe, Lockheed Martin electro-optics, a Lockheed Martin and Northrop Grumman radar system, and General Electric engines.

# EXHIBIT 3    Lockheed Martin Annual Balance Sheet
## (in millions, except book value per share)

|  | 12/31/99 | 12/31/98 | 12/31/97 |
|---|---|---|---|
| **Assets** | | | |
| Cash and equivalents | $ 455.00 | $ 285.00 | 0 |
| Receivalbes | 4,348.00 | 4,178.00 | $ 5,009.00 |
| Notes receivable | 0 | 0 | 0 |
| Inventories | 4,051.00 | 4,293.00 | 3,144.00 |
| Other current assets | 1,842.00 | 1,855.00 | 1,952.00 |
| Total current assets | 10,696.00 | 10,611.00 | 10,105.00 |
| Net property and equipment | 3,634.00 | 3,513.00 | 3,669.00 |
| Investments and advances | 2,210.00 | 0 | 0 |
| Other noncurrent assets | 0 | 0 | 0 |
| Deferred charges | 0 | 0 | 0 |
| Intangibles | 10,421.00 | 10,939.00 | 11,422.00 |
| Deposits and other assets | 3,051.00 | 3,681.00 | 3,165.00 |
| Total assets | $30,012.00 | $28,744.00 | $28,361.00 |
| **Liabilities and Shareholders' equity** | | | |
| Notes payable | $ 475.00 | $ 1,043.00 | $ 494.00 |
| Accounts payable | 1,228.00 | 1,382.00 | 1,234.00 |
| Current portion long-term debt | 52.00 | 0 | 876.00 |
| Current portion capital leases | 0 | 0 | 0 |
| Accrued expenses | 941.00 | 1,728.00 | 924.00 |
| Income taxes payable | 51.00 | 553.00 | 364.00 |
| Other current liabilities | 6,065.00 | 5,561.00 | 5,297.00 |
| Total current liabilities | 8,812.00 | 10,267.00 | 9,189.00 |
| Mortgages | 0 | 0 | 0 |
| Deferred taxes/income | 0 | 0 | 0 |
| Convertible debt | 0 | 0 | 0 |
| Long-term debt | 11,427.00 | 8,957.00 | 10,528.00 |
| Noncurrent capital leases | 0 | 0 | 0 |
| Other noncurrent liabilities | 3,412.00 | 3,383.00 | 3,468.00 |
| Minority interest (liabilities) | 0 | 0 | 0 |
| Total liabilities | $23,651.00 | $22,607.00 | $23,185.00 |
| **Shareholders' equity** | | | |
| Preferred stock | 0 | 0 | 0 |
| Common stock (par) | 398.00 | 393.00 | 194.00 |
| Capital surplus | 222.00 | 70.00 | 25.00 |
| Retained earnings | 5,901.00 | 5,856.00 | 5,173.00 |
| Other equity | (160.00) | (182.00) | (216.00) |
| Treasury stock | 0 | 0 | 0 |
| Total shareholders' equity | 6,361.00 | 6,137.00 | 5,176.00 |
| Total liabilities and shareholders' equity | 30,012.00 | 28,744.00 | 28,361.00 |
| Total common equity | 6,361.00 | 6,137.00 | 5,176.00 |
| Average shares | 384.10 | 381.10 | 427.00 |
| Book value per share | $ 16.07 | $ 15.64 | $ 13.31 |

*Source:* www.freeedgar.com

EXHIBIT 4    Lockheed Martin Segment Financial Data (in millions)

|  | 1999 | 1998 | 1997 |
|---|---|---|---|
| **Net Sales** | | | |
| Systems Integration | $10,954 | $10,895 | $10,853 |
| Space Systems | 5,825 | 7,039 | 7,931 |
| Aeronautical Systems | 5,499 | 5,459 | 5,319 |
| Technology Services | 2,261 | 1,935 | 1,989 |
| Corporate and Other | 991 | 938 | 1,977 |
|  | $25,530 | $26,266 | $28,069 |
| **Operating Profit (Loss)** | | | |
| Systems Integration | $    967 | $    949 | $    843 |
| Space Systems | 474 | 954 | 1,090 |
| Aeronautical Systems | 247 | 649 | 561 |
| Technology Services | 137 | 135 | 187 |
| Corporate and Other | 184 | (165) | 98 |
|  | $ 2,009 | $ 2,522 | $ 2,779 |
| **Profit (Loss):** | | | |
| Segment Effects | | | |
| Systems Integration | $    13 | $    4 | $    (65) |
| Space Systems | 21 | — | (60) |
| Aeronautical Systems | — | — | (31) |
| Technology Services | — | — | (12) |
| Corporate and Other | 215 | (166) | 110 |
|  | $    249 | $    (162) | $    (58) |

Military and civilian aerospace products employ this systems approach to design and construct most products. This translates into most products being produced by a lead contractor with multiple system and subsystem partners (Pope, 1999).

As a lead contractor, Lockheed competes primarily against U.S. companies for U.S. defense sales and against international and U.S. companies for defense sales in foreign countries. In the commercial satellite launching and operation business, commercial aviation, and software businesses, Lockheed must compete with international companies. As an additional constraint, Lockheed faces government scrutiny to ensure it does not transfer technology to a customer who will wittingly or unwittingly be used for military purposes against the United States or one of its allies.

## COMPETITORS AND EXTERNAL FACTORS

Boeing leads the industry and had 1999 revenues of $57.9 billion. Lockheed Martin was second in revenues in 1999 with $25.5 billion. Other industry leaders include United Technologies, Raytheon, Allied Signal, and British Aerospace. All of the industry leaders are diversified and have employed various strategies to enhance the survivability of their companies in the tenuous environment that defense contractors have operated in since the end of the Cold War.

According to *Aviation Week & Space Technology*'s "Best Managed Aerospace Performance" rankings, British Aerospace is ranked first; United Technologies is ranked third; Allied Signal is ranked eighth; Boeing is ranked fourteenth; Raytheon is ranked seventeenth; and Lockheed Martin is ranked eighteenth. This ranking compares aerospace companies' performances based on 25 financial ratios and allocates scores based on asset utilization, productivity, and financial stability (Velocci, 1999).

Boeing, since acquiring McDonald Douglas, has a very strong diversified position in both civil and military aerospace. The civilian aircraft portion of Boeing's business, despite European competition from Airbus, helps to add international sales revenues to Boeing's revenue stream. International sales for Boeing account for 47 percent of sales, and U.S. government sales account for 70 percent of Lockheed Martin sales in 1998. Additionally, although commercial aircraft sales account for 63 percent of Boeing's sales, foreign and domestic government sales account for 89 percent of Lockheed Martin sales. Boeing is a strong competitor of Lockheed Martin for satellite systems.

United Technologies is noted for building Pratt and Whitney jet engines and Sikorsky helicopters. United Technologies adopted a diversification strategy in the 1970s when it acquired Otis Elevator and Carrier. As result of this diversification strategy, the bulk of United Technologies sales are split between Carrier (27 percent), Otis (22 percent), and Pratt & Whitney (30 percent), flight systems such as Sikorsky and Hamilton Sunstrand (10 percent), and automotive parts (11 percent). Also, approximately 44 percent of United Technologies' income is derived from international operations.

British Aerospace, another strong competitor of Lockheed Martin, is similar to Lockheed Martin in that 72 percent of its sales come from its defense unit. However, BA owns 20 percent of Airbus Industries, which produces commercial aircraft and generates the remaining 28 percent of British Aerospace sales. With the scheduled acquisition of Marconi Electronic Systems, British Aerospace will become a stronger competitor. Unlike Lockheed Martin, British Aerospace only derives 11 percent of its sales from its home country, the United Kingdom. The bulk of the balance of British Aerospace sales are generated in the Middle East (38 percent), Europe (23 percent), the United States and Canada (13 percent), and the Far East, including Australia (14 percent). It has one advantage over Lockheed Martin in military sales in that it can sell military equipment to current and former Commonwealth nations without the government scrutiny that Lockheed Martin faces when it attempts to sell military products outside the United States. An additional aid to foreign military sales are the subsidiaries and affiliates in which British Aerospace participates in other countries. These include (in addition to Airbus) such companies as Eurofighter Jagdflugzeug of Germany (33 percent ownership), Matra Bae Dynamics of France (50 percent), Panavia Aircraft of Germany (43 percent), Saab-BAe Grippen of Sweden (50 percent), and Asia Pacific Training and Simulation in Singapore (63 percent). Additionally, British Aerospace is a primary member of Lockheed Martin's Joint Strike Fighter development team.

Late in 1999, the aerospace division of Daimler Chrysler combined with Aerospatiale Matra to form European Aeronautic, Defense, and Space ( EADS ). EADS has combined revenues of approximately $23 billion and is the third-largest aircraft and defense business behind Boeing and Lockheed. EADS will also have an 80 percent stake in Airbus Industries. This merger will cause renewed Pentagon concerns that the major European and American defense contractors will become competitors instead of partners in the worldwide arms sales business. These concerns include worries about the interoperability of NATO weapons systems developed separately as competitive systems by U.S. and European defense companies. Another concern involves mergers that increase the probability that U.S and European defense agencies will limit purchases to those items produced by their own countries' companies (*Wall Street Journal,* Oct. 15, 1999).

Most of Lockheed Martin's competitors have in some way managed to avoid dependence on a single market (i.e., Lockheed Martin's dependence on the U.S. government) for survival. Lockheed Martin's competitors have achieved this position by either diversification of products or diversification of customer base. Lockheed Martin's alliance with the U.S. military has enabled Lockheed Martin to develop cutting-edge technologies, but the same alliance fosters government restrictions that prohibit Lockheed Martin from taking full advantage of the technologies in the worldwide marketplace. This issue keeps Lockheed Martin from exploiting many of the advantages it has in the satellite and command, control, communications, and intelligence ($C^3I$) arenas. Lockheed Martin has acquired saleable skills in $C^3I$ that are desired for many domestic and foreign civilian business applications, but sales have been mainly to the military, FAA, the postal service, social services, and other government agencies.

## RECENT DEVELOPMENTS

Several clouds appeared on the horizon for Lockheed Martin in 1999. Congress challenged future production funding for the F-22 fighter program. Lockheed Martin is the prime contractor for the F-22 and had previously expected to reap two thirds of the $41 billion revenue stream expected to be generated by F-22 production during the next decade. Congress may decide to use current aircraft until the Joint Strike Fighter becomes available. The prime contractor for the Joint Strike Fighter has not been selected and could be either Lockheed Martin or Boeing (Cole, Squeo, and Ricks, 1999; Ricks and Squeo, 1999).

Failure of the Iridium satellite phone system caused Lockheed Martin to write off $20 million of Iridium stock. In 1999, Lockheed Martin had several unsuccessful rocket launches. Lockheed Martin's Titan IV rocket has failed on three occasions to place its payload into a correct orbit. Recent investigations have concluded that Lockheed Martin was at fault for two of the failures, and a Boeing rocket engine was at fault for the other failure (Squeo, September 9, 1999). Lockheed Martin was accountable for the poor supplier oversight and quality control that led to these failed launches. Lockheed Martin's recent loss of a Department of Defense imagery satellite contract worth $5 billion over the next decade can be partially attributed to a loss of confidence in Lockheed Martin satellite launch systems (Squeo, September 8, 1999).

Another problem for Lockheed Martin's overseas satellite sales is the new strict State Department guidelines for exporting satellite technology from the United States. The turnaround time for State Department review of satellite information before release of satellite information to foreign entities (customers, insurers, and foreign governments that launch U.S.-made satellites) is approximately 90 days. This long delay hurts the competitiveness of U.S. satellite manufacturers in the world market (Newman, 1999).

Lockheed Martin announced another sector rearrangement and asset sale in September of 1999. The new sectors will be military aircraft, space systems, systems engineering, and technology services. Additionally, several operations with sales of approximately $1.4 billion will be sold (Cole, 1999). The goal of this sector rearrangement and asset sale was to allow Lockheed Martin to concentrate on its core businesses. On the heels of this announcement, the COO and the head of Lockheed Martin's military aircraft unit both left the company, and year 2000 earnings estimates have been cut from the previous estimate of $2.15 per share to a revised estimate of $1 per share (Cole, 1999; Velocci, November 8, 1999).

## CONCLUSION

Lockheed Martin is struggling with its identity and facing a challenging future. After surviving the defense industry consolidation of the 1990s, Lockheed Martin seems to be not only having trouble maintaining its core defense business but also seems unable to take advantage of the civilian technologies it has acquired in an attempt to diversify. Lockheed Martin has had little success growing revenues and income, is holding $12 billion in debt acquired during takeover activity, and has sales and revenue problems due to quality and cost control problems associated with many of its products. As the consolidation of the aerospace and defense industry continues, Lockheed Martin must work to eliminate these problems if it is to remain a major player in this industry.

## REFERENCES

ADVANI, R. N., M. ANDERSON, S. BOWLING, D. DOANE, AND E. B. ROBERTS, "Technology Strategy in Defense Industry Acquisitions: A Comparative Assessment of Two Giants." *International Journal of Technology Management, 15* (8), 781–804.

COLE, J. "CEO at Lockheed Martin Is Only Top Official Still Remaining." *The Wall Street Journal,* November 1, 1999, p. A4.

COLE, J. "Lockheed Plans to Streamline Operations." *The Wall Street Journal,* September 28, 1999, pp. A3, A8.

COLE, J., A. M. Squeo, and T. E. Ricks. "Specter of F-22 Funding Cut Skews Lockheed's Recovery Plans." *The Wall Street Journal,* July 26, 1999, p. A4.

"Diamler and Aerospatiale Matra Agree to Combine Their Aerospace Businesses—European Firms' Accord Will Create No. 3 Firm in Aircraft and Defense." *The Wall Street Journal,* October 15, 1999, pp. A3, A4.

KANDEBO, S. W. "Lean Thinking Spurs Culture Shift at LMAS." *Aviation Week and Space Technology,* July 12, 1999, 56–63.

LOCKHEED MARTIN CORPORATION, *Annual Report,* July 12, 1999, 1998.

NEWMAN, R. J. "The Air up There—If you Build Them, Will They Fly?" *U.S. News and World Report,* November 8, 1999, p. 38.

POPE, H. "Turks Vow to Spend Heavily as Military Expands-Arms Fair Popular as U.S. Firms See Major Opportunities." *The Wall Street Journal,* October 5, 1999, p. A21.

RICKS, T. E. AND A. M. SQUEO. "Air Force Says F-22 Funding Cut May Hurt Programs, Contractors." *The Wall Street Journal,* July 27, 1999, p. A4.

SQUEO, A. M. "Boeing Is Awarded Contract to Make Imagery Satellites." *The Wall Street Journal,* September 8, 1999, p. B14.

SQUEO, A. M. "Review of Lockheed Unit's Woes Cites Poor Oversight and Quality Control." *The Wall Street Journal,* September 9, 1999, p. A16.

VELOCCI, A. L. "Lockheed Martin Faces Long, Painful Recovery." *Aviation Week and Space Technology,* November 8, 1999, 30–33.

VELOCCI, A. L. "U.K. Industry Rewarded by Focusing on 'Basics'." *Aviation Week and Space Technology,* May 31, 1999, 45–55.

# DELL COMPUTER CORPORATION—2001

**Cindy R. Smith**
**Francis Marion University**

## DELL

www.dell.com

When you think of computer systems, what is the first company to come to mind? Is it IBM? Is it Compaq? Dell Computer Corporation is making its place in the computer systems market, having experienced astronomical growth since its inception in 1984. The company is headquartered in Round Rock, Texas. Michael Dell is the computer industry's longest-tenured chief executive officer. Dell's concept is to simply cut out the middleman and sell computers directly to consumers. Consumers order Dell computers, products, and services via the Internet and the telephone.

Dell is the world's leading direct computer systems company. Revenues for the fiscal year that ended January 29, 1999, were $18.2 billion. Dell holds the number-two spot among all major computer systems companies worldwide, and it is the fastest-growing company in the computer industry.

Dell employs 29,300 employees around the globe. Dell is ranked as the number-one personal computer seller in the United States with a 17.1 percent market share. Dell's customers are made up of businesses, government agencies, educational institutions, and individuals. Their products include desktop computers, notebook computers, servers, workstations, peripheral hardware, computer software, and a full line of warranty, service, and support options. Dell currently operates manufacturing facilities in Austin, Texas; Nashville, Tennessee; Limerick, Ireland; Penang, Malaysia; and Xiamen, China. In 1999, Dell opened a manufacturing facility in Brazil. The company maintains sales offices in 33 countries worldwide and sells products and services in more than 170 countries and territories.

Dell Computer Corporation seems to be in a good strategic position. Of course, there is always room for improvement. Many industry analysts expect worldwide industry volume growth to continue at a compound annual rate of 15 percent to 20 percent over the next three to five years. Internet expansion around the world contributes to this expectation. Dell plans to move more product sales, services, and support to the Internet. It also plans to better utilize the Internet for procurement, manufacturing, and distribution. The main focus will be on product and global expansion and on partnering with "best-in-class" companies. Targeted organizations will extend, support, and leverage the Direct Model and will include companies competing in the areas of storage and enterprise technologies, communication, Internet-based services, distribution, and other technology-related investments. The goal of such relationships will be growth, profitability, and liquidity.

## HISTORY

Michael Dell's business skills emerged when he was twelve years old. He earned $2,000 operating a nationwide stamp auction. In high school, he continued to exhibit entrepreneurial behavior. By creatively using the help of classmates, he made $18,000 selling the *Houston Post* to newly married couples. Once in college, his activities changed to adding components to the unsold stock of local PC dealers and selling them to local businesses. By the spring of his first year, he was turning over $50,000 a month. In May 1984, Michael Dell formed the Dell Computer Corporation and dropped out of the University of Texas at Austin. He told his father that he would rather compete with IBM. Sales reached $180,000 the first month.

In 1985, the company introduced the first personal computer of its own design. The Turbo featured the Intel 8088 processor. Dell Computer Corporation continued to grow its products and services. The company became the first PC seller to offer next-day, on-site product service. International expansion began in 1987 with the opening of a subsidiary in the United Kingdom. In 1988, the company held an initial public offering of company stock. As growth continued, there was a need for more manufacturing capabilities worldwide. The company responded by opening a manufacturing center in Limerick, Ireland, to serve the organization's European, Middle Eastern, and African markets. Dell continued to practice product development and introduced its first notebook PC in 1991. In 1992, the company was included for the first time among the Fortune 500 roster of the world's largest companies. Of course, there were some bumps along the way.

This colossal expansion created problems for the young company. The early 1990s were plagued by weak information technology systems, a management team that lacked experience, and negative cash flows. In 1992, Dell grew 126 percent. This was a dream come true, but the establishment could no longer support itself. In 1993, Dell joined the top five personal computer manufacturers worldwide and opened subsidiaries in Australia and Japan. This expansion led to the opening of a manufacturing facility in Penang, Malaysia, in 1996. Michael Dell hired a varied management team. Morton Topfer from Motorola joined the company in 1994 along with others from the technology world. Internet sales began, and the company started its major push into the network-server market. Growth and diversification continued into 1997 with the introduction of Dell's first workstation systems. This year also marked Dell's shipment of its ten-millionth computer system. Internet sales exceeded $3 million per day in 1997. This company showed no signs of slowing in its push to become a world leader in the computer systems market.

In 1998, Dell increased manufacturing capacity in the Americas and Europe and opened a production and customer center in Xiamen, China. The PowerVault storage products were introduced in 1998 as well. With Internet sales reaching $30 million per day, 1999 proved to be no exception to this company's past success. Dell Computer Corporation has opened an on-line computer-related superstore, www.gigabuys.com and began offering an Internet-access service for Dell customers called Dellnet.

## MISSION STATEMENT

Dell's current mission statement is given below:

Dell's mission is to be the most successful computer company in the world at delivering the best customer experience in markets we serve. In doing so, Dell will meet customer expectations of:

- Highest quality
- Leading technology
- Competitive pricing
- Individual and company accountability

- "Best in Class" service and support
- Flexible customization capability
- Superior corporate citizenship
- Financial stability

## DELL AMERICAS

Dell Americas is based in Round Rock, Texas, and covers the United States, Canada, and Latin America. Manufacturing facilities are in Austin, Texas, and Nashville, Tennessee. This business segment's revenues for the fiscal year ended January 28, 2000, make up 70 percent of total company revenue at $17.8 billion. This division's operations are located in North York, Ontario, Canada; Santiago, Chile; Monterrey and Mexico City, Mexico; and Bogota, Colombia. This segment employs 19,800 employees and is in the number-two position in the United States.

## DELL EUROPE, MIDDLE EAST, AFRICA

This business segment is headquartered in Bracknell, England, and has a manufacturing facility in Limerick, Ireland. It covers European countries and also some countries in the Middle East and Africa. Revenues for this segment for fiscal year ended January 28, 2000, were $5.5 billion. This segment earned 22 percent of total company revenue and employs 7,000 employees. This division's operations are located in the following cities:

- Klosterneuburg, Austria
- Asse-Zellik, Belgium
- Prague, Czech Republic
- Horsholm, Denmark
- Helsinki, Finland
- Montpellier and Puteaux la Defense, France
- Langen, Germany
- Bray and Limerick, Ireland
- Milan, Italy
- Amsterdam, the Netherlands
- Lysaker, Norway
- Warsaw, Poland
- Johannesburg, South Africa
- Madrid, Spain
- Upplands Vasby, Sweden
- Geneva, Switzerland
- Dubai, United Arab Emirates
- Bracknell, United Kingdom

## DELL ASIA PACIFIC/DELL JAPAN

Headquartered in Hong Kong and Kawasaki, Japan, this segment has manufacturing facilities in Penang, Malaysia and Xiamen, China. Revenues from this segment are approximately $1.7 billion. It is number seven in the Asia Pacific region and number nine in Japan. This business segment employs a total of 2,400 employees. This division's operations are located in the following cities:

- Sydney, Australia
- Beijing, Guangzhou, Shanghai and Xiamen, China
- Bangalore, India
- Kuala Lumpur and Penang, Malaysia
- Auckland, New Zealand
- Singapore
- Taipei, Taiwan
- Bangkok, Thailand
- Seoul, South Korea

## OPERATIONS

### Social Responsibility

Dell is as committed to social and environmental well-being as it is to growth, profitability, and liquidity. This is obvious in its recycling efforts, its waste elimination efforts, and its generosity to society. The management team at Dell realizes it must keep the environments and societies in which they do business healthy in order to recruit and retain a highly skilled and motivated workforce.

Dell's environmental efforts can be seen through its Direct Model, products, services, and manufacturing processes. The Direct Model's build-to-order manufacturing system minimizes waste by ensuring that each product has a buyer. This reduces excess and obsolete inventory that could wind up in landfills. By selling its products directly to the consumer, the company eliminates the environmental waste associated with retail outlets or resellers. Dell's ability to keep minimal inventory allows technological advances to be brought into manufacturing more quickly. Out-of-date systems and parts do not have to be sold or discarded. Preservation is also built into Dell products. In 1996, the company introduced a new design philosophy for the OptiPlex line that extends the life cycle of the PC and has several environmentally friendly features. OptiPlex models have received such awards as the German Eco-label, Blue Angel award, and the Swedish TCO '95 certification. The services offered by Dell are also helping to preserve the natural environment. The Asset Recovery Program and European Take-Back Program are examples of such services. Support offered via the Internet and telephone curtail pollutants in the air by limiting transportation. The manufacturing process at Dell reflects the company's attitude about natural resources and the world we live in. No CFCs, HCFCs, toxins, or hazardous wastes are emitted into the environment. The Metric 12 facility uses the Reduce, Reuse, and Recycle (R3) Program. This practice also saves money.

### Corporate Structure

Dell does not publish its organizational chart. The company appears to have a divisional structure by geographic area and product line. The company allocates resources to and evaluates performance of its geographic segments based on operating income. An example of what the chart might look like is shown in Exhibit 1.

### Finance

Dell Computer Corporation's financial statements are presented in Exhibits 2, 3, and 4.

EXHIBIT 1    Dell Computer Corporation Organization Chart

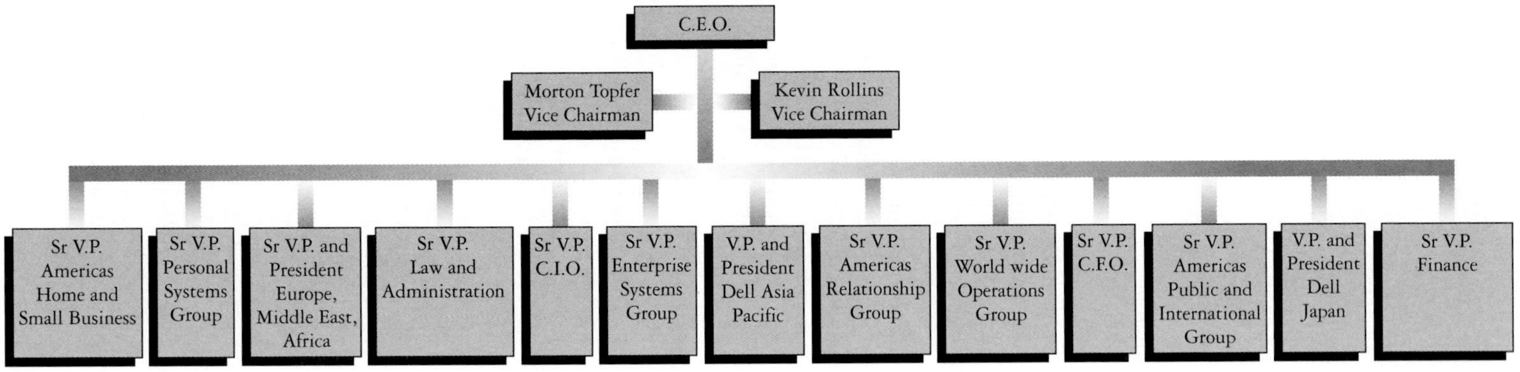

C.E.O.

Morton Topfer
Vice Chairman

Kevin Rollins
Vice Chairman

Sr V.P.
Americas Home and
Small Business

Sr V.P.
Personal
Systems
Group

Sr V.P. and
President
Europe, Middle East,
Africa

Sr V.P.
Law and
Administration

Sr V.P.
C.I.O.

Sr V.P.
Enterprise
Systems
Group

V.P. and
President
Dell Asia
Pacific

Sr V.P.
Americas
Relationship
Group

Sr V.P.
World wide
Operations
Group

Sr V.P.
C.F.O.

Sr V.P.
Americas
Public and
International
Group

V.P. and
President
Dell
Japan

Sr V.P.
Finance

# EXHIBIT 2     Dell Computer Financial Segment Data (dollars in millions)

| Fiscal Year Ended | January 28, 2000 | Percentage Increase | January 29, 1999 | Percentage Increase | February 1, 1998 |
|---|---|---|---|---|---|
| **New revenue:** | | | | | |
| Americas | $17,879 | 44% | $12,420 | 46% | $ 8,531 |
| Europe | 5,590 | 20 | 4,674 | 58 | 2,956 |
| Asia-Pacific and Japan | 1,796 | 56 | 1,149 | 37 | 840 |
| Consolidated new revenue | $25,265 | | $18,243 | | $12,327 |

# EXHIBIT 3     Dell Computer Annual Income Statement
## (in millions except earnings per share data)

| | 1/31/00 | 1/31/99 | 1/31/98 | 1/31/97 |
|---|---|---|---|---|
| Sales | $25,265.00 | $18,243.00 | $12,327.00 | $7,759.00 |
| Cost of goods | 20,047.00 | 14,137.00 | 9,605.00 | 6,093.00 |
| **Gross profit** | **5,218.00** | **4,106.00** | **2,722.00** | **1,666.00** |
| Selling and administrative and department and amortization expenses | 2,761.00 | 2,060.00 | 1,406.00 | 952.00 |
| **Income after depreciation and amortization** | 2,457.00 | 2,046.00 | 1,316.00 | 714.00 |
| Nonoperating income | (6.00) | 38.00 | 52.00 | 33.00 |
| Interest expense | N/A | 0 | 0 | 0 |
| **Pretax income** | 2,451.00 | 2,084.00 | 1,368.00 | 747.00 |
| Income taxes | 785.00 | 624.00 | 424.00 | 216.00 |
| Minority interest | N/A | 0 | 0 | 0 |
| Investment gains/losses (+) | N/A | 0 | 0 | 0 |
| Other income/charges | N/A | 0 | 0 | 0 |
| **Income from continued operations** | **N/A** | **N/A** | **N/A** | **N/A** |
| Extras and discontinued operations | 0 | 0 | 0 | (13.00) |
| **Net income** | **$ 1,666.00** | **$ 1,460.00** | **$  944.00** | **$  518.00** |

## Depreciation footnote

| | | | | |
|---|---|---|---|---|
| Income before depreciation and amortization | $ 2,457.00 | $ 2,149.00 | $ 1,383.00 | $ 761.00 |
| Depreciation and amortization (cash flow) | N/A | 103.00 | 67.00 | 47.00 |
| **Income after depreciation and amorization** | **$ 2,457.00** | **$ 2,046.00** | **$ 1,316.00** | **$ 714.00** |

## Earnings-per-share data

| | | | | |
|---|---|---|---|---|
| **Average shares** | **$ 2,728.00** | **$ 2,772.00** | **$ 2,952.00** | **$3,068.80** |
| Diluted earnings per share before nonrecurring items | 0.68 | 0.52 | 0.32 | 0.10 |
| **Diluted net earnings per share** | **$    0.61** | **$    0.52** | **$    0.32** | **$    0.10** |

*Source:* www.freeedgar.com

EXHIBIT 4   Dell Computer Annual Balance Sheet
(in millions, except book value per share)

| | 1/31/00 | 1/31/99 | 1/31/98 | 1/31/97 |
|---|---|---|---|---|
| **Assets** | | | | |
| Cash and equivalents | $ 4,132.00 | $3,181.00 | $1,844.00 | $1,352.00 |
| Receivables | 2,608.00 | 2,094.00 | 1,486.00 | 903.00 |
| Notes receivable | N/A | 0 | 0 | 0 |
| Inventories | 391.00 | 273.00 | 233.00 | 251.00 |
| Other current assets | 550.00 | 791.00 | 349.00 | 241.00 |
| Toal current assets | 7,681.00 | 6,339.00 | 3,912.00 | 2,747.00 |
| Net property and equipment | 765.00 | 523.00 | 342.00 | 235.00 |
| Investments and advances | 1,048.00 | 0 | 0 | 0 |
| Other noncurrent assets | N/A | 0 | 0 | 0 |
| Deferred charges | N/A | 0 | 0 | 0 |
| Intangibles | N/A | 0 | 0 | 0 |
| Deposits and other assets | 1,977.00 | 15.00 | 14.00 | 11.00 |
| Total assets | $11,471.00 | $6,877.00 | $4,268.00 | $2,993.00 |
| **Liabilities and shareholders' equity** | | | | |
| Notes payable | N/A | 0 | 0 | 0 |
| Accounts payable | 3,538.00 | 2,397.00 | 1,643.00 | 1,040.00 |
| Current portion long-term debt | N/A | 0 | 0 | 0 |
| Current portion capital leases | N/A | 0 | 0 | 0 |
| Accrued expenses | 1,654.00 | 1,298.00 | 1,054.00 | 618.00 |
| Income taxes payable | N/A | 0 | 0 | 0 |
| Other current liabilities | N/A | 0 | 0 | 0 |
| Total current liabilities | 5,192.00 | 3,695.00 | 2,697.00 | 1,658.00 |
| Mortgages | N/A | 0 | 0 | 0 |
| Deferred taxes/income | N/A | 0 | 225.00 | 219.00 |
| Convertible debt | N/A | 0 | 0 | 0 |
| Long-term debt | 508.00 | 512.00 | 17.00 | 18.00 |
| Noncurrent capital leases | N/A | 0 | 0 | 0 |
| Other noncurrent liabilities | 463.00 | 349.00 | 36.00 | 13.00 |
| Minority interest (liabilities) | N/A | 0 | 0 | 0 |
| Total liabilities | $ 6,163.00 | $4,556.00 | $2,975.00 | $1,908.00 |
| **Shareholders' equity** | | | | |
| Preferred stock | N/A | 0 | 0 | 0 |
| Common stock (par) | N/A | 1,781.00 | 747.00 | 195.00 |
| Capital surplus | N/A | 0 | 0 | 0 |
| Retained earnings | N/A | 606.00 | 607.00 | 647.00 |
| Other equity | N/A | (66.00) | (61.00) | 243.00 |
| Treasury stock | N/A | 0 | 0 | 0 |
| Total shareholders' equity | 5,308.00 | 2,321.00 | 1,293.00 | 1,085.00 |
| Total liabilities and shareholders' equity | 11,471.00 | 6,877.00 | 4,268.00 | 2,993.00 |
| Total common equity | 5,308.00 | 2,321.00 | 1,293.00 | 1,985.00 |
| Average shares | 2,728.00 | 2,772.00 | 2,952.00 | 3,068.80 |
| Book value per share | $     2.08 | $     0.91 | $     0.50 | $     0.36 |

*Source:* www.freeedgar.com

## Sales and Marketing

Dell's customers encompass large corporations, government agencies, medical facilities, educational institutions, small businesses, and individuals. The company uses similar sales and marketing approaches for all customers. Market prices and overall economic condition drive demand levels among all groups. The customer group is the basis on which sales and marketing teams in each region are divided. In each region the company serves relationship customers, transactional customers, and Internet customers. For its relationship customers, the company maintains a field salesforce throughout the world to call on businesses and institutional consumers and prospects. Direct sales marketing programs and services are developed specifically for these customers. The small-to-medium businesses and individuals that make up Dell's transactional customer base are targeted through the use of trade and general business publications, promotional pieces, catalogs, and customer newsletters. Internet patrons account for 40 percent of company revenues. As of March 1, 1999, www.dell.com had 2 million visits per week. Dell offers 44 country-specific sites and custom Internet sites, Premier Pages, to its Internet buyers. These amenities add to the attractiveness of on-line computer systems purchasing. Among other added services, they also offer an online source of more than 30,000 competitively priced computer-related products www.gigabuys.com.

Recently, Dell has begun to utilize television to attract potential buyers to the Dell Web page. The industry is expected to continue to grow for the next three to five years, and Dell must win consumers to sustain the growth and profitability seen in the past. Currently, it enjoys a 17.1 percent share of the U.S. PC market and an 11.6 percent share of the global PC market. This gives Dell a rank of number one in the U.S. market and number two in the global market for PC shipments.

## MANUFACTURING

Dell operates manufacturing facilities worldwide and opened an additional site in Brazil in 1999. The new facility offers Dell's full line of computer system products and services to consumers in Brazil, Argentina, Uruguay, Paraguay, and Chile. The manufacturing processes at Dell's worldwide plants include assembly, testing, and quality control of computer systems. Subassemblies, parts, and components are purchased from suppliers, tested, and held to specified quality standards. Testing is performed throughout the process and on the final product to ensure that the buyer receives a quality, defect-free product. The build-to-order manufacturing operation allows the company to take advantage of new technologies at a faster pace than competitors. This philosophy, along with the relationships Dell has with its suppliers, makes minimal inventories possible. There is no need for huge warehouses, and inventory turnover is high. All of the manufacturing facilities have been certified as meeting ISO 9002 quality standards.

## COMPETITION

### Compaq Computer Corporation

Compaq Computer Corporation, headquartered in Houston, Texas, is the largest seller of PCs in the world with a market share of 13.8 percent. The company has recently slipped to second place behind Dell Computer Corporation in the sales of PCs in the United States. Compaq distributes computer hardware, software, solutions, and services to consumers primarily through resellers. Current manufacturing facilities are located in Texas, Scotland, Singapore, Brazil, and China. In the recent past, Compac has attempted to mimic Dell's Direct Model. Its success has been limited, and this is mainly due to relationships with distributors. Most of the company's sales are to businesses, but Compaq also targets home users, government agencies, schools, and students. Compaq is currently ranked number twenty-eight in the Fortune 500 list. CEO Michael D. Capellas, in July 22, 1999, said, "Changes in the personal computer business are not just about sales and distribution models." He went on to add, "Compaq is banking on an array of upcoming computer models."

## Hewlitt Packard Company

Headquarters for Hewlitt Packard Company are in Palo Alto, California. The company is a global provider of computing and imaging solutions and services for business and home. Its focus is on taking advantage of opportunities arising due to the Internet and the proliferation of electronic services. The number-two computer company worldwide, HP has operations in the United States, Europe, Asia, and the Pacific Rim, Africa, Latin America, Canada, and the Middle East. The company is decentralized and prides itself on giving its 104 divisions decision-making authority. The number of employees around the globe totals to about 123,500. Six hundred sales and support offices and distributorships, resellers, and retailers handle distribution for the company's products. The majority of revenues come from computers plus peripherals and services. Fifty-four percent of HP's business is derived from outside the United States, and two thirds of that comes from Europe. By mid-2000, the company plans to launch Agilent Technologies as an independent corporation, which will include test and measurement, semiconductor products, chemical analysis, and healthcare solutions businesses. The company plans to restructure itself as an Internet specialist to stimulate growth. It will provide Web hardware, software, and support to corporate customers. The future outlook is positive, and the company plans to remain a major player in the computer industry.

## International Business Machines Corporation

International Business Machines Corporation is the world's top provider of computer hardware and holds 8.1 percent of the worldwide PC market. The company also makes software (ranked number two behind Microsoft) and peripherals. Thirty-five percent of IBM's sales stem from services. Although the company is headquartered in Armonk, New York, 60 percent of sales are to customers outside the United States. IBM holds a strong position in the computer industry as evidenced by the fact that its market value has grown by $146 billion since 1993. Research and development is important to the company. Products developed in 1999 generated hardware sales totaling $17.5 million. IBM also holds the record for the most U.S. patents for the past six years. Like other companies in the industry, IBM plans to revamp its image and focus on Internet business.

## GLOBAL ISSUES

The computer industry is expected to grow 15 percent to 20 percent for the next three to five years. The two major factors that led to this expectation are the Internet and global expansion opportunities. Many foreign markets are becoming accessible and attractive for computer makers and other industries. Many foreign economies are looking more favorable and 95 percent of the world's population lives outside the United States. China and Brazil are two basically untapped markets. Telephone expansion is occurring in many developing countries. On the heels of enhanced communication systems come computers and the Internet. These countries are realizing that the Internet is becoming imperative for global business. As the telephone infrastructure improves in these countries, the cost of the interacting on the Internet should also decline. The Euro should make Internet commerce more attractive for European countries. Computers are an important part of this new way of doing business, and computer companies must position themselves to gain as much of this new market as possible. Competition is heavy, and businesses must consider many factors when entering global markets.

For example, patents and trademarks are very prevalent in the computer industry, but the courts in foreign countries may not honor such agreements. Currency exchange rates, tax laws, political situations, labor conditions, environmental surroundings, and economic elements can greatly affect business relations in foreign countries. There is higher risk of loss of competitive advantages and technologies to competitors when companies expand into global markets. Precautions must be taken to minimize the negative impacts, because this expansion is necessary for companies to survive. Companies must create positive relationships with foreign countries and their inhabitants.

## CONCLUSION

Dell's major strategic focus should be on capturing more of the individual consumer market and taking advantage of the worldwide opportunities opening up to computer makers. Two thirds of the company's consumers are large organizations. Capturing the loyalties of small businesses and individuals could greatly boost Dell's position in the computer industry. Developing countries worldwide are gaining increased access to telephones. This is very significant to the producers of many products, including computer manufacturers. Once telephones are in place, the demand for computers and the Internet will skyrocket. Should Dell open operations in China and Brazil? Would a joint venture with a telephone company give Dell a competitive advantage?

Should Dell diversify with related or unrelated products? Is any diversification needed? Such products as online services may be an option for the company. Dell's philosophy has been to stick with its core competencies and partner with other "best in class" companies. Is this still appropriate?

Develop a strategic plan for the company that will enable it to capture the dollars spent on computers and related products by small businesses, individuals, and global buyers. How should the company finance your recommendations? Show the results of your plan through the development of pro-forma financial statements. Do the results look as expected? Why or why not?

---

## REFERENCES

Dell.com

HP.com

IBM.com

Compaq.com

Dell Computer Corporation's *10K Report* (1999)

BIRD, JANE. "Dell's Direct Approach." *Management Today* February 1997: 62–64.

# APPLE COMPUTER, INC.—2000

David Stanton
University of South Carolina

## AAPL

www.apple.com

Steve Jobs is back in charge at the company he cofounded, and for many fans of the company, all is again right with their world. The products are exciting; the company is profitable; the stock price is high and the prospects are bright. It has been a remarkable turnaround.

In 1997, Apple was a company in trouble. In two years, the company had lost a staggering $1.9 billion. Its revenues, market share, and stock price had plummeted. Net sales in 1998 were down more than $5 billion from 1995, a drop of almost 50 percent. But although the sales slide continued into 1998, something changed in 1997. Jobs had returned. At first, it was as de facto CEO, with no official authority, then as interim CEO as the search for a permanent CEO dragged on. Nobody wanted the position with Jobs there, but as the search stagnated, Jobs turned the company around. Apple posted a profit of $309 million in 1998.

After more than two years, Jobs ended his stint as interim CEO and announced in January 2000 that he would, after all, accept the job on a permanent basis. During his tenure as interim CEO, the company managed eight straight profitable quarters and posted a net income of $601 million in fiscal 1999.

## HISTORY

Apple was born in 1976, when Steve Jobs and Stephen Wozniak designed the Apple I computer in the garage of Jobs' parents' home in Cupertino, California. Jobs sold his Volkswagen van, and Wozniak sold his programmable calculator to finance the building of the first 50 circuit boards. The company was incorporated in 1977 and introduced a more advanced computer called the Apple II that helped to launch the era of desktop computers. The company went public in 1980 at $22 per share in the largest public offering since Ford went public in 1956.

In 1982, Apple became the first personal computer company to reach $1 billion in annual sales and entered the Fortune 500 the next year at number 411, less than five years after incorporation. The company hired former Pepsi president John Sculley as president and CEO and established a radical new direction in personal computing with introduction of the Lisa(R) computer. Although the Lisa was not a financial success, this milestone product set the industry standard for software based on a graphical user interface. Lisa technology was the foundation for the much-anticipated Macintosh(R) introduced on January 24, 1984. With icons, pull-down menus, windows, and a mouse, the Macintosh set a new standard for ease of use in the industry that continues today. It would take six more years for Microsoft to introduce a usable graphical interface for the PC.

In 1985, Jobs failed in a bid for control of the company and resigned, leaving Sculley as the head of Apple. Jobs started a new computer company, NeXT, and Wozniak resigned to start a company to develop home video products. By 1990 the market was saturated with PC-clones of every conceivable configuration, and Apple was still the only company selling Macs. In late May, Microsoft introduced Windows 3.0, which could run on virtually all of the PC-clones in the world. Apple was in trouble and considered licensing the Mac OS. There was also talk of porting the Mac OS to run on Intel-based machines. In 1992, Apple lost a copyright ruling in its lawsuit against Microsoft, essentially ending its hopes of defeating Windows in court. In 1994, Apple announced it would, for the first time, license its operating system to other computer makers.

In 1995, Apple launched a new line of laptops but had to recall them after two models burst into flames. Other companies were profiting from the PC boom, but component shortages kept Apple customers waiting. By mid-year, Apple's backlog soared to $1 billion. In January 1996, Apple posted a $69 million first-quarter loss, its first Christmas quarter loss, and announced 1,300 layoffs, or 8 percent of its workforce. Gilbert Amelio, a member of Apple's board of directors since 1994 and former CEO of National Semiconductor Corp., was elected CEO on February 5, 1996. The turnover was punctuated by a stunning loss of $740 million in the March 1996 quarter, with more than half of the loss from inventory writedowns. Amelio promised to make the company profitable in a year, a promise that would prove impossible to keep.

In December 1996, Apple announced plans to acquire Steve Jobs' NeXT Software Inc. for $400 million, reuniting the cofounder with the company. Apple had an $816 million net loss in 1996 and continued its downward spiral in 1997, posting an unexpected $120 million loss for the first quarter as sales of its flagship Macintosh model continued to fall sharply. Faced with shrinking revenues, Amelio announced plans for yet another restructuring that included layoffs of another 4,100 employees and cuts in research and development. The company lost $708 million in the second quarter. Amelio resigned, and Apple began a search for a new CEO. Jobs assumed the role of de facto CEO, fueling speculation he would take over the troubled company, but when offered the position, he declined. Weighed down by continued bad news, Apple shares slid to $12 3/4, a 12-year low. In August, after nearly a month of uncertainty, Apple and Microsoft shocked the computer world when they announced that Microsoft would invest $150 million in Apple. Apple had turned to its bitterest enemy for help, symbolically declaring defeat, but the investment provided a needed psychological boost that helped keep other software companies at bay and Mac customers from defecting.

After a period in which Jobs acted as de facto CEO, he was named interim CEO by the board, pending the completion of the search for a permanent CEO. Jobs led a fight against the "clone makers," whom he believed were hurting sales while paying too little for their Mac OS licenses. Jobs had ended Apple's short experiment with Mac OS licensing. In 1997, Apple introduced OS 8, a new operating system for the Macintosh personal computer, the most significant Mac OS upgrade since its introduction in 1984. Sales were brisk, quadrupling the company's expectations. The company also began selling many of its products directly to end users in the United States through its online store.

In 1998, in an effort to tap the growing consumer market for computers, Apple introduced the iMac, which it calls "The Internet-Age Computer for the Rest of Us." The iMac is a low-cost computer that represented a reorientation of the company toward the consumer market. The company also simplified its product line and reduced the number of its wholesale and retail channel partners. Apple's consumer efforts have driven the company's spectacular recovery.

Over the past two years, particularly since the announcement of the iMac in May 1998, software developers have demonstrated renewed interest in the Macintosh platform. Since iMac was announced, approximately 5,000 new or revised software titles have been announced for the Macintosh platform.

## OVERVIEW

Headquartered in Cupertino, California, Apple develops, manufactures, licenses, and markets computer hardware, software, and services for business, education, entertainment, scientific and engineering, and government customers in more than 140 countries. Apple owns manufacturing facilities in California, Ireland, and Singapore.

At one time, Apple dominated the personal computer market. Today, it is holding its own, saved by its restructuring, a new focus on the consumer, and the fact that Apple users are almost fanatically devoted. It has clung to an anachronistic business model. Apple is the only company in the personal computer market that makes both computers and the operating system to run them, whereas the market is dominated by computers that combine Intel processors with Microsoft operating systems.

When it comes to rank-and-file Apple users, though, hope springs eternal. Individual Apple users remain committed to the company even as corporate America moves to Wintel. Apple is not just a company to many of its customers, some of whom feel an almost religious devotion to it.

### Products

Apple has two basic lines of computers targeted at different market segments. Power Macintosh line of personal computers and PowerBook portable computers are targeted at business and professional users. The iMac computer and the iBook portable computer are targeted at the education and consumer markets. Apple also sells computer peripherals, including color monitors and the AirPort wireless networking system. The company's operating system software provides Macintosh computers with an easy, consistent user interface.

### Core Markets

Apple has traditionally held the major market share in education. According to a 1995–96 market research study by Quality Education Data, Apple's installed base of computers in K–12 public schools was 63 percent—a 4 percent increase from the previous year. Apple's dominance, however, is threatened by aggressive promotions of Windows-based systems from Compaq, Dell, and other companies. In 1999, Apple continued to lead the market but no longer dominated it. According to International Data Corp., Apple's 1999 share of overall U.S. education sales was 22.2 percent—higher than Compaq's 19.1 percent, Gateway's 17.2 percent, and Dell's fourth place showing at 15.8 percent.

Apple also leads in creative markets, defined as graphic designers, corporate design departments, ad agencies, book and magazine publishers, catalog publishers, commercial photographers, and graphic illustrators. Apple also boasts leadership in key entertainment segments, such as music production and video postproduction. However, despite the company's strong position in these specialty markets, a bigger challenge remains: how to convince other businesses to stick with the Macintosh. Many companies and organizations that once standardized on the Mac platform have phased it out in favor of Intel-based machines running Microsoft Windows.

## INTERNAL OPERATIONS

### Marketing and Distribution

Apple distributes its products through wholesalers, resellers, retailers, and cataloguers and directly to education institutions. It also sells directly to end users through its on-line store. Currently, the primary means of distribution is through third-party computer resellers. Such resellers include consumer channels such as mass-merchandise stores, consumer electronics outlets, and computer superstores. Apple increased its marketing and promotional efforts in 1999.

### Research and Development

Apple believes that continued investments in research and development are critical to its future growth and competitive position in the marketplace and are directly related to continued, timely development of new and enhanced products. Research and development expenditures totaled $314 million, $303 million, $485 million, and $604 million in 1999, 1998, 1997, and 1996, respectively. The 1996–1998 declines in total expenditures for research and development were caused by restructuring efforts that have now been completed, and Apple expects R&D expenditures to continue to rise gradually in the future.

### Finance

Apple's financial statements are provided in Exhibits 1 and 2. Note that Apple's net income nearly doubled from 1998 to 1999, and long-term debt is down from $954 million in 1998 to $300 million in 1999, the lowest level since 1995. Inventories are down substantially as well.

### EXHIBIT 1    Apple Computer Consolidated Statements of Operations
#### (in millions, except share and per-share amounts)

|  | September 25, 1999 | September 25, 1998 | September 25, 1997 |
|---|---|---|---|
| Net sales | $6,134 | $5,941 | $7,081 |
| Cost of sales | 4,438 | 4,462 | 5,713 |
| Gross margin | 1,696 | 1,479 | 1,368 |
| Operating expenses: |  |  |  |
| Research and development | 314 | 303 | 485 |
| Selling, general, and administrative | 996 | 908 | 1,286 |
| Special charges: |  |  |  |
| In-process research and development | — | 7 | 375 |
| Restructuring costs | 27 | — | 217 |
| Termination of license agreement | — | — | 75 |
| Total operating expenses | 1,337 | 1,218 | 2,438 |
| Operating income (loss) | 359 | 261 | −1,070 |
| Gains from sales of investment | 230 | 40 | — |
| Interest and other income, net | 87 | 28 | 25 |
| Total interest and other income, net | 317 | 68 | 25 |
| Income (loss) before provision for income taxes | 676 | 329 | −1,045 |
| Provision for income taxes | 75 | 20 | — |
| Net income (loss) | $  601 | $  309 |  |
| Earnings (loss) per common share: |  |  |  |
| Basic | $ 4.20 | $ 2.34 |  |
| Diluted | $ 3.61 | $ 2.10 |  |
| Shares used in computing earnings (loss) per share (in thousands): |  |  |  |
| Basic | 143,157 | 131,974 | 126,062 |
| Diluted | 174,164 | 167,917 | 126,062 |

*Source:* www.freeedgar.com

EXHIBIT 2    Apple Computer Consolidated Balance Sheets
(in millions)

|  | September 25, 1999 | September 25, 1998 |
|---|---|---|
| **Assets** | | |
| Current assets: | | |
|   Cash and cash equivalents | $1,316 | $1,481 |
|   Short-term investments | 1,900 | 819 |
| Accounts receivable, less allowances of $68 and $81, | | |
|   respectively | 681 | 955 |
| Inventories | 20 | 78 |
| Deferred tax assets | 143 | 182 |
| Other current assets | 215 | 183 |
| Total current assets | 4,285 | 3,698 |
| Property, plant, and equipment, net | 318 | 348 |
| Other assets | 558 | 243 |
| Total assets | $5,161 | $4,289 |
| **Liabilities and shareholders' equity** | | |
| Current liabilities: | | |
|   Accounts payable | $ 812 | $ 719 |
|   Accrued expenses | 737 | 801 |
| Total current liabilities | 1,549 | 1,520 |
| Long-term debt | 300 | 954 |
| Deferred tax liabilities | 208 | 173 |
| Total liabilities | $2,057 | $2,647 |
| Commitments and contingencies | | |
| **Shareholders' equity** | | |
| Series A nonvoting convertible preferred stock, no | | |
|   par value; 150,000 shares authorized, issued and | | |
|   outstanding | 150 | 150 |
| Common stock, no par value; 320,000,000 shares | | |
|   authorized; 160,779,061 and 135,192,769 shares | | |
|   issued and outstanding, respectively | 1,349 | 633 |
| Retained earnings | 1,499 | 898 |
| Accumulated other comprehensive income (loss) | 106 | −39 |
| Total shareholders' equity | 3,104 | 1,642 |
| Total liabilities and shareholders' equity | $5,161 | $4,289 |

*Source:* www.freeedgar.com

## Management

Apple's management appears to be more settled than it was a short time ago. A number of executives left the company after Jobs returned in 1997, but he put together a team that has remained fairly stable. Five of the seven top officers (other than Jobs) of the company came aboard in 1997, with one holdover from before Jobs's return and one addition in 1998. Millard S. Drexler, added in 1999, is the only new face on the board of directors since 1997.

## THE PRESENT POSITION

During 1999, Apple experienced a 25 percent rise in Macintosh unit sales, primarily attributable to the success of the iMac. Apple sold approximately 1.8 million iMacs in 1999, an increase of 730,000 units or 68 percent over sales of similar products in 1998. Apple also had improved profitability in 1999. Operating income before special charges rose 44 percent to $386 million in 1999 from $268 million in 1998.

Despite improved unit sales and profitability, net sales rose only 3 percent in 1999 to $6.134 billion, largely because of lower pricing for both iMac and Power Macintosh products and a shift in product mix towards the lower-priced iMacs. Net sales increased 3 percent to $6.134 billion in 1999 compared to 1998. As of September 25, 1999, Apple had $3.226 billion in cash, cash equivalents, and short-term investments, an increase of $926 million or 40 percent over the same balances at the end of fiscal 1998.

Apple has invested $12.5 million in Akamai Technologies, Inc. Akamai, a newly public company, is a global Internet content delivery service. The fair value of the investment in Akamai is approximately $1.2 billion. During the fourth quarter of 1999, Apple invested $100 million in Samsung Electronics Co., Ltd., to assist in expansion of Samsung's flat-panel display production capacity.

Apple is competing in one of the fastest-changing markets in the world. Computers are becoming faster and cheaper at a dizzying rate, and the companies that are doing well are those that are able to adapt to that change. Apple is one of the few large computer companies that have fared poorly. It is unique in the computer industry in that it competes in both the personal computer and operating systems markets.

## CONCLUSION

Apple's situation has stabilized, and the future is no longer dim. The shift in focus toward the consumer market has been a success. However, the company remains a shadow of its former self in terms of market share and sales. The Mac OS's share of the overall PC market seems to have stabilized, but Apple remains a niche market player. Except for a few key segments, businesses have abandoned the platform. Apple's share of the corporate market is negligible, as the mass migration to Intel-based Windows computers is complete.

In January 2000, Jobs announced expanded Web services designed to leverage the Apple brand. Most of the services are accessible only with Mac OS users, including free Web file storage and a child-friendly area designed to appeal to computer-buying parents. Apple also has invested $200 million in Earthlink, which will become the exclusive Internet Service Provider in Apple's Internet Setup Software included with all Apple Macintosh computers sold in the United States. Apple will profit from each new Mac customer who subscribes to EarthLink's ISP service.

Is it possible for Apple to regain its former dominance of the personal computer and operating system markets? Should it be content to dominate a few important niches? What does the new focus on the Internet mean for the future of Apple? What strategies would you recommend Apple pursue to increase its market share? Prepare a three-year strategic plan for the company.

# COMPAQ COMPUTER CORPORATION—2000

Maria Margiotis
Francis Marion University

## CPQ

www.compaq.com

Is it IBM compatible? That is the question that consumers ask when buying hardware or software products. Compaq Computer Corporation, a Fortune Global 100 company and a Fortune 500 company, produces laptop and desktop computers that *are* IBM compatible. Compaq is the second-largest computer company in the world and the largest global supplier of computers and other peripheral equipment. In addition to producing laptop and desktop personal computers, Compaq has a wide array of products—from hardware, software, solutions and services, and enterprise and network solutions. In order to better meet and serve the needs of the growing market, Compaq acquired Tandem Computer Company in 1997; Trace Point Technology Inc., and Digital Equipment Company in 1998. The year 1999 was pretty good [1999] for the computer and peripherals industry as demand for personal computers and mainframes continued to rise despite volatility of the industry. Sales and net income at Compaq for 1999 were $38.5 billion and $569 million respectively. Profits from sales to foreign countries declined in 1999 to $840 million from $2.12 billion in 1999.

## HISTORY

Compaq was founded in 1982 as a small company in the state of Delaware on the concept that "personal computers, like persons should be mobile". Headquartered in Houston, Texas, Compaq has five manufacturing facilities around the world. They are located in Houston, Texas; Erksine, Scotland; Singapore; Jaguariuna and Saõ Paulo, Brazil; and Shenzhen, China.

On December 9, 1983, Compaq had an initial public offering of 6 million shares at $11.00 per share to raise $66 million. In 1983, Compaq's sales that first year were $111 million. At the time, this was a U.S. record. In 1984, Compaq's sales were $329 million. This was an industry record. In 1985 the company began trading on the New York Stock Exchange under the symbol CPQ.

As the years progressed, Compaq continued to set a number of records in its industry. The company reached $1 billion in sales in 1987 and then in 1989 became the number-two supplier of business PCs in Europe. This achievement brought about an increasing demand in the international market; in 1990, Compaq's international sales surpassed its North American sales. Compaq's success continued well into the mid-1990s with the success of the Compaq Presario in 1993 and an increasing worldwide customer base.

In 1995, Compaq acquired Thomas-Conrad Corporation and Networth, Inc., providers of networking products and services. The company continued its stream of acquisitions in 1997 with the acquisition of Microcom and Tandem Computers, Incorporated. The Microcom merger cost $278 million in cash and the assumption of certain employee stock options. The Tandem merger cost $44 million in cash and 126 million shares of Compaq common stock. In 1998, Compaq acquired Digital Equipment Corporation in order to meet the increasing demand for networking business solutions. The Digital merger was considered the biggest merger in the history of the computer and peripheral industry at an aggregate purchase price of $9.1 billion— specifics of the deal included $4.5 billion in cash, 141 million shares of Compaq common stock valued at approximately $4.3 billion as well as the issuance of approximately 25 million options to purchase Compaq common stock, valued at $249 million. These acquisitions allowed Compaq to become a leading provider of technology and remote access solutions, but trouble loomed ahead.

## EXTERNAL FACTORS

Compaq is a part of a very volatile industry in which competitors vie for market share and consumer loyalty. Firms in this industry deal with aggressive pricing, changing consumer needs, growing competitors, and constant changes in technology while attempting to be low-cost producers and environmentally friendly. The competition remains fierce. A large number of personal computer companies sell directly to end users and in the United States, direct sales have become a greater percentage of the total computer market.

As the industry leader, Compaq Computer Corporation made 13.8 percent of worldwide PC shipments in 1998. Unit growth for this company jumped to 39 percent in the first quarter of 1998 but then slowed to 12 percent and 9.7 percent in the second and third quarters of 1998, respectively. The company's growth has been slowed by the challenges brought on by the integration of Digital Equipment Company.

Top competitors in the computer and peripheral industry include International Business Machines (IBM), Dell Computer Corporation, Apple Computer Corporation, Sun Microsystems, and Gateway Incorporated. Personal computers continue to be hot sellers. This trend is likely to continue as more individuals and companies increase their use of the Internet for business or pleasure. Each company feels pressure to keep low prices and tight inventory control to increase profit margins. One reason why price competition has become intense in the PC market is because Compaq instigated a 1992 shakeout in the industry by challenging the high prices of direct sellers like Dell. This shakeout, which occurred again in 1997, allowed Compaq, an indirect seller, to dominate the low end of the PC market. Industry leaders with high profit margins are Sun Microsystems, IBM, and Dell with profit margins of 11.9 percent, 8.1 percent, and 8.0 percent, respectively.

Dell Computer Corporation held the number-two spot in 1998, behind Compaq, in the U.S. PC market. However, Dell's unit growth was 61 percent in 1998, whereas Compaq's unit growth was only 13 percent. Behind Dell in growth of PC shipments in 1998 was Hewlett Packard (H-P). H-P reported the second highest growth rate in worldwide PC shipments of 26 percent. Surprisingly enough, IBM posted the slowest worldwide growth in PC sales in 1998 with only a 10 percent increase.

Aside from low costs and high profit margins, Compaq wants to increase its market share. As indicated in Exhibit 1, Compaq was the world leader in 1998 in market share of worldwide PC shipments with a 13.8 percent market share, and IBM trailed Compaq with an 8.2 percent market share. Dell followed IBM closely with a strong 7.9 percent market share in worldwide PC shipments.

A major trend in this industry is the move toward alliances and acquisitions. In September 1999, IBM and Dell, two major competitors of Compaq, formed a $16 billion deal. Dell agreed to allow IBM to integrate the products and services of the two

EXHIBIT 1    Worldwide PC Shipments in 1998—Market Share (based on units shipped)

| Number | Company | Percentage |
|--------|---------|-----------|
| 1 | Compaq | 13.8% |
| 2 | IBM | 8.2 |
| 3 | Dell | 7.9 |
| 4 | H-P | 5.8 |
| 5 | Packard Bell | 4.3 |
| 6 | Others | 60.1 |

*Source:* www.freeedgar.com

EXHIBIT 2    Worldwide Computer Hardware Revenues—1998 (based on factory shipments, in billions)

| Number | Type of Hardware | Revenues |
|--------|------------------|----------|
| 1 | PCs | $170.0 |
| 2 | Workstations | 14.7 |
| 3 | Entry-Level Servers | 25.0 |
| 4 | Mid-Range Servers | 17.6 |
| 5 | High-End Servers | 16.3 |
| 6 | High-Performance Market | 5.2 |

*Source:* www.freeedgar.com

companies in order to gain more revenue and market share as well as to broaden the service capabilities of both companies. Businesses continue to outsource noncore operations, and turn to providers such as IBM, for help in integrating their information systems and setting up their internal networks and electronic business systems.

The PC segment of the computer hardware industry is by far the largest and most competitive sector in terms of units and dollars. In 1998, the number of PC units shipped worldwide amounted to 90 million at a worth of $170 billion. As indicated in Exhibit 2, the 1998 worldwide computer hardware revenues were highest for PCs. According to International Data Corporation (IDC), desktop computers represent 80 percent of the units shipped in this segment. It is expected that this segment will continue to grow over the next several years due to Internet-driven demand, expected product and price improvements, as well as upgrades of existing computers to enhance productivity. It is expected that PCs will become more affordable, thus leading to an expansion of the PC market of an average of 15 percent over the next several years.

The Internet has created a major opportunity for growth in the computer and peripheral industry. The demand for PCs is expected to increase along with the growth of the Internet. It is projected that a large part of the forecasted demand for Internet usage is corporate demand. Businesses and other entities are seeking methods to attain competitive advantage. In today's society, in which technology and information play a major role, one way that a business can achieve a competitive advantage is through better service and support by using computers and networks that provide the necessary connections within an organization.

## INTERNAL CONDITIONS

Compaq's global presence is broken down into three segments that function as separate business units.

1. North America
2. Europe, Middle East, and Africa (EMEA)
3. Others (Asia Pacific, Greater China, Japan, and Latin America)

### North America

This segment is comprised of the United States and Canada. Products and services include printers, desktops and laptops, personal computers, client-server solutions, and various hardware and software products. Services have been expanded in this segment as a result of the increasing use of the Internet.

As indicated by Exhibit 3, the segment profit in 1999 for products and services in the North America segment increased 325 percent from $130 million in 1998 to $553 million. Compaq has facilitated its operations by providing services online for media companies and e-commerce merchants among others.

**EXHIBIT 3    Profit by Segment (6-30-99)**

| Segment | 1999 | 1998 | Percent change |
|---|---|---|---|
| **North America:** | | | |
| Revenue: | | | |
| Products | $3,841 | $2,424 | inc. 58.45% |
| Services | 631 | 151 | inc. 317.88 |
| Gross margin | | | |
| Products | 801 | 517 | inc. 54.93% |
| Services | 261 | 56 | inc. 366.07 |
| Segment profit | $ 553 | $ 130 | inc. 325.38 |
| **EMEA:** | | | |
| Revenue: | | | |
| Products | $2,614 | $2,038 | inc. 28.26% |
| Services | 818 | 193 | inc. 323.83 |
| Gross margin: | | | |
| Products | 541 | 509 | inc. 6.29% |
| Services | 252 | 60 | inc. 320.00 |
| Segment profit | $ 398 | $ 240 | inc. 65.83 |
| **Other segments:** | | | |
| Revenue: | | | |
| Products | $1,175 | $ 915 | inc. 28.42% |
| Services | 341 | 112 | inc. 204.46 |
| Gross margin: | | | |
| Products | 264 | 119 | inc. 121.85% |
| Services | 111 | 19 | inc. 484.21 |
| Segment profit | $ 153 | $ 50 | inc. 206.00 |

*Source:* www.freeedgar.com

## EMEA

Compaq first entered this market in 1984. Subsidiaries include Germany, the United Kingdom, and France. As a result of the growth in this market, some of the "newer" subsidiaries include Austria, Bahrain, Belgium, the Czech Republic, Finland, Greece, Hungary, Italy, Norway, Scotland, the Netherlands, South Africa, Sweden, Switzerland, and Poland.

This market has benefited by the introduction of the Euro into the global economy. Exhibit 3 shows a 320 percent increase in Services Revenue alone—from $60 million in 1998 to $252 million in 1999.

## Others

This segment is comprised of Asia Pacific, Greater China, Japan, and Latin America. The countries included in this segment are Australia, Malaysia, New Zealand, Singapore, and Thailand. In 1997, the Greater China region was added. The focus of this region is Hong Kong and Taiwan. In 1991, Japan announced the opening of a new Compaq subsidiary. Compaq designs and markets products exclusively for the Japanese market. Product revenues for this market have increased 28 percent—from $915 million to $1,175 million from 1998 to 1999.

## Compaq Products

Compaq products are developed through three customer-focused groups. The first is the Enterprise Computing Group, which designs mainframe workstations and a variety of business solutions such as enterprise solutions, fault-tolerant solutions, and critical solutions to name a few. Also, a variety of products are designed and developed in this group. They include Internet and networking products. This group focuses on small businesses and their needs for desktop solutions—mom and pop operations. As indicated in Exhibit 4, total product revenues for 1999 were $38.5 billion. Exhibit 5 reveals that $20.1 billion of these revenues were derived from the Enterprise Solutions and Services segment.

The second group is the Commercial PC group. This group designs commercial products such as portables, options, and small- and medium-sized business solutions. The target market is those businesses that are no longer mom and pop operations— meaning that these businesses are growing and need more sophisticated information systems. Revenue from the Commercial PC group was $12.1 billion in 1999.

The third group is the Consumer PC group, which designs products for the "regular" consumer. Products include desktops, laptops, and portables. The "average" consumer can be a college student or even someone who uses a computer at home for recreation and entertainment purposes. This target market is the fastest-growing market for Compaq's products. In 1999, the revenues from the Consumer PC group amounted to $9,580 or $5.96 billion revenues (35 percent). Revenues from Compaq products alone accounted for approximately 88 percent of Compaq's revenue.

## Compaq Services

Aside from the wide array of products, Compaq provides a number of services as well. The Compaq Services Group markets a wide variety of services, both innovative and proactive, to help consumers formulate, implement, and evaluate their work. These services include systems consulting, integration and project management, and network design. In 1999, Compaq Services comprised $6.6 billion of Compaq's revenue.

Compaq created a leasing company called Compaq Capital in 1997 to provide financing services to increase the revenues of Compaq products and services. The financial services sector is included in the income section of the "services'" statement.

EXHIBIT 4    Compaq Computer Corporation Consolidated
Statement of Income (in millions)

|  | 1999 | 1998 | 1997 |
|---|---|---|---|
| Revenue: | | | |
| Products | $31,902 | $27,372 | $24,122 |
| Services | 6,623 | 3,797 | 462 |
| Total revenue | 38,525 | 31,169 | 24,584 |
| Cost of sales: | | | |
| Products | 25,263 | 21,383 | 17,500 |
| Services | 4,535 | 2,597 | 333 |
| Total cost of sales | 29,798 | 23,980 | 17,833 |
| Selling, general and administrative expense | 6,341 | 4,978 | 2,947 |
| Research and development costs | 1,660 | 1,353 | 817 |
| Purchased in-process technology | — | 3,196 | 208 |
| Restructuring and asset impairment charges | 868 | 393 | |
| Gain on sales of business | 1,182 | — | — |
| Merger-related costs | — | — | 44 |
| Other income and expense, net | 106 | (69) | (23) |
| | 7,793 | 9,851 | 3,993 |
| Income (loss) before provision for income taxes | 934 | (2,662) | 2,758 |
| Provision for income taxes | 365 | 81 | 903 |
| Net income (loss) | $    569 | $ (2,743) | $  1,855 |
| Earnings (loss) per common share: | | | |
| Basic | 0.35 | (1.71) | 1.23 |
| Diluted | 0.34 | (1.71) | 1.19 |
| Shares used in computing earnings (loss) per common share: | | | |
| Basic | | 1,608 | 1,505 |
| Diluted | | 1,608 | 1,564 |

*Source:* www.freeedgar.com

## THE FUTURE

Since the acquisition of Digital Equipment, the company has been on unstable ground, especially internally, as a result of the many hiring and firing of top executives as well as a shaky financial situation due to the merger-related costs. In July 2000, Compaq's stock price still languished in the high 20's.

Compaq has had 17 years of experience in its industry—the Compaq trademark is well known—as well as an immense availability of facilities and other resources necessary to demonstrate its leadership through the years. Strategies for this company to implement include a focus on developing a mission statement, intensified marketing efforts into the North America and EMEA markets, modification or updating of existing products and expansion into the growing e-commerce market.

A mission statement is an important part of the strategic planning process for every organization. A mission statement allows a firm to clearly state its objectives and its purpose. In addition to a mission statement, Compaq needs intensified marketing efforts in the North American and EMEA markets. Through the years, these two regions have been the fastest-growing markets for Compaq. Increasing use of the Internet has

EXHIBIT 5    Compaq's Segment Financial Data
             (in millions)

**A. By Product**

| *Year ended December 31* | *1999* | *1998* | *1997* |
|---|---|---|---|
| Enterprise Solutions and Services | | | |
| Revenue | $20,136 | $14,488 | $ 8,731 |
| Operating income | 2,349 | 1,724 | 2,069 |
| Commercial Personal Computing | | | |
| Revenue | 12,185 | 11,846 | 11,941 |
| Operating income (loss) | (448) | (46) | 1,052 |
| Consumer | | | |
| Revenue | 5,994 | 4,932 | 3,904 |
| Operating income | 262 | 183 | 178 |
| Other | | | |
| Revenue | 210 | (97) | 8 |
| Operating income (loss) | (281) | (115) | 11 |
| Consolidated segment totals | | | |
| Revenue | $38,525 | $31,169 | $24,584 |
| Operating income | 1,882 | 1,746 | 3,310 |

**B. By Geographic Region**

| | *1999* | *1998* | *1997* |
|---|---|---|---|
| **Revenue:** | | | |
| United States | $17,351 | $13,981 | $12,593 |
| Foreign Countries | 21,174 | 17,188 | 11,991 |
| | $38,525 | $31,169 | $24,584 |
| **Fixed Assets:** | | | |
| United States | $ 2,332 | $ 2,166 | $ 1,457 |
| Foreign Countries | 917 | 736 | 528 |
| | $ 3,249 | $ 2,902 | $ 1,985 |
| **Profits:** | | | |
| United States | $    94 | $ (4,782) | $ 1,798 |
| Foreign Countries | 840 | 2,120 | 969 |
| | $   934 | $ (2,662) | $ 2,758 |

allowed for these markets to grow, especially in the EMEA market. Should Compaq continue to aggressively pursue these markets. Should Compaq continue to advertise its brand name to its loyal consumers in these markets and to improve its products and services in order to predict and react quickly to changes in the industry.

The market for e-commerce has been growing rapidly. In today's society, information plays a key role in achieving a competitive advantage. It would be in Compaq's best interest to pursue the e-commerce market. An increasing amount of communication and information exchange is handled over the Internet. More and more consumers conduct their business through the use of information technology because in today's society information plays a key role in consumers lives, and e-commerce facilitates the communication process.

These strategies are just a few of the many actions that Compaq could consider aggressively executing over the course of the next few years. For this company and this industry, growth and profitability point towards the growing international segments. With today's increasingly competitive and aggressive economy, it is important for any company to be able to predict and react quickly to the changing needs of the international market.

EXHIBIT 6    Compaq Computer Annual Income Statement
(in millions except earnings-per-share data)

| | 12/31/99 | 12/31/98 | 12/31/97 |
|---|---|---|---|
| Sales | $38,525.00 | $31,169.00 | $24,584.00 |
| Cost of goods | 29,798.00 | 23,980.00 | 17,833.00 |
| Gross profit | 8,727.00 | 7,189.00 | 6,751.00 |
| Selling and administrative and depreciation and amortization expenses | 8,001.00 | 6,331.00 | 3,764.00 |
| Income after depreciation and amortization | 726.00 | 858.00 | 2,987.00 |
| Nonoperating income | 208.00 | (3,520.00) | (229.00) |
| Interest expense | 0 | 0 | 0 |
| Pretax income | 934.00 | (2,662.00) | 2,758.00 |
| Income taxes | 365.00 | 81.00 | 903.00 |
| Minority interest | 0 | 0 | 0 |
| Investment gains/losses (+) | 0 | 0 | 0 |
| Other income/charges | 0 | 0 | 0 |
| Income from continued operations | N/A | N/A | N/A |
| Extras and discontinued operations | 0 | 0 | 0 |
| Net income | $   569.00 | $ (2,743.00) | $ 1,855.00 |

## Depreciation footnote

| | | | |
|---|---|---|---|
| Income before depreciation and amortization | $ 2,128.00 | $ 1,751.00 | $ 3,532.00 |
| Depreciation and amortization (cash flow) | 1,402.00 | 893.00 | 545.00 |
| Income after depreciation and amortization | $   726.00 | $   858.00 | $ 2,987.00 |

## Earnings-per-share data

| | | | |
|---|---|---|---|
| Average shares | $1,735.00 | $1,608.00 | $1,564.20 |
| Diluted earnings per share before nonrecurring items | 0.30 | 0.59 | 1.35 |
| Diluted net earnings per share | $    0.34 | $   (1.71) | $    1.19 |

*Source:* www.freeedgar.com

EXHIBIT 7    Compaq Computer Annual Balance Sheet
(in millions, except book value per share)

| | 12/31/99 | 12/31/98 | 12/31/97 |
|---|---|---|---|
| **Assets** | | | |
| Cash and equivalents | $ 3,302.00 | $ 4,091.00 | $ 6,762.00 |
| Receivables | 6,685.00 | 6,998.00 | 2,891.00 |
| Notes receivable | 0 | 0 | 0 |
| Inventories | 2,008.00 | 2,005.00 | 1,570.00 |
| Other current assets | 1,854.00 | 2,073.00 | 794.00 |
| **Total current assets** | **13,849.00** | **15,167.00** | **12,017.00** |
| Net property and equipment | 3,249.00 | 2,902.00 | 1,985.00 |
| Investments and advances | 0 | 0 | 0 |
| Other noncurrent assets | 0 | 0 | 0 |
| Deferred charges | 0 | 1,341.00 | 0 |
| Intangibles | 0 | 0 | 0 |
| Deposits and other assets | 10,179.00 | 3,641.00 | 629.00 |
| **Total assets** | **$27,277.00** | **$23,051.00** | **$14,631.00** |
| **Liabilities and shareholders' equity** | | | |
| Notes payable | $    453.00 | 0 | 0 |
| Accounts payable | 4,380.00 | $ 4,237.00 | $ 2,837.00 |
| Current portion long-term debt | 0 | 0 | 0 |
| Current portion capital leases | 0 | 0 | 0 |
| Accrued expenses | 1,002.00 | 1,110.00 | 0 |
| Income taxes payable | 0 | 282.00 | 195.00 |
| Other current liabilities | 6,003.00 | 5,104.00 | 2,170.00 |
| **Total current liabilities** | **11,838.00** | **10,733.00** | **5,202.00** |
| Mortgages | 0 | 0 | 0 |
| Deferred taxes/income | 0 | 0 | 0 |
| Convertible debt | 0 | 0 | 0 |
| Long-term debt | 0 | 0 | 0 |
| Noncurrent capital leases | 0 | 0 | 0 |
| Other noncurrent liabilities | 605.00 | 545.00 | 0 |
| Minority interest (liabilities) | 0 | 422.00 | 0 |
| **Total liabilities** | **$12,443.00** | **$11,700.00** | **$ 5,202.00** |
| **Shareholders' equity** | | | |
| Preferred stock | 0 | 0 | 0 |
| Common stock (par) | $ 7,627.00 | $ 7,270.00 | $ 2,096.00 |
| Capital surplus | 0 | 0 | 0 |
| Retained earnings | 4,948.00 | 4,465.00 | 7,333.00 |
| Other equity | 2,919.00 | 0 | 0 |
| Treasury stock | 660.00 | 384.00 | 0 |
| Total shareholders' equity | 14,834.00 | 11,351.00 | 9,429.00 |
| **Total liabilities and shareholders' equity** | **27,277.00** | **23,051.00** | **14,631.00** |
| Total common equity | 14,834.00 | 11,351.00 | 9,429.00 |
| Average shares | 1,735.00 | 1,608.00 | 1,564.20 |
| Book value per share | $      8.73 | $      6.68 | $      6.23 |

*Source:* www.freeedgar.com

# RESEARCH IN MOTION—2001

David Griffin
Francis Marion University

## RIMM

www.rim.net

Research in Motion (RIM) is a terrestrial wireless communications hardware and software developer and manufacturer headquartered in Waterloo, Ontario, Canada. The company is listed on the Toronto Stock Exchange under the symbol RIM and traded on NASDAQ under the ticker RIMM. Engineering and research define RIM as an extremely innovative company. RIM has enjoyed explosive growth in revenues, net income, and stock price, primarily a result of a recently introduced two-way pager. In order to support this growth, RIM has increased its employees and capital assets. Because of these changes, its successful operations need to be evaluated and tailored to RIM's new environment and internal workings. Strategic management plays an increasingly important role at RIM.

Investors have high expectations from RIM. RIM stock trades for prices in excess of 200 times earnings. It is not a trivial task to meet the expectations of its shareholders. Strategic management at RIM must use analytical tools to evaluate and perform to these expectations. The cycle of good planning and execution should, however, even exceed the expectations of RIM's stakeholders. RIM's total revenues increased to US $85.0 million for the year ended February 29, 2000, representing an increase of 80 percent over 1999. The increase was mainly due to the launch of the BlackBerry service and growth in RIM Wireless Handheld and OEM radio sales.

## HISTORY

Research in Motion was founded in 1984 as a ground-based wireless communications company. Partly funded by the Canadian government, this company invested in talented engineers and research and eventually started producing small amounts of specialty wireless products. Early products included hand-held point-of-sale terminals, alarms, and in-vehicle communication systems. In the mid-1990s, RIM began working on two-way pagers. The pager market was large, approaching 50 million in 1997 in the United States (Research in Motion, 1998 *Annual Report*). The pager market was growing, and the new pagers capable of two-way communications were expected to grow particularly fast. By 2002, the total pager market is forecast to be 80 million units, one quarter of which is expected to be two-way pagers.

RIM had been building its first two-way pager with a full qwerty keyboard. This unit was large compared to one-way pagers and had limited customer support. As RIM approached completion of its second two-way pager design, market interest in the new product was staggering. In order to raise capital to meet customer demand, the company issued shares. In 1997, RIM had its initial public offering and was listed on the Toronto Stock Exchange. RIM raised $CDN 39 million in its first year and another $CDN 116 million the following year as a publicly traded company. RIM was listed on the

NASDAQ in 1999 to appeal to a larger market and as a form of advertising to American investors, some of whom became RIM customers (Fidelity InstantBroker). Another $CDN 216 million was raised in October 1999 (Canada NewsWire, 1999). RIM's new product was a success. The company was able to secure large contracts from companies like BellSouth and Fidelity Investments. Stock prices have varied from below $CDN 5 to in excess of $CDN 56. The IPO was $CDN 7. A Canadian dollar is worth approximately $US .67.

### External Factors

Innovation drives this industry. Like many other high-technology industries, the wireless communication industry has a rapidly growing and changing market. Obsolescence is always imminent. Other technologies affect this industry, such as e-mail and the Internet. E-mail and the Internet's success and widespread use create a greater need for wireless data communication.

Currently RIM's products appear to be luxury items or discretionary expenses; RIM may be highly impacted by a downturn in the economy. The U.S./Canadian dollar exchange rate currently gives RIM an advantage. RIM has substantial U.S. dollar income with expenses in Canadian dollars. At the moment, this is a highly favorable condition since the U.S. dollar is substantially stronger than the Canadian dollar. A stock market correction could create a substantial decrease in the value of RIM stock.

Highly valued technology stocks allow for huge cash inflows for share issuance. RIM is no exception to this condition. RIM and competing companies are highly focused on narrow products; as a result, this industry is teeming with strategic alliances. In the case of RIM, companies like Intel provide customized integrated circuits. Many third-party developers are involved with RIM's success. Software and Internet sites need to be written with RIM's products in mind.

As a result of becoming publicly traded, new parties play a role in the operation of RIM. Shareholders seek shorter-term results. RIM now has a small number of customers that provide a great deal of the sales. Companies like BellSouth and Fidelity may divert RIM into new territories as a result of their buying power. Fidelity has two distinct interests and avenues of influence: Fidelity owns a great deal of RIM stock and sells RIM products to its customers.

The Canadian government provides substantial assistance and tax credits (Research in Motion, 1998, 1999 *Annual Report*). Canada subsidizes industries in which it wants Canadians to participate. High-technology firms are on the subsidy list; RIM is one of them. The assistance is primarily in the form of research grants; however, RIM has also been granted tax relief. A notable problem in Canada is the emigration of technical professionals. In addition to grants to high-tech firms, tax law changes are pending that will reduce taxes on exercising stock options and further enhance the value of employee stock options and help retain those employees. As RIM grows, it may draw attention from government anti-trust employees looking to rectify highly profitable businesses. In the United States, RIM is applying for FCC approval; this can be a long and expensive process.

RIM has a number of patents and operates in an industry with many competitive patents. Legal costs of defending patents and disputing infringements are nontrivial factors.

Some laws change the demand for RIM's products. Many people are calling for laws to control cellular phone use in moving cars. This would make asynchronous mobile communication equipment more desirable.

In general, society is moving away from synchronous communications like cellular phones. Society's growing distaste for cellular communications may further accelerate the growth of nondisruptive wireless communications.

## COMPETITORS

This industry is composed of fierce competitors, with Motorola and 3Com being major players. These competitors are large enough to make acquisitions, and RIM is at risk of becoming a takeover target.

Competitors also are clever at hiring talented employees away from other companies. RIM may see their employees lured away by competitors, and RIM's business is highly dependent on retaining highly skilled people.

Motorola does have a distinct disadvantage because it is using an older, more limited cellular network for its 1- and 2-way pagers. However, Motorola enjoys returns to scale that RIM has not achieved.

3Com's products compete less directly with RIM products. 3Com's Palm Pilot uses touch-sensitive screens without keyboards. Customers typically will prefer either the screens or keyboards. However, 3Com has the ability to enter a keyboard industry or invent a superior interface.

## INTERNAL CONDITIONS

RIM is located close to the University of Waterloo, a large Canadian University known for its engineering Co-op program. RIM often hires many Co-op students. This location and relationship allow RIM to tap a large resource of talented young engineers. Each graduating class contributes a number of new employees to RIM. The culture is ambitious, achievement oriented, and fast paced—a university atmosphere with some notable differences.

A significant difference from university life is the financial position of RIM employees. There are a large number of wealthy employees as a result of stock options. The strong stock option plan offers tremendous incentives to stay with the company. Many current employees will be able to retire when they are in their thirties a decade from now.

RIM's organizational growth is a result of backward integration. It has moved many functions in-house. For example, industrial design, mechanical engineering, and manufacturing are now internal functions.

RIM is poised to meet and exceed its growth plans. Highly motivated executives with substantial ownership in the company have insured RIM runs according to a well-laid plan. The depth of understanding based on planning allows RIM executives to rapidly exploit opportunities. RIM is geared towards high new product launch rates. RIM has established solid relationships with best-in-class manufacturers, such as Intel and Microsoft.

The organization is very fluid, but this has worked well. Currently RIM has no formal organizational chart. Many employees report to numerous managers. Employees have been empowered: To a large degree, they organize themselves. The staff is highly motivated to produce good products, and it decides how to do that. Currently RIM employs two co-CEOs and ten VPs. Should RIM publish an organization chart, it might take the appearance suggested in Exhibit 1.

Marketing and sales have grown from 15 employees to over 50 in the last year. RIM has given marketing a low priority until recently. Currently RIM's marketing is rolling out the Blackberry service, a two-way pager and airtime service and investing in marketing campaigns to support it. Blackberry gives RIM a channel to interact with end users directly. The United States and Canada account for the vast majority of sales because there is little infrastructure elsewhere to support this product. Spending on marketing, sales, and administration increased from $US 4.1 million in 1998 to $US 9.7 million in 1999. These costs are expected to continue to rise.

EXHIBIT 1     Hypothetical RIM Organization Chart

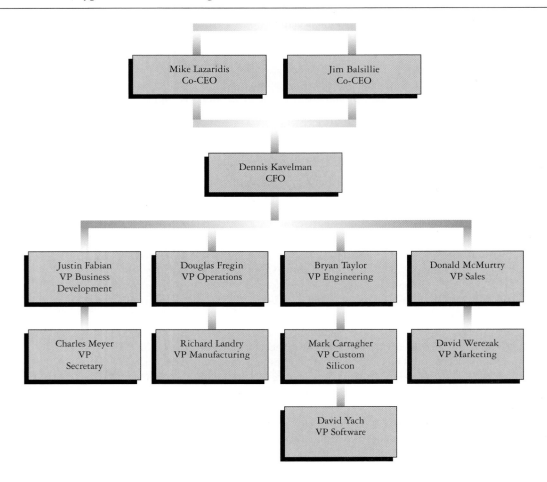

RIM is minimally forwardly integrated; sales are typically huge to distributors and retailers. RIM signed a $U.S. 90 million contract with BellSouth Wireless in 1998 (Research in Motion, 1998 *Annual Report*). BellSouth and other companies do most of the end-user marketing for RIM's products.

Finances at RIM are very impressive. RIM has been more than doubling revenue each year since 1997. Gross margins have been healthy through this period. Exhibit 2 compares financial ratios for RIM, Motorola, 3Com, the diversified communications industry, and the S&P 500. RIM is financially healthy with a couple of notable characteristics. RIM is debt free, has a very high stock price, and has cash reserves.

Research and development spending at RIM is huge. In 1999, $CDN 11.8 million was spent including $CDN 5.3 million in government grants. In 1998 gross research and development spending amounted to $CDN 6.5 million. RIM has made tremendous financial commitments to long-term technical progress. Partners like Intel give RIM an opportunity to split research and development costs and provide products with inputs from industry leaders. RIM has partnerships from universities, such as the Universities of Waterloo and Toronto and MacMaster University. RIM is planning to continue investing heavily in research and development.

# EXHIBIT 2    Financial Ratio Comparison (1999)

| | RIM | Motorola | 3COM | Industry | S&P 500 |
|---|---|---|---|---|---|
| Income/employee | $ 33,000 | $ 5,000 | $ 34,000 | $ (5,000) | $ 18,000 |
| Revenue/employee | 239,000 | 231,000 | 442,000 | 662,000 | 268,000 |
| Receivable turnover | 7.6 | 6.0 | 6.6 | 5.7 | 6.7 |
| Inventory turnover | 2.1 | 4.8 | 6.5 | 14.9 | 7.1 |
| Asset turnover | 0.6 | 1.0 | 1.3 | 0.5 | 0.4 |
| **Investment returns (%)** | | | | | |
| Return on equity | 8.7 | 4.6 | 13.8 | NE | 15.8 |
| Return on sssets | 8.4 | 2.0 | 9.9 | −0.3 | 2.7 |
| Return on capital | 8.7 | 3.7 | 13.8 | −0.4 | 7.5 |
| **Financial condition** | | | | | |
| Debt/equity ratio | 0.0 | 0.2 | 0.0 | 0.6 | 1.1 |
| Current ratio | 23.1 | 1.4 | 2.9 | 1.4 | 1.3 |
| Quick ratio | 8.8 | 7.0 | 1.4 | 1.0 | 0.7 |
| Interest coverage | N/C | 4.7 | N/C | 1.7 | 2.5 |
| Book value/share | 1.7 | 22.5 | 9.4 | 7.8 | 10.9 |
| **Price ratios** | | | | | |
| Current p/e ratio | 218.3 | 92.9 | 22.7 | 60.7 | 31.2 |
| Price/sales ratio | 30.3 | 1.9 | 1.7 | 6.1 | 2.0 |
| Price/book value | 18.9 | 4.2 | 2.9 | 4.6 | 4.7 |
| Price/cash flow ratio | 192.6 | 20.2 | 12.8 | 38.4 | 17.1 |
| **Profit margins** | | | | | |
| Gross margin | 50.4 | 36.0 | 52.0 | 54.9 | 47.7 |
| Pre-tax margin | 18.3 | 2.8 | 11.2 | 3.4 | 10.1 |
| Net profit margin | $ 14.0 | $ 2.0 | $ 7.8 | $ −0.8 | $ 6.7 |

*Source:* Media General Industry: Diversified Communication Services. Computed ratios are based on latest 12 months' results.

## CONCLUSION

Research in Motion is in an enviable position (see Exhibits 3, 4 and 5). Years of investment in wireless technology have paid off. RIM is a true wireless information company. This industry is not one to allow for complacency, and RIM must respect its future challenges, realize how the industry is changing, and continue to grow.

The company may find growth via acquisitions. Companies like Arch Communications (symbol:APGR) and MetroCall (symbol:MCLL) are countrywide chains of pager retailers. Both companies are experiencing financial difficulties and are publicly traded. Controlling interest could be purchased in either of these companies without straining Rim's financial position.

Good strategic management practice will allow RIM to maintain its success. This company needs to formulate a strategy and communicate it. A mission statement can no longer be overlooked. Internal and external audits need to be continuous. Long-term objectives must be shaped. Various strategies must be produced, evaluated, and executed. These strategies must bear polices and objectives, which require available resources. RIM needs to prevent surprises in this volatile industry. Of course, stability comes from well-behaved feedback systems. Measures need to be established and evaluated to determine if the company is on course.

Strategic management is an ongoing process. The act of performing strategic management will ensure RIM's continued success.

EXHIBIT 3    RIM's Consolidated Balance Sheet

| As at<br>(in U.S. $ thousands) | February 29,<br>2000 | February 28,<br>1999 |
|---|---|---|
| **Current Assets** | | |
| Cash and cash equivalents | $      126 | $    9,618 |
| Marketable securities | 218,116 | 56,996 |
| Accounts receivable | 33,274 | 12,515 |
| Inventory | 36,852 | 19,812 |
| Prepaid expenses | 6,014 | 3,945 |
| | 294,382 | 102,886 |
| **Deferred Income Taxes** | 3,548 | — |
| **Capital Assets** | 39,297 | 15,012 |
| **Total Assets** | **$337,227** | **$117,898** |
| **Current Liabilities** | | |
| Accounts payable and accrued liabilities | $  11,033 | $    7,764 |
| Taxes payable | 1,815 | 844 |
| Deferred revenue | 6,277 | 1,785 |
| Current portion of long-term debt | 185 | — |
| | 19,310 | 10,393 |
| **Long-Term Debt** | $    6,526 | — |
| **Shareholders' Equity** | | |
| Common shares | $293,261 | $  99,873 |
| Retained earnings | 18,130 | 7,632 |
| | 311,391 | 107,505 |
| **Total liabilities and shareholders' equity** | **$337,227** | **$117,898** |

*Source:* www.freeedgar.com

EXHIBIT 4    **RIM's Income Statements**
              **(in U.S. $ thousands, except for earnings-per-share)**

| For the year ended | February 29, 2000 | February 28, 1999 |
|---|---|---|
| Revenue | $84,967 | $47,342 |
| Cost of sales | 48,574 | 28,767 |
| | 36,393 | 18,575 |
| Research and development, net of government assistance of $4,496 (1999—$3,539) | 7,738 | 4,382 |
| Selling, marketing and administration | 13,904 | 6,546 |
| Amortization | 4,683 | 2,783 |
| | 26,325 | 13,711 |
| Income from operations | 10,068 | 4,864 |
| Investment income | 5,968 | 3,790 |
| Income before provision for taxes | 16,036 | 8,654 |
| Provision for income taxes | 5,538 | 2,245 |
| Net income | $10,498 | $ 6,409 |
| Earnings-per-share, basic | $    .16 | $    .10 |
| Earnings-per-share, fully diluted | $    .15 | $    .10 |

*Source:* www.freeedgar.com

## EXHIBIT 5  Statement of Cash Flows (in U.S. $ thousands)

|  | 2000 | 1999 | 1998 | 1997 |
|---|---|---|---|---|
| **Cash flows operating** | | | | |
| Net income for the year | $ 540 | $ 9,541 | $ 540 | $ 44 |
| Items not requiring cash outlays | | | | |
| Amortization | 2,192 | 4,144 | 2,192 | 567 |
| Deferred taxes | 0 | 0 | 0 | −118 |
|  | $ 2,732 | $ 13,685 | $ 2,732 | $ 492 |
| **Net changes in:** | | | | |
| Amounts receivable | | −$ 3,678 | −$ 3,909 | −$ 7,475 |
| Inventory | | −14,098 | 445 | −11,595 |
| Prepaid expenses | | −5,631 | −83 | −56 |
| Accounts payable | | 9,190 | 185 | 894 |
| Income taxes payable | | 1,094 | 321 | −93 |
| Deferred revenue | | 1,897 | 618 | 110 |
|  | $ 309 | $ 2,459 | $ 309 | −$17,723 |
| **Cash flows financing** | | | | |
| Income tax reduction resulting from financial costs | $ 306 | $ 775 | $ 306 | 0 |
| Government funding | 295 | 430 | 295 | $ 632 |
| Issuance of shares | 116,890 | 73 | 116,890 | 39,115 |
| Financing cost | −8,059 | −390 | −8,059 | −2,254 |
| Repayment of loans | −1,480 | 0 | −1,480 | −1,799 |
| Capital dividend paid | −390 | 0 | −390 | 0 |
| Repayment to shareholders | | 0 | 0 | −750 |
|  | $107,562 | $ 888 | $107,562 | $34,944 |
| **Cash flows investing** | | | | |
| Acquisition of capital assets | −$ 8,328 | −$ 13,191 | 0 | 0 |
| Buy marketable securities | 13,011 | −115,576 | −$ 13,011 | 0 |
| Sell marketable securities | 0 | 43,732 | 0 | 0 |
| Buy capital assets | | −13,191 | −8,328 | −8,277 |
| Total cash used investing | $ 21,339 | −$ 85,035 | −$ 21,339 | −$ 8,277 |
| Net increase in cash | **$ 86,532** | **−$ 81,688** | **$ 86,532** | **$ 8,944** |
| Cash at beginning of year | 9,476 | 96,008 | 9,476 | 532 |
| Cash at end of year | $ 96,008 | $ 14,320 | $ 96,008 | $ 9,476 |

*Source:* www.freeedgar.com

---

## REFERENCES

Canada NewsWire, "Research in Motion Commences Public Offering of Shares," October 14, 1999.

Fidelity InstantBroker, http://personal400.fidelity.com/products/stocksbonds/index.html.

Research in Motion, *Annual Report,* 1998. Research in Motion, Waterloo, Ontario, Canada.

Research in Motion, *Annual Report,* 1999. Research in Motion, Waterloo, Ontario, Canada.

# STRYKER CORPORATION—2000

**Henry H. Beam**
**Western Michigan University**

## SYK

www.strykercorp.com

Stryker Corporation is a leading maker of specialty surgical and medical products in Kalamazoo, Michigan. Although not yet a household name, Stryker is one of America's most consistently profitable growth companies. In 1999 Stryker posted record sales of $2.1 billion and a net income of $19.4 million. Since John Brown became chairman in 1977, Stryker achieved more than 20 percent annual earnings-per-share growth every year until 1998, a remarkable record. In 1998, Stryker took a "strategic detour" to take advantage of a unique opportunity to acquire Howmedica, the orthopedic division of Pfizer. Acquisition-related charges of $50 million caused Stryker's earnings to decrease by over 50 percent in 1998. CEO Brown commented, "Our long-term objective of 20 percent profit growth has been derailed by the acquisition. We are committed to getting back on track as soon as possible." The Howmedica acquisition nearly doubled Stryker's size and brought its 1999 sales slightly over the $2 billion mark. Stryker's consistent success has not gone unnoticed by Wall Street, where its stock is increasingly on the recommended list of leading brokerage firms. During a visit to Stryker's Kalamazoo facilities in 1992, President George Bush hailed the company's people as "leaders in an innovative industry that makes our country proud."

All this growth comes from making products that people hope they never have to use but are glad to have available when they need them. Stryker develops, manufactures, and markets a wide variety of surgical products and specialty hospital beds that are sold primarily to physicians and hospitals throughout the world. Stryker also provides outpatient physical therapy services in the United States.

In the 1950s and 1960s, Stryker's reputation was enhanced by good publicity about some of its unique products. Roy Campanella, the Brooklyn Dodger baseball star who had been paralyzed from injuries received in an automobile accident in 1958, was cared for with Stryker equipment. *Life* Magazine did a story about the Tennessee American Legion buying a Circ-O-Lectric Hospital Bed for Sergeant Alvin York, the World War I Medal of Honor winner who had become an invalid by the early 1960s. When Senator Edward Kennedy suffered a back injury in a plane crash in 1964, he was cared for on a Stryker turning frame and later moved to a Circ-O-Lectric Hospital Bed, both of which were pictured in national magazines during his recovery. More recently, former First Lady Barbara Bush has had Osteonics hip replacements. Such favorable publicity has enhanced the image of the company in the public's eye.

## HISTORY

The Stryker Company takes it name from its founder, Dr. Homer Stryker, a remarkable man in many respects. After serving briefly in World War I, Dr. Stryker earned his medical degree from the University of Michigan in 1925, chose orthopedics as his specialty, and located his medical practice in Kalamazoo, Michigan. Throughout his life he liked to fiddle with gadgets. During the early years of his medical practice, Dr. Stryker invented a mobile hospital bed and a cast-cutting saw. The mobile bed had a frame that pivoted from side to side so physicians could position injured patients for treatment while keeping them immobile. He won a contract to supply the Army with his beds during World War II and was soon running a small business as well as a medical practice. The contract was terminated when the war ended in 1945, but the business continued.

Dr. Stryker spoke about how he invented the cast-cutting saw:

> In 1943, the removal of a large cast was a tedious process for me and an unpleasant one at best for the patient. In search of a better way, I observed that if a small circular blade with sharp teeth was pressed firmly against the skin, or the soft cast padding used to protect the skin, and then moved back and forth, no more than an eighth of an inch of skin would move with the saw teeth, and neither the skin or the padding and skin would be cut.
>
> However, if I took the same blade and pressed against a plaster cast and moved it back and forth with the same stroke and pressure, it would cut the plaster. I took a 1/20th horsepower electric grinder, replaced the grinding stone with a 2-inch diameter saw blade and designed and attached a mechanism which would convert the rotation of the saw to oscillation, with the teeth oscillating about an eighth of an inch at about 18,000 oscillations per minute. When completed, the instrument was tested by removing a cast at the hospital. I was able to remove the cast without disturbing the patient, in about one fourth the time previously required.

This is typical of how Dr. Stryker used his creativity to improve the tools that physicians used to treat their patients. The rapid acceptance of the cast cutter by physicians and the Army for hospital beds convinced Dr. Stryker that he had more than a part-time business on his hands. In 1946 the Orthopedic Frame Company was incorporated with Dr. Stryker as its sole shareholder. Dr. Stryker continued with his medical practice and continued to develop pioneering surgical techniques. His business grew rapidly. His son, Lee, joined him in the business in 1955 after earning a bachelor's degree in business administration from Syracuse University. Lee's business sense balanced his father's desire to use the company as an outlet for his inventive talents.

In 1964 the company changed its name to the Stryker Corporation. New products came regularly, and sales reached $4.7 million in 1966. Although Dr. Stryker's medical equipment manufacturing business would make him wealthy, he gave away hundreds of ideas and techniques free of charge to other physicians, who passed them on to their patients. Dr. Stryker retired from his company in 1969. The company continued to grow under the guidance of Lee Stryker until his tragic death in an airplane crash in Wyoming in July 1976. Later that year, John Brown became president of Stryker.

Brown graduated from Auburn University in 1957 with a bachelor of science degree in chemical engineering. Prior to becoming president of Stryker in 1977, Brown held management positions with Ormet Corporation, Thiokol, and Bristol-Myers Squibb, where he was president of a subsidiary. Brown took charge of a firm with sales of $23 million and net income of $1.5 million. He swiftly took steps to decentralize the company into the autonomous divisional structure it has today. When he realized that salespeople were quitting because the compensation system had been changed from commissions to salaries and bonuses only, he restored commissions as the dominant form of compensation for salespeople. He also established goals of 20 percent growth in sales and earnings per share a year, every year. At the time, nearly 70 percent of Stryker's sales were coming from hospital beds. Building on the strength of the Stryker name with hospitals, Brown added hip implants and medical video cameras and strengthened the line of powered surgical tools.

Stryker started taking an equity position in Matsumoto Medical Instruments of Japan in 1993. In January 1999 it purchased the remaining shares of Matsumoto stock, bringing its direct ownership to 100 percent. Matsumoto, the premier distributor of medical devices in Japan and the exclusive distributor of Stryker products there, has helped Stryker achieve market leadership in hip implants, powered instruments, and endoscopic video systems in one of the world's largest and most sophisticated medical markets.

In 1996 Stryker purchased Osteo Holdings AG for $45.5 million. Osteo, based in Switzerland, produces a broad variety of high-quality trauma products. Stryker saw the acquisition of Osteo as a way to enter the $1-billion global trauma market. In December 1998 Stryker acquired the Howmedica for $1.65 billion in cash. Howmedica makes a wide variety of innovative products for the orthopedic market, including craniofacial trauma products through Leibenger, a German company it had purchased in 1996. At the time of its acquisition, Howmedica had sales of $850 million. At Stryker's 1999 annual meeting, a smiling John Brown gave his rationale for the Howmedica acquisition. "We did it to gain a better position in the marketplace. Bigger is better. We decided a boutique player would have a hard time in this marketplace in the years ahead."

No Stryker employees are covered by collective bargaining agreements. Although mainly located in Kalamazoo, Michigan, Stryker leases facilities in other U.S. cities, France, Germany, Ireland, Switzerland, Canada, and Puerto Rico. Stryker became a publicly traded firm in 1977. Officers, directors, and the Stryker family trust own about a third of the shares. Stryker's financial statements are shown in Exhibits 1 through 3. Members of the board of directors and the top corporate officers are shown in the organizational chart in Exhibit 4.

## THE U.S. HEALTHCARE INDUSTRY

The U.S. healthcare system is highly diverse. Healthcare providers deliver many different kinds of services in a wide variety of settings: acute-care inpatient general hospitals, specialty hospitals, free-standing ambulatory clinics and surgical centers, nursing homes, and patients' homes (via home healthcare services). Despite a growing proportion of elderly people in the U.S. population (about 13 percent are over sixty-five), hospital admission rates have declined for the past decade and are expected to continue to decline in the future.

In contrast, outpatient volume has increased in recent years as a result of restricted reimbursement for inpatient care and the development of diagnostic and therapeutic procedures that do not require inpatient settings. According to the American Hospital Association, over half of all surgeries performed at community hospitals are done on an outpatient basis, up from about 20 percent ten years ago.

The United States is the acknowledged global leader in the production of medical equipment and supplies, and it commands about half of the $140-billion worldwide medical device industry. Export growth in recent years has benefitted from the demand for sophisticated diagnostic equipment and a growing emphasis on the provision of quality healthcare services in countries worldwide.

Business conditions throughout the hospital industry are becoming tougher under the expanding influence of managed-care plans such as health maintenance organizations (HMOs) and constrained reimbursement from both the federal government and insurance companies. The number of hospitals in the United States has been declining for nearly two decades. With about a third of all hospital beds in the United States considered to be excess capacity, the fast pace of industry consolidations is likely to continue. As purchasing decisions in the 1980s and 1990s shifted away from physicians to

EXHIBIT 1    Stryker Corporation Annual Income Statement
(in millions except earnings-per-share data)

|  | 12/31/99 | 12/31/98 | 12/31/97 | 12/31/96 |
|---|---|---|---|---|
| Sales | $2,103.70 | $1,103.20 | $980.14 | $910.06 |
| Cost of goods | 989.70 | 472.07 | 397.77 | 392.36 |
| Gross profit | 1,114.00 | 631.13 | 582.37 | 517.70 |
| Selling and administrative and depreciation and amortization expenses | 947.50 | 442.27 | 398.39 | 383.51 |
| Income after depreciation and amortization | 166.50 | 188.86 | 183.97 | 134.19 |
| Nonoperating income | (14.10) | (128.90) | 10.48 | 26.25 |
| Interest expense | 122.60 | 0 | 0 | 0 |
| Pretax income | 29.80 | 59.96 | 194.45 | 160.45 |
| Income taxes | 10.40 | 20.39 | 70.00 | 61.65 |
| Minority interest | 0 | 0 | (0.87) | (5.66) |
| Investment gains/losses (+) | 0 | 0 | 0 | 0 |
| Other income charges | 0 | 0 | 0 | 0 |
| Income from continued operations | N/A | N/A | N/A | N/A |
| Extras and discontinued operations | 0 | 0 | 0 | 0 |
| Net income | $ 19.40 | $ 39.57 | $125.32 | $104.46 |

**Depreciation footnote**

|  | 12/31/99 | 12/31/98 | 12/31/97 | 12/31/96 |
|---|---|---|---|---|
| Income before depreciation and amortization | $ 200.40 | $ 226.45 | $217.24 | $168.84 |
| Depreciation and amortization (cash flow) | 33.90 | 37.59 | 33.26 | 34.65 |
| Income after depreciation and amortization | $ 166.50 | $ 188.86 | $183.97 | $134.19 |

**Earnings-per-share data**

|  | 12/31/99 | 12/31/98 | 12/31/97 | 12/31/96 |
|---|---|---|---|---|
| Average shares | 99.30 | 98.13 | 96.25 | 96.84 |
| Diluted earnings per share before nonrecurring items | 1.62 | 1.53 | 1.28 | 1.08 |
| Diluted net earnings per share | $ 0.20 | $ 0.40 | $ 1.28 | $ 1.08 |

*Source:* www.freeedgar.com

hospitals and buying alliances, producers of medical equipment were increasingly forced to demonstrate the cost-effectiveness of their products.

For example, in 1999, Novation signed a three-party agreement with Howmedica Osteonics, DePuy Inc., and Zimmer for hip and knee implants. Based in Texas, Novation was established January 1, 1988, through the combination of the supply programs of VHA and UHC, two national healthcare alliances. Novation healthcare organizations perform approximately 40 percent of the $2.1-billion hip and knee implant surgeries in the United States. According to terms of the agreements, VHA and UHC members will receive discounts on hip and knee implants and accessories based on local market conditions and the organization's purchasing volume. The foremost supply cost management company in healthcare, Novation serves the purchasing needs of 6,000 healthcare organizations nationwide. VHA is a nationwide network of more than 1,900 community-owned healthcare organizations and their physicians. UHC is an alliance of 80 academic centers and associate members that represents approximately 70 percent of the academic medical centers in the United States. More such buying agreements are likely in the future, as cost considerations are an increasingly important factor in Europe, Japan, and the United States, the primary places that joint replacement surgery is practiced.

EXHIBIT 2    Stryker Corporation Annual Balance Sheet
             (in millions, except book value per share)

| | 12/31/99 | 12/31/98 | 12/31/97 | 12/31/96 |
|---|---|---|---|---|
| **Assets** | | | | |
| Cash and equivalents | $ 83.50 | $ 142.20 | $351.07 | $367.57 |
| Receivables | 377.70 | 425.60 | 176.21 | 166.05 |
| Notes receivable | 0 | 0 | 0 | 0 |
| Inventories | 386.10 | 553.95 | 136.25 | 127.39 |
| Other current assets | 263.10 | 190.06 | 93.08 | 92.53 |
| Total current assets | 1,110.40 | 1,311.84 | 756.61 | 753.54 |
| Net property and equipment | 391.50 | 429.53 | 163.87 | 172.30 |
| Investments and advances | 0 | 0 | 0 | 0 |
| Other noncurrent assets | 0 | 0 | 0 | 0 |
| Deferred charges | 92.60 | 168.80 | 0 | 0 |
| Intangibles | 898.90 | 897.95 | 46.11 | 45.38 |
| Deposits and other assets | 87.10 | 77.71 | 18.49 | 22.29 |
| Total assets | $2,580.50 | $2,885.85 | $985.08 | $993.51 |
| **Liabilities and shareholders' equity** | | | | |
| Notes payable | 0 | 0 | 0 | 0 |
| Accounts payable | $ 110.40 | $ 162.43 | $ 55.03 | $ 62.43 |
| Current portion long-term debt | 106.30 | 15.01 | 73.63 | 4.40 |
| Current portion capital leases | 0 | 0 | 0 | 0 |
| Accrued expenses | 267.80 | 266.03 | 137.38 | 128.18 |
| Income taxes payable | 47.10 | 49.10 | 36.97 | 56.72 |
| Other current liabilities | 138.00 | 206.87 | 0 | 0 |
| Total current liabilities | 669.60 | 699.45 | 303.01 | 251.74 |
| Mortgages | 0 | 0 | 0 | 0 |
| Deferred taxes/income | 0 | 0 | 0 | 0 |
| Convertible debt | 0 | 0 | 0 | 0 |
| Long-term debt | 1,181.10 | 1,487.97 | 4.45 | 89.50 |
| Noncurrent capital leases | 0 | 0 | 0 | 0 |
| Other noncurrent liabilities | 58.30 | 29.61 | 29.17 | 36.03 |
| Minority interest (liabilities) | 0 | 16.73 | 35.67 | 85.87 |
| Total liabilities | $1,909.00 | $2,233.77 | $372.30 | $463.14 |
| **Shareholders' equity** | | | | |
| Preferred stock | 0 | 0 | 0 | 0 |
| Common stock (par) | $ 9.70 | $ 9.65 | $ 9.61 | $ 9.68 |
| Capital surplus | 36.80 | 10.49 | 0.02 | 5.92 |
| Retained earnings | 668.10 | 640.92 | 612.94 | 514.32 |
| Other equity | (43.10) | (9.00) | (9.79) | 0.44 |
| Treasury stock | 0 | 0 | 0 | 0 |
| Total shareholders' equity | 671.50 | 652.07 | 612.78 | 530.36 |
| Total liabilities and shareholders' equity | 2,580.50 | 2,885.85 | 985.08 | 993.51 |
| Total common equity | 671.50 | 652.07 | 612.78 | 530.36 |
| Average shares | 99.30 | 98.13 | 96.25 | 96.84 |
| Book value per share | $ 6.92 | $ 6.76 | $ 6.37 | $ 5.48 |

*Source:* www.freeedgar.com

---

## EXHIBIT 3   Stryker Corporation's Divisional Financial Data

| | Orthopedic Implants | Medical and Surgical Equipment | Physical Therapy Services | Corporate Administration | Total |
|---|---|---|---|---|---|
| **Year ended December 31, 1998** | | | | | |
| Net sales | $ 409,644 | $577,788 | $115,776 | — | $1,103,208 |
| Interest income | — | — | — | $ 16,501 | 16,501 |
| Interest expense | — | — | — | 12,181 | 12,181 |
| Depreciation and amortization expense | 16,763 | 15,987 | 4,391 | 455 | 37,596 |
| Purchased research and development | 83,296 | — | — | — | 83,296 |
| Acquisition-related charges | 52,751 | — | — | 11,193 | 63,944 |
| Income taxes | (11,463) | 33,584 | 4,027 | (5,758) | 20,390 |
| Segment net profit (loss) | (20,182) | 68,769 | 7,015 | (16,032) | 39,570 |
| Total assets | 2,157,747 | 601,406 | 71,785 | 54,914 | 2,885,852 |
| Capital expenditures | 21,825 | 23,881 | 4,450 | 1,088 | 51,244 |
| **Year ended December 31, 1997** | | | | | |
| Net sales | 375,028 | 505,099 | 100,008 | — | 980,135 |
| Interest income | — | — | — | 14,963 | 14,963 |
| Interest expense | — | — | — | 4,812 | 4,812 |
| Depreciation and amortization expense | 12,105 | 16,983 | 3,759 | 417 | 33,264 |
| Income taxes | 40,542 | 25,764 | 3,904 | (210) | 70,000 |
| Segment net profit (loss) | 69,447 | 53,264 | 6,375 | (3,766) | 125,320 |
| Total assets | 304,944 | 315,656 | 62,785 | 301,690 | 985,075 |
| Capital expenditures | 17,594 | 13,925 | 3,525 | 169 | 35,213 |
| **Year ended December 31, 1996** | | | | | |
| Net sales | 347,178 | 484,301 | 78,581 | — | 910,060 |
| Interest income | — | — | — | 13,339 | 13,339 |
| Interest expense | — | — | — | 8,349 | 8,349 |
| Depreciation and amortization expense | 12,324 | 18,420 | 3,492 | 414 | 34,650 |
| Purchased research and development | 7,500 | — | — | — | 7,500 |
| Special charges | 26,893 | 4,485 | 2,900 | — | 34,278 |
| Gain on patent judgment | 61,094 | — | — | — | 61,094 |
| Income taxes | 46,263 | 12,145 | 1,724 | 1,518 | 61,650 |
| Segment net profit (loss) | 71,892 | 39,393 | 2,809 | (9,634) | 104,460 |
| Total assets | 301,395 | 331,388 | 51,655 | 309,068 | 993,506 |
| Capital expenditures | $ 6,916 | $ 14,541 | $ 5,160 | $ 107 | $ 26,724 |

*Source:* Stryker's 1998 *Annual Report,* p. 58.

---

## EXHIBIT 4   Stryker Corporation's Organizational Chart

## STRYKER'S ORGANIZATION

Following the Howmedica acquisition, Stryker has organized itself into three major product divisions: Howmedica Orthopaedic Implants, MedSurg Equipment, and Physical Therapy Associates.

### Orthopaedic Implants

The Howmedica Orthopaedic Implants division, located in New Jersey, produces a variety of both total and partial hip and knee implants. It is a combination of the former Stryker Osteonics division and the Howmedica acquisition and is now the company's largest division. With sales of $1.2 billion for 1999, it is Stryker's largest unit, accounting for 60 percent of its sales.

Every year about 500,000 people in the United States and a comparable number abroad undergo joint replacement surgery to regain some mobility. Most hip and knee replacements result from osteoarthritis—a condition affecting the aged in which joints become painful and mobility is impaired—and rheumatoid arthritis, a disease that destroys cartilage at the joint's surface. Orthopedic research in recent years has led to the development of a broad array of prosthetic equipment and related devices, including digital cameras. Recent innovations include porous hips and knees, which allow bone to grow directly into the metal implant.

### MedSurg Equipment

The MedSurg (medical and surgical) division has three major components: Stryker Medical, Stryker Endoscopy, and Stryker Instruments. With sales of 733 million for 1999, this division accounted for 33 percent of Stryker's sales. Each MedSurg unit competes against medical equipment subsidiaries of large firms (e.g., DePuy of Johnson & Johnson, Hill-Rom of Hillenbrand Industries, Zimmer of Bristol-Myers Squibb) as well as against independent firms, such as Biomet, Midas Rex, Sofamar Danek, and U.S. Surgical.

#### Stryker Medical

It produces specialty stretchers and beds, which facilitate the transportation, transfer, and treatment of patients within the hospital. Over the past seven years, this division has designed a line of innovative stretchers as a result of a close analysis of hospital needs. It has focused on reducing the number of patient transfers (from bed to stretcher to operating table and back again) that must be performed in a hospital. It also produces accessories such as bedside stands and overbed tables.

#### Stryker Endoscopy

This division makes a broad range of medical video-imaging equipment and instruments for arthroscopy and general surgery. In an endoscopic (less invasive) surgical procedure, the surgeon removes or repairs damaged tissue through several small punctures rather than an open incision. Patients experience reduced trauma and pain, less time in the hospital, and a quicker return to health. Medical costs are also reduced. For example, less-invasive removal of the gallbladder requires a single day in the hospital followed by a week of convalescence at home. Traditional gallbladder surgery, by contrast, meant four to eight days in the hospital and a month's convalescence.

Imaging technology plays a crucial role in endoscopic procedures. Stryker is a leader in medical video-imaging systems. Through pioneering engineering work, Stryker miniaturized a three-chip video camera (with a separate computer chip for each primary color) and became the first company to offer the surgeon a broadcast-quality image. This division also makes digital cameras to assist with endoscopic procedures.

*Stryker Instruments*

This division produces a wide range of operating room equipment that is utilized primarily in orthopedic procedures, such as bone saws and drills. It is a market leader for battery-powered heavy-duty surgical instruments. Its Stryker 940 cast-removal system is the newest version of Dr. Stryker's original cast cutter. To keep pace with its growing sales volume, the Instruments division expanded its manufacturing capabilities in 1994, doubling the clean room space at its Kalamazoo facility and enlarging its facilities in Arroyo, Puerto Rico, by 50 percent. It recently began a $1.8 million addition to its Kalamazoo manufacturing and warehousing facility, bringing its total space to over 200,000 square feet.

## Physical Therapy Services

At the end of 1999, the Physiotherapy Associates division operated 185 outpatient rehabilitation centers in 20 states and the District of Columbia. Following orthopedic or neurological injury, the centers provide physical, occupational, and speech therapy to help speed a patient's return to work or full activity. With sales of $122 million for 1999, this division accounted for 6 percent of Stryker's sales.

Physiotherapy Associates generally operates multiple facilities within a single area, offering patients a choice of locations. By organizing a number of practices into a group that shares certain functions, Physiotherapy Associates is able to achieve substantial operating efficiencies. All of its facilities are leased. In the outpatient physical therapy market, Stryker's principal competitors are independent practitioners and hospital-based services. Competition is also provided by national rehabilitation companies such as HealthSouth, NovaCare/RCI, and Rehability.

## INTERNATIONAL OPERATIONS

Stryker sought to improve distribution of its products internationally by making equity investments in Matsumoto, a large Japanese distributor of medical technology. Matsumoto focuses on orthopedics, general surgery, and emergency care. In addition to Stryker products, Matsumoto also distributes devices from other leading American and European medical device makers.

Shortly after Stryker took a majority ownership position in Matsumoto in 1995, however, several medical instrument companies stopped distributing through Matsumoto because they felt uncomfortable with Stryker's majority influence. As a result, Matsumoto saw sales of non-Stryker products fall by over 50 percent from 1995 to 1996. Sales at Matsumoto have yet to return to its 1995 levels of $104.7 million. Geographic segment data on Stryker's sales are given in Exhibit 5.

## MANUFACTURING AND RESEARCH AND DEVELOPMENT

Stryker's manufacturing processes consist primarily of precision machining, metal fabrication, assembly operations, and the investment (precision) casting of cobalt chrome and finishing of cobalt chrome and titanium. The principal raw materials are stainless steel, aluminum, cobalt chrome, and titanium alloys. In all, purchases from outside sources were approximately half of the company's total cost of sales in 1999.

Most of the company's products and product improvements have been developed internally. The company maintains close working relationships with physicians and medical personnel in hospitals and universities who assist in product research and development. Expenditures for product research, development, and engineering were $56.9 million in 1998, $56.9 million in 1997, and $61.1 million in 1996. Most of this spending was under the direct control of the operating divisions, in which research and

EXHIBIT 5    Stryker Corporation's Geographic Segment Data

The company's area of operations outside of the United States, Japan, and Europe principally includes the Pacific Rim, Canada, Latin America, and the Middle East. Geographic information follows:

| | Net Sales | Long-Lived Assets |
|---|---|---|
| **Year ended December 31, 1998** | | |
| United States | $    728,948 | $    827,047 |
| Japan | 131,282 | 141,642 |
| Europe | 135,273 | 541,444 |
| Other foreign countries | 107,705 | 32,707 |
| | $1,103,208 | $1,542,840 |
| | | |
| **Year ended December 31, 1997** | | |
| United States | $633,252 | $122,635 |
| Japan | 154,308 | 68,289 |
| Europe | 104,376 | 49,278 |
| Other foreign countries | 88,199 | 2,260 |
| | $980,135 | $242,462 |
| | | |
| **Year ended December 31, 1996** | | |
| United States | $564,534 | $103,832 |
| Japan | 172,522 | 88,428 |
| Europe | 99,177 | 46,724 |
| Other foreign countries | 73,827 | 985 |
| | $910,060 | $239,969 |

*Source:* Stryker's 1998 *Annual Report,* p. 59.

development can be highly focused on the markets Stryker serves. Stryker seeks to obtain patent protection whenever possible on its products. It currently holds over 250 patents.

In 1998, *Industry Week* named Howmedica Osteonics as one of the top ten manufacturing plants in the United States. The Osteonics division is organized into vertically integrated work cells with a significant gain in efficiency. The new organization has helped Osteonics to increase teamwork, cut lead time, reduce inventory requirements, boost quality, and control costs. The cells have also enabled Osteonics to provide a rapid response to its customers' needs and orders.

## STRYKER'S CORPORATE CULTURE

Since John Brown became CEO, Stryker has developed a distinctive corporate culture that is sometimes described as "a lot like being in the Marine Corps" although senior executives try to downplay that image. Sayings representing Stryker's core beliefs are prominently written on walls in lobbies and cafeterias. One of the most common, "First be best, then be first," refers to Dr. Stryker's philosophy that Stryker should first make the best products, then seek market leadership for those products.

Although there are no time clocks visible in Stryker facilities, employees wear scanning ID cards that register when they arrive for work and when they leave. Lunch time is restricted to 30 minutes, enough time to eat in the company cafeteria but hardly enough time to go off premises to eat. Given the pressure of the 20 percent annual increase in earnings-per-share goal, the work week for white-collar workers is typically

50–60 hours. It is common for executives to work evenings or on weekends. In return for their hard work, employees are encouraged to share in the company's prosperity through a generous stock purchase plan. Employees can use up to 14 percent of their earnings to purchase Stryker stock. The company will match the first 8 percent contributed by the employees.

In the 1996 *Annual Report,* John Brown explained why 20 percent growth was so important to Stryker.

> We believe that a 20 percent growth target makes good sense for Stryker and our various constituencies. Fast-paced but consistent growth is more rewarding to our shareholders, employees and customers than is the boom-and-bust pattern typical of companies that constantly strive for spectacular growth.
>
> Through constant emphasis, our 20 percent growth target has truly become an essential part of Stryker's business culture. In our decentralized structure, Stryker's divisions pursue this goal in a multitude of ways: they invest in research and development; they launch new products; they increase the efficiency of their sales and marketing efforts; and they control or trim their manufacturing costs. Entrepreneurial in spirit and ready to meet the complex needs of their markets, our divisions strive to grow at Stryker rates. While some may fall short in any given year, we expect others will exceed the mark.

Most of the company's products are marketed in the United States directly to more than 7,500 hospitals and to doctors and other healthcare facilities. The company maintains dedicated salesforces for each of its principal product lines to provide focus and a high level of expertise to each medical specialty served. The domestic salesforce is compensated in large part by commissions. Members of the salesforce who came from Howmedica were shifted from salary to commissions. According to CEO Brown, "The beauty of commissions is there's no cap. The more the individual sells, the more he makes. The most ambitious and driven salespeople thrive in a commission environment." Stryker has been referred to as a "salesperson's paradise," where top performers can earn $200,000 or more a year. Hourly workers can earn pay increases or bonuses for meeting quality objectives. Nevertheless, some potential employees find Stryker's growth-oriented culture too demanding and choose to work for another company.

Brown sends out a monthly newsletter to top managers that ranks each division by growth and includes comments on performance, good and bad. Brown was honored as one of America's best CEOs in the September 1977 issue of *Worth,* where he is quoted as saying,

> I try to set expectations. I think I've persuaded our employees that it's a worthwhile goal. Ask any of our employees either here in Michigan or from Berlin to Osaka, and they'll tell you that what they have to do is increase sales 20 percent every year.

### THE FUTURE

Stryker has some opportunities to help it make its growth goals. It can use its strong financial position to continue making selected acquisitions to enter new markets, as it did when it entered the trauma business in 1996 with its acquisition of Osteo Holdings, or increase share of existing markets, as it did with its 1998 acquisition of Howmedica. Stryker Endoscopy can also seek new niche markets outside arthroscopy, such as instruments for ear, nose, and throat (ENT) surgeons. Few existing power tools cater specifically to the specific demands of ENT surgeons for the approximately 500,000 procedures

EXHIBIT 6    **Stryker Sales (in millions)**

|  | 1999 |
|---|---|
| Domestic | $1,228.40 |
| Foreign | 875.30 |
| Total | $2,103.70 |
| | |
| Orthopaedic Implants | $1,248.20 |
| MedSurg Equipment | 733.50 |
| Physical Therapy | 122.00 |
| Total | $2,103.70 |

*Source:* www.freeedgar.com

they perform each year. A third opportunity for growth is to add centers to its Physical Therapy Services division. Each center averages $400,000 in revenue per year.

In the past 20 years, Stryker has seen many changes as it grew from $23 million to over $2 billion in sales, and it will probably see as many more in the next 20 years. However, as long as John Brown is CEO (he turned 65 in 2000), one aspect of Stryker that isn't likely to change is the expectation that every employee will be expected to help sales and earnings increase 20 percent a year, every year.

## REFERENCES

ROYAL, WELD. "America's Best Plants: Stryker Corporation, Allendale, N.J." *Industry Week,* October 19, 1998, 72–74.

WILLIS, CLINT. "Super Chiefs: Six CEOs Who Consistently Make Companies Great and Investors Wealthy." *Worth,* September 1997, 60.

# BIOMET, INC.—2000

Satish P. Deshpande
Western Michigan University

**BMET**

www.biomet.com

Biomet, Inc., reported record sales for its fiscal year ending May 31, 1999. During fiscal year 1999, sales increased 16 percent to $757.4 million, but net income fell 7 percent to $116.4 million. Revenues reflect the continued penetration of the reconstructive device, arthroscopy, softgoods, and spinal hardware segments. Earnings were offset by a $55 million special charge in connection with the Orthofix litigation. Since fiscal year 1984, the company's net sales have grown at a 33 percent compound annual rate.

Biomet, Inc., is a specialty manufacturer, designer, and marketer of orthopedic products including reconstructive and trauma devices, electrical bone-growth stimulators, orthopedic support devices, operating room supplies, powered surgical instruments, general surgical instruments, and arthroscopy products. Biomet has its corporate headquarters in Warsaw, Indiana, and manufacturing facilities in 14 worldwide locations. The company and its subsidiaries distribute products to over 100 countries and employ over 3,000 people worldwide.

Orthopedic implant manufacturers have faced increased pressure to contain their costs as hospitals seek various ways to limit expensive inventories. Burdensome regulations, expensive product liability, and managed care have driven many manufacturers into developing and manufacturing their products abroad. On the other hand, the Food and Drug Administration (FDA) has come under increasing public and political pressure to speed up the approvals of drugs and medical devices. In Senate hearings, the FDA has been under harsh attack for failing to provide timely access to new medical technology. Congressional leaders are calling for privatization of the governmental agency. The Clinton administration has announced a number of steps to ease restrictions. These are positive signals for Biomet.

## HISTORY

Biomet, Inc., was incorporated in 1977 in Indiana by Dane A. Miller, Niles L. Noblitt, Jerry Ferguson, and Ray Harroff. Miller is president and CEO of Biomet, and Noblitt is board chairman. Miller and several other key managers worked at the Zimmer Division of Bristol-Myers before forming their own company. The company initially sold orthopedic support products through ten distributors. Biomet entered the reconstructive device market in the early 1980s by offering a titanium alloy-based hip system. Biomet further enhanced its reputation with a number of technological advances in hip replacement systems as well as in total knee replacement. Biomet was founded on the premise that major orthopedic companies, which were primarily divisions of large pharmaceutical companies, had neglected a service orientation approach to orthopedic surgeons' needs. Through a dedication to high levels of service and a variety of innovative products, Biomet has rapidly penetrated the growing market for orthopedic products.

In 1984, Biomet acquired the Orthopedic Equipment Co. (OEC), a subsidiary of Diasonics, for $8.4 million. OEC has sales of $21.5 million and was twice the size of Biomet in 1984 when acquired. The principal reason for the acquisition was OEC's large distribution network, foreign manufacturing facilities, and a complementary product line (trauma and operating room supplies). The acquisition also allowed Biomet to penetrate the European market through two manufacturing facilities in the United Kingdom. The activities of OEC, more recently, have been split among the various divisions.

In 1988, Biomet acquired Electro-Biology, Inc. (EBI), a leader in the electrical growth stimulation device field for $25.8 million. This acquisition provided Biomet with a strong presence in the electrical stimulation and external fixation markets. In 1991, a newly formed subsidiary of Biomet, Effner Biomet Corp., purchased all operations of Effner GmbH and its related companies. Effner is engaged in the manufacture and sale of orthopedic implants, general surgical instruments, and arthroscopy products with the majority of sales in Germany.

Biomet also entered a joint development agreement with United States Surgical Corporation to develop, manufacture, and market bioresorbable orthopedic products. This venture has been termed Poly-Medics and concentrates on three primary areas: bone replacement and augmentation, fracture healing, and musculoskeletal soft-tissue repair. Bioresorbable products, such as absorbable staples and sutures, essentially degrade in the body and are broken down into carbon dioxide and water. In orthopedics, bioabsorbable materials eliminate the need for a second operation to remove metal fixation parts left in the body after healing.

In 1992, Biomet purchased Walter Lorenz Surgical Instruments, Inc. (Lorenz Surgical), for $19 million. Lorenz Surgical, based in Jacksonville, Florida, was a leading marketer of oral-maxillofacial products used by oral surgeons such as orthognathic instruments (used for jaw alignment), craniofacial instruments (used to treat severe skull deformities), rigid fixation systems, TMJ instruments, exodontial instruments, and a transmandibular implant system. These products principally are used to correct deformities, assist in the repair of trauma fractures, and for cosmetic applications.

In 1994, Biomet purchased Kirschner Medical Corporation of Maryland for $38,900,000 ($13.3 million over the fair value). Kirschner, as does Biomet, produces joint replacement for hips, knees, and shoulders, along with fracture fixation products. Kirschner is a market leader in shoulder implants and also produces braces, supports, splints, and cast materials. It has four manufacturing plants in the United States and one in Spain. During the fiscal year 1996, Kirschner's orthopedic operations were consolidated into Biomet, eliminating duplicative administrative and overhead expenses. During the same period, Biomet Europe was established to coordinate manufacturing, development, and sales activities in Europe. In early 1998, Biomet entered into a joint venture agreement with Merck KgaA, a pharmaceutical and chemical company in Darmstadt, Germany. Under this agreement, both the companies contributed their European orthopedic and biomaterials business operations to form Biomet Merck. Biomet also formed an alliance with Selective Genetics, Inc., during the fourth quarter of fiscal year 1999 to develop gene therapy products for the musculoskeletal market.

Today, the majority (60 percent) of the company's business is in reconstructive devices, and almost 67 percent of its business is domestic. Biomet consists of five different strategic business units, encompassing over 1,000 sales representatives worldwide:

- **Biomet-Warsaw**—the principal strategic business unit in the United States. The product line includes a comprehensive line of reconstructive devices, internal fixation devices, and unique surgical products for the hand. Products are sold through a 400-person, distributor-based sales network.

- **Arthrotek**—the company's sports medicine division. Arthrotek offers a complete line of arthroscopy products, which are primarily distributed through Biomet-Warsaw's distribution network.
- **Electro-Biology, Inc**—the market leader in the electrical stimulation and external fixation market segments. EBI also offers products in the spinal and orthopedic support market segments. Its products are sold through the division's direct 300-person salesforce.
- **Lorenz Surgical**—a pioneer in the craniomaxillofacial market segment. The Lorenz product line includes the industry's first resorbable craniomaxillofacial fixation system. Its products are sold through its own distributor network, which encompasses 75 sales representatives in the United States.
- **BioMer C.V.**—a 50/50 joint venture between Biomet, Inc., and Merck KGaA, a German chemical and pharmaceutical company. The partnership significantly expands Biomet's presence in the European marketplace while providing the company with worldwide access to key biomaterials technologies. The joint product lines are sold through a combined salesforce, which consists of more than 200 sales representatives throughout Europe.

## COMPETITORS

Two major changes took place in the orthopedic industry at the end of 1998. In November of 1998, Johnson & Johnson acquired DePuy, Inc., and in December of 1998, Stryker Corporation acquired Howmedica, Inc. As shown in Exhibit 1, the 1999 orthopedic market in the United States was estimated to be nearly $4.745 billion. Reconstructive devices make up nearly half the orthopedic market. This $1.88 billion market segment includes total hip, knee, and shoulder replacements.

Exhibit 2 provides detailed information on the reconstructive device market in the United States. The hip market is estimated to be $805 million, and approximately 250,000 hip procedures are performed in the United States annually. Biomet is a marketplace leader in the shoulder market that is an estimated $60 million. Approximately 260,000 knee procedures are performed in the United States, and the number is growing between 3 percent to 5 percent every year. Zimmer, the leader in the orthopedics field, has over 20 percent of the reconstructive market. Biomet is the fourth-largest participant with a share of 13 percent to 14 percent of the market.

---

EXHIBIT 1    1999 Estimated U.S. Orthopedic Market $4.745 Billion (in millions)

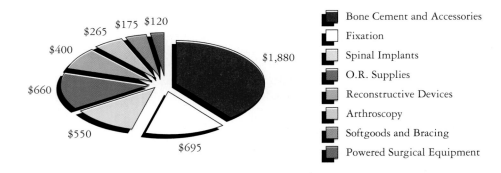

Source: Biomet *Annual Report*, 1999.

EXHIBIT 2    1999 Reconstructive Device Market
in the United States

| Major Areas | Market (in millions) | Market Growth |
|---|---|---|
| Hips | $805 | 2% to 4% |
| Shoulders | 60 | 4 to 6 |
| Knees | 995 | 3 to 5 |

*Source:* Biomet *Annual Report,* 1999.

Growth in the reconstructive market has been attributed to better products and techniques that improve surgical outcomes, cost-effective techniques, and demographic trends. Recent products last longer and require less time in the operating room, thereby lowering costs. People today are living longer, which accounts for the expanded patient pool. Life expectancies have increased by approximately 5 percent over the past two decades. Male life expectancy has increased from 67 years to 71 years, and female life expectancy has increased to 78 years. Of the estimated 37 million Americans who suffer from arthritis, approximately 14 million of them (38 percent) are between ages forty-five and sixty-four. A more active lifestyle, according to Biomet officials, has led to joint replacement at younger ages. In addition, the pool of people seventy-five and over is increasing. Clearly, the demographics are favorable for Biomet.

The general population growth rate from 1989 to 2010 is projected to be only 14 percent, but the fifty-five to seventy-four sector is expected to grow 40 percent between 1997 and 2010, an increase of 16 million people. The over-seventy-five population is expected to grow by 16 percent—to 18 million people over the same period. The over-sixty-five population segment accounts for more than two thirds of total healthcare expenditures. Competition in the implant market is primarily on the basis of service and product design, but competition in the sale of generic internal fixation devices tends to be more price sensitive. Purchasing decisions for hospitals are being made increasingly through buying groups that are able to negotiate price discounts from the manufacturers.

Two additional factors squeezing profits are: (1) the greater utilization of lower-priced implants for the elderly who require less functionality and longevity of implants, and (2) increasing cooperation of surgeons and hospital administrators in narrowing their choices of products, thereby allowing hospitals to deal with fewer manufacturers.

## PRODUCTS

Biomet's products are divided into four groups: Reconstructive products, fixation products, spinal products, and other products. Exhibit 3 gives sales by product group for the past three fiscal years ending May 31.

### Reconstructive Products

Biomet's sales of reconstructive devices worldwide increased 16 percent during fiscal year 1999 to over $450 million. These devices replace joints that have deteriorated from diseases such as arthritis or through injury. Reconstructive joint surgery involves modification of the area surrounding the affected joint and insertion of one or more manufactured joint components. Biomet's primary reconstructive products concern the hip, knee, and

EXHIBIT 3    Biomet's Sales of Reconstructive Devices for Years
Ended May 31, 1999 (in thousands)

| | 1999 | | 1998 | | 1997 | |
|---|---|---|---|---|---|---|
| | *Net Sales* | *Percent of Net Sales* | *Net Sales* | *Percent of Net Sales* | *Net Sales* | *Percent of Net Sales* |
| Reconstructive products | $450,877 | 60% | $389,483 | 60% | $347,762 | 60% |
| Fixation products | 162,825 | 21 | 144,853 | 22 | 132,875 | 23 |
| Spinal products | 45,125 | 6 | 35,902 | 6 | 31,426 | 5 |
| Other products | 98,587 | 13 | 81,167 | 12 | 68,284 | 12 |
| Total | $757,414 | 100 | $651,405 | 100 | $580,347 | 100 |

*Source:* Biomet *Annual Report,* 1999.

shoulder although the company can produce peripheral joints for the wrist, elbow, fin-ger, or large toe. A hip prosthesis consists of a femoral head, neck, and stem manufac-tured in a variety of head sizes, neck lengths, stem lengths, and configurations. Biomet's AGC Total Knee System is one of its largest-selling product groups. The product fea-tures left and right femoral components, matching tibial components, and appropriately sized patella components for resurfacing. Biomet's various major knee systems, with their variety of options, are one of the most versatile and comprehensive available in the orthopedic market. Biomet also has Patient-Matched-Implant (PMI) services group, which designs, manufactures, and delivers one-of-a-kind reconstructive and trauma devices for orthopedic surgeons. The company acquired a patent in 1990 that allows a physician to create, prior to surgery (through the use of CT or MRI data), electronic 3-D models, which are then translated into a PMI design for manufacture. The Mallory-Head Modular Calcar System, the Reach Revision Reach System, and the Finn Salvage/Oncology Revision Knee System continue to penetrate the U.S. market.

## Fixation Products

Every year, around 7 million fractures occur in the United States. The fixation market is estimated to be $695 million. It includes products used to stabilize broken bones and promote healing. EBI is a market leader in both the $120 million external fixation mar-ket segment and the $110 million electrical stimulation market. The EBI Bone Healing System Model 1200 continues to be a market leader in the domestic electrical simulation market. This product is used on fractured bones that will not heal using nor-mal methods. A coil connected to a battery-operated treatment unit is placed on the fracture. The system produces a pulsating electromagnetic field that affects the cells. Because the system is noninvasive, it poses no surgical risks and has no known side effects. Biomet introduced a compact version of the system during the fiscal year 1998 and introduced a lighter and a more patient-friendly model in 2000. With a 20 percent share of the market, the company's Lorenz Surgical subsidiary is a market leader in the $120 million craniomaxillofacial fixation market. The LactoSorb Craniomaxillofacial Fixation System comprises a co-polymer comparable in strength to existing titanium systems but which completely resorbs within 9 to 12 months. This system is especially beneficial for pediatric surgical procedures because it eliminates the need for a second surgery to remove plates and screws. But Biomet only has a small share of the $345-million internal fixation market. Overall, Biomet is the second-largest player in the fix-ation market.

Until 1995, Biomet had exclusive rights with Orthofix of Italy to distribute the Orthofix External Fixation System (OEFS) in the United States. This system is used in trauma situations in which the bone has been fractured or crushed in many places. It essentially allows the physician to hold in place complicated fractures of long bones when casts, rods, or plates are inappropriate. This exclusive distribution right expired in 1995, and in early fiscal year 1996, Biomet successfully launched the Dynafix External Fixation System. On June 2, 1997, Biomet announced that it would appeal a jury verdict entered against it in a U.S. District Court for the District of New Jersey in an action brought by Orthofix SRL against EBI and Biomet concerning the expiration of the distribution agreement. The jury found that in spite of Orthofix's refusal to renew the agreement, EBI's development of the Dynafix system prior to the expiration of the contract constituted a breach of the distribution agreement. The jury awarded Orthofix $49 million dollars in compensatory damages and $100 million in punitive damages. The jury also ruled that Orthofix breached the distribution agreement and tortiously interfered with EBI's economic relations, but only nominal damages were awarded to EBI. On June 30,1999, Biomet announced that the appellate court virtually eliminated $50 million in punitive damages assessed against the company, which reduced the judgment to $49.9 million plus interest. Accordingly, Biomet recorded a $55 million special charge against pretax earnings for the quarter and fiscal year that ended May 31, 1999.

## Spinal Products

Back injuries cost society nearly $16 billion every year. Nearly half of the over-300,000 vertebral fusion procedures performed in the United States every year utilize some type of instrumentation. Currently, EBI controls nearly 6 percent of the $660 million spinal implant market in the United States. This market is expected to grow by 15 percent every year. EBI is a market leader in the $80 million electrical segment of the spinal market. It also has a growing presence in the $330 million plates, screws, and rods segment. Its leading product is the SpF Spinal Fusion Stimulation System. This system uses cathodes to deliver small electrical currents to facilitate successful spinal fusions. EBI is currently improving the system and introduces the Omega 21 System for the lumbar spine. This is a unique rod and screw system.

## Other Products

Biomet's "other product" sales during fiscal year 1999 were approximately $98 million. This was a 21 percent increase over the previous fiscal year. This was in great part due to Arthrotek's arthroscopy products, EBI's line of softgoods and bracing products, and the Indiana Tome Carpal Tunnel Release System. Arthrotek plans to introduce a broad line of resorbable products to increase its market share in the $550 million U.S. arthroscopy market.

## OPERATIONS

### New Products and Technologies

Biomet has spent nearly $94 million on research and development in the past three years and expects this amount to increase in the future. A number of research programs are in progress, addressing reconstruction devices, bone-substitute materials and cements, cartilage substitute for repairing articular defects of the knees, and ligament replacement for anterior cruciate repair. In addition, Biomet's alliance with Selective Genetics, Inc., a gene therapy company, will provide access to their technology for orthopedic indications such as spinal fusions, fracture repair, bone-void filling, and tendon and ligament repair.

## International Operations

Biomet's international sales in fiscal year 1999 increased 31 percent to $246,339,000 from the previous level of $187,378,000 million in 1998. Biomet Merck provides Biomet with the exclusive rights to Merck KGaA's current and future biomaterials-based products. Currently it is the fourth-largest orthopedic company in Europe with a local presence in all the major markets. This is partly due to the successful integration of Biomet's and Merck KGaA's operations. Currently the joint venture has a revenue of nearly $200 million and has 1,100 employees. The European orthopedic market was nearly $2.52 billion in 1999. Exhibit 4 presents industry segment and geographic information.

## Team Biomet

According to CEO Dane Miller, the major reasons for the success of Biomet are: "(1) We remain close to the market and listen to the needs of our customer; (2) we function as a team to get the job done, and (3) our team has creative and innovative members in place to succeed." The team concept started in Biomet in 1977 and is today an integral part of the firm's philosophy. One characteristic of the concept is that Biomet has decentralized decision-making so that decisions can be made at the appropriate level. Teams are composed of employees from several functional areas—e.g., design, manufacturing, quality, and production planning. Physically, employees are located by functional areas within the facility in which routine decisions are handled. Only those decisions related to large commitments of capital expenditures or changes in strategic policies require presidential or vice presidential signatures.

Communication between subsidiaries and departments is frequent and open. Members of management interact with the workers on a daily basis in addition to attending many corporate events that foster camaraderie. When Dane Miller and his colleagues started the company, his goal was to "create an organization that could grow unencumbered by the bureaucratic structures and conservatism that he believes stifle initiative and

EXHIBIT 4    **Industry Segment and Geographic Information (in thousands)**

|  | *1999* | *1998* | *1997* |
|---|---|---|---|
| Net sales: | | | |
| North America | $535,835 | $493,877 | $465,148 |
| Europe | 204,783 | 143,615 | 110,039 |
| Other | 16,796 | 13,913 | 5,160 |
| | $757,414 | $651,405 | $580,347 |
| Operating income: | | | |
| North America | $141,194 | $166,699 | $143,522 |
| Europe | 27,030 | 9,942 | 15,131 |
| Other | 3,426 | 3,465 | 1,158 |
| | $171,650 | $180,106 | $159,811 |
| Long-lived assets: | | | |
| North America | $112,068 | $ 97,839 | $ 84,589 |
| Europe | 111,669 | 102,616 | 29,977 |
| Other | 4,204 | 2,973 | 3,940 |
| | $227,941 | $203,428 | $118,506 |

*Source: Biomet, Inc. and Subsidiaries Notes to Consolidated Financial Statements, 1999 Annual Report, Biomet Inc.*

creativity at many large firms." Although Miller and his colleagues keep an open door for employees, they are constantly on the shop floor talking to employees in their work setting. The team concept is stressed in company brochures and meetings. There is a Biomet Team Appreciation Day as well as company picnics, Christmas parties, and other special events. The quarterly in-house publication "Bio Briefs" serves as an effective communication tool to keep employees informed on corporate and product information, as well as to recognize special events such as promotions, birthdays, births, anniversaries, etc. Biomet's team concept offers every employee financial incentives including cash bonuses, company shares, and stock options. Insiders own approximately 25 percent of the outstanding stock. The team concept also extends to the medical profession. When patients face unusual circumstances, Biomet officials are often called upon to design specialty products. Biomet enjoys a healthy reputation in the medical profession for its "team effort." This concept, first announced in 1989, is reinforced in daily operations.

## Financial Information

Results in 1999 show an increase in sales of 13.9 percent and a decrease in net income of 7.1 percent. Consolidated financial information is given in Exhibit 5.

## THE FUTURE

Prepare a three-year strategic plan for CEO Dane Miller.

### EXHIBIT 5    Biomet, Inc. Consolidated Financial Information
(in thousands, except earnings per share)

|  | 1999 | 1998 | 1997 | 1996 | 1995 |
|---|---|---|---|---|---|
| **Income Statement Data** | | | | | |
| Net sales | $ 757,414 | $651,405 | $580,347 | $535,159 | $452,272 |
| Cost of sales | 229,727 | 202,235 | 185,795 | 174,364 | 142,143 |
| Gross profit | 527,687 | 449,170 | 394,552 | 360,795 | 310,129 |
| Selling, general and administrative expenses | 265,565 | 232,944 | 211,540 | 199,461 | 169,332 |
| Research and development expense | 35,472 | 36,120 | 23,201 | 24,054 | 21,770 |
| Operating income | 171,650 | 180,106 | 159,811 | 137,280 | 119,027 |
| Other income, net | 14,696 | 23,835 | 9,321 | 12,389 | 5,915 |
| Income before income taxes | 186,346 | 203,941 | 169,132 | 149,669 | 124,942 |
| Provision for income taxes | 62,527 | 79,071 | 62,678 | 55,563 | 45,742 |
| Net income | $ 116,361 | $124,726 | $106,454 | $ 94,106 | $ 79,200 |
| Earnings per share | $ 1.04 | $ 1.12 | $ .95 | $ .82 | $ .69 |
| Weighted average number of shares | 112,309 | 111,717 | 113,765 | 115,461 | 115,459 |
| **Balance sheet data** | | | | | |
| Working capital | $ 480,278 | $472,733 | $391,136 | $400,817 | $302,752 |
| Total assets | 1,067,956 | 848,739 | 628,356 | 598,469 | 539,084 |
| Long-term debt | — | — | — | — | — |
| Shareholders' equity | $ 775,947 | $667,418 | $552,828 | $534,070 | $444,617 |

Amounts after January 1, 1998 include the impact of Biomet Merck. Other acquisitions during the five-year period individually and in the aggregate have not been material to the company's operating results or financial position.
*Source:* Biomet, 1999 *Annual Report.*

# PLAYBOY ENTERPRISES, INC.—2000

Kay W. Lawrimore
Fred R. David
Francis Marion University

## PLA
www.playboy.com

Hugh M. Hefner created the first edition of *Playboy* magazine at his family's kitchen table in 1953, launched the magazine with $600 of his own cash, and created an organization that reported a net revenue of $347 million for 1999. However, net income was negative $5.33 million for 1999 as indicated in Exhibit 1. Playboy has no long-term debt as shown in Exhibit 2. Headquartered in Chicago, Illinois, Playboy Enterprises Inc. (PEI), is an international multimedia entertainment company that publishes editions of *Playboy* magazine around the globe; operates Playboy TV and Spice networks around the world and distributes Playboy programming via home video and DVD globally; operates a direct marketing business, Critics' Choice Video, Collectors' Choice Music, including Playboy and Spice catalogs and Web sites; markets Playboy-branded consumer products sold worldwide; and operates Playboy Online, which includes the Playboy.com, Playboy Cyber Club, and Cyberspice Web sites; and licenses its brand to casino hotels. Playboy Enterprises current mission statement is given as follows:

> PET is a preeminent international media and entertainment company with a worldwide recognized brand and many windows of opportunity to expand the Playboy franchise and develop other related entertainment franchises globally by leveraging Playboy's strengths of publishing, brand management, and marketing.

## MANAGEMENT

The company went public in 1971, with the family retaining 70 percent of the stock. Christie Hefner, daughter of Hugh Hefner, was named chair of the board and CEO in 1988 at the age of twenty-nine. Hugh Hefner, with 71 percent of the voting stock, has maintained control of *Playboy* magazine. At the time of the leadership change, PEI was experiencing the effect of the 1982's annual loss of $51.8 million and declining circulation of the magazine. As stated in September 1999 issue of *Chief Executive,*

> Christie didn't have CEO experience when she started, and she tried doing some things that didn't work in terms of bringing in the wrong people and putting people in the wrong places. As she got experience, she also got good at bringing people in who know what they're doing and then letting them alone to do their jobs.

The internal culture is described by analysts as very cohesive, with all working together to generate profit. The CEO believes that the growth will come from entertainment and online, with PEI positioned perfectly for the electronic age.

EXHIBIT 1    Playboy Enterprises, Inc. Annual Income Statement
(in millions, except earnings-per-share data)

|  | 12/31/99 | 12/31/98 | 12/31/97 | 12/31/96 |
|---|---|---|---|---|
| Sales | $347.81 | $317.61 | $149.54 | $79.78 |
| Cost of goods | 277.44 | 269.47 | 126.65 | 65.80 |
| **Gross profit** | 70.36 | 48.14 | 22.88 | 13.98 |
| Selling and administrative and depreciation and amortization expenses | 56.39 | 43.17 | 18.42 | 8.71 |
| **Income after depreciation and amortization** | 13.98 | 4.97 | 4.47 | 5.26 |
| Nonoperating income | (12.43) | 3.60 | 0.12 | (0.01) |
| Interest expense | 7.97 | 1.55 | 0.28 | 0.17 |
| **Pretax income** | (6.43) | 7.02 | 4.29 | 5.09 |
| Income taxes | (0.86) | 2.70 | 2.14 | 2.27 |
| Minority interest | 0 | 0 | 0 | 0 |
| Investment gains/losses (+) | 0 | 0 | 0 | 0 |
| Other income/charges | 0 | 0 | 0 | 0 |
| **Income from continuing operations** | N/A | N/A | N/A | N/A |
| Extras and discontinued operations | 0.23 | 0 | (1.07) | 0 |
| **Net Income** | $ (5.33) | $ 4.32 | $ 1.06 | $ 2.83 |

### Depreciation footnote

|  | 12/31/99 | 12/31/98 | 12/31/97 | 12/31/96 |
|---|---|---|---|---|
| Income before depreciation and amortization | $ 56.67 | $ 33.98 | $ 17.47 | $16.92 |
| Depreciation and amortization (cash flow) | 42.69 | 29.01 | 13.00 | 11.66 |
| **Income after depreciation and amortization** | $ 13.98 | $ 4.97 | $ 4.47 | $ 5.26 |

### Earnings-per-share data

|  | 12/31/99 | 12/31/98 | 12/31/97 | 12/31/96 |
|---|---|---|---|---|
| **Average shares** | $23.59 | $21.04 | $20.32 | $20.01 |
| Diluted earnings per share before nonrecurring items | 0.07 | 0.12 | 0.39 | 0.21 |
| **Diluted net earnings per share** | $ 0.07 | $ 0.21 | $ 1.05 | $ 0.21 |

*Source:* www.freeedgar.com

The CEO wants the company to have a $1 billion market capitalization by 2003. None of the approximately 773 employees are represented by collective bargaining agreements.

When Playboy Enterprises, Inc., first went public on the New York Stock Exchange in 1971, its stock certificate featured a reclining nude. Some 20,000 people purchased a single share of PEI stock just to get a copy of the certificate. Although the certificate no longer features a nude female, there are more than 20 million shares outstanding.

## ORGANIZATION

The company's divisions are Publishing, Entertainment, Marketing, Catalog, Casino Gaming, and Playboy Online. Prior to 1998 the Playboy Online results had been reported in the Publishing and Catalog groups.

EXHIBIT 2    **Playboy Enterprises, Inc. Annual Balance Sheet (in millions, except book value per share)**

|  | *12/31/99* | *12/31/98* | *12/31/97* | *12/31/96* |
|---|---|---|---|---|
| **Assets** | | | | |
| Cash and equivalents | $ 26.58 | $ 0.34 | $ 0.94 | $ 1.06 |
| Receivables | 54.89 | 49.87 | 33.32 | 34.96 |
| Notes receivable | 0 | 0 | 0 | 0 |
| Inventories | 23.83 | 25.68 | 25.37 | 22.48 |
| Other current assets | 83.49 | 76.51 | 65.55 | 57.28 |
| Total current assets | 188.81 | 152.41 | 125.20 | 115.77 |
| Net property and equipment | 9.41 | 9.15 | 10.05 | 11.19 |
| Investments and advances | 0 | 0 | 0 | 0 |
| Other noncurrent assets | 62.50 | 0 | 0 | 0 |
| Deferred charges | 5.39 | 6.52 | 8.32 | 11.59 |
| Intangibles | 137.92 | 17.29 | 14.97 | 12.47 |
| Deposits and other assets | 25.36 | 26.71 | 27.38 | 11.20 |
| Total assets | $429.40 | $212.10 | $185.94 | $162.21 |
| **Liabilities and shareholders' equity** | | | | |
| Notes payable | 0 | $ 29.75 | $ 10.00 | $ 12.00 |
| Accounts payable | $ 34.55 | 30.83 | 32.25 | 25.21 |
| Current portion long-term debt | 0 | 0 | 0 | 0.34 |
| Current portion capital leases | 0 | 0 | 0 | 0 |
| Accrued expenses | 8.83 | 15.87 | 4.49 | 4.13 |
| Income taxes payable | 0 | 0.81 | 0.62 | 1.17 |
| Other current liabilities | 76.27 | 41.71 | 51.53 | 53.57 |
| Total current liabilities | 119.67 | 118.99 | 98.91 | 96.42 |
| Mortgages | 0 | 0 | 0 | 0 |
| Deferred taxes/income | 55.22 | 0 | 0 | 0 |
| Convertible debt | 0 | 0 | 0 | 0 |
| Long-term debt | 0 | 0 | 0 | 0 |
| Noncurrent capital leases | 0 | 0 | 0 | 0 |
| Other noncurrent liabilities | 93.22 | 8.91 | 8.34 | 8.39 |
| Minority interest (liabilities) | 0 | 0 | 0 | 0 |
| Total liabilities | $268.12 | $127.90 | $107.26 | $104.81 |
| **Shareholders' equity** | | | | |
| Preferred stock | 0 | 0 | 0 | 0 |
| Common stock (par) | $ 0.24 | $ 0.22 | $ 0.22 | $ 0.22 |
| Capital surplus | 120.33 | 44.86 | 43.53 | 37.48 |
| Retained earnings | 44.24 | 49.57 | 45.25 | 26.66 |
| Other equity | (3.54) | (3.88) | (3.64) | (0.03) |
| Treasury stock | 0 | 6.57 | 6.69 | 6.92 |
| Total shareholders' equity | 161.28 | 84.20 | 78.68 | 57.40 |
| Total liabilities and shareholders' equity | 429.40 | 212.10 | 185.94 | 162.21 |
| Total common equity | 161.28 | 84.20 | 78.68 | 57.40 |
| Average shares | 23.59 | 21.04 | 20.32 | 20.01 |
| Book value per share | $ 8.34 | $ 4.10 | $ 3.83 | $ 2.83 |

*Source:* www.freeedgar.com

## Publishing

The Publishing Group includes the publication of *Playboy* magazine, other domestic publishing businesses (including specials, calendars, books, and new media), and the licensing of international editions of *Playboy* magazine. The operating income from the Publishing Group declined 28.7 percent in the quarter ended June 30, 1999. Publishing Group operating income decreased $2.1 million, 67 percent compared to the prior year primarily due to the lower *Playboy* magazine newsstand sales and advertising and newsstand special revenues, combined with the lower international royalties. Lower manufacturing costs were mostly offset by higher editorial and group administrative expenses. Operating income declined $0.5 million, or 16 percent, for the six-month period, primarily because of the lower subscription revenues, the lower international publishing royalties, higher editorial costs associated in part with the April 1999 issue and higher group administrative expenses. In early April 1999, a new president of the Publishing Group, who has experience with building strong magazine brands, was named.

*Playboy*'s editorial vitality, diversity, and cultural connection are evident in the fiction, articles, investigative reporting, interviews, celebrity profiles, and entertainment and service features that are monthly staples of the publication. Regular columns on politics, books, movies, music, style, men, women, and relationships reflect contemporary social and cultural issues and further the magazine's ongoing dialogue with its readers. With a circulation of about 3.2 million in the United States and about 4.5 million worldwide, the magazine has maintained its position as the world's leading monthly magazine for men, with a circulation greater than the combined circulation of *Rolling Stone, GQ,* and *Esquire.* However, circulation is about half what it was in the '70s and shows a decline from the 3.3 million U.S. circulation in 1998. The magazine's revenues were $105 million in the fiscal year ended in June 1997; $105.3 million in 1996; and $104.4 million in 1995. As of November 1999, *Playboy* magazine had a circulation of 3.2 million on a guaranteed rate base of 3.15 million (Exhibit 3). The median reader age is 32.7. During the 1960s, the magazine relied upon newsstand sales, but today about 80 percent of the total copies sold are subscription copies. Direct mail campaigns and

| EXHIBIT 3 | Selected U.S. Consumer Publications (in millions) | |
|---|---|---|
| | *1998 Rate Base* | *1997 Rate Base* |
| *Reader's Digest* | 15.00 | 15.00 |
| *TV Guide* | 11.80 | 13.00 |
| *National Geographic* | 8.50 | 8.50 |
| *Time* | 4.00 | 4.00 |
| *Playboy* | 3.15 | 3.15 |
| *People* | 3.25 | 3.15 |
| *Sports Illustrated* | 3.15 | 3.15 |
| *Newsweek* | 3.10 | 3.10 |
| *Cosmopolitan* | 2.30 | 2.25 |
| *Rolling Stone* | 1.25 | 1.25 |
| *Business Week* | 0.88 | 0.88 |
| *Esquire* | 0.65 | 0.65 |
| *GQ* | 0.65 | 0.65 |

*Source:* www.freeedgar.com

television advertising campaigns are used to attract new subscribers. The price of a one-year subscription depends on the source of the subscription and the length of time the subscription has been sold. Subscription copies are distributed by second-class mail. Presorting and other methods lower the cost. During the first six months of 1999, the 7 percent decrease in subscription revenue reflects in part the problems facing direct marketing stamp sheet agents.

Warner Publishing Service, a national distributor with a network of approximately 300 wholesalers, distributes the magazine to newsstands and other retail outlets. The number of issues sold in retail outlets varies from month to month, depending on the cover, the pictorials, and the editorial features. As each issue goes on sale, PEI receives a cash advance based on estimated sales. Retail outlets return unsold issues to the wholesalers who shred the returned magazines and report the returns via affidavit to Warner Publishing Services. The national distributor settles with PEI based upon the actual number sold compared to the forecasted number. The 1995 sales were impacted by the December issue with Farrah Fawcett, which set a six-year sales record. Fiscal 1997 did not have a blockbuster, and sales fell 10 percent. In 1998 the two top-selling issues featured Cindy Crawford and Olympic gold-medal winning figure skater Katerina Witt. Extraordinary sales for the April 1999 issue were due to the featured Rena Mero, the World Wrestling Federation champion. For the first six months of 1999, magazine revenues increased $1.1 million, or 2 percent, compared to the prior year. Circulation revenues increased $1.5 million, or 4 percent, primarily due to a $3.5 million, or 47 percent increase in newsstand revenues. PEI produced 23 newsstand specials in 1998 with the *Playboy's Book of Lingerie* as one of the most popular.

To attract advertisers, the U.S. *Playboy* magazine is published in 15 advertising editions: eight regional, two state, four metro, and one upper-income ZIP-coded edition. Advertising pages peaked at 1,434 in 1988 and declined to 660 in 1993, 595 in 1994 and 1995, and 569 in 1996. *Playboy's* ad pages from January through September of 1999 were up 8.6 percent, to 482 pages, compared to the same period in the previous year. *Maxim,* owned by Dennis Publishing, had 612 pages during the same 1999 period, up 59 percent. The magazine has had difficulty attracting additional advertisers but obtained new advertisers in 1997 including America Online, Aramis, Calvin Klein, HBO, Gillette, and Kawasaki. The magazine obtained 48 new advertisers in 1998, including Tommy Hilfiger, Nintendo, and Sony. A significant portion of the advertising revenue comes from companies selling tobacco products (Exhibit 4). Significant legislative or regulatory limitations on the ability to sell tobacco products materially affect the magazine's revenue.

In 1996, the U.S. Food and Drug Administration restricted publication of tobacco advertisements. PEI contends that *Playboy* qualifies as an "adult publication" and is exempt from the regulation. On April 25, 1997, the Federal District Court for the Middle District of North Carolina ruled that the FDA has no authority under existing law to restrict the advertising and promotion of tobacco products and ordered the FDA not to implement any of the restrictions. The net advertising revenues of the U.S. edition of *Playboy* magazine for the fiscal year ended June 30 in 1997, 1996, 1995, 1994, and 1993, respectively were $28.4 million, $27.4 million, $27.6 million, $28.0 million, and $30.4 million. Advertising revenue for fiscal year ending December 1998 was $30.8 million.

Paper, the principal raw material used in the production, is purchased from several suppliers. Paper prices began impacting PEI in 1994 with a 7 percent increase. For the fiscal year ended June 30, 1996, the average paper prices were 46 percent higher than they had been in 1995. Paper prices stabilized in 1997.

EXHIBIT 4    Magazine Advertising by Category, as Percent of Total
Ad Pages

| Advertising Category | 12/31/98 | *Fiscal Years Ended June 30,* | | |
| --- | --- | --- | --- | --- |
| | | 1997 | 1996 | 1995 |
| Tobacco | 25% | 21% | 24% | 20% |
| Beer/Wine/Liquor | 22 | 24 | 19 | 18 |
| Retail/Direct Mail | 23 | 23 | 25 | 31 |
| Home Electronics | 6 | 4 | 1 | 4 |
| Drugs/Remedies | 4 | 3 | 3 | 4 |
| Toiletries/Cosmetics | 6 | 7 | 9 | 9 |
| Jewelry/Optical/Photo | 5 | 4 | 3 | 3 |
| Entertainment | 3 | 3 | 2 | 1 |
| Automotives | 2 | 4 | 8 | 4 |
| Apparel/Footwear/Accessories | 2 | 4 | 3 | 4 |
| All Other | 2 | 3 | 3 | 2 |

*Source:* www.freeedgar.com

## International Publishing

In partnership with publishing companies, 17 editions of *Playboy* were produced world-wide during 1999. Overseas editions retain the distinctive style, look, and tone of the U.S. edition and include the work of the specific nation's writers and artists. Prior to 1998, PEI licensed the right to publish the magazine in Argentina, Australia, Brazil, Croatia, the Czech Republic, France, Germany, Greece, Italy, Japan, Mexico, the Netherlands, Poland, Russia, South Africa, Spain, Taiwan, and Turkey. PEI has equity interest in only one country, Poland, in which PEI owns a majority interest. Sweden was licensed in 1998. The terms of licensing vary but typically are for three or five years, have a guaranteed minimum royalty, and apply a formula for computing additional royalties based upon circulation and advertising revenue. The $5 million received from the sale of PEI's 20 percent interest in duPont Publishing is intended to strengthen the international publishing ventures.

Hefner says, "There is no cookie cutter for doing business overseas. In some countries, we've found the best way to get in is with small partners who are entrepreneurial." In Russia, the partner is a woman who established the first functional periodical distribution system in Russia and used the distribution system to start a daily paper, a woman's magazine, and then *Playboy*.

International publishing revenues decreased $0.3 million, or 9 percent, and $0.1 million, or 1 percent, for the quarter and six months ended June 30, 1999, respectively, compared to the 1998 year primarily caused by lower royalties from the Brazilian and Russian editions, principally due to economic weakness in those countries. Brazil, Germany, and Japan have typically accounted for 55 percent of the licensing revenues from overseas editions.

## Entertainment

PEI's growth strategy of taking the brand value of *Playboy* and investing in higher-margin, higher-growth electronics businesses resulted in entertainment revenues from videos, international and domestic cable, and satellite-delivered products to increase by

22 percent in 1998 to $91.0 million. After an operating loss of $7.3 million in the fiscal year ended June 1995 and a profit of $9.2 million in the fiscal year ended in June 1996, the Entertainment Group reported a profit of $18.3 million on revenue of $74.7 million in the fiscal year ended in June 1997. In 1998, the Entertainment Group reported a 41.1 percent increase in operating income, to $26.2 million. Beginning with the quarter that ended March 31, 1999, the international home video business, previously combined with international TV networks and sales results, has been combined with the domestic home video business and is now reported as worldwide home video.

### Domestic TV Networks

In 1982, PET introduced Playboy Television, available only by monthly subscription. Fee structures vary with cable systems, but PEI usually receives about 35 percent of the retail price. There are about 66 million cable television households in the United States, and PEI's cable offerings reach only the 12 million viewers with pay-per-view capabilities. As of September 30, 1999, Playboy TV was available in approximately 12.3 million analog cable households, 0.7 million digital cable households, and 11.9 million DTH households, compared to approximately 11.9 million, 0.1 million, and 9.2 million households, respectively, in 1998.

In late 1998 the U.S. District Court panel declared Section 505 of the Telecommunication Act of 1996 unconstitutional. The defendants have appealed this ruling, and the Supreme Court will hear the appeal. The law had blocked signal "bleed" that can accidentally occur on some premium and pay-per-view cable channels. Section 505 had prohibited broadcast of adult-oriented networks from 6 A.M. until 10 P.M. daily unless expensive blocking equipment was installed in cable homes. Hefner estimated that the $5 million annual revenue decline was the result of Section 505, and the effect on financial performance will continue until the case is finally decided. Cable owners have begun to use digital technology in order to upgrade cable systems and to counteract competition from DTH operators. Digital cable television offers more channels and provides a secure, fully scrambled signal. Digital technology is unaffected by the relevant sections of the Telecommunication Act.

In March 1999, PEI completed the acquisition of Spice Entertainment Companies, Inc. (a previous competitor). PEI acquired all of the outstanding shares of Spice for cash and Playboy stock. The total transaction value, including the assumption of debt, was approximately $105 million. The combination of the Spice network and PEI's AdulTVision movie channel should result in 5 million new pay television households for PEI. The second quarter 1999 reported net loss of $3 million versus a net income of $2.1 million in 1998 for the same period is attributed to the purchase of Spice and the $2.1 million increase in interest expense.

### International TV

In 1995 PEI entered its first international television programming agreement with a joint venture agreement with Flextch plc to offer Playboy Television to the United Kingdom. After the first year, Playboy Television in England lost an estimated 2.1 million pounds sterling for failing to attract enough viewers. In an attempt to maximize appeal, Playboy Television shifted its target audience from couples to males and changed advertising agencies. Recognizing that the international markets differ in the restrictions on pornography (for instance, Britain and Ireland have stricter restrictions than Germany, Portugal, and Russia), Playboy Television varies its programs in different countries.

PEI has expanded the international network by entering into an exclusive multi-year multiproduct output agreement with overseas pay television distributors. Licenses differ, but typically PEI receives license fees for programming and for use of the logo and trademark. PEI has equity agreements with the channels in Great Britain, Japan, and Latin America. Separate distribution agreements allow for U.S. home video products, with dubbing or subtitling into local languages, to be sold in 48 countries in South America, Europe, Australia, Asia, and Africa. High sales in South Korea contributed to higher revenue and profit contribution. Playboy TV Latin America was the fastest growing international network in 1998. In 1998 PEI introduced Playboy TV and AdulTVision networks in Spain and Portugal. In early 1999 Playboy TV Gmbtt Germany received a license for cable and DTH carriage in Germany. In late 1998 PEI announced the intent to form Playboy TV International, LLC with Cisneros Television Group (CTG). This venture pays $100 million to PEI to license the existing programming library for international television rights and to use the Playboy and Spice brand names. The venture owns and operates existing Playboy and Spice networks worldwide, excluding the United States and Canada, and creates additional international networks.

For the quarter and six months that ended in June 30, 1999, profit contribution from the international TV networks and sales business decreased $2.0 million and $2.1 million, respectively, primarily due to decreases in revenues of $2.4 million and $2.5 million respectively. These decreases were primarily caused by the delay in the completion of the international television joint venture with Cisneros Television Group.

## Worldwide Home Video, Movies, and Other

Following the style, quality, and focus of *Playboy* magazine, PET home videos are distributed via video (including Blockbuster Video), music, and other retail stores. Playboy Home Video finishes high on Billboard's "Top Video Sales Labels." More than 300,000 copies of a home video with Brazilian dancer, Scheila Carvalho, were sold in 1998. PEI's videos are sold in more than 60 countries and territories. In 1998 the Entertainment Group created Alta Loma Productions to produce programming for broadcast by other networks. About 150 to 200 hours of programming and about 80 movies are produced each year.

## Product Marketing

"We've also moved from being a passive licensing company to a more active brand management company," said Hefner in 1996. The name "Playboy" and the rabbit-head design are among the most recognized trademarks in the world. The company leverages the power of its brand recognition, design expertise, art collection, and loyal customer base to develop and market apparel, accessories, and other products to consumers worldwide. The movement has been toward ties and jewelry, not fuzzy dice. The value of the trademark, copyrights, and intellectual properties were protected with the judgment in a copyright infringement case between PET and Starware Publishing Corporation. Starware had thought that the images were public domain when they were downloaded. The Court awarded PEI with $20,000 for $50,000 of trademark violations.

During 1998 PEI licensed Titan Motorcycle Co. of America to produce 102 motorcycles, licensed Zippo to produce lighters, and licensed Los Angeles-based California Sunshine Activeware, Inc., to produce apparel. Special Editions, Ltd. (SEL), markets original art, limited-edition prints, posters, and art products. To increase revenue, Editions is shifting from direct sales to licensing. The trademarks and service marks of Sarah Coventry, Inc., are owned by PEI.

The Playboy and Playmate product lines consist primarily of men's and women's clothing, accessories, watches, jewelry, fragrances, small leather goods, stationery, and home fashions. In 1997, to capitalize on the cigar craze PEI formed an agreement with a world's top cigar producer, Consolidated Cigar Corporation. The cigar line is sold in restaurants, cigar bars, golf course shops, nightclubs, and wine and liquor shops. Single-tube cigars were introduced in 1998.

Products are marketed in North America, Europe, Asia, Australia, and South America, primarily through mass merchants and other retail outlets, by licensees under exclusive license agreements that authorize the manufacture, sale, and distribution of products in a designated territory. Royalties are based on a fixed or variable percentage of the licensee's total new sales, in some cases against guaranteed minimum. Asia has contributed the majority of the royalties earned from licensing PEI's trademarks. During November 1999, PEI signed a master license agreement with Mitsui & Co., Ltd., Japan's largest general trading company. Under the agreement, Mitsui & Co., Ltd., will manage the manufacture, sale, and distribution of a broad range of Playboy apparel and accessories, including sportswear, activewear, underwear, bags, small leather goods, and costume jewelry. The agreement also calls for the opening of freestanding Playboy boutiques in Japan as additional distribution outlets and brand-building initiatives. The first boutique is to open in fall 2001.

### Casinos

The Playboy Casino at Hotel des Roses on the Greek island of Rhodes opened in the spring of 1999. Hefner plans for similar partnerships with as many as 10 casinos in resorts such as Las Vegas and overseas by 2004. PEI reported licensing revenues of $0.3 million for both the quarter and six months ended June 30, 1999, as a result of the opening of the Rhodes Casino in April 1999.

### Catalog

PEI's catalog business includes the Playboy *Critics' Choice Video, Collector's Choice Music, Spice,* and *Playboy.* PEI's catalog revenues for fiscal year ended June 1997 was $75.4 million, $71.1 million in 1996, and $61.4 million in 1995. For the quarter and six months that ended June 30, 1999, PEI's catalog operating performance decreased $0.8 million and $2.2 million, respectively, on revenue declines of $0.8 million, or 5 percent, and $4.5 million, or 13 percent, respectively, compared to 1998.

The *Playboy* catalog offers fashions and accessories, home videos, gifts, calendars, art products, back issues of the magazine, and newsstand specials. *Critics' Choice Video* is one of the largest circulation catalogs of prerecorded videocassette, the fastest-growing segment of the video industry. The catalog features more than 10,000 titles, including major theatrical releases and special-interest videos. The *Critic's Choice Video* catalog generates the most sales of all PEI's catalogs. In response to competition from mass markets, which offer popular videos at deeply discounted prices, a competitive pricing strategy was introduced in the second quarter of 1996 and has continued.

Introduced in 1994, the music catalog, *Collectors' Choice Music* features more than 8,000 titles in CD and cassette formats from a wide assortment of music categories: classical, pop, rock, rhythm and blues, jazz, and country. It also offers an extensive library of hard-to-find recordings. The first Spice brand-extension effort was introduced in 1999 with a catalog offering more than 1,700 video, CD-ROM, and DVD titles.

### Playboy Online Group

PEI's homepages on the World Wide Web provide four sources of revenue: advertising, shopping, subscription, and pay per view. Hefner made Playboy Online a separate business group to give it equal status with other operating groups. During 1998, traffic on the site had increased by 70 percent, to more than 75 million page views a month. In September 1999, the traffic on the site increased to 90 million page views per month.

Revenues in 1998 increased 83.1 percent over the previous year to more than $7 million. For the third quarter of 1999, revenues nearly doubled to $3.3 million from $1.8 million in 1998. Advertising, ecommerce, and subscription showed increases. About 30,000 Cyber Club members (online subscription site) pay as much as $60 a year for access to photo archives, chat sessions, and live Webcasts from the Hefner mansion. The majority of the online visitors are in the eighteen to thirty-four age group and do not read the magazine. The Playboy/Ktel Music Store offers 250,000 music titles. The Playboy Store attracts orders from about 70 countries. The CCVideo offers more than 50,000 movies, and CCMusic offers 250,000 titles. Hefner predicts that the Web will be the company's biggest business.

## IMAGE

Popularity of the Playboy name stems from its association with fun, sexiness, and high quality. Aspiration, adventurous, and romantic are a few of the many characteristics that define the Playboy customer. Overseas, the Playboy logo benefits from its strong identification with Western freedoms, the American lifestyle, and a desire for "the good life."

## PUBLIC AFFAIRS

PEI established the Playboy Foundation in 1965 to provide financial support for organizations dedicated to protect civil rights and civil liberties, promote First Amendment rights and freedom of expression, and support research and education on human sexuality and reproductive rights. Since 1965 the foundation has contributed about $12 million. *Playboy* magazine provides free advertising space to nonprofit groups such as the Nature Conservancy, National Veterans Legal Services Program, and the Special Olympics. A basic tenet of The Playboy Philosophy is that the First Amendment is the keystone to all other rights. Playboy established the Hugh M. Hefner First Amendment Awards in 1979 to honor individuals who have championed freedom of expression.

## QUESTIONS

Answer the following questions.

Which of PEI's divisions should receive the greatest emphasis and resources?

How can PEI improve its corporate image among critics who contend its business is obscene, pornographic, and unethical?

Should PEI continue its international expansion? If yes, which new countries should be targeted?

Should PEI make a major acquisition in the near future to begin publishing other magazines, such as *Cosmopolitan, Woman's Day, Ladies' Home Journal, GQ,* or *Esquire?*

How much is the company worth today?

Can you develop a five-year strategic plan for PEI?

# READER'S DIGEST ASSOCIATION, INC.—2000

**Carol Braddock**
**Francis Marion University**

## RDA, RDB
www.readersdigest.com

Headquartered in Pleasantville, New York, Reader's Digest Association is a global leader in magazine publishing and direct marketing. The mission of *Reader's Digest* is "to inform, enrich, inspire and entertain people of all ages and cultures." The magazine is published in 49 editions and 19 languages and is read by more than 100 million readers each month in almost every country in the world. This vast distribution generated revenues of $2,532.2 million in fiscal year 1999, a decline from $2,691.2 million in fiscal year 1998 and $2,896.5 million in fiscal year 1997. Reader's Digest needs a clear strategic plan to reverse its declining revenues.

## HISTORY

In 1922 DeWitt and Lila Wallace published the first 5,000 copies of the *Reader's Digest* from their Greenwich Village apartment. These copies were sold exclusively by mail for 25 cents. The first publication contained 31 carefully selected articles including "The Future of Poison Gas," "Wanted: Motives for Motherhood," and "Advice from a President's Physician." Today, a large percentage of the *Reader's Digest* articles are written by staff writers or freelance writers. The remaining articles are selected from published sources.

In 1929, the *Reader's Digest* appeared on newsstands for the first time, and 62,000 copies were sold. Circulation passed the 1 million mark six years later.

In 1938, the magazine published its first international edition in the United Kingdom. During World War II, editions were published in Latin America and Sweden. After the war, editions were published in Australia, Belgium, Canada, Denmark, Finland, France, Germany, Italy, Norway, South Africa, and Switzerland.

In the 1950s, the *Reader's Digest* launched its condensed books in the United States and Canada. They would be introduced in Australia and the United Kingdom four years later. Paid advertising would also appear for the first time in the magazine. Today, the *Reader's Digest* carries 12,389 advertising pages annually.

In the 1960s, the company revolutionized direct marketing by introducing easy-to-enter sweepstakes. The Quality School Program became one of the largest fund-raising organizations of its kind. This organization helps over 25,000 schools and youth groups in the United States and Canada.

In the 1980s, the founders of the Reader's Digest died. DeWitt Wallace died in 1981 at the age of ninety-one, and three years later, Lila Wallace died at the age of ninety-four. Several years later, Reader's Digest entered the video business with *Why We Fight*. The company also acquired its first special-interest magazine. Today, five magazines are published with a combined readership of nearly 12 million: *The Family*

*Handyman, New Choices: Living Even Better After 50, American Health for Women, MoneyWise,* and *Walking,* which was acquired in 1997. In 1988, *Household Hints and Handy Tips* sold more than 1.2 million copies within 30 days in the United States.

In 1996, Reader's Digest established a Web site. A Thai edition was published, and later Australia, Hong Kong, India, Korea, Malaysia, New Zealand, the Philippines, Singapore and Taiwan editions were launched. Thomas O. Ryder was appointed chairman and CEO in 1998. During this time, a public hybrid equity offering of 11.8 million shares of Trust Automatic Common Exchange Securities was completed. This offering enabled six charitable organizations to combine a portion of their Reader' Digest Class A nonvoting common stock. The new issues trade under the ticker symbol RDT. Reader's Digest received none of the proceeds.

DeWitt and Lila Wallace were honored by the U.S. Postal Service for their philanthropic and cultural contributions. A postage stamp, part of the "Great Americans" series, was issued in their honor. In July of 1998, the company was globally reorganized into three business groups—Global Books and Home Entertainment, U.S. Magazines, and International Magazines as indicated in the hypothetical organizational chart in Exhibit 1.

The company offers advertisers discounts for placing advertisements in more than one edition. Worldwide revenues from advertising account for 30 percent of the total revenues of *Reader's Digest* magazine today. In the 1950s, Reader's Digest installed its first computer. Committed to leading-edge technology, the company now operates two Global Data Centers that process information worldwide. This technology has enabled the company to maintain a computerized list of prospective customers. This list consists of over 57 million households and is one of the largest direct-response lists in the United States. Music, the first nonprint product line, was launched and currently generates about 14 percent of global revenues. The classic anthology is entitled Music of the World's Great Composers.

The *Reader's Digest* is still offered by direct mail. However, in recent years other methods have also been utilized to offer the company's products to the consumer. These methods include direct-response television, catalogs, door-to-door sales, retail sales, and the Internet. Approximately 95 percent of the paid circulation of the *Reader's Digest* in the United States consists of subscriptions.

Reader's Digest has suffered a decline in financial performance. Worldwide revenues for 1999 decreased by approximately 6.9 percent from 1998. The board of directors is concerned. At their request, George V. Grune recently returned as chairman and CEO of the company. Grune had served in this capacity from 1984 until he retired in 1995.

EXHIBIT 1    Reader's Digest's U.S. Magazine Operations

| | Circulation rate base | Number of advertising pages carried |
|---|---|---|
| *Reader's Digest*—U.S. English edition | 12,500,000 | 1,137 |
| *Reader's Digest Large Edition for Easier Reading* | 425,000 | 159 |
| *The Family Handyman* | 1,100,000 | 638 |
| *American Health for Women* | 1,000,000 | 571 |
| *New Choices: Living Even Better After 50* | 600,000 | 412 |
| *Walking* | 650,000 | 366 |
| *American Woodworker* | 324,000 | 187 |

*Source:* Reader's Digest *Annual Report,* 1999.

## MISSION STATEMENT

Reader's Digest does have a mission statement; however, according to the public relations department this statement is not in writing. Many of the fundamental values of the company are outlined in the written Code of Conduct, which serves as a guide to the employees of Reader's Digest. It outlines policies to give the diverse employees a common identity and guide them in all aspects of their business lives. These policies are implemented in a manner suitable for each geographic area in which the company operates. The policies address business ethics, employee relations, and environmental protection.

## THE U.S. MAGAZINE

The *Reader's Digest* is published monthly consisting of original articles or previously printed condensed versions of general interest articles. This magazine has a worldwide circulation of approximately 25 million and over 100 million readers. Braille editions and recorded editions are published by third parties pursuant to licenses. A large-type edition for easier reading is offered in the United States. This edition contains most of the articles and all of the humor departments. Unlike the 1929 edition, this edition includes advertising and enhanced color graphics. In 1998, the magazine was redesigned for easier reading and a more contemporary style. The U.S. edition of *Reader's Digest* has the largest paid circulation of any United States magazine except those automatically distributed to all members of the American Association of Retired Persons.

The global circulation base is 27.8 million. The circulation rate base for the U.S. edition of the *Reader's Digest* was reduced from 15 million to 13.3 million copies from January to June of 1999. The rate base was also reduced in July to 12.5 million issues. This rate reduction was part of the strategic initiatives announced in 1998 to reduce the circulation rate base in the United States by 10 percent to 20 percent. Sweepstakes entries are used to promote new subscriptions by direct mail. Prizes totaled about $9 million for the 1999 edition of the sweepstakes. The largest percentage of subscriptions is sold between July and December of each year. Subscriptions can be canceled at any time, and a refund will be issued for the unused subscription. All editions of the *Reader's Digest* are printed and distributed by third parties.

Reader's Digest publishes several special-interest magazines: *The Family Handyman, New Choices: Living Even Better After 50, American Health for Women, MoneyWise, Walking,* and *American Woodworker.* These magazines provide do-it-yourself tips and information pertaining to entertainment, travel, health, and leisure-time activities. *American Health for Women* contains information on medicines, nutrition, psychology, and fitness for women. Exhibit 1 includes the circulation rate base of each of the company's U.S. magazines operations at June 30 1999, as well as the number of advertising pages carried.

Approximately 70 percent of total U.S. revenues for *Reader's Digest* are generated by circulation revenues and 30 percent by advertising revenues. Approximately 58 percent of the total revenues for the special-interest magazines are generated by circulation revenues and 42 percent by advertising revenues.

Worldwide revenues in 1999 totaled $664.3 million, $656.3 million in 1998, and $625.5 million in 1997. Operating profits in 1999 totaled $101.7, $64.9 in 1998, and $67.1 in 1997. Total revenues from this segment represent 26 percent of total revenues (see Exhibit 2).

## GLOBAL BOOKS AND HOME ENTERTAINMENT

Reader's Digest condensed books, series books, general books, recorded music collections, and series and home video products are distributed mostly by direct mail. The operations of Good Catalog Company, a subsidiary of Reader's Digest, are also included under this

EXHIBIT 2    Reader's Digest Association, Inc. Business Segment
             Financial Information (in millions)

|  | 1999 | 1998 | 1997 |
|---|---|---|---|
| **Revenues** | | | |
| Global books and home entertainment | $1,544.3 | $1,680.2 | $1,891.5 |
| U.S. magazine | 664.3 | 656.3 | 625.5 |
| International magazines | 323.6 | 354.7 | 379.5 |
| | $2,532.2 | $2,691.2 | $2,896.5 |
| **Operating Profit** | | | |
| Global books and home entertainment | $ 80.8 | $ 50.0 | $161.2 |
| U.S. magazine | 101.7 | 64.9 | 67.1 |
| International magazines | (15.5) | (14.7) | (0.5) |
| | $167.0 | $100.2 | $227.8 |

group. The condensed books are published in 16 languages and are offered in 27 countries. Worldwide revenues totaled $254.1 million in 1999 as compared to $260.4 million in 1998 and $307.0 million in 1997. Local editorial staff determine if articles printed in the U.S. edition are appropriate for their market. Six volumes are published each year in the United States, and the international editions publish from 6 to 4 each year.

The series books are offered in reading and illustration. The series can be open-ended or closed and consist of a limited number of volumes. They are published in 6 languages and offered in 11 countries. Worldwide revenues in 1999 totaled $142.8 million, $162.1 million in 1998, and $209.5 million in 1997. Operating profits in 1999 totaled $80.8 million, $50.0 million in 1998, and $161.2 million in 1997. Total revenues from this segment represent 61 percent of total worldwide revenues. (See Exhibit 2)

Additional products such as reference books, cookbooks, music packages, and television and video products are offered through direct mail. Plans are to expand video operations in the United States. Video products are marketed in the United States and 26 other countries and sold through retail establishments. Most of the original productions have been licensed to cable television networks. Several original programs have won awards of excellence. In addition, five Emmy Awards have been earned, and programs have appeared on the Disney and Discovery channel. In May 1999, Reader's Digest entered into a multiyear agreement with CBS Productions to develop television movies and mini-series based on the personal dramas chronicled in the magazine.

The company is a member of the Recording Industry Association of America and has been recognized with 49 gold, platinum, and multiplatinum certificates. Music products are marketed in 33 countries. These collections encompass a broad range of musical styles and are selected from their approximately 18,000-selection library. Music products generated worldwide revenues of $345.5 million in fiscal 1999, $377.5 million in fiscal 1998, and $404.2 million in fiscal 1997.

Good Catalog Company—which produces a catalog of home, garden, and gift-related products—was acquired in October 1998. A Web site for this company was established in July 1999 and is currently conducting e-commerce business.

## International Magazines

The International Magazines division publishes *Reader's Digest* in 48 editions and 19 languages outside of the United States. Independent contractors are licensed in Korea,

India, and South Africa. These operations publish *Moneywise,* a magazine devoted to helping families in the United Kingdom manage their finances. In August of 1999, Benchmark, Ltd., the publisher of four investment guides in Hong Kong, Taiwan, and Singapore, was acquired.

Reader's Digest World, a Web site, has been established that links the local and international Web sites. This Web site offers shopping and information about products offered. In 1999, it had over 3.9 million visitors from around the world.

Circulation and advertising data for International Magazines operations for 1999 include a circulation rate base of 12,275,585 and 11,729 advertising pages. *Moneywise* had a circulation base of 108,075 and carried 660 advertising pages.

Worldwide revenues in 1999 totaled $323.6 million, $354.7 in 1998, and $379.5 in 1997. Operating profits in 1999 totaled −$15.5 million, −$14.7 in 1998 and −$0.5 million in 1997. Revenues from this segment represent 13 percent of total worldwide revenues (see Exhibit 2).

## MAGAZINE PUBLISHING INDUSTRY NOTE

Advertising revenues in magazines rose 7.8 percent in 1998 according to the Publishers Information Bureau. Ad pages were up by 2.6 percent. The gain in advertising revenue was achieved despite the decreases in three major categories, automotive (down 6 percent), computers and office equipment (down 5 percent) and drugs and remedies (down 3 percent). However, other categories experienced substantial gains. Business and consumer services were up by 16 percent, direct response advertising by 12 percent, and retail by 22 percent. This increase in revenues would indicate that more and more advertisers are recognizing the value and effectiveness of magazine advertising. [Note: Because the PIB tallies data from roughly 200 magazines, its statistics are representative but not comprehensive.]

Higher prices for advertising, combined with modest ad page growth should cause advertising revenues to increase by 9 percent in 1999. Circulation revenues are expected to rise by approximately 6 percent over the next several years. In 1998, circulation revenues rose 4 percent due to higher cover and subscription prices. Single-copy sales remain low, and growth in subscriptions continues to remain the same. However, single-copy sales continue to rise approximately 2 percent each year.

The table from S&P Industry Surveys represents the number of magazines available, the number of magazine pages, and total advertising revenue.

|  | *1998* | *1997* | *1996* |
|---|---|---|---|
| Number of magazines | 205 | 205 | 205 |
| Number of pages | 243,000 | 230,327 | 224,490 |
| Total advertising revenue (in millions) | $14,950.0 | $13,745.0 | $12,750.0 |

*Source:* S&P Industry Surveys—Publishing, May 1999.

## RECENT DEVELOPMENTS

Reader's Digest has formed an alliance with WebMD, Inc., to expand the business into providing health information and to integrate Internet marketing into the businesses. WebMD will help develop a Reader's Digest health information Web site for consumers in the United States. This Web site was launched in the fall of 1999. Reader's Digest contemplates that WebMD will provide their magazine to its physician service subscribers by purchasing a minimum of 3,000,000 copies over the next five years. WebMD will also purchase advertising in *Reader's Digest* to promote the new Web site.

Reader's Digest has also formed an alliance with Torchmark Corporation and will market life and health insurance products to their customers in the United States and

Canada. These products will be marketed and sold by Torchmark Corporation through direct mail, telemarketing, and advertising.

## COMPETITION AND TRADEMARKS

The company owns numerous trademarks. Its two most important are the Reader's Digest and the Pegasus Logo. According to the company, name recognition, reputation, and image have enhanced customer response to Reader's Digest direct marketing sales promotions. These trademarks are important to the business and are defended aggressively. According to Reader's Digest, the name, image, and reputation as well as the customer list provide a competitive advantage over other direct marketers.

Two of Reader's Digest's major competitors are Thomas Nelson Publishers and Time Warner, Inc. Thomas Nelson revenues increased by 13 percent in 1999. In 1999, publications reached the million-unit mark and net revenues reached $261,645. Time Warner is the world's leading media and entertainment company. Time Warner's revenues increased 11 percent in 1998 to approximately $26.8 billion. In order to maintain its position in the publishing industry, Reader's Digest will need a clear strategic plan.

## CONCLUSION

Reader's Digest has initiated a three-phase strategy to create growth activities by utilizing its fundamental strengths. The key elements of the growth strategy are:

- To expand the company's presence in five targeted areas of consumer interest (home, health, family, finance, and faith)
- To sell products and services beyond publishing that fit with Reader's Digest products
- To continue geographic expansion
- To develop new channels for marketing
- To make the Internet an integral part of all the company's business

The company has identified two nonpublishing products and services that it would like to market—financial services and catalog merchandise. The initial focus in financial services is on insurance and credit cards. Reader's Digest customers aged fifty and over will be the key target market. The company will build on the success of the recently acquired Good Catalog Company to market the catalog merchandise. This business will be enhanced with Reader's Digest branding, promotion, database, management capabilities, and the Internet.

The company has experienced rapid growth in Eastern Europe, South America, and the Far East and should continue growing in these markets as well as identifying new markets. A partnership in China to open a direct market book business was established in 2000. Reader's Digest has the most extensive global infrastructure in the publishing business. To maintain this infrastructure, Reader's Digest seeks to form alliances to take other companies' products into markets where it has a presence and act as an agent for these other companies.

New marketing channels are being pursued. Nonsweepstakes direct mail is being tested. In the future, Reader's Digest plans to market all of its new, nonpublishing products without sweepstakes. The company will invest $100 million in Web sites. Marketing data provided by the company will be used to launch top U.S. sites in other markets. Reader's Digest hopes to learn more about its customers interest and needs with these online services.

Reader's Digest is a leader in publishing and direct marketing. Its strategies, if properly implemented, should secure its position in the publishing business. The company will continue to create products that "inform, enrich, entertain and inspire."

EXHIBIT 3   Reader's Digest Association, Inc. Organizational Chart

EXHIBIT 4   Reader's Digest Association, Inc. Income Statement
(in millions, except where noted)

| | Year-End 06/30/99 | Year-End 06/30/98 | Year-End 06/30/97 |
|---|---|---|---|
| Revenues | $2,532.2 | $2,691.2 | $2,896.5 |
| Product, distribution and editorial expenses | 963.5 | 1,046.6 | 1,084.2 |
| Promotion, marketing, and administrative expenses | 1,401.7 | 1,544.4 | 1,584.5 |
| Other operating items | 37.9 | 70.0 | 35.0 |
| Operating profit | 129.1 | 30.2 | 192.8 |
| Other income, net | 82.6 | 11.3 | 17.4 |
| Income before provision for income taxes | 211.7 | 41.5 | 210.2 |
| Provision for income taxes | 85.1 | 23.6 | 76.7 |
| Income before cumulative effect of change in accounting principles | 126.6 | 17.9 | 133.5 |
| Cumulative effect of change in accounting principles for pension assets, net of tax of $15.2 | 25.3 | — | — |
| Net income | 151.9 | 17.9 | 133.5 |
| Basic and diluted earnings per share | | | |
| Basic earnings per share | | | |
| Weighted-average common shares outstanding | 107.3 | 106.5 | 106.7 |
| Before cumulative effect of change in accounting principles | 1.16 | 0.16 | 1.24 |
| Cumulative effect of change in accounting principles | 0.24 | — | — |
| Basic earnings per share | 1.40 | 0.16 | 1.24 |
| Diluted earnings per share | | | |
| Adjusted weighted-average common shares outstanding | 108.0 | 106.7 | 106.7 |
| Before cumulative effect of change in accounting principles | 1.15 | 0.16 | 1.24 |
| Cumulative effect of change in accounting principles | 0.24 | — | — |
| Diluted earnings per share | $ 1.39 | $ 0.16 | $ 1.24 |

*Source:* www.freeedgar.com

EXHIBIT 5    Readers Digest Association, Inc. Balance Sheet
(in millions, except where noted)

| | 06/30/99 | 06/30/98 | 6/30/97 |
|---|---|---|---|
| **Assets** | | | |
| **Current assets** | | | |
| Cash and cash equivalents | $   413.4 | $   122.8 | $     69.1 |
| Receivables, net | 319.9 | 376.4 | 398.3 |
| Inventories, net | 94.9 | 162.2 | 167.8 |
| Prepaid expenses and other current assets | 318.3 | 311.2 | 290.6 |
| **Total current assets** | 1,146.5 | 972.6 | 925.8 |
| Property, plant and equipment, net | 148.4 | 285.4 | 314.8 |
| Intangible assets, net | 68.5 | 41.8 | 59.1 |
| Other noncurrent assets | 347.1 | 264.2 | 344.1 |
| **Total assets** | $1,710.5 | $1,564.0 | $1,643.8 |
| **Liabilities and stockholders' equity** | | | |
| **Current liabilities** | | | |
| Accounts payable | $   130.7 | $   172.1 | $   193.0 |
| Accrued expenses | 352.2 | 359.3 | 373.6 |
| Income taxes payable | 56.0 | 21.0 | 22.1 |
| Unearned revenue | 336.5 | 355.4 | 356.5 |
| Other current liabilities | 110.9 | 90.0 | 67.9 |
| **Total current liabilities** | 986.3 | 997.8 | 1,013.1 |
| Postretirement and postemployment benefits other than pensions | 146.9 | 157.6 | 153.3 |
| Other noncurrent liabilities | 195.8 | 150.0 | 131.4 |
| **Total liabilities** | $1,329.0 | $1,305.4 | $1,297.8 |
| **Stockholders' equity** | | | |
| Capital stock | $     24.8 | $     16.6 | $     29.0 |
| Paid-in capital | 146.2 | 144.8 | 141.8 |
| Retained earnings | 955.4 | 845.0 | 924.2 |
| Accumulated other comprehensive loss | (56.6) | (49.8) | (33.4) |
| Net Unrealized Losses on Certain Investments | | | (0.3) |
| Treasury stock, at cost | (688.3) | (698.0) | (715.3) |
| **Total stockholders' equity** | 381.5 | 258.6 | 258.6 |
| **Total liabilities and stockholders' equity** | $1,710.5 | $1,564.0 | $1,564.0 |

*Source:* www.freeedgar.com

EXHIBIT 6    Reader's Digest Association, Inc. Geographic financial information (in millions)

|  | 1999 | 1998 | 1997 |
|---|---|---|---|
| **Revenues** | | | |
| United States | $1,181.4 | $1,236.4 | $1,278.9 |
| Europe | 1,035.3 | 1,172.2 | 1,379.7 |
| Pacific and other markets | 424.1 | 439.8 | 445.6 |
| Interarea | (7.1) | (9.4) | (6.1) |
|  | $2,633.7 | $2,839.0 | $3,098.1 |
| **Revenues interarea** | | | |
| United States | $2.7 | $2.9 | $3.2 |
| Europe | 3.5 | 5.3 | 2.4 |
| Pacific and other markets | 0.9 | 1.2 | 0.1 |
|  | $7.1 | $9.4 | $6.1 |
| **Operating profit** | | | |
| United States | $47.3 | $133.8 | $ 16.6 |
| Europe | 11.1 | 94.1 | 110.0 |
| Pacific and other markets | 17.8 | 13.3 | 45.6 |
| Corporate expense | −46.0 | −48.4 | −62.9 |
|  | $30.2 | $192.8 | $109.3 |
| **Identifiable assets** | | | |
| United States | $ 642.8 | $ 661.0 | $ 664.9 |
| Europe | 510.9 | 542.2 | 563.4 |
| Pacific and other markets | 226.1 | 240.5 | 254.4 |
| Corporate | 184.2 | 200.1 | 421.4 |
|  | $1,564.0 | $1,643.8 | $1,904.1 |

*Source:* www.freeedgar.com

# NIKE, INC.—2000

M. Jill Austin
Middle Tennessee State University

**NKE**
**www.nike.com**

After tremendous growth from the mid-1980s through the mid-1990s, Nike, Inc. struggled in 1998 and 1999. The *Annual Report* describes these troubled years in terms of an illness.

> So if fiscal 1998 was spent in the emergency room, fiscal 1999 was spent partially in post-op and partially in rehab. We put our organization under the microscope, seeking to define what Nike needed to look like on the precipice of a new century. And while we may not feel totally healed, we believe strongly in our future and our ability to make it happen.

According to Chairman and CEO Phil Knight, the company is rebounding. Although sales and earnings are lower than desirable, the company's operations are more efficient, and sales in international markets are improving.

Nike, Inc., net income increased 13 percent to $451.4 million in 1999. For the fiscal year 1999, revenues at Nike declined by 8 percent to $8.78 billion. Net income decreased by almost 50 percent in 1998 to $399.6 million with significant declines in both U.S. and non-U.S. markets. The company reduced its selling and administrative expenses by nearly $200 million in 1999 through the downsizing of more than 1,000 employees and the reorganization of some international offices.

## HISTORY

Phil Knight, a dedicated long-distance runner, developed a plan to make low-cost running shoes in Japan and to sell them in the United States as part of his work toward an M.B.A. degree at Stanford University. After graduation, Knight teamed up with Bill Bowerman, his former track coach at the University of Oregon to make his plan a reality. Because Bowerman's hobby was making handcrafted lightweight running shoes, his expertise was very valuable to entrepreneur Knight. In 1964, Bowerman and Knight each contributed $500 and started Blue Ribbon Sports. Knight negotiated with a Japanese athletic shoe manufacturer, Onitsuka Tiger Co., to manufacture the shoes that Bowerman had designed. Blue Ribbon Sports shoes gained a cult following among serious runners because Knight distributed the shoes, called Tigers, at track meets.

In 1971, Blue Ribbon Sports received a trademark on its "swoosh" logo, and they introduced the brand name "Nike" that same year. Blue Ribbon Sports parted ways with Onitsuka Tiger in 1972 and contracted with other Asian manufacturers to produce the company's shoes. Blue Ribbon Sports officially changed its name to Nike in 1978. During the late 1970s and early 1980s, Nike researchers used their technological expertise to develop several types of athletic shoes that revolutionized the industry. The company became more and more successful every year with profits increasing steadily during this time.

In 1984, after five years of 44 percent annual growth, Nike missed the emerging market for aerobic shoes. The company had concentrated its efforts on an unsuccessful line of casual shoes. Reebok took the lead in the athletic shoe industry when it began selling large numbers of its fashion-oriented aerobic shoes to women. Nike stock prices decreased by 60 percent in 1984, and between 1983 and 1985 profits declined by 80 percent. Some analysts suggested that the decreases in stock prices and profits were the fault of managers who became complacent after the firm's early success. During the early 1980s, Phil Knight focused his attention on international operations and left daily decision making to other managers. Other top managers switched from job to job, and this lead to poor coordination between the design, marketing, and production efforts of the company. An excess inventory of 22 million pairs of shoes in 1985 forced Nike to cut prices to reduce the inventory. This excess inventory also caused Nike to release some of its manufacturing capability in the Far East. Much of this capacity was picked up by Reebok. After Nike lost the top spot in the industry, it had to lay off 350 employees in 1986.

Phil Knight took several steps to try to reestablish the dominance of Nike in the industry. He created small management teams to focus on narrow markets. He also put a stop to the job changing of top executives. New advertising campaigns stressed the technology of the shoes. Focus groups were used to determine customers' athletic shoe needs. The company also began to add touches of fashion, including color, to its many new products. All of these changes helped Nike regain a slight leadership position in the industry in 1988.

In 1988, Nike purchased New Hampshire-based Cole Haan for $64 million. The subsidiary has several brand names including Country, Sporting, Classic, Bragano, and Cole Haan. A new footwear category, Tensile Air, was introduced in 1990. The Tensile Air is a dress shoe with the Nike air-cushioning system. Nike's casual footwear business grew 16 percent the following year, lead by Cole Haan. Nike also acquired the Cole Haan Accessories Company in 1990, a distributor of premium-quality belts, braces, and small leather goods. In 1990 Nike opened its first retail store called NikeTown in Portland, Oregon. Nike acquired Tetra Plastics (now called Nike, IHM, Inc.), the manufacturer of the plastic film in Nike's air sole shoes, in 1991 for $37.5 million. Nike purchased a cap-making company called Sports Specialties (now called Nike Team Sports, Inc.) in 1993. In 1994, the Outdoor division added a new shoe called "Air Mada," and the Nike sport sandal became the top seller in the market. In 1995, Nike acquired Canstar Sports, Inc. (the world's largest hockey equipment maker) for $409 million. Canstar, now called Bauer Nike Hockey, Inc., manufactures in-line roller skates, ice skates and blades, protective gear, hockey sticks, and hockey jerseys.

## PRESENT CONDITIONS

Nike sells athletic shoes, accessories, sports equipment, and clothing for men, women, and children. The company's products are sold to approximately 20,000 retail accounts in the United States, including department stores, footwear stores, and sporting goods stores. Nike also sells its products through independent distributors, licensees, and subsidiaries in 110 countries around the world. Approximately 30,000 international retail outlets sell Nike products. Nike operates a total of 18 distribution centers in several different international markets: Asia, Canada, Latin America, Europe, and Australia. The Nike name and logo have such high consumer awareness that the company no longer includes the Nike name on its products; the swoosh logo is all that is needed.

Nike, Inc., operates 123 retail stores in the United States, including 74 factory outlets, two Nike Stores, 31 Cole Haan stores, three employee-only stores, and 13

NikeTown stores. The company's NikeTown stores are located in major cities such as Portland, Chicago, Atlanta, New York city City, Seattle, Boston, Los Angeles, and San Francisco. In 1999, NikeTown stores opened in London, England, and Berlin, Germany. NikeTown stores contain sports memorabilia, educational exhibits, basketball baskets for use by customers, and Nike products.

Non-U.S. countries that have the largest Nike businesses include: United Kingdom, Japan, France, Italy, Spain, Germany, and Canada. Revenues decreased dramatically in some of these regions in 1999. Revenues in Japan declined by 37 percent and in Canada by 22 percent. In addition, revenues in Asia Pacific decreased by 33 percent in 1999. Nike has 52 retail stores outside the United States. Domestic and international revenues for Nike are shown in Exhibit 1.

The company has several recent additions to its line of businesses. Nike launched Triax watches in 1997, and two million watches were sold by mid-1999. With the success of these sports watches, designed in-house by Nike, the company will offer six to ten new styles of watches three times each year. The watches are sold in NikeTown stores, department stores, and sporting goods stores. The Michael Jordan collection of

**EXHIBIT 1    Domestic and International Revenues for Nike (in millions)**

|  | 1999 | 1998 | 1997 |
|---|---|---|---|
| **USA region** | | | |
| Footwear | $3,244.6 | $3,498.7 | $3,753.6 |
| Apparel | 1,385.3 | 1,556.3 | 1,406.6 |
| Equipment and other | 93.8 | 84.4 | 41.4 |
| Total United States of America | $4,723.7 | $5,139.4 | $5,201.6 |
| **Europe region** | | | |
| Footwear | $1,182.7 | $1,266.6 | $1,197.1 |
| Apparel | 1,005.1 | 795.9 | 592.0 |
| Equipment and other | 68.0 | 33.6 | .7 |
| Total Europe | $2,255.8 | $2,096.1 | $1,789.8 |
| **Asia Pacific region** | | | |
| Footwear | $ 455.3 | $ 790.7 | $ 859.0 |
| Apparel | 366.0 | 453.4 | 382.8 |
| Equipment and other | 23.2 | 9.8 | .1 |
| Total Asia Pacific | $ 844.5 | $1,253.9 | $1,241.9 |
| **Americas region** | | | |
| Footwear | $ 335.8 | $ 403.0 | $ 334.9 |
| Apparel | 12.9 | 9.8 | 112.2 |
| Equipment and other | 12.9 | 9.8 | 2.1 |
| Total Americas | $ 507.1 | $ 599.0 | $ 449.2 |
| Total Nike brand | $8,331.1 | $9,088.4 | $8,682.5 |
| Other brands | 445.8 | 464.7 | 504.0 |
| Total revenues | $8,776.9 | $9,553.1 | $9,186.5 |

*Source:* Nike Form 10K, 1999.

basketball clothing was launched in 1998. In 1999, clothing designed for young men who want the "urban look" was added to the Michael Jordan collection, and sports stars Randy Moss and Derek Jeter were hired to promote the Jordan brand. The "Script" sportswear line is in the development stage. This line began selling in department stores in spring 2000.

## COMPETITION

The athletic shoe industry has changed tremendously since "sneakers" were invented. In 1873, the sneaker was developed from India rubber and canvas material. Dunlop became the dominant seller of sneakers in 1938. Keds and PF Fliers dominated the children's market in the 1960s. Adult standard brands such as Adidas and Converse were well accepted by sports enthusiasts for years. When Nike entered the market in the late 1960s, the industry changed forever. In addition to new competition, lifestyles began to change, and companies began to contract manufacturing rather than invest in plant and equipment to manufacture their own products.

The major competitors in the industry are Nike and Reebok, who hold 37 percent and 20 percent market shares, respectively. Some of the other two dozen competitors in the industry include Adidas-Salomon AG, New Balance, K-Swiss, Fila, Asics, L.A. Gear, Keds, Converse, and British Knights. Designer brands such as Tommy Hilfiger and Nautica have entered the athletic shoe market by providing shoes for fashion-minded young people. The most intense competition has been among the two industry leaders, Nike and Reebok. The secret to success for these competitors is that they contract the manufacture of shoes to low-wage factories in the Far East, allowing each company to concentrate on marketing, image, and research and development.

### Reebok International, Ltd.

Reebok designs and develops athletic shoes and clothing worldwide. The company sells 175 models of shoes in 450 different color combinations for aerobics, cycling, volleyball, tennis, fitness, running, basketball, soccer, walking, and children's footwear. The company has diversified its offerings recently to include more types of casual shoes, sports clothing, and other types of athletic shoes. The company's four product divisions are Reebok Unlimited, Greg Norman Collection, Rockport, and RLX Polo Sport (Ralph Lauren footwear).

In the early 1980s, Reebok sold aerobic shoes primarily to women, but by the mid-1980s large numbers of men were buying Reebok shoes and now account for about half of Reebok sales. The company's shoes are designed to make a fashion statement and are marketed to build on this image. Reebok CEO Paul Fireman believes that, "Reebok is basically about freedom of expression."

Reebok took the lead in revenues from Nike in 1987, but Nike regained its lead over Reebok in 1990. About this time, CEO Fireman began competing with Nike by using Nike's best strategies. First, Reebok entered the Nike-dominated men's team sports market and developed a series of marketing campaigns around sports stars in an effort to increase its market share. Some of the sports personalities who signed marketing contracts with Reebok include Julie Foudy, Venus Williams, Allen Iverson, Michael Chang, Greg Norman, and the Harlem Globetrotters. Despite Reebok's marketing efforts, the company continued to lose ground to Nike in the mid-1990s. Reebok net income decreased each year from 1994 to 1998. In 1999 President Yankowski signed Rosie O'Donnell and members of her "Chub Club" to be Reebok endorsers. Fifty thousand shoes were sold through the Chub Club promotion. Selected financial information for Reebok is shown in Exhibit 2.

EXHIBIT 2    Selected Financial Information for Reebok
(in millions except per-share amount)

| | 1999 | 1998 | 1997 | 1996 |
|---|---|---|---|---|
| Gross revenue | $2,899.8 | $3,224.8 | $3,643.6 | $3,478.6 |
| Net income | 11.1 | 47.8 | 134.0 | 139.0 |
| Long-term debt | — | 554.4 | 639.4 | 854.1 |
| Net worth | — | 524.4 | 507.2 | 381.2 |
| Net profit margin (%) | — | 1.5 | 3.7 | 4.0 |
| Earnings per share | — | — | — | .23 |

*Source:* www.freeedgar.com

## International Competition

Competition is increasing in Europe. Adidas-Salomon AG, a German company, is the number-one seller of athletic shoes in Europe and number-two worldwide. Analysts believe that doing well in the European market is crucial to the continued success of companies in the athletic shoe industry. Nike sales in Europe, Asia, Canada, and Latin America increased to $2,096 billion in 1998 and to $2,255 billion in 1999. Reebok's total international sales were about $1,434 billion in 1998. Both Nike and Reebok hope to continue increasing their presence in the international retail market.

Adidas, the top European-owned competitor, will be fighting to maintain its 12 percent worldwide share of the competitive market for athletic shoes. Founded in 1948, Adidas outfitted such sports stars as Al Oerter (1956 Olympics) and Kareem Abdul-Jabbar (NBA). Family disputes in this family-owned company threatened its success after it gained a 70 percent market share in the United States. One brother became so angry that he founded the rival company Puma. During this time, the U.S. market share dropped from 70 percent to 2 percent. The company was sold in 1989 for $320 million. The new owner became involved in other issues and neglected the company. By the time the current CEO took over in 1993, Adidas was losing about $100 million per year. When asked what he knew about the athletic shoe industry, CEO Robert Louis-Dreyfus replied, "All I did was borrow what Nike and Reebok were doing. It was there for everybody to see."

Adidas-Salomon AG brands include Adidas (footwear, balls, bags, and apparel), Erima (swimware and team sport apparel), Salomon (ski equipment and apparel, hiking boots, and in-line skates), Taylor Made (golf equipment), Mavic (cycle components), and Bonfire (winter sports clothing). Some of the sports stars who currently have endorsement contracts with Adidas include Kobe Bryant, Martina Hingis, Anna Kournikova, Napoleon Kaufman, Donovan Bailey, and Tracy McGrady. Selected financial information for Adidas is shown in Exhibit 3.

## ECONOMIC CONDITIONS

The U.S. economy has been performing well since the early 1990s, but athletic shoe manufacturers have experienced severe economic crises in some international markets. For example, recent inflation and unemployment in Asia and the Pacific Rim, Latin America, and Russia have negatively impacted athletic shoe sales in those areas. In addition the impact of foreign currency fluctuations and interest rate changes has the potential to create financial problems for athletic shoe manufacturers. The conversion to the

EXHIBIT 3    Selected Financial Information for Adidas
(DM in millions)

|  | 1998 | 1997 | 1996 |
|---|---|---|---|
| Net sales | DM 9,907 | DM 6,698 | DM 4,709 |
| Operating income | 737 | 601 | 360 |
| Net income | (322) | 465 | 314 |
| Inventories | 1,906 | 1,606 | 1,088 |
| Receivables | 2,007 | 1,158 | 818 |
| Total current assets | 4,015 | 2,827 | 1,990 |
| Total assets | 6,270 | 4,349 | 2,456 |
| Working capital | (640) | 21 | 555 |
| Total borrowings, net | 3,236 | 1,443 | 340 |
| Total liabilities | 5,289 | 2,903 | 1,506 |
| Shareholders' equity | DM 906 | DM 1,401 | DM 904 |

*Source:* http://www.adidas.com.

Euro will continue through December 31, 2001. Until this date, customers in the European community can pay for goods using either the Euro or their own country's currency. This transition may create some economic pressures in the countries that are converting to the Euro.

Most athletic shoe companies contract with manufacturing companies in the Far East to produce their shoes. Some of the countries that manufacture shoes for Nike, Reebok, and other companies include South Korea, Taiwan, China, Thailand, Malaysia, and Indonesia. The athletic shoe companies develop design specifications and new technology for the shoes in the United States and send them to the factory to be produced. The primary advantages of foreign contract manufacturing are that no capital investment is required, and the athletic shoe companies can operate with very little long-term debt. There are also several disadvantages. Some countries, such as Korea, that have produced large numbers of athletic shoes in the past are developing the expertise and contacts to begin producing more sophisticated electronics products and do not have the available capacity to continue producing athletic shoes. Some additional disadvantages of overseas production include labor unrest, political unrest, delays caused by shipping, and unreliability of quota systems (embargoes).

## SOCIAL FACTORS

Since the late 1970s, athletic shoe buyers have become much more brand conscious. Some trend watchers believe that athletic shoe companies will have some difficulty selling their products to the youth market in the next few years because of the shift to work boots and sandals on the part of young people. Large numbers of baby boomers are also interested in staying fit and healthy and have changed their diet and increased their physical activity. In the 1980s, people became obsessed with fitness, and by 1991 sales in the fitness equipment industry exceeded $30 billion. Exercise is not as popular a pasttime as it was in the early 1990s, and total athletic shoe sales decreased by 6 percent in 1998, the worst decrease since the athletic shoe boom began in the 1980s.

Since the mid-1990s women have purchased more athletic shoes than men have. In addition, more girls are involved in sports today than ever before. More than 13 million women and girls play basketball, and approximately 7 million play soccer. Generation Y children (born 1979–1994) rival the size of the baby-boom generation. They are 60 million strong and will be a significant market in the future.

## LEGAL/REGULATORY ISSUES

The global marketplace has many legal restrictions that athletic shoe manufacturers must consider. The North American Free Trade Agreement (NAFTA) and the General Agreement on Tariffs and Trade (GATT) provide better access to world trade. Companies operating in Mexico and Canada will benefit from reduced import/export duties outlined in the NAFTA agreement. GATT provides access to international markets and tariff reductions on many products. The European Union (EU) increased the power of European countries to control imports but has also provided a single, coordinated market rather than many different markets in Europe. In 1995 at the request of European footwear manufacturers, the EU imposed anti-dumping duties on athletic footwear imported to the EU from China and Indonesia. In 1995 the United States restored diplomatic relations with Vietnam, a potential high-volume producer of athletic shoes. In 1999, President Clinton awarded most-favored-nation status (MFN) to China, and Congress supported the president's decision. Because China is a major source of footwear production, it is critical for athletic shoe companies that China retain its MFN status. These legal changes, along with country-specific laws, will provide many opportunities and some threats for international business operations.

## NIKE INTERNAL FACTORS

Five primary internal factors for Nike include superior research and development efforts for the company's products, marketing and distribution expertise, social responsibility, management style and culture, and financial returns.

### Nike Research and Development

Nike spent approximately $97.5 million on product research, development, and evaluation in 1999. Nike is able to stay on the cutting edge in technology because R&D in the athletic shoe industry is largely design innovation and does not require a large investment in equipment. In 1980, the company formed the Nike Sport Research Laboratory (NSRL), which uses video cameras and traction-testing devices and researches such concerns as children's foot morphology, "turf toe," and apparel aerodynamics. In addition, NSRL evaluates ideas that have been developed by the Advanced Product Engineering (APE) group. APE is involved in long-term product development. Shoes are created for five years in the future. This group developed cross-training shoes, the Nike Footbridge stability device, inflatable fit systems, and the Nike 180 air-cushioning system. Researchers make shoe molds in the model shop and evaluate the shoe tension and adhesion in the testing lab.

In addition to their laboratory work, Nike designers visit athletes to learn more about shoe technology. In 1996 Nike staff worked with the Philadelphia 76ers to test a variety of shoes, and Nike's 1999 Air Seismic cross-trainer was the result. In 1997, Nike designers visited Mia Hamm to determine her expectations of women's soccer shoes, and the company designed a lightweight shoe with a fiber cushion and foam.

Nike continues to rely on superior technological developments to differentiate its products from those of competitors. The company presently sells approximately 300 models of athletic shoes in 900 styles for 25 different sports including basketball, tennis, cross training, baseball, hiking, cycling, cheerleading, aquatic sports, golf, and soccer. Exhibit 4 indicates the major developments of Nike technology from 1964 to present.

EXHIBIT 4    Recent Nike, Inc. Technological Developments

| Date | Development | Purpose |
|------|-------------|---------|
| 1990 | Air 180 | Air cushioning in the heel and front of the shoe; heel cushion is 50 percent larger than previous models (consumer has a 180-degree view of the heel air bag) |
| | Built-in pump shoe | Provides a tighter fit, with the convenience of a built-in pump |
| 1991 | Huarache Fit Technology | Combination of neoprene and lycra spandex that provides runners with a form-fitting, supportive, and lightweight shoe |
| 1993 | Air Max Cushioning technology | Provides 30 percent more cushioning |
| mid-1990s | Foamposite | Material that ensures no rough spots in the shoe |
| mid-1990s | Zoom Air Cushioning | Material that is used in mid-sole to absorb pounding without taking away stability or speed |
| 1998 | Air Flightposite shoe | Dual-pigmented material with metallic hues that can be molded into a shoe |

### Marketing

Because Nike does not actually produce shoes, the main focus of the company is creating and marketing the products. Nike positions its products as high-performance shoes with high technology features. The general target market for Nike athletic shoes is males and females between eighteen and thirty-four years old. Products are revamped continually, and shoe types that sell year-round are revamped quarterly. On average, Nike begins distribution of one new shoe style every single day.

Nike advertises its products in a variety of ways and targets its ads to specific groups or types of people. Advertising expenditures were $978.6 million in 1999. The company continues to spend advertising dollars on TV ads during professional and college sports events, prime-time programs, and late-night programs. Prime-time ads are intended to reach a broad range of adults, and late-night TV advertising is geared toward younger adults. Print media such as *Sports Illustrated, People, Runner's World, Glamour, Self, Tennis, Money, Bicycling,* and *Weight Watchers* are also very important in advertising Nike products. During the 1996 Olympics, Nike spent approximately $30 million on advertising and the sponsorship of individual athletes and teams. The company sponsored the U.S. women's soccer team that won the 1999 World Cup and has significant sponsorships for both the 2000 Olympics and the 2002 World Cup in Japan and Korea.

The online store, Nike.com, sells a variety of products, including shoes, equipment, and apparel. In November 1999 the company began offering NIKEiD to its online customers. Customers can personalize their athletic shoes by selecting shoe colors, a personal ID, or nickname. These custom shoes are available in two styles, Air Turbulence running shoes and Air Famished cross-training shoes. Nike adds a $10 fee for customization and will accept up to 400 personalized orders each day. The company believes its online business will be an important component of future sales. According to Phil Knight, "We absolutely believe it [the Internet] is creating an entire business revolution, and we truly intend to be a part of that revolution."

Some of the celebrity spokespersons for Nike include Michael Jordan, Andre Agassi, Monica Seles, Mia Hamm, Charles Barkley, Troy Aikman, Pete Sampras, Sheryl Swoopes, and Tiger Woods. Michael Jordan's Nike contract has, to date, been the most

EXHIBIT 5    Nike, Inc. Advertisements

| Theme | Visual Image |
|---|---|
| "Hangtime" | Air Jordan basketball shoe promotion featuring Michael Jordan and Spike Lee. |
| "Revolution" | Beatles song "Revolution" played and images of sports stars were shown. |
| "Bo Knows" | Illustrates the range of Nike shoes (20 different sport categories). |
| "Just Do It" | Shows people from many walks of life exercising in Nike shoes. |
| "Multiple Bo's" | Bo Jackson meets Sonny Bono and 14 other Bo Jacksons who represent different sports. |
| "Rock and Roll Tennis" | Andre Agassi shows his tennis skills in rock video format. |
| "Instant Karma" | Print campaign targeted to women. |
| "I Am Not a Role Model" | Charles Barkley says sports stars are not role models, but parents should be role models. |
| "Aerospace Jordan" | Cartoon characters Bugs Bunny, Looney Tunes bad guy Marvin Martin, and Michael Jordan travel to Mars. (Super Bowl XXVII) |
| "Running," "Go Slow," "Aerobics" | A series of three TV ads for women that stress comfort and developing a sense of self. |
| "Air Swoopes" | An ad with Sheryl Swoopes introducing the Air Swoopes basketball shoe and announcing Nike sponsorship of the women's U.S. Olympic basketball team. |
| "Broad-Minded" | An advertisement with Tiger Woods. The statement made is "We're not just canvas and leather shoes. We're big—and broad-minded." |
| "Nike vs. Evil" | Eight soccer stars are pitted in a fight against the devil. |
| "I Can" | Slow-motion shots of athletic competition with slogans such as "I can master pain" and "I can make you respect me." |
| "Beautiful" | Several photos of people with injuries such as callused feet and scarred knees. The song "You Are So Beautiful" plays in the background, and the Nike swoosh and "Just Do It" appear at the end of the ad. |
| "Date" | The U.S. women's soccer team says "we will take on the world as a team," and everyone on the team goes on a date with one person. |
| "Two Fillings" | The U.S. women's soccer team all want fillings when Brandi Chastain said she had two fillings. Each woman stands and says, "I will have two fillings." |
| "Chicks Dig the Long Ball" | Pitchers Tom Glavine and Greg Maddox try to get Heather Locklear's attention from Mark McGwire. |
| "Overjoyed" | Several Jordan-brand athletes are shown in slow motion: Randy Moss in a crowded hotel lobby and Derek Jeter surrounded by media in a locker room. |

lucrative endorsement contract for a professional sports player. Tiger Woods signed a reported $90 million deal in 1999 to promote Nike golf wear. It is estimated that the company spends approximately $100 million per year on endorsement fees for sports stars. Exhibit 5 lists some of Nike's advertising campaigns.

International marketing efforts continue. Nike has operations in 110 countries on six continents. Phil Knight says, "There's a pretty strong recognition that we'll be bigger in a couple of years outside the United States than inside." Nike is already number one in the overall footwear market in Spain, France, Belgium, Holland, Luxembourg,

Finland, Italy, and the United Kingdom. Some of the new markets that are now being pursued include Chile, Peru, Bolivia, India, Mexico, South Africa, and several Eastern European countries. Wieden and Kennedy, the advertising agency responsible for most of Nike's ads, has opened offices in London, Tokyo, and Amsterdam so that advertising can be developed by local people to fit local cultures.

## Distribution

Nike opened a 630,000-square-foot apparel distribution center in Memphis in 1992 that is called Nike Next Day. Footwear is distributed from centers in Greenland, New Hampshire; Beaverton, Oregon; Wilsonville, Oregon; and Memphis, Tennessee. Nike apparel is shipped from Memphis and Greenville, North Carolina. Sports Specialty products are distributed from Irvine, California, and Cole Haan and Bauer products are distributed from Greenland, New Hampshire. The company operates a "Futures" ordering program that allows retailers to order up to six months in advance and be guaranteed to receive their order within a certain time period and at a certain price. However, retailers can receive apparel orders the next day if they place their orders by 7 P.M. the day before.

Knight worries that the brand will lose its image as a technically superior sports shoe if international marketing is not monitored carefully. Nike has purchased the distribution operations of many of its worldwide distributors in an attempt to control marketing of Nike products. Some of these "Nike-owned" countries include: Singapore, Taiwan, Hong Kong, New Zealand, Korea, Japan, and Malaysia. Nike recently consolidated the operations of 31 distribution centers in the European Union countries into one distribution center in Belgium. A new distribution center is under construction in Japan.

## Social Responsibility

Nike has been criticized in the past few years for employment practices at its international manufacturing sites. Some consumers are concerned about the exploitive practices of managers in some Asian countries. The company set up a labor practices department in 1996. In 1997, former UN Ambassador Andrew Young was asked by Nike to review labor practices in Third-World factories. Ambassador Young reported that Nike was "no worse" than many other companies operating abroad, and he found "no pattern of systematic abuses." Even so, Young recommended that Nike develop ways to ensure that employees have the right to file grievances and use an outside board of observers to monitor the company's compliance with human rights standards. In 1998 Nike joined the Fair Labor Association (FLA), a sweatshop monitoring organization founded by a Presidential taskforce made up of apparel manufacturers and human rights organizations. Maria Eitel was hired as Nike's vice president of social responsibility in 1998. Nike's leadership on labor initiatives in factories producing its products is shown in Exhibit 6.

In addition to its membership in the FLA, Nike has developed a process for ensuring that its factories comply with the company's code of conduct.

Nike has developed several programs that show the company's concern about social responsibility issues, and the company has provided more than $34 million in cash and products to various charitable and non-profit organizations. Some of these contributions were made to 100 Black Men of America, INROADS, Boys and Girls Clubs of America, National Head Start Association, YWCA of the United States of America, and the Jackie Robinson Foundation. Howard White, VP of marketing for the Jordan Brand, conducts seminars called "Believe to Achieve" for at-risk youth. The seminars include a variety of local and national celebrity speakers from entertainment, sports, and business, and the seminars encourage youth to work toward success through vision, self-esteem, and commitment.

---

EXHIBIT 6    Nike, Inc. Labor Initiatives

---

- 1992—The first code of conduct in the sporting goods industry (dealing with international labor issues) was developed by Nike.
- 1994 (and following)—Independent auditors test factory compliance with the Nike code of conduct.
- 1996—A labor practices department was established by Nike. More than 1,000 production personnel in Nike contract factories work each day to monitor labor conditions.
- 1996—Nike joined President Clinton's Coalition on Fair Labor Practices. The company agreed to follow the Apparel Industry Partnership's Workplace Code of Conduct and to "help the industry eradicate sweatshops in the United States and abroad."
- 1997—Ambassador Andrew Young conducted an independent assessment of Nike labor practices. In response, for Young's recommendations, Nike adopted a termination policy for contractors who violate the code of conduct, developed penalties for violations of the code of conduct, implemented training for managers, and established training programs for U.S. managers who will work in international markets.
- 1997—Eight weeks of training in 16 Asian cities was completed to reinforce the Nike code of conduct.
- 1997—Comprehension of the code was added to the corporate audit manual as a criterion for judgment.
- 1998—Joined the Fair Labor Association (FLA), a sweatshop-monitoring organization founded by a presidential taskforce made up of apparel manufacturers and human rights organizations. Companies involved include Nike, Reebok, Liz Claiborne, and Phillips-Van Heusen. Efforts to recruit other businesses to the FLA have been unsuccessful. Most of the apparel manufacturers and some retailers are joining an effort through the American Apparel Manufacturing Association that has less stringent requirements than FLA. The group, United Students Against Sweatshops (students from 100 universities), has demanded that universities withdraw support from the FLA and create a more rigorous plan for monitoring sweatshops. The student group wants companies to publicly disclose the locations of their foreign factories so that independent investigations of labor practices can occur.

---

*Source:* "Nike Puts Its Code of Conduct in the Pocket of Workers," *PR Newswire,* September 17, 1997, "Sweatshop Reform: How to Solve the Standoff," *Business Week,* May 3, 1999.

The Nike Environmental Action Team (NEAT) was formed in 1993. This group pursues environmental initiatives in regard to recycling old athletic shoes and reusing them in new products. Nike recovers 100,000 pairs of shoes each month in its "Reuse-a-Shoe" recycling program. Nike demonstrates its concern for the environment by using the recycled materials in the soles of its new shoes and providing recycled material for sports fields and tracks. Every year Nike recycles 5 million pounds of solid wastes.

## Management Style and Culture

Phil Knight has created a strong culture at Nike, Inc., based on company loyalty and locker-room camaraderie. Most corporate employees are health-conscious young people; 41 percent of them are under the age of thirty. Knight trusts these employees to "Just Do It." He sometimes drops out of sight for months at a time and then re-emerges with some new approach for the company. His philosophy is "Play by the rules, but be ferocious. . . . It's all right to be Goliath, but always act like David." The 74-acre corporate campus of Nike, Inc., provides a sense of the culture: it has wooded areas, running trails, a lake, and a fitness center. Knight believes that people should find a "sense of peace at work."

In 1994 Tom Clark took over as president of Nike, Inc. Clark had worked at Nike for 14 years when he was appointed by Knight to replace Richard Donahue. The characteristics that should allow Clark to be successful as president include his collaborative management style, his concern about keeping lines of communication open, and his desire to facilitate decision making. Some critics suggest that Donahue, in his four years as president, added management layers that slowed the company's reaction time. Clark says, "Collaboration is in our genes, but the days when a few decision-makers can get together in the hall are over."

During 1998 and 1999, Nike restructured the company to take advantage of cost savings and to improve operating efficiency. The 1998 downsizing charge was $129.9 million, and an additional $60 million re-structuring charge was incurred in 1999. Employees were terminated from all areas of Nike including international and domestic workers. A total of 1,039 employees were terminated as part of the restructuring plan. In addition, the Asia Pacific headquarters was closed, and these operations were moved to the U.S. office.

### Finance and Accounting

Nike, Inc., income statements and balance sheets for 1993 to 1999 are provided in Exhibits 7 and 8, respectively. These statements reveal increases in sales, income, assets, and shareholders' equity. Consolidated statements of Nike shareholders' equity are shown in Exhibit 9.

EXHIBIT 7    **Nike Consolidated Statement of Income (in millions except per-share data)**

|  | 1999 | 1998 | 1997 | 1996 |
|---|---|---|---|---|
| **Revenues** | $8,776.9 | $9,553.1 | $9,186.5 | $6,470.6 |
| **Costs and expenses:** | | | | |
| Costs of sales | 5,493.5 | 6,065.5 | 5,503.0 | 3,906.7 |
| Selling and administrative expenses | 2,426.6 | 2,623.8 | 2,303.7 | 1,588.6 |
| Interest expense | 44.1 | 60.0 | 52.3 | 39.5 |
| Other (income)/expense, net | 21.5 | 20.9 | 32.3 | 36.7 |
| Restructuring charge | 45.1 | 129.9 | — | — |
|  | $8,030.8 | $8,900.1 | $7,891.3 | $5,571.5 |
| **Income before income taxes** | $ 746.1 | $ 653.0 | $1,295.2 | $ 899.1 |
| Income taxes | 294.7 | 253.4 | 499.4 | 345.9 |
| **Net income** | $ 451.4 | $ 399.6 | $ 795.8 | $ 553.2 |
| Net income per common share | $ 1.57 | $ 1.35 | $ 2.68 | $ 3.77 |

*Source:* Nike, Inc. *Annual Reports*

EXHIBIT 8    Nike Consolidated Balance Sheet (in millions)

|  | 1999 | 1998 | 1997 | 1996 |
|---|---|---|---|---|
| **Assets** | | | | |
| **Current assets:** | | | | |
| Cash and equivalents | $ 198.1 | $ 108.6 | $ 445.4 | $ 262.1 |
| Accounts receivable, less allowance for doubtful accounts | 1,540.1 | 1,674.4 | 1,754.1 | 1,346.1 |
| Inventory | 1,199.3 | 1,396.6 | 1,338.6 | 931.2 |
| Deferred income taxes | 120.6 | 156.8 | 135.7 | 93.1 |
| Income taxes receivable | 15.9 | — | — | — |
| Prepaid expenses | 190.9 | 196.2 | 157.1 | 94.4 |
| Total current assets | 3,264.9 | 3,532.6 | 3,830.9 | 2,726.9 |
| Property, plant, and equipment | 1,265.8 | 1,153.1 | 922.4 | 643.5 |
| Identifiable intangible assets and goodwill | 426.6 | 435.8 | 464.2 | 474.8 |
| Other assets | 290.4 | 275.9 | 143.7 | 106.4 |
| Total assets | $5,247.4 | $5,397.4 | $5,361.2 | $3,951.6 |
| **Liabilities and shareholders' equity** | | | | |
| **Current liabilities:** | | | | |
| Current portion of long-term debt | $ 1.0 | $ 1.6 | $ 2.2 | $ 7.3 |
| Notes payable | 419.1 | 480.2 | 553.2 | 445.1 |
| Accounts payable | 373.2 | 584.6 | 687.1 | 455.0 |
| Accrued liabilities | 653.6 | 608.5 | 570.5 | 480.4 |
| Income taxes payable | — | 28.9 | 53.9 | 79.3 |
| Total current liabilities | 1,446.9 | 1,703.8 | 1,866.9 | 1,467.1 |
| Long-Term debt | 386.1 | 379.4 | 296.0 | 9.5 |
| Noncurrent deferred income tax | 79.8 | 52.3 | 42.1 | 1.9 |
| Other noncurrent liabilities | — | — | — | 41.4 |
| **Shareholders' equity** | | | | |
| **Common stock at stated value:** | | | | |
| Class A convertible | $ .2 | $ .2 | $ .2 | $ .2 |
| Class B convertible | 2.7 | 2.7 | 2.7 | 2.7 |
| Capital in excess of stated value | 334.1 | 262.5 | 210.6 | 154.8 |
| Foreign currency transaction adjustments | (68.9) | (47.2) | (31.3) | (16.5) |
| Retained earnings | 3,066.5 | 3,034.4 | 2,973.7 | 2,290.2 |
| Total shareholders' equity | 3,334.6 | 3,261.6 | 3,155.8 | 2,431.4 |
| Total liabilities and shareholders' equity | $5,247.4 | $5,397.4 | $5,361.2 | $3,951.6 |

*Source:* Nike, Inc. *Annual Reports*

EXHIBIT 9    Nike Consolidated Statement of Shareholders' Equity (in millions)

| Date | Common Stock Class A | Common Stock Class B | Capital in Excess of Stated Value | Foreign Currency Transaction Adjustment | Retained Earnings | Total |
|------|------|------|------|------|------|------|
| 1996 | $0.20 | $2.7 | $154.8 | $(16.5) | $2,290.2 | $2,431.4 |
| 1997 | 0.20 | 2.7 | 210.6 | (31.3) | 2,973.7 | 3,155.9 |
| 1998 | 0.20 | 2.7 | 262.5 | (47.2) | 3,043.4 | 3,261.6 |
| 1999 | $0.20 | $2.7 | $334.1 | $(68.9) | $3,066.5 | $3,334.6 |

Source: Nike, Inc. Annual Reports

## FUTURE OUTLOOK

Even with limited growth and intense competition in the athletic shoe market, Nike managers expect the company will perform well in the future. According to Phil Knight,

> As we go off to get those sales and earnings up, we are reminded that ours truly is a unique business. We have similar goals as others, but different inspiration. Who else has Mia and Brandi and Michelle and Lance Armstrong to inspire them in a very personal way? How can we fail with those people in our corner?

With its innovative marketing and advertising, Nike should remain a force in the industry. It seems that Phil Knight still believes in the Nike credo—"Just Do It."

Consider the following questions regarding Nike's future:

1. Is Nike trying to supply products for too many sports? Should Nike narrow its product line in athletic shoes?
2. What types of acquisitions would you suggest to Phil Knight for Nike?
3. Should Nike begin producing some of its own products?
4. Is Nike taking the correct approach in marketing its shoes internationally?
5. What changes in product and advertising should the company pursue to appeal to the aging baby boomers? To Generation X? To Generation Y?
6. How can Nike maintain a competitive advantage over Reebok?
7. Is Nike responding correctly to concerns about the treatment of employees in international manufacturing facilities?
8. How serious are the problems Nike has faced in the last five years? Can the company create growth that is profitable and sustainable?

# REEBOK INTERNATIONAL, LTD.—2000

**Angela G. Page**
**Francis Marion University**

**RBK**
www.reebok.com

Headquartered in Stoughton, Massachusetts, Reebok International, Ltd., is a global company engaged primarily in the design and marketing of sports and fitness products, including footwear, apparel, and products for nonathletic casual use. Total sales are approximately 72 percent from footwear and 28 percent from apparel. Reebok depends upon independent manufacturers to manufacture its high-quality products. One of Reebok's most recent developments is the DMX technology, which, according to Reebok, provides a superb cushioning, utilizing an active airflow system. Another recent development is the hydromover technology for performance apparel. This technology, built into the fabric used for performance apparel, is a moisture-management system that helps to keep athletes warm in cool weather and cool in hot weather. Reebok's latest advertising campaign uses the theme of "The Human Movement" along with the catch phrase "Are You Feeling It?"

Reebok's future is uncertain, for the six months ending June 30, 1999, net sales had decreased 9 percent to $1.48 billion. Since the fourth quarter of 1997, Reebok's sales percentage has declined; earnings per share have declined, and dividends have not been declared. As of October 1, 1999, Reebok's stock price for the prior 52-week period has varied from $8.94 per share to $22.75 per share, with the most recent price being $8.94 per share. Reebok's sales and profits have been declining since 1996.

Paul Fireman, Reebok's CEO, during a 1997 angry shareholder's meeting in response to Reebok's performance during 1996, vowed to resign if he failed to turn the company around within two years. So, where is his resignation? According to *Fortune Magazine*'s cover story "CEOs in Denial," there is a fine line between denial and optimism (Sellers, 1999). The magazine's verdict on Reebok's Paul Fireman is that he is a salesman who rarely delivers; he is not a liar, just an extreme optimist. Fireman has relinquished some of his responsibilities and spotlight to his new number-two executive, Carl Yankowski, formerly of Sony. Paul Fireman is also well entrenched, owning the board and 13 percent of the stock. Because of this ownership situation, Reebok may never make the top 10 list for excellent boards.

## HISTORY

Reebok's United Kingdom-based ancestor company was founded for athletes who wanted to run faster. In the 1890s, Joseph William Foster made himself some of the first known athletic running shoes, and before long his fledgling company, J. W. Foster and Sons, became known for being used by distinguished athletes. In 1958, two of the founder's grandsons started a companion company that was named for an African gazelle, the Reedbuck—hence, the name Reebok.

In 1979, Paul Fireman, as a partner in an outdoor sporting goods distributor, participated in an international trade show, at which he negotiated for the North American distributorship of running shoes in the United States. At $60 a pair, Reeboks were the most expensive running shoes. Demand grew quickly, outpacing the U.K. plant's capacity, and new production facilities were then established. By 1981, Reebok's sales exceeded $1.5 million, and, as a dramatic move, Reebok introduced the first athletic shoe designed especially for the women's exercise of aerobic dance. The shoe was called the Freestyle, and with it Reebok transformed the athletic footwear industry. Explosive growth followed, which Reebok fueled with product extensions on the way to becoming an industry leader. The Freestyle is now a classic and is the best-selling performance aerobic shoe that has progressed through several generations.

In the 1980s Reebok began an aggressive expansion into overseas markets available in over 160 countries. In 1985, Reebok completed its initial public offering. In the late 1980s, a particularly fertile period began with "The Pump" technology being used in a host of sports and fitness activities. In 1992, Reebok began a transition to becoming a company identified principally with sports. It created a host of new footwear and apparel products for soccer, track and field, and other sports. It signed hundreds of professionals to sponsorship contracts. By the end of 1995, Reebok had established itself on the major playing fields of the world and was generating significant sales in all major sports.

## COMPETITORS

Reebok International's largest competitor is Nike. Nike holds the number-one position within the industry's ranking, and its sales are equal to 296 percent of Reebok's total sales. The athletic footwear industry's total sales have recently experienced an increased growth rate of 11.73 percent. Reebok sales for the same period decreased 11 percent, and Nike's total sales grew only by 4 percent.

## INTERNAL FACTORS

Reebok International, Ltd. used to be divided into four major divisions—Reebok, The Rockport Company, Ralph Lauren Brand, and the Greg Norman Brand. The company has recently been reorganized into six strategic business units, each of which will have the responsibility for product and marketing for the unit's business as well as responsibility for profitability and cash flow for the unit. The six strategic business units are Classic Footwear (which will focus on lifestyle footwear); Performance Footwear (which will be responsible for baseball, basketball, cross-training, football, golf, running, soccer, tennis, and adventure and outdoor footwear); Fitness (which will be responsible for men's and women's fitness and walking footwear and exercise equipment business and other related sports and fitness products); Global Apparel (responsible for sports and fitness apparel worldwide); Kid's Products (will focus on children's products sold under the Reebok and Weebok brands); Retail Operations will be responsible for retail stores as well as developing retail merchandising and promotional concepts.

Reebok has developed the DMX technology that provides superb cushioning with an active airflow system. Originally introduced in 1995, DMX has been expanded into multiple versions to meet the performance demands of various activities. Reebok has also developed the Hydromover moisture-management system technology to be incorporated into its apparel products. Reebok devotes significant resources to advertising through television, radio, and print media, utilizing its relationships with major sports figures in a variety of sports to maintain and enhance visibility for the Reebok brand. The latest brand positioning is "The Human Movement" and "Are You Feeling It?" align Reebok with the growing appeal of the human rights movements and the natural desire to feel good about ourselves.

Reebok operates nationally and internationally. The national operations use an employee salesforce as well as independent sales representatives to sell the products. The national strategy emphasizes high-quality retailers and seeks to avoid lower-margin mass merchandisers and discount outlets. The international operations are coordinated from headquarters in Stoughton, Massachusetts; there are regional offices in Leusden, Holland; Hong Kong, Delhi, India; and Toronto, Canada.

Rockport Company, a major division of Reebok designs, produces and distributes specially engineered comfort footwear for men and women worldwide that consists of casual, dress, outdoor performance, golf, and fitness walking shoes. Rockport currently markets its product through the slogan "Be comfortable. Uncompromise: start with your feet." This campaign features such famous people as a Tony nominee and the world's most famous drag queen. Ralph Lauren Brand Footwear's, another major division of Reebok, products include the RLX collection, high-performance athletic foot wear, and the Lauren collection for women. The fourth division, Greg Norman Brand, produces a collection of apparel and accessories marketed under the Greg Norman name and logo and endorsed by pro golfer Greg Norman.

The executive officers of Reebok International are: Paul B. Fireman, age fifty-five, president, CEO, and chairman of the board of directors along with Carl J. Yankowski, age fifty, executive vice president, president, and CEO of the Reebok Division and director. Officers hold their perspective office until the first meeting of the board of directors following the annual meeting of stockholders or a special meeting in lieu thereof until their respective successors are chosen and qualified. Paul B. Fireman is the founder and has served as its CEO since the company's founding in 1979 and as its chairman of the board since 1986. Yankowski was appointed executive vice president of the company and president and CEO of the Reebok Division in September 1998. Prior to that he was president and COO of Sony Electronics, Inc., a subsidiary of the Sony Corporation, from November 1993 to January 1998.

## EXTERNAL FACTORS

Trade policy affects imports from China to the United States, including footwear, which has been threatened for several years with higher or prohibitive tariff rates, either through statutory action or intervention by the Executive Branch out of concern over China's trade policies, human rights record, foreign weapons sales practices, and foreign policy. Reebok does not currently anticipate that the United States will impose restrictions on imports from China. The European Union has imposed import quotas on certain footwear from China since 1994. These quotas have not significantly affected Reebok because the quota scheme exempts certain higher-priced special technology athletic footwear, i.e., most Reebok products. In addition, the European Union has imposed anti-dumping duties against certain textile footwear from China and Indonesia. A broad exemption that covers most Reebok models from the anti-dumping duties is provided for athletic textile footwear. Various other countries have taken or are considering steps to restrict footwear imports or impose additional customs duties or other impediments that will affect Reebok as well as other footwear importers. Reebok, in conjunction with other footwear importers, is aggressively challenging such restrictions and attempting to develop new production capacity in countries not subject to those restrictions.

Sales of athletic and casual footwear tend to be seasonal in nature, with the strongest sales occurring in the first and third quarters. Apparel sales also generally vary over the course of the year, with the greatest demand occurring during the spring and fall seasons. Competition in sports and fitness footwear and apparel sales is intense.

Competitors include a number of sports and fitness footwear and apparel companies, such as Nike, Adidas, Fila, New Balance, and others, and new entrants and established companies provide challenges in every category. The casual footwear market is also highly competitive. Competitors include a number of companies such as Timberland, Bass, Clark, and Dexter. Competition has intensified as walking has grown in popularity, and athletic shoe companies have entered the market. Reebok's other product lines also continue to confront strong competition. The apparel line competes with well-known brands such as Nike, Adidas, Fila, Tommy Hilfiger, Ralph Lauren, Nautica, and other makers of men's casual sportswear. The footwear brand competes with such brands as Cole Haan, Timberland, Tommy Hilfiger, Prada, and Gucci.

The footwear and apparel industry is subject to rapid changes in consumer preferences as well as technological innovations. A major technological breakthrough or marketing or promotional success by one of Reebok's competitors could adversely affect its competitive position as could a shift in consumer preferences. Currently, the athletic footwear and apparel industry has seen some shift away from athletic footwear to "casual" product offerings. This change in preference has adversely affected Reebok's business as well as that of some of its competitors. In addition, in countries in which the athletic footwear market is mature, sales growth may be dependent in part on Reebok increasing its market share at the expense of its competitors. Competition in the markets for Reebok's products occurs in a variety of areas, including price, quality, product designs, brand image, marketing and promotion, and ability to meet delivery commitments to retailers. The intensity of the competition faced by the various operating units of Reebok and the rapid changes in the consumer preference and technology that can occur in the footwear and apparel markets constitute significant risk factors for Reebok's operations.

Reebok's business is subject to the economic conditions in its major markets, including recession, inflation, general weakness in retail markets, and changes in consumer purchasing power and preferences. Adverse changes in such economic factors could have a negative effect on Reebok. The recent slowdown in the athletic footwear and branded apparel markets has had negative effects on Reebok and its competitors.

Reebok is currently undertaking various global restructuring activities to enable it to achieve operating efficiencies, improve logistics, and reduce expenses. There can be no assurance that Reebok will be able to effectively execute its restructuring plans, or that the desired benefits will be achieved. In the short term, Reebok could experience difficulties in product delivery or other logistical operations as a result of its restructuring activities and be subject to increased expenditures and charges because of inefficiencies resulting from such restructuring activities. Reebok is currently consolidating its warehouses in Europe, which should enable it to achieve efficiencies and improve logistics. However, in the short term, benefits from this restructuring may not be achieved, and if difficulties arise in effecting such consolidation, Reebok could experience operational difficulties, excess inventory, or a decline in sales.

## CONCLUSION

For more than a decade, the semi-official corporate motto for Reebok has called for its people to always strive to "make a difference;" and one official motto of Reebok has been to become "the best, most innovative and exciting sporting goods company in the world." Thus, Reebok, after 17 years of spectacular growth around the world, has many accomplishments, continued innovation, and boundless excitement. Yet Reebok International Ltd. net sales for the year that ended December 31, 1999, were $2.891 billion, a 10 percent decrease from the year ended December 31, 1998, sales of $3.205 billion.

EXHIBIT 1    Reebok International Annual Income Statement
(in millions except earnings-per-share data)

| | 12/31/99 | 12/31/98 | 12/31/97 | 12/31/96 |
|---|---|---|---|---|
| Sales | $2,891.23 | $3,205.42 | $3,637.44 | $3,478.60 |
| Cost of goods | 1,783.91 | 2,037.46 | 2,294.05 | 2,144.42 |
| Gross profit | 1,107.32 | 1,167.96 | 1,343.39 | 1,334.18 |
| Selling and administrative and depreciation and amortization expenses | 977.12 | 1,046.62 | 1,073.59 | 1,069.20 |
| Income after depreciation and amortization | 130.20 | 121.34 | 269.80 | 264.98 |
| Nonoperating income | (52.46) | (23.62) | (47.35) | 14.93 |
| Interest expense | 49.69 | 60.67 | 64.37 | 42.25 |
| Pretax income | 28.03 | 37.03 | 158.09 | 236.67 |
| Income taxes | 10.09 | 11.92 | 12.49 | 84.08 |
| Minority interest | 6.90 | 1.17 | 10.48 | 14.64 |
| Investment gains/losses (+) | 0 | 0 | 0 | 0 |
| Other income/charges | 0 | 0 | 0 | 0 |
| Income from continued operations | N/A | N/A | N/A | N/A |
| Extras and discontinued operations | 0 | 0 | 0 | 0 |
| Net income | $    11.04 | $    23.92 | $   135.12 | $   138.95 |

## Depreciation footnote

| | | | | |
|---|---|---|---|---|
| Income before depreciation and amortization | $  135.38 | $  124.77 | $  273.96 | $  268.39 |
| Depreciation and amortization (cash flow) | 5.18 | 3.43 | 4.16 | 3.41 |
| Income after depreciation and amortization | $  130.20 | $  121.34 | $  269.80 | $  264.98 |

## Earnings per-share data

| | | | | |
|---|---|---|---|---|
| Average shares | 56.53 | 56.97 | 58.31 | 69.62 |
| Diluted earnings-per-share data before non-recurring items | 0.89 | 0.83 | 2.30 | 2.00 |
| Diluted net earnings per-share | $    0.20 | $    0.42 | $    2.32 | $    2.0 |

*Source:* www.freeedgar.com

EXHIBIT 2    Reebok International Annual Balance Sheet
(in millions, except book value per share)

| | 12/31/99 | 12/31/98 | 12/31/97 | 12/31/96 |
|---|---|---|---|---|
| **Assets** | | | | |
| Cash and equivalents | $ 281.74 | $ 180.07 | $ 209.77 | $ 232.37 |
| Receivables | 417.40 | 517.83 | 561.73 | 590.50 |
| Notes receivable | 0 | 0 | 0 | 0 |
| Inventories | 414.61 | 535.16 | 563.73 | 544.52 |
| Other current assets | 129.35 | 128.72 | 129.59 | 95.70 |
| Total current assets | 1,243.11 | 1,361.79 | 1,464.82 | 1,463.09 |
| Net property and equipment | 178.11 | 172.58 | 156.96 | 185.29 |
| Investments and advances | 0 | 0 | 0 | 0 |
| Other non-current assets | 0 | 0 | 0 | 0 |
| Deferred charges | 43.86 | 99.21 | 19.37 | 7.85 |
| Intangibles | 68.89 | 68.64 | 65.78 | 69.70 |
| Deposits and other assets | 30.13 | 37.38 | 49.16 | 60.25 |
| Total assets | $1,564.12 | $1,739.62 | $1,756.10 | $1,786.18 |
| **Liabilities and shareholders' equity** | | | | |
| Notes payable | $ 27.61 | $ 48.07 | $ 40.67 | $ 32.98 |
| Accounts payable | 153.99 | 203.14 | 192.14 | 196.37 |
| Current portion long-term debt | 185.61 | 86.64 | 121.00 | 52.68 |
| Current portion capital leases | 0 | 0 | 0 | 0 |
| Accrued expenses | 248.82 | 191.83 | 219.39 | 169.34 |
| Income taxes payable | 8.30 | 82.59 | 4.26 | 65.59 |
| Other current liabilities | 0 | 0 | 0 | 0 |
| Total current liabilities | 623.90 | 612.28 | 577.45 | 516.96 |
| Mortgages | 0 | 0 | 0 | 0 |
| Deferred taxes/income | 0 | 0 | 0 | 0 |
| Convertible debt | 0 | 0 | 0 | 0 |
| Long-term debt | 370.30 | 554.43 | 639.35 | 854.10 |
| Noncurrent capital leases | 0 | 0 | 0 | 0 |
| Other noncurrent liabilities | 0 | 16.55 | 0 | 0 |
| Minority interest (liabilities) | 41.10 | 31.97 | 32.13 | 33.89 |
| Total liabilities | $1,035.31 | $1,215.24 | $1,248.94 | $1,404.95 |
| **Shareholders' Equity** | | | | |
| Preferred stock | 0 | 0 | 0 | 0 |
| Common stock (par) | $ 0.93 | $ 0.93 | $ 0.93 | $ 0.93 |
| Capital surplus | 0 | 0 | 0 | 0 |
| Retained earnings | 1,170.88 | 1,156.73 | 1,145.27 | 992.56 |
| Other equity | (25.37) | (15.67) | (21.42) | 5.36 |
| Treasury stock | 617.62 | 617.62 | 617.62 | 617.62 |
| Total shareholders' equity | 528.81 | 524.37 | 507.16 | 381.23 |
| Total liabilities and shareholders' equity | 1,564.12 | 1,739.62 | 1,756.10 | 1,786.18 |
| Total common equity | 528.81 | 524.37 | 507.16 | 381.23 |
| Average shares | 56.53 | 56.97 | 58.31 | 69.62 |
| Book value per share | $ 9.40 | $ 9.29 | $ 9.01 | $ 6.80 |

*Source:* www.freeedgar.com

EXHIBIT 3     Reebok Sales and Assets (in millions)

|              | 1999     | 1998     | 1997     |
|--------------|----------|----------|----------|
| **Sales**    |          |          |          |
| USA          | $1,609   | $1,858   | $2,000   |
| UK           | 545      | 522      | 661      |
| Europe       | 476      | 585      | 510      |
| Other Countries | 267   | 258      | 470      |
| Total        | $2,897   | $3,223   | $3,641   |
| **Assets**   |          |          |          |
| USA          | $167     | $170     | $175     |
| UK           | 28       | 28       | 23       |
| Europe       | 40       | 30       | 14       |
| Other countries | 11    | 11       | 9        |
| Total        | $246     | $239     | $221     |

*Source:* www.freeedgar.com

## REFERENCES

"5 Hundred Largest U.S. Corporations Summary." *Fortune, 139,* 8, (1999), p. F-1.

"1 Thousand Ranked Within Industries Summary." *Fortune, 139,* 8, (1999) p. F-51.

SELLERS, PATRICIA. "CEOs in Denial." *Fortune, 139,* 12, (1999) p. 80.

SELLERS, PATRICIA. "Reebok Gets a Lift." *Fortune, 136, 4* (1997) p. 180.

"Where Companies Rank in Their own Industries Summary." *Fortune, 139, 4,* p. 80.

# UST, INC.—2000

**Marilyn M. Helms**
**Dalton State College**
**Fred R. David**
**Francis Marion University**

UST
www.shareholder.com/ust

> It is often difficult to envision a promising future when one is in an industry that is constantly under attack. We have a fiduciary obligation to manage the Company through difficult times and pursue the full range of strategies in order to best protect the interests of our stockholders. This year was no exception, and 1999, with threats of additional regulation and taxes, will likely be no different.
>
> Vincent A. Gierer, Jr.
> Chairman of the board and CEO
> UST, Inc., February 17, 1999, *Annual Report*

## UST, INC.

Vincent A. Gierer, Jr., CEO and chairman of the board for UST, Inc., formerly U.S. Tobacco, indicates that regardless of the litigation issues that plague the tobacco industry, the company is determined to continue to reward stockholders and increase its smokeless tobacco business. He notes in his letter to stockholders that young people's usage of smokeless tobacco remains low and is already below the federal government goal of 4 percent by the year 2000. He further indicates that the average retail price of a can of the company's smokeless tobacco already falls within (and in some states exceeds) the $3.30–$3.50 price range advocated by the president and public health experts as a means of further reducing youth usage of tobacco products.

### Company Products and Scope

UST, Inc., based in Greenwich, Connecticut, is a holding company for four wholly owned subsidiaries—United States Tobacco Company, International Wine & Spirits Ltd., UST Enterprises Inc. and UST International Inc. UST, through its subsidiaries, is a leading producer and marketer of moist smokeless tobacco products, including Copenhagen, Copenhagen Long Cut, Skoal, Skoal Long Cut, Skoal Bandits, Red Seal, and Rooster. Internationally, UST markets its products primarily to Canada, and sales have been both profitable and stable for a number of years. Yet recent attempts to break into Mexico and other international markets have been disappointing. This segment of company strategy is also currently being evaluated to determine if joint partnerships, among other options, would bolster international operations (UST *Annual Report,* 1998). According to *Standard & Poor's Industry Surveys,* there is a low per-capita consumption of this product on the international market.

Other consumer products marketed by the company include premium wines sold nationally through the Chateau Ste. Michelle, Columbia Crest, and Villa Mt. Eden wineries as well as sparkling wine produced under the Domaine Ste. Michelle label and premium cigars including Don Tomas, Don Tomas Special Edition, Astral, and Habano Primero as well as pipes and pipe tobacco and pipe cleaners. (UST, Inc., should not be confused with UST Corp.)

## Market Share

Of its $1.42 billion in total sales for 1998, $1.24 billion of this amount was from the tobacco segment, a 5.4 percent increase from 1997. The tobacco segment accounts for 87.5 percent of consolidated UST, Inc.'s, sales. It is the leader in the smokeless tobacco market, having captured a 77 percent share based on 1998 data. This figure is down from the company high, a near-85 percent market share in 1993. The drop is also a 3 percent slide from 1997 when UST had a near-80 percent share of the market (*Forbes,* September 8, 1997). Gierer indicated that net volume only grew at 0.2 percent, citing slowing category growth as the reason. That the company lost one point in market share is attributed to the discontinuance of some UST products.

## Financial Highlights

UST is listed among the 200 most profitable publicly held companies in the United States. Additionally, UST boasts some of the highest returns among public companies with a return on sales of 32 percent, return on assets of 52 percent, and a return on equity of 101 percent. These figures, coupled with a payout ratio of over 60 percent and a dividend yield of over 5 percent, have made UST attractive to many value investors (www.ustshareholder.com). For all of 1999, UST had sales of $1.5 billion as shown in Exhibit 1.

## Product and Market Shifts

UST, Inc., seems to be benefiting from the higher cigarette prices. As a maker of moist smokeless tobacco products, UST isn't necessarily luring new consumers who don't want to pay more for cigarettes, but the company is, instead, winning over its own customers, who, incidentally, don't want to pay more for cigarettes. About 25 percent of UST's consumers also smoke cigarettes, so instead of using both, many tobacco users are moving away from higher-priced cigarettes and buying more snuff. This resulted in a net 8.25 percent increase in sales in the third quarter of 1999. Although moist snuff volume has increased, the chewing tobacco industry has been plummeting since 1988.

## Product and Flavor Trends

One of the growing trends in smokeless tobacco, besides the cut (fine cut or long cut) is flavoring. Mint seems to be the favorite flavor amongst the younger consumers according to the president of Smokey Mountain Chew, Inc., a UST, Inc., competitor. This change in the smokeless tobacco market is consumer driven as all of the companies in the smokeless market are striving to meet the trend. Other smokeless products appearing are tobacco and nicotine-free chews. These herbal snuffs are substitutes for the standard product and smokeless tobacco in general as well as a substitute for many smokers. In mid-1995, when UST introduced their new product, the Skoal Flavor Packs, the product was marketed to "smokers who can't smoke." Skoal Bandits, a moist snuff packaged in portion packs similar to small tea bags along with other smokeless products is adding to profits.

EXHIBIT 1    UST, Inc. Annual Income Statement (in millions, except earnings-per-share data)

|  | 12/31/99 | 12/31/98 | 12/31/97 | 12/31/96 |
|---|---|---|---|---|
| Sales | $1,512.33 | $1,423.24 | $1,401.72 | $1,396.85 |
| Cost of goods | 276.35 | 257.15 | 265.19 | 272.76 |
| Gross profit | 1,235.97 | 1,166.09 | 1,136.53 | 1,124.09 |
| Selling and administrative and depreciation and amortization expenses | 459.49 | 433.81 | 425.22 | 373.20 |
| Income after depreciation and amortization | 776.49 | 732.28 | 711.31 | 750.89 |
| Nonoperating income | 0 | 2.18 | 0 | 0 |
| Interest expense | 13.53 | 0 | 7.45 | 6.36 |
| Pretax income | 762.94 | 734.46 | 703.86 | 744.53 |
| Income taxes | 293.65 | 279.18 | 264.72 | 280.53 |
| Minority interest | 0 | 0 | 0 | 0 |
| Investment gains/losses (+) | 0 | 0 | 0 | 0 |
| Other income/charges | 0 | 0 | 0 | 0 |
| Income from continued operations | N/A | N/A | N/A | N/A |
| Extras and discontinued operations | 0 | 0 | 0 | 0 |
| Net income | $   469.29 | $   455.27 | $   439.14 | $   464.00 |

### Depreciation footnote

|  | 12/31/99 | 12/31/98 | 12/31/97 | 12/31/96 |
|---|---|---|---|---|
| Income before depreciation and amortization | $ 813.50 | $ 764.00 | $ 741.80 | $ 779.21 |
| Depreciation and amortization (cash flow) | 37.01 | 31.72 | 30.49 | 28.32 |
| Income after depreciation and amortization | $ 776.49 | $ 732.28 | $ 711.31 | $ 750.89 |

### Earnings per-share data

|  | 12/31/99 | 12/31/98 | 12/31/97 | 12/31/96 |
|---|---|---|---|---|
| Average Shares | $ 175.11 | $ 186.88 | $ 185.60 | $ 192.09 |
| Diluted earnings per share before nonrecurring items | 2.70 | 2.51 | 2.37 | 2.42 |
| Diluted Net earnings per share | $    2.68 | $    2.44 | $    2.37 | $    2.42 |

Source: UST, Inc., Annual Report, 1999.

Most competitors in the smokeless category have added a discount brand. Companies like National Tobacco, Conwood, and Swedish Match have launched Durango, Cougar, and Southern Pride, respectively, to meet this market that is continuing to grow. Coupled with this bargain trend, companies like Smokey Mountain Snuff and Conwood are linking their products to sporting events as a promotional strategy. UST noted a 8.25 percent increase in sales for the third quarter of 1999 as a result of higher prices and an increase in net unit volume of 1.2 percent to 161.7 million cans. This is significant in that it was UST's Red Seal Brand, a discount product, that contributed an additional 3 million cans to the net results according to the UST shareholder information found on the Web site.

Another factor that helps to boost the trend toward moist snuff is its availability within the market. This product can be purchased in supermarkets, smoke shops, mass merchandisers, discount, and convenience stores and online at retailers like www. freshsnuff.com/orderonline.htm. Additionally, as the numbers of places where people can smoke are further restricted, moist snuff sales will grow because it is easy to use anywhere. Driving the trend further is aggressive tobacco advertising, 46.8 percent of which is directed at the moist snuff segment of the market.

EXHIBIT 2    UST, Inc. Annual Balance Sheet (in millions, except book value per share)

|  | 12/31/99 | 12/31/98 | 12/31/97 | 12/31/96 |
|---|---|---|---|---|
| **Assets** | | | | |
| Cash and equivalents | $ 74.98 | $ 33.21 | $ 6.93 | $ 54.45 |
| Receivables | 64.34 | 63.26 | 67.70 | 77.86 |
| Notes receivable | 0 | 0 | 0 | 0 |
| Inventories | 403.46 | 372.63 | 319.67 | 271.42 |
| Other current assets | 37.21 | 38.10 | 47.55 | 40.45 |
| **Total Current Assets** | **580.02** | **507.21** | **441.84** | **444.18** |
| Net property & equipment | 361.88 | 338.69 | 326.71 | 300.89 |
| Investments and advances | 0 | 0 | 0 | 0 |
| Other noncurrent assets | 0 | 0 | 0 | 0 |
| Deferred charges | 0 | 0 | 0 | 7.63 |
| Intangibles | 0 | 0 | 0 | 0 |
| Deposits and other assets | 73.74 | 67.41 | 58.16 | 54.70 |
| Total assets | $1,015.64 | $913.31 | $826.71 | $807.39 |
| **Liabilities and shareholders' equity** | | | | |
| Notes payable | $ 70.96 | 0 | $ 10.00 | $150.00 |
| Accounts payable | 144.67 | $156.69 | 119.35 | 113.64 |
| Current portion long-term debt | 0 | 0 | 0 | 0 |
| Current portion capital leases | 0 | 0 | 0 | 0 |
| Accrued expenses | 0 | 0 | 0 | 0 |
| Income taxes payable | 45.68 | 40.61 | 37.17 | 42.92 |
| Other current liabilities | 0 | 0 | 0 | 0 |
| **Total current liabilities** | **261.32** | **197.31** | **166.52** | **306.55** |
| Mortgages | 0 | 0 | 0 | 0 |
| Deferred taxes income | 0 | 0 | 0 | 0 |
| Convertible debt | 0 | 0 | 0 | 0 |
| Long-term debt | 411.00 | 100.00 | 100.00 | 100.00 |
| Noncurrent capital leases | 0 | 0 | 0 | 0 |
| Other noncurrent liabilities | 142.51 | 147.71 | 122.26 | 118.82 |
| Minority interest (liabilities) | 0 | 0 | 0 | 0 |
| Total liabilities | $ 814.84 | $445.02 | $388.78 | $525.37 |
| **Shareholders' equity** | | | | |
| Preferred stock | 0 | 0 | 0 | 0 |
| Common stock (par) | $ 104.46 | $104.04 | $103.31 | $102.08 |
| Capital surplus | 526.27 | 512.08 | 474.66 | 414.27 |
| Retained earnings | 861.81 | 684.48 | 528.52 | 388.51 |
| Other equity | (12.27) | (18.42) | 0 | 0 |
| Treasury stock | 1,279.87 | 813.91 | 668.55 | 622.84 |
| Total shareholders' equity | 200.80 | 468.29 | 437.93 | 282.02 |
| **Total liabilities and shareholders' equity** | **1,015.64** | **913.31** | **826.71** | **807.39** |
| Total common equity | 200.80 | 468.29 | 437.93 | 282.02 |
| Average shares | 175.11 | 186.88 | 185.60 | 192.09 |
| Book value per share | $ 1.17 | $ 2.52 | $ 2.38 | $ 1.54 |

*Source:* UST, Inc., *Annual Report,* 1999.

EXHIBIT 3   UST, Inc. Consolidated Industry Segment Data  (in thousands of dollars)

| | *Year ended December 31,* | | | |
|---|---|---|---|---|
| | *1998* | *1997* | *1996* | *1995* |
| **Net Sales to unaffiliated customers** | | | | |
| Tobacco | | | | |
| Smokeless tobacco | $    124484 | $  1180535 | $  1170014 | $  1119828 |
| Other tobacco products | 1268 | 7588 | 8413 | 8792 |
| | $1,245,552 | $1,181,789 | $1,178,427 | $1,128,620 |
| Wine | 148512 | 145048 | 122458 | 109453 |
| Other | 29182 | 72543 | 74508 | 70742 |
| Elimination of intersegment sales | | (3987) | (3688) | (3019) |
| Net sales | $1,423,246 | $1,395,384 | $1,371,795 | $1,305,796 |
| **Operating profit (loss)** | | | | |
| Tobacco | $ 720622 | $ 700395 | $ 751115 | $ 720965 |
| Wine | 22090 | 28178 | 19875 | 13493 |
| Other | 1712 | (1270) | (500) | (5384) |
| Operating Profit | $744,424 | $727,303 | $770,490 | $729,074 |
| Corporate expenses | (12146) | (15995) | (19600) | (21305) |
| Interest, net | 2187 | (7451) | (6364) | (3179) |
| Earnings before income taxes | $734,465 | $703,857 | $744,526 | $704,590 |
| **Identifiable assets at December 31** | | | | |
| Tobacco | $ 497623 | $ 467972 | $ 453228 | $ 431424 |
| Wine | 277249 | 230896 | 186611 | 176565 |
| Other | 87197 | 102157 | 93875 | 88847 |
| Corporate | 51250 | 25338 | 78678 | 87916 |
| | $913,319 | $826,363 | $807,392 | $784,752 |
| **Capital expenditures (dispositions), net** | | | | |
| Tobacco | $ 27696 | $ 29410 | $ 22606 | $    2266 |
| Wine | 25646 | 20135 | 11551 | 10762 |
| Other | 2470 | 6134 | 3037 | 2447 |
| Corporate | 454 | 2480 | (445) | (1473) |
| | $56,266 | $58,159 | $36,749 | $14,002 |
| **Depreciation** | | | | |
| Tobacco | $ 16100 | $ 16266 | $ 16746 | $ 17642 |
| Wine | 11953 | 10423 | 8949 | 7693 |
| Other | 1653 | 1836 | 1911 | 2386 |
| Corporate | 1665 | 1611 | 537 | 633 |
| | $31,371 | $30,136 | $28,143 | $28,354 |

*Source:* UST, Inc., *Annual Report,* 1998.

## Diversification

Over the past ten years, UST has increased its share of the moist snuff market by 57 percent. UST, like Conwood, is taking advantage of its existing warehouse and distribution networks and has diversified into other markets. UST sold an entertainment subsidiary but still operates its wineries in Washington and California. Although the wine business had a drop in sales and profits in 1998, the firm believes it is positioned for future growth due to favorable demographics and the popularity of wine and plans to expand in California internally or through acquisitions. This sector accounts for 12 percent of sales revenue. As diversification increases, a greater decentralization of operations can be expected.

Its demanding customers motivate the company's drive toward increased operating efficiencies. The company's Sales Tracking and Reporting System (STARS) is an example of UST's response to customer demand for increased efficiency. STARS provides the company's sales and marketing personnel with instant access to product and customer information. UST's server-based Logistics Information Tracking and Reporting System (LITARS) monitors order delivery and tracks shipments to customers. This client/server application utilizes Power Builder and SQL Server software. The company's plan for implementing new technologies includes a strategic planning committee, reliance on tested technologies, and the employment of windows-based LANs.

## CURRENT LITIGATION

Legal actions against UST are geared toward reimbursement of healthcare costs in addition to seeking damages and other relief for smokers. Although most cases relate specifically to cigarettes, a few relate directly to smokeless tobacco products like those manufactured and sold by UST.

Primary to the legal actions of 1998, UST signed the "Smokeless Tobacco Master Settlement Agreement" along with other leading tobacco companies. This agreement involved 46 states, which resolved all remaining claims related to smoking-related healthcare costs. Primary to this agreement, over the next 25 years, the manufacturers of cigarettes must pay out approximately $206 million to the states as reimbursement for state-filed lawsuits. This will cover the states for Medicaid expenses related to smoking. In addition, the agreement requires that the companies restrict their advertising and sponsor programs that combat tobacco usage by youth.

Another suit against UST and five other smokeless tobacco manufacturers has been filed by the City and County of San Francisco and the Environmental Law Foundation on behalf of the residents of San Francisco County and the general public. It alleges the lack of a clear and reasonable warning that the use of smokeless tobacco results in multiple exposures to substances known to the State of California to cause cancer, birth defects, and reproductive harm.

### FDA and Nicotine

In other legal matters, a federal district court ruled in 1997 that the FDA, as a matter of law, is not precluded from regulating cigarettes and smokeless tobacco as "medical devices" intended to affect the structure or any function of the body due to the effects of nicotine. Brown and Williamson, makers of Kool and Capri Cigarettes as well as Tube Rose and Bloodhound Smokeless Tobacco, joined with five other smokeless tobacco makers and sued in September 1995 to try to block the Food and Drug Administration's efforts to regulate the tobacco industry. The FDA is investigating whether to classify nicotine as an addictive drug. Studies show that snuff is habit forming. Nicotine alters mood and subjective states of feeling, improves concentration and memory, and reduces pain and anxiety. Tobacco users become dependent on the moods created by nicotine.

On August 14, 1998, the Fourth Circuit Court of Appeals ruled in favor of UST and other tobacco product manufacturers, stating that the FDA lacks jurisdiction to regulate tobacco products and that all of the regulations published by the FDA are invalid. Yet in early 1999, the FDA filed a petition seeking a review of the Fourth Circuit's ruling by the United States Supreme Court. Oral arguments began in December 1999 with a decision expected in 2000. UST is not able to predict the outcome of the appeal or assess the future effect that these FDA regulations, if implemented, may have on its smokeless tobacco business.

## THE SMOKELESS TOBACCO INDUSTRY

Since 1613, when John Rolfe sent the first shipment of Virginia tobacco from Jamestown to England, growing tobacco and manufacturing its products have been among the leading industries in America. Many products are manufactured from the tobacco plant. Among these are many brands of cigarettes, cigars, snuff, chewing tobacco, pipe tobacco, and useful chemical products, including those that kill insects or fungi. Of these products, the smokeless category of the tobacco industry is a dynamic segment facing many ethical and social changes.

Today, the U.S. tobacco industry is an approximately $53 billion industry, with cigarettes accounting for nearly 94 percent of the total. The remaining 6 percent is cigars, moist smokeless tobacco, chewing tobacco, and snuff. The cigarette industry is quite mature and consolidated, with the top four producers accounting for approximately 72 percent of industry sales.

The smokeless tobacco industry (SIC Codes 0132 & 2131) is divided into two major areas—chewing tobacco and snuff. The chewing tobacco area consists of loose-leaf, moist firm plug, and twist/roll products. The snuff group consists of dry and moist, depending on the amount of moisture added to the tobacco during manufacturing. Despite the fact that consumption patterns have shifted from loose leaf to moist snuff, a large number of consumers still use both products. Observers say this presents an opportunity for manufacturers to increase market share and sales by convincing end users to switch brands.

In 1998, snuff, the only tobacco category to show growth, had growth for the ninth straight year; production was an estimated 66 million pounds, a gain of 3 percent over 1997. Some 94 percent of this poundage is classified as moist snuff. Moist snuff leads the smokeless category with 46.8 percent of market share as compared to 45.4 percent for loose-leaf tobacco. This is primarily due to the larger amount of advertising and promotions that this product receives. This product is also more available and relatively easy to use. As compared to the chewing and spitting involved with the loose-leaf tobacco, moist snuff consumption is more discreet: The user places a small pinch between cheek and gum. There are two classifications of smokeless tobacco. The first is a flue-cured, light-colored species, which is heat dried for use. The second species is a darker leaf that requires very little advance preparation.

The aggregate tobacco industry is classed with oligopolistic industries. Implications for all firms are high capital costs, hazardous antitrust and legal action, fruitless price-cutting, and monopolistic situations if firms join in a concerted action. The U.S. tobacco products industry has undergone substantial consolidation over the years. Prompted mainly by the combined challenges of declining U.S. consumption trends in a highly developed marketplace and the steady rise in legal and regulatory burdens, many manufacturers have either joined forces with competitors or perished. The increased scale needed to compete in the industry has erected very high barriers to entry.

The smokeless tobacco industry is highly concentrated near the tobacco-producing region of the United States. The five states that have the greatest number of workers in the industry are Kentucky, Tennessee, Georgia, North Carolina, and Illinois. Georgia and Illinois have replaced Virginia and Pennsylvania as leading employers of smokeless tobacco workers. Over one-half of the employment in the industry is concentrated in Kentucky. The reasons for this geographic concentration are obvious, the first being a desire to locate factories close to raw materials. In addition, the industry is concentrated in the area of the country that has traditionally been considered the prime market for the smokeless industry—the South.

The cigarette industry dwarfs the smokeless industry, with 1996 shipments of $34,348.2 million as opposed to $2,073.7 million for the smokeless industry. In 1976, the cigar industry fell from its historic position as the second-largest segment of the tobacco business to third place, behind the smokeless industry. After growing at 2.4 percent since 1976, cigar consumption on a compound annual growth rate rose to 8.9 percent from 1991 to 1994 and zoomed to 30.6 percent from 1994 to 1995. For the fifth year in a row, the per-capita consumption of cigars by men over the age of eighteen to 37.8, and total U.S. consumption of cigars in 1998 increased to 3.7 billion units, a 6 percent increase. (*Standard & Poor's Industry Surveys,* 1999). For consumption numbers from 1992 through 1998 please see Exhibit 4. The surge of interest in cigars is straining the supply chain, from tobacco growers and cigar factories to box makers and band engravers. Magazines like *Cigar Aficionado, Cigar Insider,* and *Smoke*—smoking lifestyle magazines—are capitalizing on the stogie's neo-cool image and drawing in luxury-goods advertisers.

Although their cigar operations are small, UST, Inc., markets many recognized brands. This area of business has been affected by a substantial oversupply in the marketplace because many companies flooded the market in the effort to meet this neo-cool trend. They are currently evaluating the situation to determine their prospects and alternatives.

## Competitors

Over the past ten years, UST has increased its share of the moist snuff market by 57 percent (from 23 percent to nearly 80 percent). UST, like Conwood, is taking advantage of its existing warehouse and distribution and has diversified into other markets. As industry diversification increases, a greater decentralization of operations can be expected with more than 150 brands of smokeless tobacco products currently available in the domestic market. Conwood, which represents about 13 percent of the market, is the only company that has entries in all segments of tobacco industry. UST Inc. accounted for 77 percent of total smokeless tobacco sales, Conwood for 13 percent, and Swisher for 5 percent. The other smokeless segment players include Swedish Match (Pinkerton), National Tobacco, John Middleton, JBG Inc., RC Owen, Red Lion International, TOP Tobacco, and Nuway-Microflake, and each has less than 2 percent of the total market.

### Conwood

Conwood's major brand of chewing tobacco is Levi Garrett. Taylor's Pride and Levi Garrett Plug are their moist plug brands. Kodiak and Hawken were moist snuff brands

## EXHIBIT 4    Tobacco Products—U.S. per Capita Consumption

| Year | *Cigarettes Units | Large Cigars & Cigarillos Units | Smoking Tobacco Pounds | Chewing Tobacco Pounds | *Snuff Pounds | *Total Tobacco Product Pounds |
|------|------------|----------------|----------------|----------------|---------|------------------|
| 1998p | 2,350 | 37.8 | 0.12 | 0.64 | 0.33 | 4.5 |
| 1997 | 2,423 | 36.9 | 0.12 | 0.64 | 0.31 | 4.55 |
| 1996 | 2,490 | 35.0 | 0.12 | 0.64 | 0.31 | 4.90 |
| 1995 | 2,510 | 27.6 | 0.13 | 0.67 | 0.31 | 4.90 |
| 1994 | 2,527 | 25.3 | 0.16 | 0.67 | 0.32 | 4.90 |
| 1993 | 2,538 | 23.4 | 0.17 | 0.70 | 0.30 | 5.37 |
| 1992 | 2,641 | 24.1 | 0.18 | 0.75 | 0.29 | 4.30 |

*Consumption per capita, eighteen years and over.
p = projected
*Source:* U.S. Department of Agriculture (www.econ.ag.gov/briefing/tobacco/wk1apr98/tab02.wk1)

introduced in 1981. In 1982, the company acquired another smokeless tobacco company, Scotten Dillon and its major brands of Union Workman and Uncle Sam. Conwood has the highest market share of any company in the dry snuff and twist/roll categories, and in the moist snuff market, Conwood's 13 percent market share is second to UST. Conwood takes advantage of their existing warehouse and distribution networks and has diversified into other consumer-related products—popcorn, concession supplies, and a full line of insecticides.

### Swisher International Group Inc.

This company produces large cigars, such as Swisher Sweets, King Edward, and Optimo for the mass market. They also produce Beting, La Primadora and Siglo 21 in the premium category in addition to smokeless tobacco products, both moist and dry snuff, under the brands of Silver Creek, Redwood, and Tops and loose-leaf brands of Mail Pouch, Lancaster-Limited-Reserve, and Chattanooga Chew. This company has captured a 5 percent market share and in 1998 experienced a 3.1 percent growth in sales and a 19.8 percent growth in net income. In 1999 Swisher, controlled by William Ziegler, went private.

### Swedish Match

Swedish Match (formerly Pinkerton Tobacco Co.) in 1997 nearly doubled its pound volume to increase its market share by 1 percent. This volume increase is nearly 10 percent over its 1995 figures. The cash cow for this company in the mature loose-leaf segment is the Red Man brand, which is also available in a moist plug form. Both forms have dwindled from their 34 percent market share high in 1981. In 1993, a new entry in the moist form, High Country, was introduced.

Although Swedish Match's share of the moist snuff market is around 2 percent, it, like other tobacco manufacturers, is using the discount snuff market as a means of expanding sales. Its 1994 entry into the discount moist snuff segment was Timberwolf, which is produced in two flavors (regular and wintergreen) and two cuts (long and fine). This segment is referred to as EDLP or "everyday low price." After UST introduced its individually packaged Skoal Bandits, Renegades, a similar product, was introduced in 1989.

In the loose-leaf market, Swedish Match holds a 43 percent market share, and Conwood holds 30 percent of the 1996-pound volume. Following them is National Tobacco Company with 20 percent and Swisher at 7 percent. Fred Stoker & Sons, Inc., another producer of the loose-leaf product, gains 70 percent of its sales through mail order catalogs. This company takes advantage of flavorings with their flagship peach, apple, and cherry. They additionally market discount, or sub-brands.

## ETHICAL ISSUES

As with other tobacco products, there is concern over the health hazards associated with chewing tobacco, the major issue being mouth cancer, which includes cancer of the cheeks and gums. As early as 1761, smokeless tobacco's harmful effects were known as English physician John Hill warned consumers of the dangers of tobacco's use. Today, the American Cancer Society and the American Dental Association oppose tobacco chewing because it stains teeth as well as causes gum disease and mouth infection, which can lead to cancer.

Spit tobacco poses health hazards to users, contrary to popular notions that it is a safe alternative to smoking. The various forms of spit tobacco have been found to cause mouth cancer, a disease responsible for more than 8,000 casualties annually. Aside from oral cancer, spit tobacco also leads to bad breath, teeth stains, gum inflammation, or periodontal disease with bone loss. The concentrated nicotine absorbed orally also accelerates heart rate, increases blood pressure, and can increase the risk of coronary artery, occlusive vascular and cerebrovascular diseases, as well as stroke.

Also, dry snuff sniffed through the nostrils is considered harmful because the olfactory nerves become irritated, which lessens the ability to distinguish odors. Specifically, smokeless tobacco use increases the risk of oral cancer by 300 percent. In addition, elevated cholesterol levels and blood pressure are other harmful side effects. The elevated levels of blood pressure appear to be caused by tobacco's high sodium and sugar contents. According to the American Cancer Society, some of the major ingredients in dip and chewing tobacco are nicotine (an addictive drug), polonium 210 (nuclear waste), formaldehyde (embalming fluid), cancer-causing chemicals, and radioactive elements.

Other health problems associated with smokeless tobacco use include nausea for first-time users, cancer of the mouth and throat, leukoplakia, potential cardiovascular problems, and peptic ulcers. With the use of this variety of tobacco continuing to increase, these health problems will also increase (www.aap.org/advocacy/chmsmles.htm).

A study released in 1995 by the American Health Foundation found that a single can of smokeless tobacco contains about three times the dosage of cancer-causing chemicals found in a pack of cigarettes, and the average user of smokeless tobacco consumes three cans per week. In Kansas, a team of lawyers is preparing a nationwide class action alleging that UST and others have known for years that their products are addictive and harmful.

## CUSTOMER DEMOGRAPHICS AND MARKETING

Traditional users of smokeless tobacco products are miners, farmers, and factory workers. These workers usually need to have both hands free, and the use of lighted materials is generally prohibited because of potentially hazardous conditions. Chewing tobacco still remains predominantly a blue-collar, rural or suburban activity, but there has been some progress to new urban, inner-city markets as a result of the country-western craze. The average annual income of adult consumers of moist snuff is $37,520.

A study by the Department of Health and Human Services found that 19 percent of high school males use smokeless tobacco. Usage by the under-nineteen sector is highest in the South and the Midwest and, in particular, in the states of Tennessee and Montana. Of student athletes who used smokeless tobacco products, 57 percent played baseball, and 40 percent played football.

Over the last 15 to 20 years, consumers have generally been attracted to lighter products in all consumption areas. It is this lighter, milder, sweeter-tasting appeal that smokeless tobacco producers are selling to customers, at least for growth products like loose leaf and moist snuff. Consumers can enjoy mild tobacco taste without ever "lighting-up." Nationally, states have laws limiting smoking in public areas, according to the Health and Human Services Department. Additionally, many companies have banned smoking. All of these reasons are conducive to the purchase and use of smokeless tobacco products. In addition, smokeless tobacco manufacturers have promoted their products as the most economical form of tobacco use.

Smokeless tobacco producers are now expanding their customer base into other consumer segments, including active outdoor people, sports enthusiasts, business executives, and professional people. New younger consumers, many of whom have never used any form of tobacco before, are being attracted to smokeless tobacco products, especially the moist snuff. These younger consumers like moist snuff because it is more socially acceptable than chewing tobacco, and snuff can be used indoors as well as outdoors, because one does not have to "spit." Internationally, most find the practice of dipping and spitting to be "gross." It is not a social custom taken up by many people.

In addition to these new younger consumers, users of the more traditional forms of smokeless tobacco are switching to loose-leaf and moist snuff. The attraction of loose-leaf snuff lies in its image, flavor, and convenience; it is milder and sweeter than other available products. Smokeless tobacco producers are fervently promoting the idea of good taste and are striving to introduce milder, more flavorful formulations like mint, wintergreen, licorice, and raspberry. UST's new Skoal Flavor Packs mask the tobacco flavor and do not require spitting. Also, individually portioned packages, like Skoal Bandits and Renegades, appeal to consumers concerned with the appearance of smokeless tobacco inside the mouth. These products contain the tobacco in a tea bag-like wrapping, which prevents loose tobacco particles from getting in the user's mouth. It is this idea of a quality product, exemplified by freshness and pleasant taste, that smokeless tobacco producers feel will convince consumers to become brand loyalists.

Radio and television advertising of smokeless tobacco products was banned in 1987. Additionally, manufacturers were required to put warning labels on product packages. Furthermore, the Federal Trade Commission has proposed an amendment to the Comprehensive Smokeless Tobacco Health Education Act of 1986 to include the placement of warning labels on advertising at car races. Targets for additional labeling include cars and uniforms.

Smokeless tobacco producers use various ways to promote their products. Free product sampling is widely used by manufacturers for new and existing products. Samples are distributed to consumers at sporting events such as car races, concerts, gun and boat shows, and tobacco retailers. UST has been very successful at promoting the two largest-selling brands of moist snuff in the industry, Skoal and Copenhagen. Branded merchandise is offered by UST through its Country Western Store and concert catalog, in which items are sold for a combination of cash and proofs of purchase from Skoal products. T-shirts, knives, watches, key chains, radios, Skoal silver lids, and belt buckles are a few of the branded articles available through the store. UST's sales representatives capitalize on product awareness with one-on-one product sampling to put products directly in the hands of customers. These new potential customers, in turn, demonstrate the use of the products to their friends.

UST's leading promotion is the Skoal Bandit racing team, which it sponsors, on the NASCAR Grand National Circuit. Grand National racing commands an especially avid following in the Southeast, which is one of the fastest-growing markets for smokeless tobacco. Support promotion is comprehensive, including personal appearances at shopping malls and other locations by the Skoal Bandit racing team. Similar promotional efforts are made throughout the country, throughout the year, in connection with rodeo, skiing, and other sports events on regional and local levels as well as nationally.

## FUTURE

- Will health claims and litigation against smokeless tobacco users increase?
- With saturated markets, how can UST increase usage throughout the United States as well as target new users including women and international users? If so, what countries should they target?
- Will discount goods hurt the premium-priced brand name Skoal and Copenhagen products?
- With men aged eighteen to thirty-four declining in number, how can UST maintain their growth? Also with U.S. population growing only 1% annually, is there any hope for expanding the domestic market share?
- With the courts awarding damages to tobacco users diagnosed with cancer, should the tobacco industry try to develop its market in alternative products as tobacco has alternative uses in nutrition, drug production, antibiotics, and antiseptics?
- Will smokeless tobacco continue to be a cash cow?
- Is diversification a key to survival?